International Directory of
COMPANY
HISTORIES

International Directory of

COMPANY

HISTORIES

VOLUME 104

Editor

Tina Grant

ST. JAMES PRESS
A part of Gale, Cengage Learning

GALE
CENGAGE Learning™

Detroit • New York • San Francisco • New Haven, Conn • Waterville, Maine • London

International Directory of Company Histories, Volume 104

Tina Grant, Editor

Project Editor: Miranda H. Ferrara

Editorial: Virgil Burton, Donna Craft, Louise Gagné, Peggy Geeseman, Julie Gough, Linda Hall, Sonya Hill, Keith Jones, Jodi Nazione, Lynn Pearce, Holly Selden, Justine Ventimiglia

Production Technology Specialist: Mike Weaver

Imaging and Multimedia: John Watkins

Composition and Electronic Prepress: Gary Leach, Evi Seoud

Manufacturing: Rhonda Dover

Product Manager: Jenai Drouillard

For product information and technology assistance, contact us at **Gale Customer Support, 1-800-877-4253.**
For permission to use material from this text or product, submit all requests online at **www.cengage.com/permissions.**
Further permissions questions can be emailed to **permissionrequest@cengage.com**

Gale
27500 Drake Rd.
Farmington Hills, MI, 48331-3535

LIBRARY OF CONGRESS CATALOG NUMBER 89-190943
ISBN-13: 978-1-55862-638-6
ISBN-10: 1-55862-638-7

This title is also available as an e-book
ISBN-13: 978-1-55862-767-3   ISBN-10: 1-55862-767-7
Contact your Gale, a part of Cengage Learning sales representative for ordering information.

BRITISH LIBRARY CATALOGUING IN PUBLICATION DATA
International directory of company histories, Vol. 104
Tina Grant
33.87409

Printed in the United States of America
1 2 3 4 5 6 7 13 12 11 10 09

Contents

Preface

The St. James Press series *The International Directory of Company Histories* (*IDCH*) is intended for reference use by students, business people, librarians, historians, economists, investors, job candidates, and others who seek to learn more about the historical development of the world's most important companies. To date, *IDCH* has covered more than 10,285 companies in 104 volumes.

INCLUSION CRITERIA

Most companies chosen for inclusion in *IDCH* have achieved a minimum of US$25 million in annual sales and are leading influences in their industries or geographical locations. Companies may be publicly held, private, or nonprofit. State-owned companies that are important in their industries and that may operate much like public or private companies also are included. Wholly owned subsidiaries and divisions are profiled if they meet the requirements for inclusion. Entries on companies that have had major changes since they were last profiled may be selected for updating.

The *IDCH* series highlights 25% private and nonprofit companies, and features updated entries on approximately 35 companies per volume.

ENTRY FORMAT

Each entry begins with the company's legal name; the address of its headquarters; its telephone, toll-free, and fax numbers; and its web site. A statement of public, private, state, or parent ownership follows. A company with a legal name in both English and the language of its headquarters country is listed by the English name, with the native-language name in parentheses.

The company's founding or earliest incorporation date, the number of employees, and the most recent available sales figures follow. Sales figures are given in local currencies with equivalents in U.S. dollars. For some private companies, sales figures are estimates and indicated by the abbreviation *est.* The entry lists the exchanges on which the company's stock is traded and its ticker symbol, as well as the company's NAICS codes.

Entries generally contain a *Company Perspectives* box which provides a short summary of the company's mission, goals, and ideals; a *Key Dates* box highlighting milestones in the company's history; lists of *Principal Subsidiaries*, *Principal Divisions*, *Principal Operating Units*, *Principal Competitors*; and articles for *Further Reading*.

American spelling is used throughout *IDCH*, and the word "billion" is used in its U.S. sense of one thousand million.

SOURCES

Entries have been compiled from publicly accessible sources both in print and on the Internet such as general and academic periodicals, books, and annual reports, as well as material supplied by the companies themselves.

CUMULATIVE INDEXES

IDCH contains three indexes: the **Cumulative Index to Companies**, which provides an alphabetical index to companies profiled in the *IDCH* series, the **Index to Industries**, which allows researchers to locate companies by their principal industry, and the **Geographic Index**, which lists companies alphabetically by the country of their headquarters. The indexes are cumulative and specific instructions for using them are found immediately preceding each index.

SPECIAL TO THIS VOLUME

This volume of *IDCH* contains an entry on the leading Central European pharmaceuticals manufacturer EGIS Gyogyszergyar Nyrt and the first Mongolian company, Newcom Group.

SUGGESTIONS WELCOME

Comments and suggestions from users of *IDCH* on any aspect of the product as well as suggestions for companies to be included or updated are cordially invited. Please write:

The Editor
International Directory of Company Histories
St. James Press
Gale, Cengage Learning
27500 Drake Rd.
Farmington Hills, Michigan 48331-3535

St. James Press does not endorse any of the companies or products mentioned in this series. Companies appearing in the *International Directory of Company Histories* were selected without reference to their wishes and have in no way endorsed their entries.

Notes on Contributors

Gerald E. Brennan
Writer and musician based in Germany.

M. L. Cohen
Novelist, business writer, and researcher living in Paris.

Ed Dinger
Writer and editor based in Bronx, New York.

Paul R. Greenland
Illinois-based writer and researcher; author of three books and former senior editor of a national business magazine; contributor to *The Encyclopedia of Chicago History*, *The Encyclopedia of Religion*, and the *Encyclopedia of American Industries*.

Robert Halasz
Former editor in chief of *World Progress* and *Funk & Wagnalls New Encyclopedia Yearbook*; author, *The U.S. Marines* (Millbrook Press, 1993).

Evelyn Hauser
Researcher, writer and marketing specialist based in Germany.

Frederick C. Ingram
Writer based in South Carolina.

Carrie Rothburd
Writer and editor specializing in corporate profiles, academic texts, and academic journal articles.

Christina M. Stansell
Writer and editor based in Louisville, Kentucky.

Frank Uhle
Ann Arbor-based writer; movie projectionist, disc jockey, and staff member of *Psychotronic Video* magazine.

Ellen D. Wernick
Florida-based writer and editor.

A. Woodward
Wisconsin-based writer.

List of Abbreviations

¥ Japanese yen
£ United Kingdom pound
$ United States dollar

A

AB Aktiebolag (Finland, Sweden)
AB Oy Aktiebolag Osakeyhtiot (Finland)
A.E. Anonimos Eteria (Greece)
AED Emirati dirham
AG Aktiengesellschaft (Austria, Germany, Switzerland, Liechtenstein)
aG auf Gegenseitigkeit (Austria, Germany)
A.m.b.a. Andelsselskab med begraenset ansvar (Denmark)
A.O. Anonim Ortaklari/Ortakligi (Turkey)
ApS Amparteselskab (Denmark)
ARS Argentine peso
A.S. Anonim Sirketi (Turkey)
A/S Aksjeselskap (Norway)
A/S Aktieselskab (Denmark, Sweden)
Ay Avoinyhtio (Finland)
ATS Austrian shilling
AUD Australian dollar
ApS Amparteselskab (Denmark)
Ay Avoinyhtio (Finland)

B

B.A. Buttengewone Aansprakeiijkheid (Netherlands)
BEF Belgian franc

BHD Bahraini dinar
Bhd. Berhad (Malaysia, Brunei)
BND Brunei dollar
BRL Brazilian real
B.V. Besloten Vennootschap (Belgium, Netherlands)

C

C.A. Compania Anonima (Ecuador, Venezuela)
CAD Canadian dollar
C. de R.L. Compania de Responsabilidad Limitada (Spain)
CEO Chief Executive Officer
CFO Chief Financial Officer
CHF Swiss franc
Cia. Companhia (Brazil, Portugal)
Cia. Compania (Latin America [except Brazil], Spain)
Cia. Compagnia (Italy)
Cie. Compagnie (Belgium, France, Luxembourg, Netherlands)
CIO Chief Information Officer
CLP Chilean peso
CNY Chinese yuan
Co. Company
COO Chief Operating Officer
Coop. Cooperative
COP Colombian peso
Corp. Corporation
C. por A. Compania por Acciones (Dominican Republic)
CPT Cuideachta Phoibi Theoranta

(Republic of Ireland)
CRL Companhia a Responsabilidao Limitida (Portugal, Spain)
C.V. Commanditaire Vennootschap (Netherlands, Belgium)
CZK Czech koruna

D

D&B Dunn & Bradstreet
DEM German deutsche mark
Div. Division (United States)
DKK Danish krone
DZD Algerian dinar

E

EC Exempt Company (Arab countries)
Edms. Bpk. Eiendoms Beperk (South Africa)
EEK Estonian Kroon
eG eingetragene Genossenschaft (Germany)
EGMBH Eingetragene Genossenschaft mit beschraenkter Haftung (Austria, Germany)
EGP Egyptian pound
Ek For Ekonomisk Forening (Sweden)
EP Empresa Portuguesa (Portugal)
E.P.E. Etema Pemorismenis Evthynis (Greece)
ESOP Employee Stock Options and Ownership
ESP Spanish peseta

Et(s). Etablissement(s) (Belgium, France, Luxembourg)
eV eingetragener Verein (Germany)
EUR euro

F
FIM Finnish markka
FRF French franc

G
G.I.E. Groupement d'Interet Economique (France)
gGmbH gemeinnutzige Gesellschaft mit beschraenkter Haftung (Austria, Germany, Switzerland)
G.I.E. Groupement d'Interet Economique (France)
GmbH Gesellschaft mit beschraenkter Haftung (Austria, Germany, Switzerland)
GRD Greek drachma
GWA Gewerbte Amt (Austria, Germany)

H
HB Handelsbolag (Sweden)
HF Hlutafelag (Iceland)
HKD Hong Kong dollar
HUF Hungarian forint

I
IDR Indonesian rupiah
IEP Irish pound
ILS new Israeli shekel
Inc. Incorporated (United States, Canada)
INR Indian rupee
IPO Initial Public Offering
I/S Interesentselskap (Norway)
I/S Interessentselskab (Denmark)
ISK Icelandic krona
ITL Italian lira

J
JMD Jamaican dollar
JOD Jordanian dinar

K
KB Kommanditbolag (Sweden)
KES Kenyan schilling
Kft Korlatolt Felelossegu Tarsasag (Hungary)
KG Kommanditgesellschaft (Austria, Germany, Switzerland)

KGaA Kommanditgesellschaft auf Aktien (Austria, Germany, Switzerland)
KK Kabushiki Kaisha (Japan)
KPW North Korean won
KRW South Korean won
K/S Kommanditselskab (Denmark)
K/S Kommandittselskap (Norway)
KWD Kuwaiti dinar
Ky Kommandiitiyhtio (Finland)

L
LBO Leveraged Buyout
Lda. Limitada (Spain)
L.L.C. Limited Liability Company (Arab countries, Egypt, Greece, United States)
L.L.P. Limited Liability Partnership (United States)
L.P. Limited Partnership (Canada, South Africa, United Kingdom, United States)
Ltd. Limited
Ltda. Limitada (Brazil, Portugal)
Ltee. Limitee (Canada, France)
LUF Luxembourg franc

M
mbH mit beschraenkter Haftung (Austria, Germany)
Mij. Maatschappij (Netherlands)
MUR Mauritian rupee
MXN Mexican peso
MYR Malaysian ringgit

N
N.A. National Association (United States)
NGN Nigerian naira
NLG Netherlands guilder
NOK Norwegian krone
N.V. Naamloze Vennootschap (Belgium, Netherlands)
NZD New Zealand dollar

O
OAO Otkrytoe Aktsionernoe Obshchestve (Russia)
OHG Offene Handelsgesellschaft (Austria, Germany, Switzerland)
OMR Omani rial
OOO Obschestvo s Ogranichennoi Otvetstvennostiu (Russia)
OOUR Osnova Organizacija

Udruzenog Rada (Yugoslavia)
Oy Osakeyhtî (Finland)

P
P.C. Private Corp. (United States)
PEN Peruvian Nuevo Sol
PHP Philippine peso
PKR Pakistani rupee
P/L Part Lag (Norway)
PLC Public Limited Co. (United Kingdom, Ireland)
P.L.L.C. Professional Limited Liability Corporation (United States)
PLN Polish zloty
P.T. Perusahaan/Perseroan Terbatas (Indonesia)
PTE Portuguese escudo
Pte. Private (Singapore)
Pty. Proprietary (Australia, South Africa, United Kingdom)
Pvt. Private (India, Zimbabwe)
PVBA Personen Vennootschap met Beperkte Aansprakelijkheid (Belgium)
PYG Paraguay guarani

Q
QAR Qatar riyal

R
REIT Real Estate Investment Trust
RMB Chinese renminbi
Rt Reszvenytarsasag (Hungary)
RUB Russian ruble

S
S.A. Société Anonyme (Arab countries, Belgium, France, Jordan, Luxembourg, Switzerland)
S.A. Sociedad Anónima (Latin America [except Brazil], Spain, Mexico)
S.A. Sociedades Anônimas (Brazil, Portugal)
SAA Societe Anonyme Arabienne (Arab countries)
S.A.B. de C.V. Sociedad Anónima Bursátil de Capital Variable (Mexico)
S.A.C. Sociedad Anonima Comercial (Latin America [except Brazil])
S.A.C.I. Sociedad Anonima Comercial e Industrial (Latin America [except Brazil])

S.A.C.I.y.F. Sociedad Anonima Comercial e Industrial y Financiera (Latin America [except Brazil])

S.A. de C.V. Sociedad Anonima de Capital Variable (Mexico)

SAK Societe Anonyme Kuweitienne (Arab countries)

SAL Societe Anonyme Libanaise (Arab countries)

SAO Societe Anonyme Omanienne (Arab countries)

SAQ Societe Anonyme Qatarienne (Arab countries)

SAR Saudi riyal

S.A.R.L. Sociedade Anonima de Responsabilidade Limitada (Brazil, Portugal)

S.A.R.L. Société à Responsabilité Limitée (France, Belgium, Luxembourg)

S.A.S. Societá in Accomandita Semplice (Italy)

S.A.S. Societe Anonyme Syrienne (Arab countries)

S.C. Societe en Commandite (Belgium, France, Luxembourg)

S.C.A. Societe Cooperativa Agricole (France, Italy, Luxembourg)

S.C.I. Sociedad Cooperativa Ilimitada (Spain)

S.C.L. Sociedad Cooperativa Limitada (Spain)

S.C.R.L. Societe Cooperative a Responsabilite Limitee (Belgium)

Sdn. Bhd. Sendirian Berhad (Malaysia)

SEK Swedish krona

SGD Singapore dollar

S.L. Sociedad Limitada (Latin America [except Brazil], Portugal, Spain)

S/L Salgslag (Norway)

S.N.C. Société en Nom Collectif (France)

Soc. Sociedad (Latin America [except Brazil], Spain)

Soc. Sociedade (Brazil, Portugal)

Soc. Societa (Italy)

S.p.A. Società per Azioni (Italy)

Sp. z.o.o. Spólka z ograniczona odpowiedzialnoscia (Poland)

S.R.L. Sociedad de Responsabilidad Limitada (Spain, Mexico, Latin America [except Brazil])

S.R.L. Società a Responsabilità Limitata (Italy)

S.R.O. Spolecnost s Rucenim Omezenym (Czechoslovakia

S.S.K. Sherkate Sahami Khass (Iran)

Ste. Societe (France, Belgium, Luxembourg, Switzerland)

Ste. Cve. Societe Cooperative (Belgium)

S.V. Samemwerkende Vennootschap (Belgium)

S.Z.R.L. Societe Zairoise a Responsabilite Limitee (Zaire)

T
THB Thai baht

TND Tunisian dinar

TRL Turkish lira

TWD new Taiwan dollar

U

U.A. Uitgesloten Aansporakeiijkheid (Netherlands)

u.p.a. utan personligt ansvar (Sweden)

V

VAG Verein der Arbeitgeber (Austria, Germany)

VEB Venezuelan bolivar

VERTR Vertriebs (Austria, Germany)

VND Vietnamese dong

V.O.f. Vennootschap onder firma (Netherlands)

VVAG Versicherungsverein auf Gegenseitigkeit (Austria, Germany)

W – Z

WA Wettelika Aansprakalikhaed (Netherlands)

WLL With Limited Liability (Bahrain, Kuwait, Qatar, Saudi Arabia)

YK Yugen Kaisha (Japan)

ZAO Zakrytoe Aktsionernoe Obshchestve (Russia)

ZAR South African rand

ZMK Zambian kwacha

ZWD Zimbabwean dollar

A. Smith Bowman Distillery, Inc.

———■———

1 Bowman Drive, Suite 100
Fredericksburg, Virginia 22408
U.S.A.
Telephone: (540) 373-4555
Fax: (540) 371-2236
Web site: http://www.asmithbowman.com

Private Company
Incorporated: 1934
Employees: 350
Sales: $1,116.7 million (2007 est.)
NAICS: 312140 Distilleries

■ ■ ■

A. Smith Bowman Distillery, Inc., is a privately owned spirits company based in Fredericksburg, Virginia, specializing in handcrafted brands. The company is best known for its original product, Virginia Gentleman Bourbon, and its award-winning Virginia Gentleman 90 Proof Small Batch Bourbon. Grain mashing, fermentation, and the first two distillations are conducted at the Buffalo Trace Distillery in Kentucky; the resulting clear liquid is shipped to Fredericksburg in tankers. Here the final steps of distillation are completed in a 3,000-gallon copper pot still and the liquid is poured into charred oak barrels for proper aging, resulting in the distinctive taste and color of the bourbon. Changes in room temperature are employed to move the distilled liquid in and out of the oak.

Since the 1980s the company has produced Bowman's Vodka and Bowman's Gin. Also bottled at

the distillery is Bowman's Light, a low-calorie, 53-proof spirit. In addition, Bowman distributes Bowman's Bourbon, a Kentucky-distilled straight bourbon whiskey; Bowman's Citrus Vodka; Bowman's Mexican Tequila, a Mexican product; Bowman's Imported Rum, sourced from the Virgin Islands; Bowman's Imported Canadian Whiskey; and Bowman's Imported Scotch.

BOWMAN FAMILY MOVES TO VIRGINIA: 1927

The man who established A. Smith Bowman Distillery, Inc., was Kentucky native Abram Smith Bowman. He was a successful businessman who had owned farms in several states and Canada, as well as the People's Motor Coach Company in Indianapolis. After he sold the latter in the mid-1920s, one of his sons, DeLong, suggested that the family needed a farm. According to family lore, Bowman agreed, and because he was interested in moving back to Kentucky, he dispatched DeLong to purchase a copy of the *Louisville Courier-Journal.* The son returned with the *Cincinnati Enquirer,* however. Inside was an advertisement for 4,000 acres of land available in Northern Virginia (other sources indicated the ad was found in the pages of the *Chicago Tribune*). In any event, Bowman purchased the land in 1927, paying about $40 an acre.

In the late 1800s a New York dentist, Dr. Carl Adolph Max Wiehle, had acquired the land to build a town, but after laying out roads, digging lakes, and constructing several buildings, he abandoned the plan. A subsequent owner cleared some of the land, built a lumber mill, and established a successful dairy farm.

COMPANY PERSPECTIVES

Bowman Distillery continues the time-honored tradition of blending choice natural ingredients and the latest technology to produce its fine line of spirits.

Bowman renamed the operation Sunset Hills Farm and moved his family from Indiana to Virginia. At the time his eldest son, Abram Smith Bowman Jr., was completing his undergraduate degree at Princeton University, which was followed by a degree in architecture from Harvard University. DeLong would soon leave home and attend Princeton as well.

VIRGINIA GENTLEMAN UNVEILED: 1935

Sunset Hills was primarily a dairy farm, although the family also raised pigs and grew corn for feed. The focus would change in the 1930s as Prohibition was repealed. The ill-fated experiment to make beer, wine, and spirits illegal in the United States came to an end in 1933 with the ratification of the Twenty-first Amendment to the Constitution, which put an end to Prohibition. By the time the Virginia legislature followed suit two years later the Bowman family had already built a distillery, looking to take advantage of their resources.

They had an abundance of corn which, when mixed with rye barley, malt, and water could produce mash. There were also plenty of white oak trees to make barrels for aging, and dairy trucks that could be used for making deliveries. The mash was also used a cattle feed, which according to the family resulted in a 30 percent increase in milk production. Bowman took advantage of some of the old mill buildings on the property, which were converted into warehouses.

The eldest son, who had been working as an architect, returned home to help his father and brother run the new distillery. Relying on a formula provided by a man who had worked on the property prior to the arrival of the Bowmans, Sunset Hills produced its first finished bourbon whiskey. Younger son DeLong Bowman was credited with giving the product its name. According to the *Richmond Times-Dispatch,* he once explained the origins: "When we started making whiskey, the family was sitting around the dining room table, and I just said it was a good name for a good Virginia bourbon—Virginia Gentleman."

Virginia Gentleman, produced by Virginia's only legal distillery, soon found a regional niche. As reported by the *Times-Dispatch,* it "eventually found its way into the National Press Club and the Army-Navy Club and has been served aboard the presidential yacht, *Sequoia.*" A second brand, Fairfax County Bourbon, named for the region, was added later. More potent, it was a 100-proof whiskey.

FOUNDER DIES: 1952

In 1947 the two brothers joined their father as partners in the distillery. Smith Bowman was responsible for sales, while DeLong Bowman ran the distillery as well as the family farm. Two years later the Bowmans added another 3,200 acres, which were located adjacent to their property. As whiskey production increased, more of this land was cleared for growing corn for making mash.

After their father died in 1952 the brothers attempted to resurrect Dr. Wiehle's dream of building a town on their holdings, which was the largest farm in Northern Virginia, to take advantage of the suburbanization of the period, as the parents of the Baby Boom generation, especially military veterans taking advantage of their government benefits, looked for communities in which to raise their children. The Washington firm of Mott and Hayden developed a master plan for a 30,000-resident city in 1956, but the Bowmans found it difficult to win county approval.

In 1960 they sold nearly 6,500 acres to the New York-based Lefcourt Realty Corporation for $19.75 million, including the distillery, although the rights to run it were retained by the family. Lefcourt soon had financial problems related to its Florida real estate holdings and by the end of the year the property was once again on the block. A year later it was sold to New York developer Robert E. Simon Jr., who recognized the potential of the northern Virginia locale, less than 20 miles from the capital and close to Dulles Airport, then under construction. He eventually succeeded in gaining zoning clearance for his planned community, which would take the name of Reston. In the meantime, in 1963, the Bowman brothers also bought back some of Sunset Hills, including the distillery, for $11 million.

Virginia Gentleman continued to increase in popularity in Virginia and surrounding markets, reaching a peak in 1970 when the company sold 178,000 cases. As Americans' tastes changed, however, bourbon sales steadily declined. Also of note in 1970, Smith Bowman's brother-in-law with a prominent Virginian name joined the business: Robert E. Lee IV. Ironically the great-grandson of the famous Confederate general was born and educated in the North and lacked any trace of a Southern accent. He did, however, retain a taste for bourbon whiskey.

KEY DATES
■

1927: Abram Smith Bowman acquires Sunset Hills Farm in Northern Virginia.
1934: Bowman establishes a distillery on his farm.
1937: Virginia Gentleman bourbon is introduced.
1947: Bowman's sons become partners in the company.
1952: Bowman dies.
1970: Sales of Virginia Gentleman peak at 178,000 cases for the year.
1987: The company moves its distillery operations to Spotsylvania County.
1992: Vodka is added to company's product line.
1994: The company begins selling gin.
1998: Virginia Gentleman 90 Proof Small Batch Bourbon is introduced.
2003: The Smith Bowman distillery is sold and fermentation operations are outsourced to Kentucky.

Lee was named vice-president of marketing. In the late 1970s, in an effort to counteract shrinking regional sales of Virginia Gentleman, Lee spearheaded an effort to introduce a new whiskey to the markets of Florida and Texas, one that was slightly more potent (87.7 proof, rather than 80). The effort was not successful. As Lee recalled in a 1987 interview with the *Richmond Times-Dispatch,* "We discovered in Texas you needed money and patience. We had neither." During this period the company also tried its hand at using its corn and distilling operations to produce ethanol.

VODKA INTRODUCED: 1982

Smith Bowman Jr., the company's chairman, died from cancer at the age of 75 in 1981, leaving Lee and his brother to run Bowman Distillery. With interest in bourbon continuing to wane, the company attempt to revive the Fairfax County brand by lowering it to 90 proof. The change made no difference, as sales of the whiskey would dip below 500 cases in 1983. A year later Fairfax County was discontinued. In order to survive Bowman Distillery decided, in the meantime, to expand beyond brown spirits and become involved in clear spirits, a move that also made further use of the company's production capacity.

In 1982 the company introduced Bowman's Virginia Vodka, enjoying a stroke of good fortune when the state of Virginia launched the "We have it made in

Virginia" economic development campaign that urged residents to buy products made in Virginia. The new low-priced vodka soon became the state's best selling vodka. Buoyed by this success, the company decided to add gin to its product offerings, unveiling Virginia Gentleman Gin in the fall of 1986. It, too, found a niche in the market.

For years it had become increasingly difficult to operate a distillery in Northern Virginia, which had become a traffic-clogged, suburban extension of Washington, D.C. Gone were the area farms that had once supplied grain and served as customers for used mash. The new neighbors, mostly transplanted city dwellers, were not as forgiving as farmers when the foul smells that emanated from a whiskey factory were carried their way on a strong wind. Moreover, real estate taxes were set for residential use, not agricultural purposes, making the cost of doing business far too high for a boutique distiller like Bowman.

In 1986 the company acquired property in Spotsylvania County, Virginia, buying a former FMC Corporation cellophane plant that the county had taken over and renamed Spotsylvania County Industrial Park. In the 1920s and 1930s FMC had been the world's largest cellophane manufacturer, but in 1978 the facility was shut down. Bowman paid $1.75 million for the 25-acre site, which included more than 225,000 square feet spread across a dozen buildings.

OPERATION MOVES TO SPOTSYLVANIA: 1987

Bowman moved to Spotsylvania in 1987 and subsequently sold its 30-acre distillery site for $17 million. Only a sales office remained in Northern Virginia. For several years, while the new property was renovated and environmental concerns were addressed, the company was unable to distill any new spirits. Rather, it relied on an inventory of 27,000 barrels, about a $5\frac{1}{2}$-year supply, from which to bottle its bourbon until the still could once again be fired up in the early 1990s.

In the meantime there was a change in leadership. DeLong Bowman died from pneumonia in 1989 at the age of 78. Lee became chairman and Bowman's son-in-law, John Buchanan "Jay" Adams, took over as president and chief executive officer. Like Lee, Adams boasted illustrious forebears. He was a direct descendant of John Adams, one of the founding fathers of the United States and the country's second president.

Lee and Adams took charge of Bowman Distillery at a time of difficult business conditions. Demand for Virginia Gentleman was sagging, and only price cuts allowed the company's gin and vodka to maintain their place as a popular brand alternative.

In its new home Bowman Distillery looked for opportunities on a number of fronts. In 1990 the company added international sales when it landed an order for 50,000 cases of vodka from Poland, the largest single order for one product in its history. Sales of gin and bourbon would follow. In 1992 Bowman Distillery began selling its branded vodka in Russia, the world's largest market for the product. Because of inefficiencies Russian companies were unable to produce vodka less expensively than many newly available imports, like Bowman's Vodka. Bowman also enjoyed strong sales of 190-proof grain alcohol.

Bowman Distillery tried to generate new revenues during the early 1990s by bottling water on a contract basis for a Virginia mountain resort, Homestead. More in keeping with its primary business, the company became an importer of spirits, applying its label to Mexican Tequila, Virgin Islands Rum, Canadian Whiskey, and Scotch Whiskey.

The company also looked to the premium handcrafted category. In 1998 it introduced Virginia Gentleman 90 Proof Small Batch Bourbon. The timing for this product's introduction proved fortuitous. As the 21st century dawned, consumption of distilled spirits began to rise. In 2003 the company's handcrafted bourbon achieved some acclaim, winning "Double Gold" and "Best American Whiskey" at the 2003 San Francisco World Spirits Competition.

DISTILLERY SOLD: 2003

A number of craft distilleries were now established in Virginia. While they represented competition to Bowman Distillery in one sense, the rise of interest in handcrafted spirits bode well for the well-established producer. The operation was streamlined, with the distillery sold to a New Orleans company, Sazerac Company Inc., in 2003. Grain-mashing and fermentation were now done in Kentucky, while the final, crucial steps were completed in Spotsylvania.

In late 2008 Bowman Distillery began renovating its facilities to appeal to visitors. Plans were made to open a visitors' center, museum, and theater. Given the proximity to Civil War battlefields and the National Museum of the Marine Corps, and the major population centers of Washington and Richmond, there was every reason to believe that Bowman Distillery could enjoy the marketing benefits of directly sharing its history with consumers. Unlike wineries, however, the plant, by law, would be unable to share its whiskeys with visitors.

Ed Dinger

PRINCIPAL COMPETITORS

Beam Global Spirits & Wine, Inc.; Future Brands LLC; Pernod Ricard USA.

FURTHER READING

Barnes, Bart, "E. D. Bowman Dies at 78," *Washington Post,* October 20, 1989, p. D4.

"Bourbon Maker to Move," *Richmond Times-Dispatch,* August 9, 1986, p. B4.

Clark, Steve, "Lee's Great-Grandson Wasn't About to Use the General to Sell Gin," *Richmond Times-Dispatch,* November 25, 1986, p. 15.

Leepson, Marc, "Doing Business," *Regardie's,* June 1989, p. 210.

Lohmann, Bill, "Sightseeing—And Maybe a Sip," *Richmond Times-Dispatch,* October 24, 2008.

Marquardt, Deborah, "A New Spirit," *Richmond Times-Dispatch,* March 1, 1988, p. 15.

Rice, William, "Move Over Jack and Jim, Here Comes a Virginia Gentleman," *Washington Post,* September 3, 1978, p. K5.

Rolfe, Shelley, "The Marketing of a Gin," *Richmond-Times Dispatch,* May 16, 1987, p. B1.

Smith, J. Y., "A. Smith Bowman, Maker of 'Virginia Gentleman' Bourbon, Dies," *Washington Post,* May 8, 1981, p. B4.

Swisher, Kara, "Virginia's Own Brand of Hospitality," *Washington Post,* January 22, 1990, p. F05.

Allscripts-Misys Health-care Solutions Inc.

222 Merchandise Mart, Suite 2024
Chicago, Illinois 60654
U.S.A.
Telephone: (866) 358-6869
Toll Free: (800) 654-0889
Fax: (312) 506-1201
Web site: http://www.allscripts.com

Public Company
Incorporated: 1986
Employees: 1,155
Sales: $281.9 million (2007)
Stock Exchanges: NASDAQ
Ticker Symbol: MDRX
NAICS: 541512 Computer Systems Design Services

■ ■ ■

Headquartered in Chicago, Allscripts-Misys Healthcare Solutions Inc., which does business under the simplified Allscripts brand name, is a provider of software, services, information, and connectivity solutions for physicians and other healthcare providers. From approximately 20 locations throughout the United States, the company's 2,500-member workforce serves a customer base that includes about 700 hospitals and more than 150,000 physicians, as well as thousands of clinics, home healthcare agencies, and postacute care facilities.

Allscripts is comprised of several main business units. The company's Professional Solutions unit provides a variety of business and clinical applications targeted toward small and midsized medical practices.

These include software devoted to document management, electronic prescribing, practice management, and electronic health records. The company's Enterprise Solutions unit provides similar applications for hospitals, academic medical centers, and large physician practices. Finally, the company's Health Systems Group offers home healthcare and referral management solutions for postacute healthcare providers, and care management systems for hospitals and emergency departments.

FORMATIVE YEARS

Allscripts was incorporated in 1986. During the company's early years, it repackaged pharmaceuticals and sold them to doctors who dispensed them to patients. A pivotal development in the company's history occurred in 1997, when Glen Tullman headed a group of investors that included Morgan Stanley Venture Partners and acquired a controlling stake in Allscripts.

A native of New Providence, New Jersey, Tullman earned an undergraduate degree in economics and psychology from Bucknell University and a master's degree from Oxford University. The youngest of six children, he eventually went to work for his brother, Howard, at a computer software company named CCC Information Services Group Inc. It was there that he learned important lessons about entrepreneurship and business. Following his career with CCC, Tullman became CEO of Enterprise Systems Inc., a provider of hospital operating room management software, which he took public and sold for $300 million in 1997. At

---

COMPANY PERSPECTIVES

■

Our mission is to be the clear leader in providing innovative software, connectivity and information solutions that empower physicians and other health care providers to improve the health of both their patients and their bottom line.

---

that time, Tullman also had his own venture capital company, named Alchemy Associates, and taught an entrepreneurship course at Harvard Business School.

Following Tullman's arrival, Allscripts shifted its focus away from repackaged pharmaceuticals and onto information technology products. This development came at a time when the Internet offered new opportunities for communicating with physicians and healthcare organizations. Midway through 1997, Allscripts merged with HBO & Co., and acquired the rights to its TouchScript system. On October 20, 1997, the company changed its name to Allscripts Inc.

In March 1999, Allscripts generated $15.4 million by selling some of its pharmacy benefit management assets in a deal with Pharmacare Direct Inc., Pharmacare Management Services Inc., and Procare Pharmacy Inc. In May, the company acquired TeleMed Corp., followed by the assets of Shopping@Home Inc. in June. In mid-1999 Allscripts reincorporated in Delaware and made an initial public offering of its common stock, which generated more than $100 million in July. In September of that year, the company unveiled a new wireless handheld prescribing device called the Personal Prescriber. By the end of the year, e-commerce had become a critical component of the operations of Allscripts. In the fourth quarter alone, e-commerce accounted for half of the company's revenue ($4.1 million), compared to 29 percent of revenue during the second quarter ($1.86 million).

Glen Tullman was honored with accounting firm KPMG's Illinois High Tech Award in November 1999. Under his watch, Allscripts had successfully introduced "point-of-care" electronic prescribing technology that allowed physicians to make prescriptions using mobile devices instead of paper pads. The company's systems sent prescriptions directly to pharmacies, cross-referenced them against patients' insurance plans in order to identify the most cost-effective options, and checked for potential drug interactions.

GROWTH THROUGH ACQUISITIONS

By the dawn of the 21st century, Allscripts employed a full-time workforce of 310 people. Of these, 132 worked in support and customer service. Another 56 were employed in general or administrative roles, 56 held sales and marketing positions, 31 were employed in production roles, and 24 worked in the area of product development. At this time, the company's corporate headquarters and repackaging facilities were based in Libertyville, Illinois, where the company leased an 80,000-square-foot facility. In addition, Allscripts also leased a smaller repackaging facility in Grayslake, Illinois.

In May 2000, Allscripts parted with $160.5 million to acquire Illinois-based Masterchart Inc., a software developer that provided dictation integration technology to approximately 100 healthcare industry customers nationwide. That same month, the company acquired Medifor Inc., a provider of online patient education, in a deal worth $34.4 million.

Allscripts kicked off 2001 by changing its name to Allscripts Healthcare Solutions Inc. on January 9. Another major acquisition occurred that month, when the company snapped up ChannelHealth Inc. from IDX Systems Corp. The deal, worth approximately $200 million, involved 8.6 million shares of Allscripts stock, as well as a ten-year strategic alliance with IDX.

By 2001 the company's technology was in place at approximately 3,500 locations throughout the United States and used by more than 13,500 physicians. In October of that year, the company announced one of the largest agreements in its history to date when the University of Minnesota Physicians chose to implement its TouchWorks clinical applications suite. The deal involved 1,800 users, some 450 of whom were physicians. The company rounded out 2001 with revenues of $78.8 million, an increase of 11 percent from the previous year.

In March 2002, Allscripts was named as technology leader Intel's top wireless solution provider for 2001. Growth continued the following year. By mid-2003, the company was serving a base of more than 20,000 physicians with a workforce of approximately 300 people.

In August 2003, Allscripts acquired the document imaging, scanning, and management software developer Advanced Imaging Concepts Inc. (AIC) in an $18.98 million deal. AIC's technology had been adopted by approximately 14,000 users at 250 locations in 40 states. It was also in August 2003 that Allscripts snapped up New York-based RxCentric Inc., a developer of sales and marketing solutions for the pharmaceutical industry. All-

KEY DATES

1986: Allscripts is incorporated as a pharmaceuticals repackager.

1997: Glen Tullman and a group of investors acquire a controlling stake in Allscripts and refocus the company on information technology products; the company changes its name to Allscripts Inc.

1999: Allscripts generates more than $100 million via an initial public offering of its common stock.

2001: The company changes its name to Allscripts Healthcare Solutions Inc.

2008: Allscripts merges with Misys Healthcare Systems LLC, becoming Allscripts-Misys Healthcare Solutions Inc.

scripts saw its revenues increase 9 percent in 2003, reaching $85.8 million. Although it had yet to record a profitable year, the company recorded its first profitable quarter, with net income of $0.1 million during the fourth quarter.

CONTINUED GROWTH

Allscripts continued to expand its customer base. In April 2004 the company announced a major deal with WellPoint Health Networks Inc., which tapped the company to provide software for its 19,000 physicians. WellPoint physicians in Wisconsin, California, Missouri, and Georgia were equipped with handheld computers and began using the company's TouchScript electronic medical record product. At this point in the company's history, Allscripts benefited from federal incentives that encouraged healthcare providers who received Medicare funding to implement electronic medical record systems. A major driver behind this philosophy was the goal of reducing medical errors.

In September 2004, Allscripts announced that it would enhance its TouchScripts.NET product by integrating drug reference information from the Chicago-based company Wolters Kluwer Health. Later that year, the company also unveiled Version 10 of its TouchWorks product. Several new features were added, including one that allowed doctors to customize patient chart views.

Allscripts kicked off 2006 with another major acquisition. In January, the company announced plans

to acquire A4 Health Systems Inc. The $283.78 million deal was completed in March and gave Allscripts a product named HealthMatics Electronic Health Record, which was targeted toward smaller and medium-sized physician practices. In addition, the acquisition of A4 Health allowed Allscripts to enter several new business areas, including information systems used by hospital emergency departments, as well as systems used for physician practice management.

More customer growth occurred in August 2006, when Riverside, California-based Riverside Physician Network chose the company's TouchWorks product to connect 200 physicians practicing in various locations. By this time the company faced growing competition. In addition to Madison, Wisconsin-based Epic Systems Corp., General Electric Co. and Cerner Corp. had both acquired businesses that operated in the same market as Allscripts.

During 2007, Allscripts saw the value of its stock drop 28 percent. Meeting market growth expectations had become more challenging as the company began selling more complicated systems to larger organizations, which in turn required more complex and lengthy training. Despite this challenge, positive developments continued. In December, Allscripts acquired Extended Care Information Network Inc. for $90 million.

MERGING WITH MISYS

By early 2008, Allscripts served a customer base that included more than 700 hospitals, 7,000 postacute and home care organizations, and 150,000 physicians. In January of that year, the company announced that its Allscripts Professional Electronic Health Record Version 8.2 had been certified by the Certification Committee for Healthcare Information Technology. The announcement of another major deal followed in March 2008, at which time Allscripts revealed plans to merge with the healthcare medical software subsidiary of United Kingdom-based Misys PLC.

Misys had industry roots stretching back to 1982. That year marked the establishment of Medic Computer Systems Inc., which the Misys Group of Companies acquired in November 1997 for $922.8 million. At the time of the deal, Riley, North Carolina-based Medic Computer Systems was one of the nation's five largest healthcare information technology companies, with a workforce of more than 1,400 people and approximately 10,000 active systems used by some 50,000 physicians.

Under the ownership of Misys, Medic Computer Systems began marketing practice management systems in the United States. A series of name changes followed, as the company adopted the name Medic Computer

Systems LLC in 2000 and then Misys Physician Systems LLC in 2002. It was also in 2002 that Home Care Information Systems was acquired, leading to the formation of a business unit named Misys Homecare, which marketed software and related services to the home healthcare, private duty, and hospice segments of the healthcare industry.

After selling its Physicians Interactive online clinical education business to the investment firm Perseus Acquisitions Holding LLC in September 2008, Allscripts stockholders approved the proposed merger with Misys. On October 10, 2008, Allscripts merged with Misys Healthcare Systems LLC, resulting in the formation of a new organization named Allscripts-Misys Healthcare Solutions Inc.

On April 2, 2009, Allscripts announced that it had forged an agreement to sell its Medication Services business to A-S Medical Solutions for approximately $26 million. It was also in April 2009 that Allscripts introduced an innovative new product called Allscripts Patient Kiosk. For use by physician practices, the device allowed patients to check in for their appointments, make co-payments, update personal information, and receive health alerts. In order to ensure security, the kiosks used Fujitsu PalmSecure technology, which verified identity by using the pattern of veins in a patient's palm.

Despite dire economic conditions during the later years of the decade, the future seemed bright for Allscripts. Over the course of several decades, the company had developed a leadership position in a highly specialized field. In addition, the American Recovery and Reinvestment Act of 2009, which was signed by President Barack Obama on February 17, 2009, continued to place importance on the use of electronic health records.

Paul R. Greenland

PRINCIPAL SUBSIDIARIES

A4 Health Systems Inc.; A4 Realty LLC; Allscripts LLC; Extended Care; Information Network Inc.; Misys Healthcare Systems LLC.

PRINCIPAL OPERATING UNITS

Professional Solutions; Enterprise Solutions; Health Systems Group.

PRINCIPAL COMPETITORS

HLTH Corporation; McKesson Corporation; ProxyMed Inc.

FURTHER READING

"Allscripts Inc. Prices Initial Public Offering," *PR Newswire,* July 26, 1999.

"Allscripts Stockholders Approve Misys Transaction Proposals," *PR Newswire,* October 6, 2008.

Colias, Mike, "Closing In on Allscripts; Rivals Moving into Market for Doctor's Office Software," *Crain's Chicago Business,* December 10, 2007.

———, "Shot in the Arm," *Crain's Chicago Business,* December 10, 2007.

"MISYS Plc and Medic Computer Systems, Inc., Announce the Proposed Acquisition of Medic Computer Systems Inc.," *PR Newswire,* September 5, 1997.

Wolinsky, Howard, "High-Tech Success Is All in the Family," *Chicago Sun-Times,* May 10, 2000.

Alon Israel Oil Company Ltd.

—————■—————

PO Box 10
Europark (France Building)
Kibbutz Yakum, 60972
Israel
Telephone: (972 09) 961 85 00
Fax: (972 09) 951 43 33
Web site: http://www.alon.co.il

Private Company
Incorporated: 1989
Sales: $3.54 billion (2008)
NAICS: 447110 Gasoline Stations with Convenience Stores; 424720 Petroleum and Petroleum Products Merchant Wholesalers (Except Bulk Stations and Terminals); 445110 Supermarkets and Other Grocery (except Convenience) Stores

■ ■ ■

Alon Israel Oil Company Ltd. is a privately held holding company with operations in three areas: Energy in the United States; Energy in Israel; and Retail in Israel. The group's U.S. operations are carried out through Alon USA Energy and its retail subsidiary Alon Brands Inc., both of which are separately listed on the New York Stock Exchange. Alon USA Energy operates three petroleum refineries in Texas and California, as well as an asphalt refinery in Oregon. Most of the group's fuel output is used to supply the company's network of 1,100 Fina service stations, primarily in the southwestern region. Through Alon Brands, the company is also the largest franchise operator of

7-Eleven stores in the United States, with more than 300 convenience stores in Texas and New Mexico. Most of these stores operate as part of the group's service station network.

In Israel, Alon's Energy in Israel division operates through Dor Alon Energy, listed on the Tel Aviv Stock Exchange. Dor Alon operates 170 public service stations throughout Israel, supplies private fueling stations located at the country's kibbutz and moshav cooperatives, and is the only Israeli supplier of petroleum products to the Palestinian Territories. Dor Alon also operates the 91-strong network of Alonit and Super Alonit convenience stores. Alon's Retail in Israel division includes its 70 percent stake in Blue Square Israel (BSI), the New York and Tel Aviv operator of supermarkets under the Mega, Mega in Town, Shefa Shuk, and AMPM names. BSI also controls the Central Warehouse/Toy Village chain of general merchandise shops, and holds the Israeli franchise for the Pizza Hut and KFC restaurants chains. This division also includes publicly listed Blue Square Real Estate, which serves as the property arm for the BSI supermarket group.

Alon Israel Oil Company Ltd. started out with a single service station in 1989; 20 years later, the group's total revenues were estimated at more than $4 billion. Alon is controlled by founder and chairman David Wiessman, through Bielsol Ltd., the real estate investment group established by Wiessman and cousin Shraggi Biran. Other major shareholders include the kibbutz movement and the Africa Israel investment group.

COMPANY PERSPECTIVES

Vision: Our goal is to become a significant player in the international energy and retail markets in which we operate and to increase value for our shareholders through sustained earnings and cash flow growth. We are working to achieve this objective through: 1) Acquisitions of businesses which are within the scope of our operations, and businesses which are complementary to our retail and energy segments, with a potential for generating cash flow. 2) Geographic diversification outside of the United States and Israel in order to take advantage of opportunities in attractive retail and energy markets such as Europe. We also plan on utilizing our management's extensive knowledge in real estate in order to extend our Israeli real estate activities, primarily to the United States and/or Europe. 3) Implementing projects designed to accommodate the organic growth of our subsidiaries, such as increasing the production at our refineries and opening new supermarkets and retail outlets.

PETROLEUM DEREGULATION IN ISRAEL

Alon Israel Oil Company was established in 1989 when the ten regional bodies coordinating the activities of the country's 300 kibbutz communities joined together to take advantage of the deregulation of Israel's fuel and gasoline market. At the time, the Israeli fuel sector was dominated by a cartel established among three companies, Delek, Sonol, and Paz. The cartel established fixed market shares, of 25, 30, and 45 percent respectively. The three companies also dominated the service station sector by binding service station owners to long-term exclusive contracts of up to 30 years. The deregulation set out to break up the cartel, as well as to void many of the long-term service station contracts.

For the kibbutzim, deregulation represented a number of important opportunities. The kibbutzim would acquire control of supplying the substantial gasoline and fuel needs of the country. Moreover, the presence of kibbutzim along most of Israel's major roads offered the potential for establishing a kibbutz-owned string of service stations. Alon (the Hebrew word for "oak") initially focused on developing a network of private service stations serving the kibbutz and moshav settlements. In 1992, however, Alon decided to take the leap into ownership of public service stations. For this,

Alon turned to two up-and-coming entrepreneurs, cousins Shraggi Biran and David Wiessman.

Biran, the elder of the two, was ten years old when his parents and brother were murdered during the Holocaust. Biran survived for more than two years in the frozen woods in the region between Poland and Ukraine, and then fought alongside the Soviet forces during the liberation. After the war, Biran came to Israel, where he joined a kibbutz. However, Biran became an avid Marxist and was expelled from the kibbutz when he began to identify with the Israeli Communist Party. Biran, who went on to become a lawyer, nevertheless remained close to the kibbutz movement.

When Jerusalem became part of Israel following the Six Day War in 1967, Biran joined in the resulting construction boom of Greater Jerusalem. Biran became instrumental in negotiating the rights to build many of the new neighborhoods, such as Pisgat Ze'ev and Har Nof, created during the 1970s. This experience became an important tool for the kibbutz movement as well. Through the 1980s and into the 1990s, Biran played an instrumental role in the massive rezoning drive that allowed the country's kibbutzim and moshavim to develop their properties into high-profile residential and other construction projects. Along the way, Biran, who remained a committed Marxist, became one of Israel's wealthiest people.

ACQUIRING ALON

Biran's involvement in Israel's fuel and gasoline sector began during the mid-1970s, when he joined the family-held real estate investment company, Bielsol Ltd. There, Biran worked alongside his younger cousin David "Dudi" Wiessman, who had become Bielsol's chief executive in 1976 at the age of 21, following his service in the Israeli Air Force. Bielsol's main holding was the service station operated by Wiessman's father and uncle.

Biran and Wiessman took over the family business in 1981. Wiessman soon displayed his entrepreneurial flair, as the company acquired a property in Yavne and launched the development of a new type of service station. In addition to providing gasoline pumps, Wiessman and Biran designed the site as a full-scale commercial complex, with retail shops, a restaurant, and an office complex. This combination of fuel and retail was to become a hallmark of Wiessman's future business empire.

Yavne was at the time a small town far from Israel's main population centers. However, Bielsol recognized the town's potential as a hub between the Port of Ashdod, six miles to the south, and Tel Aviv, 25 miles to the

KEY DATES

1976: David Wiessman and cousin Shraggi Biran join Bielsol, an investment company held by their families.

1981: Wiessman and Biran take over operations of the family's service station.

1988: Dor Energy is founded to take advantage of energy market deregulation in Israel.

1989: Alon Israel Oil Company is founded by the kibbutz movement to enter the oil marketing sector.

1992: Bielsol acquires 50 percent of Alon Israel Oil Company.

1999: Alon Israel acquires control of Dor Energy.

2000: Alon acquires the U.S. refinery and service station assets of TotalFinaElf, which becomes Alon USA.

2003: Alon acquires control of the Blue Square Israel (BSI) retail group.

2009: Alon USA creates a retail subsidiary, Alon Brands, which lists on the New York Stock Exchange.

north. This led the company to invest in a second service station in Yavne, as well as contributing to the construction of a central bus station. Bielsol remained a tiny operation nonetheless, numbering just ten employees into the early 1990s. This was to change in 1992, when Biran, by then in the process of transforming the kibbutz movement through his rezoning efforts, negotiated an agreement through which Bielsol acquired 50 percent of Alon Israel Oil.

Wiessman took over as head of Alon Israel Oil and began plotting the transformation of the group from its focus on the kibbutz and moshav communities to the creation of its own network of public service stations. Toward this end, Wiessman sought to bring in additional investment capital. This came in 1993 in the form of Africa Israel Investments, another prominent Israeli real estate and investment group, which acquired a 26 percent stake in the company. Bielsol remained Alon's largest shareholder, with a 40 percent stake, while the kibbutz movement held 34 percent.

DOR ENERGY ACQUIRED

As Biran negotiated the rezoning of the kibbutz and moshav properties, Wiessman set out to challenge the

Israeli retail gasoline sector, which remained dominated by three companies, Delek, Sonol, and Paz. Wiessman began offering gasoline at a substantial discount in contrast to Alon's competitors, which had long maintained a policy of charging the maximum prices permitted by Israeli regulations. Alon also differentiated itself through its strong commitment to service as well as quality and cleanliness. The company set out to expand on Wiessman's concept of combining retail operations with filling stations, adding shopping malls, restaurants, convenience stores, and supermarkets to its sites.

Alon began developing its own convenience store format, Alonit, which later grew into Israel's largest. During the 1990s, Alon picked up a number of restaurant franchises, including the Pizza Hut, Burger King, and KFC franchises, as well as a 50 percent stake in a franchise operating Segafredo coffee shops in Israel. Also during the 1990s, Alon joined the consortium that won the bid to build the Cross-Israel Highway, as well as to operate the service stations along the completed toll road. Alon nevertheless remained a bit player in the Israeli service station sector during the 1990s. Toward the end of the decade, the company's market share barely exceeded 2 percent. However, this was to change in 1999, with the acquisition of Dor Energy Ltd.

Dor Energy had been founded in 1988 by the Dankner family in anticipation of the coming deregulation of the Israeli energy sector. Dor received its license to market fuel and gasoline products that year, but was required to wait until 1990 before the deregulation finally got under way. By the end of that year, the company had three service stations under its control. Like Alon, Dor entered head-to-head competition with the sector's "Big Three" by offering lower prices at the pumps and easier terms to its industrial customers.

A PERIOD OF GROWTH

Dor Energy's industrial supply wing took off strongly and by 1991 the company claimed a 10 percent share of the Israeli market. In that year, Dor Energy decided to bring in a foreign investor in order to increase its financial clout and raise its international profile. This led the company to sign an agreement with Shamrock Holdings, controlled by Roy Disney of the Walt Disney Company, which acquired a 33.5 percent stake in Dor. The company then announced plans to open 11 more service stations over the next year. In 1994, the Israeli government continued its reform of the energy sector, passing new rules that made it easier for operators to open new service stations. By then, the country was estimated to need between 200 and 300 new service stations in order to meet the rising demand from motorists.

Dor Energy also began exploring new markets. In 1994, the company signed an agreement with the Palestinian Authority to take over the supply of service stations in the autonomous regions. This move directly challenged the Padesco monopoly set up among Delek, Sonol, and Paz for control of the energy supply market in the Palestinian Territories. Similarly, Alon Israel reached an agreement with Jordanian company Triangle to set up eight service stations, including four in Jordan and four in the West Bank. Meanwhile, by the end of that year, Alon's Israeli network had grown to 15 stations.

The acquisition of Dor Energy not only doubled Alon's service station network, it also boosted the company's total market share in the fuel sector to 20 percent. Alon initially acquired 65 percent of publicly listed Dor Energy. In 2001, Alon completed the acquisition of 100 percent of Dor Energy, which was then delisted from the Tel Aviv exchange. In 2004, the two companies were merged together to form Dor Alon Energy. This merger came as part of an overall restructuring of Alon's operations, which resulted in the transformation of Alon Israel Oil Company into an international holding company. This restructuring had become necessary because of Alon's dramatic growth since the dawn of the new century into a major player in the Israeli retail sector, as well as a fast-growing player in the U.S. oil refinery sector.

NEW MARKETS IN THE 21ST CENTURY

Alon had joined a number of Israeli corporations seeking expansion into the United States at the beginning of the 21st century. Alon in particular recognized the opportunity to bring its expertise in service station operations to the United States. This led the company to reach an agreement in 2000 to buy the U.S. operations of the recently created TotalFinaElf, including its Big Spring refinery in Texas and more than 1,000 Fina service stations, primarily in Texas and other southwestern states. The U.S. business was then renamed as Alon USA Inc. Alon USA soon expanded, buying Southwest Convenience Stores, the largest operator of 7-Eleven convenience stores in the United States, in 2001. The purchase added another 300 sites, many including service stations, to the group's Fina service station operations. In that year, Alon USA went public, listing on the New York Stock Exchange.

Alon USA grew strongly over the next several years. The company added new refineries in Texas and California in 2006 through the acquisitions of Paramount Petroleum Corporation and Edgington Oil Company. The Paramount purchase also gave the company an asphalt refinery in Oregon. In 2008, the group added a new refinery, the Krotz Springs Refinery in Texas, boosting its capacity by 50 percent. Alon USA also expanded its retail operations, buying 40 El Paso-based convenience stores from Good Times Stores, Inc., for $27 million in 2006, and then buying Abilene-based Skinny's Inc. That company owned and operated 102 Fina convenience stores and service stations. The new stores were then converted to the 7-Eleven format. The growth of the group's U.S. retail holdings led the company to create a new subsidiary for them, Alon Brands, which was listed on the New York Stock Exchange in 2009.

Retail also became a growth market for Alon Israel back at home during the first decade of the new century. In 2003, the company reached an agreement to acquire majority control of Blue Square Israel (BSI), one of the country's top two retail groups. Under Alon, BSI began its own growth drive, leading to the acquisition of the AMPM supermarket group in 2006. That chain operated 21 stores, and had pioneered the 24-hour retail market in Israel. Alon then declared its intention to add another 20 AMPM stores before 2010.

In 2007, BSI acquired 51 percent of Eden Teva Market Ltd., which had developed a health food store format that BSI planned to expand into a network of up to 40 stores. Alon expanded its Israeli retail operations again in 2008, when it raised its control of Bee Group Retail (acquired as part of the BSI purchase) and its discount goods and retail toy stores to 85 percent. During this time, Alon Dor made its own expansion moves. In early 2009, for example, the company reached an agreement to buy 16 gas stations from Kliot Energy Ltd.

By this time, David Wiessman had received recognition for his success in building Alon Israel into a major Israeli player in both the retail and energy sectors; he was named Israel's Man of the Year at the annual Israeli Business Conference in 2005. From a single service station, Wiessman had built a major multinational company with revenues estimated at more than $4 billion.

M. L. Cohen

PRINCIPAL SUBSIDIARIES

Alon Brands Inc.; Alon Energy Inc. (USA); Alon Intrade Coffee Shops (Segafredo) Ltd.; Blue Square Israel Ltd. (70%); Blue Square Real Estate Ltd. (80%); Diners Club Israel Ltd. (37.75%); Dor Alon Energy in Israel

(1988) Ltd. (90%); Dor Alon Fuel Station Operation Ltd.; Dor Alon Gas Technologies Ltd.; Edgington Oil Company (USA); Paramount Petroleum Corporation (USA); Pizza Hut LLP; S.D. LUL Food (KFC) Ltd. (70%); Southwest Convenience Stores (USA).

PRINCIPAL DIVISIONS

USA Energy; Israel Retail; Israel Energy.

PRINCIPAL COMPETITORS

Exxon Mobil Corporation; Murphy Oil Corporation; Speedway SuperAmerica L.L.C.; AutoNation Inc.; Pilot Corporation; Flying J Inc.; BP Oil Co.; Sinclair Oil Corporation.

FURTHER READING

"Alon Gets into Supermarket Business," *NPN International,* November–December 2002, p. 8.

"Alon Takes over 147 Texas Service Stations," *NPN International,* July 2001, p. 8.

"Alon Triangle Gas Station Partnership," *Israel Business Today,* October 28, 1994, p. 11.

"Alon USA's Wiessman Israel's 'Man of the Year,'" *National Petroleum News,* January 2006, p. 10.

Baron, Lior, "Dor Alon Beats Sonol in Gas Stations Bid," *Globes,* January 26, 2009.

Bergman, Rose, "Blue Square Eyes Haredi Market with Appointment," *Globes,* April 7, 2009.

"Fina's Israeli Parent Company Steps up Search for US Refinery," *Oil Express,* December 9, 2002, p. 5.

"Gov't Won't Allow Dor Alon Oil Refineries Deal," *Israel Business Arena,* June 4, 2006.

Hayut, Ilanit, "Alon Group Buys Further Stake in Retailer," *Globes,* August 3, 2008.

"IPO for Alon C-stores to Come," *Convenience Store News,* December 10, 2008.

Lofstock, John, "A New Player on the Field," *Convenience Store News,* June 25, 2001, p. 24.

Priel, Aaron, "Blue Square Israel to Launch Health Food Chain," *just-food.com,* September 3, 2007.

———, "Bronfman-Alon Group Eyes US Supermarket Chain," *just-food.com,* October 22, 2004.

———, "Dor Alon Acquires AMPM Retail Business," *just-food.com,* November 7, 2006.

Shuster, Uri, and Roy Melzer, "Alon Israel Oil to Raise $500m in NYSE IPO," *Globes,* July 17, 2007.

"Smarts Not Size Bring Success," *World Refining,* January–February 2004, p. 44.

American Equipment Company, Inc.

———■———

2106 Anderson Road
Greenville, South Carolina 29611-6013
U.S.A.
Telephone: (864) 295-7800
Fax: (864) 295-7343
Web site: http://www.ameco.com

Wholly Owned Subsidiary of Fluor Corporation
Incorporated: 1971 as American Equipment Company, Inc.
Employees: 1,600
Sales: $550 million (2008)
NAICS: 423810 Construction and Mining (Except Petroleum) Machinery and Equipment Wholesalers; 532412 Construction, Mining, and Forestry Machinery and Equipment Rental and Leasing; 811310 Commercial and Industrial Machinery and Equipment (Except Automotive and Electronic) Repair and Maintenance

■ ■ ■

American Equipment Company, Inc., (AMECO) is a leading provider of mobile equipment and tools for construction and industry. AMECO has been ranked one of the 15 largest equipment rental firms in the United States. The company prefers to become involved in large projects early in the planning stages and supplies a very wide range of tools and materials. It is active in the construction, government, industrial, mining, and oil-drilling markets. AMECO operates globally and owns dealerships in Canada and Latin America. It is a unit of Fluor Corporation, the *Fortune* 500 construction and engineering giant based in Irving, Texas.

POSTWAR ORIGINS

AMECO began as the warehouse operations of one of the predecessors of Fluor Corporation: Daniel Construction Company of Greenville, South Carolina. AMECO counts 1947 as its launch date; it may have started even earlier as the company arranged for storage of massive amounts of equipment returning from World War II military projects. A warehouse built on Greenville's Piedmont Road became the original base for what would become AMECO.

Daniel Construction grew rapidly in the 1950s and 1960s as it built up the textile, paper, and electricity industries in the South and beyond. By 1972 it had 23,000 employees and was involved in projects around the world. Daniel International Corporation was formed on March 1, 1971 as a holding company for Daniel Construction and related businesses.

The warehouse unit had been growing too and after a few years as a division of Daniel Construction, led by Earle Daniel, AMECO was incorporated in South Carolina on December 30, 1971, as American Equipment Company, Inc. An early acquisition added Raleigh, South Carolina's Southern Industrial Supply Company; AMECO soon had branches throughout the South.

AMECO was led by P. C. Gregory III throughout the 1970s. It operated as part of the Daniel International's Industrial Services Group (the other main component being Daniel Construction Company).

The Tool Service Company affiliate was started in 1975. In 1977 AMECO's parent company, Daniel International, was acquired by Fluor Corporation. Six years later AMECO absorbed its internal FluorPort equipment division.

A CHANGING BUSINESS

Comprehensive shifts in the makeup of AMECO's business were taking place. AMECO had apparently offered limited equipment sales and rentals to the public even before it became an independent company. After years of being almost totally dependent on its parent companies, in 1987 AMECO began doing third-party work in earnest with the addition of Ogden Martin to its clientele.

AMECO also ventured into international markets, joining a local construction boom in Puerto Rico in 1989. Six years later, the company expanded its Latin American presence into Mexico, Argentina, and Chile. It entered the Canadian market in 1990. AMECO launched a formal safety program in 1991. It became ISO-9002 certified in 1994, the first among its U.S. peers to do so.

A mid-1990s expansion into the Pacific, with operations in the Philippines and Indonesia, was scrapped after just a few years in the face of the Asian financial crisis. AMECO continued to set up international offices where conditions warranted, in Jamaica in 2000 and the Middle East, including Iraq, in 2003.

Fluor Corporation executive Thomas J. Putman presided over much of this transformation as CEO of AMECO from 1990 to 1997. He would be tapped to lead rival NationsRent, Inc., through its bankruptcy reorganization a few years later.

ACQUISITION DRIVE

In the mid-1990s AMECO launched an acquisition spree focused on North America. One of the larger buys came in 1997 with the acquisition of several large U.S. equipment dealership chains from Kinnevik AB. The two companies each operated several locations in California (SMA Equipment Co., Inc.) and Georgia (SMA Stith Equipment Co., Inc.).

Also in 1997, AMECO bought S&R Equipment Co., Inc., of Toledo, Ohio, which specialized in lift equipment. Founded in 1957, S&R had 155 employees and rental revenues of $30 million a year. It was sold in 2002 to United Rentals, Inc.

In June 1997 AMECO acquired a controlling interest in Maquinaria Panamericana, S.A. de C.V. (MAPSA), from the Mexican construction and engineering company Grupo ICA. MAPSA sold and rented several leading makes of construction equipment. AMECO had opened an office in Monterrey, Mexico, several years earlier and was expanding southward for strategic reasons. AMECO also acquired the fleet of ICA/FD, a partnership between Group ICA and Fluor.

J. W. Burress Inc. of Roanoke, Virginia, was added in July 1997. The family-owned company, formed in the 1930s, sold, leased, and repaired equipment in three states. It employed roughly 135 people in eight offices.

Leaving the mid-1990s, AMECO had 900 employees at 55 locations. A quarter of them were located at its Greenville headquarters or elsewhere in South Carolina.

ON THE BLOCK

While pursuing its acquisition drive, AMECO was put up for sale by its corporate parent. In March 1998 Fluor told shareholders it was looking to sell the excellent-performing company because it believed AMECO would be worth more to shareholders as an independent entity. The plan was to use the proceeds to buy back Fluor stock while prices were low. An unnamed buyer emerged, but the deal was ultimately scrapped over a last-minute change in terms following share price fluctuations.

The Asian economic crisis of the late 1990s stalled many of Fluor's commercial and infrastructure projects. As a result the company launched a restructuring that cut 5,000 workers from its global payroll of 57,000. Operating as a unit of Fluor Global Services, in 1999 the AMECO unit had more than 2,000 employees around the world working out of 65 of its own locations or on clients' sites. It was a top ten firm according to *Rental Equipment Register* in 2001, due to its 1999 rental volume of $167 million in North America, where it still derived the bulk of its business.

KEY DATES

Mid-1940s: Daniel Construction sets up warehouse unit to store equipment returning from wartime projects.

1971: American Equipment Company, Inc., (AMECO) becomes a separate corporation.

1977: Fluor Corporation acquires AMECO's parent, Daniel International.

1983: AMECO absorbs the FluorPort equipment division.

1987: The company begins doing third-party work in earnest.

1989: AMECO begins competing internationally.

1994: AMECO is the first U.S. equipment rental firm to attain ISO-9002 certification.

1998: Fluor considers selling the profitable AMECO unit to prop up its own share price in the midst of the Asian financial crisis.

2000: AMECO is restructured into Fleet Outsourcing and Site Services divisions.

2007: AMECO celebrates its 60th anniversary and 16 million safe hours.

NEW STRATEGIES

In 1999 a new branding campaign was unveiled based around the company's acronym, AMECO. There were more substantial changes in store. The next year, the company was restructured into Fleet Outsourcing (which later became Fleet Services) and Site Services divisions.

This coincided with a new strategic emphasis in 2000. Following Fluor's shifting priorities, AMECO, led by a new executive team, started to focus more on return on equity rather than just the top line and market share growth that had been the apparent aim of its acquisition drive. Most of AMECO's equipment dealerships were transferred to Fluor to be divested. The company exited Asia and scaled back its South American operations to Chile.

The new divisions resulted from the goal of more comprehensive involvement in clients' projects, getting "inside the fence" in the planning stages rather than waiting passively outside for orders, President Gary C. Bernardez explained to *Rental Equipment Register* in 2001. Site Services expanded the range of offerings from heavy equipment to the totality of indirect supplies, including items as varied as hand tools, safety glasses, and scaffolding. Fleet Outsourcing courted end users

(typically in mining, energy, and telecommunications), promising to lower overall costs by outsourcing equipment fleets. AMECO was also investigating opportunities to take over warehousing and tool management functions.

AMECO tapped new technologies to manage such ambitious undertakings. For example, it kept track of tools distributed among hundreds or thousands of workers at job sites by marking the tools with invisible ink and sorting them in radio-frequency-tagged bins. AMECO used such data gathering to plan its equipment maintenance.

According to Bernardez, the souring economy made increased outsourcing especially relevant, as construction companies sought to minimize the colossal capital expenditures associated with large projects. According to industry sources, in 2008 AMECO owned about $500 million worth of equipment (compared to the multibillion-dollar fleets of industry leaders such as Sunbelt Rentals, Inc.). It continued to own dealerships in Canada and Latin America, including Mexico's largest dealership for Case Corporation agricultural and construction equipment. An AMECO official told the *Engineering News-Record* in 2009 that the bulk of its 11,000-piece equipment fleet was made up of Ford pickup trucks.

INCREASINGLY INTERNATIONAL

The company's business underwent a dramatic shift within a few years, noted the 2009 *Engineering News-Record* article. As late as 2003 Fluor-managed domestic projects made up the bulk of AMECO's business. By 2009 AMECO was deriving 80 percent of its trade outside the United States, working mostly for outside clients.

Revenues reached $580 million in 2006; a profile of the company several years later, as the global economy was in the throes of a severe recession, pegged the figure at $550 million. AMECO had logged 16 million safe hours over the previous six years. By 2009 the figure was up to 26 million hours. The international thrust of the company was evident in new projects in Chile, Madagascar, and Russia. AMECO's new role as a total jobsite provider was working even in the difficult economic environment, according to Bernardez in the 2009 *Engineering News-Record* article.

Frederick C. Ingram

PRINCIPAL SUBSIDIARIES

AMECO PANAMA S.A.; AMECO Services Inc.; Ameco Services, S. de R.L. de C.V. (72.6%; Mexico);

American Construction Equipment Company, Inc.; BWJ, LLC; Palmetto Seed Capital Ltd. Partnership (7.35%); SMA Equipment, LLC; Vantage Information Systems, Inc.

PRINCIPAL DIVISIONS

Site Services; Fleet Services; Equipment Distribution.

PRINCIPAL COMPETITORS

United Rentals Inc.; Hertz Equipment Rental Corporation; Rental Service Corporation; NES Rentals Holdings, Inc.; Sunbelt Rentals, Inc.

FURTHER READING

"AMECO Mexico Is Major Merger Success Story," *Advantage,* June 2003, pp. 2, 7.

"American Equipment Co. Stresses Zero-Injury Performance," *Construction Equipment Distribution,* April 1, 1999.

Canup, C. R., and W. D. Workman Jr., *Charles E. Daniel: His Philosophy and Legacy,* Columbia, S.C.: R. L. Bryan, 1981.

DuPlessis, Jim, "Fluor Mulls Sale of Greenville Subsidiary," *Greenville News,* December 16, 1997, p. 1A.

Fluor Corporation, "Fluor to Pursue Transactional Options of American Equipment Company," *Business Wire,* March 9, 1998.

"Fluor Might Divest Ameco Rental Dealerships," *Rental Equipment Register,* January 1, 2001.

"Fluor Yanks Spinoff Plan," *Financial Post* (Toronto), Sec. 1, October 8, 1998, p. 20.

Latta, John, "All That Glitters Is Not Sold … (Sometimes It's Rented)," *RentSmart!,* August 2001, pp. 38–42.

Pollack, Andrew, "Fluor to Cut 5,000 Jobs and Reorganize Operations," *New York Times,* March 10, 1999, p. C2.

Roth, Michael, "Inside the Gate," *Rental Equipment Register,* October 1, 2002, p. 10.

Van Hampton, Tudor, "As Builders Farm Out the Fleet, AMECO Tightens Its Iron Grip," *Engineering News-Record,* April 15, 2009, p. 20.

———, "Brothers Have More in Common Than a Passion for Iron," *Engineering News-Record,* August 16, 2004, p. 26.

———, "New Influx of Field Data Reveals the Cost of Ownership; Construction Machine Owners Are Revving Up for Real-Time Analytics," *Engineering News-Record,* August 16, 2004, p. 24.

Áreas S.A.

Via Augusta 21-23, Planta 6
Barcelona, E-08006
Spain
Telephone: (34 93) 240 15 15
Fax: (34 93) 240 15 18
Web site: http://www.areas.es

Private Company
Incorporated: 1968
Employees: 12,000
Sales: EUR 720 million ($900 million) (2008 est.)
NAICS: 722110 Full-Service Restaurants

■ ■ ■

Áreas S.A. focuses on providing travel hospitality and related services at airports, train stations, freeways and highways, shopping malls, hotels, and downtown locations. The company operates restaurants, retail shops and kiosks, hotels, and service stations in Spain, the United States, Mexico, Portugal, Chile, Argentina, Morocco, St. Martin, and the Dominican Republic. Spain, where the group is the market leader, remains the group's largest area of operation, accounting for 75 percent of its EUR 720 million ($900 million) in revenues in 2008. Áreas's operations span more than 100 brands, including Ars, As Hotel, Café Café, Divers, La Pausa, LDF, Medas, Minimarket, and Sibarium. The company's operations span nearly 1,200 locations.

Airports represent the group's largest business unit, accounting for 51 percent of sales. With more than 475 concessions, Áreas is the world's third largest airport concessions operator. Highways add 31 percent, while train stations and others, including city center locations and hotel concessions, make up 18 percent. Restaurant operations account for the largest share of these businesses, generating 62 percent of sales, followed by retail at 29 percent, with accommodations and other services contributing 9 percent. Áreas operates as part of a strategic partnership with France's Elior, which owns, directly and indirectly, nearly 70 percent of the company. The other major shareholder in the group is Emesa S.L. Áreas is led by CEO Bernardo Vázquez and Chairman Emilio Cuatrecasas.

ORIGINS IN CATALONIAN CONCESSIONS

Áreas was founded in 1968 in order to oversee the network of service stations along highways in the Catalonian region of Northern Spain. At first the company's operations were limited largely to a coordinating role, subcontracting out most of the operations, including accommodations and fuel supply, to third parties. In the middle of the 1970s, however, the company decided to take a more active role. Starting in 1975, the company began adding its own restaurant, hotel, service station, and retail operations. This expansion also enabled the company to compete for concessions along the numerous new highways being built in the region during this period.

The company launched its own restaurant format, called Pransor, featuring cafeteria-style service, in 1976. Áreas also targeted expansion beyond Catalonia, in 1978 gaining the contract to provide service concessions along

COMPANY PERSPECTIVES

Mission: Áreas is a private company formed by highly professional people whose mission is to provide integrated and top quality services to the traveler, while maximizing value for our shareholders, the stakeholders and society. Vision: To be globally recognized as one of the leading providers and operators of Food & Beverage and Retail services to the travel industry. Values: In order to achieve the target of our mission efficiently, we have established a set of corporate values and principles with the aim of offering the best product and excellent services to our customers and to continually strive for improvement.

the highway linking the Basque and Aragon regions. At the same time, the company had been exploring the potential for extending its range of services into other transportation markets. This led to the group's first railway station concessions in 1979.

Through the 1980s, the company's operations remained limited to Spain's northern regions. The company nevertheless began to look beyond Spain's borders with the concession to operate services at La Jonquera, also known as the Porta Catalan, on the French border. The company's first international extension came in 1992, with the launch of operations in Antua, Portugal.

Áreas in the meantime had begun developing a number of new concession brands. The company launched a new retail concept, called Divers, in 1989. Featuring a wide range of products, the first Divers store opened that year, representing the company's entry into the retail distribution market. Áreas also began positioning itself for other transportation markets in the 1990s. By 1992, the company had won its first airport concessions, rolling out the Divers brand for this market as well. The company's expertise in service station operations along Spain's provincial highways also made it a leading contender in the bid for concessions along the country's state-owned highways. Áreas won its first concession in this market in 1995.

More retail and restaurant formats followed in the middle of the decade. In 1995, the company debuted a new bakery shop, called Café Café. The following year, Áreas debuted a new all-in-one service station concept, called Ars. The new format combined retail, restaurant, and rest facilities into a single package. The first Ars sta-

tion opened at Los Monegros in 1996. Also in that year, the company created a joint venture with Renfe, called Arco Duplo, which began operating bar and restaurant concessions in Spain's train stations. The company added another new brand in 1997, debuting its La Pausa restaurant format.

GEOGRAPHIC EXPANSION

The Arco brand also proved to be the group's ticket to wider geographic expansion. In 1998, the company entered a partnership with Chilean oil company Copec to open a chain of 19 concessions in that country. In that year, the company also made two acquisitions in Spain, of General de Restaurantes, and of Serausa, which held the service station concession for Spain's A-9 freeway.

Áreas continued to build strongly as the new century dawned. The group entered Morocco in 1999, buying that country's ATASA and its network of 20 airport concessions. Áreas's thriving Chilean business also enabled it to move into neighboring Argentina. The company took its first step into this new and larger market, opening a Café Café store in Buenos Aires in 1999. The company quickly moved to solidify its presence in Argentina, buying a 75 percent stake in that country's Multimarca in 2000. In Spain, the group acquired 27 percent and management control of fast-food chain Carmen La Comida in 2000.

In order to achieve its increasingly international objectives, Áreas sought out a larger partner. In 2001, the company reached a partnership agreement with France's Elior. Under that agreement, Elior directly acquired 44 percent of Áreas, and indirectly added another 25 percent through a joint venture with Áreas's major shareholder, the steel group Emesa. In exchange, Elior turned over its own Spanish restaurant and related concessions. In this way, Áreas then became the undisputed leader in the Spanish concession services market.

With the backing of the larger French group, Áreas continued its international expansion. The company moved into Mexico in 2001, buying Latinoamerica de Duty Free, which held the duty-free retail concessions in 13 airports in that country. The acquisition, which cost Áreas EUR 98 million, gave it a network of 150 stores in Mexico. By then, Áreas had also stepped up its presence in Argentina, winning the contract to manage retail and restaurant concessions for 16 airports there, including the country's two major international airports in Buenos Aires. By the end of the year, Áreas had added its first airport concessions in Chile as well.

```
┌─────────────────────────────────────────────┐
│                                               │
│              KEY DATES                        │
│                  ■                            │
│                                               │
│  1968:  Áreas is founded in order to provide  │
│         management services to service        │
│         stations in the Catalonian region     │
│         of Spain.                             │
│  1975:  Áreas begins direct operations of      │
│         restaurants, hotels, and filling      │
│         stations.                             │
│  1978:  Áreas expands beyond the Catalonian    │
│         region and extends its operations      │
│         to include train stations.            │
│  1992:  Áreas enters airport concessions       │
│         market in Spain and adds first        │
│         international concessions in           │
│         Portugal.                             │
│  1999:  Áreas enters the Chilean market.       │
│  2001:  Áreas reaches a partnership agreement  │
│         with France's Elior, which becomes     │
│         the company's major shareholder;      │
│         Áreas enters the Mexican airport        │
│         concessions market.                   │
│  2006:  Áreas adds first airport concessions   │
│         in the United States, at Miami         │
│         International Airport.                 │
│  2008:  The company's U.S. operations extend   │
│         to Boston, Indianapolis, San Jose,    │
│         Atlanta, and Detroit.                 │
│                                               │
└─────────────────────────────────────────────┘
```

TARGETING THE U.S. MARKET

Áreas continued to build its operations through the first half of the decade. The company added 26 new restaurants in five airports in Mexico's Centro Norte region in 2002. Áreas also launched operations in the Dominican Republic that year. In Portugal, the group acquired two companies, Unitrato and Estagest, giving it 14 new concessions at the Lisbon and Oporto airports. In Chile, the group's Arco joint venture merged with Prime, an operator of city-center filling stations, adding that new market. The company also added 17 concessions at the Fira (Fair) de Barcelona in 2003. The company's international operations then gained a new market in 2006, when the company took over the network of 13 Shipwreck shops on the island of St. Martin.

During the decade, Áreas also expanded its range of brands, developing such formats as Tendido O, Stretto, Eat & Go, Tuareg Café, La Piazzeta, Meal o'clock, and Sibarium. The company also celebrated the renewal of its most important concession, for Barcelona's Barajas Airport, in 2003. This concession was extended in 2006 with the construction of 27 restaurants and five retail shops for that airport's new T4 terminal.

Áreas had also been eyeing an entry into another and still more important market, the United States. This goal was accomplished in 2006, when Áreas won its bid to operate 12 restaurants at Miami International Airport. The contract proved to be a foothold for the company's new U.S. subsidiary, Áreas USA, to extend its operations into other major U.S. cities. In 2007, Áreas received concessions to operate six restaurants in the Orlando airport and 16 restaurants in the Detroit airport. These contracts were shortly followed by a concession in the Indianapolis International Airport in 2008. By the end of 2008, Áreas had added several more U.S. cities, including Boston's Logan airport, a concession to run 30 retail shops in Atlanta's airport, and concessions in the San Jose airport.

While Spain remained its most important market, more than 25 percent of the group's business came from its international operations. The company had also succeeded in gaining leader status in most of its foreign markets. In Mexico, for example, the company acquired 100 percent control of Aerocomidas in 2006. This purchase raised Áreas to the position of leader in that country's airport concessions market. In Chile, where the company was already a leader in the service station sector, the company acquired the 17-strong Gatsby restaurant chain, boosting its presence in the airport market there.

The growth of Áreas's airport operations had by then outpaced its service station operations. By 2009, the airport sector accounted for 51 percent of the company's business. With 475 concessions in nine countries, Áreas had also raised itself to the position as the number three player in the global airport concessions market. After 40 years, Áreas had expanded from a regional business to a worldwide leader in restaurant and retail concessions, with a total network of nearly 1,200 concessions.

M. L. Cohen

PRINCIPAL SUBSIDIARIES

Aerocomidas, S.A. De C.V. (Mexico); Arco Duplo, S.A.; Áreas Argentina, S.A. (Argentina); Áreas Do Brasil Participaçoes, S.A.; Áreas Portugal-Restauraçao E Distribuiçao, S.A.; Áreas USA, Inc.; Áreas S.A. Chile Limitada; Can-Áreas, S.A. (Canary Islands); Deor Dominicana, S.A. (Dominican Republic); Elite Aeropuertos, S.A; Geresa Holding, S.A. (Argentina); Geresa México, S.A. De C.V.; Hoteleiras, S.A. (Portugal); Latinoamericana Duty Free, S.A. de C.V. (Mexico); Restauración de Aeropuertos Españoles, S.A.; Servicios y Sistemas Gastronómicos Limitada (Chile); Shipwreck Shops NV (St. Martin); Travel Retail Áreas, S.A.

PRINCIPAL DIVISIONS

Restaurants; Duty Free Distribution; Duty Paid Distribution; Convenience Stores; Hotels; Filling Stations.

PRINCIPAL OPERATING UNITS

Airports; Highways, Turnpikes and Roads; Fairs and City Center; Train Stations.

PRINCIPAL COMPETITORS

Compass Group plc; Sodexho Alliance S.A.; Accor Aramark Corporation; Autogrill S.p.A.

FURTHER READING

"Areas (Elior) Acquires Mexican Latinoamericana Duty Free Group," *European Report,* June 6, 2001, p. 600.

"Areas Opens 'The Airport Market' Supermarket," *Expansion* (Spain), April 11, 2002.

"Areas USA Wins Rights to 30 Hartsfield-Jackson Stores," *Atlanta Business Chronicle,* June 23, 2008.

"Areas Wins Concession of Restaurants in 16 Airports," *South American Business Information,* April 18, 2001.

"Areas/Hojeij Win Airport Concession Contract," *Orlando Business Journal,* June 21, 2007.

"Elior Expands in Spain and Mexico with Bid for Latinoamericana," *DFNI,* April 10, 2001.

Kabbaj, Marouane, "Atasa Investit dans Six Aeroports," *Challenge Hebdo,* April 19, 2008, p. 56.

Kauffman, Chris, "Airport Concession Fight Heats Up Again," *Orlando Business Journal,* April 18, 2008.

Ng, Melody, "Areas USA Awarded US $140 Million Worth of F&B Concessions at Indianapolis Airport," *Moodie Report,* April 24, 2008.

"Ruby Tuesday Franchise to Open at OIA," *Orlando Business Journal,* January 31, 2008.

"Ruby Tuesday Lands Deal for 5 Airport Locations," *Nation's Restaurant News,* February 11, 2008, p. 14.

Tellijohn, Andrew, "Areas USA Continues U.S. Airport Extension," *Airport Revenue News,* July 25, 2008.

Avaya Inc.

———————■———————

211 Mount Airy Road
Basking Ridge, New Jersey 07920
U.S.A.
Telephone: (908) 953-600
Toll Free: (800) 784-6104
Fax: (908) 953-7609
Web site: http://www.avaya.com

Private Company
Incorporated: 2000
Employees: 18,000
Sales: $5.28 billion (2007)
NAICS: 334210 Telephone Apparatus Manufacturing

■ ■ ■

Avaya Inc. is a leading developer of enterprise communications systems. Specifically, the company designs, builds, and manages communications networks for other businesses. Its international customer base runs the gamut of industries and ranges from small businesses of fewer than 250 employees to large organizations employing a workforce of over 1,000. The company, originally established as a division of Lucent Technologies, was taken private in 2007 when it was acquired by equity firms Silver Lake Partners and TPG Capital for $8.3 billion. Avaya's research and development efforts are led by its Avaya Labs division.

FORMATIVE YEARS

Prior to becoming a stand-alone company, Avaya operated as Lucent Technologies Inc.'s Enterprise Networks

Group. Lucent provided the company with legal and tax support, as well as financing for acquisition activities. Lucent established the business as a wholly owned subsidiary named Lucent EN Corporation on February 16, 2000. Several months later, on June 27, the company changed its name to Avaya. In the July 3, 2000, issue of *Cambridge Telecom Report,* President and CEO Donald Peterson explained: "We chose a name that would set us apart and capture what we are doing with the company, focusing on communications solutions for business customers. Avaya sounds open and fluid, reflecting a company that's open-minded and that provides seamless, effortless interconnections among people and businesses."

Prior to this time, several key developments occurred related to the company's growth. These included Lucent's acquisition of Agile Networks Inc. in October 1996 for $135 million, followed by the acquisition of Octel Communications Corporation in September 1997. Lucent grew its Enterprise Networks Group with three acquisitions in 1998. These included a $199 million deal for Prominet Corp. in January, followed by the $207 million acquisition of SDX Business Systems PLC midway through the year. In August, Lannet Ltd. was acquired for $115 million. In July 1999 Lucent merged its Enterprise Network Group with Mosaix Inc. in a transaction valued at $145 million.

Avaya's life as an independent company began from an enviable position of industry leadership. At the time of the Lucent spinoff, Basking Ridge, New Jersey-based Avaya served roughly one million business customers in 90 countries, ranging from small businesses to large corporations. In the United States, the company ranked as one of the leading players in the voice communications systems and call center markets. Globally, Avaya was a leading provider in the structured cabling solutions and messaging markets.

On September 30, 2000, Lucent's spin off of Avaya was completed and the company became an independent organization. Midway through the following month, the company formed Avaya Labs, a research arm focused on business software applications, as well as enterprise voice and data communications. In addition to CEO Donald Peterson, who had previously served as Lucent's chief financial officer, Avaya's leadership team included Chairman Henry B. Schacht, Lucent's former chairman and CEO. Another key member of the leadership team was Chief Operating Officer Homa Firouztash, Ph.D.

EARLY GROWTH

A senior leadership change unfolded in January 2001. At that time, Henry Schacht was tapped to serve as interim chairman and CEO of Lucent. His departure left a void at Avaya that was filled by Lucent Vice-President Patricia Russo, who was named chairwoman. By this time, Avaya was a $7 billion company. Avaya then proceeded to grow via acquisitions. In February 2001, a $117 million deal was made for Milpitas, California-based VPNet Technologies Inc. Two months later, the company paid $29 million for the assets of California-based Quintus Corp.

Midway through 2001, Avaya sold its manufacturing and repair facilities in Little Rock, Arkansas, and Denver, Colorado, to Toronto, Ontario-based Celestica Inc. In October, the company named Kevin Brady as its chief operating officer. In an effort to cut costs, Avaya trimmed approximately 10,000 jobs from its workforce, resulting in a savings of about $900 million. Moving forward, the company began focusing more of its research on Internet protocol-based communications systems, as opposed to traditional systems that relied upon circuit-switched technology.

Workforce reductions continued at Avaya in 2002. In order to strengthen its balance sheet, the company announced plans to trim 1,900 jobs and sell $90 million worth of new stock to the private-equity firm Warburg Pincus Equity Partners in March. A major shift occurred midway through the year when Avaya revealed a long-term strategy to move away from network hardware and focus on the development of software products.

In mid-2003, Avaya outsourced its global employee service operations to Convergys Corp., which began providing human resources support to the company's 17,000-member workforce in North America and South America, Africa and Asia Pacific, Europe, and the Middle East. Two acquisitions occurred later in the year. In October, Avaya snapped up several of VISTA Information Technologies Inc.'s business units. Late the following month, the Expanets communications services unit of NorthWestern Corp. was acquired for $152 million.

Avaya grew at a rapid pace during the first half of the decade. The company kicked off 2004 by forging a deal with CommScope Inc. for the sale of its Richardson, Texas-based Connectivity Solutions business for $250 million in cash and about 1.8 million shares of CommScope stock. In April, Avaya parted with $18 million to acquire Tata's 25.1 percent equity interest in Tata Telecom Ltd. An additional 33.6 percent of Tata Telecom was acquired in August for $24 million.

In October 2004 Avaya paid $110 million to acquire the audio and web conferencing solutions company Spectel. The following month, Avaya spent $381 million to acquire the Frankfurt, Germany-based communications systems business Tenovis GmbH & Co. KG. That deal bolstered the company's presence in Europe, and pushed its international revenues from approximately 25 percent of the total to 40 percent. Avaya rounded out 2004 by acquiring San Mateo, California-based RouteScience Technologies Inc., which produced adaptive networking software.

ACCELERATED GROWTH

In April 2005, Avaya executed some creative promotions around its employee retirement plan. The company held a 401(k) Day on April 1 (4/01). Through a tie-in with Wiley Publishing, a *For Dummies* book was created that corresponded to its retirement plan. In addition, Avaya arranged to have well-known financial expert Suze Orman present at several events. Key developments in 2005 included the $38 million acquisition of Ottawa, Ontario-based Nimcat Networks Inc. in September. Two months later, Avaya forged a strategic alliance with SAP America Inc. that focused on marketing business

KEY DATES

2000: Lucent Technologies Inc. establishes its Enterprise Networks Group as a wholly owned subsidiary named Lucent EN Corporation; name is changed to Avaya; Lucent spins off Avaya as an independent enterprise.

2002: Avaya develops a long-term strategy to move away from network hardware and focus on the development of software products.

2006: Louis D'Ambrosio succeeds Donald Peterson as CEO.

2007: The company is acquired by Silver Lake Partners and Texas Pacific Group (TPG Capital) for $8.3 billion and is taken private.

applications. For the year, Avaya recorded sales of $4.9 billion.

By early 2006 Avaya's customer base included more than 90 percent of the *Fortune* 500 companies. In the wake of slumping profits, Peterson relinquished his CEO position to Louis D'Ambrosio midway through the year. At the same time, Michael C. Thurk was named chief operating officer. In mid-2006 Avaya was one of only ten companies selected for a $4 billion initiative to overhaul data and voice communications technology at U.S. Army bases throughout the world. Late in the summer, the company rolled out a new version of its contact center software.

Peterson remained Avaya's chairman until September 30. That month GlobalConnect Australia, a subsidiary of the company's Avaya GlobalConnect business, revealed plans to acquire the converged solutions division of Sirius Telecommunications Ltd. In October 2006, CEO D'Ambrosio indicated that the company would begin to focus more on multimedia conferencing and applications for enterprise workers. In addition, plans were made to forge alliances with other technology leaders, such as Microsoft and IBM.

In the fourth quarter of its 2006 fiscal year, Avaya recorded net income of $48 million, significantly lower than the $660 million the company had earned during the fourth quarter of 2005. Impacting earnings were charges related to the elimination of 1,300 jobs as part of a restructuring effort in the United States. In November 2006, D'Ambrosio and Thurk were named to Avaya's board of directors. Midway through that month, the company acquired the Fremont, California-based enterprise mobility solutions company Traverse Networks.

NEW OWNERSHIP

Avaya kicked off 2007 by forging a partnership with Sweden-based Teleopti that intended to increase business in the Russian contact center market. Around the same time, the company revealed plans to acquire Ubiquity Software Corp. in a $144 million cash deal. In February, former Visteon Corp. Chief Information Officer Lorie Buckingham was named to the same position at Avaya. In April, the company's Avaya Global Connect business forged an alliance with Japan's Oki Electric focused on small and medium-sized businesses in India.

Midway through the year, Credit Suisse was retained by Avaya in order to explore the potential sale of the company. By this time, Avaya employed about 20,000 people and was valued at approximately $6.1 billion. On revenues of $5.12 billion, the company registered a net profit of $201 million for its 2006 fiscal year.

News surfaced that the equity firm Silver Lake Partners, as well as Nortel Networks and Cisco Systems, possibly had an interest in acquiring Avaya. In early June, the company agreed to be acquired by Silver Lake and Texas Pacific Group (TPG Capital) for $8.3 billion. Shortly after the deal with Silver Lake and TPG was announced, Avaya began seeking more lucrative bids from other buyers. In all, the company reached out to 36 other companies. However, no deals were forthcoming. Acquisition-related developments continued throughout the summer. In August, shareholder Ernst Gottdiener sued the company, claiming that the deal with Silver Lake and TPG undervalued the company. Nevertheless, the deal was completed on October 26.

Commenting on the landmark deal in an October 26, 2007, press release, Avaya President and CEO Lou D'Ambrosio said: "Today marks the beginning of an exciting new area for Avaya. As a private company, working with Silver Lake and TPG, we have an unprecedented opportunity to accelerate our strategy, act boldly in the marketplace, and serve our customers with even greater innovation and responsiveness." D'Ambrosio indicated that customers would benefit from the acquisition in a number of ways, including speedier product rollouts.

Several key leadership changes occurred in 2008. In June, D'Ambrosio resigned as CEO for medical reasons. Charles Giancarlo was named interim president and CEO, and the company retained the firm Heidrick & Struggles to find a new leader. The following month, the company named Thomas Manley as chief financial officer. In October 2008 Kevin Kennedy was chosen as

Avaya's new president and CEO, effective January 2009. Giancarlo remained with the company as chairman. Prior to joining Avaya, Kennedy had served as president and CEO of JDS Uniphase Corp.

Avaya started off 2009 by making arrangements to acquire 400,000 square feet of distribution space in Memphis, Tennessee, from New Breed Logistics, which also planned to provide Avaya with logistics services. In May 2009, the Services & Support Professionals Association honored Avaya with a 2009 SSPA STAR Award for Best Practices. The company joined a handful of other technology leaders that also were recognized, including Symantec, Xerox, EMC, and Cisco Systems. Although the uncertain economic climate presented challenges to businesses and corporations of all sizes and types in mid-2009, Avaya seemed well positioned for continued success during the first decade of the 21st century.

Paul R. Greenland

PRINCIPAL DIVISIONS

Avaya Labs.

PRINCIPAL COMPETITORS

Alcatel-Lucent; Cisco Systems Inc.; Nortel Networks Corporation.

FURTHER READING

Hooper, Larry, "Lucent Spin-off Courts Channel—$7 Billion Avaya Intent on Building Momentum in Voice and Data Networking Space," *Computer Reseller News,* January 8, 2001.

Krapf, Eric, "Avaya After a Year," *Business Communications Review,* November 2001.

"Lucent Technologies Enterprise Spin-off Unveils Name, Announces Leadership Team," *Cambridge Telecom Report,* July 3, 2000.

McElligott, Tim, "Avaya's New CEO Lays out Strategy," *Telephony,* October 10, 2006.

"Private Equity Firms Snag Avaya for $8.2 billion," *eWeek,* June 5, 2007.

Sullivan, Tom, "Avaya to Abandon Hardware Heritage; Voice Player Turns to Developing Software for Industry-Standard Servers," *InfoWorld.com,* June 5, 2002.

Barneys New York Inc.

— ■ —

575 Fifth Avenue
New York, New York 10017
U.S.A.
Telephone: (212) 239-7300
Toll Free: (800) 926-5393
Fax: (212) 450-8489
Web site: http://www.barneys.com

Private Company
Founded: 1923 as Barney's
Employees: 1,400
Sales: $104.2 million (2008 est.)
NAICS: 448110 Men's Clothing Stores; 448150 Cloth-
ing Accessories Stores; 448120 Women's Clothing
Stores; 448190 Other Clothing Stores

■ ■ ■

Barneys New York Inc. is a specialty retailer of high-
quality men's, women's, and children's clothing and accessories, as well as shoes, gifts, cosmetics, fragrances,
and housewares. It operates ten large flagship stores in
prime areas of such cities as New York, Boston,
Chicago, and Beverly Hills, California, as well as a
number of outlet stores and Barneys Co-op sites.

For decades Barneys was a single Manhattan store
for cut rate men's suits. Beginning in the 1960s it went
upscale, and by 1990 it had established a chain of stores
stretching as far as Tokyo. Because of overspending, the
family-run company fell deeply into debt and filed for
bankruptcy protection in January 1996. It emerged
from bankruptcy three years later under new ownership.

The company was acquired by Jones Apparel Group in
December 2004 for $397.3 million. Jones Apparel then
sold Barneys in a $945 million deal with the Dubai
government's Istithmar PJSC investment arm in 2007.

SEVENTH AVENUE CLOTHING STORE

Barney Pressman started out in the business by pressing
pants for three cents each in his father's clothing store.
He founded Barney's in 1923 with $500 raised by
pawning his wife's engagement ring in order to lease a
500-square-foot retail space at Seventh Avenue and West
17th Street in Manhattan, with 20 feet of frontage and
an awning on which were printed the words "Barney's
Clothes." Pressman stocked the store with 40 name-
brand suits and soon added a big sign reading "No
Bunk, No Junk, No Imitations."

Barney's was able to sell tailored clothing by noted
manufacturers at prices well below list by purchasing
showroom samples, retail overstocks, and manufacturers'
closeouts, sometimes at auctions and bankruptcy sales. It
also offered free alterations and free parking. As business
grew, floors above street level were added to the store,
beginning in 1934. Barney Pressman's son, Fred, joined
the business in 1946.

Barney Pressman knew how to publicize his wares
as well as fill his store. He claimed to be the first
Manhattan retailer to use radio and television, beginning
with "Calling All Men to Barney's" radio spots in the
1930s, a parody of the introduction to the *Dick Tracy*
show. To advertise Irish woolens he sponsored radio
programs featuring Irish tenors and bands playing jigs.

COMPANY PERSPECTIVES

As Sarah Jessica Parker once told *Vanity Fair,* "If you're a nice person and you work hard, you get to go shopping at Barney's. It's the decadent reward."

Women encased in barrels gave away matchbooks with the store's name and address. He even chartered a boat to take 2,000 of his customers from Manhattan to Coney Island.

The company had sales of about $13 million in 1965, when its name was Barney's Clothes Inc. Beginning in 1964 the store had begun to shed its discount image. Fred Pressman said in 1973, according to *Business Week,* that he became "convinced that the discount route definitely was not for us. My father and I have always hated cheap goods. ... I didn't want to sell low-end merchandise. Now, many of those who chose to are verging on bankruptcy."

NEW BUILDING, NEW IMAGE

In 1970 Barney's erected an adjacent five-story building called the International House and added another floor to the original four level store, which was renamed America House. International House, Fred Pressman promised, would feature complete collections of European designers, "from denim pants to $250 suits," not just a watered down "potpourri of fabrics and models." The renovated America House, he said, would hold merchandise from "manufacturers who are in effect designers." According to Barney's, the wings constituted the world's largest individual men's clothing store, occupying the entire Seventh Avenue block between 16th and 17th streets, with 100,000 square feet of selling space and 20 individual shops.

By 1973 Barney's had annual sales of $33 million and sales per square foot, about double the average for a men's specialty store. The store stocked 60,000 suits and employed 232 tailors for alterations. It carried full lines of such designers as Bill Blass, Pierre Cardin, Christian Dior, and Hubert de Givenchy. Barney's was the first U.S. clothing store to stock the full line of Giorgio Armani, with whom it signed an exclusive agreement in 1976. Its 13 buyers were free to reorder at any time of year. The twice per year warehouse sale, a Manhattan event for which prospective customers lined up outside the store, took care of overstocked inventory.

Barney's started carrying women's clothing for the first time in 1976, on the third floor of the international side, with fashions from more than 20 houses represented. Fred's son Gene, who was responsible for the plunge into women's wear, moved the women's area to a new top level enclosure called The Penthouse the following year. Barney's also added housewares, cosmetics, and gifts to its inventory during this period. In 1977 The Pub, the in-store restaurant that had always served only carved roast beef, was renamed The Café and began offering salads, soup, and a variety of sandwiches.

A SUBTLE NAME CHANGE

At Gene Pressman's behest the apostrophe in the Barney's name was dropped by 1979, and by 1981 the company name became Barneys Inc., while the store became known as Barneys New York. In 1981 the women's penthouse became a duplex. Some 80 percent of the women's merchandise was then imported, compared to 40 percent of the men's goods.

In 1986 Barneys completed construction of a 70,000-square-foot women's store in a row of six restored townhouses and two larger adjacent buildings along 17th Street, two years behind schedule and at a cost of more than $25 million. The new store included a unisex beauty salon and restaurant, antiques, and boutiques for accessories, gifts, and housewares. The *New York Times* report by Michael Gross on the opening described the store as, "at least the equal of the best of its kind in New York, in terms of space, design, display and merchandise." This store accounted for about one-third of Barneys' sales of some $90 million the following year.

GOING NATIONAL AND INTERNATIONAL

In 1988 Barneys opened a 10,000-square-foot store for men in lower Manhattan's swank World Financial Center. Soon after, the company announced it would build a national chain of as many as 100 clothing stores, starting with three in Manhasset, New York; Short Hills, New Jersey; and Newton, Massachusetts. The proposed new stores would offer 75 percent women's apparel and 25 percent menswear, with the company's own private-label merchandise representing about 20 percent of sales.

The stores were to be run by Barneys America, with Gene Pressman and his brother Bob as co-chief executives. (They later became co-presidents of the parent company; their father ascended to chairman, serving until his death in 1996.) To meet the ambitious goals, however, the parent company needed investors, and Wall Street looked askance at what Joshua Levine called, "several sets of financial statements, depending on who was supposed to be looking at them."

KEY DATES

1923: Barney Pressman establishes Barney's by pawning his wife's engagement ring in order to lease retail space in Manhattan.

1965: Sales at Barney's Clothes Inc. reach $13 million.

1976: The company begins selling women's clothes.

1979: The apostrophe in Barney's is dropped.

1981: The company changes its name to Barneys Inc., and the name of its store to Barneys New York.

1988: National expansion begins.

1990: The apostrophe returns to the Barney's name, temporarily.

1996: Barney Pressman dies and the company files for Chapter 11 bankruptcy.

1999: Barney's emerges from bankruptcy under new ownership.

2004: Jones Apparel Group acquires Barneys for $397.3 million.

2007: The Dubai government's investment arm, Istithmar PJSC, acquires Barneys for $942.3 million.

Barneys found the financial partner it was seeking in 1989, when it announced a joint venture with Isetan Co., one of Japan's largest retailers. The agreement provided for Isetan to hold 80 percent and the Pressman family 20 percent in stores to do business in Asia under the Barneys New York name. The first of these, which opened in Tokyo in late 1990, was the largest U.S. specialty store in Japan. Barneys would own 65 percent and Isetan 35 percent of Barneys America, with plans to open more small, upscale specialty clothing stores in malls. Around this time the parent company reinserted the apostrophe in the name, returning it to "Barney's."

The original three northeastern Barney's America stores were so intimidating to some women that a secretary visiting the Manhasset store (on Long Island's tony North Shore) called it "the kind of place you'd have to dress up to go shopping." A reporter covering this store's opening wrote, "Even the babies were dressed to the nines."

The first U.S. branches under the new agreement were opened in 1990 in Dallas, Seattle, and Costa Mesa, California. Like the three northeastern stores, they featured mostly women's merchandise and carried no men's suits. In the Seattle store blouses by the Italian

designer Romeo Gigli ranged from $275 to $480. The goods at the Costa Mesa store included what *Forbes* writer Lisa Gubernick called "items the industry generally describes as 'fashion forward'—stuff that you tend to see more in magazines than on real people," such as skin-tight synthetics by the French designer Jean Paul Gaultier.

By October 1990 Barney's America had opened a seventh store, in Westport, Connecticut, and had added tailored clothing for men. It also opened stores in Houston and Cleveland in 1991. Meanwhile a 50-50 joint venture by Barney's and Isetan was buying property for large new stores in midtown Manhattan, Chicago, and Beverly Hills, with Isetan committed to providing $236 million in acquisition and construction costs. The Chicago store opened on the city's fashionable Near North Side in 1992.

EXTRAVAGANCE IN MANHATTAN AND BEVERLY HILLS

For the new 230,000-square-foot Manhattan Barney's (the largest new store in New York City since the Great Depression) the joint venture purchased an 11 story building on Madison Avenue between East 60th and 61st streets. This structure was gutted for a 22 story building with 14 floors of offices above the store. Extravagantly furbished with flooring made of exotic woods, a marble mosaic on the lobby floor, gold leaf ceilings, and lacquered walls, the new Barney's cost $267 million, according to one account. It opened in 1993. The following year the company also opened, at a cost of $120 million, a 125,000-square-foot store in Beverly Hills, including a five story underground garage hastily built to meet an unforeseen zoning ordinance.

The Madison Avenue store did good business in spite of stiff competition in its posh locale, but some of the trade was at the expense of the downtown store. Sales at the Beverly Hills store suffered in the recession-gripped California economy. Barney's America also played poorly outside New York City; women were put off by hipper-than-thou black-on-black fashions and styling for pencil-thin models, with larger sizes sometimes hard to find. In Dallas, a flap developed when a Barney's employee said the beauty salon would not style "big hair." The Cleveland store closed in 1993. Company sales came to about $180 million that year and operating income to about $19 million.

By 1994 there were indications that finances were in serious disarray. Some of the company's more than 7,000 vendors were refusing to furnish the chain with goods because of late payments that were often as tardy as six months. The company's obsolete inventory and distribution systems were only beginning to respond to the installation of state-of-the-art computerization. There were tales about how the Pressmans, eight of them on the company payroll, helped themselves to store merchandise without accounting for it, according to the *New York Times* article "Haughty Couture" and Joshua Levine's "Let Them Wear Black." To relieve its cash flow problems, Barney's turned to insurance companies, which purchased about $45-million worth of unsecured long term notes.

FILING FOR BANKRUPTCY

In September 1995 Barney's received a letter from Isetan, which sought to take control of the company after having spent $616 million on Barney's-related affairs, including about $168 million in emergency loans, personally guaranteed by the Pressman brothers, to cover the cost overruns for the Madison Avenue and Beverly Hills stores. Barney's also owed banks nearly $170 million and others about $150 million. Instead of reaching an agreement with its creditors, Barney's filed for Chapter 11 bankruptcy in January 1996.

It was later revealed that in fiscal 1995 (the year ended July 31, 1995) the company lost $120.8 million on sales of $338.7 million. In fiscal 1996 Barney's lost $71.9 million, including a charge of $29.4 million for reorganization costs, on sales of $366.4 million. In fiscal 1997 the company lost $95 million, including a charge of $72.2 million for reorganization costs, on sales of $361.5 million.

Isetan, whose claims came to $480 million, won a judgment against the Pressmans for the loans they had personally guaranteed. It also won title to the three Barney's New York stores in New York, Chicago, and Beverly Hills. The original Barney's closed in 1997. Four Barney's America stores, including the ones in Houston, Dallas, and Troy, Michigan, also closed in 1997. "Basically," Thomas C. Shull, who was named president of the parent firm, told the *New York Times* in August 1998, "Barneys had taken a New York store and placed it in other cities without really appreciating the needs and wants by market." He concentrated on making the enterprise more customer-friendly, "hip but not haughty."

In fiscal 1998 Barneys lost $20 million on sales of $343 million but recorded operating earnings of $17.7 million, compared to an operating loss of $2.1 million the year before. By the end of the summer of 1998 only seven Barney's stores remained in existence. In early 1999 there were also about a dozen discount stores plus the distribution center in Lyndhurst, New Jersey. Gene

and Bob Pressman stepped down as chief executives of Barney's in June 1998.

REORGANIZED UNDER ISETAN OWNERSHIP

A bankruptcy plan was approved in December 1998. It acknowledged Isetan's ownership of the three big stores and also granted the company a small equity stake of around 7.3 percent, $23.2 million in cash, and $15 million in annual rent payments by Barney's for the three big stores. Some 70 percent of the stock was allotted to Whippoorwill Associates Inc. and Bay Harbour Management L.C., so-called vulture investors who had bought the company's debt at an average of 40 cents on the dollar.

In August 1998 they held $133 million (and about $149 million in December) of the estimated $320 million in secured claims and had provided, or had promised to provide, Barney's with an equity infusion of $62.5 million. They paid $240 million for their stake in the company. The Pressman family retained about 1.5 percent of the stock.

A NEW BEGINNING

A major leadership change unfolded in May 1999, when Allen Questrom was chosen as Barneys' new chairman and CEO. The experienced retail executive, who had served as chairman and CEO of Federated Department Stores, began focusing on new marketing programs, expansion efforts, service improvements, and growing the company's Co-op department, which offered items from emerging designers. Barneys, once again without the apostrophe in its name, rounded out the year with sales of $366.8 million. Midway through 2000 the company revealed that Questrom was relinquishing his president and CEO duties in order to become CEO of J.C. Penney Co. Inc. He continued, however, to serve Barneys as chairman.

As part of an ongoing effort to sharpen its bottom line, Barneys kept making improvements in 2002. In addition to store renovations and an emphasis on selling higher margin items, the company continued to slash costs. By 2003 Barneys was positioned for expansion. A core component of the company's strategy involved its Co-op concept, which focused on a younger target audience. In October of that year the company took Co-op beyond Manhattan for the first time and opened a 9,000-square-foot store in the South Beach area of Miami. Construction was underway on a similarly sized store in the Lincoln Park area of Chicago by mid-2004.

In July 2004 Barneys retained Peter J. Solomon Co. to explore the possibility of selling itself. In November

Jones Apparel Group agreed to spend approximately $400 million to acquire Barneys, beating out Federated Department Stores, Neiman Marcus, and Nordstrom. By this time the company operated stores in approximately 20 cities, and was led by Chairman, President, and CEO Howard Socol.

Against the backdrop of the ownership change, Barneys continued to roll out new Co-op locations. The company's first mall-based units opened in Atlanta, Georgia, and Costa Mesa, California, in early 2005. The company also unveiled plans for new Barneys New York stores, including a location in Tokyo, Japan. A new store opened in Boston's Copley Place in March 2006. The following month the company revealed plans to establish a three story, 85,000-square-foot store in Las Vegas. In October a new store was established in Dallas.

ACQUIRED BY ISTITHMAR

By mid-2007 Barneys' annual sales volume was approximately $600 million and a new Barneys New York store had opened in downtown Seattle. In June the Dubai government's investment arm, Istithmar PJSC, agreed to acquire Barneys for $825 million. At the time of the deal Istithmar indicated that it planned to keep Barneys' existing management team in place and avoid making significant changes to its business strategy. In July, however, Japan's Fast Retailing Co. made a sweeter, $900 million offer for Barneys. A bidding war developed, which Istithmar eventually won with a cash bid of $942.3 million. The deal was concluded on September 10, 2007.

Under its new ownership Barneys opened a new, six story, 60,000-square-foot store in San Francisco in September 2007. By this time another new store was slated to open in Scottsdale, Arizona, in 2009. Barneys kicked off 2008 by opening its new Las Vegas store in January. The three story location was situated within The Shoppes at The Palazzo Las Vegas. Midway through the year a major leadership change unfolded when Socol announced plans to resign.

By early 2009 slack economic conditions were having a negative impact on Barneys' sales. News surfaced in January that Istithmar was considering selling the company. Observers noted that Barneys would command a price of approximately $400 million—a far cry from the $942 million that had been shelled out to acquire the retailer less than two years before. In May of that year Barneys revealed plans to shutter two of its stores, including the highly publicized Las Vegas location. Heading into the 21st century's second decade

it was unclear how the dire economic climate would impact the company's performance and future.

Robert Halasz
Updated, Paul R. Greenland

PRINCIPAL COMPETITORS

Bloomingdale's Inc.; Nordstrom Inc.; Saks Fifth Ave. Inc.

FURTHER READING

Conant, Jennet, "Bringing Down Barneys," *Vanity Fair,* May 1996, pp. 74+.

Enrico, Dottie, "Barneys' Grand Opening," *Newsday,* August 21, 1989, Part III, p. 8.

Ettore, Barbara, "Barney's Seeks Uptown Image," *New York Times,* June 2, 1978, pp. D1, D11.

Gross, Michael, "Barney's Unveils Women's Store (at Last)," *New York Times,* September 2, 1986, p. B6.

Gubernick, Lisa, "So Where Are the Overcoats?" *Forbes,* June 11, 1990, pp. 178–79.

Hochswender, Woody, "Those Bold Pressman Boys," *New York Times,* December 2, 1990, Sec. 3, pp. 1, 10.

Levine, Joshua, "Let Them Wear Black," *New York,* March 1, 1999, pp. 21–29, 121.

Moin, David, "Barneys Struts Its Stuff: Boston Flagship Opening Marks New Growth Plan," *WWD,* March 9, 2006.

Morrisroe, Patricia, "Dressing Up Downtown," *New York,* October 20, 1986, pp. 38–45, 47.

Rosenbloom, Stephanie, "Possibly on Sale at Barneys: Barneys," *New York Times,* January 23, 2009, p. B5.

Sloane, Leonard, "New Barney's Wing to Open Today," *New York Times,* September 30, 1970, pp. 59, 63.

Steinhauer, Jennifer, "Barneys Is Seeking Bankruptcy, Citing Fight with Partner," *New York Times,* January 12, 1996, pp. A1, D3.

———, "Hip but Not Haughty at Barneys New York," *New York Times,* August 25, 1998, pp. D1, D6.

Steinhauer, Jennifer, and Stephanie Strom, "Haughty Couture," *New York Times,* January 21, 1996, Sec. 3, pp. 1, 10–11.

Strom, Stephanie, "Barney Pressman, Retailing Legend, Is Dead at 96," *New York Times,* August 27, 1991, p. D23.

———, "Did Barneys Overextend Itself? Not Really, It Insists," *New York Times,* July 24, 1994, Sec. 3, p. 4.

"A $33-Million Men's Shop Tries Social Climbing," *Business Week,* September 1, 1973, pp. 48–49.

Turner, Richard, "Will the Pressmans Lose Their Shirts?" *New York,* May 13, 1996, pp. 34–39.

Young, Vicki M., "Istithmar Wins Bidding War for Barneys; Dubai-Based Investment Group Comes Back with Offer of $942.3M to Acquire Specialty Retailer," *Daily News Record,* August 13, 2007.

Young, Vicki M., and Evan Clark, "With Barneys in Hand, Boneparth Seeks to Double Its Size," *WWD,* November 12, 2004.

Bauer Hockey, Inc.

———■———

150 Ocean Road
Greenland, New Hampshire 03840-2408
U.S.A.
Telephone: (603) 430-2111
Web site: http://www.bauer.com

Private Company
Incorporated: 1927 as Western Shoe Company
Employees: 950
Sales: $160 million (2007 est.)
NAICS: 339920 Sporting and Athletic Goods Manufacturing

■ ■ ■

Divested by sporting goods giant Nike, Inc., in 2008, Bauer Hockey, Inc., is a private company based in Greenland, New Hampshire, dedicated to the manufacture and marketing of ice hockey equipment for both players and goalies. Bauer skate models for players include the high-end Vapor line, followed by Supreme and Flexlite. The Supreme line also includes skates intended for goalies. Other player gear includes wood and composite sticks; gloves; shoulder, elbow, and shin pads; helmets, face masks, and visors; and pants. Bauer offers goalie sticks, gloves and blockers, goal pads, chest and arm pads, and goalie pants. In addition, Bauer produces base layer items, including shirts, shorts, and socks; protective collars, bibs, cups, and supporters; warm-up jackets, pullovers, and pants; sandals ("slides"); equipment bags for both players and goalies; as well as caps, T-shirts, hooded sweatshirts, and other lifestyle apparel. A key element of Bauer's marketing is the endorsement of National Hockey League players. Products are sold through dealers in North America and Europe.

CANADIAN ROOTS

Bauer Hockey was founded in 1927 as the Western Shoe Company by the Bauer family in Kitchener, Ontario, a hub for both hockey and shoemaking. Western, when forced to diversify during the Great Depression of the 1930s, thus began producing hockey skates. The company offered the first single unit product, a major improvement over competing skates that were simply blades strapped to boots. Dartmouth, Nova Scotia-based Starr Manufacturing Company provided the blades for the skates, marketed as the "Bauer Supreme." Overnight, the company became the top-selling skate manufacturer. Its reign was short lived, however. Later in the 1930s the Bauer Supreme was overshadowed by the Tacks skate sold by CCM, a Canadian company, originally known as Canada Cycle & Motor Company Limited, that had entered the hockey gear business by introducing the Automobile Skate some years earlier. The new CCM skate would become popular with professional players and held the distinction of being worn by every leading scorer in the National Hockey League (NHL) from 1939 to 1969. Nevertheless, Bauer held its own with amateur players and by the mid-1950s was the world's leading seller of hockey skates.

Bauer was a neglected skate brand among the professional ranks until the 1960s when a revival began following an endorsement deal with star NHL player

Bobby Hull. In 1967 the Bauer family sold the business to another Kitchener shoe manufacturer, Greb Industries. That company had been started by Charles Greb in 1910 as the Berlin Shoe Company, became known as the Greb Shoe Company six years later, and in time became Canada's largest footwear manufacturer, known for its Kodiak boots, Collins safety shoes, and Hush Puppies (Greb was the first international licensee of the revolutionary casual shoe). Under Greb, some 950,000 pairs of Bauer skates were sold.

WARRINGTON PRODUCTS ACQUIRES BAUER BRAND

The Bauer brand changed hands in 1974 when Greb was acquired by Warrington Products Ltd., a portfolio company of CEMP Investments Ltd., controlled by the Bronfman family, owners of giant liquor manufacturer Seagram Co. Warrington had been established in 1969 as W.C.R. Sports Industries Ltd. and then taken public two years later as Warrington Products. Bauer skates enjoyed a surge in popularity in the 1970s with the introduction of the TUUK blade chassis, but Warrington did not fare particularly well, more often than not posting an annual net loss into the early 1980s. Part of the problem was new competition from plastic molded hockey skates produced by Montreal newcomer Micron.

The man behind the upstart Micron was in fact an Italian, Icaro Olivieri, a product designer and self-taught engineer. In the mid-1960s he created a new ski boot buckle to replace laces. He then developed injection molding machinery to produce plastic ski boots. In 1975 he visited the Bauer skate plant while on a business trip. Seeing that Bauer still made skate boots out of stitched leather, Olivieri recognized an opportunity to apply his plastic technology to hockey skates. He set up shop in Montreal with equipment and molds he brought over from Italy and launched Micron skates, which quickly seized a large share of Bauer's market. He also manufactured Tyrol ski boots. In order to expand, Olivieri decided to join forces with Warrington; the two companies merged in 1981 with Olivieri becoming chairman.

In the 1980s Warrington expanded aggressively, acquiring several sporting goods companies and brands. The expansion proved to be too aggressive, however, and by 1987 the company was saddled with $90 million in debt. It also lost $34 million in 1987. Olivieri and the Bronfman executives disagreed over the plight of the company and in 1988 Olivieri, with financial backing from Toronto's Dundee Bankcorp Inc., bought out the Bronfmans and renamed the company Canstar Sports Inc. He stayed on as chairman but brought in turnaround expert Gerald Wasserman to serve as chief executive officer. In short order, Wasserman returned Canstar to profitability, primarily by divesting the shoe and ski businesses to focus on hockey equipment. In 1989 the company netted $6 million on sales of $71 million.

NIKE BECOMES INTERESTED

Canstar's prospects appeared bright as the 1990s dawned and the NHL established franchises in several Sunbelt communities in the United States. Moreover, in-line skates, spearheaded by the Rollerblade brand, were growing in popularity, as was roller hockey, offering new product categories to pursue that could balance out the seasonality of ice hockey gear. The Bauer in-line skate brand, Bauer Roadrollers, had been introduced in 1986, and accounted for 2 percent of Canstar's revenues in 1990, an amount that increased to 18 percent just three years later. To round out its hockey offerings, Canstar acquired the Cooper line of sticks and protective gear in 1990.

Canstar aggressively promoted roller hockey to drive sales in the early 1990s, serving as a founding sponsor of the professional Roller Hockey International League and backing amateur leagues as well. By this time, NHL teams were well stocked with European players, and as a result the league was popular across the Continent. Canstar sought to take advantage of opportunities in Europe by opening a skate plant in Czechoslovakia, producing both ice and in-line skates, and acquiring Hatersley & Davidson, a U.K. figure skate blade manufacturer.

Canstar's revenues topped $200 million in 1993, when the company also increased net income to $15.3 million. By then, ice hockey and roller hockey were piquing the interest of Nike, Inc., which in mid-1994 agreed to sponsor the NHL. The footwear giant was especially interested in the in-line skate business, which was booming at the time, and believed that by promoting the NHL it could drive interest in roller hockey, a sport whose growth would not be hindered in the United States by the scarcity of ice rinks. Canstar, as a result, became a very attractive property to Nike.

KEY DATES

■

1927: Bauer family launches Western Shoe Company, later begins manufacturing hockey skates.

1967: Bauer family sells company to Greb Industries.

1974: Warrington Products acquires Greb.

1987: Warrington is bought out and renamed Canstar Sports Inc.

1994: Nike, Inc., acquires Canstar.

2005: Canstar is renamed Nike Bauer Hockey Inc.

2008: Nike Bauer is sold and becomes Bauer Hockey, Inc.

In 1994 Nike paid $395 million for Canstar, or about 50 percent more than the company's stock had been worth in the months leading up to the deal. Ten years earlier when Nike was in the market for acquisitions and Bauer could be bought for just $35 million, Nike executives quickly dismissed the idea when it was presented to them. By this time, however, both Canstar and Nike had high hopes for the combination. Canstar's new CEO told *Sporting Goods Business,* "I have seldom seen such a perfect marriage between two companies," predicting that Canstar's sales, which totaled $160 million in 1993, would exceed $400 million by the end of the decade. The reality proved to be far different than the hope, however.

STRUGGLING TO SUCCEED

While Canstar was allowed to operate independently, it still pursued a pattern that had been successful for Nike. Bauer plants in Canada were closed and production was shifted to less-expensive plants in Asia. Canstar's corporate offices were also moved to New Hampshire. Canstar continued to produce Bauer and Cooper branded skates in Canada, but reserved the Nike brand for skates sold in the United States and international markets as well as its premium products. Nike had conquered the sneaker world in part by offering vivid styling, an approach that did not fare well in the world of ice skates, where black boots were associated with hockey and white or anything with flair was relegated to women's figure skates. Furthermore, the high-end skates sold under the Nike name were not only extremely expensive, they were not properly sized for the North American market, resulting in a product that caused blisters and all too often was returned to the retailer and then shipped back to Canstar.

In time, Nike worked through the problems with their premium skates, employing new materials and simplifying the styling, but it was too late to save the Nike brand in the hockey world. Eventually Canstar had to apply the Bauer name to the skates. The failure of the NHL to increase its popularity in Middle America proved to be a more difficult challenge, however. Despite the Sunbelt franchises, a network television contract, and the technology-induced glowing puck on Fox telecasts to help new fans to better follow the action, the game remained regional in its appeal. In cities where the sport had roots, hockey was extremely popular and local telecasts enjoyed strong ratings, but the NHL simply did not measure up to Major League Baseball, the National Football League, or the National Basketball Association in national popularity.

Even more damaging to the ambitions of Nike and Canstar was the precipitous decline in interest in in-line skates in the latter half of the 1990s, partly due to a poor marketing approach. Because skateboarding was increasing in popularity, in-line skates were pitched as another extreme pastime, involving jumps and tricks that the average person could not do and had no interest in attempting. As a result, the casual skater was ignored and the momentum for in-line skating was blunted. Roller hockey, in the meantime, found its own niche level. The professional league folded and talk of roller hockey gaining acceptance into the Olympics and surpassing ice hockey in a manner of years soon vanished.

The arrival of the new century brought little momentum to Nike's hockey aspirations. In 2005 Nike launched a new branding strategy in a last-ditch attempt to spur growth. The Nike and Bauer brands were brought together, and Canstar became Nike Bauer Hockey Inc. All products then carried the Bauer name and the Nike Swoosh logo, the first time the logo had been applied to Bauer products. The new branding strategy had little impact, however. Canstar sales totaled about $160 million in 2006, far below the $400 million mark that had been anticipated when Nike acquired the company, and a mere fraction of Nike's net revenues of $16.3 billion.

NIKE EXITS HOCKEY

Nike decided the time had come to exit the hockey business, and in September Bauer was put up for sale, a rare admission of defeat from the highly successful sporting goods behemoth. About a dozen potential buyers expressed interest, but by December 2007 the field was reduced to three, including Easton-Bell Sports and Mission-Itech. In the end the company was acquired by a Canadian expatriate, W. Graeme Roustan, who with backing from Kohlberg & Co. agreed in February 2008 to pay $200 million for Nike Bauer, or about half as much as Nike paid for Canstar 14 years earlier. Born in Canada, Roustan came to the United States in 1988 after winning a Green Card Lottery. He did well as a private investment banker but did not abandon his love for hockey, helping to bring a team to San Jose, California, and almost purchasing the Norfolk Admirals of the American Hockey League. One of his portfolio companies, Roustan United, provided support services to ice rinks and arenas.

Roustan immediately reversed the company's name from Nike Bauer to Bauer Nike and soon dropped Nike altogether, renaming the company Bauer Hockey, Inc. After the sale closed in April 2008, Roustan named Kevin Davis as president and chief executive officer. Davis had been Nike Bauer's chief financial officer and chief operating officer for the previous six years and altogether had 15 years of executive experience with Nike, Gillette, and Braun. Reinvigorated, Bauer Hockey was quick to pursue consolidation in the market, believing such an approach was the key to the long-term success of the industry. In September 2008, the company reached a deal to acquire Mission-Itech Hockey, a major manufacturer of goal equipment, facial protection, and protective apparel. Mission-Itech had focused primarily on the North American market, but Bauer planned to take the brand to the emerging markets of Eastern Europe and Russia. One business that Bauer indicated it was not interested in pursing was in-line skating.

Roustan confessed to the *New York Times,* "I really didn't understand the inline skating business, being a blade guy."

Ed Dinger

PRINCIPAL COMPETITORS

Easton Sports, Inc.; Reebok-CCM Hockey, Inc.; TPS Hockey.

FURTHER READING

Austen, Ian, "Hockey Fan, and Investor, Buys Bauer from Nike," *New York Times,* February 22, 2008.

———, "With Hockey Market Stagnant, Nike Seeks to Sell Equipment Unit," *New York Times,* February 5, 2008.

Grierson, Bruce, "Hockey Nike in Canada," *Saturday Night,* April 1997, p. 64.

Milner, Brian, "Nike Saw a Niche, but He Sees a Knockout," *Globe and Mail,* February 22, 2008, p. B1.

Munk, Nina, "Hockey in the Sun," *Forbes,* August 15, 1994, p. 95.

"Nike's Bauer Unveils New Brand Strategy," *Sporting Goods Business,* October 4, 2005.

Pesky, Greg, "Pierre Boivin: President and COO, Canstar Sports Inc. (The SGB Interview)," *Sporting Goods Business,* January 1995, p. 46.

Saporito, Bill, "Can Nike Get Unstuck?" *Time,* March 30, 1998, p. 48.

Bob's Discount Furniture LLC

---

428 Tolland Turnpike
Manchester, Connecticut 06040
U.S.A.
Telephone: (860) 645-3200
Fax: (860) 645-4056
Web site: http://www.mybobs.com

Private Company
Incorporated: 1991
Employees: 1,800
Sales: $460 million (2008)
NAICS: 442110 Furniture Stores

■ ■ ■

Bob's Discount Furniture, LLC, operates a chain of more than 30 midpriced furniture stores located in New England, New Jersey, and New York, some of which include in-store discount outlets for damaged or discontinued items. The privately held company, majority-owned by the Stamford, Connecticut, firm of Saunders Karp & Megrue, maintains its headquarters in Manchester, Connecticut, and a main warehouse complex in Taftville, Connecticut. Other warehouses are found in Nashua, New Hampshire, and North Brunswick, New Jersey. The stores offer a wide range of living room, bedroom, dining room, and home and office furniture, as well as mattresses, rugs, entertainment centers, and electric fireplaces. The family-friendly stores serve complimentary refreshments and keep children entertained with movies, miniature golf, and video arcades. Many of the stores include Häagen-Dazs ice

cream shops. Bob's advertises heavily, producing its own television commercials, which feature the company's founder, Bob Kaufman, who owns a minority stake in the business. Far from a polished actor, the normally reticent and always informally dressed Kaufman has became a minor celebrity in the Northeast, known for his "Come on down" tagline.

1976 MOTORCYCLE ACCIDENT CHANGES FOUNDER'S LIFE

Bob's founder, Robert Kaufman, grew up in West Hartford, Connecticut, the son of a longtime advertising executive, Leo Kaufman, who ran a Hartford ad agency for many years. As a youth the younger Kaufman sold magazines and sealed driveways but showed no particular zeal to become an entrepreneur. Kaufman graduated from the University of Connecticut with a degree in marketing and went to work for Radio Shack, becoming a store manager in Mystic, Connecticut, while taking electronics courses at the University of Hartford. He was content with life and Radio Shack, and he has maintained that he would have likely stayed with the company had events not intervened to change the direction of his life.

While traveling to a meeting by motorcycle one morning in 1976, Kaufman lost control while switching gas tanks and hit a utility pole. He took the full impact on his right leg, which was broken in eight places, his kneecap shattered. At first it appeared that the leg would have to be amputated, but when blood flow was restored the limb was spared. Nevertheless, Kaufman had to devote a year of rehabilitation to restore func-

COMPANY PERSPECTIVES

■

No phony gimmicks. Just pure value.

tion, and his foot remained essentially paralyzed. To provide relief to the aching leg, Kaufman, at the suggestion of a therapist, began sleeping on a water bed. This not only eased the pain but would provide entrepreneurial inspiration later in life.

NEW JOB, NEW FOCUS

After the accident and rehabilitation Kaufman became a more mature and ambitious person. Instead of returning to Radio Shack, he continued his electronics education, and by age 27 was a production line supervisor at Thomas Faria Corporation, a Montville, Connecticut-based manufacturer of tachometers. With 23 employees in his charge and demanding management to contend with, Kaufman was frequently exhausted. If he was going to work so hard, he decided he should do it for himself, take a risk, and start his own business.

In October 1981 Kaufman tendered his notice at Thomas Faria and devoted the next five months to researching business opportunities, including vending machines, a Subway sandwich franchise, lawn care, and a franchise to publish a television listings book. It was during this time that he read an article about the waterbed industry, which enjoyed strong word-of-mouth sales: For every two sales made in a store, a third was generated. Kaufman also remembered the comfort he had experienced from a waterbed during rehabilitation. Assuming that other people would find them just as desirable, he decided to sell waterbeds. To learn more about the industry he began attending West Coast trade shows.

KAUFMAN LAUNCHES WATERBED BUSINESS

To get started in the waterbed field Kaufman turned to a second cousin, Gene Rosenberg, owner of five furniture stores. Kaufman persuaded Rosenberg to allow him to set up independent waterbed departments within the stores. Kaufman would not only pay Rosenberg a percentage on each retail sale and a commission to the stores' salespeople, but also stock the departments, make deliveries, and advertise. From Kaufman's perspective, the arrangement made sense because he was spared the cost of operating a store.

Kaufman raised $60,000 in seed money, half of which he provided and the other half of which came from investors, and launched Wholesale Waterbeds. To learn firsthand what customers wanted he spent some time on the sales floor, in the process learning lessons about furniture retailing that would prove useful later. He also tapped his father, at the time retired, to help with advertising and merchandising.

Wholesale Waterbeds enjoyed steady growth and Kaufman and Rosenberg became copartners in the venture. Kaufman was able to take the department-within-a-store concept to other retailers, who were won over by the no-risk nature of the deal, retaining the right to evict Wholesale Waterbeds with 60 days notice. By 1988 the company had 24 locations throughout New England.

By 1990, however, the waterbed business fell off, leading to the closing of a major waterbed retailer, Nimbus Bedrooms, in Newington, Connecticut. Kaufman and Rosenberg decided to open their first freestanding store in this location. They did well, but the store still had about 25,000 square feet of vacant space. It was at this point that Kaufman decided to try selling a wider range of furniture rather than just waterbeds. Over the years he had observed how many of the furniture stores in which he operated had spent less on advertising for their entire store did than he did on his single department, and he thought that his more aggressive approach in merchandising might bring him success with furniture in general.

FIRST BOB'S STORE OPENS: 1991

Kaufman and his investors raised $200,000 to launch Bob's Discount Furniture. The first store opened in Newington in March 1991. The country was in the midst of a recession, a situation that played to the strength of Kaufman, who elected to focus on low- and middle-price merchandise. Kaufman continued to operate Wholesale Waterbeds but the furniture venture quickly superseded it in importance, and in 1994 the waterbed business was folded into Bob's.

Kaufman enjoyed so much success that soon landlords of former furniture stores were calling him to open Bob's Discount units in their buildings. A second store soon followed in Window, Connecticut, and a third in Willimantic. In July 1993 Bob's opened a store in Manchester, Connecticut, in a large facility that would also house the company's headquarters and provide warehouse space.

To promote his growing business Kaufman began advertising on television in 1992. He did not star in the

KEY DATES

1991: The first Bob's Discount Furniture store opens.
1993: The company adopts one-price system that means an item will be the same price in any of the company's stores.
1998: The warehouse in Taftville, Connecticut, opens.
2000: Bob's opens its first discount outlet.
2005: Saunders Karp & Megrue acquires majority control of the company.
2008: Bob's is named retailer of the year by *Furniture Today* magazine.
2009: The Yonkers, New York, store opens.

NEW WAREHOUSE OPENS: 1998

To better support the expanding chain Bob's opened a warehouse and distribution center in a former Thermos factory in Taftville, Connecticut, in 1998. The facility's location and size opened up new markets for the chain, which could support operations throughout New England as well as the New York City area. Sales totaled $94.5 million in the final year of the 1990s, and by the start of the new century all of the company's warehouse operations had been consolidated into the 300,000-square-foot Taftville location. Plans were soon underway to expand the facility; in the meantime additional storage space had to be rented in the area.

In 2000 Bob's entered the greater Boston market, and by the fall of the year it was operating 13 stores in Connecticut, three in Massachusetts, and one in Salem, New Hampshire, with a second unit set to open in Seabrook, New Hampshire. That year Bob's also began offering area rugs and opened its first discount outlet in the back of one of the chain's Connecticut showrooms. It proved popular enough that four more of the in-store outlets were opened over the next four years.

Bob's continued to enter new markets in the early 2000s. By the spring of 2004 new stores were added in Norwich and Southington, Connecticut. In Massachusetts Bob's stores opened in Saugus, Stoughton, and Worcester, while a Pittsfield store was closed. In New Hampshire two stores were added in Nashua and a third in Manchester. Bob's also entered Maine, opening a store in Portland that led to a conflict with another retailer, Lewiston, Maine-based Bob's Discount Off-Price Superstores Inc., a four-store chain that since 1991 had been selling furniture as well as other goods.

In 2004 the Maine retailer sued Bob's in federal court over trademark infringements. Connecticut Bob's had trademarked its name in 1996; Maine Bob's had not done so. Nevertheless, the court in 2005 ruled that both companies could use the Bob's Discount name in Maine. The Connecticut-based Bob's then went to court to stop the Lewiston-based company from using the name, a matter that was delayed when the smaller company filed for bankruptcy protection.

As the company continued to expand geographically and in number of stores, Bob's made plans to add to its warehousing operation in late 2004. Ground was broken on a new 217,000-square-foot building, which opened in 2006. In the meantime the warehouse facility was sold to W.P. Carey & Co. which paid $10.3 million for it and earmarked an addition $12.3 million to fund the expansion. Bob's then agreed to lease the facility for at least 20 years.

In 2005 ownership of Bob's changed hands. With Citigroup Global Markets providing advice, Bob's

initial spots, and contends that he began doing them only after he realized the person doing the voiceovers made more money than he did. "I figured if I wasn't paying him, I could afford to pay myself," he told the *Hartford Courant.* It was only then that he began to draw a paycheck. Soon the normally shy Kaufman was starring in a string of crudely produced, yet inventive, commercials that lifted the "Come on down!" line from the television game show *The Price Is Right.*

The ads aired constantly on cable television. Even though they were regarded as annoying by most viewers (although regular-looking Bob Kaufman was well liked), they drew attention and drove sales. A $500,000 production studio was established in a converted second-floor storeroom above the company's Manchester, Connecticut, headquarters. As many as a dozen commercials at a time were churned out in unrehearsed, daylong shooting sessions. The TV spots were also supported by print ads.

Bob's Discount Stores soon became their own top competitors as customers began bidding the prices in one Bob's store against another. As a result, Bob's adopted a one-price concept in 1993. Any given item would be priced the same in every store. The chain also eschewed sales, offering the same low price all the time. In just two-and-a-half years Bob's grew to nine locations and cobbled together 275,000 square feet of warehouse space. Bob's expanded into Massachusetts in 1994, opening a store in Springfield. Total sales grew to $30 million in 1994 and increased to $46.5 million a year later. After five years the chain boasted 12 units in Connecticut and two in Massachusetts.

recapitalized in order to fund further expansion. Majority control was sold to Stamford, Connecticut-based Saunders Karp & Megrue. As part of that transaction agreement, the former chief operating officer of TJX Companies Inc., Richard G. Lesser, was named to the Bob's board.

NEW OWNER: 2005

Bob's revenues grew to $280 million in 2005. A year later, with the backing of Saunders Karp, Bob's entered two new states, New York and Rhode Island, bringing the total number of units to 25. To help grow the chain further, the new owners installed a new chief executive officer, Ted English, the former president and CEO of TJX who played a key role in that company's expansion of its TJ Maxx and Marshalls retail chains. Kaufman remained president and the public face of the company, while Rosenberg stepped aside as chairman, becoming chairman emeritus.

Bob's maintained its steady expansion in 2007 with the February opening of a new store in Farmingdale, New York, on a strip of Route 100 known as Furniture Row. It was the 28th unit and the start of a push into Long Island. Over the next two years a second store opened in Freeport, as well as a store in Nanuet, north of New York City. Bob's also entered New Jersey, opening stores in North Plainfield, Paramus, South Brunswick, Totowa, and Woodbridge, and a warehouse in North Brunswick. The company continued to fill in markets in its existing territory as well. The chain's 30th unit was opened in Bellingham, Massachusetts, in August 2008.

For its stellar performance Bob's was named 2008 "Furniture Retailer of the Year" by *Furniture Today*

magazine. The company maintained it pace of expansion in 2009, opening a store in Yonkers, New York, again nipping at the edges of the lucrative New York City market. Bob's eyed the upstate New York market as well, and added a showroom in Poughkeepsie. With the financial backing of its corporate parent, a sterling reputation with consumers, a multitude of untapped markets within its territory, and opportunities in surrounding states, there was every reason to expect that Bob's was only beginning to realize its potential.

Ed Dinger

PRINCIPAL COMPETITORS

Ethan Allen Interiors Inc.; Inter IKEA Systems B.V.; Levitz Furniture.

FURTHER READING

Bessette, Claire, "Taftville, Conn., Furniture Warehouse to Expand Again," *New London (Conn.) Day,* December 30, 2004.

Carey, Mary Agnes, "Medium-Price Approach Furnishing Sales for Discount Chain," *Hartford Courant,* May 7, 1992, p. B1.

Clancy, Ambrose, "Bob's Builds Up Furniture Road in Farmingdale," *Long Island Business News,* February 16, 2007.

Marks, Paul, "New Investors Have 'Come on Down' to Bob's Discount Furniture," *Hartford Courant,* February 1, 2005.

Moran, John M., "Bob's Discount Furniture Values Its Success," *Hartford Courant,* September 6, 1993, p. 3.

Ryan, Bill, "Now About Bob and Those TV Spots," *New York Times,* November 30, 1997, p. 14CN1.

Shea, Jim, "The Man Whose Voice You Love to Hate," *Hartford Courant,* October 3, 1996, p. E1.

Spector, Joe, "Furniture Chain Buys Prime Spot Along Federal Road," *Danbury (Conn.) News-Times,* December 17, 1996.

Brenco, Inc.

2580 Frontage Road
Petersburg, Virginia 23805-9309
U.S.A.
Telephone: (804) 732-0202
Fax: (804) 732-4722
Web site: http://www.brencoqbs.com

Wholly Owned Subsidiary of Amsted Industries Inc.
Incorporated: 1949
Employees: 575
Sales: $125 million (2008 est.)
NAICS: 332991 Ball and Roller Bearing Manufacturing

■ ■ ■

Brenco, Inc., is a Petersburg, Virginia-based subsidiary of Chicago's Amsted Industries Incorporated, which focuses on freight car and locomotive undercarriage components. Brenco's role is to produce tapered roller bearings, the company controlling about 60 percent of the market in the United States. The tapered antifriction bearings consist of an inner cone, outer cup, tapered rollers between the cone and the cup, and a cage that maintains proper spacing between the rollers. The company also produces grease seals required for the use of the bearings.

Aside from railroad applications, Brenco's tapered roller bearings are used in forklifts, over-the-road trailers, construction machinery, mining machinery, oil and gas drilling rigs, and steel mill equipment. In addition, Brenco offers support services to its customers as well as the rail industry in general. Since 1989 it has sponsored

an annual rail conference, providing a technical forum where trends and developments in the rail industry can be shared, especially related to bearings, wheels, trucks, detection equipment, and monitoring equipment. The company's Virginia facility includes five production plants as well as a wastewater treatment plant.

ORIGINS IN BRONZE BEARINGS

Brenco was established by George H. Whitfield in 1949 in the east end of Petersburg, Virginia, where at a site on Puddledock Road he built a foundry and machine shop to produce bronze journal bearings for freight cars. It was an ideal location, given the intersection of three major railroads: the Atlantic Coast Line, Norfolk & Western, and Seaboard. The name Brenco was chosen because it was an acronym for Bronze Engineering Company. Providing bronze bearings to the railroads was a profitable business, as Whitfield benefited from the post–World War II economic boom that resulted in the need for more freight cars, all of which required bearings for their undercarriages. The business, however, which was dominated by the Timken Company, was not one that offered dynamic growth.

In the late 1950s Whitfield decided to take on Timken by manufacturing tapered roller bearings, which Timken had developed and were clearly more reliable and safer than bronze bearings. He knew that the railroads, rather than being at the mercy of Timken and allowing Timken to dictate prices, would be more than willing to give some business to Whitfield, no matter how small Brenco was.

COMPANY PERSPECTIVES

Continuous improvement is our commitment for success. We continually optimize the capabilities of our entire company to compete worldwide. We will improve customer value by being more efficient today than we were yesterday.

In the early 1960s Brenco built a plant to produce the new bearings, relying on rented equipment. Whitfield's timing proved perfect, as the industry was just beginning to make the switch to tapered bearings when the plant became operational in 1962. Brenco also found a customer for its bearings among Detroit automakers, who, like the railroads, were reluctant to be wholly dependent on Timken. Adoption of tapered bearings was not immediate, but Whitfield anticipated that delay, which he knew would play to Brenco's benefit, allowing the company ample time to integrate backward in order to add all phases of fabrication and ramp up production in time for an increase in demand. The addition of tapered bearings helped to drive revenues from $2.4 million in 1961 to more than $12 million in 1965.

NEW LEADERSHIP

In 1967 Whitfield stepped down as chief executive officer, replaced by George W. Meyer. Whitfield stayed as chairman until retiring in 1973. Charles Reed then assumed the chairmanship. Whitfield left behind a business that was continuing to grow in the 1970s despite a downturn in the economy, due in large measure to favorable tax laws for freight car ownership. Investment tax credits provided a tax shelter to freight car investors; production of the cars increased, as did the need for bearings. Brenco had also succeeded in establishing itself as a major provider of tapered roller bearings, controlling about half the market by the end of the decade. To keep up with demand, the company invested $11 million in an expansion program in the middle of the decade. In 1979 George Copeland, a former executive with Swedish ball-bearing company SFK, was hired as CEO.

Brenco's revenues peaked at $88 million in 1980, when the company also netted $15 million in earnings. The bubble for freight car construction then burst, however, leading to a dramatic drop in demand for tapered bearings. Because of difficult economic conditions, the overabundance of rail cars in inventory took

considerable time to be reduced. As a result of these conditions, and Brenco's relative dependence on a single market, Brenco's net income fell to $2.9 million in 1981 and $467,000 in 1982. A year later, when sales dropped to $15.6 million, Brenco found itself losing money, about $7 million from 1983 to 1985. Moreover, the price of Brenco's publicly traded stock collapsed, declining from a peak of $25 in 1980 to $3 in 1985, and three-quarters of the workforce was laid off.

A change at the helm was in order. In 1984 Reed retired as chairman and Whitfield's son, Needham Bryan Whitfield, succeeded him. A year later Whitfield became CEO as well. In his late 40s, Whitfield was a successful businessman, albeit one with a less-than-ordinary background. An English major at Princeton University, he earned a doctorate in English literature from Dublin University. Although he had always intended to teach college, while looking for a job he became interested in accounting. After earning a degree in accounting from the University of Hartford, he became a certified public accountant at Peat, Marwick & Mitchell in Hartford, Connecticut. He then joined forces with a colleague, Roger H. J. Harper, to start an accounting firm, Harper & Whitfield, P.C., Certified Public Accountants.

DIVERSIFICATION EFFORTS

Brenco held no debt when Whitfield assumed leadership, freeing it of the interest payments that might have killed off a typical manufacturer in similar straits. Whitfield had the luxury of time to recruit a new management team and create a reorganization plan that included cost-cutting measures as well as a search for new markets for the company's roller bearings, along with a diversification effort. Not every effort met with success, however. Brenco's diversification program included industrial bearings, but after a promising start the company had to contend with price-cutting competition from Japan that eliminated any hope of profit and forced Brenco to sell its industrial bearing inventory at steep discounts.

Another diversification move was the establishment of the Rail Link Inc. subsidiary. The unit offered railroad switching services to chemical plants, paper mills, and other large industrial complexes, using Brenco's ties to the railroad industry to take advantage of an opening in the market, as many rail carriers were electing to drop this service as a way to cut their own expenses. Rail Link switched cars between railroads and end customers, and would also become a short-line railroad operator. As a service business, Rail Link offered much needed earnings during periodic rail car construction slumps, providing Brenco with the financial

KEY DATES

1949: George Whitfield starts company to produce bronze journal bearings for railroad freight cars.

1962: Company switches to tapered rolling bearings.

1967: Whitfield steps down as CEO, becomes chairman.

1973: Whitfield retires from the company.

1985: Whitfield's son, Needham Whitfield, becomes CEO.

1989: Company begins hosting annual technical rail conference.

1996: Company is sold to Varlen Corporation.

1999: Amsted Industries acquires Varlen.

2003: Annual rail conference is renamed Amsted Rail Conference.

wherewithal to take advantage of lean times to acquire equipment at inexpensive prices. Other elements of the diversification effort, automotive forgings and exports, also fared well.

Brenco did well lining up overseas customers for its bearings, especially in such countries as Australia, Brazil, Canada, Korea, Mexico, and Saudi Arabia. Because most international rail systems had not yet adopted tapered bearings, overseas sales still held great potential for the future. India was especially active in making the transition, fitting all new cars with tapered bearings. Brenco was quick to sign an exclusive agreement with the Indian national railroad and then controlled 100 percent of the Indian market. The sale of bearings in the United States also picked up after the inventory of rail cars and the supply of used bearings were exhausted.

Sales grew at a steady rate in the late 1980s, increasing 53 percent in 1988 and another 40 percent in 1989, when revenues once again topped $70 million, resulting in net income of $3 million despite a $2.6 million environmental cleanup bill at Brenco's original plant. All told, the company experienced a threefold improvement in sales since the nadir of 1985. It was also at the end of the 1980s that Brenco began hosting the annual Brenco Rail Conference, creating a technical forum where rail transportation issues could be aired.

CLUTCH TECHNOLOGY ACQUIRED

With a recession in the early 1990s, the market for rail bearings again slumped, beginning in the summer of

1991, forcing Brenco to cut back on inventories and production in 1992. Business picked up again in 1993 and Brenco was able to break the 1980 sales record, posting revenues of $98.7 million and net income of $4.23 million in 1993. The results continued to improve over the next two years. Sales grew to $117.9 million in 1994 and $127.14 million in 1995, with net income increasing to $8.8 million in 1994 and $10.7 million a year later. Along the way, Brenco in 1993 acquired the rights to a one-way clutch design for automotive transmissions from Epilogics, Inc., a California design firm. The clutch was then developed as part of Brenco's Powertrain Products division.

Whitfield, approaching 60 years of age, decided the time had come to sell the business his father had founded. He and his sister owned about 20 percent of the stock. The company was quietly put up for sale in early 1996 and after six months of negotiations, Brenco was sold to Naperville, Illinois-based Varlen Corporation for $165 million, the deal closing in August 1996. Varlen, founded in 1969, provided engineered products to the transportation industry, specializing in heavy-duty truck and train parts, but held other assets as well, and with annual sales of $441.5 million was about three times the size of Brenco. Varlen had been making a number of small acquisitions over the years. The purchase of Brenco was the most ambitious deal to date, but the move into bearings was a good fit. The innovative clutch technology Brenco controlled was also an attractive pickup. For Brenco, joining forces with a larger company provided greater security and offered overseas growth opportunities, as well as greater penetration into the domestic auto market. Rail Link, on the other hand, did not fit into Varlen's plans. In November 1996 the railroad switching unit was sold to Genesee and Wyoming Inc. for $9 million and other potential proceeds.

OWNERSHIP CHANGES

Brenco operated as an independent company under Varlen for three years, Then, in 1999, publicly traded Varlen found itself the object of an unsolicited bid to buy the company from Chicago-based Amsted Industries, which offered $35 a share, or $700 million. Twice as large as Varlen, with annual revenues of $1.3 billion, Amsted was formed in 1902 when eight midwestern steel factories came together to create American Steel Foundries. Renamed Amsted in 1962, the company produced parts for rail, automotive, construction, and industrial uses. Because it served the same markets as Varlen, yet did not compete directly, Amsted considered the Varlen assets to be an excellent opportunity. Varlen executives were less enthusiastic, however, and sought other bidders. In the end, Amsted increased its offer to $42 per share, or $790 million in total, to close the deal by the end of 1999.

Brenco was brought together with a pair of Amsted assets, Griffin Wheel Company Inc. and ASF-Keystone, Inc., to form the Amsted Rail unit, although each company operated as an independent enterprise. Starting in 2003, the corporate cousins joined with Brenco to host the annual rail conference, which then assumed the Amsted Rail Conference name. It remained the industry's only technical conference that focused on bearings, wheels, and related railroad equipment.

A downturn in the economy at the start of the new century caused a slump for Brenco, but as the economy rebounded demand for rail transportation grew as over-the-road shipping costs increased. A shortage of rolling stock developed, resulting in new car production and the need for Brenco's roller bearings. A deeper economic downturn that began in 2008 forced Brenco to shed jobs at the start of 2009, but a new administration was then in charge in Washington. Part of President Barack Obama's plan to stimulate the economy was a major investment in new high-speed rail lines. Despite short-term difficulties, a new commitment to rail transportation in the United States bode well for Brenco's future.

Ed Dinger

PRINCIPAL OPERATING UNITS

Product and Performance Engineering Group.

PRINCIPAL COMPETITORS

Aktiebolaget SKF; NSK Ltd.; Timken Company.

FURTHER READING

Buettner, Michael, "Forging Ahead," *Richmond Times-Dispatch,* April 9, 1990, p. B1.

Cooper, Elliott, "Brenco Revival Getting on Track," *Richmond Times-Dispatch,* July 3, 1988, p. D1.

———, "Brenco's Prospects Turn Up," *Richmond Times-Dispatch,* April 17, 1987, p. A13.

Jones, Chip, "Brenco Expects Few Changes," *Richmond Times-Dispatch,* June 23, 1996, p. E1.

Kale, Wilford, "Brenco: A Challenge Well Met," *Richmond Times-Dispatch,* October 26, 1993, p. C1.

Loehwing, David A., "On the Ball," *Barron's National Business and Financial Weekly,* October 25, 1965, p. 3.

Morris, Thomas R., "Brenco's Latest Hope for Gain Fades," *Richmond Times-Dispatch,* January 29, 1986, p. B5.

Smith, Geoffrey N., *Sweat Equity,* New York: Simon and Schuster, 1986.

Broan-NuTone LLC

---

926 West State Street
Hartford, Wisconsin 53027
U.S.A.
Telephone: (262) 673-4340
Fax: (262) 673-8709
Web site: http://www.broan.com

Wholly Owned Subsidiary of NTK Holdings, Inc.
Incorporated: 1932 as Midwest Manufacturing Co.
Employees: 3,246
Sales: $896 million (2008 est.)
NAICS: 332313 Plate Work Manufacturing; 335211 Electric Houseware and Fan Manufacturing; 337110 Wood Kitchen Cabinet and Counter Top Manufacturing; 339992 Musical Instrument Manufacturing

■ ■ ■

Broan-NuTone LLC is one of the world's leading manufacturers of home ventilation products such as fans, heaters, indoor air quality systems, and oven range hoods. It manufactures under the Broan and Best brands, and also manufactures for other makers such as Sears. A second product line under the NuTone brand includes door chimes. Broan-NuTone controls some 90 percent of the U.S. market in range hoods and bath fans. The company operates a large facility in Hartford, Wisconsin, with other U.S. facilities in Texas, California, Illinois, and Ohio. In addition, the company operates plants in Italy, France, Germany, and Poland, in Canada and Mexico, and in China. Broan-NuTone is a subsidiary of NTK Holdings, Inc., a Rhode Island-based conglomerate with businesses in residential ventilation, home technology, and residential and commercial heating and air conditioning.

DEPRESSION-ERA START

The company that became Broan-NuTone LLC started out in 1932, the entrepreneurial dream of Henry L. Broan. Broan had been working selling building materials for a Milwaukee manufacturer when he got the idea for an improved kitchen exhaust fan. He began making fans he called Motordor, working with three part-time employees out of a Milwaukee storefront. The Motordor was quieter than other fans on the market, and had two other innovations. Instead of turning on with a pull-chain, the Motordor was operated by a wall switch, and the flap covers that vented to the outside of the house opened automatically when the fan was turned on. This was a nice selling point, since other models of the time had to be opened with a stick. Broan named his fan business Midwest Manufacturing Company.

Despite the poor economic climate, the little company expanded through the 1930s. Broan worked tirelessly, developing a network of customers who were pleased by the company's delivery and service. In addition to kitchen fans, Midwest Manufacturing began making heaters. Broan spent his days doing marketing, calling on customers or potential customers. Much of the assembly was done at night, so that Broan could return the next day with a delivery. Sales grew so much that by 1939 the company needed larger quarters, and

COMPANY PERSPECTIVES

Broan has a way of making the indoor environment a more comfortable place. A good thing, considering how much time is spent there. While you may not always know Broan products are at work, it's easy to see when they're missing: a foggy master bath, a stuffy family room, lingering aroma of last evening's dinner. But it's more than comfort; it's a home that's healthier, too. A well ventilated home minimizes mold and mildew, and removes dust, allergens and other airborne irritants, promoting good indoor air quality. Broan does all this beautifully, with high style products that are technologically advanced, quiet, and above all, dependable.

Broan bought a plant on Milwaukee's Water Street that year.

Like many industries during World War II, Midwest Manufacturing had to scale back production because of restrictions on raw materials. At the same time, home construction dwindled, so there was much less of a market for fans and heaters. Broan himself took on a government job during the war, but continued to manufacture what products he could, working out of his garage. Conditions changed, though, when the war ended. Broan and his wife Edna formed a limited partnership to reorganize the business. They bought an entire building in downtown Milwaukee, preparing for better years to come. In 1946, the Broans transformed the limited partnership into a corporation. At that time Midwest Manufacturing Co. changed its name to Broan Manufacturing Co., Inc.

Within a decade, the new corporation had outgrown its Milwaukee headquarters. In business almost a quarter-century, Broan Manufacturing had grown rapidly, and in 1956, a watershed year for the company, sales hit a record of $1 million. That year the company moved out of the city, finding new quarters in the town of Hartford, Wisconsin. Hartford was about 40 miles from Milwaukee, and the company built a 20,000-square-foot plant there. Shortly after the move to Hartford was completed, Henry Broan died of a sudden heart attack. His son, Jack, was still in college, studying engineering at Northwestern University. Henry's wife Edna stepped in as president of Broan Manufacturing. She led the company, first as president, then as chair of the firm, until 1978.

A PERIOD OF GROWTH

Broan came out with new products after the founder's death, including an innovative ductless range hood, which used charcoal filters instead of venting to the outside. The company's lines included kitchen and bathroom fans, heaters, and lights. Although the company had less than 10 percent of the total U.S. market in kitchen and bath fans, Broan studied its market carefully, and steadily expanded its share. Jack Broan joined the company a year after finishing college. He worked his way up through several positions while his mother was president. Jack became president and CEO of Broan in 1967.

Broan began calling itself "the fresh air company," as a way of summing up its various product lines. In the 1970s the company continued to make its original product line, kitchen fans, while also branching into other home devices. Broan's products added comfort to the home, principally by moving air. The company ventured into product lines such as attic ventilation fans, bathroom wall heaters, and heat recyclers that mixed hot air at the top of a room with cool air near the floor. Sales growth was as much as 20 percent a year in the 1970s, as the company found new products and new markets as well.

Broan bought an ailing line of range hoods, kitchen fans, and other equipment from appliance maker Tappan Co. in 1972. Tappan's Nautilus Industries division had been in the red, but Broan was happy to take on the Nautilus brand because it represented a new set of customers. Broan products had been aimed principally at contractors and homebuilders, but the Nautilus line was aimed at the do-it-yourself market. The purchase of the Nautilus name thus gave the company a convenient entry into a new segment. The company began selling to home center stores in 1975. Within a few years, Broan products were sold in 22 of the top 25 home center chains.

Broan also brought out new products after careful research and development. It began selling trash compactors in 1975. A year later it brought out the heat exchanger. A goal of the heat exchanger, as well as of attic ventilation fans and other Broan products that moved air, was to reduce a householder's heating and air conditioning costs. This seemed a wise strategy in the energy-conscious 1970s. Broan also increased its reach by manufacturing products for other makers, including Sears and Montgomery Ward. In the mid-1970s about 20 percent of Broan's range hood production was for Sears. With expanding product lines and greater distribution, Broan needed to expand its facilities. Between the mid-1960s and mid-1970s, Broan added onto its Hartford plant a dozen times. The company

```
┌─────────────────────────────────────────┐
│                                         │
│            KEY DATES                    │
│                 ■                       │
│ ─────────────────────────────────────── │
│                                         │
│ 1932:  Henry L. Broan founds Midwest Manufactur- │
│        ing in Milwaukee.                │
│ 1939:  Company moves into plant on Milwaukee's │
│        Water Street.                    │
│ 1946:  Midwest Manufacturing changes name to │
│        Broan Manufacturing.             │
│ 1956:  Company moves to Hartford, Wisconsin; │
│        founder Broan dies.              │
│ 1975:  The company begins selling to home center │
│        stores.                          │
│ 1981:  Broan Manufacturing is sold to Nortek. │
│ 1998:  Broan acquires NuTone.           │
│ 2000:  Broan changes its name to Broan-NuTone │
│        LLC.                             │
│ 2004:  Broan-NuTone opens a subsidiary in Hong │
│        Kong.                            │
│                                         │
└─────────────────────────────────────────┘
```

was a major employer in the area, giving jobs to some 500 people. Broan's sales had risen to $25 million by 1976.

SALE TO NORTEK

Broan continued to grow rapidly through the 1980s, but it did so under new management. The company had been closely held by members of the Broan family since its inception in 1932. Edna Broan retired as chair of the firm in 1978. Jack Broan had been working at Broan since shortly after graduating from college, and had led the company since 1967. In 1980, the family announced its decision to sell Broan Manufacturing to a Rhode Island-based conglomerate, Nortek, Inc. Broan by that time had sales of over $50 million, with a profit of $2.3 million. The company sold for $22 million in cash, plus other deferred payments.

The buyer, Nortek, had quite a diverse product mix in 1980. It was a large, publicly traded company that seemed to be in the business of buying other businesses. It had begun acquiring in 1967, and by 1980 its product lines ranged from tombstones and men's suit linings to building products and ventilators. Nortek's stock price had suffered a shock in 1978 when the company announced it would begin building and operating hotels and casinos in Atlantic City. Apparently investors were initially excited, and then skeptical that Nortek could accomplish this. By 1980, an analyst quoted in the *Wall Street Journal* (December 30, 1980) described Nortek as follows: "It's one of those

companies that's always been blurry ... it doesn't have any focus, it's hard to get the market interested."

Nortek did, however, have interests in ventilation and in other building products. Nortek greatly refined its product lines after it acquired the Wisconsin company, focusing on four loosely related product groups in home and commercial ventilation and heating and cooling. The purchase of Broan was advantageous to Nortek, giving it a kernel around which to build core businesses. At the same time, the parent company conferred advantages on Broan. With a parent with deep pockets, Broan was able to expand its product lines, move into new markets, and make some acquisitions of its own.

The sale to Nortek, announced in 1980, closed in 1981. By 1983, sales had topped $100 million, and Broan's products were nicely balanced between lines meant for homebuilders and those geared for home improvement markets. The company invested in robotic manufacturing systems, which kept its labor costs low. It continued to produce goods for major appliance manufacturers and for Sears and Montgomery Ward. When Ronald Reagan visited Broan's Hartford plant in 1987, the company could claim to have doubled in size since he took office.

MORE DIVERSIFICATION

Broan celebrated its 60th year in business in 1992. That year it brought a new $15 million fully automated range hood manufacturing system on line. Broan had become the largest range hood manufacturer in the world, and made more than 50 percent of the range hoods sold in North America. Broan was a major employer in the town of Hartford and had a strong commitment to its Wisconsin roots. Because it had installed the most up-to-date robotic equipment in the Hartford plant, Broan was able to produce on a large scale, yet keep its labor costs low. While other manufacturers turned to low-cost labor in Mexico or Asia, Broan kept over 700 people employed in Hartford.

At the same time, Broan expanded into European markets. It purchased an Italian maker of high-end range hoods in 1995, Best SpA. Best was the third largest range hood manufacturer in Europe, specializing in luxury models. It had a large distribution network in Europe and beyond. Broan took over Best's North American business, selling its products under the new "Best by Broan" label, and began making inroads into Europe as well. Broan's acquisition in 1995 of Venmar Ventilation Inc. brought Broan into a new product line, heat recovery ventilators.

Broan's parent Nortek acquired a British company, Williams plc, in 1998. Williams had multiple subsidiaries, including an Ohio company called NuTone. Nu-Tone was then folded into Broan. NuTone was founded only a few years after Broan, in 1936. It was best known for its door chimes, a product it had invented. At one time NuTone door chimes were found in 50 million U.S. homes. NuTone had changed hands multiple times since 1968, and had expanded into other product lines, including kitchen exhaust fans and bathroom heaters, so the company was in direct competition with Broan. The importance of NuTone to Broan, its new parent, was signaled in 2000 when Broan Manufacturing changed its name to Broan-NuTone. By the time of the name change, Broan had grown to employ over 4,000 people worldwide. Its product lines included central vacuum systems, bathroom cabinets, chimes and intercoms, as well as range hoods, kitchen and bathroom fans, attic fans, heaters, and trash compactors, made for both the builders market and for the do-it-yourself market.

Expanding product lines had necessitated even more expansion to the Hartford plant. Remodeling completed in 2001 more than doubled the size of the Hartford facility. The company also had manufacturing or assembly plants in several other states, and in Germany and Italy. The company moved more firmly into overseas markets, too, in the first years of the new century. It opened a subsidiary in Hong Kong in 2004, and the next year opened another in Huizhou, China. The company widened its European presence by building a new facility in Poland in 2006. This was known as Best Poland. Although the original Italian Best specialized in luxury range hoods, Best Poland made lower-end models, for sale throughout Europe. Broan also took on a new domestic subsidiary, the San Francisco-based Zephyr. Zephyr, like Best, made high-end kitchen ventilation products.

While making acquisitions and moving into new markets, Broan also brought out a slew of new products. The middle of the decade saw the introduction of over 1,000 new products. The company had started in the Great Depression with a single product, the Motordor fan. After more than 75 years in business, Broan was still headquartered in Wisconsin, and still making kitchen ventilation products. Its market by this time was global and its product lines diverse, with sales reaching toward $900 million annually.

A. Woodward

PRINCIPAL SUBSIDIARIES

Broan Building Products (Huizhou) Ltd. (China); Broan-NuTone (HK) Ltd. (Hong Kong); Best Poland.

PRINCIPAL COMPETITORS

Emerson Electric Co.; Westinghouse Lighting Corp.; BSH Bosch und Siemens Hausgerate GmbH.

FURTHER READING

Ashley, Mark, "Broan Takes Aim at Heat, Power Costs," *Milwaukee Journal,* December 12, 1976, p. 12.

Curtis, Alvin L., "Manufacturer of Fans and Range Hoods Moving at Hot Pace in Market," *Milwaukee Sentinel,* July 31, 1984, p. 1.

"Hartford Firm Gears Up for Reagan," *Wisconsin State Journal,* July 26, 1987, sec. 1, p. 9.

"Hartford, Wis.-based Manufacturer Changes Name, Plans $6 Million Addition," *Milwaukee Journal Sentinel,* October 31, 2000.

Knoche, Eldon, "Broan Led Range Hood, Fan Company," *Milwaukee Journal Sentinel,* June 25, 1997, p. 7.

"Nortek Agrees to Buy Broan Manufacturing for over $22 Million," *Wall Street Journal,* September 11, 1980, p. 19.

"Nortek Is Planning More Diversification to Achieve 'Balance,'" *Wall Street Journal,* December 30, 1980, p. 13.

Pradnya, Joshi, "Broan Buys Range-Hood Maker in Italy," *Milwaukee Journal Sentinel,* April 29, 1995, p. D1.

Rovito, Rich, "Pringle to Chinese: Bring It On," *Business Journal of Milwaukee,* July 21, 2003.

Silvers, Amy Rabideau, "Broan Expansion Aims to Secure Hartford Company's Dominance," *Milwaukee Journal,* July 11, 1992, pp. 1, 4.

———, "Broan Expansion Represents Strong Commitment to Hartford," *Milwaukee Journal,* July 11, 1992.

"Tappan to Partly Sell Unit, Then Close It," *Wall Street Journal,* June 2, 1972, p. 2.

Torinus, John, "Home-Grown Broan Has What It Takes to Compete in Global Market," *Milwaukee Journal Sentinel,* October 21, 2001, pp. 1D, 11D.

Wessels, Joe, "NuTone Co. Is Closing Its Doors," *Cincinnati Post,* July 8, 2006, p. A1.

Camp Dresser & McKee Inc.

50 Hampshire Street
Cambridge, Massachusetts 02139-1548
U.S.A.
Telephone: (617) 452-6000
Fax: (617) 452-8000
Web site: http://www.cdm.com

Private Company
Incorporated: 1970
Employees: 4,000
Sales: $1 billion (2008 est.)
NAICS: 541330 Engineering Services; 541611 Administrative Management and General Management Consulting Services

■ ■ ■

Camp Dresser & McKee Inc. (CDM) is a global consulting, engineering, construction, and operations firm based in Cambridge, Massachusetts, with more than 100 offices around the world. Focusing on environmental management, water treatment and supply, wastewater treatment, and hazardous waste, CDM divides its business among five major groups: Federal Services; Industrial Services; Public Services, North America East & Latin America; Public Services, North America West/Central & Asia; and Client Services, Europe, Middle East & Africa.

CDM's consulting services cover such areas as architecture, environmental management systems, asset management, information management and technology, security, and sustainable development. CDM offers the full complement of engineering services, including civil, electrical, mechanical, geotechnical, process, structural, automation and instrumentation, and 3D design. CDM also provides an extensive range of construction and operations services. Private clients are found in the chemical, electrical utility, food and beverage, manufacturing, and metals and mining industries. CDM also does a great deal of work for the U.S. government, including the Army Corps of Engineers, Department of Defense, Department of Energy, Department of Homeland Security, Environmental Protection Agency, Department of Transportation, and Federal Emergency Management Agency. CDM works with public agencies and utilities and universities, as well as a broad range of clients in more than 130 countries on behalf of government agencies, nongovernmental and private voluntary organizations. CDM is an employee-owned company governed by a board of directors.

POSTWAR ORIGINS

CDM was originally a partnership formed in 1947 by Dr. Thomas Ringgold Camp, Herman G. Dresser, and Jack Edward McKee. Born in 1895, senior partner Camp worked as an engineer before becoming a professor at the Massachusetts Institute of Technology (MIT), eventually becoming the head of the sanitary engineering department. While at MIT he developed a number of innovative water treatment technologies, including dual-media filters, porous underdrains, and direct filtration of municipal water supplies. Camp left MIT in 1944 to establish a consulting practice with Dresser, who served as his principal engineer.

McKee had been a student of one of Camp's friends, Gordon Fair, who, like Camp, was a leader in the field of sanitary engineering. Born in 1914, McKee earned a degree in civil engineering from the Carnegie Institute of Technology in 1936. He went to work for the Tennessee Valley Authority but when he learned that Fair was looking for teaching fellows in sanitary engineering at Harvard University, he quit to join Fair in Cambridge. McKee earned a master's degree at Harvard in 1939 and a doctorate in 1941.

During World War II McKee served in the Corps of Engineers in Europe while Camp and Dresser began their consulting practice. After he was discharged from the service, McKee conferred with Fair about his career and was directed to Camp and Dresser. McKee joined them as an associate and quickly proved his worth. In 1946, working under the aegis of Camp, he produced a study on pollution control for the Massachusetts section of the Merrimack River. This became the cornerstone of water-quality improvement for the river for the next 30 years. In 1947 the Camp, Dresser, and McKee partnership was formed, but just two years later McKee left the firm to fulfill a desire to teach. He became a professor at the California Institute of Technology in 1949.

Although McKee would work for CDM on only a part-time basis in the years to come, he remained a partner, helped to open the Pasadena office, and after the firm was incorporated, became a senior vice-president and was later named honorary chairman and consultant to the board. He made professional contributions to CDM, while Camp established the firm's high standard of technical excellence. For his part, Dresser played a key role in the firm's dedication to employee development.

JOSEPH LAWLER BECOMES PARTNER: 1952

Another key partner in the early days of CDM was Joseph Christopher Lawler, another of Gordon Fair's students. Younger than Camp, Dresser, and McKee, Lawler was born in 1920 and received his B.S. in civil engineering from Northeastern University in 1943.

With the country in the midst of World War II, he immediately joined the Navy's Civil Engineer Corps to serve with a construction battalion in the South Pacific. He enrolled at Harvard in 1946 following his discharge and studied under Fair.

After earning his master's degree a year later, Lawler joined CDM when the three principals had but eight people in their employ. Lawler demonstrated both technical ability and a strong business sense, so that in 1952 he made partner in the firm. He was then named president of CDM's international subsidiary in 1968 and chairman of the CDM board after the partnership was dissolved in favor of a corporate structure.

CDM's business through the 1950s was focused on water supply and water pollution control projects in Massachusetts, New Hampshire, and Maine. The firm began to expand internationally in the 1960s under Lawler's guidance, winning a number of major design contracts. To facilitate further growth, the firm's structure was changed to a corporation in 1970. A number of acquisitions and mergers followed, allowing CDM to add operations in California, Colorado, Florida, New York, Virginia, and Wisconsin.

During this period there was also a changing of the guard in the top ranks. Camp died in 1971, followed by McKee in 1979. Lawler took over as president and chairman of the board in 1970 and under his leadership the firm grew into an organization with offices in 15 states and another 30 offices around the world, employing more than 1,200 engineers, scientists, and support staff. CDM was listed among the top 20 on the *Engineering News-Record* list of the 500 largest engineering firms in the United States. Lawler remained chairman until his death at the age of 62 in 1982.

FIRST SUPERFUND CONTRACT: 1981

After the passing of the firm's first generation, CDM continued to grow its water and wastewater business but also became involved in hazardous waste management. A major step was taken in this direction in 1981 when the firm received one of the first major Superfund contracts awarded by the Environmental Protection Agency (EPA) in the wake of Love Canal disaster in New York in the 1970s. Congress passed the Comprehensive Environmental Response, Compensation, and Liability Act, commonly known as Superfund, to clean up abandoned hazardous waste sites. Although the Reagan administration initially neglected to provide adequate funding for the initiative, CDM received some of the early contracts.

In 1984, for example, the firm received a four-year, $168 million consulting contract from the EPA to work

KEY DATES

1947: Camp Dresser & McKee is established as a partnership.
1968: An international subsidiary is formed.
1970: The partnership is converted to a corporation.
1981: The firm receives its first Superfund contract.
1986: CDM Federal Programs Corporation is formed.
1994: The company is reorganized to become more market-driven.
2000: The Consulting Group Inc. is acquired.
2009: Three multi-country business units are created.

with several other companies in cleaning up hazardous-water dumps, the largest Superfund contract to that point. A reauthorization act finally made substantial funds available to Superfund work. Due to the requirements imposed by the federal government on contractors, the company formed CDM Federal Programs Corporation in 1986 to focus on Superfund and other federal contracts.

By the end of the 1980s CDM was generating annual revenues of $220 million. Leading the firm into the new decade was Robert C. Marini, named chairman and chief executive officer in April 1989. After earning a B.S. in engineering from Northeastern University in 1954, followed by a master's degree from Harvard University a year later, Marini went to work for CDM as a junior engineer. He worked his way up through the ranks, becoming an associate in 1964 and making partner three years later. In 1977 he became president of the Environmental Engineering Division.

Marini was responsible for implementing a "modified-matrix" system of responsibility in the organization. In short, the firm was comprised of Practices, which were entrepreneurial and technically driven, and Divisions, which were geographic in nature. According to a 1992 company profile in *Industry Week*, "The balance of power and authority between these two matrix components is constantly shifting, depending up the market situation. The Practices drive the application of innovative technology and monitor future market trends while the Divisions are the project implementors and the direct-sales interface."

A sharing of authority and resources between the practices and the divisions was key to the firm's success and ability to provide the best possible service to clients,

who fell within five market categories: environmental management, wastewater, water, solid waste, and storm water.

REORGANIZATION: 1994

With Marini at the helm, CDM continued to grow in the 1990s, striking out in several directions. To expand its environmental services in Europe, for example, CDM created a joint venture with another Massachusetts company, the major defense contract Raytheon Company, whose Netherlands subsidiary, Badger B.V., an engineering and construction company serving the chemical and petrochemical industries, joined forces with CDM in 1990.

CDM reorganized its structure again in 1994, becoming more market-driven and less geographically focused. The move also allowed CDM to grow beyond its pure design firm orientation and begin offering construction services. As a result CDM Engineers & Constructors, a construction, general contracting, and design/build subsidiary was established. Also during this time the firm built on its strengths in geotechnical services, transportation, operations, and information management. Revenues were in the $325 million range.

By the latter 1990s CDM's revenues topped $460 million, of which 15 percent, or about $70 million, was generated by its operations in more than 100 international offices. In 1998 Thomas D. Furman Jr. was selected as CEO to lead the company into the 21st century. A year later he became chairman as well. Furman had been with the firm since 1973 and had served as president since 1991.

CDM continued to grow its domestic operations in the 1990s and in the new century expanded its international operations as well. It established a full-service consultancy in Galway, Ireland, in 2001, and later that year added to its European footprint by acquiring the assets of BRP Consult GmbH, a German geotechnical, planning, environmental technology, and project management firm. CDM also looked to the Far East, in particular the growing economy of China. In 2006 the firm developed an industrial pollution control action plan for the city of Ningbo in Zhejiang Province.

RICHARD FOX NAMED
CHAIRMAN AND CEO: 2009

After leading CDM through a decade of strong growth, Furman retired in 2008, leading to a transition in leadership at the start of 2009. Replacing Furman as chairman and CEO was CDM's president since 2001, Richard D. Fox, a man with 33 years of engineering experience. At the same time that Fox took charge, CDM reorganized its structure once again to set the stage for continued growth. The operations of the International and Public Services Groups were divided into three multi-country business units: Client Services, Europe, Middle East, and Africa; Public Services, North America East and Latin America; and Public Services, North America West/Central America and Asia.

Ed Dinger

PRINCIPAL OPERATING UNITS

Federal Services; Industrial Services; Public Services, North America East & Latin America; Public Services, North America West/Central & Asia; Client Services, Europe, Middle East & Africa.

PRINCIPAL COMPETITORS

CH2M Hill Companies, Ltd.; Tetra Tech, Inc.; URS Corporation.

FURTHER READING

"Camp Dresser Receives $168 Million EPA Job to Aid Toxic Cleanup," *Wall Street Journal,* June 6, 1984, p. 1.

"Joseph C. Lawler Jr., 62, Engineering Firm Chairman," *Boston Globe,* November 20, 1982, p. 1.

"Marini New Chairman at Camp Dresser," *Boston Globe,* April 23, 1989, p. A15.

Rubin, Debra K., "CDM Realigns with Markets," *Engineering News-Record,* August 20, 1994, p. 16.

Weimer, George A., "The Business of Idealism," *Industry Week,* October 5, 1992, p. 57.

Campmor, Inc.

---

400 Corporate Drive
Mahwah, New Jersey 07430-3606
U.S.A.
Telephone: (201) 335-9064
Toll Free: (800) 525-4784; (888) 226-7667
Fax: (201) 236-3601
Web site: http://www.campmor.com

Private Company
Incorporated: 1978
Employees: 300
Sales: $82.9 million (2007)
NAICS: 451110 Sporting Goods Stores; 454113 Mail-
Order Houses

■ ■ ■

Maintaining its headquarters in Mahwah, New Jersey, Campmor, Inc., is a family-owned outdoor recreation equipment retailer. The company operates a single store, 37,000 square feet in size, on the major shopping thoroughfare of Route 17 in Paramus, New Jersey, close to New York City's George Washington Bridge. A longtime cataloger, Campmor was quick to embrace the Internet, and although the print catalog remains available, sales from the company's web site account for more than 80 percent of total revenues. The store, known for being staffed by people well versed with the equipment they sell, is divided between several departments: Winter Sports; Canoe and Kayak; Climbing, Electronics and Optics; Tents; Repair/Service; and Bike

Shop, including repair services and a wide variety of roof racks for transportation.

The Campmor catalog and web site divide its offerings among Outerwear, including jackets, vests, pants and bibs, rainwear, headwear, and gloves and mitts; Clothing, including specialty running and triathlon apparel; Footwear, including hiking boots, winter and rain boots, multisport shoes, sandals and water shoes, slippers and booties, and such casual shoes as slip-ons, jungle mocs, and deck shoes; and Gear, including tents, packs, sleeping gear, stoves, electronics, knives and tools, lights and lanterns, survival items, climbing gear, books and maps, and food and beverages packaged for outdoor treks. Founded by Chairman Morton Jarashow, Campmor is run by his son, President and Chief Executive Officer Daniel Jarashow.

POSTWAR CATALOG LAUNCH

Morton Jarashow became familiar with retailing through his father, who ran a small paint store. Jarashow had planned on a career in the law, but his education at New York University law school was interrupted by World War II. He joined the Army Air Corps in 1942 and was dispatched to England where as a gunner on a bomber he survived 33 combat missions. Following his discharge he resumed his law school studies. Jarashow's father, in the meantime, had been given some Army surplus camping gear, which Jarashow sold for him with little trouble.

Sensing a business opportunity, as well as a way to help pay the bills, he teamed up with his brother, Sanford, to start an army surplus equipment business in

COMPANY PERSPECTIVES

With over 30 years experience, we share your love of fresh air and the great outdoors. No matter what the adventure, we've got your outdoor gear needs covered.

1947, which they named Morsan Inc., drawing on the initial syllables of their first names. It consisted of a mail-order catalog and a single store located in Long Island City. In a matter of months, Sanford left the business, and Jarashow continued to run it with his wife, Irene, who managed the books. After passing his bar exam he also began practicing law while peddling surplus Army goods but eventually decided to quit the law and focus on retailing.

With the onset of the Korean War in 1950 Jarashow's goods were again needed by the military, and his supplies quickly dwindled. As a result he was forced to develop his own products and in short order turned himself into a tent design expert. Another major change that followed was his decision to relocate the store. Lacking parking, the Long Island City store held little potential for growth. While Jarashow wished to remain in the New York City area, he was loathe to pay the prevailing rents. He turned his attention to Rockland County, New York, and because every real estate agent he called was unavailable, he took a scouting trip on his own. He ventured south into northern New Jersey on the Garden State Parkway and took the Paramus exit. By sheer chance he stumbled upon a vacant building available at a price he could afford.

MORSAN SOLD: 1969

While Jarashow set up shop in Paramus, he continued to run his mail-order operation. When sales began to sag, however, he began to emphasize retail sales. Three additional Morsan surplus stores opened. In 1969 he decided to sell the four-store chain to Lionel Corporation for $3 million in stock, staying on to run the business until 1972. That year, however, he fell out with the new owners over the accelerated pace of expansion, and he quit. Although he was proven right, as the 12-store chain soon collapsed and was liquidated by 1978, it was cold comfort to Jarashow, whose stock in Lionel plummeted in value. What had been priced at $10 when he sold Morsan, was only $2 a share when he finally sold. One asset he retained was the Paramus building where he had established his store after leaving Long Island City.

CAMPMOR FOUNDED: 1978

In need of money and longing to return to a business he loved, Jarashow returned to retailing in 1978, starting Campmor Inc. and setting up shop in a former sheet-metal shop in Bogota, New Jersey. The location, near some railroad tracks, was remote, and the 9,000-square-foot, two-story structure offered a retail environment that was far from the norm, with some unusual advantages: The wooden floors allowed Jarashow to erect tents and nail them to the floor for customer inspection.

In the first year in operation, Jarashow and his lone employee rang up $300,000 in sales, mostly coming from a mail-order operation he set up. The *Reader's Digest*-sized catalog was hardly sophisticated, consisting of black-and-white drawings printed on recycled newspaper, but it was thorough and generated increasing amounts of sales, especially as catalogs of all types became popular with consumers in the 1980s.

Nevertheless, the retail store remained an important part of the company, and in 1983 Jarashow moved it from Bogota to the Route 17 location he still owned in Paramus. To support the growth of the store and catalog operation, a 40,000-square-foot warehouse was opened in 1987. Joining Jarashow to help grow the business was his son, Daniel Jarashow, who had always planned on becoming a part of Campmor and was destined to take over as chief executive. Mort Jarashow remained as chairman of the company and continued to work in his beloved tent department well past the age of 80.

As Campmor entered the 1990s the catalog continued to expand and sales continued to mount within its core serious outdoorsman/backcountry camper market. By 1994 the catalog topped 150 pages and was printed six times a year, with 15 million to 20 million copies being mailed each year. The Campmor catalog was not a threat to such catalogers as L.L. Bean, which appealed to a more mainstream market, but it was the bane of specialty sporting goods and mountaineering shops around the country that had to contend with potential customers armed with the little catalog packed with information, comparing prices, and peppering sales personnel with questions. All too often for these customers the competitors' stores were a place to see the merchandise, and the catalog was the place to buy it.

The market was also expanding because an increasing number of people were becoming interested in the outdoors. The catalog operation, the buyers and the telephone staffers who had been working in the store's back rooms, were moved in the spring of 1993 to a new corporate headquarters in nearby Upper Saddle River. A pair of new buyers, for biking accessories and children's clothing, were also added at this juncture. With the departure of the catalog sales personnel, the Paramus

KEY DATES

1947: Morton Jarashow starts an Army surplus store with brother.
1969: Jarashow sells surplus store chain.
1978: Jarashow starts Campmor, Inc., in Bogota, New Jersey.
1983: Store is relocated to Paramus, New Jersey.
1987: New warehouse opens.
1995: Campmor launches its web site.
2005: Online sales account for 70 percent of revenues.

store claimed the space to expand its offerings, as all departments increased their stock size. In addition, in-line skating products were added, and biking became a full-fledged department.

Campmor was quick to take advantage of the retail possibilities offered by the Internet. In the mid-1990s as the Web was beginning to take shape, Daniel Jarashow interviewed several New York technical firms, but settled on a small Pittsburgh, Pennsylvania-based public relations firm owned and operated by two women, Marion Lewis and Jeanette Thomas. They had been colleagues at a hospital in the early 1980s and in 1991 decided to start their own public relations firm, Thomas & Poorbaugh, their last names at the time. Because the economy soon soured they scrambled to find a niche in the marketplace and gain some press exposure for their work putting corporate brochures online, then a novelty. They decided to pursue e-business services and outsourced the technical side. Essentially on a hunch, Jarashow threw in his lot with Thomas & Poorbaugh, perhaps influenced in some small measure by a shared experience with Thomas, as both had graduated from the Pennsylvania State University.

CAMPMOR GOES ONLINE: 1995

Campmor's initial online initiative was rudimentary at best. In early 1995 the retailer began making some of its catalog offerings, about 250 products, available on the Compuserve online subscription service. An order form could then be printed, filled out, and faxed in. "We wanted to get our feet wet as soon as possible," a company spokesman told the press. "We feel that down the road," he added, in what would amount to a vast understatement, "the on-line sale will be a powerful tool in the retailing business." Campmor continued to operate its retail store, in the meantime, and soon faced

increased competition from a new Eastern Mountain Sports (EMS) store that opened next door in the fall of 1996. If anything, the new store brought more traffic to Campmor, which experienced an increase in sales following the launch of the EMS store. Parking was so limited on weekends and holidays that employees were forbidden from using any of the spaces.

It became evident by 1997 that online sales would indeed become a major marketing channel for Campmor. To extend its online reach, the company forged a marketing deal with the leading online provider of the day, America Online (AOL), in 1999 to become a tenant in the Pets, Travel and Outdoor Department of AOL's Shopping Channel, thus allowing it to directly market products, more than 10,000 in all, to AOL's 16 million members. While AOL would begin to see its business erode in the new century, Campmor continued to grow its online sales, which would overshadow stores sales and eventually the company's robust catalog business.

Helping most of the way was Thomas & Poorbaugh, and then Tachyon Solutions Inc., formed when Thomas & Poorbaugh merged with Pittsburgh Computer Consultants in 1999. Campmor's web site became increasingly more effective and efficient. Online sales soared while the back end of the system grew more robust, so that as soon as an online order was placed, the inventory system was automatically updated and shipping manifest created. By 2002 Campmor's annual revenues increased to more than $80 million, 55 percent of which were online. Mail order contributed about 30 percent, and the retail store continued to account for another 15 percent.

WEB SITE IMPROVED: 2004

In 2004 Campmor revisited its Web business with Tachyon in order to make it even more productive. Using site analytics, Tachyon studied who visited the site and for how long, and determined how many of these visitors actually became customers. It was learned that visitors often began shopping but abandoned their carts, evidence that they were having trouble finding what they were looking for on the site. As a result, Tachyon recruited a new search company to develop enhanced search capabilities. Not only did it become easier to search the Campmor site, the results, even of detailed searches, were made available in less than a second. This change to the web site led to a 35 percent improvement in online sales in 2005, thus increasing the contribution of online sales to 70 percent of the company's net revenues. Moreover, the improved web site allowed about half of all orders to go directly to the warehouse without the need of human intervention, providing additional cost savings.

Web sales increased to about 85 percent of Campmor's business by 2009. In addition to making the web site available to visitors through search engine marketing, the company also employed e-mail marketing campaigns. Because Campmor was not able to measure the effectiveness of these efforts, it contracted with StrongMail Systems, Inc., in 2009 to implement advanced marketing and transaction e-mail communications systems that allowed the company to better hone its marketing messages, which could lead to high conversions and sales. It was this commitment to every detail of its business that bode well for the continued success of Campmor.

Ed Dinger

PRINCIPAL COMPETITORS

Eastern Mountain Sports, Inc.; L.L. Bean, Inc.; Recreational Equipment, Inc.

FURTHER READING

Demarrais, Kevin G., "Campmor Outdoor Gear Company See Huge Growth Since Start in Queens," *Record* (N.J.), July 27, 2002.

McEvoy, Christopher, "Outdoor Magazines/Retailers Pedal Merchandise On-Line," *Sporting Goods Business,* May 1995, p. 21.

"Mom and Pop Camping Shop Gets E-Commerce Boost," *eWeek,* May 1, 2006.

Schooley, Tim, "Tachyon Solutions Adjust to Rapid Growth, Speed of New Tech Advances," *Pittsburgh Business Times,* May 19, 2000.

Selkirk, Scott, "Campmor Than Enough," *SportStyle,* August 1, 1994, p. 17.

Capario

Private Company
Incorporated: 1989 as ProxyMed Inc.
Employees: 170
NAICS: 518210 Data Processing, Hosting, and Related
  Services

■ ■ ■

Headquartered in Santa Ana, California, Capario is a leading healthcare technology enterprise. Held by the private-equity firm Marlin Equity Partners, the company is focused on connecting insurance companies, healthcare providers, and vendors, helping them to better manage their revenue cycles and reduce the costs associated with claims processing.

FORMATIVE YEARS: 1989–98

Capario traces its roots back to 1989, when the company was formed in Florida as a drugstore chain named ProxyMed Inc. After operating as a pharmaceutical services company for about five years, ProxyMed sold its mail-order prescription business, as well as 14 pharmacies, to Largo, Florida-based Eckerd Corp. in 1995 for $5.1 million. In September of that year, the

company also shed its home drug infusion therapy business, ProxyFusion, which was sold to National Health Care Affiliates of New York. At this time, Harold S. Blue served as chairman and CEO.

Midway through 1996, ProxyMed revealed plans to sell its subsidiary that marketed pharmaceuticals to long-term care facilities. Along with its other divestitures, this was part of a strategy to focus solely on information technology (IT). While operating as a pharmacy, ProxyMed had developed technology, dubbed ProxyNet, which allowed physicians to submit electronic prescriptions to its pharmacies.

During the mid-1990s ProxyMed was among a handful of industry players focusing on healthcare-related Internet technology. At that time, approximately 2,000 doctors in Michigan, Kentucky, New Jersey, and Florida were relying upon the company's network to submit prescriptions to roughly 15,000 pharmacies.

By 1997 ProxyMed was organized into three divisions: clinical information systems, network services, and software systems. At the time, the organization was led by President and Chief Operating Officer Jack Guinan. Early in the year, the company agreed to acquire Babylon, New York-based Clinical MicroSystems, a leading provider of software that physicians used for lab ordering and results posting.

Growth continued midway through the year, when ProxyMed snapped up the Tallahassee, Florida-based IT company Hayes Computer Systems Inc. The company also agreed to acquire an electronic prescription network owned by Walgreen Co. in a cash deal worth $3.5 million, and to include Walgreen in its network for 12 years. Also around this time, Eckerd signed a deal with ProxyMed for the use of its prescription network.

ProxyMed rounded out 1997 with net sales of $10.9 million. By this time the company's clinical network provided access to 70 percent of pharmacies in the United States. Growth accelerated in 1998, as ProxyMed parted with $27.5 million to acquire the Santa Ana, California-based electronic medical claims processing company WPJ Inc. (which conducted business as Integrated Medical Systems). That year, net sales skyrocketed 245 percent, reaching nearly $37.8 million.

EARLY GROWTH: 1999–2001

Growth continued at ProxyMed heading into the late 1990s. In January 1999 the company merged with New Albany, Indiana-based Key Communications Service Inc., a laboratory results reporting software company, gaining access to approximately 1,800 clinical laboratories that were prime prospects for ProxyMed's lab connectivity solutions.

Many new customers were acquired in 1999. Between late April and early July alone, ProxyMed gained 27 new clients, including Kaiser Foundation Health Plan of Colorado, Coventry Health Care Inc., and the University of California–Davis.

The company rounded out the 1990s with a leadership change, as John B. Okkerse Jr. was named CEO on December 1. Blue remained with the company as chairman. For the year, ProxyMed recorded a net loss of nearly $21.9 million on annual revenues of $29 million. During its first decade, ProxyMed had transformed itself from a pharmacy to an IT company providing connections between physicians and pharmacies, suppliers, insurance companies, labs, and patients, providing the means for the secure exchange of both financial and clinical data.

ProxyMed began 2000 with the news that it had enrolled its 2,000th physician in the company's Pre-Scribe electronic pharmacy management system. By April that number had increased to 2,545 physicians, who were connected to approximately 30,000 pharmacies nationwide.

Developments continued to unfold at a rapid pace throughout the remainder of 2000. In April ProxyMed announced that it had sold ProxyCare Inc., its drug dispensing business, as well as the company's Hayes network integration division. By divesting what it considered to be noncore operations, the company netted about $3.7 million.

The following month, ProxyMed announced an $8.5 million effort to cut costs. At the same time, the company cleaned out its executive suite and parted ways with its CEO, chief operating officer, chief marketing officer, and chief financial officer. Chairman Blue served as interim CEO until a more-permanent replacement could be found.

By October, Michael K. Hoover was serving as ProxyMed's chairman and CEO. That month, the company named Nancy J. Ham as chief operating officer. Following a one-for-15 reverse stock split in August 2001, at which time the value of ProxyMed's shares had dipped to less than $1, Ham assumed the additional role of president.

ACCELERATED GROWTH: 2002–04

After securing $25 million in equity financing from General Atlantic Partners in April 2002, ProxyMed shifted into growth mode. In May the Moorestown, New Jersey-based laboratory communications services provider KenCom Communications & Services Inc. was acquired. Midway through the year, Medical Data Insurance Processing Inc., a Sioux Falls, South Dakota-based claims processing company, was acquired for $2.4 million.

Acquisitions continued in 2003. ProxyMed kicked off the year by snapping up MedUnite, which focused on converting physicians' paper-based transactions to Web-based transactions. In December, plans were made to merge with the business process outsourcing services provider PlanVista Corp. The company rounded out 2003 with a $5 million net loss on record revenues of $71.6 million.

Rapid change unfolded in 2004. In March ProxyMed's merger with PlanVista was completed. Three months later the company agreed to sell its Lab Services Division's Key Electronics contract manufacturing business to A. Thomas Hardy, president of ProxyMed's Key Communications Service Inc. business.

By mid-2004 ProxyMed ranked as the second largest provider-based electronic healthcare transactions services company in the United States. At that time the company relocated its corporate headquarters from Fort Lauderdale to Atlanta, Georgia, and was added to the Russell 2000 Index of publicly traded companies.

ProxyMed capped off 2004 by instituting significant changes at the senior leadership level. In December the company announced plans to separate the roles of chairman and CEO, in the interest of more effective corporate governance. At that time, Kevin McNamara was named chairman. Hoover remained with the company as CEO. ProxyMed ended the year with a net loss of $3.8 million on record revenues of $90.2 million.

REORGANIZATION AND A NAME CHANGE: 2005

More leadership changes occurred in January 2005. At that time, CEO Hoover announced that he would retire at the end of the month. Chairman McNamara served as interim CEO until John G. Lettko, a seasoned financial and technology services industry executive, was hired in May. In early June, President and Chief Operating Officer Ham revealed plans to resign from her post in July.

In addition to the new executive team, ProxyMed completed an eight-week internal analysis in August 2005, and revealed plans to reorganize and refocus the business. This came to fruition in December, when the company began doing business under the new trade

name MedAvant Healthcare Solutions. In a December 5, 2005, *Business Wire* release, CEO Lettko explained that the new company name meant "to take appropriate measures ahead of others in our industry."

MedAvant ended 2005 with a leaner workforce, having eliminated approximately 112 jobs throughout the year. Along with its new name came a simplified corporate and technology infrastructure that combined all of the company's business units and employees under one brand. Moving forward, MedAvant shifted its focus to empowering healthcare providers to automate transactions. At the same time, the company rolled out Envision Portal for Providers, a secure, online solution focused on encouraging real-time healthcare information exchange.

DIFFICULT TIMES: 2006–09

More leadership changes unfolded in early 2006. Following the resignation of McNamara on January 30, the company named Braden Kelly as acting chairman on February 3. Only a few weeks later, MedAvant announced the acquisition of Zeneks Inc., a Tampa, Florida-based bill negotiation services company.

In mid-October, MedAvant revealed plans to acquire National Provider Network Inc. and Medical Resource LLC in a $5 million deal. That same month, the company was named as one of the fastest-growing technology companies in Georgia when it was included on the Deloitte Technology Fast 50 list. It also was in October that Kelly resigned as chairman.

MedAvant ended 2006 with an operating loss of $3.4 million on revenues of $65.5 million. In addition to a new chairman, MedAvant added several new clients to its roster in 2006, including Pekin Insurance and Adventist Health System. One key accomplishment was the transition of all of the company's transactions to a new platform named Phoenix.

In February 2007 James B. Hudak was named as MedAvant's new chairman. Midway through the year, the company took additional steps to simplify its business structure and announced the sale of its pharmacy transaction processing business to SureScripts. Another divestiture followed in November, at which time MedAvant announced that it had agreed to sell its National Preferred Provider Network (NPPN) business to Coalition America Inc. The $23.5 million cash deal for NPPN, which closed in February 2008, included subsidiaries PlanVista Solutions Inc., National Network Services LLC, PlanVista Corp., Medical Resource LLC, and National Provider Network Inc.

More leadership changes occurred in early 2008. In February Lettko resigned as CEO and was succeeded by

Peter Fleming III on an interim basis. In addition, Lonnie Hardin was named president and chief operating officer.

The leadership changes were followed by difficult times. In April the NASDAQ notified MedAvant that it had failed to maintain a minimum market value for 30 consecutive trading days. In July the company was delisted from the NASDAQ, filed for Chapter 11 bankruptcy protection, and subsequently agreed to be acquired by El Segundo, California-based Marlin Equity Partners, a private-equity firm with more than $300 million under management. Around the same time, MedAvant sold its laboratory services business to ETSec.

In September 2008 Marlin Equity was the winner in an auction for MedAvant, with a bid of $24.35 million. Following this development, MedAvant moved forward as a privately held enterprise and named Andrew Lawson as its new president. Another senior executive appointment occurred when Troy Burns was named chief technology officer in January 2009.

A significant milestone was reached on March 18, 2009, at which time MedAvant was relaunched as Capario. Three months later, Charles Lambert was named as the company's new chief financial officer. After surviving some difficult times, Capario faced the future with solid financial backing and an eye toward future expansion.

Paul R. Greenland

PRINCIPAL COMPETITORS

Emdeon Inc.; McKesson Corporation.

FURTHER READING

Chandler, Michele, "Fort Lauderdale-based ProxyMed Banking on Success of Software System," *Knight-Ridder/Tribune Business News,* June 19, 1996.

"MedAvant Healthcare Solutions Re-Launches Company as Capario," *Business Wire,* March 12, 2009.

"MedAvant Named One of Georgia's Fastest-Growing Technology Companies," *Business Wire,* October 17, 2006.

"ProxyMed, Inc. Achieves Milestone in Electronic Pharmacy Management Reaches 2,000th Physician Using PreScribe Software," *PR Newswire,* February 10, 2000.

"ProxyMed Now Doing Business as MedAvant Healthcare Solutions," *Business Wire,* December 5, 2005.

"ProxyMed to Focus Exclusively on Its Growing Healthcare-Related Businesses with Sale of Contract Manufacturing Assets; Assets to Be Acquired by ProxyMed Executive," *Business Wire,* June 28, 2004.

Carrere Group

Carrere Group S.A.

50 Avenue du Président Wilson
La Plaine Saint-Denis, 93214
France
Telephone: (33 01) 49 37 78 00
Fax: (33 01) 49 37 77 75
Web site: http://www.carreregroup.com

Public Company
Incorporated: 1986
Employees: 294
Sales: EUR 114.3 million ($145 million) (2008)
Stock Exchanges: Euronext Paris
Ticker Symbol: CAR
NAICS: 512110 Motion Picture and Video Production;
    512191 Teleproduction and Other Postproduction
    Services

■ ■ ■

Carrere Group S.A. is a diversified media company and one of France's leading producers of animated and live-action television series and films. Founded in the mid-1980s by successful music producer Claude Carrere, the company has been behind many of France's most popular television series, including such hits as *Intervilles, La Roue de la Fortune (Wheel of Fortune), Avis de Recherche, Maigret,* and *Inspector Moulin* (starring French pop star Johnny Hallyday). Films successes include the animated hits *Les Triplettes de Belleville* and *Kirikou et la Sorcière.* Carrere Group serves as the holding company for a collection of more than 50 independently run production companies, in which Carrere typically holds a majority stake of between 51 and 66 percent. In this way, Carrere has been able to diversify its production reach to encompass all the major television genres, as well as advertising, publishing, and other media businesses.

Many of the group's subsidiaries are themselves holding companies for a range of smaller production companies. Major holdings in the Carrere Group include Dune, Les Armateurs, B3Com, GD Productions, Nelka Films, Ego Productions, Dajma, as well as the company's own Carrere Active, Carrere Group DA, Septembre Productions, and Riff International Productions. Much of Carrere's expansion took place in an extended buying spree starting in 2001. This effort, however, left the group heavily saddled with debt.

By the end of 2008, faced with losses topping EUR 116 million on revenues of just EUR 114 million, in part because of write-downs on the value of the company's library, Carrere Group has been forced to seek bankruptcy protection. In January 2009, the company began a restructuring effort expected to restore its financial position within six to 18 months. Carrere Group remains under the leadership of its founder, Claude Carrere, with his sons Axel and Romain Carrere. The Carrere family holds more than 26 percent of the company, which is listed on the Euronext Paris Stock Exchange.

ORIGINS

Claude Carrere was born into a modest family in Clermont-Ferrand in the Auvergne region of France in 1936. Carrere's mother worked as a civil servant during

COMPANY PERSPECTIVES

The strategy. Federation of producers.

Thanks to the single group culture which allows producers to focus on the creative aspect of their work while benefiting from the advantages of a large group, Carrere brings together people of consequence from all over the audiovisual world. By acquiring 51% of a company, Carrere Group does not purchase that company, Carrere becomes its partner. The Group keeps the motivation and loyalty of the subsidiaries by only acquiring half the capital, the remainder being held by the minority stakeholder. The risk of the pre-eminent producer of one of the Group's subsidiaries leaving his job following such acquisition is limited. He is obliged to follow the company's orders for a specified period as stipulated in his contract, but above all because of the financial interest which still binds him. It is therefore in the interest of the subsidiary's producer to work for the success of the new unit.

the day, while working nights at the city's opera house, where she would often bring her son Claude. This exposure to music played a major role in Carrere's life; by the age of 15, he had left Clermont-Ferrand for Paris to launch his own music career. As Carrere told *Strategies:* "I was lucky that my parents, being penniless, gave me nothing but love. I had nothing when I came to Paris at the age of 15, except a wild energy and the desire to succeed on my own."

Carrere initially attempted to break into acting, landing a small part in the 1956 film *Kandara*. The following year, however, Carrere returned to music, singing his own compositions for three 45-rpm records. However, Carrere's true success came behind the scenes, first as a songwriter and then as a producer. In 1962, one of Carrere's songs enabled singer Richard Anthony to win a singing festival, providing the start for one of France's most successful songwriting careers. By the time he sold his catalog in the early 1990s, Carrere had composed more than 70 hit songs.

The start of Carrere's career as one of France's most influential music producers also began in 1962. In that year, Carrere took over the management of an unknown hairdresser and songstress named Annie Chancel. Carrere renamed the singer as Sheila, who became one of

the biggest-selling performers in French pop history. Based on Sheila's success, Carrere formed his own production company, Productions Discques Carrere, and then, in 1972, his own music distribution company, Distribution Carrere. These companies later evolved into the larger Carrere Music company. In addition to Sheila, who achieved international success as a disco singer in the late 1970s, Carrere also became responsible for helping to build the career of such French megastars as Claude François and Dalida.

FROM MUSIC TO TELEVISION

From music, Carrere entered the publishing industry, establishing his own press group. By the end of the 1970s, Carrere's magazine titles included *Hit, Girls, 30 Millions d'Amis,* and *Podium.* Carrere's interests, however, had begun to turn toward the newly developing audiovisual market. At the beginning of the 1980s, Carrere sold his press business, founding instead Carrere Video.

By the middle of the 1980s, Carrere's interests turned more solidly to the audiovisual market. This was in large part because of a revolution in the French television sector, as the French government authorized the creation of the country's first privately held television stations. The era saw the creation of TF1, the former state-owned network that became the country's dominant broadcaster, as well as upstarts Canal Plus and M6. Carrere recognized that the new proliferation of networks would stimulate demand for new television programs. In 1986, therefore, Carrere created his own production company, Carrere Television.

Carrere then began developing programming for the country's networks, at first focusing on variety and game shows, both highly popular formats in France at the time. In the early 1990s, Carrere decided that the audiovisual market held the most promise for growth and decided to sell off his music publishing and distribution business. Carrere's timing proved fortuitous, as the consolidation of the French (and later international) music industry was just getting under way at the time. In 1991, Carrere sold Carrere Music, including his entire song catalog, to Time Warner Music.

The sale enabled Carrere to focus his attention on building his television production company. Carrere Television grew quickly in the early 1990s, as the company churned out a string of hit programs. Among Carrere's early successes were *Intervilles, Avis de Recherche, La Une Est à Vous, La Roue de la Fortune,* and *Succès Fous.* These successes enabled the company to claim the position as the leading production company for French television during the decade.

KEY DATES

1986: Claude Carrere, a successful music producer, enters the television production market, founding Carrere Television.

1991: Carrere sells Carrere Music, including his entire song catalog, to Time Warner Music.

1994: Carrere decides to focus on the production of animated series.

2000: Carrere Television moves to outsource all of its production.

2001: Carrere goes public and launches an acquisition drive to become a major audiovisual group.

2008: Carrere's debt reaches EUR 60 million and its losses top EUR 116 million for the year.

2009: Carrere enters bankruptcy protection and begins restructuring its operations.

FOCUSING ON ANIMATION

If Carrere Television's initial success enabled the company to achieve strong revenue growth, Carrere recognized a fundamental flaw in the type of programming the company produced. Despite broadcasting success, the company's programming offered little in terms of long-term potential, especially in rebroadcasting rights, international sales, and ancillary product sales. In this respect, animation offered the most potential for future growth and long-term revenue streams.

This recognition led the company to turn its focus to animated production starting in 1994. In that year, the company acquired the rights to the popular novel *Poil de Carotte,* by Jules Renard, and formed a partnership with TF1 and Dupuis to develop an animated series based on the book. That series became a major success for the company, and also became Carrere's first program to enjoy international distribution.

Carrere made its name in the U.S. market the following year, when it became a partner in the production of a new animated series based on the *Flash Gordon* comic strip. This series became another international hit for the company, and was quickly followed by a number of other successful programs, such as the *Jungle Show* and *Barbe Rouge.* Over the next several years, Carrere Television's animation staff grew to more than 50, as the company added new successes, such as *Scheherazade,* a 52-part, 26-minute series that became not only a hit in France, but also in the United States.

The group's success in France continued as well. In 1997, for example, the company's released its *Dad'X* series, which recounted the adventures of the Father Christmas character, garnering a 51 percent market share for TF1. The following year, the company had a new worldwide hit with *Les Petits Castors.* Then, in 1999, Carrere's *Argai* series scored the highest-ever ratings earned by an animation series on French television to date, 74 percent. By then, the company had begun to shift its animation production from its in-house staff to an external service-provider model. Begun in 1998, this shift was completed in 2000, when the company moved to outsource all of its production.

ACQUISITION SPREE

Carrere's efforts to build off its ancillary rights business also achieved new success at the dawn of the new century, when the company acquired a two-thirds stake in V.I.P. That company controlled the French and European rights to a number of important animated characters, including Snoopy, Zorro, and Casimir. As a result of the V.I.P. acquisition, Carrere Group became the leader in France, and one of the largest in Europe, in the ancillary rights market.

The V.I.P. acquisition also seemed to whet Carrere's appetite for growth. In 2001, Claude Carrere announced plans to redevelop the company into a major audiovisual group. Toward this end, Carrere took the company public, listing its shares on the Euronext Paris Stock Exchange that year. The offering, which raised some $26 million for the company, helped fuel the start of an ambitious buying spree. Over the next five years, Carrere completed a long series of acquisitions, building a group of more than 50 production companies.

Carrere hit the ground running, buying a 51 percent stake in Les Armateurs, a highly successful production company with hits including *Kirikou et la Sorcière, L'Enfant qui Voulait Etre un Ours, Belphegor,* and *T'Choupi.* Carrere expanded its range of operations again in 2001, acquiring FX, a company focused on the postproduction sector. Other acquisitions that year included Upside, Grosse Boite Américaine, and Cosmic Peanuts. These purchases helped the company gain a major position in the European short-form animation segment.

As with Les Armateurs, Carrere's acquisition strategy involved taking only a 51 percent stake in each company. Acquired companies continued to operate independently under their existing management (and minority shareholders). Carrere itself provided central coordination and administration, while enabling the group to achieve economies of scale.

CONTINUED EXPANSION

At the end of 2001, Carrere's revenues had jumped to EUR 27 million. The company's acquisition drive continued strongly into the next year, with the addition of Auteurs Associés, Dune, producer of the popular *Maigret* series, and Ego Productions, which produced the successful series *Le Juge Est une Femme*. These purchases helped establish Carrere's expertise in the drama series category.

The company also built up a substantial position in the documentary, cultural, and news magazine segments, adding Productions Tony Comiti and Guillaume Durand Productions in 2003. By 2004, Carrere had established a position as a leading producer of telefilms as well, buying 51 percent of Nelka Films. By the end of that year, Carrere's annual revenues topped EUR 71 million.

While acquisitions continued to play a major part in the company's rising revenues, the company's past purchases allowed the company to realize significant organic growth at this time. The release of the worldwide hit film *Les Triplettes de Belleville,* which received an Oscar nomination for best animated film, helped cement the company's international status. The failure of a live-action film, *The Last Sign,* however, convinced Carrere to focus on the television market.

Carrere continued seeking out new acquisitions and new expansion targets in order to broaden its range of operations. As Axel Carrere, son of Claude Carrere and at that time company CEO explained to *Hollywood Reporter:* "We're present in all areas of production. Why? Because no one can know in four to five years' time what will be doing well in prime time. It allows us to look ahead and react."

REBUILDING FOR THE NEXT DECADE

In 2005, the company turned its attention toward the entertainment sector, buying 51 percent of B3Com, which held the rights to the French version of *American Idol.* The company also boosted its position in the series drama market, buying up PM Holding, producer of the Alain Delon vehicle *Frank Riva,* and the popular *Commissaire Moulin* series. The company also bought Communication and Programme International, which produced short subjects for French television. Another major acquisition in 2005, of Riff International, gave the company control of the popular children's series *C'est Pas Sorcier,* as well as the news program *Arrêt sur Images.* Carrere also added advertising to its range, buying up the Dassa agency in 2006.

By 2007, however, Carrere's expansion strategy appeared to be running out of steam. Through that year, the group's revenue growth remained flat, at EUR 144 million. Worse for the company, however, was its massive debt load, which neared EUR 60 million by early 2008. Part of the group's difficulties stemmed from its policy of acquiring just 51 percent of its acquisition targets, which meant that, despite the success of its subsidiaries, not enough cash reached the holding company itself.

By May 2008, Carrere had begun negotiations with its banks to restructure its debt. The company also began negotiations with a number of other audiovisual groups for a possible takeover. In August 2008, Carrere reached an agreement to be acquired by fellow French company, Moonscope. That deal ultimately fell through, however, in part because Claude Carrere refused to accept the terms of the refinancing package necessary for the acquisition's completion.

Carrere, then 76 years old, was forced to step down as the group's chairman in September 2008, but ultimately returned to the chairman's spot three months later, in time to announce that the company would seek bankruptcy protection from its creditors. That status was granted in January 2009, as the group's losses topped EUR 116 million on revenues of just EUR 114 million for the 2008 year. Trading on Carrere's stock was then suspended.

Carrere Group at this time brought in new board members, who set to work developing a restructuring plan. The company was given a period of from six to 18 months to succeed in revitalizing its financial position, at the risk of facing liquidation or a sale to one of its competitors. Having built up one of the leading audiovisual companies in France and Europe, Carrere Group found itself in a battle for survival.

M. L. Cohen

PRINCIPAL SUBSIDIARIES

Auteurs Associes (51%); B3Com (51%); Carrere Active (96%); Carrere Group D.A; Dajma (51%); Dune; Ego Productions; GD Productions (66%); Les Armateurs (66%); Nelka Films (51%); Productions Tony Comiti (51%); Riff International Productions; Scarlett Production; Septembre Productions.

PRINCIPAL OPERATING UNITS

Production; Distribution; Marketing.

PRINCIPAL COMPETITORS

Vivendi S.A.; Groupe Canal+ S.A.; France Televisions S.A.; Television Francaise 1 S.A.; Lagardere Active S.A.

S.; Metropole Television S.A.; France 3 S.A.; Pathe S.A.
S.; StudioCanal S.A.; UGC S.A.; Groupe AB S.A.S.

FURTHER READING

Baudriller, Marc, "Carrere Entre les Mains du Conciliateur," *Challenges,* June 5, 2008.

Berretta, Emmanuel, "Un Producteur Hollandais au Secours du Commissaire Maigret," *Le Point,* May 6, 2008.

"Carrere Group: C.A. 2008 en Repli de 18%," *CercleFinance. com,* March 9, 2009.

"Carrere Group: 4 Nouveaux Membres au Conseil de Surveillance," *Investir,* January 29, 2009.

"Carrere Group Multiplie les Acquisitions," *Strategies,* October 13, 2005.

"Carrere Group: 126 Millions de Pertes, Claude Carrere Démissione," *Investir,* October 6, 2008.

"Carrere Group Poursuit Sa Stratégie d'Acquisition dans le Flux," *Strategies,* October 5, 2005.

"Claude Carrere a Repris de Président du Directoire," *Boursier. com,* December 5, 2008.

"Claude Carrere: Hors norme," *Strategies,* March 7, 2003.

Hopewell, John, "French Carrere in Bankruptcy Filing," *Variety,* December 28, 2008.

Masters, Charles, "Carrere to Initiate French IPO," *Hollywood Reporter,* June 1, 2001, p. 10.

———, "It's All About Carrere Opportunities: Acquisitions Have Media Company Covering All Bases," *Hollywood Reporter,* February 14, 2006, p. 14.

"Moonscoop to Acquire Carrere Group," *Europe Intelligence Wire,* August 14, 2008.

Castorama-Dubois Investissements SCA

―――――――――■―――――――――

Pare d'Activité
Templemars, 59175
France
Telephone: (33 3) 16 75 75
Fax: (33 3) 20 1673
Web site: http://www.castorama.fr

Wholly Owned Subsidiary of Kingfisher plc
Incorporated: 1969 as Central-Castor
Employees: 21,745
Sales: £2.1 billion ($3 billion) (French operations; 2008 est.)
NAICS: 444110 Home Centers

■ ■ ■

Castorama-Dubois Investissements SCA operates a chain of do-it-yourself (DIY) and home improvement materials stores in France, Poland, and Russia. Its stores stock a wide variety of items ranging from home repair and renovation products to home, garden, and decorative items. Castorama has focused on expanding in Eastern Europe in the 21st century, opening stores in Poland and Russia. The company is a subsidiary of Kingfisher plc, the largest home improvement retail group in Europe and the third largest in the world.

AMERICAN INSPIRATION SPARKS EARLY GROWTH

Christian Dubois began his career in 1951, selling building and construction materials in the city of Lille and the surrounding region at the north of France. After a trip to the United States in the late 1960s, Dubois was inspired by a new opportunity: the idea of bringing the so-called category-killer warehouse specialty store concept, then emerging in the United States, to France's home improvement and hardware market. In 1969 Dubois opened his first large-format store, called Central-Castor (castor means "beaver" in French) in the Lille suburb of Englos. The store, which boasted 5,000 square meters, was located in a shopping mall anchored by an Auchan hypermarket. Although Auchan would later come under the ownership of Castorama's chief French competitor, Leroy-Merlin, the company would continue to seek out such shopping mall placements for many of its later openings.

The Central-Castor name was short-lived, replaced by Castorama at the start of the 1970s. The success of the concept proved more lasting. By 1974 the company had grown to four stores serving the Nord region around Lille. Castorama was then preparing to make a move toward national expansion, opening the first Castorama outside of the company's Nord home region in the Parisian suburb of Plaisir in 1975. This opening marked an important element of the company's growth strategy, aimed toward the country's larger urban areas, with a population dense enough to support the company's large-format stores. That same year saw the birth of a slogan that would become famous among France's growing ranks of do-it-yourselfers: "*Chez Casto, y'a tout ce qu'il faut!*" ("Casto's got what it takes.")

The Paris opening was the first in an aggressive expansion that would take Castorama to a 13-store chain just three years later. Expansion had become more than 45 percent in Castorama. In that year Castorama more than doubled in size when it acquired the 19-store Californie chain.

KEY DATES

∎

1951: Christian Dubois begins his career selling building and construction materials.

1969: Dubois opens his first large-format store, called Central-Castor.

1975: A new store under the Castorama name opens in Plaisir, a suburb of Paris.

1978: Carrefour purchases a shareholder position of more than 45 percent in Castorama; the company more than doubles in size when it acquires the 19-store Californie chain.

1982: Castorama-Dubois Investissements is created as a holding company.

1987: The company launches its first catalog.

1991: Castorama has 111 stores and more than 10,000 employees; sales top FRF 10 billion for the first time.

1994: Castorama-Dubois regains 100 percent control of Castorama S.A. after a stock swap agreement for Carrefour's remaining shares.

1997: The company purchases the nine-store Réno Dépôt chain in Quebec.

1998: Kingfisher plc acquires a majority interest in Castorama.

2002: Castorama becomes a wholly owned subsidiary of Kingfisher.

2003: The company exits the Canadian and German markets.

2006: The first Castorama store in Russia opens its doors in February.

2009: Castorama exits the Italian market.

CONTINUED EXPANSION

Three more Castorama stores were added over the next year. In 1979, celebrating its tenth anniversary, Castorama had grown to a 35-store chain boasting sales of FRF 1.2 billion per year and more than 2,500 employees. As the chain spread across the country, it adopted a policy of decentralization, opening regional headquarters to coordinate development. The company was also quick to add computerized inventory control to track its growing range of products. Meanwhile, Dubois had not abandoned the building and construction professional even as the Castorama chain attracted the growing ranks of DIY consumers. Dubois had also begun building a network of building supply wholesale warehouses under the Dubois Materiaux name.

At the start of the 1980s Dubois sought fresh capital for expansion. In 1982 Dubois formed a new holding company to group his parallel activities. In that year Castorama-Dubois Investissements entered the over-the-counter market on the Lille stock exchange. Three years later, the company holdings had grown to 74 stores and more than 5,000 employees, with total sales of more than FRF 3 billion (net, after taxes). Over the next ten years, the company would continue to post an impressive growth rate, averaging sales gains of nearly 16 percent per year and healthy profits as well. Added fuel for the expansion came in 1986 when Castorama-Dubois joined the Lille stock exchange's secondary market.

The individual Castorama stores were also undergoing a transformation as the company worked on refining its store concept. In 1987 the Castorama stores began a transition to a larger format, ranging from 8,000 to 10,000 square meters, while building up their range to some 50,000 products. Among these were the first products bearing the Castorama name and matching the quality of the brand names, while priced at a 10 percent to 15 percent discount. That same year brought another new feature to the Castorama customer: the company's first catalog. At 196 pages, the Castorama catalog would be distributed to 3.5 million customers.

Moving to a full listing on the stock exchange in 1988 provided Castorama-Dubois with the opportunity to increase its holding in Castorama from 52.7 percent to more than 94 percent. The company next established its first store outside of France, opening a Castorama in Milan. At the end of the decade, the company had grown to a chain of 86 Castorama stores and six Dubois

necessary; by the mid-1970s Castorama was faced with a growing number of competitors equally attracted to the large-store format. After the postwar boom years, the French economy was beginning to sour as the effects of the Arab oil crisis began to be felt. With the recession of the early 1980s looming on the horizon, tightening economic conditions gave rise to a new wave of interest in DIY home improvement; indeed, some would dub it the French national hobby.

At the same time, French consumers had become accustomed to the broad product range and discounted prices of the large-format store as the hypermarket concept swept the country. One of the leading hypermarket chains, Carrefour, would provide Castorama with the capital it needed for its own expansion. In 1978 Carrefour purchased a shareholder position of

Materiaux wholesalers, employing more than 7,500 people, for total sales (including tax) of nearly FRF 7.5 billion. The company had taken a clear lead in the French home improvement market and numbered among the largest in Europe as well. In 1989 the company took a step toward reinforcing its service commitment to its customers, opening an in-house training school for its employees.

MOVING INTO INTERNATIONAL MARKETS

The first signs of a shakeout in the DIY industry were seen at the start of the 1990s as the market consolidated into a two-tier structure: large-format stores serving primarily urban populations and smaller supply stores serving more rural populations. Castorama remained committed to the large-store format, reaching an average store size of 7,400 square meters by 1990. The company was also leading the consolidation of the industry, buying nine stores from rival Obi, owned by Belgium's GIB, and France's third largest DIY chain at the time. The following year, Castorama bought out another rival chain, Briker, including 17 stores, from another hypermarket leader, Rallye (later Casino). By the end of 1991 Castorama had grown to 111 stores and more than 10,000 employees. Sales that year topped FRF 10 billion for the first time.

The concurrent consolidation of the hypermarket industry also helped Castorama's expansion. In 1992, after Carrefour bought out rival Euromarché, Castorama saw the chance to buy the seven largest stores of Euromarché's subsidiary Bricorama (another company would acquire the Bricorama name). Consolidation among all large-format retail sectors would shortly become a necessity for expansion: a new law introduced in the early 1990s created several restrictions on new store developments, particularly in urban areas. The law, inspired in part by a desire to protect the threatened existence of the small, independent shop owner, brought such local commercial developments under national oversight. The law was to see a steady tightening over the following years, making the authorization for construction of a new large-format store a rare event.

The new law, in fact, would help solidify Castorama's position in France; the company maintained a comfortable leadership, both in store numbers and revenues, over its rivals. Castorama-Dubois took a two-pronged approach to further expansion. In France the company began to diversify, adding a new building materials concept under the Brico Dépôt name, geared toward supplying professional needs especially on the construction site. The company also branched out beyond the DIY market. In the early 1990s, it began

building a chain of large-format pet care and animal supply stores under the Amiland name. Another company project was garden supplies, under the Dubois Jardín name. Less successful was the company's attempt to enter the automotive supply market, through subsidiary Self Auto. That activity was ended in 1994. Also in 1994, however, Castorama-Dubois regained 100 percent control of Castorama S.A. after a stock swap agreement for Carrefour's remaining shares.

CONTINUED INTERNATIONAL EXPANSION

Whereas diversification would provide some growth for the company, Castorama looked beyond the French border for its main expansion thrust. After opening its first Italian store in 1988, the company added a second Italian store in Bergame in 1990, and two more stores, in Bollate and Marcon in 1992, building up its Italian branch to seven stores by the beginning of 1998. Germany was Castorama's next frontier: the company established its Castorama Deutschland subsidiary in 1990, opening its first German store in Castrop-Rauxel, near Dortmund, in 1992. Two more German stores were added that same year, followed by a store in 1994 and four Castoramas in 1995. By 1998 Castorama's German branch included seven stores. Facing an intensely competitive market, the largest in Europe, the company continued to absorb losses, despite the growth of its German revenues to more than FRF 800 million. Castorama's fortunes proved better in Italy, where its operations began turning a profit in the mid-1990s. The company planned further expansion in Italy, beginning with two stores in 1998.

Castorama's foreign expansion would serve the additional purpose of shielding the company from the potential entry of U.S. giants such as Home Depot into the European market. In 1994 Castorama moved just across the French-Belgian border, opening a store in Kortrijk. By 1996 Castorama began to look farther afield, targeting Poland as a foothold into the Eastern European market. Castorama's first Polish store, featuring its 10,000-square-meter format, opened in Warsaw in 1997, with plans to add three more stores in 1998.

The company crossed the Atlantic in 1997, targeting Brazil with an eye toward further expansion into the South American market. The company's first Brazilian Castorama opened in São Paulo in 1997. To the north, an acquisition brought a new name into the Castorama-Dubois holdings. In April 1997 the company purchased the nine-store Réno Dépôt chain in Quebec, featuring 12,000-square-meter formats. The company stated, however, that its plans for further North American expansion would remain limited to the French-speaking province.

THRIVING IN A TOUGH ECONOMY

Throughout much of the 1990s, the French economy, along with much of Europe, suffered through an extended recession. Nevertheless, the difficult economy and growing jobless rates proved to be a boon to Castorama, attracting a new wave of do-it-yourselfers. At the end of 1997 Castorama's holdings had grown to 162 stores, producing sales of more than FRF 21 billion. Between 1993 and 1997 the company had succeeded in winning authorization to open seven new French Castoramas, while also increasing the number of Brico Dépôt stores to more than ten; a ninth Dubois Materiaux center was added in 1997. Castorama also began instituting a new 12,000-square-meter format. It also ended production of its catalog, which had swelled to nearly 700 pages over its ten years, replacing it with a new publication, "Oh! Casto," modeled after consumer magazines. In 1997 Castorama also began offering its own customer fidelity credit card.

With 162 retail stores in France, Italy, Germany, Belgium, Poland, and Brazil under the Castorama name, and nine retail Réno-Dépôt stores in Quebec, Canada, Groupe Castorama had counted double-digit growth for much of its history. Its performance caught the attention of Kingfisher plc, a large retailing group that made a play for Castorama in 1998. The two companies, in an effort to grow their European operations in order to fend off foreign competitors, sealed the deal late that year. Under the terms of the agreement, Castorama acquired 293 B&Q home improvement stores while Kingfisher received a 54.6 percent stake in Castorama and the option to buy all remaining shares after 2000. The combination of B&Q plc, Britain's largest home improvement retailer, and Castorama created a global powerhouse that was among the leading home improvement retailers in the world.

MOVING INTO THE 21ST CENTURY

Kingfisher, based in London, acquired the remaining shares in Castorama in 2002, signaling its intent to focus on its DIY retailing operations. By this time, Kingfisher had positioned itself as the largest DIY retailer in Europe and the third largest in the world. Under the leadership of Kingfisher, Castorama spent the next several years exiting slow-growth regions while expanding into new areas. During 2003, the company sold its Canadian Réno-Dépôt stores in order to focus

on expansion in Europe and Asia. The proceeds of the sale were used to pay down Kingfisher debt. At the same time, it shuttered operations in Germany. The six stores located in that country had failed to meet profit expectations.

Philippe Tible, a longtime retail executive, was named Castorama's new CEO in early 2003. Under his leadership, Castorama's French operations received an overhaul and stores were modernized to shore up sales and profits. The company's next big move came in 2006, when it entered the Russian market for the first time. A store made its debut in Samara in February 2006 and a second location opened its doors in St. Petersburg in July of that year.

Castorama was also focusing on growth in Poland. By this time, Castorama was the largest DIY retailer in that country and was planning for additional expansion. The company also set plans in motion for a potential move into new Eastern European markets including Lithuania and Ukraine. Kingfisher decided to exit the Italian market in 2008 and sold its Castorama stores to Groupe Adeo in January 2009 for EUR 615 million. Overall, Castorama operated 99 stores in France, 46 stores in Poland, and seven locations in Russia by this time.

Castorama was well positioned for growth in the coming years as a subsidiary of Kingfisher, whose DIY arsenal included B&Q, Brico Dépôt, and Screwfix. Kingfisher operated 820 stores in eight countries in Europe and Asia and had over £10 billion in sales in 2008. With an eye for additional expansion, Castorama's store count in high-growth markets would no doubt continue to climb in the years to come.

M. L. Cohen
Updated, Christina M. Stansell

PRINCIPAL COMPETITORS

Bricorama S.A.; Leroy Merlin; Praktiker Bau- und Heimwerkermärkte AG.

FURTHER READING

Baverel, Philippe, "Quarante Millions de Bricoleurs," *Le Monde,* December 7, 1993, p. 6.

Braithwaite, Tom, and Lucy Killgren, "Kingfisher Quits Italy at a Premium Price," *Financial Times,* August 2, 2008.

"Castorama Stores to Mushroom in Poland," *Polish News Bulletin,* November 4, 2008.

"Castorama to Open DIY Store in St. Petersburg in July," *Prime-TASS News,* May 29, 2006.

"Castorama: Une Dimension Internationale Mesurée," *Brico-mag,* May 1995, p. 34.

Foley, Stephen, "Build on Kingfisher While the DIY Boom Continues," *Independent* (London), September 18, 2003.

"France's Castorama Defies Critics' Derision," *National Home Center News,* August 9, 1999.

"Kingfisher Announces New Castorama Chief Executive," *Pressi.com,* February 12, 2003.

"Kingfisher Sells Canadian Business for GBP 155m," *FT.com,* April 23, 2003.

"Kingfisher's Castorama to Exit Germany," *Pressi.com,* January 9, 2003.

Lupieri, Stéphane, "La Lutte pour l'Espace Vital," *Enjeux,* October 1996, p. 101.

Mason, Sophie, "Castorama Moves into Canada," *DIY Week,* March 21, 1997, p. 12.

"Mergers Alter the Balance of Power," *National Home Center News,* June 21, 1999.

Prod'homme, Gilles, "Castorama Performant Malgré l'Allemagne," *Points de Vente,* March 10, 1997, p. 18.

Smyth, Lucy, "Kingfisher's Halcyon Move," *Financial Times,* September 2, 2002.

Cegedim S.A.

BP 405
127/137 rue d'Aguesseau
Boulogne Billancourt, F-92641 Cedex
France
Telephone: (33 01) 49 09 22 00
Fax: (33 01) 46 03 45 95
Web site: http://www.cegedim.fr

Public Company
Incorporated: 1969
Employees: 8,032
Sales: EUR 849 million ($1.1 billion) (2008)
Stock Exchanges: New York Euronext Paris
Ticker Symbol: CGDM.PA
NAICS: 518210 Data Processing, Hosting, and Related
Services; 511210 Software Publishers

■ ■ ■

Cegedim S.A. is a world-leading provider of software and services to pharmaceutical companies, pharmacists, and healthcare practitioners. France-based Cegedim is the number one ranked provider of customer relationship management (CRM) software, database integration, and managing and related services in the world. The company is also leading European provider of medical management software for use by healthcare professionals and the health insurance industry. Cegedim's operations are grouped into three primary sectors. CRM and strategic data, the largest sector, generated 58 percent of the company's sales of nearly EUR 850 million ($1.1 billion) in 2008. Operating in more than 80 countries through subsidiary Cegedim Dendrite, the sector commands a global market share of 35 percent. The healthcare professionals sector represents 29 percent of group sales, providing software as well as marketing and medical information delivery services. This sector, the market leader in France and Belgium and the number two player in the United Kingdom, focuses primarily on the European markets, and covers more than 115,000 physician workstations and 15,000 pharmacists. The third sector, insurance and services, adds 13 percent to group revenues. This sector provides software solutions for health insurance professionals, primarily in France and French-speaking North Africa, as well as in Switzerland and Great Britain. The sector also operates in the banking arena, and adds software solutions for payroll and human resource applications.

France remains the company's largest market, generating 49 percent of its total business, and 27 percent of its CRM revenues. Europe adds 24 percent of total turnover, with North America accounting for 15 percent of the total, and 26 percent of CRM turnover. Cegedim is listed on the NYSE Euronext Paris Stock Exchange and is led by founder, chairman and CEO Jean-Claude Labrune, who retains control of 70 percent of the company through holding company FCB SAS.

FRENCH CRM PIONEER IN THE SIXTIES

The company was founded as Centre de Gestion, de Documentation, d'Informatique et de Marketing (Cegedim) in 1969 under the leadership of Labrune. A graduate of France's prestigious École Nationale Supérieure des Arts et Métiers, Labrune had spent several years working as a sales engineer for IBM's French operation. During this time, Labrune had worked closely with a number of major players in the French pharmaceutical industry, developing an understanding of the challenges the industry faced in bringing their products to health-care professionals and ultimately to consumers.

Labrune recognized the potential for regrouping the growing pool of documents and data generated by the country's pharmaceuticals manufacturers at a time when the information technology (IT) sector was still in its infancy. By combining these data and related resources, such as physician databases, Labrune proposed to develop databases that could assist manufacturers in their sales and marketing efforts.

Cegedim released its first databases for use that year. Over the next five years, the company continued to build up its collection of databases, while developing the software tools to manipulate the increasing mass of data. This led to the introduction of the group's first commercial services, with the launch of direct-marketing services in 1974.

The company continued to develop its own software and data management tools. In 1979 the company debuted its first CRM software platform for the French market. The growth and increasing complexity of the country's national healthcare system, one of the most comprehensive in the world, provided an important stimulus to Cegedim's growth through the next decade.

GROWTH THROUGH NEW SERVICES

Labrune added professional management in the early 1980s, in the form of Pierre Marucchi, who had started his career with Crédit Lyonnais before joining Cegedim in 1984. Marucchi became a central figure in the company's growth, assuming the role of deputy managing director for the group.

Cegedim then began targeting further growth both beyond the CRM sector and beyond France. With its growing prowess in software development, Cegedim decided to enter the wider IT services sector, with a particular focus on distribution products for the health insurance sector. Launched in 1986, the new activity formed the core of the company's Insurance & Services division.

The company also targeted growth outside of France. In 1990 Cegedim added an international sales component for its CRM business. By 1991 the group had opened its first foreign subsidiary, in Belgium. This was soon followed by subsidiaries in Portugal, Italy, and Spain in 1992; and the United Kingdom and Germany in 1994. Other countries were added in the second half of the decade, including Switzerland and the Netherlands in 1997; the Czech Republic, Greece, Hungary, and Turkey in 1998; and Poland in 1999.

ADDING MORE SERVICES IN THE NINETIES

Cegedim's range of products expanded steadily. The company added to its range of IT services during the 1990s. In 1991 Cegedim debuted a new service that permitted the exchange of data, including ordering and invoicing systems, between pharmaceutical companies and wholesalers serving the pharmacy sector. The company launched its human resources management services in 1994, positioning the company to take advantage of this fast-growing outsourcing trend among major corporations. The outsourcing market later provided the company with a new service extension, as it launched a service for managing cash receipts, as well as managing third-party health insurance payments in 1996. The group's CRM division raised its profile in 1996, when it introduced new software for the management of medical samples.

A major new market opened up for Cegedim in the mid-1990s, as the French and other European governments began converting their healthcare delivery services to computer-based systems. This effort meant that physicians were required to adopt computer-based patient database platforms, which were then linked to the centralized national healthcare system. Cegedim developed its own software platforms starting in 1994. This operation, initially focused on the French market, formed the basis for a new division, Healthcare Professionals.

Computerized access to physicians' patient data and prescribing patterns also provided the company with a new extension of its marketing services. By 1996 the company had launched a new range of services designed

KEY DATES

1969: Jean-Claude Labrune leads the founding of Centre de Gestion, de Documentation, d'Informatique et de Marketing (Cegedim) in order to develop database services for the French pharmaceuticals industry.

1979: Cegedim launches customer relationship management (CRM) services in France.

1986: Cegedim begins providing information technology services to the health insurance industry.

1990: First international sales operations are launched.

1991: Cegedim opens its first foreign subsidiary in Belgium.

1995: Company goes public with a listing on the Paris Stock Exchange.

2002: Bid to buy Synavant Inc. in the United States is unsuccessful.

2005: Cegedim's sales top EUR 500 million, with international sales generating 50 percent of the group's business.

2007: Cegedim pays $751 million to acquire Dendrite, becoming a global CRM leader.

to promote customers' pharmaceutical products to pharmacists and physicians.

The United Kingdom launched the computerization of physicians under its national healthcare system in 1998. This led Cegedim to complete that year its first foreign acquisition, In Practice Systems of the United Kingdom. Into the turn of the century, other components of the healthcare system were moved to digital platforms. In France, the insurance sector, including third-party supplemental health insurance providers, was converted to a computer-based system in 1999. The French pharmacy sector followed shortly, joining the grid in 2000. In the United Kingdom, the pharmacy industry was finally computerized in 2004.

GROWTH THROUGH ACQUISITIONS AT THE DAWN OF THE 21ST CENTURY

Cegedim's expansion through the 1990s had been fueled in part by the company's decision to go public, listing its shares on the Paris Stock Exchange in 1995. Labrune nonetheless maintained control of the company, through

Financière Cegedim (later FCB), established as a holding company in 1989 and owned by the Labrune family. Following the float, Labrune's stake in the company stood at 70 percent. Labrune's son, Laurent Labrune, joined the company in 1995, becoming the company's IT coordinator before becoming chief executive of its Cegedim SRH subsidiary. Labrune's daughter Aude Labrune-Marysse joined the company in 1999.

Into the new century, Cegedim, already a leader in France, began an effort to raise its profile among the global leaders in the pharmaceutical CRM market. The company began opening a new series of international subsidiaries, starting with Austria, Romania, and Slovakia in 2001, as well as affiliate operations in Brazil and the United States that year. Other subsidiaries created through the first half of the decade included Tunisia in 2002; Russia, Algeria, and China in 2004; and Morocco in 2005.

By then Cegedim had stepped up its international expansion effort by launching an ambitious acquisition drive. This effort started with the purchase of the CAM Group, also based in France, in 2002. CAM brought Cegedim its own market research specialty of promotional measurement tools, including tools for measuring medical representative effectiveness. CAM operated on an international level, and included most of the top 25 pharmaceutical companies as its clients.

Cegedim's became a major player in the Latin American market that year as well, when it acquired the MS Mexicana (MSM) Group from the Thomson Corporation. MSM claimed the market leadership in Mexico, with a market share of 60 percent. MSM also brought Cegedim operations in Argentina, Brazil, Colombia, Costa Rica, Ecuador, and Guatemala.

The company then set its sights farther north. In 2003 Cegedim reached an agreement to merge with the United States' Synavant Inc., then one of the global leaders in the pharmaceutical CRM market. Yet Cegedim soon found itself in a bidding war with Dendrite Inc., a fast-growing U.S.-based business that had been on its own acquisition drive since the 1990s. Dendrite ultimately won in its bid to take over Synavant, thwarting Cegedim's attempt to enter the all-important U.S. market. Cegedim, however, would soon have the last word.

REACHING EUR 500 MILLION IN 2005

In the meantime, Cegedim continued seeking new acquisition targets. The company turned to Belgium in 2003, buying HDMP, a provider of software to physicians. The following year, Cegedim entered the

Nordic market, where it acquired Pharma Marketing Norway. Founded in 1960, that company brought Cegedim operations in Norway, Sweden, Denmark and Iceland, as well as in Poland. Pharma Marketing boosted Cegedim's CRM business with its own database products, as well as sales force automation (SFA) software and market research and direct-marketing services. Also in 2004, Cegedim enhanced its U.K. pharmacy software business with the acquisitions of NDCHealth (subsequently renamed as Cegedim Rx) and Enigma.

Cegedim found its U.S. entry in 2005, when it bought that country's Target Software Inc. The purchase gave Cegedim a foothold into the U.S. CRM market, as well as Target's SFA and mobile sales software. Other acquisitions completed that year included Egyptian Trends Technology, providing the company with a base in the North African market; and Epic and Compufile, two British companies providing qualitative research on physician activity.

By the end of 2005, Cegedim's acquisitions had enabled the company's business to grow from EUR 300 million in 2001 to over EUR 500 million by 2005. Importantly, international sales had by then grown to account for 50 percent of Cegedim's total turnover. CRM and strategic data remained the company's core businesses, at nearly two-thirds of its total revenues. Nonetheless, the company's Healthcare Professionals division was also growing strongly. This was in part because of the increasing computerization of the healthcare market in the first decade of the 2000s. French paramedicals were computerized in 2006, and in that year Chile, Spain and Italy also rolled out the computerization of medical doctors.

GLOBAL LEADERSHIP IN 2007

Cegedim took advantage of these new opportunities. In 2006, for example, the company acquired RM Ingenierie, which had become the first to develop specialized software for physiotherapists in 1984. RM Ingenierie had since developed a major position in the paramedical sector, serving the range of French podiatrists, midwives, speech therapists, nurses, orthoptists, and the like. The company then turned to Spain, where it acquired that market's CRM leader Stacks in 2007. The addition of Stacks, founded in the 1980s, also gave Cegedim an entry into the Chilean market.

Already a European leader in the CRM field, Cegedim sought to extend its leadership position to a truly global level. In order to do this, the company focused on boosting its U.S. presence. This goal was quickly accomplished when, in 2007, the company reached an agreement to acquire former rival Dendrite Inc. for $751 million. Dendrite, which became Cegedim Dendrite following the merger of the group's U.S. operations, provided Cegedim not only with the leading position in the U.S. market, but also a strong presence in the Asian Pacific markets. The acquisition boosted Cegedim's sales to EUR 753 million at the end of that year.

The newly minted global leader remained on the lookout for new expansion opportunities. The company established a subsidiary in India in 2007. In 2008 Cegedim acquired Protectia, a French company focused on the third-party supplemental health insurance sector. This purchase was followed by that of 01 Santé SA, also of France, which published the MegaBaze medical software suite. Also in 2008, Cegedim acquired CRM provider Ultima in Turkey. This acquisition was followed by that of Reportive, based in France, which focused on developing business intelligence software for the healthcare and pharmaceuticals market.

These acquisitions, as well as organic growth, allowed Cegedim to raise its business again, to EUR 849 million ($1.1 billion) at the end of 2008. Despite the ongoing economic crisis, Cegedim expected to post continued strong growth into the next decade, in part because of the recession-resistant nature of the healthcare market. As one of the pioneer providers of CRM and other services to the pharmaceutical and healthcare industries, Cegedim looked forward to consolidating its position as a global leader.

M. L. Cohen

PRINCIPAL SUBSIDIARIES

Cegedim Activ SA; Cegedim Dendrite; Cegedim Dendrite (Target Software) Inc. (USA); Cegedim Dendrite Danismanlik Ticaret A.S. (Turkey); Cegedim Dendrite Inc. (USA); Cegedim Dendrite SA; Cegedim Edi; Cegedim Logiciels Médicaux; Cegedim SA; Cegedim SRH; Cegedim SRH Ltd (UK); Cegedim Srh SA (Tunisia); Cegedim Strategic Data SA; Icomed Belgium NV; In Practice Systems Ltd (UK); Stacks Consulting e Ingenieria en Softwair S.L. (Spain); Stacks Servicios Technologicos S.L. (Spain).

PRINCIPAL DIVISIONS

Healthcare and Strategic Data; Technologies and Services.

PRINCIPAL OPERATING UNITS

CRM and Strategic Data; Healthcare Insurance Services; Healthcare Professionals; Services; Technologies.

PRINCIPAL COMPETITORS

First Consulting Group Inc.; Siebel Systems Inc.; Oracle Corporation; StayinFront Inc; Acxiom Corporation; The Nielsen Company B.V.; IMS Health Incorporated.

FURTHER READING

"Cegedim Acquires NDC," *Chemist & Druggist,* November 6, 2004, p. 8.

"Cegedim Announces Acquisition of Target Software," *Customer Interaction Solutions,* May 2005, p. 45.

"Cegedim Buys Enigma Health," *Chemist & Druggist,* January 8, 2005, p. 5.

"Cegedim Dendrite Acquires Health Direction," *Pharma Marketletter,* August 13, 2007.

"Cegedim Dendrite Announces Broad Expansion of Alliance Program," *Biotech Week,* March 18, 2009.

"Cegedim Dendrite Reports Pact with Major Biotech Company," *Health & Beauty Close-Up,* May 2, 2009.

"Cegedim Recognized for Its Dendrite Acquisition," *Internet Wire,* March 18, 2009.

"Cegedim RX Set to Begin Testing," *Chemist & Druggist,* July 19, 2008, p. 4.

Iskowitz, Marc, "Cegedim Seeks Deeper US Coverage," *Medical Marketing & Media,* September 2007, p. 34.

McGuire, Stephen, "Cegedim Partnering with Microsoft," *Medical Marketing & Media,* May 2008, p. 28.

Central Parking System

2401 21st Avenue South, Suite 200
Nashville, Tennessee 37212
U.S.A.
Telephone: (615) 297-4255
Fax: (615) 297-6240
Web site: http://www.parking.com

Private Company
Incorporated: 1968
Employees: 18,000
Sales: $1.12 billion (2007)
NAICS: 812930 Parking Lots and Garages

■ ■ ■

The largest parking services provider in North America, Central Parking System provides a wide variety of services within its industry. In addition to the ownership, operation, and management of surface and multilevel parking facilities, the company provides parking notice and collection services, parking meter enforcement, toll road collections, valet and special event parking, design consultation, and customer and employee shuttle services. During the later years of the first decade of the 21st century, Central Parking oversaw roughly 1.2 million parking spaces at 2,500 facilities, including municipalities, hospitals, airports, stadiums and arenas, hotels, and office buildings.

Central Parking has brought professional management techniques to a highly fragmented, typically "mom-and-pop" industry, attaining high-profile parking contracts such as the Bush Intercontinental Airport

(Houston); the Crown Center (Kansas City, Missouri); the Los Angeles International Airport; Oriole Park at Camden Yards (Baltimore); Paul Brown Stadium (Cincinnati); Rockefeller Center (New York); Time Warner Center (New York); and Vanderbilt Medical Center (Nashville).

THE PROFESSIONAL APPROACH TO PARKING

Central Parking founder Monroe Carell Jr. held an electrical engineering degree from Vanderbilt University; his family also owned two parking lots in Nashville, Tennessee. In 1968, Carell gave up a career in engineering to manage the family's lots, incorporating the company as Central Parking Corporation. During the next decade, Carell expanded the company's operations, winning management contracts for a steadily growing number of parking facilities. The company was helped by the boom in new building construction that took place across the country during the 1970s and 1980s, as cities began urban renewal projects to revitalize their downtown areas. At the same time, more and more urban real estate was dedicated to parking garages and lots.

Central Parking stepped into the highly fragmented industry by offering a novel approach: promising, and delivering, professional service, with well-maintained facilities and well-trained staff. Under Central Parking management, a parking facility typically saw strong increases in revenues, winning the company a high customer retention rate. Central Parking's employee recruitment, training, and compensation policies were essential components of the company's growth strategy. From the start, Central Parking sought out college-educated personnel who could be groomed as company managers. Central Parking developed its own intensive training procedures, formalized in 1986, and created a specific promotion path.

The company also pursued a policy of performance-based compensation. "Since the beginning, we have paid people based on success," Carell told *Investor's Business Daily.* "Everyone has an individual contract." Managers were paid a base salary, but managers themselves held the key to their earnings potential, with performance-based bonuses capable of more than tripling their base salary. Managers were also encouraged by the company's policy of promoting from within the organization. New hires spent a year in the company's management trainee program, and then were trained for an additional year as manager of a single facility. After that year, successful managers were promoted to area managers, in charge of several facilities, and from there to operations managers and to general managers.

Central Parking's growth continued into the 1980s; once the company established itself in one facility in a city, it typically grew to capture a major share of that city's private parking spaces, allowing the company to achieve greater economies of scale. Until the end of the decade, the company's growth was based largely on winning contracts for new parking construction. However, the collapse of the new building market and a slump in the commercial real estate industry in the late 1980s led the company into new strategies for expansion.

"TAKE-AWAY" GROWTH

To continue its growth, Central Parking switched its emphasis to what Carell called a "take-away" strategy. By promising developers and other owners of parking facilities that the company could maximize parking revenues, Central Parking began increasing the number of facilities under its control by taking existing facility contracts from its competitors. At the same time, the company recognized the opportunity to shift its operating focus from management contracts to leasing arrangements, thereby not only increasing the company's profits on a facility, but also providing a more stable and predictable income. With the commercial real estate slump sending occupancy rates plunging, developers were eager to relinquish the expense of operating parking facilities for their underused properties. Central Parking, in turn, was able to cut operating costs and gain economies of scale with its increased market share. The company also began marketing itself as a consultant for developers planning parking facilities.

By 1991, Central Parking operated in 630 locations and revenues had grown to $30.6 million. In that year, the company went international, winning a contract to provide consulting services to the Canary Wharf project in London. Later that year, the company expanded its London presence by winning the contract to manage Heathrow Airport's Terminal 4 parking facility, and it soon added the airport's Terminal 1 facility. By mid-decade, the company had built its United Kingdom base to nearly 90 facilities. The company also began a new type of service in the United Kingdom, providing privatized parking meter enforcement and ticketing services for three cities. This move positioned the company for further growth domestically, as increasing numbers of communities, eyeing the successful privatization of services such as the corrections system, began to consider privatizing meter enforcement and ticketing services as well.

In 1991, the company entered a consulting agreement with Realty Parking Properties II L.P., in which the company agreed to provide information on potential parking facilities acquisitions. Central Parking received fees based on a property's acquisition cost and was required to lease and operate the acquired properties. The following year, Central Parking added significantly to its facilities base when it acquired the management contract rights of Meyers Parking, a regional parking facilities operator with 104 facilities located primarily in New York and Boston. Meyers had been generating $34 million per year in revenues, but was losing money. Central Parking paid $8 million for the contract rights and brought the Meyers system back to profitability.

By 1992, the company's move to emphasize leasing arrangements or outright ownership of its parking facilities was providing the strongest fuel for growth: the company's parking revenues from leasing or ownership rose to nearly $27 million of its $46 million in revenues, compared with $19 million from management contracts. By the end of 1993, the company leased or owned 356 of its total base of 948 facilities. Central Parking's revenues jumped to nearly $95.5 million for the year.

```
╔══════════════════════════════════════╗
║              KEY DATES               ║
║          ──────────■──────────       ║
║                                      ║
║  1968:  Monroe Carell Jr. incorporates his family
║         business as Central Parking Corp.
║  1991:  Central Parking goes international, winning a
║         contract to provide consulting services to the
║         Canary Wharf project in London.
║  1995:  The company makes its initial public
║         offering.
║  1998:  Central Parking announces plans to merge
║         with Allright Inc., the nation's second largest
║         parking services company, in a $585 million
║         stock swap.
║  2001:  Carell Jr. announces plans to step down as
║         CEO; William J. Vareschi Jr. is named vice-
║         chairman and CEO.
║  2007:  Company acquired for $733 million by an
║         investment group that included Kohlberg &
║         Co., Chrysalis Capital Partners, and Lubert-
║         Adler Partners.
╚══════════════════════════════════════╝
```

INTERNATIONAL GROWTH CONTINUES

The company's next international move occurred in 1994, when it entered a joint-venture partnership with Mexican developer Fondo Opcion to operate 16 parking facilities in Mexico. In the United States, Central Parking continued adding to its list of facilities. The company's agreement with Realty Parking Properties ended that year, and it was freed from the obligation to offer that partnership first choice at purchasing properties that Central Parking located. In 1994, the company purchased four parking facilities. By the end of 1994, it had added a net of 100 facilities, nearly 80 of which were added under leasing arrangements. With leasing and ownership producing three-quarters of the company's revenues, Central Parking's sales surpassed $112 million for the year and net earnings neared $9 million. With international sales nearing 10 percent of revenues by 1994, the company stepped up its international growth, opening a business development office in Amsterdam, Netherlands, in 1995 to expand the company's European presence.

After finishing its 1995 fiscal year with revenues topping $126 million, Central Parking went public in October 1995 to fund further expansion plans, which included not only stepping up its lease equity activities but also the acquisition of other parking services companies. The company's offering of 2.8 million shares, originally expected to trade at $15 per share, debuted instead at $18 per share and neared $21 per share by the end of the first day's trading. Shortly after the offering, the company paid $1.6 million for a Nashville garage and $10 million for property in Chicago, adding to the five facilities purchases made in the company's 1995 fiscal year.

In March 1996, the company added significantly to its European base with the announcement of a joint-venture agreement with Wisser Service Holdings AG, a leading German supplier of business services, including building security and maintenance. The joint venture, operating as Central Parking System Deutschland, would bring Central Parking into Berlin, Dresden, and Frankfurt, and help raise the company's share of revenues from its international operations to 13.6 percent, despite the loss of a number of facilities in the United Kingdom. By the end of its 1996 fiscal year, Central Parking managed 1,359 facilities, including 37 owned by the company. Revenues increased to $143 million, providing net income of $13.8 million.

ACQUISITIONS ACCELERATE

The start of Central Parking's 1997 fiscal year seemed to herald a new era of growth for the company. In November 1996, the company made a cash purchase of Civic Parking LLC, a St. Louis-based operator of four parking garages. One month later, Central Parking announced its agreement to acquire Square Industries, which, with 117 parking facilities and nearly $66 million in 1995 revenues, firmly positioned Central Parking as the leader in the U.S. parking services industry. In April 1997, Central Parking sold 50 percent of Civic Parking to a joint-venture partner affiliated with Equity Capital Holdings LLC in a $46 million cash deal. The following month, Car Park was acquired for $3.5 million. Growth continued during the latter part of the year. In October, Central Parking paid $22.2 million to acquire Diplomat Parking Corp.

More acquisitions followed during 1998. In February, Central Parking snapped up New York-based Kinney System Holding Corp. for $208.8 million. A $2.5 million deal with Property Service Corp. occurred the following month, when the company purchased the remaining 50 percent stake in Central Parking System of Louisiana Inc. In April, most of Dallas, Texas-based Turner Parking System's assets were acquired in a deal worth $3.8 million. In the southern United States, Central Parking parted with $4.3 million to acquire the assets of Atlanta, Georgia-based Sterling Parking Inc. in July.

A major deal was announced in September 1998, at which time Central Parking revealed plans to merge with Houston, Texas-based Allright Inc., which then ranked as the nation's second largest parking services company (behind Central Parking). The deal, a $585 million stock swap, stood to double the company's locations to 4,700 and bolster its parking spaces total by 53 percent, to 1.5 million. The magnitude of the Allright deal caught the attention of the U.S. Justice Department, which challenged the merger on the grounds that it would hinder competition. In order to settle matters, Central Parking agreed to sell 74 lots in 18 cities, amounting to approximately 18,000 parking spaces. Following this, the merger was completed on March 19, 1999.

LEADERSHIP CHANGES

By the dawn of the new millennium, Central Parking oversaw approximately two million parking spaces and operated a network of approximately 100 offices in 42 states and 13 countries. A number of major leadership changes occurred during the early years of the new century. In February 2001, James J. Hagan stepped down as the company's chief financial officer. The following month, founder Monroe Carell Jr. announced plans to step down as CEO but remain with the company as chairman. At that time, retired GE Engine Services President and CEO William J. Vareschi Jr. was named vice-chairman and CEO. In May, Central Parking named Hiram Cox as its new chief financial officer.

Growth continued as Central Parking acquired Fort Lauderdale, Florida-based USA Parking Systems Inc. in October 2001 for $11.5 million. That same month, the company added six western national parks to its customer base when it acquired Universal Park Holdings in a deal worth $470,000. In January 2002, the company spent $5.7 million to acquire Park One of Louisiana. Following that transaction, Central Parking generated $18.4 million by selling its 50 percent stake in Civic Parking LLC. Midway through the year, the company acquired a minority interest in the Mason, Ohio-based smart card issuer Jayd, which provided cards that motorists used to purchase blocks of parking lot time.

In January 2003, Central Parking secured $350 million in credit financing from Bank of America. Midway through the year, the company continued its growth by acquiring Sterling Parking Ltd. in a deal worth approximately $2 million. During the middle of the decade, Central Parking mulled the possibility of selling itself. In March 2005, the company retained Morgan Stanley to evaluate its options. By late April, it announced that a number of companies were interested in a deal. However, nothing materialized at this point.

In 2006 the company received a contract extension for the management of parking operations at the Bob Hope International Airport at Burbank, California, which included one of the nation's largest valet parking services. In November, the company retained the Blackstone Group to once again explore the possibility of selling itself.

NEW OWNERSHIP

In February 2007 Central Parking accepted a $733 million acquisition offer from an investment group that included Kohlberg & Co., Chrysalis Capital Partners, and Lubert-Adler Partners. The deal was concluded in May, at which time the company's stock ceased to trade on the New York Stock Exchange. By this time, Central Parking's operations had grown beyond the United States to include locations in Canada, Chile, Colombia, Greece, Ireland, Peru, Puerto Rico, Spain, Switzerland, and the United Kingdom. However, that year the company began shedding its international operations. In August, its Central Parking System business in Europe was sold to Apcoa.

In February 2008, the company's CPC Realty LLC affiliate divested its Canadian operation. Another divestiture occurred in November 2008, when CPC sold parking lots and a parking garage in Tulsa, Oklahoma, to Dallas-based TTOW properties in a deal worth $4 million. Central Parking continued to secure new business in 2008. Examples included a three-year parking facilities management contract with the city of West Palm Beach, Florida, which included 1,900 existing parking spaces, as well as nearly 1,100 additional spaces located within facilities that were under construction.

By 2009 Central Parking remained the largest parking company in the United States. Early in the year, the company announced that it had selected Jerry Skillett and Todd Nevill to serve as vice-presidents of business development. Together, these individuals were tasked with growing the company's market share in cities where it already had a presence, as well as seeking out new national accounts. It also was in 2009 that Anschutz Entertainment Group selected the company to manage parking at the Carson, California-based Home Depot Center soccer stadium. Challenging economic times prevailed in 2009. However, from its position of industry leadership, Central Parking seemed well positioned to weather the storm.

M. L. Cohen
Updated, Paul R. Greenland

PRINCIPAL COMPETITORS

ABM Industries Inc.; Imperial Parking Corporation; Standard Parking Corporation.

FURTHER READING

Carey, Bill, "Central Parking Stock Takes Off," *Tennessean,* May 27, 1996, p. 1E.

———, "Central Parking Top of the Lot," *Tennessean,* December 10, 1996, p. 1E.

"Central Parking Completes Merger for $22.53 Per Share in Cash," *Business Wire,* May 22, 2007.

"Central Parking Corporation and Allright Holdings Inc. Agree to Merge," *Business Wire,* September 21, 1998.

Maio, Patrick J., "Central Parking Corp.," *Investor's Daily Busi-ness,* September 24, 1996, p. A6.

———, "Profit Lots," *Investor's Daily Business,* January 16, 1996, p. A6.

Rudnitsky, Howard, "Take-Away Game," *Forbes,* July 29, 1996, p. 50.

Ward, Gethan, "Central Parking Buys Big Rival," *Nashville Banner,* December 10, 1996, p. D4.

"William J. Vareschi, Jr., to Join Central Parking Corporation as Vice-Chairman and Chief Executive Officer," *Business Wire,* March 1, 2001.

Clean Venture, Inc.

———————————— ■ ————————————

201 South First Street
Elizabeth, New Jersey 07206-1502
U.S.A.
Telephone: (908) 355-5800
Fax: (908) 355-3495
Web site: http://www.cyclechem.com

Private Company
Incorporated: 1977
Employees: 192
Sales: $39.3 million (2008 est.)
NAICS: 562998 All Other Miscellaneous Waste
    Management

■ ■ ■

Clean Venture, Inc. (CVI), is the flagship company of a group of environmental services companies owned by the Witte family. Serving the northeastern and mid-Atlantic states, they share a common corporate office in Elizabeth, New Jersey. CVI is a full service environmental contractor with services that include chemical and waste disposal, environmental decontamination and remediation, environmental emergency response, waste management, PCB (polychlorinated biphenyl) decontamination, waste transportation, waste treatment and management, environmental decontamination and remediation, soil, excavation, and tank removal.

CVI also works with another Witte family-owned company, Donjon Marine Company, Inc., a major marine salvage company, on removing environmental hazards from ships that are to be scuttled and scrapped as well as on disposal and dredging projects. CVI's sister environmental services companies include Cycle Chem, Inc., and General Chemical Corporation, both of which possess RCRA (Resource Conservation and Recovery Act) Part "B" permits to treat, store, and dispose of hazardous waste materials. The Cycle Chem facilities are located in Elizabeth, New Jersey, and Lewisberry, Pennsylvania, while General Chemical is based in Framingham, Massachusetts.

Another sister company, Envirotech Consultants, LLC, is a turnkey environmental company with branches in Elizabeth, New Jersey, and Baltimore, Maryland. In addition to consulting, the company offers such services as soil remediation, ground water remediation, vapor treatment, and industrial/construction remediation. CVI and its affiliated environmental services companies also sell products used in spills and cleanups: general purpose pads used to absorb oil and water-based fluids; "sorbent" pads for oil and petroleum-based fluids; five-gallon polyethylene pails and tight-fitting lids; 15-, 30-, and 55-gallon closed head or open head metal drums; 85- and 100-gallon steel overpack drums; and 30- and 55-gallon reconditioned plastic open head drums.

ORIGINS

The man behind the growth of Clean Venture and its sister companies was J. Arnold Witte, Sr. A maritime lawyer by training, practicing in New York City, he found it difficult to support his young family; he also preferred and decided to earn some extra money through marine salvage and wreck removal projects, a business with which he had some experience. His father, John J. Witte, had founded Witte Marine Equipment Company in 1931 in Rossville, Staten Island, on a 200-acre, half-mile section of the Arthur Kill waterfront opposite the better-known side of Staten Island that shared New York Harbor along with the Statue of Liberty, Ellis Island, and Lower Manhattan.

There in the waters between Staten Island and New Jersey, mostly hidden from view, the elder Witte operated a ship breaker business. Because he was loath to dismantle a ship unless there was a ready buyer for the materials, he assembled an ad hoc maritime museum including the rotting frames of old wooden sailing ships, tugs, ferries, fireboats, and other vessels. At its peak, the yard held as many as 400 vessels, the world's largest collection of historic ships, and in time historians would come in rubber rafts and small boats to view the relics. The business remained in the family even after Witte died in 1980, although the pace of dismantling increased.

Given his family background in the marine salvage trade, it was not surprising that the young lawyer should turn his attention to the business as a way to supplement his income. In 1964 J. Arnold Witte took on his first weekend project, a $5,600 contract from the U.S. Army Corps of Engineers to raise a railcar that had derailed and become submerged. It was a shoestring operation that consisted of one hired man, a station wagon, and a small launch. For the dive, Witte relied on a Sears, Roebuck paint sprayer for a compressor and a garden hose attached to a mask. This marked the humble beginning of Donjon Marine Company, named for two of Witte's children, Donna and John.

In 1967 he incorporated the business and bought his first launch and barge to create more project opportunities in New York Harbor. Over time Witte expanded the business beyond casualty-related events and also extended its reach throughout the Northeast and overseas. The company took on heavy-lift stevedoring, marine construction, and diving services. Upon the death of Witte's father in 1980, Donjon added Witte Marine Equipment.

Also in 1967 Witte joined forces with Myron L. Chase to create a steel scrapping business called Witte-Chase Corporation. Boston born, Chase had earned a degree in history from Harvard University in 1939, followed by a five-year stint in the U.S. Navy. After the war he became involved in the scrap iron and steel business by going to work for his father-in-law, Darwin Luntz, becoming a vice-president in charge of the Canton, Ohio, office of Luntz Iron and Steel Corporation. After Luntz died in 1951, his brother took charge, and because this man had sons of his own it became apparent to Chase that there was a limited future for him with the family company. In 1956 he became a vice-president at Luria Brothers of New York, a major Luntz rival in the scrap iron and steel business. Later Chase became president of Shiavone-Chase Corporation in New York before becoming president of Witte-Chase. Because of some of its recovery activities Witte-Chase had to deal with related environmental concerns, creating a natural connection to the environmental services sector.

CVI ACQUIRED

According to the *Philadelphia Inquirer,* Witte-Chase acquired CVI around 1980, three years after its founding by three men who then went on to form another company that became a competitor. For its own part, CVI became the environmental cleanup arm of the Witte family-related companies.

CVI was initially an oil spill cleanup company focused on New Jersey, but it soon expanded to include hazardous waste and chemical spills. New Jersey was a key highway and railroad corridor for the Northeast and also shared the heavily trafficked New York Harbor. The state also produced one-quarter of all chemicals produced in the United States. As a result, there was a steady source of truck turnovers on the New Jersey Turnpike, oil tanker spills in the waters surrounding the state, oil facility spills, chemical spills, and illegal hazardous waste sites to keep CVI and other firms busy year round. According to the *Record* of New Jersey, CVI went "into marshes, oceans, rivers, fields, barges, oil tanks, refineries, smelters, caves, landfills, and construction sites to get its hands on lethal materials."

In the 1980s CVI acquired a license to transport hazardous waste, but had a difficult time finding a place to dump the toxic substances collected, including acetone, acetic acid, ethyl ketones, methanol, percolates, chlorines, sodium hydroxide, cyanide, sulfuric acid, mercury compounds, liquid oxygen, phenols, and PCBs.

KEY DATES

1977: Clean Ventures, Inc. (CVI), is formed.
1980: Witte-Chase Corporation acquires CVI.
1984: Cycle Chem Inc. is formed to temporarily store toxic substances in order to recycle and dispose of them.
1995: Upgrade on Cycle Chem facilities is completed.
2000: General Chemical Corporation is acquired.
2007: Envirotech Consultants, LLC, is acquired.
2008: TPH Industries is acquired.

Almost all of the PCBs were transported to a legal dump in Arkansas, but for the most part the materials were returned to the parties responsible for the spill and stored as long as necessary. In 1984 sister company Cycle Chem Inc. was formed to temporarily store these materials in order to recycle and dispose of them. Cycle Chem found a suitable facility in Elizabeth, New Jersey, owned by the Perk Chemical Company, which it acquired in October 1985.

Clean Venture was the leading company of its kind in New Jersey, generating revenues of about $10 million by 1986. It held contracts with the Environmental Protection Agency and did a thriving business with companies that were required by law to clean up facilities before they could be sold. One of the company's largest contracts was to clean up oil spills in New York Harbor for the Clean Harbors Cooperative, formed by nine major oil companies.

PARTNER DIES

In 1987 the 68-year-old Myron Chase died of a heart attack, suffered while he was at the Harvard Club in New York City. The Wittes carried on without him, with family members taking on various posts in the affiliated group of marine salvage and environmental services companies. The need for cooperation and coordination between the units took on even greater importance following the massive oil spill of the *Exxon Valdez* tanker in Alaska's Prince William Sound in March 1989, which led to the Oil Pollution Act of 1990 that placed greater responsibilities on ships, terminal owners, and others involved in the transport of oil to prevent spills.

As CVI took on more work during the 1990s, the Cycle Chem facility had to be expanded in order to keep up with the increased amount of waste materials

brought in. A major upgrade effort was launched in 1993 and completed two years later. Improvements included a fuel blending operation, a larger tank farm, a new bulk solids consolidation-solidification facility, and the repadding of the waste process area. In addition, Cycle Chem increased its range of permits to keep pace with the growing CVI operations. A second facility, fully permitted, was added in 1999 when Cycle Chem bought a ten-acre, Part "B" treatment, storage, and disposal site in Lewisberry, Pennsylvania, south of Harrisburg, capable of storing some 900,000 gallons of hazardous wastes. It was an acquisition that expanded the geographic reach of Cycle Chem and its sister companies.

The Witte-owned group of environmental services companies continued to expand in the 21st century. In May 2000 General Chemical Corporation was acquired, adding another Part "B" treatment, storage, and disposal facility in Framingham, Massachusetts, where Cycle Chem then relocated its field services. The deal also allowed the group to extend its reach in the Northeast. Moreover, General Chemical Corporation was well established in the market. Founded in 1960, it had become the region's largest distributor/reclaimer of chlorinated and fluorinated solvents and later added waste management and environmental services. In the early years of the new century, Cycle Chem's Lewisberry facility received an upgrade, completed in November 2003 when a new residual waste building was opened. With a storage capacity of 2,500 drums and three processing pits with a total capacity of 18,000 gallons, the state-of-the-art building was able to handle the processing of residual waste entirely indoors.

In addition to working with Cycle Chem and General Chemical Corp., CVI was a joint venture partner with Donjon Marine in removing environmental hazards from ships slated to be scrapped. Together they also won contracts with the Army Corps of Engineers for dredging projects. In the early years of the decade the two companies received a contract jointly funded by the Corps and the Port Authority of New York and New Jersey to dredge and deepen New York Harbor, in particular the Arthur Kill River and the Port Jersey Channel.

The Witte companies added a consulting operation in early 2007 when Cedar Grove, New Jersey-based Envirotech Consultants, LLC, was acquired. The firm was established in 1988 and maintained site investigation, remediation, industrial, and emergency response operations. A year later, in January 2008, Envirotech grew further through the acquisition of TPH Industries.

Founded in 1990, TPH was a groundwater remediation and environmental consulting company with operations in Maryland and Delaware. As a result, CVI and its sister companies extended their reach in the mid-Atlantic region. There was every reason to expect that the need for CVI's services would continue to grow in the years to come.

Ed Dinger

PRINCIPAL COMPETITORS

Brilliant Lewis Environmental Services; Moran Environmental Recovery, LLC; Prime Environmental Inc.

FURTHER READING

Bamberger, Werner, "Ships Become Scrap on S.I.'s 'Dark Side,'" *New York Times,* April 12, 1970.

"Company Cleans Up on Toxic-Waste Spills," *Philadelphia Inquirer,* July 31, 1986, p. B11.

"Donjon: All Service, All in the Family," *Marinelink.com,* June 4, 2004.

"Donjon Marine: A Family of Maritime Services," *Marine Log,* July 1, 2004.

"Life Is Sweet for Donjon Marine," *Europe Intelligence Wire,* December 1, 2004.

Meyers, Keith, "A Lesson in History of Old Ships," *New York Times,* December 31, 1990.

"Myron L. Chase, 68, President of Scrap Metal Firm," *Boston Globe,* May 3, 1987, p. 99.

Reed, Leonard, "Spillbusters to the Rescue," *Record* (N.J.), September 24, 1985, p. B1.

The Connell Company

———— ■ ————

200 Connell Drive
Berkeley Heights, New Jersey 07922
U.S.A.
Telephone: (908) 673-3700
Fax: (908) 673-3800
Web site: http://www.connellco.com

Private Company
Incorporated: 1926 as Connell Rice & Sugar Co.
Employees: 245
Sales: $284.5 million (2008 est.)
NAICS: 551112 Offices of Other Holding Companies

■ ■ ■

Originally and perhaps best known as a major broker of rice, The Connell Company has grown to become one of the largest and most diversified privately held corporations in the United States. With three generations of the Connell family currently active, the New Jersey-based Connell Company is involved in exporting rice; exporting food processing equipment and supplies; importing, brokering, selling, and distributing canned food products; developing office buildings; leasing, distributing, and selling construction equipment; arranging financing of leased equipment and commercial property development; and offering asset management services to the technology sector. Through its subsidiaries, Connell Co. operates in over 100 countries across the globe. Grover Connell, the company's president since 1950, had an estimated net worth of $900 million in 2005 according to *Forbes* magazine.

ORIGINS AS A RICE BROKER

The Connell Company traces its origins to the 1926 founding of the Connell Rice & Sugar Co. The senior Grover Connell was a native of Texas who moved to New York City, where he established headquarters for his thriving rice distribution and export business. Connell died in 1950 and was succeeded by a son who bore the same name. By then company sales had reached $10 million a year. Connell Rice headquarters were moved in 1958 from New York to a modern building in Westfield, New Jersey, near the Connell family residence. From there, the company exported bagged rice via ship to companies around the world. The company's executives had developed their own interests in rice farms by the 1960s.

The primary business of Connell Rice & Sugar was, according to a 1967 Federal Trade Commission (FTC) document, buying and reselling commodities for its own account and acting as a broker for transactions in refined sugar, corn products, and other commodities. In addition, the company received monthly fees for studies of commodity prices and market conditions that it circulated to various industrial organizations.

In 1974 Connell Rice & Sugar, under the leadership of Grover Connell Jr., became involved in urging Congress to repeal certain legislation, in force since the Great Depression of the 1930s, designed to support rice prices by restricting production in the United States. Discussing the legislation, as well as the nature of the rice business in general, Connell told Elizabeth M. Fowler of the *New York Times* that year that the United States produced about 2 percent of the world's rice, yet was the world's largest exporter of the product. Connell attributed this irony to the fact that the world's largest rice producing nations, such as China, Japan, and India, were also experiencing sharp rises in population and thus needed even more rice to feed themselves. Connell's company was exporting rice to about 100 countries at this time, while also importing some rice and selling it domestically. All told, rice accounted for about 85 percent of the company's annual sales volume of $350 million, and Connell was reported to be the nation's largest rice exporter.

POLITICAL INVOLVEMENT LEADS TO PROBLEMS

Grover Connell's ties to two U.S. House of Representatives members became an issue during this time, when reporters revealed that Department of Justice officials were investigating charges that South Koreans were attempting to influence U.S. policies regarding rice and other export programs by bribing congressmen. According to the final report of a House investigation, Representative Otto Passman of Louisiana told a federal investigator that he forced the Koreans to hire a Connell shipping company by threatening to cut off foreign aid otherwise.

Moreover, in 1977 a Department of Agriculture officer recommended suspending Grover Connell from doing business under the department's Food for Peace program, charging that he had concealed ownership of a shipping agency representing foreign governments in the chartering of vessels carrying these food shipments. According to this official, Connell Rice & Sugar shipped 72 percent of all rice moved under the program in 1976.

Finally, Grover Connell was indicted in 1978 on six counts of violating federal law by illegally using a Korean rice dealer with ties to the South Korean government as his agent for sales to the government under the Food for Peace program. He was alleged to have paid the dealer, Tongun Park, $600,000 in commissions and

then covered up the payments by sending them to the offshore bank account of a Korean company. The firm itself was reported to have paid Park $8 million in commissions on rice sales to Korea. The charges against Connell were dismissed in 1979 after Park, who was now a prosecution witness, changed his testimony, according to the Department of Justice.

The South Korean government subsequently sought to reduce its dependence on Connell Rice & Sugar for imports of its main food staple. However, according to a *Wall Street Journal* story in 1983, Grover Connell and his allies in Congress and the U.S. rice trade were making it difficult for South Korea to buy rice from rival exporters. Korean officials attributed their problems to Connell's campaign donations to a number of Democrats in the House of Representatives, many from rice producing states. In 1982 a State Department official told Congress that Connell had threatened to use his influence to cut off foreign aid to South Korea unless the country bought his rice.

Connell Rice & Sugar's business allies in the United States included two California growers' cooperatives that were handling about 75 percent of the state's rice crop. Virtually all of the export portion of this crop was being brokered by Connell and sent to South Korea. According to a 1984 *Forbes* story, when the South Korean government ordered a shipment from another company, the cooperatives declined to sell except through Connell, which charged $35 a ton more than the other company's contract price. In 1992 Connell was cleared of allegations that it conspired to monopolize California's rice trade. The jury, however, could not agree on the broader issue of whether the company was guilty of restraint of trade. The U.S. Court of Appeals would reinstate, in 1996, this part of the lawsuit by 70 rice growers against Connell.

EXTENDING THE COMPANY'S SCOPE

Grover Connell continued to foster ties with members of Congress in the 1980s. In 1989 his company distributed more honoraria, or speaking fees, to members than any other firm: about $100,000 in all. Most of the money was being paid to members of the House and Senate agricultural committees or members from major rice- and sugar-growing states, but congressional staff members also received such payments. According to a 1990 *Washington Post* story, at least once a week Grover Connell would invite a member of Congress to company headquarters for a report on what the legislative body was doing and then pay a fee of $2,000. Connell said he and his wife were also each making the maximum $25,000 a year in personal politi-

KEY DATES

1926: The Connell Rice & Sugar Co. is established.
1950: The founder's son, Grover Connell, takes over the business upon the death of his father.
1974: Connell Rice & Sugar becomes involved in urging Congress to repeal certain legislation.
1978: Grover Connell is indicted on six counts of violating federal law by illegally using a Korean rice dealer with ties to the South Korean government as his agent for sales to the government under the Food for Peace program.
1979: The charges against Connell are dismissed after a key witness changes his testimony.
1990: The parent company changes its name to The Connell Company.
1999: Connell Rice & Sugar Co. exports domestically grown rice, as well as rice grown in the Far East and other areas, to more than 100 countries.
2001: The company receives controversial tax breaks with the passing of a $1.35 trillion tax bill.

cal donations to federal campaigns. Some $200,000 in corporate funds were donated to help build a media center for the Democratic Congressional Campaign Committee.

By this time the firm, having extended its scope of operations, had become The Connell Company, a holding company for its diverse activities. A 1988 *Forbes* story reported that Connell's expansion had begun in 1973 with leasing. In 1987 the company leased $600 million worth of railroad hopper cars, coal barges, shipping containers, aircraft, and office buildings. Connell reduced the risks of such a venture by leasing only to reliable corporate clients, handling goods with no risk of rapid depreciation, and taking payment in the form of an equity interest in the equipment at the end of the lease. Meanwhile, the lessee paid property taxes, maintenance, and insurance but realized its own benefit in the form of lower taxes.

The government of Zaire, long a client for rice shipments from Connell under the Food for Peace program, began leasing equipment for its government-run mining company, Gecamines, in the 1980s. In 1987 Connell became Gecamines' authorized supplier in the United States, with 12 U.S. companies and their subsidiaries required to sell through Connell. Grover Connell defended the country's ruler, Mobutu Sese Seko, against charges of massive human rights abuses and corruption and, when Mobutu came to the United States during 1988–89, arranged for about 50 members of Congress to attend receptions for the visitor.

Some members of Congress also visited Zaire under Connell's auspices. The company lost its contract with Gecamines later in 1990 under pressure from the World Bank, which argued that its fees were excessive. Nevertheless, Connell was said to be grossing more than $15 million a year from its dealings with Mobutu before he was overthrown in 1997.

Connell Realty & Development Co., a subsidiary, erected two office buildings in the 1980s on 107 acres in the township of Berkeley Heights, New Jersey. In 1997 this arm of the operations began construction of another office structure on an adjacent 63-acre parcel of this corporate park, with completion scheduled by the end of 1998. Plans called for more three more buildings at some future date, depending on leasing activity and demand. Connell Realty & Development had estimated operating revenue of $20 million in 1994.

COMPANY OPERATIONS: 1998–99

As the decade drew to a close, the parent Connell Company was firmly ensconced as the country's largest independent rice and sugar broker, while its heavy equipment leasing business was doing record business as well. Its nine subsidiaries represented diverse business interests at home and abroad.

Connell Rice & Sugar Co. held an estimated share of more than 20 percent of the sugar and rice export market in 1998 and exported domestically grown rice, as well as rice grown in the Far East and other areas, to more than 100 countries in 1999. Within the United States the company distributed rice to the brewing industry and to wholesalers, food processors, and retail chains. It also had longstanding relationships for storage, toll milling, and transportation.

Subsidiary Connell International Co. exported a wide range of equipment and supplies to food processing businesses in more than 100 countries. It also served as exclusive distributor for many of its suppliers and handled additional equipment and supplies on a private-label basis. These activities were served by offices in Malaysia, Senegal, Taiwan, and Thailand.

The Connell & Co. subsidiary was the largest industrial refined sugar and flour broker in the United States, providing brokerage and sales services to food companies processing and marketing sugar, flour, cocoa and chocolate, vegetable oils, and bakery seeds, and engaged in packaging and bread bag manufacturing. The sales service operated from offices in Westfield; Oak Brook, Illinois; and Omaha, Nebraska. The purchasing service was located in Oak Brook.

Connell Foods, Inc., imported canned food products from more than 50 countries for distribution to supermarkets, cooperatives, wholesale grocers, institutional distributors, food processors, and drug and restaurant chains in the United States. Its offices were in Taiwan and Thailand.

Connell Finance Co., Inc., was active in virtually all aspects of equipment, project, and real estate financing, with a portfolio of equipment having an original cost of over $800 million. The company had arranged more than $10 billion of lease financing.

Connell Equipment Leasing Co., which became a division of Connell Finance in 1997, had been providing single investor lease financing and equipment advisory services since 1982. It financed all types of long-lived, durable assets, including more than $125 million of equipment such as forklift trucks, cranes, tractors, and front end loaders.

Connell Gatco Co. worked directly with mining, quarrying, and construction companies, supplying them with parts, components, and equipment, such as bearings and loading, hauling, and dumping vehicles. It also acted as an exclusive distributor for several leading manufacturers and provided marketing, technical, and after-sales support.

Connell Realty & Development Co. developed corporate headquarters office buildings for both single and multiple tenants, arranging for both construction and permanent financing of these assets through its own funding. It had ownership positions in, or had arranged lease financing for, more than nine million square feet of commercial property space.

Connell Technologies Co. provided equipment, real estate financing, and asset management services to the technology sector. It had acted as financial adviser to a large institutional investor for a $43 million lease of semiconductor manufacturing equipment with a major computer chip manufacturer. Offices were in Westfield and California's Silicon Valley.

MOVING INTO THE 21ST CENTURY

Connell's political affiliations engendered controversy once again when it became apparent the company would benefit from a proposed tax bill in 2001. A May 2001 *Wall Street Journal* article explained the situation claiming, "Connell Co.'s success in gaining a foothold in the tax legislation—now in final negotiations among Republican leaders on Capitol Hill—illustrates how special interests are managing to hitch a ride on a bill President [Geowge W.] Bush has insisted to be dedicated to tax cuts for individuals and families."

Grover Connell, his company, and related associates had made contributions to the Democratic Party totaling $683,079 during 2000 and 2001. Connell was also a longtime friend of Louisiana Senator John Breaux, who sponsored a provision in the tax bill that included a special estate tax break that would benefit Connell. The new $1.35 trillion tax bill, passed in 2001, allowed The Connell Company to pay estate taxes over a five year period rather than in one lump sum. Such tax breaks to special interest groups had many special interest watchdog groups up in arms.

Nevertheless, the company declined to comment on the issue and continued with business as usual. The Connell Rice & Sugar Co. subsidiary began shipping rice from the Stockton port in California. During 2002, the company shipped 44,000 metric tons of rice to Uzbekistan through a federal food aid program. The Connell Company also formed a partnership with Edison International to give investment advice to its Edison Capital division, which oversaw investments in real estate and financial markets.

With roots dating back to 1926, Connell was firmly established as one of the largest privately owned companies in the country late in the first decade of the 21st century. Grover Connell, by this time in his 80s, was among the richest men in the United States and remained at the helm of the firm started by his father. The family business, with three generations actively involved, stood on solid financial footing with little debt. The company claimed to have a large capital base—as a private entity it did not have to report quarterly or annual financial results—and appeared ready to purchase assets related to its core businesses.

Robert Halasz
Updated, Christina M. Stansell

PRINCIPAL SUBSIDIARIES

Connell Rice & Sugar Co.; Connell International Co.; Connell Commodities; Connell Mining Co.; Connell Technologies LLC; Connell Real Estate & Development Co.; Connell Finance Co. Inc.; Investment Banking Group; Connell Equipment Leasing Co.

PRINCIPAL COMPETITORS

GE Commercial Finance; Riviana Foods Inc.; United Rentals Inc.

FURTHER READING

"Appeals Court Resurrects Suit," *San Francisco Chronicle,* December 3, 1996, p. E2.

Babcock, Charles R., "Controversial Rice Broker Provides Plentiful Hill Speech Fees," *Washington Post,* July 11, 1989, p. A5.

————, "The Corporate King of Honoraria," *Washington Post,* March 20, 1990, pp. Al, A9.

Cloply, Michael, "'Somebody Took the Profits,'" *Forbes,* January 16, 1984, pp. 67–68.

"Edison International Forms Strategic Relationship with The Connell Company," *Reuters Significant Developments,* January 30, 2003.

"Foremost-McKesson, Connell Rice Accept FTC Orders on Commodity Transactions," *Wall Street Journal,* April 19, 1968, p. 12.

Fowler, Elizabeth M., "Easing of U.S. Curbs on Rice Is Sought by Exporter," *New York Times,* November 4, 1974, pp. 59, 61.

Garbarine, Rachelle, "Developer Stays the Course for a Bigger Office Park," *New York Times,* June 29, 1997, Sec. 9, p. 9.

Hitt, Greg, and Shailagh Murray, "Special Interests Hitch a Ride on Tax Bill," *Wall Street Journal,* May 25, 2001.

King, Ralph, Jr., "A New Way to Beat Inflation," *Forbes,* January 11, 1988, pp. 264–65.

Lachica, Eduardo, "Seoul Runs Afoul of U.S. Rice Trader," *Wall Street Journal,* July 7, 1983, p. 26.

Pound, Edward T., "Connell Loses Lucrative Contract to Supply a Mining Firm in Zaire," *Wall Street Journal,* November 26, 1990, p. B5.

"Profile: Loopholes Inserted into New Tax Bill," *NBC News,* June 7, 2001.

"Rice Trader Indicted in Dealing with Park," *New York Times,* May 27, 1976, p. 6.

Robbins, William, "Ex-U.S. Aide Scores Main Rice Exporter," *New York Times,* May 1, 1977, p. 23.

————, "Korean Link Hinted in New U.S. Inquiry," *New York Times,* November 1, 1976, p. 3.

"Uzbekistan's Ambassador Sees Port, Rice Shipment in Stockton, Calif.," *Record,* August 8, 2002.

Cramer-Krasselt Company

733 North Van Buren Street
Milwaukee, Wisconsin 53202
U.S.A.
Telephone: (414) 227-3500
Fax: (414) 226-8710
Web site: http://www.c-k.com

Private Company
Incorporated: 1898
Employees: 165
Sales: $474 million (2008 est.)
NAICS: 541810 Advertising Agencies

■ ■ ■

Cramer-Krasselt Company ranks as the third largest independent advertising agency in the United States. It is also one of the oldest continually operating firms in the industry. Cramer-Krasselt (C-K) is a midsize advertising agency specializing in midsize accounts. In a field dominated by large global players, C-K has carved out a niche where it thrives. The company maintains offices in Milwaukee, Chicago, New York, and Phoenix. Its services are broad, from advertising in multiple media to public relations to direct and interactive marketing. Its clients span many industries, including Porsche cars, Corona beer, Master Lock, pharmaceutical brands Zantac and Rozerem, financial services TrueCredit.com and KeyBank Corporation, and consumer product lines such as Benjamin Moore paints and Burlington Coat Factory.

ORIGINS IN BICYCLING

Cramer-Krasselt was founded in Milwaukee in 1898 by two neighbors who shared a love of bicycling. Frederick "Cody" Cramer and William Krasselt met as young men in their twenties living in a boardinghouse on Milwaukee's State Street. Cramer was a typesetter and Krasselt a knife salesman. They were both members of a bicycling club, the Badger Wheelmen. They spent their spare time on their sport. They were so interested in bicycling that they founded a newsletter for fellow enthusiasts called the *Wheelman.* They formed a company they named The Pneumatic Press to publish the journal, and took out paid advertising.

Soon the partners began creating ads for the *Wheelman* as well as selling ad space. This began to seem like a promising business in itself, and the two incorporated under the new name Cramer-Krasselt Company and set up as an advertising agency. They had previously done all their work out of the boardinghouse, but at this time rented an office on Grand Avenue. They called their new quarters "The Home of Good Advertising." Among their first clients were Merkel Motorcycles and a maker of bicycle accessories, Julius Andre & Sons.

By 1910, Cramer-Krasselt had 50 employees. Early clients included prominent Milwaukee companies. As early as 1909 they created ads for Milwaukee's Miller beer using the tagline "The Champagne of Bottle Beer." Beer was a big Wisconsin industry; others were farm equipment, dairy products, leather products, automobiles, and small motors. C-K represented companies in all these areas. Some were very well known, like Miller and another Milwaukee beer, Pabst

Blue Ribbon. The company represented other products that came and went, such as the Kissel Kar. C-K's ads for this early auto called it "The Car That Stands Up."

The agency offered integrated advertising services, not only designing ads but also printing their clients' flyers, billboards, and catalogs. The company also offered clients a year's worth of weekly illustrated newspaper advertising for the all-inclusive annual fee of $50. C-K performed the service of writing and publishing corporate newsletters as well. The young company prospered, with sales growing to $500,000 in 1920. In 1927, C-K moved to new quarters on Van Buren Street. This address would remain the company headquarters into the 21st century.

SURVIVING THE GREAT DEPRESSION

Cramer-Krasselt had grown rapidly as business boomed in the Milwaukee area. It had many and varied clients, some of whom stuck with the company for many years. C-K hoped to grow beyond Milwaukee in the 1930s, but a harsh economic climate made this impossible. During the 1930s, C-K sustained itself largely through its profitable printing business. Although many clients reined in their advertising budgets, C-K had steady work printing one of the era's best-selling cookbooks, the *Settlement Cook Book*. Despite lean times, C-K opened offices in Detroit, Los Angeles, and New York during the Great Depression; however, it was shortly forced to close all three offices.

Cofounder Cody Cramer died in 1934. The new president of the company, Walter Seilert, spoke to a meeting of the Newspaper Advertising Executives' Association in 1937. He promised his audience that newspaper advertising was indeed effective at generating sales, giving the example of C-K's Norge Refrigerator Company account. Nevertheless, 1937 was a bleak year, the only year to date in the company's history in which it lost money.

The company's other founder, William Krasselt, died in 1940. The new leader, Seilert, had worked his way up through C-K, beginning as a stenographer. He understood the business thoroughly. He was able to attract prominent clients, including local companies such as Evinrude, maker of outboard motors; utility Milwaukee Gas Light Co.; and the cookware maker Mirro Aluminum. Seilert focused the agency's strategy and built it up into the largest advertising agency in Wisconsin.

Seilert's watchword was "Coordinated Advertising." This meant that C-K did not specialize in a particular advertising medium, but instead saw its task to be building a client's brand in as many ways as were effective. Thus C-K's notion of its duties was far broader than some other companies. It even built a test kitchen to help in marketing new food products.

POSTWAR YEARS

Cramer-Krasselt was also an early adopter of the new postwar medium of television. The company had one of the first television divisions of any advertising agency beginning in 1947. It produced entire shows for clients, and also ran one of the earliest local television news programs, which aired for fifteen minutes a week. C-K's media director acted as news anchorman. C-K's clients were both the television station itself and the advertising sponsors for the news program.

In the 1950s and 1960s, C-K became known for syndicated ad campaigns, meaning one national or regional campaign could be tailored to the client's local branches. Cramer-Krasselt produced a lot of such work for banks and utilities. In the 1970s, the company built advertising for prominent consumer brands. One of its best known was an ad for the Master Lock brand of padlocks. C-K produced advertising for Master Lock beginning in 1974 that featured a gunman attempting to open the lock with a gunshot. Cramer-Krasselt produced ads for Master Lock for another 20 years.

Part of C-K's strategy with Master Lock was to spend as much as one-third of the client's entire annual advertising budget on a single 30-second commercial that aired during the Super Bowl. As ad prices for the Super Bowl rose steeply over the years, Master Lock, as well as other companies, began to wonder if the high price was worth it. Cramer-Krasselt conducted consumer research on the Super Bowl that was widely shared throughout the advertising industry. This showed that indeed a 30-second spectacle had a strong impact on consumers, and therefore the high cost was justified.

C-K did business with a wealth of Wisconsin corporations and fostered many relationships of long standing. By the late 1970s, C-K was known as something of a conservative firm, doing very good work but with less zing than some of its younger, more adventurous competitors. Walter Seilert had retired in 1962, and the top job went to C. W. Faude. The baton then passed to Ted Wing in the 1970s, and the firm began to make some changes. Some of the agency's most promising admen had left in the mid-1970s to found their own shops. By the end of the decade, Wing found it necessary to bring back some talent to the Milwaukee office, and to expand into other cities as well.

BRANCHING OUT

Cramer-Krasselt opened two new offices in 1980, one in Phoenix, Arizona, and the other in Chicago. When the Phoenix office opened, it had only one account, but it grew rapidly. Within a few years, the Phoenix branch was one of the largest agencies in the Southwest, representing Southwest Airlines, among other prominent regional clients. By contrast, the Chicago office did not start small but was acquired. C-K bought two Chicago agencies, the Alex T. Franz agency and Hackenberg, Normann, Krivkovich. These two combined became C-K Chicago.

At that time, the newly expanded Cramer-Krasselt was billing just over $40 million a year, and it had 100 employees spread across its three offices. The company worked hard to change its pace. As other agencies grew through mergers, the industry became weighted with large national and international firms. C-K felt that this left a niche for a midsize company. It aimed to stay in the middle, and to court midsize companies as clients. C-K also recommitted to its earlier strategy of

coordinated advertising. Cramer-Krasselt therefore increased its capabilities in the 1980s, adding departments and employees to specialize in direct marketing, Yellow Pages advertising, research, and public relations. This led C-K to market itself to its midsize clients as having the breadth and expertise of a large agency while providing as much individual attention to clients as a small firm. The company described this philosophy as "dominating the middle market." It specialized in the $2 million account, which was considered to be precisely not too big and not too small.

With the company actively making changes to adapt to new business conditions, C-K attracted back some of its employees who had left. One of these was Paul Counsell, who left in the late 1970s and returned in 1981. He became chairman in 1985 and ran the company for the next 13 years. Counsell honed the middle market strategy, and oversaw years of double-digit billings growth. By the mid-1990s, C-K's billings had topped $200 million. The Chicago office was responsible for almost half of that. It had regional clients such as LaSalle Bank, the young suburban Chicago phone company Cellular One, minor league hockey team the Chicago Wolves, and about 40 others. The firm did not depend on any one large client. It retained its clients' business by offering complete marketing, from television to billboards. A profile of C-K in *Crain's Chicago Business* (December 18, 1995) defined the company's style as telling the consumer "more about the product than about the consumer's own desires."

The agency opened a branch in Orlando, Florida, in 1990. By the end of the decade, this branch too had shown remarkable growth. In 1998 this office employed 40 people and had attracted clients such as the Orlando/Orange County Convention and Visitors Bureau, Grendha Shoes, and other local and regional businesses in a variety of industries. Cramer-Krasselt as a whole saw double-digit sales growth in the late 1990s. Its strategy of specializing in the midsize market had done well, although its definition of midsize had swelled beyond the $2 million account to $5 million to $10 million and up. As the advertising industry consolidated and small boutique firms also proliferated, Cramer-Krasselt stood out as the solid player in the middle ground.

NEW LEADERSHIP

Paul Counsell had overseen the company's successful expansion and growth from the mid-1980s through the late 1990s. Cramer-Krasselt celebrated its 100-year anniversary in 1998, giving it an almost unprecedented age and dignity in a field full of young players. That year, Counsell retired, and Peter Krivkovich, who had headed the Chicago branch, became chief executive. Krivkovich saw no reason to tamper with the agency's direction. A panoply of clients with $10 million to $20 million to spend were snapped up by Cramer-Krasselt, where the big international ad agencies found them too small. There were hundreds of brands in the midsize category, and C-K served them well. With billings still growing as much as 20 percent from 2000 to 2001, the company set its sights on moving into New York, California, and perhaps overseas. Clients at this time included Corona beer, AirTran Airways, Hyatt Corp., and Zenith.

By 2003, Cramer-Krasselt was considered the fourth largest independent ad agency in the United States. Billings were close to $500 million, and it had almost 500 employees. The company established a presence in New York that year, acquiring the public relations firm Nichol & Company. Nichol then folded into Cramer-Krasselt's existing public relations arm, CKPR. Expanding into public relations meant C-K could offer clients a broad range of communications services, not just marketing. This included brand analysis, data systems, and long-term strategic planning, rather than a focus on a particular ad campaign or type of media.

The next year, 2004, C-K finally opened an advertising branch in New York. New York was a lucrative market, but C-K was considered an outsider there, and it was difficult and expensive to start an agency there. It called its New York branch Cramer-Krasselt/Hempel Stefanides, the latter two names belonging to two veteran New York admen. The new office shared space with the New York-based CKPR. C-K hoped to bring in more than $100 million annually through the New York shop within a few years. Krivkovich's long-term plan saw the firm growing to overall billings of $1 billion by the end of the decade.

THRIVING IN TOUGH TIMES

C-K had gained a number of impressive clients in the middle of the decade, including the GNC retail drug chain, the restaurant chain Popeyes Chicken, and the phone company Cellular South. These were well-known companies with ad billings in the $10 million to $20 million range. Pursuing the middle market still seemed to be paying off for C-K. Thus, after cutting back somewhat in 2006, the agency accelerated its efforts and grew almost 50 percent between 2006 and 2009.

It closed its Orlando branch in 2006 after watching billings fall steeply. C-K did not have enough Florida business to justify the Orlando outpost. Even some of its Florida-based clients preferred to work with the New York or Chicago offices, so Cramer-Krasselt left Florida and concentrated on its other branches. It continued to

pick up business, such as the pharmaceutical brand Rozerem in 2005. After creating memorable television ads for this sleep aid, C-K gained another pharmaceutical client a few years later with the Zantac account in 2007. Zantac was a best-selling over-the-counter heartburn medication with an advertising budget of $32 million.

Soon after, C-K took on other well-known brands, including Johnsonville Sausage, Burlington Coat Factory, and the financial planning company Edward Jones. It also began representing the country's premiere horse race, the Kentucky Derby, and the sports car brand Porsche. All these new clients added up to 20 percent growth in both 2007 and 2008. The global economy began to falter in 2008, and by 2009, many advertising firms were reporting hard times as clients cut spending. Cramer-Krasselt, however, maintained revenue growth, though at a somewhat slower pace. C-K had a long and diverse list of clients, and it was not overly dependent on the fate of any one of these. Its midsize strategy may have left it more suited to tough conditions than some of its competitors. C-K moved up from fourth to third largest independent advertising agency by 2009. The industry journal *Advertising Age* put Cramer-Krasselt on its "The Ones to Watch" list in 2009, noting the company's resilience in handling challenges and maintaining growth.

A. Woodward

PRINCIPAL COMPETITORS

W.B. Doner and Company; Wieden and Kennedy; Kirshenbaum Bond and Partners, LLC.

FURTHER READING

Barboza, David, "On My ... Desk: Peter G. Krivkovich," *New York Times,* September 5, 1999, p. BU2.

Barker, Tim, "Ad Agency Scales Back Office in Orlando," *Orlando Sentinel,* April 12, 2006.

Cahill, Joseph B., "No Mid-Sized Crisis for this Ad Agency," *Crain's Chicago Business,* December 18, 1995, p. 4.

Chura, Hilary, Kate MacArthur, and Mercedes M. Cardona, "Cramer-Krasselt Thinks Small," *Advertising Age,* September 11, 2000, p. 32.

The Cramer-Krasselt Story, Milwaukee: Cramer-Krasselt, 1998.

Elliott, Stuart, "Agency Decides to Break into the New York Market After Years of Trying—and Failing—to Buy into It," *New York Times,* September 29, 2004, p. C7.

———, "An Independent Agency Arrives in New York, Using Public Relations As a Way to Be Introduced," *New York Times,* September 19, 2003, p. C6.

"Finds Papers Effective," *New York Times,* October 19, 1937, p. 45.

Hajewski, Doris, "A Century of Ads," *Milwaukee Journal Sentinel,* October 20, 1998, pp. 1, 9.

——, "Counsell to Retire as Cramer-Krasselt Ad Agency CEO," *Milwaukee Journal Sentinel,* July 3, 1998, p. 2.

——, "Home Is Where the Ads Are," *Milwaukee Journal Sentinel,* September 28, 2003, pp. 1D, 4D.

Jensen, Trevor, "Cramer-Krasselt Brings Home ConAgra's Bacon," *Adweek,* November 8, 1999, p. 4.

Lev, Michael, "Super Bowl 25: The Football Hoopla Yields to Hype," *New York Times,* January 6, 1991, p. F5.

Mullman, Jeremy, "Ad Agency Fires CareerBuilder," *Crain's Chicago Business,* March 5, 2007, p. 20.

——, "Cramer-Krasselt: The Ones to Watch," *Advertising Age,* January 19, 2009, p. 35.

——, "Cramer-Krasselt Wins $32M Zantac Business," *Advertising Age,* March 26, 2007, p. 8.

Crum & Forster Holdings Corporation

305 Madison Avenue
Morristown, New Jersey 07960-6117
U.S.A.
Telephone: (973) 490-6600
Fax: (973) 490-6940
Web site: http://www.cfins.com

Wholly Owned Subsidiary of Fairfax Financial Holdings Ltd.
Incorporated: 1896
Employees: 1,171
Sales: $1 billion (2008 est.)
NAICS: 524126 Direct Property and Casualty Insurance Carriers

■ ■ ■

A subsidiary of Fairfax Financial Holdings Ltd., Crum & Forster Holdings Corporation is a national property and casualty insurance group based in Morristown, New Jersey, with branch offices in 11 other locations. Individual units include Crum & Forster Insurance Company, Crum & Forster Indemnity Company, Crum & Forster Specialty Insurance Company, United States Fire Insurance Company, The North River Insurance Company, Seneca Insurance Company, and Seneca Specialty Insurance Company. Products and services are marketed under the Crum & Forster name as well as Seneca and Fairmont Specialty and sold by a network of about 1,300 independent brokers in the United States. While the group writes insurance in all 50 states, two-thirds of the business is conducted in ten states. Ranked from high to low, they are California, New York, Florida, Texas, New Jersey, Pennsylvania, Hawaii, Massachusetts, Illinois, and Georgia.

Commercial property insurance products include fire and inland marine. Casualty offerings include workers' compensation, commercial automobile, commercial general liability, and risk management. Crum & Forster companies also offer umbrella coverage for lead and excess insurance. Crum & Forster Specialty Insurance Company offers property, casualty, and umbrella excess and surplus lines for risks that are difficult to determine. Other specialty products include management protection, miscellaneous professional liability, technology errors and omissions, and crime and fidelity coverage.

ORIGINS

Crum & Forster was founded as a partnership in New York City in 1896 between John A. Forster, Frederick H. Crum, and James H. Ackerman, former colleagues at North River Insurance Company. With Crum acting as the company's first president, their plan was to serve as the New York agency for Pittsburgh, Pennsylvania-based Allemannia Fire Insurance. With little more than $500 in the bank they set up shop in office space rented from North River at 95 William Street in Manhattan. In 1904 they purchased United States Fire, and two years later acquired their old employer, purchasing North River, which had suffered severe losses.

After incorporating Crum & Forster in 1907 they began representing other small fire insurers as well. In the wake of the San Francisco earthquake and fire of 1906 the stock in a number of insurance companies

COMPANY PERSPECTIVES

∎

Crum & Forster offers a broad range of commercial property and casualty insurance products including standard, specialty and excess & surplus lines and loss control services through a network of regional underwriting and claim offices located across the country.

became available at depressed prices, leading Crum & Forster to acquire stock in some of these companies. After a decade in business they were representing 26 small companies, prompting people in the industry to refer to this collection as the Crum & Forster "mosquito fleet." Starting in 1914 Crum & Forster also began organizing investment companies to purchase and hold the insurance companies the firm represented.

Crum died in 1919 and was succeeded as president by Forster. A year later the firm established the Industrial Indemnity Company to become involved in workers' compensation coverage. By 1923 the Crum & Forster fleet of insurance companies included North River, Allemannia, United States Fire Insurance Company, U.S. Merchants & Shippers Insurance Company, Richmond Insurance Company, Western Assurance Company, British American Assurance Company, New York Fire Insurance Company, Union Fire Insurance Company, Potomac Insurance Company, and the International Insurance Company. The largest was United States Fire, followed by North River. The main holding companies were Crum & Forster Insurance Shares (the manager of the fleet), which was a public company majority-owned by holding company Crum & Forster, Inc. All of the insurance companies were operated out of New York City until 1923 when a branch office was opened in Atlanta, Georgia, to provide coverage in the South.

ACQUISITION DEAL FAILS

Forster died in 1931 and was succeeded by J. Lester Parsons, who led the company through the Great Depression and World War II and into the postwar era. In 1951, Crum & Forster engineered several acquisitions and mergers to enter the property and casualty business. Parsons retired as chairman in 1956. Then leading the company on a day-to-day basis was William C. Ridgway, Jr., who had been with the firm since 1950, served as president since 1954, and ascended to the top ranks in 1962. From 1961 to 1967 he led an expansion

program that added several general agencies, through ten acquisitions as well as start-ups. The American Eagle Life subsidiary, for example, was established in 1965 to offer life insurance. An internal reorganization then converted Crum & Forster into a true holding company.

In 1968 a deal was reached to sell the company to conglomerate Walter Kidde & Co. for $400 million. The acquisition fell through, however, when Kidde shareholders failed to provide their approval a year later. In the aftermath of the collapse of the transaction, Crum & Forster engineered a two-for-one stock split, a move to disperse ownership of the company and ward off a potential hostile takeover bid. At this stage, Crum & Forster reported annual revenues of $414 million and net income of about $25 million. Ridgway was succeeded as CEO in 1970 by B. P. Russell. Under his leadership, Crum & Forster endured a down cycle in the underwriting business that culminated in a $55 million loss in 1975, although tax adjustments and investment income allowed the company to earn $1.04 per share that year. In 1977 Crum & Forster was listed on the New York Stock Exchange.

XEROX PURCHASES CRUM & FORSTER

Performance improved later in the decade, despite a price war that began in 1978, and in 1981 the company was able to increase profits to a record $5.39 per share. A recession as well as increased competition and underwriting losses hurt the performance of Crum & Forster in the early months of 1982, but as one of the largest property and casualty insurance companies in the United States, it remained an attractive property. Later in 1982 rumors circulated that a number of suitors were making bids and that the company was more than willing to listen. An anonymous analyst quoted by the *New York Times* explained, "I think there will be a deal, because Crum's top people are ready to retire rich." Interested parties included American Can; Transamerica; and Sears, Roebuck and Company, which was beginning to diversify into financial services. In the end, however, a winning bid came from an unexpected source, the photocopier giant Xerox Corporation, which in 1983 completed a $1.6 billion purchase of Crum & Forster.

In the early 1980s Xerox was facing stiff competition from Japanese copier companies and began looking for ways to diversify. Xerox launched a six-month study to identify possible areas to pursue and it was during this effort that the company became interested in Crum & Forster, which would complement Xerox Credit Corporation, established in 1979. Xerox believed that the property and casualty insurance business had finally reached bottom after a number of turbulent years and

KEY DATES

1896: Crum & Forster is established as fire insurance agency in New York City.
1923: First branch office opens in Atlanta.
1969: Deal to sell company to Walter Kidde & Co. fails.
1983: Crum & Forster is sold to Xerox Corporation.
1993: Crum & Forster Inc. becomes part of Xerox's Talegen Holdings Inc. insurance segment.
1998: Fairfax Financial Holdings Ltd. acquires Crum & Forster from Xerox.
2000: Seneca Specialty Insurance Company is acquired.
2001: Transnational Insurance Company is acquired.

was also convinced that Crum & Forster did not require any infusions of cash and would be self-financing. These assumptions proved to be wrong, however.

Xerox, unfamiliar with the insurance industry, allowed Russell to run Crum & Forster with a great deal of latitude. He retired in 1984, turning over the chairmanship and CEO post to the company's chief financial officer, John K. Lundberg, who made it clear that he was not pleased with the state of affairs in the industry at that time. He told the *New York Times,* "The insurance business is lousy. We have been cutting prices for too long, and our immediate task over the next year or two will be to raise prices."

Conditions at Crum & Forster did not improve enough in the short term, and in the fall of 1985 Xerox took steps to strengthen the insurance unit. The operations of the Industrial Indemnity Financial Corporation were terminated, while another subsidiary, L.W. Biegler Inc., a specialized insurer, received an infusion of cash to strengthen its reserves. A month later a pair of Canadian subsidiaries, Crum and Forster of Canada Ltd. and Herald Insurance Company, were sold to Kempton Investments Ltd.

CRUM & FORSTER RESTRUCTURED

More changes were to follow in the 1990s. Crum & Forster in the spring of 1990 elected to withdraw from standard personal insurance, accounting for 11 percent of the company's total business, and closed the Crum & Forster Personal Insurance unit in order to focus on

commercial insurance, specialty coverages, and reinsurance. Two years later a new CEO was brought in, Joseph W. Brown, who in December 1992 implemented a plan to reorganize the remaining operations into seven specialized business units that focused on individual market segments, rather than have the different subsidiaries in many cases write the same business.

Thus, Crum & Forster Commercial Insurance became a dedicated national property and casualty insurance company focusing on individual commercial accounts; Industrial Indemnity devoted its efforts to workers' compensation insurance; Constitution Reinsurance offered treaty and facultative reinsurance; the Coregis unit wrote professional liability, public entity, and other property and casualty coverage; the Resolution Group provided reinsurance collection services; Viking Insurance Holdings offered nonstandard personal automobile insurance; and Westchester Specialty Group handled umbrella, excess casualty, and specialty property business. Moreover, Xerox allocated $444 million for future restructuring. These moves fueled speculation that Xerox, which was enjoying a resurgence in its copier business and found insurance little more than a distraction, might be open to selling Crum & Forster, either piecemeal following the realignment of the units, or in its entirety.

At the very least the reorganization promised to make the insurance operation profitable for Xerox. Legal changes to the structure were then made the following year when the holding company, Crum & Forster Inc., was restructured as a new holding company called Talegen Holdings Inc., and the seven insurance operating groups were restructured in the 15 states where they were domiciled to become independent legal entities, provided with their own capital, loss reserves, and investment portfolios. Early in 1994 the corporate office in Morristown, New Jersey, was broken up and the 1,000-person staff allocated across the country to support the new independent units.

Xerox appeared to be poised to sell Talegen in 1994. Talks were initiated with Fund American Enterprises of Norwich, Vermont, but talks ended after two months when the two parties could not agree on a price. The major sticking point proved to be the unknown costs of future claims and pollution cleanups related to environmental liability insurance polices, some of which Crum & Forster had written in the early 1970s. Xerox was unwilling to accept a price that took these potential costs into account or protected the buyer against such claims. As a result, Fund American dropped its interest in Talegen.

XEROX EXITS THE INSURANCE BUSINESS

Xerox finally succeeded in divesting at least part of the Talegen holdings in late 1994 when it sold the Constitution Reinsurance unit to Exor America for about $400 million. A second unit, Viking Insurance, was then sold for $103 million to Guaranty National Corporation in July 1995. In December of that year a deal appeared to be made with Kohlberg Kravis Roberts & Co. to sell the rest of Talegen for $2.7 billion. For the previous few years Kohlberg Kravis had been targeting insurers it considered to be undervalued, having picked up American Reinsurance in 1992 and Canadian General Insurance Group Ltd. in 1995. By September 1996, however, the purchase of Talegen was scuttled with neither party providing an explanation.

Xerox continued to carve off Talegen units for sale. Early in 1997 Coregis Group was sold to General Electric Company for $450 and a computer services unit was sold to Andersen Consulting. Industrial Indemnity was then purchased in May 1997 by the Fremont General Corporation for $444 million. Two more units were sold in September 1997. An investor group led by the CEO of Resolutions Group Inc. bought Resolution for $612 million, and later in the month Westchester Specialty Group was sold to Ace Ltd. for $333 million.

Xerox completed its exit from the insurance business in March 1998 when it sold the Crum & Forster division for $565 million and the assumption of $115 million in debt to Toronto, Ontario-based property and casualty insurer Fairfax Financial Holdings Ltd. Also included in the transaction was $400 million of reinsurance against possible adverse loss development. Fairfax was founded in 1985 by its CEO V. Prem Watsa, a Canadian immigrant born in India who was a chemical engineer by training. After joining his brother in Canada in 1972 he earned a business degree and went to work for a Toronto life insurance company as an analyst, later becoming a portfolio manager. After gaining ten years of experience he struck out on his own as an investor, acquiring a truck insurance underwriter, Markel Insurance, which in 1984 he renamed Fairfax. Watsa then acquired a number of undervalued insurance companies in Canada and the United States, becoming known in some circles as "the Warren Buffett of the North." The acquisition of Crum & Forster was just one of several U.S. property and casualty insurers he added to Fairfax in the late 1990s.

Watsa's basic strategy was to build up Fairfax's assets in order to invest in the securities market. It was a plan that worked well until the late 1990s when losses in Europe began to drag down Fairfax. In 2000 Crum & Forster and other insurance assets performed poorly, and their inadequate reserve levels grew even worse in 2001 following the September 11 terrorist attacks that leveled New York's World Trade Center and had an adverse impact on the economy.

FACING DIFFICULTIES IN THE 21ST CENTURY

Fairfax successfully took one of its insurance companies, Odyssey Re, public in 2001, garnering $434 million in cash and notes. Watsa attempted to perform the same maneuver with Crum & Forster in 2002, but because of a lack of interest the offering was eventually scrapped despite the addition of Seneca Specialty Insurance Company in 2000 and Transnational Insurance Company in January 2001. The excess and surplus lines company was renamed Crum & Forster Specialty Insurance Company. The early years of the new century were difficult for both Crum & Forster and its parent company, due in large part to underwriting losses incurred from increased hurricane activity. In 2004 Fairfax suffered a net loss for only the second year in its history to date. The following year was even worse as record losses were caused by Hurricanes Katrina, Rita, and Wilma.

Despite tough conditions, Crum & Forster continued to grow the amount of premiums it wrote each year, increasing it from $745 million in 1999 to nearly $1.1 billion in 2005. With Nick Antonopoulos serving as CEO, the company was well on its way to a turnaround by 2006 when after seven lean years Fairfax rebounded to once again post excellent results. For its part, Crum & Forster contributed $312.3 million in net earnings. Although that amount dipped to $293.2 million in 2007, Fairfax enjoyed the best year in its history. At the end of the year, Antonopoulos retired. He was replaced as chairman and CEO by Douglas M. Libby, Seneca's former head. Libby took over a company that was on the rise, as was its corporate parent. In 2008 Fairfax posted another record year, netting $1.5 billion with Crum & Forster contributing $332.8 million of that amount.

Ed Dinger

PRINCIPAL SUBSIDIARIES

Crum & Forster Insurance Company; Crum & Forster Indemnity Company; Crum & Forster Specialty Insurance Company; United States Fire Insurance Company; North River Insurance Company; Seneca Insurance Company; Seneca Specialty Insurance Company.

PRINCIPAL COMPETITORS

American International Group, Inc.; Nationwide Mutual Insurance Company; The Travelers Companies, Inc.

FURTHER READING

Abbot, Henry W., "The Crum & Forster Fire 'Fleet,'" *Barron's,* July 6, 1936, p. 13.

"Crum & Forster Announces Plan for Restructuring Units," *Business Insurance,* December 21, 1992, p. 42.

"Crum & Forster Sets 2-for-1 Stock Split and a Dividend Rise," *New York Times,* April 12, 1969.

Cuff, Daniel F., "Xerox Reshapes Crum & Forster," *New York Times,* October 4, 1985.

Narisetti, Raju, "Xerox Agrees to Sell Crum & Forster for $565 Million," *Wall Street Journal,* March 12, 1998, p. 1.

Niedzielski, Joe, "Xerox Exits Insurance with Crum & Forster Sale to Fairfax," *National Underwriter,* March 16, 1998, p. 1.

"Profitable Portfolio: It's the Key to Crum and Forster's Steady Growth," *Barron's National Business and Financial Weekly,* April 20, 1981, p. 43.

Quint, Michael, "As Xerox's Insurance Unit Inches Toward a Sale, the Stock Rises," *New York Times,* May 19, 1994.

Sasseen, Jane, "Fairfax vs. the Shorts," *Business Week,* June 5, 2006, p. 92.

Sloane, Leonard, "Xerox to Acquire Crum in a $1.6 Billion Deal," *New York Times,* September 22, 1982.

"Takeover of Crum Is Rumored," *New York Times,* September 17, 1982.

Dave & Buster's, Inc.

———■———

2481 Manana Drive
Dallas, Texas 75220
U.S.A.
Telephone: (214) 357-9588
Fax: (214) 350-0941
Web site: http://www.daveandbusters.com

Private Company
Incorporated: 1982
Employees: 8,278
Sales: $533.4 million (2008 est.)
NAICS: 722110 Full-Service Restaurants; 722410 Drinking Places (Alcoholic Beverages); 713120 Amusement Arcades

■ ■ ■

Dave & Buster's, Inc., operates a nationwide chain of entertainment dining restaurants that offer patrons everything from pocket billiards and shuffleboard to high-tech arcade games, simulated golf, and virtual reality space combat. During 2009 the company operated 52 locations in the United States and Canada. Wellspring Capital Management LLC took the company private in 2006 and began planning for its public offering two years later.

ORIGINS IN LITTLE ROCK

The story of Dave & Buster's was the story of David Corriveau and James "Buster" Corley and started in Little Rock, Arkansas. Corriveau, whose resume included selling snow cones and cars, dealing blackjack in Las Vegas, and waiting tables, started a restaurant called Cash McCools in 1975. He sold that booming business a year later and in 1977 opened Slick Willy's World of Entertainment. The site for this 10,000-square-foot billiard and game house was in Little Rock's renovated train station.

Meanwhile, Corley had been working his way up the management ladder with T.G.I. Friday's, where he started as a waiter in 1972. By the mid-1970s he was in charge of opening new units, and he looked at the train station as a possible location. However, he had always wanted to have his own place. He approached Corriveau and others for backing and opened his restaurant, Buster's, right next to Slick Willy's in the train station. The two men became good friends and soon noticed that their customers moved back and forth between their two establishments. They began thinking about what might happen if they combined Dave's games and Buster's food under one roof and how big that roof might be. They spent about a year developing a rough design, and then Corriveau sold Slick Willy's to raise seed money and they went looking for a location.

Corriveau and Corley moved to Dallas, and in December 1982 they opened the first Dave & Buster's, in a former warehouse. They spent $3 million to make the 35,000-square-foot space into what they wanted, and it was a hit from the beginning. The establishment was packed with people playing pool, cashless blackjack, and pinball or other arcade games, while drinking and eating (burgers, steaks, finger food, salads).

Over the next several years the partners refined their "fun and food" concept, expanding the site in the process with the addition of a nine-hole simulated golf range. In 1988 they opened a second location, also in Dallas, the same size as the first. Dave & Buster's was aimed at adults. Games rented by the hour. Customers played billiards on $15,000 tables made of handcrafted mahogany and rosewood, and the shuffleboard tables met tournament-quality specifications. Full menu and bar service was available in the play areas, which were spread among several dining rooms within the complex. There was also the Million Dollar Midway, with electronic, skill, and sports-themed arcade games.

A NEW MAJORITY OWNER

Once they had the concept established, the partners were ready to open more units, and for that, they needed money. In the winter of 1989, Corriveau and Corley entered into a deal with Edison Brothers Stores, Inc., a $1 billion conglomerate operating some 2,700 retail stores, primarily in the shoe and apparel markets. St. Louis-based Edison Brothers was developing an entertainment division and invested sufficient capital in Dave & Buster's to acquire about 80 percent ownership of the company. Corriveau and Corley retained ownership of the rest.

With the financial backing available from Edison Brothers, the company began building. In 1991 Dave & Buster's opened its third location, in Houston. The new complex was 53,000 square feet, nearly 20,000 square feet larger than the first two. The following year, in 1992, Dave & Buster's opened in Atlanta. Two years later the company moved north, opening a 70,000-square-foot complex in Philadelphia. Also in 1994, the company dodged a potential legal catastrophe in Texas. A state district judge found that under a new state gambling law, arcade customers could accumulate their winnings (such as coupons at Dave & Buster's) from the arcade games they played and swap them for prizes worth more than $5.

Each new Dave & Buster's cost about $10 million to build and furnish, and this was proving to be a drain on Edison Brothers. In 1995 the majority owner spun off its interest in Dave & Buster's to its shareholders.

Following the spinoff, Dave & Buster's went public, selling nearly $30 million in stock on the NASDAQ under the symbol DANB. Andy Newman, who resigned as CEO of Edison Brothers, became chairman of the new company, with Corriveau and Corley sharing the chief executive position.

During the summer of 1995, Dave & Buster's announced that it had signed a licensing agreement with Bass plc to operate up to seven units in the United Kingdom. In addition to being the United Kingdom's largest brewer of beers, Bass operated Holiday Inn hotels, 4,000 pubs, and a network of bingo clubs, betting shops, and tenpin bowling centers throughout the country. Also that year, Dave & Buster's opened its first complex in Chicago, bringing the number of locations in the United States to six. Meanwhile, by the end of the year, Edison Brothers had filed for bankruptcy.

With money available from the Edison buyout, the stock offering, and a $28 million secondary offering late in the year, expansion picked up steam. Corriveau and Corley opened three locations (Hollywood, Florida; Bethesda, Maryland; and a second unit in Chicago) in 1996, with each unit expected to generate annual sales of from $12 to $15 million. The company also entered a joint venture with Iwerks Entertainment Inc. to develop and operate Iwerks 16-seat Turbo Ride Theatres at several Dave & Buster's locations. Customers would be able to watch major films while sitting in seats synchronized to the big-screen action.

THE "EATERTAINMENT" NICHE

Dave & Buster's was not the only company taking advantage of the American public's hunger for fun. In addition to existing theme chains such as Hard Rock Café, Planet Hollywood, and Rainforest Café, newcomers were planning restaurant prototypes such as the $11 million Laugh Factory Funhouse with comedy memorabilia and databases of jokes; Steven Spielberg's submarine-themed Dive!; music-theme eateries featuring country music or Motown; and various combinations of video arcades and virtual or real games. By mid-1996, analysts were beginning to predict oversaturation in the "eatertainment" niche and eventual consolidation.

Dave & Buster's, whose 1995 profits were up almost 27 percent, was the exception to this forecast. Although the company had a good reputation for its casual-dining food, the winning factor was its amusements, which accounted for more than 44 percent of sales. Recognizing that, Dave & Buster's constantly updated its games. "We can give [game makers] a certain amount of exposure and have a kind of most-favored national status with them," a company spokes-

KEY DATES

1982: Dave Corriveau and "Buster" Corley open Dave & Buster's in Dallas.
1988: A second location opens in Dallas.
1989: Edison Brothers Stores, Inc., acquires majority interest in company.
1995: Edison Brothers spins off Dave & Buster's and new company goes public.
1996: Dave & Buster's accelerates expansion.
1998: The company signs licensing agreements covering the Pacific Rim, Western Europe, and Canada.
1999: The company moves to New York Stock Exchange.
2002: Attempts to take the company private fail.
2004: The company purchases Jillian's restaurants and trade name.
2006: Wellspring Capital Management LLC takes the company private.
2008: Dave & Buster's announces plans to go public.

man told *Investor's Business Daily* in 1996, adding, "We're one of the first places to get new machines."

Thus the possibility of too many giant complexes going after customers' leisure dollars did not faze Corley and Corriveau. "We were ten years ahead of 'eatertainment,'" Corriveau told *Restaurant Hospitality* in 1998. "Our average customer visits ten times a year. That sets us apart from 'eatertainment,' which looks for tourists to give them a quick visit and a T-shirt sale. We set out to firmly establish and nourish a local clientele at each location."

The year 1997 saw more big names, including Disney, Spielberg, and Sony, entering the eatertainment niche and following Dave & Buster's model of giant complexes offering food and games. Meanwhile, Dave & Buster's kept opening units, including four in 1997 (in Ontario, Canada; Birmingham, United Kingdom; Cincinnati, Ohio; and Denver, Colorado). Restaurant locations were usually in metropolitan areas with a population of at least one million within a ten-mile radius, in high-profile sites close to shopping, offices, tourist attractions, and residential areas. Often the units were located in mega-malls. Opening costs at this time averaged about $11.5 million, of which 65 percent was related to the site's games areas.

To keep customers playing, the company intro-

duced the Dave & Buster's Power Card to activate its arcade games. This was a declining balance card that could be recharged as many times as wanted at conveniently located "power stations," which helped increase games revenue by 10 percent.

COURTING CORPORATE BUSINESS

In 1998 the company opened five more complexes, bringing to 17 its total U.S. locations. One of these, in Columbus, Ohio, was in the company's new "intermediate" format of 40,000 square feet aimed at metropolitan areas of less than one million people. The company also created an even smaller format, which at 30,000 to 35,000 square feet was about the size of the original Dave & Buster's. Bass plc had two locations, in Birmingham and Bristol, England, and Dave & Buster's signed additional licensing agreements, covering the Pacific Rim (Taiwan, Hong Kong, and China), Western Europe (Austria, Germany, and Switzerland), and Canada. During the year, Dave & Buster's settled litigation related to the 1995 spinoff from Edison Brothers Stores, agreeing to pay $2.244 million against all claims.

While its competitors targeted families and younger adults, Dave and Buster's continued to focus on the 24 to 44 age group. The company had always attracted some corporate business, primarily private parties. In 1998 it became more proactive in this area, instituting a "Big on Business" marketing campaign to increase sales from events ranging from conferences to product intros to office picnics. It also introduced the "Company Challenge," a team-building exercise complete with referees, team shirts, score sheets, and awards. At the end of the year, about 13 percent of the company's business was from corporate-sponsored parties. That year amusement revenue topped 50 percent of sales, which increased 42 percent over 1997.

Dave & Buster's had a popular concept. Company revenues had grown significantly each year. In fiscal 1996, with nine locations, revenues reached $88.8 million with $6.3 million in profits. In fiscal 1997, with three more sites, revenues rose to $128.5 million with $8.9 million in profits. In fiscal 1998, with 17 complexes, the company took in $182.3 million and profits of $13.6 million. Whereas the average Dave & Buster's location had a volume of $10.7 million in 1995, by 1998 the figure had moved up to $13.2 million, and sales for existing sites increased 6 percent in 1998.

FACING CHALLENGES

During 1999 the company moved to the New York Stock Exchange, taking the stock symbol DNB, and announced plans to double the number of locations in the United States (to 40) by 2002. In December, the company opened the first Dave & Buster's in Asia, in Taipei, Taiwan, and its 23rd location in the United States, in Rhode Island.

However, 1999 was a bad year for theme restaurants. Planet Hollywood filed for bankruptcy and Landry's Seafood Restaurants bought Rainforest Café after comparable store sales dropped 10 percent. At Dave & Buster's, same-store sales dropped 2.2 percent and in August 1999 lower-than-expected profits caused the company's stock to drop 45 percent in one day. "For the most part, theme restaurants have paid very little attention to food," Michael Beyard of the Urban Land Institute told the *Denver Post.* "The prevailing thought has been that it's enough to provide entertainment that is fun and visually stimulating. But without the basics, restaurants are going to fail no matter how good the theme is," he noted.

Food was only part of the picture. People also had to keep coming back. While many of the theme and eatertainment restaurants had people flocking to their doors when they opened, if customers came only once out of curiosity, or as out-of-town tourists, a location would not survive. Dave and Buster's prided itself on its food, the huge turnouts at new locations, and the repeat business at their older complexes.

After the third quarter, with a 92 percent drop in earnings and same-store sales down 6.2 percent, the company announced that it would cut back on its expansion plans and increase unit-level support. It also increased its marketing and advertising budget by $4 million, hoping to build sales that way rather than by expansion and "word of mouth." As Corriveau told *Nation's Restaurant News* in January 2000, "Our stores enjoy a great honeymoon period when they open, but after that—around 18 months to two years—they need continued attention."

CONCERNS ABOUT THE FUTURE

In December 1999, British multibillionaire Joseph Lewis bought 1.1 million Dave & Buster's shares through his Mandarin, Inc. This brought Mandarin's ownership to 10.6 percent of the company. A month later, Texas investor Lacy Harber increased his holdings to 9.8 percent of Dave & Buster's. The company board as a whole owned about 10 percent, as did Dresdner RCM Global Investors of San Francisco, the chain's biggest institutional investor.

"The people at Dave & Buster's have to be considering their own options right now, and I would think that means they have to be looking at a

management-led buyout as one of those options," Bill Baldwin of Dallas investment firm Baldwin Anthony McIntyre & Boles said in *Nation's Restaurant News.* Dave and Buster's had been around for nearly 18 years, and its concept was popular from the very beginning, as was the company's profitability. However, aside from adding new games and rides, the concept had not changed much since the first complex opened in Dallas. As one analyst told *Nation's Restaurant News,* "They might need to update and become more contemporary and hip with today rather than 1985."

Indeed, the early years of the new millennium proved to be rocky for the eatertainment chain. Its restaurants in the United Kingdom were shuttered and its European development plans were put on hold. The company's management team, along with Investcorp Bank B.S.C., attempted to take the company private but called off the deal in 2002 after they were unable to secure financing.

Dolphin Limited Partnership I, L.P., an investor group with a 9.5 percent stake in the company, voiced its concerns about the future of Dave & Buster's. With sales and profits falling, the investment firm demanded changes to the company's board. The founders defended their actions, claiming they had cut costs through layoffs and restructuring operations. Nevertheless, Corley and Corriveau gave up their shared CEO titles; Corley remained CEO and chief operating officer while Corriveau became president. The pair also took a 20 percent pay cut. Peter Edison was named chairman while the company board was expanded from eight to nine directors.

Dave & Buster's remained focused on cutting costs during 2003 and put expansion plans on hold. During the following year, however, the company purchased nine Jillian's restaurants and the Jillian's trade name from Jillian's Entertainment Holdings Inc. in a $47 million deal. Dave & Buster's also opened one new location in Arcadia, California, that year.

The Jillian's purchase proved to be a strain on the company's bottom line. The Jillian's location in the Mall of America in Minneapolis was shuttered and most of the Jillian's outlets were refitted as Dave & Buster's locations. With losses mounting, Dave & Buster's announced plans be taken private by New York-based private equity firm Wellspring Capital Management LLC in late 2005. The $375 million deal was finalized in March of the following year.

FOCUS ON SLOW AND STEADY GROWTH

Cofounder Corley left the company shortly after the change in ownership. Greg S. Feldman, founder of

Wellspring Capital and new chairman of Dave & Buster's, felt the change in management was necessary. He explained his rationale in an October 2006 *Nation's Restaurant News* article. "We bought the company knowing it had a great foundation and a unique business model. We felt that at this point, to take the company to the next level, we needed a more balanced approach and disciplined growth approach, which is a natural transition for many entrepreneurial companies such as this one." Cofounder Corriveau officially stepped down the following year.

Under new management, Dave & Buster's focused on slow and steady growth. A new location in New York City's Time Square opened in April 2006. In order to raise cash for additional expansion, the company sold three locations to National Retail Properties Inc. who agreed to lease the restaurants back to Dave & Buster's for 17.5 years. In an attempt to control overhead, the company launched a new store format, which was smaller in size and therefore lower in construction costs.

The company's new strategy appeared to pay off. With the company on solid financial footing, Dave & Buster's continued to open new outlets including a 16,000-square-foot facility in Richmond, Virginia. Additional units were also opened in Westbury, New York; Maple Grove, Minnesota; Tempe, Arizona; Arlington, Texas; and Tulsa, Oklahoma. A 32,000-square-foot restaurant was slated to open in Indianapolis in June 2009.

Meanwhile, Wellspring Capital was planning to take Dave & Buster's public once again. The firm filed with the Securities and Exchange Commission in July 2008. Shortly thereafter, the weak economy and the overall downturn in the restaurant industry put the company's $170 million public offering on hold. According to the National Restaurant Association, the number of restaurants and bars had increased 49 percent since 1990. A slowdown in consumer spending and rising food costs spelled disaster for casual-dining chains operating in a saturated market. Dave & Buster's, even in its specialized eatertainment niche, remained subject to the downturn. Its sales fell during 2008 but it was able to post a $1.6 million profit. While the company's future initial public offering remained in question, it appeared as though Dave & Buster's was well positioned to weather the economic downturn in the United States.

Ellen D. Wernick
Updated, Christina M. Stansell

PRINCIPAL COMPETITORS

Buffalo Wild Wings Inc.; Damon's International Inc.; Fox & Hound Restaurant Group.

FURTHER READING

Alva, Marilyn, "Games Good Ol' Boys Play," *Restaurant Business,* May 1, 1996, p. 68.

"Bass Launches 'Dave & Buster's' in the UK," *Universal News Services,* August 21, 1995.

Battaglia, Andy, and Richard L. Papiernik, "The British Are Coming: Buyers Eye Dave & Buster's," *Nation's Restaurant News,* January 3, 2000, p. 1.

Benz, Matthew, "Dave & Buster's Puts End to Buyout Bid," *Amusement Business,* November 11, 2002.

Donald, LeRoy, "LR-Rooted Restaurateurs Take Concept Public," *Arkansas Democrat-Gazette,* February 15, 1995, p. 1D.

Flandez, Raymund, "Dave & Buster's Faces Board Battle," *Wall Street Journal,* June 10, 2003.

Frumpkin, Paul, "Walt Disney to Unveil ESPN Zone Eatertainment Complex in NYC," *Nation's Restaurant News,* September 9, 1999, p. 4.

"Fun and Games," *Restaurant Hospitality,* September 1998, p. 60.

Garcia, Eric, "Restaurant Didn't Violate Gambling Law, Judge Rules," *Dallas Morning News,* February 26, 1994, p. 36A.

Gubernick, Lisa, and Daniel Roth, "Burp!," *Forbes,* August 12, 1996, p. 52.

Heller, Karen, "'Semi-Bored' in Philadelphia? Not at Dave & Buster's High-Tech Palace," *Albany (N.Y.) Times Union,* August 7, 1994, p. H15.

"Iwerks, Dave & Buster's Team Up," *Business Wire,* May 3, 1996.

Jaffee, Thomas, "Arrogance Goeth Before a Fall," *Forbes,* October 23, 1995, p. 128.

Johnson, Greg, "Whoever Gets the Most Leisure Dollars Wins," *Los Angeles Times,* March 23, 1997, p. D1.

"Local and State Business Briefs," *San Antonio Express-News,* February 10, 2000, p. 2E.

Martin, Andrew, "Your Table Is Ready. Please.," *New York Times,* April 4, 2009.

Martin, Richard, "Eatertainment Concepts Crowding Theme Niche," *Nation's Restaurant News,* July 29, 1996, p. 1.

Mencke, Claire, "The New America: Dave & Buster's," *Investor's Business Daily,* September 12, 1996, p. A6.

Papiernik, Richard L., "Focus on Finance: At Dave & Buster's They Play with the Bears—That's No Bull," *Nation's Restaurant News,* October 7, 1996, p. 11.

Raabe, Steve, "Reality Bites: 'Eatertainment' Leaves Sour Taste for Shareholders," *Denver Post,* November 7, 1999, p. L1.

Robinson-Jacobs, Karen, "Dave & Buster's Loses the Dave," *Dallas Morning News,* March 22, 2007.

Ruggieri, Melissa, "Dave & Buster's Allows Adults to Be Kids," *Richmond Times-Dispatch,* April 23, 2009.

Ruggless, Ron, "Dave & Buster's Goes Private in $375M Deal," *Nation's Restaurant News,* March 20, 2006.

———, "Dave & Buster's Makes Its Play to Double Its Size over Next Three Years," *Nation's Restaurant News,* June 28, 1999, p. 12.

———, "Dave & Buster's New Leaders to Take 'Slow, Steady' Growth Tack," *Nation's Restaurant News,* October 2, 2006.

———, "Dave & Buster's Posts Steep Loss," *Nation's Restaurant News,* December 19, 2005.

Sandoval, Joe, "Dave & Busters—There Is No Place Like It,"

La Prensa de San Antonio, February 7, 1999, p. 1A.

Snyder, Beth, "That's Eatertainment! As Americans Hunger for More Entertainment Value in Their Brands, a New Breed of Restaurants Prospers," *Advertising Age,* September 27, 1999, p. 18.

De Rigo S.p.A.

Zona Industriale Villanova 12
Longarone
Belluno, 32013
Italy
Telephone: (390) 4377777
Fax: (390) 437573250
Web site: http://www.derigo.com

Public Company
Incorporated: 1978
Employees: 3,800
Sales: EUR 662.7 million ($860 million) (2007)
Stock Exchanges: New York
Ticker Symbol: DER
NAICS: 339115 Ophthalmic Goods Manufacturing

∎ ∎ ∎

De Rigo S.p.A. is a leading producer and distributor of eyeglass frames, sunglasses, and other eyewear. The company is the world's third largest eyewear specialist, trailing fellow Italians Luxottica S.p.A. and Safilo S.p.A. As it does for its competitors, licensed production represents a major proportion of De Rigo's operations, capitalizing on the trend toward designer eyewear that began in the 1990s. De Rigo's list of licensed designer brands include Jean Paul Gaultier, Chopard, Escada, Loewe, Ermenegildo Zegna, Pirelli, Celine, and Fila.

At the same time, De Rigo has long distinguished itself by building up its own family of in-house brands, including the Police, Sting, and Lozza lines. In-house brands represent a significant proportion of De Rigo's

sales, helping to shield the company somewhat from the potential loss of one or more of its licensed brands. The company also develops partnerships with noted designers, including one to create Sting eyewear to complement the Yamamay line of swimsuits and lingerie. De Rigo operates its own international distribution network, with subsidiaries in the United Kingdom, Spain, Greece, Brazil, Hong Kong, Japan, and elsewhere, which helps the company reach more than 80 countries worldwide. Much of the group's sales come from the independent optician sales channel. De Rigo also operates its own retail stores, however, under the General Optica name, largely in Spain and in the United States.

In early 2009, the company agreed to merge its other retail chain, the United Kingdom's Dolland & Aitchison, into a new joint venture, Boots Opticians, with Alliance Boots. De Rigo retained a minority stake in the new company. Listed on the Milan Stock Exchange, De Rigo is controlled by cofounder and chairman Ennio De Rigo and other De Rigo family members. Michele Aracri is the company's CEO. In 2007, De Rigo posted total revenues of EUR 667 million ($860 million).

BUILDING AN OPTICAL COMPANY

The De Rigo family initially established its fortune from manufacturing industrial refrigerators. That company, called Surfrigo, was established by Walter De Rigo, who was born in 1932 and later became a senator as a member of the Forza Italia party. Surfrigo had grown to become one of Italy's leading industrial refrigerator producers by the late 1970s. While Walter De Rigo built this business, his younger brother, Ennio, born in 1940, started his own career in the construction sector.

In 1978, the De Rigos were offered the opportunity to buy out a small company manufacturing eyeglasses then owned by one of their relatives. Ennio took charge of this company, which was based in Longarone, in the province of Belluno. This region would become the heart of Italy's "Glasses Valley," so named as it would become home to many other eyeglass frames manufacturers, including Luxottica and Safilo. By the late 1990s, the Belluno region had become the world's largest source of eyeglass frames and sunglasses.

De Rigo initially focused on the contract manufacturing sector, producing eyeglass frames, sunglasses, and eyeglass components for third parties. The family soon began expanding the business, however, and increasingly targeted the new and fast-growing designer brand segment. At the same time, the De Rigos recognized an opportunity to pioneer another fast-growing branch of the eyewear sector, the production of branded sunglasses. To oversee this sideline, a new company, called Argosol, was established to operate independently.

The increasing popularity of designer labels and of branded fashions in general encouraged De Rigo to develop its own branded line of eyewear in the early 1980s. Among the group's first brands was its Charme line of sunglasses. The company's subsequent launch of the Police brand in 1983 was accompanied by a new marketing approach. Despite the fact that the vast majority of the company's products were sold through opticians and optometrists, the company launched advertising campaigns directly targeting consumers.

CONSOLIDATION IN 1992

By the mid-1980s, De Rigo had established itself as a major player in the increasingly international eyewear industry. The company generally targeted the midprice and high-end categories, while its Police brand proved an important brand in the market for younger consumers. This market by then was one of the fastest growing in the eyewear sector. As a result, De Rigo launched a second brand, called Sting, to target the segment with an edgier design aesthetic.

As Walter De Rigo's political career took off in the early 1990s, the brothers decided the time was right to merge their eyewear businesses into a single company. This consolidation took place in 1992, with Argosol becoming part of De Rigo. The company then became a clear leader in the Italian eyewear sector, while Italy itself was the leader in the global eyewear market.

The year 1992 saw another major milestone for De Rigo, with its first acquisition, of the famed Lozza brand. Lozza laid claim to being Italy's oldest eyeglasses manufacturer, with operations dating back to 1878. The purchase of Lozza helped round out the De Rigo's brand portfolio, adding Lozza's traditional appeal to the older and more conservative fashion market alongside the younger Police and youth-oriented Sting brands. The addition of Lozza also helped pave the way for De Rigo's entry into the growing market for designer eyewear. By 1993, De Rigo had signed up its first designer license, producing a line of eyewear under the Dendi name.

By the mid-1990s, De Rigo had grown into a company with more than 1,000 employees and annual sales topping ITL 100 billion per year. The company had also established an international distribution network, with more than 110 dealers, as well as subsidiaries and offices in Austria, Germany, France, Spain, the United Kingdom, and the Netherlands. Successive expansion of the company's main production facility in Longarone enabled the company to achieve annual production rates of six million pairs of glasses per year.

PUBLIC OFFERING IN 1995

De Rigo had grown strongly in the European and Middle Eastern market. The company had also established itself as a major player in such Asian markets as Hong Kong, Singapore, and the Philippines. By the middle of the 1990s, the group had become a major rival to the global sunglasses leader, Rayban.

In 1995, De Rigo decided to broaden its geographic base and take on Rayban in its home territory. By listing

KEY DATES

1978: Walter and Ennio De Rigo acquire a small eyewear manufacturer in Longarone, then found a second, separate eyewear company, Argosol.

1983: Launch of the Police eyewear brand.

1992: The De Rigos merge their eyewear operations into a single company and acquire the Lozza eyewear company and brand.

1993: De Rigo acquires its first designer license with Fendi.

1995: De Rigo goes public with a listing on the New York Stock Exchange.

1998: Company enters the retail market with the acquisition of Dollond and Aitchison in the United Kingdom.

2000: De Rigo acquires retail operator General Optica in Spain, Portugal, and the United States.

2004: Holding company is established with subsidiary De Rigo Vision as manufacturing and wholesale business.

shares on the New York Stock Exchange, the company made its name known in the United States and gained the capital for financing its entry into the U.S. market. At the same time, the company launched construction of a second factory in Longarone, expanding its capacity to meet the growing demand for its family of company-owned and licensed brands.

Sales of the Police brand in particular grew strongly during the 1990s, and the brand's designs helped in large part to set the standards for much of the sunglasses market during that period. Aiding the growth of the Police brand was the group's decision to seek out such high-profile celebrities as George Clooney, Bruce Willis, and, in 2004, David Beckham, to wear its products. At the same time, De Rigo recognized the potential for increasing the Police brand's notoriety by developing its own licensing program for the brand. As a result, it was able to launch its own Police-brand perfumes in 1997. Later Police brand licenses included watches in 2003, jewelry in 2005, and leather goods in 2007.

RETAIL OPERATIONS AT THE TURN OF THE 21ST CENTURY

De Rigo sought other avenues for expansion as well. In 1998, the company entered the retail optical market, by

acquiring Dollond & Aitchison in the United Kingdom. That company was recognized as England's oldest high street retailer, having been founded in 1750 by James Dollond. From a single shop in London, the Dollond company grew strongly, particularly after its 1927 merger with Aitchison & Co., a company founded in 1889. By the start of the 21st century, Dollond & Aitchison had become one of the United Kingdom's leading opticians chains.

Success in entering the U.K. retail sector led De Rigo to seek opportunities elsewhere, including Spain, where it acquired General Optica in 2000. This acquisition gave the company control of the leading optician chain in Spain and Portugal, with a major position in the U.S. retail market as well.

De Rigo also continued building up its portfolio of designer licenses. The group signed on La Perla in 1998, then added Givenchy, Loewe, and Celine in 2000, followed by Furla in 2002. Not all of the group's license partnerships were successful, however. In 2000, for example, the group reached an agreement to form a joint-venture licensing partnership with the Prada design house. Yet the collaboration between the two companies proved a rocky one, and by 2003 De Rigo had agreed to sell back its share of the joint venture to Prada.

Nonetheless, De Rigo's sales, protected in part by the success of its own Police and Sting brands, rose strongly into the new century, topping EUR 500 million. In 2004, the group carried out a reorganization of its operations, restructuring De Rigo S.p.A. itself as a holding company. As part of the restructuring, the group placed its wholesale and manufacturing divisions into a new company, De Rigo Vision S.p.A.

NEW LABELS

De Rigo remained on the lookout for new designer licenses in the second half of the decade. The company signed on Escada, Chopard, Ermenegildo Zegna, and Jean Paul Gaultier in 2004, followed by the Pirelli PZero brand in 2006, and Switch-It in 2007. At the same time, the group entered a cooperation agreement with U.S. eyewear distributor Viva International to distribute De Rigo's brands in the United States. The agreement also gave De Rigo the rights to distribute some of Viva's licenses, including Guess? and Tommy Hilfiger, in Italy and Greece.

With its branded and licensed businesses flourishing, De Rigo decided to reduce its exposure to the retail market. In January 2009, the company agreed to merge Dollond & Aitchison into Boots Opticians, creating the United Kingdom's second largest retail opticians group with nearly 700 stores. De Rigo retained a minority stake in the new company.

De Rigo's search for new brand opportunities continued through the end of the decade. In February 2009, for example, the company reached an agreement with Inticom S.p.A. to produce a new line of Sting eyewear for the Yamamay swimwear and lingerie brand. The new Sting for Yamamay label launched in March of that year. At the same time, De Rigo also expanded its wholesale and manufacturing division, as De Rigo Vision established two new subsidiaries in Korea and Portugal in 2008. After more than 30 years, De Rigo's vision had taken it to the top of the global eyewear market.

M. L. Cohen

PRINCIPAL SUBSIDIARIES

Bindi Investment Ltd. (Jersey); D&A contact Lenses Ltd. (Jersey); De Rigo Asia Ltd. (Hong Kong); De Rigo France; De Rigo Hellas AEE; De Rigo HK Ltd. (Hong Kong); De Rigo Japan Ltd.; De Rigo UK Ltd.; De Rigo Vision Brasil LDA; De Rigo Vision S.p.A.; Dollond & Aitchison Ltd. (UK); European Vision Ltd. (UK); General Optica Intern S.A. (Spain); General Optica Ltd. (UK); General Optica S.A. (Spain); Vantios Group Ltd. (UK); Vogart Line Italia (Spain).

PRINCIPAL DIVISIONS

Manufacturing; Wholesale; Retail.

PRINCIPAL OPERATING UNITS

General Optica.

PRINCIPAL COMPETITORS

Luxottica Group S.p.A.; Essilor International S.A.; Bausch and Lomb Inc.; Safilo S.p.A.; Grandvision S.A.; Specsavers Optical Group Ltd.; CIBA Vision Corporation; Marchon Eyewear Inc.

FURTHER READING

Colavita, Courtney, "Prada Ends De Rigo Eyewear Venture, Signs 10-Year License with Luxottica," *WWD*, July 24, 2003, p. 3.

"D&A Boosts Sales but Barely Breaks Even," *Optician*, October 1, 2004, p. 2.

"D&A Hailed as Star Performer by Parent," *Optician*, September 9, 2005, p. 5.

"De Rigo Set to Bounce Back," *Optician*, September 26, 2003, p.1.

"De Rigo Sets Up Vision Arm," *Optician*, November 12, 2004, p. 1.

"Gaultier Pulls the Shades," *WWD*, February 28, 2005, p. 24.

"Independent Key to De Rigo UK Success," *Optician*, August 9, 2002, p. 2.

Kaiser, Amanda, "Eye Drama," *WWD*, March 1, 2004, p. 22S.

"Merger Talks," *Optician*, May 14, 2004, p. 1.

"New Look," *WWD*, November 8, 2004, p. 2.

Sibun, Jonathan, "Dollond & Aitchison Agrees to Boots Opticians Merger," *Daily Telegraph,* January 30, 2009.

"Spectacular Results ... Italian Champions," *Economist*, August 18, 2007, p. 55.

Wearden, Graeme, "Optician Chain with Link Back to George III Merges with Boots," *Guardian*, January 30, 2009, p. 32.

"Wragges Sets Its Sights on Dollond-Boots Opticians Tie," *Lawyer*, February 9, 2009, p. 10.

Deutsche Messe AG

Messegelände
Hannover, D-30521
Germany
Telephone: (49 511) 89-0
Fax: (49 511) 89-32626
Web site: http://www.messe.de

State-Owned Company
Incorporated: 1947 as Deutsche Messe- und
    Ausstellungs- AG
Employees: 700
Sales: EUR 286 million ($399 million) (2007)
NAICS: 561920 Convention and Trade Show
    Organizers

■ ■ ■

Deutsche Messe AG is one the world's largest organizers of business-to-business trade shows. Roughly 60 trade shows, exhibitions, and hosted events are held annually on the company's one million square meters of exhibition grounds in Hannover, Germany, attracting up to one million visitors annually. Some of Deutsche Messe's most prominent events are the information and communication technology fair called CeBIT and the industrial and technology fair known as Hannover Messe.

Other major events hosted by Deutsche Messe include the biennial international automotive show IAA Commercial Vehicles, Europe's biggest biotechnology trade show Biotechnica, the CeMAT Hannover Fair for Intralogistics, and forestry and wood industry world fair

LIGNA Hannover. Through its international subsidiary, Hannover Messe International GmbH, Deutsche Messe also hosts some 50 trade shows per year in many regions of the world, including Turkey, China, India, Australia, South America and the United States. In addition, the company is working with the Italian trade show firm Fiera Milano to further expand its market position in China, India, Russia and Brazil. While Deutsche Messe is designated a public stock corporation, all stock is owned by the State of Lower Saxony (49.832%), the City of Hannover (49.832%), the City of Bremen (0. 207%), and Hannover County (0.129%).

BEGINNINGS IN POSTWAR GERMANY

The history of Deutsche Messe in Hannover closely mirrored the economic development of West Germany after World War II. Established on an initiative of the British military administration, Deutsche Messe- und Ausstellungs- AG was founded in 1947 to mobilize the Germans' potential to lift themselves out of the self-inflicted misery. The best way to do that, according to the British, was to show the world the industrial capabilities of the country, despite the still omnipresent devastation. On an order of General Sir Brian H. Robertson, commander-in-chief of the British occupation forces, issued on April 15, 1947, an Export Fair was to be held the same year from August 18 until September 7. After the city of Düsseldorf had rejected the idea of hosting the event, Hannover was chosen as the location for the fair.

Although the city had been severely damaged during the war, a suitable exhibition area was found in the

COMPANY PERSPECTIVES

Deutsche Messe AG is preparing to launch an ambitious strategic program dedicated to securing and expanding its position as one of the world's leading exhibition organizers over the next few years. Entitled "Hermes +", the plan is intended to realize new growth and cost-saving potential for Deutsche Messe. The program will include new exhibition themes, including within the cutting-edge sector of climate and environmental protection. Deutsche Messe plans to introduce new exhibitions and provide a range of new exhibition-related services, including consulting, in addition to its current turnkey exhibition packages.

production halls of Vereinigte Leichtmetallwerke, a light metal products manufacturer. Within ten weeks, several hundred of the company's workers dismantled and removed some 90,000 tons of machinery from the site to make space for the exhibition. In spite of the many organizational obstacles, on top of the serious lack of building materials, food, accommodations, transportation, time and expertise, the first Export Fair took place in Hannover in the late summer of 1947.

More than 700,000 visitors traveled to the city. In absence of hotel rooms, many of them stayed in one of Hannover's 23 schools or with a private host, and were brought to and from the exhibition by buses that had been gathered for this purpose from all over Northern Germany. While the many German visitors were not allowed to purchase anything, foreign visitors to the fair placed orders for goods carrying the label "Made in Germany" worth roughly $30 million, from household goods to furniture, cosmetics, clothing, and hardware, all manufactured by about 1,300 participating companies from the so-called British-American bizone. In financial terms, the fair almost broke even, with revenues of 3.6 million reichsmarks and expenditures of 3.9 million reichsmarks.

MASSIVE EXPANSION DURING "ECONOMIC MIRACLE" YEARS

After the first Export Fair's success, the Allied forces of the bizone decided to hold a second such event in Hannover in spring 1948. Again, many organizational difficulties had to be overcome, including a strike of the light metal workers turned-into Export Fair staff, who demanded better compensation for their hard work. Ad-

ditional volunteers such as students and police cadets were lined up to help before and during the exhibition, which opened its doors for visitors on May 22, 1948. This was the beginning of a world-class exhibition. The state of Lower Saxony and the City of Hannover became the principal shareholders of Deutsche Messe- und Ausstellungs- AG which, determined by its charter, was to be owned by public institutions only. According to the new guidelines defining the fair's strategic direction, it was to be a meeting place for professionals representing a comprehensive range of manufacturers of export goods from various industries.

In 1950 the first participants from other countries exhibited their goods in Hannover. Driven by the postwar economic boom in West Germany, the fair, which was renamed Deutsche Industrie-Messe (German Industrial Fair), grew very dynamically during the 1950s. The fair's location in Laatzen, a suburb at the fringes of Hannover, turned out to be an advantage, for there was plenty of space to contain the exhibition area's massive expansion. As the German Industrial Fair quickly gained in popularity, ever more modern and larger exhibition halls were mushrooming on the fairgrounds. The newly erected hall for the electrical engineering industry alone provided as much space as all the exhibition halls of the 1947 fair combined.

Many industries committed themselves to Hannover by signing long-term agreements with Deutsche Messe- und Ausstellungs- AG and invested heavily in establishing a permanent presence at the Industrial Fair. New exhibition halls were erected for luxury consumer goods manufacturers, for the electric lighting products industry, and for the office equipment industry, among others. In the fall of 1948, an Exhibitor's Advisory Committee was established to represent the exhibitors' interests. One of its first suggestions, to hold a separate trade show for consumer goods, was put into practice in 1949.

The 1950s also saw the continuous development of the necessary infrastructure, including transportation and accommodations. Huge parking areas were built to contain the estimated 50,000 motor vehicles that arrived at the fair per day. The exhibition grounds were surrounded by a ring-shaped road, followed by an expressway from the city center to the fairgrounds and a direct connection to the newly built autobahn between Hamburg and Frankfurt. The railway network was extended to the fairgrounds, followed by the opening of Hannover-Langenhagen international airport in 1952.

A pioneering video-enhanced traffic control system was installed in Hannover in the mid-1950s. Finally, the German Industrial Fair received its own runway from where an air shuttle service brought visitors and exhibi-

KEY DATES

1947: Deutsche Messe- und Ausstellungs- AG is founded and the first Hannover Export Fair takes place.

1961: Hannover Fair becomes the trade fair's official name.

1970: The International Machine Tool Exhibition is held in Hannover for the first time.

1981: Hannover Fairs International (HFI) is established as a new business division.

1984: Hannover Fair enters the *Guinness Book of Records* as the "Fair of Superlatives."

1986: The first computer and office machines fair CeBIT takes place.

1987: The company is renamed Deutsche Messe AG.

2000: World exhibition Expo 2000 is held in part at Hannover Fairgrounds.

2007: A Hannover Fair is held in Bangalore, India.

tors to and from Hannover airport in small aircraft or helicopter. Bed and breakfast accommodations in thousands of private homes became a mainstay in Hannover's exhibition hospitality sector during the fair. Messe Gastronomie Hannover, the catering and restaurant subsidiary of Deutsche Messe, was established in 1959.

RAPID GROWTH, COMPETITION, AND RECESSION CAUSE CRISIS

At the beginning of the 1960s, the German Industrial Fair, officially renamed Hannover Fair in 1961, emerged as a major international trade show that attracted some 5,000 exhibitors per year on average, with roughly one-fifth of them coming from other countries. Among the most prominent industries at the fair were the mechanical and electrical engineering, iron and steel, chemical, construction machinery, and office equipment industries. However, as the mega-trade show continued to grow, exhibitors had to vie for the limited space, and some of them even had to be turned down.

While Deutsche Messe's revenues soared in the 1960s, a growing number of exhibitors expressed their concern about rising costs, resulting in discussions about establishing separate trade shows for different industries to solve the mounting problems. In addition, Hannover had to face the growing competition from other West German trade show centers. A major loss for Hannover

Fair, for example, was the early departure of the automotive industry, which moved to the Frankfurt Motor Show. The emerging microelectronics industry, on the other hand, was heavily courted by Munich's trade show company, which also managed to attract major construction machinery exhibitors to its Bauma trade show.

To keep other major industries in Hannover, Deutsche Messe invested heavily in new and modernized exhibition halls in the early 1970s that were exclusively dedicated to certain industries. One of the new facilities was the Centrum für Büro und Informationstechnik or the Center for Office and Information Technology (CeBIT), the construction of which convinced the industry to remain under the roof of the Hannover Fair. The machine tool industry, on the other hand, established its own international trade show in Hannover, which took place in 1970 for the first time.

In the same year, however, 29 manufacturers of consumer goods, such as cutlery and products made from china and glass, pulled out of Hannover. After Deutsche Messe's attempt to establish the new consumer goods show "Interfachmesse" in 1974 flopped, the last exhibitors of such goods moved away from Hannover four years later. As the first oil price crisis in 1973 caused a severe recession in Western Europe thereafter, Deutsche Messe witnessed significant declines in the numbers of visitors and exhibitors. On the positive side, the new separate trade show for the woodworking machinery industry, LIGNA, was successfully launched in 1975. Two years later the "Research and Technology" showcase featuring results of companies involved in high-tech industries was established. By 1978, the size of Hannover Fair had shrunk to the level of 1962. However, that year marked the end of the 1970s crisis.

THE FAIR OF FAIRS CONCEPT AND CEBIT

With a new concept and under new management, Deutsche Messe was off to a successful new start in 1980. The 29 major exhibition themes that had emerged during the 1970s, and each of which constituted a mini-trade show of its own, were regrouped into ten main categories. Hannover Fair's new tagline, the Fair of Fairs, communicated the new concept of holding ten separate trade shows under one roof, which catered to the trend of increasing specialization and allowed for cross-networking opportunities at the same time.

Five of the ten new fairs, including Electrical Engineering, CeBIT, Plant Engineering and Iron and Steel, Mechanical Engineering and Power Transmission and Control, and Materials Handling, became the biggest events in their industry worldwide. The fact that the 1980 Hannover Fair was again fully booked and turned up a record sales figure was proof of the success of the new concept. The new format was supplemented by the new "Youth and Technology" program, allowing young adults to attend the trade show, and of the Partner Country program, featuring the economy and culture of one industrially developing country at each Hannover Fair.

Another pillar of Deutsche Messe's new strategy was to contain all further expansion within the existing limits of the exhibition grounds by using the existing space and by means of modernization. For example, a new CeBIT hall was built on the site of the former consumer goods building, while other existing facilities, such as vacated halls of the shrinking steel industry, were remodeled and put to new uses.

Still, as the redesigned fair was growing to new heights, it once again reached its limits of growth. The 1984 Hannover Fair made it into the *Guinness Book of Records* as the "Fair of Superlatives," including the record number of 740,000 visitors and 6,610 exhibitors from 119 countries; the largest fairgrounds and the biggest exhibition space containing the single biggest exhibition hall; the world's largest parking space and the largest onsite passenger railway station. Even the launch of the second largest investment program in the history of Deutsche Messe, which earmarked DEM 124 million for the further upgrading of the fairgrounds' facilities and infrastructure in the mid-1980s, could not solve the problem of overcrowding.

Therefore, the management board of Deutsche Messe, with the approval of major exhibitors, decided to spin off the fast-growing Hannover Fair, CeBIT, from Hannover Fair Industry. Despite a fire that destroyed one of the major exhibition halls in January, the first independent computer, office, and information technology fair CeBIT was held four weeks before the Hannover Fair in 1986. In the years that followed, CeBIT almost doubled in size while Hannover Fair Industry grew slightly and added the Industrial Automation and New Materials trade shows to its program. However, only ten years after the split, CeBIT once again reached the limits of the fairgrounds. Again, the popular trade show was split into two—one for businesspeople and one for consumers. Named CeBIT Home Electronics, the biennial consumer show was launched in 1996 and attracted 200,000 visitors in its first year. Yet, when major exhibitors stayed away from the event, it was canceled in 2000.

DIVERSIFICATION AND INTERNATIONAL EXPANSION

In the meantime, Deutsche Messe added new formats to its program of events, including the sheet metal trade show EuroBlech, the biotechnology show Biotechnica, the agricultural machinery fair Agritechnica, and the carpet and floor coverings show Domotex. By the mid-1990s the company was grossing DEM 400 million per year. Yet, it was the consequent internationalization of the company's activities that opened up a brand-new chapter in the history of Deutsche Messe. As early as in 1981, Hannover Fairs International (HFI) was established as a new subsidiary that began to organize trade exhibitions and showcases abroad. However, the fall of the Berlin Wall in 1989 and the following opening of the Eastern European and Asian economies to the West provided for unprecedented business opportunities in these parts of the world.

At first, HFI helped European clients who were increasingly looking to get their foot into new markets abroad, such as in Turkey, Mexico, China, and Vietnam. Then, the subsidiary began to organize its own trade shows, such as PTC Power Transmission and Control in Peking, China. Deutsche Messe also invested in its own fairgrounds in Istanbul, Turkey, where a number of regular trade shows for the Arab region was successfully established, and participated in a joint venture of several German trade show companies that built the Shanghai International Expo Centre in China. Finally, HFI began to export Deutsche Messe's own successful products in the form of regional versions of CeBIT to other parts of the globe, including Istanbul, Shanghai, Sydney, and New York. After the first CeBIT in China was held, the number of Chinese exhibitors in at CeBIT in Hannover grew fivefold. By 1999 HFI was organizing 33 trade shows abroad that attracted over 93,000 visitors.

MANAGING CRISIS WITH SHAREHOLDERS' HELP

As the 20th century came to a close, a combination of trends resulted in an increasingly difficult market environment for Deutsche Messe. In a stagnating and more and more fragmented trade show market, competition between the major German players intensified, resulting in shrinking profit margins and in Deutsche Messe's loss of a few major fairs to competitors. The company's flagship shows, Hannover Fair and especially CeBIT, were struggling with dwindling numbers of visitors and exhibitors, resulting in shrinking revenues. At the same time, major trade show organizers in other European countries were trying to gain a larger piece of the market. Deutsche Messe's involvement in the world exhibition Expo 2000 helped the company further improve its transportation infrastructure at Hannover

Fairgrounds, including a new railway station, better connections to the autobahn, and several new exhibition halls. However, the DEM 250 million investment also significantly weakened the company's financial position.

To defend Hannover Fair's position as the world's most important trade show event for industry, Deutsche Messe adopted the new Process and Factory Automation concept, covering the entire value chain from raw materials processing to final product manufacturing in two alternating fairs. The renewed positioning as a comprehensive industrial fair and at the same time as a marketplace for research and development with a sharpened focus on cutting edge technologies was to be strengthened by the coverage of emerging technologies such as nanotechnology and hydro technology, and themes such as global climate change and environmental protection; and by focusing more on exhibits of practical applications, such as machines and equipment in action, for which the large Hannover Fairgrounds provided an ideal setting.

In 2002 Deutsche Messe began to record losses, at first in the one-digit millions. Between 2001 and 2006, the booked exhibition area at CeBIT shrank by 30 percent and the number of exhibitors decreased by one-quarter. As the numbers of CeBIT visitors and exhibitors went down, the company's sales diminished by 25 percent from 2005 to 2006. To reverse the critical situation, Deutsche Messe worked on redesigning the CeBIT concept and on cutting costs for exhibitors. The 2008 financial crisis further worsened the situation as the number of CeBIT visitors and exhibitors further decreased, resulting in a heavy EUR 14 million loss.

In March 2009 Deutsche Messe's two main shareholders, the city of Hannover and the state of Lower Saxony, pledged to boost its capital base by EUR 250 million to help the struggling company get out of this critical situation. For the short term, Deutsche Messe's management was planning to significantly cut fairgrounds maintenance costs, possibly by reducing the number of exhibition halls. To secure the long-term future of the company, Deutsche Messe entered a strategic partnership with Italian trade show firm Fiera Milano to strengthen the market position of both companies in China, India, Russia, and Brazil, in January 2008.

Evelyn Hauser

PRINCIPAL SUBSIDIARIES

Hannover Messe International GmbH; Fachausstellungen Heckmann GmbH; Messe Gastronomie Hannover GmbH; Travel2Fairs GmbH: Robotation Academy GmbH; Hannover Fairs Australia; Hannover Fairs USA Inc.; Hannover Fairs South America Ltda.; Hannover Fairs India Pvt. Ltd.; Hannover Fairs China Ltd.; Hannover Messe International Istanbul (Turkey).

PRINCIPAL COMPETITORS

Messe Frankfurt GmbH; Messe Düsseldorf GmbH; Messe München GmbH; Koelnmesse GmbH; Messe Berlin GmbH.

FURTHER READING

"Bangalore Chosen as Venue for Hannover Fairs," *PTI—The Press Trust of India Ltd.,* October 18, 2007.

"CeBIT Will Hold Shows in Istanbul and Shanghai," *Shipping Digest,* June 23, 2008.

"Deutsche Messe Acquires Stake in Moscow Vehicle Show," *Tradeshow Week,* November 6, 2006, p. 4.

"Deutsche Messe AG to Hold Industrial Exhibitions in Shanghai," *Alestron,* August 31, 2004.

"Deutsche Messe Cancels CeBIT America 2005," *Europe Intelligence Wire,* August 4, 2004.

"Deutsche Messe Moves into Dubai," *Asia Africa Intelligence Wire,* November 10, 2005.

"Deutsche Messe Returns to the Black," *Europe Intelligence Wire,* December 19, 2005.

"Deutsche Messe Still Faces Burden from Expo 2000," *Europe Intelligence Wire,* January 18, 2007.

"Deutsche Messe Suffers Further Loss for 2003," *Europe Intelligence Wire,* January 23, 2004.

"First CeBIT Australia Trade Fair to Open Tuesday," *AsiaPulse News,* May 27, 2002.

Hart, Michael, "Biotechnica, Interphex to Collocate," *Tradeshow Week,* May 7, 2007, p. 1.

Helmer, Wolfgang, "50 Jahre Hannover Messe: Ein militärischer Befehl machte Hannover zur Messestadt," *Frankfurter Allgemeine Zeitung,* April 9, 1997, p. 23.

"Hot News from the Streets of the World," *Design News,* June 26, 2006, p. 18.

Mather, Joan, "Deutsche Messe Works with Subsidiaries and Other Trade Fairs to Open Worldwide Markets, " *Tradeshow Week,* February 5, 2001, p. 34.

"Milan, Hannover Team Up," *Tradeshow Week,* February 11, 2008, p. 4.

Tasch, Dieter, *Face to Face with the Future. Trade Fairs in Hannover: 1947–1997,* Hannover, Germany: Deutsche Messe AG, 1997, 156 p.

"Trade Fair Leader Sees Growth Eastwards," *New Straits Times,* June 28, 1999.

Tufel, Gary, "Deutsche Messe Grows Its Shows," *Tradeshow Week,* December 19, 2005, p. 4.

Wimberly, Rachel, "Big Exhibitors Bailing Out of CeBIT 2007: Motorola, Nokia, BenQ Join Sony, Canon, Philips in Abandoning ICT Show," *Tradeshow Week,* October 2, 2006, p. 1.

Do it Best Corporation

6502 Nelson Road
Fort Wayne, Indiana 46803
U.S.A.
Telephone: (260) 748-5300
Fax: (260) 748-5620
Web site: http://www.doitbestcorp.com

Cooperative
Incorporated: 1945 as Hardware Wholesalers, Inc.
Employees: 1,549
Sales: $2.65 billion (2008)
NAICS: 421310 Lumber, Plywood, Millwork, and
   Wood Panel Wholesalers; 421320 Brick, Stone, and
   Related Construction Material Wholesalers; 421330
   Roofing, Siding, and Insulation Material Wholesal-
   ers; 42139 Other Construction Material Wholesal-
   ers; 421710 Hardware Wholesalers

■ ■ ■

Founded in 1945 as Hardware Wholesalers, Inc. (HWI),
Do it Best Corporation is one of the largest dealer-
owned cooperatives in the United States and one of
Indiana's largest privately owned businesses. From an
initial membership of 75 hardware and building and
lumber supplies dealers, the cooperative had grown to
include more than 4,100 member-retailers throughout
the United States and 47 foreign countries by 2008. Do
it Best distributes some 65,000 different hardware and
building supplies items from eight retail service centers
and five regional lumber offices.

ORIGINS AND DEALER-OWNED COOPERATIVES

Hardware Wholesalers, Inc. (HWI), was founded in
1945 by Arnold Gerberding as a member-owned
cooperative. It was established to serve independent
hardware and building materials dealers. By combining
the purchasing power of its members, HWI helped the
independent dealer face intense competition from
discount stores, warehouse outlets, and big chain
operations.

Born in Fort Wayne, Indiana, in 1900, Gerberding
went to work for the Pfeiffer Hardware Co. after
graduating from high school. After several years he took
a job with Schafer Hardware Co. in Decatur, Indiana, at
the urging of his uncle, who was the firm's treasurer.
Schafer was a small hardware wholesaler that served
both hardware and building materials dealers within a
100-mile radius.

Gerberding spent nearly two decades with Schafer,
primarily as a buyer. During the 1920s and 1930s, the
wholesale middlemen, also known as jobbers, dominated
the flow of goods from the manufacturer to the local
retailer. The jobbers not only added a layer of expense
for the independent retailer, they also controlled the
retailers to some extent.

Independent hardware dealers, who faced growing
competition from national catalog and retail chains such
as Sears and Montgomery Ward, fought to be competitive by forming associations and using the pooled
resources of the group to buy directly from
manufacturers. These groups typically tied themselves to
a "cost-plus" store that would act as a buyer for the

```
COMPANY PERSPECTIVES

Our mission is the make the best even better. Our
philosophy is to serve others as we would like to be
served. Our goal is to help our members grow.
```

group, then sell merchandise to the associated stores at cost plus a standard handling fee. Using another model, Ace Hardware, formed in 1925, gained combined strength through a franchise of stores that all carried the same name and products.

While working for Schafer, Gerberding developed his own vision for creating a dealer-owned company. Dealer-owned cooperatives had been springing up around the country to break the power of the wholesalers over the independent dealers. The first hardware cooperative wholesaler, Franklin Hardware Co. of Philadelphia, had appeared in 1906. The first truly dealer-owned cooperative was the American Hardware & Supply Company of Pittsburgh, founded in 1920. It was soon followed by others. There were nearly two dozen such cooperatives by the end of the 1930s, but most did not survive.

FOUNDING MEMBERSHIP: 1945

By the early 1940s Gerberding realized he had to leave Schafer to pursue his vision of establishing a dealer-owned company. Influenced by the ideas of William Stout, head of the American Hardware & Supply Company, and George Hall, founder of the Hall Hardware Company, Gerberding joined the Auburn Hardware Company of Auburn, Indiana, in 1943 as its general sales manager. Auburn Hardware was one of the wholesale operations that operated on a cost-plus basis.

From 1943 to 1945 Gerberding contacted several area dealers to explore the possibility of creating the organization that became Hardware Wholesalers, Inc. (HWI). He left Auburn Hardware in 1945 and founded HWI on June 28, 1945. A group of independent dealers became the heart of the organizing board of directors of the new company.

The original organizing plan for HWI called for finding 75 dealers to become members. Each member was asked to invest $1,000 by purchasing 20 shares of common stock in the company, with an initial payment of $50 and the balance due upon call from the board of directors. When the meeting to incorporate was held on June 28, 1945, there were 96 subscribers. Nearly half of

the new members turned out to be lumber and building materials dealers, with the rest being independent hardware dealers. This mixture became a defining characteristic of HWI and a source of strength for the firm in its early years.

FIRST YEARS OF A FLEDGLING COOPERATIVE

The directors decided to locate HWI in Fort Wayne, Indiana, not only because that was Gerberding's hometown and the home of the businesses of several of the board members, but also because it was the region's rail and truck center. Moreover, Fort Wayne was a rapidly growing community. That made it an ideal place to locate a wholesale distributor to the independent hardware and lumber dealers who were serving a growing number of homeowners.

An office and warehouse site was selected. Three additional warehouses were added in 1946. All of the early warehouses were small, and the company's equipment was primitive. For example, the company displayed merchandise at various state hardware and lumber shows that were usually held in January and February—and the company's truck did not have a heater.

Acquiring merchandise also posed a problem for the fledgling firm. It faced opposition from the established wholesalers, who would "blackball" merchants and manufacturers who dealt with dealer-owned organizations. Fearing retaliation, some members joined HWI under fictitious names. There was also a shortage of hardware and building materials following the end of World War II. For many years HWI had to deal with secondary manufacturers, until its growth attracted the interest of the leading companies.

Although faced with many difficulties, HWI saw its revenue increase from $171,069 in 1946 to $546,275 in 1948, while membership increased from 75 to 112 dealers. In 1947 the firm constructed its first warehouse facility in Fort Wayne. From 1952 to 1966 this facility would see expansion through six additions. In 1948 HWI moved its merchandise market from local meeting halls to its new warehouse in conjunction with an open house that allowed the members to see and use the new facility as well as view the increasing range of products. The merchandise markets were held in the warehouse until 1955, when a huge tent was erected on the company's parking lot.

THE SECOND DECADE

By 1955 HWI was an established and rapidly growing regional wholesale distribution company. It served more than 200 member hardware and lumber dealers and of-

KEY DATES

1945: Arnold Gerberding establishes Hardware Wholesalers Inc. as a member-owned cooperative.

1947: The firm constructs its first warehouse facility in Fort Wayne.

1955: Revenues are nearly $3 million, and rebates to members amount to nearly $170,000.

1966: Revenues reach $31.5 million, rebates to members are $1.2 million, and the number of members grows to 619.

1971: A new 300,000-square-foot facility opens in Missouri.

1974: A distribution center opens in Illinois.

1977: Another distribution center is built in Medina, Ohio.

1980: A facility opens in Waco, Texas.

1982: The Do it Center program is introduced.

1998: HWI and Our Own Hardware Co., Inc., merge; the company changes its name to Do it Best Corp.

1999: A full-fledged e-commerce site, billed as "The World's Largest Hardware Store," is launched.

2006: Sales surpass $3 billion; the company's eighth retail service center opens in Nevada.

fered several major lines of hardware products. In 1955 revenues were nearly $3 million, and rebates to members amounted to nearly $170,000.

During the next decade HWI would acquire more major lines of manufactured goods, expand its building materials business, recruit more members, expand its member services, and increase its warehouse space. By 1966 revenues reached $31.5 million, rebates to members were $1.2 million, and the number of members reached 619.

As HWI began to expand beyond the immediate Fort Wayne area, it used commercial carriers to ship products. In 1955 it created its own fleet, initially consisting of two trucks, to make deliveries. The drivers were paid a percentage of the value of products they hauled rather than an hourly wage. As the company began to use larger trucks, an incentive program was introduced, and HWI's drivers were among the best paid in the United States.

In 1964 the company replaced its punch-card system with an IBM computer to handle data. The computer enabled HWI to expand its member services and, perhaps more importantly, offer its members variable pricing based on margins specified by the members themselves.

EXPANDING VISION

HWI entered its third decade with new leadership. Its founder, Gerberding, retired on September 30, 1967, at the age of 67. He remained an honorary executive vice-president and consultant to HWI until his death in 1977. The directors appointed Don Wolf, one of their own employees, to succeed Gerberding. Wolf, who worked his way up the ranks of HWI to merchandise and sales manager before his appointment, would lead HWI for the next 25 years.

The 1970s brought more competition for independent hardware and building materials dealers. Established chains such as Sears were expanding their hardware and remodeling departments. Discount store chains such as Kmart, Wal-Mart, and Target, which had appeared in the 1960s, were beginning to flourish. Specialty discount stores that focused on one category of product highlighted another aggressive retail concept. A variety of other retailers were starting to carry housewares and home hardware items.

Perhaps the biggest competitive threat to HWI came from the new lumber, building supply, and hardware cash and carry stores. These giant retail centers were the forerunners of big-box stores that boasted no-frills, super-discount prices in a warehouse setting. Other competition came from regional buying groups that were growing and seeking to become national in scope, including Ace Hardware and True Value, among others.

In order to meet these competitive threats, Wolf believed that HWI needed to grow beyond a one-warehouse company. The firm preferred to remain independent, although the possibility of merging with another company existed. In order to grow, HWI needed to formalize its planning process and articulate the concepts it stood for. As its basic operating philosophy, HWI adopted the slogan, "Serving others as we would like to be served."

GEOGRAPHIC EXPANSION BEGINS

At first the board of HWI resisted the development of regional centers, because it would double HWI's cost of operation and exposure. Financing was also problematic, as HWI did not have a strong cash position at the time. Previous warehouse expansions on a much smaller scale had been financed by selling bonds to the members. The new facility was ultimately financed by the Lincoln National Life Insurance Company, based in Fort Wayne, through industrial revenue bonds.

Cape Girardeau, Missouri, was selected as the site for the new 300,000-square-foot facility. The city was strategically located to serve the southern and western regions as well as the St. Louis area. Two years before the facility opened in 1971, HWI began recruiting stores in the St. Louis area, so that Cape Girardeau would be immediately profitable when it opened.

HWI grew dramatically in the early 1970s, and a new distribution center was built in Dixon, Illinois, to service the Great Lakes region and, especially, Chicago, Minnesota, and Wisconsin. Again, new members were recruited in the region before the distribution center opened in 1974. In 1977 another distribution center was built in Medina, Ohio, that became HWI's highest-volume distribution facility.

To keep up with HWI's growth, additional distribution centers were built in Waco, Texas, in 1980; Lexington, South Carolina, in 1986; and Woodburn, Oregon, in 1991. These six large distribution centers (the Fort Wayne warehouse had been closed in 1980 following a labor dispute) served more than 3,500 members in the United States and several other countries in the 1990s.

HWI enjoyed dramatic growth throughout the 1970s. Sales reached $455 million by the end of the decade, and the number of members increased to nearly 1,000. Home-building and remodeling, in addition to do-it-yourself maintenance, was the fastest-growing retail market of the decade. Home centers (retail stores that joined hardware with lumber and building supplies) played an important role in HWI's growth in the 1970s and beyond.

By 1976 HWI's merchandise market events had become too large for Fort Wayne, and they were moved to Indianapolis. These three-day events gave members a chance to view new products and take advantage of sales and special deals from vendors. Members could also take the time to meet with HWI staff to discuss areas of concern and new merchandising ideas. Members usually left the events with a six-month marketing plan.

DO IT CENTER REVOLUTION

HWI's sales more than doubled in the 1980s, from $470 million in 1981 to over $1.1 billion in 1990, and membership increased to over 3,000. It was a decade of tremendous growth in the hardware and lumber and building supplies industry, as retail space increased

overall by 50 percent. Discount chain stores expanded rapidly, and big-box stores exceeding 100,000 square feet, such as Home Depot and Builders Square, opened.

HWI's members were able to keep pace, though, and several members more than doubled their number of stores. In fact, most of HWI's growth came from established members selling more products and buying more from HWI. During the 1980s HWI was committed to creating a total retail marketing strategy for its members. Its "Do it Center" program helped "ignite the resurgence in hardware retailing," according to the *National Home Center News,* and HWI was named Hardware Merchandiser of the Year in 1985 by *Hardware Merchandiser* magazine.

The Do it Center concept was developed by merchandising expert Don Watt, who had first impressed CEO Wolf and other HWI people with his presentation at a 1978 industry convention. The Watt Group, headquartered in Toronto, Ontario, was recognized as the leading design and communications group in North America. At the invitation of Don Wolf, Watt attended all 27 of the HWI district meetings in 1979. At each meeting Watt made a one-hour presentation on worldwide marketing trends and modern merchandising. Six months later he returned to HWI headquarters with a two-hour slide presentation that revealed the similarities among contemporaries Sears, HWI, Ace, and True Value stores. As a result, HWI retained Watt to develop an innovative marketing concept that would set HWI apart from its competition.

Watt came up with the Do it Center program, which included bright, aggressive colors and signage to create a warm and exciting atmosphere. Floor layouts included "power aisles" that allowed customers to take a short walk and see all of the store's departments. Similarly, employees could easily walk the power aisles to see who needed service. Seasonal and new items were displayed at end caps, the end of shelving units dividing departments.

Many members were reluctant to try such sweeping change. However, the concept was tested in 1981, and the results from the first store were good. When four stores implemented the changes, sales in each increased 50 percent in the first year. More importantly, the concept was a hit with customers and employees alike. Customers responded positively to features and sales. Employees took pride in working in such an innovative environment, and Do it Centers became a favored place to work.

The Do it Center program was introduced at the fall market in 1982. With many of the dealers remaining skeptical and others wanting to adopt only part of the program, HWI headquarters established strict mandatory guidelines for opening a true Do it Center. It was agreed that members who chose not to participate in the program would not be penalized in any way.

RECOGNITION, GROWTH, AND LEADERSHIP

HWI's sales nearly doubled again in the 1990s, from $1.1 billion in 1991 to more than $2 billion in fiscal 1999 (ending June 30). At the beginning of the decade HWI was competing successfully with the big chain discount and warehouse stores. Management guru Tom Peters, author of *In Search of Excellence* and *Liberation Management,* was so impressed with HWI's performance that he changed his keynote address at the Home Center Trade Show at McCormick Place in Chicago in 1989 to focus on the strength and dynamics of such dealer-owned organizations as HWI.

Like many other industries, the wholesale hardware, lumber, and building materials industry was affected by globalization. In the 1990s HWI led international cooperation efforts among dealer-owned firms in the formation of Interlink, a global association of dealer-owned companies. After HWI began working with the two largest dealer-owned organizations in Canada, an organization called Alliance was formed in 1993 to pool buying power and develop programs for members across North America.

Don Wolf stepped down as CEO in 1992 and retired in July of the following year. As part of a planned succession, executive vice-president Mike Mc-Clelland became president and CEO of HWI in October 1992. Bob Taylor, who owned five Do it Center stores in Virginia Beach, Virginia, became chairman.

HWI celebrated its 50th anniversary in 1995. "Serve others as you would like to be served" continued to be the company's guiding philosophy. When McClelland became president, he added a mission statement: "We're going to make the best even better." That year HWI separated its sales and marketing division into two divisions, with marketing covering advertising, retail merchandising, store design, special events, and communications. Sales would focus on domestic and international sales.

Through its Canadian joint venture, Alliance, HWI had positioned itself as a total North American buying group. McClelland indicated he wanted to eventually form a holding company with the two Canadian partners, Home Hardware Stores and Le Groupe Ro-Na Dismat, and merge into one company with three marketing identities. The group engineered 35 "common buys" in the first half of 1995 and entered into 200 "common alliances" with manufacturers.

CONCEPT FLEXIBILITY AND AN INTERNET PRESENCE

A new store format, Do it Best Vision, was introduced in October 1995. The flexible program allowed smaller retailers with limited resources to buy into Do it Best with varying degrees of financial commitment. Do it Express, which focused on quicker customer service, was introduced in 1996. The company expected that 80 percent or more of its members would choose one of the three available store programs: Do it Center, Do it Best Vision, or Do it Express. In addition, HWI offered its members three private-label brands: Do-it, Do-it Best, and Master Touch.

HWI initially established its web site in May 1996. Later in the year it made its catalog of 61,000 products available on CD-ROM as well. In 1997 HWI contracted with the Internet division of QVC to sell some 4,000 to 5,000 products over the Internet, making them available to an international market. However, none of the firm's private-label brands, which members felt gave them a competitive advantage, was offered over the Internet.

In May 1998 the firm's INCOM Distributor Supply division debuted a new web site for members. A full-fledged e-commerce site, billed as "The World's Largest Hardware Store," was launched in July 1999. It offered more than 70,000 hardware and building products and featured an online encyclopedia of how-to advice and project tips.

MERGER AND A NEW CORPORATE NAME

In October 1997 HWI and Our Own Hardware Co., Inc., announced their intention to merge and form a single co-op. At the time HWI had 3,500 members, while Our Own Hardware had 900 members. HWI's annual sales for fiscal 1996 (ending June 30) were $1.6 billion, compared to $218 million for Our Own Hardware. The proposed merger was quickly approved by Our Own's members, and the two co-ops officially became a single buying group effective January 1, 1998. By the end of the year HWI had fully integrated former Our Own members.

HWI officially changed its name to Do it Best Corporation on March 16, 1998. The new name better reflected the co-op's membership, which included hardware stores, home centers, and building supply stores—the entire home improvement retail sector. The Do it Best retail identification program, first introduced in 1996, included the name in HWI's private-brand products, truck fleet, and company web site. HWI encouraged members to adopt the Do it Best retail identity.

Sales for fiscal 1998 reached $1.9 billion, a 5 percent increase over fiscal 1997. The firm ended the year with about 4,000 members, including about 900 that joined following the merger with Our Own Hardware. Not counting purchases from new members, sales were relatively flat, reflecting the rest of the industry. In August 1998 the company broke ground for a new distribution center in Montgomery, New York. Scheduled to open in October 1999, the company's seventh distribution center had 360,000 square feet, which could be expanded by an additional 125,000 square feet of warehouse space if necessary.

For fiscal 1999 Do it Best reported a 16 percent increase in sales, which topped $2.2 billion. The company remained focused on helping members identify and implement new marketing strategies. More than 1,000 stores had signed up to implement the Do it Best or Do it Center retail designs. After five years the Do it Best Rental Center program had its 500th member join the program. At the end of the 20th century Do it Best was committed to expanding member services, such as a recently introduced guarantee of 100 percent customer satisfaction with its private-label products, and to remaining focused on operating efficiencies.

MOVING INTO THE 21ST CENTURY

Do it Best spent the early years of the new millennium focused on international growth. The company added 30 Thai retailers to its fold during 2001 as part of a partnership with the Siam Cement Group. During the company's 2002 Spring Market event, potential members from Mexico, Grenada, Micronesia, the West Indies, and Vanuatu attended.

McClelland retired in August 2002 and Bob Taylor took the helm as president and CEO. Under new leadership, the company worked to control costs and make technological improvements. Its Waco, Texas, facility was upgraded in 2004, making it the largest of the company's distribution centers. It also launched RetailSTART, a program that helped members pinpoint where and when to open new stores.

Voice-picking technology was tested at company distribution centers and new product offerings continued to be added as well. Sales increased in 2003 to $2.42 billion, earning the company the number two position in the U.S. hardware and building materials market, ahead of competitor True Value Company and just behind Ace Hardware Corp.

Sales continue to grow over the next few years and surpassed a record $3 billion in 2006. The company

opened its eighth retail service center that year in Mesquite, Nevada, and also opened two buying offices in China. The company's Signature Store Design Program was also launched, which could be tailored to each member's home market to boost sales. In 2008, recognizing the value of "green" products, Do it Best began offering Perf Go Green biodegradable trash and garbage bags to its members.

CHALLENGES THROUGHOUT THE INDUSTRY

The company, however, began to feel the effects of a severe downturn in the housing industry in the United States, a slowdown in the overall economy, and skyrocketing oil costs. Sales declined in 2007 but even as these challenges threatened to derail the company's bottom line, Do it Best issued a record $126.2 million rebate to its members. Its operating overhead was 2 percent, which the company claimed to be the lowest in the industry. Taylor explained the company's success in a September 2007 *Home Channel News* article: "By providing our member owners with innovative programs to increase their performance at retail, and by continuing our relentless focus on improving operational efficiency, we have been able to return a consistently high year-end rebate to help our members reinvest in and grow their independent businesses."

Sales fell 5.6 percent over the previous year in 2008 while net income also declined by 8 percent. Despite these declines, fiscal 2008 was the company's third most profitable year in its history. The company added 135 new members during 2008 and remained dedicated to providing exceptional product distribution and easy-to-use retail programs that could help members secure revenues and increase brand awareness. With zero long-term debt on its books and a solid strategy in place, Do it Best appeared to be on track for success in the years to come.

David P. Bianco
Updated, Christina M. Stansell

PRINCIPAL COMPETITORS

Ace Hardware Corporation; The Home Depot Inc.; True Value Company.

FURTHER READING

Canlen, Brae, "Do it Best Members Reap Largest Rebate Ever," *Home Channel News,* November 5, 2001.

———, "Housewares, International Expansion Share Spotlight at Do it Best Market," *Home Channel News,* June 3, 2002.

Copeland, Mike, "Waco, Texas' Do it Best Distribution Center Is Now Company's Largest," *Knight-Ridder/Tribune Business News,* May 6, 2004.

Cory, Jim, and Cheryl Ann Lambert, "Efficiency Rules at HWI.," *Home Improvement Market,* June 1996, p. 36.

"Do it Best Corp. Reports Jump in Sales," Knight-Ridder/Tribune Business News, July 27, 1998.

"Do it Best Corp. to Open New York Distribution Center," *Do-It-Yourself Retailing,* August 1998, p. 33.

"Do it Best Introduces Two New Member Programs," *Do-It-Yourself Retailing,* June 1998, p. 23.

"Do it Best Sets Sights on $2 Billion," Do-It-Yourself Retailing, November 1998, p. 15.

Girard, Lisa, "Wholesale Sales Decline 7 Percent at Do it Best," *Home Channel News,* September 24, 2007.

"Hardware Wholesalers Inc. and Our Own Hardware Agree to Merge," *Do-It-Yourself Retailing,* October 1997, p. 29.

"Hardware Wholesalers Inc. Changes Name to Do it Best Corp.," *Do-It-Yourself Retailing,* April 1998, p. 23.

Hromadka, Erik, "Bob Taylor," *Indiana Business Magazine,* June 2008.

"HWI and Our Own Hardware to Merge," Home Improvement Market, October 1997, p. 12.

"HWI Catalog Now on the Internet," Do-It-Yourself Retailing, October 1996, p. 25.

"HWI Introduces Convenience-Oriented Do-it Express Store Format," *Chilton's Hardware Age,* December 1993, p. A-8.

"HWI Separates Sales and Marketing Divisions," Do-It-Yourself Retailing, April 1995, p. 27.

"HWI Teams Up with QVC to Sell Hardware on the Internet," *Do-It-Yourself Retailing,* March 1998, p. 19.

Kelly, Joseph M., and Laurie Shuster, "Flexibility Fuels Do it Best Vision," *Home Improvement Market,* June 1996, p. 42.

Lambert, Cheryl Ann, "HWI Discusses Competitive Strategies," *Home Improvement Market,* July 1995, p. 14.

———, "HWI—Our Own Merger Approved by Members," *Home Improvement Market,* January 1998, p. 9.

Lasek, Alicia, "HWI at 50: Ready for the Next Era," Building Supply Home Centers, May 1995, p. 22.

LeDuc, Doug, "Fort Wayne, Ind.-based Hardware Cooperative Raises National Sales Ranking," *Knight-Ridder/Tribune Business News,* August 13, 2003.

Sutton, Rod, and Alicia Lasek, "HWI Poised for Next 50 Years," *Building Supply Home Centers,* May 1995, p. 30.

"True Value and HWI Join Ace in Hardware Cyberspace," *Do-It-Yourself Retailing,* July 1996, p. 76.

Wolf, Don, with Michael C. Hawfield, *HWI: People ... Building a Great American Success Story,* Fort Wayne, Ind.: Hardware Wholesalers, 1995.

E. & J. Gallo Winery

---

600 Yosemite Boulevard
Modesto, California 95354-2760
U.S.A.
Telephone: (209) 341-3111
Toll Free: (877) 687-9463
Fax: (209) 341-3208
Web site: http://www.gallo.com

Private Company
Incorporated: 1933
Employees: 5,000
Sales: $3.15 billion (2007 est.)
NAICS: 312130 Wineries; 111332 Grape Vineyards

■ ■ ■

E. & J. Gallo Winery is the largest family-owned wine-maker in the world and the second largest winery based on volume. Gallo owns seven wineries and over 15,000 acres of vineyards throughout California. The company markets more than 60 brands of table and sparkling wines, malt beverage products, dessert wines, and distilled spirits. Some of its labels found on store shelves in the United States include Gallo Family Vineyards, Ecco Domani, Carlo Rossi, Louis M. Martini, Bella Sera, Dancing Bull, Rancho Zabaco, and Turning Leaf. As the largest exporter of California wine, its products can be found in more than 90 countries. E. & J. Gallo celebrated its 75th anniversary as a family-owned company in 2008.

EARLY HISTORY

Gallo's phenomenal success rests on the shoulders of the brothers Ernest and Julio Gallo, who founded the winery in Modesto, California, in 1933. Ernest was regarded as the marketing and distribution expert, while Julio oversaw wine production. The Gallos' contribution to every aspect of their business is widely acknowledged throughout the industry. Ernest is credited with almost singlehandedly increasing domestic demand in the 1960s and 1970s, while Julio's technical innovations include the widespread adoption of stainless steel fermentation tanks to replace the traditional wood casks for all but the most expensive wines.

The growth of the Gallo winery parallels the emergence of California winemaking as a world-class industry. California had been successful in international competitions as far back as the early 1900s, but with the arrival of Prohibition in January 1920 the thriving industry was almost destroyed. Thousands of acres of carefully cultivated wine grapes were uprooted and replaced with cash crops such as apples and walnuts. When Prohibition was repealed on December 5, 1933, a mere 160 of California's original 700 wineries were intact, and federal and state taxation and legislation had decimated domestic wine consumption.

In 1933 Ernest and Julio Gallo, aged 24 and 23 years, respectively, entered the wine business. They had worked since childhood in the modest vineyards of their immigrant Italian father, and after the death of both their parents, they decided to start making their own wine. Their technical expertise was gleaned from two pre-Prohibition wine pamphlets in the Modesto Public

COMPANY PERSPECTIVES

Our mission is to remain a family company that will be the leader in the U.S. wine industry and a leading provider of New World wines in select markets outside the U.S.

Library. Ernest and Julio obtained the necessary government license, purchased winemaking equipment on credit, and leased a small Modesto warehouse for $60 a month. They then visited local growers, offering them a share of the profits in return for the use of their grapes. By the time of Prohibition's repeal in December 1933, Ernest had made his first sale of 6,000 gallons of wine to Pacific Wine Company, a Chicago distributor. Profit in the first year was $34,000, a sum that was immediately plowed back into the business.

The first Gallo winery was built at Dry Creek in Modesto and until the late 1930s sold table wine to local bottlers, who marketed it under a variety of labels. In 1940, however, the first Gallo-labeled wine was introduced, and business increased substantially. Bottled in Los Angeles and New Orleans, the original selection consisted of the varietal wines Zinfandel and Dry Muscat, in addition to sherry and muscatel. It was during this early period that Ernest developed the strategic vision that would make him renowned throughout the industry. Realizing that consumption would never rise as long as wine was relegated to a secondary position behind hard liquor, he introduced the novel concept of salespeople who sold wine exclusively, a highly successful idea that was soon widely imitated. He recruited a team of zealous salespeople to push Gallo products and guarantee them high visibility on liquor store shelves. From the beginning, Gallo followed a strategy of expansion into new markets only when existing markets were conquered. Twenty-five years later, Gallo brands were available nationwide, and the company's distribution system was regarded as its greatest competitive strength.

ACCOMPLISHMENTS IN WINEMAKING

The company was also admired for its enological accomplishments. The Prohibition era had wreaked havoc on crops of better varieties of wine grape, which had been largely supplanted by inferior table and raisin varieties. The Gallo brothers addressed this problem with the purchase in 1942 of 2,000 acres of land in Livingston, California. Starting in 1945, they pursued an ambitious research and experimentation program that covered all aspects of viticulture, from rootstocks to irrigation methods. Grapes grown on the Livingston land were transported to a special research winery in Modesto for further testing. When a particular variable was determined to be beneficial, it was introduced into day-to-day winery operations. Many of the experiments, such as an innovative pest control system, were well ahead of their time and had far-reaching beneficial effects on the entire industry. In 1958 a research laboratory went into operation. By 1993 the research staff of 20 included chemical engineers, microbiologists, and biochemists, and a total of 50 research papers had been submitted by the winery to the American Society of Enology and Viticulture. The company also maintained a technical library designed to keep researchers and growers abreast of the latest developments in their respective fields.

In 1957 the Gallo brothers built a customized glass plant in Modesto, a step in the process of vertical integration that would eventually encompass the Fairbanks Trucking Company, an intrastate transportation company established in 1961; and Midcal Aluminum, an aluminum bottle cap and foil manufacturing plant founded the same year. In 1957 the company introduced Thunderbird, a citrus-flavored fortified wine that reflected consumer tastes of the period. Over the years, the brand began to sell particularly well in depressed neighborhoods because of its high alcohol content and low price. Although Thunderbird was undoubtedly one of Gallo's early marketing successes, it also contributed to the company's down-market image. By 1989, in the face of public concern over alcoholism and internal family pressure, Gallo had asked distributors not to sell its flavored fortified wines to retailers in low-income neighborhoods.

Consumption of table wine in the United States increased more than sixfold between 1960 and 1980, corresponding to a period of great growth for the Gallo company. Production techniques were developed to provide high quality at lower cost than the competition. Wine industry experts unanimously praised Gallo's achievement in "bringing new wine drinkers to the fold" with their clean, consistent, and competitively priced product. As early as 1972 the wine critic of the *Los Angeles Times* identified Gallo Hearty Burgundy, priced at $1.25 a bottle, as "the best wine value in the country today." This wine was credited with influencing Americans to buy more California jug wines.

In 1965 Julio Gallo established a Grower Relations staff of wine professionals who continued to work with growers, recommending new technologies and practices developed largely at Gallo's research facility. Among the

KEY DATES

1933: Prohibition is repealed; brothers Ernest and Julio Gallo establish a winery in Modesto, California.

1940: The first Gallo-labeled wine is introduced.

1942: The Gallo brothers buy 2,000 acres of land in Livingston, California.

1945: An ambitious research and experimentation program begins that covers all aspects of viticulture, from rootstocks to irrigation methods.

1957: A customized glass plant in Modesto is built; the company introduces Thunderbird, a citrus-flavored fortified wine.

1976: The Federal Trade Commission charges Gallo with unfair competition; the winery signs a consent agreement restricting its ability to control its wholesalers.

1981: A premium Chardonnay is launched.

1985: The Bartles & Jaymes wine cooler is launched.

1995: Turning Leaf makes its debut.

2002: The company acquires the Louis M. Martini Winery and Mirassou Vineyards.

2004: Bridlewood Estate Winery is purchased.

2005: The company buys Barefoot Cellars.

2007: William Hill Estate is acquired; founder Ernest Gallo dies at the age of 97.

2008: E. & J. Gallo celebrates its 75th anniversary.

most important developments of this period was a quality drive initiated by the company with California growers in 1967. In exchange for replacing existing grapes with grape varieties of Gallo's choice, growers were offered ten- to 15-year contracts guaranteeing them a fair price for their harvest. More than 100 growers signed contracts, thus ensuring the reemergence of such classic grapes as Chardonnay, Cabernet Sauvignon, and Sauvignon Blanc. As a result of the increasing supply of true wine grapes, Gallo was able to discontinue use of the inferior Thompson seedless grape in 1972.

In 1976 the Federal Trade Commission charged Gallo with unfair competition, and the winery signed a consent agreement restricting its ability to control its wholesalers. The consent order was designed to prevent Gallo from vertically integrating to a point such that competitors would be unable to distribute their products effectively. In September 1982, Gallo successfully filed a petition to have the order set aside, arguing that "dramatic changes in the wine industry," specifically the entry of conglomerates such as Coca-Cola and Seagrams, had rendered the terms of the original order obsolete.

MOVE INTO PREMIUM WINES

During the 1980s Gallo made a strong move into the premium wine market. In 1981 a premium Chardonnay was launched, to be followed one year later with a vintage-dated Cabernet from 1978. In late 1988, having dropped some of its original cork-finished varietals, Gallo introduced others, such as a successful new "blush" category. A vintage year was added across the Wine Cellars label, a trend the winery had resisted for many years. Given the company's production, marketing, and distribution expertise, no one in the industry was surprised when Gallo quickly took a leading role in the premium wine market.

At the same time, Gallo was experiencing great success with the Bartles & Jaymes wine cooler, a beverage containing a mixture of wine, fruit juices, and carbonated water, and having less alcohol than table wine. The Bartles & Jaymes product was introduced in 1985 and within a year had become a market leader in a highly competitive and burgeoning segment. Many analysts attributed its success to an inspired ad campaign by Hal Riney and Partners, featuring a pair of eccentric characters named Frank Bartles and Ed Jaymes. The wine-cooler phenomenon was short-lived, however; by 1993 demand had plummeted and Gallo and Seagrams were the only wine-cooler producers left in the market. Advertising expenditure dropped accordingly. New introductions in the 1990s included the Eden Roc champagne brand, priced somewhat higher than the company's market leader, André champagne.

In April 1986 Ernest and Julio filed suit against their younger brother Joseph, charging him with trademark infringement. Joseph had begun to market cheese under the Gallo name. The case was important because it brought into question the right of an individual to use a personal name that had already been registered as a trademark by someone else. Several months later, Joseph filed a countersuit, claiming that he had been deprived of his rightful one-third share of their parents' winery, in effect a substantial share in the E. & J. Gallo Winery itself. Ernest and Julio's defense rested on the assertion that their winery was completely self-funded and had nothing to do with their parents' estate. In September 1988 Joseph's counterclaim was dismissed. In June 1989 a U.S. district court judge settled the trademark infringement case in favor of the plaintiffs, and Joseph Gallo was given 30 days to stop using the Gallo name on his cheese.

SECOND GALLO GENERATION TAKES OVER

Ernest and Julio Gallo headed the winery they founded into their 80s. By the early 1990s the winery's leadership finally passed on to the second generation. Julio died in 1993 at the age of 83 from a broken neck he suffered when he overturned his jeep on a family ranch. Ernest, stricken by the loss, soon thereafter gave up day-to-day management, remaining involved only in long-range planning as Gallo chairman. Gallo was thereupon run by four copresidents: David Gallo, eldest son of Ernest, in charge of domestic marketing and advertising; Joe Gallo, also a son of Ernest, head of domestic and international sales; Bob Gallo, son of Julio, head of vineyards and winemaking; and Jim Coleman, Julio's son-in-law, responsible for warehouses and bottling plants. David died in March 1997 of a heart attack, leaving Joe Gallo fully in charge of sales. According to an article in the *Los Angeles Times Magazine,* 15 of Ernest's and Julio's 20 grandchildren were employed by the winery in 1997, making it likely that Gallo family members would remain in leadership positions for years to come.

In the 1990s consumers continued to gravitate toward more expensive wines, and Gallo sought new ways to capture the midpriced and premium categories. Despite the winery's efforts to escape its longstanding image, Gallo was still perceived as a low-end brand. To counter this, the Gallo winery began producing varietal wines under new brand names, with the Gallo name appearing nowhere on the label. In 1995 Turning Leaf made its debut, with Gossamer Bay debuting the following year. Gallo positioned both of these brands in the $5 to $10 per bottle range, the midpriced area typical for supermarket-sold wine. By the fall of 1996 Turning Leaf had become one of the top 12 varietal wines sold in supermarkets.

Both Turning Leaf and Gossamer Bay were made at the Modesto winery; the inclusion of "Made in Modesto" on their labels was the only clue to their Gallo parentage. Nevertheless, Gallo was able to achieve an even greater distancing with wines produced in California's Sonoma County, where Gallo had been buying up vineyards and had a winery in Healdsburg. Varietal wine vinted and bottled by Gallo in Sonoma County was sold under a number of different brands, including Indigo Hills, Rancho Zabaco, Anapamu, Marcellina, and Northern Sonoma, and labeled "Made in Healdsburg." Some varieties sold for as much as $40 a bottle, placing them well into the premium category.

Gallo wines finally began to receive serious attention from wine critics.

The move upmarket was not without its difficulties. Gallo was the object of a much-publicized lawsuit filed in April 1996 by Kendall-Jackson Winery Ltd., on behalf of their Vintner's Reserve, the number one Chardonnay in the United States. Kendall-Jackson contended that Gallo had copied the packaging of Vintner's Reserve for that of the Turning Leaf line of Chardonnay and other varietals. Gallo prevailed in federal court in 1997 as well as in a federal court of appeals in 1998.

At the turn of the 21st century, the Gallo winery was well-positioned from the low to high ends of the wine market. Even under the direction of the second generation of Gallo family leadership, the winery was clearly following the direction of its founders—Ernest Gallo once said, "We don't want most of the business. We want it all."

SUCCESS IN THE NEW MILLENNIUM

The Gallo winery spent the early years of the new millennium focusing on growth. The $50 billion U.S. wine industry as a whole was experiencing a wave of consolidation brought on by intense competition during this period. Gallo saw a unique opportunity for expansion as smaller vineyards sought larger partners. Its first significant purchases of the decade were made in 2002 when the company added the Louis M. Martini Winery and Mirassou Vineyards to its holdings. Two years later, it acquired the Bridlewood Estate Winery.

Meanwhile, competitor Constellation Brands Inc., based in New York, was also growing at a rapid pace. Through its 2003 acquisition of Australia's BRL Hardy and the 2004 purchase of Robert Mondavi Inc., Constellation knocked Gallo from its number one position as the world's largest winery. Gallo, however, remained the largest family-owned winery.

Undeterred, Gallo continued to make strategic purchases. During 2005 the company bought Barefoot Cellars from owner Grape Links Inc. Two years later, the William Hill Estate winery, which made Chardonnay and Cabernet Sauvignon, was acquired. Along with its acquisition strategy, Gallo also began focusing on importing international wines from Argentina, Australia, France, Germany, Italy, New Zealand, Spain, and South Africa. It launched Bella Sera, a line of Italian wines, in 2001. Red Bicyclette, a French line, made its debut in 2004. Plans for the future included an expansion into hard liquor, including tequila, and expanding into China and Russia.

COFOUNDER AND WINERY HONORED

Cofounder Ernest Gallo died on March 6, 2007. The U.S. Congress passed a resolution in April of that year honoring Gallo's life and accomplishments. California Senator Barbara Boxer's comments regarding Gallo were published in an April 2007 *US Fed News* report: "Ernest was an American success story and an embodiment of the entrepreneurial spirit that makes this country so great," the senator claimed. "He founded one of the most successful wineries in the world and helped put California wines on the map. The Gallo Family business has done so much for the State's economy. Ernest will be missed—but his legacy lives on." Indeed, with Joe Gallo, Bob Gallo, and Jim Coleman remaining at the helm, E. & J. Gallo Winery celebrated its 75th anniversary as a family-owned company in 2008.

Gallo marked its anniversary with its first television campaign in ten years, which showcased its affordable Gallo Family Vineyards line. With the U.S. economy in a downward spiral, many consumers of wine had turned to purchasing bottles that cost less than $10 to consume at home. This bode well for Gallo, whose products fit this niche. The company sold over 70 million cases during 2007, and sales remained strong into 2008. That year the company was named "California Winery of the Year" by industry analyst Jon Fredrikson at the Unified Wine & Grape Symposium held in Sacramento. The award was based on overall sales growth in U.S. retail outlets.

Joe Gallo summed up his company's success over the years in a September 2008 *Modesto Bee* interview. "We had certain principles that we've always been guided by. One is to stay independent and be master of our own destiny. Run the company conservatively. Don't take on too much risk. Invest in innovation … and be very attuned to what the customer wants." With this strategy firmly in place, E. & J. Gallo Winery would no doubt remain securely ensconced as the largest family-owned winery in the world in the years to come.

Moya Verzhbinsky
Updated, David E. Salamie; Christina M. Stansell

PRINCIPAL COMPETITORS

Constellation Wines U.S. Inc.; Foster's Americas; Kendall-Jackson Wine Estates Ltd.

FURTHER READING

"American Wine Comes of Age," *Time*, November 27, 1972.

Boone, Virginie, "E&J Gallo Goes Global," *Santa Rosa (Calif.) Press Democrat*, March 23, 2005.

———, "The Face of Gallo," *Santa Rosa (Calif.) Press Democrat*, June 18, 2008.

Fierman, Jaclyn, "How Gallo Crushes the Competition," *Fortune*, September 1, 1986.

Fisher, Lawrence M., "The Gallos Go for the Gold," *New York Times*, November 22, 1992.

Fujii, Reed, "Wine Sales Slow, but Rebound Expected," *Ventura County Star*, April 25, 2009.

Gallo, Ernest, and Julio Gallo, with Bruce B. Henderson, *Ernest and Julio: Our Story*, New York: Times Books, 1994, 358 p.

Hamilton, Joan O'C., "Grapes of Wrath," *Business Week*, April 15, 1996, p. 50.

Hawkes, Ellen, *Blood and Wine: The Unauthorized Story of the Gallo Wine Empire*, New York: Simon & Schuster, 1993, 464 p.

Himelstein, Linda, "This Merlot's for You," *Business Week*, September 20, 2002.

Holland, John, "Gallo Named Winery of the Year," *Ventura County Star*, February 27, 2009.

King, Ralph T., Jr., "Grapes of Wrath: Kendall-Jackson Sues Gallo Winery in a Battle over a Bottle," *Wall Street Journal*, April 5, 1996, p. B1.

Laube, James, "Gallo Brothers' Growing Stake in Sonoma," *Wine Spectator*, May 31, 1991.

Priai, Frank J., "From the Top of the Barrel: Gallo Powers Its Way into the Premium Wine Market," *New York Times*, September 4, 1997, pp. D1, D4.

———, "Passing the Jug," *New York Times Magazine*, November 15, 1992.

Sbranti, J. N., "It Started in Red Jug Wine; Now Gallo Sees a Future in China and Tequila," *Modesto Bee*, September 21, 2008.

"Senate Passes Resolution to Honor Life of Ernest Gallo," *US Fed News*, April 19, 2007.

Shanken, Marvin R., "Gallo's Dramatic Shift to Fine Varietals," *Wine Spectator*, September 15, 1991.

Stavro, Barry, "A New Vintage Gallo," *Los Angeles Times Magazine*, March 2, 1997, pp. 12–17, 28.

Stecklow, Steve, "Gallo Woos French, but Don't Expect Bordeaux by the Jug," *Wall Street Journal*, March 26, 1999, pp. A1, A14.

Steinriede, Kent, "New Gallo Brands Aim High," *Beverage Industry*, December 1998, p. 19.

———, "Technology Meets Tradition," *Beverage Industry*, December 1998, p. 22.

"Surprising Moves by Gallo," *Wines & Vines*, November 1, 2002.

Van Der Meer, Ben, "Gallo Adds Premium Brand to Mix," *Modesto Bee*, July 31, 2007.

"Who Owns What," *Wines & Vines*, June 1, 2004.

EBX Investimentos

Praia do Flamengo 154
Rio de Janeiro, 22210-903
Brazil
Telephone: (55 21) 2555-5500
Fax: (55 21) 2555-5550
Web site: http://www.ebx.com.br

Private Company
Founded: 1983
NAICS: 551112 Offices of Other Holding Companies

■ ■ ■

EBX Investimentos is the holding company for Eike Fuhrken Batista, Brazil's wealthiest individual. The company's most important holdings are majority stakes in four public corporations that are holding companies themselves: MMX Mineração e Metálicos S.A. (minerals and mining), OGX Petróleo e Gás Participações S.A. (oil and natural gas); MPX Energia S.A. (electrical energy generation); and LLX Logística S.A. (transport). Batista is chairman of all these companies as well as of EBX. They form a synergy of infrastructure designed to support one another's activities and reduce dependence on companies outside the group.

EBX's wealth comes principally from the sale of stock in these enterprises, which in 2008 were basically start ups with little in operational revenues. Other companies in what is commonly called Grupo EBX are engaged in activities such as forestry, real estate, and entertainment. Batista calls the "X" at the end of all the companies that he controls the symbol for the potential to generate and multiply businesses; the "EB" in EBX stands for his initials.

HITTING PAY DIRT

Eike Fuhrken Batista was born into Brazil's elite as one of the seven children of Eliezer Batista da Silva, the nation's minister of mining and power, and later, president of Companhia Vale do Rio Doce (CVRD), the world's leading producer of iron ore. Eike's mother was German, and he grew up mostly in Germany and Belgium, where the family lived after his father was ousted from his cabinet post by the senior military officers who overthrew the Brazilian government in 1964. Exile left the family in reduced circumstances, and Eike sold insurance policies door-to-door while attending college.

After receiving a degree in metallurgical engineering in Germany, the younger Batista returned to Brazil in 1979 or 1980, intent on making a fortune. He started out by exporting food products such as tomatoes and corned beef but soon, tipped off by an acquaintance identified only as Adolfo, cast his eye on a far more lucrative commodity—gold. Hundreds of thousands of hardscrabble prospectors, armed with only a pan, pick, and shovel, were combing the Amazon jungle for alluvial deposits at a time when double-digit inflation had raised the price of the metal on world markets to as high as $900 an ounce.

Batista raised a grubstake of $500,000 from several Rio de Janeiro jewelers and gave it to Adolfo, who returned a few days later with over 60 pounds of gold dust. After eight more trips over two months, Adolfo disappeared, so Batista entered the jungle himself with another borrowed $500,000. Overcoming all hazards, including a miner who shot him in the back, he established a network of village chiefs who would do the buying for him and accumulated $5 million in profit by the end of 1980.

Not content with this bonanza, Batista next began buying thousands of acres of properties far up the Amazon basin in order to establish a mechanized gold mining operation. He and his partners ran through almost $6 million before hitting pay dirt. A second operation also became productive. In 1982 the British-based RTZ Corporation plc made Batista its local partner in a gold mine in central Brazil.

GOLD TYCOON

By 1983, when the EBX holding company was established to oversee the various operations, Batista owned the mining rights to 10 million hectares (almost 25 million acres) in Brazil. His track record and his father's connections enabled him to find backing from a group of Canadian investment bankers and entrepreneurs who took control of a public company named Treasure Valley Explorations Ltd. (TVX). These Canadians in turn pulled in bankers and portfolio managers who made more money available after junkets to Brazil that included visits to Rio de Janeiro's notorious sex clubs.

TVX spent $12 million before finding any gold, but in 1985 it secured more funds by merging with another Canadian firm to establish Consolidated TVX Mining Corporation. Batista, the largest shareholder, became its chairman and chief executive officer in 1986. The following year he personally purchased a Chilean gold mining company for $30 million and paid another $30 million to settle claims, later selling it to Consolidated TVX and Placer Dome Inc., another Canadian corporation. The extraction of gold and silver deposits at this La Coipa open pit mine began in 1991.

TVX Gold Inc. was established in 1991 from the $650 million merger of Inco Gold Inc., a subsidiary of

Inco Limited, with Consolidated TVX. Inco took 62 percent of the shares and Batista, who had only 13 percent, soon chafed at being subject to his partner's more conservative ways. A group of investors bought Inco's holding for $385 million in 1993.

Batista, then freed from Inco's suffocating embrace, vowed to double TVX's gold production within three years. In 1995 the company purchased a Greek property with large reserves of gold and silver for $46 million. However, the prophetically named Kassandra mine proved ill fated and consumed at least $200 million without producing any precious metal as TVX fought in vain to overcome violent protests by villagers and secure a construction permit from the government. TVX also lost $30 million on a Siberian mining venture that fell victim to the Russian mafia.

By this time Batista had worn out his welcome in Canada, where, according to a *Canadian Business* article by Paul Kaihla, his path was "strewn with recently burned TVX shareholders, fired executives, acid relations with former partners ... and, according to Batista himself, at least one corpse" (the miner who shot him and was in turn killed by Batista's bodyguards). By 2001 he had sold his shares for some $800 million.

SOUTH AMERICAN VENTURES

When not wooing North American investors, Batista was leading a colorful life in Rio de Janeiro. He won the powerboat offshore world championship on his own 48-foot catamaran in 1990 and married the city's Carnival queen, Luma de Oliveira, an actress, model, and samba school drum majorette (they later separated). Batista used her celebrity to create a franchised product line of 160 shampoos, lotions, perfumes, and cosmetics sold door to door and on the Internet, but the enterprise failed to thrive and was purchased cheaply by a Portuguese group in 2002.

Batista's other Brazilian initiatives also did poorly in the 1990s. EBX Express, a delivery service, became the leader in its field but could not compete with the post office and went bankrupt in three years. JBX was a firm that was manufacturing Jeeps furnished with a French army engine under license and was selling them to the Brazilian army. This undertaking was undercut by cheaper foreign rivals despite success in international Jeep rallies and was closed down in 2002, after ten years. Batista also lost $10 million selling Labatt's beer to service stations in Brazil's major cities.

In all, Batista lost about $160 million on these ventures. However, he would soon become a billionaire many times over by focusing on Brazilian infrastructure. AMX, a holding company, included a firm named Geo-

KEY DATES

■

1983: Eike Batista founds EBX as holding company for his operations.

1986: Batista becomes chairman and chief executive of TVX, a mining enterprise.

2001: Batista sells his shares in TVX for about $800 million.

2006: EBX takes public MMX, a company proposing to extract iron ore in Brazil.

2007: EBX collects over $1 billion in an initial public offering (IPO) of MPX shares.

2008: LLX raises about $650 million in its IPO; OGX brings in about $3.6 billion, the most ever to date for a Brazilian IPO.

2009: Batista's net worth is estimated at $7.5 billion.

plan that was drawing water from underground aquifers below most of Brazil's major cities and stood to benefit from the impending privatization of the nation's facilities for treating and distributing water and disposing of sewage. Geoplan was sold to a unit of Enron Corporation in 2001, but it set the standard for EBX's future activities.

The next big thing for Batista, opening an iron ore mine and building a steel mill in Bolivia, turned out to resemble the Kassandra disaster. This venture lasted only nine months. After investing $65 million, Batista was expelled in 2006 by the country's left wing president, Evo Morales, and the business was nationalized. This left him unfazed, however. "Failure doesn't bother him," a friend told Samantha Lima for an article in the Brazilian business magazine *Exame*. "But he can't tolerate sharing power."

IRON ORE SUCCESS

Batista's next venture was much more successful. Once again engaging in mining, he founded MMX Mineração e Metálicos S.A. in December 2005 to extract iron ore from properties in three states in Brazil. Of the first 100 executives contracted by the firm, 90 came from CVRD, the giant producer in this business segment. Batista's father, once CVRD's chief executive, became chairman of MMX.

Even before any ore had been taken out of the ground, MMX went public, collecting BRL 1.1 billion ($460 million) in July 2006 for the 32 percent of the

shares sold on the São Paulo stock exchange. Batista soon sold some $240 million more of shares in the company, which had a market value of $5.2 billion in October 2007; by the end of the year MMX shares had more than tripled in a year and a half since the originally offering. By mid-2008 this had grown even further, to $10.5 billion.

In 2007, the U.S. company Cleveland Cliffs Inc. purchased 30 percent of the MMX complex in the state of Amapá, including a pig iron plant, for $133 million. Later in the year, Anglo American plc purchased 49 percent of the complex in the states of Minas Gerais and Rio de Janeiro, including a pellet plant, slurry pipeline, and port, for $1.15 billion. MMX used some of this money to buy AVG Mineração for $224 million. This company was mining iron ore in Minas Gerais.

In January 2008 Batista sold Anglo American the remaining 51 percent of the Minas-Rio complex and the 70 percent of the Amapá project not sold to Cleveland Cliffs for $5.5 billion. This price reflected the rise of commodity prices over the last few years, in great part because of the rise in Chinese demand for building materials. Even so, it seemed truly amazing since MMX had not yet extracted a single ounce of iron ore. As the majority stockholder, about $3.3 billion of this sum went directly into Batista's pocket. This raised his net worth to $6.6 billion, making him the third richest individual in Brazil, according to *Forbes*. Other MMX executives shared in the bonanza; 27 of them shared $440 million, with the director general receiving 10 percent of that sum.

The sale left MMX considerably stripped down in size and scope. Limited production of iron ore began in 2008 from two mines in the state of Mato Grosso. The company also held three mines in southeastern Brazil and was planning production of cast iron and semifinished products.

BRINGING IN BILLIONS

In December 2007 Batista was back at the stock exchange to sell shares of MPX Energia S.A. Founded in 1998 as MPX Soluçãos de Energia, the company, in partnership with another firm, had a diesel-powered electricity generating plant in Brazil and licenses to build and operate several coal-fired plants in Brazil and one in Chile. It also owned a Brazilian coal mine and was prospecting for coal deposits in Colombia. A major investor was Energias do Brasil, controlled by the Portuguese company EDP. MPX Energia brought in at least $1.2 billion from the public for 35 percent of the shares.

LLX Logística S.A., established in 2006, was planning to build two ports in Brazil—one of them for MMX—and one in Chile, as well as the MMX slurry pipeline. LLX already had as a major investor the Ontario Teachers' Pension Plan, which bought 15 percent of its shares for $185 million. Batista's 51 percent holding was estimated at $1 billion in value in January 2008. Six months later, LLX made an initial public offering (IPO) of stock on the São Paulo exchange that collected about BRL 1.2 billion (about $650 million).

In January 2009 LLX won a BRL 1.32 billion ($561 million) loan from the Brazilian development bank BNDES to develop a port in the state of Rio de Janeiro (Porto do Açu), and two months later the bank paid BRL 150 million (about $80 million) for 12 percent of the stock. LLX was also building Porto Sudeste near Itaguaí, Rio de Janeiro, which was part of MMX's system to bring to market iron ore and products from southeastern Brazil.

Even before these three initial public offerings of stock, Batista had founded another company, OGX Petróleo e Gás Participações S.A., with an initial investment of $1.3 billion—at least $300 million from Batista and the rest raised from investors such as the Ontario Teachers' Pension Fund. This company's goal was to obtain licenses to explore and drill for oil off the Brazilian coast and in Bolivia, Ecuador, and Angola. Staffed by executives recruited from state-owned Petróleo Brasileiro S.A. (Petrobras), Brazil's giant oil company, OGX had as its mission to find nine billion barrels of petroleum by the end of 2012.

In December 2007 OGX paid BRL 1.57 billion (about $800 million) for drilling rights to 21 offshore oilfields. It was then Brazil's largest private sector oil and gas company in terms of its offshore exploration area. The company's value was estimated at over $9 billion at the end of 2007, when Batista held 75 percent of the stock, having sold the remainder for about $1 billion. OGX's initial public offering of stock in June 2008 was oversubscribed by nearly tenfold and raised BRL 6.7 billion ($3.6 billion)—the most ever in Brazil from an IPO to that time—even though the company still had only a skeleton staff and had not yet begun drilling for oil.

CHALLENGES AND ASPIRATIONS

By this time Batista's net worth was estimated to be as high as $20 billion. His wealth was soon to take a hit from the world economic crisis, but even before then shares of Grupo EBX's public companies dropped 10 percent on the news in July 2008 that federal police had raided his headquarters by Rio de Janeiro's Guanabara Bay, and his mansion, which featured a half-million-dollar silver Mercedes-Benz in the living room. The police said they had evidence of possible fraud with regard to MMX's 20-year concession to operate a railway line connecting iron ore mines with the port of Santana, Amapá. They said they were also investigating whether EBX companies had evaded taxes on gold produced in Amapá. Next, Anglo American said it was suspending its payment for the purchased MMX assets, and MMX was fined millions for using illegal fuel supplies in its mills.

Batista immediately returned from a vacation in the United States and the next day, flanked by his directors and some counselors, he held the first of three teleconferences, all in English, to calm investors and restore the image of his group. He also enlisted the support of prominent politicians, especially President Luiz Ignácio Lula da Silva, who described the raid as an abuse of authority. The situation soon eased.

In the following months EBX's market value dropped by half, but share prices were recovering early in 2009. Batista voiced confidence that he could tap non-invested cash in the United States and Japan and said he was ready to shop for assets himself. Batista was rated the richest person in Brazil in March 2009 by *Forbes,* which estimated his wealth at $7.5 billion.

Other EBX companies included BFX, a forestry enterprise by means of which Batista hoped to produce alcohol from cellulose; toward this end, ten million seedlings were planted in west-central Brazil. Grupo EBX also remained active in the field of water resources. It was searching for water in arid northern Chile for use in mines such as La Coipa. It was also engaged in water treatment for Brazilian mining and energy enterprises such as Petrobras and CVRD.

Other EBX assets in 2009 included the 630-room Hotel Glória, located behind the marina where the group's luxury tourist ship, *Pink Fleet,* was anchored, and Mr. Lam, a Chinese restaurant. Other holdings included MDX Day Hospital, a Rio medical center, and La Cañada de Pilar, a residential condominium in Argentina. Batista was planning to invest $200 million into movies, perhaps creating what he called "Riollywood," and to establish a line of Japanese restaurants named for chef Nobu Matsuhisa. One of Batista's goals was to make his beloved Rio de Janeiro the envy of its great rival, São Paulo, the largest city in South America and the business and financial capital of Brazil. His personal goal was to be the richest man in the world in five years. Whether he would achieve these goals remained to be seen.

Robert Halasz

PRINCIPAL SUBSIDIARIES

LLX Logística S.A.; MMX Mineração e Metálicos S.A.; MPX Energia S.A.; OGX Petróleo e Gás Participações S.A.

FURTHER READING

Gaspar, Malu, "Reação ao bombardeio," *Exame,* August 13, 2008, pp. 60–62.

————, "O vendedor de sonhos," *Exame,* October 24, 2007, pp. 80–82.

Hayward, Chloe, "Batista Tries to Maintain His X Factor," *Euromoney,* March 2009, pp. 60–62.

Kaihla, Paul, "Mayhem Man," *Canadian Business,* April 9, 1999, pp. 36–37, 39–46, 48, 50, 57.

Lima, Samantha, "O nanico que sonha grande," *Exame,* December 6, 2006, pp. 50–51.

Lima, Samantha, and Carolina Meyer, "Sou o homem mais rico do Brasil," *Exame,* January 30, 2008, pp. 88–93.

Maher, Kris, "Anglo American May Buy Brazil Projects," *Wall Street Journal,* January 18, 2008, p. A9.

McDougall, Bruce, "Inco Meets Indiana Jones," *Canadian Business,* March 1991, pp. 70–73.

Regalado, Antonio, "Brazil Oil IPO Lures Investors," *Wall Street Journal,* June 12, 2008, pp. B1–B2.

————, "Brazil's Richest Man Attracts Federal Probe," *Wall Street Journal,* July 12, 2008, p. A6.

Shirai, Dan, "The X Factor," *LatinFinance,* June 2008, pp. 12–14.

Eclipsys Corporation

———■———

Three Ravinia Drive
Atlanta, Georgia 30346
U.S.A.
Telephone: (404) 847-5000
Toll Free: (800) 869-8300
Fax: (404) 847-5700
Web site: http://www.eclipsys.com

Public Company
Incorporated: 1995 as Integrated Healthcare Solutions
   Inc.
Employees: 2,800
Sales: $515.8 million (2008)
Stock Exchanges: NASDAQ
Ticker Symbol: ECLP
NAICS: 541512 Computer Systems Design Services

■ ■ ■

Headquartered in Atlanta, Georgia, Eclipsys Corporation provides hospitals and healthcare systems with information solutions that are used to manage a variety of functions. The company offers clinical solutions devoted to areas such as analytics, acute care, ambulatory care, critical care, emergency care, and medication management. It offers a variety of financial solutions, in areas such as decision support, enterprise registration and scheduling, and patient financials. At the departmental level, Eclipsys markets tools devoted to health information management, medical imaging, surgery, and laboratory. The company also provides out-

sourcing solutions, as well as consulting and education services.

FORMATIVE YEARS

Eclipsys was established in December 1995 as Integrated Healthcare Solutions Inc. Based in Delray Beach, Florida, the company was formed in order to commercialize a clinical information system named BICS, which had been developed internally at Brigham and Women's Hospital in Boston. BICS was comprised of 80 different software applications, and had been developed by approximately 30 programmers over the course of seven years.

In January 1997, Integrated Healthcare Solutions changed its name to Eclipsys Corporation when it acquired Alltel Healthcare Information Services Inc. from Atlanta-based Alltel Information Services. The $154 million deal included the TDS 7000 Series clinically oriented information system, which Little Rock, Arkansas-based Alltel Corporation had acquired in an $80 million deal with TDS Healthcare Systems in 1993. The TDS 7000 system had existed for approximately 20 years, and was in use by some 200 organizations.

Moving forward, the company revealed plans to integrate the two systems, and successfully met the challenge of merging older technology with newer technology. Following the Alltel merger, the organization included a mix of newer programmers, as well as information systems professionals who had worked in the healthcare industry for more than 20 years. Leading Eclipsys was President and CEO Harvey Wilson, who had cofounded a company named Shared Medical Systems Corporation in 1969.

Although Alltel had exited the healthcare information management field, the company maintained a presence on Eclipsys's board, and agreed to supply the company with technical support.

Eclipsys grew at a steady pace during the late 1990s. Midway through 1997, the company parted with $16.5 million to acquire SDK Computer Services Corp. In January 1998, Motorola Inc.'s Emtek HealthcareDivision was acquired in a deal valued at $11.7 million. Established in 1985, Tempe, Arizona-based Emtek developed point-of-care clinical information software that was used to capture information from patient-monitoring devices.

The following month, Eclipsys forged a strategic partnership with Seattle, Washington-based Health Systems Technologies Inc. that centered on the resale of the latter company's Trillium Managed Care System Products. In April, Eclipsys shelled out $5.6 million to acquire a 4.9 percent stake in the home healthcare software and service company Simione Central Holdings Inc.

It was around the same time that Eclipsys unveiled its Enterprise Master Person Index, a product that allowed healthcare providers to track and identify patients at different points throughout their organization, regardless of the software system being used.

A major development unfolded in June, when Eclipsys announced plans for an initial public offering (IPO) of its common stock. Trading under the symbol ECLP on the NASDAQ, the company completed its IPO on August 7, 1998; it sold 4.2 million shares at $15 per share.

Eclipsys rounded out 1998 with another acquisition. On December 31, the company snapped up the healthcare outcomes-enhancement software and services provider Transition Systems Inc. (TSI). TSI had just itself acquired the Santa Rosa, California-based healthcare software company HealthVISION.

EARLY DEVELOPMENTS

Following the acquisition of TSI, Eclipsys ranked as one of the healthcare industry's leading information technology companies. By this time its products were in place at roughly 1,300 healthcare provider organizations throughout the world, in locations such as Australia, North America, the United Kingdom, the Eastern Rim, and Western Europe.

Progress continued as the 1990s came to a close. In February 1999 Eclipsys acquired the enterprise resource planning software firm PowerCenter Systems Inc. in a deal worth $35 million. Specifically, PowerCenter offered applications for functions such as accounts payable, budgeting, general ledger, package tracking, human resources, materials management, and surgery scheduling.

A major leadership change also occurred in February when James E. Hall was promoted to president and chief operating officer. Harvey Wilson continued to lead the company as chairman and CEO.

More growth occurred during the early part of the year when Eclipsys acquired two of SunGard Data Systems's subsidiaries. In a cash deal worth $25 million, Med Data Systems Inc. and Intelus Corp. were both acquired in March. The acquisitions allowed Eclipsys to further enhance its Sunrise product suite.

Midway through the year, Eclipsys snapped up Atlanta, Georgia-based MSI Solutions Inc. for $53.6 million. The company also unloaded the Med Data business it had acquired from SunGard earlier in the year, selling it for $5 million.

Eclipsys ushered in the new millennium by making an unsolicited, $2 billion stock offer for Malvern, Pennsylvania-based Shared Medical Systems (SMS), which Eclipsys Chairman Harvey Wilson had helped to establish in 1969. SMS immediately rejected the offer.

Another potentially large deal emerged on March 30, when Eclipsys and Healthvision, a company it had formed in 1999 with VHA Inc., agreed to be acquired by the Santa Clara, California-based online medical supply company Neoforma.com in a stock deal worth approximately $2.1 billion. However, when the value of Neoforma.com's stock plummeted 70 percent, the deal was canceled.

Eclipsys had difficult times of its own during the early 2000s. Midway through 2002, the company's stock fell 45 percent following news of a projected second-quarter loss. The financial shortfall was attributed to several customers who failed to sign new contracts.

However, analysts were soon singing the company's praises as more hospitals and healthcare systems began

KEY DATES

■

1995: The company is established as Integrated Healthcare Solutions Inc.

1997: Integrated Healthcare Solutions changes its name to Eclipsys after acquiring Alltel Healthcare Information Services Inc.

1998: Eclipsys goes public and lists on the NAS-DAQ under the symbol ECLP.

2006: The International Association of Outsourcing Professionals names Eclipsys to its Global Outsourcing 100 list of the world's leading outsourcing service providers.

implementing software applications such as those offered by Eclipsys, which helped to reduce errors and costs. In 2003 the company forged sales agreements with hospitals connected to the likes of Cornell University, Johns Hopkins University, and Columbia University.

PRODUCT AND CUSTOMER GROWTH

A major accomplishment unfolded in early 2004, when Dallas, Texas-based Baylor Health Care System chose Eclipsys to design an electronic medical record system. The system was part of a major, $119 million information technology overhaul that spanned Baylor's 11 hospitals, 69 clinics, and numerous other locations.

It also was in early 2004 that Eclipsys made another acquisition, shelling out approximately $5 million to obtain CPM Resource Center Ltd. Later in the year, Eclipsys established a new partnership with the Johns Hopkins University School of Nursing to develop and test new information technology applications for use in nursing school curriculums. By serving as a test site, Johns Hopkins University was able to familiarize students with Eclipsys technology, which already was used in its hospital.

Eclipsys rounded out 2004 by finalizing its acquisition of the Montreal, Canada-based radiology information system company eSys Medical Inc. for $2.3 million. In addition to its Montreal headquarters, eSys also had offices in Toronto.

By late 2004 Paul L. Ruflin was serving as Eclipsys's president and CEO. The company's technology was used by approximately 1,500 healthcare facilities throughout the world.

The company continued to introduce new products and services in 2005. Examples included Pocket Sunrise 4.0 XA and Remote Access Services 4.0 XA, which allowed users to access the company's technology from more locations throughout the patient care environment. In addition, approximately 450 enhancements and new features were added to the latest version of Eclipsys's flagship product, Sunrise Clinical Manager 4.0.

In October 2005, another major leadership change occurred at Eclipsys. At that time, the company named R. Andrew Eckert as its president and CEO. Eugene V. Fife, who had been functioning as president and CEO on an interim basis, remained with the organization as its chairman. Eclipsys capped off the year with revenues of $383.3 million, an increase from $309.1 million in 2004.

AN INDUSTRY LEADER

By 2006, Eclipsys's operations had grown to include 15 offices nationwide. Early that year, the company announced plans to eliminate 5 percent of its workforce, or 100 employees, in an effort to reduce costs. In all, Eclipsys hoped to save between $10 million and $12 million per year as a result of the job reductions.

In addition to developing and marketing technology solutions, Eclipsys also was providing a variety of information technology services to organizations on an outsourced basis. These ranged from help desk and desktop services to the complete management of information technology operations. In early 2006 the company was recognized by the International Association of Outsourcing Professionals, which named Eclipsys to its Global Outsourcing 100 list of the world's leading outsourcing service providers.

Eclipsys continued to grow via acquisitions in 2006. Midway through the year, the company parted with $3.7 million in order to obtain the assets of Sysware Health Care Systems Inc., as well as its Mosum Technology (India) Private Ltd. operation. Eclipsys rounded out the year by acquiring Phoenix, Arizona-based Van Slyck & Associates Inc., a developer of staffing software for nursing managers, for $1.5 million.

By 2007 Eclipsys's computerized physician order entry system, which physicians and residents used to place orders, had become the most widely adopted solution of its kind in the healthcare industry. In April of that year, the company announced that New York University (NYU) Medical Center was using the technology at all three of its hospitals. Specifically, NYU activated the Eclipsys Sunrise Clinical Manager product, as well as Sunrise Emergency Care and Sunrise

Pharmacy modules. Collectively, some 5,000 users relied upon the technology to process about 95,000 transactions per day.

Eclipsys ended 2007 by selling its Clinical Practice Model Resource Center product to the Philadelphia-based medical reference publisher Elsevier Inc. in a cash deal valued at $25 million.

GROWING IN DIFFICULT TIMES

Growth continued in 2008. In April, Eclipsys acquired the St. Louis, Missouri-based financial decision support software company Enterprise Performance Systems Inc. (EPSi) in a $53 million deal. Two months later, the company forged an alliance with Yonkers, New York-based Emerging Health Information Technology to supply health information technology to hospitals and long-term care facilities in Connecticut, New York, and New Jersey.

In October, Eclipsys acquired the physician practice information solutions company MediNotes for approximately $45 million. The deal gave Eclipsys cost-effective, Web-based practice management and electronic medical records software that allowed doctors to better communicate with hospitals and healthcare systems.

Another sizable transaction took place in late December, when Eclipsys acquired the Farmington, Connecticut-based patient flow software company Premise Corporation for $38.5 million. Following the deal, which was completed in January 2009, Premise's products were renamed Sunrise Patient Flow. Eclipsys's new offerings helped hospitals use their existing emergency department and inpatient beds in the most efficient way. This was expected to benefit the company during the challenging economy during this time, as many hospital expansion projects had been put on hold.

Another new offering that held the potential to help hospitals make important decisions in difficult economic times was a new integrated strategic planning/budgeting solution that was introduced in March 2009. Sunrise EPSi's Strategic Product Budgeting module aided hospitals and healthcare systems in deciding whether to establish, maintain, or discontinue certain services.

By continuing to offer new products that met the needs of its customers, especially during challenging times, Eclipsys seemed to be positioned for continued growth during the second decade of the 21st century.

Paul R. Greenland

PRINCIPAL SUBSIDIARIES

Eclipsys (India) Private Ltd.; Eclipsys (Mauritius) Ltd.; Eclipsys Canada Corporation; Eclipsys Healthcare IT (Singapore) Pte. Ltd.; Eclipsys Holding 1 Corporation; Eclipsys International Corporation; Eclipsys LIS Holdings LLC; Eclipsys RIS Canada Inc.; Eclipsys Solutions Corporation; Eclipsys Technologies Corporation; Enterprise Performance Systems Inc.; HVC Holdings Canada Ltd.; HVision Inc.; Van Slyck & Associates Inc.

PRINCIPAL COMPETITORS

Cerner Corporation; GE Healthcare; McKesson Corporation.

FURTHER READING

Bazzoli, Fred, "Merging Two Systems into New Product Line," *Health Data Management,* May 1997.

"Eclipsys Appoints R. Andrew Eckert President and Chief Executive Officer," *PR Newswire,* October 20, 2005.

"Eclipsys Completes Acquisition of Premise, Adds Patient Flow Solutions to Enterprise Performance Management Solution Set," *Business Wire,* January 5, 2009.

"Eclipsys Corporation Completes Initial Public Offering," *PR Newswire,* August 12, 1998.

Hensley, Scott, "Neoforma.com in E-Commerce Megadeal," *Modern Healthcare,* April 3, 2000.

Morrissey, John, "Deal Spawns Eclipsys Information Systems," *Modern Healthcare,* February 3, 1997.

"New York University Medical Center Successfully Activates Eclipsys Sunrise Clinical Manager, One of the Industry's Largest Ever Big-Bang Activations," *PR Newswire,* April 11, 2007.

Egis Gyogyszergyar Nyrt

Kereszturi ut 30-38
Budapest, H-1106
Hungary
Telephone: (36 06 1) 265 5555
Fax: (36 06 1) 265 5529
Web site: http://www.egis.hu

Public Company
Incorporated: 1913 as Dr. Wander Gyógyszer-és Tápszer-
  gyár Rt.
Employees: 3,836
Sales: HUF 24.28 billion ($568.4 million) (2008)
Stock Exchanges: Budapest
Ticker Symbol: EGIS
NAICS: 325412 Pharmaceutical Preparation Manufac-
  turing; 424210 Drugs and Druggists' Sundries
  Merchant Wholesalers

■ ■ ■

Egis Gyogyszergyar Nyrt, or Egis Pharmaceuticals PLC, is Hungary's leading pharmaceuticals manufacturer and a leading pharmaceuticals player in the Central European region. The Budapest-based company is active in pharmaceuticals development and production and is a major producer of generic drugs. The company manufactures active ingredients and other raw materials used in pharmaceutical production, as well as finished products in tablet, capsule, injectable, and syrup form. The company's product portfolio includes more than 44 active ingredients covering a broad spectrum of diseases and medical conditions. Egis also has a strong product pipeline of drugs under development. The company operates three production facilities in Hungary, as well as a fourth in Russia operated in partnership with France's Servier.

Egis also boasts an extensive distribution network, with subsidiaries in Poland, the Czech Republic, Slovakia, Bulgaria, Romania, Ukraine, Latvia, Lithuania, Azerbaijan, Kazakhstan, Armenia, Turkey, Uzbekistan, and, farther abroad, in Vietnam. Hungary represents 34.5 percent of the group's annual revenues, which reached HUF 24.28 billion ($568.4 million) in 2008. The European Union, particularly Germany, the United Kingdom, and France, adds another 31.5 percent to group sales, while other European markets, including the Commonwealth of Independent States (CIS), adds 30 percent. The company also markets its generic drugs in the United States and Japan. Egis is listed on the Budapest Stock Exchange; Servier, through its ATP subsidiary, has been the majority shareholder, with a 51 percent stake, since 1995. Egis is led by CEO Agnes Gal.

SWISS ORIGINS

Egis traces its operations back to the founding of a laboratory in Bern, Switzerland, by Georg Wander and his associate Albert Lohner in 1865. Wander's research interests focused on nutrition, particularly on the nutritional imbalance of people's diets at the time. The existence of vitamins had not yet been established and the understanding of the role of minerals was only in its beginning stages. Nonetheless, Wander recognized that certain foods offered important nutritional advantages.

KEY DATES

◼

1913: A subsidiary of Switzerland's Dr. Alfred Wander AG is formed in Hungary in order to market that company's nutritional supplements, including Ovomaltine.

1937: The company's research and development efforts result in the launch of Ronin, an antibiotic.

1950: The company is merged with six other companies to form EGYT (United Pharmaceutical and Food Preparations Company).

1967: The company launches its first in-house product since the war, a vasodilator used for circulatory disorders.

1985: EGYT changes its name to Egis Pharmaceuticals Company.

1994: Egis is privatized and listed on the Budapest Stock Exchange.

1995: Servier, through its subsidiary ATP, gains majority control of Egis.

2002: Egis joins consortium to acquire control of Hungaropharma.

2007: Egis acquires control of Serdix, which opens a packaging facility in Russia.

Wander developed a number of nutritional supplements through the end of the nineteenth century. From the start, Wander began working with barley malt, which had been used as a natural remedy for many centuries. Wander began seeking ways to combine malt with other ingredients, in order to provide a broad spectrum of nutrients. Wander had also developed the idea that by combining ingredients, the nutrient potential of the individual components might be reinforced.

By the end of the century, Wander's malt products were a mainstay in many Swiss homes. However, it was under Wander's son Albert, who took over the company after his father's death in 1897, that the company's true success began. Albert Wander continued to refine his father's formulations by seeking new combinations of malt and other ingredients. By 1904, Wander had hit upon a method of combining dried egg powder with barley malt extract, which could then be mixed with milk. The main ingredients gave the beverage its name: Ovomaltine. The addition of cocoa provided additional flavor.

Ovomaltine (which would later be known as Ovaltine in English-speaking markets) proved a swift success in Switzerland, and by 1906 the company had launched its first exports, to the United Kingdom and Italy. In 1907, Wander incorporated the company as Dr. Albert Wander AG. By 1913, the success of the drink, particularly in the United Kingdom, led Wander to open its first foreign factory, in London. That year also marked Wander's arrival into the Hungarian market, then still part of the Austro-Hungarian Empire. In 1913, Wander opened a new company in Budapest, called Dr. Wander Gyógyszer- és Tápszergyár Rt. The Hungarian subsidiary launched its own manufacturing operations for Wander's line of nutrients and supplements.

LABORATORY SUCCESSES

The outbreak of World War I, the collapse of the Austro-Hungarian Empire and the subsequent creation of an independent Hungarian state put a temporary hold on Wander's Hungarian subsidiary. In the 1920s, however, the company successfully brought Ovomaltine to the Hungarian market. At the same time, it began importing the active ingredients for Ovomaltine and other products so that it might begin producing finished nutritional and pharmaceutical products.

In fact, the Hungarian subsidiary developed its own strong research and development operations. This resulted in the launch of its own product, Hordenzym, a nutritional supplement that was considered a major breakthrough in infant health at the time. In the early 1930s, the Hungarian laboratory also became the first to isolate the chelidonin alkaloid, used as an antispasmodic. The company had also broadened its product range, adding the production of cosmetics and cleaning products starting in 1929. Through the decade, the company continued to build its research and development capacity. This led to a new breakthrough in 1937, when the company launched a new product, Ronin, the first heterocyclic sulfonamide. This antibiotic was used especially for skin infections.

World War II represented a new disruption to the company's operations. Following the war, as Hungary fell within the Communist bloc, the company, like the rest of the country's pharmaceuticals sector, became nationalized. In 1950, the Wander company was merged with six other small Hungarian pharmaceutical companies to form Egyesult Gyogyszer- es Tapszergyar (United Pharmaceutical and Food Preparations Company, or EGYT).

Under government control, EGYT grew into one of Hungary's largest pharmaceutical producers. The company's initial focus, in 1955, was on the production of generic drugs, as well as drugs produced under license. The company rapidly built up a large portfolio of medicines and by the mid-1960s included more than 100 products.

RESEARCH AND DEVELOPMENT

EGYT also sought to continue its earlier heritage of research and development work. This effort led to the launch of the company's first in-house product since the war, bencyclane fumarate. Introduced in 1967, the company marketed this drug, a vasodilator used for circulatory disorders, under the name Halidor. EGYT developed a number of other active ingredients through the 1970s and 1980s. Among the company's areas of special interest were central nervous system therapy, and the respiratory and cardiovascular fields. Through the 1980s, EGYT also maintained its original product line of nutritional supplements, including infant foods. In 1970, this division was expanded with the construction of a new factory in Körment, near the Austrian border.

Branded generics remained EGYT's main business, however. In the 1980s, the company emerged as a major exporter of generic drugs, particularly to the other members of the Soviet bloc. During this time, the company's leading product was Tensiomin, a reproduction of Bristol-Myers Squibb's Capoten. An ACE inhibitor used for the treatment of hypertension, Tensiomin became EGYT's flagship product. Tensiomin continued to account for some 20 percent of the group's total pharmaceutical sales into the mid-1990s.

In order to remain competitive, the company built its own galenic formulation facility in the 1980s. In this way the company was able to develop new and more effective formulations. The move allowed the company to produce pharmaceuticals in a variety of formulations, including tablets, capsules, syrups, and injectables.

Later in the decade, EGYT also invested in its packaging capacity, adding a new packaging facility. This addition came as a means of making the company more competitive as well, particularly on the export market. In another move designed to enhance its stature on the international market, the company decided to change its name in 1985. The name EGYT had often led to the company being mistaken as an Egyptian company in the international market. Instead, the company chose the name Egis, from the Greek *aegis,* or shield.

OPPORTUNITIES AND CHALLENGES

The collapse of the Soviet Union and the resulting creation of free market economies throughout the former Eastern bloc provided new opportunities and challenges for Egis. In order to meet them, the company launched construction of a new factory in Budapest, built to meet the industrial standards demanded by the European Union. The new facility incorporated the company's packaging facility, as well as its injectables production. The factory, located on Budapest's Bokeny-foldi Street, also became the site of the company's pre-clinical research department.

The construction of the new factory came ahead of the Hungarian government's decision to convert the company's status from a state-owned enterprise into a business association. As such, the group's name changed again, becoming Egis Gyógyszergyár Részvénytársaság, or Egis Pharmaceuticals Ltd., in 1991. The change in incorporation status proved a first step toward the privatization of Egis. In 1993, the Hungarian government sold a 30 percent stake to the European Bank for Reconstruction and Development. Then in June 1994, the government sold out its remaining stake in the company. Half of the government's shares were sold to foreign investors, while the other half were listed on the Budapest Stock Exchange.

Like most pharmaceutical companies in post-Soviet Eastern and Central Europe, Egis was too small in size to conduct an active pharmaceutical research program. In response, the company went in search of a larger partner, finding Servier SA, one of France's leading privately held pharmaceuticals groups. By December 1995, Servier, through its subsidiary ATP, had gained majority control of Egis, with a 51 percent stake.

With Servier's backing, Egis launched a new international expansion effort. The company began developing its foreign sales and marketing network, starting with Poland, where it established a subsidiary in 1995. This was shortly followed by the opening of a subsidiary in the Czech Republic that same year, and then a move into Slovakia in 1996. In Hungary, meanwhile, Egis established itself as a leading player in the country's wholesale pharmaceuticals distribution sector when it acquired 50 percent control of Medimpex Nagyker, formerly part of the state-owned Medimpex, in partner with its chief rival Richter Gedeon Nyrt. When Medimpex was broken up in 1997, Egis gained control of its network of 24 warehouses, which operated throughout the CIS region.

BUILDING THE GENERICS PORTFOLIO

By this time, Egis had begun making progress in its efforts—backed by Servier—to establish its generic drugs business in the West. The expiration of Bristol-Myers

Squibb's patent on Capoten in 1995 provided Egis with the opportunity it needed. In that year, Egis launched Tensiomin as a branded generic for the German market, quickly building up an impressive 7 percent market share. Exports to the United Kingdom followed soon after. Servier helped Egis enter the French generics market as well, starting in 1999. By then, the company's manufacturing facilities had gained approval from the U.S. Food and Drug Administration (FDA), allowing the company to begin marketing its generic products in the United States as well.

However, Egis was far from the only company marketing its generic version of Capoten, and the company was faced with the impending collapse of its core product, Tensiomin. In response, the company renewed its efforts to build its generic product portfolio. In 1998, the company gained a five-year agreement to supply the then-generic methyldopa to Merck, which had originally developed that active ingredient. The deal also served to raise the profile of Egis as a supplier of bulk active ingredients to other major pharmaceutical companies.

In 1999, the company became the first in Hungary to launch a generic version of Losec, the omeprazole-based blockbuster drug developed by Astra. The following year, Egis became one of a group of companies approved by the FDA to sell generic versions of buspirone, a blockbuster drug developed by Bristol-Myers Squibb and marketed as Buspar.

Egis's own research and development efforts had also begun to show some promise. In the late 1990s, the company teamed up with Finland's Orion Oy to begin clinical trials testing Egis's deramciclane. The new compound offered strong potential as an antidepressant. However, development of the compound hit a snag in the early years of the new century after early trials failed to produce positive results. Egis nevertheless remained in expansion mode. The group solidified its Hungarian wholesale arm, joining a consortium to acquire control of Hungaropharma from the Hungarian government in 2002. By 2003, Egis's own stake in that company had risen past 19 percent. One year later, Egis raised its stake again, to 30 percent.

Egis also joined with majority shareholder Servier to target expansion into Russia in the first decade of the 21st century. In 2002, the companies announced plans to form a joint venture, Serdix, and to build a pharmaceutical packaging facility near Moscow. That factory was completed in 2007, at a cost of nearly $50 million. By then, Egis had gained majority control of the Serdix business. The next year, Egis acquired control of another joint venture with Servier, Anpharm, based in Poland. By the end of the decade, Egis had established itself as one of Hungary's leading pharmaceuticals groups.

M. L. Cohen

PRINCIPAL SUBSIDIARIES

Egis Bulgaria EOOD; Egis Ilaclari Limited Sirketi (Turkey); Egis Polska Dystrybucja Sp.z o.o.; Egis Polska Sp.z o.o.; Egis Praha spol. s r.o. (Czech Republic); EGIS Rompharma S.R.L. (Romania); Egis Slovakia spol. s r.o.; Ingatlankezelo Kft.; Medimpex Irodaház; Medimpex Kereskedelmi Zrt.; Medimpex UK Ltd.

PRINCIPAL COMPETITORS

Pfizer Inc.; Crucell N.V.; Gedeon Richter plc; Humet Nyrt.; Phylaxia Pharma Nyrt; PharmaFarm S.A.

FURTHER READING

"CEO of Hungarian Pharma Company Egis Retires After 23 Years," *Hungary Business News,* December 14, 2005.

"Egis Nyart," *MondayMorning,* January 26, 2009.

"Egis Plans to Build Pharmaceuticals Plant in Russia," *Inzhenernaia Gazeta,* June 18, 2002, p. 3.

"Hungarian Egis Not Ready to Give Up on Anti-Anxiety Drug," *Asia Africa Intelligence Wire,* August 12, 2003.

"Hungarian Pharma Egis Announces Death of CEO," *Hungary Business News,* January 19, 2006.

"Hungarian Pharma Egis Expects New Russian Factory to Recover Investment in 6–7 Years," *Hungary Business News,* August 2, 2007.

"Hungarian Pharma Egis May Lose at Least HUF 3.6 Bln on Planned Gov't Subsidy Reforms," *Hungary Business News,* November 9, 2006.

ENCHO

Encho Company Ltd.

2-12 2-chome Chuo-cho
Fuji-shi
Shizuoka, 417-0052
Japan
Telephone: (81 0545) 57 0808
Fax: (81 0545) 57 0811
Web site: http://www.encho.co.jp

Public Company
Incorporated: 1962 as Endo Zaimokuten Co., Ltd.
Employees: 1,300
Sales: ¥49,540 million ($431.8 million) (2008)
Stock Exchanges: Tokyo
Ticker Symbol: 8208
NAICS: 444130 Hardware Stores; 444120 Paint and
    Wallpaper Stores

■ ■ ■

Encho Company Ltd. is one of Japan's pioneering operators of do-it-yourself (DIY) home centers. The company, which originated as a lumber supply company in the late 1930s, operates 33 stores under the Jumbo, Home Assist, Assistpro, and Casa banners. Jumbo is the company's primary retail format, with 23 stores in operation. The Jumbo stores feature a wide range of hardware and DIY goods, as well as interior decoration, gardening, household goods, pet and animal care, and other supplies. The Jumbo stores represent a midsize retail format that ranges in size from approximately 19,000 square feet to nearly 65,000 square feet. Encho has also experimented with a large-scale retail format,

called Home Assist. This type of store features sales space of more than 104,000 square feet.

In addition to its DIY home centers, Encho has developed a network of home furnishings specialty shops under the Casa name. These stores, which range in size from 3,000 square feet to more than 8,000 square feet, offer a selection of furniture, kitchenware, interior decoration, and other items. In 2005, Encho extended the Casa network with the opening of an Asian-design store, Cosa Oriente. The company also operates an Assistpro store, focused on the professional carpenters and builders market. A public company listed on the Tokyo Stock Exchange, Encho remains controlled by the founding Endo family. Takeo Endo is the group's president and, since May 2009, its chairman. The company, which struggled through Japan's decade-long recession, saw its revenues slip from a high of more than ¥60,000 million to ¥49,500 million ($432 million) in 2008.

FROM LUMBER SUPPLY TO DIY

Encho Company originated as a lumber supply shop opened by Chotaro Endo in Japan's Fuji City in 1939. The extension of the business led to the company's incorporation as Endo Zaimokuten Co. Ltd. in 1962. At the time, the group was valued at ¥1 million. Japan's rising economy during the 1960s, as the country emerged as a new industrial and technological powerhouse on the global market, led to a surge in demand for new construction. The corresponding rise in demand for lumber products encouraged Endo to focus its operations on the professional sector. In 1970, the company reoriented its sales to the construction industry, serving building contractors and carpenters. At this time, the group's retail operation adopted the name Encho Center.

Despite the focus of its existing operations on the professional sector, Endo also played the role of pioneer in a newly emerging retail market in Japan. In the early 1970s, the do-it-yourself (DIY) market remained almost entirely undeveloped. By 1973, however, the country witness the appearance of the first DIY home centers—stores specialized in distributing tools, materials, and other products needed by homeowners seeking to carry out improvements on their own homes.

Endo Zaimokuten recognized the opportunity to expand into this new retail category. The company set to work developing its own retail DIY home center format. By 1974, the company had opened the doors to its first DIY retail store, in Fuji City. The new store opened under the Jumbo Encho name and later grew into one of the largest in the company's retail network, with sales space of more than 64,000 square feet.

By the mid-1970s, Endo Zaimokuten's operation had become more popularly known under the Encho name. This prompted the company to adopt Encho as its corporate name in 1975. The success of the initial Jumbo store also encouraged the company to add new DIY shops.

EXPANDING THE DIY SECTOR

The second Jumbo store opened in Numazu at the end of 1976. The store, which featured more than 18,750 square feet, was followed six months later by a larger store in Shizuoka. The company's third store was nearly 35,000 square feet. The growth of the group's DIY activities led the company to create a dedicated subsidiary to oversee these operations. In 1978, the company incorporated a subsidiary, Jumbo Co. Ltd.

Encho, and the Endo family, also played a major role in helping to expand the retail DIY sector in general. The company launched a home improvement lecture series in 1980. This activity was expanded with the launch of a television program in 1982, *Dial 110*, focused on DIY subjects. Encho also recognized the

need to staff its store network with experienced and knowledgeable sales staff in order to help consumers purchase the needed tools and materials for their home improvement projects. In order to ensure a level of expertise in its sales staff, the company established a new staff category of "DIY Advisors." In order to qualify for this status, employees were subject to examinations. The first of these, held in 1983, identified a first group of 16 DIY Advisors. By the 21st century, the company's retail network numbered more than 400 DIY Advisors.

By then, Encho had opened a new store, in Kakegawa. This store was nearly 53,000 square feet in size. The new store, like the company's other stores, was located in Japan's central region. In the ensuing years the group would remain focused on this region and would concentrate its expansion there. This was in keeping with Japan's retail DIY sector as whole. Despite the growth of several major groups, some with 300 stores or more, none reached a truly national level. This was the result of the marked differences in consumer habits and preferences within the DIY and home centers in Japan's various regions.

Nonetheless, the retail DIY chains often worked together, notably in the creation of the Japan DIY Industry Association in 1978. The Endo family became particularly involved in this body, and Toshiharu Endo, who had taken over from his father as head of Encho by the 1980s, later became president of the industry association. Endo also later served as president of the country's International Hardware and Houseware Association.

GOING PUBLIC

Encho's retail network remained relatively modest through most of the 1980s, with no new Jumbo store openings until the end of the decade. Instead, the company focused on strengthening its existing operations, adding computerized support functions in the early 1980s. These were brought under a new subsidiary, Systech Co., established in 1984. The company also introduced its own credit card, called Casa, in cooperation with the Central Finance Company, in 1985. Also that year, the company added architect services.

By the end of that year, Encho had rolled out the Casa brand into a new retail format. The Casa stores, based on a retail concept developed in Europe, focused on the interior decoration sector, offering furniture, decorative items, kitchenware, and other home furnishings. The first Casa store opened in Shimizu in 1985. Encho then opened a second Casa store in Shichikencho the following year.

Encho went public in 1986, listing its shares on the Tokyo and Nagoya stock exchanges. The offering valued

```
┌─────────────────────────────────────────────┐
│                                               │
│              KEY DATES                        │
│              ■                                │
│  ───────────────────────────────────────      │
│                                               │
│  1939:  The company is founded by the Endo    │
│         family as a lumber supply store in    │
│         Fuji City, Japan.                     │
│  1962:  The company incorporates as Endo      │
│         Zaimokuten Co.                         │
│  1974:  Endo opens its first retail do-it-    │
│         yourself (DIY) store, called Jumbo     │
│         Encho, in Fuji City.                   │
│  1975:  The company changes its name to       │
│         Encho.                                 │
│  1978:  The Japan DIY Industry Association     │
│         is formed.                             │
│  1985:  Encho goes public on the Tokyo and    │
│         Nagoya stock exchanges; the Casa       │
│         home furnishings retail store format   │
│         is introduced.                         │
│  1988:  Encho moves to new headquarters in    │
│         Shizuoka-shi.                           │
│  1997:  Encho debuts its superstore format,    │
│         Home Assist.                            │
│  2006:  Encho introduces a new store format,   │
│         Assist-pro, for the professional       │
│         builders and carpenters market.        │
│                                               │
└─────────────────────────────────────────────┘
```

the company at ¥804 million. The following year, the company issued another ¥2 billion in convertible bonds. The sale of shares and the bond offering provided the company with the treasury to enter into a new growth phase.

Encho moved to new headquarters in Shizuoka-shi in 1988. From there, Encho launched a major expansion of its operations, becoming a major regional DIY and home center player. The company's growth drive took off in 1989 with the opening of a new Jumbo store in Yoshida. The following year, the company opened a Jumbo store in Hamakita. In 1991, the company entered into a cooperation agreement with two other companies, Tel Wel Home Center Co. and the Denki Tsushin Kyosaikai Foundation. Tel Wel, founded to operate its own DIY shop in 1988, then came under Encho's management. By 1998, Encho had taken full control of Tel Wel, which became a separate Encho subsidiary.

The Jumbo chain continued to grow strongly through the 1990s. In 1992, the company added stores in Narumi and Fuji Nishi, followed by Fujinomiya in 1993. Three more stores joined the group's network, adding a total of more than 150,000 square feet of selling space, in Hamamatsu, Shiroi, and Kanie. Encho, through an affiliated company, also added a new store format called Swen in 1993, specialized in outdoor

furnishings and materials. The first of these shops opened in Fukuroi, in Shizuoka Prefecture.

SURVIVING THE JAPANESE RETAIL SLUMP

After decades of unparalleled growth, the Japanese economy slipped into a profound recession in the mid-1990s. While most retail sales plummeted through the end of the decade and into the next century, the DIY sector continued to grow. Part of the reason for this was the increasing willingness of Japanese homeowners to carry out their own home repair and home improvement projects, in an effort to save money.

In response to the growing demand, Encho added a number of new stores through the end of the decade. These included a store in Hamamatsu Minami in 1995, and stores in Kosai and Fujeida in 1996. Two more stores followed in 1998, in Fujeida and Gotenba. The company also opened stores in Kozoji in 1999, Okazaki in 2000, and Shimizu Torisaka in 2003.

Encho also participated in a new trend among the Japanese DIY home center market, which had begun developing new superstore formats. Encho debuted its own superstore format, called Home Assist, in 1997. The new store featured sales space of more than 104,000 square feet. Leading the company by then was Takeo Endo, who became company president in 1995. His father, Toshiharu Endo, remained as the group's chairman.

Into the middle of the first decade of the new century, Encho focused on developing its Casa retail format. The company added a new Casa store in Fuji in 2002. Also in that year, the group debuted an extension of the Casa brand, called Cosa Oriente, which featured Asian-style furniture and decorative items. Encho opened several more Casa stores, including in Hamamatsu Ichino, Chuo-Rinkan, and Nagatsuta in 2005; and in Fuji-Yoshida in 2006. In that year, also, Encho debuted a new store format, Assistpro, with an initial location in Hamamatsu. The new format represented a return of sorts to the company's roots, targeting exclusively professional builders and carpenters.

The recession that had affected the rest of Japan's retail sectors had by then caught up to the DIY home center sector. Encho, too, found itself suffering from the weakness of the Japanese economy. As a result, the group's sales had peaked at nearly ¥57,000 million in 2000. From there, the group's revenues entered a steady decline, bottoming out at less than ¥47,000 million in 2005.

By mid-decade, the expansion of the Casa chain began to contribute to the company's sales. Further challenges to the economy toward the end of the decade once again encouraged consumers to turn to the DIY market. As a result, by the end of 2008, Encho had managed to restore its business to more than ¥49,000 ($431 million). Toshiharu Endo stepped down as the company's chairman in May 2009. The Endo family nonetheless remained in control of the company, with Takeo Endo taking the company's lead. As a pioneer of Japan's retail DIY home center sector, Encho remained a major player in the central Japan region.

M. L. Cohen

PRINCIPAL SUBSIDIARIES

BROS Co. Ltd.; J.E. Service Co. Ltd.; Jumbo Co. Ltd.; Systech Co. Ltd.; Tel Wel Home Center Co. Ltd.

PRINCIPAL DIVISIONS

Hardware; Housing-Related Business.

PRINCIPAL OPERATING UNITS

DIY Home Center; Home Interior Speciality Store.

PRINCIPAL COMPETITORS

Joyful Honda Co., Ltd; Komeri Co., Ltd.; Cainz Corporation; Sekichu Co., Ltd.

FURTHER READING

"Encho Co., Ltd., Announces Resignation of Chairman," *Reuters Key Development,* May 25, 2009.

"Encho Co., Ltd., Lowers Full-Year Consolidated Outlook for FY Ended March 31, 2009," *Reuters Key Development,* April 27, 2009.

"Encho Co., Ltd., Raises Consolidated Mid-Year Profit Outlook for H1 of FY Ending March 31, 2009," *Reuters Key Development,* October 24, 2008.

"Product Market Study 2008: Japanese DIY Products Market," *Matrade Tokyo,* May 2008.

EP Henry Corporation

201 Park Avenue
Woodbury, New Jersey 08096-3523
U.S.A.
Telephone: (856) 845-6200
Toll Free: (800) 444-3679
Fax: (856) 845-0023
Web site: http://www.ephenry.com

Private Company
Incorporated: 1913 as E.P. Henry & Son
Employees: 300
Sales: $224 million (2007 est.)
NAICS: 327331 Concrete Block and Brick Manufacturing; 327991 Cut Stone and Stone Product Manufacturing

∎ ∎ ∎

A family-owned company based in Woodbury, New Jersey, and primarily serving a market that stretches from New York to Virginia, EP Henry Corporation is a major manufacturer of concrete masonry blocks and hardscaping products, attractive interlocking stones used to make paths, patios, and walls. EP Henry's original business was the production of standard gray concrete blocks. These masonry units are still sold under the Profile label and are more varied in appearance and style, available with a weathered look produced by sandblasting, a cut-stone polished appearance, a natural stone look, and a blend that resembles brick and natural stone. The company also offers ten split-and-fluted styles of blocks that are available in more than 50 colors.

EP Henry's main business, however, is its hardscaping products, which account for 85 percent of all sales. The company offers paving stones in a multitude of shapes and colors, and wall systems for gardens and retaining walls.

EP Henry products are not for the do-it-yourself customer. Rather, they are installed professionally, and the company has expended a great deal of time and money to train a network of installers to properly use its products. Each year EP Henry sponsors the Mid-Atlantic Hardscaping Trade Show, the primary mission of which is to educate hardscaping contractors on the latest company products and developments in the industry, providing both classroom and hands-on training. EP Henry operates a pair of manufacturing plants in Woodbury as well as operations in Vineland and Wrightstown, New Jersey; Parker Ford, Pennsylvania; and Capitol Heights, Maryland. The company is run by the fourth generation of the Henry family, making it the oldest family-owned-and-operated manufacturer of unit concrete products in the United States.

CINDER BLOCK ORIGINS

The man who gave EP Henry its name was Edward Pitcher Henry, whose family came to the Philadelphia, Pennsylvania, area during the Revolutionary War. He was descended from a British army officer who served with a mercenary troop of Hessian soldiers and grew sympathetic to the cause of the breakaway colonies. He deserted the British army, threw in his lot with the rebels, fought for them, and made his life in the young

COMPANY PERSPECTIVES

As the oldest family owned and operated manufacturer of unit concrete products in America, EP Henry has long been committed to being the market leader in both consumer and commercial Hardscaping. Our commitment goes beyond just having the highest quality and broadest product offering. EP Henry ensures that you get not only the best product but the best finished project. EP Henry is 100% USA made, owned and operated.

country. Edward P. Henry brought the clan to Woodbury, New Jersey, around 1888, and it was there, a short distance across the Delaware River from Philadelphia, that he worked as a contracting stone mason, involved in all manner of projects in Gloucester County, New Jersey, including homes, schools, and churches.

Around the dawn of the 20th century, as concrete gained increasing acceptance in construction, he recognized the potential for building blocks produced from portland cement. During the winter months he was largely idle due to the weather, and starting in 1903 he began taking advantage of this time to produce cinder blocks in the basement of his home. He poured cement into wooden molds and tamped down the material to produce the blocks one at a time.

Henry became a supplier of concrete products to area contractors and soon after was joined in the business by his son, James Carlton Henry, resulting in a company called E.P. Henry & Son. The younger Henry was born near Woodbury in Paulsboro, New Jersey, in 1890, and was educated at Woodbury High School. He then enrolled at the University of Pennsylvania in Philadelphia, graduating with a degree in civil engineering in 1910. He then went to work for the Pennsylvania Railroad in Wilmington, Delaware, before returning home to Woodbury in the spring of 1913 to join his father. It was in 1913 that the younger Henry incorporated the business. In addition to the manufacture of cinder blocks, the Henry family continued to work as builders, involved in general lines of construction, including the Paulsboro High School, and later making a specialty of concrete highway bridges. A prominent businessman, Edward Henry also became involved in banking, serving as president of the First National Bank and Trust Company in Paulsboro.

REACHING A TURNING POINT

Edward P. Henry died in early 1936, leaving the cinder-block business in the hands of his son. James Henry was in turn joined by his son, James Carlton Henry Jr., who graduated with a degree in engineering from Cornell University in 1949. Over time, the family left the construction trade and focused solely on the manufacture of concrete blocks for builders. The products were architect specific, the size, shape, and color predetermined and custom made. It was a business cyclical in nature, so that during building slumps the company suffered. A possibility for a different business model began to emerge in the 1960s and 1970s when the European trend of using concrete blocks for consumer landscaping and outdoor projects made its way to the United States and began to enjoy steady growth.

Thus a market emerged for stone products for use in making patios, walkways, driveways, and retaining walls. Interlocking block systems also proved increasingly popular because the stones, which did not rely on mortar or any other kind of binder, could shift with temperature changes, making them less likely to crack than cement or asphalt. Moreover, deicing salt that often caused concrete slabs to chip did not impact the stones because the saltwater could drain between them. The stones could also be taken up to allow for work on plumbing or utilities and then be reinstalled. Finding a new source of income was of further importance for the company (by this time known as EP Henry Corporation) because the demand for basic concrete blocks was slipping. For decades EP Henry had depended on demand remaining steady because cinder blocks were the lowest-priced structural material on the market, but beginning in the 1970s, poured concrete, wood, metal, and glass siphoned off sales at a steady rate.

EP Henry reached a turning point in the early 1980s, both in terms of leadership and business focus. In 1981, after graduating from Cornell University with a degree in engineering, James Carlton Henry III joined the family business. He was familiar with the operation, having worked for EP Henry during high school and while on summer vacation in college. He would eventually succeed his father as chief executive officer, while his father assumed the chairmanship, and would be joined in the business by his brother, Shafer Henry.

SHIFT TO HARDSCAPING

The infusion of new blood in the early 1980s was also a key factor in the company's shift into the hardscape industry. The PaverWorks unit was established in 1981 and began installing paving stones produced by other

KEY DATES

1903:	Edward P. Henry begins manufacturing cinder blocks.
1913:	Henry's son, James C. Henry, joins company.
1936:	Edward P. Henry dies.
1981:	James C. Henry III becomes fourth generation to join family business.
1989:	Plant focusing on hardscape products opens.
2000:	Company begins hosting trade show.
2004:	Distribution center opens in Landover, Maryland.

manufacturers, a business that in effect tested the waters for EP Henry, which was content at this stage to act as a distributor for products made by other companies. Convinced that there was an opening in the market for consumer concrete paving stones, the company in 1986 introduced its own line of these materials aimed at the family backyard. In 1989 the company constructed a second Woodbury plant to focus on the manufacture of concrete paving stones.

EP Henry was new to the consumer sector and therefore had to invest heavily in marketing to advertise its products with the primary target customers, the affluent suburban homeowner and institutional markets. In turn, the company had to make sure there were contractors available and trained to use the stones, which were not intended for the do-it-yourself market, to make patios, walks, and walls. The individual stones were quite heavy, requiring more brawn than most homeowners possessed. Even professional landscapers and masons, the people most likely to serve as contractors, were not ready to properly install the stones. According to the *Philadelphia Business Journal,* "Few knew how to turn a pile of cement blocks into a retaining wall or a patio, a tricky process that involves tying the soil mass to the wall, or, with surface applications, laying the right base materials at the right depths." Without a proper base, these projects were destined for serious problems.

EP Henry won some major public paving contracts, including the installation of interlocking paving stones for 300,000 square feet of runways at Dallas County Airport, and in Baltimore, Maryland, the company installed several hundred thousand square feet of stones for dockside loading facilities. For the most part, EP Henry continued out of necessity to install its products through PaverWorks, but began holding training seminars to develop a network of capable installers. The classes were initially held at the company's Woodbury

headquarters, but were later held elsewhere, extending the reach of the program. EP Henry later joined the Interlocking Concrete Pavement Institute, founded in 1993 to certify installing contractors. Once there were enough certified installers in the field, EP Henry was able to exit the installation business and cease competing against its customers.

OPENING NEW PLANTS TO MEET INCREASING DEMAND

In the early 1990s EP Henry opened another manufacturing plant for paving stones, located in Vineland, New Jersey. By this juncture, interlocking paving stones accounted for about 20 percent of revenues while retaining walls, a new product, added another 5 percent. Once the province of railroad ties and poured concrete, the new retaining wall systems, relying on clips and inserts, were much less expensive to install, maintenance free, able to be constructed 30 feet high, and were available in a variety of colors and looks that emulated brick, stucco, and other finishes. To broaden its product offerings the company in 1991 also began importing European-style paving and garden wall stones. At the same time, EP Henry continued to develop its own products, introducing a sandblasted concrete block that offered a distinctive look, a combination of marble and stone.

By 1995 EP Henry was selling its products through a network of about 50 dealers located in a territory that stretched from southern New York to northern New Jersey and ranged inland about 60 miles west of Philadelphia. They included garden centers, home centers, and masonry-product dealers. The demand for hardscaping products continued to enjoy strong growth in the United States, reaching 140 million square feet in 1994, a dramatic increase over the market of six million square feet that existed in 1980. About 75 percent of EP Henry's market was residential. The most popular paving stones were shaped and colored like bricks but made from concrete instead of clay.

To keep up with increased demand, EP Henry began making plans to build a new manufacturing facility. Rather than add another plant in New Jersey, already saturated with paving manufacturers, the company elected to move into Pennsylvania, constructing a plant near Pottstown, Pennsylvania, about 30 miles west of Philadelphia. Another plant followed in Capitol Heights, Maryland, to better serve the company's southern territory. There was also a need for trained installers, an increase of which was a further necessity in growing the company. In 2000 EP Henry hosted its first Mid-Atlantic Hardscaping Trade Show in order to encourage contractor development, attracting 600 contractors. A year later that number jumped to 1,600 and reached 2,100 in 2003.

INTRODUCING NEW PRODUCTS

Although the economy cooled off in 2001 and slipped into recession following the terrorist attacks against the United States of September 11, 2001, EP Henry became the beneficiary of the sudden reluctance of Americans to travel far on vacations. Rather, they spent more time at home and looked to improve the quality of their backyards by building patios. In addition, property values were on the rise while interest rates were low, making home-improvement projects such as patios and garden walls even more attractive. Unlike wooden decks that required maintenance, patios required little continuing effort on the part of homeowners. For those people who were expressing concern about the over-paving of the country and the problems caused by storm water runoff, EP Henry introduced the Eco-Pave line of interlocking blocks, which provided wide spaces between blocks for ample drainage.

More new products followed in the early years of the new century. In 2003 EP Henry introduced the Chameleon Cast Wall System, a panel that, as the name suggested, offered a range of looks in tilt-up construction projects. The Chameleon masonry was embedded in the face of the tilt-up panel during construction. Designers could then finish the walls with a wide variety of colors, shapes, and textures, including completely new patterns. Again to keep pace with demand, EP Henry made plans for a sixth manufacturing facility, acquiring 57 acres of land in Wrightstown, New Jersey, in early 2004. Ground was then broken on a 140,000-square-foot plant. In late 2004 the company also added a distribution center in Landover, Maryland, to better serve the Washington/Baltimore metro market. A company that at one time was devoted exclusively to the production of cinder blocks had transformed itself into a leading hardscaping company. By 2009 about 85 percent of its business came from paving bricks. There was every reason to believe that EP Henry would continue to prosper as a leading independent in its field.

Ed Dinger

PRINCIPAL UNITS

EP Henry Pavers; EP Henry Wall Systems.

PRINCIPAL COMPETITORS

The Belden Brick Company; Belgard Hardscapes; Keystone Retaining Wall Systems, Inc.

FURTHER READING

Austin, Gene, "A Concrete Change," *Philadelphia Inquirer,* April 28, 1995, p. F1.

Cory, Jim, "EP Henry: Building Its Business One Block at a Time," *Philadelphia Business Journal,* March 4, 2002.

"E.P. Henry: From Concrete Blocks to Paving Stones," *Cherry Hill (N.J.) Courier-Post,* January 31, 2008.

Heavens, Alan J., "Patios, Pavers Make Comeback with Americans," *Philadelphia Inquirer,* August 3, 2003.

Heston, Alfred Miller, *South Jersey: A History, 1664–1924,* New York: Lewis Historical Publishing Company, 1924.

Ruth, Joao-Pierre S., "Keeping It in the Family," *NCBIZ,* October 20, 2003.

Vanaman, Joyce, "A Rock-Solid Business," *Press of Atlantic City,* February 22, 1998, p. F1.

VanderWerf, Pieter, "Masonry or Tilt-Up?" *Concrete Construction,* November 2003, p. 45.

Werner, Tom, "E.P. Henry Is Paving New Masonry Niche," *Philadelphia Business Journal,* June 3, 1992, p. 20B.

Europcar

Europcar Groupe S.A.

3 avenue du Centre, Immeuble Les Quadrants
St. Quentinen Yvelines, 78881
France
Telephone: (33 30) 449-000
Fax: (33 30) 449-445
Web site: http://www.europcar.com

Private Company
Incorporated: 1927 as Motor-Verkehrs-Union Kommanditgesellschaft auf Aktien
Employees: 8,000 (2008)
Sales: EUR 2.1 billion ($3.1 billion) (2008)
NAICS: 532111 Passenger Car Rental; 532120 Truck, Utility Trailer, and RV (Recreational Vehicle) Rental and Leasing; 485320 Limousine Service

∎ ∎ ∎

With over 5,300 locations in more than 150 countries and with a fleet of roughly 225,000 vehicles, Europcar Groupe S.A. is Europe's largest car rental company for passenger cars and one of the leading global players in the industry. Holding a strong market position in Germany, the United Kingdom, France, Spain, Italy, Portugal, and Belgium, Europcar Groupe's global network of outlets includes 600 airport locations in big cities around the world. In addition to renting passenger cars, SUVs, vans and trucks globally under the Europcar brand, the company also operates rental car outlets under the National and Alamo brands in Europe, the Middle East, and Africa. With 45 percent of its revenues generated by leisure travelers, Europcar cooperates with over 80 partners in the travel industry, including TUI and Accor, and major airlines such as easyJet, All Nippon Airways, American Airlines, and Delta Air Lines. The company also has partnerships with auto manufacturers Daimler, Fiat, Peugeot, Volkswagen, General Motors, and Hyundai as well as with financial services providers such as American Express and with insurance companies such as AXA. In 2008 Europcar formed a strategic alliance with American car rental company Enterprise Rent-A-Car. The company is owned by the French equity firm Eurazeo.

MODEST BEGINNINGS IN PARIS AFTER WORLD WAR II

At the end of the postwar years in Europe a small car rental company named Europcar was founded in Paris in 1949. After two decades of slowly building a national presence in France, the company was acquired by French car manufacturer Renault in 1970. Still a relatively small operation, Europcar then grossed about $3.4 million annually. Determined to establish a serious competition for the two unchallenged European car rental market leaders, Hertz and Avis, Renault invested heavily in Europcar's growth, while getting more of its own cars on the road at the same time. During the first half of the 1970s Europcar began to expand beyond France under the leadership of CEO Jean Ordner, a Renault executive.

New subsidiaries were established in Belgium, the Netherlands, Germany, and Switzerland, and business operations were started in Saudi Arabia in 1973. In 1974 Europcar became active in Spain and acquired the

Italian branch of Budget Rent-A-Car. In the same year the company signed a mutual representation agreement with National Car Rental. Europcar served National's customers in Europe; National represented Europcar in the rest of the world. By 1977 Europcar's revenues had risen to about $40 million, the equivalent of almost one-fifth of Europe's quickly growing car rental market. Trying to set itself apart from its American competitors, the company created the slogan "Rent Europcar, Rent European."

JOINING THE GLOBAL TOP LEAGUE THROUGH BETTER SERVICES AND BRITISH ACQUISITION

By the 1980s Europcar had emerged as one of Europe's largest car rental companies. Sales reached new heights in the late 1970s, amounting to approximately $200 million per year at the end of the decade. To achieve that position Europcar had worked relentlessly at creating persuasive offers for its customers and partners in a highly competitive market. Renting a vehicle from Europcar cost about 10 percent less compared to what Hertz and Avis were charging at the time. Targeting business travelers in particular, Europcar sweetened the deal by offering volume discounts and by sending commercial customers just one bill per month for all of their company's rentals.

Associated travel agents received their commissions from Europcar without delay. A special Europcar credit card for regular customers allowed renting clerks to immediately access all the necessary information for such customers, thereby speeding up rental processing and shortening wait time. Last but not least, Europcar managed to hire experienced personnel away from its American competitors by offering more attractive career opportunities. To emphasize its focus on customer service and to stress its global presence, Europcar changed its slogan to "Everywhere Europcar Super Service."

In 1981 Europcar took over Britain's leading car rental company, Godfrey Davis, including an 8,000-vehicle-fleet and a network of about 200 locations across the country, including more than 25 airport locations.

This strategic acquisition propelled Europcar into the global top league of its industry, making it one of the world's largest car rental companies and the third largest in Europe. The company's network had grown to 2,300 locations around the globe and included 120,000 vehicles. Renault cars accounted for about 60 percent of the total rental fleet. Godfrey Davis Europcar, as the new subsidiary was named, offered car rentals at 75 intercity stations under an exclusive contract with British Rail.

FRENCH-GERMAN MERGER AFTER RECESSION

As the Western European economy went through a recession in the early 1980s, interest rates skyrocketed, resulting in much higher costs for purchasing new vehicles while the prices for used cars plummeted at the same time. This cut sharply into car rental companies' profit margins. Godfrey Davis Europcar was hit hard because the company's fleet consisted mainly of Ford makes manufactured in Britain. As Ford offered enormous discounts on new Ford models to car buyers in Britain to boost new car sales during the recession, prices for used Ford makes went into free fall, raising depreciation costs by 30 percent for Europcar's British subsidiary. Furthermore, Europcar was confronted, as were all other players in the industry, with a major drop in demand caused by slimmed-down corporate expense budgets.

In 1988 Renault sold Europcar to French tourism group Compagnie Internationale des Wagons-Lits et du Tourisme which in turn sold a 50 percent share to Volkswagen AG. Volkswagen, the owner of West Germany's number one rental car company, interRent Autovermietung, had a vital interest in Europcar. While interRent held a leading position in Europe's largest car rental market, Europcar was number one in Britain, the second largest European market, and held a strong position in France as well. Joining forces of the two enterprises was Volkswagen's strategic step to gain a competitive edge over the leading American rivals in a joint European car rental market. Consequently, in 1989 Europcar merged with interRent, a company with roots going back to the late 1920s.

GERMAN ROOTS GO BACK TO 1927

InterRent got started in 1927 when a group of businessmen in Hamburg founded Motor-Verkehrs-Union Kommanditgesellschaft auf Aktien. In 1928 the renamed Selbstfahrer Union Deutschland GmbH started its car rental activities with 150 vehicles at ten different

KEY DATES

1927: Motor-Verkehrs-Union is founded in Hamburg.

1939: Selbstfahrer Union is Germany's largest car rental company.

1949: A car rental company named Europcar is founded in Paris.

1970: Renault takes over Europcar and Volkswagen acquires a majority stake in Selbstfahrer Union.

1981: Europcar takes over Britain's leading car rental company Godfrey Davis.

1989: French car rental company Europcar merges with interRent.

1999: Volkswagen AG becomes Europcar's sole owner.

2003: German subsidiary interRent offers low-budget rentals in Germany.

2006: European investment firm Eurazeo acquires Europcar.

2007: Vanguard Car Rental Inc.'s operations in Europe, the Middle East, and Africa are taken over.

2008: A strategic alliance with Enterprise Rent-A-Car is formed.

locations. After the company had succeeded in pushing German authorities to accept driver's licenses from foreign countries and to significantly shorten approval processing time for motorists from abroad, Selbstfahrer Union's service became very popular among Americans traveling from Hamburg, where they arrived by ship, to Berlin, their final destination.

Soon the idea of cross-regional car rental attracted additional investors, including German car manufacturer Adler Automobil-Werke, transatlantic shipping company Hamburg-Amerikanische Paketfahrtgesellschaft (HAPAG), Deutsche Bank predecessor Norddeutsche Bank, and two large travel agencies. By the end of the 1930s Selbstfahrer Union was Germany's largest car rental company. In 1933 its network included 30 locations in 25 German cities and its fleet had grown to about 700 vehicles.

The beginning of World War II put a sudden end to the company's growth. By 1941 all of Selbstfahrer Union's vehicles had been confiscated by Adolf Hitler's *Wehrmacht* and the company barely managed to survive the war and the immediate postwar years by offering garage and miscellaneous repair services in Hamburg's Rotherbaum district. Since there were almost no private car owners in the mid-1940s, the company specialized in repairing rubber boots, raincoats and bicycle tubes using its inventory of motor vehicle tires. Equipped with fresh capital from three private investors and starting with two hidden-away vehicles from its fleet and with six Jeeps from the American military, Selbstfahrer Union resumed the car rental business in 1948.

In the 1950s the company began to rebuild its network of locations and invested in a new fleet which consisted mainly of German cars by Volkswagen and Daimler-Benz. The number of locations grew from nine in 1950 to 59 in 1962. In 1955 Selbstfahrer Union started a pilot project with the German railway for renting cars to railway passengers. In 1959 the first airport location opened in Hamburg. In addition to expanding its own network of locations to roughly 200 in 1960, Selbstfahrer Union signed several cooperation agreements with internationally active car rental companies, such as the American firm Dollar Rent-A-Car. Five years later the company added trucks to its fleet.

In 1970 Volkswagen AG took control over Selbstfahrer Union when it acquired a majority stake in the company, which was renamed SU interRent in 1971 and three years later changed its name to interRent Autovermietung. During the 1970s interRent expanded massively within as well as outside of Germany. By 1977 the company had locations in 35 countries and its national network had grown to more than 330 stations.

Throughout the 1980s interRent continued to expand its fleet, services, and network of locations. In 1988 the company employed 1,650 workers and operated a fleet of roughly 11,500 passenger cars, 4,000 trucks and 300 recreational vehicles. Generating about $200 million in annual sales, interRent had achieved a 23 percent market share in Germany. However, the fierce price wars between car rental companies had significantly cut into the company's profits.

MERGER CREATES EUROPEAN LEADER

The 1989 merger of French Europcar and German interRent created one of Europe's largest car rental enterprises with annual sales of roughly $500 million, about 40 percent of which originated in Germany; a workforce of about 4,000, operating a network of roughly 950 locations in nine European countries; and a combined fleet of approximately 40,000 vehicles. The new entity was headed by the French holding Europcar International S.A. and all of its subsidiaries were renamed Europcar while green and white became the company colors. In 1992 the French hotel chain and tourism group Accor took over Wagon-Lits, including the company's 50 percent share in Europcar.

Determined to become a global player, Europcar intensified its efforts to further extend its network in and beyond Europe. Most importantly, the company negotiated long-term cooperation agreements with U.S.-based National, with the Canadian car rental firm Tilden, and with the Japanese Nippon Rent-A-Car. In 1989 Europcar was the first to set up a car rental joint venture—Trojka-Europcar, a cooperation with the Moscow Chamber of Commerce—in the former Soviet Union. After the fall of the Berlin Wall in the same year, Europcar was the first car rental company to open five locations in former East Germany. Fifteen locations were added within the following two years. By 1994 Europcar had also built a strong foothold in Saudi Arabia with a fleet of 1,500 cars.

In the years following the merger Europcar fought a fierce battle with Avis Europe Plc, the former European division of the American car rental giant, which also claimed market leadership in Western Europe. With many economies going through another recession, car rental companies' rates stagnated while interest rates rose and business volume shrunk by up to 15 percent. Europcar successfully attracted additional business by entering strategic alliances with international tourism giant TUI, with Euro-Disney in Paris, and with ADAC, the German equivalent of the AAA. The company also opened new outlets in smaller cities to gain additional business and signed agreements with franchisees in Bulgaria, Hungary, Yugoslavia, Poland, Romania, Slovakia, and the Czech Republic. As a result, Europcar operated the most closely knit network of locations in Europe.

GETTING OUT OF FINANCIAL DIFFICULTIES WITH SHAREHOLDERS' HELP

After the Europcar-interRent merger, the company streamlined its operations, cut costs, and generated new business in an extremely competitive market. However, the company slipped into the red in 1993, mainly due to mounting problems with a custom-designed central computer system that was to integrate the various systems used by different Europcar subsidiaries. The $100 million system was supposed to give Europcar a competitive edge. Instead, it increased the company's information technology costs to roughly ten times the industry average. This was a major reason that Europcar fell behind its competition, and that the company struggled through four years of financial and organizational difficulties.

As Europcar was producing losses in the two-digit-millions in 1993 and 1994, shareholder Volkswagen announced in mid-1995 that it might put its 50 percent share up for sale. However an almost-finalized deal with Europcar's main German competitor, Sixt, fell through at the last minute. One of the problems was that French shareholder Accor was not interested in selling its share in Europcar at the time, which prevented any potential buyer from taking full control over the enterprise. Volkswagen and Accor decided instead to do whatever it took to make Europcar profitable again. To free the company from its mounting debt, they boosted Europcar's capital base. Volkswagen's financial arm, Volkswagen Financial Services, also took on the financing of Europcar's fleet, which made the company much less dependent on the goodwill of commercial banks.

In a booming European car rental market and under new management, Europcar achieved a turnaround in the second half of the 1990s. In 1997 the company started cooperating with Euromobil, the car rental enterprise of German Volkswagen and Audi dealers with 1,400 locations across Germany. In the same year the company announced a worldwide marketing alliance with Chrysler subsidiary Dollar Rent-A-Car, after Europcar's long-term partnership with National Car Rental suddenly ended when the latter was taken over by Republic Industries. The new partnership enabled U.S. customers to make reservations through Dollar for rental cars in Europe, the Middle East, and Africa, while Europcar customers were able to book Dollar rentals in the Americas.

In 1998 Europcar's German subsidiary launched its web site, which enabled customers to book rental cars over the Internet. One year later the company entered a partnership with German airline Lufthansa through which Europcar rentals earned travelers frequent flyer miles. In Britain Europcar acquired BCR Car & Van Rental, the fastest-growing short-term car rental firm in the country. The company also optimized its automated self-service rentals and online bookings. By the late 1990s Europcar was back in the black.

BECOMING A MAJOR GLOBAL PLAYER WITH NEW SHAREHOLDER

In December 1999 Volkswagen took over Accor's 50 percent share in Europcar and became the company's sole owner. Europcar was already a major Volkswagen customer, with approximately 16,000 vehicles that were replaced about twice a year. Having potential auto buyers test-drive the auto manufacturers' latest models for a few days was also seen as an important marketing tool.

In addition, Volkswagen products were often featured in Europcar's advertising.

After Europcar's partnership with Dollar ended in spring 2000, the company entered a similar cooperation agreement with the American Budget Group. As a growing number of smaller operators in the industry had to give up, for example, in Italy and Spain, Europcar's business volume increased. Shrinking revenues in the business traveler's segment was offset by growing numbers of leisure travelers. To attract even more of the latter, Europcar relaunched interRent as a separate low-budget car rental brand, starting out in five large German cities, in 2003. In the same year Europcar sealed exclusive cooperation agreements with tourism groups TUI and Accor and with low-budget airline easyJet. In addition, the company was successful in generating new business by becoming a partner of Payback, a rebate system through which customers could collect points for their car rentals with Europcar which could later be redeemed for rebate vouchers, frequent flyer miles or cash.

In spring 2004 Europcar announced that it had regained its leading position in the European market. Two years later Volkswagen sold the company to the French investment firm Eurazeo for an estimated $3.95 billion, roughly two thirds of which was assumed debt. Following the new shareholder's declared goal to significantly strengthen Europcar's global presence, the company acquired the National and Alamo brands business in Europe, the Middle East, and Africa for roughly $850 million from Vanguard Car Rental in 2007. The deal not only boosted Europcar's market position in the United Kingdom from 6 to 25 percent, roughly double as much as the company's closest competitors, it also gave Europcar direct market access outside of Europe for the first time.

After Enterprise Rent-A-Car's acquisition of the National and Alamo brands in the United States, the American company announced a strategic alliance with Europcar in 2008, creating the largest car rental network in the world. That year Europcar implemented a "Green Charter" with various environmental commitments regarding fleet, fleet maintenance, and the education of customers and employees. In 2009 the company teamed up with Nissan to jointly market electric vehicles by 2010.

Evelyn Hauser

PRINCIPAL SUBSIDIARIES

Europcar International SASU; Europcar Holdings S.A. S.; Europcar Inti S.A. und Co OHG (Germany); Eu-

ropcar Autovermietung GmbH (Germany); Europcar U.K. Ltd.; Europcar France SAS (99.9%); Europcar Italia SSTA (Italy); Europcar IB (Spain); Europcar Inti Aluguer de Automoveis S.A. (Portugal; 99.9%); Europcar S.A. (Belgium; 99.9%).

PRINCIPAL COMPETITORS

Avis Europe plc; The Hertz Corporation; Sixt AG.

FURTHER READING

"Accor's Europcar to Be First Int'l Car Rental Co in China," *AsiaPulse News,* August 2, 1999.

"Autovermiet-Riese in den Startlöchern für Europa," *Süddeutsche Zeitung,* March 23, 1989.

"Der Autovermieter Europcar moechte 1995 wieder Gewinne erzielen," *Frankfurter Allgemeine Zeitung,* May 27, 1994, p. 23.

Bray, Roger, "Europcar Teams Up with Budget," *Financial Times,* February 7, 2000, p. 14.

Buchan, David, "Accor, VW Agree on Europcar," *Financial Times,* January 5, 1996, p. 20.

"Dollar Rent A Car and Europcar Alliance Takes Off," *PR Newswire,* January 29, 1998.

"Enterprise Rent-A-Car and Europcar Expand Strategic Alliance to Create the World's Largest Car Rental Network," *Business Wire,* September 4, 2008.

"Europcar hofft auf bessere Zeiten," *Frankfurter Allgemeine Zeitung,* April 18, 1995, p. 18.

"Europcar will mit Interrent neue Anbieter abschrecken," *Frankfurter Allgemeine Zeitung,* July 19, 2004, p. 12.

Gaines, Lisa, "Europcar Interrent Has High Hopes for Automation System," *Travel Weekly,* June 24, 1993, p. E10.

Harris, Derek, "Car Hire Firms Find Small Is Beautiful," *Times,* January 21, 1991.

———, "Europcar Fine-Tunes to Rejoin Race for World Rental Market," *Times,* May 4, 1992, p. 26.

Iftikhar, Ahmed, "Special Report: The Thriving Rent-a-Car Business," *Moneyclips/Saudi Gazette,* August 6, 1994.

"International Business; World Roundup: Europe," *Business Week,* June 13, 1977, p. 51.

"InterRent/Europcar wird erster Autovermieter in der Sowietunion," *Frankfurter Allgemeine Zeitung,* March 25, 1989.

"McCann Steers Europcar Drive," *Campaign,* August 24, 1990.

"National Car Rental Becomes National Interrent; Enters New Era with Global Partners," *PR Newswire,* April 14, 1992.

"Renault's Europcar Moves into 3rd Place Among Car Renters," *New York Times,* May 7, 1981, p. D5.

Robertson, David, "Europcar Expands in UK with Euro 670m Brands Deal," *Times,* November 14, 2006, p. 43.

"Rocky Roads for Car-Hire Firms," *Economist,* September 11, 1982, p. 71.

"Volkswagen Gets Green Light to Take Over Europcar Rental Group," *European Report,* February 23, 2000.

"VW, Wagons-Lits Merge Rental Firms," *Automotive News,* March 28, 1988, p. 16.

Wallmeyer, Andrew, "Eurazeo to Buy VW's Europcar Unit for Euros 3.3bn," *Financial Times,* March 10, 2006, p. 30.

"Warum Accor und Volkswagen Europcar sanieren muessen," *Frankfurter Allgemeine Zeitung,* January 11, 1996, p. 16.

Fisher Auto Parts, Inc.

—■—

512 Greenville Avenue
Staunton, Virginia 24401-4755
U.S.A.
Telephone: (540) 885-8901
Fax: (540) 885-1808
Web site: http://www.fisherautoparts.com

Private Company
Incorporated: 1929 as Coiner Parts Inc.
Employees: 1,900
Sales: $243 million (2007 est.)
NAICS: 423120 Motor Vehicle Supplies and New Parts
Merchant Wholesalers

■ ■ ■

A private company based in Staunton, Virginia, Fisher Auto Parts, Inc., is an automobile parts retailer catering to both professional installers and do-it-yourself customers. The company operates about 300 stores in Delaware, Illinois, Kentucky, Maryland, Massachusetts, Missouri, New Hampshire, New York, North Carolina, Pennsylvania, Tennessee, Vermont, and Virginia. Product groups include brake and chassis; chemicals and oils; electrical; engine and drive train; exhaust; fuel systems; heating and cooling; ignition and emission; lighting and safety; paint and body; tire care and repair; tools and equipment; as well as miscellaneous tools, hardware, and other items. Fisher stores carry a wide variety of brands, including those of Federated Auto Parts, an allied company under the same management as Fisher.

Federated is an auto parts distribution network of 3,800 stores across the United States and also includes a network of independently owned repair shops marketed under the Federated Car Care Center banner. The shops work together to provide a national warranty on work, so that a customer who is more than 25 miles from a shop that performed the work can be serviced at no extra charge by a participating Federated member. Federated also advertises its own brand, supported in part by the sponsorship of race cars and stock car races, and provides professional training to member car care center personnel. Both Fisher and Federated are owned by the Fisher family and led by Chief Executive Officer Arthur Jay "Bo" Fisher III.

FAMILY ORIGINS

Fisher Auto Parts was founded in 1929 by Blair C. Coiner as Coiner Parts Inc. in Staunton, Virginia, an area his family had helped to settle. The patriarch of the clan was born Michael Keinadt (also spelled Koinath and other variations) in Winterlingen, Germany, in 1720, and 20 years later he immigrated to the United States, settling in Lancaster, Pennsylvania, where he fathered 13 children. In 1789 two of his sons moved to Augusta County, Virginia, where Staunton was located, and he soon followed, purchasing a large amount of acreage that his family would farm for generations. The family name would be anglicized and his descendants adopted varying spellings, including Koiner, Coyner, and Coiner, names heavily represented throughout Augusta County and the United States in general.

Blair Coiner was born in 1900. According to family lore he inherited the money that set him up in business in the 1920s. He initially pursued the taxicab business, buying a pair of cars that served the Staunton area. He then began buying and selling batteries, according to Fisher spokesperson Ken Cox, and soon began dealing in a wider range of auto parts. With the use of a Model T one-ton truck Coiner began distributing his wares to area car dealers, garages, and service stations. In a matter of four years his one truck grew into a fleet of six specialty delivery vehicles, capable of holding hundreds of auto parts while also carrying the tools necessary to offer machine shop services. In this way Coiner salesmen could bring replacement parts to remote areas and had the capability of staying out on the road for a week at a time before returning home to Staunton for rest and replenishment of supplies.

In time, the rural deliver business gave way to auto parts stores and Coiner Parts became a wholesale distributor. Blair Coiner also became involved in other ventures, such as purchasing a 49-room Staunton hotel that eventually became the Ingleside Resort & Country Club. He was, in fact, better known as a hotelier than a purveyor of aftermarket auto parts. Coiner Parts was a relatively modest business by the 1960s, comprised of just a single store in Staunton. The man who was responsible for growing the business into a regional concern was Coiner's son-in-law, Arthur Jay Fisher, Jr.

Art Fisher was born in Delton, Michigan, in 1938. After graduating from Hope College in Holland, Michigan, in 1960, Fisher taught school in Holland at West Ottawa High School for four years. He married Mary Louise Coiner, Blair Coiner's daughter, and in 1964 the couple moved to Staunton. Fisher gave up teaching and went to work for what was then known as Coiner Auto Parts. In that same year the business relocated from a downtown site to the outskirts of Staunton on Greenville Avenue, where it had more room for expansion. After Blair Coiner died in 1968, his daughter inherited the business and Fisher became chief executive officer and chairman of the board, and

began to take advantage of the extra space to grow Coiner Auto Parts.

FEDERATED AUTO PARTS FORMED

Given how much Fisher had grown the company, it was fitting that in 1983 the business was renamed Fisher Auto Parts. It was a period of rapid consolidation in the aftermarket parts industry and Art Fisher responded by aggressively acquiring stores in order to compete in larger markets. He also looked to join forces with other wholesale distributors to leverage their size and improve their collective marketing strength. In May 1985 he brought Fisher and 23 other wholesale distributors together to form Federated Auto Parts Distributors, Inc.

Federated was actually part of a second wave of programmed distribution groups that brought together wholesale distributors, but unlike the others, which were just buying groups, Federated started out as a nonprofit marketing group. The company urged its members to embrace common product lines, and even before Federated was formed, Fisher had put in place a preferred vendor program. Only with common lines could the members effectively market together, a concept that members would eventually embrace. "We knew from the beginning," Art Fisher told *Automotive Marketing* in 1998, "that to accomplish what we wanted to in our marketing efforts, we had to have one voice." One of the first marketing programs was a monthly wholesale magazine, the *Competitive Edge*. Federated also produced a weekly retail flyer named the *Advantage*.

Federated introduced a full range of programs, allowing members to create a program that worked best in their markets, including logo programs, and inventory and stock level programs developed in conjunction with manufacturers. Members were also encouraged to open and acquire stores to grow the network. Fisher Auto Parts led the way in this effort and Art Fisher also acquired wholesale distributors and jobbers to expand Federated. In 1988, for example, Fisher added three small job chains, bringing the total number of Fisher Auto Parts stores to 120. It also acquired distribution centers. Moreover, Federated developed a private-label strategy offering its own line of products under the Federated name to improve margins, while simultaneously pursuing a co-labeling program, building up the Federated name by joining it with such well-known brands as BWD, Moog, Anco, Champion, Raybestos, and Monroe.

BO FISHER NAMED PRESIDENT

Helping Art Fisher to grow Fisher Auto Parts and Federated Auto Parts was his son, Arthur Jay "Bo" Fisher III.

KEY DATES

1929: Blair C. Coiner forms Coiner Parts Inc.
1964: Coiner's son-in-law, Arthur Fisher, joins company; the business relocates to larger site.
1968: Blair Coiner dies; Fisher becomes CEO and chairman.
1983: Coiner Auto Parts is renamed Fisher Auto Parts.
1985: Art Fisher establishes Federated Auto Parts Distributors, Inc.
1992: Fisher's, son, Bo Fisher, is named president.
1995: Federated launches its first national marketing campaign.
2004: Art Fisher dies; Bo Fisher succeeds him as CEO and chair.

In 1992 Bo Fisher was named president of Fisher Auto Parts, which enjoyed strong growth in the early 1990s. By the fall of 1995 the chain had grown to more than 200 stores and 14 distribution centers, of which 12 were bought from other companies. Generating net sales of about $150 million, Fisher ranked No. 13 on *Automotive Marketing*'s Top 100 list of auto parts stores in 1995. It was by far the largest member of Federated. The second largest member was Cincinnati, Ohio-based KOI Warehouse, operating 52 stores that generated a combined $125 million.

After a decade of growing the Federated brand through local and regional advertising, Federated in the fall of 1995 launched its first national marketing campaign. It focused on radio and television spots that ran on programming that appealed to the target audience, such as motor sports, hunting, and fishing programming on ESPN. As Federated's national marketing strategy evolved, advertising was tied into the sponsorship of a truck in the NASCAR Truck Series and a NASCAR truck race in Nashville, Tennessee. National retail flyers were also produced for the spring and fall as part of a jobber program, distributed by Fisher Auto Parts stores and other Federated members.

The Fisher family continued to expand Fisher Auto Parts in the second half of the 1990s. Fisher Auto Parts increased sales to $193 million in 1996, of which 80 percent was wholesale. Much of that growth was due to further acquisitions, bringing the total number of stores to 240. In 1997 the company maintained the pace by acquiring Shepherds Auto Supply, Inc., adding two stores in Roanoke, Virginia, to reenter a market it had

exited some years earlier. Shepherd stores were also operated in nearby Salem and Christiansburg, Virginia. The deal brought another $10 million in annual revenues to Fisher Auto Parts. A year later, Knoxville, Tennessee-based Motor Products Company was acquired, bringing with it ten auto parts stores located throughout eastern Tennessee and a Knoxville warehouse. The Fisher chain then reached the 250-store mark and stretched across 14 states.

Federated also sustained its strong growth in the late 1990s. No longer was it efficient to run everything out of the Staunton office, and in 1997 regional managers living around the country were hired, some of whom also worked for a Federated member. By the summer of 1998 Federated had 93 warehouse distributor members operating 144 distribution centers, mostly catering to professional installers. The Federated family also included some 2,000 Federated Car Care Centers, which Federated supported by providing illuminated outdoor signage and a management package that included an electronic ordering and cataloging system. In 1998 Federated began running national TV ads to promote the Car Care Centers; the spots were later made available to members for local use.

GROWTH IN THE 21ST CENTURY

The Fisher enterprises maintained steady growth as the new century dawned. In 2000 Fisher Auto Parts, then 265 units in size supported by 17 distribution centers, acquired Federated members Quinsig Automotive Parts Inc. and Christie & Thomson, which they consolidated. The new Worcester, Massachusetts-based company operated 15 stores in central and western Massachusetts, supplied by a warehouse in Worcester. Also in 2000 Fisher expanded its Staunton operation to support the expanding Fisher and Federated businesses. A building purchased in 1999 for $1.5 million was opened in August of the following year to house a parts store, automotive machine shop, automotive glass shop, and a fleet maintenance shop, and to provide warehousing for Federated. Administrative offices and a warehouse remained at the Greenville Avenue site. Altogether, Fisher Auto Parts at this time had 365,000 square feet of administrative and warehouse space in Staunton.

Bo Fisher was then serving as chairman of Federated, which by 2001 included 85 wholesale distributor members, 3,800 jobbers, 2,400 Federated Car Care Repair Centers, and 147 distribution centers. Despite ongoing consolidation in the automotive aftermarket industry, Federated continued to enjoy strong growth, regularly bringing outside jobbers and distributors into the fold. Bo Fisher would take on additional responsibilities as well. In early 2004 his father died at the age of 65, succumbing to cancer after a lengthy fight. Art Fisher left behind the Fisher Auto Parts chain of more than 300 stores and 18 warehouses along with 3,800 Federated Auto Parts Stores. The former schoolteacher had also been an industry leader, having served as chairman of Automotive Warehouse Distributors Association. In 2001 he had been honored by being inducted into the Automotive Hall of Fame.

Following the death of his father, Bo Fisher was unanimously elected CEO of Fisher Auto Parts and chairman of the board. He was well prepared to take the helm, having already played an important role in both the Fisher Auto Parts and Federated operations, which continued to grow under his leadership. In 2007, for example, Fisher added four stores in Maryland by acquiring Hayden's Auto Supply, Inc., a Federated member since 1999. In 2009 Fisher celebrated its 80th anniversary by opening new stores in West Virginia and Pennsylvania and building up its presence in New Hampshire by acquiring the 12 store Robbins Auto Parts chain and centralized distribution center. Robbins was one of the original Federated members and at this time generated about $30 million in annual revenues. Plans were also in the works to add two new distribution centers. There was every reason to expect that Fisher Auto Parts and Federated were well positioned to enjoy further success in the years to come.

Ed Dinger

PRINCIPAL SUBSIDIARIES

Blankenship Auto Parts; Shepherds Auto Supply; Manlove Auto Parts; Daniels Auto Supply; Phillips Auto Parts.

PRINCIPAL COMPETITORS

Advance Auto Parts, Inc.; AutoZone, Inc.; Genuine Parts Company.

FURTHER READING

DiSalvo, Kristie, "Fisher Expands to Statler Boulevard," *Staunton (Va.) Daily News Leader,* August 11, 2000, p. 3A.

"Federated Celebrates Decade as Full Line Marketing Group," *Automotive Marketing,* September 1995, p. 9.

"Federated Continues to Target Traditional Market," *Automotive Marketing,* June 1998, p. 15.

"Federated Keeps Building Tradition in the Traditional Marketplace," *Automotive Marketing,* December 2001, p. 21.

"Group Sees Strong Marketing as Key to Growth," *Automotive Marketing,* June 1998, p. 20.

Langley, Maria, "Staunton Auto Parts Store Founder Dies at 65,"*Staunton (Va.) Daily News Leader,* January 16, 2004, p. 1A.

Peyton, J. Lewin, *History of Augusta County,* Staunton, Va.: Samuel M. Yost & Son, 1882.

Schnabel, Megan, "Staunton Chain Buys Shepherds," *Roanoke Times,* October 3, 1997, p. A5.

Gallup, Inc.

901 F Street N.W., Suite 200
Washington, D.C. 20004
U.S.A.
Telephone: (202) 715-3030
Toll Free: (877) 242-5587
Fax: (202) 715-3041
Web site: http://www.gallup.com

Private Company
Founded: 1935
Employees: 2,000
Sales: $180 million (2008 est.)
NAICS: 541611 Administrative Management and General Management Consulting Services; 541910 Marketing Research and Public Opinion Polling

■ ■ ■

Gallup, Inc., was created in 1958 by George Gallup, whose name worldwide is all but synonymous with public opinion polling. The Gallup Poll, which monitors political and economic trends, has been conducted since 1935. Some 2,000 professionals, including leading scientists in fields such as sociology, economics, management, and psychology, work at 40 Gallup locations throughout the world. Toward the end of the first decade of the 21st century, the company operates Gallup Consulting, a research-based consultancy; Gallup University, a provider of both degree and non-degree programs; and a publishing arm called Gallup Press.

EARLY POLLING METHODS

Although George Gallup did not invent public opinion polling, he virtually created the image of the "pollster." He helped to incorporate scientific methodology in the mid-1930s, but almost as important was his gift for promoting the field and himself. The scores of pollsters working in politics as well as in market research in the 21st century have all benefited from his pioneering efforts.

Political polls were conducted in the United States long before Gallup. The first published presidential poll, based on a straw vote, appeared on July 24, 1824, in the *Harrisburg Pennsylvanian*. Newspapers at the time were little more than vehicles for the political parties, but as economic pressures forced publishers to become less partisan in order to expand readership, objectivity became a virtue. Straw polls were, by definition, objective; and by the beginning of the 20th century they had become a staple of newspapers.

The way straw polls were conducted, however, did not lend itself to accuracy. Some newspapers and magazines printed the ballot within its pages. Readers mailed in or hand delivered their votes, and they were encouraged to stuff the ballot box by purchasing more copies of the publication. Reliable results were willingly sacrificed for a spike in sales. A later technique, the mail ballot, selected names from such sources as telephone directories, registered voter lists, and automobile registrations. A sample was then created by pulling names at certain intervals, such as every tenth one. It was more difficult to stuff the ballot box, but the sample had an inherent bias against the lower economic strata.

The personal canvass proved to be the most reliable method for conducting straw votes. Under this method, solicitors would hand out pencils and ballots to people on the street and collect the votes on the spot. Some newspapers made an attempt to sample a cross section of voters by creating quotas for their solicitors, for example requiring a certain number of white-collar voters from one community and blue-collar voters from another. Although arrived at intuitively, this technique anticipated the scientific polling that Gallup and others would refine.

PREDICTING RESULTS

Most of the early newspaper polls were local or regional. The *New York Herald Tribune* and collaborating newspapers began to conduct wider pre-election polls in the 1890s. By 1912 they polled in over 35 states. The Hearst newspapers attempted nationwide polling in 1924. Although 43 states were covered, the average error rate was a high 6 percent. In 1928, however, Hearst had an error rate of less than three points in 46 states.

By the 1930s the publication with the greatest reputation for accurate polling was the *Literary Digest*—the *Time* or *Newsweek* of its day. The *Digest* mailed out an incredible 20 million ballots and covered all 48 states. Although some critics questioned the sample, maintaining that the *Digest* overemphasized the higher income brackets, the results of the 1932 election silenced all doubters. The straw poll predicted a Franklin Roosevelt win with 59.85 percent of the popular vote. The election results gave Roosevelt the win with 59.14 percent of the vote. The straw poll also predicted that Roosevelt would win 41 states, totaling 474 electoral votes. The actual results were 42 states and 472 electoral votes.

The *Literary Digest* did not hesitate to boast about its accomplishment and was very confident in its ability to predict election results. Then in the summer of 1936, more than six weeks before the *Digest* began its massive mailing to poll for the winner of the Roosevelt–Alf Landon presidential race, a little-known pollster from Princeton, New Jersey, predicted that the *Digest* would be wrong, and he had the further audacity to predict their final numbers. That pollster was George Gallup.

Gallup had attended the University of Iowa, where he became editor of the campus newspaper. While working one summer for a St. Louis advertising agency that was researching reader satisfaction with the *St. Louis Post-Dispatch,* Gallup decided that there had to be a more efficient way to measure opinions than to go from door to door, neighborhood after neighborhood. He wondered if he could use techniques similar to the ones employed by government inspectors who might test a crop of wheat or a supply of water by taking several small samples and then extrapolate the quality of the entire amount.

While teaching journalism at Iowa, Gallup earned his M.A. and Ph.D. His doctoral dissertation, "A New Technique for Objective Methods for Measuring Reader Interest in Newspapers," outlined what would simply become known as the "Gallup Method." He began to conduct surveys and publish the results in trade magazines, drawing the attention of the newspaper world. In 1932 the New York advertising agency Young & Rubicam hired him as director of research. He would work for the company until 1947.

GALLUP PREDICTS ROOSEVELT TO WIN IN 1936

It was also in 1932 that Gallup's mother-in-law was elected Iowa's secretary of state, under unusual circumstances. She had been placed on the ballot in honor of her husband who had died during a run for governor in 1926. Despite running as a Democrat in a heavily Republican state, and without even mounting a campaign, she was swept into office with a Roosevelt landslide. Gallup began to wonder if his sampling methods could be used to forecast such drastic changes in public opinion. He used the congressional elections of 1934 as a test and came within one percentage point of predicting the overall returns. A Chicago agent, Harold R. Anderson, recognized the potential to make money out of the technique and partnered with Gallup to create the American Institute of Public Opinion in 1935. They set up shop in Princeton, New Jersey, with the hope that the prestigious Princeton postmark might influence people to mail back their questionnaires to the "Institute" that was in actuality a one-room office in which a handful of workers hand counted ballots.

In 1935 Gallup began writing a syndicated column using his poll results, titled "America Speaks." To sweeten his pitch to newspapers, Gallup offered a

KEY DATES

1935: George Gallup begins syndication of "America Speaks" column; founds the American Institute of Public Opinion.

1936: Gallup's reputation is made by predicting Roosevelt's win over Landon in the presidential election.

1948: Pollsters, including Gallup, predict Dewey to defeat Truman.

1958: The Gallup Organization is incorporated and the many companies founded by George Gallup are brought under the one umbrella organization.

1984: George Gallup dies.

1988: The Gallup Organization is sold to Selection Research Inc. but maintains Princeton, New Jersey, headquarters.

1999: Gallup produces its first best-selling book called *First, Break All the Rules*.

2001: The quarterly *Gallup Management Journal* is introduced, as well as a subscription-based electronic news magazine named the *Gallup Poll Tuesday Briefing*.

2003: The 50-acre Gallup University Riverfront Campus in Omaha, Nebraska, is developed.

2004: A book publishing arm named the Gallup Press is established to produce the company's own business titles.

2008: Gallup begins offering a daily consumer confidence indicator.

money-back guarantee that he would prove more accurate than the illustrious *Literary Digest* poll in predicting the presidential election of 1936. His partner was then able to place "America Speaks" with 42 newspapers. More than pride was then on the line. Given the cost of a poll sample of 15,000 respondents, ten times the size of what he would one day use, Gallup faced financial ruin. The *Digest,* suffering so much from the effects of the Great Depression that it was forced to reduce its mailing to ten million pieces, was more than eager to defend its franchise and to ridicule Gallup's charge that by drawing its sample mostly from the ranks of people who owned telephones and automobiles the *Digest* would undercount lower-income voters.

The final *Digest* poll results were within one percentage point of Gallup's earlier forecast. The *Digest* gave the election to Landon with 57 percent of the vote. Gallup gave it to Roosevelt with 54 percent. In reality Roosevelt won another landslide victory, taking 61 percent of the popular vote. Gallup was off by seven points, much to his dismay, but at least he picked the winner. The *Literary Digest* put on a brave front, refusing to acknowledge its errors, but its reputation was shattered, and within a year the magazine folded.

POLLING RESULTS DISPLAY BIAS

The career of Gallup, as well as those of Elmo Roper and Archibald Crossley, who also predicted the Roosevelt victory, flourished. However, it was Gallup who became the best known of the new scientific pollsters. "America Speaks" would eventually be carried by 200 newspapers. He founded the British Institute of Public Opinion, as well as polling operations in dozens of other foreign countries, making Princeton, New Jersey, the public opinion polling capital of the world. The Audience Research Institute, which Gallup founded in 1937, studied public reaction to movie titles, casts, and stories. He began to keep tabs on questions that would be taken for granted in the 21st century, but provided a historical perspective on the American public and its officials. He kept track of presidential popularity. He was the first to ask, "Who would you vote for if the election was held today?" He asked Americans if they believed in God and how often they went to church. When Senator Joseph Lieberman was selected to run as the Democratic vice-presidential candidate in 2000, journalists could report how the country had changed in its willingness to vote for a Jewish American, because the Gallup Poll had been asking the question since the 1930s.

Gallup continued to refine his techniques, determined to avoid the large margin of error in his polling of the 1936 election. He no longer relied on mail ballots, because higher-income voters were more likely to return them, which he felt would favor Republican candidates. He sent his people into the field to interview respondents, with quotas based on demographic categories, such as age, sex, geography, and income. The interviewers, however, were given too much latitude. Rather than embarrass respondents by asking their age or income, they often guessed. Interviewers also tended to seek out respondents with whom they felt most comfortable, with the result that working-class interviewers and white-collar interviewers were getting different results.

Overall, the Gallup Poll was displaying a systematic bias in favor of Republican positions over Democratic ones, enough to prompt Congress to call in Gallup to explain his election results of 1940 and 1944 that underestimated the Democratic vote in two-thirds of the states. A technical committee criticized him for using a quota system instead of "probability" sampling, a method that would give everyone an equal chance of being included in a poll. However, probability sampling was both complicated and extremely expensive. Gallup felt that the difference between quota and probability sampling was not large enough to justify the cost. Only in a very close election would it even matter; as it happened, such an election was at hand.

REPUTATION TARNISHED IN 1948 ELECTION

The presidential election of 1948 would prove almost as devastating to Gallup as the 1936 contest was to the *Literary Digest.* Because the Democratic Party was splintered, with Henry A. Wallace running for president on the Progressive Party ticket and Strom Thurmond representing the Dixiecrats, Harry Truman appeared to have little chance to retain the White House against the bid of the Republican nominee, Thomas Dewey. Gallup and the other major pollsters believed that public opinion only showed dramatic change when responding to important events. Political campaigns were not considered important enough; a poll taken after the political conventions would surely predict the winner. Gallup stopped polling in mid-October, and although he noted a surge in support for Truman, he felt confident that Dewey would win the election. All the experts agreed with him. Truman did not stop campaigning, however; he beat the odds, and won the election.

"The pollsters became national laughingstocks," according to Michael Wheeler, author of *Lies, Damn Lies and Statistics,* "and Gallup, the most famous pollster of them all, took the hardest fall. Others were more graceful in their embarrassment, but Gallup was indignant. How, he sputtered, could scientific surveys be expected to take into account 'bribery of voters' and 'tampering with ballot boxes.'" Gallup was also accused of favoritism, a charge that could prove devastating to a man whose business depended on impartiality. Although Gallup vehemently denied that he rigged polls to favor Dewey, he admitted that he considered Dewey to be a close friend and had been in contact with him throughout the 1948 campaign.

There was no doubt, however, that Gallup's reputation had been tarnished. Many newspapers, unwilling to accept his explanation that this was an election that would happen only once in a generation, threatened to cancel their contracts. Gallup managed to survive, became more scrupulous about maintaining distance from political candidates, and improved his polling methods. Still, the influence of political polling in America was diminished until the 1960s.

CONTINUED CONTROVERSY

While other polling operations began to focus on the more profitable area of market research, Gallup maintained his academic approach. Finally in 1958 he created the Gallup Organization and moved his company into market research, but he never achieved a significant share of the business. Although in 1966 his son, George Gallup Jr., became president of the Gallup Organization, the elder Gallup continued to serve as chairman of the board and was actively engaged in its day-to-day operations. He vowed that he would never retire, and he never did. He died in 1984 of a heart attack at his summer home in Switzerland.

Gallup's final years were not, however, without controversy. In 1968 two of Gallup's interviewers were discovered to have falsified data in a poll of Harlem residents conducted for the *New York Times.* More troubling were charges that Gallup's people maintained improper ties to the Nixon administration. Poll numbers were provided before publication, allowing Richard Nixon to prepare the public and to put the best possible spin on the results. Nixon's aides also suggested questions for the Gallup Poll, thus influencing public opinion from the outset. The Nixon administration used both Gallup and rival Louis Harris, misleading the pollsters' associates into thinking that Nixon would not make improper use of early poll results. At the very least the pollsters were naive. The fact that Gallup officials met with Nixon aides only in a hotel rather than at the White House was a tacit admission that public knowledge of such contact would compromise the company's reputation for objectivity.

With the loss of its founder in 1984, the Gallup Organization struggled. According to George M. Taber writing for *Business News New Jersey,* "One of the most difficult transitions any corporation faces is to move away from the structure and style established by the founding father and become a company that has a life bigger than he. Corporations as large as the Ford Motor Company and as small as a country grocery store have faced that challenge. It was a transition, however, that the Gallup Organization did not successfully make."

NEW OWNERSHIP

The Gallup name did retain brand value, and in 1988, after discussing a merger for three years, the Gallup family sold its private company to Selection Research, Inc., a selection and marketing research firm based in

Lincoln, Nebraska. Gallup's data processing and interviewing operations were moved to Lincoln, but the company's headquarters remained in Princeton, considered the "epicenter of the polling world," according to a 1997 article in *Business News New Jersey.* The Gallup Organization continued to produce the Gallup Poll in conjunction with print and television news organizations, and became more aggressive in performing surveys for corporations and marketers.

Under its new parent, led by Chairman Don Clifton and President Jim Clifton, as well as the leadership of the Gallup Organization cochairmen Alec Gallup and George Gallup Jr., the founder's sons, the Gallup Organization saw increasing revenues in the late 1990s at an estimated annual rate of 30 percent. In a 1997 interview for *Marketing News,* the two men discussed the future of the research industry in an age of rapid technological advancement, agreeing that although the polling process had become quicker and more sophisticated, the "fine art of crafting a good question" remained integral to successful polling. Regarding Gallup's prominence in its field, one in which competition was heating up in the late 1990s, Alec Gallup noted, "We do have an advantage—and it's an important one and we exploit the hell out of it—and that is the fact that the Gallup name is well-known and has credibility."

Gallup rounded out the decade by introducing a management consulting tool called Q 12, which for the first time identified the link between engaged employees and financial outcomes through 12 key questions. The tool gave corporate leaders insight into issues that impacted workplace morale and productivity. Around the same time, the company produced a best-selling book called *First, Break All the Rules,* which focused on the importance of employee engagement.

EXPANDED CAPABILITIES

Gallup ushered in the new millennium by relocating 100 employees from its Maryland office to 49,000 square feet of office space in a building in the East End of Washington, D.C. Around the same time, the company also developed a management theory called the Gallup Path, which determined how business outcomes were impacted by human nature. The Gallup Path would eventually become the organization's premier management consulting model.

In early 2001, Gallup introduced the quarterly *Gallup Management Journal,* which drew upon the company's management science research to provide analysts, investors, government leaders, and business executives with informative articles about relevant issues. The company also introduced a subscription-based

electronic news magazine named the *Gallup Poll Tuesday Briefing,* which summarized the latest Gallup Poll results. It also was in 2001 that Gallup signed a $3 million technology leasing agreement with U.S. Bancorp Oliver-Allen Technology Leasing, allowing it to equip its workforce with the latest computer technology. That same year, Donald O. Clifton, Ph.D., and other Gallup scientists developed a program called the Clifton StrengthsFinder. Relying upon a web-based talent assessment tool that focused on individual strengths, the program helped people to discover their strengths and maximize their potential.

Gallup kicked off 2002 by announcing a publishing agreement with Warner Business Books. The deal, which netted the company a seven-figure advance, followed Gallup's best-selling business books *First, Break All the Rules* and *Now, Discover Your Strengths,* which had been published by Simon & Schuster. Gallup agreed to publish at least five books with Warner as part of the deal. In October 2002, the Gallup Brain was introduced, providing subscribers to the *Gallup Poll Tuesday Briefing* with access to searchable survey results and content dating back to 1935. Gallup designed the new resource with world leaders in mind, equipping them with a tool to improve their decision-making abilities.

In 2002, Gallup generated approximately $200 million in revenue. Of this amount, about 40 percent came from market research, while 3 percent came from its syndicated public opinion polls, which were purchased by the likes of *USA Today* and CNN. At this time, Gallup was experiencing rapid growth in the area of management consulting. Following its success with business books, the company focused on marketing more of its own information. As Chairman James K. Clifton explained in the July 21, 2003, issue of the *New York Times,* "We want to turn into our very own media outlet."

CONTINUED GROWTH

The 50-acre Gallup University Riverfront Campus in Omaha, Nebraska, was developed in 2003. The following year, a book publishing arm, the Gallup Press, was established to produce the company's own business titles. Gallup's growth also was marked by physical expansion during the middle years of the decade. For example, during the first quarter of 2005, the company agreed to occupy the 12th floor of the Adelphi, an Art Deco building in London. Later that year, Gallup signed a contract to use the Kiewit Institute's new supercomputer, located at the Holland Computing Center at the University of Nebraska on Omaha's South Campus.

In 2005 Gallup began a 100-year survey project known as the Gallup World Poll. With ongoing research projects in more than 150 countries and nationally representative polling in at least 130 of them annually, Gallup began collecting and analyzing information about the well-being and conditions of 95 percent of the world's population. Gallup planned to use the new supercomputer to run its World Poll.

In 2008 Gallup began interviewing a nationally representative sample of 1,000 American adults every single day on their well-being, economic issues, and political issues. The survey offered a daily measure on various indexes, including life evaluation, economic outlook, health, personal finance, and consumer confidence, providing economists with tools to quickly gauge and measure the impact of various events and economic developments in real time. Gallup also began using the Oracle Business Intelligence Suite, Enterprise Edition, software in 2008, giving its business users self-service analytical and reporting tools.

By 2009 Gallup had expanded the scope of its organization well beyond its polling roots. By drawing upon the wisdom and data it had gathered over the course of many decades, and combining it with experience in the areas of research, education, and consulting, Gallup appeared to be uniquely positioned for continued success.

Ed Dinger
Updated, Paul R. Greenland

PRINCIPAL DIVISIONS

Gallup Poll; Gallup Consulting; Gallup University; Gallup Press.

PRINCIPAL COMPETITORS

The Boston Consulting Group Inc.; Harris Interactive Inc.; McKinsey & Co.

FURTHER READING

Coy, Peter, "Consumer Pain Is Gallup's Gain; Gallup's New Tool Gauges Consumer Confidence Daily. Right Now, 85% of Americans Say Economic Conditions Are Getting Worse," *Business Week Online,* April 9, 2008.

Gallup, George Horace, *The Pulse of Democracy,* New York: Greenwood Press, 1968.

"'Gallup Management Journal' Launched by the Gallup Organization," *Business Publisher,* March 16, 2001.

"The Gallup Organization Has Launched a Subscription-Based News Service Called the Gallup Poll Tuesday Briefing," *Online,* March–April 2003.

Jacobs, Lawrence, and Robert Y. Shapiro, "Presidential Manipulation of Polls and Public Opinion," *Political Science Quarterly,* Winter 1995/1996, p. 519.

McCullough, David, *Truman,* New York: Touchstone, 1992.

Miller, Cyndee, "Gallup Brothers Analyze the Research Industry," *Marketing News,* January 6, 1997, p. 2.

Moore, David W., *The Super Pollsters,* New York: Four Walls Eight Windows, 1992.

Pace, Eric, obituary, *New York Times,* July 28, 1984, pp. 1, 9.

Smith, Richard D., "In Polling, It All Started with Gallup," *Business News New Jersey,* April 21, 1997, p. 5.

Spiro, Leah Nathans, "Gallup, the Pollster, Wants to Be Known for Its Consulting," *New York Times,* July 21, 2003.

Sussman, Barry, obituary, *Washington Post,* July 28, 1984, pp. A1, A7.

Taber, George M., "Gallup Polls Sells Out to a Nebraska Company," *Business News New Jersey,* October 11, 1988.

Wheeler, Michael, *Lies, Damn Lies and Statistics,* New York: Liveright, 1976.

Gertrude Hawk
Chocolates Inc.

—■—

9 Keystone Industrial Park
Dunmore, Pennsylvania 18512
U.S.A.
Telephone: (570) 342-7556
Fax: (570) 342-0261
Web site: http://www.gertrudehawk.com

Private Company
Founded: 1936
Employees: 1,000
Sales: $90 million (2008 est.)
NAICS: 311330 Confectionery Manufacturing from Purchased Chocolate; 311320 Chocolate and Confectionery Manufacturing from Cacao Beans

■ ■ ■

A top-ranked national candymaker, Gertrude Hawk Chocolates Inc. operates more than 75 retail stores in New York, New Jersey, and Pennsylvania, and employs a workforce that ranges from 300 to 625 persons during peak seasons. The company is a major economic force in northeastern Pennsylvania and has a reputation for being one of the Northeast's most successful and visible privately owned companies. The company's own brand accounts for only about 40 percent of its sales; the rest comes from contract or private-label manufacturing of chocolates and the sale of chocolate-based ingredients to other confectioners.

HOME-BASED ORIGINS

The company's history may be traced to early 20th-century Pennsylvania, where, after her father died, and with her mother being invalid, Gertrude Jones began work to help support herself and her family. In 1915 at age 12 she learned to make candy in a little neighborhood shop on the west side of Scranton, Pennsylvania. It was a skill she was later to perfect for her own profit. After marrying Elmer Hawk and giving birth to two sons in the 1920s, Gertrude Hawk began life as an entrepreneur. In 1936, during the Great Depression, she established a candymaking operation. Hawk developed a small, steady business selling chocolates and other confections from home; her molasses coconut treats proved a bestseller into the 1940s.

When Gertrude's son Elmer Hawk returned home after service in World War II, he partnered with his parents and invested in machinery to help automate and build his mother's chocolate business. At this time the business was still very small and barely profitable. Gross sales for 1946 totaled just under $3,000, and direct sales were conducted in the living room of the Hawk home, which became a little busier during the holiday season. However, the Hawks soon hit upon an idea that would make growth possible.

CARVING OUT A NICHE IN THE BUSINESS

Gertrude Hawk's decision to direct marketing efforts to local churches seeking to hold fund-raisers proved seminal to her company's future growth. A Methodist church and a Lutheran church, both in Scranton, were

COMPANY PERSPECTIVES

For over 70 years the company has grown to become a nationally respected manufacturer and distributor of fine quality chocolates. Dedicated crafts people blend the finest, freshest ingredients using time tested recipes to create mouth-watering chocolates. Every box of delicious chocolates contains a personal guarantee of satisfaction.

the first to contract with Hawk for fund-raiser chocolates. The orders were delivered by Elmer Hawk, who, because of his aptitude with mechanics, also took care of finding and repairing machinery, much of it secondhand, to make the candy. Elmer's wife Louise also became involved in the business, keeping the books and records.

From the late 1940s to the early 1960s, Gertrude Hawk Chocolates grew steadily. By 1959 the company was reporting annual sales of $125,000. Also that year, the family learned that the Hawk house was to be demolished in order to make room for a bridge on Interstate 81. The time was right for the company to move into bigger facilities. The Hawks spent a little over $6,000 for four acres of land in nearby Dunmore and arranged for the construction of the first Gertrude Hawk factory. Construction was completed in 1962 and the factory became operable in November of that year. The retail section of the facility, comprising a full-service restaurant, opened the following year.

In 1971, the third generation of Hawks entered the business. Elmer's son, Dave Hawk, had been interested in the company from a very early age. According to his recollections in a 2005 *Candy Industry* article, as a child he liked to visit the plant, which then employed fewer than 30 workers, with his father on Saturdays. Upon his graduation from Pennsylvania State University with a degree in business in 1971, he joined Gertrude Hawk Chocolates and helped the company evolve from a family business to a midsized corporation. Father and son worked side by side as co-owners of Gertrude Hawk Chocolates from 1972 until the early 1990s when Elmer Hawk retired. In 1973, the Gertrude Hawk restaurant was shuttered and the space was used to set up a retail candy shop. Also during this time, Elmer Hawk bought out his parents' interest in the company.

In 1982, Dave Hawk contacted the home sale cosmetics company Avon, which was thinking about selling chocolate in its catalog, and Gertrude Hawk

Chocolates entered into a two-year arrangement to make 25,000 units of candy per day for the new customer. "The truth is we had never made 25,000 units daily in our lifetime," confessed Hawk in a 2005 *Candy Industry* article. "It was way more than we could bite off. ... We put all our resources into it and did it well." The account forced the company to "become a real manufacturer. ... [W]e learned how to put in a second shift, how to set up standards, improve our quality control and put in a real manufacturing line. Becoming a modern-day manufacturer wasn't the reason we did those things, but that's what happened as a result."

When Avon opted out of selling candy in 1984, a marketing company that focused on fund-raising approached Gertrude Hawk with a proposal for making chocolates. Gertrude Hawk called its fund-raising segment Chocolate Specialties, and by 1989 this segment represented 35 percent of Gertrude Hawk's revenues. Another key development during the 1980s was the company's decision to establish a chain of retail outlets for Gertrude Hawk chocolates.

GROWTH AND DIVERSIFICATION

After completing construction on a new 175,000-square-foot plant with ten one-shot molding lines in 1992, the company realized its need for outside help and hired David Speakman from ConAgra in 1992 as chief operating officer to blend "'big company' thinking and systems onto a small chassis." Speakman helped put in a sophisticated management information systems program, financial controls, and improved marketing and quality control. With his background in foodservice, he made it easier for Hawk to court and do business with large clients.

In 1994, Gertrude Hawk diversified, adding an ingredients business and making chocolate and compound bits and inclusions for ice cream manufacturers. The segment quickly expanded into baking, beverage, snacking, and foodservice applications, and in 1997, by which time David Hawk had taken over as president and CEO, the company began a three-year effort to develop innovative concepts in retailing and diversification. In 1999, in another move to recruit business, the company entered into a contract to make Frango mints for department store retailer Marshall Fields.

With fiscal year 2000 sales of about $64 million, 625 factory employees, and 350 employed in its 41 stores in Pennsylvania, New York, and New Jersey, Gertrude Hawk began positioning itself for a decade of growth. "We want to continue to grow the business," explained Dave Hawk in a 2000 *Northeast Pennsylvania*

Business Journal article. "We're redefining the business as an ingredients business rather than just [a maker of] ice cream inclusions." The company also opened a new type of retail store in Deptford, New Jersey, just east of Philadelphia, in mid-March 2000. At 1,700 square feet, with a country store feel and pictures of Gertrude Hawk, this retail outlet was markedly different from other Gertrude Hawk stores, more welcoming and homey by design.

Around this time, Dave Hawk decided that the company needed to hire a new leader from outside the Hawk family. His reasons were twofold: most of the fourth generation of Hawks were still young adults, and changing market conditions demanded a change of management to move the company toward new levels of success. When David Speakman went into semiretirement in 2003, Hawk hired Bill Aubrey of Kraft Foods as chief operating officer. Aubrey had been president of the cheese division of Kraft Foods in Chicago, Illinois. He had also served as Kraft's director of strategy for all brands.

CREATING A NATIONAL PRESENCE

It soon became evident that Aubrey was president in all but name, and his job title was changed to president and chief executive officer in 2004. Aubrey and Hawk worked together closely and shared responsibilities, Hawk being "the chocolate guy" involved in research and development and Aubrey "the management guy." "Dave believes that a strong management team rounds out the skill sets necessary to move the company to the next level. We have very similar belief systems about fundamental issues, such as how people should be treated, and we're like hands in a glove. We both believe two sets of thoughts together make a better team," Aubrey was quoted in a 2004 *Northeast Pennsylvania Business Journal.*

Despite having a non-relative at the company's helm, the Hawk family remained very involved in the business. Two of Dave Hawk's sisters were in charge of public relations and brand management respectively, and his brother supervised maintenance of the retail stores. "Our family members are always matched to their skills," was the way in which Dave Hawk explained his family's policy on employment in the 2004 *Northeast Pennsylvania Business Journal.* "They are paid a fair market value for the positions they hold, and they must earn their employment."

The local public, however, was not as sanguine about the change. It objected strenuously after Aubrey took the reins, spreading rumors that Dave Hawk was terminally ill. Hawk was forced to reassure the public, explaining in a 2004 *Northeast Pennsylvania Business Journal* article, "[t]he simple fact that Bill was the right person for the company at the right time. I made it clear ... that there was absolutely no need to be nervous."

The benefits of having Aubrey on board were apparent almost immediately. During his first 18 months, Gertrude Hawk added 100 new jobs, and for fiscal year 2004, the company's volume increased 40 percent over the previous two, with fiscal 2004 sales approaching $90 million. In 2005, Gertrude Hawk launched a web site, creating a national presence for the formerly exclusively East Coast company. The new site also extended the company's gift programs, including corporate gift giving and fund-raising.

ADDING PANNING OPERATIONS

All told, from 2003 to 2005 the company grew 33 percent in sales volume; by mid-decade the company, which had about 600 employees, was divided into three segments: fund-raising sales, ingredients (which included contract manufacturing and wholesale), and retail. Shortly after Dave Hawk won the 60th Kettle Award for his contributions and accomplishments in the candy industry in 2005, the company added a $1.5 million Dumoulin automated panning system for its ingredients segment.

Panning, a process in which a small kernel or center is wrapped in successive layers of coating, allowed Gertrude Hawk to take advantage of opportunities to expand inclusions for ice cream makers. "With the automated panning system, we can produce such inclusions as pretzel particles that are coated with a jalapeno cream cheese or honey mustard flavors," said Hawk in *Candy Industry* in 2005 of the Dumoulin. The company could also coat particles as fine as coconut shreds.

During the several years preceding the acquisition of the Dumoulin, the company had driven its growth through geographic expansion and had reached a total of 74 units in Pennsylvania, New Jersey, and New York. With the addition of the Dumoulin in 2005, management turned its investment emphasis to ingredients, and its goal became to break the $100 million sales mark in fewer than five years. Firmly committed to innovation, or what it called "ideation," Gertrude Hawk would continue to complete an annual plan and would spend more than $3 million on capital improvements annually with 40 percent dedicated to maintenance and the rest to innovation. "We need to continue originating new ideas, simultaneously tightening up the process we have to bring them out to our customers," said Aubrey in 2005 in the *Candy Industry* article.

By 2007, chocolates accounted for 70 percent of Gertrude Hawk's product line. Despite the economic downturn of 2008, sales at Gertrude Hawk's retail stores were comparable to 2007 as people continued to indulge in affordable luxuries. "It's a funny thing and I'm pleasantly surprised—it doesn't seem the economy is affecting us," Hawk noted in a 2008 *Citizen's Voice* article. Whether the same would be true for the years to come remained to be seen.

Carrie Rothburd

PRINCIPAL DIVISIONS

Retail; Ingredients/Inclusions, Fundraising; Contract Manufacturing.

PRINCIPAL COMPETITORS

World's Finest Chocolates; Helen Grace Chocolates Inc.

FURTHER READING

Falchek, Dave, "Luxuries Weather Downturn," *Wilkes-Barre (Pa.) Citizens' Voice,* December 14, 2008, p. A1.

———, "Not Just a Family Affair," *Scranton (Pa.) Times-Tribune,* November 20, 2005, p. H1.

Gardner, Dave, "Sweet Succession," *Northeast Pennsylvania Business Journal,* September 1, 2004, p. 1.

Moore, John L., "Candy Company Positioned for Decade of New Growth," *Northeast Pennsylvania Business Journal,* April 1, 2001, p. 59.

Pacyniak, Bernard, "Living the Plan," *Candy Industry,* July 2005, p. 18.

Gomez Inc.

10 Maguire Road, Suite 330
Lexington, Massachusetts 02421-3110
U.S.A.
Telephone: (781) 778-2700
Toll Free: (877) 372-6732
Fax: (781) 778-2799
Web site: http://www.gomez.com

Private Company
Incorporated: 1997 as Gomez Advisors
Employees: 237
Sales: $32.6 million (2007 est.)
NAICS: 511210 Software Publishers

■ ■ ■

Based in Lexington, Massachusetts, Gomez Inc. is a leading provider of web site testing software. The company's technology is used to test web site functionality under a variety of conditions and from multiple locations. Thousands of companies throughout the world use the company's Gomez ExperienceFirst platform; customers include leading financial service companies, retailers, industrial firms, and social networking providers.

FORMATIVE YEARS

The origins of Gomez Inc. date back to May 1997, when former Forrester Research analysts Julio Gomez and John M. Robb established the company as Gomez Advisors. Initial funding of $1.5 million was provided

by Ashton Technology Group Inc. A graduate of Princeton University, Gomez had built a reputation as a leading online brokerage expert, serving as senior analyst in Forrester's Money & Technology Strategies Service. Prior to that time, his 15-year career in the financial services sector included stints in bank loan syndications, executive management, investment banking, securities sales and trading, and regulatory reporting.

Likewise, Robb also had developed an impressive resume. After attending Yale University and earning an undergraduate degree in astronautical engineering from the U.S. Air Force Academy, Robb served as a command pilot in the Air Force and worked for the research firm Gartner. At Forrester, he served as a senior Internet technology analyst, working on Internet strategies for companies such as Microsoft and Netscape.

Gomez and Robb established Gomez Advisors in order to offer strategic counsel to financial institutions such as banks, brokerages, and mutual funds. Specifically, their new enterprise offered services such as web site design, implementation, and evaluation; strategic planning; and marketing/retail account acquisition. The firm served existing brokerages with its Internet and Broker Site Evaluation service, which used a scorecard tool to evaluate customer relationships, as well as attributes such as reliability and ease-of-use.

In August 1997, Dr. Alexander D. Stein joined Gomez and Robb in the corporate suite as a principal. Stein, who held a PhD in computer science from Carnegie Mellon University, brought expertise in the area of online financial product design and development to Gomez Advisors. Steady progress continued throughout the remainder of the 1990s. However, profitability remained elusive. For its fiscal year ending March 31, 1999, Gomez Advisors lost $17.9 million on revenues of $1.5 million.

EARLY CHALLENGES

By the dawn of the 21st century, Gomez Advisors was functioning as a provider of e-commerce Internet portals. Specifically, the firm operated a consumer portal that provided news, tools, ratings, and more. In addition, its GomezPro business-to-business portal provided data, analysis, and tools to approximately 800 e-commerce companies in about 25 industries. The company kicked off the new millennium with news that it had secured approximately $30 million in venture capital funding. Announced in February, the third-round funding was led by BancBoston Ventures Inc., as well as other noteworthy investors, including the John Hancock Global Technology Fund and Softbank.

In April 2000 Gomez Advisors revealed plans for an initial public offering (IPO) of its common stock, from which the company hoped to generate as much as $60 million. However, these plans were tabled in the wake of sluggish economic conditions. During the early years of the decade, the workforce at Gomez Advisors grew to include roughly 135 people. In addition to compiling content for the company's scorecards and portals, staff also generated sales leads for other Internet firms by directing traffic from its web site. Gomez Advisors generated the bulk of its revenues from a handful of main customers, including E*Trade, which represented about 19 percent of sales.

By 2001 Gomez Advisors had changed its name to Gomez Inc. In April of that year, the company eliminated approximately 40 jobs from its workforce, mainly in the consulting and market research departments. In addition to slashing costs, Gomez reined in plans to broaden its focus on various e-commerce sectors to concentrate mainly on financial services as it pursued a goal of reaching profitability quickly.

Conditions worsened throughout 2001. By August, Gomez had shuttered its office in the United Kingdom and began focusing more on its web site performance evaluation offerings as opposed to its ratings business. This shift in focus became necessary as many dot-com firms were failing, and a more conservative operating approach became necessary. In addition to a struggling economy, 2001 became especially challenging when terrorist attacks were made against the United States on September 11 of that year. Following this tragedy, businesspeople and consumers flocked to the Internet for information about investments, travel, news, and more.

In the midst of this situation the company used its Gomez Performance Network to monitor the availability and performance of leading travel and financial web sites and to provide regular updates. Around the same time, the company added a service called Gomez Load Performance Testing, which evaluated a web site's scalability. Late in the year, Gomez benefited from an additional $3.5 million in venture funding.

PERFORMANCE MANAGEMENT FOCUS

Conditions improved in 2002. Building upon its existing range of web site performance indices, including its Banking Performance Index, Gomez announced plans to unveil a new performance index for mortgage industry web sites in September. The company rounded out the year with news that it had secured an additional $750,000 in funding from its investors.

Gomez furthered its growth in early 2003, when it acquired two United Kingdom-based companies. In addition to the reseller ActualIT, the company acquired the web site monitoring firm Web Perform. At this time, Gomez served the United Kingdom and surrounding areas via its Gomez Europe arm. Progress continued during the latter part of 2003, when $6.1 million in equity funding was secured to support international expansion, product development, and channel distribution initiatives. The additional funding came on the heels of eight consecutive quarters of revenue growth for the company's Internet Performance Management (IPM) business.

During 2003, Stein was serving as president and CEO of Gomez. Billing itself as The Internet Performance Management Company, Gomez served a customer base that had grown to include the BBC, Eastman Kodak, Motorola, Audi, Bristol Myers-Squibb, Citibank, and Hasbro. In October, the company secured Ruder Finn to serve as its public relations agency.

During the third quarter of 2003, Gomez saw its sales skyrocket 93 percent over the same period in 2002.

KEY DATES

1997: Former Forrester Research analysts Julio Gomez and John M. Robb establish the company as Gomez Advisors.

2000: Plans for the company's initial public offering (IPO) are tabled due to sluggish economic conditions.

2001: Gomez Advisors changes its name to Gomez Inc.

2003: Gomez receives the Editor's Choice Award from *Network Computing Magazine.*

2004: The company sells its Gomez Pro benchmarking and web site assessment business unit to Watchfire Corp. in order to focus exclusively on Internet Performance Management (IPM).

2008: Gomez files with the U.S. Securities and Exchange Commission for its IPO.

Driving its growth was the addition of 90 new customers, including eBay, Bell Canada, T-Mobile, Virgin Mobile, Royal Bank of Scotland, Lands' End, Prudential Insurance, and Visa international. Growth was especially strong in the company's IPM business, subscriptions to which surged 84 percent during the fourth quarter and 51 percent for the year. Gomez capped off the year on a high note when it received the Editor's Choice Award for ranking first in a three-month Internet performance monitoring service test hosted by *Network Computing Magazine.*

Following strong growth within its IPM business, a key milestone in Gomez's history occurred when the company decided to focus exclusively in that area. As part of this strategy, its Gomez Pro benchmarking and web site assessment business unit was sold to the online business management software and services company Watchfire Corp. in March 2004.

Around the time of the Watchfire deal, Gomez created a new executive vice-president of worldwide operations position in order to strengthen its IPM business. Bruce Reading was hired to fill the new role. Another highlight in 2004 occurred when Gomez CEO Stein received the New England Entrepreneur of the Year Award in the Web Infrastructure and Services, Information Technology category from Ernst & Young. Stein left Gomez at the end of the year, in order to establish Boxborough, Massachusetts-based Hybrid Power Solutions. However, he remained a strategic adviser to the company.

LEADERSHIP CHANGES

The introduction of new services continued at Gomez during the middle of the decade. In February 2005 the company rolled out Gomez Performance Index for Credit Cards. Published in the magazine *American Banker,* the new index allowed financial services companies to understand how customer behavior, experience, and satisfaction were affected by the availability and speed of online credit card applications.

A number of leadership changes also occurred. In March 2005 technology industry executive Jill Smith was named as the company's CEO, filling the void left by the departure of Stein. By September of that year, Reading had been elevated to the position of president and chief operating officer. That month, the company hired Michael Bromilow to lead its international growth efforts and fill the role of managing director for Europe, the Middle East, and Asia.

Midway through that year, a new office was established in Beijing, China, where the company planned to employ product development and engineering personnel. Shortly thereafter, Gomez indicated it would hire a direct sales and support staff to focus on Southeast Asia. By this time, Gomez was providing its services to approximately 500 companies throughout the world. The company provided web site monitoring, benchmarking, performance measurement, and more from some 12,000 monitoring sites around the globe.

Gomez began 2006 by naming Jaime W. Ellertson as CEO. Prior to joining Gomez, Ellertson had served as CEO of the software firm S1 Corp. During the second quarter, Gomez achieved record sales, bolstered by the addition of approximately 50 new customers. One reason for the popularity of the company's web site management and monitoring services was that they were delivered via a "software as a service" model, meaning that clients did not have to install and manage their own software. Gomez rounded out 2006 by announcing that its revenues had increased more than 45 percent from 2005. More than 180 new customers had come on board during the year, including Thomson Corp., ShopNBC.com, Autodesk Inc., eHarmony.com, Janus Capital Group Inc., and Avon products Inc.

STRONG GROWTH CONTINUES

During 2007 Gomez saw its customer base reach the 750 mark. That year, new quality-assurance applications were introduced, including the company's Reality XF solutions, which enabled developers to test web applications before they were deployed based upon a range of different variables, including connection types, operating systems, browsers, and geographies.

Other noteworthy developments in 2007 included the formation of a reseller partnership with the content delivery network provider Panther Express Corp., which began offering Gomez's performance management solutions. Midway through the year, Gomez launched a new, enhanced version of its web site. At the same time, the company also announced that the e-business solutions provider Ecetera would begin reselling its services in both New Zealand and Australia. Gomez finished 2007 with a 45 percent raise in revenue from the previous year, bolstered by the addition of 400 new customers.

In early 2008 Gomez established a referral partner agreement with Rackspace, a leading web site hosting company. That April, the company announced that the network of desktop computers upon which it relied to measure web site performance had reached the 40,000 mark. In May, Gomez filed with the U.S. Securities and Exchange Commission for an IPO it hoped would generate $80.5 million. Following the proposed offering, the company expected its shares to trade on the NAS-DAQ Global Market; the process was still pending in 2009.

Heading into the end of the decade, Gomez continued to expand it global footprint. In early 2009 the company forged a reseller partnership agreement with Inetasia Solutions Ltd., an Internet consulting firm that agreed to sell Gomez ExperienceFirst products in Hong Kong, Thailand, Singapore, and Malaysia. Gomez moved toward the 21st century's second decade as an established leader within the technology sector. The company served approximately 2,000 customers, and seemed well positioned for continued success.

Paul R. Greenland

PRINCIPAL COMPETITORS

BMC Software Inc.; Hewlett-Packard Ltd.; Keynote Systems Inc.

FURTHER READING

"The Ashton Technology Group, Inc., Announces Dr. Alexander D. Stein, Co-Founder of FarSight Financial Services Joins Gomez Advisors," *PR Newswire,* August 13, 1997.

"Gomez Advisors Raises $30 Million in Venture Funding," *Business Wire,* February 16, 2000.

"Gomez Announces 2007 Financial Results; Reports 45 Percent Year-over-Year Revenue Growth," *PR Newswire,* January 10, 2008.

"Gomez Inc. Wins Internet Performance Monitoring Face-off; Network Computer Magazine Names Gomez First Among Industry Players Like BMC and Keynote," *PR Newswire,* November 19, 2003.

"Jaime W. Ellertson Named Chief Executive Officer at Gomez Inc.," *PR Newswire,* January 23, 2006.

"Julio Gomez and John Robb Form Gomez Advisors," *Business Wire,* June 23, 1997.

Sweeney, Phil, "Gomez Inc. Keeps Going After the e-Commerce Fall," *Boston Business Journal,* August 3, 2001.

Grafton Group plc

Heron House
Corrig Road
Sandyford Industrial Estate
Dublin, 18
Ireland
Telephone: (353 1) 216 0600
Fax: (353 1) 295 4470
Web site: http://www.graftonplc.com

Public Company
Founded: 1902 as Chadwicks
Employees: 9,000
Sales: EUR 2.67 billion
Stock Exchanges: Dublin London
Ticker Symbols: BOOMZ44; GFTU.L
NAICS: 444110 Home Centers; 444190 Other Building
    Material Dealers

■ ■ ■

Grafton Group plc is a group of companies that do
business in the wholesale, retail, and manufacturing sectors of the construction trades in the United Kingdom
and the Republic of Ireland. Based in Dublin, the
Grafton Group is Ireland's largest distributor of plumbing and other builders' materials, which are sold from
62 locations of its Chadwicks and Heiton Buckley
outlets. Another Grafton construction materials
wholesaler is Macnaughton Blair, which serves Northern
Ireland with 20 outlets. Grafton is the fourth largest
distributor in the U.K. market with approximately 430
locations.

Builders Merchanting serves the general construction market from 219 locations with products under the
Buildbase trade name; Plumbers Merchanting distributes
its Plumbase brand products from 211 outlets. Grafton's
Woodie's DIY is the leading retail home center in
Ireland with 41 stores located throughout the Republic.
Grafton produces its EuroMix dry mortar in nine
factories in England and Scotland. Grafton also
manufactures paints, plastics, and windows. Britain accounts for approximately 65 percent of the Grafton
Group's total revenues, with the rest coming primarily
from Ireland.

CONSTRUCTION SUPPLIES FIRM
FOUNDED IN DUBLIN

The Grafton Group plc traces its history back to 1902,
when William Thomas Chadwick launched a building
supplies company called Chadwicks in Dublin, Ireland.
The firm imported cement and plaster from continental
Europe and sold it to construction companies in
Ireland. The Chadwick family business was a successful
one. It remained a supplier until 1930, when with the
takeover of a customer that made concrete blocks and
roofing tiles, it became involved in manufacturing. One
year later that subsidiary, Concrete Products of Ireland
(CPI), became a private limited company (plc). When
the founder passed away in the mid-1940s, control of
Chadwicks and CPI passed into the hands of his sons,
Terence and Finton Chadwick.

The middle 1960s witnessed a major organizational
shake-up at the Irish company. CPI went public in 1965
and shortly afterward purchased the Chadwicks building

COMPANY PERSPECTIVES

The Group's strategy is consistent and focused. It aims to achieve above average long term returns for shareholders by: building on strong positions in businesses serving the UK and Irish construction markets; developing in other Irish markets; growing outside Ireland in businesses with which the Group is familiar. This strategy is underpinned by key Group strengths which include: growth through acquisition and organic development; leading market positions and brands in Ireland and the UK; dedicated and highly motivated management teams and staff; a profit-orientated growth philosophy; unique acquisition and integration skills; a portfolio of highly cash generative and profitable businesses; a strong balance sheet and financial capacity.

good distributors from the Chadwick family. Around the same time, Marley Ltd., a company that had held a minority share in CPI for about 20 years, acquired a 51 percent controlling interest. The Chadwick family retained important positions in both CPI and Chadwicks, however, and in 1985 Michael Chadwick was named the executive chairman of The Group, as the two companies had been renamed.

By 1987 Marley had adopted a new strategic plan to focus its efforts on producing rather than selling construction supplies, and as a result, it divested itself of The Group, selling its holding to institutional investors and a management team from The Group. Once independent, The Group expanded its own activities into retailing building materials and other products to homeowners interested in doing their own home improvements. The company opened its first do-it-yourself outlet, known in the United Kingdom and Ireland as a DIY store, in Walkinstown, Ireland, in 1987. It was the first store of the Woodie's DIY chain. The store was an immediate hit and the second location was opened just a year later in Glasnevin.

THE FIRST U.K. EXPANSION

In 1988 The Group adopted a new name for itself, Grafton Group plc. Around the same time it launched the first of a series of bold acquisitions, moves that would extend over the following 20 years, when it acquired a heating and plumbing firm that served the British construction industry. It was a significant

acquisition, as it represented the company's first foray into the United Kingdom's lucrative construction market. While the Grafton Group expanded aggressively in the Republic of Ireland as well as Northern Ireland, British companies would be its prime takeover targets during the following decade and a half.

At beginning of the 1990s, the Grafton Group was operating two main lines of business. The first was its Woodie's DIY retail chain, which catered primarily to Irish homeowners. The third and fourth Woodie's stores were opened in 1990, one in Sallynoggin and the other in Cork. The Cork store was the first Woodie's superstore that was modeled on the big American home centers, such as Home Depot, and offered a significantly larger range of products than the first stores. Grafton's second line of operations was the distribution of building materials to companies in the construction trades. It purchased Macnaughton Blair, an old construction supply company located in the Northern Irish capital Belfast, in 1990. Later the same year, Grafton acquired Dublin-based Joseph Kelly & Son Limited.

The firm added two new Woodie's stores in Ireland in 1993, bringing the total in the chain to seven. Woodie's was a phenomenon in Ireland as sales rose that year by some 76 percent over 1992, and Grafton had an eighth branch on the drawing board that would open in April 1994. Despite the success of DIY retailing for the company, 1993 revealed Grafton's weak point. During the first half of the year, the demand for construction in the country—which accounted for approximately 85 percent of Grafton's annual revenues—fell dramatically. The result was a drop in company profits of 35 percent.

FURTHER INROADS INTO THE BRITISH MARKET

In early 1994 Grafton launched a major offensive on the British market. In February 1994 it purchased the Thrower Brothers Group for £2.5 million. Thrower's main subsidiary, H. Bradley, supplied plumbing, heating, and sanitary supplies to the British construction industry. Bradley represented more than 75 percent of Thrower's £7.3 million in annual revenues. With nearly 50 years of experience, Bradley provided Grafton with immediate access to the London professional heating and plumbing market. Thrower's other subsidiary, Nalex, also supplied the construction trade as well as being a wholesaler to DIY stores and home centers. It was a small part of the Thrower company, but with more than 1,000 customers in Britain, Nalex was the leader in its market.

Grafton made its second major inroad into the British market in November 1994 when it acquired Lumley & Hunt, a heating and plumbing supplier based in

```
┌─────────────────────────────────────────────┐
│                                               │
│              KEY DATES                        │
│          ■                                    │
├─────────────────────────────────────────────┤
│ 1902: William Thomas Chadwick founds Chad-    │
│       wicks in Dublin.                        │
│ 1930: Chadwicks acquires manufacturer of      │
│       concrete blocks and roofing tiles.      │
│ 1931: Manufacturing subsidiary, Concrete      │
│       Products of Ireland (CPI), becomes a    │
│       private limited company (plc).          │
│ 1965: CPI becomes a public company and        │
│       acquires ownership of Chadwicks.        │
│ 1966: Marley Ltd. assumes a controlling       │
│       interest in CPI.                        │
│ 1967: MFP plumbing goods distributor is       │
│       founded.                                │
│ 1987: Parent company Marley divests itself    │
│       of its controlling interest in The      │
│       Group, as CPI has been renamed.         │
│ 1988: Firm is renamed Grafton Group plc.      │
│ 1990: Macnaughton Blair and Joseph Kelly &    │
│       Son Ltd. are acquired.                  │
│ 1995: P.P.S. Mortars of Glasgow, Scotland,    │
│       is acquired.                            │
│ 2003: Jackson Building Centres in England is  │
│       acquired.                               │
│ 2005: Heiton Holdings, Grafton's biggest      │
│       competitor in Ireland, is acquired.     │
│                                               │
└─────────────────────────────────────────────┘
```

England's Sussex area with annual revenues of about £6.5 million, for £1.6 million. The U.K. strategy was proving to be a successful one for Grafton; its total revenues from Britain and Northern Ireland rose approximately 53 percent in 1994. By the end of the year, those areas accounted for nearly a quarter of the Grafton Group's total sales.

Grafton's acquisition spree in Britain continued during the following four years. In 1995 it purchased P.P.S. Mortars, a mortar maker located in Glasgow, Scotland. The plant was converted to produce EuroMix mortar, which Grafton had first introduced to the Irish market in 1994. In 1996 it acquired Boormans, a plumbing and heating materials dealer that was immediately integrated into Grafton's Lumley subsidiary. Later in the year, it obtained its first British builders supply company, R.J. Johnson, located in Oxford. Grafton went on to add another six small companies to its portfolio that year. The decade between 1986 and 1996 had been, in general, a healthy one financially for the Grafton Group, with an average annual growth in sales of 18 percent.

A FORCE TO BE RECKONED WITH IN BRITAIN

As it approached the new millennium, the Grafton Group continued its remarkable string of acquisitions. In 1998, with the acquisition of British Dredging plc for £33.9 million, it became the first Irish company ever to purchase a British limited company that was listed on the stock exchange. British Dredging's size with 23 locations also made it one of Grafton's largest acquisitions ever. The company added an astonishing 40 additional purchases between 1998 and 2001 in both the United Kingdom and Ireland, expanding both its retail and wholesale operations. Grafton's business was not only growing, it was prospering as well. In 1999 it reported a 35 percent increase in pretax profits. The following year its wholesale revenues in Ireland jumped by 15 percent, reaching EUR 105.9 million. Business at the Woodie's DIY chain rose 23 percent to EUR 33.5 million annually. The changeover in Ireland to the euro also helped Grafton's results. The company started purchasing goods in the euro zone in continental Europe to take advantage of the favorable exchange rate with the British pound.

As the new century started, Grafton was a healthy company operating in a highly favorable economic climate in both Ireland and Britain. In 2001 it added another 170 U.K. outlets to its empire. In 2002 the company set a new company record, acquiring 15 new construction materials and plumbing firms in England. A year later it made its largest acquisition to date when it purchased the English enterprise Jackson Building Centres for EUR 131 million. That same year it purchased Scotland's largest independent plumbers' merchant, Plumbline.

By 2003 the Grafton Group had become the fourth largest building materials company in the United Kingdom, behind Woolsey, Saint Gobain, and Travis Perkins. While Grafton had only about 5 percent of the £9 billion British market, it was the fastest-growing player there with annual growth rates of 25 percent. Investors were also showing their faith in Grafton, pushing its stock price steadily upward. In July 2003 alone its shares increased in value by some 30 percent. Aided by its new subsidiary Jackson Building Centres, Grafton was able to report a 27 percent increase in profits for 2004. The company leadership reported that if Grafton continued to perform at the pace of the previous few years, it could continue to increase its share of the U.K. market by one percentage point annually.

MAIN IRISH RIVAL ACQUIRED

Beginning in March 1999, when it bought a 4.9 percent share in construction materials firm Heiton Holdings,

Grafton had been slowly acquiring shares in its biggest competitor in Ireland. By March 2004 Grafton had increased its Heiton holdings to 29 percent, just below the amount at which it would have been required to make an offer to buy the company outright. Market observers were divided in their opinion as to why Grafton was going after Heiton. Some wondered if the company was merely establishing a defensive position to guard against the possibility that a British company might attempt a takeover of Heiton, while others wondered if Grafton had an ultimate takeover of its own in the works.

Finally, in June 2004, Grafton announced that it intended to acquire Heiton. The only hurdles it had to overcome were two: satisfying institutional investors holding Heiton shares with a competitive offer for their stock, at a time when Heiton was performing particularly well, with profits up 25 percent and its stock price climbing steadily; and getting approval of the deal from the Competition Authorities, the Irish antitrust regulators. In August 2004 Grafton offered EUR 336 million, a price almost 40 percent higher than the prevailing market price of Heiton shares. By January 2005 the Competition Authorities had given its approval and the acquisition was consummated.

The merger immediately raised Grafton's share of the EUR 2 billion Irish construction materials market from 9 percent to 19 percent. Heiton brought Grafton 50 new outlets, some 1,900 additional employees, and additional annual revenues estimated at more than EUR 500 million. Grafton and Heiton had been the two leaders in the Irish DIY market, with shares of about 9 percent and 7.5 percent respectively. Joining forces was crucial at a time when another company, Dairygold, was about to invest EUR 30 million in a new DIY chain in Ireland.

Grafton organized a bond offering in 2005 to raise money to pay off some of its EUR 474 million in debt acquired in the course of its decade-long chain of acquisitions. The well-being of the firm was reflected in the eagerness of investors to participate in the offering. The first issue worth about EUR 127 million was vastly oversubscribed, so Grafton decided to increase its value to EUR 265 million.

A DOWNTURN IN FORTUNES

After nearly a decade and a half of rapid, uninterrupted growth, the Grafton Group experienced a major turnaround after 2005, when the previously booming Irish economy ground to a sudden halt and the British economy turned stagnant as well. In March 2006, profits in the United Kingdom flattened out and

Grafton was forced to start laying off workers. The following year new home construction in Ireland began a long, precipitous decline. With housing construction in the Republic accounting for some 12.5 percent of the Grafton Group's total annual revenues, the trend's impact on the company was harsh, and as a result, analysts at two major banks revised their outlook for Grafton stock and predicted further drops in the company's earnings over the next 12 months.

The situation worsened at the beginning of 2008 when the pound went into a free fall in relation to the euro. This represented a serious state of affairs for Grafton because more than half of all its operating profits were from Britain where all income was in pounds. The situation was no better in Ireland, where business was done in euros. The rate of new home construction had dropped to a point lower than any time since the 1980s; by mid-2008 sales of construction materials had dropped approximately 26 percent. With the Irish economy nearing a recession, consumer spending was dropping significantly as well, which translated into a decline in Grafton's DIY business in the Republic. Altogether in the first 11 months of 2008, the Grafton Group's revenues dropped 14.5 percent to EUR 2.35 billion, and in early 2009 the Group announced that its profits the year before had declined 73 percent from 2007.

In response, the Group inaugurated stringent cost-cutting measures. In 2008 acquisitions were curtailed sharply. In the first six months of the year the firm spent EUR 25.3 million on new companies; in the last six months only EUR 2.8 million. The firm closed outlets that had been losing money and cut 1,500 of about 10,500 employees. The measures ended up saving Grafton about EUR 45 million. However, until the British and Irish economies emerged from the financial crisis that was gripping most western nations and construction picked up once again, the outlook for the Grafton Group was a bleak one.

Gerald E. Brennan

PRINCIPAL SUBSIDIARIES

Woodie's DIY and Garden Centres; Chadwicks Ltd.; Macnaughton Blair Ltd.; CPI EuroMix; MFP Sales Ltd.; Circle Syntalux Ltd.; Heiton Buckley Builders Merchants; Atlantic Homecare; Wright Window Systems Ltd.; Jackson Building Centres; Buildbase Ltd.; Plumbase Ltd.

PRINCIPAL COMPETITORS

CRH; Wolseley Ireland plc; Saint Gobain plc; Travis Perkins Trading Company.

FURTHER READING

Beesley, Arthur, "Decline in Sterling Value Hits Grafton's Earnings Outlook," *Irish Times,* March 11, 2008, p. 20.

"Differing Views on Grafton's Fortunes," *Irish Times,* December 7, 2007, p. 22.

"Grafton's Making a Name for Itself," *Irish Times,* January 24, 2003, p. 54.

"Grafton's Rise Reflects Housebuilding Strength," *Irish Times,* August 29, 2003, p. 55.

Hancock, Ciaran, "Grafton Group Set to Restructure UK Outlets with Loss of 200 Jobs," *Sunday Times* (London), March 19, 2006, p. 2.

McCaffrey, Una, "Grafton Shows Its Hand at Last," *Irish Times,* June 18, 2004, p. 53.

———, "Grafton Spends E40m on Purchases in State and UK," *Irish Times,* October 7, 2003, p. 19.

———, "Purchases Help Push Grafton's Profits up 27%," *Irish Times,* March 11, 2004, p. 18.

McManus, John, "Grafton Gets August 6th Deadline for Heiton Bid," *Irish Times,* July 22, 2004, p. 19.

Murdoch, Bill, "Acquisition in UK Costs Grafton £13.5m," *Irish Times,* April 7, 1999, p. 17.

———, "Grafton Buys Builders' Merchants in Britain for £2.5m Sterling," *Irish Times,* February 10, 1994, p. 15.

———, "Grafton Continues British Expansion," *Irish Times,* February 2, 2000, p. 21.

O'Halloran, Barry, "Grafton Says It Faces Difficult Year After Fall in Profits of 73%," *Irish Times,* February 28, 2009, p. 19.

———, "Turnover at Grafton Group Falls 14.5% in Tough Trading Conditions," *Irish Times,* November 20, 2008, p. 21.

Paul, Mark, "What Price a Private Grafton?" *Sunday Times* (London), May 11, 2008, p. 9.

Grupo Martins

———■———

Rua Jataí 1150
Uberlândia, Minas Gerais 38400-632
Brazil
Telephone: (55 34) 3218-1305
Toll Free: (0800) 729-3400 (Brazil)
Fax: (55 34) 3232-4290
Web site: http://www.martins.com.br

Private Company
Founded: 1953 as Armazém Martins
Employees: 4,609
Sales: BRL 3.43 billion ($2.04 billion) (2007)
NAICS: 424210 Drugs and Druggists' Sundries Merchant Wholesalers; 424410 General Line Grocery Merchant Wholesalers; 522210 Credit Card Issuers; 522220 Sales Financing

■ ■ ■

Grupo Martins is the name commonly used for the largest independent general-line wholesale distributor in Latin America. Its fleet of vehicles delivers more than 19,000 product items, including groceries and construction and electronic materials, to every city and town in Brazil. Farma Service, one of the group's newest companies, is the only medical distributor present in every Brazilian municipality. Through Smart Varejos Ltda., Martins sponsors a network of retail stores that collectively rivals even the biggest supermarket chains in annual sales. Most of the group, which also includes a financial arm named Banco Triângulo S.A. (Tribanco), is controlled by the holding company Almart Adminis-

tração e Participações S.A., which in turn is held by a family company, Almart Participações Ltda.

RETAIL TO WHOLESALE

Martins began in 1953, when 18-year-old Alair Martins do Nascimento persuaded his parents to sell the family farm so that he could found a small general store in Uberlândia, Minas Gerais. Working from 6:30 in the morning until 11 at night, he took in the equivalent of $110,000 in the first year of the store that was originally called Armazém Borges Martins. Martins entered wholesaling in 1956 by selling surplus stock to other merchants and in 1959 acquired a small fleet of used trucks.

Uberlândia was becoming a major distribution center because of its location, nearly equidistant from Brasília, Rio de Janeiro, and São Paulo, and in 1964 Martins became exclusively a wholesale distributor. A new warehouse store was added in 1972. Martins's annual revenue was below $1 million at the time, but by 1975 sales had reached $16.5 million, and the company was present in northern as well as central Brazil. A year later, Martins founded Metalgrampo, a nonalloyed staple and nail factory, and acquired Rádio Visão, Uberlândia's audience leader.

Martins's annual revenue reached $73.4 million in 1982. By that time it was serving retailers throughout northeastern Brazil and was also present in São Paulo. Volkswagen Brasil Ind. de Véhiculos Automotores Ltda. was supplying its trucking fleet. Brazil's so-called lost decade—the 1980s—took a heavy toll on wholesalers, but by 1988 Martins had once again more than tripled its revenues. The company opened Tele Martins, a telemarketing call center, in 1989.

In 1990 Grupo Martins established its own bank, Tribanco, to finance its customers and suppliers. Among the former was the major discount chain Lojas Americanas. Also that year, the group established a retail and distribution trades "university" for its clients, with the goal of helping them develop the tools to grow their businesses. It was the largest independent wholesaler in Latin America at the time.

WHOLESALE LEADER, INFLUENTIAL GROUP

By 1992 Martins was in every one of Brazil's states. Its sales had more than doubled again in only four years. The only wholesale distributor in Brazil larger than Martins at this time was Makro Atacadista S.A., but this firm was tied to the Dutch group SHV and the Mesbla retail chain and supplied big city customers who paid cash and carried their merchandise home. Other big wholesalers specialized in a single line of business, such as fuels distribution. By contrast, Martins distributed a variety of goods to thousands of points of sale, including general stores, grocery stores, pharmacies, and bazaars, in the vast Brazilian interior.

Martins was, moreover, beginning to make an impact in the major population centers by supplying convenience stores. In late 1992 it became the principal supplier for Shell Brasil Ltda.'s 20 Express and 23 Algo Mais convenience stores, as well as the 14 7-Eleven outlets. Martins was buying consumer items in bulk directly from major firms such as Nestlé Brasil Ltda. and Procter & Gamble do Brasil S.A. Martins's properties included 1,303 trucks in 1993. Marbro Logística Integrada, the group's transport and auto assembly company, was manufacturing some of its largest vehicles.

Martins was aided by one of the best computerized data systems in Brazilian commerce, including the best IBM mainframe computer for large businesses and more than 200 microcomputers. This was essential in order to distribute efficiently 7,000 different products to 164,000 customers. Orders and sales were registered, and the distribution center in Uberlândia was notified when items were running out of stock. Computers also determined what routes the company's trucks should take and the history of the clients doing business with the firm.

By this time Martins was not a single company but a group of 13 companies, including the radio station, a transport firm, and a Volkswagen dealership. Alair Martins worked six days a week and maintained two company jets in Uberlândia for business trips, but had never even set foot in some of these businesses. Tribanco, with assets of $45 million, was financing more than 100,000 contracts every month, the great majority with customers being supplied by Martins. Marbro received most of its revenues from Martins's own suppliers.

Marketing was also essential to Martins's success. The company published monthly a 300-page illustrated catalog and maintained a sales force of 2,600, trained not only to sell but also to make suggestions to retailers on how to stock their shelves and expand their own sales. Courses on commercial management were offered in different regions of the country.

A project was underway to aid small stores to survive competition from the growing number of supermarket chains. Empório da Gente, in Uberlândia, a cross between a convenience store and a supermarket, was established in 1992 as a pilot project, or retail laboratory. By 1995 there were three of these ultramodern stores, offering bargain prices and prizes. The first of these stores was taking in twice as many dollars per square meter of selling space as the average for the 20 largest supermarket chains.

Martins's revenues reached BRL 1 billion ($640 million) in 1994. In partnership with Visa International, it was introducing a credit card for the 188,000 retailers it was supplying. The company was offering 11,500 items, including, for the first time, automotive products, medications, and even IBM microcomputers. A fleet of 1,804 trucks, tracked by satellite, plied the nation's roads and highways. Some 80 percent of Brazil's 600 convenience stores were being supplied by Martins.

A MORE CHALLENGING MARKETPLACE

Five years later, the picture was not so rosy for Martins, whose revenues came to only $816 million in 1999. The last years of the 20th century were a slow growth period for Brazil, but, more to the point, the wholesaler-distributor was beset both by competition in its field

KEY DATES

1953: Alair Martins do Nascimento founds a small general store in Uberlândia.

1956: This enterprise enters wholesale distribution by selling surplus stock to other merchants.

1964: Martins becomes a wholesale enterprise exclusively.

1982: The company has widespread operations in northern as well as central Brazil.

1988: Martins's annual sales have passed $200 million a year.

1990: As the largest independent wholesaler in Latin America, Martins founds its own bank.

1992: Martins, a group of 13 companies, is doing business in every Brazilian state.

1994: Grupo Martins's annual revenue has passed BRL 1 billion.

2000: Smart, a network of retailers dealing directly with Martins, is founded.

2001: Farma Service, a nationwide distributor of medications, is established.

2008: Grupo Martins has grown an annual average of 12 percent since 2003.

such as Wal-Mart Stores, Inc.'s cash-and-carry Sam's Club and by the difficulties of its main customers, the small retailers being swallowed by big chains such as Wal-Mart itself, the Portuguese chain Sonae, and the Dutch chain Royal Ahold.

In addition, the Internet had become a rival, threatening to usurp Martins's role as a middleman. In early 2000 the company began to sell to its customers in a virtual mode and to establish new subsidiaries to offer services to digital enterprises and to companies seeking to adjust to the digital era. Intercom, a joint venture with J.P. Morgan & Co. Incorporated, was established to provide logistics over the Web, offering to supervise the flow of goods from factories to stores, financing, and postsale activities. Martins was also using the Internet in other ways. Among three specialized sites—called vertical portals—was one offering construction materials in the name of associated retailers. The others sold the company's stocks of home appliances and pet food not only to stores but also directly to the final consumer.

Another of Martins's 22 projects under consideration in 2000 was Smart, developed by the company's university of retailing. This institution, which had trained thousands of small entrepreneurs in administration, marketing, and technology, was considering uniting such retailers under a common banner. Financing of BRL 300 million ($164 million) was to be provided by the government development bank BNDES.

SMART AND FARMA SERVICE

Smart was up and running by the end of 2000. Three years later, it was present in nine out of 26 states, plus the federal district of Brasília, with 512 stores nationwide at the end of 2003. The merchants enrolled were, by means of this network, able to pool their resources and deal collectively with Martins, which was offering more than 19,000 items to its 207,000 customers—more than half of all Brazilian retailers. Members were under no obligation to buy from the company, but a program of incentives was offered, including lower prices and a lengthier period of payment. Smart also functioned as a marketing cooperative.

Farma Service was founded by Grupo Martins in 2001 as a distributor of medications, including both prescription and over the counter items and also health and beauty products. By 2005, as an aid to Farma Service's growth, Grupo Martins was part-owner of Vidalink, which was supplying low-income Brazilian employees with a magnetic card to pay for medications, with a predetermined limit on credit based on salary. Vidalink, the largest pharmacy benefits management company in Latin America, had signed pacts with 18 drug manufacturers to sell 1,500 medications to 3.5 million people at discounts of as much as 70 percent.

GRUPO MARTINS IN 2008–09

Grupo Martins was growing an average of 12 percent a year since 2003, far greater than the wholesaling market as a whole. The most important subsidiary was Martins Comércio e Serviços de Distribuição S.A., which was engaged in the sale and distribution, both wholesale and retail, of durable and nondurable goods, including pharmaceuticals and similar products and Martins's own private-label merchandise. This company, through its subsidiaries, was also responsible for the transport of cargo and integrated logistics. The 1,116 vehicles in the transport fleet were traveling about 52 million kilometers (32 million miles) per year. Martins also made use of about 200 contracted vehicles and boasted that it was not only serving every municipality in Brazil but arriving in many places before the mail.

Martins Comércio e Serviços de Distribuição was subdivided into three strategic business units with independent management. Food retail was the segment that gave origin to Martins. Electro invested in catalogs, advertising campaigns and publications, awards, and communication in general, including the Internet via the web site www.efacil.com.br. Construction-Vet was the largest wholesale distributor of construction and veterinary materials in Brazil. The Logistics division consisted of three warehouse centers and 43 branches and offices.

Tribanco was extending credit to more than 39,000 small retailers for such purposes as financing store improvements. This accounted for more than 80 percent of the bank's lending, but it was also providing consumer credit to the customers of these retailers. Tribanco also was providing retailers the opportunity to offer their shoppers branded credit cards and was the biggest issuer of private-label credit cards in Brazil, its principal one being Tricard, with 3.2 million in circulation. Tribanco was also in the process of offering services that might include medical, dental, and home insurance.

Rede Smart, by the end of 2008, had 1,210 dues-paying member stores in 16 Brazilian states and the federal district. These stores had combined annual sales of BRL 5.2 billion ($2.83 billion), which was higher than the totals of all but three supermarket chains. Farma Service was the only distributor of medicine present in every Brazilian town. Farma Service and the university (Universidade Martins de Varejo) belonged to a larger grouping of the family-owned enterprise named Sistema Integrado Martins.

At age 75, Alair Martins continued to be president of the Martins group. As active as ever, he exercised every morning in a gym under the direction of a personal trainer. His goal for Grupo Martins was to double revenues every four years. Of his three eldest sons, Juscelino Fernandes Martins had long been the heir apparent, in charge of the group's day-to-day operations and president of Tribanco by the time he was 30, but now having entered middle age.

Martins was considered one of the best companies to work for in Brazil. Its founder affected an informal style, with an open-door policy for employees, weekly "happy hours," and access to a beauty salon and video viewing as well as a subsidized cafeteria. The company paid part-tuition for university courses both in Brazil and abroad and bonuses for goals met. There was a company pension plan, and the median salary was above average for Uberlândia, one of Brazil's more prosperous cities.

Robert Halasz

PRINCIPAL SUBSIDIARIES

Martins Agropecuária S.A. (52%); Martins Comércio e Serviços de Distribuição S.A. (90%); Martins Overseas Limited (British Virgin Islands); Martins Participações Ltda.; Metalgrampo Comércio e Serviços Ltda.; Smart Varejos Ltda.

PRINCIPAL COMPETITORS

Peixoto Comércio, Industria, Serviços e Transportes S.A.; Proforma Distribuidora de Produtos Farmacêuticos S.A.

FURTHER READING

Carvalho, Sandra, "Como se faz um rei do atacado," *Exame,* March 17, 1993, pp. 40–45.

Correa, Cristiane, "O Compadre do Varejo," *Exame,* December 10, 2003, pp. 36–39.

Filgueiras, Maria Luíza, "Card Linked to Salary Takes Off in Country," *Gazeta Mercantil,* December 20, 2005.

———, "Martins quer dobrar receita a cada 4 anos," *Gazeta Mercantil,* May 19, 2008, p. C5.

Furtado, José Maria, "Atacado digital," *Exame,* May 17, 2000, pp. 104–06.

———, "Trem doido, sô," *Exame,* March 19, 1995, pp. 42–43.

"Martins," supplement, *Exame,* August 23, 2000, p. 122.

Vasconcelos, Yuri, "O modelo que vem de fora," *Exame,* April 27, 2005, p. 64.

HALMA

Halma plc

———■———

Misbourne Court, Rectory Way
Amersham, HP7 0DE
United Kingdom
Telephone: (44 01494) 721111
Fax: (44 01494) 728032
Web site: http://www.halma.com

Public Company
Incorporated: 1894 as The Nahalma Tea Estate Company Ltd.
Employees: 3,663
Sales: £395.1 million ($566.8 million) (2008)
Stock Exchanges: London
Ticker Symbol: HLMA
NAICS: 551112 Offices of Other Holding Companies

■ ■ ■

Halma plc is a holding company focused on the niche engineering sector. The Amersham, England-based company serves as the administrative hub for more than 20 companies operating more or less independently throughout the world. Halma's operations fall into three primary divisions: Infrastructure Sensors; Health and Analysis; and Industrial Safety. The Infrastructure Sensors division, with operations in more than 20 countries, contributed 42 percent of the company's £395.1 million ($566.8 million) in revenues in 2008. This division produces smoke detection and other security sensors, as well as automatic door and elevator safety sensors.

The Health and Analysis division includes a wide range of companies developing safety and environmental

analysis systems. This division includes subsidiaries in nine countries and contributes 34 percent to the group's turnover in 2008. Industrial Safety adds 24 percent of group sales, and focuses on four primary areas: gas detection; bursting discs; safety interlocks; and asset monitoring. Most of Halma's companies focus on the research and development, design and engineering, and assembly phases, turning to outside manufacturers for the components required for their products. Halma has been listed on the London Stock Exchange since 1981 and has been led by CEO Andrew Williams since 2005.

FROM RUBBER COMPANY TO ENGINEERING INVESTMENTS

Halma originated as The Nahalma Tea Estate Company, set up by British interests in Ceylon (later known as Sri Lanka) in 1894. The company later listed its shares on the London Stock Exchange, but remained a small, if profitable, business. Throughout the 1920s Nahalma began investing in rubber plantations, and by 1937 had converted its operations entirely to that product. The company changed its name that year to The Nahalma Rubber Estate Company. When the newly independent Ceylon emerged from British colonial rule in the 1950s, however, the new government nationalized the country's rubber industry. This forced the Nahalma company to sell its more than 650 acres of rubber plantations in 1955.

With the proceeds of more than £33,000 from the sale, the company's directors established a new company, called Halma Investments in 1956. Halma initially sought to operate only as an investment trust, announc-

COMPANY PERSPECTIVES

Our objective is to create shareholder value based on five principles: Operate in specialised global markets offering long-term growth underpinned by robust growth drivers; Build businesses which lead specialised global markets through innovative products differentiated on performance and quality rather than price alone; Recruit and develop top quality boards to lead our businesses and nurture an entrepreneurial culture within a framework of rigorous financial discipline; Acquire companies and intellectual assets that extend our existing activities, enhance our entrepreneurial culture, fit into our decentralised operating structure and meet our demanding financial performance expectations; Achieve a high return on capital employed to generate cash efficiently and to fund organic growth, closely targeted acquisitions and sustained dividend growth.

ing its intention to buy shares in publicly listed securities and companies, without seeking to gain major or controlling stakes in any of its investments. While the company maintained this policy through the end of the decade, Halma nonetheless carried out a capital increase at the end of 1959. This set the stage for Halma's emergence as an engineering-oriented holding company.

In 1961 another investment group, Vakusa Investments, acquired 75 percent of Halma, marking the beginning of a new era in the company's development. Among the company's investments at the time were Wheeler & Tilling, a company specialized in cadmium and zinc-based electroplating. Under Halma's ownership, Wheeler & Tilling diversified, acquiring the electrical engineering and contracting group Thorpe & Thorpe in 1965. Wheeler & Tilling then changed its name to Mansell Thorp while T. H. Tilling became chairman of Halma. By then Halma had completed its own acquisition, of Farmers' Investment Trust, in 1964.

THE BARBER ERA BEGINS IN 1972

Halma continued to focus its investments on the engineering sector in the 1960s. The company acquired the Fletcher, Brock and Collis engineering group in 1966, paying £200,000. That business made its own acquisition two years later, paying £15,000 for Dalston Plating Works.

The acquisition of Power Equipment Company in 1971 represented a new milestone for Halma. At £412,000, the acquisition was the company's largest to date. More significant, however, was the addition of Power Equipment's focus on designing and manufacturing specialized safety and environmental security products. These became part of Halma's core focus into the next century. Power Equipment, which included its subsidiary Castell Locks, added a number of new product lines, including acoustic control and industrial safety systems.

That acquisition also signaled the arrival of David Barber, who took over as Halma's managing director and CEO in early 1972. Barber remained as head of the company for nearly 30 years, guiding its constant expansion. Acquisitions played a significant role in Halma's growth, as Barber put into place a policy of acquiring relatively small engineering companies that targeted niche markets in which there were few competitors. Barber remained notoriously tight-lipped about his strategy, however, and rarely gave interviews. As Barber later explained to the *Financial Times:* "If I spelled out our business model [I was afraid] we would spawn a number of competitors or pretend competitors."

From the start, however, acquisitions formed the heart of Barber's strategy, and he completed an impressive series of some 100 acquisitions by the 1990s. In 1972, for example, Halma paid £360,000 for privately held Argosy Engineering, which manufactured specialized components for the ventilation and air conditioning industry. The following year, the company added Standard Engineering, including several subsidiaries, paying £750,000. As the company completed its shift from investment trust to a focus on the environmental control and specialized engineering, it changed its name again, becoming Halma Investment that year.

INTERNATIONAL GROWTH IN THE 1980S

Halma's acquisitions enabled the company to post impressive gains into the middle of the 1970s. By 1974 the company had nearly doubled its revenues to £5.3 million. The company's revenues climbed again, past £9.6 million in 1978. By then Halma had launched its first international expansion effort, buying a stake in the Netherlands' Handelsbureau de Sleutel in 1976.

The United States, however, became the company's primary foreign focus at the end of the decade. In 1979 Halma made its first U.S. acquisition, buying Post Clover, part of Philadelphia-based ESB that year. For this the company paid $1.8 million, while adding Post Clover's own $3.2 million in annual sales.

KEY DATES

1894: The Nahalma Tea Estate Company is founded to exploit tea plantations in Ceylon.

1937: Nahalma refocuses on rubber production, becoming Nahalma Rubber Estate Company.

1955: Nahalma is forced to sell off its rubber plantations and become Halma Investment.

1973: David Barber becomes CEO and redevelops Halma as a specialty engineering conglomerate and becomes Halma Ltd.

1981: Halma goes public as Halma PLC.

1985: The company's sales reach £25 million.

1995: Barber steps down as CEO (and as chairman in 2003).

2002: Halma completes its largest acquisition to date, of BEA in Belgium.

2008: Halma posts revenues of £395 million ($567 million).

PICKING UP AT THE START OF THE 21ST CENTURY

By the turn of the century Halma's operations spanned the United States, the Netherlands, France, Germany, Australia, Italy, Canada, Malaysia, and Singapore, as well as the United Kingdom. The company's holdings then consisted of some 90 subsidiaries. While Halma's focus remained on specialty and niche engineering markets, its product range had grown significantly, to include smoke and other sensors, such as elevator door sensors, ultrasonic cleaning equipment, control devices for heat treatment furnaces, and other industrial safety equipment. In many of its product categories, such as smoke detectors, Halma had achieved leading worldwide positions.

Barber began preparing his succession in the 1990s, turning over the CEO spot to Stephen O'Shea in 1995. Barber remained as chairman of the company until 2003, when he was succeeded by Geoff Unwin. By then Halma had weathered a rough patch as its revenues and profits were hit by the strong British pound in the late 1990s.

The company's growth through acquisition strategy remained in full swing, however. In 1998, for example, the company earmarked some $100 million for acquisitions in the United States alone. By the end of 1999 the company had completed a number of acquisitions, including elevator safety specialists e-Motive in Singapore and TL Jones in New Zealand States, and Oseco, a U.S.-based producer of safety devices for pressurized environments.

The following year the company spent nearly £30 million to acquire five more companies. This total included $7.7 million to acquire power resistor producer Cutler-Hammer, based in Milwaukee. Other purchases during this period included France's Hydreka, which designed flow and leakage detection software and equipment, and the United States' Vandal-Proof Products Inc., which produced vandal-resistant emergency voice communication devices. By then the company's sales had grown to £233.5 million.

Halma's growth remained somewhat muted, however, amid the overall economic downturn at the beginning of the new century. The company's prospects brightened, however, in the wake of the September 11, 2001, terrorist attacks against the United States, which initiated a surge in demand for safety and security products.

NEW ACQUISITIONS AND A NEW STRATEGY

Halma made its largest acquisition to date in 2002, buying Belgium's Bureau d'Electronique Appliquée (BEA)

Over the next decades Halma completed nearly 20 acquisitions in the United States alone. Other acquisitions during the decade included Hannovia Group, in 1981, which boosted the group's total sales to £16. 5 million. In 1985 the company acquired another company, Microphax, paying £700,000.

The company also pruned its growing portfolio of companies, shedding a number of noncore and underperforming subsidiaries. Nonetheless, the group's turnover continued to build, nearing £25 million in 1985. Indeed, the group's commitment to its operational focus, and its insistence on ROCE (return on capital employed) rates of at least 40 percent, were two strategic elements behind the company's success.

Halma emerged as one of the stars of the London Stock Exchange in the early 1990s, posting more than two decades of steady profit and revenue growth. The company's acquisition appetite had remained strong, as the company completed a string of eight acquisitions through 1992 and 1993. These helped raised the company's turnover to £116 million. Despite his secretive nature, Barber laid out part of his company's acquisition strategy to the *Independent,* saying: "They [the acquired companies] tend to add to things we already have, and we are pretty content with our formula of going forward primarily through organic growth rather than making big acquisitions in other sectors."

and its subsidiary. The purchase, for an initial EUR 72 million and a maximum price of EUR 95 million made Halma the world's leading producer of automatic door sensors, and added EUR 42 million to its total revenues.

After completing the integration of BEA, Halma returned to the acquisition trail. The company bought United Kingdom-based Radcom Technologies in 2003, the United States' Diba Industries and Ocean Optics in 2004, Holland's Netherlocks Safety Systems and United Kingdom-based Radio-Tech Limited and Texecom Ltd. in 2005, and Germany's Mikropack GmbH and the United Kingdom's Tritech Holdings in 2006. Leading the charge by then was Andrew Williams, who took over as group CEO in 2005.

While Halma's revenue growth remained strong, nearly all of it was fueled by acquisitions. After taking over the company's lead, Williams set out a new strategy designed to improve the company's organic growth efforts, boosting spending on research and development. This effort soon showed results, with organic growth reaching 6 percent at the end of 2005 compared to zero in the year before.

As part of its growth efforts, Halma announced its intention to develop a "hub" in Shanghai, China, in order to take advantage of that country's strong growth. Williams also reversed a company policy against taking on debt in order to complete acquisitions, securing a £60 million debt facility to fuel further purchases at the end of 2006. The first of these came soon after, with the purchase of New Hampshire-based Lapshere in 2007. By the end of that year the company had completed the acquisition, for more than $70 million, of Germany's Rudolf Riester GmbH.

Through 2008, Halma remained buoyant, despite the flagging economic climate. The company completed several new acquisitions, including Nester, a maker of handheld medical and eye testing equipment, for £40 million; Sonar Research & Development, a producer of industrial safety components; and, in September 2008, Fiberguide Industries Inc., in the United States, which produced complex optical fiber cables. By then Halma's revenues had climbed to £395.1 million ($566.8 million), making the company one of the leading specialty engineering groups in the United Kingdom and the world. Halma had come a long way from its beginnings as a 19th-century tea company.

PRINCIPAL SUBSIDIARIES

Air Products and Controls Inc. (USA); Apollo Gesellschaft für Meldetechnologie mbH (Germany); Aquionics Inc. (USA); B.E.A. Inc. (USA); Berson Milieutechniek B.V. (Netherlands); Bio-Chem Fluidics Inc. (USA);

Bureau d'Electronique Appliquée S.A. (Belgium); Diba Industries, Inc. (USA); E-Motive Display Pte Limited (Singapore); Fortress Systems Pty. Limited (Australia); Halma Holdings Inc. (USA); HF Sécurité S.A.S. (France); Hydreka S.A.S. (France); Janus Elevator Products Inc. (USA); Labsphere, Inc. (USA); Netherlocks Safety Systems B.V. (Netherlands); Ocean Optics, Inc. (USA); Oklahoma Safety Equipment Co. Inc. (USA); Perma Pure LLC (USA); Rudolf Riester GmbH & Co. KG (Germany); SERV Trayvou Interverrouillage S.A.S. (France); TL Jones Limited (New Zealand); Volk Optical Inc.

M. L. Cohen

PRINCIPAL DIVISIONS

Infrastructure Sensors; Health and Analysis; Industrial Safety.

PRINCIPAL OPERATING UNITS

Asset Monitoring; Automatic Door Sensors; Bursting Discs; Elevator Safety; Fire Detection; Fluid Technology; Gas Detection; Health Optics; Photonics; Safety Interlocks; Security Sensors; Water.

PRINCIPAL COMPETITORS

LG Group; VINCI S.A.; Abengoa S.A.; Johnson Controls Inc.; Tata Sons Ltd.; ABB AB; Panasonic Electric Works Company Ltd.; Safran; L-3 Communications Holdings Inc.; Danaher Corp.; Hashmira Security Technologies (1971) Ltd.

FURTHER READING

Cookson, Robert, "Halma in $15m US Acquisition," *Financial Times,* September 9, 2008, p. 22.

"Halma Remains Positive," *Acquisitions Monthly,* July 2008, p. 61.

"Halma Restructures to Improve Transparency," *Finance Week,* November 2, 2005, p. 7.

"Halma's Rocky ROCE Claim," *Investors Chronicle,* February 25, 2005.

Hofmann, Julian, "Halma Dampens Its Outlook," *Investors Chronicle,* February 13, 2009.

———, "Tip of the Year Review: Halma," *Investors Chronicle,* January 5, 2009.

Joliffe, Alexander, "BEA Deal Is Halma Pointer to Expansion," *Financial Times,* October 17, 2002, p. 26.

Kavanagh, Michael, "Health and Safety Bolsters Halma," *Financial Times,* November 28, 2008, p. 18.

Kavanagh, Michael, and Toby Shelley, "Halma Thriving in Safety-First World," *Financial Times,* June 18, 2008, p. 20.

Marsh, Peter, "Manufacturing Success Comes Quietly for Halma," *Financial Times,* July 28, 2003, p. 21.

———, "A Very Secretive Success Story," *Financial Times,* August 17, 2004, p. 12.

Odell, Mark, "Halma to Set Up Chinese City Hubs," *Financial Times,* June 21, 2006, p. 27.

O'Doherty, John, "Halma Builds War Chest for More Acquisitions," *Financial Times,* December 6, 2006, p. 24.

Sekhri, Rajiv, "Local HQ Girds for Major Expansion," *Business Courier,* December 11, 1998, p. 1.

Stafford, Philip, "Halma Coping with Organic Growth Problems," *Financial Times,* December 7, 2005, p. 28.

HANG LUNG GROUP

Hang Lung Group Ltd.

28/F Standard Chartered Bank Building
4 Des Voeux Road Central
Hong Kong
Telephone: (852) 2879 0111
Fax: (852) 2868 6086
Web site: http://www.hanglung.com

Public Company
Incorporated: 1960
Employees: 2,155
Sales: HKD 10.55 billion ($1.29 billion) (2008)
Stock Exchanges: Hong Kong
Ticker Symbol: 0010
NAICS: 531210 Offices of Real Estate Agents and
  Brokers

∎ ∎ ∎

Hang Lung Group Ltd., which is primarily active through its listed subsidiary Hong Kong Properties Ltd., is one of Hong Kong's top ten property development companies. Founded in 1960, Hang Lung has played a prominent role in building the Hong Kong skyline, especially in the development of the residential, office and commercial properties above the island's Mass Transit Railway (MTR) stations. Hang Lung operates in both the property leasing and property development sectors. The company's residential portfolio includes Burnside Villa, near Repulse Bay on Hong Kong Island; The Summit, in the Mid-levels district; and Kornhill Apartments, above the Tai Koo MTR station in Quarry Bay. Commercial properties include the Peak Galleria,

Park-In Commercial Centre in Mongkok; Amoy Plaza in Ngau Tau Kok; and One Grand Tower in Mongkok. Altogether, the company oversees nearly 885,000 square meters of properties in Hong Kong.

Hang Lung was also an early mover into the mainland Chinese market, guiding the construction of two major Shanghai developments: the Grand Gateway, a multipurpose site including residential and office properties, as well as one of the city's largest shopping centers; and the office and commercial site Plaza 66. Hang Lung Group is listed on the Hong Kong Stock Exchange and is led by Ronnie C. Chan, chairman and son of the company's founder. Chan is also chairman of Hang Lung Properties, also listed on the Hong Kong Stock Exchange. In 2008 the group's total revenues reached HKD 10.55 billion ($1.29 billion).

BUILDING HONG KONG

Hang Lung Group Ltd. was founded by Thomas Chen and his brother in 1960 as Hang Lung Development Company Ltd. Chen had wide-ranging business interests, and his family later became major investors in Hong Kong's dynamic high-technology sector. Among Chen's initial investments was a dry cleaning and laundry company, operated as a joint venture with Japan's Hakuyosha. That company started operations in 1964.

Chen was joined by son Ronnie C. Chan, who returned to Hong Kong after several years in the United States, where he completed bachelor's and master's degrees in biology at California State University, and then a master's degree in business administration from

COMPANY PERSPECTIVES
—

We will continue not only to expand our presence in mainland China, but also to invest in our portfolio in Hong Kong, with an aim of becoming the most established property developer active in both markets.

the University of Southern California. The latter degree proved the most useful to Chan as the company turned its attention toward the blossoming Hong Kong property development industry. As Chan pointed out in an interview, the property development market "was different then. The tallest building in Hong Kong was about 20 stories tall."

As part of its new real estate focus, Hang Lung went public in 1972, listing its shares on the Hong Kong Stock Exchange. The following year, the company made its first move into the property market, buying an existing property in Mongkok. The company then launched a redevelopment of the site, which was renamed as Argyle Centre.

Joint ventures were a common feature among Hong Kong's property development groups as the rush to rebuild the island's skyline kept pace with Hong Kong's emergence as a major Asian financial center. Hang Lung participated in its own range of joint ventures including one set up in 1976 to development the site above the Kowloon Bay Station of the city's Mass Transit Railway (MTR). Over the next decade projects to develop properties along the MTR line were among the city's largest.

ACQUIRING A PROPERTY INVESTMENT SUBSIDIARY IN 1980

Hang Lung also began building up its own land bank amid the rush to claim the increasingly rare properties on the mainland. While the property development companies received the right to build on the sites, their ownership nonetheless remained with the island's government. The situation existed even after the United Kingdom returned control of Hong Kong to China in the 1990s, as the Chinese government maintained a similar ownership position on land in the mainland. Hang Lung acquired its own large scale site in 1977 with a property on Kowloon Bay. That site had previously been operated as a factory by The Amoy Canning Corporation.

The acquisition of the Kowloon Bay site soon led the Chen family to acquire the Amoy Canning Corporation itself. In 1980 Hang Lung bought a 63 percent stake in Amoy Canning. As its name implied, that company originated as a cannery in Amoy (now Xiamen) in China in 1908. Amoy initially produced soy sauce, but later branched out into dairy products, and then began producing other local foods, becoming a major exporter to such markets as Indonesia, the Philippines and Singapore. The company opened a number of factories over the next decades. In 1929 Amoy merged with a rival group, Ta Tong, which brought Amoy its first operations in Hong Kong. This location became the company's headquarters after war broke out in China in 1938.

Following the war and the Communist takeover of the mainland, Amoy refocused its operations on the Hong Kong market. By 1949 the company had reincorporated as The Amoy Canning Corporation (Hong Kong) Limited, then listed on the Hong Kong Stock Exchange in 1954. Over the next decades Amoy Canning developed its own property arm, Amoy Properties Ltd.

After its acquisition by Hang Lung, Amoy was restructured to focus entirely on the property market, and was renamed as Amoy Properties in 1987. At that time Hang Lung transferred its portfolio of investment properties (the company's rental, leasing, and real estate sales businesses) into Amoy Properties. Hang Lung then focused its own operation on property development.

RESTRUCTURING IN 1987

By then Hang Lung had emerged as one of Hong Kong's top ten property groups. The company had taken a major step in this direction earlier in the decade. In 1981 the company had taken the lead of a consortium that successfully bid for the development rights of nine of the island's MTR stations. The company expanded its range of holdings to include a number of Hong Kong hotel properties.

As a result, Hang Lung became not only a major property group, but also a major figure among the Hong Kong investment community. This position was confirmed in 1985 when the company was admitted to the Hong Kong Exchange's prestigious Hang Seng Index. By then the company also had a changing of the guard, as Thomas Chen stepped down as head of the company. This position was filled by his brother, then was turned over again to Ronnie Chan at the end of the 1980s.

As part of the restructuring of its operations in 1987 Hang Lung acquired a new, vacant site, held by

KEY DATES

1960: Thomas Chen founds the company as Hang Lung Development Company Ltd.

1972: Hang Lung goes public and begins to focus on the property development sector.

1980: Hang Lung acquires the Amoy Canning Company and its Amoy Properties Limited subsidiary.

1987: Hang Lung restructures, and Amoy Properties becomes the group's main property investment operation.

1992: Hang Lung enters the mainland China market with the acquisition of two sites in Shanghai.

2001: Amoy Properties changes its name to Hang Lung Properties.

2005: Hang Lung begins expanding its mainland China operations beyond Shanghai, acquiring sites in Shenyang, Jinan, Wuxi, Changsha, and Tianjin.

2008: The company holds groundbreaking ceremonies for most of its new mainland developments, with the first properties expected to be completed by 2010.

Amoy Properties, in Tsuen Wan. The company then launched the development of the location into the Bay-view Garden residential complex. The following year Hang Lung added a new group of hotel properties to its portfolio, acquiring, through Amoy Properties, control of Local Property Company Ltd., which was subsequently renamed as Grand Hotel Holdings. Hang Lung then transferred its existing hotel properties to Grand Hotel; in exchange, Grand Hotel's non-hotel properties were transferred to Amoy Properties.

By the beginning of the 1990s Hang Lung's operations and revenues, were primarily carried out through Amoy Properties. The group gained a new high-profile property in 1989, paying HKD 1.6 billion for the Daimaru site in Causeway Bay. That property was subsequently redeveloped as Fashion Island/Fashion Walk/Fashion Square by the company. In 1990 the group bought another site, called the Peak, for HKD 328 million, and then launched development of a new residential and commercial complex, The Peak Galleria.

Hang Lung completed several more Hong Kong property acquisitions in the 1990s including the Grand Hotel site in 1991; the Star Centre in Kwai Chung, a shopping mall and parking garage complex in Laguna City, and the Standard Chartered Bank Building in the Central district in 1992; and, in 1993, the Park Building in Cheung Sha Wan; and the Mid-levels district's No. 2 Garden Terrace.

ENTERING CHINA IN THE EARLY NINETIES

By the early 1990s the Hong Kong real estate market was both highly volatile and increasingly mature. In order to provide for new growth, Hang Lung began to look elsewhere for expanding its operations. The mainland Chinese market became an obvious target, particularly as the introduction of new economic reform policies, which began in the late 1970s, had begun to create an emerging middle class.

Hang Lung initially targeted three cities for potential expansion, including Guangzhou, which lay across from Hong Kong and which had been the first of China's cities to develop under the new economic reforms; Beijing, the capital city; and Shanghai, which had long played a central role in the country's economic development. In the end Hang Lung chose to focus its mainland China expansion on the Shanghai market.

The group's entry came in 1992 when the company acquiring an existing residential complex then under development, the Hanson Garden, in Shanghai's Hongkou District. Hang Lung, however, targeted an entry into the property development market project. This led the company to become the lead partner in the acquisition of a site in the city's Xuhui District. This location became the site of the company's largest project to date, the Grand Gateway, a multipurpose residential and commercial complex. These acquisitions were shortly followed by the purchase of a new site in Nanjing Xilu, which the company developed as the Plaza 66 office complex and shopping mall.

EXPANDING BEYOND SHANGHAI

While Hang Lung's focus was on its two Shanghai developments, the company carried out further property acquisitions in Hong Kong. These included the 9 Wing Hong Street office and industrial complex, acquired in 1993, the CNT Group Building, located in Cheung Sha Wan, in as well as the Ritz Building in Mongkok, and 14 floors in the Shui On Centre in Wanchai, in 1994. Altogether, the company spent more than HKD 6 billion on property purchases in the first half of the decade. These also included HKD 860 million for the right to develop a new site on Stubbs Road, which became The Summit residential and commercial complex.

Despite this spending spree, Hang Lung had also begun building a treasury through the 1990s. This decision proved a wise one, as the Hong Kong market collapsed amid the general economic crisis that swept through the Asian region in the late 1990s. As the city emerged from the crisis, Hang Lung was in a strong position to profit from a new boom in the property market spurred by the fast-growing dot-com sector.

Hang Lung continued to add new properties to its portfolio through the first decade of the 2000s. In 2001 its main subsidiary Amoy Properties changed its name, becoming Hang Lung Properties. By then Hang Lung Properties had taken over all property development activities from Hang Lung Group, in addition to its property investment business. The company also celebrated the opening of both of its key Shanghai developments early in the decade.

Hang Lung then deemed that the time was right to begin expanding its mainland property holdings beyond Shanghai. In 2005 the group began acquiring sites elsewhere, starting with a site zoned for commercial use in Tianjin. By September of that year the company had also added a 35,000-square-meter lot in Shenyang City. This was followed in 2006 by the rights to build a shopping mall in the city of Jinan, as well as a 92,000-square-meter property in Shenyang City, a 37,000-square meter lot in Wuxi, and, in 2007, a second site in Jinan. By then, too, Hang Lung had become interested in the relatively underdeveloped inland market, acquiring the site for a proposed 500,000-square-meter office, shopping mall and residential complex in Changsha.

By the end of 2007 the company held groundbreaking ceremonies for the first of its new sites in Shenyang, and by the end of 2008 construction was underway at all of the company's mainland sites. Hang Lung's mainland holdings had grown to cover more than twice the total surface area of its Hong Kong properties. Hang Lung sought to extend its status as one of the top ten Hong Kong property groups in the Chinese mainland in the new century.

M. L. Cohen

PRINCIPAL SUBSIDIARIES

Akihiro Company Ltd.; Antonis Ltd.; Hong Kong AP Properties Ltd.; AP Universal Ltd.; Dokay Ltd.; Glory View Properties Ltd.; Hang Lung (China) Ltd.; Hang Lung Property Management Ltd.; Levington Ltd. (British Virgin Islands); Promax Ltd.; Prosperland Housing Ltd.; Rago Star Ltd.; Rioloy Ltd.; Stanman Properties Ltd.

PRINCIPAL DIVISIONS

Hong Kong–Property Leasing; Hong Kong–Property Development and Sales; Mainland China–Property Leasing; Mainland China–Projects Under Development.

PRINCIPAL COMPETITORS

Hutchison Whampoa Ltd.; Orient Overseas (International) Ltd.; China Resources Enterprise Ltd.; Sun Hung Kai Properties Ltd.; China Overseas Land and Investment Ltd.; CITIC Pacific Ltd.; Kerry Properties Ltd.; Cheung Kong (Holdings) Ltd.; Agile Property Holdings Ltd.

FURTHER READING

Joseph, Tara, "Hang Lung's Chan Bullish on Apartment Sales," *Standard,* October 30, 2003.

Ko, Kenneth, "Sales Strategy Pays Off for Developer," *South China Morning Post,* October 31, 2008.

Li, Sandy, "Hang Lung Aiming for Fresh Focus," *South China Morning Post,* April 14, 2000.

———, "Hang Lung Pulls Sale of Flats at Discount," *South China Morning Post,* November 8, 2008.

———, "Hang Lung, Swire in Mainland Push," *South China Morning Post,* February 23, 2007.

———, "Hang Lung's Mainland Income to Outpace HK," *South China Morning Post,* August 15, 2008.

———, "Shanghai May Hurt Hang Lung Rental Income," *South China Morning Post,* February 12, 2009.

Liu, Alfred, "Hang Lung to Invest $13b in China Projects," *Standard,* February 11, 2009.

———, "Hang Lung Upbeat on Leasing," *Standard,* February 12, 2009.

Man, Joyce, "Hang Lung Group Chairman Says No Job Losses," *South China Morning Post,* November 26, 2008.

"Ronnie Chan Tops Developers' Pay List with Cool $11.8m," *Asia Africa Intelligence Wire,* November 5, 2005.

Sito, Peggy, "Hang Lung Turns Towards Mainland," *South China Morning Post,* August 29, 2003.

Sito, Peggy, and Sandy Li, "Developers Step Up China Foray," *South China Morning Post,* November 15, 2006.

Wong, Foster, "Hang Lung to Concentrate on Retail Properties in the Mainland," *South China Morning Post,* June 7, 2006.

Harry Winston Inc.

718 Fifth Avenue
New York, New York 10019
U.S.A.
Telephone: (212) 245-2000
Fax: (212) 765-8809
Web site: http://www.harrywinston.com

Wholly Owned Subsidiary of Harry Winston Diamond Corporation
Incorporated: 1932
Employees: 200
Sales: $281 million (2008 est.)
NAICS: 448310 Jewelry Stores

■ ■ ■

Harry Winston Inc. is one of the world's most prestigious luxury jewelers. The global operation is run from a Fifth Avenue location in New York City, where the company not only maintains a salon open to a select clientele but also operates workshops that design jewelry and cut, polish, and set gems. In addition to its eight U.S. locations, Harry Winston salons are found in Paris, London, China, Japan, Hong Kong, Taiwan, and Dubai. Canadian mining firm Aber Diamond Corporation purchased a majority interest in Harry Winston in 2004 and then acquired all remaining shares in 2006. Aber, the new holding company, changed its name to Harry Winston Diamond Corporation the following year.

HARRY WINSTON AND THE BIRTH OF HIS COMPANY: 1890–1939

When Harry Winston established his business in 1932, he already had many years of experience in the jewelry business. His father, a Ukrainian immigrant named Jacob Winston, had opened a jewelry retail and repair shop in Manhattan's upper west side in 1890. His mother died when Harry was seven, and a year later he and his father, who suffered from asthma, moved to the West Coast for health reasons and opened a jewelry store in the center of the Los Angeles business district at a time when the film industry was just beginning to establish itself in the area.

According to lore, Harry early on demonstrated an ability to recognize valuable stones when at the age of 12 he noticed a two-carat emerald ring on a tray of junk jewelry in a pawnshop window. He bought the ring for 25 cents and resold it two days later for $800. He dropped out of high school at the age of 15 and went to work for his father to devote himself full-time to the store as well as to visit boomtown saloons, where he sold gems to oil prospectors who struck it rich.

At the age of 18, Harry moved back to New York with his father, who opened another Manhattan jewelry store, which he would operate until just before his death in 1929. With $2,000 saved from his California enterprises, Harry began to operate entirely on his own, buying and selling in the New York Diamond Exchange, which required sound, quick decisions and the boldness of a gambler.

COMPANY PERSPECTIVES

The company will build on its established reputation and expand its market position by introducing new product offerings to serve the needs of a growing number of affluent clients in the diamond jewelry market.

In 1916, at the age of 19, he started his own company, The Premier Diamond Company, located at 535 Fifth Avenue. In a matter of just two years, Winston was able to parlay his limited capital into a stake of $10,000 in cash and jewelry worth another $20,000. Unfortunately, an employee ran off with all of his money and inventory. With the help of bank financing, Winston was able to maintain his independence and rebuild his business. Because at his first appointment bank management mistook him for a messenger, he subsequently hired a distinguished-looking gentlemen to serve as a front.

He soon turned to the estate sales of the wealthy to buy jewelry that had gone out of fashion. He removed the stones and, to prepare them for resale, had them recut and reset to offer greater brilliance in a modern setting. His first major estate sale occurred in 1925, after which his activities gained notice in newspaper society columns. Winston achieved a national reputation in December 1930 when he bought the famous jewelry collection of mining tycoon B. J. "Lucky" Baldwin, which included the largest diamond ever sold in a U.S. public auction, a 39-carat-emerald-cut diamond. Although the collection also included a 26-carat ruby that was one of the largest rubies in the world, Harry Winston became linked to diamonds, especially large ones.

In 1932, Winston closed down Premier Diamond and established Harry Winston, Inc., in order to begin producing his own line of jewelry. He sought to highlight the jewels' own shapes by minimizing the setting. He was supposedly inspired one Christmas season when he observed how a holly wreath was shaped by its leaves, then applied the concept to jewelry design, relying on light platinum settings that allowed for the three-dimensional arrangement of stones so that they, rather than the metal, dictated the design.

Winston had a particular dislike for the yellow-gold used in older settings, which he felt distorted the color of the gems. His flair for new designs and penchant for publicity allowed Winston to flourish during the Depression years, when he became a major figure in the New York diamond business and in many ways was personally responsible for keeping the industry afloat in the city. He boosted New York while at the same time he gained an international reputation when in 1935 he paid $700,000 to De Beers Company for the 726-carat Jonker diamond, named after a South African man, Jacobus Jonker, who found the stone on a farm. Winston's plan to split the diamond into smaller stones for reselling was so fraught with peril that even Lloyd's of London would not insure the company for damage. He essentially risked his entire investment, which only added greater emphasis to his decision to have the work done in New York rather than Europe. It was the first major stone, in fact, to be cut in the United States.

After several European experts examined the diamond and indicated precisely where it should be divided, Winston turned to Lazare Kaplan, a Russian-born immigrant, to do the work, paying what was at the time an incredible sum of $30,000. After nearly a year of study, Kaplan concluded that if he followed the advice of the European experts he would destroy the Jonker diamond. He determined his own plan and successfully split the giant stone into 12 diamonds, the largest at 126.65 carats. Winston was then able to sell the results for a total of $2 million, realizing a hefty profit on his investment.

ACQUIRING THE HOPE DIAMOND: 1949

Over the ensuing decade Winston acquired other large, uncut diamonds, including the 726.6-carat Vargas, discovered in Brazil in 1938, and the 155-carat Liberator, discovered in Venezuela in 1943. Winston also continued to purchase cut stones through estate sales. In 1949, Winston paid $1 million for the world's most famous diamond, the sapphire-blue Hope Diamond, notorious because of a curse supposedly attached to it. According to the myth, the Hope Diamond was originally part of a 112.5-carat diamond stolen from the statue of a Hindu goddess in India in 1642 and smuggled out of the country by Jean-Baptist Tavernier, a French gem merchant. He sold it to the king of France, Louis XIV, who had the stone cut down to 67 carats. Louis subsequently died of smallpox and Tavernier at the age of 80 was attacked and devoured by wild dogs.

Louis XVI and his wife Marie Antoinette then inherited the throne and the diamond and were ultimately beheaded during the French Revolution. These deaths established a foundation for a later belief that the Hope Diamond was cursed and anyone who touched it would come to a disastrous end. A recut 44.5-carat stone surfaced in London some 30 years after

KEY DATES

■

1896: Harry Winston is born in New York City.

1916: Winston establishes his first company, The Premier Diamond Company.

1930: Winston buys the B. J. "Lucky" Baldwin collection of jewels, which includes largest diamond ever sold in a U.S. public auction.

1932: Harry Winston Inc. is formed.

1935: Winston acquires the 726-carat Jonker diamond.

1949: Winston acquires the Hope Diamond.

1957: Paris Salon opens.

1958: The Hope Diamond is donated to Smithsonian Institution.

1978: Harry Winston dies.

1980: The tradition begins of lending jewels to be worn at the Academy Awards.

1986: The Beverly Hills salon opens.

2000: Harry Winston's son Ronald buys out his brother Bruce Winston's share of business.

2004: Aber Diamond Corporation purchases a majority stake the company.

2006: Aber buys all remaining shares.

2007: Aber changes its name to Harry Winston Diamond Corporation.

the death of Louis XIV and Marie Antoinette. It was purchased by merchant Henry Thomas Hope, whose name has been attached to the diamond ever since. He gave it to his wife, who ran off with another man, and eventually was forced to sell it to fend off bankruptcy. A succession of ill-fated owners of the Hope Diamond followed.

In 1911, the famous Paris jeweler Pierre Cartier sold the stone to Washington socialite Evalyn Walsh McLean and, according to some, essentially used the "curse" as a marketing ploy, going so far as to insert a clause in the sales contract stating if any fatality occurred in the family within six months, the Hope Diamond could be exchanged for jewelry equal to the $180,000 McLean paid for the stone. She had her share of family troubles over the next 46 years and in fact died of pneumonia wearing the Hope Diamond, but the curse did not scare off Harry Winston. He acquired it as part of McLean's jewelry collection for an estimated $1.5 million.

Winston then combined the Hope Diamond with several other jewels to create a touring exhibit called the Court of Jewels, which traveled around the country for the next four years. Although it was good showmanship and garnered excellent publicity, the tour, and others that followed, were very much an expression of Winston's deep love of gems. Because so many of the finest examples were in private hands, he simply wanted the public to have a chance to share his joy in appreciating beautiful stones. In 1958, he donated the Hope Diamond to the Smithsonian Institution's Hall of Gems and Minerals, sending it by registered mail in a plain wrapped package. Over the years, he donated more gems to the Smithsonian, gems that one day would be housed in the Winston Gallery that serves as an entrance to the Janet Annenberg Hooker Hall of Geology, Gems, and Minerals.

For uncut stones, Winston, like other diamond dealers, was reliant on "The Syndicate," De Beers Consolidated Mines, Ltd. De Beers controlled around 85 percent of diamond production and could essentially determine who could buy diamonds and name the price. In the 1940s, Winston sought an independent source of uncut stones by funding a South American jewel-hunting expedition. Other attempts followed, including one in Sierra Leone that almost resulted in the severing of his relationship with De Beers. The parties settled their differences and Winston was able to negotiate a better deal with De Beers. He would become the Syndicate's largest customer.

Winston opened a Geneva salon in 1955, followed two years later by a Paris salon. His reputation as the King of Diamonds during this period was reflected in the song "Diamonds Are a Girl's Best Friend," made famous by Marilyn Monroe, who uttered the tagline, "Talk to me, Harry Winston." He was friends with Hollywood royalty as well as actual royalty and was a frequent guest for tea with the queen of England. Although known for big diamonds and showrooms with drawn shades where salespeople often outnumbered the few customers permitted to enter, Winston had other operations that contributed to his business. He sold industrial diamonds, as well as less expensive engagement rings that could be purchased through such pedestrian channels as Montgomery Ward mail-order catalogs. By the early 1960s, Winston was estimated to generate as much as $50 million in annual revenues. Because he was such a private man, the accuracy of this amount could not be verified. Winston was so private that he refused to allow his photograph to be taken, claiming that this decision was at the behest of his insurer, Lloyd's of London.

As Harry Winston aged, he faced the question of passing on the business to his two sons, who proved to have divergent personalities. He was known to proclaim,

"I have two sons, one a genius, one a moron." The eldest, Ronald, eagerly learned about the jewelry business from his father. He graduated from Harvard University with majors in both chemistry and English, then studied rocket propulsion at New York University before honoring his father's request that he help him run the family business.

Younger brother Bruce, on the other hand, showed little inclination for academics and was far less ambitious than his brother. Concerned that Bruce might squander his inheritance, Winston wrote a will that split the business between his sons, but Ronald was to be awarded his stake outright, while Bruce would have his shares held in trust. Every five years, 20 percent would be turned over to Bruce, who would also receive a living wage from a trust run by his brother and two trustees.

DEATH, SUCCESSION, AND THE FUTURE: 1970–2000

Harry Winston died at the age of 84, and Ronald took over the family jewelry business. He talked about the need to make the salons more accessible to a younger clientele, a theme that he would repeat periodically but never actually act upon. Ronald Winston was, however, credited with starting the practice of lending jewelry to actresses for the Academy Awards, which served as the firm's most overt effort at publicity. He also oversaw the opening of a new salon in Beverly Hills in 1986 and Tokyo in 1988. In addition he launched Winston's Ultimate Timepiece Collection, which created and sold watches in the $100,000 price range.

When Harry Winston's wife died in 1986, Ronald attempted to get his brother more involved in the business, naming him to the board of directors. For the most part, however, Bruce remained uninterested, reportedly signing whatever documents that required his signature without even reading them and generally preferring to spend his time sailing and driving his collection of sports cars. According to his attorney, Edward Wohl, Bruce in 1989 began to question Ronald's running of the company, especially in light of several years of reported losses. Moreover, during this period Ronald increased his salary from $350,000 a year, the same amount Bruce drew, to $1.13 million. Ronald claimed he was entitled to the money because he actually ran the company. Bruce went to court in 1990, seeking a full accounting of Harry Winston, Inc., and Ronald responded in January 1991 by calling a special meeting of the board of directors in order to claim the 50 percent of company stock promised to him by his father's will, then promptly dismissed his brother from the board. This act set off a bitter, decade-long legal battle.

The Winston brothers wasted few opportunities to castigate one another in the press, creating a public relations nightmare for a company that traded on decorum and taste. Ronald accused Bruce of being under the control of his attorney, Wohl, whom he claimed would realize more money in legal fees than Bruce if he simply sold his share of the business in a reasonable settlement. Bruce, on the other hand, accused Ronald of using company assets for his personal benefit. He pointed to Ronald's charging of expenses incurred in Beverly Hills during a somewhat unexpected effort to train for the 1988 Olympics; Ronald hoped to represent the Marshall Islands in the 100-meter sprint at the age of 47, but the country failed to qualify for the games. He insisted that the expenses charged to Harry Winston Inc. were related to the opening of the company's salon on Beverly Hill's Rodeo Drive. Nevertheless, Ronald further revealed an eccentric nature during legal proceedings. Like his father, he was reluctant to be photographed and insisted that a Lloyd's of London policy forbade pictures for security reasons. During one videotape deposition he wore a plastic pig mask and in another he donned a Lone Ranger costume.

To settle the suit Ronald offered his brother $4.5 million, which he subsequently increased to $17 million, and finally $28 million in September 1997. Bruce refused these offers, and eventually the court forced Ronald to return his stock to trustees and abide by their decision on the selling of the company. In the end, Ronald acquired complete control of Harry Winston Inc., buying out his brother for $54.1 million in the summer of 2000. In order to finance the deal Ronald took on a partner, the private equity investment firm Fenway Partners.

With the squabble finally ended, Ronald planned to take Harry Winston into a new era. He hired a new marketing firm to create an ad campaign to position the company as a lifestyle brand. Looking to bring in executive talent that had shied away from the company in recent years, he then hired Patricia Hambrecht, formerly with Christie's, to serve as president. He also hoped to attract new customers by offering more jewelry that cost less than $100,000, lowering the minimum price from $6,000 to $4,000. Even the idea of perfume, handbags, and eyeglasses under the Harry Winston label were entertained.

The company looked to open as many as 15 salons in such major cities as Chicago, Las Vegas, London, and Hong Kong, as well as to renovate the older Fifth Avenue and Paris locations. Overall, Ronald hoped to soften the image of Harry Winston, a task that would entail a wholesale change in attitude for its sales personnel.

EXPANSION IN THE 21ST CENTURY

Harry Winston gained a valuable partner in 2004 when Canadian mining firm Aber Diamond Corporation purchased a 51 percent stake in the company for $85 million. Aber owned 40 percent of Diavik Diamond Mines, one of the richest diamond mines in the world, and was eyeing Harry Winston as an important piece in its strategy to link its mining operations with luxury retail. The union with Aber gave Harry Winston the capital to fund further expansion as it planned to open up to 45 new salons over the next eight years.

Aber acquired all of the remaining shares of Harry Winston it did not already own in 2006 for $157 million. Shortly after the deal, Ronald Winston retired and was named honorary chairman. His departure marked the first time in company history that a Winston family member did not play a role in the business. Ronald's comments about the change in ownership were reported in a September 2006 *Women's Wear Daily* article. "I think the company is given a certain immortality beyond me and a destiny beyond me, and I think it's in good hands, I wish Aber continued success," he stated. Ronald's two-year-old son Blaise retained an option to be a Harry Winston jeweler for one day a year to preserve the family's legacy.

Under the leadership of Chairman and CEO Robert A. Gannicott and President Thomas J. O'Neill, Harry Winston forged ahead with its growth plans. In 2005, new salons opened in Hawaii and Florida. During 2006, the company opened salons in Dallas, London, and Tokyo, and also announced plans to launch a men's collection of cuff links, rings, various jewelry, and timepieces by designer Thom Browne. Additional salons made their debut in Osaka, Beijing, and Chicago the following year. A salon in Costa Mesa, California, opened in August 2008 while a Harry Winston watch boutique made its debut in Dubai in early 2009. By that time, the company's store count had climbed to 18 locations.

The company's link with its new parent, which adopted the Harry Winston Diamond Corporation name in late 2007, proved successful. Sales and profits were on the rise with revenues growing from an estimated $128 million in 2004 to an estimated $191 million in 2006. Sales growth in its key markets hit a snag in 2007, however, when the global economy began to weaken. While the company worked to revamp operations, disaster struck in December 2008 when the Harry Winston salon in Paris was robbed by four thieves suspected to be part of a gang called the Pink Panthers. The thieves took approximately $105 million in jewels in under 15 minutes in one of the largest jewel heists in history. The same store had been robbed a year earlier when thieves walked away with over $13 million in jewels.

While luxury goods such as diamonds were generally considered to be recession-proof, the company cut costs and laid off employees in an attempt to shore up profits. With demand continuing to fall in its key U.S. and Japanese markets, the prestigious Harry Winston fell victim to the faltering global economy despite its luxury brand status. As the slowdown in the luxury goods sector threatened to temporarily take the shine off of Harry Winston, company management was confident its growth in Europe, the Middle East, and Asia over the previous several years had positioned it for success in the years to come.

Ed Dinger
Updated, Christina M. Stansell

PRINCIPAL COMPETITORS

Bulgari S.p.A.; Cartier S.A.; Compagnie Financière Richemont A.G.; Tiffany & Co.

FURTHER READING

Berman, Phyllis, "Touch of Class; A Tiny Canadian Diamond Mine Buys Legendary Harry Winston," *Forbes,* May 24, 2004.

Burleigh, Nina, "The Trouble with Harry Winston," *New York,* January 18, 1999, pp. 46–53.

Carvajal, Doreen, "The Heist at Harry's," *New York Times,* December 14, 2008.

Chabbott, Sophia, "An Era Ends: Winston Sells Off to Aber," *Women's Wear Daily,* September 14, 2006.

Clark, Evan, "Harry Winston Hit by Luxe Spending Falloff," *Women's Wear Daily,* June 8, 2009.

Conroy, Sarah Booth, "Hope & Despair: The 'Curse' of the Diamond," *Washington Post,* September 29, 1997, p. D2.

Covert, James, "Jeweler Aims to Raise Its Profile," *Wall Street Journal,* November 21, 2007.

Haber, Holly, "Harry Winston Brings Its Bling to Dallas," *Women's Wear Daily,* December 11, 2006.

Karimzadeh, Marc, "Harry Winston Mining Its Way to the Top," *Women's Wear Daily,* September 13, 2004.

Parr, Karen, "Harry Winston Buffs Its Image," *Women's Wear Daily,* July 13, 1998, p. 8.

Posnock, Susan Thea, "Aber Acquires Full Ownership of Harry Winston," *National Jeweler Network,* November 1, 2006.

Scott, Sarah, "The Odd Couple," *National Post,* May 1, 2004.

Shor, Russell, "New York Judge Orders Sale of Harry Winston," *Jewelers Circular Keystone,* March 1998, p. 78.

Wade, Lambert, "Gems in the Rough: Sibling Feud Tarnishes the Diamond Empire Built by Harry Winston," *Wall Street Journal,* February 14, 1996, p. A1.

Wadler, Joyce, "Tranquility Elusive for Famed Jeweler's Heir," *New York Times,* October 17, 2000, p. B2.

Well, Melanie, "Reconstructing Harry," *Forbes,* October 1, 2001, p. 93.

Hastings Entertainment, Inc.

———■———

3601 Plains Boulevard, Suite 1
Amarillo, Texas 79102
U.S.A.
Telephone: (806) 351-2300
Fax: (806) 351-2424
Web site: http://www.gohastings.com

Public Company
Incorporated: 1972 as Hastings Books and Music, Inc.
Employees: 5,774
Sales: $538.7 million (2008)
Stock Exchanges: NASDAQ
Ticker Symbol: HAST
NAICS: 451211 Book Stores; 451220 Prerecorded Tape,
    Compact Disc, and Record Stores; 451120 Hobby,
    Toy, and Game Stores; 453310 Used Merchandise
    Stores; 722213 Snack and Nonalcoholic Beverage
    Bars; 454111 Internet Retail Sales Sites

■ ■ ■

A pioneer in multimedia home entertainment, Hastings Entertainment, Inc., sells, rents, and trades items for home entertainment, including new and used books, CDs, videos, and video games through a network of superstores. The stores, which are usually located in medium-size communities with populations of less than 250,000, also sell consumer electronics such as video game consoles and DVD players, magazines, and a variety of items ranging from T-shirts to posters to guitar strings. The company also operates www.gohastings.com, an online retail site. In 2009 Hastings operated 153 superstores in 21 states, primarily in the West and Midwest.

WHOLESALE ORIGINS

Hastings developed from an enterprise named Western Merchandisers, Inc., founded by Sam Marmaduke. Regarded as an pioneer in the wholesale industry, Marmaduke started his career as a rack jobber in 1946 when he arrived in Amarillo, Texas, to take over the wholesale business left to him by his late father. In his mid-20s at the time, Marmaduke transformed his father's small business, West Texas News Agency, into a family fortune, creating an expansive wholesaling business that later spawned Hastings, the retail arm of his wholesale business.

Initially, Marmaduke achieved success by keeping operating costs down, an important aspect of his managerial approach and a characteristic Hastings would later inherit. More significantly, it was Marmaduke's diversification into other product categories that propelled his wholesaling company forward and cemented his reputation as an industry maverick. "They said I was crazy," Marmaduke recalled, describing his colleagues' reaction when he diversified into wholesaling record albums in 1959. The bold, innovative move succeeded, however, leading to the incorporation of Western Merchandising, Inc., in 1961, the book and music wholesaling enterprise from which Hastings developed.

Hastings was formed in 1968 when the first Hastings Books & Music retail store opened in Amarillo. Marmaduke, who later confessed he made a belated entry into retail, succeeded in retail as he had in wholesale, cross-merchandising decades before other bookstores or music retailers. Along with Tower Records, Hastings was among the first chains to offer books and music within it stores. Marmaduke's unique approach was emulated by his son John, who was named president of the Hastings business in 1973 and watched over the company's first decade of expansion. By the end of the 1970s there were 22 Hastings stores in Oklahoma, Texas, Arkansas, and Kansas, all situated in small towns, a trademark of Hastings that the company employed as its expansion strategy in the years to come.

Growth picked up pace for Hastings at end of the 1970s as John Marmaduke and his father decided to expand by acquiring other retail chains. In 1979 Hastings purchased 29 stores that sold music exclusively and that were located in regional shopping malls. Converted to the company's cross-merchandising strategy, the stores acquired in 1979 were followed by other acquisitions in 1981, 1983, and 1985. Expansion through acquisitions was coupled with internal expansion, as the Marmadukes used their profits to establish additional retail outlets, both freestanding units and strip-mall stores. The first chapter of Hastings's corporate history ended at this point, with dozens of retail units located in small towns scattered throughout the Southwest and Midwest.

LARGER MULTIMEDIA DISCOUNT STORES

The next era began in the mid-1980s, when strategic changes were implemented that altered Hastings's business philosophy and changed the characteristics of the chain that had developed between 1968 and 1985. The strategic repositioning of the company stemmed from the influence of Western Merchandisers' biggest customer, Wal-Mart.

As Hastings developed into a regional retail chain, Western Merchandisers achieved prominence and robust financial growth by becoming a primary supplier to the Wal-Mart chain of discount retail stores. Hastings was similar to Wal-Mart in that both formats sold a variety of merchandise rather than a single product category, although Wal-Mart's merchandise diversity was greater, to be sure. In 1985, however, Hastings increased the breadth of its cross-merchandising approach, adding video rentals to the books and music it retailed. The addition of a video department led to a new name, Hastings Books, Music & Video, Inc., and, more importantly, signaled the company's decision to embrace the entertainment superstore concept.

The first store to offer the three product categories, touted as the company's first "triple combo" unit, opened in 1985 in Amarillo's Wolfin Village Shopping Center. Equally as important as the foray into videos was a change in the company's pricing strategy, an alteration that underscored the chain's similarity to Wal-Mart. In 1986, searching for ways to beat back mounting competition, Hastings began discounting its merchandise.

The experiment worked wonders, driving sales upward and convincing the Marmadukes that Hastings's future lay as a discount chain. By the end of the 1980s the company's strategy was firmly set. The larger, all-media discount units the company was operating were realizing greater profits and sales. In response the Marmadukes turned away from adding any more mall-based stores. Mall store leases were allowed to expire, and the company sold its mall stores to Camelot, directing management's focus on Hastings's blueprint for the 1990s: discount, triple combo, superstores.

A FOCUSED STRATEGY FOR NEW LOCATIONS

With a prototype for future expansion established, the company pursued physical growth in its unique way. The prevailing characteristic of the chain was the location of its stores, nearly all of which were situated in small towns with populations ranging between 10,000 and 50,000. The company's niche was in towns such as Warrensburg, Missouri; Marshalltown, Iowa; and Stephenville, Texas, communities where competition was limited and residents often were delighted to have the opportunity to purchase a broad selection of books, music, and videos close to home.

"When we go to open a new store in a small town," John Marmaduke explained, "and the people learn we are from headquarters, they don't just want to meet us—they want to hug us!" For these small rural towns, isolated from the wealth of merchandise showered upon their urban counterparts, Hastings offered what one company official described as "discovery opportunities" by cross-merchandising. From a practical standpoint, the intent was simple, effective, and profitable: "We want to

```
┌─────────────────────────────────────────────┐
│                                             │
│              KEY DATES                      │
│                  ▬                          │
│  1961:  Sam Marmaduke incorporates wholesaler│
│         Western Merchandising.              │
│  1968:  The first Hastings Books & Music retail store│
│         opens in Amarillo, Texas.           │
│  1973:  John Marmaduke is named president of Hast-│
│         ings business.                      │
│  1985:  With the addition of video rentals, the│
│         company is renamed Hastings Books, Music│
│         & Video, Inc.                       │
│  1992:  The company begins selling used CDs.│
│  1994:  Hastings and Western Merchandising sever│
│         ties.                               │
│  1998:  Hastings Entertainment goes public. │
│  2008:  The company celebrates its 40th anniversary.│
│                                             │
└─────────────────────────────────────────────┘
```

sell mysteries to people who come in and buy music, and we want to sell music to people who come in to by mysteries," explained Marmaduke.

SEPARATING HASTINGS AND WESTERN MERCHANDISERS

The company used this approach to expand rapidly during the 1990s, a decade that began with Hastings's sister company, Western Merchandisers, falling under the control of another company. Although separate companies, Hastings and Western Merchandisers were woven closely together, with the fate of one company having an equal effect on the other. Accordingly, when Wal-Mart acquired Western Merchandising in 1991, the corporate life of Hastings was affected as well.

Following Wal-Mart's acquisition of its primary wholesaler, Hastings remained under the ownership of its founder and chairman, Sam Marmaduke, but both companies shared the same president and chief executive officer, John Marmaduke. Western Merchandisers and Hastings also shared overhead, distribution services, and headquarter support, and held their annual conventions together. Under this arrangement, the two companies prospered in the shadow of the sprawling Wal-Mart chain, but the close-knit relationship between Western Merchandisers and Hastings did not last. The numerous ties connecting the two companies were strained not from poor performance by either company, but from the success of each.

Under the agreement reached with Wal-Mart in 1991, John Marmaduke was supposed to divide his time evenly between Western Merchandisers and Hastings. As Wal-Mart expanded its operations vigorously during the early 1990s, however, Western Merchandisers was forced to keep pace with the distribution demands of a fast-growing retail chain, which required an increasing amount of Marmaduke's attention. He was spending two-thirds of his time matching the gallop of Wal-Mart, leaving Hastings, whose all-media superstore concept was demonstrating encouraging success, without the full attention it required. "When you dance with an 800-pound gorilla," Marmaduke remarked, "the gorilla leads."

However, even devoting only one-third of his time to Hastings, Marmaduke continued to introduce innovations in the industry. Principal among these at the time was getting into the used CD business in 1992. A customer could walk into a store and sell a CD for cash or a credit for a future purchase, or buy a used disc at a discounted price. As Marmaduke explained, "Used product allows us to double our customers' reasons for visiting the store, while trading drives additional and often impulse purchases."

After several years the two sister companies could no longer effectively share the familial ties that had characterized their relationship since Hastings's creation in 1968. By the end of 1993, several months after Sam Marmaduke died of a massive heart attack, John Marmaduke decided not to renew his contract with Western Merchandisers and Wal-Mart. In the wake of Marmaduke's decision to forgo stewarding both companies, Wal-Mart sold Western Merchandisers to Anderson News Corp., one of the country's largest distributors of consumer magazines. For the first time in its history, Hastings was going to be a truly independent entity.

INDEPENDENCE FUELS EXPANSION

The divestiture was completed in August 1994, giving Hastings the freedom to pursue its own path. The chain, at this critical juncture in its history, comprised 95 stores spread throughout 13 states in the Southwest and the Rockies. Together, the stores generated approximately $300 million in revenue a year. With all his attention focused on this enterprise for the first time in years, Marmaduke faced a fundamental, pressing problem. Hastings lacked sufficient infrastructure to support its existing operations and future expansion, having shared centralized functions with Western Merchandisers.

To resolve this dilemma, Marmaduke organized a new purchasing staff, spent roughly $3 million to develop a management information system, and replaced other services and support previously provided by Western Merchandisers. Undaunted by this essential undertaking, Marmaduke concurrently announced expansion plans, targeting markets in Missouri and Nebraska as sites for future Hastings stores. Immediate plans called for the establishment of 20 new stores in 1995, as well as the expansion of 12 existing stores. The success of this initial expansion and the trouble-free separation from Western Merchandising instilled confidence for more ambitious expansion to follow.

As Hastings pushed forward into secondary markets with limited competition, "running to daylight," as Marmaduke described it, the company did so in a low-cost manner, continuing to embrace Sam Marmaduke's focus on keeping operating costs to a minimum. Instead of buying property or constructing new stores, the company expanded by taking on shorter-term leases on vacant buildings. The strategy increased flexibility, allowing the company to move from one location to another with greater ease, and it reduced the capital required for expansion.

Following this mode of expansion, Hastings fleshed out its presence in the western half of the United States during the mid-1990s, establishing nearly a dozen new stores a year. All expansion was financed internally, using the profits gleaned from existing stores. Between 1995 and 1997, Hastings opened 23 new stores, giving the chain 114 stores scattered among 15 states. Some units measured as much as 47,000 square feet, generally the stores located in areas with populations in excess of 250,000, but most averaged between 20,000 square feet and 25,000 square feet, representative of the typical small-town Hastings store.

In 1997 Marmaduke accelerated Hastings's expansion plans for the remainder of the 1990s. He announced plans to double the chain's size to 200 by 2000, with immediate plans calling for the establishment of 20 units in 1998, the most in one year in the company's history. As this expansion program was laid out, the company also began an extensive remodeling program scheduled to renovate all existing Hastings stores during the ensuing two years.

GOING PUBLIC

For the resources to implement his expansion plans, Marmaduke turned to Wall Street through an initial public offering (IPO) of stock in June 1998. Although he had previously vowed to keep Hastings a private company, the financial demands of his proposed expansion campaign could not be met without a substantial infusion of cash. The IPO netted the company $36 million, with Hastings's stock debuting on the NASDAQ at $13 per share.

Following the IPO, Hastings immediately began opening new units, providing evidence that the company's future would be filled with frenetic expansion activity. Five new stores were opened in a five-week period, giving the company 129 stores in 18 states by late 1998. In May 1999 Hastings launched a new electronic-commerce web site on the Internet featuring more than ten million new and used multimedia products. The launch of www.gohastings.com, which was supported by a national advertising campaign, and the company's expansion plans suggested Hastings's future financial growth would far eclipse the rate of growth achieved during the company's first 30 years of business. Marmaduke, it appeared, was intent on transforming Hastings from a regional competitor into a national force.

Within a year, Hastings was operating 149 superstores (20,000 square feet) in 22 states. The company continued to focus on communities with populations under 250,000, and primarily in small markets with populations of 30,000 to 50,000. In such markets a store could be a destination shopping experience, and there was relatively little competition. Beyond the merchandise for sale and rent, stores offered other attractions, including free gourmet coffee and soda, children's reading areas, book signings, and comfortable chairs for reading.

Located near residential neighborhoods, the stores' video rental offerings drew foot traffic. The company's video rental business accounted for one-quarter of its revenues at a time when other stores that offered music and videos were cutting back on rental offerings. In keeping with its strategy to provide what the customers need, the company added new departments offering DVD equipment and software for sale and rent.

The company had a rough 2000, announcing in March that it would have to restate its earnings for part of 1999 and for the previous four years due to an accounting error that understated the cost of goods. This resulted in overstated pretax earnings.

ADJUSTING TO CHANGES IN MUSIC INDUSTRY

As the decade began, the music industry faced sharply dropping sales due to CD burning, file sharing, and the discounting of prices at big-box merchants. Hastings's initial defense was to increase its mix of offerings so that it was less dependent on music. In 2001 the stores expanded its "used" product offerings, adding DVDs and video games to used CDs products, buying or trading those of customers. The company introduced a new store design, which offered three separate departments.

At the center of the store was a secure "bullpen" containing music, video games, and accessories. To one side of this was the video and DVD section, and to the other, books, magazines, and a café.

In January 2003 Hastings and five other music retailers formed Echo, a joint venture to sell downloaded music over the Internet. However, Echo could not compete with Apple Computer's iTunes Music Store when it appeared on the scene three months later, and the millions of dollars required to create a comparable service was more than the partners were able to raise. By 2004 the consortium had dissolved. Although iTunes knocked out Echo, it did cause recording labels to loosen their hold on the licensing of music in their collections. This made it much easier for individual retailers to offer digital downloading options without having to band together for leverage.

However, Hastings decided not to jump on the digital music bandwagon. Its web site remained fairly basic, offering what was in its stores and announcing special store events. There were no music downloads and no online DVD rentals, and there were no download kiosks in the stores.

Rather, Hastings continued to diversify its product offerings. In 2004 customers were able to trade in and/or buy used books. Hastings's marketing concept for all its used products was to combine new and used items. Thus customers found used titles right beside new CDs, videos, video games and books. The company also honed the offerings of its stores in smaller markets, with fewer than 50,000 people. Targeting local interests, these stores offered, for example, Christian music or items in Spanish.

SURVIVAL BY INNOVATION AND EVOLUTION

In 2002 music accounted for 30 percent of Hastings business, books were 25 percent, and video rentals were 21 percent. By 2006 music represented only 20 percent, books had dropped to 22 percent, and rentals to 17 percent. Replacing those losses were gains in video games, electronics, "trends" such as T-shirts, sports merchandise, posters, stationery, and licensed movie memorabilia, and the company's Hardback Coffee Café and other consumable items.

The company survived by continuing to innovate. It introduced a children's department, which included categories ranging from children's books to toys, games, clothing, and starter musical instruments. In 2009 there were plans to test a new line of baby products. The area of consumer electronics expanded to include not only Blu-ray players and digital converter boxes, but also musical instruments.

In 2008 the company saw increases in revenues from books (23 percent of sales), videos (22 percent), video games (from 9 percent in 2006 to 11 percent), trends (from 4 percent to 5 percent) and electronics, (from 3 percent to 4 percent). In September Hastings celebrated its 40th anniversary with its sixth consecutive quarter of profit.

As the economy weakened, the company's total revenues dropped, despite cost cuttings that included layoffs. However, Hastings believed that its rental, used, and discount offerings in particular would prove attractive to customers cautious about spending. Further, in 2009, the company planned to introduce a revamped gohastings.com web site, which would offer enhancements such as social networking and digital downloads. Having been a pioneer in offering multimedia entertainment and embracing used CDs, locating in markets underserved by other media retailers, conducting extensive research, and continuing to evolve to serve its communities, Hastings appeared to be in good shape to weather the economic downturn.

Jeffrey L. Covell
Updated, Ellen D. Wernick

PRINCIPAL SUBSIDIARIES

Hastings Internet, Inc.

PRINCIPAL COMPETITORS

Wal-Mart Stores, Inc.; Borders Group Inc.; Best Buy Co., Inc.; Amazon.com; Blockbuster Inc.; Barnes & Noble Inc.

FURTHER READING

Albright, Max, "Amarillo, Texas-based Book-Music Store Chain Plans Public Stock Offering," *Knight-Ridder/Tribune Business News,* May 14, 1998.

"Anderson News to Acquire Western Merchandisers," *Publishers Weekly,* June 20, 1994, p. 23.

Ault, Susanne, "Casting a Wider Web: Music Downloads, Social Networking Part of New Site," *Publishers Weekly,* September 29, 2008, pp. 36–37.

———, "Key Innovations at Hastings: These Five Achievements Have Contributed to Hastings' 40 Years of Success," *Publishers Weekly,* September 29, 2008, p. 33.

Banerjee, Scott, and Ken Schlager, "As Echo Fades, Stores Go It Alone," *Billboard,* June 26, 2004, pp. 5–6.

Benz, Matt, "Hastings Making Turnaround," *Billboard,* April 14, 2001, p. 56.

Christman, Ed, "Anderson News to Western Confab: Embrace Change," *Billboard,* October 22, 1994, p. 55.

————, "Hastings Find Strength in Diversity: CEO Relates How a Variety of Product Keeps the Specialty Music Chain Afloat," *Billboard,* November 16, 2002, p. 89.

————, "Hastings Turns 40 Ruling Retail: Innovative Multimedia Chain Hastings Entertainment Celebrates Four Decades of Retail Success," *Billboard,* September 27, 2008, pp. 31–34.

————, "How Did Hastings End Up Restating Earnings?" *Billboard,* April 1, 2000, p. 86.

————, "The Majors Missed Everything from MTV to Downloading," *Billboard,* March 6, 2004, p. 74.

Facenda, Vanessa L., "Small Towns, Big Media: Hastings Entertainment Offers Small Town Consumers the Opportunity to Buy, Sell, Trade or Rent Packaged Entertainment," *Retail Merchandiser,* April 2006, pp. 32–33.

"A Family Affair: John Marmaduke Reflects on the Growth and Future of Hastings Entertainment," *Billboard,* September 27, 2008, pp. 32–33.

Frankel, Daniel, "Six Retailers in Tune for Music Downloads: Echo Venture Seen As a Way to Boost CD Sales, Not Destroy Them," *Video Business,* February 3, 2003, pp. 8–9.

Garrett, Lynn, "The Small-Town Strategy," *Publishers Weekly,* August 25, 1997, p. 29.

"Hastings to Launch New www.gohastings.com E-Commerce Internet Web Site," *PR Newswire,* April 1, 1999, p. 2538.

Magiera, March, "For CEO Marmaduke, Hastings Is a Work in Progress," *Video Business,* September 29, 2008, pp. 1–3.

Netherby, Jennifer, "Change for the Good: Retailer Stays Competitive with Constant Modifications, Consumer Knowledge," *Publishers Weekly,* September 29, 2008, pp. 39–40.

Scally, Robert, "Hastings Hits Growth Spurt, Plans 50 Units by End of '99," *Discount Store News,* November 23, 1998, p. 4.

Villa, Joan, "At Hastings, Business Is a Convenience Thing," *Video Business,* December 13, 1999, p. 42.

Hills Industries Ltd.

944-956 South Road
Edwardstown, S.A. 5039
Australia
Telephone: (61 08) 8301 3200
Fax: (61 08) 8297 4468
Web site: http://www.hills.com.au

Public Company
Incorporated: 1946 as Hills Hoist Ltd.; 1957 as Hills
   Industries Ltd.
Employees: 2,999
Sales: AUD 1.18 billion ($785.3 million) (2008)
Stock Exchanges: Australia
Ticker Symbol: HIL
NAICS: 332999 All Other Miscellaneous Fabricated
   Metal Product Manufacturing; 332321 Metal
   Window and Door Manufacturing; 333112 Lawn
   and Garden Tractor and Home Lawn and Garden
   Equipment Manufacturing; 334290 Other Com-
   munication Equipment Manufacturing

■ ■ ■

Hills Industries Ltd., inventor of the iconic Hills Hoist, is a leading Australian diversified manufacturer of consumer and industrial products. The Edwardstown-based company operates through three main divisions: Electronic Security and Entertainment Products; Home, Hardware and Eco Products; and Building and Industrial Products. The Building and Industrial Products is the group's largest division, accounting for more than 54 percent of the company's AUD 1.18 billion ($785 million) in revenues in 2008. This division produces steel tubing, metal roofing and fencing products, carports and sheds, and steel door frames, among other products. Subsidiaries in this division include Orrcon, Fielders, and Korvest.

The Electronic Security and Entertainment division encompasses a wide range of products, from antennae and closed circuit television systems; satellite dishes and set-top boxes; professional audio equipment; consumer audio and video appliances; automation and control systems; and fiber-optic networks for housing estates. This division's subsidiaries include Hills Antenna, Hills Signal Master, DGTEC, Opticom, Direct Alarm Supplies, and Hills Sound Vision and Light. The Electronic Security and Entertainment division generates 26 percent of group sales.

Lastly, the Home, Hardware and Eco division produces 19 percent of group turnover and encompasses the group's original business producing outdoor clothes-drying apparatus, as well as ironing boards; childproof barriers; playground equipment; wheelbarrows; ladders and scaffolds; rainwater collection and storage systems; hospital, home care, and mobility equipment; and plumbing products. Subsidiaries include Hills, Bailey, Oldfields, Kelso, Kerry Equipment, and K-Care. Hills Industries is listed on the Australia Stock Exchange. Jennifer Hill-Ling, granddaughter of one of the company's founders, is the group's chairman. Graham Twartz is CEO.

COMPANY PERSPECTIVES

Vision and Values: Hills is a diversified company operating in three industry segments, namely Electronic Security and Entertainment; Home, Hardware and Eco; and Building and Industrial Products. We aim to be market leader in the industries in which we operate, supplying innovative, quality products to our customers and to achieve superior financial performance that provides strong shareholder value.

BUILDING A BETTER CLOTHESLINE IN 1945

Rotary clotheslines offered a distinct advantage over traditional clotheslines, in that they provided more line in less space. The rotary clotheslines could also turn with the wind, allowing clothing to dry more quickly. A number of Australian inventors had begun to seek ways of raising the rotary line, in order to take advantage of the stronger wind flow above ground. An early rotary hoist design appeared in 1912, designed by Gilbert Toyne. By 1925 Toyne had patented his design, which featured a windup mechanism. Production of the rotary clotheslines was handled by the L.L. Lambert company.

The Lambert clothesline remained expensive, however, and production was limited. This was particularly true during World War II, when Australia faced a shortage of raw materials. One day on an Adelaide train in the early 1940s, Lance Hill, a motor mechanic, overheard two women discussing the difficulties in finding a rotary clothesline. Hill, whose wife had complained of this as well, decided to build his own rotary clothesline.

Hill based his design on the Toyne design, which saw its patent expire in 1946. Hill's design used a single central pole supporting a series of steel ribs, which in turn supported the rustproof wire from which the clothing would be hung. Hill's hoist mechanism boasted two improvements over Toyne's design. First, Hill attached a handle, making it easier to lift the hoist. Second, he added a windup mechanism that permitted the entire clothesline to be easily raised into the air.

The Hills Rotary Hoist, as the product became famously known, was largely perfected by 1945. Hill was quickly besieged with requests from neighbors for their own rotary hoists. Hill obliged them, building the clotheslines in the garage of his home. Then, in 1946 he was joined by his brother-in-law and neighbor, Harold Ling, a bookkeeper who had just returned to Adelaide after serving as a clerk in the Australian Imperial Force during the war.

Ling and Hill became partners and secured the patents for Hill's designs in 1946. The partnership then rented a factory in Fullerton and launched large-scale production for the first time. Finding materials remained difficult during the postwar period, as Australia remained under wartime restrictions. Hill also faced resistance from the country's largest tube steel producer, British Tube Mills, to supply the company. This led the partners at first to buy salvaged tubing, and then to begin importing tubing from France.

BRANCHING OUT

As word spread about the Hills Rotary Hoist, demand soared. The company soon began filling orders beyond South Australia. Into the end of the 1940s, the company took steps to develop itself on a national level. This led Hill and Ling to reincorporate the company as Hills Hoist Ltd. and to buy the Fullerton factory in 1948. For this, Hill and Ling borrowed money from their families, as well as from some of the company's employees. In exchange, employees received shares in the company—a policy that became a permanent fixture at the company. Hill served as the company's chairman, while Ling became managing director. Over the next two decades, Ling succeeded in building the company into a multimillion dollar business.

Demand for the clothesline remained strong despite its relatively high price, which reached the equivalent of two weeks of the average salary. In order to maintain its supply of materials, the company expanded, acquiring its own tube manufacturing and steel galvanizing operations in 1950. The company also opened a number of sales agencies across Australia, as well as in New Zealand and in London.

Despite the success of the clotheslines, Ling recognized the opportunity for extending the group's line of products. During the early 1950s, the company began introducing new products, such as ironing boards, folding chairs, strollers, and playground equipment, based on the use of tube steel. In 1955 the group built a new factory, in Edwardstown, which became the central site for all of its manufacturing operations. The new facility allowed the company to launch production on an industrial level. It also permitted the group to continue to expand its product range.

Television antennae were a major new product line for the company starting in 1956. Ling had correctly recognized the coming impact of television, and the

KEY DATES

1946: Lance Hill and his brother-in-law Harold Ling form a partnership to produce and sell a rotary hoist clothesline developed by Hill.

1948: Hills Hoists Ltd. reincorporates and buys its first factory.

1958: The company, which had expanded into television antenna production and other tube steel-based products, goes public on the Adelaide Stock Exchange.

1965: Bob Hill-Ling takes over as managing director and leads the company for 27 years.

1986: The company begins expanding through acquisition, including a 46 percent stake in Korvest.

1992: David Simmons becomes managing director and leads the company on 16 years of revenue growth.

2002: Hills acquires K-Care and its line of mobility products for senior citizens.

2006: Hills forms Hills Eco business unit based on its acquisition of Team Poly.

2009: Hills announces revenues of more than AUD 1.18 billion ($785 million).

company had begun manufacturing television antennae, which were closely related in design to the group's clotheslines, in anticipation of the launch of broadcast television in Australia. In this way, the company became the leading supplier of antennae in the country. By the end of the decade, the company's turnover had topped AUD 5 million.

NEW GENERATION IN 1966

The company's expanding product range led the company to change its name to Hills Industries Ltd. in 1957. The following year, the company went public, listing its shares on the Adelaide Stock Exchange. The company shifted its listing to the Australian Stock Exchange in 1962.

By then, Hills had begun expanding beyond its tube-based products. In 1959, for example, the company launched a television repair service, Hills Telefix. This operation was to remain as part of the company until it was sold in 1996. In the meantime, the Telefix operation provided the basis for what was to become one of the group's core divisions at the dawn of

the 21st century, the Electronic Security and Entertainment division. During the 1960s, also, Hills's tube manufacturing business grew to become an Australian leader and soon began supplying third parties.

A new generation came into the group's leadership in 1965 when Bob Hill-Ling took over from his father, Harold Ling, as managing director. Hill-Ling had joined the company as a youth, becoming its first cadet engineer in 1952, before completing an engineering degree at Adelaide University in 1957. Under Hill-Ling, Hills Industries expanded to become a major Australian manufacturing force.

ACQUISITIONS

Hills's growth remained strong through the 1960s and into the 1980s. The company began targeting further growth that decade, leading to a series of acquisitions. These including a 46 percent stake in metal products producer Korvest Ltd. in 1986, and a 30 percent share of Radio Frequency Systems Pty Ltd., which produced a range of antennae and radio-frequency equipment and systems for the commercial broadcast sector.

During the 1980s Hills added wheelbarrow production, acquiring the Kelso brand. In 1990 Hills boosted this business with the purchase of Wesbarrows, a producer of wheelbarrows based in West Australia. Wesbarrows was then merged into the Kelso business. The company also expanded into the production of ladders, taking over Brisbane-based Baileys.

Hills underwent another changing of the guard in 1992 when Bob Hill-Ling stepped down as the group's managing director. That position was then filled by David Simmons, who had joined the company in 1984 as its finance director. Under Simmons, who led the company until 2008, Hills experienced its strongest growth.

Acquisitions continued to play an important role in the group's expansion through the turn of the century. The company added security doors in 1994, taking over Gaylit Pty Ltd. By then, the company had also expanded its steel production, acquiring hot-rolled steel products specialist Rydal Steel in 1992, and Western Australia-based sheet metal producer Du Feu in 1996.

NEW MARKETS IN THE 21ST CENTURY

Hills continued to seek out new markets at the dawn of the 21st century. In 1999, for example, the company acquired Triton, a producer and distributor of products for the do-it-yourself and woodworking sectors. After several years of disappointing results, however, the company sold Triton in 2005.

More promising for the company was its acquisition of K-Care in 2002. This Perth-based company allowed Hills to move into the production and distribution of mobility equipment, particularly for senior citizens. K-Care's products included powered wheelchairs and electric scooters, lifting mechanisms, walking frames (walkers), and hospital beds.

The company also had been building a new subsidiary, Orrcon, founded as a joint venture through a merger between Hills Tubing and Welded Tube Mills of Australia in 2000. In 2002 Orrcon opened a new pipe and large-tube factory in Wollongong, a move that allowed Hills to add structural steel products to its Industrial Division's range. Hills acquired full control of Orrcon in 2005, paying AUD 58.5 million for the 50 percent it did not own. Bob Hill-Ling, in the meantime, had retired as the group's chairman, turning over that position to his daughter, Jennifer Hill-Ling in 2005.

Another important acquisition came that year, with the purchase of 75 percent of Team Poly, based in Adelaide, which produced tanks for water, septic systems, and other fluids. Team Poly formed the basis of a new Hills business unit, Hills Eco, created in 2006. The company then launched its first product, a line of rainwater collection tanks, that year.

Hills showed no signs of slowing down into the second half of the decade. The company was buoyed by its 2004 acquisition of Access Television Services, a major provider of satellite and subscription television services in Australia. In 2006 the company acquired the rights to a solar water heater, which Hills then redeveloped and launched under the Hills Solar (Solar Solutions for Life) brand in 2007. The following year, the group's Eco operations expanded again with the launch of a new brand, Hills Water, in order to launch Team Poly's product line for the urban market.

MANUFACTURING IS SENT OVERSEAS

For all its success, Hill remained under pressure during the first decade of the 2000s, as it faced rising competition from low-priced imports from China and elsewhere. By 2006 Hills was forced to give in to the pressure, shifting much of its own manufacturing overseas.

Simmons retired as managing director in 2008, after having successfully led the company throughout 16 years of continued growth. Between 2004 and 2008 alone, the company's sales had grown from AUD 718

million to nearly AUD 1.2 billion ($785 million). Taking Simmons's place was the group's former finance director, Twartz. The company then announced its intention to maintain the pace of acquisitions that had helped transform the company into one of Australia's most diversified industrial companies. Hills and its iconic Hills Rotary Hoist remained an Australian success story in the new century.

M. L. Cohen

PRINCIPAL SUBSIDIARIES

Audio Telex Communications Pty Ltd; Bailey Aluminium Products Pty Ltd; Crestron Control Solutions Pty Ltd; Fielders Australia Pty Ltd; Hills Finance Pty Ltd; Hills Hoists Pty Ltd; Hills Industries Limited (New Zealand); Korvest Ltd; Opticomm Co Pty Ltd (50%); Orrcon Holdings Pty Ltd; Orrcon Tubing Pty Ltd; Pathfinder (Edwardstown) Pty Ltd (Singapore); Step Electronics Pty Ltd; Team Poly Pty Ltd; Woodroffe Industries Pty Ltd.

PRINCIPAL DIVISIONS

Electronic Security and Entertainment Products; Building and Industrial Products; Home, Hardware and Eco Products.

PRINCIPAL OPERATING UNITS

Access Television Services; Consumer Products; Fielders; Hills Antenna & TV Systems; Hills Eco; Hills Electronic Security; Hills Healthcare; Hills Sound, Vision and Lighting; Korvest; Opticomm; Orrcon; Woodroffe Australia.

PRINCIPAL COMPETITORS

Futuris Corporation Ltd.; Dexion Ltd.; ARB Corporation Ltd.; MCK Holdings Proprietary Ltd.; Saferoads Holdings Ltd.; Oldfields Holdings Ltd.

FURTHER READING

"Australia's Hills Industries Buys Perth-Based K-Care Group," *AsiaPulse News*, October 1, 2002.

"Australia's Hills Industries Posts 31% Drop in Net Profit," *AsiaPulse News*, February 4, 2009.

"Australia's Hills Industries Seeks Growth via Acquisition," *AsiaPulse News*, November 9, 2007.

"End of the Line for 87 Workers as Hills Imports from Asia," *Advertiser*, April 3, 2006.

"Hills Industries to Target Green Sectors to Grow," *TendersInfo*, September 9, 2008.

Hopkins, Philip, "Future Looking Bright, Says Hills," *Australasian Business Intelligence,* August 7, 2007.

Macey, Richard, "It's Lost a Little Hoist, but You Can Still Take a Hills for a Spin," *Sydney Morning Herald,* October 4, 2002.

"No Surprises Please," *Australasian Business Intelligence,* April 14, 2009.

O'Neil, Bernard, "Ling, Harold Eustace Hill (1907–1966)," *Australian Dictionary of Biography,* Vol. 15, Melbourne: Melbourne University Press, 2000, pp. 100–01.

Home Product Center plc

96/27 Moo 9, Bangkhen, Muang
Nonthaburi, 11000
Thailand
Telephone: (66 02) 832 1000
Fax: (66 02) 832 1400
Web site: http://www.homepro.co.th

Public Company
Incorporated: 1995
Employees: 5,000
Sales: THB 18.54 billion ($570 million) (2008)
Stock Exchanges: Thailand
Ticker Symbol: HMPRO
NAICS: 444130 Hardware Stores; 444220 Nursery and
   Garden Centers

■ ■ ■

Home Product Center plc (HomePro) is the leading operator of retail home improvement and do-it-yourself (DIY) centers in Thailand. The company operates 35 large-scale HomePro stores, with plans to add up to four more stores by the end of 2009. Seventeen of the group's stores are located in the heavily populated Bangkok region; most of the remainder target the more rural "upcountry" markets. Since the middle of the first decade of the 2000s, HomePro has been targeting Thailand's tourism markets with a new Market Village shopping center format. The first of these opened in Hua Hin in 2006 and features more than 60,000 square meters of selling space, including a supermarket, a multiplex cinema, a bowling alley, and restaurants. The

company plans to add new shopping centers in Pattaya, Phitsanulok, Samui, and elsewhere. HomePro stores feature a range of 60,000 products, including more than 1,000 products produced under the company's own brand names. These include Homebase, Bathtime, Home Concept, Estetik, Spring, Purity, Parno, Furdini, and Elektra.

A major sales-generating event for the company is its annual Home Expo, during which the company sells many products at discounts of up to 50 percent, and others as high as 80 percent off. HomePro is listed on the Thailand Stock Exchange. The company is led by Chairman Anant Asavabhokin and Managing Director Khunawut Thumpomkul. Major shareholders include Land & Houses PLC and Quality Houses PLC, both of which are controlled by Asavabhokin.

WESTERN-STYLE DIY IN 1995

Asavabhokin had already established himself as Thailand's leading homebuilder, through Land & Houses PLC, founded with his mother in the early 1970s. Land & Houses's focus remained largely on the Bangkok region. Into the middle of the 1990s, however, Asavabhokin began seeking to expand his business operations. Land & Houses targeted a number of overseas ventures in the second half of the 1990s.

Closer to home, Asavabhokin, who had earned a degree in civil engineering at the Illinois Institute of Technology in 1973, recognized the potential for extending his relationship with Thailand's growing numbers of homebuyers. Asavabhokin decided to develop a retail DIY and home improvement concept

COMPANY PERSPECTIVES

The Company has the goal to become a leader in retail business in home improvement market for the goods of construction, decoration, and refurbishment of houses and residence places together with the provision of complete services as One Stop Shopping to attain highest customer satisfaction. At present the Company has more than 60,000 items of products. In addition, it has established a Training Center to develop the personnel at all levels so that they will have knowledge and ability to provide good services to customers.

patterned after Western-style superstore formats such as Home Depot.

For this project, Land & Houses teamed up with American International Assurance Co. and Pong Sarasin, a member of one of Thailand's wealthiest and most politically influential families, to found Home Product Centers in 1995. The new company then began developing its retail concept, creating the HomePro name. The first HomePro store opened in Rangsit in 1996.

HomePro took advantage of the booming Thai housing market as the country experienced an economic boom through the mid-1990s. This period came to abrupt halt in 1997, however, as the entire Asian region became caught up in a dramatic economic crisis. In Thailand, the housing market more or less collapsed, with hundreds of building contractors declaring bankruptcy and leaving homebuyers in the lurch. The crisis nearly toppled Land & Houses as well.

PUBLIC OFFERING IN 2001

As the Thai economy pulled out of the crisis toward the end of the decade, HomePro too started to grow. The company opened a new store in Bangkok's Seri Center shopping mall in May 2000, followed a store in Bang Khae two months later. The company also expanded its retail concept, developing its own supercenter format featuring 6,000 square meters of selling space. The expanded store format allowed HomePro to expand its range of products and services as well, as the company moved from a focus on the DIY market to position itself as a home improvement retailer. This provided the company with a larger umbrella. The company soon added home appliances, including televisions, stereo

equipment, and furniture, as well as interior decorating items.

In support of its growing operations, HomePro added a new warehouse and distribution facility in 2000. At that time, the company also instituted an electronic ordering and purchasing system, linked to a growing network of more than 1,000 suppliers. By the end of that year, HomePro had opened its sixth Bangkok region store.

As Thailand's main population center, Bangkok remained HomePro's primary market. The company laid plans to open two new stores through 2001 and into 2002, including a store at the Wave Place commercial complex. HomePro also turned its attention toward expanding into Thailand's "upcountry" provincial market. The company opened its first store outside of Bangkok in April 2001, in Nakhon Ratchasima.

The success of this venture encouraged HomePro to step up its expansion. HomePro announced plans to open as many as four new stores per year into the middle of the decade. In order to finance this objective, the company went public, listing its stock on the Thailand Stock Exchange in September 2001. Land & Houses and its affiliated company, Quality House PLC, retained control of the company, combining to hold more than 50 percent of HomePro's stock.

SHOPPING CENTER IN 2005

The initial public offering enabled the company to boost its store network to 11 sites by late 2002. At the same time, the company had launched construction of four new Bangkok-region stores, with another two in the planning stages. The company then announced its intention invest THB 1 billion ($23 million) to raise its store network to as many as 30 stores nationwide by 2005.

The new housing boom, and a buoyant economy in general, provided HomePro with even greater growth prospects into the middle of the decade. The company continued to roll out new stores in order to meet the growing demand both for building and DIY supplies and home furnishings. The company's sales soared, rising by an average of 42 percent per year in the first five years of the 21st century. Earnings grew even more strongly, with compound annual growth of 89 percent.

Part of the group's success was the changing nature of Thai consumer habits in the early years of the new century. More and more Thai shoppers had begun to abandon their traditional market-based purchases in favor of the Western-style retail environment. HomePro

KEY DATES

1995: Land & Houses PLC leads the creation of Home Product Center (HomePro), which opens its first HomePro retail store in 1996.
2001: HomePro goes public on the Thailand Stock Exchange.
2004: Company launches construction of a new Market Village retail complex, which opens in 2006.
2009: HomePro opens its 35th store.

met this demand with new stores openings. By the end of 2004, the company boasted a network of 18 stores, with the construction of four more completed in 2005. The company's revenues grew from less than THB 7 billion in 2004, to more than THB 12 billion in 2005.

HomePro also began developing a new retail concept, launching the construction of a new THB 1 billion shopping center complex in Hua Hin, a major tourism destination. Called Market Village, the complex, built on four stories with a total retail floor space of 60,000 square meters, expanded the HomePro format to 10,000 square meters. Market Village also added a range of other retail operations and services, including a Tesco Lotus supermarket, restaurants, a karaoke bar, a five-screen movie theater, and a bowling alley.

When the Hua Hin Market Village opened in February 2006, HomePro had greater ambitions for the new retail mall concept. The company announced its plans to develop a series of Market Village malls, targeting other tourist destinations, including Pattaya, Phitsanulok, and Samui.

THAI HOME IMPROVEMENT LEADER IN THE NEW CENTURY

HomePro met its objective for 30 stores by the end of 2007, including some five stores completed that year. Nearly half of the group's retail network was located outside of the Bangkok region. Yet this expansion represented something of an end of the line for the group, as it began to draw near to limitations put into place on future retail store openings by the Thai government. Nonetheless, the company managed to secure permission for five new stores, boosting its total network to 35 stores by May 2009. New sites included Phuket, a popular tourist destination.

More troubling for the company was the softening economy as a new economic crisis begun in the United States, destabilized the global economy. The company also suffered the effects of the growing political instability in Thailand. As consumer confidence waned and spending fell through 2008, the company launched a THB 50 million incentive campaign. For this the company reduced prices on a wide range of items, with some prices dropping as much as 80 percent.

Although HomePro continued to post revenue growth, the difficult economic climate forced it to postpone plans to open at least two more stores by the end of 2009. The company's own financial position, however, remained sound, with sales rising to THB 18.5 billion ($570 million) and profits of THB 959 million ($30 million) in 2008.

Into 2009 the company took steps to shore up its operations, launching the refurbishment of a number of its existing stores. HomePro also sought to differentiate itself by emphasizing its services, including new training initiatives for its personnel. This effort led to the unveiling of a new marketing campaign, based on the slogan "We Know." As the leader of Thailand's DIY and home improvement market, Home Product Center had constructed a solid foundation for future growth.

M. L. Cohen

PRINCIPAL SUBSIDIARIES

Market Village Co., Ltd.

PRINCIPAL COMPETITORS

HomeWorks Plc; Siam Global House Plc.

FURTHER READING

Asawanipont, Nitida, "Home Pro's BT50 Million Business Reviver," *Nation*, August 27, 2008.

"Home Pro Invests One Billion Baht in Hua Hin Branch," *Asia Africa Intelligence Wire*, December 20, 2004.

"Home Product Center Emphasises Integrated and Tailor-Made Services," *Thai Press Reports*, March 5, 2009.

"Home Product Center Forecasts Sharp Revenue Rise," *Thai Press Reports*, March 3, 2006.

"Home Product Center Opens Hua Hin Store," *Thai Press Reports*, February 23, 2006.

"Home Product Center Renovates Store on Ratchaphruek Road," *Thai Press Reports*, May 13, 2009.

"Home Product Center Sets Up Exposition," *Thai Press Reports*, October 23, 2006.

Pinijparakarn, Sucheera, "HomePro Banking on Increase in House-Brand Products Sales," *Nation,* February 27, 2009.

"Thai Retailer to Expand," *Home Channel News Newsfax,* November 25, 2002, p. 2.

"Thailand's Home Pro Hopes for Annual Growth of 28 Percent," *Asia Africa Intelligence Wire,* August 10, 2005.

"Thailand's Home Product Center Plans IPO," *Bangkok Post,* September 11, 2001.

Iron Mountain, Inc.

———————— ■ ————————

745 Atlantic Avenue
Boston, Massachusetts 02111
U.S.A.
Telephone: (617) 535-4766
Toll Free: (800) 935-6966
Fax: (617) 350-7881
Web site: http://www.ironmountain.com

Public Company
Incorporated: 1951
Employees: 20,100
Sales: $2.73 billion (2007)
Stock Exchanges: New York
Ticker Symbol: IRM
NAICS: 49311 General Warehousing and Storage

■ ■ ■

Iron Mountain, Inc., is one of the largest records and information management companies in the world. The company provides a full range of records storage and management services to more than 100,000 clients across the globe. Iron Mountain's major business segments include Records Management, Data Protection and Recovery, and Information Destruction. The company operates more than 1,000 offices in 38 countries throughout North America, Europe, Latin America, and the Asia-Pacific region. Iron Mountain's revenues have grown substantially over the years, increasing from $209 million in 1997 to $2.7 billion in 2007.

EARLY HISTORY

Iron Mountain was established in 1951 by a group of dedicated visionaries who understood the nature of the modern business era. Through the end of World War II, records for all types of business activities were recorded by hand. If the company was organized and prosperous enough, the records were later typed and then filed in a filing cabinet or appropriate container, often a heavy-duty cardboard box. As time passed, older records were then stored in a basement or warehouse, whichever was most convenient and least damp.

The entrepreneurs who decided to open a records management firm understood the old-fashioned methods and knew that these methods would not be able to keep pace with the burgeoning economy and the rise of the consumer product era in postwar America. How could a company that sold millions and millions of items keep records of all the transactions and inventory by hand? How could a firm with thousands of employees ensure that they received their paychecks in the exact amount at the right time? How could hospitals maintain patient information for rapid retrieval and analysis? As businesses expanded, how could management be sure that their ventures met with the regulatory standards set by state and federal government agencies?

As laborious and time-consuming in-house record keeping began to drain valuable resources away from the primary focus of a company, managers began to search for new ways to store and manage their records while retaining easy access to critical information. At first, Iron Mountain was contracted by large businesses within and around the Boston metropolitan area to provide consulting services for records management. Soon, however, the consulting services turned into an operational activity when Iron Mountain started its business records storage and management system. Iron Mountain assisted a company in gathering and organizing records; establishing a file system by date, product, or topic; and then providing a cost-effective method to manage the entire system that had been established. By the end of the 1950s, Iron Mountain had gained a reputation for providing reliable, efficient, highly organized, cost-effective solutions to the problems faced by both small and large companies in managing their records.

Throughout the 1960s, management at Iron Mountain focused on providing high-quality consulting services, as well as assisting firms in the storage and management of business records. During this time, the company began to expand the range of its services. Active file management became one of the services that was most sought after, especially by larger firms, and Iron Mountain came up with the innovative idea to use customized retrieval labels so that any record could be routed from a manager's or supervisor's desk in the administrative office to the receiving dock with minimal effort and maximum efficiency. As management in larger firms began to realize the importance of controlling critical information and having access to it at a moment's notice, Iron Mountain began to develop new and even more efficient methods to meet customer needs, including such techniques as sealing files to protect their contents and a new way to refile records quickly and accurately.

EXPANSION: 1970–89

During the 1970s and 1980s Iron Mountain expanded its operations across the United States and into Europe. Having established the nation's first underground center for records storage in 1951, the year the company was founded, Iron Mountain was inundated with requests from *Fortune* 500 firms to assist them in their manage-

ment and storage of an ever-increasing number of records. To meet this demand, the company embarked upon a comprehensive strategy to expand across the United States. While maintaining its headquarters in Boston, the company opened offices in New York City and throughout the state of New York, as well as in Arizona, California, Connecticut, Delaware, Florida, Indiana, Kentucky, Nebraska, New Hampshire, New Jersey, North Carolina, Ohio, Pennsylvania, Rhode Island, Texas, and Virginia. This was only the first round of the company's expansion program. Additional offices followed in Alabama, Colorado, Georgia, Louisiana, Maine, Maryland, Michigan, Minnesota, Missouri, Nevada, New Mexico, Oregon, Utah, and Washington. By the end of the 1980s, Iron Mountain provided a wide variety of records storage and management services to nearly one-third of the companies on the *Fortune* 500 list, as well as to a host of start-ups, small firms, and midsized companies.

During the 1980s Iron Mountain expanded its services dramatically in the field of medicine, becoming the nation's leading provider of records storage to a wide spectrum of doctors, hospitals, and insurance companies within the healthcare industry. The specialized services that the company provided involved open-shelf filing, onsite indexing projects, onsite purges, stat (quick) and regular schedule deliveries of patient records, and radiology file management. Iron Mountain worked with some of the country's busiest hospitals and largest research laboratories, as well as small clinics and group practices, to provide safe record storage and management. Perhaps the most innovative and useful of all the services provided by the company included the stat delivery of patient records. Iron Mountain operated and maintained its own storage facilities for hospitals that were able to deliver hundreds of medical files throughout the day and night at a moment's notice in the case of a life or death matter.

It was also during the 1980s that the company grew into the leading provider of records storage services for the legal profession. Although Iron Mountain had been providing such services to lawyers from its inception, during the 1980s the company developed customized searching, sorting, and selection criteria that enabled law professionals to either broaden or narrow the scope and range of their search for legal records and documents. Iron Mountain also developed a filing system for lawyers based on customer needs, including access to files by attorney, date, client, issue, or any other field that was requested. This aspect of the company's services grew rapidly throughout the decade, and most of the firm's offices around the United States were provided some sort of legal file storage and management. As the 1980s drew to a close, Iron Mountain was providing state-of-

<table>
<tr><td colspan="2" align="center">## KEY DATES
■</td></tr>
<tr><td>**1951:**</td><td>Iron Mountain opens for business in Boston.</td></tr>
<tr><td>**1955:**</td><td>Company expands legal profession records storage and management services.</td></tr>
<tr><td>**1960:**</td><td>Active file management services are expanded.</td></tr>
<tr><td>**1970:**</td><td>Underground records storage facilities are enhanced.</td></tr>
<tr><td>**1994:**</td><td>Major growth through acquisitions strategy begins.</td></tr>
<tr><td>**1998:**</td><td>Company makes first oversees acquisition, British Data Management, Ltd., and reports revenues of $423 million at the end of the fiscal year.</td></tr>
<tr><td>**1999:**</td><td>Iron Mountain acquires its top competitor Pierce Leahy.</td></tr>
<tr><td>**2005:**</td><td>Iron Mountain gains a foothold in the Australian and New Zealand markets with its $87 million acquisition of Pickfords Records Management.</td></tr>
<tr><td>**2006:**</td><td>The company forms a joint venture with Singapore-based Transnational Company Pte. Ltd.</td></tr>
</table>

the-art legal file storage and management services to some of the most prestigious law firms in the United States.

GROWTH CONTINUES: 1990–2000

By the early 1990s, Iron Mountain offered a full range of services, including business records storage and management, software escrow, healthcare records storage and management, active file management, vital records protection, data security services, records management consulting, facilities management, film and sound archive services, destruction services, disaster recovery support, and storage cartons and supplies. By the mid-1990s, Iron Mountain was clearly the dominant company within the industry, and continuing to grow at a record pace. The firm had 30 million square feet of storage space and was providing its services to over 25,000 customers, including an ever-increasing number of *Fortune* 500 firms.

Ambitious as ever, and ready to take an even larger share of the market, management at the company decided to implement one of the most aggressive growth through acquisitions strategies in modern corporate history. During four years beginning in 1994, Iron

Mountain acquired no less than 62 companies, enabling the firm to establish a new presence in 46 markets. In 1998 alone the company made 12 purchases, some of the more notable including the Arcus Group, Inc., which expanded Iron Mountain's data security service business and propelled it to number one within the industry; National Underground Storage, located in Pennsylvania, which significantly enhanced and strengthened the company's vital records and film and sound archive storage services; and a number of companies in the Pacific Northwest, which resulted in Iron Mountain becoming the leader in the region.

All of these acquisitions were reorganized and incorporated into Iron Mountain's administrative and regional operations. In addition, Iron Mountain made a foray into Europe, acquiring British Data Management, Ltd., one of the two leaders in providing records storage and management services throughout the United Kingdom. Although Europe remained behind the United States in outsourcing records storage and management services, Iron Mountain's management saw the market as having great potential for the future and viewed the acquisition of British Data Management as a step toward further expansion on the continent, including France, Germany, and the Netherlands.

By the end of fiscal 1998, Iron Mountain could justifiably lay claim to the title of "The World's Largest Records Management Company." The company counted offices in nearly 70 cities across the United States, with additional offices planned due to the continuing acquisitions program. Most impressively, the company reported a 103 percent increase in revenues from 1997 to the end of 1998. Revenues for 1998 reached $423 million.

In October 1999, the company announced a deal to merge with its chief rival, Pierce Leahy Corporation, in a stock swap valued at around $1.1 billion. This reverse merger was completed in February 2000, with Pierce Leahy assuming the Iron Mountain name. Together, the two powerhouses boasted over 115,000 clients through their 77 facilities in the United States, nine Canadian operations, and joint ventures in Mexico, South America, and Europe.

The new Iron Mountain assumed its former rival's debt of about $570 million as well as the costs incurred in the transaction, while Pierce Leahy shareholders acquired about 35 percent of the new entity's stock. Prospects for 2000 looked just as bright. Early in the year, the company announced the acquisition of Data Storage Centers, Inc., of Jacksonville, Florida, which would give the company a greater presence in the southeastern states. With the global business sector generating ever-greater amounts of data and information, whether paper or electronic, the demand for Iron Mountain's services continued to increase.

MOVING INTO THE NEW MILLENNIUM

During the early years of the 21st century, Iron Mountain focused on increasing its digital offerings. Clients demanded new ways to store and retrieve electronic files as well as access old paper files that had been transferred to electronic images. To allow its customers to access stored files, the company operated data centers in Boston, Pennsylvania, and—according to reports—at a secret location in a mine 280 feet underground in New York State. In addition to digital archiving, Iron Mountain also saw an increase in its information destruction operations. The company destroyed 260,000 tons of documents in 2001, nearly double the amount destroyed in 2000.

The company continued to grow during this period by making strategic acquisitions. Arcemus, a domain name records management company, was acquired in May 2004. Arcemus and DSI Technology Escrow Services joined together to form Iron Mountain Intellectual Property Management Inc. later that year. Data storage software manufacturer Connected Corporation was also purchased in 2004. Iron Mountain gained a foothold in the Australian and New Zealand markets with its $87 million acquisition of Pickfords Records Management the following year.

Iron Mountain formed a joint venture with Singapore-based Transnational Company Pte. Ltd. in 2006, allowing it to further serve the Asia-Pacific region. Additional investments were made abroad that year including a joint venture in India with Mody Access Info Pvt. Ltd. and the purchase of Melbourne-based DigiGuard. Joint ventures secured in 2007 allowed the company to expand in Turkey and Greece. Xepa Digital LLP, a converter of analog audio and video to high-resolution digital files, was acquired in 2007, allowing the company to strengthening its position in the film and sound industry. The company also purchased Stratify Inc., a provider of electronic discovery services for the legal field, that year.

Robert T. Brennan, the company's president and chief operating officer, was named CEO in 2008 after Richard Reese relinquished his duties. Reese remained chairman of the company and with Brennan, began to shift focus away from a growth-through-acquisition policy to place more emphasis on internal growth and expanding its core physical storage business. The company also planned to continue increasing its international footprint, looking for opportunities in untapped markets. With a solid strategy in place and sales and profits rising consistently, Iron Mountain appeared to be positioned for success in the years to come.

Thomas Derdak
Updated, Christina M. Stansell

PRINCIPAL DIVISIONS

Records Management; Data Protection; Information Destruction.

PRINCIPAL COMPETITORS

Anacomp Inc.; Cintas Corporation; SOURCECORP Inc.

FURTHER READING

Bray, Hiawatha, "Salvation and Destruction," *Boston Globe,* August 26, 2002.

Dillon, Paul, "Iron Mountain Adds to Records Storage Empire," *Orlando Business Journal,* August 23, 1996, p. 4.

Kerber, Ross, "Happily, Business Is in Shreds," *Boston Globe,* April 18, 2002.

"Iron Mountain Buys Four Records-Management Companies," *New York Times,* April 14, 1999, p. C19(E).

"Iron Mountain CEO Stepping Down, Replacement Named," *FinancialWire,* February 28, 2008.

"Iron Mountain Expands in Asia Pacific with Transnational Company Joint Venture," *PR Newswire,* December 14, 2006.

"Iron Mountain, Inc.," *New York Times,* May 10, 1999, p. C14.

"Iron Mountain, Inc.," *New York Times,* July 9, 1999, p. C4.

"Iron Mountain Listing Change," *Wall Street Journal,* April 26, 1999, p. C19.

Preimesberger, Chris, "Iron Mountain Acquires Digital Conversion Company," *eWEEK,* November 19, 2007.

ITV plc

200 Gray's Inn Road
London, WC1V 8HF
United Kingdom
Telephone: (44 20) 7156 6000
Web site: http://www.itvplc.com

Public Company
Incorporated: 1934 as Granada Theatres Ltd.; 1983 as
    Carlton Communications plc
Employees: 4,000
Sales: $2.94 billion (2008)
Stock Exchanges: London
Ticker Symbol: ITV
NAICS: 51312 Television Broadcasting

■ ■ ■

ITV plc is the United Kingdom's largest advertising-funded broadcaster. The company's network arsenal includes ITV1, the country's largest commercial television channel, as well as digital channels ITV2, ITV3, and ITV4. The company's ITV Studios arm produces content for ITV channels as well as other U.K. broadcasters. Among the most popular programs on ITV1 are *Britain's Got Talent* and the long-running *Coronation Street.* The company was formed in 2004 by the merger of Granada plc and Carlton plc. Since that time, ITV has struggled with falling advertising revenues and dwindling audiences, reporting losses of £2.7 billion in 2008.

GRANADA ORIGINS

Granada traces its roots to the early 1900s when, shortly after the turn of the century, Alexander Bernstein opened the Edmonton Empire music hall. During the 1920s his sons Sidney and Cecil started up a chain of movie theaters. The Bernstein brothers approached their business with an innovative spirit and a desire to bring their deep appreciation of cinema to larger audiences. They actively promoted many kinds of films, conducted surveys to determine the kinds of films people most wanted to see, and initiated children's matinees.

The theater chain adopted the name Granada in 1930. The name was chosen by the well-traveled Sidney Bernstein, who felt that its exotic connotation fit with the image he wanted for the theaters. Following the formation of Granada Theatres Limited in 1934, which consolidated all activities into one group, the company made its first public stock offering in 1935 on the London Stock Exchange.

Over the next three years, Granada opened a new theater almost every three months, including "super cinemas" with seating capacity for as many as 3,000 patrons. Created by leading architects, artists, and theatrical designers of the period, the super cinemas offered live programming as well as films in elegantly appointed surroundings. As theatergoing habits changed with the times, however, Granada gradually phased out this concept in favor of theaters with either single or multiple screens and converted others into bingo and social clubs. The firm moved cautiously into bingo, even though it was lucrative, maintaining a low profile until the 1968 Gaming Act legalized bingo and permitted the company to feel more comfortable about its business involvement and the longevity of the game's consumer appeal.

A FOCUS ON TELEVISION

By the late 1940s, Granada's attention gradually had turned away from theatrical entertainment toward the fledgling television industry. After requesting a license to operate an independent television station in 1948, the company finally received the contract in 1954 to broadcast five days a week in all of northern England, becoming one of the four founders of Britain's Independent Television Network. Granada subsequently made its first black-and-white transmission on May 3, 1956, with a program called *Meet the People.* This development was particularly well-timed, since it offered Granada a new growth area to offset continuing declines in its theatrical operation. In November 1956 the company introduced a new show, *What the Papers Say,* which later became the country's longest-running weekly program on current events. Two years later, Granada became the first network to provide live coverage of a local election, despite strong official opposition, and later it pioneered broadcasts of the annual meetings of the country's major political parties and trade unions.

As the first television company in the country to construct its own studio rather than to use existing facilities built for other purposes, Granada also brought widely acclaimed plays to audiences who had never before had such viewing opportunities. Another program, *Coronation Street,* whose characters captured the regional flavor of northern England, began production in 1960 and continued as one of the country's longest-running series well into the new millennium.

To reflect its evolving focus, the company changed its name in 1957 to Granada Group Limited. Management remained under the tight control of the Bernstein family, with Sidney's eye for opportunities and insistence on quality and creativity to drive the company's business operations.

DIVERSIFICATION BEGINS

One of Granada's major areas of growth in the early 1960s was the television rental business. Granada first opened showrooms under the name Red Arrow to handle rentals of televisions and other merchandise such as record players, washing machines, refrigerators, and vacuum cleaners. Granada also expanded into book publishing in 1961 as an extension of its involvement in the visual media. This business was sold eventually to William Collins & Sons in 1983, since it no longer fit the company's business focus.

In 1963 Granada Television introduced *World in Action,* a weekly program that broke with broadcasting tradition by addressing the subject of current events without a host or moderator. Later that year, the company expanded its activities into furniture rental with the formation of Black Arrow Leasing, a business that was sold in 1971.

In 1964 Granada began to export television programming through Granada Overseas Ltd. (later renamed Granada Television International before becoming British Independent Television Enterprises Ltd. [BRITE] in 1995). That year Granada also acquired Barranquilla Investments, a real estate developer, and formed Granada Motorway Services to sell food and fuel to highway travelers across Britain. This business stood in marked contrast to Granada's other ventures in the media area and almost folded within its first six years because of high leasing costs and low profits.

Seven years after the introduction of its domestic television rental business, Granada expanded into the West German market under the name Telerent Europe. Additional showrooms were opened in France, Spain, Italy, Sweden, Switzerland, and North America as Granada looked to establish a television rental market in areas where the concept had never before been introduced.

Granada Group Services also was formed in 1968, initially to provide computerized support to the firm's own businesses, but later to develop systems for outside clients as well. In the meantime, Granada Television continued to prosper and grow technologically. Having been awarded a new seven-days-a-week contract for Great Britain's northwest region, the company began broadcasting programming in color for the first time in September 1969.

The 1970s brought two additional businesses into the Granada fold. Novello and Company, a music publisher founded in 1811, and L'Etoile, a 70-year-old Belgian insurance company, were acquired in 1973 and

KEY DATES

1934: Granada Theatres Ltd. is created.

1935: Granada goes public on the London Stock Exchange.

1954: Granada receives a contract to broadcast five days a week in all of northern England, becoming one of the four founders of Britain's Independent Television Network.

1956: Granada makes its first black-and-white transmission on with a program called *Meet the People.*

1957: The company changes its name to Granada Group Ltd.

1960: *Coronation Street* begins production.

1983: Carlton Communications plc is incorporated and lists on the London Stock Exchange.

1988: Carlton acquires Technicolor and is listed on the NASDAQ.

1993: Carlton produces its first broadcast of Carlton Television.

1997: Carlton forms a partnership with Granada called British Digital Broadcasting.

2000: Granada merges with Compass Group.

2001: Carlton sells Technicolor to Thomson Multimedia; Granada Compass demerges leaving Granada plc as a pure play media company.

2004: ITV plc is created upon completion of the merger between Granada and Carlton.

1974, respectively, followed by the 1981 purchase of a second Belgian insurance company, Eurobel, which was merged with L'Etoile. The insurance business was sold a decade later after incurring consistent losses; Novello was sold in 1988 because it no longer fit with the company's core businesses.

In 1979 Sidney Bernstein retired as chairman of Granada and turned over leadership of the company to his nephew Alex. Alex Bernstein inherited an organization whose television rental operation had grown to represent more than 60 percent of the company's profits by 1979, but was threatened by a marked decline in business. The company's overall long-range planning system was erratic and informal at best. He gradually instituted a more decentralized management structure to give Granada's subsidiaries greater operating autonomy.

CONTINUED DIVERSIFICATION

Continued expansion in the motorway services business in the early 1980s was accompanied by similar success in the television production area. Granada's programming franchise was renewed in 1982 for another eight years—it was the only independent TV contractor in Great Britain to hold onto its license. Its critically acclaimed dramatic series *Brideshead Revisited* was broadcast with resounding success in the United States, and Granada Cable and Satellite was formed in 1983 to capitalize on new broadcasting technology.

The firm also embarked upon another new venture in 1983, Granada Microcomputer Services, to market computer hardware to businesses through retail outlets. Granada Microcomputer Services began with a single store and from the start met heavy competition from a number of other retailers, making the undertaking less lucrative than it first promised. Granada decided to reposition its shops as business centers that could package microcomputer hardware and software programs into customized systems for small businesses. This operation, however, was sold in 1987 as Granada reorganized and shifted away from computer retailing toward providing computer maintenance services for businesses through Granada Computer Services.

In 1984 Granada made a major move to consolidate its position in the rental business with the acquisition of Redif-fusion, a major rental competitor. Although the television rental market had been declining for several years, the Rediffusion purchase increased Granada's cash flow, market share, and profits and also gave it a stronger position in VCR and movie rentals. After the Rediffusion outlets had been consolidated and integrated with its own, Granada made a second major decision: to begin selling TVs and video recorders to offset declines in the rental area. That same year Granada Television scored a major programming success in the production area with the premiere of the award-winning series *The Jewel in the Crown.*

In February 1986 Granada received an unwelcome merger offer from the Rank Organisation, a British company with similar interests in the television, entertainment, and leisure industries. At the time, Granada had broken off merger negotiations with the Ladbroke Group because of a difference in opinion over Granada's net worth. The Independent Broadcasting Authority, Britain's regulator of broadcasting licenses, blocked the takeover, much to Granada's relief, by ruling that Rank's offer would illegally shift ownership of Granada's television franchise. Rank withdrew its bid a month later, after exhausting its legal appeals.

This incident appeared to sharpen the company's outlook on the future. Shortly thereafter, Granada began refining its planning systems with an eye toward growing in several directions at the same time. This approach contrasted with the Bernsteins' original managerial style, which had focused on personal pet projects, whether or not they fit with the company's strengths and resources.

The new strategy backfired to a certain degree in July 1986 when Granada's plan to acquire Comet, an electrical appliance retailer, fell through. This purchase was part of an intricate arrangement in which Dixons Group sought to acquire Woolworth Holdings and then sell Woolworth's Comet subsidiary to Granada. When the Dixons takeover attempt failed, Granada was prevented from making a major move into electrical retailing.

Granada overcame this setback the following year, when it made the largest single acquisition in its history at the time. In November 1987 Granada launched and successfully completed a $450 million bid for Electronic Rentals Group PLC. This purchase gave Granada a stronger presence in the consumer rental and retail markets in the United Kingdom, with two chains, and also served as a springboard for renewed growth in the European rental business. The 1987 acquisitions of NASA in France and Kapy in Spain provided additional retailing strength in those countries. The Granada Hospital Group also was formed during the year to oversee the company's television rentals to hospitals in Canada and the United States.

Granada made another significant purchase in June 1988 when it bought DPCE, a European-based computer maintenance company. Integrated with the company's existing maintenance businesses under the Granada Computer Services International umbrella, DPCE gave the company a larger customer base and a wider range of services to make it a more competitive player in the industry.

By the late 1980s, Granada defined its overall business in terms of four major areas: rental and retail, television, computer services, and leisure. This latter area encompassed not only the original motorway services operation and bingo clubs, but also bowling centers, travel and tour activities, and theme parks and holiday villages managed by Park Hall Leisure, a 1986 acquisition.

TRANSFORMATION INTO MEDIA AND HOSPITALITY GROUP

The 1990s brought a host of changes to Granada, dramatically transforming it once more. The decade began inauspiciously with the company in dire straits largely because of the expansion into computer maintenance. This unit was losing money and its growth

through acquisition had burdened Granada with a heavy debt load. The company was forced to make a £163 million stock offering in May 1991 to stay afloat. Granada also sold its bingo clubs to Bass plc for £147 million. To mollify its stockholders, the company forced Derek Lewis out as chief executive. In October 1991 Gerry Robinson, who had been chief executive of catering specialist Compass Group, was brought in to replace Lewis. Robinson, who has been credited in large part with the quick turnaround that followed his appointment, brought with him from Compass his right-hand man, Charles Allen, to run Granada's television and leisure sectors—the two sectors that within a matter of a few years would become the company's core areas. In March 1996, Alex Bernstein retired as chairman, Robinson replaced him, and Allen took over the chief executive slot.

During the 1990s Granada's television sector continued to develop its satellite pay television operations through the company's involvement in Granada Sky Broadcasting and British Sky Broadcasting (BSkyB). The company was also in the forefront of the nascent digital television industry, through British Digital Broadcasting plc (BDB), a 50-50 joint venture of Granada and Carlton Communications. BDB launched a digital television service in late 1998 requiring only a set-top box and receiving digital signals for a maximum of 30 channels through existing television antennae. Meanwhile, in August 1997 the company's independent television and television programming operations received a boost through the acquisition of Yorkshire-Tyne Tees Television (YTT) for about £700 million. The addition of YTT's independent television licenses gave Granada a dominant position in independent television in northern England, while YTT's programming arm bolstered Granada's standing as the largest commercial television production company in the United Kingdom.

By the time of this acquisition, Granada had made some critical divestments. The company's near-disastrous foray into computer services came to an end when that unit was jettisoned through an £89 million management buyout. In rental, Granada during fiscal 1997 decided to focus its resources on its core U.K. operation, and thereby sold off its North American and German (Telerent) rental businesses.

However, it was Granada's leisure sector that underwent the most dramatic transformation of all in the 1990s. By mid-decade the core of this sector was the motorway service areas (the market leader in the United Kingdom), a chain of Granada Lodges with a total of 1,400 rooms, and a contract catering operation (the bowling centers and travel unit having been divested in 1995). In January 1996 Granada boldly paid £3.9 billion ($6 billion) for Forte PLC, the second largest hotel group in Europe, in a fierce hostile takeover. Granada gained the Travelodge chain of budget hotels in the United Kingdom (to which were added the Granada Lodges, converted to the new brand); 147 "provincial" hotels located outside of London, under the business-traveler-oriented Posthouse and the more historic Heritage brands; 17 London "trophy" hotels in the Savoy Hotel group, in which Granada owned a 68 percent stake; and 103 Meridien and Exclusive luxury hotels, mainly located overseas.

Also added through the Forte purchase were a chain of 400 Little Chef roadside family restaurants and 21 Welcome Break motorway service areas in the United Kingdom, which were sold for antitrust reasons in February 1997 for £473 million to Investcorp, a Bahrain-based investment group. In December 1997 Granada sold the French motorway service areas, also included in Forte, for FRF 820 million (£83 million) to Autogrill, an Italian roadside restaurant chain. In April 1998 Blackstone Hotel Acquisition Co., a U.S. investment company, agreed to buy the Savoy Group for £520 million ($866.5 million).

The Exclusive hotels were also divested, leaving Granada with four core lodging brands: Travelodge, Posthouse, Heritage, and Meridien. With such a strong presence in what was called the hospitality sector (instead of leisure), Granada in mid-1997 considered de-merging its media operations, but decided not to for the time being. Such a move likely would have led also to the divestment of the rental operation. In any case, Robinson and Allen had changed Granada into a company that in fiscal 1997 generated only 17 percent of its revenues and 21 percent of its profits from media, while hospitality operations generated 69 percent of revenues and 64 percent of profits (with rental responsible for nearly all of the remaining 14 percent of revenues and 15 percent of profits). Having progressed through its history from film to television to rental, Granada Group had now clearly staked its future to hospitality.

Major change was on the horizon as Granada however, as it entered the new millennium. During 2000, the company joined with Compass Group in a merger that proved short-lived. The complex deal allowed Granada to forgo a hefty £1.5 billion tax bill and ultimately ended in a demerger the following year. A December 2000 *Guardian* article summed up the process claiming, "The transaction goes like this: two companies merge, spin off Granada Media to leave a focused hospitality group and then sell off all Granada's hotels."

When the dust settled and the demerger took effect in 2001, Granada plc was left as a pure play media/

broadcast company while Compass Group plc continued on with the hospitality portion of the business and eventually became the largest contract foodservices provider in the world with operations in more than 50 countries. By then, the Forte hotels were sold as well as the Le Meridien chain.

HISTORY OF CARLTON COMMUNICATIONS

Michael Green, the man who brought Carlton Communications from obscurity into the league of $1 billion companies, grew up in a business-oriented family. Rather than relying on higher education as he left public school at age 17, Green benefited from contacts through the family of his wife, Janet Wolfson, whom he married in 1972. Those contacts included Janet's brother David, with whom Green established a printing and photo-processing company dubbed Tangent Industries, and Lord Wolfson, Green's father-in-law, who owned Great Universal Stores, which hired Tangent to reproduce its catalogs.

After 15 years with Tangent, Green bought Transvideo, which was renamed Carlton Television Studios, in 1982. Fleet Street Letter soon became part of the fold, and the group of companies went public as Carlton Communications. The Moving Picture Company (MPC), Europe's largest video facilities provider, joined Carlton in a joint venture soon thereafter, acquiring the U.K. subsidiary of California's International Video Corporation for £400,000. Carlton acquired MPC itself in July 1983 for £13 million. MPC's Mike Luckwell remained as managing director in the new company and became Carlton's largest single shareholder.

Carlton acquired more than a dozen companies at a cost of over £600 million in the remainder of the decade, all related to either television and film or electronics. Importantly, Green valued cash flow and strict financial controls. When companies were acquired, existing managers were trained to practice strict accounting practices. The result was profits and success. By 1985, Carlton was producing projects as diverse as commercials, rock music videos, and corporate videos. The £30 million purchase of Abekas Video Systems in 1985 made Carlton a manufacturer of video editing gadgets (the division was sold ten years later to Scitex Corporation for $52 million). Carlton grossed £38.1 million in 1985.

The goal of acquiring a broadcasting station took several years to realize and divided the partnership of Green and Luckwell. The two had differing strategies for acquiring Thames after Britain's Independent Broadcasting Authority (IBA) thwarted Carlton's attempts to gain a controlling interest (Luckwell preferred to defy the IBA), and Luckwell left the company in 1986, selling his shares for £25 million. The IBA interfered with Green's bid for his next target, London Weekend Television, allowing him only a 10 percent share. In response, Green sold his existing 5 percent share for £1 million.

After failing in a group bid for a direct satellite broadcasting service, Green finally succeeded in acquiring a stake in a broadcast network, gaining 20 percent of Central Television in exchange for £18 million and stock. D.C. Thomson and Pergamon Holdings owned equal 20 percent shares. Green had previously hired Bob Phillis away from Central Television to replace Luckwell as Carlton's managing director; Phillis was able to return to his seat on the Central Television board of directors after the deal. Soon afterward, Carlton moved into film production with the £7.3 million acquisition of Zenith Productions; Carlton later had to sell much of Zenith so the company could stay independent.

Sometimes Carlton seemed a bit ahead of its time, as in the 1986 purchase of satellite dish manufacturer Skyscan, which was sold in 1988 due to poor sales. Carlton's biggest buy of the decade proved more fortuitous. The company paid $780 million for Ronald Perelman's U.S.-based Technicolor, the world market leader in videocassette duplication and motion picture film processing. Despite the 1987 stock market crash, Green was able to raise the necessary funds. In five brisk years, Green transformed Carlton from a relatively obscure company into an international corporation that garnered half its revenues (since the Technicolor purchase) from U.S. operations.

INTO THE LIVING ROOM 1991–96

In 1989, Carlton's stock took a serious fall, from a high of £9.60 a share to a low of £2.98 in the course of a year. Pretax profits grew just 13 percent in 1990, a lackluster performance for Carlton, and the market shuddered. Carlton won a 1991 bid for a London weekday broadcasting license, in spite of competition from Thames and a David Frost/Richard Branson coalition (CPV-TV), which outbid Carlton by £2 million but were denied the license as the Independent Television Commission (ITC) was unconvinced about the quality of their programming (Branson's Virgin Group later did outbid Carlton for MGM's British cinemas). The deal signaled a recovery for Carlton.

Besides the annual license fee, Carlton agreed to pay 15 percent of advertising revenue (estimated to be approximately £50 million per year) to the British government for the ten-year duration of the contract. The *Daily Telegraph* and Italian publishers Rizzoli Corri-

ere della Sera each bought 5 percent of Carlton's stock prior to the bid, worth £43.2 million. The Daybreak consortium, in which Carlton held a 20 percent share, lost the bid for the breakfast television license to the Sunrise consortium of LWT, Scottish Television, the *Guardian*'s newspaper company, and Walt Disney. Carlton, optimistic about the future of morning television, promptly bought a 20 percent share in Sunrise for £5.4 million.

At the end of 1993, Carlton announced it would buy Central Independent Television for £624 million ($925 million), thereby combining the first and third largest independent television companies in Britain. The timing could have helped both of them escape being consumed by European companies when ownership restrictions were relaxed in 1994. In 1995, Carlton was Britain's largest broadcaster, controlling 30 percent of ITV (channel three, the United Kingdom's first commercial channel) advertising revenues through its London and Midlands stations. The *Economist* reported Carlton's biggest challenge would be expanding into foreign broadcasting markets, in which Green expressed interest, as well as into newspapers and other types of media.

Although Carlton aborted a venture with the German station Vox, it invested in two other overseas ventures in 1995. France Tele Films, a cable channel launched in cooperation with France Television, would rely on programming from Carlton's CTE library (stocked with 4,000 hours as of 1995, including 200 films) as well as that of France Television. Carlton also entered a partnership with Singapore's Channel KTV, also cable-based, which prepared to add two karaoke channels to its existing services.

Almost half of Carlton's profits came from broadcast television in 1995. In spite of the growth of satellite and cable services, Carlton remained optimistic about the importance of free-to-air broadcasting. Nigel Walmsley, Carlton's director for Broadcasting, told shareholders in a 1995 annual report that only terrestrial broadcasting reached mass audiences since cable and satellite channels "tend to take audience share from existing minority channels, thus fragmenting the total cable and satellite audience."

A 1 percent increase in turnover (to £169.1 million) boosted operating profits for the Video and Sound Products division by 43 percent in 1995 to £32.5 million. Its primary components, Quantel and Solid State Logic, produced equipment for making special effects. Both companies were market leaders based on such state-of-the-art technologies as Quantel's digital visual effects editing systems (Henry for television and Domino for film) and Solid State Logic's Axiom and

9000-J Series digital audio consoles. Quantel supplied the printing industry with its Graphics Paintbox system.

Notably, the acquisition of Cinema Media extended Carlton's advertising sales capability from television onto the big screen. Cinema Media, renamed Carlton Screen Advertising, quickly became a market leader distributing promotional materials to cinemas throughout the United Kingdom. Carlton's acquisition of Westcountry Television expanded their coverage to 39 percent of the U.K. population. The acquisition of Action Time brought one of Europe's most successful producers of entertainment programs into the Carlton fold.

FOCUS ON INTERACTIVE AND DIGITAL MEDIA

In 1997, Carlton formed a partnership, British Digital Broadcasting (BDB), with longtime competitor Granada. BDB was awarded three principal digital terrestrial television licenses. These licenses allowed BDB one half of the digital terrestrial capacity in the United Kingdom, and in November 1998, the partnership launched ONdigital, the world's first multichannel service through an aerial. ONdigital, which was eventually renamed ITV Digital, moved Carlton into the lucrative pay-television market.

In 1998, Carlton launched ITV2, to complement ITV1, their mainstay terrestrial channel. ITV2 allowed their viewers to see rebroadcasts of the ITV1 program and also broadcast a range of original programs. Carlton also invested in television program and film libraries. By the end of 1999, Carlton was the world's largest distributor of classic British films television programs, offering 18,000 hours of television programs and 2,000 films to over 100 countries.

Technicolor benefited in the 1990s as Hollywood studios issued large-scale releases (for example, *Batman Forever* opened simultaneously on 4,500 screens), which required many duplicates. Declining currency values brought Film and Television Services turnover down to £251.8 million in 1995, although operating profit increased 9 percent to £41.6 million. Beside Technicolor, the division boasted some of the largest postproduction facilities in the world, such as The Moving Picture Company in London and Complete Post in Los Angeles. In 1995 when sales for the Video Production and Duplication division (including Technicolor and Carlton Home Entertainment) were £474.2 million (profits down 9 percent to £60.7 million), a new one-million-unit-per-day videocassette facility was under construction in Michigan. Beginning in 1996, digital video discs offered Technicolor a new format to master.

The company also produced CDs and CD-ROMs through Technicolor Optical Media Services. In 1999, Technicolor continued its expansion internationally and started the development of digital cinema. Carlton sold Technicolor to Thomson Multimedia in 2001.

CREATING ITV

Granada plc, fresh off its demerger with Compass and looking to expand its media holdings, tapped Carlton as a partner in 2002. By that time, Granada owned six regional broadcasting licenses while Carlton owned five. The boards of both companies gave the nod in October of that year and the complex process of uniting the two companies began. Over the next year, the deal was subject to scrutiny by both investors and Britain's Competition Commission. At the same time, Granada was feeling the effects of a downturn in advertising, which was wreaking havoc on profits and revenues. ITV Digital (the venture created in 1998 by Granada and Carlton) was shuttered in 2002 after its poor performance.

The £5.2 billion merger gained approval and in February 2004 Granada and Carlton joined to form ITV plc. The years immediately following the union however, proved challenging. In order to protect advertisers after the Granada and Carlton merger, the Competition Commission had issued the Contracts Rights Renewal (CRR) set of rules that limited the rates that ITV could charge its advertisers. As United Kingdom's largest advertising-funded broadcaster, the company relied heavily on such proceeds. With ad revenues continuing to fall, ITV management believed the regulations set forth by the CRR were too harsh. The CRR was slated for review in late 2009.

In the meantime, the company worked to revamp its operations while the global economy faltered. The company sold off unprofitable ventures and those not related to its core broadcasting business. Granada Learning was sold in 2006 as well as its stake in Seven Network and TV3. In March 2008, it sold the majority of Carlton Screen Advertising. In order to expand its business, it launched ITV3 in November 2004 and then ITV4 the following year. A 25 percent stake in GMTV was acquired in 2004, and U.K. digital terrestrial television operator SDN was purchased in 2005. The company also added several independent producers to its fold including Mammoth in 2007 and Silverback in 2008.

Despite the company's efforts, advertising revenue was dwindling and its network was losing viewership. By 2006, the company had become a takeover target. BSkyB secured a position as ITV's largest shareholder when purchased a 17.9 percent stake in the company for £135 per share later that year. BSkyB's purchase put takeover speculation to rest. At the same time, Michael Grade, the former BBC chairman, was tapped to head ITV in 2006. The company's board hoped his charismatic personality and expertise in the industry would pump new life into ITV.

Grade immediately set out to improve programming on ITV channels in order to win back audience members. Shows including *Britain's Got Talent, X Factor,* and *Dancing on Ice* improved audience numbers, but intense competition and the continuous fall in advertising revenue placed ITV in a perilous position. Losses in 2008 reached £2.7 billion, forcing Grade to implement a cost cutting program that included cutting its production budget and the loss of over 1,000 jobs.

ITV scored a small victory in June 2009 when over 19.2 million viewers—nearly three-quarters of the entire U.K. television audience—tuned into to ITV1 for the finale of *Britain's Got Talent.* The show featured Susan Boyle, a 48-year-old singer who gained instant worldwide recognition after her first appearance on the show in April 2009 thanks to replays on such Internet sites as YouTube.com.

At the same time, Grade announced he would step down from his executive chairman position in 2010 amid speculation that his strategy to focus on content did little to pull the company out of its downward spiral. As the company looked for his replacement, ITV would no doubt continue to face challenges on the road ahead.

Sandy Schusteff, Frederick C. Ingram
Updated, David E. Salamie; C. J. Gussoff;
Christina M. Stansell

PRINCIPAL DIVISIONS

Broadcasting; Global Content; Online.

PRINCIPAL COMPETITORS

British Broadcasting Corporation; Channel Four Television Corporation; RDF Media Group plc.

FURTHER READING

Blackhurst, Chris, "It's Going to Take More than Buckets of Charisma to Make the Grade at ITV," *Evening Standard* (London), March 5, 2009.

Burton, Patrick, "C5 and the Threat of London TV Monopoly," *Marketing,* January 14, 1993, p. 15.

Carter, Meg, "ITV Takes Seats for the Big Fight," *Marketing Week,* July 9, 1993, pp. 20–21.

Cassell, Michael, "Serving Up a Recipe for Revival," *Financial Times,* July 27, 1996, p. 6.

Clarke, Steve, "Merger Hold-off Taunts U.K. Biz," *Variety,* October 1, 2001, p. 62.

"Compass Loses Direction in Granada Deal," *Guardian* (London), December 14, 2000.

Cunliffe, Peter, "Grade Focuses on ITV Revival Plan," *Daily Express* (London), December 29, 2006.

Daneshkhu, Scheherazade, and Raymond Snoddy, "Granada Finds That Good News Isn't Enough," *Financial Times,* June 14, 1997.

Davidson, Andrew, "The Davidson Interview: Gerry Robinson," *Management Today,* June 1995, pp. 48–50, 55.

———, "The ITV Chairman's Got Talent," *Sunday Times* (London), June 7, 2009.

Dawtrey, Adam, "Regulators Prodded by U.K. Mega-Merger," *Variety,* November 29, 1999.

DuBois, Peter C., "Worth the Trip," *Barron's,* February 20, 1995.

Fisher, Liz, "Set on Broadcasting Its Ambitions," *Accountancy,* January 1992, pp. 17–19.

"Fortissimo?" *Economist,* November 25, 1995, pp. 59+.

Foster, Anna, "Behind the Carlton Screen," *Management Today,* April 1989, pp. 52–56.

Gapper, John, "Vision of the Future Is Down to Earth," *Financial Times,* November 25, 1997, p. 35.

"Greenland," *Economist,* December 4, 1993, pp. 68–69.

Guyon, Janet, "UK Broadcaster Carlton Makes Bid for Rest of Central," *Wall Street Journal,* November 30, 1993, p. 12.

Hewlett, Steve, "What Does the Michael Grade Move Mean," *Guardian* (London), December 4, 2006.

Higham, Nick, "Green Shoots of Discovery?" *Marketing Week,* April 29, 1994, p. 19.

Jackson, Tony, "Stand and Deliver," *Financial Times,* August 21, 1997, p. 12.

Larsen, Kay, "Granada Walks Tenuous Line on Merger Issue," *Wall Street Journal Europe,* January 12, 2004.

Lorenz, Andrew, "Worth More Together … or Apart?" *Management Today,* November 1997, p. 56.

Marcom, John, Jr., "Is This One for Real?" *Forbes,* July 24, 1994, p. 252.

Mistry, Tina, "Shock as Unilever Dumps Carlton TV," *Campaign-London,* January 7, 1994, p. 1.

"NTL Pullout Averts ITV Battle," *Guardian Unlimited,* December 6, 2006.

Plender, John, "A Risk of Indigestion," *Financial Times,* December 7, 1995, p. 25.

"Profile: Cresswell's Mission Impossible?" *Media Week,* March 10, 2009.

Robinson, Jeffrey, "The Modest Media Magnate," *Business-London,* October 1990, pp. 100–04.

Snoddy, Raymond, "Bernsteins Take Final Bow from Granada," *Financial Times,* October 4, 1995, p. 21.

Sorkin, Andrew Ross, "British Media Merger," *New York Times,* November 27, 1999, p. B3(N).

"The Wearing of the Green," *Economist,* July 8, 1995, p. 68.

Wilkinson, Amanda, "ITV Roadshow to Woo Top Clients," *Marketing Week,* January 24, 2002, p. 13.

Johanna Foods, Inc.

20 Johanna Farms Road
Flemington, New Jersey 08822
U.S.A.
Telephone: (908) 788-2200
Fax: (908) 782-8192
Web site: http://www.johannafoods.com

Private Company
Incorporated: 1944 as Johanna Farms
Employees: 540
Sales: $112.2 million (2007 est.)
NAICS: 311421 Fruit and Vegetable Canning; 311510
   Dairy Product (Except Frozen) Manufacturing

■ ■ ■

Johanna Foods, Inc., is a Flemington, New Jersey-based manufacturer of chilled juices and beverages, aseptic beverages, and yogurt, sold under its own stable of brands as well as private labels. Chilled juices are sold under the Tree Ripe brand in 59-ounce, 32-ounce, 16-ounce, and 6-ounce containers and include several varieties of orange juice, organic apple juice, and organic grape juice. Refrigerated drinks, available in 64-ounce and 6-ounce sizes, are sold under the Ssips label and include iced teas, orangeade, lemonade, and fruit punch. Tropical drinks and nectars such as guava mango and piña colada are offered under the Ssips Sabor Latino banner. A wide variety of refrigerated 6-ounce drink boxes are also available under the Ssips and the Ssips Sabor Latino labels. In addition, Johanna offers the La Yogurt brand of 6-ounce and 32-ounce plain and flavored yogurts, and La Yogurt Sabor Latino items in flavors targeting Hispanic customers. The company also uses its excess production capacity to produce drinks and yogurt on a contract and private-label basis. Products are distributed primarily on the East Coast. Johanna is privately held and majority owned by its president and chief executive officer Robert A. Facchina.

DAIRY FARM ORIGINS: 1927

Johanna Foods started out as a poultry and dairy farm located near Pennington, New Jersey, established by Max and Julius Piser in 1927 (some sources claim 1912). They called the enterprise Johanna Farms, named for their niece Johanna Neustadt. In 1944 they sold a half-interest in the farm to the Eugene Goldman and Leo Honig families. Goldman and his wife Marie had been farmers in Austria but because they were Jews fled their homeland after it was overrun by Nazi Germany in 1938, and they found their way to the United States. Also refugees, the Honigs provided financial backing for the Goldmans to return to farming in their adopted country. Eugene Goldman ran the farm with Marie tending the books.

Johanna Farms bottled and sold its own milk, and in 1953 the company elected to sell its herd in order to focus on bottling and distributing milk, which was provided by other farms in New Jersey and Pennsylvania. Two years later the Goldman and Honig families bought out their partners and gained full control of the business, which took the name Johanna Dairies. In 1958 Eugene Goldman passed away, and his son, Kurt Goldman, took over as general manager, eventually named president in 1976. Marie Goldman, in the meantime, served as company treasurer, a post she held in her 80s.

JOHANNA AND OTHERS FINED FOR BID RIGGING: 1980

Focusing on milk sales, Johanna Farms grew into one of the largest dairy operations in the Northeast and ranked the second largest in New Jersey by the mid-1970s. Milk was a highly competitive and low-margin business, however, especially after supermarket sales drove the home-delivery segment out of business. Making matters worse was a steady decline in the consumption of milk, which by the mid-1980s fell to 20 gallons per person annually. Consumption of soft drinks, on the other hand, increased to 42 gallons, about double the amount of the 1960s.

A major source of milk sales came from schools and other public institutions and in the 1970s several of New Jersey's largest dairies consolidated to carve out territories for one another in which they would become the sole supplier, further agreeing not to underbid one another outside their designated territories. It was not an arrangement the state would countenance, and in 1980 Johanna Farms and eight other New Jersey dairies were fined $2.5 million for bid rigging from the period 1974 to 1978.

To help remain profitable, Johanna began offering yogurt and juice products and using its production capacity to serve as a private-label packager for wholesale distributors and supermarket chains. Johanna Farms fared better than most dairies, which, when faced with lower demand and escalating operating costs, lacked the financial wherewithal to modernize their plants and eke out what margin there was in the business.

Thus, the smaller dairies fell by the wayside, snapped up by the larger dairies, like Johanna Farms. In 1984, for example, Abbotts Dairy Products, a century-old Philadelphia milk-bottling company, filed for Chapter 11 bankruptcy protection. Abbotts controlled 20 percent of the Philadelphia milk market, compared to Johanna's 40 percent. Johanna was able to cherry-

pick Abbotts' assets and gain a dominant market share, paying $2.16 million for the Abbotts logo, plus the company's customer list, refrigeration equipment, vending machines, and milk cases. It was also allowed to collect notes receivables that Abbotts held.

LABATT ACQUIRES COMPANY: 1985

Johanna became an acquisition target itself in 1985 when the family owners elected to sell the business to John Labatt Ltd., a Canadian brewery and food conglomerate. Concerned about limited growth possibilities, Labatt had initially expanded into the United States in 1968, acquiring frozen-pizza maker Chef San Francisco, but it was not until the 1980s that Labatt made a concerted push for other acquisitions, picking up a wide variety of assets, including pasta and pizza ingredient manufacturers, and Pennsylvania's Latrobe Brewing, maker of Rolling Rock beer. The addition of Johanna provided Labatt with a foundation in the United States to expand its dairy and juice operations. The deal also brought about $300 million in annual sales.

With Labatt's deep pockets Johanna grew even larger. In March 1986 it acquired its main competitor, Atlantic Processing, Inc., adding three milk plants in Pennsylvania and two in Maryland. Johanna then acquired Union, New Jersey-based Tuscan Dairy in January 1988, thus providing entry into the New York City market. For years the city's milk business had been regulated, a situation that came to an end in January 1987. Thus, Johanna's timing was poor, as New York milk prices began to fall, making the Tuscan deal increasingly less advantageous.

Labatt's dairy operation was a $2 billion business by the early 1990s (Johanna accounted for $900 million of that total), providing 55 percent of Labatt's total revenues, it proved to be a drag on the more profitable side of the business, namely beer and entertainment. The company looked to cut costs across its dairy operations. In 1992 Johanna closed its Flemington, New Jersey, milk plant, but that move did little to alleviate the problem. In September 1992 Labatt announced its intention to divest the dairy operations. Labatt tried to spin off Johanna and the Canadian milk operation as a single unit, but that plan was abandoned in 1993 due to Johanna's poor performance. Labatt hoped to sell Johanna alone but found no buyers.

ROBERT FACCHINA BUYS THE COMPANY: 1995

Finally in 1995 Johanna's president, Robert A. Facchina, bought Johanna Dairies. Not included in the deal was

KEY DATES

1927: The Piser family names its dairy farm after Johanna Neustadt.
1944: The Goldman and Honig families acquire half interest in Johanna Farms.
1953: Johanna Farms sells its dairy herd.
1955: The Goldman and Honig families acquire the remaining interest in the company.
1985: John Labatt Ltd. acquires Johanna Farms.
1995: Robert Facchina buys the business and renames it Johanna Foods.
2000: A state-of-the-art filling operation is completed.
2004: Pasco Beverage assets are acquired.

Lehigh Valley Dairies, part of the 1986 Atlantic Processing deal. Facchina had grown up in Washington, D.C., his family involved in the construction business. His goal was to become an architect, but after his application to the University of Maryland school of architecture was rejected, he worked in construction for two years before enrolling at Maryland to study food science, graduating in 1977. He then went to work as a plant manager trainee for Embassy Dairy, owned by 7-Eleven convenience store parent Southland Corporation.

Facchina joined Labatt in 1986 and would hold positions at all of the U.S. dairy operations, most of the time dealing with a malignant skin cancer, which was diagnosed in 1987. Through immunotherapy and other treatments and a dietary regimen, Facchina overcame his cancer and continued to be promoted through the Labatt dairy operation, eventually becoming Johanna's president.

As owner and chief executive, Facchina renamed Johanna Dairies as Johanna Foods, Inc., an indication that he planned to exit the low-margin milk business and focus on the juice and yogurt products sold under the Ssips and La Yogurt labels that had been added in the previous 15 years. In the final years of the decade, the company spent $30 million in plant improvements. It also invested in product development to stay current with changing consumer tastes and demands.

In 1999, after more than a year of effort, Johanna introduced La Yogurt low-fat yogurts fortified with calcium as well as vitamins A, C, D, and E. While the private company did not have to disclose its financial results, Facchina revealed to a reporter in 1999 that Johanna at this stage produced 80 million gallons of yogurt, 50 million gallons of juice, and 300 million boxes of box juices and drinks each year.

EXPANDING CAPACITY AND FUELING GROWTH

The 21st century brought further plant advancements and product introductions. Work was completed in 2000 on the Flemington facility's high-volume filling operation, making it the country's first processing and packaging plant dedicated to extended-shelf life, high-acid, and chilled beverages. This extra capacity allowed the company to extend its distribution to institutional channels and recreational outlets. Later in the year Johanna began work on an additional expansion of the Flemington site, resulting in another 160,000 square feet of space, including a new beverage processing plant and a dry storage facility for yogurt cups, boxes, and shrink-wrap.

The first year of the decade also brought a new serving size for juice packs. Johanna introduced a 16-ounce gabletop juice pack for the Tree Ripe label. Because of the larger size, the company marketed the new six-flavor line more to teens and adults than to young children, the primary consumer of the traditional 6-ounce juice boxes. Also in 2000 Johanna became the exclusive licensee of the aseptic juice products of the Chiquita brand in the United States and Canada.

New space and equipment allowed Johanna to revamp its yogurt line in 2002. Not only were the flavors reformulated, but the company also upgraded its packaging equipment so that the La Yogurt products, 40 stock-keeping units in all, were presented in colorful shrink-wrap packaging that helped consumers to quickly and easily identify their favorite flavors and varieties.

ODOR CAUSES PUBLIC RELATIONS PROBLEM: 2002

While Johanna generally maintained good relationships in the Flemington community, the company had to deal with a public relations problem in June 2002 when about 10,000 gallons of orange-mango juice were inadvertently spilled into its outdoor wastewater treatment lagoon, upsetting the delicate balance of the microbes in the ecosystem used to break down wastes. A foul odor resulted that lingered for weeks, angering the plant's neighbors. Because it did not address the problem in a timely fashion, Johanna was fined by the Department of Environmental Protection. To address the problem, the company had to invest $1 million to upgrade the treatment facility.

Johanna grew through acquisition in 2004. At the start of the year it closed on the purchase of Dade City, Florida-based Pasco Beverage Company, LLC., a private-label juice and juice beverage supplier. Johanna picked up Pasco's private-label chilled juice business, including orange juice, other fruit juices, and juice blends. In 2007 the company also acquired the refrigerated orange juice and chilled beverage business of Spokane, Washington-based Olympic Foods Inc.

Johanna pursued further internal growth in the new century. Because of the fast-growing Hispanic market, the company continued to expand its beverage and yogurt offerings aimed at this population under the Sabor Latino banner. In 2006, for example, Johanna introduced a pair of new yogurt flavors: Dulce de Leche and Horchata. Another area of opportunity was organic juices, which had grown increasingly popular with health-conscious consumer. Organic versions of orange, apple, and grape juice were introduced under the Tree Ripe label, and in 2007 the company added a Light Probiotic Pomegranate Berry Medley yogurt flavor.

Ed Dinger

PRINCIPAL COMPETITORS

Apple & Eve L.L.C.; Country Pure Foods Inc.; Stonyfield Farm, Inc.

FURTHER READING

"Former Johanna Managers Return to Posts," *Hunterdon County Democrat* (Flemington, N.J.), July 1, 1993.

Hicks, Jonathan P., "A Test for Labatt's U.S. Expansion," *New York Times,* August 3, 1988.

"Johanna Sets $1M Project to Fix Waste Lagoon," *Hunterdon County Democrat,* August 8, 2002.

Lin, Jennifer, "Court Will Allow Johanna to Buy Assets of Abbotts," *Philadelphia Inquirer,* September 13, 1984, p. C1.

——, "Johanna Farms Is Fast Consuming Its Milk Competition," *Philadelphia Inquirer,* April 14, 1986, p. D1.

——, "Two Leading Local Dairies Are Merging," *Philadelphia Inquirer,* March 1, 1986, p. A1.

"Marie Goldman Dies at 87," *Hunterdon County Democrat,* August 1, 1991.

"9 Jersey Dairies Fined Total of $2.5 Million for Rigging Milk Bids," *New York Times,* February 22, 1980.

"Renewal at Work and Life—Robert A. Facchina Has Revitalized Hunterdon County's Johanna Foods Inc.," *Easton (Pa.) Express-Times,* September 26, 1999, p. D1.

Wright, Terry, "CEO Buys Johanna from Conglomerate," *Hunterdon County Democrat,* April 6, 1995.

Jos. A. Bank Clothiers, Inc.

———————— ■ ————————

500 Hanover Pike
Hampstead, Maryland 21074
U.S.A.
Telephone: (410) 239-2700
Toll Free: (800) 285-2265
Fax: (410) 239-5700
Web site: http://www.josbank.com

Public Company
Incorporated: 1945
Employees: 4,040
Sales: $695.9 million (2008)
Stock Exchanges: NASDAQ
Ticker Symbol: JOSB
NAICS: 448110 Men's Clothing Stores

■ ■ ■

Jos. A. Bank Clothiers, Inc., is a designer and retailer of men's tailored and casual wear with over 460 stores, nationwide. The company also sells through quarterly catalogs and via the Internet. Bank sells only the company's own branded lines of clothing, which are priced 20 to 30 percent lower than goods of comparable quality offered by competitors.

BEGINNINGS

Jos. A. Bank traces its origins to the end of the 19th century, when Lithuanian immigrant Charles Bank opened a small tailor shop in Baltimore, Maryland. In 1898 his grandson Joseph A. Bank joined the firm,

which had evolved into a trouser manufacturing company. Joseph, who had started working at the age of 11 as a cloth cutter, became a salesman over the next decade, and in 1912 he married Anna Hartz, a saleswoman for a rival company. He then joined forces with his new mother-in-law to form L. Hartz and Bank, which manufactured and suits in the Baltimore area and sold them at wholesale.

The company continued in this form over the next several decades. In 1940 a building was purchased in Baltimore to house its offices, showroom, and cutting and shipping departments. In 1945 Joseph Bank and his son Howard bought out the Hartz family interest, renaming the company Joseph A. Bank Clothiers. At this time the Banks decided to focus on making clothing for businessmen, in an "understated, conservative" style, as there was a shortage of men's business and professional wear following World War II.

Bank's move into retailing took place when Howard Bank began selling the company's suits out of the factory, initially hanging them for display on a pipe rack, as legend has it. With interest in retail sales sparked, the company reached an agreement with a store named Louie's in Washington, D.C., to market the company's goods. Out-of-town customers had also begun writing to request cloth swatches and to order clothes, and in 1960 a catalog was introduced to allow sales over a wider geographical area. The company continued to manufacture men's clothing for the wholesale market as well.

Beginning in the late 1960s more retail outlets were opened, with the location of catalog customers often

COMPANY PERSPECTIVES

Jos. A. Bank is not just another menswear retailer. What makes us unique is also what has attracted customers to our stores for 104 years; a heritage of quality and workmanship, an extensive selection of beautifully made, classically styled tailored and casual clothing, and prices typically 20 to 30 percent below our competitors'. Add to that an expert staff of sales professionals who prize service and customer satisfaction above all, and you get the idea.

giving the company an idea about where to open a new store. Bank's line of clothing continued to feature men's suits that were well-manufactured and conservative in design. In 1977 the company branched out into women's professional clothing, introducing a line of skirts and suits.

VARIOUS OWNERS 1981–90

In 1981 the Bank family, enticed by an offer of some $20 million, sold Jos. A. Bank to the Quaker Oats Company. At this time the company had 11 stores and several manufacturing facilities. Leonard Ginsberg, who had been with the company for a number of years, was retained as president. Under Quaker, Bank embarked on a campaign of expansion, opening 20 more locations within the next five years. Annual sales reached a peak of $112 million by 1986.

By then, however, Quaker had decided to get out of retail and concentrate on its core strengths of food products and toys. The parent company sold Jos. A. Bank and two other chains it owned in December of that year. Bank was purchased for $105 million in a leveraged buyout (LBO) by a group that included McKinley Holdings, Eli S. Jacobs, and Bank management. Much of the financing came from Drexel Burnham Lambert.

Over the next several years Bank began to experience difficulties from both the debt generated by the LBO and soft sales in a weakening retail environment. In addition, the workplace was changing. The less-formal style of the baby boom generation, which was moving into management, and the growing numbers of workers in computer industry, with its casual ethos, led increasing numbers of companies to relax their dress codes.

In 1988 CEO Ginsberg retired and was succeeded by David Waters, a veteran of Brooks Brothers and other major retailers. The company was still performing poorly, and losses continued to mount. In May 1989 Bank was restructured, and the company's lenders were given new bond notes and stock shares in exchange for accepting a delayed payment plan. McKinley Holdings, Jacobs, and Bank company management all essentially wrote off their investments, with one insider telling Warfield's that the purchase price had been $20 million too high. Bank reported a loss of $48 million for the year.

COMPANY NEARS BANKRUPTCY 1990–91

In early 1990 the company's board proposed to the bondholders that they exchange their bonds for equity in Jos. A. Bank. The offer was rejected, and shortly afterward a number of senior managers left the company, including CEO Waters. Bank was on the verge of bankruptcy, and the board sought out a crisis management company, The Finley Group, for help. Timothy Finley, founder and president of that company, agreed to take the reins of Bank and try to get it back on its feet.

Finley, age 47, had been an accountant for Cannon Mills and Deloitte, Haskins & Sells before founding his crisis management firm in 1985. One of his team of eight associates would take charge of failing companies, and, in a period typically ranging from 6 to 18 months, either nurse them back to health or liquidate their assets. Finley was known for his quick decision making, which he sometimes characterized with the motto, "Ready, Fire, Aim."

After examining Bank's situation, he came to the conclusion that its problems were not merely caused by the debt load of some $70 million, but by a loss of overall purpose and some bad marketing decisions. Although the company had always stood for quality at a fair price, it had been upgrading its stores into elegant, plush showrooms that gave customers the impression that the clothing cost more than it actually did. There were also production problems within Bank's factories, as well as other issues.

Once in charge, Finley quickly let 250 employees go and also tried once more to renegotiate with the company's lenders. In 1991 an agreement was reached in which they took an equity stake in Bank in exchange for their bonds. As part of this arrangement, Finley agreed to stay on for three years, something he had never done before. To address the company's image and marketing problems, he hired Henry "Chick" Schwartz to serve as president and oversee merchandising. Schwartz, who had many years of clothing industry

KEY DATES

1905: Joseph A. Bank's grandfather Charles Bank formally establishes his clothing business.

1912: Joseph A. Bank forms L. Hartz and Bank Co. with his mother-in-law.

1945: Joseph and Howard Bank buy out Hartz's interest; the company is renamed Joseph A. Bank.

1950s: Company enters retailing, first at its Baltimore factory, and then with a Washington, D.C., store.

1960: Joseph A. Bank begins catalog sales.

1977: A line of women's clothing is introduced.

1981: The Bank family sells the company to the Quaker Oats Co.

1986: Quaker Oats refocuses on core businesses, and McKinley Investments and others exercise a leveraged buyout of Joseph A. Bank.

1990: Nearly bankrupt, Bank hires Timothy Finley as a crisis manager/CEO.

1994: The company goes public.

1995: The women's clothing line is dropped in favor of an increased line of men's casual wear.

1998: The company introduces its first web site.

1999: A new management team, headed by Robert Wildrick as president and CEO, takes over.

2001: A new store prototype is introduced.

2004: The company begins to sell clothes at QVC.com and opens a storefront at Amazon.com.

2008: The company posts record revenues of $696.9 million for the year.

experience, set about lowering prices and adding more contemporary flair to the suits. The company also began to run national advertisements to build brand awareness outside of its Baltimore stronghold. Plans were soon being made to open additional stores in Florida, and move or upgrade others in Philadelphia, St. Louis, and Louisville, Kentucky.

In the summer of 1991 Bank moved its corporate headquarters from Owings Mills, Maryland, to its distribution warehouse in Hampstead, and instituted a new computer system for its stores that enabled improved gathering of data on customer preferences. In the fall the company introduced its own credit card, with General Electric Credit handling the operation of this service. The stores, which had featured other brand names along with Bank-made products, began to drop all but the company's own lines from their shelves.

INITIAL PUBLIC OFFERING FOLLOWS RETURN TO PROFITABILITY 1992–94

In 1992 Bank opened a prototype store in Oak Brook, Illinois, which featured a modified "Shaker" look, as opposed to the fancier, upscale style that had been introduced in the late 1980s. The chain soon had the new design in five other stores of the 43 it owned, with more to follow. The cost of the simplified interior was half that of the more luxurious style it was replacing. For 1992 Bank reported sales of nearly $150 million and profits of close to $3 million, its first time in the black since 1989. In 1993 the company began to expand more aggressively, opening 11 more stores over the year in widespread locations including Kansas, Connecticut, and Texas.

With its financial situation stabilized and a renewed emphasis on growth, the company's management went to Wall Street to secure more capital for expansion. In May 1994 an initial public offering of two million shares of stock was made on the NASDAQ, with an additional million shares sold by the lenders who had become part owners in 1991. The response from investors was mixed, with prices lower than expected, and the value of the stock declined over the following months.

The company kept refining its approach. Plans were made to open a small number of catalog stores in towns where full showrooms were not warranted, but which had shown a good response from customers ordering by mail. These 1,100-square-foot outlets displayed the company's wares but did not stock merchandise for sale. Customers could try on the styles and have their purchases shipped to them via overnight delivery. Catalog stores were opened in locations such as Portland, Maine; Bedford, New Hampshire; and Montgomery, Alabama. Bank was also considering introducing specialty catalogs that featured only certain types of clothing, such as ties or sportswear. The company was accelerating its development of the latter category for its stores to meet the demand brought on by "casual Fridays" in the business world. Availability of big and tall sizes was also being expanded.

In September 1994 Bank opened its first store in New York City, on the corner of 46th Street and Madison Avenue, just blocks from the flagship stores of many of its major competitors. The 9,000-square-foot showroom was expected to do as much as $8 million in business the first year. Radio advertisements for the new location featured the tag line, "There's no status in overpaying." The company's expansion plans had begun slowing down, however, and Bank announced that it would be opening fewer stores than previously expected so it could concentrate more on its catalog, which accounted for about 15 percent of sales. The catalog, which had been a useful source of information on where to open new stores, was also serving as a trend-spotter. Items such as vests, which showed sudden surges of catalog orders, were highlighted in stores with good results.

SPORTSWEAR SALES SPUR GROWTH 1995–99

In early 1995 Chick Schwartz stepped down as president, and Finley added that job to his other duties. Several months later, in May, the company announced that it was dropping women's clothes from its lineup by year's end. Men's casual wear was expected to fill the space in stores, in a new department to be named Joe's Casuals. Bank's casual clothing would continue to be purchased from outside suppliers, as its women's line had been, rather than manufactured in its Baltimore and Hampstead, Maryland, plants.

In late 1995 Bank officials announced the closing of the Hampstead sewing factory and the loss of 100 jobs, as well as several store closings. The period since the stock offering had been a tough one, with national clothing sales declining and casual workplace trends increasing. The company reported losses for fiscal 1995 of $13.2 million, two-thirds of which were restructuring costs.

The year 1996 saw a turnaround in sales, with the expanded sportswear offerings doing particularly well, and the company managed a slim profit of $300,000. Bank had found a replacement for Schwartz in Frank Tworecke, formerly of Merry-Go-Round stores, who was named president in September. The company also reached an agreement with golf pro David Leadbetter to feature his casual wear line in Bank stores.

In 1997 the company resumed its expansion, opening ten stores within a 12-month period. New locations were often added in existing markets so the company could get better bang for its advertising dollar. In February 1998 Bank announced it was selling its sole remaining factory, becoming the last major U.S. men's business and formal wear maker to leave this end of the business. M.S. Pietrafesa LP, the buyer, announced it would continue to operate the plant to produce clothing for Bank as well as other customers. Numbers for fiscal 1997 delivered more good news, with $2.5 million in profits reported on $172 million in sales.

In 1998 the company introduced a web site where customers could order clothing, and additional stores were also opened. More than 100 were in business by year's end, located in 28 states and Washington, D.C. Ten were franchise outlets, while the rest were company-owned. Bank also established a Corporate Sales division, which sold monogrammed clothing and other products directly to businesses for use as gifts or as employee uniforms. In May 1999 Timothy Finley stepped down after nearly nine years as CEO. He was widely credited with saving Bank from the scrap heap. However, the company he left was experiencing declining sales.

EXPLOSIVE GROWTH 1999–2004

The board of directors set up a search committee, and in October 1999 convinced one of its members, Robert Wildrick, to join the company as president and CEO. As Wildrick took control, he and his management team looked seriously at whether to sell the company or to grow it. Once they decided to go with growth, they developed a strategic plan that focused on quality, customer service, and supply.

The company implemented several major changes in operations, including the return to the company's design and manufacturing base. Rather than continue to buy from various manufacturers and put its label in a suit, Bank established strict design and manufacturing specifications for the producers of its merchandise. It invested more in its catalog and Internet channels. It trained it sales associates on how to develop relationships with customers to keep them coming back, such as writing thank you notes.

Bank also began a serious program of opening new stores. Among these was the new prototype introduced in 2001 in Charlottesville, Virginia. That 5,000-square-foot model, which aimed to present a more casual corporate environment, was more open and lighter and featured creams and greens in place of Bank's standard of burgundy and hunter green, brass, and dark woods. That year, casual sales increased to 47 percent of sales, while suits accounted for just 27 percent of sales. Suits had represented 42 percent of sales only a few years before.

In January 2002 Bank had 136 stores in 29 states and the District of Columbia. Twenty-four months later, there were 200 Bank stores, including the first ones in California. Wildrick indicated that the company planned to operate 500 stores by 2007, and to continue to pay for the openings with money from profits, not by taking on debt. During this period, the men's clothing industry was declining an average of 2 to 3 percent per year. Several chains closed, others moved into women's clothing.

Bank, however, continued to grow, with quarter after quarter of record earnings per share. Stores were being added and the company's web site and catalog sales were doing well. Bank also began offering new products and introduced its trio concept, which included a suit jacket, a pair of matching pants, and a pair of coordinated pants. At the end of 2004 it launched a nationwide advertising campaign. This followed its partnership with QVC through which Bank sold its products on QVC's web site. The company also launched a storefront on Amazon.com. Also that year, Bank settled a suit with the New York State attorney general and agreed not to advertise items at discounted prices unless those "sale" items had been offered at higher prices for a "substantial" time. The company paid $475,000 in penalties and costs.

CONFRONTING A COLLAPSING ECONOMY

In January 2005 Bank opened its new 280,000-square-foot distribution center near its headquarters in Maryland, which gave the company the capacity to supply 580 stores. The new facility was designed to handle hanging merchandise, leaving the older facility to deal with flat items. Bank continued to introduce new products, including its Stays Cool suits and Traveler all-cotton, stain resistant pants and all-cotton, wrinkle-free sport shirts.

A significant portion of company sales came as men, particularly younger men, were again buying suits and sport coats to wear in the workplace. Bank offered "Three Levels of Luxury," based on, for example, the wool in a suit or sports coat. Whether a suit was from the original Executive collection, the high-end Signature, or the exclusive Signature Gold, Bank was able to achieve healthy gross margins, enabling it to discount a suit at 70 percent.

Meanwhile, the economy was weakening, with the real estate market collapsing and gas prices jumping. The economic situation may have contributed to a move by customers toward more professional attire. Whether it did or not, the company's suit sales surged, increasing 30 percent in 2008. Bank continued to open new stores and announced a new target of 600 stores by the end of 2012. In December 2008, Wildrick retired as CEO, taking over as chairman. R. Neal Black, Bank's president and chief merchandising officer, succeeded him as CEO and director. That year the company posted revenues of $696.9 million, an annual record in more than a century of operation.

UNIQUE PROMOTIONS IN CHALLENGING TIMES

As the national economy worsened, and unemployment climbed, Bank offered appropriate promotions. Under the "Risk Free Suit" program, if a customer bought a suit during a three-week period in the spring of 2009 and involuntarily lost his job at some point in the next few months, Bank would rebate the cost of the suit up to $199. The customer would get to keep the suit to help in his job hunt. This promotion was followed with a buy-one-get-two-free offer on suits. The company also increased its television advertising, appearing on cable financial and news networks as well as ESPN. It hinted, however, that it might not try to open as many stores as previously announced. Bank appeared to have found the secret to retail success, even in a recession. With experienced leadership able to manage quality control, value, and supply as well as keep the company's debt low, Bank was in an enviable situation.

Frank Uhle
Updated, Ellen D. Wernick

PRINCIPAL SUBSIDIARIES

Joseph A. Bank Mfg. Co., Inc.; RS Servicing Co., Inc.; IS Servicing Co., Inc.; TS Servicing Co., Inc.

PRINCIPAL COMPETITORS

Brooks Brothers; Macy's Inc.; The Men's Wearhouse, Inc.

FURTHER READING

Ariano, Alexis, "Jos. A. Bank Joins Ranks of Retailers Capitalizing on Online Shopping Growth," *Baltimore Daily Record,* February 1, 1999, p. 7A.

"Bank Tries to Get Casualwear Right," *Catalog Age,* January 2000, p. 6.

Bowie, Liz, "A Seamless Commitment," *Baltimore Sun,* March 30, 1997, p. 1F.

D'Innocenzio, Anne, "Finley's Bailout Plan: Re-Define Bank's Image," *Daily News Record,* March 28, 1991, p. 2.

Embrey, Alison, "Tailoring to Men," *Display & Design Ideas,* November 2003, pp. 36–38.

Fickes, Michael, "Life Lessons," *Chain Store Age,* March 2008, pp. 142–47.

Forseter, Murray, "As Recession Wears On, Value Is Back in Vogue," *Chain Store Age,* April 2009, p. 58.

Girard, Peter, "More Bank Books, More Bank Bucks," *Catalog Age,* March 15, 2000, p. 12.

Gogoi, Pallavi, "Men Dress for (Retail) Success," *Business Week Online,* January 20, 2006, p. 8.

Haeberle, Matthew, "Taking It to the Bank," *Chain Store Age,* January 2002, pp. 51–52.

Hall, Jessica, "Bank's Fashions a Turnaround," *Baltimore Daily Record,* March 22, 1994, p. 1.

————, "Jos. A. Bank Public Offering Falls Far Short of Projections," *Baltimore Daily Record*, May 4, 1994.

Hancock, Jay, "Jos. A. Bank Adopts a More 'Casual' Approach," *Baltimore Sun*, December 1, 1994, p. 9C.

————, "Jos. A. Bank Alters Line, Management," *Baltimore Sun*, March 16, 1995, p. 13D.

————, "Jos. A. Bank: On the Mend," *Baltimore Sun*, May 22, 1994, p. 1D.

Hinden, Stan, "Jos. A. Bank Clothiers Seeks a Suitable New Look," *Washington Post*, March 28, 1994, p. F29.

"Jos. A. Bank Clothiers, Inc. (JOSB)," *Wall Street Transcript*, March 14, 2005, pp. 42–44.

Krieger, Dale, "Hanging by a Thread," *Warfield's*, February 1, 1991, p. 38.

Mayer, Caroline E., "Bank Clothiers Is Fashioning Expansion Plans," *Washington Post*, April 11, 1988, p. F05.

Medina, Alison Embrey, "The Ageless Boomer," *Display & Design Ideas*, October 2008, pp. 26–29.

Mirabella, Lorraine, "Clothier Loses the Man Who Mended It," *Baltimore Sun*, May 22, 1999, p. 12C.

————, "Jos. A. Bank Bets on Corporate Casual," *Baltimore Sun*, September 21, 1999, p. 1C.

————, "Jos. A. Bank Sells a Plant, Ends an Era," *Baltimore Sun*, February 19, 1998, p. 1C.

Murray, Shanon D., "Clothier Sells 2 Operations in City," *Baltimore Sun*, April 22, 1998, p. 1D.

"No 'Sale' at the Bank: Retailer Will Change Ads," *Newswire*, September 20, 2004.

Owens, Jennifer, "You Can Take It to the Bank; Jos. A. Bank CEO Tim Finley Has Strong Growth Plans." *Daily News Record*, September 8, 1997, p. 7.

Palmieri, Jean E., "The First Bank of New York: Jos. A. Bank Opens Its First New York Retail Store Today," *Daily News Record*, September 1, 1994, p. 8.

————, "Men's Wearhouse, Jos. A. Bank Garner Attention from Wall Street," *WWD*, April 29, 2009, p. 8.

————, "Putting Jos. A. Bank Back in the Black," *Daily News Record*, December 27, 1993, p. 4.

Pepper, Tara, "Wish You Looked Cooler in a Suit?" *Newsweek*, October 31, 2005, p. E4.

Pressler, Margaret Webb, "Jos. Bank Suits Up to Win in Retailing Fray," *Washington Post*, April 26, 1996, p. F05.

"Robert Wildrick," *Chain Store Age*, December 2003, pp. 72–74.

"Robert Wildrick," *Chain Store Age*, December 2004, pp. 30–32.

Roland, Kara, "Billion in Sales Seen for Clothier," *Washington Times*, September 18, 2007, p. C11.

Singletary, Michelle, "Jos. Bank Pins Turnaround Hopes on Ad Campaign," *Baltimore Evening Sun*, March 18, 1991, p. B1.

Smalley, Suzanne, "An Aggressive New Cut," *Newsweek*, June 10, 2002, p. 37.

Speer, Jordan K., "Gearing Up for Growth: Jos. A. Bank," *Apparel Magazine*, January 2006, pp. 18–19.

————, "Jos. A. Bank Sets the Bar High," *Apparel Magazine*, May 2003, pp. 20–22.

Sundius, Ann, "Interview with the Chairman of Jos. A. Bank Clothiers from the Wall Street Forum Institutional Investor Conference" [transcript], *MSNBC Private Financial Network*, June 24, 1997.

Sway, RoxAnna, "Robert Wildrick, the Dean of Men's Apparel," *Display & Design Ideas*, November 2003, p. 34.

Talley, Karen, "Jos. A. Bank Takes Unusual Path as Retailer with Record Results," *Dow Jones Newswires*, April 8, 2009.

Wilson, Marianne, "Jos. A. Bank Sharpens Image," *Chain Store Age Executive with Shopping Center Age*, October 1, 1992, p. 86.

Joy Global Inc.

100 East Wisconsin Avenue
P.O. Box 554
Milwaukee, Wisconsin 53201-0554
U.S.A.
Telephone: (414) 319-8500
Fax: (414) 319-8520
Web site: http://www.joyglobal.com

Public Company
Incorporated: 1884 as Pawling & Harnischfeger
Employees: 11,800
Sales: $3.4 billion
Stock Exchanges: NASDAQ
Ticker Symbol: JOYG
NAICS: 333131 Mining Machinery and Equipment
  Manufacturing

■ ■ ■

Joy Global Inc. is a world leader in the manufacture, marketing, and servicing of mining equipment for both surface and underground operations. The company is represented in markets around the world, including Europe, Latin America, Australia, and Southeast Asia, as well as in South Africa, Canada, and the United States. Through its three operating divisions, Joy Global manufactures specialized equipment for underground mining (Joy Mining Machinery), equipment for surface extraction of ores and minerals (P&H Mining Equipment), and equipment for crushing and moving material (Continental Crushing and Conveying). A significant portion of the company's income comes from servicing mining equipment worldwide and providing spare parts.

MACHINE SHOP ORIGINS

Joy Global Inc. grew out of the Harnischfeger Corporation. Like many U.S. enterprises more than a century old, Harnischfeger traced its origins to an industrious immigrant with a dream. In 1884 Henry Harnischfeger was working at a sewing machine company in Milwaukee, Wisconsin. Born in Germany, Harnischfeger had worked previously as a locksmith, a machinist, and a machine maker. He was a foreman in the sewing plant when the company appeared about to go under. Forming a partnership with Alonzo Pawling, a pattern maker in the same plant, Harnischfeger launched a small machine and pattern shop in Milwaukee.

It was a modest beginning. The company had one milling machine, one drill press, one planer, and two lathes. After each snowstorm, someone had to shovel the flat roof so it would not collapse. Wind whistled in through the building's cracks. Milwaukee was bustling at the time, however, and before long the reputations of Pawling and Harnischfeger as craftsmen brought business to their door. Located in the midst of many booming manufacturing companies on Walker's Point, Pawling and Harnischfeger soon were building machines for knitting, grain drying, stamping, brick making, and milking, as well as conducting their regular repair work. The company was called Pawling & Harnischfeger and was commonly known as P&H. The small shop was soon expanding.

Harnischfeger's dream was to build a line of machinery that the company could produce and market itself. His chance came in 1887 after a tragedy occurred at a nearby plant, when another manufacturer's overhead crane fell, killing a workman. An engineer at that plant, H. A. Shaw, designed a more durable, safer crane powered by three electric motors. P&H soon hired Shaw, and their first electric overhead crane was shipped in 1888. It was a risky investment for the small company, which had built a three-story brick plant and large foundry and hired more workers.

In 1892 Shaw left with his patent to form his own company, and 1893 saw the onset of a severe economic downturn. Struggling beneath debt and with little work, the foundry was kept in operation by an order from the Pabst Brewery for six grain dryers. A few years later Shaw lost exclusive rights to manufacture the electric crane, and P&H immediately jumped back into production. Adding a line of electric hoists, essentially, smaller versions of the crane, as well as electric motors and controls, the company was prospering by the dawn of the 20th century, with nearly 100 employees.

GROWING PRODUCT LINES

In 1903 a fire destroyed the main shop of P&H; the following year the company built a new plant in West Milwaukee on land that had been purchased for expansion. Covering 20 acres, the plant was state-of-the-art at the time; it eventually became the world's leading manufacturer of overhead cranes. Soon after moving to the new facility, P&H began streamlining its operations and making the parts it had previously purchased from suppliers. Eventually the company designed, manufactured, and repaired every component of every product it sold, demonstrating self-reliance and accountability that brought repeat business from its customers.

Throughout the company's growth, Harnischfeger oversaw the business affairs while Pawling handled the engineering. Pawling's health declined in 1911, and he asked Harnischfeger to buy out his share of the business. Three years later, Pawling died and the company became Harnischfeger Corporation, retaining P&H as its trademark out of respect for its cofounder.

The heavy equipment industry, notoriously cyclical, alternated boom with bust. The year Pawling's health began to fail was a bust year. During those times, the company was saved by an order from J.I. Case Company for 1,000 gasoline tractor engines. The demand for cranes resumed in 1913, and then skyrocketed with the start of World War I a year later.

In the meantime, Henry Harnischfeger was looking for other products to help even out the cycles of the heavy equipment market, and he eventually settled on excavating and mining equipment. After the war, the company's engineers designed the world's first gasoline-powered dragline, a truck-mounted machine that could lift, pile-drive, clam, and drag. They also created a backhoe and a shovel-type excavator mounted on crawlers. With ample applications in both mining and construction, the products were instantly successful, and Harnischfeger became well known in those industries throughout the world. The main plant was expanded to handle this manufacturing; by 1930 the number of employees had grown to 1,500. Founder Henry Harnischfeger died in 1930, and his son Walter became president.

This modest diversification, however, did not offset the effects of the Great Depression. There was no market for Harnischfeger products, and the company lost money every year from 1931 to 1939. Harnischfeger was forced to offer used equipment that had been returned because customers could not afford to keep it at fire-sale prices just to raise cash. In 1937 and 1938 the company's workers struck and, eventually, formed a union.

POSTWAR INDUSTRIAL BOOM

Despite the weak market demand, Walter Harnischfeger continued to innovate and to improve the company's products. Harnischfeger replaced the rivets in its cranes with all-welded design and fabrication in the 1930s, creating cranes and excavators that were stronger, lighter, and less costly. Harnischfeger also sought more ways to diversify in the 1930s and 1940s, making welding machines, welding electrodes, diesel engines, and even prefabricated houses. Other Harnischfeger innovations changed the industry, while not exactly becoming household words. These included the electromagnetic brake and control system, Magnetorque, designed by Harnischfeger's engineers in 1946.

KEY DATES

1884: Milwaukee entrepreneurs Alonzo Pawling and Henry Harnischfeger go into business together, launching a small machine and pattern shop.

1914: Pawling dies; company is renamed Harnischfeger Corp.

1919: Joseph Francis Joy incorporates Joy Mining Machinery.

1956: Harnischfeger Corp. stock is listed on the American Exchange.

1971: Company stock is listed on the New York Stock Exchange.

1986: Harnischfeger acquires Beloit Corporation for $175 million.

1994: Harnischfeger buys Joy Technologies.

1999: Company files for Chapter 11.

2000: Harnischfeger sells Beloit division.

2001: Harnischfeger Industries completes reorganization and changes its name to Joy Global Inc.

2006: Company buys Stamler manufacturing division of Oldenburg Group.

2008: Joy Global acquires N.E.S. Investment Co. and its subsidiary, the Continental Global Group, and China's Wuxi Shengda.

World War II rocked the world, but revived the U.S. economy. Harnischfeger's plant was operating at full capacity again, and the company spent millions on plant additions. The company's cranes lifted tanks and heavy artillery in defense plants, its hoists positioned planes on aircraft carriers, and its excavators dug foundations for new buildings. Despite the burgeoning demand, chronic material shortages, a lack of skilled workers, and increased government regulation made it a difficult time for the company.

Harnischfeger hit its stride during the postwar industrial boom. From $29 million in sales in 1946, Harnischfeger grew steadily to $86 million by 1957, despite periodic economic downturns. New plants were built in Michigan, Illinois, and California, and plants were added and expanded in Milwaukee. Harnischfeger had also developed a market overseas, and companies were licensed abroad to build Harnischfeger cranes and excavators. Agreements were signed with Rheinstahl Union Brueckenbau of West Germany in 1952 and Kobe Steel, Ltd., of Japan in 1955. In 1951 Harnisch-

feger borrowed $5 million to develop better products. In 1956 it joined the American Exchange, opening itself up to more shareholders. Previously, the company had been primarily a family-owned company, although listed on the Midwest Stock Exchange.

In 1959 Walter Harnischfeger became chairman of the company and his son, Henry, became president. During this period industries were becoming more complex, and Henry Harnischfeger felt challenged to choose between being an average competitor in several tough fields or the leader in two or three. Between 1964 and 1968, Harnischfeger streamlined its operations. The prefabricated home and diesel engine lines were dropped, and the road-building equipment and welding product divisions were all dropped or sold as well.

By the late 1960s Harnischfeger had two divisions. The Construction and Mining Division produced digging and lifting machines, such as electric and hydraulic excavators, and truck- and crawler-mounted cranes, while the Industrial and Electrical Division manufactured overhead cranes and hoists, as well as the electrical motors and controls needed to power them. The two divisions were run, essentially, as separate companies, with individuated engineering and marketing responsibilities. From there, product lines were broadened and improved, especially for the larger products.

A GLOBAL COMPANY

Between 1969 and 1979 the average capacity of Harnischfeger's mining equipment doubled. In 1964 the company introduced stacker cranes to serve material handling markets. In 1967 it offered a new line of hydraulic backhoes and cranes for the booming hydraulic construction equipment market. Easier to operate and more mobile, these machines were very successful in the industry.

Harnischfeger's global presence also grew, with 25 percent of its production being exported in 1965 and 40 percent of U.S. output being exported a decade later. The company's licensed overseas partners and subsidiaries continued to grow, the largest being Harnischfeger GmbH, based in Germany, with distribution in Europe, the Middle East, and North Africa.

The restructuring of the 1960s left the company well poised for growth in the 1970s. After the oil embargo of 1973, new coal reserves were opened and oil pipelines and mass transit systems were built, increasing sales of Harnischfeger machinery. Annual sales grew from $150 million in 1970 to $646 million in 1981, excluding nearly $200 million sourced from overseas licensees. The company's stock was listed on the New

York Stock Exchange for the first time in 1971. The company continued to borrow funds to fuel growth, pouring nearly $200 million into upgrading its plants and equipment, as well as into research and development, between 1975 and 1980.

In the late 1970s, however, economic recession and high interest rates hit the company hard. Unhappy with its balance sheet, Harnischfeger sought to bring its debt-equity ratio into better focus by lowering capital requirements and cutting production costs. In 1979 Harnischfeger's interest bills alone came to about $28 million, and debt was roughly 40 percent of total capital in 1980.

The heavy equipment industry was hit hard by the recession, and Harnischfeger lost money for the first time since the end of the Depression in 1938. Harnischfeger also fell victim to political change abroad; the company had been about to ship a $20 million order to Iran when the Ayatollah Ruhollah Khomeini came to power, halting all trade between Iran and other countries. At the same time, the inflated deutsche mark was dulling the competitive edge of Harnischfeger's German subsidiary. The recession spread across the globe and by 1981 had depressed many of Harnischfeger's primary markets.

MAJOR CHANGES

In 1982 Henry Harnischfeger became chairman and CEO, and the position of president was assumed by William Goessel, formerly of Beloit Corporation, a manufacturer of papermaking machinery. For the first time in its nearly 100 years, Harnischfeger's president was not a Harnischfeger. The year Goessel became president was one of the company's darkest, with some plants operating at less than 20 percent of capacity. In his first week on the job, Goessel was told the company would run out of cash in six weeks; he then learned that the company was in technical default on $175 million of debt. Goessel closed some operations, slashed the workforce, sold excess inventory, and set about restructuring Harnischfeger's finances. He shifted the focus of operations from old technologies to computerized systems. The ailing construction equipment business, which had accounted for about half of Harnischfeger sales at one point, was sold.

The heavy equipment industry was going through vital changes at the same time, with the crane market shrinking while competition was increasing both at home and abroad. Leveraged buyouts and closings threatened several of the major construction crane manufacturers. In 1984 Harnischfeger announced that it would be buying virtually all of its construction cranes

from Kobe Steel, which then owned about 10 percent of Harnischfeger's stock. Family interest in Harnischfeger had been reduced to 5 percent. Between debt restructuring, public stock offerings, and cash from liquidations, Harnischfeger was able to pay its debts to private lenders by 1984 and report a profit that year. With the pressure diminished, at least until the ten-year notes came due in 1994, the company was again free to shift its focus back to growth.

The new focus was on material handling. In 1983 sales of mining, construction, and material handling equipment and systems were about equal, but the automated factory systems market seemed to be booming. Many factories were modernizing and retooling, using computerized systems to upgrade efficiency in production lines. In 1984 Harnischfeger formed a new subsidiary, Harnischfeger Engineers, to tap this market; by year's end General Motors and Nabisco Brands were customers.

Automated material handling systems were computer-controlled complexes of machinery that unload raw materials at the receiving dock, steer work through the factory, and send finished goods out for shipping. The systems included stacking cranes that retrieved parts in inventory and vehicles that were automatically guided by electric wires embedded in a factory floor. Harnischfeger seemed an unlikely competitor in the industry, but by the end of 1984 Harnischfeger Engineers was building a $5 million automated warehouse at a General Electric jet engine plant in Massachusetts.

DIVERSIFYING

One of the company's most notable milestones was the 1986 acquisition of Beloit Corporation. A manufacturer of pulp and papermaking machinery, Beloit was founded in 1858 and was also family run. The purchase was made for $175 million during a down cycle in the paper industry. About seven months later, at the onset of a boom in papermaking equipment and pulp and paper systems, the newly formed holding company, Harnischfeger Industries, sold a 20 percent stake in Beloit to Mitsubishi for $60 million. By 1988 Beloit was Harnischfeger's largest and most profitable unit, and by 1990 Beloit's sales were nearly $1.1 billion. It was a timely acquisition for Harnischfeger Industries and gave the parent company cash to reinvest in all its units.

Also purchased that same year was Syscon Corporation, for $92 million. This company provided software to the defense industry and was a leader in information systems integration. Harnischfeger's Systems Group, which included Syscon and Harnischfeger Engineers, was conceived as a counterbalance to the cyclical nature of mining equipment and papermaking machinery sales. Much of Syscon's work was with the U.S. Department of Defense, making it vulnerable to military cutbacks, but the company's work increasingly involved computer-based information systems designed to reduce paperwork and, therefore, could be of use in all federal departments as well as large companies. By 1990 Syscon was developing systems for the U.S. Departments of Labor and Education.

Harnischfeger was prospering in 1988, thanks to these acquisitions, the paper boom, and the improving climate in the mining industry. It was a record year, ending with doubled earnings. Two more common stock offerings were made in 1987 and 1988 to help bolster the balance sheet. In 1989 income from operations was up 65 percent over 1988. By 1990 roughly 60 percent of Harnischfeger's sales and earnings stemmed from papermaking machinery. Beloit equipment was used in producing 70 percent of the world's newsprint and writing and printing grade papers, as well as half of the world's tissues, towels, and napkins. Replacement parts for these machines was a thriving business as well.

A NEW CEO

The company announced in 1990 that it was shopping for new acquisitions. That same year, the paper cycle began a downturn. Although orders for papermaking machines dropped, a quarter of Beloit's paper machine manufacturing had been subcontracted to avoid the expense of expanding, so even with business decreasing, Beloit maintained presentable margins. Meanwhile, the Mining Equipment Division was still expanding, with sales of its massive electric-powered shovels growing nearly 20 percent in the first half of 1990. The poorest performing unit was still the material handling business, which supplied overhead cranes and hoists. Harnischfeger announced plans to buy a stake in Measurex Corporation in 1990 but not more than 20 percent over the next seven years by agreement between the companies. A Cupertino, California-based company, Measurex made industrial process-control systems, primarily for the paper industry. Beloit and Measurex entered a joint agreement on marketing, sales, and development.

William Goessel passed the reins to Jeffery T. Grade in 1991. Grade, then president, became CEO, and Goessel stayed on as chairman of the board. The paper slump continued and Beloit's paper machine orders suffered in 1992, hurt by industry overcapacity and a lingering global recession. Mining equipment sales were strong that year, while the material handling division had an increase in sales but a dip in operating profits.

Stalled defense contracts hurt Syscon in 1992, but caused the company to broaden its commercial and federal agency business bases. Goessel retired as chairman in early 1993, and Grade became chairman and CEO.

Grade was by all accounts a dashing and flamboyant leader, who claimed to have been a fighter pilot in Vietnam, hero of dangerous night landings on aircraft carriers, who had been shot down deep in enemy territory and fought his way to safety. He was a notoriously flashy dresser, with three company cars and a company jet at his disposal. He enraged Wall Street by continually falling short of earnings expectations, a feat he accomplished for 14 out of 24 quarters while he was CEO. A profile in *Barron's* for July 12, 1999, revealed that Grade had no Navy record, and Grade revised his story to say that he had been a passenger on some practice flights while a college student enrolled in the Navy ROTC.

EXPENSIVE ACQUISITIONS

Whereas Grade's predecessor William Goessel had cut Harnischfeger's debt as much as he could, Grade expanded it. The company's debt-to-overall-capital ratio climbed to 45 percent at the end of Grade's first year as CEO, and to 53 percent by 1997. The company bought Joy Technologies in 1994. Started as Joy Mining Machinery by Joseph Joy in 1919, the latest acquisition made equipment for underground mining. This was a new area for Harnischfeger, but Grade's ultimate goal was to get into areas that would balance the dangerous cyclical nature of its paper equipment and other product lines. In 1996, Harnischfeger bought an ailing British mining equipment firm, Dobson Park Industries, for $322 million. Neither Dobson nor Joy was doing particularly well, and Joy's slump caused it to close nine plants in 1996.

In 1997 Harnischfeger launched an unsuccessful hostile takeover bid for a machine-tool manufacturer, Giddings & Lewis, taking the company to court to force its board to consider the deal. Harnischfeger's stock began to fall in spite of record quarterly earnings, and Grade insisted Wall Street was overreacting to an announced year-end earnings shortfall. "We are the global leaders in everything we do. ... We haven't lost any customers; we haven't lost any market share," Grade insisted to the *Milwaukee Journal Sentinel* (May 22, 1997).

Nevertheless, the company's stock slid as news came in of a disastrous deal the company had undertaken in Indonesia. Harnischfeger had sold the Singapore-based Asia Pulp & Paper four huge papermaking machines, and the company was so eager to make the sale that it agreed to manage construction of the plants in Indonesia for which the machines were destined. This was not something Harnischfeger had done before, and complications soon forced sizable cost overruns, leading Asia Pulp & Paper to stall on payments. The Asian economic downturn of 1998 made the situation worse. A disastrous third-quarter loss in 1998 led Harnischfeger to lay off 20 percent of its workforce. That same year, Harnischfeger had sold 80 percent of its material handling division to Chartwell Investments.

INTO AND OUT OF BANKRUPTCY

By January 1999, Harnischfeger's stock was ranked the worst performing on the S&P 500. In May 1999, Jeffery Grade had left, and in June Harnischfeger filed for reorganization under Chapter 11 of the U.S. bankruptcy code. John Nils Hanson succeeded Grade and worked to put the company back together. The company's mining equipment division was still profitable, though far less so in 1998 than it had been in 1997, dropping from more than $200 million in operating profit to $82 million. The pulp and paper division, stung by the ongoing Indonesian debacle, lost more than $368 million. To get out of bankruptcy, Harnischfeger put its pulp and paper division, Beloit Corp., up for sale. Beloit was sold off piecemeal in 2000, with proceeds going to the company's creditors.

By late 2000, Harnischfeger had filed a plan to emerge from Chapter 11 as a pared down company concentrating on the manufacture of mining equipment. Its two principal divisions were P&H Mining Equipment, specializing in surface mining equipment, and Joy Mining Machinery, making and servicing equipment for underground mining. Even without its papermaking equipment unit, Harnischfeger remained a large company with a strong global presence.

On July 12, 2001, the company completed its financial reorganization and changed its name to Joy Global Inc. The company's stock initially began trading over the counter and then on the NASDAQ. Hanson moved the company's headquarters from its posh location on Lake Michigan to P&H's hometown of Milwaukee.

Joy Global emerged from bankruptcy at a promising time. The Bush administration had announced an energy policy that strongly supported the use of coal and other fossil fuel. Coal stockpiles were at 30-year lows, although the United States depended on coal for over half of its electricity. At Joy Mining Machinery, 90 percent of its sales were to coal mines, with over 40 percent of U.S. coal mines using the company's machines. At P&H, coal mines generated about one-third of business, with the mining of copper, iron ore, and sands accounting for the rest. In addition to domestic accounts, Hanson wanted to focus on two other areas: increasing revenues from overseas markets, which stood at about 40 percent of sales, and continuing to grow the company's parts and service sales, which accounted for 63 percent of revenues.

COMMODITIES BOOM

Across the globe, countries, particularly emerging markets such as Chile, Russia, China, and India, wanted commodities such as coal, copper, oil, and iron ore to meet their development and industrialization needs. The demand drove up the prices of metals, which in turn led mining companies to start new mining projects, which required more equipment.

In 2004, Joy Global entered the hard rock mining market when it signed a distribution agreement with Oldenburg Group. At the same time, the company began supplying equipment to a coal producer in Siberia and had new-equipment sales of $125 million in China, up from $25 million in 2001. Furthermore, Hanson's goal of increased service and maintenance revenues was being met as that channel brought in 70 percent of total sales.

By 2006, management announced a stock repurchase and later that year announced the acquisition of the Stamler manufacturing subsidiary of Oldenburg Group. The company was experiencing nearly 25 percent growth, with revenues of $2.4 billion. Net profits jumped from $148 million in 2005 to $416.4 million. In January 2007, Hanson stepped down as president and CEO, succeeded by Michael Sutherlin, president and COO of Joy Mining Machinery. Hanson kept his position as the company's chairman.

As the commodities boom continued, so did Joy Global's fortunes. Orders were at record levels, leading to sales of $2.6 billion and profits of $473 million in fiscal 2007. Under Sutherlin, the company increased its capacity, first by building new factories in low-cost countries. Then, in 2008, it made two major purchases: N.E.S. Investment Co. and its subsidiary, the Continental Global Group, which made conveyor systems; and Wuxi Shengda, a Chinese manufacturer of longwall shearing machines.

As the world economy contracted, the big question was how much, and when, the demand for commodities, and the resulting call for mining machinery, would drop. Joy Global had expanded its product offerings and moved aggressively into international markets. Perhaps its biggest defense in the uncertain commodities market was that over 60 percent of its sales came from its aftermarket—service, parts, and maintenance—business. Thus even if customers cut back on new purchases, or canceled, as one Chinese mine did, they would still need Joy Global to keep their existing machines operating.

Carol I. Keeley
Updated, A. Woodward; Ellen D. Wernick

PRINCIPAL SUBSIDIARIES

Joy Technologies Inc.; Joy Global Ltd. (UK); P&H Mining Equipment Inc.; N.E.S. Investment Co.; Continental Conveyor and Equipment Company; China Mining Machinery; Wuxi Shengda.

PRINCIPAL DIVISIONS

Joy Mining Machinery; P&H Mining Equipment; Continental Crushing and Conveying.

PRINCIPAL COMPETITORS

Bucyrus International, Inc.; Ingersoll-Rand Company, Ltd.; Caterpillar, Inc.

FURTHER READING

"Back from the Brink," *Industry Week,* July 9, 1984, pp. 16–17.

Barrett, Rick, "Mining Equipment Makers Ponder Uncertain Future," *JSOnline* (Milwaukee Wisconsin Journal Sentinel), February 14, 2009.

Bettner, Jill, "Digging Out," *Forbes,* June 18, 1984, pp. 110–11.

Briggs, Jean, "Those Deadly Words—Too Soon," *Forbes,* October 27, 1980, p. 149.

Byrne, Harlan, "Harnischfeger Industries, Inc.," *Barron's,* March 5, 1990, p. 53.

"A Centennial History of the Harnischfeger Corporation," Milwaukee: Harnischfeger Industries, Inc., 1984.

Daykin, Tom, "Earnings Below Estimates for Wisconsin's Harnischfeger Industries," *Knight-Ridder/Tribune Business News,* September 12, 1996.

Dayrit, Anthony, "Joy Global, Inc.," *Morningstar Analyst Report,* March 3, 2009.

"A Failing Grade," *Business Week,* June 7, 1999, p. 42.

"Firm Plans to Buy Stake, Possibly 20%, of Measurex," *Wall Street Journal,* May 31, 1990, p. A4.

"From Old Tech to High-Tech," *Financial World,* November 14, 1984, p. 107.

Geer, John F., Jr., "Dig It: Why Harnischfeger Has Been Buying into Underground Mining Equipment," *Financial World,* February 26, 1996, p. 52.

Goodman, Jordan, "Scaling the Wall of Adversity," *Money,* May 1985, pp. 103–04.

"Harnischfeger Expects Lower Fiscal '93 Profit Than Analysts Predict," *Wall Street Journal,* January 14, 1993, p. B4.

Huber, Robert, "Do You Want to Cook Hamburgers?" *Production,* December 1988, pp. 34–39.

"Huge Layoff at Harnischfeger," *Business Week,* September 7, 1998, p. 42.

Jerenski, Laura, "The Naked Truth," *Forbes,* May 18, 1987, pp. 86–87.

"Join Hands," *World Mining Equipment,* July–August 2004, p. 4.

"Joy Global Buys Equipment Builder," *Forging,* January–February 2009, p. 11.

"Joy Global CEO to Retire in 2007," *Diesel Progress North American Edition,* May 2006, p. 65.

"Joy Global Inc.," *Mining Journal,* July 20, 2001, p. 51.

"The Joy of P&H After Chapter 11," *Business Journal–Milwaukee,* July 27, 2001, p. 58.

Kirchen, Rich, "Goessel Continues to Turn on the Juice at Harnischfeger," *Business Journal–Milwaukee,* March 19, 1990, p. 13.

Laing, Jonathan R., "Grave Digger," *Barron's,* July 12, 1999, pp. 25–28.

Lank, Avrum D., "Wis. Machine Tool Maker Rejects Harnischfeger Offer," *Knight-Ridder/Tribune Business News,* May 9, 1997, p. 509B1252.

Lazo, Shirley, "Speaking of Dividends," *Barron's,* March 14, 1988, p. 79.

———, "Speaking of Dividends," *Barron's,* December 10, 1990, p. 64.

McFadden, Michael, "Prospering Merchants of Productivity," *Fortune,* December 10, 1984, p. 50.

"Measurex Corp.," *Insider's Chronicle,* July 30, 1990, p. 3.

"Measurex Corp.," *Wall Street Journal,* August 15, 1990, p. B2.

"Measurex Corp.," *Wall Street Journal,* October 15, 1990, p. A5.

Nelson, Brett, "The Big Dig," *Forbes,* August 17, 2001, p. 74.

———, "Mined over Matter," *Forbes,* December 13, 2004, p. 56.

Peer, Melinda, "Shiny Outlook for Miners," *Forbes.com,* April 27, 2009.

Pinkham, Myra, "Steel Digs the Commodities Boom," *Metal Center News,* July 2008, pp. 16–19.

Rose, Robert, "Laden with Cash, Harnischfeger Seeks Acquisition," *Wall Street Journal,* March 19, 1990, p. B3.

Rottenberg, Dan, "Adrenaline in the Rust Belt," *Business Month,* May 1990, p. 43.

Rudolph, Barbara, "Construction, Mining, Rail Equipment," *Forbes,* January 2, 1984, pp. 190–93.

"Sale of Final Beloit Units Approved," *Pulp & Paper,* April 2000, p. 15.

Sharma-Jensen, Geeta, "Harnischfeger Stock Falls After Firm Reports Record Profits," *Knight-Ridder/Tribune Business*

News, May 22, 1997.

Siegel, Matt, "The Worst Stock on the S&P 500," *Fortune,* January 11, 1999, p. 196.

"Stake in Measurex Increased to 14%," *New York Times,* August 28, 1990, p. D4.

Stires, David, "Digging for Dollars," *Fortune,* March 31, 2008, pp. 49–50.

"Supplier Companies," *Pulp & Paper,* December 1991, p. 129.

"13D Highlights," *Insider's Chronicle,* April 24, 1989, p. 2.

Wrubel, Robert, "Harnischfeger: Paper Profits," *Financial World,* June 26, 1990, p. 16.

KLM Royal Dutch
Airlines

———————■———————

Amsterdamseweg 55
Amstelveen, 1182 GP
Netherlands
Telephone: (31 20) 649 9123
Fax: (31 20) 649 2324
Web site: http://www.klm.com

Wholly Owned Subsidiary of Air France-KLM S.A.
Incorporated: 1919 as Koninklijke Luchtvaart
Maatschappij
Employees: 33,002
Sales: EUR 8 billion ($12.3 billion) (2008 est.)
NAICS: 481111 Scheduled Passenger Air Transporta-
tion; 481120 Scheduled Freight Air Transportation;
488190 Other Support Activities for Air Trans-
portation

■ ■ ■

KLM Royal Dutch Airlines, formerly known as Koninklijke Luchtvaart Maatschappij, N.V., and best known
simply as KLM, is the world's oldest scheduled airline.
In 2004, as the result of a merger, it became part of Air
France-KLM S.A., the largest airline company in
Europe. Under the new structure, KLM operates as an
independent carrier but coordinates operations with Air
France. KLM has three business areas: passenger
transportation, cargo transport, and maintenance and
engineering. Its passenger transport division includes
charter airline KLM Cityhopper and low-cost subsidiaries transavia.com and Martinair. As of April 2009, KLM
operated 114 planes serving over 130 destinations. Con-

nections through its network of partners and alliances
provide access to 905 destinations in 169 countries on
six continents.

ROYAL BEGINNINGS

KLM was organized by a young aviator lieutenant
named Albert Plesman. In 1919 Plesman, with the
financial support of an Amsterdam shipping company,
sponsored the "Elta" aviation exhibition in Amsterdam
to satisfy the public's fascination with the airplane. Over
half a million people attended the air show. When it
closed, several Dutch commercial interests decided to
establish a Dutch air transport company, and Plesman
was nominated to head the company.

The Royal Dutch government lent its support to
Plesman's project by offering to allow him use of the
title "Koninklijke," meaning "Royal," in the company's
name. On October 7, 1919, the Koninklijke Luchtvaart
Maatschappij (KLM) was founded in The Hague. It was
one of the world's first commercial airline companies.

In 1924 the airline made its first intercontinental
flight, from Amsterdam to Batavia, and 8,700-mile trip
that took 11 days. Soon KLM was transporting passengers, freight, and mail to a growing number of
European destinations linking Dutch cities with
London, Paris, Oslo, and Athens. At that time the
Netherlands had a worldwide empire with colonies in
Asia and the Caribbean. Soon KLM was charting routes
to link these colonies with Holland. In 1934 the airline
made its first transatlantic flight, from Amsterdam to
Curaçao. Services to Trinidad soon opened as well.

COMPANY PERSPECTIVES

Offering reliability and a healthy dose of Dutch pragmatism, KLM provides customers with innovative products and safe, efficient and service-oriented operations paying proactive attention to the environment and corporate social responsibility. Since four years, Air France KLM is the leading airline in the Dow Jones Sustainability indexes, and the only airline in the "Global 100" list.

At the start of World War II German armies invaded the Low Countries and closed KLM operations. Plesman was upset by the occupation and frustrated with his inability to persuade the Germans to relax their grip on the Netherlands. One summer night Plesman's determination to take action led him to awaken one of his houseguests, a Swedish KLM pilot named Count von Rosen. Plesman reportedly asked the count, "What can I do to stop this?," and Von Rosen replied, "You could talk to my Uncle Hermann." Suddenly Plesman realized he was speaking to the nephew of the German Reichsmarschall Hermann Göring. A few days later Plesman was in Berlin discussing with Göring the possibility of a peace treaty between England and Germany.

Plesman formulated a document that was later forwarded to Winston Churchill's office in London. The peace terms would leave the British Empire intact but give Germany control of the European continent and the United States control of the Americas. The matter was "studied with much interest" and receipt of the document was acknowledged by Lord Halifax. Göring, however, became displeased with Plesman's initiative and later had him jailed. Plesman was released in April 1942 and told to remain at his house in Twenthe in the woods of eastern Holland until the end of the war. During this time he kept himself occupied by formulating strategies for the postwar operation of KLM.

POSTWAR EXPANSION

When the war ended in the spring of 1945 Plesman was largely forgiven by the public for his attempts to make peace with the Germans earlier in the war. Soon afterward he traveled to the United States to negotiate the purchase of surplus warplanes for KLM. The company wasted no time rebuilding its network, but since the Dutch East Indies were in a state of revolt, Plesman's first priority was to reestablish KLM's route to Batavia. By the end of the year KLM was again flying to Indonesia. In 1946 the airline began flying to New York. By 1948 services were opened to places in Africa, North and South America, and the Caribbean. Also during the immediate postwar period, the Dutch government expressed interest many times in gaining a controlling stake in KLM. Plesman, however, was a fiercely independent man and kept the company under private control while conceding only a portion of KLM's ownership to the government.

Indonesia (formerly the Dutch East Indies) gained its independence from the Netherlands in 1949. The following year the Indonesian government established its own national airline called Garuda. KLM assisted Garuda from the time of its inception and continued to aid the company with technical and financial assistance until 1982. KLM later helped to establish several other airlines in developing nations, including Philippine Airlines, Nigeria Airways, Viasa (Venezuela), Egyptair, and Aerolineas Argentinas.

In 1950 KLM entered into an agreement with Swissair and Belgium's Sabena airlines that led to the establishment of a spare-parts pool. The BeNeSwiss agreement laid the ground for a future maintenance pool called the KSSU group, which included KLM, Scandinavian Airlines, Swissair, and the privately operated French airline UTA. KLM also continued to modernize and expand during the 1950s. It was the first European airline to fly new versions of the Lockheed Constellation and Electra. In addition, several destinations in western North America were added to KLM's route structure. In 1954 the company created KLM Aerocarto N.V., an aerial survey and photography service.

Plesman died on December 31, 1954, at the age of 64. Praised and decorated as a hero of the Netherlands, Plesman also received decorations from Denmark, Belgium, Sweden, Czechoslovakia, Greece, Tunisia, Lebanon, and Syria. The company he left behind was entering a difficult period in commercial aviation history. A sudden and unexplained decline in ridership caused financial reverses at KLM and most of the world's other airlines. The company also faced the burden of financing a costly conversion to jet airplanes. Moreover, by this time the government had increased its ownership of the company to two-thirds by purchasing new KLM stock issues. The board of directors, however, remained under the control of the private shareholders.

ENTERING THE JET AGE

In 1961 KLM reported its first year of losses. The company's president, I. A. Aler, resigned and was replaced by Ernst Hans van der Beugel. The change in

KEY DATES

1919: Koninklijke Luchtvaart Maatschappij (KLM), the Royal Dutch Airlines for the Netherlands and its colonies, is founded.

1924: KLM's first intercontinental flight, from Amsterdam to Jakarta, is the world's longest-distance scheduled service at the time.

1934: Company's first transatlantic flight is from Amsterdam to Curaçao.

1946: KLM initiates scheduled service between Amsterdam and New York.

1960: Company introduces its first jet plane, the Douglas DC-8.

1966: NLM (Netherlands Airlines), precursor of NLM Cityhopper, is founded.

1989: KLM acquires 20 percent interest in Northwest Airlines.

1991: Flying Dutchman, first frequent flyer program on the Continent, is introduced.

2004: Air France and KLM form Air France-KLM Group S.A.

2008: KLM becomes 100 percent owner of Martinair.

leadership, however, was not enough to reverse the company's financial difficulties. Aler returned to active participation and enlisted McKinsey & Company, an airline consulting firm, to make recommendations for restoring the company to profitability. Their study concluded that KLM should reduce its staff and number of airplanes. Aler, however, had already reduced the staff by one-seventh and refused to release any more personnel. In January 1963 Aler left KLM and later, suffering from exhaustion, checked into a hospital.

KLM's board of directors then elected Horatius Albarda to the company's presidency. Albarda initiated a reorganization of the company that involved further cutbacks in staff and air services. Albarda's tenure as president ended when he was killed in a private plane crash in 1965. Albarda was succeeded by KLM's Deputy President Gerrit Van der Wal, who would adopt Plesman's attitude toward government involvement in KLM. Before his appointment to KLM Van der Wal reached an agreement with the government that, despite its major financial holding in the company, KLM would be run as a private enterprise without interference from the government. By 1966 the Dutch government's interest in KLM had been reduced to 49.5 percent.

In 1965 the airline created a subsidiary called KLM Helicopters to transport oil workers to and from oil drilling rigs in the North Sea. The division was eventually expanded in its range of operations to include specialized and chartered airlift services. KLM created another subsidiary in 1966, called NLM (Netherlands Airlines) to operate domestic passenger air services in the Netherlands. It connected a number of smaller Dutch cities with the nation's international airports in Rotterdam and Amsterdam. KLM later included flights to other European cities, and in 1976 the division's name was changed to NLM Cityhopper.

In an attempt to better utilize its facilities at Amsterdam's Schiphol Airport, KLM initiated a promotion during this time called Distrinet, in conjunction with some Dutch shipping and transport companies. Distrinet was intended to coordinate these various Dutch companies in order to establish Amsterdam as the primary continental port of entry and distribution for European cargo.

DIVERSIFICATION AIDS SURVIVAL

KLM was a regular customer of the McDonnell Douglas Corporation during this time. When the airline introduced jet service in 1960, it decided to employ the Douglas DC-8 rather than the Boeing Company's 707, and in 1969 the company purchased DC-9s rather than Boeing's similarly configured three-engine 727. In 1971, however, KLM purchased the first of several Boeing 747 jumbo jets. McDonnell Douglas campaigned very hard to prevent KLM from purchasing more Boeing products, but KLM opted to remain neutral, preferring to recognize the unique qualities of each company's product and avoid becoming the exclusive customer of any one company.

In 1972 KLM purchased the first of several of McDonnell Douglas's new DC-10s to provide the airline with a more flexible fleet. Boeing and McDonnell Douglas, however, soon had more than just each other for competition. Airbus, the European aerospace consortium, began developing a new plan. KLM ordered ten Airbus A-310 passenger jetliners scheduled for delivery beginning in 1983.

Difficult economic conditions caused by the oil crisis in 1973–74 forced KLM to seek government assistance in arranging debt refinancing. In return for the government's money, KLM issued additional shares of stock to the government. By the late 1970s the government held a 78 percent majority of KLM stock. Company management, however, remained under the control of private shareholders.

Sergio Orlandini, whose father was Italian and his mother Dutch, became KLM's president in 1973. Upon taking office he was confronted with a problem common to all international carriers at that time: overcapacity. KLM was flying planes with too many empty seats. The solution at other airline companies was to offer discounted fares in the belief that some income from a given seat was better than none at all. Orlandini chose another approach. His idea was to reconfigure KLM's 747s, with their huge capacity for passengers, so that they could carry a combination of passengers and freight. A partition separated the passenger cabin from the cargo hold in the rear of the airplane. Later 747s delivered to KLM, called "combis," were specifically designed for combinations of passengers and freight. KLM competed with Federal Express and DHL by specializing in high-end operations such as shipping live horses and global sourcing.

In the mid-1980s, one-sixth of KLM's earnings came from non-airline operations, which included management consulting, technical services, staff training, hotels, duty-free shops, catering, and ground handling. The company's diversity enabled it to survive difficult periods in the airline passenger market. The Dutch government's share of KLM was reduced to 54.8 percent in 1986. Also during this time, KLM began cooperating with British Airways and several U.S. airline companies in lobbying to relax airline regulations in Europe.

MARKET LIBERALIZATION

Airlines worldwide were hurt by the Persian Gulf crisis and sluggish economy that opened the 1990s. In order to survive the decade's sharp competition, KLM aimed for at least a 10 percent share of the markets served by itself and its affiliates. KLM invested heavily in its fleet, bringing its debt and lease obligations to the $2 billion level. In the short term, the carrier configured its combis to carry more freight. However, KLM still lost money as the dollar and yen fell in value and was unable to turn a profit for 1990–91.

KLM started a three-year restructuring plan in 1990. The plan eliminated about 1,000 staff positions and focused the company on its core operations, with hopes of cutting expenses 15 percent a year. However, productivity increases were the most important component of the regimen. Pieter Bouw, a longtime KLM veteran, became its chairman in 1991. The reforms begun under Bouw were estimated to improve productivity by 60 percent within a few years. *Business Week* noted that passenger traffic rose by half without a further loss of jobs. Among the initiatives were the introduction of Flying Dutchman, the continent's first

frequent flyer program, begun in 1991, and World Business Class, introduced on KLM and Northwest Airlines (NWA) intercontinental flights.

As the European market liberalized, KLM developed its Amsterdam hub, feeding it with traffic from 50 affiliated airlines. The most newsworthy of its partnerships was that with NWA. KLM owned a 20 percent equity holding in NWA and although the two reaped significant benefits from their cooperation, the relationship proved notoriously difficult at times, culminating in an aborted takeover attempt on the part of KLM. Still, the relationship gave KLM the global reach it found necessary for survival in the deregulated international environment. An "open skies" agreement between the United States and the Netherlands allowed KLM and NWA to operate virtually as a single airline. The pair cut transatlantic fares and offered U.S. passengers discounts and easy connections to KLM's European and North African destinations. Even so, profits were not instantaneous for NWA, which would suffer numerous labor crises, and KLM was compelled to write off its original $400 million investment made in 1989.

KLM had its own labor concerns as well. Pilots made some concessions in 1993 in the face of further losses, when management contemplated moving back office operations from The Hague to a lower-cost area such as India. KLM finally saw another profit in 1993–94, of $42 million on revenues of more than $5 billion. Cargo operations contributed $800 million. In 1993–94 KLM was 38.2 percent owned by the Dutch government but received no subsidies, unlike other European counterparts such as Air France, which received nearly $4 billion that year. In 1994 the partnership with NWA brought in an extra $300 million per year to the two carriers. KLM increased its stake in NWA to 25 percent, the legal limit.

EXPANDING ALLIANCES

In December 1995 KLM successfully bid for a 26 percent share of newly privatized Kenya Airways. The two shared codes, as Kenya Airways implemented KLM's customer service procedures and benefited from new economies in purchasing and other areas. By the end of the decade, KLM had also teamed with Eurowings, Braathens, Malaysia Airlines, Nippon Cargo Airlines, and others. Air Engiadina and Air Alps Aviation operated flights under the brand "KLM Alps." KLM Cargo formed an alliance with EAC Logistics, based in Beijing.

This type of alliance had become very popular within the industry. As Scott M. Gawlicki explained in a

2000 article in *Investment Dealers' Digest,* "Alliances allow airlines to expand their global reach while attaining many of the cost-saving synergies of a merger without actually bringing two or more airlines together. Generally speaking, the airlines keep their separate identities but provide point-to-point service by integrating global networks."

An operating loss of $86.8 million in 1996–97 followed high fuel prices and weak Dutch currency. The next year, however, brought reported income of $389 million. KLM's internal regimen appeared to be working under new President and CEO Leo van Wijk. KLM's 1998 contract with its seven unions allowed for three bonuses and a permanent pay raise.

In 1997 KLM agreed to sell its shares back to NWA for $1.1 billion, an investment that was originally worth $400 million. The takeover issue set aside, the two signed a ten-year extension to their mutually beneficial arrangement. That same year saw the deregulation of the industry in the European Union. This meant that any airline could then fly into and within any European country.

Relatively flush with cash, KLM in 1998 completed its privatization process as it bought back the remaining regular shares from the Dutch government. The state continued to own preferential shares for a total of 14 percent of the company. Nearly 15 million passengers flew KLM that year, more than double the number carried ten years earlier, and the company ordered $1.2 billion of Boeing aircraft to meet the new demand.

In November 1998 KLM and Alitalia SpA, the Italian airlines, announced a joint venture. The deal would allow the two companies to get around regulatory barriers regarding foreign ownership of an airline because there would not be any equity ownership or financial stake. They would, however, run their passenger and cargo operations under a single management. Over the next 18 months, the two airlines moved toward a full merger, reorganizing networks and fleets, combining sales offices, and making broad strategic plans.

FACING INDUSTRY CHANGES

Then, in mid-2000, just as the industry expected an announcement detailing the process for completing the KLM-Alitalia merger, the partnership collapsed. Soon afterward KLM and British Airways began merger talks to create the world's third largest airline, but these ended within three months due to opposition from regulators. However, merger was not the only change KLM was exploring. With low-cost airlines gaining market share, KLM modified some of its operations to offer low-budget options. It created no-frills carrier Ba-

siq Air by selling some of the capacity of leisure airline Transavia, of which KLM owned 80 percent. Transavia sold seats primarily to tour operators within Europe, and Basiq offered individual seats from Amsterdam to Barcelona and Nice.

The terrorist attacks on the United States in September 2001 caused the demand for air traffic to decline and, combined with rising fuel prices and stricter security regulations, passenger travel and air cargo business dropped significantly. To improve its cargo costs, KLM partnered with TNT International Express, a subsidiary of the Dutch postal entity. KLM stopped leasing freighters for European deliveries, turning instead to sharing capacity on TNT flights from Amsterdam to Dublin, Budapest, and Helsinki.

Within a year of the attacks, KLM announced its cargo traffic had grown 8 percent. Rather than use sales agents, the airline focused on four target industries: high tech, automotive, pharmaceuticals, and fashion. As the company posted a record net loss of $474 million for fiscal 2002, its cargo operation was outshining passenger operations. That growth was largely attributable to KLM's continuing reliance on its combi airplanes. These were fairly easy to reconfigure to replace lost passenger traffic with cargo. Additionally, the airline had moved aggressively into the fast-growing Far East cargo market, so that by 2003, that area accounted for 50 percent of KLM's cargo capacity (compared to 25 percent for its transatlantic routes) and 60 percent of cargo revenues. The company also purchased three new 747-400 freighters, each with 112 tons of capacity.

By 2003 KLM was again holding joint-venture discussions with British Airways as well as with Air France. The domestic population of the Netherlands was too small for KLM to survive without forming alliances. The company pioneered such a partnership with its joint venture with NWA and later with alliances that often involved purchasing a financial stake. KLM's strategy was two pronged. First, it aimed to strengthen its individual situation, undertaking significant cost cutting, with layoffs and restructuring. It then looked for a profitable partner with which it could increase its presence in growing long-haul markets. In September, KLM announced its decision to go with Air France in forming the first cross-border European alliance.

MERGER WITH AIR FRANCE

The merger of Air France and KLM was completed on May 5, 2004, with the formation of Air France-KLM Group S.A., the largest airline company in Europe and one of the largest in the world to date. Chief Executive Jean-Cyril Spinetta and Deputy Chief Executive van

Wijk headed the new holding company. Each airline continued to operate as an independent carrier, maintaining its separate identity. This was especially important to KLM, for although it had been privatized, it was still the Dutch national carrier, laden with history and much national pride.

The Dutch public was not eager to see the name disappear within Air France. However, the two companies were united under a single management and quickly integrated their cargo transport activities and began coordinating other operations, particularly joint buying, aircraft maintenance, and financial planning. Passengers saw increased flexibility, such as being able to fly one line to a destination and the other back, as well as more connections to more destinations through the two networks and the SkyTeam alliance. KLM (and NWA) soon joined the SkyTeam alliance, whose members included Korean Air Lines, Alitalia, Delta, Aeroflot, China Southern Airlines, and Continental. When CEO van Wijk retired in July 2007, Peter Hartman was named CEO for KLM, later adding the position of president.

Consolidation within the airline industry continued. In April 2008 Delta and NWA merged, simplifying a transatlantic joint venture combining Air France-KLM and the new Delta entity, which was signed in May 2009. Under that agreement, the three partners offered customers 200 flights and some 50,000 seats daily. Also in December 2008, KLM acquired the remaining 50 percent of Martinair from the A.P. Møller-Maersk Group; Air France-KLM acquired 25 percent of Alitalia in January 2009. As KLM celebrated its 90th anniversary with a rebranding that reinforced its Dutch heritage, the airline continued to face major challenges, including increasing fuel prices, a shrinking world economy, and long-haul competition in Asia and the Middle East.

Updated, Frederick C. Ingram; Ellen D. Wernick

PRINCIPAL SUBSIDIARIES

KLM UK/Cityhopper; transavia.com; Martinair.

PRINCIPAL COMPETITORS

AMR Corporation; British Airways plc; Deutsche Lufthansa AG.

FURTHER READING

"Airline of the Year," *Air Transport World,* February 1998, pp. 39–40.

Allen, Roy, *Pictorial History of KLM, Royal Dutch Airlines,* London: Ian Allen, 1978.

Barnard, Bruce, "KLM Cargo Holds Its Own," *Journal of Commerce,* May 19–25, 2003, pp. 38–39.

Buyck, Kathy, "Cityhopper Knows the Business," *Air Transport World,* June 2001, pp. 142–43.

———, "The Reluctant Dutchess," *Air Transport World,* February 2001, pp. 41–44.

Churchill, David, "A Marriage Made in Heaven," *Business Travel World,* August 2006, pp. 22–23.

Condom, Pierre, "Obstacle Course," *Interavia Business & Technology,* October 2000.

Cottoli, Ken, "KLM, Alitalia Join Forces," *Traffic World,* December 7, 1998, pp. 37–38.

Del Canho, Dave, and Joeri Engelfriet, "Flying Higher— Together," *Business Strategy Review,* Spring 2008, pp. 35–37.

"End of KLM/Alitalia Merger Creates Uncertainty in Industry," *World Airline News,* May 5, 2000.

Feldman, Joan M., "Potential Realized," *Air Transport World,* December 1996, pp. 44–47.

Freedman, Michael, and Deborah Orr, "The Long Haul: How Does the Biggest Carrier, Air France-KLM, Thrive amid a Global Airline Slump? Lots of Connections," *Forbes Global,* February 28, 2005, pp. 22–27.

Gawlicki, Scott M., "Virtual Mergers," *Investment Dealers' Digest,* January 31, 2000, pp. 16–19.

"Going Dutch," *Air Cargo World,* November 2001, pp. 22–23.

Hill, Leonard, "80 Years Young," *Air Transport World,* October 1999, pp. 44–47.

"KLM Royal Dutch Airlines," *Aviation Week & Space Technology,* December 11, 2006, p. 9.

"Martinair Falls to KLM After 50 Years," *Air Cargo World,* January 2009, pp. 4–5.

McKenna, James T., "Northwest/KLM Package Challenges Competition," *Aviation Week and Space Technology,* February 15, 1993, p. 31.

Michaels, Daniel, "Behind Easing of Airline Rules, KLM's 20-Year Urge to Merge," *Wall Street Journal Eastern Edition,* September 5, 2006, pp. A1–A6.

Morais, Richard C., "They Ship Horses, Don't They?" *Forbes,* November 7, 1994, pp. 45–46.

Ott, James, "KLM Boosting Productivity and Debt to Survive Airline Wars of 1990s," *Aviation Week and Space Technology,* May 27, 1991, pp. 81–82.

———, "Top Airline Competitors Share Growth Strategy," *Aviation Week and Space Technology,* August 10, 1998, pp. 53–58.

Samuels, David, "You Also See the Ugly Side," *International Commercial Litigation,* May 1998, pp. 10–13.

Shiffrin, Carole A., and Pierre Sparaco, "European Carriers Regroup As Alcazar Hopes Fizzle," *Aviation Week and Space Technology,* November 29, 1993, pp. 29–30.

Thornton, Chris, "End of the Affair," *Airline Business,* October 1, 2000, p. 7.

Toy, Stewart, et al., "Flying High," *Business Week,* February 27, 1995, pp. 90–91.

Trepins, Dagmar, "A Ray of Hope for Europe's Airfreight Industry," *Logistics Management,* November 2002, pp. 72–73.

Tully, Shawn, "Northwest and KLM: The Alliance from Hell,"

Fortune, June 24, 1996, pp. 64–72.

Wahyuni, Sari, and Luchien Karsten, "How Successful Will the KLM-Air France Partnership Become?" *Problems and Perspectives in Management,* January 2006, pp. 111–23.

Koninklijke Reesink N.V.

Postbus 20, Loskade 6
Zutphen, NL-7200 AA
Netherlands
Telephone: (31 0575) 59 93 01
Fax: (31 0575) 59 93 04
Web site: http://www.royalreesink.com

Public Company
Incorporated: 1878 as H.J. Reesink en Compagnie
Employees: 357
Sales: EUR 198.9 million ($249 million) (2008)
Stock Exchanges: Euronext Amsterdam
Ticker Symbol: ALRRE
NAICS: 423710 Hardware Merchant Wholesalers; 423820 Farm and Garden Machinery and Equipment Merchant Wholesalers; 423830 Industrial Machinery and Equipment Merchant Wholesalers

■ ■ ■

Koninklijke Reesink N.V. is a wholesale trading group operating in three primary industry sectors: Retail, Industrial, and Green (agriculture, parks, and woodlands). The company's Green division represents the group's largest operation, generating nearly 44 percent of its annual sales of nearly EUR 199 million ($250 million) in 2008. This division imports and distributes agricultural machinery, including tractors, harvesters, hay tedders, balers, spraying machines, feed mixing machines, and other equipment for use in the agricultural sector, as well as in the maintenance of parks and woodlands. The major subsidiaries of this division include Reesink Technische Handel, Packo Agri and Kamps de Wild. Major brands include Kuhn, Rauch, McHale, Posch, and Claas.

Reesink's Industrial division focuses primarily on the import and distribution of rolled steel products for industrial use, through Reesink Staal B.V. This division also includes Safety Center International, a distributor of work shoes and related equipment. The industrial division accounted for more than 31 percent of group sales in 2008. The third division, Retail, focuses on supplying do-it-yourself (DIY) products to independent DIY retailers in the Netherlands. The main subsidiary in this division is Reesink Retail, which also oversees the Fixet franchise network of more than 150 independent hardware stores. Through subsidiary Bureau Voor Dienstverlening The Pentagon B.V., Reesink also operates its own e-commerce DIY website at www.handig.nl. The retail division generated 25 percent of group sales in 2008. Reesink is listed on the Euronext Amsterdam Stock Exchange's Alternext index. Gerrit van der Scheer took over as group CEO in May 2009.

18TH-CENTURY ORIGINS

Reesink's involvement in the Netherlands' wholesale trade sector stemmed from a village smithy in operation in the late 18th century. Hendrik Reesink, son of a blacksmith in the village of Warnsveld, apprenticed at a another blacksmith's shop west of there in Zutphen. When his master died, Reesink, then 21 years old, took over the shop's operation; he married the blacksmith's widow several months later. In this way, Reesink became the shop's new owner, and in 1786 he joined the blacksmith's guild as a master blacksmith.

We are not a group that always sings the same tune just because it has only one trading activity. In our case the complementary trading companies, which distribute technical goods from stock, add up to a harmonious whole. As a group we intend to continue this combined effort, in which each of the trading activities clearly shows its own, individual strong focus.

Reesink's son Jan was born that same year; he would grow up to take over the smithy. By then, the elder Reesink had begun to diversify, trading in coal and developing a business as a wholesaler for steel products and smithy tools and equipment. The younger Reesink took up this business as well, expanding the import operation to include steel products from England, Sweden, and Germany.

In the first decades of the 19th century, Reesink's wholesale business grew to become the family's primary focus. In 1843, the next generation, under Johan Gerhard Reesink, took over the business. Under Johan Reesink the family's smithy was spun off into a separate business, which was then operated by one of Hendrik Reesink's other grandchildren.

EXPANDING THE WHOLESALE TRADE

Reesink ran into difficulties in the 1870s. Faced with bankruptcy, the company was forced to turn over half of the business to its creditors. Johan Reesink then turned over what remained of the business to his son, Herman Johan Reesink, and son-in-law Hendrik Willem Massink. The partners reincorporated the company as H.J. Reesink en Compagnie in 1878. The following year, the company moved to larger quarters, taking over three buildings that had been newly constructed on Zutphen's Stationsplein. By then, too, the family had paid off its debts and once again regained full control of the recovering wholesale business.

Reesink began trading an ever-growing assortment of farm implements, machinery, and equipment in the years that followed. The company also expanded its range of goods to include stoves, furnaces, chimneys, and the like. This growth prompted the company to expand its warehousing facilities at the end of the century, with the construction of three new warehouse

buildings on Havenstraat, on Zutphen's Noorderhaven port. Over the next three decades, Reesink continued to grow strongly. Into the 1930s, Reesink's operations stretched the length of the Havenstraat.

By then, the company had come under the leadership of a new generation of the family led by Hendrik Willem Reesink. In 1927, Reesink reincorporated the company as a limited liability concern called H.J. Reesink & Co. NV. Over the next decade, Reesink expanded beyond Zutphen. During the 1930s, the company bought Amsterdam-based Van den Berg & Co. At the same time, it established a presence in Rotterdam, opening an office in that city.

REBUILDING AFTER WORLD WAR II

Reesink suffered along with the rest of the Netherlands under the Nazi occupation during World War II. Hendrik Reesink was himself interned for a time in a German camp. By the end of the war the company had suffered major damage both from Allied bombing raids and the Nazi scorched-earth policy during the German retreat. Nevertheless, Reesink immediately launched the reconstruction of its operations, a process that was completed ten years later. By then, Hendrik Reesink had turned over the company's reins to his son Herman Johan Reesink and his half-brother Adrianus Reesink.

The reconstruction of the Netherlands and the subsequent postwar economic boom represented a new era of opportunity for the company. In order to take advantage of the expanding markets, Reesink went public in 1959, listing its shares on the Amsterdam Stock Exchange. The listing generated funds that allowed the company to expand its wholesale trade operations into a number of new areas, such as pipes and tubing, while also enhancing its longstanding trade in agricultural machinery, equipment, and tools.

This business grew especially strongly during the 1950s, as the wholesale industrialization of the agricultural sector got underway. During this decade, Reesink became the exclusive importer for the French farm machinery maker, Kuhn.

The company added garden furniture and household appliances, including washing machines, to its product line in the 1960s. In support of its growing range, the company opened a series of showrooms, with shops in Zutphen, Amsterdam, 's Hertogenbosch, Hoensbroek, and Rotterdam.

Other strong areas of growth for the company were the fast-emerging do-it-yourself (DIY) and home

KEY DATES

1786: Hendrik Reesink takes over a blacksmith shop in Zutphen.

1878: Brothers-in-law Herman Johan Reesink and Hendrik Willem Massink incorporate the company as a partnership, H.J. Reesink en Compagnie.

1927: The company incorporates as a limited liability company, H.J. Reesink & Co. N.V.

1959: Reesink goes public on the Amsterdam Stock Exchange.

1968: Reesink acquires G.F. Wolters Technische Handelmaatschappij and then steel trading group Leeuwenberg Zonen the following year.

1985: Bernard Ten Doescahte becomes CEO, and the company introduces its first DIY franchise formats: De Vakman and Knap-'t-Op.

1997: Reesink merges its franchise formats into a single brand, Fixet.

2005: Reesink fights off hostile takeover attempt by real estate group Van Herk.

2009: Ten Doeschate retires and is replaced by Gerrit van der Scheer.

gardening sectors. In the mid-1960s, Reesink launched its own brand of garden tools and supplies called Hendrik Jan de Tuinman. Backed by a series of television commercials, the brand soon achieved national prominence. Over the next several decades, Reesink would continue to expand its range of hardware and gardening supplies, becoming a major wholesale partner for the Netherlands' independent retailers.

Reesink's expansion remained solid through the end of the 1960s. The company completed several acquisitions, including Groningen-based G.F. Wolters Technische Handelmaatschappij in 1968. The following year, the group expanded its steel trading business with the purchase of Amsterdam-based Leeuwenberg Zonen.

In a more challenging economic climate in the 1970s the company's aggressive growth stalled. In fact, Reesink was forced to shut down its network of showrooms in the early 1980s as a result of flat sales and corporate belt-tightening. In 1983, Adrianus Reesink, the last of the Reesink family to lead the company, stepped down. The company then hired a management consulting team to devise a new strategy for the company.

NEW LEADERSHIP

In 1985, the company named Bernard Ten Doeschate to take over as head of the company. Ten Doeschate moved quickly to refocus the company around its core operations as a wholesaler. By then, the country's independent hardware and garden supply sector faced new competition from a growing number of national and internationally operating chains. So in response Reesink decided to develop its own franchise formula, providing the independent retailers with the greater purchasing power of a large-scale group. In 1986, the company launched its first two franchise formats, De Vakman and Knap-'t-Op.

Reesink faced a crisis in its farm machinery market during this time, as manufacturer Kuhn, confronted with its own financial difficulties, opened its Dutch imports to other wholesale groups. Faced with the loss of part this business, Reesink moved to expand its own range of brands. This led to the 1987 takeover of Kamps de Wild, based in Zevenaar, which held the Dutch franchise for the Claas farm equipment brand. Two years later, Reesink acquired Stierman Soest, providing it with a range of tools and equipment for the parks and woodlands sector.

FIXET FORMULA IN 1997

Into the 1990s, the company also sought a further expansion of its retail trade operations. The slump in the housing market at the end of the 1980s and a new recession at the start of the 1990s had served to stimulate both the DIY and home gardening markets. At the same time, many consumers increasingly came to view home improvement and gardening as hobbies, further stimulating the retail channel's expansion.

These trends led Reesink to boost its own trade in the sector. In 1992, the company bought Hadva-Koelink, a company based in eastern city of Enschede, which had developed two retail franchise formats: Plus Klus and Happy Hobby. In the second half of the 1990s, the company's network included more than 320 franchisees. The company also expanded its wholesale business with purchase of 's Hertogenbosch-based Dutec, a small, regionally focused company dealing in industrial and engineering components and tools.

Reesink encountered new difficulties in the middle of the 1990s. Specifically, the group suffered from a slowdown in its farm machinery branch, and profits declined. The company moved to streamline its franchise business by merging its different store formats under a single new brand, Fixet, in 1997. The move met with disapproval from many of the group's franchisees, and their numbers declined. By 1998, the Fixet franchise network numbered just 170 stores. Many of the group's former franchisees remained customers of the company's wholesale operations, however.

HOSTILE TAKEOVER ATTEMPT IN 2005

Reesink moved to new facilities in 2003, a process Ten Doeschate had begun shortly after taking over as the group's CEO in 1985. Ten Doeschate at first sought to remain in Zutphen, but after several years of negotiating with the city, he was unable to find a suitable site. Nonetheless he promised to build the company's new facility near Zutphen, so that its employees would still be able to travel to work. A site was settled on in Apeldoorn, near the Zutphen border, but relations with that city soon soured, causing a long delay in Reesink's move. Authorization for construction of the new facility was finally approved in 2002, and the company completed its move in 2003. In that year, the company was also granted "royal" status by the Netherlands government, becoming Koninklijke Reesink BV.

Despite the move to Apeldoorn, Reesink maintained possession of its buildings in Zutphen. These holdings, however, caused the company to face into a new challenge in 2005. In that year, the company received a takeover offer from Dutch real estate group Van Herk, which offered to buy out the company's shareholders at 60 Euros per share. The bid, and a subsequent bid at 70 euros, represented a premium over the group's share price, which averaged 43 euros per share at the time.

However, Reesink management, which suspected the Van Herk's true interest was the acquisition of the company's Zutphen properties, judged the price too low. When the Van Herk bid turned hostile, Reesink continued to resist the takeover. In the end, Ten Doeschate helped sway the company's shareholders, who backed the group's continued independence.

Reesink was able to return its attention to building its core operations. In 2006, the company acquired Packo Agri, based in Zedelgem, near the Belgian border. That company, founded as a blacksmith shop in the early 20th century, had become a prominent regional dealer of Kuhn farm machinery. The addition of Packo's operations enabled Reesink to reclaim the position as the largest Kuhn dealer in the Netherlands.

TARGETING THE INTERNET IN 2007

In 2007 the company reorganized its operations to focus more strongly on its three core operations of steel trad-

ing, so-called green equipment (for the agricultural and parks and woodlands sectors), and retail trade. As a result, the company sold its Dutec BV operation that year but maintained Dutec's mail-order Technical Supplies Catalogue operations.

Instead, Reesink turned its attention to expanding its DIY and garden supply operations into new territories. In 2007, the company activated a dormant subsidiary, Bureau voor Dienstverlening The Pentagon BV, which then became the group's "incubator" for developing new businesses, especially e-commerce Internet operations. The company debuted the first of these sites, www.handig.nl, in that year. The new site offered a range of 1,000 DIY, gardening, and home improvement items. The Pentagon began developing a second online operation, which debuted in 2008, at www.tic.biz, and was based on the group's Technical Supplies Catalogue.

Reesink was confronted with global recession at the end of the decade. While the group's industrial and agricultural machinery division maintained their growth through 2008, the group's retail operation, like the rest of that sector, continued to slip. Given the uncertain times, Ten Doeschate raised eyebrows with his suggestion that Reesink would inevitably acquire rival DIY group Doe-het-zelf Groep Nederland (DGN), which served as wholesaler to its own chain of Multimate-branded DIY franchises. Ten Doeschate retired in May of that year, however, replaced by Gerrit van der Scheer, former head of the group's industrial trade division. After 223 years, Reesink remained an important part of the Dutch wholesale steel, agricultural, and hardware markets, poised to prosper as global economies recovered.

M. L. Cohen

PRINCIPAL SUBSIDIARIES

Bureau Voor Dienstverlening The Pentagon B.V.; Interlogica B.V.; Kamps De Wild B.V.; Packo Agri N.V.; Recobel B.V.; Reesink Retail B.V.; Reesink Staal B.V.; Reesink Technische Handel B.V.; Safety Centre International B.V.

PRINCIPAL DIVISIONS

Agriculture, Parks and Woodland; Retail Trade; Industry.

PRINCIPAL COMPETITORS

Intergamma B.V.; Cooeperatie Agrifirm U.A.; Kooijman N.V.; BCC (Elektro-Speciaalzaken) B.V.

FURTHER READING

"Bedrijfsresultaat Reesink Een Derde Gedaald," *Trouw,* May 11, 2009.

Leeflang, Gep, "Krachtenbundeling van Doe-Het-Zelvers," *De Stentor,* May 11, 2009.

Meijsen, Joep, "Fikse Botsing Fixet en Multimate," *Elsevier Retail,* May 12, 2009.

Nobelen, Paul, "Lak aan de Eisen," *Management Scope,* June 30, 2006.

"Reesink Eind Dit Jaar Als Eerste Naar Alternext," *Trouw,* June 28, 2006.

"Reesink Rondt Overname Packo Agri Af," *Trouw,* February 10, 2006.

Van den Berg, Marjan, "Onder Reesinks Puin en Stof Glinsteren Miljoenen," *De Volkskrant,* March 9, 2005.

"Winstdip Reesink door Doe-Het-Zelvers Fixet," *De Volkskrant,* December 16, 1998.

Krombacher

Krombacher Brauerei Bernhard Schadeberg GmbH & Co. KG

Hagener Strasse 261
Kreuztal, D-57223
Germany
Telephone: (49 2732) 880 0
Fax: (49 2732) 880 254
Web site: http://www.krombacher.de

Private Company
Incorporated: 1896 as Hasbrauerei Eberhardt und Cie
Employees: 866
Sales: EUR 642.5 million ($963.7 million) (2008 est.)
NAICS: 312120 Breweries; 312111 Soft Drink Manufacturing

■ ■ ■

Krombacher Brauerei Bernhard Schadeberg GmbH & Co. KG is Germany's largest privately owned brewery. Located in Kreuztal near Siegen in Southern Westphalia, Krombacher Brauerei puts out about 5.7 million hectoliters of beer annually. The company's flagship brand, Krombacher Pilsener or "Pils," is Germany's most popular pilsner beer brand and accounts for roughly 70 percent of the brewery's total output. About one-sixth of that volume is sold in kegs to bars and restaurants.

Krombacher Brauerei also sells other types of beer under the Krombacher brand name, including Krombacher Weizen, a wheat beer, Krombacher Radler, a combination of beer and soda pop, and nonalcoholic versions of these products. The beer brands Rolinck, Eichener, Rhenania Alt, and Vitamalz also belong to the group. In addition, the brewery makes a number of mixed beverages containing beer, such as its Cola & Beer and Lemon & Beer lines, under the Cab brand name. Krombacher Brauerei also manufactures a variety of nonalcoholic soft drinks under the Schweppes brand name, which contribute roughly 10 percent to the Krombacher group's total sales. Krombacher Brauerei is owned by the Schadeberg family.

ORIGINS AND EARLY GROWTH

While the precise founding date of Krombacher Brauerei is not certain, researchers have traced the brewery's first mention in print to the 1803 existence a local inn owned by the father of Johannes Haas. Located directly on the main transportation route to Cologne and the Ruhr, the town of Krombach had been home to breweries since the 1300s and became a popular stop for coachmen passing through hauling goods, mail, and travelers across the country in their horse-drawn carriages. The local economy was dominated by ore mining operations and related business activities such as smelting and forging, works that as a side effect produced thirsty crowds of beer drinkers.

Having grown out of a small family business, brewing beer became the sole activity of Krombacher Brauerei in the early years of the 19th century. Taking advantage of its favorable location at one of the region's main traffic routes, the brewery soon began to expand its reach beyond its small hometown. Industrialization in the second half of the 19th century revolutionized beer production. The discovery of the fermentation process made it possible to produce much larger batches and new cooling technologies allowed the beer to be preserved and stored and to be transported over long distances. Krombacher Brauerei secured the capital needed to purchase state-of-the-art brewing equipment for that time and became one of the region's largest and most modern breweries.

While Krombacher Brauerei expanded brewing capacity dramatically during the second half of the 19th century, the brewery's market grew very quickly as well. Due to rapidly advancing industrialization, the population of Siegen County, according to *Weihrauch,* doubled between 1850 and 1900. The number of establishments selling beer grew rapidly as well. Furthermore, the rapid expansion of the German railroad network made the long-distance shipping of large quantities of beer in barrels possible. After the Ruhr-Sieg-Bahn railroad line in 1861 connected the region around Siegen with the Ruhr, one of the fastest-growing industrial centers, Krombacher Brauerei began to conquer the huge market there, where most of western Germany's largest breweries were based. In 1896 Johannes Haas sold the brewery to Otto Eberhardt, an entrepreneur in Dortmund, who renamed the company Hasbrauerei Eberhardt und Cie and transformed the business into a limited partnership until it became a public stock corporation in 1905. By the end of the 19th century, the brewery was putting out over 30,000 hectoliters of beer annually.

BUILDING BRAND RECOGNITION

In the 1890s the brewmasters at Krombacher Brauerei began to brew a new kind of beer called pilsner, a clear beer with a golden yellow color named after the Bohemian city Plzeň where it was developed in the mid-1800s. After a few years of experimenting, Krombacher Brauerei launched its own pilsner brew, which quickly became popular among the regional beer consumers.

Around the dawn of the 20th century the brewery began to promote its new brew with ads in Siegen's local newspaper, stressing the excellent quality of the hops, malt, and spring water used to produce the popular beverage. To start building brand recognition, the brewery chose the newly built tower on the Kindelsberg, the mountain at the foothills of which the brewery was located, to symbolize the region where the beer originated. The tower became part of the company's coat of arms, which from then on was printed on every beer bottle label that left the brewery. In 1908 Krombacher Brauerei distributed promotional flyers stressing the superior characteristics of Krombacher Pilsener in comparison to competing brands.

The beginning of World War I in 1914 ushered in an era of political and economic turmoil in Germany and a period of severe hardship for the country's population. Prices for raw materials increased significantly and exports came to a sudden halt. As the war progressed, the necessary ingredients became so scarce that the brewery was forced to lower the barley content, resulting in a below standard, thinned down product. Germans in turn, rather than drinking the low quality "thin beer," as they called it, cut back on their beer consumption altogether.

ENDURING ECONOMIC DEPRESSION AND WORLD WAR II

The galloping inflation that followed the war further decreased Germans' thirst for beer. According to *Weihrauch,* per capita consumption of the country's most popular beverage dropped roughly 60 percent in the decade between 1913 and 1923. In 1922, when hyperinflation was in full force, Eberhardt's son-in-law, maltster and brewer Bernhard Schadeberg, took over the brewery. Krombacher Brauerei's sales recovered somewhat in the second half of the 1920s, but did not return to prewar levels.

Sales of Krombacher's Export brand continued to drop drastically as well during the 1920s, from approximately 60 percent to a meager 20 percent. At the same time, the brewery's pilsner brand, Krombacher Pilsener, became the company's most important product. Krombacher Brauerei also produced another beer brand, Märzen, which accounted for roughly 10 percent of the brewery's sales. In addition, the company manufactured a sweet-tasting malt beer that contributed between 2 percent and 5 percent to Krombacher Brauerei's revenues.

The Great Depression, which reached Germany in the early 1930s, left the brewery once again struggling with sharply dropping sales. Within only two years the

KEY DATES

■

1803: A brewery is in operation in the German town of Krombach.

1896: The Krombach brewery is sold to Otto Eberhardt, who renames it Hasbrauerei Eberhardt und Cie.

1908: The brewery begins to market Krombacher Pilsener as a brand name beer.

1953: Bernhard Schadeberg's son Friedrich joins Krombacher Brauerei as managing partner.

1961: Friedrich Schadeberg and Barbara Lambrecht-Schadeberg become co-owners of the enterprise.

1972: Krombacher Brauerei reports an output of over one million hectoliters.

1980: Günter Heyden joins the company as CEO.

1995: The "Krombach Eleven" crate with 11 rather than the usual 20 bottles is introduced.

1999: A nonalcoholic pilsner beer and the six-pack as a new packaging unit are launched.

2001: New CEO Bernhard Schadeberg begins to expand the company's branded product portfolio.

2002: Krombacher Brauerei becomes German market leader in the premium beer segment and introduces Krombacher Radler.

2006: The company acquires a license for the Schweppes line of branded nonalcoholic soft drinks.

2007: Krombacher Brauerei takes over the Westphalian brewery Rolinck and launches the wheat beer Krombacher Weizen.

brewery's output shrank by more than 30 percent. Sales recovered again later in the decade, partly due to the brewery's efforts to further expand distribution into other parts of the country.

However, the beginning of World War II in 1939 was another major setback. Again, raw materials were restricted by the Nazi government and the brewery was forced to produce a below-standard product. As the war progressed, growing barley for making bread took precedence over using the grain for brewing beer. In 1943 Krombacher Brauerei discontinued the manufacturing of its pilsner brand, but continued to put out some 28,000 hectoliters of "wartime beer" per year until the war ended in 1945.

MASSIVE GROWTH IN THE RECONSTRUCTION ERA

Securing enough food for survival was a daily struggle in postwar Germany. The British military government issued a ban on using barley for brewing beer within its zone, including the Siegerland, for some time. Consequently, beer consumption in Germany dropped 70 percent in the late 1940s compared to prewar levels. In addition to barley, malt was also in short supply and Krombacher Brauerei began to produce substitute beverages containing hops, as well as synthetic aromas and colors. In 1949 the brewery reached the bottom of the postwar recession with an output of 19,000 hectoliters.

Beginning in the 1950s, when Germany entered its postwar reconstruction boom, and the rationing of raw materials finally ended, beer consumption started to increase again. In 1953 Bernhard Schadeberg's son Friedrich joined Krombacher Brauerei as managing partner. Within the next 20 years under the younger Schadeberg's leadership, Krombacher Brauerei emerged from a local brewery to be one of Germany's largest private brewers, due mainly to two major strategic decisions. First, Schadeberg decided to pursue a one-product strategy by focusing on Krombacher Pilsener. Second, he envisioned Krombacher Pilsener as a brand name product that had to be built by substantial investments in regular advertising campaigns.

As a symbol for its home region, and also for a healthy natural environment, the company chose the idyllic image of a small island in the middle of a pristine lake, surrounded by a range of mountains overgrown with lavish green forest, as a key visual for its advertising. Riding the wave of the growing popularity of pilsner beer in Germany, beer consumers were enticed into choosing Krombacher Pilsener over any other pilsner brand with the legendary invitation, "Friends, let's krombacher one together (*Freunde, lasst uns einen krombachern*)," uttered by a forester in green uniform raising his glass invitingly.

Two additional critical success factors that helped propel Krombacher Brauerei into the top league of German breweries during the 1950s and 1960s were the willingness to invest significant amounts into state-of-the-art technology and the determination to systematically expand its circle of customers beyond its home region. As the Germans' beer consumption gradually returned to and later exceeded prewar levels, Krombacher Brauerei's production and storage facilities were constantly expanded and modernized. As a result of these combined efforts, the brewery's output rose from about 70,000 hectoliters in 1953 to roughly 500,000 in 1967. The percentage of bottled beer being sold climbed continuously, reaching about half of Krombacher Brauerei's output by 1960.

In the early 1970s Krombacher Brauerei was one of the first breweries to introduce large-tank-fermentation technology, which allowed producing much larger batches in shorter periods. In addition to extending its advertising campaigns into the neighboring regions, the brewery's sales organization was expanded as well. In 1972 Krombacher Brauerei reported an output of over one million hectoliters. Although two-thirds of the brewery's product was still sold to customers within a radius of 60 kilometers, one-third was being shipped to regions outside of southwestern Westphalia, mainly to the Sauerland and the southern Ruhr.

QUADRUPLING OUTPUT UNDER NEW CEO

That Krombacher Brauerei managed not only to survive but to thrive in the unpredictable and increasingly competitive beer market of the 1980s was mainly due to the company's continued strategy to position Krombacher Pilsener as a premium consumer brand. When Günter Heyden, the former director of marketing at German coffee manufacturer Melitta, whom Friedrich Schadeberg had persuaded to join his company, came to Krombacher Brauerei as CEO in 1980, the brewery had entered a period of stagnating and even decreasing sales. Under Heyden's direction the company conducted thorough research on consumer trends and preferences. Based on that research, Krombacher Brauerei invested heavily in consumer advertising, stressing Krombacher Pilsener's high-quality, exquisite taste, and easiness on the stomach.

In addition, the company put considerable effort into extending product distribution in the hospitality industry and in supermarkets, with a main focus on larger retail outlets where the majority of bottled beer was sold. As a result of these combined measures, Krombacher Brauerei witnessed a surge in demand for Krombacher Pilsener beginning in the mid-1980s. As the brewery's sales continued to climb, the company outgrew its original site and built a new bottling plant and shipping center in Kreuztal. In 1987 Heyden succeeded Schadeberg as head of the company's management board. Three years later Krombacher Brauerei reported sales of over two million hectoliters for the first time in its history.

The reunification of West and East Germany in 1990 immediately created a new market with several million potential Krombacher Pilsener consumers. Krombacher Brauerei jumped at the chance to conquer the new market and quickly extended its activities to the new eastern German states. Within the next five years, the brewery's output doubled, reaching more than four million hectoliters in 1995.

PRODUCT INNOVATION

In the second half of the 1990s, Krombacher Brauerei continued to invest in a variety of marketing measures to further expand its market share. To increase brand recognition on the national level, the brewery invested heavily in sponsoring sports teams and live television broadcasts of sports events, including Formula 1 races, the national soccer league, handball, hockey, tennis, athletics, skiing, and water sports. At the same time Krombacher Brauerei spent some DEM 20 million annually on advertising campaigns in national print titles and on television to strengthen its pilsner brand. To communicate the only slightly modified positioning of Krombacher Pilsener as a "pearl of nature," a synonym for high value and indulgence, naturalness, and freshness, the product was presented in the pristine nature scene with the legendary lake, underscored by sequences from George Gershwin's "Rhapsody in Blue."

While Krombacher Brauerei's continued investment in consumer marketing strengthened brand recognition on a national level, it was a bold step in product innovation that helped the company's success in the difficult market environment of the mid-to-late 1990s. Due to changes in consumer preferences, beer consumption was stagnating, resulting in growing competition among Germany's beer brewers for a shrinking number of beer drinkers. In addition, retail chains started selling brand-name products at extremely low prices to boost their sluggish sales. In 1995 the company introduced the "Krombach Eleven," a crate that contained only 11 instead of the usual 20 multiuse half-liter bottles. The new crate was designed to cater to the needs of the rising number of single-person households as well as to younger and to female beer consumers who preferred smaller packaging.

The "Krombach Eleven" was not only much easier to handle for customers, but also more attractive for retail outlets because the packages sold faster. Its name induced associations with a soccer team, which consisted of 11 players, thus capitalizing on the Germans' sympathy for the popular sport. Variations of the name "Krombach Eleven" were successfully used in promotion campaigns to boost sales. Looked at rather suspiciously by competitors and retail outlets at first, the novelty became a big success and was soon copied.

Despite aggressive competition among breweries in the premium segment, Krombacher Pilsener resisted the general trend of lowering its prices. On the other hand, the company only hesitantly began to offer Krombacher Pilsener in half-liter cans in 1995, because beer in cans was more often subject to price wars between brewers as well as retailers. The percentage of canned beer was kept at below 5 percent, compared to 20 percent on average for the whole beer market in Germany.

DIVERSIFICATION AND CHANGE

As Krombacher Brauerei's long-pursued one-product strategy seemed to have reached its limits of growth in the continuously shrinking German beer market of the late 1990s, the company began to expand its product range. In the summer of 1999 the brewery launched a nonalcoholic version of Krombacher Pilsener under the name Krombacher Alkoholfrei, after the technology was refined enough to produce a beer that matched the brewery's high standards for its pilsner in taste and aroma. The company also introduced new packaging units, including a six-pack, a "Star-Pack" with 18 bottles, and a five-liter party keg with a tap.

When CEO Heyden retired in 2001, he left behind an impressive legacy. Under his direction, the brewery's output more than quadrupled while sales grew almost sixfold, the result of a consistent focus on brand building and steadfastness in keeping prices relatively high. The volume of beer sold in bars and restaurants had roughly quadrupled since 1980. In 1999 Krombacher Pilsener for the first time sold more beer through retail outlets than its longtime competitor Warsteiner. Three years later Krombacher Brauerei became Germany's leading premium beer brewer.

Heyden was succeeded by Friedrich Schadeberg's 36-year-old son Bernhard Schadeberg, who had joined the company as director of finances in 1993. In response to new consumer trends, Krombacher Brauerei expanded its portfolio of branded products under Schadeberg's leadership. Targeting younger consumers, the brewery launched Cola & Beer under the brand name Cab in 2001. Later in the decade the Cab line of mixed beverages containing beer was further extended. Two major highlights were the introduction of Krombacher Radler, a combination of beer and soda pop, in 2002, and the launch of Krombacher Weizen, a wheat beer, in 2007. In 2003 Krombacher Brauerei acquired Eichener Brauerei, a local brewery in Kreuztal, followed in 2007 by the takeover of the Westphalian brewery Rolinck based in Steinfurt. The company also acquired a 49 percent stake in MBG International Premium Brands, a distributor of beverages to popular cafés and bars.

As sales of Krombacher Pilsener began to decrease late in the decade, the brewery took the next strategic step when it entered the market for nonalcoholic beverages by acquiring a license for the Schweppes line of nonalcoholic soft drinks for Germany and Austria in 2006. With an output of roughly 700,000 hectoliters of Schweppes Original Bitter Lemon, Lemon Light, Indian Tonic Water, and American Ginger Ale, the leading German brand in the bitter nonalcoholic soft-drinks segment brought in about EUR 65 million in sales in 2007. In the increasingly competitive and consolidating German beer market, it remained to be seen if the family-owned brewery would be able to stand its ground among about a dozen large premium beer brewers, including the global brewery giants whose takeover offers Krombacher Brauerei's owners, until then, had refused to accept.

Evelyn Hauser

PRINCIPAL SUBSIDIARIES

MBG International Premium Brands GmbH (49.8%); Privatbrauerei A. Rolinck GmbH & Co. KG; Eichener Gebr. Schweinsfurth GmbH.

PRINCIPAL COMPETITORS

Anheuser-Busch InBev; Carlsberg A/S; Bitburger Holding GmbH; Brau Holding International GmbH & Co. KGaA; Karlsberg Brauerei KG Weber.

FURTHER READING

"Absatz von Krombacher stagniert," *Lebensmittel Zeitung,* December 24, 1998, p. 8.

Baumann, Hans, "So zapft der Bier-Guru seine Erfolge; Günter Heyden kreierte den Krombacher-Kasten," *Welt,* March 22, 1999.

"Das Unternehmergespräch," *Frankfurter Allgemeine Zeitung,* July 8, 2002, p. 13.

"Friedrich Schadeberg 80 Jahre," *Frankfurter Allgemeine Zeitung,* April 22, 2000, p. 17.

Keun, Christian, and Martin Scheele, "Eine Perle aus dem Rothaargebirge," *Manager Magazine Online,* June 23, 2003.

"Krombacher ueberholt Warsteiner," *Frankfurter Allgemeine Zeitung,* February 3, 2000, p. 31.

"Krombacher uebernimmt Markenrechte fuer Schweppes in Deutschland und Oesterreich," *News Aktuell Schweiz,* May 12, 2006.

"Krombacher übernimmt westfälische Privatbrauerei Rolinck," *VWD Wirtschaftsnachrichten,* January 5, 2007.

"Krombacher will kräftig in die Marke investieren," *Frankfurter Allgemeine Zeitung,* January 19, 2005, p. 21.

Pilar, Gabriel von, "Aufstieg zum Fernsehbier," *Lebensmittel Zeitung,* November 3, 2000, p. 38.

Roth, Frank, "Mehr als nur Bier," *Bestseller Magazin,* April 25, 2006.

Vossen, Manfred, "Krombacher stoesst an die Grenzen," *Lebensmittel Zeitung,* October 17, 2008, p. 14.

Weihrauch, Franz-J., "Kurze Geschichte der Krombacher Brauerei," in *Krombacher: Brauwesen im Siegerland,* Christian W. Thomsen ed., Siegen, Germany: Vorländer GmbH & Co. KG, 2005, 123 p.

Land and Houses PCL

———■———

37-38/F Q House Lumpini Building
1 S Sathorn Road
Tunghamek, Sathorn
Bangkok, 10500
Thailand
Telephone: (66 02) 343 8900
Fax: (66 02) 237 9861
Web site: http://www.lh.co.th

Public Company
Incorporated: 1983
Employees: 450
Sales: THB 16,008 million ($482.3 million) (2008)
Stock Exchanges: Thailand
Ticker Symbol: LH
NAICS: 237210 Land Subdivision

■ ■ ■

Land and Houses PCL (LH) is Thailand's leading residential property development group. The company operates through a network of nine subsidiaries, four of which, Quality Houses, Polar Property, and Land & Houses Property Funds 1 and 2, are directly active in property development. LH is also the main shareholder in two related businesses, Quality Construction Products, a producer of concrete blocks, and Home Product Center, Thailand's leading do-it-yourself (DIY) and home improvement retailer. Based on a "mass customization" concept, the company sells fully completed properties, including furniture, appliances, decoration, and even landscaping.

In 2008 the company sold more than 58,000 properties, primarily in the greater Bangkok region, as well as in other major Thai urban centers, including Chiang Mai, Khon Kaen, Nakhon Ratchasima, and Phuket. Detached houses account for nearly 92 percent of its revenues, followed by condominiums and apartments (2.3 percent) and town houses (1.7 percent). Other businesses controlled by LH include Kasemrad Prachachuen Hospital; Asia Asset Advisory Co.; and Land and Houses Retail Bank, which is expected to complete a public offering in 2009. Land and Houses PCL is led by founder and chairman Anant Asavabhokhin and is listed on the Thailand Stock Exchange. The company posted revenues of THB 16,008 million ($482.3 million) in 2008.

THAI HOUSE BUILDER IN 1973

Anant Asavabhokhin completed a bachelor's degree in civil engineering at Thailand's Chulalongkorn University, and then traveled to the United States, where he received a master's degree in industrial engineering from the Illinois Institute of Technology in 1973. Asavabhokhin returned to Thailand, where he later earned a master's degree in business administration from Thammasat University as well. In the meantime Asavabhokhin went to work for his mother, Piangjai Harnpanich, who owned land in the Bangkok region. The mother-son team launched their first development project, called Baan Srirubusik in 1973. That project targeted Thailand's small but growing middle class with a series of modest single-story houses.

This endeavor nearly ended Asavabhokhin's real estate career. The oil crisis of the early 1970s caused

Thailand's budding housing market to collapse,
especially as interest rates soared past 20 percent. As a
result Asavabhokhin struggled to sell the Srirubusik
properties. Sales finally picked up toward the end of the
decade. This encouraged Asavabhokhin and his mother
to launch a number of new housing projects, including
Baan Thanintorn, Baan Prachachuen, and Baan
Suknatee. By then the family was one of many builders
in what remained a highly fragmented construction
industry. At the same time much of the country's housing market remained dominated by landowners, who
often launched construction projects as a side business.
As a result the Thai housing sector suffered from a lack
of professionalism.

HOMEBUILDING U.S.-STYLE IN 1983

Asavabhokhin's experience in the United States had
exposed him to Western homebuilding concepts, and
notably the focus on constructing subdivisions, rather
than focusing on individual properties. An important
moment in Asavabhokhin's career came in the early
1980s when he met and became friends with Bruce
Karatz. Karatz had recently returned to the United
States from France, where he helped establish the
Marseille and Lyon branches of building giant Kaufman
& Broad (later KB Homes). In 1980 Karatz was appointed president of KB's California business, which he
helped expand into one of the United States' largest
home developers. By 1985 Karatz had gained the CEO
spot at KB. He later became the group's chairman, a
post he held until early 2009, when he was indicted for
securities fraud and pleaded guilty to obstruction of
justice charges.

In the early 1980s, however, Karatz often received
Asavabhokhin on his trips to the United States, allowing
him to study KB's fast-growing Los Angeles operations.
Asavabhokhin recognized the potential for introducing
the U.S.-style subdivision concept into the Thai market.

In 1983 he set up a new company, called Land and
Houses (LH), as well as a project development
subsidiary, Quality Houses. The company became one
of the first in Thailand to focus solely on the homebuilding market.

With an initial capital base of just $200,000 Asav-
abhokhin acquired his first project in August of that
year, when he bought the Prueksachart housing development from a subsidiary of Thai Farmers' Bank. Asavabhokhin then turned his attention to developing the
company's first full-scale project. Based on market
research LH introduced what it called a "Consumer
Oriented" approach to homebuilding. The result was
the launch of Nuntawan, a subdivision of single-family
homes designed after the American style, established in
Chiang Mai, the second largest city in Thailand.

STOCK LISTING IN 1989

Bangkok quickly became LH's primary market,
however, as the company rushed to supply homes to the
city's booming and increasingly wealthy population. LH
also adapted to the rapidly changing homebuyer market
in Thailand. Where previously several generations of a
family lived under the same roof, the new generation of
urban, upwardly mobile Thais had begun to seek out
separate homes. At the same time the increasing wealth
of the middle and upper-middle classes brought about
new consumer demands. The relatively simple homes
that had been built during the 1970s gave way to
increasingly elaborate properties.

LH kept abreast of these changes, responding with
the launch of a new subdivision development, the Siwa-
lee, in Rangsit, in 1984. The success of the project,
completed in 1986, helped establish LH as one of the
country's leading independent homebuilders. The
company also inspired a wave of competitors who
sought to capitalize on LH's business model. Yet many
among this new wave of builders proved highly unreli-
able, often delivering homes after excessively long delays
that suffered from poor workmanship, and even lacked
features and equipment that had been part of the
purchase price.

LH actually benefited from this sort of competition
because the company had established a strong reputation
for the high quality of its homes. Thia reputation also
helped ensure the success of its initial public offering
when the company listed on the Thailand Stock
Exchange in 1989. The group's Quality Homes
subsidiary, which branched out into developing serviced
apartments in 1990, also went public, in 1993. The
company's strong reputation helped attracted a number
of high-profile institutional investors including Fidelity

KEY DATES

1983: Anant Asavabhokhin founds Land and Houses, and Quality Houses, in order to build American-style residential subdivisions in Thailand.

1989: Land and Houses goes public on the Thailand Stock Exchange.

2001: Land and Houses launches its "mass customization" concept of fully completed home sales.

2005: Land and Houses forms Land and Houses Retail Bank.

2009: Land and Houses Retail Bank announces plans to go public.

Emerging Markets and Merrill Lynch Dragon for both listings.

NEW MARKETS

By the middle of the 1990s LH was building more than 3,000 homes per year, with prices ranging widely from $40,000 to as high as $1 million. The company's sales had grown dramatically, jumping from THB 500 million ($16 million) in 1989 to more than THB 10,000 million ($320 million) by the end of 1994. The company's market capitalization had grown similarly, from THB 200 million in 1989 to THB 100 billion. Asavabhokhin's own net worth was estimated at THB 50 billion.

Asavabhokhin attributed the company's success that year to its strong research and its willingness to adapt to consumer demand. As he explained to *Forbes:* "We treat houses as a consumer product. You have to be close to the client because people's lifestyles change fast."

LH leveraged its success in the mid-1990s with an extension into a number of new areas. In 1995 the group invested in building materials, becoming the major shareholder in Quality Construction Products Co., which manufactured the cement blocks used to build the company's homes. At the other end of the home sales spectrum, LH joined in the founding of Home Products Center Co., which began developing the HomePro network of retail DIY and home improvement stores.

LH also sought to replicate its success in other markets. The company targeted other Thai cities, such as Phuket, the popular tourism destination, acquiring a 55 percent stake in the Muangmai Group there in 1995.

The company also joined an investment consortium, which included the Government of Singapore Investment Corporation and OCBC Capital Management, to launch a housing development operation there. Similarly, the company targeted the Philippines, forming a joint venture, ML&H Corporation, with Manuela Corporation there.

REBUILDING INTO THE 21ST CENTURY

Land and Houses, like the rest of the Thai building market, faced a new test in the late 1990s. Thailand was among the hardest hit by the economic crisis that swept through the Asian region from 1997. Almost overnight, LH's share price plummeted by some 10,000 percent, reducing its market capitalization to just THB 200 million. The company also found itself heavily burdened by its exposure to the foreign currency markets through its debt load, which was primarily denominated in yen and U.S. dollars. As a result, the company's debt soared from just THB 4 billion to more than THB 25 billion.

LH teetered on the verge of disaster as the company remained confronted with the collapse of the Thai housing market. The crisis had sent many of the country's homebuilders into bankruptcy stranding large numbers of homebuyers with unfinished or nonexisting properties. Despite the precarious condition of his own company, Asavabhokhin remained determined to keep the business afloat. As he explained to *Worldsources Online:* "I realised that if I did nothing then we would eventually have to close down our business altogether."

Asavabhokhin was able to negotiate with the company's banks, which agreed to extend credit to the company's customers. He also renegotiated the interest payments of the group's debts, a move which saved enough money to allow the company to maintain all 500 of its employees on its payroll. The company then took advantage of the lack of home sales to revamp the group's information technology system, establishing a new infrastructure and database that would provide the heart of the group's future growth.

The company had to find a way to market an inventory of 500 finished homes. LH took the unusual step of shutting down its sales offices, choosing instead to print a catalog containing photos of these homes, which was then placed in newspaper. The result exceeded expectations: within two days, the company had sold all 500 properties.

INVENTING A NEW HOME SALES MODEL

Asavabhokhin recognized the potential of developing an entirely new sales model. Instead of building homes based on architectural drawings, the company decided to shift its sales approach to offering only completed homes including interior decorations, landscaping, furniture and appliances. Toward this end, the company conducted new market research to determine consumer demand, and developed a number of different home models. This effort led to the development of the company's Baan Sabai design concept in 1999.

By building and finishing homes before selling them, the company was able to achieve strong cost reductions while also guaranteeing the quality of the finished product to wary homebuyers. Fueling the company's new business strategy was its decision to pay down its debt. For this, the company raised new capital, selling a stake in the LH to Government Investment Corporation of Singapore.

By 2001 LH had shifted its single home sales strategy entirely to the Baan Sabai complete house concept. LH became credited with almost single-handedly restarting the Thai housing market, as its sales strategy inspired a new wave of home buyers. The company also refined its construction techniques, developing its Pre-Fabricated Wall technology in 2003. The success of the Baan Sabai sales concept encouraged the company to roll out the strategy to other properties, including condominiums in 2004. Single family homes nonetheless remained the group's primary activity, accounting for nearly 75 percent of the more than 3,000 properties the company sold each year, and nearly 92 percent of group revenues.

LH, together with Quality Houses, also sought to extend its operations into the financial sector. In 2005 the company's finance arm, Land & Houses Credit Foncier merged with Book Club Finance. The operation was then renamed as Land and Houses Retail Bank. The new bank at first focused on the home mortgage sector before expanding its operations to become a full commercial bank in the later years of the first decade of the 2000s. LH Bank then made plans to go public before the end of 2009.

The political upheavals in Thailand in 2008, coupled with the global economic collapse, caused a new slowdown for LH, which saw its revenues slip by nearly 16 percent in 2008. However, the company remained financially solid and in early 2009 unveiled plans to launch 12 new residential projects worth more than THB 16 billion. The company intended to sell 3,300 properties in 2009—73 percent of which were slated to be single-family homes, with 11 percent town houses, and 16 percent condominiums. LH—which, combined with Quality Houses, claimed to have the largest combined market share on the Thailand Stock Exchange—remained Thailand's leading homebuilder.

M. L. Cohen

PRINCIPAL SUBSIDIARIES

Asia Asset Advisory Company Ltd. (39.99%); Home Product Center Public Company Ltd. (30.23%); Kasemrad Prachachuen Hospital; LH Muang Mai Co., Ltd. (55%); Quality Construction Products Public Co., Ltd.; Quality Houses Public Co., Ltd. (24.86%); Atlantic Real Estate Co., Ltd. (99.99%); Bangkok Chain Hospital PCL (28.73%); L&H Property Co., Ltd. (60%); L&H Sathon Co., Ltd. (99.99%); Land and Houses Retail Bank PCL (42.12%); LH Asset Co., Ltd. (99.99%); LH Real Estate Co., Ltd. (99.99%); Pacific Real Estate Co., Ltd. (99.99%); Polar Property Holdings Corporation Co., Ltd. (25%); Polar Property Holdings, Corporation (Philippines); Pt Anekagriya Buminusa Co., Ltd. (Indonesia); Pt Putra Prabukarya Co., Ltd. (Indonesia); Siam Tanee Property Co., Ltd. (99.99%); Siam Tanee Real Estate Co., Ltd. (99.99%).

PRINCIPAL DIVISIONS

Construction Material Business; Consultantcy Investment/Bank Business; Hospital Business; Property Business.

PRINCIPAL OPERATING UNITS

Condominiums; Detached Houses; Land; Townhouses.

PRINCIPAL COMPETITORS

Central Group of Cos.; Sansiri PCL; Sojitz (Thailand) Company Ltd.; Sumitomo Corporation Thailand Ltd.

FURTHER READING

"Anant Asavabhokhin, President, Land & Houses, Thailand," *Business Week*, June 9, 2003, p. 55.

Chanjindamanee, Siriporn, and Thanong Khanthong, "Rebuilt from the Ground Up," *Worldsources Online*, June 14, 2004.

Katharangsiporn, Kanana, "Confident LH to Invest B4.6bn," *Bangkok Post*, February 27, 2008.

———, "Land & Houses Keeps Investing Despite Slump," *Bangkok Post*, August 17, 2005.

———, "LH to Vary Units for Growth," *Bangkok Post*, March 3, 2009.

———, "Thailand's Land & Houses Brings Pre-Built Approach to Condos," *Bangkok Post*, June 1, 2004.

"Land & Houses CEO Offers Ideas on How to Revive Economy," *Thai Press Reports,* March, 16, 2009.

"Land & Houses Diversifies Types of Residential Units for Sale," *Thai Press Reports,* March 3, 2009.

"LH Bank Expects IPO in 2009," *Bangkok Post,* August 20, 2008.

Parnsoonthorn, Krissana, "LH to Spend B8bn on Expansion," *Bangkok Post,* November 18, 2003.

Parnsoonthorn, Krissana, and Darana Chudasri, "Land & Houses Bank to Open Early in 2006," *Bangkok Post,* August 5, 2005.

"Price Is Always Rights at L&H," *Worldsources Online,* December 8, 2004.

Tanzer, Andrew, "A Yuppie Is a Yuppie, Wherever He Lives," *Forbes,* November 7, 1994, p. 60.

"Thai Property Developer Land & Houses to Launch 13 Projects This Year," *Thai Press Reports,* March 3, 2005.

Larry H. Miller Group of Companies

9350 South 150 East, Suite 1000
Sandy, Utah 84070-2721
U.S.A.
Telephone: (801) 563-4100
Fax: (801) 563-4198
Web site: http://www.lhm.com

Private Company
Incorporated: 1979 as Larry H. Miller Toyota
Employees: 7,000
Sales: $3 billion (2009 est.)
NAICS: 551112 Offices of Other Holding Companies; 441110 New Car Dealers; 441120 Used Car Dealers; 711211 Sports Teams and Clubs; 512131 Motion Picture Theaters (Except Drive-Ins); 513112 Radio Stations; 513120 Television Broadcasting; 522220 Sales Financing; 532112 Passenger Car Leasing; 233110 Land Subdivision and Land Development; 448190 Other Clothing Stores; 531120 Lessors of Nonresidential Buildings

■ ■ ■

The Larry H. Miller Group of Companies comprises roughly 80 subsidiaries and ranks as the one of the largest auto dealer groups in the United States. It includes 40 auto dealerships in six states (Utah, Arizona, Colorado, Idaho, New Mexico, Oregon). From acquiring his first dealership in 1979 to his death in 2009, company founder Larry Miller sold about one million cars of more than 20 different brands. Related businesses include a motorcycle and ATV dealership in Portland, Oregon, and auto-finance companies. In 2005 the group opened the Miller Motorsports Park to the west of Salt Lake in Tooele, Utah.

The family-owned group is involved in more than just vehicles. Its influence is so pervasive that virtually every resident of the Salt Lake Valley does some form of business with one of the Miller companies. The group also owns the Utah Jazz team in the National Basketball Association (NBA) and the Salt Lake Bees, a minor league baseball team. Miller built Salt Lake City's EnergySolutions Arena (formerly the Delta Center), the home of the Jazz, which is also used for concerts, other entertainment, and business conferences. Miller's additional business holdings include KJZZ-TV and a pair of AM radio stations, the Jordan Commons office/entertainment complex in suburban Salt Lake City, roughly 25 Fanzz sports apparel stores, and several theaters along the Wasatch Front. The group's charities have funded education in particular, sponsoring hundreds of scholarship students and building an entrepreneurial center for the local community college system.

MILLER'S BACKGROUND

Born in 1955, Larry H. Miller grew up in Salt Lake City, the son of an oil refinery worker and a homemaker. Even in the sixth grade, Miller demonstrated his entrepreneurial bent by using money from his paper route to acquire more marbles, baseball cards, stamps, pennies, and pigeons than any other kid on his block. After he graduated from West High School in 1962, he worked as a framer in his uncle's

COMPANY PERSPECTIVES

The company that began in 1979 as a single Toyota Dealership has blossomed into one of the nations 200 largest privately owned companies in the United States. From the nucleus of a single location with fewer than 30 employees has become a collection of businesses ranging from Automobiles to Racetracks. In 27 years the organization has grown to over 7,000 employees in six states. Generating over $3 Billion in revenue and showing little signs of slowing down.

construction company. However, in November 1963, with the end of the building season, Miller found a job at American Auto Parts as a driver and apprentice counterman. In 1968 he took another position as a parts manager at Peck & Shaw Toyota in Murray, a Salt Lake City suburb.

In the meantime, Miller honed his skills as an outstanding softball pitcher for Salt Lake City adult teams. To play in a fast-pitch league, he moved to Denver, where he became the parts manager of the Stevenson Toyota dealership. In three years Miller turned around that dealership's parts operation from one of the poorest in sales to become Toyota's national leader. It became the first Toyota dealership in the nation to sell $1 million in parts and then $2 million in one year. "Larry did a phenomenal job," said Gene Osborn, a partner in the Denver dealership, in the May 2, 1999, *Salt Lake Tribune,* adding, "He was intense and committed to his job."

In his mid-thirties, Miller worked 90 hours a week as the operations manager of five Denver Toyota dealerships, but bigger opportunities soon arose for the ambitious man with a growing family. In 1979 Miller was looking for something new after Gene Osborn left to start a solo dealership. While in Salt Lake City to attend a wedding, Miller visited Hugh Gardner, a friend who was a partner in Universal Toyota in Murray. After years of asking Gardner if he would sell his dealership, Miller was surprised when Gardner finally consented.

THE EARLY CAR DEALERSHIPS

On April 6, 1979, Miller paid Gardner $20,000 in earnest money. He also used the rest of his own savings and a $200,000 bank loan to pay Gardner, and then agreed to pay the balance of the $3.5 million price in $17,000 monthly payments for ten years. Deep in debt,

Miller risked much in 1979 when he began buying his first dealership. "If I'd stopped to think about it, it would have scared me and I probably would not have done it," recalled Miller in the May 2, 1999, *Salt Lake Tribune.* Later in 1979 he purchased a second dealership in Spokane, Washington, but later sold it. In 1980 he bought an undercapitalized dealership in Phoenix that turned out to be his best-selling operation. In 1983 Miller paid about $2 million for Gordon Wilson Chevrolet in Murray, and by 1984 he owned six dealerships.

According to the Utah Division of Corporations, on December 30, 1986, the new Larry H. Miller Corporation was created as a Utah corporation. It consolidated Cottonwood Chrysler-Plymouth, Inc; Miller Imports Ltd.; Larry H. Miller Hyundai; Larry H. Miller Leasing; and Larry H. Miller Toyota.

In October 1990 the Larry H. Miller Lexus dealership was officially dedicated at 5701 South State Street in Salt Lake City. The new $2.8 million, 16,000-square-foot dealership offered two cars made by the Toyota division: the smaller, less-expensive ES 250, and the upscale LS 400 that competed with Mercedes-Benz, Jaguar, BMW, and the Nissan Infinity. By 1990 Miller owned 16 dealerships in Utah, Colorado, New Mexico, and Arizona, and was ranked as Utah's largest car dealer and the 17th largest in the nation. He employed 1,500 in the four states. In 1989 he sold 21,953 cars and recorded gross revenues of $310.77 million.

Such fast-paced growth required some changes, however. "We made a major change in our management style about two years ago," said Miller in the November 1990 *Utah Holiday.* "For the first eight years, we managed primarily on a basis that we would be successful if we continued to market and merchandise aggressively, and continued to grow and control expenses reasonably well. The last two years taught us we couldn't do that. We've made a lot of adjustments and started to utilize very stringent cost control methods." Because of the tough times, Miller said there had "been a certain number of casualties. ... And I don't think there's any question that there are too many dealers."

OWNERSHIP OF THE UTAH JAZZ

Meanwhile, the professional basketball team Miller would eventually buy struggled on the court and at the box office. Original owner Sam Battistone in 1974 had started the New Orleans Jazz and named the club for the birthplace of jazz music. Although the team had star "Pistol" Pete Maravich, in five seasons in New Orleans it failed to win even half its games. Battistone moved the franchise to Salt Lake City, where in its initial 1979–80 season it continued its losing ways.

KEY DATES

1979: Larry H. Miller buys his first auto dealership in a suburb of Salt Lake City.

1985: Miller acquires a half-interest in the Utah Jazz basketball franchise and buys the remainder the following year.

1991: The Delta Center opens as a venue for Jazz games and other events.

1998: Work begins on Jordan Commons office complex.

2005: Miller Motorsports Park opens in Tooele, Utah.

2006: The Delta Center is renamed EnergySolutions Arena.

2009: Larry Miller dies; his son Greg Miller carries on as CEO.

Colorful Frank Layden, who became head coach in 1981, helped to turn things around eventually. Key players drafted during this period were Mark Eaton, the center from the University of California–Los Angeles, in 1982; Thurl Bailey from North Carolina State in 1983; and little-known guard John Stockton from Gonzaga University in 1984. The Utah Jazz in the 1983–84 season achieved their first winning record and for the first time went to the NBA playoffs.

In spite of the winning season, by 1985 Sam Battistone had lost $17 million after 11 seasons of owning the Jazz. Larry Miller was concerned about the persistent rumors the Jazz might leave small-market Salt Lake City for greener pastures. In 1985, as a successful car dealer, he was asked if he would like to be one of several investors each putting up $200,000 to support the team and become limited partners. Miller declined because he felt that piecemeal approach would not work, but he negotiated another deal. On April 11, 1985, he purchased half of the Utah Jazz for $8 million from Battistone. Then 14 months later Miller paid about $14 million for the second half of the Jazz franchise. He borrowed much of that money, thus assuming major debts for the second time in his career.

Miller's first season as the Jazz owner, 1985–86, was also the first for Karl Malone, drafted in 1985 after playing at Louisiana Tech. Initially, Malone knew little about Utah and was disappointed with the draft result. Author Clay Latimer wrote, "When Karl Malone arrived in Salt Lake City in 1985, he couldn't make a free throw, hit a jumper, decipher a game plan, and he

lacked the emotional resources and ruthlessness to make himself into a first-rank power forward, according to his plentiful critics. The Utah Jazz, meanwhile, was a burlesque of an NBA franchise."

Jazz Coach Frank Layden saw Malone's potential, which eventually earned him the nickname of "The Mailman" for delivering what the team needed. By his third season, Malone averaged more than 25 points per game. With guard John Stockton racking up record numbers of assists, Jazz fans loved to hear the phrase "Stockton to Malone" again and again. After putting together a winning combination, Layden early in the 1988–89 season resigned as the Jazz coach to become its president. Assistant Coach Jerry Sloan, a former NBA star, took over as head coach.

THE DELTA CENTER

With his car dealerships and Jazz ownership a success, Larry Miller decided to go into debt for a third time to build a new sports and entertainment arena called the Delta Center. The Salt Palace simply was not large enough to hold a sufficient number of Jazz fans. In 1990 Miller invested $5 million of his own money and borrowed $66 million to build the new sports/entertainment center that seated more than 19,000.

Jay Francis, senior vice-president for marketing, negotiated with Smith's Food & Drug Centers and Franklin Quest (later renamed Franklin Covey) before the Jazz sold Delta Air Lines the rights to use its name on the new facility. Owner Larry Miller disliked such commercialization of sports but realized it was an economic necessity as the cost of players' salaries and operating expenses escalated faster than ticket prices. Francis also played a crucial role in selling the Delta Center's 56 luxury suites. Originally, in 1990 and 1991, one could buy a suite for $50,000 to $95,000 a year. However, like everything else in the NBA, including season tickets and players' salaries, the cost of the suites increased, to between $78,000 and $130,000 in 1999.

On October 9, 1991, the Delta Center was dedicated, and the Utah Jazz played their first game in the new arena that fall. On October 22, 1991, the Delta Center held its first rock concert when the group Oingo Boingo came to Salt Lake City. President J. C. O'Neil of United Concerts, in the September 19, 1991, *Salt Lake Tribune,* said the new building's seating capacity, along with better power sources and improved access for those with disabilities, made such concerts possible.

Another feature was the Sony Jumbotron Video System, a four-sided 9-by-12-foot screen that showed both live performances and instant replay, more important for sports teams. Scott Williams, the Delta

Center's general manager, reported that its designers took good ideas from other sports arenas and that it closely resembled Milwaukee's Bradley Center. Although the Delta Center hosted mainly sports and entertainment, large business meetings were also held there. For example, Dexter Yager, a major Amway distributor, held annual conventions in the Delta Center, attracting thousands of people who booked most of the city's hotels.

In January 1993 Miller finally realized that his business success had cost him a lot of time away from his wife Gail and their children. In line with his Mormon beliefs, Miller found more time for his children and grandchildren as the decade progressed, while still promoting his businesses. A popular speaker, Miller once spoke at a college symposium for 11 hours straight. He even said in the November 1996 *Home-Court* magazine, a Jazz publication, that he did not sell cars or own the Jazz for a living: "What I do for a living is talk."

OTHER VENTURES

After five years of owning the Golden Eagles, a professional hockey team in Salt Lake City, in 1994 Miller sold the team that had lost about $1 million each year. The franchise left the city and became the Detroit Vipers. To promote his businesses, including the Utah Jazz, his car dealerships, the Delta Center, KJZZ-TV, Pro Image retail stores, and Salt Lake City's Thrifty Car Rental, in 1995 Miller started his own in-house advertising agency called LHM Advertising. Working out of the Jazz headquarters in the Delta Center, Jay Francis, the Jazz marketing vice-president who managed the new ad agency, said it used direct mail and telephoning to market the businesses, in addition to more traditional methods such as radio, billboard, and TV advertising.

In 1996 the NBA Board of Governors approved the formation of the Women's National Basketball Association (WNBA), and Salt Lake City was chosen as one of the eight cities to sponsor charter teams. Larry Miller's Utah Starzz thus helped make women's basketball history. In June 1999 the WNBA's 12 teams started the league's third season. After a rocky start, the league was maturing. For example, its teams enjoyed an average attendance of 10,000 fans per game in the 1998 season, far more than had been expected.

The retail division of the Utah Jazz had started in March 1987 when the Jazz purchased four Pro Image shops that sold sports apparel and other gifts and souvenirs. In 1996 the Jazz ended any association with Pro Image and changed the name of their stores to Fanzz. By March 1999, 28 Fanzz stores, including 15 stores in Idaho, California, Colorado, and New Mexico, sold items with the Jazz logo, as well as hats, shirts, and other items promoting the Utah Starzz, Utah's college teams, professional teams in other cities, and two teams not owned by Larry Miller, the Utah Grizzlies professional hockey team and the Salt Lake Buzz minor league baseball team.

Although retail sales were a minor part of Larry Miller's businesses, the Fanzz stores were profitable. Shauna Smith pointed out in 1999 that, "Few NBA teams have ventured into the retail business. Teams like the Phoenix Suns, Detroit Pistons, and Orlando Magic are involved in the business, but no team comes even close to the retail involvement of the Utah Jazz."

BUILDING FOR THE FUTURE

In 1999 the financial world considered the Utah Jazz to be one of the NBA's best-managed franchises. In March, Morgan Stanley along with First Security Bank of Utah helped refinance the $50 million that Larry Miller still owed on the Delta Center. Investors were encouraged by the Jazz's strong fan base, aided by the team's *Home-Court* magazine started in 1998 and increased season ticket sales. Investors also knew that the Utah Jazz had gone to the NBA finals two years in a row in the late 1990s and consistently for many years participated in the playoffs, thus making them one of the NBA's best teams. Standard & Poor's Corporate Rating Service gave the March 1999 refinancing a "low-A" grade, the highest it had ever given for a sports or entertainment deal. In addition to Miller's Delta Center debts, in 1999 he also owed about $92 million for buildings and land used by his car dealerships.

After opening his first Sandy car dealership a few years earlier, Larry Miller sought ways to promote business and entertainment in the Salt Lake City suburb. He and other car dealers invested in a huge auto mall in Sandy. In addition, in 1997 Miller purchased and then demolished the old Jordan High School on 9400 South State Street in Sandy. At a West High School assembly, Miller told the students that in 1962, his senior year at West High, the school lost the state basketball championship to Jordan High School. "It has been a burr under my saddle," added Miller jokingly in the January 17, 1998, *Salt Lake Tribune.* "So, I bought the old Jordan High and tore that sucker down. It took 35 years, but we got even."

Miller then began construction of a new office and entertainment building called the Jordan Commons. It was to include 270,000 feet of office space, a 35,000-square-foot Mexican restaurant, and a 17-screen multiplex theater. The project was completed in 1999 for a price tag of $110 million.

CONTINUED SUCCESS

In late 1998, also in Sandy, Miller began construction of a two-story Larry H. Miller Entrepreneurship Training Center in partnership with Salt Lake Community College. Miller planned to give the $7 million building, land, and accompanying parking lot to the college. Sterling Francom, director of the college's entrepreneurship program that started in 1990, said in the November 12, 1998, *Deseret News* that the new facility would "be able to accommodate upwards of 5,000 to 7,000 people annually through the training program. … There's no other place in the country that will have such a thing as this."

"I have to consider myself fortunate," said Larry Miller in the November 1990 *Utah Holiday.* "It's proof the American dream is alive and well." To encourage others to take the risks necessary to fulfill their dreams of owning their own business, Miller supported Salt Lake Community College and other programs with not only funding but also his time. For example, he taught a graduate class on entrepreneurship at the Brigham Young University School of Management.

In 1999 Miller's companies were overseen by two men. Richard Nelson served as president of the Larry H. Miller Group of Automotive Companies. Dennis Haslam, who had founded the law firm of Winder and Haslam, had served since 1997 as the president of the Larry H. Miller Group of Sports and Entertainment Companies.

Although Miller took numerous risks trying new business ventures, his management style also included long-term relationships. For example, he helped veterans John Stockton and Karl Malone start their own dealerships in the late 1990s. Three of his vice-presidents by 1999 had served a combined 54 years with the Utah Jazz: David Allred, vice-president, public relations; Jay Francis, senior vice-president, marketing; and Grant Harrison, vice-president, promotions and game operations. Jazz President and Utah Starzz Coach Frank Layden also spent many years with the Jazz. "Hot Rod" Hundley was the voice of the Jazz on both radio and TV for about 25 years. Such continuity, somewhat rare among other professional teams and businesses, might have seemed old-fashioned, but it was part of Miller's formula for continued success.

The center of the group, the dealerships, continued to expand. In July 2000 Miller added a pair of family-owned dealerships near Albuquerque, New Mexico, to three existing ones he owned or co-owned there. In 2001 Miller bought back four dealerships Ford Motor Co. had two years earlier compelled him to surrender to its short-lived Utah Auto Collection experiment, a collection of a dozen manufacturer-owned stores. The Miller Group ranked as high as the tenth largest car dealership in the nation. By 2008 the auto group alone had sales of $2.5 billion or more.

SUCCESSION

Larry H. Miller's son Greg was named CEO of the group in June 2008 after his father suffered a heart attack that put him in the hospital for two months. The company was governed by a 13-member advisory board; Larry Miller's other children were involved in various areas of the business; and Gail Miller remained co-owner.

Greg Miller, a baseball fan and avid cyclist, had been working at the dealerships since his father bought the first one in 1979. After doing odd jobs around the sales lot, Greg Miller moved to the parts department and spent most of the next decade and a half working in the automotive group. He ran his own graphics business for several years before returning to the family business working at KJZZ-TV and then the company's minor league hockey franchise, the Golden Eagles (later sold).

Greg Miller then headed the company's construction efforts for a few years before being placed in charged of several underperforming auto lots. With the help of a mentor within the group, these were eventually restored to profitability. By 2005, Larry Miller was specifically grooming his oldest son to ultimately take over leadership of the company, according to the *Deseret News.* In June 2006, after a year at corporate headquarters, Greg Miller was named senior vice-president of operations, and chiefly tasked with overseeing the Miller Motorsports Park, which opened in September 2005 to the west of Salt Lake City in Tooele, Utah.

After 2008 Larry Miller remained involved in the business, but his health continued to deteriorate due to complications of type 2 diabetes. He died February 20, 2009, at the age of 64. Miller left behind an empire employing 7,000 people and touching literally millions of lives. It was estimated that his dealerships had sold one million cars during his thirty years in car sales. He was known for sending hundreds of students to college on scholarships and had recently donated a $50 million entrepreneurship center to Salt Lake Community College.

While the succession issues were playing out, a number of visible changes had taken place. The Delta Center was renamed EnergySolutions Arena in

November 2006 after a nuclear-waste management company acquired naming rights. Larry H. Miller Group took over the Mexaplex 8 at Lehi's Thanksgiving Point in January 2005, its third theater complex to date. It then opened its giant Megaplex 20 on the outskirts of Salt Lake City in May 2006. With 5,594 seats in all, it cost $30 million to build. A 13-screen theater was added in Ogden, Utah, a year later. In January 2009 the group sold its Mayan and Spaghetti Mama's restaurants to Atlantic Restaurant Consultants of South Carolina, who had originally been hired to turn them around.

The group was not immune to the general malaise affecting the economy at the time, and the worldwide credit crunch prompted many customers to defer new car purchases. However, this was at least partially offset by improving theater attendance and revenues; 4.5 million people visited the group's theaters in 2008, Greg Miller told the *Wall Street Journal Online.*

David M. Walden
Updated, Frederick C. Ingram

PRINCIPAL SUBSIDIARIES

Prestige Financial Services, Inc.; Larry H. Miller Corporation–Oregon; Larry H. Miller Dodge, Inc.; Larry H. Miller Education Foundation; Larry H. Miller Fleet/Lease, Inc.; Larry H. Miller Luxury Cars; Larry H. Miller Restaurants, Inc.; Larry H. Miller Theatres, Inc.; Larry H. Miller Used Car Supermarket, Inc.; Larry H. Miller Communications Corporation; Larry H. Miller Corporation–5650 South State; Larry H. Miller Corporation–90th South; Larry H. Miller Corporation–Avondale; Larry H. Miller Corporation–Boise; Larry H. Miller Corporation–Denver; Larry H. Miller Corporation–Colorado Inc.; Larry H. Miller Corporation–Colorado South; Larry H. Miller of Colorado Springs Inc.; Larry H. Miller Corporation–Mesa; Larry H. Miller Arena Corporation; Prestige Financial Services, Inc.; Larry H. Miller Corporation–New Mexico; Larry H. Miller Corporation–Oklahoma.

PRINCIPAL DIVISIONS

Dealerships; Sports & Entertainment.

PRINCIPAL COMPETITORS

Burt Automotive Network; Penske Automotive Group, Inc.; Lithia Motors, Inc.; Mark Miller Auto Group.

FURTHER READING

Bailey, Jeff, "Driven (Legacy: Larry H. Miller, 1944–2009)," *Inc.,* May 2009, p. 116.

Buttars, Lori, "Delta Center to House Rock Concerts in Addition to Jazz," *Salt Lake Tribune,* September 19, 1991, p. B6.

Cates, Karl, "Larry's World: An Interview with Larry H. Miller," *Deseret News,* April 28, 1994.

———, "Long Live the Jazz," *Deseret News,* May 12, 1996, pp. A1, A8.

———, "Unknowns Suit Up for the Jazz," *Salt Lake Tribune,* May 14, 1999, pp. A1, A15.

Corcoran, Greg, "Long Toss: Questions for: Greg Miller—The Utah Jazz CEO Discusses the NBA, the Economy and Taking Over the Family Business on Short Notice," *Wall Street Journal Online,* January 14, 2009.

Dewell, Thomas R., "Miller Rides High with 15 Stores and the Utah Jazz," *Automotive News,* February 11, 1991, p. 96.

Free, Cathy, "Life with Larry: Off the Court and Showroom Floor, Miller Is Your Basic Family Man," *Salt Lake Tribune,* June 10, 1990, pp. B1–B2.

Horowitz, Alan S., "Off the Court: Jazz Greats in the Business Arena," *Utah Business,* November 1996, pp. 38–42.

House, Dawn, "Utah Mogul Expresses Faith in Sons," *Salt Lake Tribune,* Business sec., August 8, 2008.

Hundley, Rod, with Tom McEachin, *Hot Rod Hundley: "You Gotta Love It, Baby,"* Champaign, Ill.: Sports Publishing, 1998.

Kratz, Gregory, "Encouraging Entrepreneurship," *Deseret News,* November 12, 1998.

Latimer, Clay, *Special Delivery: The Amazing Basketball Career of Karl Malone,* Lenexa, Kans.: Addax Publishing Group, 1999.

Lewis, Michael C., *To the Brink: Stockton, Malone, and the Utah Jazz's Climb to the Edge of Glory,* New York: Simon and Schuster, 1998.

Pentz, Michelle, "Larry Miller Building Huge Auto Complex," *Albuquerque Journal,* November 2, 2000, p. 7.

Rattle, Barbara, "Larry H. Miller Acquires Super Ford Store, Ford Truckland," *Enterprise,* December 17, 2001, p. 1.

Robinson, Doug, "Destiny of a Dynasty," *Deseret Morning News,* September 21, 2008, p. A1.

Ryan, Kevin, "Driven to Succeed," *Utah Holiday,* November 1990, pp. 50–54, 62.

Sahm, Phil, "Miller Built Empire on Calculated Risks," *Salt Lake Tribune,* May 2, 1999.

Smith, Shauna, "Fanzz Stores Are Big Hit," *HomeCourt,* March 1999, pp. 56–57.

Snyder, Jesse, "'Always a Teacher'; His Legacy: 6-State Dealer Group That's Growing, Thanks to Succession Plan," *Automotive News,* March 2, 2009.

———, "How the Kid Got in the Picture; When Larry Miller Suffered a Heart Attack in June, the Country's 4th-Largest Private Dealership Group Had to Make a Change at the Top," *Automotive News,* August 25, 2008, p. 3.

Sorensen, Dan, "A Man of Parts," *HomeCourt,* November 1996, pp. 19–21, 64.

Swensen, Jason, "Miller Complex Halfway Complete," *Deseret News,* January 20, 1999.

Wodraska, Lya, "On Top of Utah: Miller's Influence Not Just Limited to Sports," *Salt Lake Tribune,* July 17, 2005, p. C1.

The Lewin Group Inc.

3130 Fairview Park Drive, Suite 800
Falls Church, Virginia 22031-4517
U.S.A.
Telephone: (703) 269-5500
Fax: (703) 269-5501
Web site: http://www.lewin.com

Wholly Owned Subsidiary of Ingenix, Inc.
Incorporated: 1970 as Lewin & Associates, Inc.
Employees: 200
Sales: $400 million (2007 est.)
NAICS: 541611 Administrative Management and
   General Management Consulting Services

■ ■ ■

The Lewin Group Inc. is a healthcare and human policy research and consulting firm based in Falls Church, Virginia, and especially well known for the work it performs for federal government clients. The firm also serves the needs of local and state governments, foundations, insurance companies, pharmaceutical and biotechnology companies, hospitals, and other healthcare providers. Lewin prides itself on being so widely respected that in some cases it provides studies that are employed by advocates on both sides of an issue.

Lewin offers modeling, statistics, and actuarial analysis to help clients cut costs and provides information useful in healthcare reform efforts. The firm's policy research and data analysis skills are geared to policy makers and advocates. Another important service is program evaluation in healthcare and human services,

valuable in implementing programs and policies. The firm's strategic planning services help clients with competitive market pricing, market sizing, product positioning and pricing, consensus building, and mergers and acquisitions. In addition, Lewin provide technical assistance and training.

Lewin's areas of expertise include aging and disability; children, youth, and family policy; chronic disease, cost of illness, emergency preparedness and response, health reform, Medicaid and CHIP; Medicare; mental health and substance abuse; and program integrity. Lewin Group is part of Ingenix, Inc., a major healthcare information company, which in turn is a subsidiary of giant U.S. health insurer UnitedHealth Group Inc.

FOUNDER, MEMBER OF JOHNSON ADMINISTRATION

The history of Lewin Group may be traced through that of founder Lawrence Stephen Lewin. Born in New York City in 1938, Lewin earned an undergraduate degree from Princeton University's Wilson School of Public and International Affairs, graduating cum laude in 1959. Following three years in the U.S. Marine Corps, he enrolled at the Harvard Business School, receiving a master's of business administration in 1964. Lewin then moved to the nation's capital. According to the *Wall Street Journal*, Lewin "decided he wanted to come to Washington after John Kennedy was slain and became involved in Lyndon Johnson's War on poverty."

From 1964 to 1968 Lewin served as administrative assistant to the postmaster general. After two years in

COMPANY PERSPECTIVES

The Lewin Group is a premier national health care and human services consulting firm. We understand the industry and provide our clients with high-quality products and insightful support.

the private sector he struck out on his own in 1970, forming a Washington consulting firm under the name Lewin & Associates, Inc. Lewin provided consulting services in the healthcare and energy fields. The firm was especially strong in the oil and natural gas industries, but the focus switched heavily to healthcare in the 1980s.

The energy sector underwent a major slump as oil and gas prices plummeted, forcing numerous companies out of business, a situation made worse by the poor performance of coal companies during this period. On the other hand, the increased role of the U.S. government in supervising the healthcare system created greater opportunities in the healthcare consulting market in the 1980s. Lewin & Associates became well respected during this period for its strategic planning and management expertise. By the mid-1980s the firm's annual revenues from energy consulting fell to about $4 million while the healthcare practice increased to approximately $5 million.

MERGER WITH CHIEF RIVAL: 1987

In 1987 Lewin & Associates joined forces with one of its chief rivals, ICF Inc., agreeing to be acquired by its fellow Washington-based consulting firm in a stock transaction, a move that rounded out each company's capabilities. A larger concern, ICF was led by Dr. Robert J. Rubin. After earning his M.D. from Cornell University Medical College, Rubin had served as assistant secretary in the Reagan administration's Health and Human Services Department. He then left to start a consulting firm, which, like Lewin & Associates, maintained healthcare and energy practices but also did consulting work in the engineering services and information systems fields. ICF derived about $3 million in annual sales from its healthcare practice and about $6 million from energy, in particular coal and electric utilities. Where ICF held a significant edge over Lewin & Associates was in its sophisticated data processing and computer modeling geared toward the healthcare sector.

The combined company took the name Lewin-ICF Inc., with both Larry Lewin and Robert Rubin assuming leadership roles in the organization. The firm also continued to develop the ICF computer modeling technology, which led to the creation of the Health Benefits Simulation Model, a program that not only provided an edge over competitors but was also more robust than anything the government had to offer. It made the company an ideal consultant to Washington policy makers, as well as an attractive property.

COMPANY SOLD: 1992

In late 1992 Lewin-ICF was sold to Value Health Inc., a managed care services company focused on certain niches, including mental health, drug benefits, and foot care. The addition of Lewin-ICF was part of a larger effort to help Value Health better compete in the rapidly consolidating managed-care industry.

Simultaneous to the Lewin-ICF deal, Value Health acquired a mail-order pharmacy company, struck a deal to buy an Arizona insurance company, and bought a stake in Complete Pharmacy Network with an option to buy the rest of the company later in the year. It also agreed to fund the development of another company that would analyze claims for large employers. Lewin-ICF was an attractive property because the health data analysis business was fast growing in light of changes in the country's health policy. Renamed Lewin-VHI Inc., the company continued to be run by chairman and CEO Larry Lewin and maintained its Virginia headquarters.

Healthcare policy became an even more hotly debated subject when U.S. President Bill Clinton took office in 1993 and his administration introduced a new comprehensive healthcare plan that would provide universal coverage. On its own initiative and without sponsorship, Lewin-VHI applied its sophisticated modeling software to the Clinton plan, reportedly losing about $200,000 in potential income to complete the task. It issued an assessment, concluding that while the plan could indeed pay for itself as the president maintained, it would cost employers and individuals more than what was projected.

Both advocates and opponents of the plan accepted Lewin-VHI's evaluation as a good-faith effort, indicative of how highly regarded the firm was in Washington, especially in light of Larry Lewin's position as a member of the Clinton transition team. Helping to balance the scales, of course, was Rubin's Republican convictions. There was also a standing policy in the firm that whenever dealing with something politically sensitive, both Lewin and Rubin had to review and concur on the

KEY DATES

1970: Lawrence Lewin founds Lewin & Associates, Inc.
1987: Lewin acquired by ICF Inc.
1992: Value Health Inc. acquires Lewin-ICF.
1996: Quintiles Transnational Corporation acquires Lewin-VHI and company is renamed The Lewin Group.
1998: Technology Assessment Group is acquired.
2008: Ingenix, Inc., acquires The Lewin Group.

final product. In 1994 Rubin told the *Wall Street Journal*, "We're at the point now where people say our reputation for being fair is such that we're just not going to do something in a half-baked way."

In the early 1990s, in fact, a Lewin-VHI study in hand was almost mandatory for an interest group to be taken seriously. "The days of wine, women and song are over," one healthcare lobbyist told the *Wall Street Journal* in describing the current way to influence Congress. He continued, "I don't go anywhere in this town without being armed with a Lewin-VHI study. You can't win without it." Because of its Health Benefits Simulation Model, the firm was able to offer high-quality information quickly. The analysis on the Clinton health plan, for example, required little more than a month to complete. A comparable effort conducted by the Congressional Budget Office took three times as long.

In some cases, groups on differing sides of an issue brandished Lewin-VHI studies to support their positions. Backers of the Clinton plan, for example, contended that on the basis of the firm's findings the average American could save $695 per year in healthcare expenses, while the Heritage Foundation, on the other side of the debate, pointed to their Lewin-VHI study to assert that families on average saved just $31 and that more than half of all American would actually experience an increase in healthcare costs.

The data were not tailored to suit the differing clients. Rather, the clients highlighted information from different years to make their points. To make sure that its information was not grossly distorted, Lewin-VHI retained the right to review press releases based on its research and to issue its own press release to clarify the record if necessary. From a bottom-line perspective, the healthcare reform debate and the demand for supporting data was a boon for the fortunes of Lewin-VHI, which

enjoyed a 30 percent increase in revenues to total about $20 million in 1993.

NEW OWNER: 1996

Lewin-VHI was a valuable asset for Value Health Inc., but in time the subsidiary's success had a detrimental impact as competitors began to argue that Value Health should not be awarded lucrative government contracts due to conflicts of interest related to Lewin-VHI's government work.

As a result, Value Health lost a pair of contracts it had originally won. In 1994 the company had a mental health contract for the Iowa Medicaid program taken away and awarded to another firm because Lewin-VHI had performed some policy work for Medicaid in Iowa. A year later Value Health lost a $200 million, five-year military healthcare contract because Lewin-VHI had played a role in preparing the contract's proposal request. Given that Lewin-VHI represented less than 5 percent of Value Health's annual profit, the unit cost the parent company more in lost revenue than it made. Thus, in 1995 Value Health agreed to sell Lewin-VHI to Quintiles Transnational Corporation for about $30 million in a deal that closed in July 1996. North Carolina-based Quintiles was a contract research organization, providing product development services to pharmaceutical and biotechnology companies.

Lewin-VHI was renamed The Lewin Group upon the completion of the sale, but little else changed under new ownership. Larry Lewin continued to serve as chairman and CEO, while Rubin remained president and chief operating officer. The new owner and the subsidiary hoped to generate new opportunities in the field of disease management, but for the most part it was business as usual. Lewin Group did, however, develop a new tool in 1996 to analyze state healthcare spending utilization, demographics, and government programs. Working in conjunction with the National Pharmaceutical Council, Lewin Group developed an interactive software database system that drew on more than 30 sources of information, including census data, government surveys, and proprietary data from a number of sources. The information could then be sorted by state for purposes of comparison on a variety of issues, printed out, or downloaded to disk.

Quintiles also used its deep pockets to help bolster Lewin Group through acquisition. In 1998 the firm's parent company acquired Technology Assessment Group and folded it into the medical technology/health economics practice of Lewin Group. Based in San Francisco with offices in Boston and Oxford, United Kingdom, Technology Assessment Group was an international health outcomes assessment company with expertise in patient registries and the evaluation of economic, quality-of-life, and clinical effects of drug therapies and disease management programs. In 2000 Quintiles reorganized its operation, and The Lewin Group became part of the Commercial Development service group, a member of the Commercial Development practice.

About two-thirds of Lewin Group's revenues came from government organizations that provided human and healthcare services. The remainder of its business in the new century was often associated with debatable positions taken by its private-sector clients. According to a 2007 profile in *Modern Healthcare,* Lewin Group had "earned a reputation as the 'go to' firm for beleaguered organizations in need of reports and research to support sometimes controversial positions and issues."

Examples included the 2002 and 2003 studies commissioned by the Health Industry Group Purchasing Association to calculate the savings that hospitals and other healthcare providers could derive from group purchasing organizations (GPOs), undertaken at a time when GPOs were subject to congressional scrutiny for possible anticompetitive practices. In 2004, when hospitals were under fire by Congress for aggressive billing practices, an American Hospital Association–sponsored study calculated the economic benefits hospitals brought to communities. A year later the same organization offset criticism of skyrocketing healthcare costs with a Lewin Group study that attributed the problem to increased demand for hospital services, the rising costs of goods, and a workforce shortage that led to higher wages.

INGENIX ACQUIRES LEWIN GROUP: 2008

The work conducted by The Lewin Group received greater scrutiny after Quintiles elected to sell the unit in 2007 to Ingenix, Inc., a deal that was consummated in the spring of 2008. Ingenix was a health information technology company launched by health insurer United-Health Group Inc. in 1996 to manage and analyze medical claims. Starting with a database purchased from the Health Insurance Association of America, Ingenix acquired scores of companies over the next decade to emerge as one of the country's largest health data and technology companies, boasting annual revenues of $1.3 billion and playing a key role in determining how much doctors are to be paid when patients receive care outside of their health plan's network. Critics, including New York Attorney General Andrew Cuomo, claimed that

Ingenix manipulated data so that doctor reimbursements were low and patients obligations high. While Ingenix contributed a minor portion of UnitedHealth's annual sales of more than $75 billion, it was a fast-growing, high-margin business, and one that UnitedHealth was willing to enhance through acquisitions, such as the purchase of Lewin Group.

Ingenix officials pledged that Lewin Group would maintain its editorial independence. At the very least, the new property would bolster Ingenix's methodologies and analytics. For its part, Lewin Group looked to benefit from access to Ingenix's deep pool of financial and clinical data and information technology. Whether Lewin Group would continue to maintain its reputation for unbiased independence remained to be seen, but for the time being at least, the Lewin brand remained the gold standard in healthcare analysis. Given the election of a new president, Barack Obama, in 2008, and a renewed effort to bring some form of universal healthcare to the United States, it was all but certain that demand for Lewin Group studies would remain unabated in the short term.

Ed Dinger

PRINCIPAL COMPETITORS

Active Health Management, Inc.; Covance Inc.; Health Management Systems, Inc.

FURTHER READING

Becker, Cinda, "Ingenix Acquires Lewin Group," *Modern Healthcare,* June 18, 2007, p. 13.

Chandler, Clay, "Consulting Firm Agrees to Acquisition," *Washington Post,* August 27, 1987, p. E1.

Stout, Hilary, "Go Figure: One Company's Data Fuel Diverse Views in Health Care Debate," *Wall Street Journal,* June 28, 1994, p. A1.

———, " Health Plan Cost Outlook Is Too Rosy, but Basic Financing Works, Firm Says," *Wall Street Journal,* December 1993, p. A2.

"Value Health Inc. Sells Lewin-VHI to Avoid Potential Conflict of Interest," *Health Care Strategic Management,* June 1996, p. 4.

"Value Health to Sell Its Lewin-VHI Unit," *Wall Street Journal,* August 1, 1995, p. B6.

Winslow, Ron, "Value Health to Buy 4 Firms to Bolster Growth of Managed Health-Care Unit," *Wall Street Journal,* November 3, 1992, p. B4.

Yee, Chen May, "Mystery Player in the Spotlight: Ingenix Who?" *Minneapolis Star Tribune,* March 16, 2008, p. 1D.

Loewe S.A.

—•—

Carrera de San Jerónimo 15
Madrid, E-28014
Spain
Telephone: (34 91) 360 61 00
Fax: (34 91) 360 15 50
Web site: http://www.loewe.es

Wholly Owned Subsidiary of LVMH Moët Hennessy Louis Vuitton SA
Incorporated: 1872
Employees: 190
Sales: $137.9 million (2008)
NAICS: 315992 Glove and Mitten Manufacturing; 316991 Luggage Manufacturing; 316992 Women's Handbag and Purse Manufacturing; 316993 Personal Leather Good (Except Women's Handbag and Purse) Manufacturing

■ ■ ■

Loewe S.A. (pronounced Lew-ay-vay) is one of Spain's most well-known luxury brands and a prominent component of the LVMH Moët Hennessy Louis Vuitton SA (LVMH) luxury-brands empire. Madrid-based Loewe is especially prized for its leather goods, including its famous handbags, as well as coats and jackets, ties, belts, and other accessories. Stuart Vevers was named the company's creative director in 2008, the first time the company has filled this position since the departure of legendary designer José Pérez de Rozas, who guided the company's design from 1945 to 1978. The company's Perfumes Loewe subsidiary develops and distributes its

own range of fragrances for both men and women, including the scents Solo and Quizas Quizas Quizas, released in 2008. Loewe also designs a line of ready-to-wear women's fashions, and a limited range of menswear.

Loewe continues to oversee most of its manufacturing, with a staff of experienced, traditional craftspeople based at its Madrid headquarters. The company also operates an international chain of approximately 135 stores. These include a new boutique format, designed by Peter Marino, the first of which opened in Valencia, Spain, in early 2009. Loewe is grouped under LVMH's Fashion and Leather Goods division, while Perfumes Loewe is included in LVMH's Perfumes division. Albert Puyol serves as the company's chairman.

LEATHER EXPERTISE IN THE 19TH CENTURY

Loewe's origins trace back to the middle of the 19th century. In 1846 a group of Madrid-based leather craftsmen decided to join together to form their own workshop on what was then Calle Lobo in the commercial district of the city's center. The workshop became noted for the fine quality of its workmanship, producing tobacco pouches, wallets, bags, and the like.

The workshop's fortunes changed with the arrival of German immigrant Enrique Roessberg Loewe, who had trained as a leather craftsman in Germany before moving to Madrid in 1872. Impressed by the quality of the workshop's products, Loewe proposed a partnership, marrying the precision of German production techniques with the Spanish flair and sensibility. By the start of the 20th century, the E. Loewe name was already well known throughout the city. Part of the secret of the company's success was its use of a Spanish sheepskin, manufactured from a breed of sheep that lived in the Pyrenées Mountains. The leather produced from these sheep was reputed to be the finest and most delicate in the world.

The company flourished with the next generation, under the leadership of Enrique Loewe Hilton. A commitment to quality brought the company further recognition, when King Alfonso XIII named the company as an official supplier to the royal family in 1905. This recognition enabled the company to gain a national reputation, and soon allowed the company to expand beyond its single Madrid store. In 1910 the company had opened a second shop, in Barcelona.

Madrid remained the heart of the group's operations, however, and in 1923 the company opened a second shop in the Spanish capital. Over the next decade, the company opened several more stores in the Madrid region. The next generation of the Loewe family, under Enrique Loewe Knappe, took over in 1934 and continued the company's expansion, adding a new series of stores. These included a new store on Madrid's Gran Via, opened in 1939.

START OF THE PÉREZ DE ROZAS ERA

Loewe marked a new milestone with the arrival of a new creative director, Pérez de Rozas, who joined the company in 1945. Pérez de Rozas had a profound influence on the company's product line, which he guided for more than 30 years. Among his earliest successes was the creation of the "boxcalf" handbag in 1945. This became one of the company's most enduring signature products. Throughout the 1950s the company also attracted the attention of a number of international personalities, such as Ava Gardner and Ernest Hemingway.

The Loewe name itself remained somewhat confidential during the era, in large part because of the nationalistic economic policies of the Franco regime. Few outside of Spain knew of the company, and few inside the country could afford its products. During the 1950s, however, Pérez de Rozas found a way to enhance the company's reputation, launching a tradition of fanciful window dressing in the company's Gran Via store.

Loewe received a boost on the international fashion scene with the arrival of a number of Hollywood stars, including most famously Gardner, then married to Frank Sinatra, who had first come to Madrid to shoot the film *Pandora and the Flying Dutchman* in 1951. According to one story, Gardner's friend Hemingway introduced her to Loewe later in the decade, taking her to visit the Gran Via shop. Gardner walked out of the store carrying one of Loewe's handbags, and set off a new style trend in Hollywood. Other stars noted for their Loewe purchases included Sophia Loren, Anthony Quinn, Cary Grant, and Gary Cooper.

By then, Loewe had come under the leadership of the fourth generation of the Loewe family as Enrique Loewe Lynch took charge of the company's growth. Loewe recognized the opportunity to capitalize on the brand's growing overseas' reputation, opening its first international store, in London, in 1963. Loewe also sought to expand the brand's range beyond leather goods for the first time. This led to the launch of the company's own ready-to-wear line in 1965.

INTERNATIONAL EXPANSION

Although the Franco regime's policy of economic isolation had negative consequences for Spain as a whole, the same policies provided some benefits to Loewe. Perhaps the most important of these was that the company faced little competition from other luxury brands, including Hermès and Vuitton, which had grown strongly in the postwar era, but were blocked from entering Spain directly. Instead, Loewe gained an additional benefit by becoming one of the few in Spain to sell international designer labels from its own stores.

By the time the foreign labels began to appear more widely in Spain, Loewe had not only established itself as one of the country's preeminent brands, but had also developed its own international store network. This network was later brought under a dedicated subsidiary, Loewe International. After adding new stores in Europe, including one in Brussels and a second in London, the company turned to the Asian market, opening its first store in Japan in 1973. The Asian market proved to be particularly interested in the group's products. Within

KEY DATES

1846: A group of leather craftsmen join together to found a workshop in Madrid, Spain.

1872: German immigrant Enrique Roessberg Loewe forms a partnership with the Madrid workshop, founding E. Loewe.

1905: Under son Enrique Loewe Hilton, the company becomes the official supplier to the Spanish crown.

1910: The company opens its first store outside of Madrid, in Barcelona.

1945: José Pérez de Rozas becomes creative director, a position he will hold for more than 30 years.

1963: Loewe opens its first international store in London, and later creates Loewe International to oversee its foreign growth.

1973: Loewe opens a store in Japan.

1983: Loewe enters the United States with a store in New York City.

1987: Louis Vuitton acquires 95 percent of Loewe International.

1996: LVMH acquires full control of Loewe.

2008: Stuart Vevers is named the company's first creative director since 1978.

ten years the company's Asian store network had become its largest, with 30 stores in operation.

Loewe continued to develop new product lines into the 1970s. One of the best-selling and longest lasting of these was the company's collection of scarves and handkerchiefs. In 1972 the company joined another trend among luxury-goods groups, launching its first perfume, L. Loewe. This was followed by the group's first men's cologne, Loewe Loewe pour homme, introduced in 1975.

CHANGES IN THE EIGHTIES

The departure of Pérez de Rozas in 1978 ended an era at Loewe. For the next 30 years, the company declined to name a new creative director responsible for the entirety of its product development. Instead, the separate product areas were handled by different designers, such as Renzo Zengiaro, who debuted his Napa collection in 1979.

Loewe's shareholding was also undergoing changes. Through the 1970s, a rift developed between members of the Barcelona-based branch of the Loewe family, which favored a more conservative expansion strategy, and the Madrid branch, led by Enrique Loewe, who sought a more ambitious expansion. The rift led to the Barcelona branch finally agreeing to sell its stake to fast-growing conglomerate Ramusa, allowing that company to gain control of Loewe by 1981.

Ramusa collapsed soon after and was nationalized by the Spanish government. Enrique Loewe then lobbied to buy back the company, succeeding in 1983. With the company more fully under his control, Loewe launched a new step in the group's expansion. In that year, the company entered the United States for the first time, opening a store at the Trump Tower in New York City.

Into the 1980s, Loewe introduced its first men's fashions. The success of the line led the company to open a dedicated retail shop, Loewe Man, with the first store opened in Madrid in 1986. The company's perfumes were also enjoying success during the decade, particularly following the launch of Aire Loewe in 1985. That fragrance became a bestseller for the company.

Rising competition in the international designer and luxury-brand market brought Loewe to align itself with a larger partner in order to ensure its own future expansion. In 1987 the company reached an agreement to sell 95 percent of Loewe International to the Louis Vuitton, part of the LVMH group. That company was shortly to grow into one of the world's leading luxury-products groups.

JOINING LVMH IN 1996

LVMH soon sought take a stake in Loewe itself, achieving this aim with the purchase of 10.75 percent of the company in 1990. LVMH then boosted its share to 23 percent, with an agreement to add another 7 percent during the decade. In the meantime, Loewe found itself in financial difficulties amid the worldwide recession of the period. By 1992 the company's majority shareholders, including the Loewe family, had reached an agreement to complete a capital increase meant to allow the Cartier luxury group to acquire a stake in Loewe.

The move was meant mostly as a symbolic gesture of support from Cartier for the Spanish label. Nonetheless, LVMH and other minority shareholders persuaded Loewe to abandon the deal. At the same time, Loewe continued to struggle and in 1992, as the weak dollar caused its sales in the United States to plummet, the company shut down its New York store.

The company's fortunes brightened as the economy began to grow again, and by 1995 the company's sales neared $140 million, compared to just $45 million in 1990. The rising strength of the Loewe brand, stimulated in part by LVMH's success in expanding Loewe International onto a worldwide level, led the champagne and luxury-products company to launch an offer to buy out full control of Loewe. This sale was completed in 1996. Loewe joined LVMH's impressive stable of some of the world's most prized luxury brands.

NEW DIRECTIONS IN THE NEW CENTURY

LVMH brought in a new management team, led by Gerald Mazzalovo, formerly with Salvatore Ferragamo, as chairman and CEO of Loewe. The company then brought in Narciso Rodriguez to head the design team for the company's flagging ready-to-wear collection. Rodriguez debuted his first collection for the company in 1997. Under Rodriguez the ready-to-wear line's focused especially on the use of leather, underscoring its relationship with the company's historic core.

In the meantime, Mazzalovo continued Loewe's international expansion, bringing the company's retail network into Russia and other markets. These included the United States, which the company reentered in 1998 with a store on New York's Fifth Avenue. By the end of the next decade, the company boasted nearly 135 stores worldwide. Into the 21st century, Loewe also sought a new brand extension, launching a bath and beauty line in 2001.

The company's ready-to-wear operation, which had picked up under Rodriguez, took a hit in that year when Rodriguez decided to leave the company in order to launch his own design group. In his place was named José Enrique Oña Selfa, a Belgian of Spanish descent. Oña Selfa struggled, however, to infuse new growth into the ready-to-wear collection, as the global economy was again hit by a slowdown at the turn of the century.

Loewe itself was described as something of a "sleeper" through the 1990s, as other luxury leather brands, including Hermès, Gucci, and Vuitton, captured international attention. The company took steps to regain momentum in 2007, when it terminated Ona Selfa's contract. In his place, the company named an up-and-coming designer, 35-year-old Stuart Vevers, who joined Loewe in January 2008.

Vevers had begun his design career with Calvin Klein in the United States, before moving to London, where he made a name for himself as the handbag and clothing designer for Mulberry. Under Vevers, the Mulberry bag became a major fashion accessory throughout much of the first decade of the 2000s. This experience led Loewe to name Vevers not merely as

designer for its ready-to-wear line, but as the creative director for all of the group's products marking the first time the company had named a creative director in 30 years. With a new global design leader, Loewe looked forward to raising its profile as one of the world's most respected luxury brands.

M. L. Cohen

PRINCIPAL SUBSIDIARIES

Loewe Hermanos (UK) Ltd.; Loewe Italiana SRL; Manufactuas Loewe S.L.; Perfumes Loewe S.A.

PRINCIPAL DIVISIONS

Leather Goods; Loewe Fragrances; Men Skincare; Novelties; Ready to Wear.

PRINCIPAL OPERATING UNITS

Product; Sales; Branding and Communication; Visual Merchandising and Architecture; Finance; Operations; Human Resources.

PRINCIPAL COMPETITORS

PPR S.A.; Gucci Group N.V.; Hermès International S.C.A.; Alkali Group of Cos.; Remploy Ltd.; William Prym GmbH and Company KG; Antichi Pellettieri S.p.A.

FURTHER READING

Argullol, Rafael, et al., *Loewe 1846–1996,* Madrid: Loewe, 1996.

Costello, Brid, "Loewe's Lady in Red," *WWD,* August 9, 2002, p. 10.

Huckbody, Jamie, "The King of Leather," *Independent* (London), October 17, 2002.

Hume, Marion, "Bag Man," *Time,* November 17, 2008.

"Loewe and Narciso Rodriguez Extend Their Agreement Until 2001," *Business Wire,* September 30, 1999.

"Loewe Has Designs on Gaudi, Even After 150 Years," *Cosmetics International,* April 25, 2002, p. 12.

Long, Carola, "New King of Spain," *New Zealand Herald,* May 7, 2009.

"LVMH in Talks to Buy Loewe," *WWD,* October 23, 1995, p. 20.

Morris, Bernadine, "Loewe Leather Arrives," *New York Times,* September 21, 1983.

Socha, Miles, "Ona Selfa Brings Passion to Loewe," *WWD,* March 6, 2002, p. 16.

Thilmany, Jean, "Loewe Gets up Close on Inventory," *Daily News Record,* August 4, 1999, p. 12.

Wilson, Eric, "Loewe Opens U.S. Effort," *WWD,* September 29, 1998, p. 10.

The Louis Berger Group, Inc.

———■———

412 Mount Kemble Avenue
Morristown, New Jersey 07960-6654
U.S.A.
Telephone: (973) 407-1000
Fax: (973) 267-6468
Web site: http://www.louisberger.com

Private Company
Incorporated: 1953
Employees: 4,000
Sales: $448 million (2003 est.)
NAICS: 541330 Engineering Services

■ ■ ■

Maintaining its headquarters in Morristown, New Jersey, The Louis Berger Group, Inc., is a global family of infrastructure engineering, environmental science, and economic development consulting firms. All told, the company maintains more than 140 offices around the world. Louis Berger Group includes Berger, Lehman Associates, P.C., in the United States; Louis Berger S.A.S., a Paris, France-based engineering consulting firm serving Eastern Europe, the Middle East, and Africa; Florida's BergerAvart, Inc.; CHELBI Engineering Consultants, Inc., a Chinese engineering consulting joint venture; Berger/ABAM Engineers, Inc., providing services from offices in the northwestern United States as well as Las Vegas, Nevada, and Houston, Texas; New York City-based Ammann & Whitney, a structural, civil, architectural, mechanical, and electrical engineering company; Klohn Crippen Berger Ltd. in Canada; Berger

Devine Yaeger, Inc., a Kansas City, Missouri-based architectural, engineering, and planning company serving a wide range of domestic and international clients; and The RBA Group, Inc., in Parsippany, New Jersey.

FOUNDER BORN 1914

The founder of The Louis Berger Group was Dr. Louis Berger. Born in 1914 in Lawrence, Massachusetts, he was the son of a small businessman and worked odd jobs to help support his family. Determined to become an engineer he enrolled at Tufts College in 1931. A shortage of funds forced him to leave school and work for a year, but he eventually graduated with a degree in civil engineering in 1936. While he was at Tufts he became interested in soil mechanics, which became the focus of his career. After earning a master's degree in soils and geology from the Massachusetts Institute of Technology in 1940, Berger went to work for the U.S. Soil Conservation Service to supervise the construction of a pair of dams in southern Illinois. He then worked with the U.S. Army Corps of Engineers and the U.S. Department of Agriculture.

Soon after the United States entered World War II, he enlisted with the U.S. Coast Guard as a civil engineer and designed Mississippi waterfront facilities. Following the war Berger earned his doctorate in soil mechanics from Northwestern University. While completing his thesis on landslides, he joined the Pennsylvania State University engineering faculty in 1948, teaching soil mechanics as well as highway engineering and foundation engineering.

COMPANY PERSPECTIVES

The Louis Berger Group's objective is to continue to be one of the leading infrastructure engineering operations in the world.

Berger's academic career came to an end in 1953 when, at the age of 39, he opened a consulting engineering practice in Harrisburg, Pennsylvania. After establishing his firm in soil testing and foundation design, Berger became involved in transportation engineering, his first major assignment the design of a portion of the Northeast Extension of the Pennsylvania Turnpike. He then opened a second office in East Orange, New Jersey, where he hoped to attract clients from the New York City area as well as overseas.

In time, the New Jersey office would replace Harrisburg as the firm's headquarters. The East Orange branch quickly paid dividends, as Berger won its first assignment from the New Jersey State Highway Department, followed by a major project: designing 13.5 miles of Interstate 80.

FIRST INTERNATIONAL
CONTRACT AWARDED: 1959

In 1959 Berger received his first international assignment, directing a team of engineers in designing a 435-mile road from Rangoon to Mandalay in Burma. That same year in the United States, Berger designed several highway bridges in the Buffalo, New York, area. His company then expanded its services and in the 1960s was able to tackle some projects that spanned from concept to construction to operation. Berger Group was thus able to win a number of major international contracts in the 1960s.

The company began work on Nigeria's "Highway of Progress," designing and supervising the 210-kilometer road that included a major bridge over the Calabar River and took 14 years to complete. In South America, Berger Group designed the 2,000-mile Trans-Amazon Highway during the 1960s. Moreover, the firm continued to secure work from Asian countries, including the 600-mile East Pakistan Road in what is now Bangladesh, a country that became the firm's first long-term client state. In Thailand the Berger Group worked with the U.S. government in the 1960s, building a major military base. The company also designed and constructed the Kittikachorn Stadium in Bangkok as part of Thailand's bid to land the Olympic Games.

The 1970s brought expansion into Europe for Berger Group. Through Stockholm-based subsidiary Brokonsult, the firm began doing business in Norway and Sweden, taking on such projects as an extension of the Stockholm Subway System and a wharf in Narvik, Norway. In 1975 Louis Berger S.A.S. was established in Paris, France, and would do business in the Middle East and Africa and later in Eastern Europe. Other major international projects taken on by Berger Group in the 1970s included the Philippines' Flood Damage Control and Rehabilitation Project, the Highway Organization and Maintenance Study in Sudan, and a national transportation study for Haiti.

LOUIS BERGER DIES: 1996

In the 1980s Louis Berger ended his management responsibilities, although he continued to work on projects for the firm. He oversaw the construction of the $4 billion Second Bangkok International Airport and played a key role in the firm's efforts to incorporate a computer-aided design system. Berger passed away in 1996 at the age of 82. During his tenure, the company was responsible for the design and construction of more than 100,000 miles of highways, 3,000 bridges, 100 airfields, 2,000 miles of railroads, and a host of dams, seaports, water supply systems, and other projects. Altogether Berger Group completed nearly 7,000 projects in 140 countries.

During the 1980s the firm continued to grow without Berger's direct leadership, establishing several subsidiaries. BergerAvart Inc. was formed in Miami in 1981 to serve a wide range of public sector clients in Miami-Dade and Broward counties, including transportation authorities, public works, water and sewer agencies, parks, and schools. CHELBI, Inc., was created in 1985 as a joint venture with China's Highway Planning and Design Institute. Based in Beijing, the partnership not only provided consulting engineering services but helped to introduce computer design services and other state-of-the-art techniques to China.

GROWTH THROUGH
ACQUISITION AND INNOVATION

Berger Group also grew through acquisition. In 1988 ABAM Engineers, Inc., was brought into the fold. Founded in 1951, ABAM was especially well known for its efforts in prestressed concrete and port designs. Under Berger it expanded its planning, management, environmental, and engineering services. Maintaining its headquarters in Federal Way, Washington, ABAM would also maintain offices in Vancouver and Seattle,

KEY DATES

1953: Louis Berger founds an engineering consultancy firm.
1959: The company's first international contract is awarded.
1975: Louis Berger S.A.S. is established in Paris, France.
1985: Joint venture CHELBI, Inc., is formed.
1988: ABAM Engineers, Inc., becomes a group member.
1996: Louis Berger dies.
1999: Klohn Crippen is acquired.
2007: RBA Group, Inc., is acquired.

Washington; Portland, Oregon; Las Vegas; and Houston.

Noteworthy projects of the 1980s for Berger Group included design and construction work on Israel's Ovda Airbase, an important element of the Camp David peace agreement between Israel and Egypt. Berger was hired in 1986 to serve as a technical adviser for the Channel Tunnel, providing design, cost, risk analysis, and schedule monitoring services for the eight-year project that connected the United Kingdom to Europe.

In the United States, in the meantime, Berger Group designed a portion of Interstate 295 in New Jersey, a project that proved challenging because one of the bridges spanned a sensitive wetland area as well as the landmark Abbott Farm near Trenton, a site that coupled prehistoric settlements with early American farmsteads and had become one of the East Coast's largest archaeological excavations. To address the needs of this sensitive area, Berger established a Cultural Resource Group to conduct subsurface testing in order to locate, excavate, and preserve many Native American artifacts.

MORE UNITS ACQUIRED IN THE NINETIES

Two more units were added to the Berger Group family in the 1990s. Ammann & Whitney was brought into the fold in 1994. Based in New York City, this company had been founded in 1946. It served both public and private clients from New York and additional offices in Philadelphia and Pittsburgh, Pennsylvania; Boston, Massachusetts; Washington, D.C.; and Richmond, Virginia. The company provided architectural, civil, electrical, mechanical, and structural engineering services for such projects as highways, bridges, transit stations, airports, and military installations.

In 1999 Klohn Crippen, a high-value-added consulting services firm mostly catering to mining clients, joined Berger Group. Founded in Canada in 1951, it grew from a geotechnical and water resources engineering firm into a major designer of dams, hydroelectric power plants, and tunnels, offering a wide range of seismic, environmental, geotechnical capabilities. In addition to its Vancouver, British Columbia, headquarters, Klohn Crippen maintained offices throughout Canada as well as Lima, Peru; and Brisbane, Australia.

HIGH-PROFILE PROJECTS WORLDWIDE

Significant projects for Berger Group in the 1990s included the Second Bangkok International Airport project and the redevelopment of the Newark International Airport in New Jersey, which included a new international terminal, improved access roads, and a monorail system. Another important contract was the design of the 41-kilometer Buenos Aires–Colonia Bridge that connected Argentina and Uruguay.

Berger expanded beyond engineering services as well, branching into economic revitalization services. In the Philippines island of Mindanao, Berger organized a growth program that helped small business development and provided job training for workers while attracting foreign investment. Similar expertise was applied by the firm in Eastern Europe where countries struggled to adapt to post-Communist political and economic systems. Berger was involved, for example, in war-torn former Yugoslavia on a variety of fronts. It reconstructed the Sloboda Bridge in Serbia, rebuilt police stations in Bosnia and Kosovo, and participated in a variety of projects in Croatia and Macedonia.

As the 21st century dawned, Berger Group was well positioned to continue plying its capabilities around the world, often finding itself at the site of international conflict. Following the terrorist attacks that struck the United States on September 11, 2001, Berger was called in to assist in the aftermath of the World Trade Center collapse in New York City. The firm helped to rebuild damaged structures and restore the transportation system of lower Manhattan, in particular the Port Authority Trans-Hudson (PATH) train station beneath the World Trade Center. Moreover, Berger maintained an important database that kept track of plans, budgets, and schedules of the many projects taken on to recover from the attacks.

AFGHAN HIGHWAY COMPLETED: 2003

After the United States took military action in Afghanistan in the wake of the September 11 attacks, Berger Group once again was called upon to help rebuild a country ravaged by war. The firm was responsible for the design and construction of the refurbished 300-mile-long highway that linked Kabul and Kandahar. Completed in 2003, the project came with a human price tag that included four deaths and a pair of kidnappings.

Following the U.S. military invasion of Iraq, Berger Group received contracts in that country as well, to help in the reconstruction of transportation and communication systems as well as the building of schools, hospitals, police stations, and courts. At the same time, Berger was heavily involved in projects in Asia to help develop environmental codes and improve construction standards.

The family of Berger subsidiaries expanded further in the new century. In 2007 RBA Group, Inc., was added. The Parsippany, New Jersey-based firm had been established in 1968 and maintained offices in New York City, Long Island, and Columbia, Maryland. Its focus was on urban planning and downtown restorations, environmental impact analysis, and the design of parks, bicycle and pedestrian trails. Given its manifold capabilities and history of success, there was every reason to expect that Berger Group would continue to grow and win contracts around the world, as demonstrated by projects it undertook in Serbia and Qatar in 2009.

Ed Dinger

PRINCIPAL SUBSIDIARIES

Berger, Lehman Associates, P.C.; Louis Berger SAS; BergerAvart, Inc.; CHELBI Engineering Consultants, Inc.; Berger/ABAM Engineers, Inc.; Ammann & Whitney; Klohn Crippen Berger Ltd.; Berger Devine Yaeger, Inc.; The RBA Group, Inc.

PRINCIPAL COMPETITORS

Bechtel Group, Inc.; Jacobs Engineering Group Inc.; Parsons Brinckerhoff Inc.

FURTHER READING

Deutsch, Claudia H., "Louis Berger, 82, Who Built Engineering Concern," *New York Times,* August 19, 1996.

"Global Rebuilding Efforts," *Construction Today,* November 2006, p. 132.

"Louis Berger, Who Built Large Firm, Dies at 82," *Civil Engineering,* October 1996, p. 74.

Morley, Hugh R., "N.J. Firm to Help Rebuild Iraq," *Record* (Bergen County, N.J.), August 8, 2003, p. B1.

———, "300-Mile Highway in Afghanistan Had Foundation in N.J.," *Record* (Bergen County, N.J.), December 19, 2003, p. B1.

Weingardt, Richard G., "Louis Gerber," *Leadership and Management in Engineering,* October 2005, p. 94.

Madelaine Chocolate Novelties, Inc.

96-03 Beach Channel Drive
Rockaway Beach, New York 11693
U.S.A.
Telephone: (718) 945-1500
Toll Free: (800) 332-1505
Fax: (718) 318-4607
Web site: http://www.madelainechocolate.com

Private Company
Incorporated: 1949
Employees: 450
Sales: $45 million (2002 est.)
NAICS: 311330 Confectionery Manufacturing from Purchased Chocolate; 311320 Chocolate and Confectionery Manufacturing from Cacao Beans

∎ ∎ ∎

Madelaine Chocolate Novelties, Inc., which also does business as The Madelaine Chocolate Company, manufactures molded chocolate candies that it wraps in brightly colored foils from Italy. It also sells gourmet chocolate-covered fruits, nuts, and specialty centers, and provides private-label manufacturing and packaging services for some of the largest domestic candy companies. The company's products sell to retailers throughout the United States, Puerto Rico, and in Canada, as well as overseas. Its own brands include

Madelaine, Hatchers, Gooey Ghouls, Love & Kisses, Fiesta, Penny Lane, and Grand Estate.

ORIGINS

Madelaine Chocolate Novelties was founded in 1949 by Jack Gold and Henry Kaye, two brothers-in-law, and Jacob Pludwinski. The partners had immigrated to the United States after surviving the Holocaust in concentration camps. They worked briefly in a chocolate factory, and then rented 2,500 square feet in a lower Manhattan warehouse where they started making boxed chocolates. They named their company Madelaine after a well-known screen star of the time because they felt her name suggested sophistication. "We figured if we don't start now, we never will," Gold recalled in a 1999 *New York Daily News* article, speaking of their decision to invest $1,000 in the new business.

In the beginning, Madelaine produced 400 to 500 pounds of chocolate per day. As the business grew, it needed more space, and in the mid-1950s, it moved to the Canarsie section of the borough of Brooklyn in New York City. There the owners discovered that it could not compete with the large manufacturers of boxed chocolates, so they invested in molding and foil-wrapping machinery.

With this shift in focus, Madelaine became the first domestic chocolate company to manufacture chocolate novelties, such as foil-wrapped Santas, snowmen, and Easter bunnies. Its brightly colored foils, which it imported from Italy, the fine detail of its molded chocolates, and its modest prices, caught the attention of buyers from retail shops nationwide, and the company grew steadily. "The finest details interplay to create a product that connoisseurs love, and have always loved," explained company Chief Executive and President Jorge Farber on the Madelaine web site. To accommodate its growth, the company moved to Rockaway Beach in the New York City borough of Queens in 1967, where it quickly became a neighborhood establishment, drawing almost all of its employees from the surrounding communities.

From 1969 to 1976, employment in the New York City candy industry dropped from about 4,000 to around 1,600, the result of competition-led mergers, computerized machinery, and high New York City taxes and energy costs. However, as the number of New York City-based candy manufacturers continued to decline into the late 1970s, Madelaine continued to grow.

THE SECOND GENERATION TAKES OVER

After Henry Kaye died in 1989, the company passed to his daughter Vivian and her husband, Jorge Farber, and Jack Gold and his son, Norman Gold. The second generation of managers at Madelaine Chocolate Novelties had grown up in the business, Vivian putting together displays as a young adult, Norman loading trucks. During the early to mid-1990s, demand for Madelaine's products increased dramatically, and by 1996, the company was bringing in $24 million in sales and was making 100,000 pounds of chocolate daily in three shifts, using more than ten million pounds of chocolate annually.

During this time, the company considered moving its business to a different state to take advantage of lower operating expenses outside of New York. The city and state then offered the company $3.2 million in incentives to stay in Rockaway Beach, and in 1997 Madelaine began construction of a multimillion-dollar factory and warehouse expansion on land adjacent to its factory. "You need long production lines to be efficient. You need long buildings," explained Vivian Kaye Farber about the need for more space to remain competitive in the $20 billion candy industry in a 1997 *Daily News* article. The new factory promised to add up to 100 jobs, increasing employment in the community.

Another change took place in the candy industry during the 1990s with which Madelaine Chocolate Novelties had to contend: growing consumer interest in premium dark chocolate. In light of the information that chocolate contained many antioxidants that made it good for one's health, more and more people were purchasing premium chocolate even at its higher price point as a small indulgence as the economy slowed.

After enjoying steady above industry-average growth of between 5 percent and 10 percent throughout the 1990s, Madelaine invested nearly $7 million to expand capacity and capability from 1997 to 2000. It upgraded existing equipment and purchased new molding, demolding, and foiling equipment. Part of this investment went to the construction of a new 56,000-square-foot warehouse that it completed in 1998. Overall, the company boosted capacity by about 50 percent during the decade.

INVESTING IN INFRASTRUCTURE

By the dawn of the new century, Madelaine's more than 400 employees were producing not just the molded and foil-wrapped products for which it had earned its reputation, but items for private-label companies as well. "Our strategy is to maintain a healthy balance, with one-third of our sales coming from co-manufacturing, one-third from private label, and one-third from our own Madelaine line," explained Jorge Farber, who became president and chief executive in 2001, in a 2002 *Candy Industry* article. The momentum for the company's growth was its co-manufacturing business; with contracts in place, management could predict a portion of revenues and plan for ongoing expansion.

As the seasonal novelty business increased in strength throughout the early years of the first decade of the 21st century and chocolate novelties moved into the mass merchandising arena, Madelaine Chocolate Novelties continued to invest in its infrastructure, spending another $5 million on the latest technology and upgrades in equipment between 2000 and 2007. These investments paid off as its private-label and contract manufacturing business both grew. In 2002, the company's revenues were estimated at $45 million annually; it had 450 employees and 13 molding lines in a 200,000-square-foot, three-building facility.

KEY DATES

1949: Jack Gold, Henry Kaye, and Jacob Pludwinski found Madelaine Chocolate Novelties. The company moves to the Canarsie section of the borough of Brooklyn in New York City.

1967: The company moves to Rockaway Beach in Queens, New York.

1989: Henry Kaye dies; the company passes to his daughter Vivian and her husband, Jorge Farber, and to Jack Gold and his son, Norman Gold.

1998: New 56,000-square-foot warehouse is completed.

2003: Madelaine Chocolate Novelties purchases Fiesta Nut and Confection Corp.

2007: Jorge Farber, president and chief executive, wins the 62nd annual Kettle Award.

Although the company's customer list by this time exceeded 5,000, Vivian Farber, vice-president and general manager, still knew at least two-thirds of all accounts by name. "Customers really appreciate a personal phone call. We insist on maintaining a personal relationship; success hasn't spoiled our personal touch to the business," Farber announced in a 2002 *Candy Industry* article. The company assigned a production supervisory person to accounts with special requirements to assure its personalized touch and held weekly meetings of its quality action committee consisting of production staff.

ENTERING NEW MARKETS IN THE 21ST CENTURY

As lines between mass and upscale markets continued to blur and as consumers began to celebrate more holidays throughout the year, Madelaine Chocolate Novelties entered new markets, "actively cementing the Madelaine brand by developing clearly identifiable packaging that impresses the consumer with the quality of the chocolate," according to Barbara Berg, the company's marketing manager in a 2008 *Professional Candy Buyer* article. In 2003, Madelaine Chocolate Novelties diversified its product base with the purchase of Fiesta Nut and Confection Corp., a manufacturer of panned, or coated, items, such as chocolate-covered nuts, fruits, and malt centers. In order to increase Fiesta's production capacity, Madelaine relocated Fiesta and expanded its panning operations. By 2007, Fiesta had tripled its sales.

In 2007, when Jorge Farber, the company's chief executive office, was the winner of the 62nd annual Kettle Award, the candy industry's highest honor, the company still divided its business among branded, private-label, and contract manufacturing items. However, it was focused on expanding the Madelaine line of chocolates to account for 50 percent of its sales. As it did so, it planned to take advantage of the popularity of dark chocolate to expand into markets that had traditionally been closed to gourmet items. "We've expanded our line with both dark chocolate as well as high cocoa content chocolates and watched our sales grow," announced Jorge Farber in a 2008 *Professional Candy Buyer* article.

At the same time, the company was striving to streamline its operations. "Our goal is to minimize the number of processes involved in making an item," explained Jorge Farber in *Professional Candy Buyer* in 2008. By 2008, Madelaine offered Easter bunnies, Halloween treats, Thanksgiving turkeys, Advent calendars, chocolate cigars, crayons, golf balls, poker chips, hearts, and its signature chocolate rose in its catalog of products. The company continued to contend with rising costs in ingredients, packaging, equipment, and labor, but maintained its quest to change "the idea of novelties as cheap chocolate," according to Farber on the company's web site.

As the third generation of Golds and Kayes were entering the business, the company offered close to 500 items for sale online, focused on new gourmet chocolate gift packaging as the way toward ongoing revenue growth. "Consumers are more aware of quality today and expectations are that chocolate of all kinds should be high quality, even novelties," explained Farber.

Carrie Rothburd

PRINCIPAL COMPETITORS

Lindt & Sprungli; R.M. Palmer Co.; SweetWorks, Inc.; The Hershey Company; Mars, Inc.; Sherwood Brands; Zachary Confections.

FURTHER READING

"Chocolate Adds Seasonal Profits," *Professional Candy Buyer,* March 2008, p. 12.

Colangelo, Lisa, "Sweet Smell of Biz Success: Rockaway Chocolate Factory Fills Mold," *New York Daily News,* August 31, 1999, p. 4.

Grant, Peter, "Candy Company Gets Dandy Deal to Stay; Hundreds of Jobs Saved in Queens," *New York Daily News,* March 19, 1997, p. 51.

"Plenty New at Madelaine," *Candy Industry,* June 2002, p. 24.

"Premium Chocolate Edges Mainstream," *Professional Candy Buyer,* November 1999, p. 18.

"Rockaway Beach's Renaissance Man," *Candy Industry,* November 2007, p. 3

Serant, Claire, "Delicious News for Company: Chocolate Maker to Stay in Boro," *New York Daily News,* February 9, 1997, p. 1.

"Success Stories," *Crain's New York Business,* April 9, 2007, p. 22.

Martha White Foods Inc.

———■———

P.O. Box 751030
Memphis, Tennessee 38175
U.S.A.
Telephone: (330) 682-3000
Toll Free: (800) 663-6317
Web site: http://www.marthawhite.com

Wholly Owned Subsidiary of J. M. Smucker Company
Incorporated: 1899
Sales: $150 million (2008 est.)
NAICS: 311211 Flour Milling

■ ■ ■

Headquartered in Nashville, Tennessee, Martha White Foods Inc. manufactures and distributes 19 muffin, three brownie, eight cornbread, and three biscuit mixes, as well as pizza crust and hush-puppy mixes, five varieties of corn meal, and both self-rising and all-purpose flour. The company has gone through many changes of ownership since 1899, but remains true to its roots in southern cuisine and its commitment to convenience in the kitchen. Martha White has a long association with country music and the Grand Ole Opry, of which it has been a sponsor since 1948.

EARLY YEARS

Richard Lindsey Sr. founded Nashville's Royal Flour Mill in 1899 and named his company's finest flour Martha White after his three-year-old daughter. Although the company did not have an official logo at the time, Martha's face on a round paper label used on 100-pound barrels of flour graced its original barrelhead. Martha White was to become the company's best-selling flour, putting Royal Flour in competition with the slightly older White Lily Flour. White Lily would remain the company's major southern competitor throughout many decades. Both White Lily and Royal Flour were distributed primarily in the South where people made more quick breads than yeast breads and used more self-rising than all-purpose flours. According to experts on southern cuisine, southern flour was more like cake flour than its northern equivalent because of its low gluten content (8 percent as opposed to 12 percent). This difference was responsible for making fluffier cakes and biscuits.

In 1941, the Williams family, led by Cohen E. Williams, acquired the Royal Flour Mill and changed its name to Martha White Flour. The newly renamed company benefited from the family's strong leadership; Williams served as chairman while his son, Cohen T. Williams, was president. Martha White Flour experienced rapid growth under the Williams family. Cohen E. Williams made the strategic decision to associate his company with country music and radio. The people who bought Martha White's products were, he reasoned, largely rural; they ate biscuits and cornbread, and most listened to the Grand Ole Opry. Thus, starting in 1947, Martha White sponsored the 5:45 morning show, called "Martha White Biscuit and Cornbread Time," on Nashville's WSM radio.

The program helped many Grand Ole Opry performers, such as Chet Atkins and Marty Robbins, get their start in Nashville. Martha White also began to sponsor Nashville's famed Grand Ole Opry in 1948 and soon became a fixture there. In 1953, Nashville songwriter Pat Twitty wrote the company's jingle, "You Bake Right with Martha White," which became a standard at the Opry and a favorite among bluegrass music artists and fans.

Also in 1953, the company hired Lester Flatt, Earl Scruggs, and the Foggy Mountain Boys, who went on to become the nation's number one bluegrass music group, to perform in a tour called Bluegrass Express as musicians and as coupon-dispensing spokesmen for Martha White. Over the years Flatt and Scruggs became closely associated with Martha White, and during an appearance at Carnegie Hall, they played the famous Martha White jingle in response to shouted requests from the audience.

INNOVATIONS AND EASY-TO-USE MIXES

It was not just country music that was responsible for Martha White's growth in the 1950s, however. Cohen E. Williams also started a test kitchen in 1952, which led to the company's pioneering introduction of self-rising flour and self-rising corn meal. These items contained Hot Rize, a secret ingredient mixed in with the flour that made it rise. Innovation continued into the 1960s. In 1961, the company introduced cake mixes to which the customer simply added water; in 1963, the first in its line of family-serving-size packages, BixMix, offered an easy way to make the southern favorite, homemade biscuits. The company advertised BixMix as "the world's best biscuits," and targeted busy young homemakers as its potential customers. A full line of pouch-mix products followed, including southern hot bread, and in the late 1960s, strawberry and blueberry muffin mixes and macaroni and cheese.

In 1967, the younger Williams became chairman with James R. King and later Robert V. Dale assuming the presidency of Martha White. H. C. Cole Milling Co. acquired Martha White in late 1970. Cole's Omega

brand was the dominant brand in the Memphis and St. Louis areas. Under Cohen T. Williams, operations at the company's Steeleville, Illinois, mill and an older cake mix plant were transferred to Cole's large, modern St. Louis mill and its cake mix facility, creating substantial savings for Martha White. By the late 1960s, 100 salesmen represented the company in its major markets, with brokers selling its products elsewhere. Martha White had sales offices in Philadelphia and Chicago and was beginning to spread into the Midwest and the Northeast. During this period, the company also went public and completed a distribution facility in Nashville, which added to its more than 20 warehouses.

During the early 1970s, Martha White flour and cornmeal were among the best-selling brands in the Midwest and the South. However, while revenues reached a high of $49.3 million in 1971, up from $46 million in 1970, $44 million in 1969, and $40 million in 1968, profits experienced a downturn. Cake mixes and other prepared foods accounted for roughly a quarter of these sales with private-label business contributing another 50 percent. To make up for lower profits, the company instituted across-the-board price increases for its products, which were put into effect toward the end of fiscal 1971.

In its first significant departure from radio country music as a form of advertising, Martha White invested in print ads in women's magazines and in television spots in 15 markets during the 1970s, allocating about $1 million to its advertising budget. After Flatt and Scruggs disbanded, Tennessee Ernie Ford became the spokesman for Martha White in 1972. Ford's easygoing, country personality and musical popularity helped Martha White reach out to both rural and urban consumers, and Ford's association with the company continued through the 1980s.

CHANGES IN OWNERSHIP

The independent company continued to pioneer its "convenience in a pouch" in the 1970s with the addition of ready-to-make fruit muffins. Then, in 1975, Martha White merged with Beatrice Companies. It remained a wholly owned subsidiary of the Chicago-based firm until 1987 after Beatrice was taken private, and the new owners spun Martha White off as part of a consumer products division called E-II Holdings, which went public in July. American Brands bought E-II Holdings in 1988 and sold Martha White.

During the mid-1980s, the popularity of southern foods was in full swing throughout the United States. While more than 75 percent of domestic cornmeal consumption occurred in the southeastern United States,

KEY DATES

1899: Richard Lindsey founds the Royal Flour Mill and names its finest flour after his daughter.

1941: Cohen E. Williams buys the mill and changes its name to Martha White Flour.

1945: The Williams family coins the company's tagline: "Goodness Gracious, It's Good!"

1948: Martha White becomes a sponsor of the Grand Ole Opry.

1952: The company opens its test kitchen.

1953: The company begins to sponsor the Bluegrass Express music tour of the South; Nashville songwriter Pat Twitty composes the company's jingle.

1961: The company introduces cake mixes to which the customer must simply add water.

1970: H.C. Cole Milling Co. acquires Martha White.

1975: Martha White merges with Beatrice Companies.

1987: Beatrice is taken private and Martha White is spun off as part of E-II Holdings.

1988: American Brands buys E-II Holdings.

1989: Windmill Holdings acquires Martha White.

1994: The Pillsbury Company acquires Martha White.

2001: International Multifoods purchases Martha White.

2004: The J. M. Smucker Company purchases Martha White.

Martha White moved into the Southwest and initiated distribution in the Midwest and the East. It introduced newer convenience mixes for cornbread, pancakes, and brownies, as well as two-cup-measure flour pouches, and a mix for microwaves. Nationwide, sales of muffin, bread, and roll mixes went from $207 million in 1983 to $215 million in 1985. Competition remained fierce between White Lily and Martha White during this decade, with major national brands such as Gold Medal and Pillsbury entering the South as well.

In 1989, Windmill Holdings acquired Martha White. As part of updating its packaging, the company metamorphosed Martha White from a child of three into a young woman. This was the first change to occur in packaging since the company was founded, and the intention behind the new Martha White, shown holding a steaming pie, was, according to company literature, to

"embody the warmth of home cooking" and to tie all of the company's products together.

Dale remained president of Martha White until The Pillsbury Company, Grand Metropolitan's American subsidiary, purchased it in 1994. At this point, the company had sales of $165 million and controlled 5.2 percent of the baking-mix market. The acquisition put Pillsbury, with a 20 percent market share of the American dessert and baking product mix, in the number two position after Betty Crocker of General Mills, Inc.

The company's identification with Tennessee and the South remained strong throughout these changes in ownership. Martha White sponsored the 1996 and 1997 tours of Alison Krauss and Union Station, carrying on its long tradition of support for country and bluegrass music. In 1996, it joined forces with Lodge Manufacturing, one of the only remaining domestic manufacturers of cast iron, to sponsor the first National Cornbread Cook-Off. In 1999, in celebration of its 100-year anniversary, Martha White released its *Southern Traditions* cookbook and invited 27 bluegrass bands to compete for the honor of playing the Martha White jingle at the Grand Ole Opry.

BACK TO THE COMPANY ROOTS

After General Mills purchased Pillsbury during the summer of 2001, International Multifoods acquired Pillsbury's dessert and specialty products including Martha White. Deciding to invest once again in its folksy image, Martha White worked on building the brand from the ground up. Before the sale closed, it hosted a bluegrass bash for retailers at the Grand Ole Opry that included resurrecting the Bluegrass Express Tour Bus for a 150-concert tour. The effort improved sales by more than 20 percent and reestablished Martha White as a prominent brand in the South.

In 2004, The J. M. Smucker Company purchased Martha White as part of the foodservice and bakery products business of Multifoods. Smucker also acquired White Lily in 2006. Martha White continued to maintain its own management, identity, and web site under Smucker, as well as its dedication to southern-style cooking. Still committed to innovation, the company in 2008 invited bakers to take part in the Martha White Muffin Mix Challenge to create an original recipe using at least one of its 19 muffin mixes in a new way or as an adaptation of a traditional scratch recipe. With three brownie, eight cornbread, and three biscuit mixes in addition to 19 muffin mixes, as well as pizza crust and hush-puppy mixes, five varieties of corn meal, and self-rising and all-purpose flour, Martha White promised to keep southern cooks busy in the kitchen into the next decade.

Carrie Rothburd

PRINCIPAL COMPETITORS

The White Lily Foods Company; Gold Medal Products Co.

FURTHER READING

Auchmutey, Jim, "27 Bands Rise to the Occasion for Martha White Anniversary," *Atlanta Journal and Constitution,* August 1, 1999, p. 1M.

"Higher Price Tags Help to Spur Turnabout at Martha White Foods," *Barron's National Business and Financial Weekly,* October 4, 1971, p. 23.

Kennedy, Tony, "Pillsbury to Rise to No. 2 Spot by Buying Martha White; Acquisition of Retail Baking Mix Firm the Biggest Since Becoming Part of Grand Met," *Minneapolis Star Tribune,* July 20, 1994, p. 1D.

Kinsman, Matthew, "Retailgating," *Promo,* March 2002, p. 4.

Wassell, Irene, "Martha White Grows Up: New Image Updates a Southern Classic," *Arkansas Democrat-Gazette,* January 17, 1990.

Marubeni Corporation

—■—

4-2, Ohtemachi 1-chome
Chiyoda-ku
Tokyo, 100-8088
Japan
Telephone: (81 3) 3282-2111
Fax: (81 3) 3282-4241
Web site: http://www.marubeni.co.jp

Public Company
Incorporated: 1949 as Marubeni Co., Ltd.
Employees: 5,359
Sales: ¥4.16 trillion ($41.6 billion) (2008)
Stock Exchanges: Tokyo Nagoya Osaka
Ticker Symbol: MARUY
NAICS: 551112 Offices of Other Holding Companies;
523910 Miscellaneous Intermediation; 523920
Portfolio Management; 523130 Commodity
Contracts Dealing

■ ■ ■

Marubeni Corporation is one of the largest of Japan's general trading companies, known as *sogo shosha*. With a global network of almost 115 representative offices in 70 countries, Marubeni is involved in a wide variety of activities, including domestic, import, export, and offshore trade; investment activities; and product development operations, ranging from development of natural resources and raw materials to the marketing of finished products. The company consolidated its operations in the first decade of the 2000s, managing approximately 14 divisions whose interests include foods, forest products, chemicals, metals and minerals, real estate development, and energy.

EARLY HISTORY

In 1872 a young merchant named Chubei Itoh established a small store called Benichu in Osaka to serve as an outlet for his commercial trading business, C. Itoh & Company, which he had founded in 1858. A symbol for the store was created that placed the word *beni* (Japanese for "red") inside a circle, or *maru*. In 1883, as the Itoh trading company expanded, the Marubeni store was made its head office.

Over the next 20 years, C. Itoh & Company took over an increasing number of duties from foreign trading agents and established its own international trading network. The company experienced particularly strong growth after Japan asserted its military dominance in the region by defeating Chinese armies in 1895 and the Russian navy in 1905. At the outbreak of World War I, C. Itoh & Company took advantage of several opportunities in international trading, created when companies in Europe redirected their energies toward production of war materials.

Japan allied itself with the Entente later in the war, and when Germany was defeated in 1919 Japan was awarded German colonies and commercial rights in Asia. Within two years, however, uncontrolled economic expansion caused a serious recession that threatened hundreds of companies with financial collapse. C. Itoh & Company was forced to reorganize in 1921. The company itself was renamed Marubeni Shonten, Ltd., and several divisions belonging to its larger subsidiary C.

Marubeni Corporation, as a business enterprise, will actively pursue its business interests through the exercise of fair and legal competition. As a company, Marubeni will also continue to play its part in the enlargement of the global economy, while always striving to enrich the society within which it operates.

Itoh Trading became a new company called Daido Trading. Marubeni was mainly involved in textile trading, but expanded over the course of the decade to include a wider variety of industrial and consumer goods.

WORLD WAR II YEARS

In the early 1930s a group of right-wing militarists within the Japanese armed forces initiated a rise to political power based on subversion and terrorism. As strong opponents of Communism, these militarists were natural allies of the Nazi and Fascist governments of Germany and Italy. After taking control of the government they declared a "quasi-war economy" in preparation for the Japanese conquest of East Asia and the western Pacific.

Large Japanese conglomerates known as *zaibatsu* (Mitsui, Mitsubishi, and Sumitomo) and companies such as Iwai, C. Itoh, and Marubeni were viewed by the militarists as self-interested institutions of laissez-faire capitalism. One widely recognized goal of the militarists was the nationalization of these companies. At the time, however, nationalization was not possible. These companies were responsible for virtually all of the weapons, machinery, and provisions needed to maintain the Japanese occupation of Korea, Manchuria, and China, and to conduct subsequent military campaigns.

In 1941, as part of an effort to increase the scale and raise the efficiency of Japanese industries, Marubeni was merged with C. Itoh Trading and Kishimoto & Company to form a larger firm called Sanko Kabushiki Kaisha. On December 1 of that year Japanese forces attacked British colonies in Asia, and on December 7 attacked American forces in the Philippines and Hawaii.

Initially, Sanko performed better than most Japanese companies in the war economy. Later in the war, however, Japanese forces failed to consolidate their gains and the war turned in favor of the United States. Additional demands were placed on the economy in

general and companies such as Sanko in particular. In 1944, the year the Japanese mainland became exposed to American bombing raids, Sanko was merged forcibly with Daido Boeki and Kureha Spinning to form a new company called the Daiken Company. Chubei Itoh II, the son of Marubeni's founder, was placed in charge of Daiken as its president. The companies that formed Daiken, and even those that formed Sanko, were forced to perform under such extraordinary circumstances that none of them had an opportunity fully to integrate their operations with the other companies. Daiken existed more as an industrial group than a company.

POSTWAR RECONSTRUCTION

When the war ended in the late summer of 1945 most of the country's industrial capacity had been destroyed. An Allied occupation authority under General Douglas MacArthur initiated a plan for reconstruction and the general reorganization of Japanese industry. Large conglomerates, particularly the *zaibatsu*, were divided into hundreds of independent companies in an effort to eliminate monopoly practices and encourage greater competition. In 1949 Daiken, which was not a *zaibatsu*, was divided into Kureha Spinning, C. Itoh & Company, Marubeni, and a small manufacturer of nails called the Amagasaki Company. Marubeni was given authority to conduct international trade. Under the leadership of President Shinobu Ichikawa, the company utilized its strength in textiles to finance diversification into nontextile items such as food, metals, and machinery.

When the Korean War broke out in June 1950, Marubeni became one of thousands of Japanese companies whose services were urgently needed by the United Nations forces. Marubeni reacted quickly to new opportunities created by the war and as a result experienced faster growth than many other companies. The postwar Allied occupation transformed Japan into a cooperative ally of the United States with a focus on its development as an industrial nation.

The Korean War ended in 1953, and many United Nations supply contracts with Japanese companies were terminated. This caused a serious recession in Japan and forced many companies, including Marubeni, to reorganize operations and management. Nonetheless, the company declared itself fully recovered from both World War II and the recession in 1955.

On February 18, 1955, Marubeni merged with Iida & Company, an established name in Japanese business that operated several large department stores under the name Takashimaya. To emphasize its equality with Iida, the Marubeni Company changed its name in September to Marubeni-Iida. The Ministry for International Trade

KEY DATES

1872: Chubei Itoh establishes a small store in Osaka.

1921: C. Itoh & Company is forced to reorganize; the company is renamed Marubeni Shonten, Ltd.

1941: Marubeni merges with C. Itoh Trading and Kishimoto & Company to form a larger firm called Sanko Kabushiki Kaisha.

1944: Sanko is forced to merge with Daido Boeki and Kureha Spinning to form the Daiken Company.

1949: Daiken is divided into Kureha Spinning, C. Itoh & Company, Marubeni, and the Amagasaki Company.

1955: Marubeni merges with Iida & Company and changes its name to Marubeni-Iida.

1966: Marubeni-Iida merges with the Totsu Company.

1972: The company's name is changed to Marubeni Corporation.

1973: Nanyo Bussan is acquired.

1997: Marubeni launches its first fund, the MBI Fund.

2001: Marubeni-Itochu Steel Inc. is created.

2006: Marubeni forms a joint venture with the government of the Emirate of Abu Dhabi to create a general trading house in United Arab Emirates.

and Industry (MITI), the Japanese government's coordinating body for the nation's industries, selected Marubeni-Iida to handle trading activities for Yawata Iron & Steel and Fuji Iron & Steel (merged in 1970 to become Nippon Steel). As a result of this decision, Marubeni occupied a leading position in the field of silicon steel and iron sheets, which were being consumed in greater quantities by the growing Japanese appliance and automobile industries.

Marubeni-Iida's newly established machinery trade group was awarded several contracts over a short period during the late 1950s, firmly establishing the company in the area of engineering. These contracts included a nuclear reactor for the Japan Atomic Energy Research Institute, a fleet of aircraft for the Japanese defense agency, and a number of factories that produced components for the electronics industry.

Marubeni-Iida entered the petrochemical industry in 1956 when it helped a leading chemical fertilizer and aluminum company called Showa Denko to secure chemical production licenses from American companies. The company fostered relationships with other chemical companies and later became a leading importer of potassium and phosphate rock.

In the ten years from 1949 to 1959 Marubeni had reduced its concentration in textiles from 80 percent of sales to 50 percent. During the 1960s Marubeni-Iida acted as a supplier of materials for Japanese companies as well as a marketing agent for their products. In addition to textiles, metal products, and chemicals, Marubeni-Iida was active in trading light and heavy machinery and rubber products.

REORGANIZATION

In 1966 Marubeni-Iida merged with the Totsu Company, a leading metal and steel trading firm that was closely associated with the future Nippon Steel. The merger substantially increased the company's size and strengthened its position in metals. With the addition of Totsu's 1,380 employees to Marubeni-Iida's 8,000, the new company became a *sogo shosha,* a large general trading firm like the former *zaibatsu* companies. To cope with its new position as one of Japan's primary instruments for industrialization and growth, the new Marubeni-Iida initiated a general reorganization of its management and planning systems.

When the reorganization was executed in 1968, the company made greater efforts to develop raw material sources overseas, including petroleum products, coal, metal ores, industrial salt, foodstuffs, and lumber. During this time Marubeni-Iida improved its transportation and marketing networks and also improved upon the coordination of its various trading activities.

President Richard Nixon's decision to remove the U.S. dollar from the gold standard in August 1971 resulted in a worldwide disruption of currency values known as the "Nixon shock," or in Japan, *shokku.* The value of the dollar dropped steeply, which made it more difficult for Japanese companies such as Marubeni-Iida to export products to the United States. The company's operations were affected so adversely that it was again forced to reorganize. The company entered promising new lines of business, emphasized its more profitable existing operations, and divested itself of unprofitable slow-growth enterprises. The following January the company's name was changed to the Marubeni Corporation.

In August 1973 Marubeni acquired Nanyo Bussan, a trading firm that handled copper, nickel, chrome, and other metals from the Philippines. The acquisition increased Marubeni's share of the nation's copper imports from 0.8 to 7 percent, and refractories (hard to melt metals) from 0 to 30 percent. The addition of Nanyo Bussan to Marubeni further diversified the company's operations and strengthened its position in metals.

OVERCOMING SCANDALS

In February 1976 it was reported that Marubeni illegally diverted commissions from the sale of Lockheed aircraft to officials of the Japanese government. Marubeni was accused of bribing officials for their support of Lockheed sales in Japan. Marubeni, Lockheed's agent in Japan, initially denied any complicity in the scandal. Marubeni Chairman Hiro Hiyama, however, resigned in an effort to preserve the company's integrity. The former vice-chairman of Lockheed, Carl Kotchian, testified that Hiyama advised him to bribe the Japanese officials, in accordance with "Japanese business practices." Hiyama later denied Kotchian's testimony. By July prosecutors arrested nearly 20 officials of Marubeni and All Nippon Airways, including Hiyama, who was accused of violating Japan's foreign exchange control laws.

The Lockheed scandal came only three years after Marubeni was accused of profiteering in rice by hoarding supplies on the Japanese black market. Marubeni was seriously damaged by its unfavorable public image; more than 40 municipalities canceled contracts with Marubeni, and several international ventures were terminated.

Marubeni's president, Taiichiro Matsuo, who had served in the government's MITI, assumed the chairman's responsibilities. After declaring that it no longer represented Lockheed, the company implemented a reform of its management structure to improve upon checks and balances at the executive level. In a move toward decentralization, many of the president's administrative responsibilities were redistributed to a board of senior executives.

Marubeni recovered quickly from the Lockheed scandal. In 1977 the company's trading volume was double the figure in 1973. As the third largest of Japan's *sogo shosha*, Marubeni consolidated its international trading network and expanded its business in the United States, Australia, Brazil, Britain, West Germany, and Sweden. Marubeni also opened or expanded offices in the Soviet Union, the People's Republic of China, the Middle East, and Africa. The company later came to operate offices in more than 100 foreign countries. Through the early 1980s Marubeni was involved in the development of coal mines in the United States and Australia, a copper mine in Papua New Guinea, and nonferrous metal mines in Australia and the Philippines.

When President Ferdinand Marcos of the Philippines was forced into exile in the United States in February 1986, he brought with him 2,300 pages of documents that were seized by the U.S. government. Officials of the U.S. Congress later revealed that some of these documents detailed illegal payments by Japanese companies to President Marcos and several of his friends and associates. Once again, Marubeni was identified as a major participant.

Called into question was the Japanese "aid-for-trade" policy, which promised aid to foreign countries on the condition that Japanese companies performed the work. Whereas the Lockheed scandal brought down the government of Kakuei Tanaka and involved several suicides, the Marcos scandal merely damaged Japanese-Philippine relations. For Marubeni it was an unwelcome revelation that further compromised its public image. In addition, the company had suffered a ¥900 million appraisal loss due to the company's close association with the financially troubled Sanko Steamship Company.

CHALLENGES AND OPPORTUNITIES

The bursting of the late 1980s Japanese economic bubble led to prolonged difficulties for Marubeni in the 1990s. Nearly all of the *sogo shosha* had diversified aggressively into financial investments during the speculative bubble years, in large part because their traditional activity of marginally profitable commodity trading had been in a deep decline for years, a development compounded by a trend toward Japanese companies handling their international operations themselves. In desperation the trading companies built up large stock portfolios and became dependent on the revenues they could gain through arbitrage (or *zaiteku* in Japan). Once the bubble burst, the *sogo shosha* were left with huge portfolios the worth of which had plummeted, and all of the trading companies were forced eventually to liquidate much of their stock holdings. Marubeni's troubles were even greater because the company had made large real estate purchases near its Osaka headquarters during the bubble. In 1995 the company wrote off ¥45 billion ($542 million) from portfolio losses, declines in the value of real estate, and the liquidation and restructuring of both domestic and overseas subsidiaries. Further streamlining moves came in April 1996 when operations were reorganized into 21 divisions within eight business groups, and in April

1997 when the number of divisions was reduced to 19. In late 1997 Marubeni wrote off an additional ¥17.5 billion ($143.8 million) in portfolio losses.

As Marubeni recovered from the burst bubble, and as it operated within the environment of a prolonged 1990s Japanese recession, it pursued a variety of new revenue streams. In March 1996 Marubeni spent about ¥27 billion ($230 million) to purchase a 30 percent stake in the U.S.-based Sithe Energies, Inc., the seventh largest independent power producer in the world at the time. In May 1996 Marubeni and Toho-Towa Co., Ltd., Japan's largest film producer, announced that they would invest up to ¥13 billion ($125 million) over a three-year period in films produced by Paramount Pictures, a subsidiary of Viacom. The consortium's first release was *The Relic,* which opened in the United States in January 1997. In September 1997 Marubeni and France's Cie. Generale des Eaux S.A. announced they would invest ¥100 billion ($828 million) in a joint venture aiming to develop drainage and sewer infrastructure projects in Asia.

Beginning in late 1996, Marubeni began to investigate ways that it could take advantage of the forthcoming Japanese "big bang," the long-anticipated deregulation of the financial sector, a prime opportunity to secure new revenue sources. Targeting the consumer-financial industry, Marubeni launched its first fund, the MBI Fund, in July 1997 and planned for more.

Marubeni had weathered fairly successfully the variety of challenges it had faced in the 1990s, but confronted additional serious problems resulting from the Asian financial crisis, which began in 1997. The company had numerous operations throughout Asia, including significant activities in the troubled nations of Indonesia and Thailand. The crisis affected Marubeni and its bottom line, but the company had shown on more than one occasion in its history the ability to adapt to the fluctuations of the global economy.

MOVING INTO THE 21ST CENTURY

Marubeni focused on reducing debt and controlling costs during the early years of the new millennium. Commodity trading, natural resources, and foreign power generation remained at the forefront of its investment strategy. The company's first bold move of the decade came when it teamed up with Itochu Corporation and agreed to merge its steel products division with Itochu's operations. Marubeni-Itochu Steel Inc. was created in 2001.

Meanwhile, restructuring charges wreaked havoc on Marubeni's profits. During 2001, the company reported

a substantial loss, prompting Chairman Iwao Toriumi to step down. Shortly thereafter, the company faced an embarrassing public scandal when subsidiary Marubeni Chikusan Corporation was found guilty of falsely labeling over 100 tons of imported chicken as domestic.

Determined to rebound, Marubeni management implemented an aggressive new course titled "Vitalize Plan" in 2003. Under the leadership of Chairman Tohru Tsuji and President Nobuo Katsumata, the company worked to restore profitability. During the early years of the new century, Marubeni and most of its trading house peers successfully overcame Japan's economic woes. Through lucrative global partnerships, the trading houses positioned themselves in the upper echelon of Japan's business world. In fact, an April 2005 *Wall Street Journal* article claimed that Japan's top *sogo shosha* had fundamentally "transformed themselves into modern-day merchant banks, investing in ventures from Australia to Chile. They are crucial suppliers of capital, a sort of private-equity industry in themselves, though they often provide services, from financing to consulting, to go along with their investments." The article went on to report that the trading houses stood among the fastest-growing and most profitable companies on the Tokyo Stock Exchange.

During this period, the company remained steadfast in its plan to expand business while increasing profits over the next several years. During 2006, Marubeni formed a joint venture with the government of the Emirate of Abu Dhabi. The agreement would allow for the creation of a general trading house designed to capitalize on investment opportunities in the United Arab Emirates. In 2007, Marubeni and Mitsui & Co. Ltd. announced their intention to merge their liquefied petroleum import and wholesale businesses. A consortium led by Marubeni purchased Singapore-based Senoko Power Ltd. in a $2.8 billion deal in 2008.

During fiscal 2007, the company reported its fifth consecutive year of record profits. Teruo Asada assumed the presidency of Marubeni in 2008 while Katsumata was named chairman. The company remained focused on business opportunities in the Middle East and North Africa, in countries with economies that were expected to grow at a rate similar to those in Brazil, Russia, India, and China (also known as the BRIC countries). However, the global economy was faltering, with the United States and Europe experiencing rapid declines. Nevertheless, company management believed Marubeni was poised for success in the years to come. With 150 years of history under its belt, the *sogo shosha* stood well positioned to weather new economic challenges.

Updated, David E. Salamie;
Christina M. Stansell

PRINCIPAL DIVISIONS

Food; Lifestyle; Forest Products; Chemicals; Energy; Metals & Mineral Resources; Transportation Machinery; Power Projects & Infrastructure; Plant, Ship & Industrial Machinery; Real Estate Development; FT, LT, IT & Innovative Business; Iron & Steel Strategies and Coordination; Abu Dhabi Trade House Project; Overseas Operations.

PRINCIPAL COMPETITORS

Itochu Corporation; Mitsubishi Corporation; Mitsui & Co. Ltd.; Kanematsu Corporation.

FURTHER READING

Dawkins, William, and Alice Rawsthorn, "Japanese Groups Announce Plan to Invest in Paramount," *Financial Times,* May 14, 1996, p. 28.

Hayashi, Yuka, "New Tricks for Japan's Old Dogs," *Wall Street Journal,* April 7, 2005.

Iwao, Ichiishi, "Sogo Shosha: Meeting New Challenges," *Journal of Japanese Trade & Industry,* January/February 1995, pp. 16–18.

The Japanese Edge: The Real Stories Behind a Sogo Shosha—One of Japan's Unique New Class of Global Corporations, Tokyo: Marubeni Corporation, 1981.

"Marubeni Chief Sees Opportunity in Mideast Power Industry," *Nikkei Report,* October 29, 2008.

"Mitsui & Co.: Deal with Marubeni will Merge LPG Units," *Wall Street Journal,* June 13, 2007, p. A16.

Nakamoto, Michiyo, "Marubeni Heads for the Red," *Financial Times,* November 9, 2001.

Paris, Costas, and John Jannarone, "Marubeni-Led Consortium Prevails in Senoko Auction," *Wall Street Journal,* September 8, 2008.

Rosario, Louise do, "Lose and Learn: Japan's Firms Pay Price of Financial Speculation," *Far Eastern Economic Review,* June 17, 1993, pp. 60–61.

Sato, Kazuo, ed., *Industry and Business in Japan,* White Plains, N.Y.: Croom Helm, 1980.

Spindle, Bill, "Japan's Turmoil Opens Opportunities for Outsiders in Finance," *Wall Street Journal,* December 18, 1997, p. A19.

Terazono, Emiko, "Marubeni Writes Off ¥45bn for Closed Units," *Financial Times,* April 12, 1995, p. 29.

"Trader Marubeni Raided over Meat Mislabeling Scandal," *Jiji Press English News Service,* July 26, 2002.

The Unique World of the Sogo Shosha, Tokyo: Marubeni Corporation, 1978.

Yonekawa, Shin'ichi, ed., *General Trading Companies: A Comparative and Historical Study,* Tokyo: United Nations University Press, 1990.

Yoshihara, Kunio, *Sogo Shosha: The Vanguard of the Japanese Economy,* Tokyo: Oxford University Press, 1982.

Young, Alexander K., *The Soga Shosha: Japan's Multinational Trading Companies,* Boulder, Colo.: Westview Press, 1979.

Maruzen Company Ltd.

9-2, Nihombashi 3-chome
Chou-ku
Tokyo, 103-8244
Japan
Telephone: (81 3) 3272-7032
Fax: (81 3) 3272-7266
Web site: http://www.maruzen.co.jp

*51.28% Owned Subsidiary of Dai Nippon Printing Co.
Ltd.*
Incorporated: 1869 as Maruya Shosha
Employees: 856
Sales: ¥102.5 billion ($963.62 million) (2008)
Stock Exchanges: Tokyo
Ticker Symbol: 82360
NAICS: 451211 Book Stores; 453210 Office Supplies
and Stationery Stores; 448110 Men's Clothing
Stores; 448120 Women's Clothing Stores

■ ■ ■

Maruzen Company Ltd. is one of Japan's best-known
booksellers. From its initial concentration in the
importation and sale of books and journals, the
company has expanded into consumer merchandise, online and electronic content, and information systems. In
2008 over 54 percent of the firm's sales went to public
institutions such as schools and universities, with the
remainder generated via retail book stores, publishing,
and other businesses. The company's retail store business, which included approximately 50 outlets, suffered
during the early years of the new millennium as book

and magazine sales faltered. Dai Nippon Printing Co.
Ltd. gained controlling interest in the company in 2008
and planned to merge it with another subsidiary,
Junkudo Co., in late 2009.

19TH-CENTURY ORIGINS

Maruzen's roots stretch back into the late 1860s, an era
when Japan was evolving out of a 200-year period of
feudal government under the Tokugawa shogunate.
After years of isolation ended by the arrival of American
Commodore Matthew Perry in 1853, Japan entered a
period of rapid modernization that brought about
sweeping social, economic, and political change.
Established in 1869, Maruzen straddled the cusp of this
cultural shift. Maruzen founder Yuteki Hayashi was
urged to establish a bookstore by Yukichi Fukuzawa, an
educator and stalwart proponent of Westernization. Hayashi sought out, translated, published, and sold seminal
works of the Western world. The company's first store,
located in Yokohama, was joined by an outlet in Tokyo's
Nihonbashi section in 1870.

Hayashi's relationship with Fukuzawa, who founded
Japan's first private system of elementary and secondary
schools as well as Keio University in Tokyo, formed the
basis of Maruzen's strong sales to educational
institutions. Over its decades of service to schools and
universities, the company developed a comprehensive array of scholarly periodicals. By the mid-1890s, sales to
these markets constituted more than half of the
company's annual revenues. As Japan's own educational
and research institutions developed, Maruzen was also
well-prepared to print and distribute Japanese journals
overseas.

DAWN OF THE 20TH CENTURY BRINGS DIVERSIFICATION

Maruzen did not limit its imports to intellectual properties. After the start of the 20th century, it began to import contemporary business machines from the United States and Europe. The company got a foothold in the fledgling information technology industry in 1918, when it started importing and selling Wellington typewriters and American-made Monroe calculators. These early activities laid the foundation for Maruzen's later involvement in computerized databases and networks.

Maruzen also began trading in consumer goods early in the 20th century. The company started in this vein with domestic and imported stationery and office supplies. The firm expanded into clothing with an emphasis on brand-name, mostly British, apparel. In 1914 it received the country's first shipment of the world-famous Burberry raincoats. Maruzen later manufactured its own clothing, which was sold in company-owned stores and independent department stores as well as by mail order. Western-style liquor, eyewear, and even golf equipment and accessories were later added to the merchandise mix. By the mid-1900s Maruzen was importing furniture and supplies for offices and libraries, computers, office automation equipment, educational equipment, and teaching materials.

EXPANSION CONTINUES

During the 1960s and 1970s, Maruzen began to broaden its activities into the fields of arts and electronic information services. The company's involvement in the arts began in the early 1960s, when it hosted an exhibit of international art books. From this rather meager effort evolved the country's biggest art book fair. As it had in the past, Maruzen focused on making Western art and cultural institutions accessible to the citizens of Japan. Maruzen encouraged and assisted major museums from around the world in building Japanese annexes to their institutions. The Japanese retailer parlayed its relationships with the world's museums into a new profit center by reproducing and selling works of art. A 1990 agreement with the British Museum exemplified these efforts.

Maruzen established itself as an innovator in Japan's electronic information services industry in the late 1970s when it teamed up with Knight-Ridder Information Inc. to offer Japanese citizens their first opportunity for online access to an overseas database, specifically Knight-Ridder's DIALOG database of scientific documents. Maruzen enhanced its service to libraries with the development of the Computer Assisted Library Information System (CALIS) in 1984. CALIS provided library purchasing and cataloging departments with the information they needed to select, order, and catalog books and journals. This service made it easy for libraries to choose Maruzen as their book supplier. A selection of about 1,100 CD-ROMs and electronic books rounded out Maruzen's computer hardware and software offerings.

By combining its vast data resources with its computer networking expertise, Maruzen was able to design, install, and support local access networks (LANs) and other information management systems for its existing pool of library and museum clients. Augmenting this, by the early 1990s the company was designing physical environs as well, offering an integrated package including design, furnishings, computer hardware and software, and audiovisual equipment. The company later tailored these services for businesses and even competing publishers. Maruzen claimed that its computer division had "been offering an MIS (management information systems) package for publishers for nearly 30 years."

Maruzen expanded its operations into the preservation and conservation of rare books and documents, many of which were printed on rapidly deteriorating acidic paper, in the late 1980s. The company started a microfilming program in 1989, and had duplicated some 160,000 volumes by 1993. Maruzen completed the filming of the National Diet Library Collection (comparable to the U.S. Library of Congress) in 1991, thus preserving over 150,000 Meiji Era books. Maruzen, which characterized this project as "a feat as yet unmatched by any other library around the world," also won a contract with the National Diet Library to sell the film collection to other libraries. The union of Maruzen's computer know-how and preservation expertise facilitated the development of a sophisticated storage and retrieval system that allowed "multiple access

KEY DATES

1869: Yuteki Hayashi opens a book store under the name Maruya Shosha.

1914: Maruzen receives the country's first shipment of world-famous Burberry raincoats.

1918: The company begins to import and sell Wellington typewriters and American-made Monroe calculators.

1984: Maruzen enhances its service to libraries with the development of the Computer Assisted Library Information System (CALIS).

1991: The company completes the filming of the National Diet Library Collection, thus preserving over 150,000 Meiji Era books.

2000: Maruzen digitizes the National Diet Library's collection of books and pamphlets from the Showa Era.

2008: Dai Nippon Printing Co. Ltd. becomes Maruzen's largest shareholder with a 51.28 percent stake.

2009: Maruzen announces plans to merge with Junkudo Co., another subsidiary of Dai Nippon.

to up to 200 reels of microfilm in a LAN environment," according to the company's web site.

COMMITMENT TO KNOWLEDGE AND KEEPING PACE

In order to highlight its preservation program and commemorate its 120th anniversary, Maruzen spent more than $5.39 million to buy one of the fewer than 50 Gutenberg Bibles in existence in 1987. Maruzen's acquisitions of other rare books including the Hyakumantā Darani (Buddhist incantations to ward off disasters) saluted the company's blending of Eastern and Western cultures. The company said that these books "are representative of Maruzen's commitment to the dissemination of knowledge and are lasting symbols of the key role that the printed word has played in the development of cultures around the world."

From its earliest days, Maruzen strived to keep pace with the ever-changing field of information dissemination. This effort helped the company evolve from a retail bookseller into a provider of very advanced information services. During 1997 the company launched a new Internet service that enabled libraries to select, order, and organize collections while controlling costs. Knowledge Worker, an academic information database, made its debut two years later. The company's creation of a retail outlet in Singapore addressed one of its most apparent weaknesses during the 1990s, a lack of internationalization.

MOVING INTO THE NEW MILLENNIUM

The company's preservation expertise was called upon once again in 1999 when plans were set in motion to digitize over 80,000 science books and various publications from the period of 1926 to 1989, known as the Showa Era. The collection, owned by the National Diet Library, was launched on CD in 2000.

The early years of the new millennium proved challenging for Maruzen, however, as book and magazine sales faltered. By 2006 industry-wide sales had fallen by nearly 2 percent each year since 1998, and Maruzen's sales and profits were taking a hit. A January 2006 *Forbes* article explained the situation claiming, "Instead of reading, the Japanese are prey to the same time-consuming infatuation with the Internet and mobile phones as Americans."

At the same time, Maruzen became embroiled in an accounting scandal in early 2007 when it announced that an employee had inflated profits by approximately $7.4 million over the preceding five years. While the company worked to correct the problem and establish a system of internal controls to prevent future accounting irregularities, it continued to face hardships amid the slowdown in Japan's publishing industry.

Dai Nippon Printing Co. Ltd., owner of a 25.59 percent stake in Maruzen, increased its holding to 40.6 percent in 2008. It upped its stake to 51.28 percent later that same year. As the majority shareholder, Dai Nippon took control of the company and restructured it as a subsidiary. Under Dai Nippon's direction, Maruzen began to focus heavily on its academic and education-related business while cutting costs and restructuring its internal customer management system. It also partnered with am/pm Japan Co. Ltd. to open convenience stores on university campuses. The first store, Yamanashi Gakuin Maruzen, opened in April 2008.

Dai Nippon, one of Japan's largest diversified printing companies, had spent several years bolstering its publishing holdings; it also controlled TRC Inc., a provider of database, consulting, and operational supports services to libraries, as well as Junkudo Co., another Japanese bookseller. With sales in a downward spiral, Japan's publishing industry was consolidating and Dai Nippon appeared to be taking the lead. Indeed, the company announced in early 2009 that Maruzen and Junkudo would partner together in several ventures and eventually merge. The union, slated for completion in late 2009, would make Maruzen one of Japan's largest publishing concerns.

April Dougal Gasbarre
Updated, Christina M. Stansell

PRINCIPAL SUBSIDIARIES

Maruzen System Service Co. Ltd.; Maruzen Bookmates Co. Ltd.; Maruzen Mates Co. Ltd.; Olmo Co. Ltd.; Daiichikotetsu Kogyo Co. Ltd.; Maruzen Trycom Co. Ltd.; Kyocera Maruzen Systems Integration Co. Ltd. (27.3%).

PRINCIPAL COMPETITORS

Amazon.com Inc.; CSK Holdings Corporation; Tohan Co. Ltd.

FURTHER READING

"Corporate Profile: Maruzen," Tokyo: Maruzen Co., Ltd., 1993.

"Dai Nippon Printing to Sponsor Maruzen," *Nikkei Report,* April 21, 2008.

"Dai Nippon Printing to Turn Maruzen into Subsidiary," *Nikkei Report,* August 1, 2008.

"English Books in Japan," *Publishers Weekly,* June 3, 1988, pp. 50–51.

Gorsline, George, and Wyley L. Powell, "UTLAS-Japan Communications Link," *Information Technology and Libraries,* March 1983, pp. 33–34.

"How Distribution Works; Japanese Distributors and Importers Are Fast, Efficient, and Perform a Multitude of Tasks for Their Money," *Publishers Weekly,* January 12, 1990, pp. S27–S31.

Izumi, Sachi, "Japan Bookseller Maruzen Says Inflated Profits," *Reuters News,* January 19, 2007.

Kelly, Tim, "Iconoclast; How a Japanese Bookseller Has Avoided an Industry Slump," *Forbes,* January 9, 2006.

"Maruzen, am/pm Tie Up on Campus Stores," *Jiji Press English News Service,* January 30, 2008.

"Maruzen, Junkudo Eye Merger to Create Giant Bookseller," *Asia Pulse,* March 25, 2009.

"Maruzen to Integrate Biz with Library Service Firm," *Jiji Press English News Service,* December 16, 2008.

"Showa Texts Slated for Digital Publication," *Daily Yomiuri,* September 22, 1999.

Taylor, Sally A., "Asia: The Now & Future Book Market," *Publishers Weekly,* March 14, 1994, p. 34.

———, "Book Fairs Are a Growth Market in Asia This Year," *Publishers Weekly,* March 11, 1996, p. 18.

Marvelous Market Inc.

—■—

2825 Dorr Avenue
Fairfax, Virginia 22031-1504
U.S.A.
Telephone: (703) 964-5500
Fax: (703) 282-9830
Web site: http://www.marvelousmarket.com

Private Company
Incorporated: 1990
Employees: 500
Sales: $25 million (2008 est.)
NAICS: 445110 Supermarkets and Other Grocery
(Except Convenience) Stores

■ ■ ■

Marvelous Market Inc. is a Fairfax, Virginia-based chain of company-owned and franchised gourmet convenience stores, located mostly in the Washington, D.C., area, including eight units in the District and three in Northern Virginia. Marvelous Market is best known for its breads, especially sourdoughs, but also dark breads, flavored breads, flat breads, rich breads, and a variety of white breads. Other bakery items include muffins, scones, cookies, brownies, gingerbread, pastries, crackers, and a wide variety of cakes, pies, and tarts. The stores also carry gourmet cheeses, spreads, olives, and coffee, and offer sandwiches, salads, and such entrees as beef stew, chicken pot pie, lasagna, and spinach and feta chicken. No cooking or baking is done onsite. Rather, the stores rely on central commissaries and bakeries, and

all items are prepackaged, thus simplifying store operations and improving customer convenience.

Because of the range of its products, Marvelous Market is able to accommodate five day parts: breakfast, lunch, snack time, dinner, and catering. Efforts to successfully franchise the Marvelous Market concept have proved less than successful. Thompson Hospitality Corporation Inc. took over the chain in late 2008 with promises to reinvigorate the franchising program.

FOUNDER, A MEMBER OF THE KENNEDY ADMINISTRATION

The founder of Marvelous Market, Mark H. Furstenberg, originally came to baking as a hobby, not a business. He enjoyed a varied career and passed the age of 50 before turning his attention to baking bread as the cornerstone of his Marvelous Market venture. He started out in the public sector working on the war on poverty in the Kennedy administration. He went on to serve on presidential commissions studying crime and violence in America, became personnel director of the Boston Police Department, and then ran Reading Tube Corporation, a copper tubing manufacturer.

In the late 1980s Furstenberg was a Washington management consultant looking to start his own company, preferably related to food. He conducted market research in the District, sending surveys to 900 families in well-to-do neighborhoods. While many expressed interest in a deli and high-quality produce, there was overwhelming passion for good bread, a product that the area simply lacked in high quality.

Furstenberg traveled around the country for further research, making his way to California where he visited coastal bakeries. It was at "Celebrity Bread" on La Brea Avenue in Los Angeles that his quest came to an end when he sampled owner Nancy Silverton's sourdough rolls. "I had never tasted bread like that before," he told the *Washington Times*. Furstenberg trained with Silverton, working in the bakery for a week. Silverton then provided him with three jars of white, rye, and wheat sourdough "starter." She had created them four years earlier by soaking organic grapes in flour and water. All that was necessary to create a culture from which to produce his own sourdough bread was to mix the starter with flour and water in separate barrels.

Upon his return to Washington, Furstenberg borrowed $95,000 from friends and secured a Small Business Administration loan, altogether raising $300,000. He used the money to purchase the best available French baking equipment, leased a shop in northwest Washington on upper Connecticut Avenue, and hired a pair of experienced bakers, Eugene Gathright and Stanley Bosefski. The two men were then dispatched to Celebrity Bread to participate in a monthlong apprenticeship with Singleton to learn more of her techniques.

MARVELOUS MARKET OPENS: 1990

Marvelous Market opened its doors for the first time in July 1990, although the debut party was not held until September. The store's initial baked goods included a variety of baguettes, boules, and sourdough loaves. Washingtonians, starved for quality breads, quickly embraced Marvelous Market, which also carried a range of deli items, including Vermont cheeses, Virginia smoked trout and salmon, sausages, and an assortment of condiments.

The bread was the star attraction, however, and the reason why customers lined up outside the shop for a chance to make a purchase. Able to bake only 1,700 loaves per day, the shop was generally sold out by midday, prompting Furstenberg to institute a two-loaf limit on customers. He increased production to 2,000 loaves a day, but quality began to suffer.

To meet high demand Furstenberg established a central baking facility in a warehouse in Silver Spring, Maryland, which opened in October 1991, and added three retail outlets, in Union Station and Dupont Circle in the District plus one in Alexandria, Virginia. In addition the company provided catering and about 20 other area stores carried Marvelous Market breads as did a number of restaurants. Furstenberg sold off a quarter of the company in order to finance these moves.

He expanded too quickly, however. Marvelous Market lacked enough cash in the bank to support such rapid growth. The company soon was unable to keep up with payments to suppliers and as a result was forced to file for Chapter 11 bankruptcy protection in April 1994, listing $1.72 million in assets and $2.66 million in liabilities. The company's success also created a wealth of new competition. Marvelous Market continued to prosper but demand was not strong enough to fully utilize the production capacity of its large, new central baking facility.

COMPANY SOLD: 1996

Marvelous Market reorganized, granting 20 percent of the company to creditors and emerging from bankruptcy protection. Furstenberg's troubles were far from over, however. He had personally guaranteed loans to Marvelous Market and when the company continued to struggle, he lost his own assets and was forced to personally file for liquidation under Chapter 7 of the federal bankruptcy code in February 1995. Although he contended that his 43 percent stake in Marvelous Market had no particular value, the bankruptcy court put it up for sale.

The person to make the first bid, offering $63,000, was the man Furstenberg had just hired to serve as president, Jonathan Malbin, a New York food industry consultant. Malbin's move ruptured the relationship between the two men, leading to a struggle for control of the company. It culminated in March 1996 when Malbin's final offer for the company was rejected by Marvelous Market's board of directors and shareholders. Several months later another offer to buy the company was accepted by shareholders and Malbin was fired. The deal then received the necessary approval from the bankruptcy court, which was still overseeing the company's affairs.

NEW OWNERSHIP

Paying $525,000 for a 70 percent interest in Marvelous Market were 31-year-old Michael Meyer and 32-year-old Christopher Brookfield, along with a group of nine

KEY DATES

1990: Mark Furstenberg founds Marvelous Market.
1994: The company files for Chapter 11 bankruptcy protection.
1996: The company is sold; Furstenberg leaves.
1999: Marvelous Market begins pursuing the gourmet convenience store concept.
2006: The first franchised unit opens in Washington, D.C.
2008: Thompson Hospitality Corporation Inc. acquires Marvelous Market.

other investors. The two were former friends at the Darden School of Business at the University of Virginia, where they both received M.B.A. degrees in 1992. Meyer then went to work for Boston's Wellington Management as portfolio manager for a growth fund, investing in the likes of AOL, Netscape, and Starbucks.

As he dealt with entrepreneurs and high-growth companies, he began to nourish a desire to develop his own concept. Brookfield, in the meantime, had been working in Eastern Europe, opening a sales office for AMF Corporation in the former Soviet bloc countries that were new to capitalism. While home for the Christmas holidays, he met with Meyer and the two decided to go into business, in particular the boutique bakery business, which they believed could be to bread what Starbucks was for coffee. They targeted Marvelous Market, and began wooing its board of directors, a courtship that culminated in an agreement seven months later.

CHANGE IN COURSE PLOTTED: 1999

Meyer and Brookfield planned to better control costs and expand more slowly than had Furstenberg. Nevertheless, they harbored ambitions of ultimately spreading the Marvelous Market brand across the country. Furstenberg stayed on as a consultant for a brief period before leaving the company he founded, but he was far from ready to retire. In 1997 he opened The Breadline, another Washington bakery focusing on bread, and would later serve as a bakery and restaurant consultant.

The new owners of Marvelous Market faced difficult challenges in achieving their goals. They pared down the store's offerings, eliminating the gourmet products and focusing on the bread. Unlike coffee,

however, bread was difficult to replicate on a large scale. Moreover, there was a great deal more competition. The days of customers driving long distances to wait in line for the privilege of buying two loaves of bread were a distant memory. Not only was there a plethora of small bakeries offering high-quality breads, but local supermarkets and specialty stores had also entered the market.

Out of necessity Marvelous Market became as much an eatery as a bakery, but the bakery café concept was also becoming a saturated field. Around 1999 Meyer and Brookfield took stock of Marvelous Market, surveying customers to learn what they valued the most about the stores. Learning that it was actually the quick side of the business that held the most appeal, the partners elected to convert Marvelous Market into a hybrid operation that combined bakery, coffee shop, gourmet food shop, and convenience store under a single roof.

FOCUSING ON RETAIL: 2005

By 2004 Marvelous Market was operating nine Washington-area stores, supported by a pair of commissaries, generating total annual sales in the $10 million range. The company began taking steps to expand the concept nationally through franchising, expressing a belief that the market potential for its concept could be as large as 1,000 to 2,000 stores. Rather than invest money in a new central bread bakery to support growth, Marvelous Market elected to sell its bread baking facility in June 2005 and exit the wholesale business.

Instead, it turned to an area company, Uptown Bakery, which had just opened a new baking operation, to supply it with bread, allowing Marvelous Market to concentrate on its retail operations. The company chose, however, to retain a Fairfax, Virginia, pastry production unit. French baguettes were provided by Breadline, briefly reuniting Furstenberg with the company he founded. Furstenberg soon sold Breadline, which continued to supply Marvelous Market with baguettes.

Marvelous Market opened its first franchise unit in the Capitol Hill area in November 2006. The company hoped that it would be the first of about 50 franchised stores to open in the next $2\frac{1}{2}$ years, but growth could not keep pace with aspirations. The chain receded to the nine-unit level in the summer of 2008 when the company decided to sell its Bethesda Row, Maryland, store to focus on more profitable units. Nevertheless, management continued to express optimism that it would have more than 50 stores by 2010. By the end of the year, however, the chain was on the selling block.

BUSINESS SOLD: 2008

In November 2008 Thompson Hospitality Corporation Inc., the largest U.S. minority-owned food service company, agreed to purchase Marvelous Market for an undisclosed amount of money. Marvelous Market's new parent company was founded by Warren M. Thompson, a hospitality industry veteran, who in 1992 acquired 31 Bob's Big Boy restaurants from Marriott Corporation. He converted some of the units to Shoney's and developed some proprietary brands while also creating a contract food service business, which in 1995 became the company's focus.

Thompson Hospitality changed gears once again in 2007 when it acquired the Washington, D.C.–area Austin Grill Tex-Mex restaurant chain as part of a diversity program that included a franchising plan that emphasized minority participation. Marvelous Market became a part of this effort to encourage minority business ownership. While the financial backing of Thompson promised to help Marvelous Market realize its national aspirations, it remained to be seen if the concept would indeed enjoy broader appeal.

Ed Dinger

PRINCIPAL COMPETITORS

Firehook Bakers Inc.; Panera Bread Company; Starbucks Corporation.

FURTHER READING

Baum, Geraldine, "Wonder Bread," *Los Angeles Times,* October 23, 1990, p. 1.

Davis, Sabrina, "Ones to Watch: Marvelous Market," *QSR Magazine,* September 2007.

Day, Kathleen, "Bankruptcy Judge Allows Sale of Marvelous Market," *Washington Post,* October 12, 1996, p. H2.

Eddy, Kristin, "Bread to Be Simply Marvelous," *Washington Post,* September 19, 1990, p. E1.

Estrada, Louis, "Marvelous Market Files Chapter 11," *Washington Post,* April 23, 1994, p. C1.

"Going from Marvelous to Organic in Bethesda," *Washington Post,* July 21, 2008, p. D2.

Haberkom, Jen, "Fairfax Market Planning Growth," *Washington Times,* September 18, 2006, p. A15.

Hedgpeth, Dana, "Too Many Bakers, Too Few Buyers," *Washington Post,* February 23, 2002, p. E1.

Lesly, Elizabeth, "As the Long Bread Lines Testify, Marvelous Market Fills a Knead," *Washington Times,* June 1, 1992, p. B2.

Mui, Ylan Q., "More Than Bread Rises Between 2 Area Bakers," *Washington Post,* September 25, 2006, p. D1.

O'Reilly, Brian, "What's Next?" *Fortune Small Business,* May 2004, p. 65.

Pressler, Margaret Webb, "At Marvelous Market, a Spoiling Pair," *Washington Post,* October 7, 1995, p. H1.

Townes, Glenn, "Thompson Hospitality Buys Marvelous Markets," *Black Enterprise,* November 2008, p. 30.

Webb, Margaret, "A Little Dough and a Fresh Approach Make for Rising Hopes," *Washington Post,* November 4, 1996, p. F10.

Weinraub, Judith, "Bread Changes at Marvelous Market," *Washington Post,* June 15, 2005, p. F1.

McLanahan Corporation

200 Wall Street
Hollidaysburg, Pennsylvania 16648
U.S.A.
Telephone: (814) 695-9807
Fax: (814) 695-6684
Web site: http://www.mclanahan.com

Private Company
Incorporated: 1857 as McLanahan-Stone Machine
  Company
Employees: 224
Sales: $57 million (2008 est.)
NAICS: 333131 Mining Machinery and Equipment
  Manufacturing; 331511 Iron Foundries

■ ■ ■

A sixth-generation family-owned-and-operated company, McLanahan Corporation is a manufacturer of mineral processing and aggregate processing equipment, and also provides maintenance and repair services. The company offers customized roll crushers for coal, limestone, gypsum, salt, and other low silica materials; rotary breakers for further processing; pug mill mixers; hammer mills; sizers, used to size and separate materials; and feeders to convey materials for crushing and processing. McLanahan's Aggregate Processing Division manufactures equipment used to crush and scrub rock, process sand, and remove contaminants, as well as water management equipment needed for aggregate processing.

Also part of the McLanahan family is the HSS Sampling Division, provider of sampling equipment for the aggregate, coal production, and power generation industries. McLanahan's Agricultural Division offers dairy manure management equipment, including containers, augers for conveyance, pumps, and sand separation systems. Finally, McLanahan's Contract Sales Division makes use of its nearly 200-year-old foundry, the oldest family-run foundry in the United States, to offer custom-made castings and patterns. McLanahan's headquarters and main facility are located in Hollidaysburg, Pennsylvania, in the Allegheny Mountains of Central Pennsylvania. The company also maintains a manufacturing facility in Gallatin, Tennessee, and an office in Newcastle, Australia, for sales and engineering personnel.

FOUNDRY ORIGINS

The history of the company may be traced to James Craig McLanahan, who was born in 1794. He learned the iron business at Cove Forge in Pennsylvania and eventually became the manager of the Bedford Forge. In 1846 moved his family to Central Pennsylvania's Hollidaysburg, named after the Irish brothers, Adam and William Holliday, who first settled the town. In the 1830s Hollidaysburg had become a commercial center because it served as an important link between Philadelphia and Pittsburgh with the connection between the Pennsylvania Main Line Canal and the Allegheny Portage Railroad. McLanahan bought an interest in the Bellorophon Foundry in nearby Gaysport (later a part of Hollidaysburg) and established a machinist business with a partner named Michael Kelly.

The region became a center for the iron industry not only because of the transportation assets but also the presence of significant iron ore deposits, the abundance of hardwood trees that could be used to produce charcoal for smelting, and limestone that could be quarried for fluxing. Also available was coking coal, which would become important later when charcoal was replaced by coke, thus allowing these Central Pennsylvania foundries to continue to be viable producers of iron. One of a dozen foundries in the area, the Bellorophon Foundry had been established in 1835, a crude affair that relied on a blind horse circling a center hitch to power the blast for the foundry's cupola furnace. McLanahan acquired majority ownership of the foundry in 1848 and moved it to Hollidaysburg. A year later James Craig's 21-year-old son, John King McLanahan, who had been serving an apprenticeship in Philadelphia with Baldwin Locomotive Works, joined him to run the foundry.

TAKING ON A PARTNER

John King was steeped in the iron trade. His middle name, King, was the maiden name of his mother, whose father was a great iron master in Bedford County, Pennsylvania. At the age of 16 John King went to work as a clerk at Sarah Furnace and then entered his apprenticeship at Baldwin to further his knowledge of all aspects of the iron business. One year after he joined his father, the foundry was destroyed by a fire, and the younger McLanahan designed a new, improved foundry. He left in 1851 to serve as superintendent of Cincinnati's Shock Steam Fire Engine Works, where he designed the first steam fire engine in Ohio. He returned to Hollidaysburg in 1855 and became involved in a variety of concerns in addition to the family foundry, designing a furnace for Watson, White and Company and trying for a time to make a go of a fine pottery manufacturing operation.

In 1857 the McLanahan foundry took a new partner, with William Stone replacing Michael Kelly,

resulting in the McLanahan-Stone Machine Company, for which John King McLanahan served as president and Stone vice-president. Born in Philadelphia in 1819, Stone had learned the iron business as an apprentice molder. In 1853 he became foreman of the McLanahan foundry. It also around the time Stone became a partner that John King McLanahan's younger brother, Samuel Calvin McLanahan, began putting his inventive talents to work for the family. At just 14 years of age he created an accounting system for the company and began designing machines.

The foundry was always a financially precarious business. Several times the operation was destroyed by fires and rebuilt. In 1863 water from a nearby cresting river managed to seep beneath the foundry floor, meet the hot iron, and cause an explosion that destroyed the entire foundry as well as the shop. Once again, the McLanahan family rebuilt, adding in 1866 the first coke oven ever built in the United States. The previous year, James Craig McLanahan died, leaving the business completely in the hands of his sons. It was Samuel, around 1890, who used his mechanical genius to make the family less dependent on the foundry operation. Then in charge of McLanahan-Stone, he began inventing equipment, the manufacture of which would become the foundation of the McLanahan Corporation.

MOVING INTO EQUIPMENT MANUFACTURING

The McLanahan family owned phosphate deposits in Florida, but had to contend with wet clay that adhered to the rock. To address this problem, Samuel McLanahan invented what he called the Log Washer, for which he secured a patent in January 1891. It was a long box that inside had cast-iron paddles attached to wooden logs. The sticky phosphate rocks were placed inside, where they were washed and scrubbed free of the clay. This invention then led McLanahan to seek a way to make the rocks smaller before introducing them into the Log Washer. The result was the Single Roll Crusher, which used a roll and a solid plate not only to produce sticky feed the proper size for the Log Washer but could also be employed as a general-use crusher. During the early 1890s Samuel McLanahan also worked with inventor Hezekiah Bradford to build rotary breakers used to size coal. In addition to the Bradford Breaker, McLanahan Corporation eventually produced a complete line of rotary equipment for the coal trade, including scrubbers and screens. The machinery built by the McLanahan brothers quickly gained a reputation for performance and durability, leading to requests from others to produce machinery for them. As a result, a process equipment manufacturing operation took shape and steadily superseded the foundry in importance.

William Stone died an octogenarian in 1902, while John King McLanahan died at the age of 90 in 1918. He was followed in death by his brother Samuel ten years later. It was the latter's son, Craig "Ward" McLanahan, who then led the company. Ward McLanahan was also a track and field star, who in the 1904 Olympics finished fourth in the pole vault and also participated in the 110-meter hurdles. He was succeeded as head of the family business by his own son, Craig McLanahan, and then passed away in 1974. During this period the company, in 1961, adopted the McLanahan Corporation name. A year later a fifth generation of the McLanahan family joined the business, Michael W. McLanahan. Like his predecessors, he grew up in the business, paying visits to the shop as a child and as a teen working as a laborer in the shop during the summer months. After graduation from college he took a position in the sales department, beginning a grooming process that would lead to his taking the helm of the company in the late 1980s.

Under Michael McLanahan's leadership, McLanahan Corp. entered a new phase in its history. Not only was money spent to modernize the company's infrastructure, McLanahan diversified, adding product lines both through acquisition and licensing agreements. In 1988, for example, the company secured a license to sell multi-deck vibratory screens from Morgensen of Sweden, maker of sizing equipment. The following year

McLanahan added steel castings to its product offerings. Further expansion would take place in the following decade.

ROOTS OF AGRICULTURAL BUSINESS

McLanahan's Agricultural Division took shape in 1996 when it began to manufacture and sell dairy manure handling equipment and systems. Two years later the division debuted its sand-manure separation equipment, first installed at the Green Meadow Farms in Elsie, Michigan, addressing a longstanding problem for dairy farmers. Sand was used as stall bedding for the cattle, about 50 pounds of which would be kicked in the free-stall alley each day, intermixed with another 115 pounds of manure each animal produced. With a herd of 2,000 cows, Green Meadow Farms was producing well over 360,000 pounds of a sand and manure mixture each day.

McLanahan's separation equipment was able to recover as much as 90 percent of the sand passing through it. In addition, the removal of sand was the first step in reducing odor and eliminating pollutants. In order to separate the sand, however, the raw mix had to be properly delivered to the separator. As a result, McLanahan developed a complete system of manure-handling equipment, including an auger mechanism to replace a gutter cleaning system that could not keep up with the capabilities of the separator. McLanahan's sand-manure separation equipment quickly found a market with dairy farmers of all sizes around the world.

To better serve its customers, McLanahan entered the sampling business in 1998. On January 1 of that year, the company completed the acquisition of Hebden, Schilbe & Smith, a company that since 1964 had been designing sampling systems for such bulk materials as aggregate, coal, coke, and salt. McLanahan then added its own capabilities to provide customers with an even greater range of custom-designed sampling systems, able to capture materials as small as a grain of sand, whether wet or dry, and suitable for a wide range of needs. Service of the systems was also provided.

EXPANSION IN THE 21ST CENTURY

McLanahan continued to expand in the new century. A license agreement was struck in 2000 to sell German-made Allgaier Tumbler Screens, grading systems mostly used for powders, granulates, and small-grained bulk goods. The line of highly efficient screening machines performed in a circular, three-dimensional manner and could be adjusted to take into account material tendencies. A year later McLanahan acquired the sand and gravel and aggregate process technology product line of Linatex Corporation of America, which included cyclones, separators, hindered settling classifiers, pumps, dewatering screens, jigs, thickeners, and belt filter presses, all of which could be integrated to create custom systems. The assets were housed in a new unit called LPT Group Inc., which operated out of a facility in Gallatin, Tennessee, where Linatex Corp was based. Heavy fabrication and equipment assembly, however, was assigned to the highly capable McLanahan shops at Hollidaysburg. Serving as the president of the group was Michael McLanahan's son, Sean K. McLanahan. In May 2004 he was named executive vice-president and chief financial officer, poised to one day become the sixth generation of the McLanahan family to lead the company.

In 2003 McLanahan again added to its product offering through a licensing agreement that aligned itself with another German firm, KHD Humboldt Wedag AG, to sell KHD's jig and flotation equipment in North America. Also in 2003, McLanahan extended its reach overseas, complementing the business it was doing in Europe by opening a sales, engineering, and maintenance office in Newcastle, Australia, in order to serve the needs of Australia and other Pacific Rim countries. As a result a company tucked away in the Allegheny Mountains of Pennsylvania was growing into a major international player in its field. In keeping with this trend, McLanahan in 2008 struck a deal with Italian firm Matec to distribute throughout North America

plate and frame filter presses for aggregate processing. Given the reputation of the company, the scope of its products, and continuity that came with six generations of continuous family management, there was every reason to believe that McLanahan Corporation would continue to enjoy steady growth in the years to come.

Ed Dinger

PRINCIPAL DIVISIONS

Aggregate Processing; Mineral Processing; HSS Sampling; Agricultural Systems; Contract Sales.

PRINCIPAL COMPETITORS

Caterpillar Inc.; Metso Corporation; Telsmith Inc.

FURTHER READING

"John King McLanahan, Hollidaysburg Resident Dead," *Altoona Times,* December 16, 1918.

"McLanahan Corp.," *Pit & Quarry,* December 2002, p. 62.

"McLanahan Corporation," *Pit & Quarry,* December 1999, p. 96.

"McLanahan Corporation Offers Inventions and Innovations," *North American Quarry News,* April 1, 2007.

"The Pioneer Foundries of America," *Foundry Management & Technology,* September 1, 1992.

"Quality Since 1835," *Coal Leader,* May 2003.

Schoonmaker, Kimberlee, "Recovered Sand Solution," *Dairy Herd Management,* August 8, 2001.

Media Sciences
International, Inc.

8 Allerman Road
Oakland, New Jersey 07436-3324
U.S.A.
Telephone: (201) 677-9311
Toll Free: (888) 376-8384
Fax: (201) 677-1440
Web site: http://www.mediasciences.com

Public Company
Incorporated: 1987 as Cadapult Graphic Systems Inc.
Employees: 67
Sales: $24.2 million (2008)
Stock Exchanges: NASDAQ
Ticker Symbol: MSII
NAICS: 334119 Other Computer Peripheral Equipment

■ ■ ■

Media Sciences International, Inc. (MSII), is an Oakland, New Jersey-based manufacturer of generic color toner cartridges and solid ink for color business printers and industrial printers, serving as an inexpensive alternative to the supplies offered by such brand manufacturers as Brother, Dell, Epson, Konica, Minolta/Minolta-QMS, OKI, Ricoh, Tektronix, and Xerox. The company does not produce color ink-jet cartridges, too expensive an approach on a per-copy basis for businesses, which prefer instead color laser and solid ink printers. The first requires four individual color cartridges rather than the single black cartridge used in monochrome printers, while solid ink printers, just 5 percent of the color business printer market, rely on four solid ink sticks. Aside from saving business customers about 30 percent over branded toners and inks, MSII offers its INKlusive free office printer program, which along with automatic shipments of color supplies provides technical support.

In addition to the office printer market, MSII supplies solid ink to industrial printers, used by manufacturers to print bar, date, and lot codes and other package information. Unlike business printers, these coders rely on a single color at any one time, albeit in extremely high volumes. MSII offers two colors, black and blue, used in the Markem 9000 and 5000 series coders, and also supplies inks for two industrial printer manufacturers. Products are either sold under the Media Sciences label (70 percent) or in a generic white box. They are shipped to U.S. customers, representing about 78 percent of sales, from the Oakland, New Jersey, facility. A third-party logistics provider in the Netherlands handles distribution to Western European customers, who account for the remainder of the company's revenues. Led by its founder, Michael W. Levin, MSII is a public company listed on the NASDAQ.

FOUNDER STARTS BUSINESS WHILE IN COLLEGE

Media Sciences was founded in 1987 as Cadapult Graphic Systems Inc. by Michael Levin while he was still a mechanical engineering student at Lehigh University in Bethlehem, Pennsylvania. He started out to provide consulting services for computer-aided design (CAD) systems, primarily the high-end systems, having

COMPANY PERSPECTIVES

We didn't invent the idea of generic printer supplies. We just believe that color printer users should be able to have a cost effective choice in the marketplace versus the higher priced printer manufacturer's brand.

become interested in the field during his days at Lehigh. His customers were the companies he had encountered during college internships. After graduating summa cum laude he moved back to his parents' home in Ridgewood, New Jersey, operating his consulting business out of a basement office, funded by a loan cosigned by one of his parents.

Levin's consulting business grew and naturally evolved from advising companies on CAD software to the installation of graphic arts systems. Cadapult then began servicing the color printers that were a major part of such systems. The company extended its reach throughout the northeastern United States, beginning in 1996 with the opening of a sales office in Boston, Massachusetts. Two years later, in March 1998, another shift in direction took place when Cadapult acquired Boston-based BBG Technologies, Inc., a computer products reseller with $2 million in annual sales. No longer just a consultancy, Cadapult was then a provider of computer graphics systems, peripherals, supplies, and services, primarily catering to computer graphics professionals in advertising agencies, design firms, marketing companies, industrial designers, corporate graphics communications departments, and quick printers. It also served digital-media studios and film and animation studios, as well as the broad business-to-business market for color printers and copiers.

In 1998 Levin took Cadapult public by merging it with a shell corporation, the only tangible asset of which was its public listing. This entity had been formed in Utah in 1983 as Communitra Energy, Inc. Two years later the name was changed to Seafoods Plus, Ltd., but the enterprise was essentially out of business from 1988 to June 28, 1998, when it acquired Cadapult. The company was then reincorporated in Delaware as Cadapult Graphic Systems, Inc. Cadapult then had the ability to raise funds through the sale of stock, or to use its stock in making acquisitions. The company completed a pair of stock transactions in the first six months of 1999 to add to its reseller operations. In January of that year it purchased the assets of Tyngs-

boro, Massachusetts-based Tartan Technical, Inc., a company that sold and serviced computer graphics and imaging equipment and also sold supplies. Next, in June 1999, Cadapult bought select assets of a similar company, WEB Associates, Inc., based in Norristown, Pennsylvania.

COLOR INK BUSINESS ADDED

In a profile by the *Record* of Bergen County, New Jersey, in 2007, Levin advised people starting a new business to "be open to ideas and opportunities that present themselves even when they are not what you've originally set out to do." It was advice he drew from firsthand experience, having followed opportunities to become involved in the installation of graphic arts systems and then a reseller of the equipment and supplies. He was also quick to seize upon the potential of the Internet to drive sales, forming eCadapult to pursue this avenue through three services: an online store for selling products and supplies; the Sampleprint.com site to provide potential buyers of color printers and copies a chance to print sample files and compare the results from different equipment; and GraphicsAuction.com, an online auction site for computer graphics equipment. Cadapult also looked to host a site where graphics professionals could post their portfolios to line up jobs.

In 1999 Levin recognized another business opening, providing a lower-price alternative in the highly profitable ink-cartridge refill business. In August of that year he formed a subsidiary called Media Sciences, Inc., to manufacture and distribute digital color printer supplies. A month later Media Sciences acquired Cadapult's ink vendor, UltraHue, Inc., a Redmond, Washington-based manufacturer of color printer cartridges and solid ink sticks used by Tektronix printers. UltraHue was the world's only independent manufacturer of color toner and solid ink for business color printers.

Media Sciences got off to a rocky start, as Tektronix, in the process of being acquired by Xerox, tried to undercut the UltraHue business, leading to a lawsuit in which Cadapult alleged that Tektronix illegally terminated its reseller franchise because it was selling a non-Tektronix product: UltraHue solid ink. UltraHue had 3 percent of the solid ink market, which was essentially limited to Tektronix printers. Tektronix controlled 97 percent of the market and was determined to see no further erosion in this high-margin business by hindering Cadapult's ability to promote UltraHue's cheaper alternative. Another practice that came under fire was the denial of service for printers that used non-Tektronix supplies, despite the fact that it was illegal to

```
┌─────────────────────────────────────────────┐
│                                             │
│              KEY DATES                       │
│                   ■                          │
│                                             │
│  1987:  Michael Levin founds Cadapult Graphics│
│         Services, Inc.                       │
│  1996:  Boston sales office opens.           │
│  1998:  Levin takes Cadapult public by merging it│
│         with a shell corporation.            │
│  1999:  Cadapult forms Media Sciences, Inc., which│
│         then acquires ink manufacturer UltraHue,│
│         Inc.                                 │
│  2002:  Cadapult changes name to Media Sciences│
│         International, Inc.                   │
│  2008:  Plant in China opens.                │
│                                             │
└─────────────────────────────────────────────┘
```

tie warranties to the use of original equipment manufacturer supplies.

NO-CAP COLOR PROGRAM INTRODUCED

Cadapult clashed with Tektronix and Xerox on another front as well. In 1999 Cadapult launched its No-Cap Color program that provided free high-quality workgroup color printers, with retail values as high as $6,600, to customers willing to sign a two-year minimum supply purchase agreement. Three months later Tektronix introduced its own free color printer program, although not as broad as the one offered by Cadapult. Cadapult developed the free printer concept further by adding the INKlusive program, which provided a free printer for a two-year supply commitment to small businesses, nonprofits, schools, and similar-size customers.

In May 2001 Cadapult reached a settlement on its litigation with Tektronix and Xerox. While the details of the deal were not made public, the settlement had to be considered a victory for Cadapult, which not only remained in business but also continued to enjoy strong growth. It was soon marketing supplies for 14 Tektronix-Xerox printer models. Sales increased from $13.5 million in fiscal 2000 to $17 million a year later, and $23 million in fiscal 2002 when net income totaled $1.8 million.

To keep pace with growth, Cadapult, following the settlement of its legal difficulties, moved its headquarters in 2001 to a 15,000-square-foot, Allendale, New Jersey, facility, where it also had additional manufacturing capacity. A year later, in April 2002, the company decided to change its name as well, switching from

Cadapult Graphic Systems, Inc., to Media Sciences International, Inc. (MSII). It was a move that not only reinforced the Media Sciences brand, but also demonstrated the growing importance of the color printer supply business, which in each of the past two years had increased 60 percent. MSII was looking for larger accommodations, as well as to expand its product offering beyond Tektronix-Xerox printers.

In June 2004 MSII announced several new products that expanded the company's reach to two more top workgroup color printers, Minolta QMS and Epson. Later in the year MSII moved to even larger accommodations to house its rapidly growing business, relocating to a 42,000-square-foot facility in Oakland, New Jersey, which offered more manufacturing as well as distribution space.

GOING GLOBAL

By this time the company's focus had clearly shifted to the replacement toner and ink business. In May 2005 Cadapult's electronic prepress systems sales and service operations, the bulk of the subsidiary's business, was discontinued. Service contracts were sold and inventory written off, and in September 2007 all of Cadapult's operations came to an end. Without Cadapult's contribution to the balance sheet, MSII's revenues totaled $18 million in fiscal 2005.

MSII made a greater fiscal commitment to research and development, increasing the budget 73 percent, or $500,000, in fiscal 2006. Several new products were introduced in fiscal 2006, including color toner cartridges for the Oki 5000 series of color printers; solid ink sticks for the new Xerox Phaser 8500 and 8550 printers; color toner cartridges for the Ricoh 3800; and high-capacity cartridges for the Xerox Phaser 7300 and 6250, Oki 9300 and 9500, Konica Minolta Magicolor 3300, Epson AcuLaser C4100, Brother HL-4200CN, and Konica 7830 office color printers. These new products helped MSII to improve revenues 18 percent to $21.6 million in fiscal 2006. A year later, in fiscal 2007, MSII added $700,000, or 60 percent, to its research and development budget. It also hired additional personnel for the team.

A significant achievement in fiscal 2007 was MSII's ability to introduce a compatible ink for the new Xerox 8560 printer virtually as the model was introduced. All told, the company added products for 22 business color printer models. For the year sales improved 5 percent to $22.5 million, a disappointment to management, which had hoped for better results. Midyear actions were taken to rectify the situation. In particular, the top ranks of the sales organization were replaced by more seasoned professionals better suited to driving growth in Europe, the Middle East, and Africa. MSII also decided that in order to maintain future growth it had to develop its own xerographic manufacturing capacity, a move that would not only make it less dependent on vendors but also decrease product development time. As a result, MSII made plans to open a manufacturing plant in China and hired a managing director of Asian operations.

In 2008 MSII added European logistical capabilities and opened a plant in China, major steps in making the company a global concern. Revenues increased 8 percent to $24.24 million in fiscal 2008. Again, management had hoped for even better results, and in order to better align the operation with actual sales, the company trimmed its workforce. Nevertheless, the company, with its new plant in China and strong research and development effort, was well positioned to continue its growth on a global basis.

Ed Dinger

PRINCIPAL SUBSIDIARIES

Cadapult Graphic Systems, Inc.; Media Sciences, Inc.; Media Sciences UK Ltd.; Media Sciences (Dongguan) Company Ltd.

PRINCIPAL COMPETITORS

Konica Minolta Holdings, Inc.; Seiko Epson Corporation; Xerox Corporation.

FURTHER READING

Fitzgerald, Beth, "Smaller Name in Printer Ink Takes a Big Step Forward," *Newark (N.J.) Star Ledger,* March 27, 2007, p. 48.

"Forty Under 40: Michael Levin," *Business News New Jersey,* March 11, 2002, p. 30.

"Made in New Jersey: Media Sciences International, Inc.," *Newark (N.J.) Star-Ledger,* February 20, 2003, p. 46.

"Maker of Printer Color Is No Mere Copycat," *Record* (N.J.), May 17, 2007, p. B4.

McAleavy, Teresa M., "Media Sciences Moving Headquarters to Oakland," *Record* (N.J.), October 6, 2004, p. B3.

Savastano, David, "Media Sciences Makes Strides in Color Work Group Market," *Ink World,* May 2003, p. 60.

Menard, Inc.

———————■———————

4777 Menard Drive
Eau Claire, Wisconsin 54703-9604
U.S.A.
Telephone: (715) 876-5911
Fax: (715) 876-2868
Web site: http://www.menards.com

Private Company
Incorporated: 1972
Employees: 40,000
Sales: $7.9 billion (2008 est.)
NAICS: 444130 Hardware Stores; 444190 Other Building Material Dealers

■ ■ ■

Menard, Inc., is the United States' third largest home improvement supply chain. A rarity among retailers, Menards (as the company's stores are called) also operates its own manufacturing facility. The cost-saving measure is representative of founder and owner John Menard's penchant for keeping prices low. The regional chain faces market pressure from national players such as Home Depot and Lowe's, which have increased their presence in the Midwest.

FOUNDER'S VALUES: BEDROCK FOR BUSINESS

John Menard, the eldest of eight children, worked his way through the University of Wisconsin–Eau Claire by building pole barns with some fellow students. In col-

lege, he majored in business, math, and psychology, but his work philosophy was influenced by his upbringing. "Menard remains a farm boy at heart, anchored by a few simple beliefs," the *National Home Center News* (*NHCN*) stated in a 1996 profile. His parents, both teachers and dairy farmers, instilled in him "the principles of frugality and, in Menard's words, common sense."

Alert to opportunity, Menard expanded the boundaries of his late 1950s construction business. He began buying wood in bulk and then reselling it to builders scrambling to find materials on the weekends, a time when lumberyards typically were closed. In 1960, Menard added to his building supply line. A decade later, when the building supplies generated a majority of his revenues, Menard sold the construction end of the business. He founded Menard, Inc., in 1972, just in time to catch the building wave of do-it-yourselfers.

Deviating from the standard lumberyard format, Menards stores featured wide aisles, tile floors, and easy-to-reach shelves, a design similar to mass merchandisers. During the 1970s and 1980s, Menard opened building supply stores in a five-state area: Wisconsin, Iowa, North Dakota, South Dakota, and Minnesota. Menard snapped up vacated retail sites that were inexpensive but well situated. Seconds, overstocks, and closeout items were peppered among the product mix. By 1986, Menard ranked 15th among the top home improvement chains, with estimated sales from the 34 outlets approaching the half billion mark.

To support the growing company, in the early 1990s Menard opened a huge warehouse/distribution center and a manufacturing plant. Menard moved into Nebraska in 1990, the Chicago area in 1991, and Indiana and Michigan in 1992. The economic downturn in the early 1990s slowed home turnover and boosted sales on the home repair and improvement front.

EXPANSION DRIVE

By the fall of 1993, 12 Menards stores served suburban Chicago and were in direct competition with the 28-unit, Illinois-based Handy Andy chain, as well as Builders Square and HomeBase. Anticipating the arrival of Atlanta's Home Depot, Menard announced a major expansion drive. The company planned to open up to 18 additional stores in three different formats. The regional chain ended 1993 with a total of 88 stores and $1.7 billion in revenues. The $9 billion home improvement supply leader, Home Depot, entered the Chicago market in September 1994.

John Menard, meanwhile, based on a net worth of close to $400 million, qualified for the *Forbes* 400 list in 1994. His personal wealth allowed him to finance a longtime hobby. In 1979, along with two friends, Menard had purchased a $65,000 racing car, which Herm Johnson drove in the Indianapolis 500. Team Menard cars had become perennial entries in the event; Menard spent millions on car and engine development. In 1994, Menard qualified two out of the three cars he sponsored for the Indy 500 and placed 8th and 20th. "He'll need to do a lot better than that to succeed in Chicago," wrote Frank Wolfe for *Forbes* magazine in June 1994.

By the end of 1995, Menard operated 115 outlets and produced $2.7 billion in sales. The company's rapid growth in the Chicago area played a significant role in the demise of Handy Andy and Courtesy Home Centers according to *NHCN*. The privately held Menard funded its growth through cash flow generated by the stores: "That cash flow is sustained by aggressive cost containment policies that come directly from its president, whom vendors will describe as 'tenacious, frightening, entrepreneurial and paranoid,' all in the same breath," reported *NHCN* in May 1996. Sole owner John Menard's business practices served the company well; Menard, Inc., claimed the 44th spot on the *Forbes* list of the largest private U.S. companies in 1996 and held third place in the home improvement industry.

KEEPING PRICES LOW

In spite of the company's increasing size, Menard retained the flavor of a family business. One of John Menard's brothers, a daughter, a son, and a nephew held prominent management positions, and day-to-day policies reflected the owner's worldview. Employees put in six-day workweeks, both in stores and at the more than 600-acre corporate headquarters in Eau Claire. Store workers built gondolas, bulk displays, and checkout counters. Scrap wood was used for store signage, and carpet remnants covered displays. The company's buyers played hardball with suppliers when negotiating allowances, discounts, and price increases.

Menard tenaciously held to his low price strategy, including in head-to-head competition with Home Depot, even when it meant slim margins. Staple products such as studs and paint sold consistently below Home Depot's prices, sometimes just by a penny. Conversely, Menard was trying to upgrade its image in order to draw in more middle and upper income shoppers. In the familiar 120,000-square-foot format, Menards stores were reminiscent of 1970s discount stores, but in upscale neighborhoods the company needed to cater to customers more concerned with quality than cost.

Menards stocked better-quality product lines in areas such as kitchen and bath; more employees walked the sales floor. In 1996, a new 165,000-square-foot format was introduced although the department store–like design was retained. The company also upped its advertising expenditures and offered its first private-label credit card that year. Despite the changes, the dominant advertising theme remained the same: "Save Big Money at Menards."

Menards stores, furthermore, were considered a rarity among retailers by depending on vertical integration as a cost-saving measure, according to *NHCN*. The products Menard manufactured in its plant accounted for about a quarter of items sold. In-house production cut an estimated 10 percent off the cost of going through a supplier for a steel door. Among others items, Menards stores offered the company's own line of Formica countertops, dog houses, and picnic tables. The company had $45 million invested in the state-of-the-art manufacturing facility, according to a 1997 *Forbes* article.

Menard's across-the-board control helped him produce the highest sales per employee ratio among industry leaders. On the other hand, Menard's penchant

KEY DATES

1960: John Menard begins reselling lumber as a side business to pole barn building.
1972: Menard, Inc., is founded.
1991: The company enters the Chicago market as part of an expansion drive.
1996: Menard ranks 44th on *Forbes* magazine's list of largest private U.S. companies.
1999: The company enters into direct competition with the two largest home improvement chains in several key markets.
2000: The company opens its 150th store.
2001: Menard begins focusing on larger stores that carry appliances.
2003: Plans to introduce a private-label credit card are announced.
2005: Menard pleads guilty to disposing of pollutants into Wisconsin waters without a permit.
2008: The company has 240 locations in 11 states.

for being in charge generated lawsuits from disgruntled ex-employees, as well as customers and suppliers. Few, though, could ignore his bottom line; 1996 after-tax profits were $93 million, up 15 percent from 1995, according to *Forbes*. The 128 Menards stores produced $3.1 billion in sales for the year.

PRESSURE BUILDING

The onslaught of larger players had brought other home improvement concerns to their knees while Menard flourished. Kmart closed its five Minneapolis-area Builders Square stores when Home Depot entered the market. By contrast, Menard's properties produced higher per square foot sales than Home Depot's midwest offerings.

In a February 1997 *Forbes* article, James Samuelson said John Menard attributed part of his success against Home Depot to the sheer size of the industry leader's stores. "He believes that many do-it-yourselfers, especially the weekenders, feel pressed for time and are put off by Home Depot's cavernous, cement-floored superstores, where the merchandise is stacked high in the air." Menards offered a comparable number of items, an average of 50,000 per store, in a smaller space by rapidly restocking shelf items from ample warehouse and stockroom space adjacent to each store.

The company distinguished itself from Home Depot via advertising as well. While Home Depot's

promotions had some glitz, Menard's television ads, shot in the flagship store, had a down-home feel. "The spots feature a 70-year-old Ray Szmanda, a longtime employee from Eau Claire who simply goes on the air to point out Menard's low prices on hammers and shower curtains and other household gear that appeals to local do-it-yourselfers," wrote Samuelson. The company used its midwest roots to encourage customer loyalty.

In the latter half of 1997, rumors circulated regarding Menard's future as an independent entity. Some Wall Street analysts suggested the number two home improvement retailer was interested in buying Menard to gain a foothold in the Midwest. North Carolina-based Lowe's Companies Inc. operated 402 stores and reported 1996 sales of $8.6 billion. At the time, number one Home Depot had sales of $19.5 billion. Both of the industry leaders were in expansion drives. John Menard denied the rumors.

Also in 1997, Menard received a fine of $1.7 million for violating Wisconsin laws regulating the disposal of hazardous waste. The company had also been fined in 1989 and 1994. In other legal action, Menard faced off against fellow contenders in the $150 billion home improvement market over advertising claims. Sears sued Menard and Menard in turn sued Home Depot.

PRESSURE CONTINUES AT DECADE'S END

Home Depot entered another one of Menard's midwest strongholds in 1998. The four Milwaukee-area Menards stores, thanks to the company's regional roots, held market leadership. A number of independent retailers also had a strong following among area consumers. Menard planned to add more Milwaukee stores in response to Home Depot's challenge. In 1998, Home Depot's 888 stores earned nearly $40 billion; Lowe's 550 stores produced sales of about $16 billion; and number three Menard's 139 stores followed behind with $4 billion in sales.

In 1999, number two Lowe's entered the Chicago market with plans to open 20 to 30 stores. Menard had 25 Chicago outlets. Home Depot operated 31 units and was poised to add ten to 20 more. The entry of Lowe's was expected to spark a price war in the nation's largest hardware market. Menard had cut prices 10 percent during a 1998 price war with Home Depot.

Lowe's pending entry into the Chicago area rekindled some speculation about a merger with Menard. However, in a December 1999 *Crain's Chicago Business* article, John Caulfield, executive editor of *National Home Center News* in New York, indicated that a merger with Lowe's was unlikely, given Menard's emphasis on lower-priced items, and a different approach to store layout.

Menard celebrated the opening of its 150th store in early 2000. At the time, Christopher Menard, vice-president of distribution, announced that the company would be phasing out the sale of products made out of wood cut from endangered forests. Menard followed the action of other home improvement dealers such as Home Depot.

Just as the industry had been under pressure by environmentalists, Menard felt the squeeze of market leaders Home Depot and Lowe's. Industry observers generally agreed that only two big chains could thrive in a particular market. Given John Menard's competitive nature, it was clear that he intended to hang on to his share of the midwest home improvement scene. This was evident in early 2001 when Menard and Home Depot went head-to-head in West St. Paul, Minnesota, where the latter company had plans to build a 170,000-square-foot store.

SUPERSIZING

Menard itself began focusing on newly constructed, larger stores that carried a range of appliances and spanned anywhere from 161,000 square feet to 171,000 square feet. Menard also announced plans to build its largest Wisconsin store, on the site of a racetrack in the town of Franklin. In addition, large-sized stores were slated for construction in Fort Wayne, Indiana, and Grand Forks, North Dakota. The company rounded out 2001 with estimated sales of $5.2 billion.

By mid-2002, Menard had opened a total of ten large-sized, next-generation stores, bringing the size of its chain to 165 locations. The company moved forward on a path of steady, measured growth, and an emphasis on even larger stores. In the Chicago market, plans were made to begin building several suburban locations that were as large as 225,000 square feet.

In early 2003 Menard revealed plans to introduce a private-label credit card in partnership with Household International. By October of that year, the company's chain of stores had increased to 184 locations in ten states. At that time, John Menard found himself involved in an entanglement with the Internal Revenue Service (IRS), which claimed he owed $78 million in back taxes. Specifically, the IRS claimed that money paid to Menard in the form of salary, a tax-deductible business expense, and to his Team Menard racing team, should have instead been considered dividends paid to Menard.

Menard kicked off 2004 on a high note, announcing plans to build its largest store to date, a 250,000-square-foot location in Duluth, Minnesota. That September, the U.S. Tax Court issued a ruling in its case against John Menard. After evaluating the salaries paid to the CEOs of competitors Lowe's and Home Depot, a judge ruled that John Menard's $20.64 million salary was excessive. Specifically, the judge found that Menard was entitled to a salary of $7.07 million, and that the remainder of his compensation was considered a dividend. In all, Menard was ordered to pay the IRS $5.72 million in additional taxes, along with a penalty of nearly $188,296.

CHALLENGING TIMES

Difficulties continued that November, when the Wisconsin attorney general's office alleged that the company improperly disposed of hazardous materials, based on an investigation by the Department of Natural Resources. Specifically, the complaint alleged that Menard had disposed of neutralized battery acid, solvent, oil, and spray paint down a floor drain in its distribution center for a period of five years.

Midway through 2005, Menard pleaded guilty to disposing of pollutants into Wisconsin waters without a permit. By doing so, the state dropped an additional hazardous waste dumping charge. Following a hearing in August, the company was fined $2 million for the incident. Despite this setback, progress continued as Menard continued to open new stores. By mid-2007 the company had more than 200 locations in Wisconsin, Illinois, Michigan, Iowa, Indiana, Nebraska, Missouri, Ohio, South Dakota, and North Dakota. That year, *Forbes* estimated John Menard's worth at $7.3 billion, making him the richest person in Wisconsin.

By May 2008, Menard had increased its base of retail stores to 240 locations in 11 states. At that time, the company began pursuing a strategy to develop residential subdivisions located in close proximity to existing or new Menards retail stores. Some observers considered the strategy, which allowed Menard to forge new relationships with homeowners and builders, to be unusual, especially in light of weakening economic conditions. Nevertheless, the company moved forward with plans for subdivisions in Urbana, Illinois, and Warsaw, Indiana.

In March 2009, John Menard claimed victory when the Seventh U.S. Circuit Court of Appeals reversed the U.S. Tax Court's decision regarding his liability for more than $5 million in taxes. Heading toward the second decade of the 21st century, his business held onto its third-place position in the ultra-competitive home improvement retail sector. Although the company moved forward into an uncertain economic climate, marked by high unemployment and a slowdown in the housing market, Menard seemed to be well positioned for continued success.

Kathleen Peippo
Updated, Paul R. Greenland

PRINCIPAL DIVISIONS

Menards; Midwest Manufacturing Division.

PRINCIPAL COMPETITORS

The Home Depot, Inc.; Lowe's Companies, Inc.; True Value Co.

FURTHER READING

"Builders Square Closing 34 Units," *Chicago Tribune,* February 11, 1999.

Carlo, Andrew, "Menard Beefs Up to Compete," *National Home Center News,* July 2, 2001.

———, "Menard Reveals Strategy for Slow, Steady, Regional Growth: Retailer Keeps Rolling Out Bigger Stores," *Home Channel News,* June 17, 2002.

Daykin, Tom, "Menard Breaks New Ground; Retailer Hopes Developing Subdivisions Will Pay Off," *Milwaukee Journal Sentinel,* May 5, 2008.

Demaster, Sarah, "Depot's Entry Did Not Shake Rivals in Milwaukee Market," *National Home Center News,* May 3, 1999.

Freeman, Laurie, "Menards John Menard," *Advertising Age,* June 30, 1997, p. S23.

"Home Center Mogul Keeps a Low Profile," *St. Paul Pioneer Press,* September 3, 1997, p. 7B.

"John Menard," *National Home Center News,* December 16, 1996.

Klobuchar, Jim, "Disabled Girl's Dad Loses Job by Building House with Ramps," *Minneapolis Star Tribune,* June 3, 1992, p. 3B.

McAuliffe, Bill, "FYI: The Menards Guy Is Calling It Quits," *Minneapolis Star Tribune,* November 17, 1998, p. IB.

"Menard Has No Trouble Playing with the Giants," *National Home Center News,* May 20, 1996, p. 68.

"Menard Prepares for Aggressive Chicago Push," *Building Supply Home Centers,* October 1993, p. 20.

"Menards Hops onto Eco Bandwagon," *National Home Center News,* February 21, 2000, p. 4.

"Menards Is Fined for Mishandling Hazardous Waste," *Minneapolis Star Tribune,* December 11, 1997, p. A6.

"Menards Pleads Guilty to Illegal Dumping," *Home Channel News NewsFax,* May 31, 2005.

Moore, Janet, "Menard Discounts Speculation About Buyout by Lowe's," *Minneapolis Star Tribune,* September 11, 1997, p. Dl.

Murphy, H. Lee, "Lowe's Builds for Area Expansion: Hardware Retailer Aims to Nail Menard's, Home Depot," *Crain's Chicago Business,* December 20, 1999, p. 3.

"The NHCN Top 10: A Five-Year Perspective: Menard Inc.," *National Home Center News,* May 25, 1998, p. 84.

"The NHCN Top 10: A Five-Year Perspective: Menard Inc.," *National Home Center News,* May 24, 1999, p. 58.

"No. 3: Menard," *National Home Center News,* May 26, 1997, p. 80.

Novack, Janet, "The Do-It-Yourself Billionaire," *Forbes,* October 6, 2003.

Reusse, Patrick, "The Right Stuff," *Twin Cities Business Monthly,* August 1999.

Samuelson, James, "Tough Guy Billionaire," *Forbes,* February 24, 1997, pp. 64, 66.

Walker, Dan, "Menard Wins Case on Appeal; Tax Court Decision on Billionaire's Salary Reversed," *Milwaukee Journal Sentinel,* March 12, 2009.

Wolfe, Frank, "Rearview Mirror," *Forbes,* June 20, 1994, p. 138.

The Middleby Corporation

1400 Toastmaster Drive
Elgin, Illinois 60120
U.S.A.
Telephone: (847) 741-3300
Fax: (847) 741-0015
Web site: http://www.middleby.com

Public Company
Incorporated: 1985
Employees: 1,779
Sales: $651.9 million (2008)
Stock Exchanges: NASDAQ
Ticker Symbol: MIDD
NAICS: 333294 Food Product Machinery Manufacturing

■ ■ ■

The Middleby Corporation is a leading designer, manufacturer, and marketer of a wide range of commercial and institutional foodservice equipment. Its products include heavy-duty cooking equipment such as ranges, convection ovens, broilers, grills, and fryers used in restaurants and other institutional kitchens; commercial toasters, mixers, griddles, and other cooking equipment used in fast-food, casual, and full-service restaurants; and other innovative and energy efficient foodservice products that Middleby manufactures and distributes. The company launched a major restructuring effort in late 1999 under the leadership of CEO Selim Bassoul and has since secured a position as a global leader in the foodservice equipment industry with products found in over 100 countries across the globe.

INCORPORATED IN 1985

The Middleby Corporation was incorporated in Delaware on May 14, 1985, as a successor to TMC Industries Ltd. From 1978 to 1985 TMC Industries was the parent company of WWG Industries, Inc., a Georgia-based carpet manufacturer. TMC Industries had acquired WWG Industries in 1978 for $100 million from Champion International Corporation. High interest rates and a collapsing housing market forced WWG Industries into Chapter 11 bankruptcy protection in the early 1980s. When it emerged from Chapter 11 protection in 1983, largely under the guidance of William F. Whitman Jr., a former PaineWebber executive, WWG Industries acquired the Middleby Marshall Oven Co., Inc., in a highly leveraged deal.

Middleby Marshall was a well-established manufacturer of conveyor ovens with a reputation for high-quality products. It was founded in 1888 by Joseph Middleby, who owned a bakery-supply firm, and John Marshall, a licensed engineer. The business was created to produce custom designed movable ovens. Up to the time it was acquired in 1983, the company specialized in developing and introducing new innovations in baking technology and equipment. In 1976 descendants of the founding families sold the company to Stewart Systems, Inc., a Dallas-based baking systems engineering firm.

The 1983 sale of Middleby Marshall was engineered by William F. Whitman Jr. and David P. Riley, who

COMPANY PERSPECTIVES

The Middleby Corporation believes in the importance of social responsibility in its business practices. We strive to reach the highest standards in serving our communities, supporting our customers and employees and caring for the environment. We believe this brings sustained, collective value to our shareholders, our employees, our customers and society.

managed the unit for Stewart Systems. Riley first saw the possibility of splitting off Middleby Marshall from Stewart in 1982 and contacted an investment banker about a possible leveraged buyout. A year later Whitman emerged as a partner after steering WWG out of bankruptcy. Following the acquisition of Middleby Marshall by WWG, Whitman held 51 percent of the new company and became chairman of the board, and Riley was named president and, later, chief executive officer. Recalling the acquisition, Whitman told *Crain's Chicago Business,* "I liked the company because of its proprietary, patented oven, with its strong margins. The company also has a sterling, almost Rolls Royce, reputation."

The leading pizza chains, notably Domino's Pizza Inc. and Pizza Hut Inc., recognized the superiority of Middleby Marshall's conveyor ovens, whose greater cooking speed and patented cooking methods enabled them to guarantee faster pizza deliveries. With WWG Industries as Middleby Marshall's parent company, Middleby Marshall benefited from WWG's net loss carry-forward tax benefits, which were valued at $50 million, and its status as a public company.

FIRST YEARS DIFFICULT FOR THE MIDDLEBY CORPORATION

The first two years for Middleby were marked by flat sales and earnings, and the company reported a net loss of $1.1 million on net sales of $24.8 million in 1986. Cooking ovens were the company's core business, accounting for approximately 75 percent of net sales. Its acquisition of Reynolds Electric Co. for $1.4 million in cash gave Middleby a presence in the commercial mixer business, but it was facing stiff competition from Hobart Corporation, which held an 80 percent share of the $100 million commercial mixer market. Middleby looked to its core business for future growth and enjoyed 40 percent margins on the sales of its cooking ovens.

In November 1986 Middleby divested itself of its revolving tray oven business, Culter Industries, Inc., for $200,000. The unit had been a significant drag on earnings, accounting for only 12 percent of sales while occupying some 35 percent of manufacturing space. Following the sale, earnings improved with the help of other cost-cutting measures, and in 1987 Middleby reported net income of $629,000 on net sales to $29.1 million, a 17 percent increase in net sales over the previous year.

ACHIEVED RECORD SALES AND NET INCOME IN 1988

Middleby posted record sales in 1988, up 18 percent over the previous year to $34.2 million, and net income of $4.2 million, a peak it was unable to match in subsequent years (through 1996). Middleby was able to improve its balance sheet and eliminate much of its debt, significantly reducing interest expense and improving the bottom line of its income statement. At the end of 1986, debt had accounted for 97 percent of Middleby's capital structure. In November 1987 the company was able to refinance and reduce debt to 61 percent, with 25 percent preferred stock and 14 percent shareholders' equity accounting for the company's remaining capitalization. Middleby's strong performance in 1988 then allowed it to prepay all of its revolving bank debt more than four years ahead of schedule, so that by year-end 1988 debt represented only 34 percent of the company's capitalization.

On July 13, 1988, the company's stock, which had been trading on NASDAQ over-the-counter markets, was listed on the American Stock Exchange (AMEX). In December the company began a cash dividend program, starting with a $0.02 quarterly dividend and a special year-end dividend of $0.03 per share. To improve the liquidity and marketability of the company's stock, a five-for-four common stock split was effected June 1, 1988. The dividends would be suspended in 1991, however, and no further dividends have been paid.

At this time, the company's principal product was the Pacesetter oven, which was sold to what was then called "fastfood chain" markets and, especially, pizza makers. Middleby's strategy was to broaden the acceptance of Pacesetter ovens in other foodservice markets, while at the same time broadening its product base. Other products included conventional deck ovens (Middleby entered the market in 1988 with a South Korea–manufactured product), a proprietary oven ventilation system (introduced in 1987), and Titan brand commercial electric food mixers and related accessories.

Looking ahead, overall market conditions were promising. Foodservice sales were $213 billion in 1988,

KEY DATES

1888: Middleby Marshall Oven Co., Inc., is established by Joseph Middleby.

1978: TMC Industries Ltd. acquires WWG Industries, Inc.

1983: WWG Industries buys Middleby Marshall.

1985: The Middleby Corporation is incorporated as a successor to TMC Industries Ltd.

1988: Middleby posts record sales, up 18 percent over the previous year.

1989: The company acquires the Foodservice Equipment Group of Hussmann Corporation.

1990: Middleby purchases a majority interest in Asbury Associates Inc., a foodservice equipment manufacturer and distributor based in Manila, Philippines.

1997: Middleby sells Victory Refrigeration Company.

2000: Selim A. Bassoul is named CEO.

2001: G.S. Blodgett Corporation, a cooking equipment manufacturer, is purchased.

2007: The company makes five acquisitions including Jade Products Company and New Star International Holdings Inc.

2009: TurboChef Technologies Inc., a maker of high-speed cooking equipment, is purchased in January.

or about 5 percent of the gross national product (GNP). Fast-food chains were the fastest-growing subgroup with $63 billion in sales projected for 1989. Pizza sales were greater than $20 billion annually, and the two largest chains, Pizza Hut and Domino's, were Middleby's two largest customers.

MAJOR ACQUISITION IN 1989

Full of confidence in the future growth of the foodservice market and not anticipating the recession of the early 1990s, Middleby acquired the Foodservice Equipment Group of Hussmann Corporation, a subsidiary of Whitman Corporation, for $62.5 million on July 14, 1989. The acquisition included four established businesses with well-known industry brand names: Southbend (heavy duty cooking equipment), Toastmaster (cooking and warming equipment), Victory (refrigeration), and Seco (holding and serving systems). An unaffiliated company, Toastmaster, Inc., owned the rights to the Toastmaster brand name for consumer products;

Toastmaster products manufactured by Middleby were limited to commercial products for the foodservice industry.

To finance the acquisition, Middleby took on a significant amount of debt, again raising its annual interest expense. It entered into a $77.5 million credit agreement with a major lending institution. It reduced its debt somewhat by applying the proceeds from the sale of its Southern Equipment Company Division of St. Louis in February 1990 for $7.9 million in cash to a group of private investors that included managers of the company.

After the acquisition, the new businesses reported a $10 million loss for the first half of 1989, three times the amount originally forecast. In 1990 Middleby brought a lawsuit against Whitman, parent of Hussmann, over the Foodservice Equipment Group acquisition. The suit was settled in Middleby's favor in October 1992, when the jury awarded Middleby $27 million. The award was later set aside by a judge on a technicality, but Middleby and Hussmann reached a $19.5 million cash settlement out of court in 1993.

In the suit, Middleby claimed that Hussmann's overly optimistic financial projections led it to pay too much for the companies. The losses greatly affected Middleby's financial performance over the next several years. Even though 1989 sales more than doubled to $72.2 million from $34.2 million in 1988, net income dropped 86 percent to only $573,000. While the reduction of net income was due in part to the poor performance of the newly acquired subsidiaries, Middleby had also assumed a gigantic debt in the acquisition and was saddled with $3.6 million in interest expense in 1989, more than three times its 1988 level of about $1 million.

Middleby's growing interest expense continued to batter the company's bottom line in 1990, a year in which the company also experienced flat sales volume in a highly competitive environment. Interest expense grew to $8.3 million in 1990. Despite drastic cost-cutting measures that reduced the workforce at continuing operations by 22 percent and slashed administrative and overhead costs by 25 percent, Middleby reported a net loss of $978,000 on record sales of $113 million for 1990.

INTERNATIONAL GROWTH

In April 1990 Middleby acquired a majority interest in Asbury Associates Inc., a foodservice equipment manufacturer and distributor based in Manila, Philippines. It was a key step in building an international organization. Middleby increased its interest in Asbury to 80 percent in 1991, and it was soon expanded from serving the Pacific basin to become Middleby's export distributor throughout the world, except Canada, where Middleby owned a distributor called Escan. In 1991 Asbury established a separate unit, Fab-Asia, Inc., in metropolitan Manila to fabricate kitchen equipment for the Asian market and to produce some components for Middleby's domestic factories. Asbury's new corporate headquarters were opened in Miramar, Florida, in October 1992.

In 1991 international growth was offset by declining domestic sales. International business increased 33 percent over 1990, accounting for 21 percent of Middleby's total sales in 1991. The next year Asbury's sales doubled as it expanded sales in Latin America, the Middle East, and Europe. Middleby reported higher net sales in 1992 of $110 million, up from $103 million in 1991, and reduced its net loss for the year to $1.9 million from $7.5 million in 1991.

On August 21, 1992, Middleby completed the sale of its Seco division, which was one of the units acquired from Hussmann in 1989, to a newly formed company called Seco Products Corporation. Net proceeds of $11 million were used to reduce debt. Middleby retained a minority interest in the new company, which it later sold in 1995 for $1.4 million net of expenses.

During the first half of 1992 Middleby consolidated its foodservice equipment divisions, closing plants in Niles and Morton Grove, Illinois, and consolidating production at an Elgin, Illinois, facility to save nearly $2 million in annual overhead expenses. The previous year Middleby had consolidated the Middleby Marshall and Toastmaster divisions into a newly formed Cooking Systems Group. During 1991 Middleby had also closed its Montreal manufacturing operations and dissolved its U.K. distribution center.

MIDDLEBY COOKING SYSTEMS GROUP ESTABLISHED IN 1993

In 1993 management was consolidated at the Elgin-based Middleby Cooking Systems Group, the company's largest operating unit. David P. Riley, parent company Middleby's president and CEO, also assumed presidency of the newly formed Middleby Cooking Systems Group. Middleby Marshall became part of Middleby Cooking Systems, with Middleby Marshall's General Manager John Hastings named corporate executive vice-president, chief financial officer, and vice-president of administration. Two other financial executives left the company as part of the consolidation. Hastings told *Crain's Chicago Business,* "The management changes have basically been driven by the desire to reduce

overhead and streamline decision-making."

As part of its strategy to introduce new products into a relatively flat foodservice equipment market, Middleby formed a joint venture in 1993 with Rational GmbH, a German manufacturer of high-tech oven equipment that combined steam and convection cooking capabilities. The joint venture, called Rational Cooking Systems International, Inc., and headquartered in Schaumburg, Illinois, targeted the expanding U.S. market for high-tech ovens. Middleby would distribute the German company's product under the trade name Rational Combi-Steamer. Middleby marketed both compact floor and countertop units that were capable of multiple cooking processes, including cooking, baking, roasting, steaming, poaching, blanching, boiling, basting, grilling, and pressure cooking.

RETURN TO PROFITABILITY IN 1994

Middleby did not return to profitability until 1994, reporting net income of $3.0 million on net sales of $130.0 million. It noted in its annual report that results from operations confirmed the expansion of margins and operating income increased fivefold. (Middleby had reported net income of $3.4 million in 1993, but that was helped by a one-time $7.7 million income item related to the settlement of its 1990 lawsuit with Hussmann and Whitman.) The balance sheet was restructured with an influx of new capital, and a new incentive system was put into place to link managers' compensation directly to shareholder return.

Middleby also noted in its annual report that it had repositioned itself to participate "in the rapid worldwide expansion of the hotel and fast-food restaurant chains." Through its export management company, Asbury Associates, Middleby had the "unique capacity to offer turnkey, 'concept to kitchen floor' packages worldwide." In 1994 international sales accounted for one-quarter of total sales.

As part of a major expansion of the company's manufacturing capabilities in the Philippines, Middleby Philippines Corporation (MPC) was incorporated in 1995. Middleby owned 80 percent of MPC, with the remaining 20 percent in the hands of local management. MPC's predecessor, Fab-Asia, Inc., was formed in 1991, with Middleby owning a majority interest. Middleby increased its ownership to 80 percent in 1994, and the operating assets of Fab-Asia were transferred to MPC on January 1, 1996. In April 1996 it moved to a new facility. MPC primarily served the Asian operations of major foodservice chains and hotels.

PUBLIC STOCK OFFERING IN 1997

On January 23, 1997, Middleby sold its Victory Refrigeration Company to an investor group led by local management at Victory for approximately $11.8 million. Middleby had acquired Victory as part of its Foodservice Equipment Group acquisition in 1990. When Middleby's previous years' earnings were restated to exclude Victory, international sales accounted for an even greater proportion of the company's earnings. For fiscal 1996, international sales accounted for approximately 37 percent of total sales, up from 36 percent of the previous year's restated sales. With operations organized under two international business units and two domestic units, Middleby reported net earnings from continuing operations of $473,000 on net sales of $124.8 million in 1996. Earnings were adversely affected by one-time losses from discontinued operations (Victory) of approximately $1.1 million. Income from operations was $8.7 million, more than enough to offset the company's interest expense of $4.4 million.

Recognizing the need to improve its capital structure by reducing debt and increasing shareholder equity, Middleby announced a public offering of stock in September 1997 at a price of $10 per share. Management hoped to raise approximately $18.5 million, which would be used in part to reduce debt. The company's stock had been trading on the NASDAQ National Market since November 1995, when it switched from the American Stock Exchange. The reason for the switch was to "provide broader liquidity for our shareholders and offer greater coverage within the investment community," according to Chairman Whitman. Following Middleby's 1997 public offering, at least one investment firm began covering the stock, giving it an "outperform-significantly" rating.

RETOOLING FOR THE 21ST CENTURY

The company's move to the NASDAQ failed to produce significant changes in the company's bottom line and Middleby found itself in a precarious situation during the latter half of the 1990s. A new management team was brought in and the company was forced to retool under the helm of Selim A. Bassoul, who took over as CEO in 2000. Bassoul reflected on the company's position during this period in a 2008 *Smart Business Chicago* article. "We had very limited resources and capital, we were running out of cash, we were very reliant on three customers that generated more than 60 percent of the sales," he told the magazine. In addition to its poor financial outlook, Bassoul also claimed, "We lacked innovation, and the products we were generating or creating were very me-too products. The competitors were stealing our best employees, and the turnover at Middleby was more than 33 percent. Roughly 30 percent of the orders were not shipped on time, so we had a case study of a lousy company."

Bassoul immediately set out revamp Middleby's operations. He quickly cut products that were not related to the company's core business: cooking and warming equipment. Middleby's research and development team focused on creating energy efficient or 'green' products that quickly cooked or warmed food in less time than competing products. New products launched over the next several years were designed to cut energy consumption by nearly 40 percent; this would provide significant cost savings on customers' utility bills.

GROWTH THROUGH ACQUISITION AND OVERSEAS EXPANSION

During the decade Middleby also focused heavily on the fast-food and casual dining segment, international expansion, and growing its business through key acquisitions. During 2001 Middleby acquired G.S. Blodgett Corp., a cooking equipment manufacturer selling products to hamburger and chicken fast-food chains. Houno A/S, a Denmark-based manufacturer of steam ovens, was purchased in 2006. Five acquisitions were made in 2007 including Jade Products Company and New Star International Holdings Inc. The latter purchase added the Star, Holman, and Lang brands to Middleby's arsenal.

The company made two key European purchases in April 2008 including Frifri aro SA, a frying system supplier, and Giga Grandi Cucine S.r.l., a range, oven, and steam cooking equipment manufacturer. TurboChef Technologies Inc., a maker of high-speed cooking equipment, was purchased in January 2009.

Under the leadership of Bassoul, Middleby had transformed itself into a major player in the foodservice equipment industry. The company's market share had grown from 6 percent in 2000 to nearly 20 percent in 2008 and it ranked as the first or second largest manufacturer in every market it served. Sales had grown significantly from $242 million in 2003 to nearly $652 million in 2008. Profits were climbing as well, reaching $52.6 million in 2007 and then rising to $63.9 million in 2008. The company claimed that one of every three cooking appliances used in a commercial kitchen in the United States was a Middleby-owned brand. With international sales accounting for nearly 20 percent of the company's overall revenues, Middleby appeared to have secured a substantial foothold abroad as well.

David Bianco
Updated, Christina M. Stansell

PRINCIPAL SUBSIDIARIES

Alkar Holdings, Inc.; Alkar-RapidPak, Inc.; Alkar-RapidPak Brasil, LLC; Blodgett Holdings, Inc.; Carter-Hoffmann LLC; Chef Acquisition Corporation; Cloverleaf Properties, Inc.; Fab-Asia Inc. (Philippines); frifri LTD. (Switzerland); G.S. Blodgett Corporation; Giga Grandi Cucine S.r.l. (Italy); Holman Cooking Equipment Inc.; Houno A/S (Denmark); Houno Holdings LLC; Houno Svenska AB (Sweden); Jade Range LLC; MagiKitch'n Inc.; Meat Processing Equipment LLC; Middleby Asia Ltd. (Hong Kong); Middleby China Corporation; Middleby Cooking System Manufacturing (Shanghai) Corporation; Middleby Espana SLU (Spain); Middleby Europe SL (Spain); Middleby Marshall Holding, LLC; Middleby Marshall, Inc.; Middleby Mexico S.A. de CV; Middleby Philippines Corporation; Middleby U.K. LTD.; Middleby Worldwide, Inc.; Middleby Worldwide Korea Co., LTD.; Middleby Worldwide Philippines; Middleby Worldwide (Taiwan) Co., LTD.; New Star International Holdings, Inc.; Pitco Frialator, Inc.; Star International Holdings, Inc.; Star Manufacturing International Inc.; Wells Bloomfield LLC.

PRINCIPAL DIVISIONS

Commercial Foodservice Equipment Group; Food Processing Equipment Group; International Distribution.

PRINCIPAL COMPETITORS

Aga Rangemaker Group plc; Illinois Tool Works Inc.; Manitowoc Foodservice Companies Inc.

FURTHER READING

Alva, Marilyn, "Professional Cooking Equipment Maker Digests New Acquisitions," *Investor's Business Daily,* October 15, 2008.

Brandstrader, J. R., "This Oven Maker Is Really Cooking," *Barron's,* March 30, 2009.

Bremner, Brian, "Oven Firm Reheats: Middleby Eyes Sizzling Growth," *Crain's Chicago Business,* August 10, 1988, p. 1.

Carroll, S. R., "Middleby Corp. Is Really Cookin'," *Chicago Tribune,* September 24, 1995.

Cottrill, Mike, "Changing the Menu," *Smart Business Chicago,* September 2008.

Durgin, Hillary, "Middleby Turning Up Heat with Joint Venture," *Crain's Chicago Business,* September 20, 1993, p. 40.

Elstrom, Peter J. W., "Debt Restructuring Will Fuel Oven Maker's Market Growth," *Crain's Chicago Business,* May 9, 1988, p. 59.

———, "Disputed Buyout Cooks Oven-Maker," *Crain's Chicago Business,* June 18, 1990, p. 1.

Isaac, David, "Middleby Corp. Elgin, Illinois Technology Is a Key Ingredient in Its Success," *Investor's Business Daily,* April 13, 2004.

"Middleby Acquisition of TurboChef Complete," *Foodservice Equipment & Supplies Specialist,* February 1, 2009.

"Middleby Adopts Management Stock Ownership Plan," *Business Wire,* March 4, 1994.

"The Middleby Corporation Reports Financing Package," *Business Wire,* January 10, 1995.

"The Middleby Corporation to Move to NASDAQ from AMEX," *Business Wire,* November 14, 1995.

Murphy, H. Lee, "Court Ruling Bolsters Ailing Middleby Corp.," *Crain's Chicago Business,* October 19, 1992, p. 33.

———, "Middleby Makes Strategic Buys," *Crain's Chicago Business,* May 19, 2008.

———, "Middleby's Managers to Take Its Performance Personally," *Crain's Chicago Business,* March 28, 1994, p. 40.

Ott, James F., "The Middleby Corporation Wins $27,000,000 Verdict Against Hussmann," *Business Wire,* September 28, 1992.

MN Airlines LLC

1300 Mendota Heights Road
Mendota Heights, Minnesota 55120
U.S.A.
Telephone: (651) 681-3900
Toll Free: (800) FLY-N-SUN; (800) 359-6786
Fax: (651) 681-3970
Web site: http://www.suncountry.com

Wholly Owned Subsidiary of Petters Group Worldwide LLC
Incorporated: 1982
Employees: 1,035
Sales: $119.6 million (2008)
NAICS: 481111 Scheduled Passenger Air Transportation

■ ■ ■

Headquartered in Mendota Heights, Minnesota, MN Airlines LLC, which conducts business under the name Sun Country Airlines, is a subsidiary of Petters Group Worldwide. The company conducts operations from a hub in Minneapolis/St. Paul, flying to approximately 30 locations throughout North America and the Caribbean with a fleet of about 12 Boeing 737-800 aircraft, including the environmentally friendly 737 NG. The company also offers services targeted toward business travelers, including charter services and group sales, as well as cargo services.

PILOTS TAKE OFF: EARLY 1980S

Sun Country Airlines, the brainchild of former Braniff International pilots, took flight in January 1983. Follow-

ing the shutdown of Braniff in 1982, Ken Sundmark sought out Bob Daniels, his former neighbor and cofounder of Mainline Travel Inc. Sundmark proposed they establish a charter service, combining the assets of Mainline and the airline expertise of the now unemployed Braniff crew. "They needed outside financing, and they also needed a reliable market, something more steady than the topsy-turvy world of post-deregulation scheduled services," wrote Peter Reed in a February 1987 *Corporate Report Minnesota* article.

Mainline, which owned MLT Vacations Inc., had already toyed with the idea of owning its own plane to serve its vacation travel market and willingly signed on for the ride. Mainline's principal owners, Daniels and MLT CEO Warren Phillips, retained 51 percent of ownership. Eleven Braniff pilots, two cabin attendants, an attorney, and a financial consultant shared the remaining 49 percent.

Sun Country Airlines was incorporated in July 1982 but implementation of service was delayed by higher than expected start-up costs. Airport facilities, fuel suppliers, maintenance contractors, and airplane lessors all required large deposits on their goods and services. MLT committed additional funds, in the form of a letter of credit for the deposit on the airplane and a cash loan of $250,000, to get Sun Country's inaugural flight, from Sioux Falls to Las Vegas, in the air. At first, Sun Country flew just one aircraft, a Boeing 727-200.

Within six weeks, according to the Reed article, the company became profitable and was able to pay back MLT's loan within eight months. Net income was $180,413 for the first fiscal year and $1.47 million for

COMPANY PERSPECTIVES

As part of Sun Country's commitment to a healthy, "green" environment, our fleet is comprised of current-generation aircraft, resulting in maximum fuel efficiency, decreased noise and reduced environmental impact. The 737NG is the most environmentally friendly and has the lowest carbon emissions per seat of any aircraft in its class. In addition, Sun Country's aircraft offers a great experience from inflight entertainment to comfy leather seats.

fiscal 1984. Headquarters were less than glamorous. Sun Country operated out of an old freight building. That space and the rented hanger had once been Braniff's—the defunct airline frequently housed planes overnight at Twin Cities International, then flew them out as charters.

During the early days and from the top on down, Sun Country employees had multiple roles to perform. Company executives flew aircraft. Flight attendants acted as receptionists and baggage handlers in a pinch. Pilots updated manuals and even pitched in to clean the company's aircraft.

SHARED RESPONSIBILITY FOR FINANCIAL HEALTH

In addition to sharing the workload, Sun Country's employees shared the knowledge that they were responsible for the financial health of the business, the fate of Braniff and other airlines was still fresh in their minds. Sundmark, Sun Country vice-president of finance, gained his financial know-how while serving as a representative of the Air Line Pilots Association. Peter Reed wrote, "Sundmark's formula for Sun Country's success is simple: 'Cost control, cost control, cost control.'"

To survive, Sun County and every other airline had to keep its seat-per-mile cost down. The seat-mile measurement was tied to a number of factors. Key among them was the number of seats being filled. During the first three-and-a-half years of operation Sun Country's average load exceeded 90 percent, thanks to MLT. The travel company purchased seats from Sun Country, packaged the air travel with hotel and a variety of other services, and then sold the packages via travel agencies. Consequently, Sun Country had no marketing costs, and by leasing its aircraft, terminal, and office space, the tiny airline kept debt service costs off its books.

Sun Country, unlike other U.S. charter companies, depended primarily on vacation travel business; other charters gained revenue by seizing opportunities to fly military, cargo, and summer vacation charters to Europe. Although Sun Country had remained profitable from the start, their business was highly seasonal, concentrated around the Midwest's peak tourist season, January through mid-April.

Attempting to balance the seasonal flux of revenue, Sun Country added new destinations and flights originating from cities with different travel patterns. The Dallas/Fort Worth area, for example, generated a travel market to Las Vegas even during the summer months. More importantly in terms of revenue growth, Sun Country increased capacity during winter months by leasing additional planes from a British carrier whose peak times occurred during the summer.

Sun Country began with one additional 727 in December 1983, increased to two planes during the next two years, and moved to three during the 1986–87 winter travel season. In January 1986, to accommodate growth, Sun Country moved into a new facility. In June, the company leased its first wide-bodied plane, a DC-10, which offered larger capacity and longer flight time than the 727s.

TURBULENT AIR, NEW OWNERSHIP

As Sun Country operating officers pushed to keep the airline growing, the majority owners at Mainline were increasingly concerned with the small charter service's ability to compete in an increasingly tough market. Major airlines had begun discounting fares, placing them in line with what Mainline paid for Sun Country seats. In that light, Phillips and Daniels struck a deal with NWA Inc., parent company of Northwest Airlines, to sell both Mainline Travel and Sun Country Airlines.

Members of the Braniff ownership faction felt the deal overvalued Mainline and undervalued Sun Country ($22 million and $5.5 million, respectively) and sued to block the purchase. A compromise deal was reached but rejected by two of the shareholders. The sale of Mainline was completed in 1985, but NWA dropped the bid for Sun Country. Sun Country eventually tried to force the dissenting shareholders to sell their shares to the company; the matter was tied up by litigation for several years. In late 1988, Midwest banker B. John Barry purchased majority ownership of Sun Country from the original investors.

Publicity shy Barry, who owned 12 Minnesota and Wisconsin banks with combined assets of $530 million,

KEY DATES

1982: Sun Country Airlines is incorporated.

1988: Midwest banker B. John Barry purchases majority ownership of Sun Country.

1997: Mark Travel Corp. owner Bill La Macchia acquires a majority interest in the company.

2001: The airline lays off most of its 900-member workforce in December and temporarily closes its doors.

2002: An investment group named MN Airlines LLC acquires ownership of Sun Country.

2006: Petters Aviation, a subsidiary of Petters Group Worldwide, and the investment firm Whitebox Advisors, acquire the company.

2008: In separate matters, Sun Country files for bankruptcy, and the CEO of parent company Petters Group Worldwide faces legal charges of obstruction of justice and other wrongdoing.

maintained a low profile over the next several years. The Gulf War changed all that. Thanks largely to military charters, Sun Country's revenue increased 38 percent to $109 million, and net income more than doubled to $9.7 million for the 12 months ending June 30, 1991.

Sun Country's bottom line had also been aided by a decline in the number of charter companies. About 15 carriers had been in operation during the mid-1980s, but only a handful remained viable, including American Trans Air (Indianapolis), Tower Air Inc. (New York), and Key Airlines Inc. (Georgia). Sun Country was the third largest charter airline in the United States.

Historically, Sun Country had expanded conservatively, a practice which had helped the airline weather the industry downturn. The company had no long-term debt. Barry, encouraged by the year's growth, pushed forward with an aggressive expansion plan. He intended to add two DC-10s and four or five 727s to the aircraft already in service.

RESTRUCTURING ALLIANCES

While the military charters had produced a good-sized blip on Sun Country's revenue screen, MLT continued to be a very important customer. The small carrier was also closely tied to MLT's sister company Northwest Airlines. Sun Country leased both airport facilities and a number of its planes from Northwest. (The Sun

Country hanger had been purchased by NWA at the time of the MLT deal.) However, the relationship between the two companies was changing.

In late 1990, NWA had notified Sun Country that it would not be renewing its lease on the facility or on some of its planes. Significantly, Northwest Airlines had begun operating its own quasi-charter service which it sold via Mainline; discounted tour seats and vacation packages were booked on regularly scheduled Northwest flights.

The changes in climate with NWA factored into Sun Country's declining numbers in 1992. When NWA chose not to extend its DC-10 lease agreement with Sun Country, the smaller operation was forced to pump out dollars for repair and maintenance costs associated with the return of the aircraft sooner than anticipated. Also eating into Sun Country's profitability was a rebound of competition in the charter industry. A drop in aircraft leasing prices had encouraged start-up companies to join the fray.

Sun Country, on the other hand, was still carrying higher rates. Moreover, a price war among the major carriers forced fares downward in all categories. On a positive note, passenger numbers remained solid, and NWA decided to extend the facility lease after all.

Even as Sun Country grew, however, charter demand fell, as more large airlines offered comparable services. Sun Country launched its own vacation travel package program late in 1995. Doug Iverson reported in December 1995 for *Knight-Ridder/Tribune News* that some industry observers speculated the "move could be the beginning of a major rift" between Sun Country and NWA. "In the past, Sun Country flights to 12 cities were marketed through MLT. Since Northwest was essentially getting a cut, observers believe the airline didn't fight back and allowed cheaper flights to such destinations as Detroit, Chicago, Cleveland and Newark."

HEAD-TO-HEAD COMPETITION
WITH NORTHWEST

In early March 1996, Sun Country moved into direct competition with Northwest by offering discounted summer fares to locations such as Boston and J.F.K. in New York. Sun Country hoped Twin Cities travelers, who, according to American Express Domestic Airfare Index, paid 25 percent more than the national average for flights, would flock to their gates. Northwest, which controlled 80 percent of the Twin Cities air market, was quick to respond to the challenge. The giant airline slashed its fares. Sun Country had to reduce its fares, thus putting their profit margins in jeopardy.

In August Sun Country announced that it had lost 50 percent of its MLT business for the 1996–97 winter vacation season. The airline said that the cut-back was related to the reallocation of resources to scheduled flights. The business with MLT had been producing 25 percent of the charter company's annual revenue of more than $200 million.

TRAVEL MOGUL AT THE HELM

Mark Travel Corporation owner Bill La Macchia purchased Barry's majority interest in Sun Country in the spring of 1997. Barry retained some shares and remained on the board of directors as did founding pilot and CEO John Skiba. (The Barry family and Skiba had been the only stockholders prior to the sale.) La Macchia's Funjet vacation package firm had been doing brisk business with Sun Country since the mid-1980s. At the time of the sale Sun Country employed 1,000 people and operated flights from 23 cities. Privately held Mark Travel, based in Milwaukee, generated annual revenue of about $600 million.

Sun Country was on the slide when La Macchia took over. Operating profits which had been about $9.57 million in 1994, fell to $2.1 million in 1995, and plummeted again in 1996. Barry's venture in scheduled service had nosedived, scuttled by the combination of a meager marketing effort and Northwest's aggressive response to the competition.

"They got beat up terribly," La Macchia said of Sun Country's initiative against Northwest, in an April 1997 *Minneapolis Star Tribune* article by Tony Kennedy. "My focus is not scheduled service. I'm in the package business."

La Macchia's son, Bill Jr., called back from a nine-year stint of working in the Las Vegas hotel and casino business, was named chief operating officer of Sun Country. Six months later he was promoted to president. "Since then, La Macchia has steered the privately held company out of crisis and driven its growth by booking travel directly rather than relying on charter sales to wholesale tour operators," wrote John Rosengren and Paul Duncan for *Corporate Report Minnesota* in February 1999.

The turnaround was aided by a 15-day strike by Northwest pilots in late August 1998. Seizing the opportunity, Sun Country added seats and new business destinations, and backed the effort with a $1.5 million advertising campaign. Bookings tripled and bolstered a traditionally slow period. The airline maintained pre-strike prices in an effort to earn the goodwill of frustrated Northwest travelers. Sun Country ran a two-for-one post-strike promotion hoping to bring back customers gained during the Northwest walk-out, but the bigger player countered with its own two-for-one ticket special.

CHARTING A NEW COURSE

In January 1999, Sun Country was offering 81 nonstop flights to 23 domestic destinations plus winter travel flights to five Caribbean Islands. The majority of the 2.6 million travelers the airline had carried in 1998 had been vacationers. The charter business still brought in more than 80 percent of sales, but the La Macchias were positioning themselves to change all that. Sun Country planned to alter the scheduled service to charter service ratio to 60/40, respectively.

The new plan was a far cry from the course La Macchia Sr. had in mind when he took over the struggling airline. The change in direction was due to "economics," according to Sun Country marketing director Lori Barghini. "As a charter we don't have the option of doing anything to our schedule," she said. "And charter operators want to fly on a Friday or a Sunday. We have to fly every day to make a profit."

La Macchia was used to making a profit. Mark Travel's estimated fiscal 1998 net profit was $20 million. *Leisure Travel News* had named La Macchia one of the 25 most influential tour and travel industry executives on three different occasions. He had deep pockets. "I could probably support the needs of Sun Country for a long time," La Macchia said in an April 1999 *Star Tribune* article by Kennedy, "but we have to make a profit. The community has to support Sun Country to enjoy a competitive market."

After putting $41 million on the table for 75 percent of Sun Country's stock, La Macchia saw net losses of $11.7 million in fiscal 1997. It was more than he had expected. Eager for total control, he purchased the remaining Sun Country shares in the summer of 1998. Now the profits and losses were all in La Macchia's hands.

TAKING ON NORTHWEST AGAIN

La Macchia was going into direct competition with the nation's fourth largest airline, and Northwest had a history of driving small carriers out of the market. Sun Country, according to Rosengren and Duncan, faced some internal barriers to success as well. The airline lacked a frequent flyer program, was viewed as a vacation airline by business travelers, had to contend with cramped terminal conditions, and had limited listing in the central reservation system used by travel agents.

Aware of its internal weaknesses, Sun Country had a frequent flyer/loyalty program in the works and tapped into Mark Travel's sophisticated computer resources for its reservation system. The existing Hubert H. Humphrey charter terminal at Twin Cities International was receiving a makeover, and a new terminal, with Sun Country as the anchor tenant, was scheduled to open in 2001.

DETERMINING TO FLY HIGH IN THE FUTURE

Sun Country positioned itself as an underdog fighting giant Northwest. Playing off of ex-wrestler Jesse Ventura's unexpected victory in the 1998 Minnesota's governor's race, a billboard read: "Jesse Did It—Why Can't We?" The billboard campaign was just one piece of a multimillion-dollar marketing push. Print ads featured a mail-in coupon offering a chance to win a year of free travel. Company president Bill La Macchia Jr. appeared on the small screen peddling his family business door-to-door. Radio ads emphasized low fares and cultivated a connection with the flying public.

With about 500 daily flights and 410 planes, Northwest badly outgunned Sun Country, which had just 15 planes and flew a maximum of one time per day to the 15 cities it served. Eric Torbenson wrote on the eve of scheduled service, "La Macchia Sr. knew going in that he couldn't compete on price, nor on the number of flights. He hopes to win over Twin Cities travelers with great service. With just a few more than 1,200 employees companywide, compared with 50,000 at Northwest, Sun Country feels the camaraderie of its flight crews will help set it apart from Northwest."

FLYING IN THE FACE OF RISK

As the low airfare battle with Northwest heated up during the early summer, La Macchia made some other moves. Mark Travel purchased Trans Global Tours and strengthened its position in the Twin Cities market. The Twin Cities-based vacation charter business ranked second to NWA-owned MLT Inc. Sun Country announced the addition of state-of-the-art Boeing 737-800 series aircraft to its fleet beginning in January 2001, and that it would become a signatory carrier in Seattle, thus receiving a terminal location comparable to the larger airlines.

These victories were small in comparison to the risks it faced in its fight with Northwest. In April 1999 La Macchia told the *Star Tribune* he was willing to spend up to three years building the Sun Country business, but his task was daunting. Although no other larger carrier had successfully bridged the gap from charter to scheduled airline, La Macchia was determined to give it his best shot, and on June 1 of that year Sun Country became a scheduled carrier. However, the competition that followed was fierce, leading to losses of $62 million by 2000.

TROUBLED TIMES

In May 2001, the company named former AirCal President and Chief Operating Officer David Banmiller to serve as its chief operating officer. La Macchia remained with the organization as CEO. The following month, eight new Boeing 737-800 aircraft arrived at Sun Country, signifying what La Macchia referred to as a new era for the airline. The planes, which were the first new aircraft the company had ever purchased, arrived as it relocated to the new Hubert H. Humphrey terminal and made flights accessible to travel agents via the computerized Sabre reservation system. In order to improve the company's financial position, Sun Country shed 25 percent of its non-union employees and reduced its budget by approximately $8 million.

Although these were positive developments, the terrorist attacks against the United States on September 11, 2001, further exacerbated Sun Country's difficult financial condition. By October, Banmiller was serving as president and CEO. That month, the airline announced that it was eliminating 250 jobs and scaling back its flight schedule by 26 percent. The airline laid off most of its 900-member workforce on December 7, and ceased to offer scheduled services the following day. Shortly thereafter, Sun Country temporarily closed its doors.

After ceasing regular operations, Sun Country stopped functioning as a charter carrier for Mark Travel Corp. In order to maintain its flight certification from the Transportation Department, six of Sun Country's managers were retained, along with five flight crews to provide Saturday charter flights. The company revealed plans to offer charter flights for the military, leisure travelers, sports teams, as well as other tour operators.

NEW LIFE, NEW CHALLENGES

A positive development occurred in March 2002, at which time the federal bankruptcy court allowed an investment group named MN Airlines LLC to acquire ownership of the Sun Country name, as well as some of its assets. In May the U.S. Department of Transportation announced that it had approved the transfer of Sun Country's operating certificate to MN Airlines, signifying the transaction's completion.

Banmiller stepped down as Sun Country's CEO on May 31, but remained with the company as a consultant through December. Banmiller was succeeded by Jay Salmen. The company moved forward by establishing a presence on the World Wide Web and offering a blend of scheduled and charter flights. Revenues totaled $108.5 million in 2003, with some 27 percent of ticket sales coming from the Web that year.

By early 2004, the company had a workforce of 550 people who operated a fleet of nine Boeing 737 aircraft. A major leadership change occurred the following year, when Shaun Nugent was named CEO. For 2005, Sun Country recorded a loss of $11 million on sales of $204 million. The company was challenged by skyrocketing fuel prices, which increased 94 percent that year.

PETTERS TAKES CONTROL

By mid-2006, Sun Country's workforce had grown to about 700 people. An ownership change occurred in November of that year, when Petters Aviation, a subsidiary of Petters Group Worldwide, and the investment firm Whitebox Advisors, acquired Sun Country. Owned by business mogul Tom Petters, Petters Group Worldwide consisted of approximately 60 different companies, including Sunbeam Appliances, Fingerhut, and Polaroid. Sun Country ended the year by setting a new company record for passenger volume in late December.

More change was in store for Sun Country in 2007. In April, Stephen M. Spellman was named chief operating officer and chief financial officer. That same month, CEO Nugent left the company, and was temporarily succeeded by Salmen. In November, Petters Group Worldwide bought out its partners and acquired full ownership in Sun Country. By this time, the airline employed approximately 1,100 workers.

Profitability remained elusive as Sun Country moved into the later years of the first decade of the 2000s. In 2007, the company recorded a net loss of $34 million on revenues of $234 million. In an effort to turn things around, roughly $10 million was devoted to marketing efforts.

In March 2008 the company hired AirTran Airways Chief Financial Officer Stan Gadek, who also had spent 13 years working for competitor Northwest, as its new CEO. Difficult times led the airline to scale back its workforce by approximately 30 percent. In October, Gadek was named both chairman and CEO. The promotion was bittersweet as Sun Country filed for bankruptcy that same month.

Beyond the difficulties at Sun Country, major problems were unfolding at parent company Petters Group Worldwide in the fall of 2008. After stepping down as CEO in September, Petters was arrested early the next month on charges of obstruction of justice, mail fraud, money laundering, and wire fraud. Prosecutors, who considered him to be a potential flight risk, alleged that he had stolen as much as $3 billion from investors.

Around the time of Petters' arrest, Sun Country found itself short of cash. The company had been hoping for a loan from Petters to cover operational costs until the busy winter travel season. In order to keep the company alive, employees agreed to wage cuts as high as 50 percent in October. Late that month, the company appealed to the U.S. Bankruptcy Court for permission to obtain a loan from fellow Petters Group Worldwide company Elite Landings, which also was in bankruptcy.

AN UNCERTAIN FUTURE

Conditions were improving at Sun Country toward the end of 2008. In late December the company announced that it was paying back 40 percent of the wages that it had cut in early October to its employees. After scaling back the size of the company's fleet, eliminating both union and non-union jobs, doing away with unprofitable flights, lining up new military and charter contracts, and increasing passenger fees, Sun Country finished 2008 with a profit of $1 million in the fourth quarter, on revenues of $49.5 million.

In April 2009, the U.S. District Court established a trial date of September 14 for Tom Petters. Sun Country had successfully weathered another difficult period in its history. In the wake of tumultuous economic conditions, they moved forward, establishing nonstop service between the Boston Logan International Airport and the Minneapolis–St. Paul International Airport on May 1.

Kathleen Peippo
Updated, Paul R. Greenland

PRINCIPAL COMPETITORS

Allegiant Travel Company; AMR Corporation; Northwest Airlines Corporation.

FURTHER READING

"Acquisition of Sun Country Complete," *Europe Intelligence Wire*, November 1, 2006.

"Airline Flies Charters to Stay Aloft," *Travel Weekly*, December 13, 2001.

Causey, James E., "Mark Travel Corp. Owner to Buy Twin Cities Airline," *Knight-Ridder/Tribune Business News*, April 17, 1997.

Fedor, Liz, "Petters Buys All of Sun Country," *Minneapolis Star Tribune*, November 16, 2007.

———, "The Reborn Airline's Message to Potential Flyers: Cheap, Fun & Easy," *Minneapolis Star Tribune*, February 25, 2004.

———, "Sun Country Reports $1 Million Profit," *Minneapolis Star Tribune*, January 29, 2009.

Iverson, Doug, "Minnesota's Sun Country Airlines Challenges Northwest with Air Fare Cut," *Knight-Ridder/Tribune Business News,* March 8, 1996.

———, "Sun Country Airlines Aims to Outshine Northwest with Latest Low Fares," *Knight-Ridder/Tribune Business News,* May 31, 1996.

———, "Sun Country Airlines Begins to Offer Packages Similar to Major Customer," *Knight-Ridder/Tribune Business News,* December 20, 1995.

Kennedy, Tony, "Bill La Macchia: Sun Country Money Man," *Minneapolis Star Tribune,* April 25, 1999.

———, "Competition Promises to Make Summer Air Fares a Breeze," *Minneapolis Star Tribune,* April 24, 1999.

———, "Sun Country Airlines to Be Sold," *Minneapolis Star Tribune,* April 16, 1997, p. 1D.

———, "Sun Country Loses Charter Business," *Minneapolis Star Tribune,* August 8, 1996, p. 1D.

Kurschner, Dale, "Financial Situation Gets Cloudier at Sun Country," *Minneapolis/St. Paul City Business,* October 23–29, 1992, p. 12.

———, "Sun Country Takes Off," *Minneapolis/St. Paul City Business,* October 28, 1991, pp. 1, 21.

———, "Sun Country to Construct Headquarters," *Minneapolis/St. Paul City Business,* December 30, 1991, pp. 1, 16.

Maler, Kevin, "MAC Clears Sun Country Improvements for Takeoff," November 25–December 1, 1994, p. 8.

"MN Airlines Takes Control of Sun Country," *Airfinance Journal,* May 2002.

Reed, Peter, "The Little Airline That Did," *Corporate Report Minnesota,* February 1987, pp. 68–72.

Rosengren, John, and Paul Duncan, "Up, Up, and Away," *Corporate Report Minnesota,* February 1999, pp. 24–29.

"Sun Country Airlines," *Corporate Report Fact Book 1999,* p. 577.

"Sun Country Airlines Becomes Signatory Carrier," *PR Newswire,* July 6, 1999.

Torbenson, Eric, "St. Paul-based Airline Buys Tour Company," *Knight-Ridder/Tribune Business News,* June 23, 1999.

———, "Sun Country Aims to Be Jesse Ventura of the Skies," *St. Paul Pioneer Press,* May 6, 1999, p. 1B.

———, "Sun Country: Little Airline That Could?" *St. Paul Pioneer Press,* May 30, 1999, p. 1A.

Welbes, John, "Petters in Jail: Family Man or Flight Risk?" *America's Intelligence Wire,* October 8, 2008.

Ylinen, Jerry, "Court Dispute Focuses on Control of Innovative Charter Airline," *Travel Weekly,* July 20, 1987, p. 35.

———, "Shareholders Appeal Ruling to Force Sale of Sun Country Stock," *Travel Weekly,* December 14, 1987, p. 14.

Mövenpick Holding

Postfach 465
Luzernerstrasse 9
Cham, 6330
Switzerland
Telephone: (41 041) 784 00 93
Fax: (41 041) 784 00 99
Web site: http://www.moevenpick.com

Private Company
Incorporated: 1948
Employees: 16,246
Sales: CHF 1.45 billion ($1.3 billion) (2008 est.)
NAICS: 721110 Hotels (Except Casino Hotels) and
Motels; 551112 Offices of Other Holding
Companies; 722110 Full-Service Restaurants

■ ■ ■

Mövenpick Holding is a Switzerland-based international operator of hotels, resorts, restaurants, and wine shops; the company also markets a range of fine foods under the Mövenpick brand. Mövenpick is structured as a holding company for five autonomously operating business units: Mövenpick Hotels & Resorts, Marché International, Mövenpick Restaurants, Mövenpick Wein, and Mövenpick Fine Foods. Mövenpick Hotels & Resorts (MHR) is the group's largest operation, generating approximately 60 percent of the group's annual revenues of CHF 1.45 billion ($1.3 billion) in 2008. MHR provides management services to nearly 70 hotels and resorts, including 29 in Switzerland, Germany, the Czech Republic, and other European locations; 18

properties throughout the Middle East region; 16 properties in Africa; and three in India and other Asian region markets. The company also operates its own fleet of Nile River cruise ships. In 2009 MHR adopted an ambitious expansion program designed to raise its total hotel portfolio to 100 by 2010 and to 115 by 2012. Mövenpick Holding's stake in MHR stands at 60.67 percent, in partnership with Kingdom Holding, of Saudi Arabia.

Mövenpick's restaurant operations are divided into two separate business units. Marché International operates 115 informal dining restaurants under the Marché, Marché Bakery, Marché Bistro, Cindy's Diner, and Mövenpick Restaurants names. This division includes businesses in Switzerland, Germany, Austria, Hungary, Norway, Croatia, Slovenia, Singapore, and Indonesia, as well as franchises in South Korea and Malaysia. The Mövenpick Restaurants division includes the group's original restaurant format, which operates in 20 locations in Switzerland and Germany. Mövenpick Wein is a chain of 26 wine cellars in Switzerland and Germany, plus an additional location in Liechtenstein. Lastly, Mövenpick Fine Foods oversees the marketing of a wide range of food items under the Mövenpick brand, including coffee, smoked fish, salads, and jams. The company sold its internationally known ice cream division to Nestlé in 2003. Mövenpick Holding is led by Guido Egli, chief executive.

DEVELOPING A NEW RESTAURANT CONCEPT

The son of a Swiss hotel owner, Ueli Prager was no stranger to the hospitality industry when he decided to

COMPANY PERSPECTIVES

Our mission. All areas invariably show the typical characteristics of the Mövenpick brand: "giving pleasure," "pampering guests," and "preserving the authentic." We strive to be extraordinary in the sphere of the ordinary. After all, it is the small things that make life worth living. We invite our guests to share precisely these precious little moments with us—at home, while travelling or during their holidays. We want to surprise our customers with unique pleasures, let them know how important they are to us through thoughtful gestures and with our delicacies put them in the mood to try new things. Pampering people is our passion.

open his own restaurant in the years following World War II. Prager, born in 1916, developed a novel idea for his restaurant, having recognized that eating habits had begun to change in the postwar period. Diners had traditionally come to restaurants for large multicourse meals that often lasted for a long time. Prager recognized the potential for developing a restaurant offering lighter, yet still high quality, meals served more quickly.

Prager, then 32 years old, opened his first restaurant in 1948 on Zurich's Dreikönigstrasse, to the consternation of the local restaurant industry. The name Prager chose for his restaurant, Mövenpick, raised eyebrows as well. According to Prager, his walks along Lake Zurich, where he watched the gulls fly down to pick their food, inspired the name. Prager modified the German word for "seagull," *Möwe*, replacing the *W* with a *V* as an attention-getter, and added the word *pick*. The name accurately described Prager's goal for the dining experience he hoped to offer his customers.

The Mövenpick format was a hit with Zurich diners, and by 1950 Prager had opened his second restaurant in the city. This was soon followed by a third Zurich restaurant, as well as the first outside the city, in Lucerne, both in 1952. Through the end of the decade, Prager added several new locations, including one in Bern in 1953, and two more restaurants in Zurich. Prager also entered the French-speaking Swiss market, establishing a new company, Mövenpick Genève SA, in partnership with a friend. That company developed a new format, Baron de la Mouette (the French word for "seagull"), opening restaurants in Geneva and Zurich.

Prager continued to develop new restaurant concepts, setting up the first Silberkugel restaurant on the Löwenstrasse in Zurich in 1962. Prager had also been building up a wine distribution business, an effort that had started in the mid-1950s with the creation of a "Wine of the Month" subscription program. Prager added a new layer in 1962 when he opened his first cash-and-carry store. This business led Prager to develop a retail wine format as well, as the company began developing its "Celliers" shop format. The Wine Cellars, as the chain became known, later expanded across Switzerland and into Germany.

MOVING INTO HOTELS

Germany became a major market for Mövenpick in the mid-1960s, with the company adding its first restaurant there in 1965. This restaurant, in Frankfurt, became the first of many as Germany grew into the company's largest single market. The company also added a site at the Swiss Centre in London during the decade.

Prager had by then also recognized the potential for developing the Mövenpick name itself as a brand. This effort started with the launch of the group's own "Heavenly" coffee line in 1963. The company began looking for other brand extensions, targeting the premium luxury segment. Mövenpick initially produced its own food items; in 1966 the company opened its own salmon smoking facility. This was followed in 1971 by the establishment of a central manufacturing plant, which produced the group's smoked salmon, as well as its own line of ice cream, launched in 1969, and salad dressings, added in 1972.

The company also moved into roadside restaurant operations, opening a Silberkugel in Dietlingen in 1968. In 1972, the company added a shopping and restaurant complex built on a bridge across a highway near Würenlos, the first of its kind in Switzerland. Also that year, Mövenpick introduced a new restaurant concept, called Cindy's Diner, based on the popular American restaurant format.

Prager's growing range of business interests led him back to his roots in the hospitality industry. In the mid-1960s, the company launched construction of its first hotel. Mövenpick's hospitality division started off modestly, focusing on the motorist market with the opening of the Jolie Ville Motor Inn outside of Zurich in 1966. The company later sold that site to Ibis. Instead, Mövenpick sought to move its hospitality division upscale. This led the group to build two new hotels targeting the business traveler segment at the Zurich airport. The Mövenpick Hotel Zurich-Airport and the Mövenpick Zurich-Regensdorf both opened in 1973

KEY DATES

1948: Ueli Prager opens his first Mövenpick restaurant in Zurich, Switzerland.
1966: Mövenpick opens its first hotel.
1974: The company begins licensing food with ice cream line.
1976: Mövenpick adds its first hotel in Cairo, Egypt.
1992: Prager sells the company to Germany's Baron August von Finck.
1998: Mövenpick is restructured as a holding company for five autonomously operating divisions.
2003: Mövenpick sells its ice cream brand and operations to Nestlé.
2009: The company announces plans to add more than 30 hotels in the next three years.

and provided the foundation for the later growth of the company's premium-class hotel chain.

EXPANDING BRANDS AND MARKETS

While the company continued to produce some of its own goods, the early 1970s marked the start of the company's licensed foods program. This effort was launched in Germany in 1974, when the company granted a license to produce its ice cream line to Nuremberg-based Theo Schöller. By the end of the decade, the company had added licenses for mayonnaise, salad dressings, and coffee. In the 1980s, however, Mövenpick's ice cream brand became the major ambassador for its food products, and a major publicity generator for the company itself. Toward this end, the company formed a new company, Premium Ice Cream International Licensing, in 1982.

A major milestone in Mövenpick's hotel operations came in 1976 when the company established its first location in Cairo, Egypt. The opening of the Jolie Ville Cairo marked the company's expansion beyond Europe and the start of its expansion through the Middle East/ North African market. This region grew to become one of the company's core markets by the beginning of the 21st century. The Cairo hotel also represented the first Mövenpick hotel to be operated as a managed property, as opposed to company-owned. The success of this venture led Mövenpick to focus much of its later hotel expansion on a contract management basis.

Success in Egypt encouraged the company to introduce its hotel brand into Germany as well. The company launched its first German hotel operation in Neu Ulm in 1980. By then, the company's hotel portfolio included 17 locations. That year also marked the company's entry into the North American market with the opening of two Mövenpick restaurants, one in Toronto and one in New York. Soon after, the group opened a restaurant in Paris as well.

CHANGE IN OWNERSHIP

Through the 1980s, Mövenpick continued to expand its range of businesses. In 1982 the company launched Marché, a new fresh produce–oriented restaurant format, with a first restaurant in Stuttgart, Germany. The Marché brand was then brought to Switzerland, with a first restaurant there in 1987. The Marché brand grew into one of the company's most successful, and later spawned related formats under the Marché Bakery and Marché Bistro names. Mövenpick also developed its own ice cream shop format, Mövenpick Ice Cream Boutique, with a prototype store opening in 1985.

Ueli Prager, then 72 years old, decided to retire in 1988, turning over operation of the company to his wife, Jutta, who had joined the company in 1968 and married Prager just 18 months later. Jutta Prager had taken over the operation of an underperforming restaurant in Zurich in 1980; by 1983, she had taken charge of all of the group's Swiss restaurants. Two years later she was placed in charge of the group's entire restaurant division.

Under Jutta Prager the company continued its international growth, building its turnover past CHF 1 billion into the next decade. The company opened a hotel in Beijing in 1990 and also added a new hotel at the Munich airport that year. That property featured the group's new Cadett format, targeting the midpriced hotel range. During this time the group also introduced a budget hotel range, the BenjamInn. While the company maintained a number of four- and five-star hotels in its portfolio, the group's hotel operations targeted growth in these lower-priced segments during the 1990s. The company also introduced its own Nile River cruise ship service in 1991, later building up a fleet of five cruise ships.

Jutta Prager's tenure as the head of the company was short-lived, however. By the end of 1991, she had stepped down as the group's managing director. The following year, the Pragers agreed to sell their stake in the company to Germany's Baron August von Finck. Under its new management, Mövenpick carried out a restructuring of its operations through the 1990s. This effort resulted in the creation of Mövenpick Holding in 1998. The holding company provided oversight for essentially autonomous business units: Mövenpick Hotels & Resorts; Mövenpick Gastronomy (later Mövenpick Marché), Mövenpick Wine; and Mövenpick Fine Foods. As part of the restructuring, Mövenpick also agreed to sell a one-third stake in Mövenpick Hotels & Resorts to Saudi Arabian-based Kingdom Holding.

EXPANDING THE HOTEL SEGMENT

Mövenpick began reorienting its hotel business to focus more strongly on the premium business traveler segment, as well as targeting expansion into the luxury resort sector. Among the group's new projects was the opening of its first golf hotel, in Egypt's Sharm El Sheikh in 1999. The company had already expanded into the Southern Africa market, buying 55 percent of South Africa's Karos Hotels group in 1998. The deal boosted Mövenpick's portfolio to more than 50 properties. In 2001 Mövenpick opened a hotel in Tangiers, Morocco, and then added a site in Tunisia as well. The company also added properties in the Netherlands, as well as its first in Prague, Czech Republic.

The company's food operation in the meantime added operations in New Zealand, buying Chateau Crème Delight Ice Cream Company in 2000. The purchase gave the company the leading share of that country's superpremium ice cream segment. However, in 2003 Mövenpick agreed to sell its ice cream operations, together with the Mövenpick Ice Cream brand, to Nestlé.

Hotel operations continued to drive the company's growth. The Middle East, including the Persian Gulf region, became a major focus for the company's expansion during the decade. By 2003, the company added a hotel in Kuwait, two more in Egypt, and the contract to manage the Dubai Pearl Hotel, which opened in 2005. Other hotels were added in Egypt, Turkey, Berlin, Saudi Arabia, Lebanon, Paris (at Disneyland Paris), and Rome, as well as a second site in Dubai. The company extended into India in 2006 with the contract to operate a five-star hotel in Bangalore for MS Ramaiah Hotels, which opened for business in 2008. In that year the company also opened its first hotel in Yemen, and signed a deal to operate two hotels under development in Abu Dhabi, in partnership with Aldar.

Under new CEO Guido Egli, who took over in 2006, Mövenpick stepped up its ambitions. The company announced plans to add more than 30 hotels between 2009 and 2012. This expansion was expected to increase the group's portfolio to more than 100 hotels by 2010 and to 115 by 2012. These projects included hotels in new markets such as Israel, the Palestinian Territories, the United Arab Emirates, Libya, and Thailand. Other parts of the Mövenpick group prepared to follow its hotel flagship in its international expansion. In April 2009, for example, the Marché division opened its first Marché restaurant in Jakarta, Indonesia. Despite the global recession at the end of the decade, Mövenpick remained optimistic for the success of its future expansion program.

M. L. Cohen

PRINCIPAL SUBSIDIARIES

Marché International Ltd; Mövenpick Restaurants & Dienstleistungen AG; Mövenpick Wein AG.

PRINCIPAL DIVISIONS

Hotel & Resorts; Restaurants; Wine; Food.

PRINCIPAL OPERATING UNITS

Mövenpick Hotels & Resorts; Marché International; Mövenpick Restaurants; Mövenpick Wein; Mövenpick Fine Foods.

PRINCIPAL COMPETITORS

S.V. Ag; Touring Club Suisse; Hapimag; Swissotel Hotels and Resorts; Victoria-Jungfrau Grand Hotel and S.p.A.; Weisse Arena AG; Davos Klosters Bergbahnen AG.

FURTHER READING

"August 2007 Opening for Mövenpick Ramallah," *MEED Middle East Economic Digest,* August 11, 2006, p. 27.

Diamond, Kerry, "Mövenpick's New President Is Focusing on Operations and Development in His First Year," *Travel Agent,* November 18, 1996, p. 52.

Farmer, Colin, "Mövenpick Flies the Flag," *SwissBusiness,* September–October 1993, p. 60.

Frewin, Angela, "Who's Who … Mövenpick Hotels & Resorts," *Caterer & Hotelkeeper,* May 15, 2003, p. 26.

"Jeddah Group to Build Moevenpick," *MEED Middle East Economic Digest,* December 10, 2004, p. 21.

"Mövenpick Hotels & Resorts Has Entered into a Strategic Alliance with Property Developer Aldar to Operate a High-End Resort in the Al Seef Precinct in Abu Dhabi's Upcoming Al Raha Beach Development," *Business Traveller Middle East,* November–December 2008, p. 10.

"Mövenpick Hurt by German Sales Slump," *Caterer & Hotelkeeper,* August 15, 2002, p. 8.

"Mövenpick Kick-Starts Revamp," *Travel Trade Gazette UK & Ireland,* May 28, 2001, p. 39.

"Mövenpick to Add Düsseldorf Property," *Hotels,* March 2006, p. 32.

"Mövenpick to Mix It with Bigger Rivals," *Travel Trade Gazette UK & Ireland,* March 27, 2000, p. 38.

"Mövenpick to Open Business Hotel in Bangalore," *Hotels,* April 2006, p. 28.

"Mövenpick Transfers Chocolate License," *just-food.com,* January 29, 2008.

"Mövenpick's Sales Rise 19%," *Travel Trade Gazette UK & Ireland,* April 11, 2008, p. 14.

Sheridan, Elizabeth, "Mövenpick Moves into Southern Africa," *Hotel & Motel Management,* October 5, 1998, p. 6.

Strauss, Karyn, and Jeff Weinstein, "Mövenpick to Manage 450-Room Hotel in Dubai," *Hotels,* March 2003, p. 34.

"Swiss Ice Cream Firm Bought by Nestle," *Frozen & Chilled Foods,* March 2003, p. 4.

"What's New in Mövenpick Hotels and Resorts," *Leisure Travel News,* July 26, 1999, p. 43.

Wicks, John, "At the Sign of the Seagull," *SwissBusiness,* July–August 1990, p. 6.

Mrs. Fields' Original Cookies, Inc.

———■———

2855 East Cottonwood Parkway, Suite 400
Salt Lake City, Utah 84121-7050
U.S.A.
Telephone: (801) 736-5600
Fax: (801) 736-5970
Web site: http://www.mrsfields.com

Private Company
Founded: 1977
Employees: 6,614
Sales: $354.4 million (2008 est.)
NAICS: 722213 Snack and Nonalcoholic Beverage Bars;
   31181 Retail Bakeries

■ ■ ■

Mrs. Fields' Original Cookies, Inc., operates as one of the largest franchisers in the United States specializing in cookies, brownies, and soft-serve frozen yogurt outlets. From one store started by Debbi and Randy Fields in 1977, the firm has expanded to over 1,200 stores throughout the United States and in 22 foreign countries. The company also sells baked products and gifts through its web site. The rise of Mrs. Fields' Original Cookies stands as a true success story of an American homemaker who overcame numerous obstacles to create an international business. However, like many companies that began as family businesses, it later reorganized under outside leadership and ownership. Mrs. Fields was acquired by Capricorn Holdings in 1996 and Debbi Fields ended her consultancy with the company in 2000. Mrs. Fields' Original Cookies filed for Chapter 11 bankruptcy protection in August 2008 and emerged in October of that year.

EVERYBODY SAID SHE WOULD FAIL

Debbi Fields grew up in a Catholic working-class family in Oakland, California. Her father was a welder and her mother raised Debbi and her sisters to become good wives and mothers. Growing up, Debbi held a burning desire to be special. Although she was a mediocre student, she learned to work hard and sought a way to fulfill her dreams. Debbi graduated from high school, then worked at various jobs before marrying Randy Fields, a Stanford University–trained economist, in 1976.

For about a year as a new wife, Mrs. Fields tried to fit into her husband's world as a dutiful spouse by hosting visitors and making polite conversation. However, a painful incident in which she tried to pretend she was a sophisticated person made her decide to do something else with her life. In her book, *One Smart Cookie,* she wrote, "at last I understood that I had to do something that was mine. ... I gave up, in that moment, the desire to succeed in other people's eyes and realized that first I had to succeed for myself." She elaborated, "I couldn't be Randy's shadow any more, his tagalong. ... Somehow I would have to change, to become an independent, self-respecting individual able to stand on my two feet."

Debbi Fields decided to start a business based on a skill she had acquired as a girl. From age 13 she had baked delicious chocolate chip cookies for her family and friends. She gradually improved the basic recipe pioneered in the 1930s by Toll House.

Her husband's business acquaintances loved her cookies, so she asked them what they thought about starting a cookie business. "Bad idea," they said with their mouths stuffed full of cookies. "Never work," they said, "Forget it." Debbi's mother, her in-laws, and her friends and fellow students at Los Altos Junior College also said she would fail.

Her husband went along with the idea, but deep down he did not really believe his wife could succeed in the business world. For one thing, market studies showed that consumers strongly preferred crispy cookies. Debbi's cookies were soft and larger than normal and would have to be sold at much higher prices than regular bakery cookies.

TAKING A CHANCE

She went ahead anyway but needed financial backing from a bank. She and Randy approached the Bank of America, their home mortgage lender. Their banker Ed Sullivan trusted the young couple to pay back a business loan, even though he expected the cookie business would fail. Debbi said in her book that the bank "trusted us, not cookies. ... As things turned out, Ed Sullivan and his bank built Mrs. Fields' Cookies."

So at age 20 Debbi Fields started her first cookie store at Liddicoat's Market in Palo Alto. She signed the lease under the name Mrs. Fields' Chocolate Chippery. On August 18, 1977, she opened her store at 9 A.M., but by noon nobody had bought even one cookie. Frustrated and afraid to fail, she took samples to people on the streets. They liked the samples so returned to actually buy cookies. Providing free samples to potential customers remained a cornerstone of her business in the years to come.

EARLY EXPANSION

Debbi Fields initially was content with her one store. Then Warren Simmons, the builder of the Pier 39 shopping area in San Francisco, told her he loved the cookies and invited her to open a store in Pier 39. She at first turned him down, then a year later changed her mind. Pier 39 had reserved a prime space for Mrs. Fields' Cookies. Employees at her first store kept asking for opportunities to grow. Since her employees were like family, Fields felt a responsibility to them. With additional loans, the second store was opened in 1979. The Pier 39 store was so successful with its long customer lines that it caused problems for nearby businesses. The pressure was on to open more outlets.

An early crisis illustrates how the young company operated. Mrs. Fields refused to replace higher cost raisins with less costly but also less tasty dates. Fields explained, "The point wasn't to make money, the point was to bake great cookies, and we sacrificed for that principle. From the very first, I set up a policy that we still follow today. Our cookies had to be warm and fresh and when they were two hours out of the oven, what hadn't been sold was donated to the Red Cross to be given to blood donors, or to other deserving charities, and we baked a new batch. We guaranteed everything we sold."

THE CHALLENGES OF EXPANSION

By 1979 the company had three stores but had reached a turning point. Working 16 hours per day to oversee everything, Debbi Fields said, "The cookie business had become a monster, demanding and demanding." She was so busy she had to schedule times to see her husband. She and Randy offered the rights to the company outside of California to Foremost McKesson, a large ice-cream maker, for $150,000, but the firm turned them down. Despite their disappointment they managed to survive the burdens of expansion. Eventually they received but turned down better offers for their firm, for they were learning how to handle a growing business.

Not all of Mrs. Fields' stores were immediately successful. In 1980 the company opened its new store in the Ala Moana Shopping Center in Honolulu, but initially it failed miserably. Debbi Fields decided to invite a kahuna or priest of the native Hawaiian culture bless her store. "The day after the ceremony," she wrote, "crowds of cookie buyers appeared; since that day, the Ala Moana location has been one of our most successful and profitable stores." A few months later the firm reached a major milestone when it opened its first Utah store, in the Crossroads Mall in Salt Lake City.

By the spring of 1981 the company operated 14 stores. In 1982 Mrs. Fields' Cookies recorded sales of

Although combined revenues from these firms were just over $150 million in 1983, profit margins ran higher than in other industries, partly because of inexpensive materials. For example, batter for five pounds of cookies cost only $1.50, and cookies were relatively easy to produce. Frank Bonanno, quoted in *Forbes,* estimated that, "Pretax profits run anywhere between 10% and 20%."

For several years Debbi Fields rejected the idea of franchising her stores. She realized the cookies and other products could be duplicated but not the atmosphere of "love and caring" that was so important to the business. She also said in her book that she did not "want anyone else to get his hands on it." Although in 1987 she intended to retain total control over all aspects of business growth, economic necessity would change that approach in just a few years.

STRONG REPUTATION AFTER A DECADE IN BUSINESS

By 1987 Debbi Fields had created 14 different kinds of cookies: Pecan Whites; Milk Chocolate with and without walnuts; Semisweet Chocolate with and without walnuts; Semisweet Chocolate with and without macadamia nuts; Coco-Mac with coconut and macadamia nuts; Oatmeal Raisin Nut, called Debra's Special; Peanut Butter Dreams; Triple Chocolate that combined white and dark chocolate; Raisin Spice; White Chunk with macadamia nuts; and Royal Pecan. Her stores also sold five kinds of brownies, her own ice cream, candy, and muffins.

In 1987 Mrs. Fields' Cookies did well financially. It earned a profit of 18.5 percent on sales of $87 million, up from $72.6 million in 1986. In 1987 the company purchased La Petite Boulangerie, a chain of 119 French bakery/sandwich stores, from PepsiCo for $15 million. In just four weeks Randy Fields used specially developed software to help him and his wife reduce La Petite Boulangerie's administrative staff from 53 to just three individuals.

COMPUTERIZATION CREATES A NEW ENTREPRENEURIAL MODEL

Several articles in business and computer magazines in the late 1980s praised Mrs. Fields' Cookies' innovative use of computer software to run its expanding cookie operations. The firm equipped each of its stores with inexpensive IBM-compatible computers that were linked by modems to the company's larger system in Park City. Computerization allowed the firm's retail stores to plan daily production schedules, monitor stocks and order

---

KEY DATES

1977: Debbi Fields opens her first store in Palo Alto.
1979: A second store opens at Pier 39 in San Francisco.
1983: The company moves to Park City, Utah, and operates 70 stores from Honolulu to Chicago.
1986: Mrs. Fields goes public on London's Unlisted Securities Market.
1987: La Petite Boulangerie, a chain of 119 French bakery/sandwich stores, is purchased.
1990: Mrs. Fields' Cookies announces an agreement with the Marriott Corporation.
1993: The company is delisted from London's stock exchange; new owners reorganize the company.
1996: Capricorn Investors II, L.P. acquires Mrs. Fields.
1998: Pretzelmaker Holdings Inc. is acquired.
2000: TCBY Enterprises Inc. is purchased; Debbi Fields ends her consultancy with the firm.
2001: Mrs. Fields Famous Brands Inc. is formed.
2008: The company files for Chapter 11 bankruptcy protection and emerges in October.

---

about $30 million. By early 1983 the company had moved to Park City, Utah, and operated 70 stores, from Honolulu to Chicago. Only then did it decided to open its first store in New York City.

TAKING STOCK OF THE COMPETITION

When the firm began in the late 1970s about 100 independent stores sold gourmet or specialty cookies. By 1983, according to *Forbes,* competition in this niche industry had resulted in just a few main companies. Mrs. Fields' Cookies competed against the Famous Amos Chocolate Chip Cookie Corporation, started in 1975 by Wally (Famous) Amos. By 1983 Famous Amos began a program to franchise 100 stores within two years. David Liederman began David's Cookies with a store in Manhattan and soon dominated the New York City market for specialty cookies. Other key firms included The Famous Chocolate Chip Cookie Company, headed by President Frank Bonanno; the Original Cookie Company, owned by Cole National Corporation; and Original Great American Chocolate Chip Cookie Co., led by President Arthur Karp.

materials automatically, communicate with headquarters using electronic mail, improve employee training, and handle payroll and other accounting tasks. Store managers spent about five minutes each hour and 20 minutes before and after work using their computers to help run their outlets. Headquarters staff in 1988 remained low at about 130 persons.

Although Mrs. Fields' Cookies management structure on paper included levels of middle management, Tom Richman in an October 1987 *Inc.* article wrote: "Randy Fields has created something entirely new—a shape if not the shape, of business organizations to come. It gives top management a dimension of personal control over dispersed operations that small companies otherwise find impossible to achieve. It projects a founder's vision into parts of a company that have long ago outgrown his or her ability to reach in person." Richman continued: "In the structure that Fields is building, computers don't just speed up old administrative management processes. They alter the process. Management ... becomes less administration and more inspiration. The management hierarchy of the company feels almost flat."

After Randy Fields computerized Mrs. Fields' Cookies, he began selling his artificial intelligence/store management software through a subsidiary, Fields Software Group. Burger King Corporation became one of the first software customers in 1990.

AWARDS FOR PHILANTHROPIC ACTIVITY

In the meantime, Debbi and Randy Fields were a highly visible couple who were recognized with numerous honors for their community involvement and support. In 1988 the Utah Chapter of the National Conference of Christians and Jews honored the couple with its Brotherhood/Sisterhood Award for their many community contributions in business and philanthropy. As the president of a firm with over 700 outlets worldwide, Debbi Fields told the National Conference attendees that, "We are very proud to receive this award, but you must remember that each time you've enjoyed Mrs. Fields' Cookies, you're the one who's allowing us to give."

Debbi Fields also served on the boards of the Cystic Fibrosis Research Foundation, the Park City Educational Foundation, and Salt Lake City's LDS Hospital. She and her husband founded Mrs. Fields' Children's Health Foundation and donated millions to study children's diseases. Randy Fields was president of Riverview Financial Corporation, the Fields Investment Group, and the Fields Consulting Group.

The company, however, had a bad year in 1988, when it lost $19 million and closed 85 of its 500 stores, mostly in the eastern and southeastern United States. Some argued that these problems began in 1986 with Mrs. Fields' Cookies' initial public offering on London's Unlisted Securities Market. British investors purchased only 16 percent of the 30 million shares offered at $2.46 per share. After the company said it had set up a $15 million reserve to pay for store closings, its stock price decreased to just 44 cents per share.

The company also closed its Park City candy factory in order to concentrate on building its La Petite Boulangerie bakery business in Carson, California. To integrate the new subsidiary, Mrs. Fields' Cookies transitioned from cookie stores to full-service bakeries. Randy Fields admitted this was a difficult situation, particularly with overseas investors. In the February 13, 1989, issue of *Fortune,* he said, "We've been very ineffective at telling the British what we're trying to do." Some British food industry analysts said investors felt deceived after they were told it was a cookie company and then it changed directions.

DEVELOPMENT BEYOND THE BUSINESS

In spite of these challenges, Randy and Debbi Fields continued to play a major role in developing the rapidly growing community of Park City, where more celebrities and about 300 *Fortune* 500 executives decided to move or build condominiums in the 1980s. For example, the couple developed the Summit County Industrial Park, anchored by tenant Lucas Western's $40 million aerospace manufacturing plant. They also owned Park City's Main Street Mall, home of their corporate headquarters, the Egyptian Theatre, and other properties. In 1988 they closed their ice-cream parlor so they could use the former Dudler Building for Mrs. Fields' Cookie College.

Gregg Goodwin, head of Park City Area Chamber of Commerce economic development, cited Randy and Debbi Fields as an example of corporate leaders who had moved their family and company to Park City to enjoy the area's high education levels, strong work ethic, low rates of alcohol use, and other lifestyle advantages.

In 1989 the company rebounded from a poor performance the year before. Revenues for the parent company, Mrs. Fields' Inc., increased 8 percent from $120.4 million in 1988 to $129.7 million in 1989, while the firm recorded a 1989 net income of $1.5 million, a major improvement from 1988's loss of $19 million.

That year Mrs. Fields' Cookies began making frozen cookie dough at its Carson, California, plant and then shipping it to selected stores in Utah. Previously it had been the only major cookie maker that did not use frozen dough. In December 1989 the company began the process of selling its Carson plant to Van den Bergh Foods, a Unilever Group subsidiary. However, Mrs. Fields' Cookies kept the part of the plant that made its cookies.

Mrs. Fields' Inc. reorganized in 1989 by redistributing certain management roles. A new executive committee included Chairman Randy Fields, President Debbi Fields, Larry Holman, Paul Baird, and Tim Pierce. Holman, an attorney, had joined the company as a senior vice-president in October 1989 to manage corporate development and real estate. Director of Operations Baird took over much of the responsibility of managing the firm's cookie stores, thus allowing Debbi Fields to emphasize development and marketing. Pierce was a CPA and company vice-president of finance. Even more significant changes would occur in the years to come, but in the meantime the company had to deal with damaging rumors and stories circulating among the public.

THE URBAN LEGEND

University of Utah Professor Jan Brunvand and other scholars have shown that tales or stories about modern companies are sometimes told so often they become urban legends. Usually without a basis in fact, they spread because they are told by a friend of a friend in a chain of communication. For example, in the 1950s, a story called "Red Velvet Cake" was told about a customer who paid New York City's Waldorf-Astoria Hotel a large sum of money for a red cake recipe. The story, which began spreading in 1983 had mutated so that Mrs. Fields' Cookies was the culprit. In this version, "someone had called the Mrs. Fields' company and asked for their recipe. When told that it was available for 'two-fifty,' the caller supposedly told the phone representative to send the recipe and charge it to her credit card, learning later that the price was $250 rather than the expected $2.50."

Then, according to this tale disseminated by photocopies, the corporation's victim became upset and thus sent many bitter letters with the supposed secret recipe, and encouraged others to send out even more copies.

Debbi Fields acknowledged in her book that by 1987 the rumor had caused damage to the company. She responded to this persistent tale by placing notices in all her stores denying that the company had ever sold its recipe. Denunciations from the top usually had little impact and the story continued to be told well into the

early 1990s. Fortunately for Fields and her company, however, exactly the same rumor was spread about other firms such as Chicago's Marshall Field's, New York City's Macy's, St. Louis' Union Station, and Neiman Marcus, thus blunting its negative effect on her business.

Dr. Brunvand, a leading expert on urban legends, wrote about this story in his fourth book, *Curses! Broiled Again.* He said in his 1991 newspaper column that this story about Mrs. Fields' Cookies and other companies was a "classic recipe-scam story that refuses to die, no matter how often I debunk it or how vigorously companies deny it. ... [It] illustrates two things: that many people love stories about corporate ripoffs, and that few can resist chocolate chip cookies."

A DECADE OF CHANGE: 1990–99

In 1990 Mrs. Fields' Cookies announced an agreement with the Marriott Corporation that allowed Marriott to own at least 60 stores to bake and sell the popular bakery products. Marriott gained the exclusive right to build Mrs. Fields' Cookies stores in airports, hotels, and highway travel plazas and pay the cookie company approximately 5 percent of its gross sales.

By 1990 there were 45 Mrs. Fields' stores internationally, in Canada, Australia, Japan, Hong Kong, and the United Kingdom, and the company planned to expand further through joint ventures and licensing contracts. By 1992 the firm had added stores in Thailand and Mexico City, the latter through a licensing agreement with Pastelería El Molino S.A.

In 1990 the company also began remodeling some stores to allow more display space for new packaging products, cookie jars, and tins. To stimulate gift buying as well as cookie purchases, teddy bear maker Gund was commissioned to make little bears like those on the cookie tins. With new designs and decor, Debbi Fields intended to create boutiques or European-style cafés that were more colorful and exciting. The biggest change was yet to come however.

In 1993 Mrs. Fields' Cookies stock was removed from the London Stock Exchange, and new owners reorganized the company. Four lenders, led by the Prudential group, acquired almost 80 percent of the firm in exchange for writing off $94 million in company debt, while Debbi Fields retained a minority interest, remained board chairman, and accepted a salary cut of $150,000 to $450,000. Thomas Fey, formerly with Godiva and Pepperidge Farm, replaced Debbi Fields as president and CEO. The refinancing allowed the company to plan a major expansion of 100 new company-owned and franchised stores within the next year. Started in August 1991, the company's franchise option was praised by at least three publications: *Success, Entrepreneur,* and *Self* magazine.

THE CASE FOR CHANGE IN TOP MANAGEMENT

Although the company survived and retained the name of its founder, many wondered why Debbi and Randy Fields lost control. As Max Knudson, the business editor of Salt Lake City's *Deseret News* wrote in 1998, the couple "seemed to have it all: beauty, brains, ambition, family values, a business growing exponentially—people couldn't get enough of them."

Three reasons accounted for the company's huge debt and the loss of control to outsiders. First, the company expanded too fast, and many of these stores could not afford their expensive rents. In many cases, the company had purchased property for its mall stores. Second, the nation's economic downturn in the early 1990s hurt Mrs. Fields' Cookies. Many customers decided they could no longer could afford these treats (about $1 per cookie), and the value of her real estate declined, as well.

Last but not least, Debbi Fields' insistence on hands-on personal management and her reluctance to franchise did not work. Francorp's Don Boroian, a Chicago franchising consultant, quoted in the July 1993 *Working Woman* magazine, said he told Mrs. Fields' Cookies to franchise when it was still a young firm. "When you're trying to expand as they did, with units in malls, you can't provide close enough supervision. By the time they decided to franchise, the concept wasn't strong enough because of increased competition, fewer customers, higher rents and a downturn in the economy. They needed to add more products, and they're finally doing that now." By 1993 the company had added yogurt, coffee, and diversified with other products, but it had also closed most of its mall stores by then.

EXPANSION THROUGH FRANCHISING OVERSEAS

Chairwoman Debbi Fields announced in early 1995 that the company planned to add 100 new stores overseas. At that time 5 percent of the firm's 617 stores were located outside the United States. Fields said the company had franchise agreements in Indonesia, Australia, the Philippines, Canada, and the Middle East. European and South American markets were also under consideration. Fields said the firm's long-term goal was to franchise all overseas operations.

Like many other firms, Mrs. Fields' Cookies used the Internet to stimulate sales during the 1990s. The company was one of more than 100 businesses included on the Utah-based virtual mall called iShopper, which was started in July 1996.

In the 1990s the company moved its headquarters from Park City to offices on Bearcat Drive in Salt Lake City. In the summer of 1998 it moved to a new 30,000-square-foot complex in Salt Lake City's Cottonwood Corporate Center. However, it kept its facilities on Bearcat Drive and Lawndale Drive for about 40 employees. Its mail-order operation remained on Bearcat Drive.

Meanwhile, the family that started the business ended in divorce. Debbi Fields married Michael Rose, the retired chairman of Harrah's Entertainment, on November 29, 1997, and moved from Park City to live with her husband in Memphis, Tennessee. Debbi Fields Rose served as a consultant to the firm she founded and also participated in a public television show called *Great American Desserts.* Randy Fields continued to live in Park City and work in the software industry.

The company continued to expand in 1998 under the ownership of Capricorn Investors II, L.P., which purchased the company in 1996, and the leadership of Chairman Herbert S. Winokur Jr. and President/CEO Larry A. Hodges. Effective November 23, 1998, Mrs. Fields' Original Cookies purchased Denver-based Pretzelmaker Holdings Inc. This acquisition added 229 pretzel stores to the firm's existing 1,324 cookie and pretzel stores. The company also purchased Pretzel Time Inc. and the Great American Cookie Company Inc. during this period.

MOVING INTO THE NEW MILLENNIUM

Under Capricorn's leadership Mrs. Fields' continued to focus on expansion during the early years of the new millennium. In 2000 the company purchased TCBY Enterprises Inc. in a $140 million deal, adding a chain of nearly 3,000 frozen yogurt outlets to its holdings. Capricorn then formed Mrs. Fields' Famous Brands Inc. to oversee the operations of its cookie, pretzel, and yogurt stores. Growth continued in 2002 with the launch of the first Mrs. Fields' franchise in Tokyo.

As the U.S. economy began to falter in the early 2000s, however, Mrs. Fields' saw a decline in store sales. With profits waning the company was forced to revamp its expansion strategy. It continued to sell most of its company-owned locations in order to focus on its franchise locations. In 2003 CEO Larry Hodges resigned and Stephen Russo was named his replacement. Under new leadership, Mrs. Fields' worked to shore up profits and control costs. During 2006 the company launched a new store design and several new menu items, including a line of specialty coffee drinks, in an attempt to lure new customers.

In order to focus on its core cookie and yogurt business, Capricorn sold its Pretzelmaker and Pretzel Time business to NexCen Brands Inc. in 2007. NexCen purchased the Great American Cookie Co. for $93.7 million the following year. Meanwhile, consumer spending continued to decline while food costs reached record highs. With debt mounting, Mrs. Fields' found itself in a precarious financial position.

BANKRUPTCY AND REORGANIZATION

In August 2008 the company announced that it was filing for Chapter 11 bankruptcy protection in order to cut nearly $145 million in debt from its books. Founder Debbi Fields, who had ended her professional consultancy with the firm in 2000, issued a press statement later that month concerning the bankruptcy. "Hopefully, reorganization will allow Mrs. Fields' Cookies to do what it was built to do: make the best cookies in the world, serve happy and loyal customers, and never compromise on the quality of its product or its people. These are the principles that made the brand great and what I believe will allow Mrs. Fields' Cookies to delight customers for generations to come."

Mrs. Fields' Original Cookies emerged from bankruptcy in October of that year with lofty goals. It expected to open 40 new franchised stores in 2009, expand its gifting and branded retail business by 15 percent and its licensing business by nearly 30 percent. Under the leadership of co-CEOs Michael R. Ward and John Lauck, the company indeed had its work cut out for it in the years to come.

David M. Walden
Updated, Christina M. Stansell

PRINCIPAL COMPETITORS

1-800-FLOWERS.COM, Inc.; Auntie Anne's, Inc.; Yogurt Ventures U.S.A., Inc.

FURTHER READING

Berta, Dina, "Mrs. Fields Bakes Up New Look," *Nation's Restaurant News,* November 6, 2006.

———, "Mrs. Fields' Co-CEOs Bring Multitasking to the C-Suite," *Nation's Restaurant News,* December 8, 2008.

Brunvand, Jan Harold, "Fresh Batch of Kooky Cookie Stories Is Served," *Deseret News,* October 25, 1991.

"Capricorn Closes Deal for TCBY," *Wall Street Journal,* June 2, 2000.

"Chips and Chocolate," *Economist,* July 23, 1988, p. 56.

Fields, Debbi, and Alan Furst, *One Smart Cookie: How a Housewife's Chocolate Chip Recipe Turned into a Multimillion Dollar Business: The Story of Mrs. Fields' Cookies,* New York: Simon and Schuster, 1987.

Funk, Marianne, "Mrs. Fields' Is Transforming Some Stores into Boutiques," *Deseret News,* July 16, 1990.

Kercheval, Nancy, "Mrs. Fields Files for Bankruptcy," *Deseret Morning News,* August 26, 2008.

Knudson, Max B., "Fields Cookie Without the Mrs. or Mr.?" *Deseret News,* May 20, 1998.

———, "Marketing Plan for Park City Is Imaginative," *Deseret News,* December 17, 1989.

———, "Mrs. Fields' Cookies Says It Has Accord to Fuel Growth," *Deseret News,* February 17, 1993.

Madden, Stephen, "Tough Cookies?" *Fortune,* February 13, 1989, p. 112.

Mao, Vincent, "The Queen of Mrs. Fields Cookies," *Investor's Business Daily,* February 17, 2009.

McKanus, Kevin, "The Cookie Wars," *Forbes,* November 7, 1983, p. 150.

Moulton, Tina, "Fieldses Honored for Compassion and Service to the Community," *Deseret News,* May 8, 1988.

"Mrs. Fields' Cookies Goes East," *Fortune,* February 7, 1983, p. 9.

"Mrs. Fields Inc. Back on Track with '89 Income of $1.5 Million," *Deseret News,* April 11, 1990.

Newquist, Harvey P., III, "Experts at Retail," *Datamation,* April 1, 1990, p. 53.

"NexCen Pays $93.7M for Second Mrs. Fields Chain," *Nation's Restaurant News,* February 11, 2008.

Pogrebin, Robin, "What Went Wrong with Mrs. Fields?" *Working Woman,* July 1993, p. 9.

Richman, Tom, "Mrs. Fields' Secret Ingredient: The Real Recipe Behind the Phenomenal Growth of Mrs. Fields' Cookies Cannot Be Found in the Dough," *Inc.,* October 1987, p. 65.

"Statement from Debbi Fields Regarding the Announcement from Mrs. Fields Famous Brands, LLC that the Company Plans to File for Chapter 11 Bankruptcy Reorganization," *Business Wire,* August 19, 2008.

Williams, Jean, "Send in the Clones: Top Secret Recipes," *Deseret News,* June 18, 1996.

Munir Sukhtian Group

—————— ■ ——————

P.O. Box 1027
Amman,
Jordan
Telephone: (962 06) 5688888
Fax: (962 06) 5601568
Web site: http://www.sukhtian.com

Private Company
Incorporated: 1933
Employees: 780
Sales: $1.03 billion (2007 est.)
NAICS: 424210 Drugs and Druggists' Sundries
Merchant Wholesalers; 312111 Soft Drink
Manufacturing; 325620 Toilet Preparation
Manufacturing; 423450 Medical, Dental, and
Hospital Equipment and Supplies Merchant
Wholesalers; 424910 Farm Supplies Merchant
Wholesalers

■ ■ ■

The Munir Sukhtian Group, along with its affiliated
company Munir Sukhtian International, is a leading
Jordan-based conglomerate involved in a number of
diversified industries. Founded as a single pharmacy in
1933, Munir Sukhtian remains active in the para-
pharmacy and pharmaceuticals sector both as a
manufacturer and as a distributor. The group's holdings
in this area include United Pharmaceuticals, a producer
of generic drugs for the Middle East, North African,
European and other regions; Tabuk Pharmaceuticals,
based in Saudi Arabia in partnership with the Astra

Group, and its Algeria-based subsidiary El Kendi
Pharmaceutical Manufacturing Co.; and the Beit Jala
Pharmaceutical Manufacturing Company in the
Palestinian Territories.

Since 2007 the group has also become a supplier of
materials and equipment for neurological applications
through its medical division. Related manufacturing
operations include Household and Toiletries
Manufacturing (HTM), which produces a wide range of
soaps, shampoos, toothpaste, disinfectants, paramedical,
and first-aid products, among many others, including
many under license for the Schwartzkopf and Fumakilla
brands. The company's general trade division distributes
these as well as third-party products, including for Henkel, Boots, and Heinz. Among the other divisions are
agriculture, including the production and distribution of
fertilizers, pesticides, seeds, and plant tissue cultures;
flower and plant auctions, through Jordanian Flower
and Plants Marketing Company; and greenhouses and
poultry houses under the Rayyan and Dajjan names.

More recently, the company has entered the
telecommunications and information technology (IT)
sectors, with holdings including Nour Communications
in Saudi Arabia, Nour USA, and WaTanServe in
Algeria, as well as telecommunications operations under
the Munir Sukhtian name in Sudan, Egypt, Bangladesh,
and Algeria. Munir Sukhtian's Jordanian operations are
led by Nadil Sukhtian, while the family's international
holdings are led by his brother Ghiath Sukhtian. A third
brother, Munjed Sukhtian, is also active in the privately
held company, which posted revenues of more than $1
billion in 2007.

PHARMACY ORIGINS

The Munir Sukhtian Group was founded by Munir Sukhtian, who completed a degree in pharmacy at the American University of Beirut in the early 1930s. Sukhtian's family was already active in the pharmacy business, and in 1933 Sukhtian returned to his native Palestine, where he bought his father's pharmacy in Tulkarm. That business was to provide the foundation for the company's growth into one of the region's major conglomerates.

Sukhtian's business interests spread beyond the pharmacy following the war with Israel in 1948. In 1950, Sukhtian launched his own import/export operations, as well as becoming a major wholesaler for the region, with offices based in Nablus and Amman, Jordan. These operations later grew into three of Munir Sukhtian Group's main divisions: Chemicals, General Trade, and Medical Equipment and Consumables. Over the following decade, the group's trading business expanded to include a wide variety of goods, ranging from personal care products to cleaning supplies and detergents, medical equipment and supplies, paints, chemicals, and pharmaceuticals.

The 1950s also saw the creation of Jordan Chemical Laboratory, in Beit Jala, near Bethlehem. The operation focused on generic drug production, with a range of tablets and capsules, syrups, and suppositories, as well as ointments and creams. This business, which began producing eye drops in 1978, became known as Beit Jala Pharmaceutical Manufacturing Company and later joined the Munir Sukhtian Group. By this time, the Munir Sukhtian Group had begun to position itself as a major player in the Palestinian and Jordanian economies.

Munir Sukhtian himself did not live to see the growth of the company he had founded. Following his death at the age of 50 in 1960, the company's operations were taken over by Sukhtian's three sons. Taking the most active roles were Nidal Sukhtian, who became head of the group's Amman office, and his younger brother Ghiath, who took over the Nablus office, and later guided the growth of the family's international operations.

DIVERSIFICATION FOLLOWING THE SIX DAY WAR

The Israeli takeover of the West Bank territories following the Six Day War in 1967 had a major impact on the Sukhtian family's operations. Tightening import policies cut the company off from its normal supply channels. Instead of buying products from Israeli sources, the Sukhtians took the different approach of launching their own manufacturing operations.

For this, Ghiath Sukhtian installed a small laboratory in the garage of his mother's home. With a small team of pharmacists and lab technicians, Sukhtian began producing its first medicines. With the friendly support of local pharmacists and physicians, Sukhtian was able to establish a new presence as a supplier of medicines and other products. Soon after launching production, for example, Sukhtian learned the process for removing the odor from kerosene. This permitted the group to launch its own line of disinfectants. The success of this product provided the foundation for the group's growth into a major regional producer of household cleansers and toiletries. In 1972 Sukhtian founded a new subsidiary, Household and Toiletries Manufacturing, or HTM, which expanded its range to include toothpaste, cosmetics, disinfectants, and detergents.

The Arab oil embargo, and the resulting economic boom in the Middle East, provided new opportunities for the company. The Sukhtian Group then began to extend its reach beyond its core pharmacy trade and manufacturing sectors into a variety of new industries. Communications provided one early source for diversification as the company established a number of activities in the sector, leading to the creation of a new division, Communications and Security Systems, in 1977. Based in Jordan, that operation later became a prominent supplier of communications and other equipment to the Middle East region.

The region's harsh growing conditions and limited supply of fresh water provided another business stream for the growing group. In 1980 the company founded Jordan Greenhouses Manufacturing Company. That company helped pioneer the greenhouse market for the Middle East, marketing its greenhouses and systems. These later came under the Rayyan name. The company launched production of poultry houses as well, under the Dajjan name. The greenhouse business grew increasingly international and over the next two decades the

KEY DATES

1933: Munir Sukhtian buys a pharmacy from his father in Tulkarm, in Palestine.

1950: Sukhtian launches import/export operations and becomes a major wholesaler for the region.

1960: Sukhtian dies at the age of 50 and his sons take over the operation of the company.

1967: The company launches its own manufacturing business.

1972: The company adds the production of household products and toiletries.

1980: The group founds Jordan Greenhouses Manufacturing Company.

1989: Sukhtian founds a new pharmaceutical company, United Pharmaceuticals (UPM), for the production of generics.

1994: Tabuk Pharmaceutical Manufacturing Company is formed in partnership with Astra Group in Saudi Arabia.

2005: Tabuk and UPM found El Kendi Pharmaceutical Manufacturing Co. in Algeria.

2007: A new division is created to market medical equipment and supplies.

group completed a number of turnkey greenhouse projects across the Middle East, the Persian Gulf region, and North Africa, as well as in Greece, Cyprus, Romania, and other markets.

AGRICULTURAL EXPANSION

The Jordanian government's decision to block flower imports into Jordan led the Sukhtian family in another direction. In 1984 the company teamed up with Mazen Ghalayini to create the Amman Flower Auction House, based in Rabia, in West Amman. This auction initially focused on native Jordanian flowers and plants and then played an important role in marketing and exporting the country's products into other Middle East markets. The flower auction operation also added support operations for the country's farmers, providing seedlings and technological support and information. The success of the venture led to the opening of several branches, including at King Abdullah Gardens in West Amman, and in Fuhais and Irbid. In support of the company's growing sales to the Persian Gulf region, the company added an international branch as well, in Qatar.

The Sukhtian Group deepened its interest in agriculture in the late 1980s. In 1988 the company joined in the creation of Astra Agricultural Company Ltd., in partnership with Saudi Arabia's Astra Group. Based in Riyadh, Astra Agricultural was founded as a marketing and distribution group for fertilizers, agrochemicals, and other agricultural supplies in the Middle East region. In 1996 the Astra partnership launched its own fertilizer blending facility, called Astrachem, in Saudi Arabia's Eastern Province.

In the meantime, the plant and flower wing of the business had undergone its own extension, with the founding of Sukhtian Tissue Culture Labs and Nurseries and Celtis Labs in 1989. This business initially focused on producing commercial plant tissue cultures. Over the next decade and a half the laboratory began a research and development effort to create a rootstock capable of tolerating the high salinity of the region's soil, while at the same time providing disease-resistance qualities. This effort resulted in the successful launch of the group's ASAAS rootstock. ASAAS supported fruit plant grafts from watermelon, melon, and tomato plants, while eliminating the need for the use of chemical treatments, such as methyl bromide.

POSITIONED FOR PROFIT

The Munir Sukhtian Group continued its growth through the 1990s. The company added its own IT operations in the mid-1980s, with the creation of Arabian Office Automation (AOA) in 1986. This was one of the first companies in Jordan to provide IT services to the local market. AOA grew especially strongly after reaching an exclusive agreement with Xerox Corporation to deploy that company's office equipment and technology in the Jordanian market.

The growing family-owned conglomerate joined in partnership again with Astra to found Nour Communications Company in 1989. This business focused on providing design, engineering, and installation of telecommunications systems and equipment. Nour soon expanded beyond Saudi Arabia, setting up operations in a number of markets, including Bangladesh and the United States.

Into the next decade, Munir Sukhtian's position in Jordan placed it in a strong position to profit from the political situation surrounding Iraq following the Persian Gulf War. Jordan had not joined the international coalition against Iraq during the war. The country also did not participate in the international blockade of Iraq following the war. As a result, Jordan became the sole conduit of goods into and out of Iraq. The country also played a key role in the so-called oil-for-food trade with Iraq during this period. The situation allowed the Sukhtian Group to expand its trade operations with Iraq and position itself as a presence in Iraq following the U.S. invasion of that country in 2003.

Munir Sukhtian also expanded its pharmaceuticals operations through the 1990s. The company took a major step forward in this industry with the 1989 creation of a new company, United Pharmaceuticals (UPM), in order to produce generics. With an initial investment of $30 million, the company established a state-of-the-art manufacturing complex that ultimately grew to cover 15,000 square meters. UPM quickly received authorization to market its products in the European Union, becoming the first in Jordan to do so. Exports, particularly to Germany, played a major part in UPM's growth, and by the middle of the next decade represented 90 percent of UPM's sales.

THRIVING IN THE 21ST CENTURY

In the 1990s, the company's partnership with Astra grew again with the founding of a new Saudi Arabia-based pharmaceuticals company, Tabuk Pharmaceutical Manufacturing Company. This company, like UPM, launched production of generic medicines, initially for the Middle East market, before gaining its own license to market its products in Europe. Tabuk and UPM also joined together to begin marketing their products in Algeria in the late 1990s. Over the next decade, the companies developed a strong business in that market. This led to the decision to launch manufacturing operations based in Algeria, which would also serve other African markets. In 2005 the companies founded El Kendi Pharmaceutical Manufacturing Co., which began construction of its factory the following year.

UPM made a number of its own expansion moves at the dawn of the new century. In 2002, the company established a European presence, buying Stowic Resources Ltd. in the United Kingdom. This company specialized in the production of transdermal patches for drug delivery. UPM also eyed a move into the South American market. This led the group to Brazil, where it received authorization to market its range of generic tablets and capsules. UPM then went on to form cooperation agreements with Tabuk, which had a strong expertise in injectables, and Jordan Chemical Laboratory, which soon after changed its name to Beit Jala Pharmaceutical Manufacturing Company.

Trade remained an important component of the Munir Sukhtian Group as well. In 2002 the company

decided to enter the food distribution sector. For this the company founded a new food division and began importing a range of chilled, frozen, and dry foods from the United States and Europe. Also in that year, Munir Sukhtian took full control of Zayyan Metal Furniture, which had been founded in 1991 in Irbid to produce metal exterior furniture before moving to Amman in 1997.

By the later years of the first decade of the new century, the Munir Sukhtian Group boasted total revenues of more than $1 billion. Brothers Nadil and Ghiath Sukhtian continued to oversee the family's holdings, which had been restructured into two main holding companies, Munir Sukhtian Group, which represented the family's Jordanian holdings, and Munir Sukhtian International, which, guided by Ghiath Sukhtian, operated its foreign businesses. The restructuring came ahead of a possible initial public offering, as the Sukhtian brothers prepared the company's succession.

The family's appetite for expansion remained as strong as ever. In 2007, for example, the company created a new medical division, which focused on marketing medical equipment and supplies, with an emphasis on neurology products. At the same time, the group announced its plans to extend its HTM trade operation into the Latin American market. For this, the company again targeted the Brazilian market, first launching its Hi-Geen branded line of hand-cleaning products, while planning a general rollout of its other product lines. After more than 75 years, Munir Sukhtian's legacy had created a thriving Jordanian business empire.

M. L. Cohen

PRINCIPAL SUBSIDIARIES

Al Kendi Pharmaceutical Manufacturing Company (Algeria; 75%); AnwarNet (Algeria); Arab Supply and Trading Corporation (Saudi Arabia); Arabian Office Automation Company; Astra Agricultural Company (Saudi Arabia); Beit Jala Pharmaceutical Manufacturing Company (Palestinian Territories); Celtis Labs; Greenhouse Manufacturing Company; Households and Toiletries Manufacturing Company; Munir Sukhtian for Telecommunications (Egypt); Nour Communications (Saudi Arabia); Nourbangla Communications Company (Bangladesh); Ogier Electronics–Libya; Palestine Plastic Industries Company; Sukhtian Brothers Company (Palestinian Territories); Sukhtian International Trading Company (Algeria); United Pharmaceutical Manufacturing Company; Watanserve Communications–Algeria; Watanserve Communications–Pakistan.

PRINCIPAL COMPETITORS

Entreprise de Distribution de Produits Chimiques S.p. A.; General Foreign Trade Organization; Omar Zawawi Establishment; Union Trading Company WLL; Teva Pharmaceutical Industries Ltd.; Perrigo Israel Pharmaceuticals Ltd.

FURTHER READING

"Jordanian Company Seeks Distributor in Brazil," *IPR Strategic Business Information Database,* August 7, 2007.

"Jordanian Group Wants to Conquer Brazilian Market," *IPR Strategic Business Information Database,* August 29, 2007.

Newcom Group

———————————— ◾ ————————————

8th Floor, 8 Zovkhis Building, Seoul Street 21
Ulaanbaatar, 14251
Mongolia
Telephone: (976 11) 313183
Fax: (976 11) 318521
Web site: http://www.newcom.mn

Private Company
Incorporated: 1993
Employees: 1,000
Sales: $927 million (2008)
NAICS: 513322 Cellular and Other Wireless Telecommunications; 481111 Commuter air carriers, scheduled; 221119 Power generation, wind electric.

◼ ◼ ◼

Newcom Group, under the auspices of its parent company Newcom LLC, is the leading privately owned holding company in Mongolia with interests in the telecommunications, aviation, real estate, energy, and financial sectors. Newcom's primary holding is its stake in Mobicom Corporation, the country's leading mobile telephone services provider. Launched in 1996 in partnership with Japan's Sumitomo and KDD, Mobicom offers a full range of cellular telephone services, including broadband services rolled out in 2009. Mobicom also provides prepaid and subscription services, short message service (SMS) and voice-mail service, as well as wireless loop service. Another of Newcom's fast-growing investments is Eznis Airways, founded in 2006. Eznis Airways provides domestic air transport services, as well as flights to Russia, Kazakhstan, and China. Eznis's fleet consists of three Saab 340B aircraft. In 2009

the company signed a letter of interest to acquire seven Bombardier C-series aircraft starting in 2013. Newcom Property LLC, founded in 2005, combines real estate investment and development operations with property management and maintenance services.

In the later years of the first decade of the 2000s, Newcom has also developed an interest in the energy sector, most notably wind-power generation through subsidiary Clean Energy Company. This subsidiary participated in the construction of Mongolia's first wind farm, expected to come online in 2009. Newcom also operates in the security services sector, through Newsec LLC, and provides financial services, including home loans and salary advances, to its employees through Newfund LLC, launched in 2005. Newcom LLC was founded in 1993 as a telecommunications provider. The company is led by CEO B. Unenbat and chairman Tserenpuntsag Boldbaatar.

FOUNDING A PRIVATE COMPANY IN 1993

The collapse of the Soviet Union in the late 1980s led to Mongolia's own peaceful revolution as the country replaced decades of Communist Party domination with a parliamentary democracy and a free market system in 1992. The new economic landscape encouraged the emergence of an entrepreneurial class seeking to build on Mongolia's wealth of natural resources. At the same time, the country witnessed the growth of the various services sectors.

Telecommunications was an especially promising market, given the low number of telephone lines put in place by the country's Ministry of Communications during the Soviet Era. Into the early 1990s, the total number of telephone lines stood at less than 50,000, for a population of more than 2.5 million. In 1992 the Ministry of Communications was broken up into regulatory and operational components. The former telephone monopoly was then reincorporated into Mongolian Telecommunication Company (MTC).

The need to upgrade and expand the country's telephone network, and its telecommunications sector in general, stimulated the appearance of a number of new companies. Among these was Newcom LLC, founded in 1993 by N. Tuya in order to supply telecommunications equipment and services. Although MTC was to maintain the monopoly over the country's domestic and international landlines, other areas of the telecommunications market, including cellular telephony services and Internet access, opened to competition.

Newcom's first success came soon after, when the company won a bid to supply the equipment as part of MTC's effort to digitize the country's largely analog telephone network. By 1995 the company had also begun importing and distributing two-way radios for Motorola in Mongolia.

CELLULAR PIONEER IN 1995

At the same time, Newcom had been looking for partners to assist it in achieving its true objective of becoming Mongolia's first cellular telephone operator. Japan, which had gained the lead both in mobile telephone technology and in cellular telephone uptake, provided no shortage of potential partners for Newcom. By September 1995 the company had reached agreement with two Japanese companies, operator KDD and equipment supplier Sumitomo, to set up a joint venture for Mongolia, called Mobicom Corporation.

Mobicom officially launched its operations just six months later, providing service based on the GSM (global system for mobile communications) standard to the capital city of Ulaanbaatar. Over the next year, the company built up its network in that market. By 1997 Mobicom was ready to expand its services to other markets in Mongolia. The company opened branches in Darkhan, Sukhbataar, and Erdenet in March of that year. By the end of the decade, Mobicom had extended its coverage to Nalaikh and Altanbulag, followed by Zamiin-Uud in 2000, and Arvaikheer and Dornogovi in 2001. The company also rolled out a range of services, including its prepaid MobiCard service in 1998; international roaming, voice mail, and SMS texting in 2000; and Internet access in 2001.

While Mobicom took charge of building a national cellular telephone infrastructure, Newcom founded a mobile telephone services subsidiary, Newtel, in 2000. Newtel then began building a national network of agencies, while also developing a range of telephone services.

During this time, Newcom developed into a major supplier of telecommunications equipment and products. The company became Mongolia's supplier of a number of Toshiba products, including its electronic cash register starting in 1999. In 2001 the group began importing the bank note detection and counting systems developed by Japan's JCM. These were followed by the import contracts for a range of products from France's Alcatel, including its PBX systems and mobile telephone handsets. The company also became the supplier of Bulgaria-based Datecs' electronic cash registers.

EXPANDING OPERATIONS INTO THE TURN OF THE 21ST CENTURY

Newcom continued to explore new investment opportunities into the turn of the century. The company founded a new subsidiary, NewcomTel, in 2001 to develop a range of telecommunications-based products and services. This led to the launch of voice over Internet protocol services in partnership with Japan's NTT Communications later that year. The following year, the company founded Newtelcard LLC, which served as retail distributor for prepaid mobile services.

Newtelcard played an important role in Mobicom's success, allowing the company to triple the number of prepaid telecommunications customers. This market was all the more important for Mobicom as it appealed to lower-income users. The difficult transition to a free market economy, which had put the country through several crises during the 1990s, was only slowly beginning to transform the country's profile. During the first decade of the 2000s, average incomes remained very low. As a result, prepaid services represented the only possibility for many citizens to gain access to the telephone grid.

first and only cellular telephone provider to boast national coverage.

Nonetheless, Mobicom continued to fill in coverage, adding services to Guulin and Delger in 2003; Tosontsengel and Bor-Undur in 2004; and Berkh, Tsagaannuur, Tsogt-Ovoo, Bayanchandmani, Hui Doloon, Daschinchilen, among others, in 2005.

Mobicom had also expanded its services components, extending its network of service branches to nearly 150 by the end of the decade. The company added such telephony services as SMS-based banking, and the RBN-509 text-based ticker, in 2002; a Web2SMS service, as well as InternetEASY, a prepaid mobile Internet access service, and messenger services between Mobicom customers and customers of rival Skynet, in 2003.

Newcom remained on the lookout for new investment opportunities. The rising growth of Mongolia's industrial and corporate sectors, as well as its increasing attractiveness as a tourist destination, led Newcom to investigate the possibility of entering the aviation sector. Toward this end, the company launched feasibility studies in 2004.

The results of that study led the company found its own airline, called Eznis (a name that combined the sound of the English word *easy* with the Mongolian word for "fly") in January 2006. The company signed on GE Aviation to provide engine maintenance services, then acquired two Saab 340B commuter jets from American Eagle Airlines in July of that year. By November the company had completed its first test flights. Eznis launched full commercial operations in December, providing flights to Mongolia's rural areas, as well as a number international flights to China, Russia, and Kazakhstan.

MONGOLIA'S CORPORATE LEADER

Eznis continued to grow through the end of the decade. By the end of 2007, the company laid claim to being Mongolia's leading domestic carrier, carrying 60 percent of all domestic passenger traffic. To accommodate its growing passenger lists, the company added a computerized reservation system in 2008. Then, in January 2009 the company announced a major expansion of its fleet, with the signing of a letter of interest to acquire seven Bombardier C-Series aircraft. The company expected to sign the purchase order by 2010, with delivery of the first C-Series projected to be in 2013.

Newcom's Clean Energy subsidiary had also been making progress in the second half of the decade. In 2007 the company announced its decision to proceed

---

KEY DATES

1993: Newcom LLC is created to develop operations in telecommunications equipment and services in Mongolia.

1996: Newcom launches the Mobicom mobile telephone service in partnership with Japan's KDD and Sumitomo.

2000: Mobile telephone services subsidiary Newtel is founded.

2004: Newcom launches wind energy subsidiary Clean Energy Co.

2006: Newcom enters the aviation sector with the founding of Eznis Airways with three aircraft.

2009: Clean Energy begins operations on Mongolia's first wind farm; Eznis signs letter of interest to acquire seven more aircraft starting in 2013.

Newcom's range of businesses grew strongly in the middle of the first decade of the 21st century. The company founded Newsec in May 2004, to provide security services to both the private and professional markets. Also in 2004 the company took its first steps into energy generation with the launch of Clean Energy LLC. This company at first focused on conducting feasibility studies for the proposed construction of Mongolia's first wind farm project.

Also at the end of 2004 Newcom joined with Mobicom to enter the financial services market, forming NewFund as a joint venture. NewFund focused on providing home loans and financial aid services, including salary advances, to employees of both companies. In 2005 the company created another joint venture, Newcom Systems, to offer information technology systems integration services. Newcom then extended into the real estate and property development sector, founding Newcom Property.

TAKING TO THE SKIES IN 2007

The growth of the mobile telephone market, and of Mobicom, in Mongolia benefited Newcom in other ways. In 2005, for example, the company opened its TEDY Center, featuring a one-stop shopping concept for GSM-based telephone services, equipment, and accessories. Mobicom, in the meantime, had continued expanded its network. By 2003, with the extension of services to Uvs and Hövsgöl, the company became the with the construction of Mongolia's first wind farm, to be built on Salhit Mountain, in Sergelen. The farm, expected to be commissioned in 2009, was slated to provide 116 kilowatt-hours of electricity per year.

Although these and other Newcom businesses continued to grow, Mobicom remained the group's primary source of revenues, which neared $1 billion by 2009. Mobicom remained committed to its own expansion, signing a contract with Alcatel in 2007 to extend its cellular network. The company also began developing its own high-speed mobile network, working with Ericsson to introduce its high-speed packet access technology. Mobicom officially launched its high-speed mobile services in April 2009. By then, the company had also teamed up with Alcatel-Lucent and Research in Motion to launch Blackberry wireless support in Mongolia, starting in March of that year. In just 15 years, Newcom had grown into Mongolia's largest private corporation.

M. L. Cohen

PRINCIPAL SUBSIDIARIES

Clean Energy Company; Eznis Airways LLC; Mobicom Corporation; Newcom Property LLC; Newsec LLC.

PRINCIPAL DIVISIONS

Domestic Aviation; Financial Services; Information Technology; Real Estate; Retail; Telecommunication.

PRINCIPAL COMPETITORS

MAGICNET Co., Ltd; MIAT Mongolia Airlines; MICOM Co., Ltd.; Mongolian Telecommunication Company; Skytel Co., Ltd.

FURTHER READING

"Ericsson and Mobicom Bring Mobile Broadband to Mongolia," *Europe Intelligence Wire,* April 27, 2009.

"Eznis Airways Flies High," *Mongol Messenger,* December 7, 2007.

"Eznis Airways Places Aircraft Order," *Auto Business News,* January 9, 2009.

"Japan's KDD Plans to Launch Service in Mongolia," *Mobile Phone News,* September 25, 1995, p. 5.

"Mobicom Corporation," *Mongolia Business,* February 1, 2008.

"Mobicom to Launch Blackberry Solution in Mongolia with Support from RIM and Alcatel-Lucent," *Corporate IT Update,* March 17, 2009.

"Mobicom to Market Wireless GPRS Data Cards Under Capitel Brand," *China Business News,* October 17, 2002.

"Mongolia Mobile Advertising Reaches Mongolia," *TendersInfo,* July 2, 2008.

"Mongolian Mobile Phone Network Set Up in Tourist Area," *BBC Monitoring International Reports,* August 12, 2005.

"'Reliable Domestic Flights Needed to Develop Tourism Industry,' Says Eznis," *Mongolia Web,* September 8, 2006.

Odwalla Inc.

120 Stone Pine Road
Half Moon Bay, California 94019-1783
U.S.A.
Telephone: (650) 726-1888
Toll Free: (800) 639-2552
Fax: (650) 726-4441
Web site: http://www.odwalla.com

Wholly Owned Subsidiary of Coca-Cola North America
Incorporated: 1985
Employees: 900
Sales: $187.9 million (2008 est.)
NAICS: 311411 Frozen Fruit, Juice, and Vegetable
    Manufacturing

■ ■ ■

Odwalla Inc. manufactures and sells juices, juice drinks, soy beverages, and nourishing food and protein bars. Its products can be found across the United States and in Canada in natural food stores, supermarkets, and specialty outlets. Its products are known for their unique names including C Monster, Mango Tango, Mojito Mambo, and Mo Beta. Odwalla overcame a devastating *Escherichia coli* (*E. coli*) outbreak in 1996 and was purchased by The Coca-Cola Company in 2001. Odwalla operates as a subsidiary of its Coca-Cola North America division.

ORANGE JUICE ORIGINS

In 1980, 25-year-old George Steltenpohl and two fellow musicians, Gerry Percy and Bonnie Bassett, were in Santa Cruz casting about for ways to make money without much capital. They also wanted to contribute something positive to their community. A business guidebook gave them the idea of selling fruit juices and thus Odwalla was launched in a shed in Steltenpohl's backyard in September 1980. The company's name came from a character in an Art Ensemble of Chicago song-poem called "Illistrum." Odwalla delivered the "people of the sun" from the "gray haze." The group set out to do the same with a secondhand $225 juicer and a 1968 Volkswagen van. Local restaurants were the first clients for the fresh-squeezed orange juice.

Business was brisk. The company was incorporated in California in September 1985. It expanded into San Francisco in 1988. Steltenpohl, who earned a degree in environmental science from Stanford University, attributed Odwalla's success to the fact that consumers were becoming more quality-conscious in general. In fruit drinks, this translated to the taste, nutrients, and enzymes available only in fresh, nonpasteurized juice. This total reliance on fresh produce left the company somewhat at the whim of nature, though, and subject to unexpected losses.

In 1992, *Inc.* magazine reported on the pride and passion that rallied Odwalla's 80 employees around the product. The company kept workers informed about the nutritional benefits of the juices and involved them in taste testing and product naming. A pint of juice (two for drivers) was part of the daily salary. The company marketed about 20 different types of juices at the time, which sold for about $1.50 to $2.00 a pint.

Steltenpohl aimed for more than simple enthusiasm

COMPANY PERSPECTIVES

Odwalla is a juice company that for 25 years lived by three key principles ... Make great juice. Do good things for the community. Build a business with a heart.

through empowerment. "If you can take wage earners and instill an entrepreneurial drive, that translates into much greater productivity," he told *Nation's Business*. People were essentially trained to manage themselves, he said. Employees could also design their own jobs to an extent. The location of corporate headquarters a couple of blocks from the surf in Davenport, California, also was considered a motivator.

GOING PUBLIC

Odwalla operated 35 delivery trucks in 1993, when sales were about $13 million a year. It invested in state-of-the-art handheld computers for its drivers, who served as de facto public relations representatives as they escorted the juice along the "cold chain" to the "O-Zone"—the company's distinctive in-store coolers. The company launched its initial public offering (IPO) in December 1993, when it had slightly fewer than 200 employees. The RvR Securities ("risk-versus-reward") arm of San Francisco investment bank Hambrecht & Quist Inc. had begun investing in the company in 1992, acquiring a 16 percent stake. The group was impressed by Odwalla's strong customer loyalty and its distribution network. Soon after the IPO, the company expanded into the Pacific Northwest via the acquisition of Dharma Juice. It then bought Just Squeezed, based in Denver.

In 1994, Odwalla moved production to a renovated plant in Dinuba, California, surrounded by produce fields. It moved its corporate headquarters to Half Moon Bay, California, the next year. Odwalla by then dominated Northern California's fresh juice sales, holding half the market. Its products were sold in 1,400 locations.

Odwalla began selling bottled water in the mid-1990s. It was supplied by Idaho's Trinity Springs, whose aquifer held water carbon-dated from the Stone Age 16,000 years earlier. This new line was very much the opposite of its highly perishable, nonpasteurized fruit drinks. Water did not require refrigeration and could be sold in more outlets, offering a distinctive growth opportunity.

Revenues for fiscal year 1996 were $59.2 million. Odwalla supplied 4,000 locations in seven states (California, Colorado, Nevada, New Mexico, Oregon, Texas, and Washington) and British Columbia. Its largest customer was the Safeway grocery chain. The natural foods market was growing at a rate of 25 percent a year. Steltenpohl estimated that the company would reach $100 million in sales around 1999. He and Co-CEO Stephen Williamson told shareholders: "Our objective, our passion, is to lead the fresh beverage revolution." The company spent heavily to get on Texas shelves in October 1996. Odwalla was on the verge of becoming a national brand.

FACING DISASTER

As part of its sanitation process, the company cleaned its fruit with a phosphoric acid wash and whirling brushes. However, this failed in October 1996. An outbreak of food poisoning caused by *E. coli* 0157:H7 killed a toddler in Denver and sickened 66 other people in the West, and the problem was traced to Odwalla apple juice. Pure apple juice accounted for a tenth of the company's revenues; it also was used in blended drinks, which accounted for a majority of its business.

Investigators speculated that Odwalla might have been sent fallen apples (or "grounders") that had come into contact with animal feces (the microbe lives primarily in the digestive tract of cattle). Another possibility was that the contamination might have come from carrots harvested from the earth. The *Seattle Times* reported that Odwalla's sanitation was substandard in the week the tainted juice was produced.

Odwalla officials stated that they believed this strain of *E. coli*, only discovered in 1982, could not survive in cooled, acidic apple juice. The microbe appeared to be evolving. Steltenpohl pointed out that it could also be spread on fresh lettuce. Even minuscule amounts of the germ could spread infection. This was the same virulent pathogen that in 1993 had killed three people in Washington State who had eaten insufficiently cooked hamburgers at the Jack in the Box chain.

Odwalla responded by recalling its juices containing apples or carrots, which were processed on the same line. It offered to pay medical bills for consumers made ill by the juice. The public relations problem was serious. As Steltenpohl later told *Forbes*, "Children's health problems are ranked as the worst thing that can happen to a company." Damage control took many forms. Aside from holding press conferences and setting up an 800 number hotline, Odwalla used the Internet to disseminate information about the health problem and Odwalla's response to it. Edelman Public Relations

KEY DATES

1980: Odwalla begins juicing in Santa Cruz.
1994: First shipments are delivered outside of California.
1996: An *E. coli* outbreak is traced to the company's apple juice.
1998: Odwalla returns to profitability.
2000: The company buys Fresh Samantha Inc.
2001: The Coca-Cola Company buys Odwalla.
2003: Odwalla stops producing the Fresh Samantha line.
2008: The company launches its Odwalla Plant a Tree program.

had a web site devoted to the crisis running on the same day Odwalla received word of the contamination. The site received 20,000 hits in the first two days. Links to authorities like the Centers for Disease Control helped firm Odwalla's credibility.

Odwalla's stock fell 40 percent. It would not be considered an attractive takeover candidate by the major fruit juice brands. Its brand name was damaged. There were also numerous lawsuits, which the company faced with $27 million worth of insurance and $10 million in cash. (The Jack in the Box *E. coli* lawsuits of 1993 cost Foodmaker $56 million in legal costs.) Most of the suits were settled within a year. Sales fell 90 percent in the immediate wake of the crisis. Odwalla laid off 10 percent of its 650 workers by December 1996 and posted a loss of $11.3 million for the fiscal year ending February 28, 1997. In December Odwalla announced plans to flash-pasteurize its apple juice.

MITIGATION

The crisis affected not just Odwalla; grocery store chains dropped other fresh juice producers as well. Growers across the country grappled with the issue of pasteurization as the Food and Drug Administration (FDA) considered making it mandatory. Most felt that the process destroyed the freshness with which they differentiated their offerings, in addition to adding another set of costs. Some growers in the Apple Hill area of California were among the first to implement a 23-point quality-assurance plan that, among other things, forbade the use of "grounders," or fallen apples. These guidelines were referred to as Hazardous Analysis Critical Control Point (HACCP) rules.

Fresh juice accounted for only 2 percent of the total juice market in the United States. Some producers resented attempts by Odwalla, the media, and government to deflect criticism to the industry as a whole. "Let's not lose track of the real issue," one told the *San Mateo Times,* "Odwalla got animal poop on its apples and failed to wash it off." According to FDA statistics, the fresh juice industry overall reported only 447 illnesses (including the one fatality) for more than 500 million servings between 1993 and 1996.

Nevertheless, the agency required juice marketers to label fresh apple juice with the following warning beginning in September 1998 (and all other fruit and vegetable juices by November): "WARNING: This product has not been pasteurized and, therefore, may contain harmful bacteria which can cause serious illness in children, the elderly, and persons with weakened immune systems." Juice produced to the HACCP standard was exempt from the labeling requirement. The fresh juice industry naturally railed against the labeling, believing it would scare away consumers. They complained that it was "more aggressive" than that required even on raw pork.

Although Odwalla's openness in the face of the crisis was commended by many, the company received the highest food injury penalty ever to date in what was reportedly the country's first criminal conviction in a food poisoning case. The company was levied a $1.5 million fine after it pleaded guilty to 16 counts of delivering adulterated food products into interstate commerce, a misdemeanor. At Odwalla's suggestion, one-sixth of the fine was earmarked for the Safe Tables Our Priority charity and to researchers at the University of Maryland and Penn State University. The resolution of this case made Odwalla stock safe again for institutional investors, who owned about 28 percent of the company before the crisis. That would fall to a low of 4 percent in 1998.

REBUILDING

Product offerings proliferated as the company pulled out all the stops to win back consumers. A new type of liquid lunch debuted in May 1997. Odwalla's Future Shake, designed to appeal to a younger market than that of nutrient-fortified Ensure, was marketed as a "drinkable feast" made from "real food" such as oats, almonds, soy, banana, and mango. Not a diet drink (one pint contained 12 grams of fat), it offered a lunchtime alternative to fried fast food. The shakes were offered in Inner Chai, Dutch Chocolate, and Café Latte flavors. Odwalla introduced an energy bar, its first solid product, in September 1998, entering the company in a $900-million-a-year market. There was also a new line of "Nutritionals" enhanced with proteins, herbs, vitamins, and fruits. Redesigned packaging appeared in September 1999. The new bottles featured bolder graphics and a sturdier cap but held slightly less juice. Odwalla also introduced pasteurized versions of its citrus drinks.

Odwalla announced that it was again profitable by the third quarter of 1997–98, posting a profit of $140,000 versus the previous year's $1.8 million loss for the period. Analysts believed there was still life left in its brand name. The company continued to expand geographically, entering Philadelphia and Washington, D.C., markets. This expansion was soon followed by entry into the Chicago, Detroit, Minneapolis, and Phoenix markets. Analysts thought it wise for the company to get a toehold in these new markets before someone else did, even if it came at the expense of bottom line profits. Odwalla's revenues were up 12 percent in 1998, to $59.1 million.

MOVING INTO THE 21ST CENTURY

Odwalla entered the new millennium focused on growth. During 2000, the company acquired competitor Fresh Samantha Inc., an East Coast manufacturer of fruit and vegetable juices as well as soy shakes and frozen fruit bars. Odwalla began producing its own soymilk the following year.

By this time, it was apparent that Odwalla had successfully overcome the *E. coli* disaster and its products were securing premium space on store shelves. During 2001, sales reached $128.3 million, up 37 percent over the previous year. Its solid financial record made it attractive to The Coca-Cola Company. Coca-Cola, eyeing non-carbonated beverages as crucial to its growth strategy, made a $181 million play for Odwalla in 2001 and added the company to its fold late in the year. Odwalla became part of its Minute Maid division; the division was eventually reorganized as Coca-Cola North America.

Under Coca-Cola's wing, Odwalla had access to a major distribution network. At the time of the deal, the company's products were found in approximately 8,000 retail outlets in the United States while Coca-Cola products were found throughout the world. Odwalla management believed it could capitalize on Coca-Cola's distribution expertise and expected to significantly increase overall revenues. During 2002, Odwalla launched four new beverages in the Southeast region of the United States including Blueberry Smoothie, Protein Tropicale, Passionate C, and Organic Orange Juice. The company also began selling its products in Wal-Mart and Publix stores.

As demand for Odwalla products grew, the company's Fresh Samantha juice line was faltering. The company stopped producing the line in 2003 in order to focus on its Odwalla products. During 2006 it launched a new soymilk product found in retailers' dairy cases in 64-ounce cartons. In 2009 its Light Lemonade and Light Limeade, made with pure-squeezed juice and Truvia sweetener, hit store shelves.

Odwalla stood well positioned for growth in the coming years as Americans continued to demand health and wellness products. The company's involvement with the world's largest soft-drink firm did little to dampen its mission of producing great products while protecting the environment and operating as a socially conscious business. During 2008, the company launched its Odwalla Plant a Tree program and provided over 60,000 trees to state parks in the United States. The initiative, which allowed people to visit a web site and to donate a tree to one of 11 participating state parks free of charge, was continued in 2009. A May 2009 company press release summed up Odwalla's intent: "The Odwalla Plant a Tree program is part of our commitment to respecting the earth and nourishing the body, mind, and spirit. ... The Plant a Tree program allows us to support something we all believe in—a healthy environment for generations to come."

Frederick C. Ingram
Updated, Christina M. Stansell

PRINCIPAL COMPETITORS

Hansen Natural Corporation; Snapple Beverage Corporation; South Beach Beverage Company Inc.

FURTHER READING

Bianchi, Alessandra, "Best Love of Product: True Believers," *Inc.,* July 1993, p. 72.

Evan, Thomas J., "Odwalla," *Public Relations Quarterly,* Summer 1999, pp. 15–17.

Fryer, A. P., "Fresh Fears: The Odwalla Crisis Has Put a Hard Squeeze on Local Makers of Fresh Juice," *Puget Sound Business Journal,* November 8, 1996, p. 1.

Groves, M., "Firm Might Stop Making Apple Juice," *Los Angeles Times,* November 12, 1996, p. D2.

———, "Juice Left in Odwalla: Company Posts Loss, but Sales and Cash up Despite Recall," *Los Angeles Times,* January 8, 1997, p. D1.

Isaacs, Marc, "The Fresh Juice Industry: An Industry in Transition?" *Beverage Industry,* August 1998, p. 29.

Joyce, Andee, "Odwalla's Pickup Line of the Future: How About a Meal with that Shake?" *Beverage World,* September 30–October 31, 1997, p. 17.

Kaufman, Steven B., "Freshness by the Bottle," *Nation's Business,* February 1994, p. 14.

King, W., "How Sleuths Traced Source of *E. coli* to Odwalla Juice," *Seattle Times,* October 31, 1996, p. A1.

———, "Odwalla's *E. coli* Error: Acid," *Seattle Times,* November 3, 1996, p. A1.

Kokmen, L., "Odwalla Can Learn from Jack-in-the-Box Eatery; Chain Showed What Not to Do, Experts Say," *Seattle Times,* November 7, 1996, p. A21.

Martinelli, Kathleen A., and William Briggs, "Integrating Public Relations and Legal Responses During a Crisis: The Case of Odwalla, Inc.," *Public Relations Review,* Winter 1998, pp. 443–60.

Masters, Greg, "All Juiced Up," *Discount Merchandiser,* July 1999, pp. 107, 109ff.

Moore, Brenda L., "Time May Be Right to Take Bite of Odwalla," *Wall Street Journal,* August 19, 1998, p. CA1.

Murphy, Edward D., "Fresh Samantha Makes One Last Move—Off the Shelves," *Portland Press Herald,* July 29, 2003.

"Odwalla Teams with State Parks Across the Nation for Greener Future," *Business Wire,* May 27, 2009.

Postlewaite, Kimbra, "Comeback in a Bottle," *Beverage Industry,* March 1999.

Rapaport, Richard, "PR Finds a Cool New Tool," *Technology's 100 Richest* (supplement to *Forbes*), October 6, 1997, pp. 101–08.

Rice, Eric, "Local Investors Bullish on Odwalla's Future," *Half Moon Bay Review,* July 8, 1998, p. 10A.

Richards, Bill, "Odwalla's Woes Are a Lesson for Natural-Food Industry," *Wall Street Journal,* November 4, 1996, p. B4.

Shopes, Rich, "Coca-Cola Buying California Juice Company," *Sarasota Herald-Tribune,* October 31, 2001.

Sinton, Peter, "Odwalla OKs Acquisition by Coca-Cola," *San Francisco Chronicle,* October 31, 2001.

Theodore, Sarah, "Odwalla: Growing Naturally," *Beverage Industry,* March 2006.

Thomsen, Steven R., and Bret Rawson, "Purifying a Tainted Corporate Image: Odwalla's Response to an *E. coli* Poisoning," *Public Relations Quarterly,* Fall 1998, pp. 35–46.

Veverka, Mark, "Odwalla Still Faces Some Problems That Could Make It a Risky Bet," *Wall Street Journal,* December 4, 1996, p. CA2.

Wyatt, Edward A., "H&Q Lite," *Barron's,* September 5, 1994, p. 19.

ORIX Corporation

Mita NN Building
4-1-23, Shiba
Minato-ku
Tokyo, 108-0014
Japan
Telephone: (81 3) 5419-5042
Fax: (81 3) 5419-5901
Web site: http://www.orix.co.jp

Public Company
Incorporated: 1964 as Orient Leasing Company, Ltd.
Employees: 18,702
Sales: ¥1.15 trillion ($11.62 billion) (2008)
Stock Exchanges: Tokyo Osaka New York
Ticker Symbol: IX
NAICS: 52231 Mortgage and Nonmortgage Loan
    Brokers; 52421 Insurance Agencies and Brokerages;
    52222 Sales Financing; 522292 Real Estate Credit

■ ■ ■

ORIX Corporation began as a Japanese-American joint venture in the mid-1960s, and helped introduce Japanese business to the idea of leasing equipment instead of owning it. Now a global corporation and one of Japan's largest financial services firms, ORIX is involved in leasing, corporate finance, real estate–related finance and development, life insurance, and investment and retail banking. The company provides its services through a vast network of subsidiaries that serve corporate and retail clients in 26 countries and regions across the globe.

EARLY GROWTH

In 1964 Nichimen Company—later known as Nichimen Corporation—and the United States Leasing Corporation established the Orient Leasing Company (OLC) in Osaka. Backed by the Sanwa Bank, the company began with an initial capital of ¥100 million. At this time, leasing was very new in Japan. Growth was slow throughout the 1960s as Japanese business adjusted to the idea. OLC spent much of the 1970s establishing itself throughout Asia, developing a pattern of growth either through ties with well-established local businesses or through heavy investment in local companies. In 1970 OLC was listed on the second section of the Osaka Stock Exchange; by 1973 it was on the first section in Tokyo, Osaka, and Nagoya. In 1971 the company established its first wholly owned subsidiary, Orient Leasing (Asia), in Hong Kong. The subsidiary handled mortgage loans, finances in multiple currencies, and leased such major items as ships and planes.

In 1972 OLC established its first major subsidiary in Japan, Orient Leasing Interior Company. That same year, OLC established the Korea Development Leasing Corporation and Orient Leasing Singapore, which leased vehicles, machinery, furniture, medical and dental equipment, and vessels. In 1973 OLC entered Malaysia; in 1975, Indonesia; in 1977, the Philippines; and in 1978, Thailand. OLC also established subsidiaries in South America during the 1970s, entering Brazil in 1973 and Chile in 1977.

OLC began to lease commercial aircraft in 1978, when the company purchased a DC-10 from McDonnell Douglas and two Boeing 747 passenger jets for lease to Korean Air Lines. The company purchased another aircraft in the same deal for lease to Thai Airways International. This deal, part of a joint venture with Nippon Shinpan Company, came at a time when U.S. aircraft manufacturers were complaining that limited export funding was making it difficult for them to compete internationally. According to the *Wall Street Journal,* the purchases were arranged in an effort to show genuine Japanese concern for reducing its trade surplus. Later in 1978, OLC purchased two wide-bodied airbuses with C. Itoh & Company for lease to Greece's Olympic Airways.

INTERNATIONAL EXPANSION

Although OLC spent the 1970s establishing itself in Asia, the 1980s were a time of expansion in the United States, Europe, and China, one still untapped Asian market. OLC brought leasing to a developing China in 1981. In partnership with two Chinese companies, China International Trust and Investment Corporation and Beijing Machinery and Equipment Corporation, OLC founded the China Orient Leasing Company. Leasing in China boomed in the following years, as state-owned enterprises demanded machinery for their outdated factories.

In 1984 China Orient Leasing Company wrote $40 million in contracts, three times the amount it had written just two years earlier, for equipment as varied as plant machinery, film development apparatus, and printing presses. In 1982 OLC opened a representative office in Greece, and in 1983 the company established Orient Leasing (UK) in London, its first step toward an independent presence in Europe. Growth continued in 1986 with the establishment of Lombard Orient Leasing

Ltd., a partnership between OLC and Lombard North Central, the largest finance company in the United Kingdom. In 1988 OLC expanded further into Europe when it made an agreement to form a leasing company in Spain to lease Japanese computers and office equipment.

In the United States, OLC set up Orient Leasing USA Corporation in 1981 and Orient-U.S. Leasing Corporation in 1982. In the late 1980s OLC began to diversify, investing in the Hyatt Group, a hotel chain, and Rubloff Inc., a major Chicago real estate company. With the Hyatt Group, OLC arranged financing for hotels in Chicago, Illinois; Greenwich, Connecticut; and Scottsdale, Arizona. Most of the equity financing came directly from OLC and Hyatt; OLC assembled Japanese investors to cover the rest. In 1987 OLC entered the U.S. real estate market when it bought a 23.3 percent interest in Rubloff. Willard Brown Jr., the chairman of Rubloff, told the *Chicago Tribune* in 1987, "[OLC] has a substantial appetite, and [Rubloff's] job will be to create the right investments for them." OLC entered the housing loan and mortgage security loan markets in the early 1980s. OLC also diversified into securities in 1986, surprising the leasing community with the purchase of Akane Securities Company, Ltd., a small Japanese brokerage firm. Although lease financing was its core business, through this purchase the company announced its intention to initiate "new operations in related, high-potential fields."

NAME CHANGE AND FURTHER DIVERSIFICATION: 1989–95

As part of its plan to diversify, OLC renamed itself ORIX in 1989, the company's 25th anniversary. According to company officials, the name ORIX was adopted as an abbreviation of the word *original,* with the "X" added to symbolize a future of "flexibility and diversity." As part of a campaign to increase recognition of its new name, ORIX bought a Japanese baseball team, the Hankyu Braves, and renamed it as the ORIX Braves. The leasing business soared in Japan in the late 1980s, fueled by heavy capital investments by Japanese industry. It became such an attractive business, in fact, that many new companies entered the field, pushing profit margins below 1 percent even for industry-leader ORIX, according to the *Economist.* The firm's name change signaled the most visible part of the company's move to broaden the financial services it offered in an effort to decrease its reliance on the leasing business.

Despite a weakening Japanese economy and instability throughout the entire Asian region, ORIX remained intent on diversification throughout the 1990s. Aiding in its efforts was its status as a leasing

KEY DATES

1964: Nichimen Co. and the United States Leasing Corp. establish the Orient Leasing Company (OLC).

1970: OLC lists on the second section of the Osaka Stock Exchange.

1972: Subsidiaries Orient Leasing Interior Co., Korea Development Leasing Corp., and Orient Leasing Singapore are formed.

1978: OLC begins leasing commercial aircraft.

1981: The firm enters the Chinese market and forms Orient Leasing USA Corp.

1983: Orient Leasing (UK) is established.

1986: The company acquires Akane Securities Company, Ltd.

1987: OLC enters the U.S. real estate market through a 23.3 percent purchase of Rubloff Inc.

1989: The firm officially adopts the name ORIX Corporation.

1990: ORIX begins selling commodities funds in Japan.

1993: Shanghai Yintong Trust Co. is established as China's first joint consumer credit company.

1994: Company announces plans to set up a joint-leasing venture in Vietnam.

1997: ORIX enters the Egyptian market.

1998: ORIX lists on the New York Stock Exchange; it also acquires Yamaichi Trust & Bank Ltd.

2000: The company's management restructures; Yasuhiko Fujiki is named company president and chief operating officer; Yoshihiko Miyauchi remains CEO and is named chairman.

2001: The real estate firm Nihon Jisho Corp. is acquired.

2006: Houlihan Lokey Howard & Zukin Inc. is purchased.

company—a status that allowed it to report to Japan's Ministry of International Trade and Industry, whereas banks and securities brokers were forced to report to the strict Ministry of Finance. The trade ministry's liberal policy enabled ORIX to pursue diverse expansion options. Building upon its 1989 investment in U.S.-based Stockton Holdings Ltd., the company began selling commodities funds in Japan in 1990 and entered the investment management business by creating ORIX

Commodities Corp. The firm also purchased outright—rather than financed—74 Airbus Industrie jets from Braniff Airlines Inc. ORIX then sold or leased the jets to different airlines.

In 1993 the company established Shanghai Yintong Trust Co. to operate as one of the first joint consumer credit companies in China. The following year ORIX teamed up with the Bank for Investment and Development of Vietnam to create ORIX BIDV Leasing Co. Ltd., the first leasing company in Vietnam. The firm also focused on its real estate operations and in 1995 partnered with Daikyo, Inc., an apartment management service company, to expand and develop real estate and lending opportunities. Also in 1995, in order to increase its presence in Taiwan, ORIX acquired two leasing credit firms, Sun Leasing Corp. and Sun Credit and Trading Corp. Having entered the region in 1990 with the creation of subsidiary ORIX Taiwan Corp., the firm eyed Taiwan as a lucrative market because of the financial deregulation initiated by the Taiwan government that enabled leasing and credit sales firms to embark on lease financing ventures.

GLOBAL EXPANSION CONTINUES: 1996–99

As the Asian economy fell under financial crisis in the mid- to late 1990s, ORIX continued its global expansion efforts. The firm announced plans to enter the Egyptian market in 1997, and continued to take advantage of U.S.-based opportunities. That year, ORIX began a joint venture with Banc One Corp. and formed the commercial mortgage firm Banc One Mortgage Capital Markets. In 1998 General Electric Capital Services Inc. entered Japan's leasing market, dramatically increasing competition because of its financial size and expertise in leases related to industrial machinery. Although ORIX held an 8 percent share of that market and stood as the leader, the firm faced fierce competition and continued to look for ways to bolster profits outside of the leasing arena. ORIX acquired Yamaichi Trust & Bank Ltd. that year, broadening its line of financial services that by that time included insurance and brokerage, along with leasing operations.

ORIX also listed on the New York Stock Exchange (NYSE) in September 1998, the first Japanese company to list on the NYSE since 1994. In 1999 ORIX began take advantage of the burgeoning e-commerce world. The firm teamed up with Softbank Corp. and Fuji Bank to create a joint Internet-based leasing venture that offered financial services to small-to-midsized companies in technology industries. The Japanese government deregulated fixed commissions on stock transactions in October 1999, allowing ORIX to begin online trading.

Through its ORIX Securities subsidiary, the firm secured 12,600 online accounts by November of that year.

FOCUS ON DIVERSIFIED FINANCIAL SERVICES IN THE NEW MILLENNIUM

As ORIX entered the new millennium on strong ground, the company management was restructured. Yoshihiko Miyauchi relinquished the role of president, remaining CEO and taking on the job of chairman; Yasuhiko Fujiki became president and chief operating officer. In January 2000 the firm formed an alliance with U.S.-based Enron Corp., allowing it to enter the Japanese retail power market with plans to form new power generation facilities. The partnership was dissolved upon Enron's demise in 2001.

Nevertheless, ORIX continued to develop and diversify its product and service offerings. The real estate firm Nihon Jisho Corp. was acquired in 2001, broadening ORIX's reach in the real estate and management industry. It also made key investments in Aozora Bank Ltd., Fuji Fire and Marine Insurance Company, Korea Life Insurance Co. Ltd., and Daikyo Inc. It expanded its motor vehicle leasing and rental company business through the purchase of IFCO Inc. in 2001 and Japaren Co. Ltd. in 2003.

The firm increased its Internet-based offerings with the launch of e-Direct Deposit, allowing its customers to conduct business transactions via the Web. Its auto leasing business also began a program titled e-ERG, which allowed leasing customers to manage their accounts online. It purchased the Internet Research Institute Inc., a Japanese information technology firm, in 2007.

With sales and profits on the rise, ORIX continued its growth efforts, especially overseas. The company expanded its international network in 2001 by moving into Saudi Arabia and South Korea. The following year ORIX opened an office in the United Arab Emirates. A new office opened in China in 2004 and a location in Kazakhstan was established in 2005. The company eyed future expansion in India and the Middle East as crucial to its growth platform.

The company created ORIX M&A Solutions in 2003 to strengthen its offerings in investment banking and financial advisory services, which included services related to merger and acquisition activity. During 2006 the company acquired the investment bank Houlihan Lokey Howard & Zukin Inc. in order to strengthen its foothold in the U.S.-based corporate finance market. It also began to move into real estate development markets.

The company's efforts to expand its investment banking business paid off significantly over the next few years. The company reported a record net profit of ¥54 billion in fiscal 2003 and its financial position continued to strengthen. Profits peaked at ¥196.5 billion in fiscal 2007. The company up until this point had remained somewhat immune to the subprime loan crisis in the United States and the weakening of global economies. It began to feel the effects of what it called "an unprecedented global financial crisis," in a 2009 press release, however, and profits fell 14 percent in fiscal 2008. The company experienced a sharp decline the following fiscal year when net income fell by 87 percent to ¥21.9 billion. With real estate–related companies filing for bankruptcy and the overall downturn in credit markets, ORIX began to lose money on many of its investments.

As the company worked to shore up profits, it reevaluated its investment strategy and began cost-cutting measures to stem future losses. Plans were in the works to sell 51 percent of ORIX Credit Corporation to Sumitomo Mitsui Banking Corporation. The deal was expected to go through by the end of 2009. Although management anticipated a slow and steady recovery, ORIX's position as one of Japan's largest diversified financial services firms left it subject to future fluctuations in the real estate and credit markets.

Angel Abcede
Updated, Christina M. Stansell

PRINCIPAL SUBSIDIARIES

ORIX Alpha Corporation; ORIX Auto Corporation; ORIX Rentec Corporation; ORIX Trust and Banking Corporation; ORIX Asset Management & Loan Services Corporation; ORIX Estate Corporation; BlueWave Corporation; ORIX Real Estate Corporation; ORIX Life Insurance Corporation; ORIX Insurance Services Corporation; ORIX Credit Corporation; ORIX Capital Corporation; ORIX Securities Corporation; ORIX Baseball Club Company Ltd.; ORIX Computer Systems Corporation; ORIX USA Corporation; ORIX Asia Ltd.

PRINCIPAL COMPETITORS

GE Commercial Finance; Mitsubishi UFJ Financial Group Inc.; Sumitomo Corporation.

FURTHER READING

Asanuma, Naoki, "ORIX Would Do Well to Paint More Detailed Financial Picture," *Nikkei Weekly,* November 5,

2007.

"GE Capital Strategy Keys on Acquisition," *Nikkei Weekly,* August 3, 1998.

Ibata, David, "Tokyo Firm Buys Stake in Rubloff," *Chicago Tribune,* August 4, 1987.

Jarman, Max, "Banc One, ORIX Form Commercial Mortgage Firm," *Arizona Business Gazette,* April 3, 1997, p. 3.

Lau, Shirley, "ORIX Launch Aimed at Doubling Customer Base," *South China Morning Post,* March 14, 2000, p. 2.

"Leasing Company Begins Negotiating to Acquire Yamaichi Trust Bank," *Nikkei Weekly,* December 29, 1997, p. 13.

"ORIX Acquires Two Taiwan Leasing, Credit Firms," *Japan Economic Newswire,* August 16, 1995.

"ORIX Corp. to Take Over IRI," *Asia Private Equity Review,* July 1, 2007.

"ORIX Corporation to Sell Shares of Subsidiary," *Reuters Significant Developments,* May 7, 2009.

"ORIX Launches China's First Consumer Credit Business," *Japan Economic Newswire,* October 7, 1993.

"ORIX Profit Dives 87% on Fall in Loans, Leasing to Corporate Borrowers," *McClatchy–Tribune Business News,* May 8, 2009.

"ORIX to Enter Investment Management Business," *Japan Economic Newswire,* January 31, 1990.

"ORIX to Enter Retail Power Market," *Nikkei Weekly,* January 10, 2000, p. 19.

"ORIX to Set Up Vietnam Lease Joint Venture," *AFX News,* December 16, 1994.

Plender, John, and Gillian Tett, "The Shareholder Fundamentalist: Interview Yoshihiko Miyauchi," *Financial Times* (London), March 30, 2000, p. 14.

Sterngold, James, "Japanese Lessor Thrives Under Loose Regulation," *New York Times,* July 27, 1990, p. D1.

Tudor, Alison, "ORIX Set to Expand Advisory Service Across Asia," *Reuters News,* May 15, 2006.

Orkin, Inc.

2170 Piedmont Road Northeast
Atlanta, Georgia 30324-4135
U.S.A.
Telephone: (404) 888-2000
Toll Free: (866) 949-6097
Fax: (404) 888-2662
Web site: http://www.orkin.com

Wholly Owned Subsidiary of Rollins Inc.
Founded: 1901
Employees: 7,500
Sales: $895 million (2007 est.)
NAICS: 561700 Exterminating and Pest Control
Services

■ ■ ■

Orkin, Inc., is one of the world's leading termite and
pest control companies. It fields one of the best-known
brand names anywhere; the "Orkin Man," in all his
various incarnations, has long been a U.S. advertising
icon. Orkin made business history in 1964 when it was
acquired by the precursor of Rollins, Inc., in what is
considered the world's first leveraged buyout. In 1997
Rollins, a publicly traded, family-controlled company,
sold off its other holdings to focus on the pest control
business.

ORIGINS

Otto Orkin, born in 1886, immigrated from Latvia to
America at a young age. As one of six children growing

up on his family's farm near Allentown, Pennsylvania,
he was tasked with rat control on a sprawling property
dotted with junk heaps. After buying arsenic and mixing
his own formulations, he began peddling the baits to his
neighbors in 1901, first for $1 and then for $3 per one-
pound bag. As in later years, he typically started
relationships with a free sample.

Otto Orkin was far from the first to sell pest
control products or services in the United States. Some
writers have maintained that he learned the trade from
David "Red" Kramer, who also immigrated from the
Old World, although the official company version and
others discount this possibility. Described as intelligent
and perceptive, if somewhat quirky, Otto Orkin was the
picture of an obsessive, hard-working entrepreneur; he
would later spend hours poring over administrative
records such as listings of closed accounts.

In 1909 Orkin traveled south and set out to build a
trade in Richmond, Virginia. This was significant not
just as the start of a geographic expansion, but as the
beginning of a change in Orkin's business to a service-
based model. Instead of selling poison, he offered
freedom from the property damage and disease brought
by pests. Orkin started in Richmond by offering to rid
the F. A. Saunders tobacco and food warehouse of a
severe rat infestation. With a combination of baits,
traps, and shotgun he succeeded, keeping that particular
customer for 25 years.

As business slowed in the early 1920s, Orkin
expanded his scope beyond rodents to pests such as
roaches and bedbugs. The company was fumigating by
1929. In the mid-1920s, Orkin was paying technicians

$10 per each six-day workweek of ten- to 12-hour days. Managers made three times as much. By the 1950s, regional managers would be earning six figures.

EVOLVING IMAGE

Having established himself as a nattily attired business success, Orkin married the first of three wives in 1912. Over the ensuing years, he would divorce this woman and then another who bore him four children. A significant early milestone for his business during this time was a successful 1925 bid to provide rat control for the construction of the Wilson Dam in Muscle Shoals, Alabama.

By the time an office opened in Atlanta in 1926, Orkin, who had previously promoted himself as "The Rat Man," was ready for a more sophisticated image. The company's trademark diamond logo was introduced, reportedly designed through a bartering arrangement with a newspaper's advertising department. The pictures of vermin that had once adorned Orkin's ads were gradually reduced to a minimum, although the concept later resurfaced around 2000 in television commercials featuring a roach scurrying across the screen. Instead, Orkin began to appeal to customers through images suggesting cleanliness, sanitation, and professionalism.

Around 1937, according to *The Making of the World's Best Pest Control Company,* Orkin began to impose standardization on his rapidly growing business. Orkin ended the decade with revenues of about $1 million a year and had 50 offices in 14 states by 1940. He preferred to expand via states adjacent to existing territories. A necessary detail in national expansion was buying out an independent exterminating business one of Otto's nephews had set up under the Orkin name in Norfolk, Virginia.

Like many other companies, Orkin found itself scarce on material and personnel resources during World War II. However, being officially recognized by the government as an essential service helped the business continue to grow. The war effort led to a number of technical innovations for the pest control industry. Orkin was among the first commercial companies to use the new chemical DDT. It also introduced chlordane, originally known as 1068, which was the leading termite treatment until banned by the Environmental Protection Agency (EPA) in 1988.

Wartime austerity did not stop the company from reaching new levels. Sales were a record $2 million in 1945 and by 1951 Orkin was operating nationwide and had revenues of $7 million. The termite business was growing particularly quickly, accounting for $3 million of the total. The 1950s represented the peak of Otto Orkin's career. In 1960 he lost control of the company to the next generation, including his children Sanford, Billy, and Bernice, and son-in-law Perry Kaye, who had him committed to an asylum for three months. They also pushed aside scores of dedicated upper-level managers, including Ted Oser, general manager since 1939. Otto Orkin died February 11, 1968, at the age of 82.

FIRST KNOWN LEVERAGED BUYOUT

Otto Orkin had always exhibited a flair for advertising. Like medieval ratcatchers who toted examples of their quarry on poles through town, in the early years Orkin constructed window displays featuring stuffed rats or timbers infested with termites. After World War II, Orkin exploited the powerful new medium of television with a cartoon "Orkin Man." Originally an anthropomorphized insecticide sprayer, this figure evolved over the years to the robotic "Exterminator" of the 1980s and finally to the approachable Orkin Man recognizable from real life, replete with pressed khakis and branded shirt. (Orkin received many requests for company uniforms for use as Halloween costumes, but denied them due to the potential for misuse.)

A massive $1.8 million headquarters facility opened in Atlanta in 1963. Although the Sears department store chain was making an attempt to field a pest control business, Orkin was by far the largest player in the industry. By the fiscal year ended October 31, 1963, Orkin had earnings of $3 million on revenues of $37.3 million. It served 700,000 customers with its 2,900 employees at 800 offices in 29 states. Assets were valued at $18 million.

Such figures caught the interest of O. Wayne Rollins, an Atlanta entrepreneur who had developed a knack for turning around distressed companies. The cornerstone of his empire was Rollins Broadcasting, Inc., of Wilmington, Delaware, which included ten radio and television stations, but he had also added a citrus farm

KEY DATES

1901: Otto Orkin sells rat poison door-to-door to farmers near Allentown, Pennsylvania.

1909: Richmond, Virginia, is the site of the first office in the South, and the place where Orkin shifts to a service business model.

1926: After successfully landing a rat-control contract at Alabama's Wilson Dam, Orkin opens offices in Atlanta.

1937: Otto Orkin seeks to standardize branch operations as annual sales approach $1 million.

1960: Otto Orkin loses control of the company to some of his children and their spouses.

1964: Orkin is acquired by Rollins Broadcasting, Inc., in the world's first known leveraged buyout.

1997: Rollins, Inc., sells lawn care, plantscaping, and protective services businesses to focus on pest control.

2003: Orkin Exterminating Co., Inc., is renamed Orkin, Inc.

REALIZING THE POTENTIAL OF THE ORKIN BRAND

Rollins was right about Orkin's potential for growth. It had annual revenues of about $200 million by 1982, when there were more than 5,600 employees at 300 locations. Rollins also leveraged the Orkin name and reputation into a number of ancillary service ventures. Rollins Lawn Care, a small unit launched in 1976, was renamed Orkin Lawn Care around 1983. It grew to $30 million over the next several years.

In June 1984 the parent company spun off two of its businesses, Rollins Communications and RPC Energy Services, on the New York Stock Exchange. This left Rollins Protective Services and Orkin Lawn Care as sister divisions to Orkin Termite and Pest Control. In 1990 Rollins applied the Orkin name to another venture, Orkin Plantscaping, which supplied indoor tropical foliage to businesses. By 1994, the interior plant business was the second largest in the country, with annual sales of $18 million. The four divisions together had revenues of $436 million and reached nearly 1.4 million customers. The commercial business had been relatively neglected, compared to the advertising-driven consumer side. In the mid-1990s Orkin renewed its commitment to commercial pest control; this segment's revenues reached $150 million in 1997.

After decades of involvement in a number of different businesses, Rollins, Inc., pared down its activities to termite and pest control. Orkin Lawn Care, Orkin Plantscaping, and Rollins Protective Services were all sold in 1997. The Delaware corporation for the main pest control business, Orkin Exterminating Co., Inc., adopted the simplified name Orkin, Inc., in 2003.

Orkin offered its own termite control services; however, this market had begun to prove troublesome. In 1988 the EPA pulled the leading termite treatment, chlordane, from the U.S. market over health concerns. Orkin found replacement chemicals did not work as well and the company struggled as the amount of claims doubled to $20 million in 1996. This led the company to reduce the term of its termite guarantees to a fixed period of years, rather than offering lifetime protection.

In 1992 the company had sponsored the O. Orkin Insect Zoo at the Smithsonian National Museum of Natural History, covering most of its cost with a $500,000 donation; in 2001 as part of its centennial celebrations, Orkin gave $1.2 million to the Smithsonian National Museum of Natural History to sponsor the O. Orkin Insect Safari, a traveling exhibit. Orkin had plenty to celebrate at the time of its 100th anniversary, and it claimed the title of "World's Best." However, Memphis-based rival Terminix, which had begun in 1927 by providing treatments for termites, had

and an ethnic hair-care products supplier. Founded in 1948, Rollins had gone public in 1961. Rollins liked Orkin's return on assets and the steady income stream. Further, there was plenty of room for growth into other states.

In the spring of 1964 New York investor Lewis B. Cullman engineered the deal that valued Orkin at $62.4 million, or $26 a share, when its stock was trading around $24. Prior to the transaction, the acquiring company, Rollins Broadcasting, had sales of just $9.1 million and earnings of about $1 million. The disproportionate size of the takeover—the first known leveraged buyout—stunned the business press.

Rollins was not finished buying. It added Waukegan, Illinois-based Arwell, Inc., a specialist in pest control for the commercial market, in May 1965. This was considered a clever, and ambitious, play to open up to Orkin new territory in nine midwest states. Founded by Wellington W. Scott in the 1920s, Arwell had grown to employ 300 people. It was profitable on annual revenues of $4 million when Rollins acquired it for $3 million; the purchase included $1 million worth of shares Arwell owned in public companies.

overtaken Orkin as the world's largest pest control company around 1990.

Annual revenues of parent company Rollins, Inc., reached $1 billion in 2008, and the bulk of this was supplied by Orkin, which counted more than two million customers worldwide. Orkin had begun to offer pest control franchises for the first time in the mid-1990s. These were used as a vehicle to expand the brand internationally, particularly in the Middle East and Latin America. Orkin had about a dozen international franchises in 2008.

Frederick C. Ingram

PRINCIPAL SUBSIDIARIES

PCO Services, Inc. (Canada).

PRINCIPAL OPERATING UNITS

Pest Control; Termite Control.

PRINCIPAL COMPETITORS

Terminix, Inc.; Ecolab Inc.; Rentokil Initial plc.

FURTHER READING

Barnes, Scottie, and Heather Gooch, "Tracking Orkin's Bottom Line: GPS-Based Fleet Tracking Is Helping Orkin to More Effectively Dispatch Pests and Multiply Profits," *Geospatial Solutions,* May 1, 2004, p. 26.

Cullman, Lewis B., *Can't Take It with You: The Art of Making and Giving Money,* New York: Wiley, 2004, pp. 4–21, 109–110.

Gooch, Heather, "Otto Orkin Took His Business to the Top," *Pest Control,* November 1999, p. 40.

Hildebrandt, Peter, "Orkin's Uniforms Have Worked Well for a Long, Long Time," *Made to Measure,* Fall/Winter 2008.

Kirk, Margaret O., *The Making of the World's Best Pest Control Company,* Atlanta: Rollins, Inc., 2005.

Pifer, Drury, "Making History," in *Hanging the Moon: The Rollins Rise to Riches,* Newark: University of Delaware Press, 1983, pp. 153–159.

Reckert, Clare M., "Rollins Proposes to Acquire Orkin for $62.4 Million," *New York Times,* June 20, 1964.

"Rollins to Acquire Western Industries," *Pest Control,* April 1, 2004, p. 12.

Snetsinger, Robert, *The Ratcatcher's Child: The History of the Pest Control Industry,* Cleveland: Franzak & Foster, 1983.

Pacific Sunwear of California, Inc.

—■—

3450 East Miraloma Avenue
Anaheim, California 92806-2101
U.S.A.
Telephone: (714) 414-4000
Fax: (714) 414-4251
Web site: http://www.pacsun.com

Public Company
Incorporated: 1979
Employees: 11,000
Sales: $1.25 billion (2008)
Stock Exchanges: NASDAQ
Ticker Symbol: PSUN
NAICS: 448110 Men's Clothing Stores; 448120 Women's Clothing Stores; 448140 Family Clothing Stores

■ ■ ■

Pacific Sunwear of California, Inc., sells casual apparel as well as a limited variety of footwear and accessories designed for teenagers and young adults in more than 930 stores under the names Pacific Sunwear and PacSun throughout 50 states and Puerto Rico. Merchandise brands carried in the company's stores include Billabong, Element, Quiksilver, Roxy, DC Shoes, Fox Racing, Volcom, and Hurley. Pacific Sunwear also sells private-label brands including Bullhead, Kirra, Kirra Girl, Vurt, and Nollie. During 2008, the company generated 42 percent of its revenues from its juniors line, 41 percent from its young men's merchandise line, while accessories and footwear garnered the remaining

17 percent of sales. Pacific Sunwear started as a surf shop, broadened its merchandise to include casual young men's apparel in 1990, and began retailing young women's apparel and footwear in 1995.

Against the background of these strategic alterations, the company expanded vigorously, increasing its store count from 21 units in 1988 to 344 units by the beginning of 1999. Up until 2007, the company averaged 50 new store openings per year. Annual sales during the 1990s swelled from $18 million to $321 million, and surpassed $1 billion in 2003. Like many retailers, PacSun experienced a decline in sales and profits as the U.S. economy weakened in 2007 and 2008. In response, the company significantly slowed its expansion efforts, closed unprofitable Pacific Sunwear locations, shuttered its d.e.m.o. and its One Thousand Steps stores, and began to focus on its core PacSun casual apparel concept.

SURFING ORIGINS

The roots of Pacific Sunwear's business originated in Newport Beach, California, where Tom Moore opened his first shop catering to surfers in 1980. The opening of another small surf shop in Southern California was not a remarkable event, but the success of the Newport Beach store did lead to a novel development in surf shop history. Hoping to secure year-round business, Moore and his partners opened a second shop the following year in a mall—the exclusive domain of Pacific Sunwear stores for the next 17 years.

The location proved a winner, generating more than $1 million in sales in 1982. The success of the first mall

COMPANY PERSPECTIVES

Our mission is to be a leading lifestyle specialty retailer rooted in the youth culture and fashion vibe of Southern California. Our objective is to be a "Branded House of Brands" that sells casual apparel with a limited selection of accessories and footwear designed to meet the needs of teens and young adults. We believe our customers continually seek newness in their everyday wear and want to stay current with, or ahead of, emerging fashion trends.

store, located in Santa Monica Place, spawned the establishment of ten more stores, all in proximity to the coast and all situated in malls. With the financial backing of venture capitalists in 1987, the chain grew to 21 stores, collecting $18 million in sales in 1988.

By all measures, the concept was a success, thriving during a decade in which the bright, neon shorts and shirts of the surfer lifestyle were popular, trendy apparel items among non-surfers as well. Quick success, however, turned to quick failure when the company began to expand outside of California. Sales plunged sharply at stores on the East Coast and in Minnesota, for example, where a company store located in the Mall of America struggled to sell shorts when the thermometer outside read 17 degrees below zero. According to a company official, the typical customer reaction was, "This is a cool store, I'll be back when it's summer." In response, new management was brought in to inaugurate the new decade, led by Michael W. Rayden, whose chief task was to transform the chain into a profitable retailer able to expand outside of Southern California.

STRATEGY CHANGES

A retail veteran, Rayden joined Pacific Sunwear in 1990 after working for Stride Rite, Eddie Bauer, and Liz Claiborne. During the early 1990s, Pacific Sunwear registered two money-losing years and closed eight underperforming stores, as the company suffered along with the decline in popularity of the surfer "look." Of the stores closed, four were in the company's mainstay California market and the other four were located in new markets: two units in Texas and two in Washington, D.C.

Pacific Sunwear had faltered in its first bid to become a national retailer, but the company did not

make the same mistake twice. Rayden devoted his first years with the company to developing a new merchandising strategy and forming a more prudent real estate plan to support geographic expansion. Rayden's new merchandising strategy revamped the Pacific Sunwear concept. He broadened consumer appeal (thereby increasing the company's customer base) by adopting a new focus for the retailer. Instead of relying on shorts, shirts, and hats, Rayden shaped Pacific Sunwear into a young men's casual apparel retailer, a chain that carried fashionable brands such as Stussy, Mossimo, Quiksilver, Rusty, and Billabong.

Rayden was trying to attract a specific customer: white, suburban, teenage males. The intense focus on attracting this type of customer proved successful. By early 1993, there were 60 Pacific Sunwear stores in operation, with 47 units located in California and the remaining 13 units spread among Arizona, Connecticut, Florida, Nevada, New Jersey, and Washington, all in regional malls. Annual sales in 1992 were up more than 30 percent from the previous year's total, and profitability was sound. Profitability had been sustained for seven consecutive quarters, and Rayden was ready to expand in earnest.

The signal informing outside observers of Rayden's readiness to expand on a grand scale arrived in March 1993, when Pacific Sunwear filed with the Securities and Exchange Commission for an initial public offering (IPO) of stock. The company hoped to raise $14.4 million in proceeds from the IPO, and earmarked $4.2 million of the total to expand. News of the IPO arrived at the same time the company announced its expansion plans for the immediate future; between 18 to 20 store openings were planned for 1993, and 25 store openings were slated for 1994.

PUBLIC OFFERING FUELS EXPANSION

In the wake of the IPO, Pacific Sunwear expanded at a vigorous pace, exceeding its own projections. By late 1994, there were 118 stores in 17 states, including 46 new stores added to the chain in 1994, nearly twice as many new store openings as announced in early 1993. On the heels of this prodigious growth spurt, plans were announced for the expansion of the chain by 35 percent, or 50 new stores, in 1995. In 1995, the square footage of the entire Pacific Sunwear chain increased 45 percent over the retail space occupied by the company in 1994. During the year 55 new stores debuted, for a total of 128 stores opened over a three-year period. Remarkably, profitability was sustained during this period of prolific growth, as Pacific Sunwear recorded positive net income for 15 consecutive quarters.

KEY DATES

1980: Tom Moore opens his first shop catering to surfers in Newport Beach, California.

1981: Moore and his partners open a second shop in a mall.

1987: The chain grows to 21 stores and collects $18 million in sales.

1993: Pacific Sunwear goes public.

1994: The chain expands to include 118 stores in 17 states.

1995: Footwear and junior women's apparel begin appearing in Pacific Sunwear stores; 55 new stores open.

1997: The company acquires the Good Vibrations chain.

1998: The first d.e.m.o. stores open.

1999: The company launches its first national advertising campaign.

2003: Sales surpass $1 billion.

2007: Pacific Sunwear closes its One Thousand Steps stores.

2008: The last d.e.m.o. store closes its doors; losses for the fiscal year reach $39.4 million.

Amid the frenzied expansion activity in 1995, the first currents of a movement to fundamentally alter Pacific Sunwear's concept emerged. At a two-and-a-half day executive retreat in May 1995, Pacific Sunwear officials discussed broadening the chain's customer appeal again. The executives who had gathered at Rancho Valencia discussed introducing new types of merchandise into the stores, making the stores bigger to house the new merchandise, and increasing the percentage of private label merchandise within the stores. In the months following the executive retreat, footwear and junior women's apparel began appearing in Pacific Sunwear stores, as the stores themselves became larger. The square footage in new stores was increased 50 percent to 3,000 square feet. With these changes, the company began to stray from its tight focus on white, suburban, teenage males in order to embrace a broader customer base, thereby making the transition from a niche-oriented retailer to a more broadly defined specialty retailer.

As the company maneuvered through this transition, its most profound change since Rayden arrived in 1990, unexpected news took industry pundits and analysts by surprise. On January 30, 1996, Rayden an-

nounced his resignation from Pacific Sunwear, sending a shockwave through the financial community that caused the company's stock value to fall 15 percent. Rayden left the company to join Ohio-based women's apparel retailer The Limited, where he was named president of Limited Too, a division that sold casual sportswear for girls. While an executive search firm looked for a replacement for Rayden, Greg Weaver, Pacific Sunwear's chief operating officer, took over as president.

NEW LEADERSHIP

Weaver's temporary stewardship of Pacific Sunwear occurred at a critical juncture in the company's history and at a time of great opportunity for astutely managed, young men's apparel retailers. During the previous three years, more than 2,500 young men's stores were closed, as such retailers as Merry-Go-Round, Edison Bros., and Clothestime either exited the business or reduced the size of their chains. Fewer stores left more business for existing retailers to capture, business that Weaver estimated at $2 billion. Enticed by the potential, Weaver was intent on capturing the lion's share of the abandoned business.

"Our mission," Weaver said in September 1996, "is to become the dominant, national specialty retailer of teenage apparel, footwear, and accessories." A month after setting this lofty goal, Weaver was named chief executive officer of the company, having, according to Pacific Sunwear's chairman of the board, "demonstrated great success since assuming operational control." The search for Rayden's successor was over; it was Weaver's responsibility to lead the company toward national dominance.

As Weaver set out in pursuit of his objective in September 1996, Pacific Sunwear operated 198 stores in 33 states. By the end of 1996, 30 new stores had been established during the year. This was a relatively slow pace of expansion for the company, limited by the problems associated with its transition into a specialty retailer, but 1996 proved to be only a temporary lull. In 1997, 50 new stores were slated to open and another 50 stores scheduled for 1998, with expansion aided by a stock offering in June 1997 that raised $29 million.

As Pacific Sunwear began fulfilling its expansion goals, opening an average of two new stores each month, the company achieved additional growth in a new way. For the first time in its history, Pacific Sunwear completed an acquisition, purchasing a 15-unit, young men's and juniors chain named Good Vibrations for $9.2 million in September 1997. Similar to Pacific Sunwear, Good Vibrations was a regional mall-based retailer of casual young men's apparel, accessories, and footwear, whose annual sales, collected from the company's stores in Florida, amounted to $17 million. Following the acquisition, the Good Vibrations name was retained, with Good Vibrations and Pacific Sunwear stores in many cases operating within the same mall.

MOVING INTO URBAN MARKETS

Pacific Sunwear broke with tradition in another way in 1997, opening its first non-mall, freestanding store. Located in Greenwich Village, the 6,000-square-foot store was evidence of Weaver's conviction, as expressed to the *Daily News Record* in September 1997, that Pacific Sunwear "can take this store prototype anywhere in the country." The Greenwich Village store was the first of what was expected to be several Pacific Sunwear units in the lucrative New York City market. Following the debut of the Greenwich Village store, the company began researching other potential store locations in densely populated urban environments, specifically in Chicago and Boston.

As the company entered 1998, it announced plans to expand on another front. In February, Pacific Sunwear revealed its intentions to launch a second retail concept whose merchandise would duplicate Pacific Sunwear merchandise to a very limited extent. Named "d.e.m.o.," the new concept was expected to offer, according to the company, "popular and emerging cross-cultural brands," catering to urban fashion tastes rather than retailing the clothing trends of suburbia. After initial experiments proved positive, Good Vibrations stores were converted to the d.e.m.o. format. A majority of the 15 stores planned for the first wave of expansion were expected to be opened before the 1998 school season, with stores slated for malls in California, Florida, Illinois, Louisiana, New Jersey, New York, and Michigan. Between April and August, 15 d.e.m.o. stores were opened in time for the back-to-school season, recording sufficient success to prompt the company to expand further.

As Pacific Sunwear reached the end of a prodigious ten-year growth period, the company showed no sign of slowing its pace of expansion. In 1999, 108 stores were scheduled to be opened, including the 25 new d.e.m.o. units. To assist in this ambitious expansion, the company launched its first national advertising campaign in February 1999, placing advertisements in the *Sports Illustrated* swimsuit issue, *Teen People* magazine, and *Seventeen* magazine. Said Weaver, according to a February 1999 *Business Wire* report, "With our aggressive growth plans to add 108 stores in 1999 we felt it was the right time to aggressively step up our marketing efforts." On this note, Pacific Sunwear

prepared for the work ahead, intent on becoming the dominant national retailer for the youth of America.

OVERCOMING CHALLENGES IN THE 21ST CENTURY

Under Weaver's guidance, Pacific Sunwear's growth continued at breakneck speed during the early years of the new millennium. The company was averaging 50 new store openings per year and sales surpassed $1 billion in 2003. Weaver caught Wall Street analysts as well as company employees off guard in 2004 when he announced he was turning day-to-day operations over to Seth Johnson, an executive from competitor Abercrombie & Fitch Co. Claiming he wanted more free time, Weaver stayed on as chairman until his retirement in April 2006. Johnson's tenure at Pacific Sunwear was short-lived. Citing differences with the board, Johnson left his post in September 2006 and Sally Frame Kasaks, Pacific Sun director, was named interim CEO and eventually took over permanently in 2007.

By this time, the company's stellar growth had caught up with it and fierce competition was eating into store sales. During fiscal 2006, same store sales fell 4.7 percent and profits were falling as well. Up until 2007, the company had opened an average of 50 new stores per year. This slowed considerably in 2008 when just 16 new Pacific Sunwear locations opened their doors. Over the next three years, the company planned to close 35 to 50 unprofitable locations each year and open under five new locations each year.

With Kasaks at the helm, Pacific Sunwear refocused on its core casual apparel business. It set plans in motion to close all of its d.e.m.o. stores by 2008 and also shuttered its One Thousand Steps footwear stores, which had opened in 2006 and had nine locations. The company also closed its distribution center in California, relying solely on its facility in Kansas for its distribution needs. It gave its existing Pacific Sunwear stores a makeover, making them less cluttered, brighter, and easier to shop in an attempt to attract young female shoppers.

Meanwhile, the company found itself embroiled in a proxy battle with Adrenalina Inc., a small, four-store chain that owned approximately 3.2 percent of Pacific Sunwear. Adrenalina offered to buy the company in 2008 but its advances were rejected. The company's CEO then nominated four candidates for election to Pacific Sunwear's board and called for the resignation of Kasaks. The Pacific Sunwear board stood behind Kasaks and in 2009, Adrenalina gave up its fight.

Most retailers faced a harsh operating environment during this period and Pacific Sunwear was no exception. With the U.S. economy faltering and consumer spending in a tailspin, the company saw a 3.9 percent decline in revenue for fiscal 2008 while posting a $39.4 million loss. Nevertheless, management believed the company had a solid strategy in place to overcome the challenges that lay ahead.

Jeffrey L. Covell
Updated, Christina M. Stansell

PRINCIPAL SUBSIDIARIES

Pacific Sunwear Stores Corporation; Miraloma Corporation.

PRINCIPAL COMPETITORS

Abercrombie & Fitch Co.; Aéropostale, Inc.; American Eagle Outfitters Inc.

FURTHER READING

Barron, Kelly, "CEO Steps Down at California Retailer Pacific Sunwear," *Knight-Ridder/Tribune Business News,* January 31, 1996.

———, "Cool It," *Forbes,* November 2, 1998, p. 218.

———, "Pacific Sunwear's Future Looks Bright Despite Departure of CEO," *Knight-Ridder/Tribune Business News,* February 10, 1996.

Bellatonio, Jennifer, "Pacific Sunwear Looks to Surf Roots for Sales," *Orange County Business Journal,* December 17, 2007.

———, "Replacement Hunt Over, PacSun Chief Exhales," *Orange County Business Journal,* October 18, 2004.

D'Innocenzio, Anne, "Pacific Sunwear Chain Planning to Go Public," *Daily News Record,* March 3, 1993, p. 10.

"Greg Weaver Promoted to CEO of Pacific Sunwear of California," *Daily News Record,* September 26, 1996, p. 2.

Hardesty, Greg, "California's Pacific Sunwear to Expand Urban-Themed Clothing Stores," *Knight-Ridder/Tribune Business News,* September 15, 1998.

Harmon, Andrew, "Kasaks to 'Reinvent' PacSun," *DNR,* May 28, 2007.

Harmon, Andrew, and Jean E. Palmieri, "PacSun Puts Focus on Flagship Chain," *DNR,* March 3, 2008.

Kaplan, Don, "Pacific Sunwear, Gadzooks Drive to Nab $2B Void in YM Market," *Daily News Record,* September 12, 1996, p. 3.

La Franco, Robert, "Pacific Sunburn?" *Forbes,* May 5, 1997, p. 190.

"Pacific Sunwear Launches National Ad Campaign," *Business Wire,* February 3, 1999.

"Pacific Sunwear Launching New Chain," *Daily News Record,* February 13, 1998, p. 4.

"Pacific Sunwear of California Sets '95 Store Expansion Plan," *Daily News Record,* October 7, 1994, p. 4.

"Pacific Sunwear Stock Rises," *Daily News Record,* December 19, 1996, p. 10.

"PacSun to Close all d.e.m.o. Stores," *Women's Wear Daily,* January 7, 2008.

Palmieri, Jean E., "Fads Don't Fit Pacific Sunwear's Fashion Focus," *Daily News Record,* August 28, 1995, p. 14.

———, "Pacific Sunwear Acquires Good Vibrations; $17 Million, 15-Unit Men's Chain Will Retain Name," *Daily News Record,* September 10, 1997, p. 16.

Smith, Elliot Blair, "Stock Sale Reaps Pacific Sunwear $29 Million to Fund Expansion," *Knight-Ridder/Tribune Business News,* June 12, 1997.

Steigrad, Alexandra, "Adrenalina Withdraws PacSun Nominees," *Women's Wear Daily,* April 6, 2009.

Tschorn, Adam, "Johnson: Board Had Its Own Vision," *DNR,* October 9, 2006.

Zimmermann, Kim Ann, "Controlled Growth: Pacific Sunwear's New Network Will Keep the Company on the Expansion Path While Cutting Costs," *Footwear News,* February 23, 1998, p. 17.

———, "Pacific Sunwear Preps for E-Commerce," *Daily News Record,* January 13, 1999, p. 14.

Parsons Brinckerhoff Inc.

One Penn Plaza
New York, New York 10119
U.S.A.
Telephone: (212) 465-5000
Fax: (212) 465-5096
Web site: http://www.pbworld.com

Private Company
Incorporated: 1975
Employees: 11,500
Sales: $2.3 billion (2008)
NAICS: 234110 Highway and Street Construction;
234120 Bridge and Tunnel Construction; 541330
Engineering Services; 551112 Offices of Other
Holding Companies

∎ ∎ ∎

Parsons Brinckerhoff Inc. operates as one of the world's
leading engineering consulting firms, involved in the
planning, design, and construction of transportation,
power, building, and telecommunications systems.
Although the company has long been the leading
consulting engineer firm for transportation projects in
the United States, it also has a presence in nearly 80
other countries through a network of 150 offices across
the globe. Originally organized as a partnership, Parsons
Brinckerhoff incorporated in 1975, with all of its shares
being employee owned. The company has been involved
in contracts ranging from the infamous Big Dig project
in Boston, to the Beijing Olympic Green Convention
Center, which was used for the 2008 Summer
Olympics.

TRANSPORTATION SPECIALIST: 1885–1935

The history of Parsons Brinckerhoff may be traced to
1885, when William Barclay Parsons, the company
founder, opened an office as a consulting engineer in
lower Manhattan. Parsons's had earned an engineering
degree from Columbia University in 1882. Business
grew steadily, and in 1900 he was awarded a major
project: the design and engineering of the New York
City subway. By 1904 the first stage of the project was
opened, offering transportation from Manhattan to
Harlem. Eugene Klapp and Henry M. Brinckerhoff
joined Parsons in 1906 in what would become known as
the firm of Barclay Parsons and Klapp by 1909. Brinckerhoff would gain fame as being integral to the invention of the "third rail," a concept that would revolutionize rapid transit. Another associate, Walter J. Douglas,
joined the firm in 1908. During this time, Parsons and
Brinckerhoff were responsible for transportation
projects, while Klapp and Douglas focused on building
bridges. In addition, Douglas and Parsons oversaw
power plants and dam projects.

In 1914 Parsons was named chief engineer in the
construction of the Cape Cod Canal. Following the
completion of that project, however, Parsons scaled back
his involvement in the engineering firm in order to
focus on the war effort. Parsons founded and led a
special regiment during World War I known as the
"fighting engineers." First, he was instrumental in

COMPANY PERSPECTIVES

∎

PB will be a positive and highly influential force in the development and operation of infrastructure around the world. Through service to our clients and collaboration with colleagues, we will create a lasting legacy that improves the lives of people and communities. Our vision will only be achieved by living our values, and it will be sustained by our culture of employee ownership. Taken separately these standards of behavior are not unique to PB, nor are they new. But by making a commitment to them together we will find new strength. Our values are: we behave ethically, acting with integrity and respect; we work with our clients to contribute to their success; we care for our colleagues, encouraging their development, engagement and achievement; we share knowledge with our colleagues to deliver professional excellence; and we act in a socially and environmentally responsible manner, committed to high standards of safe performance.

organizing the Eleventh Engineers Regiment of the First Army, and then he went abroad, being among the first to land in Europe, where he studied and made recommendations for improving railway systems, ports, shipping terminals, and the like. At war's end, at the age of 60, Parsons was detached from his engineering corps and returned to New York, where he resumed his work at the firm while also writing several books on engineering and serving as a trustee for such prominent organizations as Columbia University, the New York Public Library, and the Carnegie Institute.

While Parsons had served abroad, Brinckerhoff had remained on the home front, directing the construction of naval dry docks to support the war effort. Brinckerhoff and Douglas were eventually made partners after the war, and the firm became known as Parsons Klapp Brinckerhoff & Douglas. Between 1920 and 1939 the firm completed more than $50 million of work, including railroad and harbor terminals and manufacturing plants.

Parsons died in 1932 and was succeeded as senior partner of the firm by Douglas; the company would, however, continue to bear the name of its famous founders, even after the passing of Brinckerhoff. After the completion of the Detroit-Windsor Tunnel linking Michigan and Ontario in 1930 and a tunnel under the

Schelde River for Antwerp, Belgium, completed in 1931, the firm fell upon lean times because of the Great Depression.

DEPRESSION ERA AND POSTWAR PROJECTS: 1936–56

Between 1936 and 1940 net income totaled only $293,010. Still, the company managed to secure important projects, among them construction of the network of roads for the 1939 World's Fair in New York. This project was headed by Brinckerhoff and John P. Hogan, who became senior partner that year. In 1943 Hogan and Eugene Macdonald replaced Klapp and Douglas, who were both deceased by that time, as name partners in the firm. During World War II virtually the entire staff worked on designing the U.S. Navy's fixed and floating dry docks, including those for the Brooklyn Navy Yard.

Hogan retired in 1947 and was succeeded as senior partner by Macdonald. Projects in the immediate postwar years included tunnels, bridges, airports, and highways, culminating in New Jersey's 173-mile-long Garden State Parkway, for which the firm served as the general engineering consultant. This project was completed in 1955 at a cost of $330 million. Also noteworthy was the firm's construction of the first Hampton Roads Bridge-Tunnel, completed in 1957. Upon his retirement in 1956, Macdonald was succeeded as managing partner by Maurice Quade, who was assisted by Walter S. Douglas, son of Walter J. Douglas. The firm became Parsons Brinckerhoff Quade & Douglas (PBQD).

GROWTH AND END OF PARTNERSHIP

During the ensuing years the firm designed and supervised the construction of the headquarters for the U.S. Air Force's North American Air Defense Command (NORAD) Center, which was completed in 1964. This facility was built underground, beneath Cheyenne Mountain in Colorado. By 1965 the firm had branch offices in four cities and field offices in nine. A joint venture of PBQD and Tudor Engineering Co. had begun work on a public rail system centered around San Francisco and Oakland for the Bay Area Rapid Transit District (BART). This undertaking included nine miles of subway, 14 miles of single-bore tunnel, a three-mile twin rock tunnel, and a 3.5-mile tube tunnel under San Francisco Bay that was, at the time, the longest underwater tunnel in the world. The $1.6 billion, 71-mile system was not completed until 1974—five years behind schedule. The same joint venture constructed a

KEY DATES

1885: William Barclay Parsons opens an engineering office in New York City.

1900: Parsons breaks ground for his New York City subway system project.

1906: Henry Brinckerhoff joins the firm.

1916: Parsons founds and leads the Eleventh Engineers Regiment of the First Army in World War I; on the home front, the firm constructs facilities to support the war effort.

1930: The firm completes the Detroit-Windsor Tunnel.

1939: Brinckerhoff and the firm design the road network for the New York World's Fair.

1964: Firm completes the NORAD underground command center for the U.S. Air Force in Colorado.

1974: In a joint venture, the firm completes the Bay Area transit system.

1975: The firm converts from a partnership to a corporation.

1979: Parsons Brinckerhoff Inc. (PB) is established as a holding company.

1987: PB, in a joint venture, begins work on a Boston transportation project that becomes the most expensive in the world.

1998: Staff grows 45 percent after four acquisitions.

2006: The company reorganizes operations into three divisions; Milena Del Valle dies after the ceiling of a Big Dig tunnel collapses.

rapid-transit system for the Atlanta metropolitan area that opened in 1979.

PBQD had been incorporated in the early 1950s to meet the licensing requirements of certain states, but it continued to operate as a partnership until 1975, when it transformed itself into an employee-owned corporation in order to foster further growth and to meet increased competition and combat rising costs. Shares were offered annually to middle and senior managers, based on nominations made to a corporate committee, with the shares accumulated to be sold back to the company over a ten-year period following an employee's departure or retirement. There were 83 shareholders in 1982.

The change from partnership to corporation affected company culture as well as organization. Henry

Michel, the firm's president in 1983, told *Management Review* that year: "The partnership structure endowed individual partners, each of whom specialized in one technical area, with absolute decision-making power in their respective fields of expertise. ... The partners were almost controlling little fiefdoms." Under the new corporate structure, however, the partners found their power somewhat diminished. The company felt that sharing the decision-making controls allowed, according to Michel, "the best technicians and the best managers to concentrate on what they do best." Of the new employee-ownership status, Michel noted that employee-owners were more likely to keep an eye out for cost overruns, as witnessed by a 350 percent increase in business since 1974. The change to corporate status also allowed the firm to retain earnings and thus ease the borrowing needed for expansion.

OVERSEAS WORK INCREASES

Parsons Brinckerhoff Inc. (PB) was established in 1979 as the holding company for several subsidiaries. PBQD continued to be responsible for the firm's traditional transit, highway, and bridges and tunnels projects. Parsons Brinckerhoff International was charged with servicing clients abroad and also acted as a holding company for foreign subsidiaries. In addition, PB oversaw Parsons Brinckerhoff Construction Services and Parsons Brinckerhoff Development Corporation. By 1982, 20 percent of the company's business was coming from overseas, including projects in Singapore and Hong Kong. PB also established a subsidiary for the alternative energy facilities that the company was designing, building, and operating for third-party clients, including cogeneration, hydroelectric, and waste-to-energy projects in New England and California.

In 1985, PB's centennial year, the company was at work on no fewer than 14 subway systems and won nine of the 11 major projects on which it had made proposals. It was also designing and managing construction of the Fort McHenry Tunnel in Baltimore Harbor—at 8,000 feet in length and eight lanes in width, the largest underwater tunnel in the world at the time. PBQD, along with Morrison Knudsen Corporation and CRSS Inc., won a contract valued at $1.6 billion in 1990 to design and build the tunnels, service areas, roads, campus, utilities, and experimental facilities for the world's largest atom smasher. (This Texas-based high-energy-physics project was later canceled, however.)

In fiscal 1993 PB reported operating income of $13.9 million on revenues of $343.1 million, both company records. The number of employees—3,575— was also a record. The four major operating subsidiaries were in charge of infrastructure, construction services, facilities, and international work. The second largest of the company's more than 80 offices was in Hong Kong, and a Shanghai office also was opened in 1993. By late 1996 one-fifth of PB's workforce was based in five East Asian offices. PB also had clients in eastern Europe and had formed a Madrid-based transportation company with a Spanish partner. In seeking to gain access to Asia's lucrative and developing private power market, PB acquired Merz & McLellan Holdings Ltd., a British-based power consultant, in 1994. The company also opened a Vienna office that year.

LARGE-SCALE PROJECTS: 1996–99

When work began in 1996 on the 2,400-megawatt Sabiya power plant in Kuwait—one of the largest in the world—Merz & McLellan was responsible for the design, project management, and site supervision. PBQD was in charge of project management services for the H-3 highway, the largest construction project in Hawaii history, completed in 1997. That year it won a contract, with CH2M Hill Ltd., for the planning, design, construction, and project management of a $6 billion deep-tunnel sewage collection, treatment, and disposal system in Singapore. PBQD was the prime engineering consultant for the construction of Pearl Harbor Naval Station's Ford Island Bridge, which opened in 1998. It was managing the construction of Cairo's subway, which began in 1986 and was scheduled for completion in 2003.

PB's revenues reached a record $698 million in fiscal 1998. Net income came to nearly $9 million, and the company enjoyed its 23rd consecutive year of increased value per share of stock. Its number of employees grew 45 percent, to 7,700. Four new acquisitions were made during the year, including Booker Associates Inc., a St. Louis-based engineering and architectural firm, and Kennedy & Donkin Group, a British engineering firm. In addition to the aforementioned undertakings, the projects in which PB was taking part at this time included London's $1.4 billion Heathrow Airport Terminal 5; Saudi Arabia's $1.2 billion Ghazlan II Power Station; and Brazil's $500 million Castello-Raposo, Lot 12 toll road.

PB's main job, and its biggest headache in the 1990s, was its work with Bechtel Group, Inc., as project manager for Boston's Central Artery/Third Harbor Tunnel project—also known as the Big Dig—the largest civil engineering project in U.S. history. Authorized in 1987 as a mile-long portion of Interstate 93 that would run through downtown Boston underground, it was also intended to link the Massachusetts Turnpike (Interstate 90) to Logan Airport by means of a third tunnel through Boston's inner harbor. The Big Dig was

originally planned for completion in 1994 and the cost estimated at $2.5 billion. By the time the 1.6-mile Ted Williams Tunnel opened in late 1995, the estimate had reached nearly $8 billion. A report by an independent consultant charged that Bechtel/PB managers had allowed costs to spiral needlessly by not delegating authority to area managers in a position to control spending. The project had fallen behind schedule and over budget because managers had failed to test the soil properly before designing the tunnel. The next part of the job involved establishing a link between the turnpike and the tunnel. In just 1,150 feet, nine lanes of highway had to be threaded under eight sets of railroad tracks bringing 40,000 people into South Station each working day, and just inches above 81-year-old tunnels through which ran a rapid-transit line. By early 2000, cost estimates had reached $12.2 billion, with completion of the project not expected until 2005.

This domestic challenge notwithstanding, PB was widely recognized as the leader in American transportation engineering and by the late 1990s was truly a global concern with offices in Europe, South Africa, China, Australia, and South America. Achieving such prominence in servicing all types of infrastructure, in addition to its flagship transportation services, remained its goal for the next century.

MOVING INTO THE NEW MILLENNIUM

While the company worked toward that goal in the early years of the new millennium, the Big Dig proved to be a dark spot in its history. Most of the work was finished in late 2005 and early 2006, but costs had climbed to nearly $15 billion and there were major leaks in the tunnel. Disaster struck in July 2006 when four three-ton concrete slabs fell from a tunnel ceiling, killing 38-year-old Milena Del Valle. The woman's death and other Big Dig issues sparked a series of lawsuits against project manager Bechtel/PB and other construction companies. In the end, Bechtel/PB agreed to a $458 million settlement with the Federal Highway Administration, the U.S. attorney, and the Massachusetts attorney general.

During this period, PB focused on overcoming the negative publicity surrounding its involvement with the Big Dig project. It focused on securing new contracts, expanding its international business, and also revamped its operating structure. PB restructured into three divisions in 2006. The Americas division oversaw business in North and South America; the International arm included Europe, Africa, the Middle East, Asia, and Australia; and the company's new Facilities division was responsible for facility operations and maintenance and its U.S. government contracts.

The company was part of several projects that reached completion in 2008 including Phoenix's METRO light rail; the reconstruction of 23 miles of the Katy Freeway in Houston; the Abu Dhabi Taweelah B power and desalination plant expansion; construction of a new complex at Catholic Medical Center in Seoul, South Korea; and the Bundamba Advanced Water Treatment plant project in Australia. PB also played a role in the development of JetBlue Terminal 5 at John F. Kennedy International Airport in New York and the Beijing Olympic Green Convention Center, which was used for the 2008 Summer Olympics and then converted into China's largest convention venue in 2009.

PB's strategy to expand its business and secure international contracts appeared to be paying off. During 2008 revenue increased 26 percent over the previous year, due in part to its growth overseas. Its international arm was also responsible for a 19 percent increase in net income for the year. PB was named to conduct an integrated rail transit study for Dubai in early 2009. In May of that year, PB was chosen by the California Department of Transportation and the San Diego Association of Governments to manage the public works plan for its I-5 North Coast Corridor project. In addition, PB landed a contract to provide construction supervision services for the New Jersey Turnpike Authority's project to construct a new bridge for the Garden State Parkway over the Mullica River. With additional construction bids in the works, including projects for the 2012 Olympic Games in London, PB appeared to be well positioned for additional growth in the years to come.

Robert Halasz
Updated, Christina M. Stansell

PRINCIPAL DIVISIONS

Americas; International; Facilities.

PRINCIPAL COMPETITORS

HNTB Companies; The Louis Berger Group Inc.; URS Corporation.

FURTHER READING

"Acquisition Puts PB in World Power Play," *Engineering News-Record,* October 24, 1994, p. 24.

"BART District Sues for Damages of $237.8 Million," *Wall Street Journal,* November 20, 1974, p. 15.

Belluck, Pam, and Katie Zezima, "4 Ceiling Panels in Boston's Big Dig Fall, Killing Woman in Car," *New York Times,* July 12, 2006.

Bobrick, Benson, *Parsons Brinckerhoff: The First 100 Years,* New York: Van Nostrand Reinhold, 1985.

"Employee Ownership As a Corporate Strategy," *Management Review,* June 1983, pp. 4–5.

Gersten, Alan, "US Group to Run Singapore Sewer Project," *Journal of Commerce,* July 31, 1997, p. 6A.

Green, Peter, "Money Flows Through Boston Aorta," *Engineering News-Record,* July 21, 1988, pp. 22–23.

Howe, Peter J., "Threading the Needle," *Boston Globe,* May 20, 1996, pp. 45, 48.

Korman, Richard, "Taking a Lot More 'Prudent Risks,'" *Engineering News-Record,* June 13, 1994, pp. 34–37.

Kosowatz, John J., "A-E and Management Team Named for Superconducting Supercollider," *Engineering News-Record,* March 1, 1990, pp. 10–11.

"No Federal Debarment for Bechtel/Parsons Brinckerhoff," *Engineering News-Record,* December 15, 2008.

Palmer, Thomas C., Jr., "Mismanagement Blamed for Costs, Delays in Big Dig," *Boston Globe,* December 12, 1995, pp. 1, 18.

"Parsons Brinckerhoff Builds on Project Expertise," *Project Finance,* October 1998, p. 8.

"Parsons Brinckerhoff to Assess Dubai Railway Network," *Middle East Economic Digest,* February 13, 2009.

"Parsons Brinckerhoff's High Stakes Players," *Engineering News-Record,* September 30, 1982, pp. 22–24.

"PB Redesigns Its Own Structure," *Real Estate Weekly,* March 29, 2006.

"Providing Careers Prospects for Engineers and Technicians," *Management Review,* February 1981, pp. 29–31.

"Shoddy Work, Big Settlement," *Boston Globe,* January 24, 2008.

Vennochi, Joan, "The O'Neill Name and the Big Dig—All in the Family," *Boston Globe,* July 30, 2006.

Yamin, Rebecca, "Pioneering Transit Engineering Firm Celebrating Centennial Year," *Mass Transit,* January 1985, pp. 8–10, 26–27.

Zutell, Irene, "Parsons Engineering New Blueprint in Asia," *Crain's New York Business,* November 14, 1994, p. 17.

Petróleos Mexicanos (PEMEX)

Avenida Marina Nacional
329 Colonia Huasteca
Mexico City, DF 11311
Mexico
Telephone: (55) 1944 2500
Fax: (55) 1944 9378
Web site: http://www.pemex.com

State-Owned Company
Incorporated: 1938
Employees: 141,146
Sales: $103.99 billion (2007)
NAICS: 221210 Natural Gas Distribution; 486210
  Pipeline Transportation of Natural Gas; 486110
  Pipeline Transportation of Crude Oil; 486910
  Pipeline Transportation of Refined Petroleum
  Products; 32411 Petroleum Refineries

∎ ∎ ∎

Petróleos Mexicanos (PEMEX) operates as a government-owned oil company responsible for nearly one-third of Mexico's federal budget. The company is involved in exploration, production, refining, and petrochemicals and is ranked the sixth largest oil company in the world in terms of barrels per day of output. During 2007, the company produced approximately three million barrels of crude oil per day, a decline of 5 percent over the previous year. Throughout its history as a state-owned entity, PEMEX has seen its share of corruption, scandal, and controversy. PEMEX has been plagued by high debt and falling production since 2005, forcing the Mexican government to rethink its longstanding nationalistic strategy and potentially allow foreign investment in its oil fields.

EARLY HISTORY

PEMEX was founded in 1938 as a decentralized agency of the federal government of Mexico, with direct responsibility for all aspects of the country's oil and gas industry, since 1959 including basic petrochemicals. Oil has been known in Mexico since ancient times and the country was one of the earliest oil-and-gas-producing countries in the Western Hemisphere. The first significant commercial exploitation was started in 1901 by Edward L. Doheny, with an oil well located at El Ebano, in the eastern part of the state of San Luis Potosí. Up to 1938, production was largely controlled by U.S. and British interests, including Royal Dutch/Shell, Exxon, the Pearson family, Sinclair, and Gulf Oil. Production increased considerably during World War I, reaching a peak of 530,000 barrels per day. In 1921 Mexico was the second largest oil producer in the world after the United States, and produced about a quarter of the world's oil supply.

Around 1910, in order to ensure adequate supplies of fuel for its locomotives in the early 20th century, the National Railways of Mexico created a petroleum division to exploit the hydrocarbons found on its lands in the rich El Ebano and Panuco oil fields. Soon afterward it became apparent that the government itself, in order to meet its oil demand, would have to develop the oil fields found on its federal lands, not including the land belonging to the railway company. At the end of

December 1925 the Control de Administración del Petróleo Nacional (Control of the Management of National Petroleum) was set up in order to simplify government participation in the development of its reserves by concentrating it in one entity. This government entity competed directly with private capital in the production and refining of crude oil but at the same time regulated the domestic price of petroleum products.

THE OIL INDUSTRY IS NATIONALIZED

In December 1933, a congressional decree established Petróleos de México S.A. (Petromex), a publicly traded company in which only Mexican nationals could purchase equity, with the specific purpose of supplying the fuel requirements of the National Railways in particular and the domestic market with petroleum products in general. It also regulated the domestic petroleum markets and trained Mexican personnel in all aspects of the industry. Petromex lasted only until September 1934, when it was wound up owing to a lack of interest on the part of the investing public, and the assets and shares of the company were transferred to the Control de Administración del Petróleo Nacional. In November 1936 a law was passed which expropriated for the state all assets considered to be of public utility, including oil and natural gas, and in January 1937 the state-owned Administración General del Petróleo Nacional was created to explore and develop the national reserves that were assigned to it.

As a result of long-existing conflict between the oil workers' union and the companies, which at one stage threatened to bring the oil industry to a standstill, President Lázaro Cárdenas nationalized the oil industry on March 18, 1938. A number of reasons were given for this drastic measure, among which the most important were the following: that the foreign-owned companies had adopted inadequate conservation measures for existing reserves; that there was a lack of interest on the part of the companies in exploring for new reserves; and that the companies had used unfair labor practices.

On March 19, 1938, the day after expropriation, the Consejo Administrativo del Petróleo (Petroleum Administrative Council) was established, with nine government members, to administer the assets it had taken over. In June the administration of the country's oil and gas industry was split between two government agencies: Petróleos Mexicanos (PEMEX), which took over the properties and functions assigned to the Petroleum Administrative Council, and the newly created Distribuidora de Petróleos Mexicanos, which distributed and marketed petroleum products. By August 1940, however, it became obvious that this delegation of responsibilities was not working, because of conflict between the two agencies, and it was decided that all matters related to hydrocarbons should become the sole responsibility of PEMEX. The Administración del Petróleo Nacional and the Distribuidora de Petróleos Mexicanos were abolished.

OPERATING AS A STATE-OWNED ENTITY

With the creation of PEMEX, Mexico faced an economic boycott instigated by the governments of the expropriated companies, which included an economic blockade to prevent the company from selling its oil in world markets; a ban on selling raw materials, replacement parts, and equipment needed by PEMEX; pressure on shipping lines to refuse transportation of Mexican oil; legal action to embargo the oil that PEMEX managed to export through other countries; and a massive withdrawal of bank deposits held in Mexico by foreign companies. After long and strenuous negotiations, the Mexican government finally agreed to indemnify the foreign oil companies for $114 million, with the first payment beginning in 1940 and the last one in 1962.

PEMEX's original brief from the Mexican government was to supply the Mexican market with oil, gas, and petrochemical products at the lowest possible cost. The mandate was not profit-motivated, and there was a strong desire on the part of the government to improve the living standards of its employees.

Beginning in 1940, PEMEX's board of directors was headed by the secretary of patrimony and industrial development with five other government representatives—the secretary of finance, the secretary of commerce, the deputy secretary of patrimony and industrial development, the director general of the Federal Electricity Commission, and the director general of the Nacional Financiera, a financial institution—as well as five union representatives. The executive officers of the company were headed by a director general and seven sub-directors in charge of production, refining, finance, sales, exploration, personnel administration, and project

KEY DATES

1901: Oil is discovered in El Ebano.

1938: President Lázaro Cárdenas nationalizes Mexico's oil industry; Petróleos Mexicanos (PEMEX) is founded as a decentralized agency of the federal government of Mexico.

1971: Fisherman Rudesindo Cantarell discovers oil in Campeche Sound.

1974: The company launches a major exploration and development plan.

1992: PEMEX is restructured with four main subsidiaries; a series of explosions in Guadalajara's sewer system kills nearly 200 people.

2000: Vicente Fox is elected Mexico's president and pledges to modernize PEMEX while keeping it government-owned.

2002: PEMEX announces plans to invest $4.5 billion in its Ku-Maloob-Zaap offshore oil field.

2006: Felipe Calderón is elected Mexico's president; Jesús Reyes Heroles is appointed director general of PEMEX.

2007: Members of the Popular Revolutionary Army (ERP) claim responsibility for blowing up natural gas pipelines owned by PEMEX.

administration. The number of employees rose tenfold from 1938 to the late 1980s.

About 72 percent of Mexico's surface area of 2.5 million square kilometers was covered by sedimentary basins—potentially oil-producing areas—and only about 10 percent of this area was explored. The proved hydrocarbon reserves were located mainly in the Chicontepec basin in the northern part of the state of Veracruz, the Tabasco-Chiapas Mesozoic area in the continental shelf of the Gulf of Campeche, and the Sabinas basin in the states of Coahuila and Nuevo León.

CRUDE OIL PRODUCTION

In 1938 PEMEX inherited total reserves of 1.276 billion barrels of oil equivalent (boe), including oil and gas, from the expropriated oil companies. This increased steadily to reach 5.568 billion boe in 1960, undergoing a spectacular rise in the 1980s to 60.126 billion boe in 1980, and at the end of 1990 standing at 64.96 billion boe.

After the first commercial exploitation of the country's reserves at El Ebano, production was concentrated in the zone of Tuxpan in the northern part of the state of Veracruz, where the famous Golden Lane complex, dating from the first two decades of the 20th century, was located and where the productivity of the wells was legendary. Between 1910 and 1937 the Potrero del Llano well produced 117.3 million barrels of crude oil and the Cerro Azul well produced an average of 261,400 barrels per day of crude oil in the early stages.

At the time of nationalization, PEMEX's production averaged 104,110 barrels per day of crude oil and liquid natural gas (LNG), increasing to just over 197,260 barrels per day in 1950 and undergoing a spectacular rise in the 1980s to an average of 2.54 million barrels per day of crude oil and LNG. Fisherman Rudesindo Cantarell discovered oil in Campeche Sound in 1971. The area proved to be one of the largest offshore reservoirs in the world and moved PEMEX into the forefront of world crude oil production. PEMEX reached its production plateau of 2.5 million barrels per day of crude oil and almost 400,000 barrels per day of LNG in 1989. That year over two-thirds of PEMEX's crude output was heavy Maya crude from the offshore Gulf of Campeche, while the lighter Olmeca and Isthmus blends came from onshore areas where reserves were declining.

Most of PEMEX's gas production was associated with crude oil production, although there were also natural gas fields independent of oil fields. Gas production at the time of nationalization was 600 million cubic meters per annum and in 1990 stood at around 36 billion cubic meters. PEMEX's oil fields historically produced much higher ratios of gas per barrel of oil than was previously estimated.

In 1976 PEMEX launched an ambitious program for gas treatment plants to enable the company to handle the large amounts of gas produced from the oil fields that were being developed. Most of the gas was processed by PEMEX's petrochemical complexes in southern and central Mexico, and a proportion of it was fed into Mexico's gas system. The gas was transported through PEMEX's 12,788-kilometer network of gas pipelines.

A CALL FOR EXPLORATION AND DEVELOPMENT

Until 1938 Mexico was one of the world's largest oil exporters, but with the international boycott and increased domestic consumption PEMEX was not able to export significant quantities of oil until the mid-1970s. Until 1971 Mexico was self-sufficient in crude oil and natural gas, as well as being a net exporter of refined products. In the early 1970s, in order to meet its domestic consumption requirements, PEMEX became a net importer, importing 64,600 barrels per day of crude oil in 1973. After that, there was a radical adjustment of PEMEX's role, which up until then had been to provide energy to the ever-increasing domestic market at low prices.

When the country's balance of payments was adversely affected in 1974, PEMEX was forced to double the prices of its products to dampen down demand, and a decision was made to allow the company to invest more money in exploration and development in order to reestablish itself as a major oil exporter. PEMEX was called on by the government to export oil, gas, and petrochemical products, and to become the cornerstone of Mexican industrial development. The 1974–76 $3 billion development plan was the largest in Mexico's history and called for $240 million to be spent on geological and seismic studies and $728 million to be invested in drilling development and exploration wells.

This plan was followed by an even bigger one in 1977 when PEMEX approved an ambitious $15.5 billion development program with the aim of increasing by 1982 the company's production in the following areas: crude oil to 2.2 million barrels per day; gas to 113.3 million cubic meters per day; crude oil exports to 1.1 million barrels per day; refining capacity to 1.7 million barrels per day; and petrochemical output to 15.5 million tons per annum. Almost half the budget would be spent on the drilling of 2,152 development wells, and $1.2 billion would be spent on drilling 1,324 exploration wells. The plan called for the surveying of 1.2 million square kilometers of prospective oil-bearing areas.

The exploration and development effort led to a spectacular increase in reserves and production in the 1980s. With increased production, PEMEX managed to export between 1.3 million and 1.5 million barrels per day of crude oil during the 1980s, with exports in 1989 at just under 1.3 million barrels per day. Since 1976 the Mexican government operated a ceiling on exports of 1.35 million barrels per day to keep its prices high in world markets. PEMEX had three main export markets, with the United States being by far its largest customer, taking 57 percent of its exports in 1989, followed by Spain with 15 percent and Japan with 13 percent.

MEETING DOMESTIC NEEDS

During the 1980s, PEMEX's crude oil reserves remained remarkably static despite a significant reduction in the number of exploration wells drilled during the period—from 305 in 1983 to 123 in 1989—because of the

country's austerity program, which involved a reduction in government expenditure.

PEMEX also followed a policy of self-sufficiency in the downstream and petrochemical side of the oil business. Production in these two sectors evolved to meet domestic demand. In 1938, PEMEX produced 92,229 barrels per day of products, increasing to 481,135 barrels per day in 1970 and 1.403 billion barrels per day in 1988. PEMEX operated nine refineries with a primary capacity—not including upgrading—of 1.679 million barrels per day, and with the following upgrading facilities: 82,000 barrels per day thermal operations, 267,000 barrels per day catalytic cracking, and 157,800 barrels per day catalytic reforming. The expansion of cracking and reforming facilities was a direct response to the increase in production of heavy Mayan crude since the mid-1970s. Heavy Mayan crude was put through the refineries in order to leave the lighter crudes for export. The refineries were served by an oil pipeline network of 4,784 kilometers.

Domestic demand at this time was heavily geared toward transport fuel, such as gasoline and fuel oil, which accounted for 32 percent and 33 percent respectively, out of total consumption of petroleum products in 1989 of 1.3 million barrels per day. Exports of products in 1989 declined by 31 percent to 83,000 barrels per day, from 121,000 barrels per day in 1988, because of higher internal consumption.

After its first investment overseas, a small investment in the early 1980s in Petronor, a Spanish refiner, PEMEX decided to concentrate on expanding its domestic refining business, which it hoped to increase by 300,000 barrels per day during the early 1990s. It later exchanged its stake in Petronor for a 2.9 percent stake in Repsol, the privatized Spanish oil company, increasing PEMEX's share of the Spanish market for its products beyond the 150,000 barrels per day of crude it supplied.

EXPANSION AND DEVELOPMENT

In 1977 PEMEX embarked on an expansion program intended to triple its petrochemical output by 1982. It aimed to be self-sufficient in basic petrochemicals by 1979 and subsequently to develop large volumes of feedstocks—raw or part-processed products destined for further processing—for export. This policy was successful, with basic petrochemicals production increasing from 1.931 million imperial tons in 1980 to 16.9 million tons in 1989. Private capital was allowed to account for up to 40 percent of total issued capital in the petrochemical industry mainly because of PEMEX's lack of technological expertise.

In 1989, petrochemicals exports climbed by 50 percent to $110.4 million, while imports declined to $21.7 million. Export earnings from petrochemicals represented only 1.4 percent of PEMEX's total export earnings, but their growth helped to offset the company's deteriorating trade in refined products, which accounted for 6 percent of PEMEX's gross exports. PEMEX operated a shipping fleet that grew from 6,438 deadweight tons in 1938 to 618,780 deadweight tons in 1988.

Although Mexico was not as dependent on oil as some South American countries, in the early 1990s, this commodity accounted for 70 percent of its foreign exchange and provided around 45 percent of government tax receipts. Crude oil exports also enabled the country to keep up with the repayment of its $103 billion of foreign debt. As a decentralized public agency of the Mexican government, PEMEX paid 18 percent tax on total revenues from oil and gas, 13 percent on total revenues from petrochemicals, and a 50 percent corporation tax. In 1989 PEMEX made an international trading surplus of $7.03 billion between oil sales and product imports, an increase of 15.3 percent compared with the previous year, representing 46 percent of non-oil exports.

Total oil exports were up to $7.84 billion and oil imports just $800.4 million. The deficit on product trade of 38,000 barrels per day (the amount Mexico had to import) in 1989 stemmed from burgeoning domestic demand, particularly for gasoline, jet fuel, and fuel oil. In 1989 PEMEX generated pretax profits of $7.9 billion, all of which—with the exception of $7 million—was sent to the Mexican government. PEMEX provided 32 percent of total government tax receipts in 1989, slightly below the level of 1985, when the company contributed 36.8 percent of total government tax income.

During the early 1990s, PEMEX underwent an internal reorganization, with the company being divided into five separate operating units, leaving PEMEX as a holding company. One part of PEMEX, international marketing, was split off in June 1990. Named Petróleos Mexicanos Comercio Internacional, the subsidiary was responsible for the marketing of crude oil, refined products, and petrochemicals. The other four subsidiaries included PEMEX Exploración y Producción, PEMEX Refinación, PEMEX Gas y Petroquímica Básica, and PEMEX Petroquímica.

OVERCOMING CHALLENGES

Throughout its history, PEMEX had seen its share of problems, controversy, and scandal as a government-

owned entity. Its infrastructure was aging and its pipelines were often the cause of oil spills and explosions. In 1992, a series of explosions in Guadalajara's sewer system killed nearly 200 people. Four PEMEX executives were charged with negligent homicide after failing to respond to complaints about gas fumes prior to the explosions.

The PEMEX union came under fire in 2000 after it was revealed that the union illegally spent nearly $50 million to support the candidate of the Institutional Revolutionary Party—the party lost the election for the first time in 71 years in 2000 when Vicente Fox was elected Mexico's president. Raúl Muñoz Leos, named director general of PEMEX by Fox, was forced to resign in 2004 after it became public that he had paid nearly $700 million to the PEMEX union without receiving approval from the company's board. In addition, Muñoz used company funds to pay for his wife's liposuction.

During 2007, the Popular Revolutionary Army, or Ejército Popular Revolucionario (ERP), claimed responsibility for blowing up several natural gas pipelines owned by PEMEX. The guerrilla warfare group, created to overthrow the Mexican government, carried out the hostile action believing the government had kidnapped two of its members. The bombings called into question the security of Mexico's natural gas infrastructure as well as its oil supply.

Despite the controversies and setbacks, PEMEX's focus during the early years of the new millennium was on shifting its image from a nationalistic and poorly run government entity into a modern global corporation. The company trimmed its workforce, sold its air fleet holdings, allowed open bidding for major projects, and slowly began to increase spending on exploration, development, and refining. During 2002, PEMEX announced plans to invest $4.5 billion in its Ku-Maloob-Zaap offshore oil field.

FACING AN UNCERTAIN FUTURE

While the company worked to revamp its operations, it remained subject to government control and continued to be the backbone of the Mexican economy. Nevertheless, it was often criticized for corruption and mismanagement. "PEMEX is a necessary evil. It harms us, but it is good for many people. It builds roads, hospitals, schools," claimed a Mexican citizen in a January 2005 *Dow Jones International News* report. Indeed, the Mexican government continued to rely heavily on PEMEX for income. Sales in 2006 were $97 billion; of that total $79 billion went to the government. Overall, PEMEX revenues accounted for nearly 40 percent of Mexico's federal budget.

A major problem, however, became apparent during this period. The company had failed to invest properly in exploration and development, and production at the Cantarell field, one of the largest oil fields in the world, was dwindling. Cantarell was once responsible for nearly 60 percent of the company's output, but production had fallen by 13.5 percent in 2006 and continued to fall over the next several years. The company's crude oil production averaged just over three million barrels per day in 2007, which was a 5 percent decline over the previous year. It was estimated that Mexico had tens of billions of barrels of untapped oil reserves but PEMEX lacked funds and the technological expertise for deep underwater exploration. Mexico was the third largest crude oil exporter to the United States and its ability to provide an oil supply to its northern neighbor appeared to be in jeopardy.

Felipe Calderón was elected Mexico's president in 2006 and placed Jesús Reyes Heroles in charge of PEMEX. Calderón immediately set out to pass energy reform bills that would begin to allow foreign investment in developing Mexico's oil fields. While advocates argued that PEMEX needed to seek out joint ventures with foreign oil companies to increase production, this strategy faced major opposition from those who wanted to keep PEMEX and Mexico's oil fields government-owned. At the same time, analysts speculated that the company's future as an oil exporter was in question unless the company increased production. With debt mounting and production and reserves waning, the future of PEMEX would no doubt remain a hotly contested topic in Mexico for years to come.

Brian S. McBeth
Updated, Christina M. Stansell

PRINCIPAL SUBSIDIARIES

PEMEX Exploración y Producción; PEMEX Refinación; PEMEX Gas y Petroquímica Básica; PEMEX Petroquímica; PMI Comercio Internacional, S.A. de C.V.

PRINCIPAL COMPETITORS

Exxon Mobil Corporation; Petróleos de Venezuela S.A.; Royal Dutch Shell plc.

FURTHER READING

Baker, George, *Mexico's Petroleum Sector: Performance and Prospects,* Tulsa, Okla.: PennWell Publishing Co., 1984.

Bermudez, Antonio J., *The Mexican National Petroleum Industry. A Case Study in Nationalization,* Stanford, Calif: Stanford University Press, 1963.

DeCordoba, Jose, "Guerillas in the Mist," *Wall Street Journal,* November 14, 2007.

———, "Mexican Gas Pipelines Attacked Again," *Wall Street Journal,* September 11, 2007.

Lyons, John, and Neil King, Jr., "Mexico's Allure to Big Oil Is Uncertain," *Wall Street Journal,* April 10, 2008.

Malkin, Elisabeth, "Leader of Mexican Energy Monopoly Resigns," *New York Times,* November 2, 2004.

———, "Output Falling in Oil-Rich Mexico, and Politics Gets the Blame," *New York Times,* March 9, 2007.

McKinley, James C., Jr., "State Oil Industry's Future Sets Off Tussle in Mexico," *New York Times,* April 8, 2008.

"Mexico—Pemex Changes Ahead of Election," *Petroleum Economist,* September 30, 1999.

"Mexico's PEMEX Faces Crumbling Infrastructure, Spills," *Dow Jones International News,* January 18, 2005.

"PEMEX to Invest $4.5-Bil to Triple Field's Production," *Platts Oilgram News,* August 27, 2002.

Philip, George, *Oil and Politics in Latin America,* Cambridge: Cambridge University Press, 1982.

Randall, Laura, *The Political Economy of Mexican Oil,* New York: Praeger, 1989.

Sepulveda, Isidro, "PEMEX in a Dependent Society," in *US-Mexican Energy Relationships,* by Jerry R. Ladman, Deborah J. Baldwin, and Elihu Bergman, Lexington, Mass.: Lexington Books, 1981.

Szekely, Gabriel, *La economía política del petróleo en Mexico, 1976–1982,* Mexico City: El Colegio de México, 1983.

Williams, Edward J., *The Rebirth of the Mexican Petroleum Industry,* Lexington, Mass.: Lexington Books, 1979.

Plow & Hearth.

Plow & Hearth, Inc.

———————— ■ ————————

1107 Emmet Street North, Suite C
Charlottesville, Virginia 22903-4840
U.S.A.
Telephone: (434) 977-3707
Toll Free: (800) 494-7544
Web site: http://www.plowhearth.com

Wholly Owned Subsidiary of 1-800-FLOWERS.COM,
Inc.
Incorporated: 1980
Employees: 425
Sales: $180 million (2008 est.)
NAICS: 454113 Mail-Order Houses

■ ■ ■

A subsidiary of 1-800-FLOWERS.COM, Inc., Plow & Hearth, Inc., is a retail, catalog, and Internet seller of home, hearth, yard, and garden products, as well as apparel, footwear, and jewelry catering to outdoor enthusiasts and nature lovers. The company strives to offer handmade products that use uncommon materials, sourcing the items from manufacturers and artisans around the world. Plow & Hearth owns other brands as well, including Problem Solvers, focusing on practical solutions, including kitchen organizers, cleansers and spray-on protectors, and handy tools for the car, home, and garden. Mostly geared toward weather buffs, the Wind & Weather brand offers thermometers, rain and wind measurement instruments, barometers and hygrometers, and electronic "weather stations" that offer an assortment of meteorological data and real-time

warnings. Other brands include HearthSong and Magic Cabin, the former offering children's toys and the latter classic toys.

Plow & Hearth maintains its corporate headquarters in Madison, Virginia, where a service center and distribution center are also operated. Other distribution centers are located in Vandalia, Ohio, and Reno, Nevada. In the early years of the 21st century, the company has paid more attention to retail outlets, which offer some products unique to the stores. At the start of 2009 there were eight Plow & Hearth stores, four located in Virginia, three in Maryland, and a single unit in North Carolina.

COUNTRY-STORE ROOTS

Plow & Hearth began as a small country store founded in 1980 by longtime president Peter G. Rice, his wife Peggy, and partner Michael Burns. Rice was familiar with start-up companies, and this new venture was essentially a sideline to pursue close to home. After earning an undergraduate degree from Williams College and a master of business administration from the University of Virginia's Darden School, Peter Rice used his passion for the outdoors to found Blue Ridge Mountain Sports, an outdoor apparel and equipment retailer, and to cofound Phoenix Kayaks, maker of kayaks and accessories.

The original Plow & Hearth store, established in Madison, Virginia, on Route 29 in the foothills of the Blue Ridge Mountains near Shenandoah National Park, billed itself as Essentials for Country Living. At the time, fuel prices were high and interest was growing in a lifestyle that combined alternative energy with self-reliance. The store both served consumers who embraced this philosophy and embodied the principles itself. The earth-bermed, passive-solar building relied on a single wood stove for heating. The store offered such products as wood stoves, food preparation and preservation equipment, country kitchen items, bulk seeds, gardening tools, bird-watching gear, and a library of books detailing the back-to-basics lifestyle.

After the store proved successful, Rice decided to use a spare outbuilding, a former granary at his farm, to launch a companion mail-order business. In the fall of 1981 the first *Plow & Hearth* catalogs, 100,000 copies in all, were mailed across the country, featuring primarily items carried by the store. Peggy Rice and her sister, Marty, filled the orders in the old granary. The catalog was hardly an overnight success, the mailing lists generating a low response rate and low average orders, but the $228,000 in sales it generated was enough to prompt the partners to continue the operation and move fulfillment to the back of the store.

The timing for the launch of a catalog business proved ideal, however, as catalogs of all sorts prospered in the 1980s. Using different mailing lists in 1983, Plow & Hearth enjoyed much better success, and a year later the company mailed catalogs to 250,000 names. The acceleration of Plow & Hearth's catalog sales prompted a move out of the store in 1983, and the catalog operation was relocated to downtown Madison in the former Farmers' Cooperative building, where a computerized operation was established. The catalog also began to expand its range of product offerings, as revealed by the change in tagline from "essentials for country living" to "products for country living."

While the catalog business grew at a steady rate, a second Plow & Hearth store was opened in Ivy, Virginia, in 1984, and the following year the original store was closed. The catalog quickly became Plow & Hearth's primary business, the success of which launched the young company onto *Inc.* magazine's list of the 500 fastest-growing private companies in the United States, at number 301 with a five-year growth

rate of 723 percent. To keep pace with demand, the catalog operations were moved once again, taking over an 80,000-square-foot renovated textile mill in nearby Orange County in 1989 that also served as corporate headquarters.

NEW DISTRIBUTION CENTER OPENS

Strong growth continued in the 1990s. The Ivy store, in search of even more traffic, was moved to the new Barracks Road Shopping Center in Charlottesville, Virginia, in 1990. By this time Plow & Hearth was mailing nine million catalogs each year. Like other catalog operations the company had to contend with regular postal rate increases. Another increase in 1990 prompted Rice to hire a consultant to improve the order-filling process and cut costs. Despite rising shipping costs and a downturn in the economy, Plow & Hearth catalog sales continued to climb, and the company looked to expand further through the acquisition of other catalogs. *Green River Tools,* a special tool catalog, proved to be a profitable addition, but less successful was the *Kemp George* gift catalog. Nevertheless, the company once again outgrew its facilities. In 1993 land was purchased on Route 230 in Madison and a year later a 120,000-square-foot distribution center and headquarters facility opened there.

While the new facility was under construction, Plow & Hearth looked for a way to increase its response rate and profitability. The company had relied on the recency, frequency, and monetary (RFM) method of organizing its mailing list database, which pigeonholed customers according to the date of their most recent purchase, frequency of purchases, and the amount they spent on average. It was hardly the most effective way to focus mailing lists, but Plow & Hearth could not afford the statistical models that larger competitors commissioned to predict consumer spending. By chance, Plow & Hearth was given the opportunity to serve as a beta subject for a new artificial intelligence system in development by Advanced Software Applications. As a result Plow & Hearth was able to take advantage of neural networking software at a reasonable cost ($20,000), which not only took into account RFM data but also such variables as age, gender, and product affinity to create a scoring model that allowed the company to more accurately rank its customers from most likely to least likely to buy.

Having the ability to determine the people to whom it was worth the expense of mailing a catalog became even more crucial in 1995. Not only did Plow & Hearth face another postal increase, but paper prices were increasing rapidly as well. Another significant

KEY DATES

1980: Plow & Hearth established as country store.
1981: First *Plow & Hearth* catalog printed and mailed.
1990: Plow & Hearth store opens in Charlottesville, Virginia, shopping center.
1994: New 120,000-square-foot distribution facility and headquarters opens.
1998: Plow & Hearth acquired by 1-800-FLOWERS.COM, Inc.
2001: *HearthSong* and *Magic Cabin* catalogs acquired.
2002: *Problem Solvers* catalog launched.
2004: Company begins opening new retail stores.
2006: Distribution center opens in Reno, Nevada.

change in the mid-1990s was the expansion of the types of products Plow & Hearth carried. Footwear was added, but only brands that appealed to core customers were offered, such as Birkenstock, Dansko, and Ugg. Later the catalog began carrying apparel and food items as well, all of the new categories helping to drive growth in holiday sales. By 1998 Plow & Hearth was generating about $42 million in annual sales.

COMPANY SOLD

Many of Plow & Hearth's customers urged the retailer to launch a web site, but the company, lacking the necessary resources, was hesitant to take on this additional burden. In order to maintain its growth, in fact, Plow & Hearth was in need of a larger partner. This was found in 1998 in Westbury, New York-based 1-800-FLOWERS, Inc., which in April of that year acquired an 80 percent stake in the business. Originally a Dallas business, 1-800-FLOWERS was a struggling nationwide florist marketing service losing about $400,000 a month that began to turn around in 1987 when it was acquired by James McCann, who had built up a small chain of flower shops under the Flora Plenty name. McCann made 1-800-FLOWERS into a profitable, technology-savvy operation that achieved $100 million in annual revenues by 1993. A year earlier it established an online presence, well before the emergence of web browsers, setting up a store site on the CompuService Electronic Mall.

While excelling in telemarketing and Internet sales, 1-800-FLOWERS fell short in its limited catalog effort. The complementary strengths and needs of Plow &

Hearth and 1-800-FLOWERS thus made them an ideal fit. Moreover, many of Plow & Hearth's 32 shareholders, including Peter and Peggy Rice, were interested in liquidity. They had considered both a public offering of stock and a complete sale of the company, but in the end opted to sell a major portion to 1-800-FLOWERS, whose stock was publicly traded, a deal concluded after five months of negotiations.

Peter Rice continued to run Plow & Hearth, but he and his staff also worked with 1-800-FLOWERS to help grow its other catalog operations. In the meantime, the new parent company helped Plow & Hearth to launch its first e-commerce web site in 1998, and financed a 60,000-square-foot addition to the Madison distribution center, which opened later in the year. The two companies also took advantage of the overlap in their customer databases, exchanging their lists and creating cross-promotions. The customer names were especially helpful to Plow & Hearth, which had about 400,000 buyers over the course of a year, compared to four times that number doing business with 1-800-FLOWERS. Thus, Plow & Hearth received a large new pool of potential customers to which its sophisticated customer segmentation model could be applied.

Plow & Hearth soon launched another catalog to take advantage of its expanded mailing list and modeling. In 1999 it introduced *Plow & Hearth Country Home,* which focused on home furnishings and decorative accents. The company mailed more than three million catalogs in the first year, generating over $4 million in sales. To keep pace with the company's growing business, another 115,000 square feet were added to the Madison fulfillment center as the decade came to a close. The facility then approached 300,000 square feet.

CATALOGS ADDED AT START OF 21ST CENTURY

At the start of the new century the enlarged fulfillment center was reengineered to incorporate the latest materials handling systems to make the order fulfillment process both faster and more accurate. To better serve customers in the Midwest and western states, Plow & Hearth opened a second distribution center in Vandalia, Ohio, in 2001. The extra capacity would also prove useful with the acquisition of two children's catalogs in 2001, *HearthSong* and *Magic Cabin.* Plow & Hearth introduced another catalog in 2002, *Plow & Hearth Problem Solvers,* offering a wide variety of home organization products.

Plow & Hearth made a return to its roots in 2004. The company had been running a pair of retail stores, located in Charlottesville and Madison, Virginia, as well as a Madison outlet store, but the stores accounted only for less than 4 percent of total sales. Because it was difficult to continue to grow catalog circulation, retail expansion was seen as a key to ongoing growth. A decade had passed since the last store opening, and then in October 2004 Plow & Hearth opened a store in the Promenade Shops near Richmond, Virginia's, Short Pump Town Center. A month later another store opened its doors in Fairfax, Virginia. Rather than simply mirror what the *Plow & Hearth* catalog had to offer, the stores offered a large selection of merchandise that was only available at those locations. In 2006 the first stores outside of Virginia opened and soon there were Plow & Hearth stores in Raleigh, North Carolina, and in Hagerstown, Hunt Valley, and Rockville, Maryland.

As Plow & Hearth celebrated its 25th anniversary in 2005, the company experienced changes on two fronts. It acquired another catalog, *Wind & Weather,* featuring weather-related instruments and gifts. In October this operations was moved to Madison. At the close of 2005 Peter Rice retired from the business after 25 years at the helm. He left behind a well-established business that continued to grow after his departure. In 2006 the Problem Solvers web site was launched, and in that same year a third distribution center opened in Reno, Nevada, to better serve West Coast customers. Given its extended record of success, there was every reason to expect Plow & Hearth to remain a valuable part of 1-800-FLOWERS for many years to come, and

in all likelihood the company's branded retail stores would spread throughout and beyond the Mid-Atlantic region.

Ed Dinger

PRINCIPAL OPERATING UNITS

HearthSong; Magic Cabin; Plow & Hearth; Problem Solvers; Wind & Weather.

PRINCIPAL COMPETITORS

The Country House; Reiman Publications; The Sharper Image.

FURTHER READING

Chevan, Parry, "Databases That Learn to Be Smarter," *Catalog Age,* January 1995, p. 45.

Gilligan, Gregory J., "Plow & Hearth Turns Attention to Stores," *Richmond-Times Dispatch,* November 1, 2004, p. D3.

Miller, Paul, "Flowering Hearth," *Catalog Age,* May 1998.

Schafer, Sarah, "Software That Thinks," *Inc.,* December 1996, p. 109.

Tode, Chantal, "Plow & Hearth Reaps Its Rewards," *DMNews,* March 24, 2006.

Willis, Gerri, "Catalog Retailers Deliver the Goods," *Norfolk Virginian-Pilot,* April 9, 1990, p. 14.

Radiant Systems Inc.

3925 Brookside Parkway
Alpharetta, Georgia 30022
U.S.A.
Telephone: (770) 576-6000
Fax: (770) 754-7790
Web site: http://www.radiantsystems.com

Public Company
Incorporated: 1985 as Softsense Computer Products Inc.
Employees: 1,354
Sales: $301.6 million (2008)
Stock Exchanges: NASDAQ
Ticker Symbol: RADS
NAICS: 541512 Computer Systems Design Services

■ ■ ■

Headquartered in Alpharetta, Georgia, Radiant Systems Inc. develops and markets software and hardware products used by the retail and hospitality industries. Specifically, the company offers systems focused on site management, back-office management, and point-of-sale. Radiant Systems' products are used to administer electronic gift card systems, customer loyalty programs, self-service kiosks, e-commerce initiatives, and more. By the later years of the first decade of the 2000s, the company's technology had been installed at more than 100,000 locations in approximately 100 countries.

FORMATIVE YEARS

Radiant Systems traces its origins to August 1, 1985, when Erez and Alon Goren formed Softsense Computer

Products Inc. in New York. As teenagers, the Israeli brothers had initially saved money to buy new dirt bikes. However, they purchased an Atari 800 computer system instead and began developing video games.

In 1983, at the age of 17, Alon was featured in a *New York Times* article that described Microvations Inc., a business venture he had established with Evan Grossman, a classmate at Long Island's Great Neck South High School. By the time the article appeared the enterprise had sold some 500 games to a distributor. Providing employment for approximately 30 students, who helped develop the games, Microvations generated between $400 and $2,000 for each game that it developed, allowing its high school-aged partners to earn salaries in the neighborhood of $20,000 to $30,000.

This early success ultimately led the Gorens to establish another enterprise, which focused on developing inventory and transaction management software for video rental stores. In time, the technology was adopted by gas stations, convenience stores, and oil change businesses.

Recalling the company's humble beginnings in the April 26, 2000, issue of the *Atlanta Journal and Constitution,* Erez Goren remarked: "We were on a starvation diet. For the first five years we took home less than $10,000 a year each. Then we took $30,000. We took the minimum and worked the maximum. No instant millionaires here."

Softsense grew at a measured pace during its first decade of operations. The company then reincorporated in Georgia on October 27, 1995, and began growing at a faster pace. Liberty Systems International Inc. was acquired in mid-1996. Following that deal, Softsense changed its name to Radiant Systems Inc. on November 13, and rounded out the year by acquiring full ownership in a business called PrysmTech, which served the entertainment market.

By this time Radiant Systems' solutions were used at approximately 2,500 locations worldwide. The company moved forward with Softsense and PrysmTech as its main operating divisions. In addition to its Georgia headquarters, Radiant Systems also had operations located in Dallas, Texas; Denver, Colorado; Malaysia; and London.

EARLY PROGRESS

Radiant Systems had a very busy year in 1997. In February the company offered 2.9 million shares of its common stock via an initial public offering. By this time Radiant Systems was marketing a variety of retail automation solutions to the convenience store market. These included point-of-sale systems, back-office management systems, and consumer-activated ordering systems. Along with the technology, the company provided customers with related planning, design, and implementation services. Radiant Systems claimed that its solutions could be installed quickly, and required minimal staff training.

During the late 1990s Radiant Systems had plans to enter the quick-service restaurant (QSR) market. This was realized in April 1997, when the company announced an alliance with the Atlanta-based restaurant chain Chick-fil-A, which agreed to evaluate its new Radiant QSR technology as part of a pilot program. The following month, Radiant Systems was honored by Microsoft Corp. with two Retail Application Development Awards. Specifically, among more than 100 applicants, the company was ranked first in both the hospitality and convenience store categories.

It also was in May that Radiant Systems merged with Pleasanton, California-based Restaurant Management and Control Systems (ReMACS), which served leading restaurants such as Ruby Tuesday's, Applebee's,

Arby's, Taco Bell, KFC, Burger King, Boston Market, Longhorn Steaks, and Dunkin' Donuts. Following the $18.5 million deal, the company combined its QSR operations with those of ReMACS, a provider of back-office and corporate management systems that already had technology in place at approximately 12,000 locations.

One final development that month occurred when Radiant Systems acquired Dallas-based Twenty/20 Visual Systems, which provided full-service restaurants with table management systems and point-of-sale systems, for $3.7 million.

ACQUISITIONS, EXPANSIONS, AND AWARDS

Radiant Systems rounded out 1997 by acquiring both Equilease Financial Services Inc. and Hillsboro, Oregon-based RapidFire Software Inc. in October, followed by Atlanta, Georgia-based Logic Shop Inc. in November. The latter deal allowed the company to begin providing management software to companies within the automotive service center sector. Also in November Radiant Systems announced plans to build a new headquarters campus in Alpharetta, beginning with an 110,000-square-foot facility. By this time the company employed 550 workers and continued to be led by the Goren brothers.

Radiant Systems began 1998 with recognition from *Forbes ASAP,* which included the company on its Dynamic 100 list of technology companies, ranking it 13th in the software category. In April the company opened an office in Prague, Czech Republic. That October, Radiant Systems announced that it had developed a point-of-sale lottery ticket dispensing systems in partnership with Interlott Technologies Inc. Erez Goren served as co-chairman and CEO of Radiant Systems, while Eric Hinkle fulfilled the role of president and chief operating officer.

PRODUCT EXPANSION AND GROWTH

Several key developments occurred at Radiant Systems in 1999. As part of its AOL Anywhere initiative, America Online Inc. purchased $10 million of Radiant Systems stock and invested $25 million in the company, which agreed to put AOL technology on its point-of-sale terminals, thus allowing customers at gas stations, convenience stores, and restaurants to access their e-mail remotely. Radiant Systems also agreed to work with AOL subsidiary MovieFone Inc. to develop new point-of-sales systems.

KEY DATES

1985: Erez and Alon Goren establish Softsense
Computer Products Inc.

1995: The company reincorporates in Georgia.

1996: Softsense changes its name to Radiant
Systems Inc.

1997: Radiant Systems goes public, and plans for a
new headquarters campus in Alpharetta,
Georgia, are announced.

2002: John Heyman is named CEO.

2004: Radiant Systems splits off BlueCube Software,
its Enterprise Software Systems business, to
Erez Goren, and begins focusing exclusively
on the point-of-sale market.

2006: Company ranks as one of the state's fastest-
growing technology firms.

2009: A new office is established in Shanghai,
China.

In addition, BP Amoco Corp. agreed to buy next-generation gas pumps from Fort Wayne, Indiana-based Tokheim Corp. that included Radiant Systems' technology. Specifically, the Internet-connected pumps provided customers with traffic and weather information and also communicated sales volume and service-related issues back to BP.

Radiant Systems capped off 1999 on a high note. That year the value of its stock had increased about 500 percent. In order to support the company's growth, it made plans to expand operations by occupying two additional facilities in Alpharetta. Radiant Systems ended the decade with revenues of $130 million.

ENTERING THE 21ST CENTURY

By the dawn of the new millennium Radiant Systems technology was in place at approximately 40,000 retail locations worldwide. Since its inception the company had been profitable and managed to grow without venture capital funding. The company's workforce included 945 people. Erez Goren served as co-chairman and CEO, while Alon Goren fulfilled the role of co-chairman and chief technology officer. Like many other technology companies at this time, Radiant Systems offered unique perks to employees, including an onsite café with free food and drinks, as well as a company rock band.

Radiant Systems continue to grow via acquisitions during the 21st century. Midway through 2000

TimeCorp was acquired in a deal valued at approximately $6.4 million. In early 2001 the company acquired the Australia-based transaction-processing company Breeze Software Pty Ltd. for $2.8 million. In July of that year, Radiant Systems parted with $2.9 million to acquire assets from HotelTools Inc.

In January 2002 John Heyman was named as Radiant Systems' CEO. Late that year the company received a $496,300 contract to provide Middlesex County, New Jersey, with a new jail management computer system. That same month Radiant Systems expanded its intellectual property base when it shelled out $400,000 in cash to acquire software source code from ICON Software Ltd. Growth continued in 2003 as sales reached $93.9 million.

POINT-OF-SALE FOCUS: 2004

In January 2004 Radiant Systems split off BlueCube Software, which had served as its Enterprise Software Systems business, to Erez Goren, who no longer held a leadership position at the company. The deal allowed Radiant Systems to focus exclusively on the point-of-sale market, and to rid itself of a business unit that had lost money for several years.

Around the same time the company acquired Aloha Technologies Inc. in a $48.9 million deal, followed by the assets of E-Needs Inc. for about $700,000. Radiant Systems ended the year with revenues of $134.9 million, a 43.6 percent increase from 2003.

Progress continued during the middle years of the first decade of the 2000s. In early 2005 the company's Radiant Point-of-Sale technology was certified for use on ConocoPhillips' credit card network, allowing it to be used at gas stations operating under the Phillips, Conoco, and 76 brand names.

GROWTH THROUGH ACQUISITION

A major deal unfolded in October 2005 when Radiant Systems acquired MenuLink Computer Solutions Inc., the largest supplier of back-office software for the hospitality industry, in a deal worth $12.8 million. MenuLink's technology already had been installed in more than 280 chains and 9,000 locations.

In early 2006 Radiant Systems parted with about $19.5 million in cash to acquire the assets of Synchronics Inc. In October Deloitte & Touche LLP added the company to its Georgia Technology Fast 50 list, ranking it as one of the state's fastest-growing technology firms. By this time Radiant Systems employed about 1,000 people throughout the world, and had offices in the

United States, Asia, Australia, and Europe. Its technology was used in more than 100 countries, at approximately 6,000 sites.

By 2007 Radiant Systems was serving clients such as Burger King, Morton's Restaurant Group, and Chipotle Mexican Grill. In November of that year the company announced that it was renewing its stock repurchase program. Specifically, the company planned to buy back up to one million shares of its common stock by November 2009. Radiant Systems rounded out the year with sales of $253.2 million, a 14 percent increase from 2006.

SUCCEEDING IN DIFFICULT TIMES

Radiant Systems kicked off 2008 with a major deal. In January, the company's RADS Australia Holdings Pty Ltd. subsidiary acquired Quest Retail Technology Pty Ltd. in a cash deal worth $54 million. The acquisition of Quest Retail Technology allowed Radiant Systems to begin serving arenas, stadiums, parks, and related entertainment venues with point-of-sale technology.

Despite worsening economic conditions during the later years of the first decade of the 2000s, Radiant Systems continued to grow at a healthy pace. In April 2008 the company announced that Batteries Plus, the nation's largest battery retail chain, had chosen to use its technology at its 300 retail locations. More growth occurred in July, at which time the company forged a deal with the convenience store chain Wawa Inc. to install point-of-sale terminals at more than 570 locations throughout Delaware, New Jersey, Maryland, Virginia, and Pennsylvania.

Around the same time the company's Radiant Systems GmbH subsidiary parted with $30.85 million to acquire Salzburg, Austria-based Orderman GmbH, which ranked as the largest manufacturer of wireless handheld ordering and payment devices for the hospitality industry. At the time of the deal the company had approximately 50,000 handheld devices in place at some 20,000 restaurants in 45 countries around the globe. In December 2008 Burger King franchisee Goldco LLC announced that it had completed the installation of Radiant Systems' point-of-sale technology at more than 60 of its restaurants.

Radiant Systems began 2009 with a focus on international expansion. In February the company formed a wholly owned foreign entity in China and established a new office in Shanghai. Although its office was new, the company had been doing business in China for several years. Moving forward, plans were in place to deploy Radiant Systems' point-of-sale technol-

ogy at roughly 200 Chinese restaurants.

After establishing its new office, Radiant Systems announced a major deal with the Minor Food Group, one of the largest hospitality and leisure companies in the Asia-Pacific region, which called for the installation of its technology in approximately 600 restaurants over the course of three years. The Minor Food Group operated leading restaurants such as The Pizza Co., Sizzler, The Coffee Club, Dairy Queen, and Swensen's.

Based on its past performance, Radiant Systems' prospects for continued success during the 21st century's second decade seemed promising.

Paul R. Greenland

PRINCIPAL SUBSIDIARIES

Estorelink.Com Inc.; Quest POS Ltd.; Quest Retail Technology Inc.; Quest Retail Technology Pty Ltd.; Radiant Enterprise Software LLC; Radiant Hospitality Systems Ltd.; Radiant Systems Asia-Pacific Pty Ltd.; Radiant Systems Central Europe Inc.; Radiant Systems International 2 S.e.n.c.; Radiant Systems International S.e.n.c.; Radiant Systems Retail Solutions Pte Ltd.; Radiant Systems Retail Solutions S.L.; Radiant Systems s.r.o.; Radiant Systems UK Ltd.; Radiant Systems, International Inc.; RADS Australia Holdings Pty Ltd.; RADS Holding Corporation; RADS International S.a.r. l.; RetailEnterprise LLC.

PRINCIPAL COMPETITORS

MICROS Systems Inc.; NCR Corporation; VeriFone Holdings Inc.

FURTHER READING

"Radiant Systems Expands Global Reach with Opening of New Office in Shanghai; Increasing Demand for End-to-End Technology Solutions Drives Growth Plans in Asia Pacific Region," *Business Wire*, February 18, 2009.

"Radiant Systems, Inc., Announces Initial Public Offering of 2,900,000 Shares of Common Stock," *PR Newswire*, February 13, 1997.

"Radiant Systems, Inc., Recognized As a Top 100 Dynamic Company by Forbes ASAP Magazine," *Business Wire*, February 13, 1998.

"Radiant Systems to Buy Quest Retail for $54 Million in Cash, Deal to Close in 1st Quarter," *Associated Press*, December 11, 2007.

Watkins, Steve, "Alpharetta, Georgia; Manufacturer of Restaurant Computer Gear Gobbles Up a Winner," *Investor's Business Daily*, February 23, 2006.

Wells, Susan, "Radiant Managing to Succeed; Software Company Founders Help Businesses Run More Efficiently," *Atlanta Journal and Constitution,* April 26, 2000.

Wilbert, Tony, "Radiant Systems Grows in Alpharetta; Tech Firm to Lease Two More Buildings," *Atlanta Journal and Constitution,* December 31, 1999.

Rautakirja Oy

———————————————————— ■ ————————————————————

PO Box 1, Koivuvaarankuja 2
Vantaa, FIN-01641
Finland
Telephone: (358 09) 85 2 81
Fax: (358 09) 85 28 511
Web site: http://www.rautakirja.fi

Wholly Owned Subsidiary of Sanoma Corporation
Incorporated: 1910 as Rautatiekirjakauppa Osakeyhtiï
Employees: 8,395
Sales: EUR 866.6 million ($1.12 billion) (2008 est.)
NAICS: 451212 News Dealers and Newsstands; 722110
     Full-Service Restaurants

■ ■ ■

Rautakirja Oy is a Finland-based trade and services company focused on four primary sectors: Kiosks; Press Distribution; Bookstores; and Cinemas. Rautakirja's Kiosk division operates nearly 1,800 newsstand kiosk shops in Finland, Estonia, Latvia, Lithuania, Russia, and Romania. All of the company's 712 Finnish stores, as well as its 200 Estonian, 112 Russian, and 30 Romanian shops operate under the R-Kiosk name. Other kiosk brands are Narvesen and Preses Apvieniba in Latvia, and Spaudos Vilniaus in Lithuania. The company's Press Distribution division holds leading positions in all of these markets, as well as in the Netherlands, serving more than 24,000 retailers.

Rautakirja's Bookstores division operates the leading bookstore chain in Finland, Suomalainen Kirjakauppa, with 62 stores across Finland, as well as an online

bookstore, a direct-mail operation, and nine Apollo Raamatud stores in Estonia. Rautakirja's Entertainment division focuses primarily on movie theater operations, with 16 Finnkino multiplex cinemas in Finland, and a total of nine Forum cinemas in Estonia, Latvia, and Lithuania. Rautakirja is a fully owned subsidiary of Finnish publishing giant Sanoma, serving as the parent company of the Sanoma Trade division. In 2008, the company's revenues neared EUR 866.6 million ($1.12 billion). Rautakirja is led by President and CEO Timo Maenty and Chairman Hannu Syrjaenen.

ORIGINS

In 1910, a group of Finnish publishing companies, including the future members of the Sanoma Corporation, joined together to form a distribution joint venture based on the retail format pioneered by WH Smith in the United Kingdom. The new company was called Rautatiekirjakauppa Osakeyhtiö, Finnish for "Railway Bookstore Ltd." The company opened its first 30 kiosks at the beginning of 1911, and another six through the rest of the year. The company also debuted an onboard distribution service, hiring a team of boys to sell newspapers on the trains themselves.

Rautatiekirjajauppa expanded its operations in the 1920s, adding a wholesale press distribution service in 1922, and launching subscription sales from its growing ranks of kiosks. These topped 100 locations at the beginning of the decade, and by the end of the 1920s had reached 140 in number. Another extension of the group's operations came in 1924, when the company bought its first bookstore, Suomalainen Kirjakauppa, in downtown Helsinki.

In the 1930s, the company expanded its kiosk business beyond the country's railway stations and terminals. The company was also increasingly adding new products to its operations, such as candy and tobacco products, film, and, beginning in 1940, lottery tickets. By the middle of that decade, the group's newspaper distribution operations had grown to more than 50 million copies per year. Rautatiekirjakauppa's kiosk business continued to grow strongly in the postwar period, and by the beginning of the 1970s had topped 500 locations. By then, the company's kiosk network had achieved national recognition under the R-Kiosk brand, first introduced in 1958.

The company launched the expansion of its bookstore operations in the mid-1960s. The company added a second Suomalainen Kirjakauppa bookstore in 1965, and then began building that company into a nationally operating chain. By the end of the century, Suomalainen Kirjakauppa had grown into Finland's largest bookstore operator.

Rautatiekirjakauppa also began to explore new press distribution venues. Through the 1960s, the company developed a new service supplying newspaper and magazine stands to supermarkets and other retailers. By the end of that decade, Rautatiekirjakauppa counted more than 7,500 customers. In 1969, the company created a new format, Lehtipiste, for its in-store kiosks.

Rautatiekirjakauppa also began looking beyond the publishing world, and in 1972 acquired majority control of Kauppa Hallenberg Oy, one of Finland's major wholesale groups. That purchase led the company to build a new headquarters, combining its press distribution and wholesale operations into a single facility in 1974. In that year the company changed its name to Rautakirja Oy, in order to reflect its more diversified operations. In 1976, the company expanded its

wholesale operations with the opening of a Merkur-branded Cash & Carry store in Vantaa.

PUBLIC OFFERING

Rautakirja reorganized its growing bookstore business into a dedicated subsidiary in 1979. That company then took over Rautakirja's newspaper and magazine subscription business. New growth for the bookstore chain came in 1987, when WYSOY sold its 13-store Yliopistokirjakauppa chain to Suomalainen Kirjakauppa.

The R-Kiosk chain had also been growing strongly, nearing 700 stores by the mid-1970s, and then reaching 800 stores by 1985. Part of this group came from the incorporation of video rental services into the R-Kiosk shops, starting in 1982. Rautakirja recognized the potential of this sector and in 1985 acquired the Kotikatsomo video rental chain. The company also expanded its wholesale operations that year with three acquisitions.

Another acquisition, of Oy Paletti AB in 1987, added the wholesale distribution of cards, games, and related items. By this time, Rautakirja had also ventured into the operation of restaurants and service stations, through its Eurostrada subsidiary. That company developed a small chain of service stations, which included their own café-style restaurants, along Finland's roadsides. At the same time, Eurostrada operated a number of other restaurant concessions, including a restaurant at Helsinki International Airport.

By the late 1980s, Rautakirja had become a joint-venture partnership between the Sanoma and WYSOY companies. Rautakirja then prepared to launch a new diversification effort. Toward this end, Sanoma and WYSOY decided to take Rautakirja public, listing its shares on the Helsinki Stock Exchange in 1988. While Sanoma's Erkko family then became Rautakirja's dominant shareholder, the public offering provided the company with the capital backing for its next expansion phase.

BECOMING PART OF SANOMAWYSOY

Rautakirja's new strategy got off to a strong start in 1989, when the company acquired 7.6 percent of Finnish cinema operator Finnkino. The company soon turned this foothold into a full-scale takeover, and by 1994 Rautakirja had gained 100 percent of Finnkino's shares. Next, Rautakirja targeted a move into the retail stationery and gifts sector. For this, the company bought Tukkutiimi Oy and its Swedish subsidiary Tukkutiimi AB, giving the company control of the 98-strong Tii-

KEY DATES

1910: Rautatiekirjakauppa Osakeyhtiö is formed to operate newsstands in Finland's railway stations.

1924: The company buys its first bookstore, Suomalainen Kirjakauppa, in downtown Helsinki.

1958: Rautatiekirjakauppa Osakeyhtiö rebrands its kiosks as R-Kiosks.

1965: Rautatiekirjakauppa Osakeyhtiö acquires second Suomalainen Kirjakauppa bookstore in Helsinki.

1969: The company creates a new format, Lehtipiste, for its in-store kiosks.

1974: The company changes its name to Rautakirja Oy.

1985: The company acquires the Kotikatsomo video rental chain.

1988: Rautakirja Oy lists on the Helsinki Stock Exchange.

1993: The company makes its first international expansion, into Estonia.

1998: Rautakirja becomes a subsidiary of SanomaWYSOY.

2003: SanomaWYSOY acquires full control of Rautakirja.

2008: SanomaWYSOY changes its name to Sanoma Corporation and rebrands its operations; Rautakirja becomes the parent company of the Sanoma Trade division.

mari retail chain. The vast majority of Tiimari shops operated in Finland; by the early 1990s, however, Tukkutiimi had opened five Tiimari stores in Sweden.

Rautakirja revisited its diversification strategy during the 1990s. The company sold its Paletti wholesale cards and games business in 1993. In that year also the company sold off much of the Eurostrada restaurant operations in order to refocus that business on its eight service stations including the latest station opened on the Finnish-Russian border in 1995. The company also exited the wholesale market, selling its Merkur Cash & Carry store at the beginning of 1996.

Rautakirja returned to the restaurant sector later in the decade, buying through Eurostrada, the ten-strong chain of Pizza Hut restaurants in Finland in 1998. However, by 2006 the company had sold the Pizza Hut operation as well. Meanwhile, in 1998, Rautakirja sold off the Tiimari retail cards and gifts in a management buyout backed by CapMan Capital Management Oy.

That year also marked the start of a new era for Rautakirja, as its parent companies, Sanoma and WYSOY, reached an agreement to merge their operations, together with those of Helsinki Media Company (HMC), as well as the shareholdings in Sanoma and HMC of a holding company, Devarda. The deal created SanomaWYSOY, the largest media group in Finland and the second largest in the Scandinavian region. The combination of Sanoma's and WYSOY's stakes in Rautakirja gave SanomaWYSOY more than 54 percent of the company.

ESTONIAN EXPANSION

As part of one of Europe's leading publishing and media empires, Rautakirja then found itself in a position to turn to the international market for its future growth. The company had begun this effort earlier in the decade, entering Estonia in 1993 with the opening of its first R-Kiosks in Tallinn. The company's Finnkino subsidiary, which had built up a network of 31 theaters in nine cities in Finland, as well as a chain of 17 Kotikatsomo video rental stores, also targeted international growth. By the mid-1990s, Finnkino operated three cinemas in Latvia, through subsidiary Baltic Cinema SIA.

Rautakirja's interests turned to Latvia at the end of the decade. In 1999, the company teamed up with Narvesen ASA, the leading kiosk operator in Norway, to create Narvesen Baltijas Sia, a company formed to develop kiosk, café, and retail cosmetics operations in Latvia. Rautakirja also bought a 10 percent stake in Narvesen, with the announced goal of acquiring full control of its Norwegian counterpart.

The joint venture got off to a strong start, buying 85 percent of Preses Apvieniba, a company with 450 kiosks throughout Latvia. However, Rautakirja's relationship with Narvesen soured after the latter company merged to form Reitan Narvesen, ending Rautakirja's own hopes of adding the Norwegian kiosk market to its operations. Nevertheless, Rautakirja maintained its stake in Narvesen Baltijas Sia, raising its share to 50 percent in 2001.

Rautakirja's operations elsewhere continued to grow strongly. The company solidified its presence in Estonia, buying two of that country's largest kiosk chains and raising its total number of kiosks there to 200. The company then formed AS Lehepunkt, a press distribution joint venture with Estonia's newspaper leader Ekspress Grupp. By the end of 1999, Rautakirja had also expanded into the Estonian cinema market, launching construction of the country's first multiplex cinema, in Tallinn. Other Estonian investments included a 90 percent stake in Megapanus, a sports betting business, and full control of film distributor and cinema group MPDE.

INTERNATIONAL OPERATIONS IN THE 21ST CENTURY

The company's bookstore business completed its own expansion drive in the years that followed. In 1999, that subsidiary acquired control of rival Pohjalainen Kirjakauppa from the Info retail group, and then acquired a major stake in another bookstore operator, Kirjavölitys Oy. After launching its e-commerce site in 2002, Suomalainen made its own entry into Estonia, acquiring 60 percent of bookseller Astro Raamatud. The company then acquired the remaining 40 percent in 2003.

In 2003, SanomaWYSOY bought out Rautakirja's minority shareholders, and Rautakirja became a fully controlled subsidiary of the Finnish media giant. The purchase enabled Rautakirja to step up its international expansion objectives. In 2004, the company acquired majority stakes in Romania's Hiparion Distribution and Lithuania's UAB Impress Teva, allowing the company to position itself in the press distribution market in both countries.

The next year, 2005, the company bought kiosk operator Lietuvos Spauda, which distributed to more than 540 kiosks in Lithuania. Rautakirja also made its Russian debut in 2005, acquiring Moscow-based press distributor TK Pressexpo. By 2007, the company had also added kiosk operations there, through its 70 percent control of the OOO R-Kiosk joint venture. The company then bought up Press Point International, a press distributor, and HDS CIS, a kiosk operator, further raising the company's profile in Russia.

The company also added a new foreign market that year, buying a 65 percent stake in the Aldipress press distribution group in the Netherlands, formerly part of Sanoma Magazines International. Less successful was the group's attempt to enter the Czech market, through a joint venture with France's Hachette formed in 2004. Rautakirja exited that business in 2005. By then, Rautakirja had also sold its Eurostrada operations to Neste Oy. The company had also made a small entry into Germany, acquiring D+J Arena in Hamburg, but sold that business in 2007.

SanomaWYSOY changed its name to Sanoma Corporation in 2008, launching a restructuring of its organization. As a result, the company rebranded most of its operations under the Sanoma brand, as well as creating the new Sanoma Trade division. Rautakirja

retained its name, becoming the parent company of the Sanoma Trade division. Backed by its powerful parent, Rautakirja was positioned to continue to seek new expansion opportunities in the next decade.

M. L. Cohen

PRINCIPAL SUBSIDIARIES

Aldipress BV (Netherlands); Apollo Raamatud AS (Viro); Finnkino Oy; Forum Cinemas AS (Estonia); Forum Cinemas Home Entertainment AS (Estonia, Latvia, Lithuania); Hiparion Distribution S.A. (Romania); Jokerit HC Oy; Kirjavälitys Oy; Lehepunkt AS (Estonia); Lehtipiste; OOO Press Point International (Russia); OOO R-Kiosk (Russia); OOO TK Pressexpo (Russia); Printcenter Oy; R-Kiosk Eesti AS (Estonia); R-Kiosk Romania S.A. (Romania); R-Kiosks; SIA Forum Cinemas (Latvia); SIA Narvesen Baltija (Latvia); SIA Preses Serviss (Latvia); Suomalainen Kirjakauppa Oy; Suomalainen.com Oy; UAB Forum Cinemas (Lithuania); UAB Impress Teva (Lithuania); UAB Lietuvos Spaudos; Vilniaus Agentura (Lithuania).

PRINCIPAL OPERATING UNITS

Bookstores; Corporate Finance and Administration; Entertainment; Kiosk Operations; Press Distribution.

PRINCIPAL COMPETITORS

Reitangruppen A.S.; Kolporter S.A.; Tisak d.d.; Magyar Lapterjeszto Zrt; Reitan Servicehandel Sverige; PSG Prima Service GmbH; UAB Lietuvos spauda; Stilke Buch- und Zeitschriftenhandelsgesellschaft mbH; Axxe Reisegastronomie Gmbh.

FURTHER READING

"Finland's Rautakirja to Sell D+J Arena Hamburg GmbH in Germany," *Nordic Business Report,* October 25, 2007.

"Finnish Rautakirja Pulling Out of Czech Market over Brand Feud," *Helsingin Sanomat International Edition,* November 5, 2005.

Jury, Jennifer, "CapMan Leads MBO of Leading Retailer Tiimari," *European Venture Capital Journal,* May 1, 1998.

"More than 500 ATMs to Be Installed in R-Kiosks Across Finland," *Helsingin Sanomat International Edition,* March 14, 2008.

"Rautakirja Enters Russian Press Distribution Market," *Nordic Business Report,* June 27, 2005.

"Rautakirja Group Divests Pizza Hut Restaurants in Finland to Icelandic Entrepreneurs," *Nordic Business Report,* June 15, 2006.

"Rautakirja Oy Merges into SanomaWYSOY Oyj," *Nordic Business Report,* March 3, 2003.

"Rautakirja's President Erkki Järvinen Takes Up New Responsibilities," *Euroinvestor,* October 24, 2008.

"SanomaWYSOY Corporation Acquires Finnish Printcenter Oy," *Nordic Business Report,* January 5, 2007.

"SanomaWYSOY Corporation Subsidiary to Form Joint Venture in Romania," *Nordic Business Report,* December 20, 2007.

"SanomaWYSOY Subsidiary Expands Its Kiosk Operations to Russia," *Nordic Business Report,* March 15, 2007.

"SanomaWSYOY Unit Eyes Controlling Stake in Polish Peer Ruch," *AFX News Limited,* August 6, 2007.

"SanomaWYSOY's Rautakirja Division Sells Its Restaurant Operations," *Nordic Business Report,* December 23, 2004.

Raymarine plc

Anchorage Park
Robinson Way
Portsmouth, Hampshire PO3 5TD
United Kingdom
Telephone: (44 0 23) 9269 3611
Fax: (44 0 23) 9269 4642
Web site: http://www.raymarine.com

Public Company
Incorporated: 2001
Employees: 539
Sales: $195.3 million (2008)
Stock Exchanges: London
Ticker Symbol: RAY
NAICS: 334511 Search, Detection, Navigation, Guidance, Aeronautical, and Nautical System and Instrument Manufacturing

■ ■ ■

Raymarine plc is a United Kingdom-based manufacturer of consumer marine electronics, such as chart plotters for navigation, fish finders, and devices that combine chart plotters and fish finders. Raymarine is a pioneer in integrating high-definition (HD) digital technology into its fish finders, offering a picture far clearer than devices using analog technology. When combined with chart plotting capabilities, Raymarine units are able to locate fish, or shipwrecks, and then help navigate a vessel to these target points.

Raymarine also offers marine instruments, measuring such factors as wind, speed, depth, and direction; marine radar systems; autopilots; navigation systems; marine weather display systems; radios and hailers; marine cameras; man-overboard pendants and monitoring systems; and marine satellite television systems capable of bringing music and television programming to ships at sea. Raymarine products are available through a dealer network as well as online through dealers and the company's web site. Raymarine also offers repair, warranty, and software and firmware updates and upgrades.

The company's U.S. headquarters is located in Merrimack, New Hampshire, a key operation given that the bulk of the company's sales are derived from the United States, where half of all pleasure boats in the world are purchased. Another office for sales and engineering is maintained in Fort Lauderdale, Florida, while a New South Wales, Australia-based subsidiary serves the Southeast Asia and Australia market.

1922 FOREBEARS

Raymarine grew out of the Recreation Marine Division of Raytheon Company, a major U.S. defense contractor that converted many of the technologies it developed for the military to commercial applications. Raytheon was established in 1922 by civil engineer Laurence Marshall and Harvard University physicist Charles G. Smith, who had invented a noiseless home refrigeration system using compressed gases. Although the two men initially went into business together to develop Smith's refrigeration system, they soon decided instead to latch onto the growing popularity of radio and began manufacturing radio tubes in 1925. The partners had planned to use the American Appliances name for their manufacturing company, but because that name was already claimed they came up with the name Raytheon, Greek for "god of life."

The seeds of a marine business were planted when the company launched its first depth sounder. The company eventually diversified, designing and manufacturing transformers, power equipment, and electronic auto parts. Profits were used to support research and development efforts in microwave communications and industrial electronics. During World War II the company played an important role in the development and manufacture of ship radar systems.

APPLIED ELECTRONICS COMPANY ACQUIRED: 1958

During the post–World War II era, while Raytheon continued to develop radar systems, it also became involved in sonar as well as missile guidance systems. The company sold its radio and television units in the 1950s but continued to pursue consumer appliances, most notably the Radarange microwave oven. In the 1960s the company made a concerted effort to become less dependent on government contracts, diversifying further by introducing a countertop microwave oven under the Amana brand name, a product that would revolutionize the way Americans cooked.

Although Raytheon grew through acquisition, its primary means to achieve diversification was the application of its military technology for civilian use. As a result the Raytheon Marine Products unit developed electronic gear for amateur boaters that emphasized safety, such as radar systems, depth finders, radiotelephones, and autopilots. The products were sold under the Raytheon and Apelco labels, and some were manufactured by Japan Radio Company. The Apelco name had been added when Raytheon acquired San Francisco-based Applied Electronics Company in 1958.

The marine unit took the name Raytheon Marine Company and made its headquarters in Manchester,

New Hampshire, where in 1970 a new plant was opened. Until 1986 the marine operation shared the plant with another Raytheon unit, Switchcraft, a maker of industrial electronic and electromechanical components that also produced electronic components in Gibson electric guitars.

Raytheon Marine added a U.K. operation in 1990, acquiring Nautech Ltd., manufacturer of marine electronics products for recreational sailboats and power boats under the Autohelm name. In addition to autopilots, Nautech, founded in 1974, produced instrumentation, handheld digital compasses, and electronic chart plotters. In 1984 the company had introduced the first autopilot that made use of digital control systems. The British company added $25 million in annual sales to Raytheon Marine, as well as an important manufacturing capability in the United Kingdom. With the backing of Raytheon, the innovative Nautech could grow into a truly international company. In 1991 it introduced the Autohelm NavCenter, an electronic chart plotter.

In the early 1990s, with the end of the Cold War, the United States looked to cut defense spending, a move that prompted Raytheon to focus even more on commercial markets. Engineers who had devoted their time to defense technology were available to Raytheon Marine, resulting in new product developments. In 1992, for example, the company was able to integrate global positioning technology into its navigation, instrument, and autopilot control systems. More money was also made available to grow the recreational marine business through further acquisitions.

In 1995 German company Anschutz was acquired, bringing with it products for big ships, including autopilots, bridge controls, and gyros. A year later Standard Radio of Sweden was acquired, adding medium-frequency and high-frequency communications technology. It was also during this period that Raytheon began to sever its relationship with Japan Radio Co., which came to an end in 1998. A year earlier the Pathfinder Radar system had become the first leisure marine radar to be designed and built outside of Japan since the early 1980s. In 1999 the marine unit was able to integrate high-resolution radar and chart plotters, and a year later it acquired Kiwitech to launch Ray Tech PC software packages.

RAYMARINE FORMED: 2001

Recreation products were just one division of Raytheon Marine, accounting for $141 million in 2000. Some of the unit managers with financial backing from European venture capital firm Mercury Private Equity acquired the business for $108 million in 2001, renaming the

```
┌─────────────────────────────────────────┐
│                                         │
│           KEY DATES                     │
│              ■                          │
│  ──────────────────────────────────     │
│  1922:  Raytheon is founded.            │
│  1958:  Apelco is acquired.             │
│  1974:  Nautech Ltd. is founded.        │
│  1990:  Raytheon acquires Nautech.      │
│  2001:  Raytheon sells Recreation Marine│
│         Division, resulting in          │
│         Raymarine plc.                  │
│  2004:  Raymarine is floated on the     │
│         London Stock Exchange.          │
│                                         │
└─────────────────────────────────────────┘
```

company Raymarine. The company's headquarters was established in Portsmouth, England, where a manufacturing plant was also operating. Just prior to the sale, Raytheon had elected to close the New Hampshire plant that produced fish finders, sell the building, and move manufacturing to Spain. Raymarine elected to keep the Spain operation intact, while sales, distribution, and customer services operations were retained in New Hampshire.

Although the economy began to stall, Raymarine experienced an increase in sales during its first year of independence to about $150 million. Profits were bolstered by the fact that management no longer had to tailor its efforts to fit in with the corporate plan of its parent company or go through channels to make a decision. Soon after its formation, Raymarine spent $2 million on improvements in manufacturing and another $2 million on a marketing campaign, mostly consisting of boating magazine ads.

The company was also able to adapt more quickly to changing business conditions and had the ability to listen to customers and make changes without the encumbrance of corporate bureaucracy. In 2001 the company introduced its Advanced Steering technology inboard autopilot course computers. The research and development budget also enjoyed a healthy increase to help keep the product pipeline well stocked. The budget grew from 5.7 percent of sales in 2001 to 9 percent in 2003, as Raymarine pursued a strategy of developing innovative new products that could be used a wide range of vessels.

NEW CEO INSTALLED: 2003

In January 2003 Raymarine brought in a new chief executive officer, Malcolm Miller, a man with a quarter-century of experience in consumer electronics. He was the former CEO of SEGA Europe and from 1997 to 2002 was chief executive of Pace Micro Technology plc.

Under his leadership Raymarine continued to enjoy steady growth, and in 2004 he prepared to float Raymarine on the London Stock Exchange, primarily as a way to allow HGCapital, the former Mercury Private Equity, which held a 70 percent stake, to realize some profit. Raymarine shares were placed privately with institutional investors. No new money was raised for the company, but Raymarine benefited from a higher profile and a greater diversity of shareholders, while HGCapital retained a significant interest in the company.

Sales increased 14 percent to £106 million in 2004, as Raymarine's strategy of making versatile products paid off. The company also benefited from a marketplace populated by older, affluent consumers who were willing to pay for the latest high-tech safety and navigation devices, and from the decision to pursue the higher end of the leisure boat market. Some of the new products included a high-definition fish imaging system, "smart pilot" course computers employing advanced steering software, and entertainment systems.

Raymarine outsourced manufacturing to Eastern Europe and Mexico in order to reduce costs and bolster profits, as well as to remain competitive with its chief competitors, Simrad from Norway and Gamin from the United States, which had already outsourced manufacturing to Taiwan. Hence, a Portsmouth factory was closed, replaced by an operation in Hungary, which produced printed circuit boards, a move that was completed in 2006. Furthermore, the growing economies of Eastern Europe, along with China, were expected to be a new source of customers for Raymarine. Leisure boating was also growing in popularity in the Middle East.

To support ongoing growth, Raymarine introduced about a dozen new products in 2006. One was a new satellite television antenna system, the 60STV, especially suited for tracking satellites in parts of the globe that received weaker signals, allowing larger yachts to receive digital music and video programming far out at sea. Raymarine also unveiled the LifeTag wireless man-overboard-system, which could act as a stand-alone system or be incorporated into a boat's instrument or multifunction display system. A base system could monitor as many as 16 LifeTags, which could be worn around the neck on a lanyard, attached to clothing, strapped around a wrist, or even attached to a pet's collar. Should a wearer venture beyond the protected zone, such as falling overboard, an alarm sounded, and if integrated with the boat's other systems the device could mark the location of the wearer so the boat could be navigated to that spot. The LifeTag alarm could also be activated by the wearer holding down a button on the device for three seconds.

DISTRIBUTORSHIPS ACQUIRED

The price of Raymarine's stock kept pace with its growth in revenues until the 2007. The key U.S. market then faltered, due in part to a weak dollar, but also because the company had overstocked in late 2006. The company sought to improve its competitive position in 2007 by acquiring important distributorships. The first came in April of that year when SDM Electronique SAS of Paris, France, was added. It was followed by the addition of E.E. Eissing KG, a German distributor. More distributors were brought into the fold in 2008, including DeckMarine S.p.A., the sole Italian distributor of Raymarine products, and NavSystems Oy of Finland.

In the meantime, Raymarine continued to roll out new products to provide those distributors with the merchandise they needed to attract sales. In 2008, for example, Raymarine introduced a new generation in course computers, the new SPX Autopilot Range, available in versions to accommodate all types and sizes of vessels. An enhanced series of SPX Autopilots followed a year later. Raymarine also unveiled a new HD digital radar system in 2008.

These new products helped Raymarine to maintain strong sales through the bulk of 2008, but as the global economy began to struggle late in the year, the company implemented some cost-cutting measures. Raymarine also had to contend with management transitions, when CEO Miller left the company in October 2008. The company's chairman, Peter Ward, replaced him on a temporary basis, and a search was then initiated for a permanent replacement. Although economic conditions remained challenging on a short-term basis, Raymarine was confident that its expertise in new product development would keep it on track for long-term growth.

Ed Dinger

PRINCIPAL SUBSIDIARIES

Raymarine Inc.; Raymarine Asia Pty Ltd.

PRINCIPAL COMPETITORS

Gamin Ltd.; L-3 Communications Holdings, Inc.; Navico Holding A.S.

FURTHER READING

Allison, Kevin, "Raymarine Launches Pounds 125m Float Plan," *Financial Times,* November 9, 2004, p. 25.

Auchincloss, Louis, "All Shipshape at Raymarine," *Engineer: The Professional Bulletin for Army Engineers,* March 11, 2005, p. 22.

Bailey, Anthony, "Strategy Kept on Course," *Financial Times,* September 12, 1997, p. 15.

Blackwell, David, "Raymarine Profits Hurt by Credit Crunch," *Financial Times,* March 2, 2009.

———, "Raymarine Rides Weaker US Sales," *Financial Times,* February 26, 2008, p. 22.

———, "Raymarine to Launch 12 New Products," *Financial Times,* February 28, 2006, p. 24.

Fales, Dan, "Raytheon's Renaissance," *Motor Boating & Sailing,* May 1997, p. 98.

Kennedy, Eileen, "Nashua, N.H.-based Marine Equipment Company Sees $150 Million in Sales," *Nashua (N.H.) Telegraph,* January 6, 2002.

Muspratt, Caroline, "Raymarine Boosted by Russian Wealth," *Daily Telegraph* (London), August 22, 2006, p. 6.

"Raytheon Sells Recreational Unit for $108 Million," *New York Times,* January 31, 2001, p. C4.

Thomaszewski, Walter, "Amateur Boatman Is Spending More on Electronic Gear," *New York Times,* May 4, 1969.

Urquhart, Lisa, "Raymarine Sees Promise in the East," *Financial Times,* August 16, 2005, p. 20.

Rollins, Inc.

2170 Piedmont Road Northeast
Atlanta, Georgia 30324
U.S.A.
Telephone: (404) 888-2000
Toll Free: (800) 800-6756
Fax: (404) 888-2662
Web site: http://www.rollins.com

Public Company
Incorporated: 1948 as Rollins Broadcasting, Inc.
Employees: 10,049
Sales: $1.02 billion (2008)
Stock Exchanges: New York
Ticker Symbol: ROL
NAICS: 561700 Exterminating and Pest Control
    Services

■ ■ ■

Rollins, Inc., is a leading service company in the United States, providing termite and pest control services to more than 1.7 million residential and commercial customers. Rollins derives the bulk of its revenues and profits from Orkin, Inc., with 400 locations in North and South America, the Middle East, and Asia. The acquisition of Orkin by Rollins in 1964 made business history as the first recorded leveraged buyout. Once a diversified conglomerate with origins in TV and radio broadcasting, Rollins spun off its protective services, lawn care, and interior tropical plant units in 1997 in order to focus on pest control. The company listed shares publicly in 1961 but has continued to be led by the Rollins family.

ROLLINS BROADCASTING

Rollins, Inc., began as Rollins Broadcasting, Inc., in the 1940s, although the company's Orkin Pest Control business is older, having been founded in 1901 and acquired by Rollins in 1964. Rollins Broadcasting was cofounded by O. Wayne Rollins, who was raised in rural Georgia and worked in a cotton mill during the Depression era, and his brother, John Rollins. Together they formed Rollins Broadcasting, a partnership based on a simple strategy: Wayne Rollins would acquire a small Virginia radio station that would advertise his brother's car dealership.

Wayne Rollins became president of Rollins Broadcasting and guided an expansion of its media interests, which by 1960 included six radio stations and three television stations in the eastern United States. In 1961, the company went public and was listed on the American Stock Exchange. Also that year, the company began diversifying, acquiring Tribble Advertising Company of Texas and launching its outdoor advertising/billboard business. In 1962, Rollins acquired its tenth broadcasting station with the purchase of its first West Coast media operation, KDAY radio station in Los Angeles.

In 1963, Rollins expanded its outdoor advertising business farther south when it acquired Vendors S.A., a Mexican company that marked the entry of Rollins into international operations. During the first half of 1964, Rollins acquired Satin Soft Cosmetics and also entered the citrus-fruit growing business, planting groves on acreage it had acquired in south-central Florida during the late 1950s.

In mid-1964, Wayne Rollins led what is believed to have been the first leveraged buyout in history, when his rapidly diversifying company acquired Orkin Exterminating Company for $62.4 million, a figure nearly seven times that of Rollins Broadcasting's revenues that year. At the time of the Orkin acquisition, the family-run Atlanta-based pest control business was beset with squabbles that at one juncture led family members to commit the company founder, known as "Otto the Rat Man," to a mental institution. Although Wayne Rollins knew little about pest control, he used his connections with Delaware's Du Pont family to help secure financing from the Chase Manhattan Bank and Prudential Insurance Company, which funded most of the acquisition costs.

NAME CHANGE

With more than 800 offices in 29 states and Washington, D.C., Orkin gave Rollins a service company to which Rollins could apply advertising and merchandising operations. For a time the buyout served as a case study at the Harvard Business School, representing the first time that large institutional investors backed a smaller firm buying a larger company and lent money on the basis of potential earnings rather than on the base value of Orkin, setting the stage for an acquisition that Wayne Rollins compared to "Jonah swallowing the whale." The deal also became emblematic of other future Rollins acquisitions, with Rollins later acquiring several family-owned businesses based in southern states that offered cross-marketing opportunities.

Soon after acquiring Orkin, Rollins entered the professional building maintenance service business with the acquisition of another Atlanta-based business, L.P. Martin Maintenance Corp. (renamed Rollins Services), with operations in ten southern states. In 1964 and 1965 Rollins also took over several smaller pest control firms, including Dettlebach Pesticide Corp., a manufacturer of pesticides, insecticides, and rodenticides; and Arwell, Inc., a Midwestern termite and pest control firm.

With the name Rollins Broadcasting no longer reflecting the company's scattered interests, in 1965 the company changed its name to Rollins, Inc. By 1966, Orkin's operations had been expanded to 1,000 offices and had followed the Rollins billboard business into Mexico. The following year, Rollins, Inc., relocated its corporate offices from Wilmington, Delaware, to the Orkin headquarters in Atlanta, and in 1968 Rollins began trading on the New York Stock Exchange. Moreover, the company also entered the wall covering and decorating business with the purchase of the Atlanta-based wholesale distribution firm Dwoskin, Inc., and its subsidiary Dwoskin Decorating Company.

In 1968, the Federal Communications Commission (FCC) refused to renew the operating license of one the 12 radio stations owned by Rollins at that time, WNJR in Newark, New Jersey, one of the first radio stations in the United States to tailor programming specifically to African-American audiences. In failing to renew the license, the FCC cited gross misconduct and fraud by station managers who concealed the relationship between the station and an advertising agency and charged that home office officials failed to exercise adequate control and supervision over the station. The FCC ruling was later upheld when the U.S. Supreme Court refused to hear a Rollins appeal.

CONTINUED DIVERSIFICATION

In 1969, company sales rose above $100 million for the first time. By the end of the decade, the company had formed Rollins Protective Services (RPS), initially a subsidiary, which became a pioneer in the security field after developing one of the first affordable wireless early-warning burglar and fire alarm systems in the 1970s.

During the early 1970s Rollins continued diversifying by acquiring the consumer cooperative United Buying Service and the oil and gas field services operation of Patterson Services, a leading supplier to oil and gas companies and drilling contractors in the Gulf Coast area. During the same period, Rollins also expanded its home decorating operations with the acquisitions of Star Wallpaper & Paint Company, Carole Textile Company, and Marks Custom Draperies, Inc. In 1973, the

KEY DATES

1901: Otto Orkin begins his namesake pest control business.

1948: Rollins Broadcasting is incorporated.

1964: Rollins acquires control of Orkin in what is believed to be the first leveraged buyout.

1968: After seven years as a public company Rollins lists shares on the New York Stock Exchange.

1984: Rollins Communications, Inc., and RPC Energy Services, Inc., are spun off to shareholders.

1997: Rollins, Inc., divests lawn care, plantscaping, and protective services businesses in order to focus on pest control.

2004: Purchase of Western Industries for $110 million is the largest acquisition by Rollins since Orkin.

2008: Total revenues exceed $1 billion.

company's Dwoskin division, which had become the country's largest wholesale distributor of wall coverings, began serving as the sole distributor of Ultra-Ease, a pre-pasted vinyl-coated wall covering developed by the Du Pont Company.

By the end of 1973—Rollins's 25th year in business—the company's media interests included a growing cable television system in Wilmington, Delaware (a state that had no commercial television station), as well as three television stations and six radio stations operating in Virginia, West Virginia, Alabama, Illinois, California, and New York. Rollins was also operating the nation's fourth largest outdoor advertising firm and an expanded collective buying service involved in the sale of such items as furniture, major appliances, cars, and boats, and boasting one of the largest operations of its kind. Additionally, Rollins Services, the company's building maintenance division, was the largest such operation serving commercial and institutional customers in the Southeast and Southwest and had expanded its services to include janitorial, building management, security and polygraph, engineering, hospital laundry and carpet care, and air sanitization services. Moreover, the company's leading service business, Orkin, was the world's largest termite and pest control company, having grown to serve more than one million customers through offices in 35 states, Mexico, and Jamaica.

SECOND GENERATION OF FAMILY LEADERSHIP

R. Randall Rollins, son of Wayne Rollins, succeeded his father as president in 1975 while the company cofounder remained as chairperson and chief executive. In 1975, the company sold Dwoskin operations and closed the year recording revenues of $213 million and earnings of $19 million.

In early 1976, Rollins became the first American company to formally announce that it had made and would continue to make payoffs to local Mexican government officials (which was not illegal under U.S. law) in order to conduct business across the border. In a voluntary disclosure statement filed with the Securities and Exchange Commission (SEC), the company reported that it had paid Mexican officials $127,000 over a five-year period, helping the billboard business earn about $10 million. After receiving negative publicity from the disclosure, in late 1976 Rollins announced that it would discontinue questionable payments to Mexican officials.

In 1977, Rollins began operating its second cable television system, in New Haven, Connecticut, and about the same time the company completed a new, expanded Plattsburgh, New York, television station, which began broadcasting across the northern U.S. border to Montreal. In 1977, Orkin Pest Control, hoping to benefit from another cross-marketing opportunity, launched a lawn care operation to compete for business in that growing industry. Rollins, between 1978 and 1981, abandoned its consumer cooperative, business services, and custom drapery operations by discontinuing the business of United Buying Service and selling Rollins Services, Carole Textile Company, and Marks Custom Draperies.

In 1980, the company's annual sales surpassed $400 million for the first time—after nearly doubling in five years—as earnings rose above $35 million. In 1982, drawing on Orkin's history of serving residential customers in environmentally sensitive markets, Rollins created a separate lawn care entity, Orkin Lawn Care, offering fertilization, weed and insect control, seeding, and aeration services.

During the early 1980s, Rollins began acquiring and operating numerous cable television franchises in Massachusetts and Rhode Island. In 1982, a local attorney representing Rollins in Danvers, Massachusetts, was convicted of offering a town official a $50,000 bribe to help Rollins secure a franchise there. Rollins was never implicated in the bribe, and following the conviction, the Danvers Town Council voted to grant a franchise to Rollins, although the cable license was revoked in 1983 by a state consumer agency.

SPINOFFS AND ACQUISITIONS

During this time, Rollins acquired about three million shares of its common stock as the Rollins family increased its stake in the company to about 43 percent. During the same period, the company's earnings, which had increased on an average of more than 20 percent per year since the company went public, dipped with falling profits from oil and gas services. In 1984, seeking increased shareholder value and expanded business opportunities for family members, Wayne Rollins split his company into three public units: a new Rollins, Inc., operating strictly as a consumer services business offering pest control, lawn care, and security services; a media business, Rollins Communications, Inc. (RCI), controlling television and radio stations and cable television franchises; and RPC Energy Services (RPC), focusing on oil and gas field services. RCI and RPC were then spun off to shareholders, with Rollins family members retaining significant stakes in each. Wayne Rollins remained chair and chief executive of Rollins, Inc., and became chair and chief executive of RCI; Randall Rollins became senior vice-chair of Rollins, chair and chief executive of RPC, and president of RCI; and Gary, the younger son of Wayne Rollins, became president of Rollins, Inc., assuming the bulk of operational control over the new Rollins, Inc.

With the ability to channel capital which its service divisions had earned back into the company, Rollins, Inc., bought back more than a million of its shares for acquisition purposes and purchased companies operating in all three of the company's principal business segments. In 1985, RPS increased its scope of operations in Cincinnati, Columbus, Dallas, Houston, and St. Louis with the acquisition of Warner Amex Security Systems, a home security business that provided Rollins with a hardwired security system product line (generally used in commercial application) to add to the company's established line of wireless systems. The company's pest control business also expanded in 1985 through acquisitions, including that of Ace Pest & Termite Control Company, which gave Orkin an entrance into the Southern California market.

Between 1984 and 1987, Orkin Lawn Care, in an attempt to pull its operations out of the red, expanded its reach from the Southeast across seven Sun Belt markets from North Carolina to Texas. In 1987, the lawn care division further extended operations into the Midwest and Northeast with the acquisition of Amcare, Inc., which gave Orkin Lawn Care an additional 24 branches and doubled to more than 40 the division's number of locations.

LEADING SERVICE COMPANY

Also in 1987, the company acquired two pest control firms, including Abalene, the largest operation in New York and New England. By this time, Orkin controlled about 10 percent of the U.S. pest control market—followed by Terminix with about 6 percent—and accounted for about 90 percent of the revenues and earnings of Rollins. After media properties became a hot commodity on Wall Street, the Rollins family sold its interest in RCI for $600 million, propelling Wayne Rollins into the ranks of the world's 400 wealthiest. Moreover, *Forbes* magazine named Rollins, Inc., the nation's top-performing service company in 1986, a distinction it would hold for several years. However, within a few years rival Terminix, Inc., would eclipse Orkin as the world's largest pest-control company.

The Federal Trade Commission (FTC) soon ruled that Orkin Exterminating had unfairly raised its renewal fees in 1980 after earlier guaranteeing certain customers fixed fees. The company was ordered to roll back fees, although it was allowed to retain the $7.5 million it earned as a result of the increases. Orkin, which had cited inflation as the impetus for its fee increases, appealed the decision, which was ultimately upheld when the Supreme Court let the FTC ruling stand. After the initial FTC ruling, a federal court found Orkin guilty of improper use of pesticides during a home fumigation—which allegedly caused the death of a Virginia couple—and was fined $350,000. In 1988, Orkin's pest control operations were hurt by industry-wide regulatory changes after the U.S. Environmental Protection Agency banned chlordane, a widely used termiticide. Rollins responded to the new regulations, which took effect in the midst of Orkin's research into a new foam termiticide, by establishing new customer relations and public relations departments that focused their efforts on public education.

During the late 1980s, Orkin Lawn Care acquired Village Green, Inc., operating in Connecticut and New York, and Easy-Lawn, Inc., operating in South Carolina. Initially Orkin Lawn Care treated lawns with sprays, but in 1988 it converted its treatment process to a combination of wet and dry granular applications, allowing the company to change its vehicle fleet from tankers to smaller and more economical vans. Despite having expanded to a peak of 56 branches by 1988, Orkin Lawn Care had generated little profit since its formation six years earlier. Faced with an industry slump and increased competition, the lawn care division began consolidating some operations and added a complete tree and shrub program to its services. Continuing to persist toward a goal of profitability, in 1989 the lawn care division entered the commercial market while pushing its territory westward, acquiring Yearound Lawn Care Experts, a West Coast company with branches in San Diego, Los Angeles, Sacramento, Portland, and Seattle.

A PERIOD OF SLOW GROWTH

Around the same time, RPS opened an expanded Technical Center in Atlanta, upgraded the computerized operating systems at its three alarm monitoring centers, acquired two security firms, and entered the Chicago residential security market. In 1989, Orkin, the only pest control business maintaining a continuous national television and outdoor advertising program, launched its "Exterminator" advertising campaign designed to reinforce the recognition of Orkin's name while using the robotic Exterminator to suggest that the firm was the service company of the future. For 1989, Rollins company sales climbed above $400 million (for the first time since the 1984 spinoffs) while profits remained flat due to unusual weather conditions that reduced the termite swarm period and delayed the start-up season for lawn care.

During the slow-growth period of the late 1980s, Rollins began focusing on lowering turnover among both customers and employees by initiating a program that increased employee recruiting, training, and compensation. Early the following decade, Rollins initiated a total quality improvement plan, beginning with corporate management and designed to eventually touch the company's entire workforce with additional quality training.

Rollins entered the 1990s introducing a new division, a new foam termiticide, and new security systems. In 1990, Rollins formed Orkin Plantscaping to sell and rent flowering and green plants principally to commercial customers such as upscale hotels, office buildings, and shopping malls. Also that year, Orkin Termite and Pest Control division, after four years of development work, became the first business in its field to employ a foam termiticide. The pest control division, seeking ways to develop low-cost sales leads, also introduced a toll-free phone line—offering free termite inspections—in conjunction with its Exterminator commercials. In 1990, RPS launched a new automated alarm monitoring system and introduced the Rollins System VI and the hardwired Vista LX System. The System VI, consisting of a network of alarm sensors and devices communicating directly with one of the company's three, 24-hour alarm monitoring centers, featured one-touch system activation, multiple zone security, and house lighting controls while the Vista LX system combined hardwired and wireless features.

In 1991, O. Wayne Rollins died unexpectedly after entering a hospital for a pacemaker implant. A near-billionaire and one of Florida's largest landowners and biggest cattle ranchers, Rollins had an estimated net worth of $930 million and had been one of Atlanta's most generous philanthropists. Randall Rollins succeeded his father as chairperson and chief executive while Gary Rollins remained president.

ORKIN LAWN CARE CONTINUES TO STRUGGLE

In 1991, the company launched a "Zero Pest" guarantee designed to attract premium commercial pest control accounts from sources such as upscale restaurants and major hotels as well as to complement the company's toll-free inspection hotline, which was generating increasing numbers of residential sales leads. In 1991, RPS introduced its Quality-Plus system, targeting the middle-income family and small business markets, and the following year the security division expanded its cross-marketing programs with other Rollins operations and opened new commercial offices. In 1991, Orkin Plantscaping acquired operations in Dallas, Nashville, and Denver, and the following year purchased operations in Portland, San Diego, and Seattle, as it became the second largest plantscaping concern in the country. In 1992, with increased sales generated by three of its four divisions, the company's revenues rose more than $50 million and climbed above $500 million for the first time—to $528 million—while net income rose to $38 million.

While the company's pest control, security, and plantscaping services were growing during the early 1990s, Orkin Lawn Care continued to struggle, resulting in further departures from unprofitable markets. In 1991, Orkin Lawn Care abandoned California and the following year bowed out of parts of the Northeast and Midwest. A slowing of industry growth and an increase in competition caused the lawn care operation to boost its prices and redirect marketing activities to focus on direct sales and forced the operation to retreat from some of its territory. By 1993, the lawn care division had been pared back to a 32-branch area, largely in territory familiar to Rollins: the Southeast and the Sun Belt region.

In 1993, Orkin Plantscaping, then serving 16 states, opened a new Dallas distribution center to consolidate purchasing, warehousing, and distribution of plants and supplies. Also that year, Orkin Pest Control introduced a 24-hour hotline and launched a new agri-business service designed to help dairy farmers in the control of the common fly. In September 1993, the insect zoo at the Smithsonian National Museum of

Natural History was renamed the O. Orkin Insect Zoo after the company donated $500,000 for its expansion and renovation. Also in 1993, taking aim at its core residential market, RPS introduced a midpriced security system product, Protector. Moreover, Orkin Lawn Care introduced its Total Lawn Care (TLC) service, an expanded all-inclusive lawn service, and began a training school for its lawn care technicians and managers. For 1993, Rollins, for the seventh consecutive year, was ranked by *Forbes* as the nation's best services company, as revenues rose to more than $575 million and net income increased to $44.5 million, marking the company's fourth consecutive year recording double-digit earnings increases.

CHANGE IN STRATEGY

Rollins, Inc., moved into the mid-1990s with the Rollins family owning in excess of 41 percent of the company's common stock and occupying three of the company's seven director seats. The Orkin Pest Control division continued to pace the company's revenues and earnings and had only one national competitor in the nearly $4 billion pest control industry, which was fragmented and growing, and still in the process of slowly consolidating.

Rollins anticipated increased acquisition activity—which had slowed considerably during the late 1980s and early 1990s due to high asking prices—particularly in the area of local and regional pest control operations and possibly those which could extend operations into Canada and Europe. Rollins Protective Services, generating about 10 percent of the company's revenues, appeared to be gaining momentum as it increased cross-marketing programs with other company divisions and expanded its product line in both residential and commercial market segments. Rollins was also hoping that its plantscaping operation, generating about 5 percent of the company's annual sales, could become the first national concern of its kind.

Rollins changed its strategy in 1997, however, divesting the lawn care, plantscaping, and protective services businesses in order to focus on pest control. It continued to acquire smaller companies, adding Prism and Redd Pest Control in the United States. It also bought PCO Services, Inc., Canada's largest pest control business, which had been formed in 1952. The PCO buy and other acquisitions were aimed at growing the relatively neglected commercial side of the business.

Orkin was still dealing with a termite crisis resulting from the less-effective chemicals used to replace the banned chlordane. There were numerous lawsuits and Orkin modified its lifetime guarantee policies to cover fixed terms instead. Orkin continued to innovate in this area, however, and by 2008 it was offering certain West Coast communities a service to kill termites by applying heat.

Rollins, Inc., counted $677 million in revenues in 2003 as its chief rival Terminix approached the $1 billion mark. Glen Rollins, the son of Gary Rollins, became president and chief operating officer of the Orkin subsidiary in February 2004. He had been involved with the business since beginning as a teenager as a termite technician's assistant and boasted experience at a wide variety of jobs within the company. He was expected to eventually succeed his father as CEO of Rollins.

WESTERN INDUSTRIES ACQUIRED

In March 2004 Rollins made its largest acquisition since buying Orkin, paying $110 million for Western Industries of Parsippany, New Jersey. Western was established in 1928 and had been run by the Sameth family. The deal, which brought with it Western Pest Services and Western Fumigation, boosted Orkin's business in the Northeast, where it previously had relatively little penetration. Western had pest control revenues of $72 million in 2003. The Western deal also included a chemicals business, Residex Corp., which was soon divested. Gary Rollins told *Business to Business* he intended to keep making acquisitions among the dozens of smaller, family-owned pest control companies that had sprung up since the 1950s.

Rollins continued to strengthen its commercial segment. In 2005 it acquired the Industrial Fumigant Company (IFC). Based in Olathe, Kansas, IFC specialized in the food and commodity industries and had been started in 1937. Rollins had revenues of $802 million in 2005 and net income of $52.8 million. Revenues exceeded $1 billion in 2008 as net income reached $68.9 million. The company was slowly adding international Orkin franchises, particularly in the Middle East and Latin America.

Acquisitions continued in the United States. In April 2008 Rollins bought HomeTeam Pest Defense, Inc., and associated companies for $134 million. Home-Team was one of the nation's largest residential pest control businesses. It had been formed in 1996 and boasted a unique in-wall system that it marketed to builders. The deal added 1,500 employees while boosting residential sales by one-fifth.

In December 2008 Rollins acquired Crane Pest Control, Inc., a San Francisco firm that dated to 1930. Crane operated in Northern California and the Reno,

Nevada, area and had annual revenues of more than $10 million. Orkin announced Crane would be allowed to operate independently under its own brand name, said to inspire a great deal of loyalty in its home market.

As a global economic recession took hold and deepened in 2008 and 2009, forcing many businesses to restructure and scale back in order to survive, Rollins was able to boast a strong balance sheet. The company reported its highest sales and profits up to that time in 2008 and paid investors a dividend for the year of $0.25 per share. Moreover, the company's financial strength allowed it to remain committed to its agenda of further acquisitions and expansion.

Roger W. Rouland
Updated, Frederick C. Ingram

PRINCIPAL SUBSIDIARIES

Orkin, Inc.; PCO Services, Inc. (Canada); HomeTeam Pest Defense; Western Pest Services; Industrial Fumigant Company; Crane Pest Control, Inc.

PRINCIPAL COMPETITORS

Terminix, Inc.; Ecolab Inc.; Rentokil Initial plc.

FURTHER READING

Barry, Tom, "Energy and Experience," *Business to Business,* September 2004.

Calonius, Erik, "Cable Conniving: Fight for TV Franchise in New England Town Elicits Big Bribe Offer," *Wall Street Journal,* September 22, 1981, pp. 1, 8.

"FCC Refuses to Renew a Radio License of Rollins Unit, Charges Improper Moves," *Wall Street Journal,* November 29, 1968, p. 4.

"Ghouls' Choice," *Forbes,* January 20, 1992, pp. 134–35.

Haddad, Charles, "O. Wayne Rollins Lets Go," *Georgia Trend,* November 1988, p. 42.

Hannon, Kerry, "Bugs, Burglars and Sod," *Forbes,* July 25, 1988, p. 168.

Ho, Rodney, "On the Prowl for Acquisitions," *Atlanta Constitution,* May 31, 1994, p. D1.

Kirk, Margaret O., *The Making of the World's Best Pest Control Company,* Atlanta: Rollins, Inc., 2005.

McKenna, Jon, "Rollins' Sons Absorbed Dad's Lessons: Steady, Careful Management," *Atlanta Business Chronicle,* October 21, 1991, p. 3A.

———, "Wayne Rollins' Fortune: What's Charity's Stake in $930 Million," *Atlanta Business Chronicle,* November 11, 1991, p. 1.

Miller, Andy, "Lawsuits, Depressed Stock Price Weaken Atlanta-Based Pest-Control Company," *Atlanta Journal-Constitution,* September 27, 2000.

Neill, Carol P., "For Rollins, a House Divided Is Good News," *Business Atlanta,* January 1986, p. 22.

"Nobody's Fool," *Forbes,* January 30, 1984, p. 46.

Paul, Bill, "Rollins Payoffs: Perils of Candor," *Wall Street Journal,* October 1, 1976, p. 10.

"Residex Becomes Independent Company," *Pest Control,* May 2004, p. 12.

"Rollins Broadcasting Plans to Buy Orkin, Pest-Control Firm, for $62.4 Million Cash," *Wall Street Journal,* June 22, 1964, p. 7.

"Rollins to Acquire Western Industries," *Pest Control,* April 2004, p. 12.

Schonbak, Judith, "Randall Takes Rollins' Reins," *Business Atlanta,* December 1991, p. 12.

Sanrio Company, Ltd.

———————■———————

6-1, Ohsaki 1-chome
Shinagawa-ku
Tokyo, 141-8603
Japan
Telephone: (81 3) 3779 8111
Fax: (81 3) 3779 8054
Web site: http://www.sanrio.co.jp

Public Company
Incorporated: 1960 as Yamanashi Silk Center Co., Ltd.
Employees: 796
Sales: ¥73 billion ($73.5 million) (2008 est.)
Stock Exchanges: Tokyo
Ticker Symbol: 81360
NAICS: 339932 Game, Toy, and Children's Vehicle
   Manufacturing; 713110 Amusement and Theme
   Parks; 511120 Periodical Publishers; 511130 Book
   Publishers; 512110 Motion Picture and Video
   Production; 512131 Motion Picture Theaters
   (Except Drive-Ins); 722110 Full-Service
   Restaurants; 451120 Hobby, Toy, and Game Stores

■ ■ ■

Japan's Sanrio Company, Ltd., offers what are called social communication gifts. The company designs, manufactures, markets, and distributes a vast range of gifts and greeting cards and also has operations in the publication of books and magazines and the production and distribution of videos and DVDs. Sanrio also runs restaurants and theme parks, and is involved in the production of theatrical works. By far the most popular of Sanrio's characters is Hello Kitty, which has inspired some 22,000 different products and even a themed maternity hospital in Taiwan. Hello Kitty is responsible for nearly $500 million in sales annually. Sanrio, trading on the Tokyo Stock Exchange, is run by founder Shintaro Tsuji, who serves as president and CEO.

BRINGING CUTENESS TO THE WORLD

Sanrio Company, Ltd., began business in 1960 as Yamanashi Silk Center Co. Founder Shintaro Tsuji, who had raised ¥1 million to launch his company, had ambitious plans for building what the company called "the Social Communication Business." Built around the Japanese culture's tradition of gift giving, Tsuji's company quickly turned to producing the gifts themselves. In 1962 the company began decorating its gift products with Strawberry, the first of what was to become a long string of company-designed characters. The Strawberry character enabled Tsuji to take his company's products overseas, finding success in the United States. The success of the character, which was able to capitalize as well on worldwide hit "Strawberry Fields Forever" by the Beatles, inspired the company to open a retail store in San Francisco, dubbed the Strawberry Shop. Strawberry also inspired the company to begin production and publication of its own newspaper, *Strawberry News.*

The company opened a new retail store concept in Tokyo in 1971, the Gift Gate store. Two years later, the company changed its name to Sanrio Company, Ltd. In that year, the company began production of a new magazine, *Shi to Meruhen* (Poetry and Fairytales). The

COMPANY PERSPECTIVES

Small Gift, Big Smile. It's more than just a catchy phrase; it's the foundation of everything we do, and we're proud to say we've been creating smiles for over 40 years. At Sanrio we believe that a gift is more than just a gift. Rather, a gift is a means of expressing our heartfelt feelings for others. This philosophy guides all Sanrio activities, whether we're designing a stationery set, a theme park, a retail store or an animated television series. From Sanrio boutiques showcasing the ultimate Sanrio collection to smaller assortments in other shopping environments, we invite all our friends and guests to experience the magic of these four simple words.

company also was preparing the launch of what was to become its greatest success, even becoming an icon in Japan.

In 1974, the company introduced two new characters, Patty and Jimmy. These characters were joined by another new character, a pink and white somewhat expressionless cat with a bow behind its ear. Dubbed Hello Kitty, the new character initially was marketed toward young girls, especially at the ages of five and six. Hello Kitty quickly proved to be a hit far beyond her original target audience.

MARKETING HELLO KITTY

As with all of its characters, Sanrio marketed Hello Kitty on nearly every product imaginable. By the end of the century, Sanrio had placed the Hello Kitty character on more than 15,000 products, including a condominium complex built in celebration of Hello Kitty's 25th anniversary. Licensees brought Hello Kitty to such diverse products as toasters, telephones, watches, and even specially designed automobiles, as Hello Kitty quickly became as ubiquitous a cartoon icon as Mickey Mouse in Japan. With Hello Kitty, Sanrio had tapped into the Japanese mania for *kawai,* or cuteness, a quality that sometimes sufficed as a product's primary marketing tool. Sanrio also was to find the Hello Kitty image easily exportable, particularly in the United States, where fashion trends would legitimize the cat for a whole new generation of teenagers and even older consumers.

While Hello Kitty came to represent half of Sanrio's annual sales, the company continued to produce new

characters and new products, as well as to branch out into other industries. In 1974, Sanrio created a subsidiary in the United States, Sanrio Communications, Inc., which began producing animated films for the U.S. market, as well as handling distribution of Sanrio's products. In 1975, the company launched a new magazine, *Strawberry News.* That same year, the company released its first commercial animated feature film, called *Little Jumbo.*

Until the mid-1970s, Sanrio's characters were featured on products manufactured by Sanrio itself. In 1976, however, Sanrio began to build on the success of the Hello Kitty character, signing the first of a long series of licensing agreements to add Hello Kitty and many of its other characters to products such as credit cards and toys included in McDonald's children's meals. In that year, also, the company set up a new subsidiary, Sanrio, Inc., based in San Jose, California, to oversee its U.S. development. The Sanrio Communications company was reorganized as a subsidiary under Sanrio, Inc. The company later moved its U.S. headquarters to San Francisco. Meanwhile, Sanrio also was achieving recognition for its film production, winning the Academy Award for Best Documentary Film for 1978 for the Sanrio-produced *Who Are the Debolts and Where Did They Get 19 Kids?* The company also released the film *The Glacier Fox* in 1978.

CONTINUED EXPANSION

Sanrio continued to produce new characters and the products and toys to feature them. In 1975, the world met such characters as My Melody, Robby Rabbit, and Little Twin Stars. The end of that decade saw the appearance of Giga Chibiko Gang (the Milky Way Gang) and Sanrio's own version of the Snow White crew, Seven Silly Dwarfs. The early 1980s brought a host of new characters as Sanrio stepped up the pace of its launches, with such names as Mellotune in 1981, Zashikibuta in 1983, and Dachonosuke and Little Wonder Story in 1985.

Sanrio also followed the somewhat standard approach to international growth established by many Japanese companies. After building up its first overseas business in the U.S. market, the company next turned to the European market, more difficult to master because of the different languages and cultures. The company first moved into Europe in 1980, opening up a branch office in West Germany to prepare the company's introduction into the European market. Then, in 1983, Sanrio set up a full-fledged European subsidiary, choosing Hamburg, Germany, to form Sanrio GmbH. In the United States, meanwhile, Hello Kitty's popularity reached still greater heights when the

KEY DATES

1960: The company is founded as Yamanashi Silk Center Co., Ltd.
1962: The Strawberry character is introduced.
1969: Strawberry Shop is opened in San Francisco.
1971: The company opens first Gift Gate store in Japan.
1973: The company changes name to Sanrio Company, Ltd.
1974: Hello Kitty is introduced; Sanrio Communications is launched in the United States.
1976: Licensing of characters begins; Sanrio, Inc., is established in San Jose, California.
1983: A West German subsidiary is established.
1987: A Brazilian subsidiary is established.
1990: Puroland theme park opens; Sanrio Far East Co., Ltd., is established.
1991: Harmonyland theme park is launched.
1992: The company establishes Taiwan subsidiary.
1994: The company establishes Hong Kong subsidiary.
1999: Hello Kitty celebrates 25th anniversary.
2003: Sanrio establishes an advertising department for the first time.
2004: Hello Kitty celebrates 30th anniversary.

character was named UNICEF's child ambassador to the United States. In that year, also, the company began to produce and sell videos, as the new media began to go mainstream in technology-hungry Japan.

In the late 1980s and early 1990s, Sanrio pursued further international expansion. The company started up a subsidiary in Brazil in 1987 for the vast Latin American market. At the beginning of the 1990s, Sanrio's expansion target widened to include the huge and dynamic Asian market. In 1990, the company established the subsidiary Sanrio Far East Co., Ltd. Two other subsidiaries were opened in the first half of the 1990s, in Taiwan in 1992 and in Hong Kong in 1994. If older generations in many of the Asian countries had been somewhat hostile to Japanese culture in the previous 50 years, new generations of children and teenagers eagerly embraced the country's love of *kawai,* especially Hello Kitty.

A CULT ICON IN JAPAN

Back home, Sanrio was building toward its, and Hello Kitty's, biggest success to date. The company founded its own amusement park, Puroland, in 1990. Dedicated to Hello Kitty, the amusement park quickly began to attract surprising numbers of adults as the Hello Kitty phenomenon began to break out of the children's market to become a cult icon throughout the whole of Japanese society. With the Japanese economy dipping into a deep recession for the first time in some 40 years, consumers eagerly adopted Hello Kitty and other Sanrio characters, perhaps in a mass display of nostalgia for a simpler, less stressful period in history. At the same time, Sanrio, which had courted young girls as its primary market, had its first crossover success with the introduction of its frog-shaped character Keroppi in 1988. That success inspired the company to create a series of other "gender-neutral" characters, helping the company gain increasing popularity in the young boys market as well.

Puroland was followed quickly by the opening of a second Sanrio-based theme park, Harmonyland, featuring characters from across the Sanrio spectrum, which opened in 1991. As the recession in Japan reached crisis proportions, Sanrio's characters and the products they were designed to support helped boost the company to the top ranks in Japan. In 1994, Hello Kitty was named child ambassador for UNICEF for Japan. Although Sanrio faced competition from such new arrivals as Nintendo's Mario Bros. and Bandai's Pokémon characters, as well as such fads as the Tamagotchi virtual pets, Hello Kitty continued her long-running reign as "queen of cuteness" in that country. In the United States and other parts of the world, meanwhile, Hello Kitty also was transcending age barriers and generation gaps, being adopted—often ironically—as a fashion statement among teenagers and even older consumers.

The economic crisis in other parts of the Asian world also helped to spur on the Hello Kitty craze in such countries as Thailand, Singapore, and Taiwan (where riots broke out among people waiting in line for a McDonald's Hello Kitty promotion). In the meantime, Japan and Sanrio geared up for the celebration of Hello Kitty's 25th birthday, in 1999. That occasion was marked by the launch of two of the most unusual Hello Kitty licensed products. The first, offered by Daihatsu Motor Co., was a car featuring such "standard" equipment as Hello Kitty door locks, dashboard, and upholstered seats. The second was condominium apartments, sold by Itochu Housing, decorated according to the Hello Kitty theme. The Hello Kitty craze, which had only just begun to gather momentum in many parts of the world, promised Sanrio a leading role in the world's cuteness market in the new century.

MOVING INTO THE 21ST CENTURY

Indeed, international demand for Hello Kitty products continued to grow at breakneck speed during the early years of the new millennium. Sales of Hello Kitty products in the United States alone grew 30 percent from 1999 to 2002. By the time Hello Kitty celebrated her 30th birthday on November 1, 2004, she was a $1 billion global brand. A June 2006 *Business Week* article commented on her popularity, claiming, "Today, the fabulous feline is embraced by Parisian fashion houses, U.S. pop divas such as Mariah Carey and Christina Aguilera, and legions of fashion-conscious women in rich world markets."

Despite Hello Kitty's growing popularity abroad, demand for Sanrio's products slowed in its home market. At the same time, Sanrio's bottom line was suffering due in part to bad investments made by founder Tsuji. The company's operating profit in 2001 was reportedly ¥6.2 billion but its losses from stock trading activities reached nearly ¥5 billion. During fiscal 2003, the company reported a ¥19.3 billion loss from the sale of various securities holdings. With Japan's economy stagnant, the company's theme parks were also experiencing a decrease in revenues.

For the first time in its history, Sanrio established an advertising department designed to promote new products and characters, including Cinnamoroll, a dog with a tail shaped like a sweet roll that debuted in 2002. Advertising, which historically had not been part of Sanrio's strategy, signaled a change in the company's promotion efforts for its products. Launched in 2003, the department's first task included designing magazine ads for its Cinnamoroll character.

With sales and profits faltering in Japan, Sanrio looked to new Hello Kitty products and growth in foreign markets to bolster its bottom line. The company joined with Bank of America to launch a Hello Kitty credit card; new Fender Hello Kitty guitars and accessories hit the market; and high-end jewelry and accessory lines were designed by Kimora Lee Simmons and Judith Leiber. A Hello Kitty–themed maternity hospital opened in Yuanlin, Taiwan, in 2008, and a MAC cosmetics line was slated to launch in 2009. Overall, nearly 600 new Hello Kitty products were launched each month in the early 2000s.

Sanrio's new management plan, Project2010, focused on improving its domestic sales while cutting costs, as well as international expansion, especially through licensing deals related to its theme parks. In May 2008, Hello Kitty was named by Japan's Tourism Ministry as its Goodwill Tourism Ambassador to China and Hong Kong. While Sanrio struggled to revive its financial record in its home market, the Hello Kitty brand was poised to remain a cornerstone in the company's growth strategy in the years to come.

M. L. Cohen
Updated, Christina M. Stansell

PRINCIPAL SUBSIDIARIES

Sanrio Puroland Co., Ltd.; Kokoro Co., Ltd.; Sanrio Far East Co., Ltd.; Harmonyland Co., Ltd.; Sanrio Car Lease Co., Ltd.; Sanrio Enterprise Co., Ltd.; Sanrio Music Publications Co., Ltd.; Sanrio Wave Co., Ltd.; Pantry Co., Ltd.; Sanrio, Inc. (USA); Sanrio Entertainment Inc.; Sanrio do Brasil Comerico e Representacoes Ltda. (Brazil); Sanrio Taiwan Co., Ltd.; Sanrio GmbH (Germany); Sanrio (Hong Kong) Co., Ltd.; Sanrio Korea Co., Ltd.; Sanrio Shanghai International Trading Co., Ltd. (China); Sanrio Asia Merchandise Co., Ltd. (Hong Kong); Sanrio Wave Hong Kong Co., Ltd.; San-Byte Taiwan Co., Ltd.

PRINCIPAL COMPETITORS

4Kids Entertainment, Inc.; Hasbro, Inc.; Mattel, Inc.

FURTHER READING

Bellman, Eric, "Heard in Asia: Hello Kitty Has Sweet Purr, but Her Master Likes to Bet," *Wall Street Journal Asia,* July 15, 2002, p. M1.

Bremner, Brian, "Kitty Glitter: Saving Hello Kitty," *Business-Week,* June 26, 2006.

Hosaka, Tomoko A., "Hello Kitty Is New Face of Tourism Campaign," *Commercial Appeal,* May 20, 2008.

Huang, Annie, "Hello Kitty Frenzy," *Dallas Morning News,* August 19, 1999, p. 1D.

Ikenberg, Tamara, "A Cool Cat," *Newsday,* November 15, 2000, p. B31.

Kanellos, Michael, "Hello Kitty's Guide to Business Success," *CNET News.com,* June 21, 2005.

Matchan, Linda, "Kitty on Top; Her Unparalleled Popularity at 30 Keeps on Showing that She Had Us at Hello," *Boston Globe,* October 28, 2004.

Naughton, Julie, "MAC Saying 'Hello' to Kitty Collection," *Women's Wear Daily,* November 21, 2008.

Parker, Ginny, "Japan Specializes in Cute," *Minneapolis Star Tribune,* December 16, 1999, p. 33A.

Parry, Richard Lloyd, "Hello Kitty," *Independent,* October 28, 2000, p. 1.

"Pawing in Enough to Be a Fat Cat," *Japan Times,* June 10, 2008.

"PR Juggernaut Supports New Toys," *Nikkei Weekly,* June 16, 2003.

Tomisawa, Ayai, "How Sanrio Leader Expanded Gift-Giving in Japan," *Wall Street Journal Asia,* October 15, 2007.

Wong, Martin, "I Was a Cat," *Yolk,* September 30, 1995.

SCHMOLZ + BICKENBACH
Providing special steel solutions

Schmolz + Bickenbach AG

Emmenweidstrasse 90
Emmenbrücke, CH-6020
Switzerland
Telephone: (41 41) 209-5000
Fax: (41 41) 209-5104
Web site: http://www.schmolz-bickenbach.com

Public Company
Incorporated: 1919 as Dörrenberg Stahl-Gesellschaft
Employees: 11,184
Sales: EUR 4.1 billion ($6.1 million) (2008)
Stock Exchanges: SIX Swiss Exchange
Ticker Symbol: STLN
NAICS: 331111 Iron and Steel Mills; 331512 Steel
    Investment Foundries; 331513 Steel Foundries
    (Except Investment); 331221 Rolled Steel Shape
    Manufacturing; 331222 Steel Wire Drawing;
    332312 Fabricated Structural Metal Manufacturing

■ ■ ■

Swiss-based Schmolz + Bickenbach AG is the largest
manufacturer, processor, and distributor of special steel
long products (such as bars, rods and wires, and tubes)
in the world. The company leads the market for stainless long steels and tool steels and holds a strong position in high-alloy special and engineering steels.
Schmolz + Bickenbach's production subsidiaries Deutsche Edelstahlwerke, Ugitech, Swiss Steel, and A. Finkl
& Sons operate high-capacity steelworks in Germany,
Switzerland, France, and the United States, as well as

steel processing plants in Denmark, Germany, Italy,
Switzerland, and Turkey.

Schmolz + Bickenbach is a supplier mainly to the
automotive, mechanical engineering and metal forming
industries. The company's sales network spans across
about 25 countries in Europe, North America, South
Africa, Australia, and Asia, including China. North
American subsidiary Schmolz + Bickenbach USA
distributes specialty stainless bar products to the U.S.
market from its warehouses in New Jersey, Illinois,
South Carolina, Texas, California, Ohio, and Ontario,
Canada, and is building a state-of-the-art stainless steel
bar processing plant in Batavia, Illinois. The company is
controlled by members of the German founding families
Schmolz and Bickenbach.

COMMERCIAL SUCCESS AFTER WORLD WAR I

When Arthur Schmolz and Oswald Bickenbach
established Dörrenberg Stahl-Gesellschaft, a company
selling steel products in Düsseldorf in 1919, the German steel industry was in a severe crisis. Germany had
lost World War I and was obliged to pay enormous
reparations while the country's currency began to lose
value; raw materials were in short supply and the large
orders from the military had suddenly stopped.
However, with many years of experience in the steel
trade under their belt (Schmolz was the former director
of administration at steel products manufacturer Stahlwerke Ed. Dörrenberg Söhne; Bickenbach was a traveling salesman for the same company) the two business
partners began selling the products of their former

COMPANY PERSPECTIVES

In the heart of Europe we produce high-grade steel that our customers need to be successful in their toughly contested markets. Our unique corporate concept with its three pillars of production, processing, and distribution and service qualify us as a solution provider and technology driver—and above all as a reliable and quality-conscious partner to our customers worldwide. Our goal is to create a stable, robust, and globally based group of companies which, thanks to its own sources of supply and service as well as cross-regional compensation, reacts only minimally to external market fluctuations. As a single-source provider of solutions, know-how and service for steel, we want to constantly further expand and strengthen our position.

employer. Over time the two entrepreneurs won additional steel product manufacturers clients who preferred to put selling their goods in the hands of experienced salespeople. In 1922 the company was renamed Schmolz + Bickenbach.

Schmolz and Bickenbach were convinced that steel products would always be in demand, even in the midst of economic crisis and galloping inflation. After Germany's currency reform in 1923 their business began to flourish as a growing number of small businesses such as lathe operators and blacksmiths began to buy their supplies at Schmolz + Bickenbach. In the second half of the 1920s the company opened a warehouse at the Rhine harbor and set up subsidiaries in Bremen, Cologne, Bielefeld, and Chemnitz. In 1929 the company acquired Speemann & Vollmann, a steel drawing plant based in Dahl near Düsseldorf where a workforce of about 60 produced bright steel. Schmolz + Bickenbach continued to thrive during the years of the Great Depression and opened additional subsidiaries in Remscheid and Velbert near Düsseldorf, and in Berlin. When the Dahl factory's output was not sufficient anymore to satisfy demand, bright steel production was moved to a larger, state-of-the-art plant in Neuss south of Düsseldorf in 1936. Two years later the company added a cold rolling mill to its production facilities. With the beginning of World War II in 1939, the production and distribution of steel came under the control of the Nazis and became a crucial part of Adolf Hitler's war economy.

RAPID GROWTH AFTER WORLD WAR II

Because Schmolz + Bickenbach's Düsseldorf headquarters had been destroyed during the war, the two company founders, now in their 60s, began to build the business from the ground up again after the war. At first they set up an office in Ründeroth and once again began selling steel products. After the remaining machinery was spared the common fate of being dismantled, and after an official permit was secured from the British military administration, Schmolz + Bickenbach was the first German drawing plant that resumed production after the war. The postwar years also marked a generation change. In 1949 company founder Arthur Schmolz died. Oswald Bickenbach died four years later. The company remained under the control of their heirs.

As the German economy entered the postwar reconstruction boom, Schmolz + Bickenbach witnessed a period of rapid growth. In the early 1950s the company moved into its newly built Düsseldorf headquarters. To keep up with the surge in demand, new production facilities were set up for stainless steel round bars and structural steel, two of the product categories Schmolz + Bickenbach decided to specialize in. Again, subsidiaries were established in large German cities. In 1954 the company expanded into the neighboring Netherlands.

By the mid-1950s, the company's annual sales passed the DEM 100 million mark and climbed to three times that amount by the late 1960s. While the demand for ordinary steel products began to slow down in the second half of the 1960s, the market for stainless steel products continued to grow. Five warehouses were built in Düsseldorf and additional subsidiaries were established in Stuttgart and Bochum. In 1973 Schmolz + Bickenbach's sales reached DEM 500 million.

CONTINUED GROWTH DURING STEEL INDUSTRY CRISES

The first oil crisis of 1973 put a sudden end to Schmolz + Bickenbach's dynamic growth. The surge in oil prices pushed the costs for the energy-intensive steel production through the roof while the demand for stainless steel products dropped. Because production capacities of the European steel industry exceeded the size of the market by far, the crisis persisted into the 1980s. In the rapidly consolidating industry Schmolz + Bickenbach, however, continued to grow. In 1981 the company acquired one of its financially struggling suppliers, Krefeld-based foundry Körver & Nehring. Two years later Schmolz + Bickenbach's sales passed the DEM 1

```
┌─────────────────────────────────────────┐
│                                           │
│            KEY DATES                      │
│                 ■                         │
│  1919:  Arthur Schmolz and Oswald Bickenbach │
│         establish Dörrenberg Stahl-Gesellschaft. │
│  1922:  The Schmolz + Bickenbach name is adopted. │
│  1937:  The company becomes a private limited │
│         partnership.                      │
│  1954:  Schmolz + Bickenbach opens a subsidiary in │
│         the Netherlands.                  │
│  1959:  Another subsidiary is established in │
│         Switzerland.                      │
│  1981:  The company acquires Krefeld-based foundry │
│         Körver & Nehring.                 │
│  1998:  Schmolz + Bickenbach's new Vienna │
│         subsidiary coordinates activities in Eastern │
│         Europe.                           │
│  2003:  The company buys a majority stake in Swiss │
│         Steel.                            │
│  2006:  The company merges with Swiss Steel and is │
│         renamed Schmolz + Bickenbach AG.  │
│                                           │
└─────────────────────────────────────────┘
```

billion mark for the first time. By the end of the decade the company had about 2,000 workers on payroll and grossed roughly DEM 1.5 billion.

The unexpected opening of the Iron Curtain that separated the Eastern bloc countries in 1989 also opened a new potential market for Schmolz + Bickenbach. In the early 1990s the company set up three sales offices in former East Germany, in Berlin, Chemnitz, and Erfurt. In 1998 the company established a subsidiary in Vienna that coordinated business activities in Eastern European countries, including Hungary, Croatia, Slovenia, Slovakia, and the Czech Republic. However, the progressing liberalization of world trade also had a downside, namely low-cost imports of steel products that threatened to undermine the profitability of Western European manufacturers during the 1990s. Yet thanks to the company's focus on high-quality specialty steels and steel products, Schmolz + Bickenbach was able to largely resist the mounting pressure on prices.

2003 CREATION OF A SPECIALTY STEEL GROUP

After the turn of the 21st century Schmolz + Bickenbach went on a buying spree that added five large steel production and processing enterprises to its operations. The first acquisition in 2003, Schmolz + Bickenbach

together with Swiss partner Gebuka bought a 50.5 percent stake in Swiss Steel AG.

The history of the Swiss steelmaker based in Emmenbrücke north of Lucerne reached back to the 19th century. In the 1820s the von Moos family, which owned a hardware store in Lucerne, began to produce simple iron products such as nails in small workshops. In 1842 the business was acquired by the two brothers Ludwig and Franz Xaver who invested in new equipment for mass production and focused on manufacturing brand-name shoe nails. A decade later the Xaver brothers decided to produce the raw iron in their own factory, which was built in Emmenbrücke. To secure additional capital, the company was transformed into a public company, called von Moos'sche Eisenwerke AG, in 1887.

As cheap imports of semifinished steel products from Germany flooded the Swiss market early in the 20th century, von Moos'sche Eisenwerke suffered major financial losses and closed down its Siemens-Martin steel plant. The situation changed during World War I when von Moos'sche Eisenwerke became a contractor for the Swiss Army and the company's workforce doubled to over 700. The company continued to grow during the following three decades, reaching a workforce of 2,500 in the mid-1960s. Thereafter, however, the Swiss steel industry stagnated and entered a long crisis period. In 1996 the company was merged with Von Roll Stahl, another Swiss steel products manufacturer, to form Swiss Steel AG.

After the Schmolz + Bickenbach takeover in 2003, the acquired shares in Swiss Steel were transferred to SBGE Stahlholding, in which Schmolz + Bickenbach held 80 percent. In 2005 the company reorganized its production subsidiaries under the umbrella of Swiss Steel which raised Schmolz + Bickenbach's stake to 60 percent.

PRODUCTION OF STAINLESS STEEL STRUCTURAL STEEL BEGINS

In a second takeover, Schmolz + Bickenbach, through Swiss Steel, bought Edelstahlwerke Südwestfalen GmbH, a manufacturer of stainless steel products headquartered in Geisweid, north of Siegen in southern Westphalia, in 2004. Founded by the two entrepreneurs H. A. Dresler and Friedrich Klein as H. A. Dresler senior OHG in 1846, the company started manufacturing raw steel using the large supply of iron ore in the region around Siegen. About 70 workers operated a foundry, a forging workshop, and a rolling mill. Despite the strong competition from England and the Ruhr,

Dresler and Klein successfully claimed a stake in the market. A second company that later became a part of Edelstahlwerke Südwestfalen was Asbeck, Osthaus & Co. in Wehringhaus. Established in 1853 it later became Harkort-Eicken-Edelstahl. In the 1870s the Geisweid factory was transformed into Geisweider Eisenwerke AG, a public corporation that by then put out some 20,000 tons of high-quality steel.

In the early 20th century the company was a supplier to the German shipbuilding industry, survived the Great Depression, set up an electric arc furnace that allowed the use of scrap metal as raw material in the early 1930s, and began to specialize in high-quality stainless steel for ball bearings, which were in high demand before and during World War II. In 1946 Geisweider Eisenwerke merged with Stahlwerke Hagen AG. Through the reconstruction boom of the 1950s the renamed Stahlwerke Südwestfalen in Geisweid invested in new production facilities and its workforce grew quickly to 4,000.

In 1974 the company became part of the German steel conglomerate Krupp, which invested heavily in modernizing Geisweid's production facilities. However, as cheap imports from overseas caused a severe crisis of the European steel industry, the company began to generate losses. In 1994 Stahlwerke Südwestfalen was restructured and significantly downsized and spun off as Krupp Edelstahlprofile GmbH, a specialized manufacturer of stainless steel structural steel. After Schmolz + Bickenbach acquired the company from ThyssenKrupp in 2004, its name was changed to Edelstahlwerke Südwestfalen GmbH.

THE ADDITION OF STAINLESS STEEL LONG PRODUCTS

One year after the Krupp Edelstahlprofile takeover the Schmolz + Bickenbach group acquired a second steel products manufacturer with a longstanding tradition from ThyssenKrupp—Edelstahl Witten-Krefeld GmbH. Located in Witten, in the heart of the Ruhr, the company was founded in 1854 by merchant Carl-Ludwig Berger who, with no technical training, had conducted numerous experiments on making high-quality cast steel in the basement of his home. One of the main customers of his company, Gussstahlfabrik Berger & Co, was the state of Prussia, which Berger supplied with premium-quality steel for blades and sabers as well as with parts for rifles. Soon Berger shipped his steel parts for handguns to customers in Europe and the United States. Within a decade the company, which also started to manufacture cannons, employed some 300 workers who operated about five dozen furnaces. In the early 1870s the company was

transformed into a public corporation which in 1900 acquired its own smelter to secure raw materials supplies.

At the beginning of the 20th century the factory in Witten that focused on defense contracts was one of the most modern and productive in Europe and employed about 2,000 workers. In 1930 the company became part of Witten-based Ruhrstahl AG. In the decade that led up to World War II the steel manufacturer's output more than doubled and the factory became an important part of the German war economy. In 1947 the company regained its independence as Gusstahlwerk Witten AG.

Three decades later, in 1975, Gusstahlwerk Witten was merged with Krefelder Stahlwerke AG and became Thyssen's long stainless steel products division, Thyssen Edelstahlwerke AG. Founded in 1900 by German steel tycoons Peter Klöckner and August Thyssen, Krefelder Stahlwerke in the western Ruhr was a state-of-the-art manufacturer of high-quality tool steel that grew very rapidly. In 1937 Europe's largest electric arc furnace with a capacity of 30 tons was installed there. The company thrived during the postwar reconstruction boom, and specialized in long stainless steel products after it ended. In 1994 Thyssen Edelstahlwerke was spun off as an independent private company and renamed Edelstahl Witten-Krefeld, which was acquired by Swiss Steel in 2005. Two years later Edelstahlwerke Südwestfalen and Edelstahl Witten-Krefeld were merged and renamed Deutsche Edelstahlwerke.

GLOBAL EXPANSION CREATES NICHE MARKET LEADER

Schmolz + Bickenbach continued its rapid expansion through acquisitions. In 2006 the company took over Ugitech, a manufacturer of stainless steel and nickel alloy long products, such as semis, bars, wire rod, and drawn wires, from the French Arcelor group. Founded in 1908 in Ugine, France, the company put out about 200,000 tons of steel products and generated roughly EUR 630 million in annual sales with a workforce of 2,000 in 2005. The acquisition gave Schmolz + Bickenbach access to one of the company's main target markets, the United States, where Ugitech had begun to establish a distribution network in 1990 with the takeover of Alloy & Stainless, a stainless steel products distributor based in Colmar, Pennsylvania.

In February 2007 Schmolz + Bickenbach took a second major step to strengthen its presence in the United States when the company acquired Finkl & Sons Co., a Chicago-based manufacturer of hot work die steels, plastic mold steels, forged tool steels, large-dimensioned forged parts, and custom open die forgings for clients in the automotive, aviation, and mining industries. With roots going back to 1879 when the Bavarian immigrant Anton Finkl set up a blacksmith shop in Chicago, the company remained under the control of the Finkl family into the 2000s. At the time of the takeover, the company generated about $260 million in annual revenues, employed 900 workers worldwide and put out up to 160,000 tons of crude steel per year. The company's operations included a second production plant in Quebec, Canada, and sales offices in Mexico, Thailand, and the United Kingdom.

The Finkl & Sons acquisition positioned Schmolz + Bickenbach as a globally leading producer of tool steels. To further strengthen Schmolz + Bickenbach's position in North America, the company was building in a brand-new processing plant for stainless steel bars in Batavia, Illinois. According to the company's strategy to focus on high-value products Schmolz + Bickenbach sold its 65 percent share in Swiss reinforcing steel specialist Stahl Gerlafingen in spring 2006. A few months later Schmolz + Bickenbach transferred most of its activities to Swiss Steel and merged with the Swiss company. The new Swiss-based and publicly traded parent company was named Schmolz + Bickenbach AG in which majority shareholder Schmolz + Bickenbach Holding AG held a 74 percent stake.

Altogether, the company's annual sales roughly quadrupled between 2002 and 2008, primarily through acquisitions, about three-quarters of which originated in Germany and Western Europe. However, in the wake of the 2008 worldwide financial crisis, the company witnessed a sharp decline in orders received, in particular from its main customers in the automotive industry, and expected demand to recover only slowly. Looking ahead, Schmolz + Bickenbach was planning to further increase the percentage of high-value products and to expand its business activities in Eastern Europe and Asia, especially China, where the company had established four distribution centers by spring 2009. The company was also aiming at offering additional services to its customers, such as the complete handling of the procurement, warehousing and distribution, and customization of steel-related products.

Evelyn Hauser

PRINCIPAL SUBSIDIARIES

Deutsche Edelstahlwerke GmbH (Germany); Ugitech S.A. (France); A. Finkl & Sons Co. (USA); Swiss Steel AG; Schmolz + Bickenbach Blankstahl GmbH (Germany); Schmolz + Bickenbach A/S (Denmark);

Trafilerie Bedini Srl. (Italy); Steeltec AG; Schmolz + Bickenbach Çelik A.S. (Turkey); Boxholm Stål AB (Sweden); Schmolz + Bickenbach Guss GmbH & Co. KG (Germany); FSG Automotive AG (Germany); Schmolz + Bickenbach Stahlcenter AG; Schmolz + Bickenbach Distributions GmbH (Germany); Schmolz + Bickenbach France S.A.S.; Schmolz + Bickenbach Italia/STEELTEC TOSELLI (Italy); Günther + Schramm GmbH & Co. KG (Germany); Panlog AG; Schmolz + Bickenbach USA Inc.; Schmolz + Bickenbach UK Ltd.; Schmolz + Bickenbach AG (Austria); Schmolz + Bickenbach Oy (Finland); Bickenbach Portugal S.A.; Schmolz + Bickenbach China Ltd.; Schmolz + Bickenbach Hong Kong Co. Ltd.; Schmolz + Bickenbach (Czech Republic); Schmolz + Bickenbach Baltic OÜ (Estonia); Schmolz + Bickenbach Acélkereskedelmi Kft. (Hungary); Schmolz + Bickenbach B.V. (Netherlands); Schmolz + Bickenbach Sp. z o.o. (Poland); Schmolz + Bickenbach Romania Srl; Schmolz + Bickenbach Russia; Schmolz + Bickenbach Slovakia; Schmolz + Bickenbach Ibérica S.A. (Spain); Schmolz + Bickenbach Australia Pty. Ltd.; Schmolz + Bickenbach do Brasil Ltda.; Schmolz + Bickenbach Middle East FZCO (Dubai); Schmolz + Bickenbach Canada Inc.; Schmolz + Bickenbach Malaysia Sdn. Bhd.; Schmolz + Bickenbach Mexico S.A. de C.V.; Schmolz + Bickenbach Singapore Pte. Ltd.; Schmolz + Bickenbach South Africa (Pty.) Ltd.

PRINCIPAL COMPETITORS

Mittal Steel Company N.V.; Böhler-Uddeholm AG; AFV Acciaierie Beltrame S.p.A.

FURTHER READING

"A. Finkl & Sons Co. Signs Agreement to Be Acquired by German Steel Producer," *PR Newswire*, December 7, 2006.

Blum, Dieter, and Werner Schmidt, *Schmolz + Bickenbach: Providing Special Steel Solutions*, Düsseldorf, Germany: Schmolz + Bickenbach AG, 2007, 409 p.

Burgert, Philip, "Former TK Unit Sporting New Swiss Steel ID," *American Metal Market*, October 3, 2005, p. 6.

"Exclusive Negotiations Between Arcelor and Schmolz + Bickenbach for Ugitech," *Business Wire*, March 10, 2006.

"German Firm to Purchase Finkl & Sons," *Chicago Tribune*, December 8, 2006.

"Merger of Swiss Steel and S+B to Go Ahead (Stahlfusion bei S+B ist perfekt," *Europe Intelligence Wire*, September 22, 2006.

"Record Year for Schmolz + Bickenbach (Schmolz + Bickenbach trumpft auf)," *Europe Intelligence Wire*, March 19, 2007.

"Schmolz + Bickenbach and Gebuka Acquire Majority in Swiss Steel (Schmolz + Bickenbach ubernimmt Swiss Steel),"

Europe Intelligence Wire, May 27, 2003.

"Schmolz + Bickenbach to Expand in Asia and Eastern Europe (Schmolz + Bickenbach will im Ausland zukaufen)," *Europe Intelligence Wire,* August 21, 2006.

"Schmolz + Bickenbach USA," *Production Machining,* February 2008, p. 38.

"Specialist Steel Company S+B Sells Majority Stake in Stahl Gerlafingen (Schmolz + Bickenbach trimmt das Portfolio)," *Europe Intelligence Wire,* May 23, 2006.

"Technical Member Profile: Schmolz + Bickenbach," *Production Machining,* March 2008, p. 20.

"Ugine Stainless & Alloys Becomes UGITECH USA," *PR Newswire,* October 27, 2006.

"Ugitech—Stainless Steel Solutions Provider for the Medical Sector," *Eurotec,* April 2007, p. 17.

"UGITECH USA Completes Construction of Bar Mill," *PR Newswire,* May 31, 2007.

"Umbau der früheren Swiss Steel ohne öffentliches Kaufange-bot," *Associated Press Worldstream,* November 16, 2006.

"Vom Handelshaus zum integrierten Stahlkonzern," *Frankfurter Allgemeine Zeitung,* July 31, 2006, p. 12.

"World Business Briefing Europe: Switzerland: Steel Maker Acquires Units," *New York Times,* March 25, 2005, p. C4.

Shed Media plc

---

2 Holford Yard
London, WC1X 9HD
United Kingdom
Telephone: (44 0207) 239 1010
Fax: (44 0207) 239 1011
Web site: http://www.shed-media.com

Public Company
Incorporated: 1998
Sales: £81.9 million ($119 million) (2008)
Stock Exchanges: London AIM
Ticker Symbol: SHDP
NAICS: 512110 Motion Picture and Video Production

■ ■ ■

Shed Media plc is one of the United Kingdom's leading independent producers of television programming. Founded in 1998, Shed has grown on the basis of a number of hit programs, including the long-running *Bad Girls* and *Footballers' Wives* drama series. Listed on the London Stock Exchange's alternative investment market (AIM) since 2005, Shed Media has completed several acquisitions. These include Ricochet Productions, a leading producer of factual and reality television programming, including the international success *Supernanny*, as well as such fare as *My Crazy Life, It's Me or the Dog, Sex Tips for Girls, Open House,* and, for the U.S. market, *The Real Housewives of New York City.* Twenty Twenty, acquired by Shed in 2007, focuses on documentary, historical, drama, and current affairs programming. This subsidiary has produced such

programs as *The Choir, The Sorcerer's Apprentice, Wakey Wakey Campers, Brat Camp,* and *How to Divorce Without Screwing Up Your Children*. Wall to Wall, founded in 1987, adds its production of event specials, factual programming, and science and history programming to Shed's portfolio. Wall to Wall titles include the genealogy program *Who Do You Think You Are?, New Tricks,* and *Filth: The Mary Whitehouse Story*. Wall to Wall's first feature-length documentary, *Man on Wire* (2008), won an Oscar. Shed Media produced a total of 215 hours of programming, including 64 hours for the U.S. market, in 2008. The company also operates its own global distribution subsidiary, Outright Distributions Ltd. Shed Media is led by CEO Nicholas Southgate.

RISE OF U.K. INDEPENDENT TELEVISION PRODUCERS

Shed Media was founded by a team of former Granada executives led by Eileen Gallagher in 1998. A native of Scotland, Gallagher's career in British broadcasting began in the 1980s after a stint as a journalist for the *Glasgow Herald*. In 1984 Gallagher joined Scottish Television as a junior press officer, but by the end of the 1980s rose to become the station's director of broadcasting.

In 1993 Gallagher left Scottish Television to become the managing director of London Weekend Television, one of the United Kingdom's oldest ITV Network's broadcasters. When that company became part of Granada TV, one of the largest members of the ITV Network, Gallagher became Granada Broadcasting's deputy managing director.

COMPANY PERSPECTIVES

Shed Media is a leading creator and distributor of television content. The Group produces long-running television brands in drama, factual, documentary, factual entertainment and history. Shed Media owns and fully exploits the rights to its extensive programme library worldwide, through its in-house distribution company, Outright Distribution.

Gallagher had begun dreaming of a new career as a producer of television programming. She was encouraged by the rising strength of the independent television producers in the United Kingdom. This sector had received a kick-start in 1990 when the U.K. government passed a new communications bill. The new legislation forced the British Broadcasting Corporation (BBC) to open its broadcast schedule to independent programming for the first time. With a quota of at least 25 percent of the BBC's schedule to be filled by third-party producers, the United Kingdom saw the appearance of a growing number of nonaffiliated production houses.

GOING INDEPENDENT IN 1998

Despite an already crowded market, Gallagher, together with colleagues Maureen Chadwick, Ann McManus, and Brian Park, decided to leave Granada and form their own production company, called Shed Media in 1998. From the start, the company decided to focus on the drama genre, considered to be the most difficult in the television programming sector. The team immediately set to work developing their first series, a prison drama called *Bad Girls*.

Bad Girls was picked up by the ITV Network, and started broadcasting that same year, quickly becoming a hit for the television network and for Shed Media. By the end of its first year, the company had posted a profit of £700,000 ($1.1 million). The success of the first season brought Shed Media the commission for a new season and consistent renewals after that. By the end of its run, *Bad Girls* had aired for eight years and more than 100 episodes.

PACT VICTORY IN 2003

Shed Media soon placed a second hit vehicle, again for ITV, called *Footballers' Wives*. The show, described by *Hollywood Reporter* in 2006 as "a tale of glamour, sex and intrigue set in the world of English premier league soccer," became another highly watched and long-running series for Shed Media. The company continued to produce new episodes for the series until 2007, when ITV declined to renew it.

By then, however, Shed Media had emerged as one of the leading independent television producers in the United Kingdom, with a thriving business in the United States as well. In addition, Gallagher had become one of the most well-known and respected people in the U.K. television industry.

By 2000 Gallagher had been approached by U.K. satellite television leader Sky to take up a prominent place in its management. Yet Gallagher preferred to remain at the head of her fast-growing company and challenge the BBC's program commissioning policies.

Although the BBC had opened its airwaves to independent productions, and had respected its quota, it nonetheless insisted in taking control of all rights, including future broadcast and international rights, to the programs it acquired. This situation meant that although a company might enjoy success with sale of a program, it held no assets to ensure a future revenue stream and continued growth. As Gallagher pointed out to *Daily Variety* in 2007: "Without rights we are just a service industry."

Gallagher decided to lead the charge for a revamping of the BBC's purchasing policies, and took up the position as the chairperson of the producers' lobby Pact (Producers Alliance for Cinema and Television) in 2002. Over the next year, Gallagher waged an intensive lobbying campaign with the British government, leading negotiations with the BBC. Surprisingly, Gallagher met with a degree of resistance within the ranks of independent producers, who worried that adding a profit motive would denature the industry.

As Gallagher explained to the *Guardian* in 2007: "There is almost a British embarrassment about profits and popularity. I think it's old Britain. As much as I was brought up as a good Scottish socialist, I'm very much an entrepreneur. I'm proud that we make good profits and have good margins and that we can reward people well." Gallagher added: "The vast majority of programme-makers want to make brilliant programmes. ... Just because you're part of an organisation that has to make a profit doesn't diminish that absolute core objective. ... If there was no profit in this country, there would be no public sector and no BBC."

Gallagher's efforts paid off when, in 2003, the British government agreed to revise the legislation governing the audiovisual sector and pass the 2003 Communications Act. The new legislation provided a number of important boosts to the independent production sector.

KEY DATES

1998: Eileen Gallagher leads a group of former Granada executives in the creation of a television programming production company, Shed Media.

2002: Gallagher becomes chairman of Pact and helps negotiate new programming terms for independent producers from the BBC.

2005: Shed Media goes public and acquires Ricochet Productions.

2006: Shed acquires its own distribution operation, Outright Distribution.

2007: Shed acquires productions houses Twenty Twenty and Wall to Wall.

2008: Gallagher steps down as company CEO, replaced by Nicholas Southgate.

2009: Shed Media's board of directors reject a management buyout proposed by Gallagher and Southgate.

For one, producers were able to keep the rights to the programs they sold to broadcasters. For another, the BBC agreed to raise to 50 percent the level of programming commissioned from independent producers.

GOING PUBLIC IN 2005

The new legislation inaugurated a new era in the British television production sector, sparking a wave of consolidation as a number of larger producers bought up or merged with their smaller rivals acquiring their libraries as well. In 2005 Shed decided to join in on the consolidation. In March of that year, the company listed its stock on the London Stock Exchange's AIM, in a highly successful floatation that valued the company at £44 million ($83 million).

Next, Shed began looking for its first acquisition candidate. For this, the company, which maintained its focus on the drama segment, sought to expand its range of production offerings. This search led the group to Ricochet Productions in November 2005. Ricochet had been founded in 1995 and was another highly successful production company, particularly with commercial broadcaster Channel 4.

Ricochet focused on the factual, reality, and entertainment segments, and had created a number of highly popular programs. These included *Sex Tips for Girls* and *Nigella Bites* in 2000; *The Ultimate Rule*

Breakers, More Sex Tips for Girls, and *Why Pay Men for Sex* in 2002; *Wanted: New Mum and Dad* in 2005; and especially the long-running and international hit reality series, *Supernanny.* Shed paid $50 million to acquire Ricochet in 2005, while its managing director, Southgate, took up the position as chief financial officer for Shed Media.

NEW TARGETS IN THE UNITED STATES

The expansion of the group's library, and the success exportation of a number of series, particularly the *Supernanny* franchise into international markets, including the United States, encouraged Shed to establish its own international distribution arm. For this, the company bought U.K.-based distribution group Screentime Partners, subsequently renamed Outright Distribution, in 2006.

Shed Media increasingly turned its attention to expanding its operations in the United States. The company sought both to adapt its existing program formats for the U.S. market, as well as pitch new series developed specifically for that market. In support of these efforts, Shed Media continued to seek to expand its range of programming offerings.

This led the group to its next acquisition, of Twenty Twenty, for £19 million ($38 million) in September 2007. Twenty Twenty was an award-winning production house established in 1982. Twenty Twenty added its own expertise in the production of documentaries, current affairs programs, drama, and history series, before branching out into children's programming as part of Shed Media. The purchase added such ongoing hit series as *That'll Teach 'Em, Bad Lads Army,* and *Brat Camp.* The latter quickly attracted the attention of U.S. buyers, and was sold to ABC Television in 2008.

Two months after acquiring Twenty Twenty, Shed Media paid £20 million ($40 million) to acquire another well-respected producer, Wall to Wall. That company had been founded in 1987 by Alex Graham, also from Scotland and a good friend of Gallagher. Wall to Wall brought its own catalog of hit series, including the genealogy program *Who Do You Think You Are?* and the ongoing series *New Tricks.* Wall to Wall added its own range of programming interests, including event specials, entertainment shows, science and history programming, as well as factual and documentary programs. In 2008 Wall to Wall branched out from television, producing its first feature-length documentary, *Man on Wire.* That film went on to win both the British Academy of Film and Television Arts award for Outstanding British Film and the Oscar for Best Documentary Feature.

Shed's acquisitions helped cushion the blow as ITV declined to renew its two longest-running series, *Bad Girls* and *Footballers' Wives*. Nonetheless, Shed had continued to develop a range of new programs, including the hit school-age drama *Waterloo Road*, and part-fiction, part-reality music program, *Rock Rivals*, developed in cooperation with Simon Cowell, of *American Idol* and *Britain's Got Talent* fame.

At the end of 2008, Gallagher decided to step down as Shed Media's CEO in order to return her focus to developing new programs as head of Shed Productions. Southgate was then named to take the CEO spot. By then, the company's annual sales had climbed to nearly £82 million ($119 million). By then, too, the company had achieved a good balance among its U.K., U.S., and intellectual property (IP) rights operations. The company's IP business was especially strong, generating nearly 45 percent of the group's gross profits. Although the group's position in the U.K. market remained solid, the United States offered the most attractive prospects for future growth. In April 2009, for example, the company celebrated the 100th episode of the U.S. *Supernanny* series.

Despite its success, Shed Media's share price languished at the end of the decade, slipping to below its initial floatation price. This led Gallagher, Southgate, and other members of the company's management to propose a buyout of the company in February 2009. The proposal was rejected, however, by the company's board of directors.

Instead, Shed turned its focus toward seeking new expansion opportunities. For this, the company looked toward the U.S. market, where Shed announced its interest in entering the lucrative game-show segment. By the end of 2009, the company expected to see more than 40 percent of its revenues generated by its U.S. business. In just a decade, Shed Media had become one of the most successful and most international players in the United Kingdom's independent television production sector.

M. L. Cohen

PRINCIPAL SUBSIDIARIES

Off the Grid Limited; Outright Distributions Ltd; Ricochet Limited; Ricochet Productions Limited; Ricochet Television Inc; Shed Productions (Jailbirds) Limited; Shed Productions Ltd; Spring Place Services Ltd; Supernanny USA Inc; Twenty Twenty Brighton Ltd; Twenty Twenty Productions Ltd; Wall to Wall (Egypt) Ltd; Wall to Wall (Holdings) Ltd; Wall to Wall (New Tricks) Limited; Wall to Wall Drama Ltd; Wall to Wall Inc (USA); Wall to Wall Media Ltd; Wall to Wall Television Ltd.

PRINCIPAL DIVISIONS

Programme Revenue (UK); Programme Revenue (U.S.); IP Revenue.

PRINCIPAL OPERATING UNITS

Shed Media US; Wall to Wall; Twenty Twenty; Ricochet.

PRINCIPAL COMPETITORS

ALL3MEDIA Ltd.; Incepta Group PLC; Endemol UK PLC; The Sanctuary Group Ltd.; HIT Entertainment Ltd.; RDF Media Group PLC; Dorling Kindersley Ltd.; Avesco Group PLC; ITV Wales and West Ltd.; Entertainment Rights PLC; The Television Corporation Ltd.

FURTHER READING

Andreeva, Nellie, "Shed Media Adds Execs in New British Invasion," *Hollywood Reporter,* April 3, 2009, p. 8.

Andrews, Amanda, "Shed's Management in Second Buy-Out Bid," *Daily Telegraph* (London), February 20, 2009.

Clarke, Steve, "Brit Indies Pair Up," *Daily Variety,* September 20, 2007, p. 6.

———, "Shed Shores Up US Biz," *Daily Variety,* April 3, 2009, p. 4.

Creamer, Jon, "Bill of Rights," *Televisual,* June 2003, p. 18.

"Eileen Gallagher on the Success of Television Production Company Shed Media," *Telegraph,* March 10, 2009.

Gibson, Owen, "'Grow Up—We Have to Make Money,'" *Guardian* (London), November 26, 2007, p. 5.

Gleeson, Bill, "Shed Media Expands Its Programme of Takeovers," *Daily Post* (Liverpool), November 30, 2007, p. 25.

"Good Times for Shed Media," *Investors Chronicle,* April 6, 2009.

Hasell, Nick, "Shed Media," *Times* (London), April 3, 2009, p. 57.

"'I've Had a Few Cheque Books Waved at Me,'" *Guardian* (London), May 29, 2000, p. 8.

Mason, Rowena, "Southgate Is New Chief Executive at Shed Media," *Daily Telegraph* (London), December 4, 2008.

"New Deal for Shed on Waterloo Road," *Evening Standard* (London), March 9, 2009, p. 30.

"The Shows Go on for Production Company As Figures Rise," *Daily Post,* May 1, 2008, p. 17.

Thompson, Susan, "Shed Media to Adopt Maker of BBC's *Who Do You Think You Are?*" *Times* (London), November 26, 2007, p. 42.

Turner, Mimi, "Taken to the Shed," *Hollywood Reporter,* February 18, 2006, p. 14.

"TV Production Firm Shed Beats Forecasts," *Evening Standard* (London), April 2, 2009, p. 28.

Sikorsky Aircraft Corporation

━━━■━━━

6900 Main Street
Stratford, Connecticut 06615
U.S.A.
Telephone: (203) 386-4000
Fax: (203) 386-7300
Web site: http://www.sikorsky.com

Wholly Owned Subsidiary of United Technologies Corporation
Incorporated: 1923 as the Sikorsky Aero EngineeringCorporation
Employees: 13,000
Sales: $5.37 billion (2008)
NAICS: 336411 Aircraft Manufacturing; 336412 Aircraft Engine and Engine Parts Manufacturing

■ ■ ■

For much of the time since its founder first tinkered with helicopter design, the Sikorsky Aircraft Corporation has stood for the leading technology in vertical flight. The company designs, manufacturers, and services military and commercial helicopters as well as fixed-wing aircraft. The firm also provides spare parts and maintenance, repair, and overhaul services. Sikorsky helicopters are used by all branches of the U.S. military as well as militaries and civil firms in 40 countries across the globe. The U.S. Army and the U.S. Navy are heavily

dependent on Sikorsky H-60 models—the Black Hawk and Seahawk helicopters.

A PIONEERING HERITAGE

Igor Sikorsky was in a sense born to a pioneering family. His father, Ivan, was a researcher in the infant field of psychiatry during the late 19th century. As a boy, Sikorsky's interest in aviation was propelled by reading Jules Verne, particularly his *Clipper of the Clouds,* which described a hypothetical vertical flight machine.

In 1908, Sikorsky's imagination was further stoked by seeing the Zeppelin dirigible in Germany and by hearing accounts of the Wright brothers' heavier-than-air flying machine, which was then touring Europe. Sikorsky had meanwhile studied at the Naval Academy in Saint Petersburg and Polytechnic Institute of Kiev, and had attended lectures in France as well. He returned to Russia in 1909, entering the passionate center of the nascent aviation community, where he was inspired by meeting legendary aviators Louis Bleriot and Ferdinand Ferber, who told Sikorsky his idea for a flight machine was unattainable.

Sikorsky's sister purchased for him the same type of engine that had powered Bleriot's channel-crossing flight, and Sikorsky returned to Kiev the next spring to build a helicopter. His first two attempts failed, however, and he turned to designing conventional aircraft. Sikorsky's fifth plane, appropriately dubbed the S-5, actually flew, though poorly. His next three designs, comprising the S-6 series, would both cement his reputation and attract a patron.

COMPANY PERSPECTIVES

We produce products and services that safeguard and delight our customers. We work in a safe, ethical and friendly environment that fosters continual learning and growth. We hold ourselves accountable for the commitments we make to our customers, our shareholders and each other. We have the skills and the motivation to embrace impossible challenges, confident of our success. We work together in a collaborative fashion, respecting each other's ideas and diversity. We behave, at all times, at the highest levels of business and human integrity. We are citizens of our community and accept our leadership role with humility and resolve. We are aligned and committed to our vision. "We pioneer flight solutions that bring people home everywhere ... every time."

AN AWARD-WINNING REPUTATION

M. V. Shidlovskiy, impressed with the potential of both the airplane and Sikorsky himself, placed him in charge of the St. Petersburg aviation factory of the Russ-Baltic Wagon Company. There, in addition to building airsleds, Sikorsky built two streamlined aircraft that won competitions against France's most advanced military planes.

His next project was truly a gargantuan undertaking. The idea of multiple engines was viewed with some suspicion at the time, but Sikorsky began building a giant, four-engine flying machine which received several appellations. First called the *Ruskii vityaz* (Russian knight) by its designer, the aircraft picked up the tag the "Petersburg Duck" from skeptics before it had flown and eventually became known as the Grand. The stable craft proved that multiengine flight was viable, even with the loss of one or more engines.

The Grand was damaged while parked when a lesser aircraft's engine fell out of the sky and through its wing. Its successor, the Il'ya Muromets, succeeded on an even grander scale and brought Sikorsky worldwide acclaim. In 1914, one of its most memorable achievements was to fly, in stages, a 1,600-mile round-trip between St. Petersburg and Kiev. Eventually 70 of these aircraft were built for use as bombers in World War I, bringing in the age of the heavy bomber. As would become a tradition for aircraft designers in Russia,

Sikorsky was given the rank of general during the conflict.

REVOLUTION IN RUSSIA AND A MOVE TO AMERICA

Sikorsky fled the Bolsheviks in February 1918; his patron, Shidlovskiy, was captured and executed. The impoverished Sikorsky soon made his way to France, where he won a contract to build military bombers. When the Great War soon came to an end, Sikorsky sailed for America.

Despite an unsuccessful venture with other émigrés in New York, in 1919 Sikorsky won a contract with the U.S. Army Air Service and moved to Washington, D.C. However, the plan was soon dropped for lack of funding, and Sikorsky returned to New York with a new focus on commercial aviation. A second attempt to form a partnership in 1920 also failed, and Sikorsky began teaching night classes to Russian immigrants to supplement his income. On March 5, 1923, Sikorsky formed the Sikorsky Aero Engineering Corporation with help from his predominantly Russian expatriate supporters. Most of the shares were worth $100, but the esteemed composer Sergei Rachmaninoff gave Sikorsky $5,000, allowing him to rent hangar space at Roosevelt Field.

A chicken farm housed the company's first workshop, where Sikorsky's motivated team transformed a piece of junk (actually many pieces of salvaged materials such as hospital beds) into an aircraft dubbed the S-29-A. Despite such inauspicious beginnings, the craft did get off the ground, although it quickly proved underpowered and its first attempt resulted in a crash landing.

With new engines, the 14-passenger S-29-A finally overcame gravity on September 25, 1924. A tour and numerous publicity stunts ensued, earning the fledgling company a place in the American imagination. Four years later the S-29-A (A for "America") ended its service life in the hands of another eminent aviation enthusiast, Howard Hughes, who destroyed it for a film stunt in the picture *Hell's Angels*.

FUELING IMAGINATION AND BUILDING A BUSINESS

Aviation dominated the American imagination in the Jazz Age. Airplanes became a popular Art Deco design motif and the airways became a stylish way to travel. The Sikorsky firm produced several designs for air races, including one for the Orteig transatlantic crossing prize that Charles Lindbergh eventually claimed. However,

KEY DATES

1923: Igor Sikorsky forms the Sikorsky Aero Engineering Corporation.

1924: The 14-passenger S-29-A aircraft flies for the first time.

1929: United Aircraft and Transport Corporation buys the company.

1931: Sikorsky patents a design for a single-rotor helicopter.

1939: The VS-300, with three tail rotors, flies for the first time.

1941: Sikorsky lands a contract to build the XR-4 helicopter for the U.S. Army.

1962: Sikorsky introduces its CH-53, which is designed to carry troops for the Marine Corps and is the largest helicopter in the world at this time.

1974: The Black Hawk helicopter makes its first flight.

1975: Sikorsky's parent changes its name to United Technologies Corp.

1998: Helicopter Support Inc. is acquired.

2002: The company purchases Derco Aerospace Inc.

2005: Sikorsky loses its Marine One contract.

2007: The company secures a $7.4 billion order for approximately 540 military helicopters.

this plane, the S-35, was destroyed in a disastrous accident.

In spite of this setback, the company moved to a better equipped facility in College Point, New York. It settled in to producing clippers—the long-range amphibious aircraft that became a staple of international airlines such as Pan American. The fact that they were essentially flying boats naturally made them popular with aviators concerned about safety while flying overseas routes. The S-38, the most successful of the lot, also appeared in corporate and military roles.

The company had become the Sikorsky Manufacturing Corporation in 1925 and was led by Massachusetts businessman Arnold Dickinson as president. The company expanded quickly, relocating to Stratford, Connecticut, and reorganizing as the Sikorsky Aviation Company in 1929. It was promptly taken into the folds of the United Aircraft and Transport Corporation, which would be reorganized as the United Technologies Corporation in 1975.

WHIRLING INTO THE NEXT DECADE

The refined S-42 outclassed all of its clipper competitors upon its appearance in 1934. However, the heyday of the flying boat was rapidly coming to an end, and the company would have to scramble to stay in business.

Sikorsky persuaded United Aircraft management to let him revisit his old studies on developing a practical vertical flight apparatus. Some headway had been made since Sikorsky abandoned his projects. Engines and building materials had become lighter and stronger, and the autogiro, essentially a conventional aircraft with a large free-rotating propeller on top instead of a fixed wing, first flew in the 1920s. As a result, in 1939 Sikorsky began to work on the project again at the Vought-Sikorsky plant in Stratford, Connecticut.

Although Sikorsky had patented a design in 1931 for a single-rotor helicopter, others had outpaced him by the time he reentered the field. The World War I aviator Heinrich Focke had built a twin-rotor helicopter in 1936, and others in Germany and France were also producing working models. In fact, Anton Flettner's Fl-282 Kolibri (Hummingbird) became operational in the German military in 1940.

As a helicopter's rotor turns one way, opposite forces swing the body the other. Some balance is needed in order to keep the machine stable—usually either another, counter-rotating rotor or a small vertically mounted tail rotor. Sikorsky was unique in devoting his efforts to the single-rotor philosophy, which he erroneously believed he had originated. (In fact, his countryman Boris Yuriev had developed such a design in 1912.)

Sikorsky borrowed the main rotor design from the autogiro developed by Juan de la Cierva, which was by then being made in the United States. The first models of the VS-300 actually had three tail rotors; a number of different configurations were tried.

The VS-300 first flew on September 14, 1939, the dawn of World War II. It was just a short, tethered flight, but it confirmed the viability of the craft. After a change of engines and other adjustments over the next several months, it became capable of extended flights, although controllability in forward flight remained a problem.

MILITARY HELICOPTERS' HEYDAY

Nevertheless, the progress of the VS-300 earned Sikorsky Aircraft a contract to build a model for the U.S. Army in January 1941, to be dubbed the XR-4. In May, the refined VS-300-A set a stunning endurance record, hovering for one hour and 30 minutes. Sikorsky, and the United States, stood at the forefront of vertical flight. The new technology would soon be put to wartime use.

Sikorsky built 131 of the R-4 series during World War II; over 200 other models were also built. The British firm Westland built a version of its successor, the R-5, under license, dubbing it the Dragonfly. The helicopters were used for reconnaissance and rescue missions right away. In 1944, an R-4 flying in Burma made the first combat aerial rescue. Soon these types of missions were being flown routinely, since the helicopter could reach places that no fixed-wing aircraft could, and its hovering ability made it practical to pluck people from harm's way. R-4s were used extensively in the Korean War.

The R-4 spawned the company's first civil helicopter, known as the S-51. In spite of its unparalleled military and civil applications, the helicopter never became the consumer item that Sikorsky envisioned after the war. Every man, it turned out, would not one day have a helicopter in his backyard, as illustrated in one of the company's wartime promotional films.

POSTWAR PROSPERITY

For a time in the 1950s and 1960s three commuter airlines serving New York, Chicago, and Los Angeles operated aircraft such as the large S-61 twin-rotor helicopter to ferry passengers from the outlying airports of the jet age to urban centers. Due to the high cost of flying the helicopters ($3.68 per seat per mile in 1954), these operations were heavily subsidized (half the average fare, or a total of $4.3 million in 1965). The flights were consigned to history after the subsidies were eliminated in 1970, although the popularity of the flights had grown and the per-seat cost had fallen to only $0.32 per mile by 1964.

The S-64 "flying crane," a huge, powerful helicopter specifically designed to carry large loads, created its own unique heavy-lifting niche. The copter was unique in that it did away with the cargo compartment that would otherwise limit its lifting capacity, instead latching onto containers. It first flew in 1962, but never developed into the modular commuter vehicle Sikorsky had envisioned. Of 98 aircraft made, 88 were used in military applications. Among the few commercial customers, U.S. Steel tested the concept of lifting manufactured houses to remote locations with these aircraft.

Sales of helicopters to the U.S. military during the Vietnam War peaked in the mid-1960s, when corporate orders were also rising. Between 1953 and 1996, Sikorsky sold 1,444 of its S-58 models to the U.S. government. The commercial sector was dominated by competitor Bell Aerospace, which also sold thousands of its military UH-1 series. In 1962 Sikorsky introduced its CH-53, designed to carry troops for the Marine Corps. At the time it was the largest helicopter in the world. Sikorsky faced some Soviet competition in South America for military and oil industry clients.

PASSING OF A LEGEND

Sikorsky, who had retired in 1957, died on October 26, 1972. By the time of his death, the helicopter had become well established in the civilian world. By 1970 almost 300 hospitals in the United States relied on helicopters for ambulance duties, and the number of heliports had grown within a decade from about 360 to more than 2,300.

Passenger helicopters were still being used by some commuter carriers, and the industry as a whole (including entrants such as Bell, Hughes, and Boeing's Vertol division) shipped more than 500 units per year to the commercial sector. Growth was expected in several areas, such as servicing offshore oil platforms, which remained a viable area, as well as serving in corporate fleets. Sikorsky sought to increase its exports.

In the mid-1970s the company promoted its S-67 Black Hawk attack helicopter as a replacement for the Vietnam-era Bell AH-1 Cobra. Although its testing program suffered a lethal crash in 1974, the machine eventually became a favorite of the U.S. armed forces. Sikorsky continued to dominate the military marketplace throughout the 1970s.

Military contracts kept coming during the Reagan years, including a $950 million contract for 294 UH-60 helicopters. By 1982 Sikorsky had grown into a military giant, with total sales of $1 billion and 12,000 employees.

In the mid-1980s Boeing and Sikorsky entered into a joint venture to develop the $22 billion LHX program of light helicopters. They were awarded the military contract in 1991, ensuring both companies a place in attack helicopter niches as well as the prospect of future international sales. At the time, the company was producing only four models: the Black Hawk, Seahawk, S-76, and CH-53. However, its research interests were diverse, including studying materials for a hypersonic aircraft.

Sikorsky sought international manufacturing partners throughout the 1980s. In 1984 the company succeeded in selling two dozen commercial helicopters to China. Nevertheless, only a fraction of sales, which totaled $1.5 billion in 1987, came from foreign sources.

NEW HORIZONS: 1990–99

The company remained dependent on military contracts, a liability in the 1990s. It laid off nearly 2,000 workers in the first two years of the decade. The S-92 carried Sikorsky's hopes for the future in the commercial medium helicopter segment, where the company expected the most growth.

In July 1997 Sikorsky announced an agreement to supply the U.S. Army, Navy, and Air Force with helicopters for five more years. The Army ordered 58 UH-60L Black Hawks, while the Navy ordered 42 CH-60 assault helicopters, and the Air Force ordered eight HH-60G Pave Hawk helicopters for search and rescue.

In 1994 international clients accounted for one-third of the company's $2.1 billion in sales. Sikorsky produced 18 different models in order to satisfy the divergent demands of the international marketplace. The company also looked abroad, specifically in Turkey, to develop relationships with foreign suppliers.

In 1997 Korean Air Lines Co. joined Sikorsky in a six-year, $400 million agreement to develop general purpose helicopters. Sikorsky also shared technology with De Bono Industries of Malacca as part of a $20 million helicopter sale to the Malaysian government. In 1998 the company acquired Helicopter Support Inc.

FLYING INTO THE 21ST CENTURY

Despite some major setbacks, Sikorsky Aircraft focused on growth during the early years of the new millennium. While recent years had proved difficult, with employee layoffs and plant consolidations, the company stood to benefit from the U.S. Army's modernization plan, announced in April 2000, which named the UH-60 Black Hawk as the core of its fleet. The U.S. Navy also received authorization to purchase up to 237 MH-60S Seahawk aircraft through 2010.

In addition to military contracts, the company pursued growth through key acquisitions. It purchased Derco Aerospace Inc. in 2002, which provided military fixed-wing logistics, overhaul, and repair services. Two years later it added Schweizer Aircraft Corp. to its arsenal, giving it a foothold in the unmanned aerial vehicle (UAV) market. Its next deal was made in 2005 when it bought Keystone Ranger Holdings Inc., a custom installation and service firm based in Pennsylvania. Keystone could customize aircraft, providing various interior and equipment needs for Sikorsky's diverse customer base, which included not only military branches, but very important clients, offshore oil customers, and *Fortune* 500 customers.

During 2005 Sikorsky lost its bid to produce the Marine One fleet, helicopters used by the president of the United States. It lost out to an international team led by Lockheed Martin Corp., which provided a model with a larger cabin. The program was put on hold in 2009, however, after the U.S. Navy revealed that it had fallen seriously behind schedule and that costs had skyrocketed. The grounding of the Lockheed contract led to speculation that Sikorsky would have a chance to re-bid on the Marine One project.

MILITARY RELATIONSHIP CONTINUES

During 2006 the National Brotherhood of Teamsters launched a strike at Sikorsky's production facilities in Fairfield County, Connecticut. The strike halted production and left the company subject to criticism from the Pentagon. The negative press was short-lived. Indeed, during 2007 the company signed a $7.4 billion contract to provide over 500 Black Hawk and Seahawk helicopters to the U.S. Army and U.S. Navy.

Meanwhile, the company agreed to pay the U.S. government $2.9 million in 2009 to settle a case related to charges the company committed fraud by installing armored plates on Black Hawk helicopters that had not been tested for combat-readiness as required by contract. The settlement, while embarrassing, did little to mar the relationship Sikorsky had with the U.S. military. In March of that year the company delivered its 100th UH-60M Black Hawk helicopter to the Army. It was expected that the Black Hawk fleet would log over one million hours of combat duty in Iraq and Afghanistan from 2003 through 2009.

With sales and profits on the rise, Sikorsky appeared to be well positioned for additional growth. The company believed its new X2 technology, which significantly increased the airspeed of helicopters, had the potential to generate substantial profits. With a longstanding history of innovation and a steady stream of military contracts, Sikorsky would no doubt continue to play a major role in the aviation industry for years to come.

Frederick C. Ingram
Updated, Christina M. Stansell

PRINCIPAL COMPETITORS

AugustaWestland; Bell Helicopter Textron Inc.; Eurocopter S.A.

FURTHER READING

Bartlett, Robert M., *Sky Pioneer: The Story of Igor I. Sikorsky,* New York: Charles Scribner's Sons, 1947.

Brown, David A., "US Helicopter Lead Threatened," *Aviation Week and Space Technology,* May 28, 1973, pp. 179–81.

Cochrane, Dorothy, Von Hardesty, and Russell Lee, *The Aviation Careers of Igor Sikorsky,* Seattle: University of Washington Press for the National Air and Space Museum, 1989.

Dawkins, Pam, "Dodd Shows Support at Sikorsky Visit," *Connecticut Post,* April 16, 2009.

DeLear, Frank J., *Igor Sikorsky: His Three Careers in Aviation,* New York: Dodd, Mead and Company, 1969.

Driscoll, Lisa, "It'll Take More Than Saddam for Sikorsky to Soar Again," *Business Week,* October 1, 1990, p. 37.

Finne, K. N., *Igor Sikorsky: The Russian Years,* edited by Carl J. Bobrow and Von Hardesty, translated and adapted by Von Hardesty, Washington, D.C.: Smithsonian Institution Press, 1987.

Hughes, David, "Boeing Sikorsky Fantail Demonstrates Unprecedented Maneuverability," *Aviation Week and Space Technology,* July 8, 1991, pp. 45–49.

Kandebo, Stanley W., "Sikorsky Boosts Quality, Cuts Costs with Kaizen," *Aviation Week and Space Technology,* May 1, 1995, pp. 39–40.

Kastner, J. "Sikorsky's Helicopter: A Flying Machine Which May Some Day Be Everyman's Airplane," *Life,* June 21, 1943, pp. 80–84.

"Military Helicopter Production Reaches Peak," *American Aviation,* May 1967, p. 139.

"New Markets Give Helicopter Industry a Whirling Future," *Industry Week,* February 22, 1971, pp. 18–20.

Phillips, Edward H., "Sikorsky Forging Ahead with S-92 Program," *Aviation Week and Space Technology,* January 5, 1998, pp. 48–49.

Ropelewski, Robert R., "Blackhawk Future Pondered After Crash," *Aviation Week and Space Technology,* September 9, 1974.

"Sikorsky Aircraft Pays $2.9 Million to Settle False Claims Act Allegations," *US Fed News,* May 1, 2009.

Sikorsky, Igor I., *The Invisible Encounter,* New York: Charles Scribner's Sons, 1947.

———, *The Message of the Lord's Prayer,* New York: Charles Scribner's Sons, 1942.

———, *The Story of the Winged-S: An Autobiography,* New York: Dodd, Mead and Company, 1938 (rev. ed. 1958).

"Sikorsky Marks 100th Delivery of Newest Black Hawk," *New Haven Register,* March 29, 2009.

Siuru, Bill, "Igor Sikorsky: Aviation Pioneer and Engineering Entrepreneur," *Mechanical Engineering,* August 1990, pp. 60–63.

Smart, Tim, and Stan Crock, "Choppy Winds at Sikorsky," *Business Week,* May 27, 1996, p. 40.

Soule, Alexander, "For Sikorsky, a $7B Cap on a Very Good Year," *Fairfield County Business Journal,* December 24, 2007.

———, "Sikorsky Seeks to Avoid Repeat of '06 Job Action," *Fairfield County Business Journal,* February 2, 2009.

Varnon, Rob, "Lockheed's Marine One Grounded," *Connecticut Post,* May 16, 2009.

———, "Sikorsky's X2 Copter May Suit Army's Need for Speed," *Connecticut Post,* May 6, 2009.

Velocci, Anthony L., Jr., "Boeing Sikorsky Could Reap Bonanza in Foreign Military Sales After LH Win," *Aviation Week and Space Technology,* April 15, 1991, pp. 72–73.

Wetmore, Warren C., "Sikorsky Pushes Export of S-67 Gunships," *Aviation Week and Space Technology,* July 29, 1974, pp. 39, 42, 47.

Wright, Robert A., "Helicopter Firms to Seek Big Commercial Market," *New York Times,* October 22, 1967, p. F1.

Solo Cup Company

1700 Old Deerfield Road
Highland Park, Illinois 60035
U.S.A.
Telephone: (847) 831-4800
Fax: (847) 831-5849
Web site: http://www.solocup.com

Private Company
Incorporated: 1936 as Paper Container Manufacturing
    Company
Employees: 7,100
Sales: $1.8 billion (2008)
NAICS: 326122 Plastics Pipe and Pipe Fitting
    Manufacturing; 322299 All Other Converted Paper
    Product Manufacturing; 326150 Urethane and
    Other Foam Product (Except Polystyrene)
    Manufacturing

■ ■ ■

Solo Cup Company is a leading manufacturer of disposable food and beverage containers. It makes paper, plastic, and foam cups, plates, and bowls, as well as beverage lids, drinking straws, disposable cutlery, and food containers. It serves both retail markets and the foodservice industry, with major customers in global food chains such as McDonald's, Starbucks, and Yum Brands. Its brand names include Sweetheart, Trophy, and Solo. The company has manufacturing facilities across the United States and in Mexico, Canada, Panama, and the United Kingdom. The private company was run by members of the founding Hulse-

man family until 2007. The company's major stockholder is the New York-based private-equity firm Vestar Capital Partners.

EARLY YEARS

Solo Cup Company began its life as the Paper Container Manufacturing Company. It was founded by Leo Hulseman in Chicago in 1936. Hulseman had been an employee of the Dixie Cup Company, maker of the familiar disposable Dixie cup. Hulseman's company spent much of its first years fighting off a patent infringement suit from Dixie. The suit was filed in 1938, and dragged through the courts for the next ten years, with most of the charges eventually withdrawn. Court records alleged that Dixie had cut prices on its cups solely in order to undercut Hulseman, and that Dixie also bought up competitors when it could, in order to hold on to the paper cup market. Undeterred by Dixie, the Paper Container Manufacturing Co. found customers for its brand name Solo cup, a paper cone that Hulseman offered to local purveyors of bottled water. The Solo brand became so well known that in 1952 the company changed its name to Solo Cup Company.

WELL-KNOWN PRODUCTS

The company manufactured many products that became ubiquitous in U.S. homes and businesses. It made waxed paper cups for cold beverages in the 1950s that were used especially by drive-in restaurants of the era. Its Cozy Cup became a standard in offices in the 1960s, where it replaced old-fashioned ceramic coffee mugs in corporate lunchrooms and kitchenettes. In the 1970s, Solo moved from paper-coated disposable cups into plastic cups. It made a certain red plastic Solo cup that became something of an American icon. These cups had a large retail market.

Promotions of Solo cups for a time featured recordings by Hulseman's wife, Dora Hall. Hall had been a singer and actress in her youth, but cut short her career to marry the entrepreneur. When she made her recordings, and even starred in a syndicated television program alongside Frank Sinatra and other famous singers of the day, she was a grandmother. Hulseman himself was a dashing figure, known for his keen interest in polo. He was a championship player, and trained a Solo Cup polo team in California for many years.

The Solo Cup Company was evidently a comfortably profitable business throughout Leo Hulseman's career. The family owned several homes, and could afford to spend $400,000 on Mrs. Hulseman's television debut, as well as large sums on other television advertising for Solo. Hulseman's sons were involved in the business, too, and the family owned all the stock. When Leo died in 1989, his son Robert L. Hulseman took over. The company still manufactured out of its original Chicago plant, although it also had other facilities in Illinois, and later across the United States.

EXPANDING FACILITIES AND MARKETS

A decade after the founder's death, Solo was still considered a low-profile company in Chicago. The Solo brand was well known, although the company itself did not often make news. Yet it had grown considerably. By the late 1990s, Solo employed approximately 4,200 people. Half of these worked in factories in Illinois, where Solo had its original Chicago facilities as well as plants in Urbana and Wheeling. The company also had facilities in Maryland and elsewhere in the United States. Annual revenues stood at about $650 million.

In the late 1990, Solo embarked on several major expansions. In 1997, it began building a $15.5 million distribution facility in Maryland. Then in 1999 Solo bought a 107-acre plot of land on Chicago's Southeast Side for another new plant. This Chicago real estate had been the site of steel mills owned by U.S. Steel, which by the 1990s went under the name USX. The mills dated back to the 1880s, and had been shut down in 1992. USX had tried to unload the entire site, which stretched to close to 600 acres, to a single buyer for $85 million. When that price proved too high, the company sold a smaller portion to Solo. Solo paid only $6.5 million, while the city and state chipped in roughly $30 million in assistance to develop the site. Solo's new factory to be built on the site was to cost about $75 million.

Solo worked closely with Illinois government officials interested in promoting the state's trade. In 2000, Solo inked a deal with the fourth largest brewery in the world, South African Breweries PLC. The brewery planned to buy over 15 million Solo cups over the next five years. This huge deal was brokered under the auspices of a trade mission sent by the governor of Illinois. By this time, Solo was involved in global markets, selling to worldwide companies such as McDonald's and Starbucks. By 2004, the company also had made several small acquisitions abroad, buying in Japan and the United Kingdom.

ACQUISITIONS CHANGE COMPANY'S PATH

While it was expanding and refurbishing its plants in the 1990s, Solo also began making acquisitions. Solo spent $140 million in 1998 to buy Clear Shield National Inc., a subsidiary of Envirodyne Industries. Clear Shield made plastic cutlery and drinking straws, product lines Solo did not carry. Clear Shield had five U.S. manufacturing facilities, with two in Wheeling, Illinois and others in the East, South and West. It seemed a nice match for Solo. By that time, Solo was the second largest manufacturer in the plastics category called thermoforming. Its sales were higher than that of Clear Shield's parent, Envirodyne. In addition, both Clear Shield and Solo were major Illinois employers. At the time of the acquisition, a Solo spokesman told industry journal *Plastics News* that plans were to keep the operations of Clear Shield and Solo separate.

Solo also made forays abroad. In 2000 it acquired the British-based company Insulpak. It renamed its new purchase Solo Cup Europe. The next year, Solo bought a Japanese manufacturer of disposable containers, Sanyo Pak. This became Solo Cup Asia Pacific. These were relatively small acquisitions that gave

```
┌─────────────────────────────────────────────────┐
│                                                   │
│              KEY DATES                            │
│                    ■                              │
│  ────────────────────────────────────────         │
│                                                   │
│  1936:  Company is founded as Paper Container      │
│         Manufacturing Company.                     │
│  1952:  Name is changed to Solo Cup Company.       │
│  1989:  Founder Leo Hulseman dies; leadership passes│
│         to son Robert.                             │
│  1998:  Clear Shield is acquired.                  │
│  2004:  Sweetheart Cup Company is acquired.        │
│  2007:  Vestar takes control of board.             │
│                                                   │
└─────────────────────────────────────────────────┘
```

the company a foothold in the overseas market. The really large acquisition, which in many ways changed the company's course, came in 2004. That year Solo bought its biggest competitor, the Sweetheart Cup Company.

Sweetheart had had a tangled history, beginning life in 1911 as an ice cream cone bakery. In the 1930s, it began making straws and developed the Sweetheart brand. It moved into the disposable products market after World War II, and expanded rapidly. It had somewhat broader product lines than Solo, making cups, straws and cutlery, and also disposable food packaging for hospitals, and food containers such as ice cream boxes and juice boxes. It went public in 1961, but remained in the hands of the founding Shapiro family until the 1980s. When it was sold in 1983 to the Fort Howard Paper Co., the company was known as Maryland Cup, and it ran more than 30 manufacturing plants employing some 10,000 people.

When Fort Howard Paper was itself acquired in 1988, its Maryland Cup subsidiary was spun off into a private firm then known as Sweetheart Holdings. The holding company ran Sweetheart Cup, as well as other businesses such as a bakery, a holdover from the company's earliest years. The company had lost profitability as it changed hands rapidly. It was sold again in 1993, to the investment firm American Industrial Partners. In the early 2000s, the company was recording sales of $1.3 billion, but was still not profitable and was hampered by debt.

Sweetheart needed a buyer, and Solo leapt at the chance to combine with its competitor, forming a new company that would be the biggest in the market, with combined sales of over $2 billion. Solo would gain access to Sweetheart's superior distribution network and its large foodservice market. To buy the bigger company, Solo needed $917 million. It got $240 million of that from a New York venture-capital firm, Vestar Capital Partners. Vestar put up the cash in exchange for a one-

third interest in the company, along with two seats on Solo's board and an option to gain further control of Solo if certain financial goals were not met down the road. Solo borrowed $650 million, too. As of February 2004, Solo found itself a much expanded company, with over 30 manufacturing facilities, new product lines, and a huge task of integrating the two former competitors.

MERGER DIFFICULTIES

It was much more difficult to bring the two companies together than Solo had thought. On top of that, the cost of plastic resin Solo needed as raw material for its disposable products began to rise. Solo poured money into consultants, but more than two years after the merger closed, Solo and Sweetheart were still using different, incompatible software for ordering, tracking, and invoicing. The companies operated as two separate entities, meaning that all the savings that were to have come from integration were not realized.

In 2005, Solo was forced to return to its bankers and borrow more money. This gave it long-term debt of $1 billion. The company lost $8.2 million in 2005. This was an improvement over the almost $50 million loss of 2004, but things seemed not to be going well. Company president Ronald Whaley resigned in early 2006. Finally in August 2006, the founder's son, Robert Hulseman, stepped down as Solo's chief executive. Hulseman was then in his 70s, and had worked at the company for 50 years, beginning as a machine operator. Leadership of the company was turned over to a much younger former Sweetheart executive, Robert Korzenski.

The company abandoned its plans to build a huge new plant on the USX site in Chicago. It reduced its factories from more than 30 into 20, and cut its number of warehouses by almost half. Its integration costs had come to some $35 million, while its raw materials costs had gone up more than 15 percent in 2005. Its bonds were downgraded to junk status, and Solo was in the red. Solo began looking into the compensation it paid Hulseman family members, who had been collecting advisory and consulting fees, as well as dividends. Korzenski predicted that the worst was over when he took the top job in 2006. Nevertheless, a year later, Vestar moved on the commitments it had gotten when it invested in the merger, and took control of the board of directors. This move displaced board chairman Robert Hulseman, as well as his brother John.

By that time entirely out of family hands, Solo continued to cut costs. It sold its Japanese subsidiary in 2007 in order to pay down debt, and closed and consolidated factories. Solo also sold a Wisconsin-based subsidiary, Hoffmaster, in 2007. Hoffmaster made paper goods such as napkins, placemats, and table cloths, primarily for restaurants and hotels. The sale, for about $170 million, gave Solo more cash for paying down its debt. Within a year of the Hulseman family leaving the board, Solo had managed to cut its debt from $1.1 billion to $786 million. Its credit rating was upgraded as it continued to consolidate operations and dispose of obsolete equipment.

The company had been through several extremely challenging years when recession hit the global economy in earnest in 2008. Raw material costs had gone up significantly over the summer of 2008, when petroleum rose to an all-time high. By the fall of that year, the banking and auto industries were in crisis in the United States, and consumer spending dropped dramatically. Oddly enough, Solo was well prepared for the recession because it had already done so much work to cut costs. It had reduced its debt significantly, and instituted a lean, cost-cutting culture. In a March 2, 2009, interview with the *Chicago Tribune,* Solo's chief executive Korzenski mused that without the merger, neither Solo nor Sweetheart would have been able to manage the recession. "I'm not sure if either of those two companies would have been around today if they hadn't done this," he said.

Although the merger had been difficult, Solo now had an economy of scale that worked to its advantage. The food industry market was affected by the cutback in consumer spending, as fewer people were eating out. This put pressure on Solo, which did a lot of business with big foodservice customers. So things were not rosy for Solo. Yet all in all, the timing seemed to have been right for the merger. The company looked forward to persevering through difficult times with a newly stable structure and increased mindfulness of costs.

A. Woodward

PRINCIPAL SUBSIDIARIES

Solo Cup Canada Inc.; Solo Cup Operating Corporation.

PRINCIPAL COMPETITORS

Dart Container Corporation; Huhtamaki Foodservice, Inc.; WinCup, Inc.

FURTHER READING

Antosiewicz, Frank, "Solo Cup Selling Japanese Units," *Plastics News,* October 29, 2007, p. 3.

Berk, Mechele, "Uncle Joe's Sweetheart Legacy," *Baltimore Business Journal,* August 18, 2000, p. 25.

Burns, Greg, "Solo Cup Keeping Head Above Water in Recession," *Chicago Tribune,* March 2, 2009.

Corfman, Thomas A., "South Works Comeback Odds Grow," *Crain's Chicago Business,* June 14, 1999, p. 3.

Esposito, Frank, "Solo Cup Co. Relocating to New Ill. Site," *Plastics News,* June 14, 1999, p. 1.

Finnigan, Joseph, "Hubby Spent $400,000," *TV Guide,* August 21, 1971.

"$5,400,000 Suit Filed Against Dixie Cup Co.," *New York Times,* November 13, 1948, p. 21.

Lambert, Emily, "Flying Solo," *Forbes,* December 10, 2007, p. 42.

———, "Party's Over," *Forbes,* November 27, 2006, pp. 158–62.

"Leo Hulseman, 90, Founder of Solo Cup Co.," *Chicago Sun-Times,* September 18, 1989, p. 42.

Merrion, Paul, "Profile: Ex-Southwest Sider Toast of Solo Cup Co. in Africa," *Crain's Chicago Business,* June 26, 2000, p. 15.

Murphy, H. Lee, "Blemishes Tarnish Solo's Sweetheart," *Crain's Chicago Business,* January 19, 2004, pp. 4, 26.

Pryweller, Joseph, "Solo Cutting 4 Sites, 654 Jobs As It Blends in Sweetheart Biz," *Crain's Chicago Business,* February 21, 2005, p. 7.

———, "Solo Plans Purchase of Rival Sweetheart," *Plastics News,* January 5, 2004, p. 1.

Roeder, David, "Solo Cup Boss Steps Down 2 Years After Acquisition," *Chicago Sun-Times,* April 18, 2006, p. 59.

"Rules in Cup Patent Suit," *New York Times,* July 25, 1948, p. F1.

Smith, Sarah S., "Solo Buying Clear Shield for $140 Million," *Plastics News,* June 15, 1998, p. 1.

"Solo Cup Sells Unit to Private Equity Firm," *Arlington Heights (Ill.) Daily Herald,* September 11, 2007, p. 1.

"Solo Expanding, Transforming Operations," *Plastics News,* June 9, 1997, p. 3.

Tita, Bob, "Solo Cup Slips Out of Family's Hands," *Crain's Chicago Business,* January 8, 2007, p. 2.

———, "Solo, Sweetheart off to a Rocky Start," *Crain's Chicago Business,* August 28, 2006, pp. 3–10.

Specsavers Optical Group Ltd.

La Villiaze
Saint Andrews
Guernsey, GY6 8YP
United Kingdom
Telephone: (44 0 1481) 236 000
Fax: (44 0 1481) 235 555
Web site: http://www.specsavers.com

Private Company
Incorporated: 1984
Employees: 17,000
Sales: £1.02 ($1.46 billion) (2008 est.)
NAICS: 446130 Optical Goods Stores; 339115 Ophthalmic Goods Manufacturing

■ ■ ■

Specsavers Optical Group Ltd. is the United Kingdom's leading provider of optical services. The Guernsey-based company claims to fit one in three eyeglasses in the United Kingdom, for a total market share of 35 percent. Specsavers oversees a network of nearly 900 optical shops in the United Kingdom. These shops operate under a unique joint-venture partnership model, in which the shops' owner-operators retain store profits, while Specsavers provides marketing, manufacturing, supply, and other support functions for a management fee. Since the 1990s Specsavers has been rolling out its retail model to other markets, starting with Ireland before moving to the European continent in 1997. Other markets include the Netherlands, Spain, Norway, Denmark, Sweden, Finland, Iceland, Australia, and New Zealand. Altogether the group's global network tops 1,600 stores.

Beginning in 2008, Specsavers has been rolling out hearing services to its optical chain. The Specsavers web site also offers customers the ability to order eyeglasses that are then fitted at one of its optical shops. The group generated total revenues of £1.02 billion ($1.46 billion) in 2008. Specsavers remains a privately owned company, owned and led by the Perkins family. Founders Doug and Mary Perkins are company directors, joined by their three children, Cathy, Julie, and John.

EARLY BUSINESS SUCCESS

Specsavers was founded by Doug and Mary Perkins in 1984, but the company was not the couple's first successful venture into the optical field. Mary Perkins, born Mary Bebbington, had grown up in the optical world, helping out from an early age at her father's Bristol, England, optical shop in the late 1950s and early 1960s. As she explained to the *Bristol Evening Post:* "When I was 13 or 14 I used to help him on the reception on Saturdays. People would be coming in to collect their glasses, so from a very early age I learned how to fit them."

Bebbington went on to earn her degree in ophthalmic optics at Cardiff University, where she met and later married another optometry student, Doug Perkins. Following their studies, Bebbington and Perkins moved to Bristol, taking over the business from Bebbington's father, who retired and moved to Guernsey in 1967. Perkins bought out Bebbington's main daytime shop.

COMPANY PERSPECTIVES

Trust the experts. When you choose Specsavers Opticians you are in safe hands—every year, for seven years running, the readers of Readers' Digest have voted us the most trusted opticians' brand in the UK. We always completely follow the guidelines set out by the General Optical Council—this means that all our glasses whether bought online or in one of our stores are professionally fitted under the supervision of a qualified optician. Every pair of glasses is individually made to meet your vision requirements and lifestyle needs—your dispenser will check that your new glasses fit properly and that you have clear, comfortable vision, making any necessary adjustments to ensure a perfect fit. With a network of over 600 stores throughout the UK you have the reassurance of a Specsavers optician in a location near you.

Bebbington's father then gave his daughter a second, smaller practice, located over a bakery, which opened for business three nights per week.

Bebbington and Perkins Opticians grew rapidly to become a major chain in the Bristol region. Through the 1970s, the company expanded, building up a network of 23 shops throughout Bristol and into Exeter, Plymouth, and South Wales. The growth of the business soon attracted the interest of some of the larger optical groups in the United Kingdom, including Dolland & Aitchison, the country's oldest and largest at the time. In 1980, Doug and Mary Perkins made the decision to sell the business and move to Guernsey to join Mary's family. The couple sold their company for £2 million that year. Most of the couple's original shops were eventually acquired by Dolland & Aitchison, with many still in operation at the dawn of the 21st century.

TRANSFORMATION IN THE EYEWEAR MARKET

Under the terms of the sale, which also provided an annual income for the couple, Mary and Doug Perkins agreed to a three-year non-compete clause. Instead, the couple began preparing their next venture, taking business classes and traveling to the United States to study the optical market there. The early 1980s represented a time of important change in the United States, as a new generation of major regional and nationally operating chains, which primarily operated as franchises, had begun to transform the eyewear market, dramatically lowering the prices for prescription eyewear.

The Perkinses were eager to adopt these new ideas for the U.K. market. By 1984, they had worked out their own retail concept, called Specsavers, based on a low-price, high-volume model. The couple also adapted the traditional franchise formula, creating a unique joint-venture partnership format. Independent opticians retained ownership of the shops, rather than paying a franchising fee to open a new shop, as well as all profits generated at their store. Specsavers provided the manufacturing, logistics, marketing, and other support services, in exchange for a management fee.

Specsavers launched in 1984. The company's timing proved fortuitous, as that year marked the introduction of new legislation that deregulated the optical market in the United Kingdom. Specsavers quickly took advantage of the new freedoms, including the right to advertise. The Perkinses decided to open the first Specsavers stores themselves, in Guernsey and Bristol. New stores in Bath, Plymouth, and Swansea followed shortly. In this way, they were able to attract potential joint-venture partners by providing proof-of-concept not only in branding and styling, but also in the financial viability of the sales model. The company launched advertisements in trade magazines, and the couple traveled around the country meeting with prospective partners.

While Doug and Mary Perkins operated their own shops, Specsavers focused on developing the support operations for the retail front. For this the Perkinses initially set up shop in a spare bedroom, and both Mary and Doug Perkins took charge of driving to frame and lens manufacturers, including to France and Italy, to acquire stock for the retail shops. At first, Specsavers sold eyeglasses under its own brand. The Specsavers concept represented something of a revolution in the United Kingdom, where the majority of eyeglasses had been dispensed under the former National Healthcare System (NHS). Specsavers offered quality eyeglasses at low prices.

FRANCHISE LEADERSHIP

Specsavers launched its first advertising campaigns in 1989. Rather than turn to an advertising agency, the company developed its own ad campaigns. This strategy paid off, as the company created a number of iconic slogans over the next two decades, including the "should've gone to Specsavers" tagline, which quickly entered the British vernacular.

Around the same time, Specsavers also introduced two more important features that contributed to its success. In 1989, the company became the first in the United Kingdom to offer a two-for-one package on eyeglass purchases. This was followed in 1990 with the group's "complete price" offering, in which the purchase of certain eyeglass frames included free single-vision lenses. For this, the company worked out the average price of all the lenses sold in its shops, and then added that price to the displayed frame price. In this way, customers knew exactly how much they would pay before delivery, an advantage rarely available elsewhere.

The company's business model attracted both joint-venture partners and customers. In the early 1990s, Specsavers had become the biggest and fastest-growing franchise-based optical chain in the United Kingdom. The company had also entered Ireland, capturing the lead in that market as well. By 1992, the company's network counted 200 shops, with plans to double that number before the end of 2003. The company's annual sales followed suit, growing an average of 25 percent per year, and topping £100 million pounds.

The early goals set by Specsavers proved a bit ambitious, with the company's store network reaching just 300 stores by 1995, and 400 stores by 2000, including a new flagship store opened on Tottenham Court Road in London in 1999. Nonetheless, the group remained on course to achieve its long-term goal of becoming the leading optical chain in the United Kingdom, and one of the largest in Europe.

In the second half of the 1990s, the Perkinses, by then joined in the business by their three children, Cathy, Julie, and John, sought new horizons for the company's expansion. The lowering of trade barriers among European Union members in the early 1990s led the company to explore the potential for extending its retail model to the continent.

BRAND EXTENSION

The company chose the Netherlands as its first target, opening its first joint-venture store in Haarlem, near Amsterdam, in 1997. At first, the company entered the Dutch market under a new name. The company quickly recognized this as a mistake, however. As Mary Perkins explained to *Management Today:* "Another bad decision: when we started in the Netherlands ten years ago, we were advised by consultants that Specsavers wasn't a good name, so we entered the Dutch market under another name. Within two months, I realised it was a huge mistake and reverted to the Specsavers name. When you're a marketing company, to bring in another brand is ridiculous; half the people there knew the Specsavers name anyway. Since then we have gone into all the other countries as Specsavers and it has been fine. I should have gone on my gut instinct."

The first Dutch store was followed by stores in Gouda and Breda. In the next decade, the Specsavers name achieved national coverage in the Netherlands. By 2002, the company had opened more than a dozen stores there, and toward the end of the decade, had grown into the third largest optical chain in the Netherlands.

The Perkinses had also begun to seek to extend their joint-venture business model into other areas. In 1999, the company launched an attempt to enter the dental market, a move designed to counter the entry of rival optical group Boots into that market. Specsavers announced plans to spend some £20 million and open as many as 100 Specsavers Dental Practices within three years. However, the company's dental ambitions hinged on proposed changes to the NHS which would have allowed patients greater freedom to choose their own dentists. The changes failed to be enacted, and Specsavers quickly dropped its own dental plans.

Specsavers next considered a brand extension closer to its core optical operation. In 2000, the company announced its plans to begin offering cataract operations including lens replacement surgery and laser eye surgery at its shops. However, the cost of acquiring equipment and personnel and of achieving competency requirements deterred the company from pursuing this market.

In 2002, Specsavers found a better fit for its optical shops. In that year, the company acquired HearCare, based in Leicester, which operated eight audiology and hearing aid fitting centers in the United Kingdom. The market for hearing aids, particularly the newer generation of digital hearing aids, fit in more neatly with the overall customer demographic of Specsavers, which skewed toward the elderly. Many of the group's existing optical shops could easily be extended to include an audiology section. The company also laid plans to open as many as 100 separate audiology centers.

CONTINUED INTERNATIONAL EXPANSION

Specsavers also resumed its international expansion in the new century. The company entered Sweden in 2004, buying the 34-store Blic Optik chain. This acquisition was followed by the purchase of Tva Bla, a chain of 19 shops. The company's Swedish stores were then placed under the Specsavers Blic Optik brand. Also in 2004, Specsavers announced plans to open another 40 stores in the United Kingdom, raising its total to 500 shops.

Specsavers extended its reach into the Scandinavian market in 2005, buying Denmark's Louis Nielsen optical chain. This addition was followed by the announcement to launch operations in Norway as well, with plans to add 21 Specsavers Optikk stores in that country through the end of the decade. These formed part of the company's goal to add several hundred European shops by 2010.

Specsavers also entered the Finnish market, opening its first shop there in 2007. The company quickly ramped up its presence there, opening another 60 stores by the end of 2008, and then acquiring the 26-store chain of Eyen optical shops in December of that year. The purchase helped raise the group's total number of stores to 1,000 for the first time at the beginning of 2008. By this time, the company had entered the southern European market as well, establishing its first shops in Spain in 2006.

The company had also been eyeing the Australian and New Zealand markets for some time. In 2007, the company established an optical products supply subsidiary in Port Melbourne. This operation soon proved to be the group's beachhead as it launched a full-on expansion into the Australian market in 2008.

The entry of Specsavers into Australia became its most successful to date. By the end of 2008, the company's network there topped 153 shops, making Specsavers the number two player in that market. The company promised to maintain its momentum through 2009, backed by the construction of a new 13,000-square-meter manufacturing plant in Port Melbourne.

Specsavers also entered New Zealand in 2008, opening its first six stores, with plans to add another 50 there.

Doug and Mary Perkins remained at the head of a retail empire with 1,600 stores that achieved sales of £1.02 billion ($1.46 billion) in early 2009. Mary Perkins, granted the title of Dame Mary Perkins for her charity work, and husband Doug remained at the head of the company. Specsavers remained resolutely family-owned, and the Perkinses were preparing to turn the business over to their children.

M. L. Cohen

PRINCIPAL SUBSIDIARIES

Specsavers Optical NV (Netherlands); Specsavers Australia Pty Ltd.

PRINCIPAL COMPETITORS

HAL Investments B.V.; Pearle Europe B.V.; OPSM Proprietary Ltd.; Synoptik A/S; Vision Express UK Ltd.

FURTHER READING

Davidson, Andrew, "Specsavers Founder in the Frame," *Sunday Times,* July 10, 2005.

"Decisions: Dame Mary Perkins—Specsavers Optical Group, Co-Founder of the Opticians' Chain," *Management Today,* January 1, 2008, p. 26.

"Doug and Mary's Model," *Optician,* July 8, 2005.

Flanagan, Martin, "Specsavers in Danish Move," *Scotsman,* July 7, 2005, p. 54.

"42 Specsavers Optical Superstores," *Sunday Times,* March 8, 2009, p. 47.

"Free Varifocals," *Optician,* April 10, 2009.

"Marking 25 Years of Optical Excellence," *Daily Record,* May 6, 2009, p. 8.

Nelson, Fraser, "Specsavers Sees Bright Future in Providing Dental Care," *Times,* May 31, 1999, p. 45.

"Perkins Appointed Joint MD," *Optician,* August 10, 2007.

Rees, Jon, "Specsavers Sparks Fury over Web U-turn," *Mail on Sunday,* December 16, 2007, p. 3.

"Specsavers Acquires 26 Retail Shops in Finland," *Nordic Business Report,* December 11, 2008.

"Specsavers Focuses on Future with New Stores," *Evening News,* March 11, 2002, p. B1.

"Specsavers Notches Up Record Turnover," *In-Store,* July 8, 2005, p. 17.

"Specsavers Opens '100 Stores in 100 Days,'" *Inside Retailing,* March 17, 2008.

"Specsavers Spies Gap in Market," *New Zealand Herald,* November 26, 2008, p. 3.

"Specsavers to Create 200 Aust. Jobs, Open More Stores in 2009," *AsiaPulse,* January 29, 2009.

"Specsavers' 20 Years of Optical Care in the City," *Derby Evening Telegraph,* December 12, 2008.

"Spec-tacular Success," *Bristol Evening Post,* July 26, 2005.

Sperian Protection S.A.

BP 50288, ZI Paris Nord II
33 rue des Vanesses
Roissy CDG, F-95958 Cedex
France
Telephone: (33 01) 49 90 79 79
Fax: (33 01) 49 90 79 80
Web site: http://www.sperianprotection.com

Public Company
Incorporated: 2001 as Bacou-Dalloz
Employees: 6,190
Sales: EUR 751 million ($970 million) (2008)
Stock Exchanges: Euronext Paris
Ticker Symbol: SPR
NAICS: 339115 Ophthalmic Goods Manufacturing;
322299 All Other Converted Paper Product
Manufacturing; 339113 Hard Hats Manufacturing

■ ■ ■

Sperian Protection S.A. is one of the world's leading specialists in the personal protection equipment (PPE) industry. The France-based company claims the number one position in the eye protection and fall protection markets, and the number two spot in the world market for hearing protection. Sperian's operations are organized into two main divisions: Head Protection, which accounts for 52 percent of the group's revenues and includes its hearing, eye and face, and respiratory business segments; and Body Protection, which includes its fall protection, shoes, clothing, and gloves business segments, for 48 percent of group sales.

Sperian markets its products under four primary brands: the main Sperian brand, as well as the Uvex, Miller, and Howard Leight brands. Sperian operates on a global scale, with subsidiaries in the United States, Canada, Australia and New Zealand, Germany, the Netherlands, Spain, Italy, Switzerland, Russia, Hungary, and China, among other markets. The EMEA (Europe, Middle East, Africa) market represents 50 percent of Sperian's sales, while the Americas add 43 percent, with the Asia-Pacific region completing its revenue base with 7 percent of sales. The company was formed in 2001 through the merger of Bacou SA, together with its publicly listed subsidiary Bacou USA, and Christian Dalloz. The company adopted the Sperian name in 2007 in an effort to increase its market visibility. Henri-Dominique Petit is the company's chairman, and Brice de la Morandiere is chief executive officer. Sperian Protection is listed on the Euronext Paris stock exchange. In 2008, Sperian posted revenues of EUR 751 million ($970 million).

ORIGINS

Sperian Protection was created through the merger of two prominent French manufacturers of personal protection equipment (PPE), Bacou SA and Christian Dalloz. Both companies had grown through a string of acquisitions, emerging as major players in the ongoing consolidation of the highly fragmented global PPE industry. The merged company, initially called Bacou-Dalloz SA, became one of the world's leading PPE specialists.

Henri Bacou's career in the safety equipment industry began when he joined Jallatte, a world-leading maker of safety shoes based in the Gard region in the south of France, in the early 1960s. By the early 1970s, Bacou had risen to become the company's managing director. In 1974, after more than 17 years with Jallatte, Bacou decided to found his own company. In that year, he moved to Annonay, in the Ardeche region.

Ardeche had long been a major tannery center in France. In the 1970s, the sector had been undergoing a major crisis, in part because of shifting trends in the footwear market toward manmade materials. Bacou began working with a local tannery to convert its production from leather goods to the production of safety shoes. Backed by state subsidies, Bacou's safety shoe business grew strongly through the end of the decade. In the meantime, the tightening of work safety rules, a trend started in the United States and soon adopted in Europe, meant that companies would be required to invest in new types of equipment in order to protect their workers. Bacou recognized the potential to establish his company as provider of the full range of "head to toe" safety protection.

Rather than develop new business lines from scratch, Bacou targeted acquisitions of existing companies in order to accomplish this goal. Bacou launched its first acquisition in 1980, picking up work-clothes manufacturer Commeinhes-Remco. Other acquisitions soon followed, including glove maker Sofraf in 1984 and clothing producers Delta Protection and Mutexil in 1986, and fall protection specialist Antec in 1989.

ENTERING THE UNITED STATES IN 1992

By the end of the 1990s, Bacou had completed more than 40 acquisitions. The most important of these came in 1992, when Bacou acquired a two-thirds stake in Uvex Winter Optical, the U.S. subsidiary of Germany's Uvex Winter Holding based in Rhode Island. Uvex (which stood for "ultraviolet excluded") had been founded in the 1960s as a producer of sunglasses for skiing and other sports, before extending its operations into the industrial safety sector. Uvex's entry into the

United States had come in 1980, with the opening of a factory in Smithfield, Rhode Island.

The sale of the U.S.-based safety eyewear division came as part of Uvex Winter's decision to exit the industrial safety sector in order to focus solely on its sports products lines. Over the next year, Bacou bought the remainder of the Uvex U.S. business, establishing a new subsidiary, Bacou USA, for the purpose. The Uvex acquisition cost Bacou FRF 300 million ($45 million), but helped boost the company's total revenues from FRF 800 million ($120 million) to more than FRF 1.3 billion ($200 million). Bacou then claimed the position as one of Europe's leading safety products groups, as well as the leading position in industrial safety eyewear in the United States.

Bacou's acquisition drive enabled the company to build an extensive line of PPE products, which in turn enabled the company to develop a strong list of major multinational companies as its clients. The company quickly built its own international network of operations, with subsidiaries in Germany, the United Kingdom, Italy, Spain, the United States, and elsewhere. At the same time, the company invested strongly in new product development, opening two research and development centers, as well as a research center specialized in developing respiratory products. Bacou also established a number of high-profile partnerships, including with the National Aeronautics and Space Administration for the Freedom space station; diving equipment for Comex; and specialized equipment for the military in France, the United States, and elsewhere.

Tragedy struck the company with the death of Henri Bacou at the age of 60 in 1996. Taking his place was his son Philippe, who had joined the company in the mid-1980s. Under Philippe Bacou, the company continued its growth, adding a number of new acquisitions through the end of the decade, including Survivair, a respiratory specialist, in 1997; hearing protection group Howard Leight in 1998; welding safety group Optrel in 1998; and glove makers Perfect Fit, Whiting & Davis, and Platinum in 1999 and 2000. Along the way, the company listed its U.S. subsidiary on the New York Stock Exchange in 1996. Bacou also targeted an entry into the Asian region, and in 1997 established a base in Shanghai, China.

MERGING WITH DALLOZ

Bacou had played its own part in the consolidation of the international PPE industry during the 1990s; by the dawn of the new century, however, the company was faced with increasing competition from a growing number of large players, including French compatriot

KEY DATES

1957: Christian Dalloz founds a company producing injection-molded plastic products.

1974: Henri Bacou founds a company producing safety shoes.

1980: Bacou launches an acquisition strategy, starting with Commeinhes-Remco.

1985: Dalloz begins focusing on the production of safety products.

1989: Dalloz acquires WGM Safety Corp.

1992: Bacou acquires two-thirds stake in Uvex Winter Optical in the United States.

1996: Bacou USA lists on the New York Stock Exchange.

2001: Bacou and Dalloz merge, forming Bacou-Dalloz.

2007: The company refocuses its operations entirely on the personal protection equipment sector, becoming Sperian Protection.

Christian Dalloz. By this time, Bacou SA's family-based management structure, and its closely held shareholding, had become obstacles to its future expansion. Rather than dilute their holding, the Bacou family instead decided to sell the entire operation, including Bacou USA. After completing its control of Bacou USA, the company was put up for sale in 2000.

However, Bacou struggled to find a buyer for the company. Instead, in May 2001, Bacou announced that it had reached an agreement to merge with French rival Christian Dalloz, forming one of the world's leading PPE specialists. The new company claimed a workforce of more than 7,000 worldwide, and annual revenues of more than $770 million.

Christian Dalloz had founded a company producing injection-molded plastics products in 1957. In the 1960s, Dalloz began to shift its focus to eyewear, producing sunglass lenses, and in the 1970s became one of the first to develop polycarbonate-based lenses. It was not until 1985, however, as the company sought a new means of growth, that Dalloz began targeting the safety products market.

Fueling the group's new strategy was a stock market listing, completed in 1986, and a partnership agreement with fast-growing lens producer Essilor. At the end of the 1980s, Dalloz had largely achieved its goal, acquiring the larger WGM Safety Corp. in 1989. The WGM purchase transformed Dalloz into a leading player in the international occupational safety equipment market. The United States then became the company's primary market, accounting for 90 percent of its revenues.

The first half of the 1990s proved difficult for Dalloz. The WGM purchase came ahead of the global recession, sending the group's revenues and profits into a downward spiral. Dalloz also invested heavily in an attempt to enter the market for intraocular lenses at the beginning of the decade, only to be forced to exit that sector in 1992. Then, in 1996, Christian Dalloz, who had no children, was killed in an automobile accident. Dalloz's wife Ginette took over as head of the company as well as its majority shareholder.

Dalloz recovered its momentum in the second half of the decade, as it launched its own acquisition drive. The purchase of Sweden's Bilsom, a hearing protection specialist, helped reduce the group's overdependence on the U.S. market. The company then turned to the United Kingdom, buying eye and face specialist Pulsafe, and fall protection group Troll in 1996. Other acquisitions included Komet (France, fall protection) in 1997, Moxham (Australia, fall protection) in 1998, and Fendall (United States, eyes) and Söll (Germany, fall protection) in 2000.

BECOMING SPERIAN PROTECTION

Bacou-Dalloz, which included both Philippe Bacou and Ginette Dalloz as cochief executives, emerged as the world's leading PPE specialist in the early years of the new century. By 2002, the company had largely completed the integration of its operations. Also in that year, the company announced its plans to spin off its money-losing distribution business into a new company, Abrium, which was then put up for sale. Abrium finally found a buyer in 2004, for just one euro, in Butler Capital Partners, resulting in a loss of more than EUR 36 million for the company, and a drop in the group's revenues from EUR 796 million to EUR 678 million at the end of 2004. Bacou-Dalloz continued its streamlining through the decade, selling its Christian Dalloz SunOptics sunglass lens division in 2006.

Refocused entirely on its core PPE product manufacturing operations, Bacou Dalloz continued to see strong growth through the decade. By 2003, the company had once again returned to the acquisition trail, in the United States buying Securitex, a producer of protective clothing for firefighters and emergency rescue personnel. This was followed by the purchase of Brazil's Epicon, a producer of disposable face masks.

The purchase not only gave the company a base in South America for the first time, it also positioned the company to respond to the growing demand for face masks. The outbreak of the SARS epidemic, and fears of a bird flu epidemic in the middle of the decade, caused a surge in demand for face masks, bringing Bacou-Dalloz an order for 12 million masks from the French government. Similarly, the potential outbreak of a swine flu pandemic in April 2009 was expected to bring a new surge of orders for the company.

The company's acquisitions continued into the end of the decade. In 2007, the group acquired Nacre, based in Norway, a maker of "intelligent" earplugs. The following year, the group completed three more acquisitions, of Argentina's Musitani, a fall protection specialist; Combisafe, another leading fall protection group; and DoseBusters, a hearing protection group.

By this time, Bacou-Dalloz had been forced to recognize that, despite its position as a global leader in many of its product segments, the company's name lacked international recognition. This led the group to adopt a new name, Sperian Protection (meant to evoke the words *experience* and *expertise*) in 2007. Sperian then carried out a reorganization of its more than 50 brands, streamlining to just four core brands: the main Sperian brand, as well as Uvex, Miller, and Howard Leight, which were each complemented by the addition of "by Sperian." The company also held a license for the Timberland Pro footwear brand in Europe.

Sperian's sales climbed to EUR 754 million ($970 million) at the end of 2007. However, the company bore the brunt of the global economic downturn, as the industrial slowdown reduced demand for its products. By the end of 2008, and despite its acquisitions, the group's revenues had slipped back to EUR 751 million. Nonetheless, the foundations of Sperian Protection's business remained strong as the company looked forward to renewed growth in the future.

M. L. Cohen

PRINCIPAL SUBSIDIARIES

Auralguard Pty Ltd (Australia); Glendale Protective Technologies, Inc. (USA); Gloves Plancher Bas SAS; Logandene Ltd. (UK); Moxham Safety Pty Ltd (Australia); Nacre AS (Norway); OPMA Arbeitsshutz GmbH (Germany); Pulsafe Europe Holding BV (Netherlands); Safety Eyewear Ltd. (UK); Sperian Fall Protection Deutschland Gmbh & Co KG; Sperian Fall Protection France SAS; Sperian Hearing Protection de Mexico S. de R.L. de C.V.; Sperian Produtos de Seguranca Ltda. (Brazil); Sperian Protection (China) Co., Ltd; Sperian Protection Australia Pty Ltd.; Sperian Protection Deutschland GmbH & Co Kg; Sperian Protection Europe SAS; Sperian Protection Footwear Givors SAS; Sperian Protection France SAS; Sperian Protection Gloves Morocco; Sperian Protection Holding (UK) Ltd.; Sperian Protection Hong Kong Ltd.; Sperian Protection Hungaria Kft.; Sperian Protection Iberica S.A.; Sperian Protection India Private Ltd.; Sperian Protection Netherlands BV; Sperian Protection Sweden AB; Sperian Protection USA, Inc.; Sperian Protection Verwaltungs GmbH (Germany); Sperian Protection Workwear Dorno Srl; Sperian Protective Apparel, Ltd. (Canada); Sperian Safety LLC (Russia).

PRINCIPAL DIVISIONS

Head Protection; Body Protection.

PRINCIPAL OPERATING UNITS

Clothing; Eye and Face; Fall Protection; Gloves; Hearing; Respiratory; Shoes.

PRINCIPAL COMPETITORS

Jalatte-Almar S.A.; Cofra Holding AG; Morning Pride Manufacturing LLC; Lion Apparel Inc.

FURTHER READING

"Bacou-Dalloz a Payè Cher la Vente de Sa Filiale Abrium," *Les Echos,* September 9, 2004, p. 20.

"Bacou-Dalloz Confiant pour l'Avenir," *L'Expansion,* March 8, 2006.

"Bacou-Dalloz: Le Directeur Général Remercié," *Les Echos,* April 6, 2004, p. 27.

"Bacou-Dalloz Plans to Revitalize Its Hand Protection Business Unit and Focus on Growth and Profitability in the North American Market," *Industrial Safety & Hygiene News,* March 2007, p. 65.

"Bacou-Dalloz Rachète l'Américain Securitex," *Les Echos,* April 9, 2003, p. 12.

"Bacou-Dalloz Souffre de la Faiblesse du Dollar," *Les Echos,* September 8, 2003, p. 22.

"Bacou Grandit avec le Marché," *Les Echos,* November 9, 1994, p. 24.

Bayle, Nadine, "Bacou-Dalloz Prêt pour de Petites Acquisitions," *Les Echos,* December 26, 2002, p. 11.

———, "Bacou-Dalloz Vise 1 Milliard d'Euros de Chiffre d'Affaires d'Ici à Quatre Ans," *Les Echos,* March 2006, p. 24.

———, "Un homme de Kodak aux Commandes de Bacou-Dalloz," *Les Echos,* May 19, 2004, p. 26.

Benjamin, Jeff, "Bacou SA Calls on Bacou USA," *Investment News,* October 2, 2000, p. 29.

"Christian Dalloz change de dimension," *Les Echos,* August 3, 1994, p. 6.

"Christian Dalloz Sunoptics Quitte le Giron de Bacou-Dalloz," *Les Echos,* September 19, 2006, p. 22.

"Des Gants Malins," *L'Expansion,* February 1, 2008.

Du Guerny, Stanislas, "Grippe Aviaire: Bacou-Dalloz Investit 10 Millions d'Euros à Plaintel," *Les Echos,* January 13, 2006, p. 16.

Holman, Kelly, and Josh Kosman, "French Companies Play It Safe," *Daily Deal,* May 30, 2001.

"La Grippe A (H1N1) Dope la Production de Masques de Sperian," *Reuters,* May 4, 2009.

"New Name in Welding Safety," *Plant & Works Engineering,* January 2009, p. 42.

"Smithfield, R.I., Safety-Equipment Maker Seeks Security in Sale of Company," *Providence Journal,* July 11, 2000.

"Sperian Protection S.A. Appoints Brice de La Morandiere," *EHS Today,* April 2009, p. 12.

Sutcliffe, Virginia, "Bacou USA, Bacou SA Merge with Christian Dalloz," *EHS Today,* May 31, 2001.

"12 Millions de Masques Contre la Grippe Aviaire pour l'Etat Français," *Les Echos,* October 14, 2005, p. 20.

"Uvex Safety Becomes a Full Subsidiary of the Bacou Group," *Business Wire,* December 20, 1994.

Walter, Laura, "Bacou-Dalloz Becomes Sperian Protection," *Occupational Hazards,* November 2007, p. 16.

Stagecoach Group plc

10 Dunkeld Road
Perth, PH1 5TW
United Kingdom
Telephone: (44 1738) 442 111
Fax: (44 1738) 643 648
Web site: http://www.stagecoachgroup.com

Public Company
Incorporated: 1980 as Stagecoach
Employees: 30,000
Sales: £1.76 billion ($3.94 billion) (2008)
Stock Exchanges: London
Ticker Symbol: SGC
NAICS: 485113 Bus Services, Urban and Suburban;
485210 Bus Line Operation, Intercity; 487110
Buses, Scenic and Sightseeing Operation; 485510
Charter Bus Industry; 482111 Passenger Railways,
Line-Haul

■ ■ ■

Stagecoach Group plc operates as an international transportation group with bus, train, tram, and express coach operations in the United Kingdom, the United States, and Canada. The company serves 2.5 million passengers each day and controls the largest commuter network in the United Kingdom through its contract to operate the South West Trains line. Stagecoach's U.K. bus operations include 19 regional companies that oversee 7,000 vehicles serving 100 cities throughout the United Kingdom. Stagecoach pursued an aggressive expansion-by-acquisition policy in the late 1990s and

has since curtailed such activity while selling off many of its international holdings to focus on its operations in the United Kingdom as well as North America through its Coach USA arm.

HUMBLE BEGINNINGS

Company founders Ann Gloag and younger brother Brian Souter grew up in council flats (the equivalent of the housing projects in the United States) in Perth, Scotland. Their father was a driver for the local community's bus lines. Buses played a large role in their lives; Brian Souter would later recall playing with buses on the floor of the family's home. As Ann Gloag, who had a 20-year career as a nurse before founding Stagecoach, said, as related by *Time International:* "Buses were what the family knew. My father, my husband, and my brother had all worked on them."

The Thatcher era in the United Kingdom brought a wave of deregulation and privatization of industries that had formerly been government controlled. Among the first of the industries to be privatized was the public transportation sector, and specifically the bus routes in the United Kingdom. Gloag and Souter were quick to recognize the potential of this newly opening market. In 1980, using their father's £25,000 severance paycheck, Gloag and Souter bought two small buses. Just days after the bus line deregulation was enacted, the brother and sister were ready to begin operations. They called their company Stagecoach and offered service between Dundee and London.

Stagecoach was not the only new bus operator to ply the roads in the United Kingdom. However, the

COMPANY PERSPECTIVES

The key elements of Stagecoach Group's business strategy to deliver long-term shareholder value are: To deliver organic growth across all of the Group's operations; To acquire businesses that are complementary to the Group's existing operations, in areas where the Group's management has proven expertise and which offer prospective returns on capital in excess of the Group's weighted average cost of capital; In addition to organic and acquisition growth, to maintain and grow the Group's UK Rail division by bidding for selected rail franchises and to seek to secure new franchises where the risk/return trade-off is acceptable. This part of the strategy includes working with VRG to secure an acceptable renegotiated West Coast Trains franchise. A fundamental objective underlying this strategy is the continued provision of safe and reliable services to passengers.

brother-sister team hit upon a service formula that kept customers coming back: offering sandwiches (prepared by their mother), blankets, and tea, while also charging lower fares than their competitors. Soon after the company began operations, it was able to add a second route, between Glasgow and London. By the mid-1980s, Stagecoach operated along a growing number of Scotland's roadways.

If privatization had opened the way for Stagecoach, the deregulation of the busing industry in the middle of the decade brought the company its greatest opportunities. The breakup of the formerly government-run National Bus Company into its regional subsidiaries created 70 independent bus companies, which were generally sold to their management. While content to be government employees, many of the new bus line owners were uncomfortable in this position, or were otherwise eager to cash in on the growing interest in private bus companies.

Stagecoach was quick to recognize the potential opportunity of the National Bus Company breakup: Souter and Gloag embarked on their own acquisition tour, making nearly 40 acquisitions between 1985 and 1999. Among the first acquisitions were those of Cumberland Motor Services and United Counties Omnibus, both made in 1987 and both counted among the company's largest purchases to date. The fast-growing company continued to extend its holdings throughout

the United Kingdom. In 1989, Stagecoach took another leap forward when it bought East Midland Motor Services. At the same time, the company became one of the first bus lines to operate a global strategy: in 1989, the company entered Africa, buying a 51 percent stake in United Transport of Malawi. Further African expansion followed with the purchase of Kenya Bus Services in 1991.

STRATEGY FOR SUCCESS

The company's strategy proved simple and highly effective. New acquisitions were placed through rigorous cost-cutting measures, including drastic reductions in management levels as the subsidiary operations were placed under parent Stagecoach's control. The company was also careful to position its own people in key management positions, assuring a cohesive strategy. The company's acquisition drive itself helped improve profit margins, as the company began to realize economies of scale. Stagecoach also made shrewd use of the real estate acquired through its acquisitions. Many of the former National Bus Company regional subsidiaries had operated from depots and offices in downtown locations. Stagecoach quickly sold these valuable properties, moving operations to less expensive locations. With the cash gained, the company was able to return to the acquisition trail.

At the same time as Souter and Gloag were buying up the United Kingdom's bus routes, they were careful not to neglect passengers. Bus lines added to the Stagecoach family were quick to see fare reductions, often drastically undercutting their rivals, and even operating for limited times for free. These practices, which included hiring away conductors from other local companies, were to bring negative repercussions to the company as it rapidly became one of the largest players on the public transport scene in the United Kingdom. Under frequent investigation by the country's Monopolies and Mergers Commission, Stagecoach was found to have acted, at least in one instance, in a manner that was "predatory, deplorable and against the public interest." Nevertheless, in the deregulated, highly competitive public transportation market, none of Stagecoach's activities were illegal.

Moreover, for whatever aggressiveness Stagecoach brought to bear on its rivals, the company was careful to treat its passengers well. When a bus company was added to the Stagecoach stable, its fleet was usually outfitted with an array of new buses, allowing Stagecoach to claim one of the youngest bus fleets in the country. Apart from lower fares, Stagecoach also added other services (although the hot tea and sandwiches seemed to have fallen by the wayside). As its network of

KEY DATES

1980: Ann Gloag and younger brother Brian Souter buy two buses and establish Stagecoach.
1987: Cumberland Motor Services and United Counties Omnibus are acquired.
1989: Stagecoach buys East Midland Motor Services; the company enters Africa, buying a 51 percent stake in United Transport of Malawi.
1993: Stagecoach goes public on the London Stock Exchange.
1996: The company buys the rights to operate South West Trains; Stagecoach pays £825 million for Porterbrook.
1999: The company acquires Coach USA.
2006: The London bus operations are sold.
2007: The company wins a contract to operate the Manchester Metrolink tram network.

bus companies grew, the company began innovating with hub-and-spoke style express coach services, which were much appreciated by the company's passengers. Stagecoach also began operating open-top buses on some of the company's more scenic commuter routes; these buses proved popular with passengers, both commuters and sightseers alike. In addition, where other companies avoided sparsely populated, and expensive, rural routes, Stagecoach began introducing new routes. These were quick to provide linkups into the company's other lines, bringing even more passengers on board.

PUBLIC TRANSPORT GOES PUBLIC

Stagecoach continued its acquisition drive into the 1990s, buying more and more bus lines that were struggling under the economic recession. Among its early 1990s purchases were two prominent Scottish bus operators, Fife Scottish and Bluebird Buses, acquired in 1991. The following year, Stagecoach formed its Stagecoach South subsidiary, combining a number of its southern England operations into a single, cost-effective entity. The company made a similar move in western England, after buying up Western Travel in 1993. This operation was renamed Stagecoach West. Meantime, Stagecoach moved to a new continent, with the purchase of New Zealand's Wellington City Transport. Through the rest of the decade, Stagecoach continued to

build its position both in New Zealand and in Australia, making it a prominent player in that region.

The year 1993 also marked a new milestone for Stagecoach. Having reached annual sales of £100 million, the company went public, taking a listing on the London Stock Exchange. The listing made millionaires out of Souter and Gloag, who were then counted among the England's top 100 wealthiest people. Access to new capital enabled Stagecoach to continue its growth-by-acquisition campaign. The deregulation of the London bus industry opened the country's most important market, and Stagecoach established its presence with two key purchases, those of the South East London & Kent Bus Company Ltd. (Selkent) and East London lines, in 1994. In that same year, Stagecoach strengthened its position in the northern regions of Scotland and England, making a number of important acquisitions.

The company was well on its way to becoming the leading coach bus operator in the United Kingdom. Additional lines in Cambridge in 1995, and in Exeter and Manchester in 1996, firmly established the company's leadership position. Stagecoach was also boosting its foreign position, first with the start-up operation of Portugal's Rodoviaria Lisboa in 1995, and then with the £230 million purchase of the formerly state-run Swedish bus operator, Swebus, in 1996. That purchase, the company's largest to date, forecasted Stagecoach's future expansion on the European continent, as more and more countries studied privatization of their bus routes.

By 1996 Stagecoach had swelled to annual revenues of more than £1 billion per year, with operations in nine countries, and a 17 percent share of the bus market in the United Kingdom. With acquisition opportunities becoming rare in the U.K. bus sector—and with large-scale purchases likely to bring the company fresh difficulties with the Monopolies and Mergers Commission—Souter and Gloag then looked to diversify their operations. The privatization of the country's train system opened up a new route to Stagecoach. In 1996 the company bought the rights to operate South West Trains (SWT), which enabled the company to offer bus-rail linkup services to its southern region and London operations. In the same year, Stagecoach paid £825 million for Porterbrook, a rolling stock leasing company that owned some 30 percent of the country's passenger railroad vehicles.

ACQUIRING COACH USA

By 1997 Stagecoach's operations of SWT were being called into question, as the company faced a high rate of daily cancellations and passenger complaints. While the company pledged to turn operations around, Stagecoach nevertheless found itself threatened with the loss of the SWT franchise and the possibility of fines for substandard services reaching into the millions of pounds. Stagecoach was also chafing under shrinking expansion possibilities in the United Kingdom. As Souter told *Investor's Chronicle* in 1997: "We don't intend to make any more U.K. acquisitions. The U.K. has moved very quickly. We got in early when there was still a bob in it. But we want value for shareholders and are getting out of a market that is overpriced."

Stagecoach's U.K. railroad ambitions were also being thwarted, when it lost its bid to operate the West Coast Mainline and ScotRail railroads, which went to National Express and Virgin Rail. In response, in 1998 Stagecoach turned to new sectors for development. After losing a bid to chief U.K. competitor FirstGroup to run Hong Kong's main bus franchise, Stagecoach nonetheless found entry into the rapidly developing Chinese market. In 1998 the company made the surprise purchase of a 22 percent stake in Road King Infrastructure, a Hong Kong-based toll-road builder, with operations chiefly on the Chinese mainland. The following year, Stagecoach achieved its ambition, when it took over operations of Hong Kong's Citybus operations, which, with 1,200 buses and more than 4,000 employees, gave Stagecoach the number two position in that city's bus market. Meanwhile, the company was preparing to abandon its money-losing operations on the African continent. When Ann Gloag stepped down from day-to-day operations, the company hired Mike Kinski as CEO.

In June 1999, the company announced its intention to acquire Coach USA, the largest passenger coach service in the United States. Based in Houston, Texas, Coach USA had taken an early lead in consolidating the charter and tour bus industry in the United States.

Founded by venture capitalist Steven Harter in 1995, and run by CEO Lawrence King, Coach had rapidly built a fleet of some 3,500 sightseeing buses, as well as an equal number of taxis and other vehicles. After going public in 1996, the company went on a buying spree, making more than 50 acquisitions across the United States, with particular emphasis on Texas, Florida, and the midwestern and eastern regions. By the time Coach entered into talks with Stagecoach, the U.S. company was posting revenues of more than $800 million. The acquisition agreement with Stagecoach, which left King in place as the head of the U.S. operation, cost the U.K. operator more than $1.8 billion, including the assumption of some $600 million in Coach's acquisition-induced debt.

MOVING INTO THE 21ST CENTURY

The company's decision to buy Coach proved costly during the early years of the new millennium. With tourism in the United States hitting a slowdown, Coach's bus operations were faltering and Stagecoach was forced to take a £575 million charge in 2002 to cover losses from its 1999 purchase. Brian Souter stepped in to restructure Coach and worked to revamp the U.S. company's operating structure. Staff at the U.S.-based headquarters was cut by nearly 40 percent and over 300 buses were permanently taken out of service. Unprofitable businesses were also sold off. Overall, Stagecoach's shares lost nearly 70 percent of their value during 2002 as a result of the company's steep profit decline.

In response, Stagecoach set a new strategy in motion and began to focus on organic growth while making key, but much smaller, acquisitions. It also began to divest certain business, including its Hong Kong operations, its interest in Scotland's Prestwick Airport, and Porterbrook. Its bus and ferry business in New Zealand as well as its London bus operations were sold in 2005 and 2006, respectively. Some of its acquisitions included Glenvale Transport Limited's bus operations in Merseyside as well as bus operator Traction Group.

Megabus.com, an inexpensive and no-frills bus line with tickets sold only online, was launched in 2003. During 2006, Stagecoach secured the new South Western rail franchise for a period of ten years. It landed the East Midlands rail franchise for a period of approximately seven years in June 2007. In July of that year, Stagecoach became the sole operator of the Manchester Metrolink tram network in a ten-year contract that positioned it as Britain's largest tram operator.

Under the direction of cofounder Souter, Stagecoach's efforts to rebound from its Coach USA purchase were paying off. The company was seeing increased numbers onboard its routes as rising fuel costs and environmental concerns made public transportation an attractive alternative to personal transportation. Stagecoach launched a number of "green" initiatives during this time period including a program that allowed customers to exchange used cooking oil for discounted bus travel. The first bio-buses were launched in the United Kingdom in October 2007. Stagecoach launched Scotland's first carbon-neutral bus network the following year.

With passenger numbers rising, the company's revenues and profits began to climb. During 2008 company revenues increased 17 percent over the previous year while profits grew nearly 8 percent. With nearly 2.5 million passengers choosing Stagecoach as a means of transportation each day in the United Kingdom, Canada, and the United States, the company appeared to be on track for success in the years to come.

M. L. Cohen
Updated, Christina M. Stansell

PRINCIPAL DIVISIONS

Stagecoach UK Bus; Stagecoach Rail; North America.

PRINCIPAL COMPETITORS

Arriva plc; FirstGroup plc; National Express Group plc.

FURTHER READING

Flanagan, Martin, "A Cultural Revolution in Buses," *Scotsman,* March 20, 1999.

Gibson, Helen, "Boom Times for Buses," *Time International,* October 21, 1996, p. 52.

Griffiths, Ben, "Stagecoach on the Road to Recovery," *Herald,* December 11, 2003.

Harrison, Michael, "Bus Firm that Took the Fast Route to Trouble," *Independent,* March 15, 1997, p. 10.

Hawkes, Steve, "Stagecoach Is Running Right off Track in U.S.," *Journal,* December 5, 2002.

MacNamara, William, and Maggie Urry, "Passenger Surge Bolsters Stagecoach," *Financial Times,* June 28, 2007.

Nag, Arindam, "Britain's Stagecoach Buys Ticket to Ride U.S. Market," *Reuters Business Report,* June 14, 1999.

O'Connell, Dominic, "The Next Stage for Stagecoach," *Sunday Times,* August 20, 2006.

———, "Stagecoach on Track for Rail Deal," *Sunday Times,* September 17, 2006.

Smith, Mark, "Souter Shares Credit for Surge in Stagecoach Value," *Herald,* August 30, 2008.

Stevenson, Tom, "Stagecoach Offers an Exciting Ride," *Independent,* October 10, 1996, p. 26.

Wright, Robert, "Buses Take Stagecoach 'Back to Roots,'" *Financial Times,* March 1, 2004.

Yates, Andrew, "Souter Eyes Wider Stage," *Investor's Chronicle,* February 14, 1997.

Thumann Inc.

———————■———————

670 Dell Road, Suite 1
Carlstadt, New Jersey 07072-2201
U.S.A.
Telephone: (201) 935-3636
Fax: (201) 935-2226
Web site: http://www.thumanns.com

Private Company
Incorporated: 1949
Employees: 220
Sales: $115 million (2008 est.)
NAICS: 311612 Meat Processed from Carcasses

■ ■ ■

Thumann Inc. is a family-owned company based in Carlstadt, New Jersey, that manufactures, markets, and distributes premium-quality deli meats, cheeses, and salads under the Thumann's label. The products are distributed to supermarkets, gourmet delicatessens, convenience stores, and sandwich shops in 36 states, Puerto Rico, and the Bahamas. Manufactured in the company's 150,000-square-foot facility, all Thumann products are certified gluten free, display the heart symbol indicating they meet the American Heart Association's standards for saturated fat and cholesterol, and are certified by the Feingold Association as suitable for people on sensitive diets.

Deli-counter meats include smoked liverwurst and several varieties of bologna, such as beef, beef and pork,

garlic, ring, and lower-sodium. Italian meats include mortadella; stick and sandwich-style pepperoni; prosciutto; sopressata; and Genoa, hard, and cooked salami. Thumann also offers a wide variety of roast beef, ham, and corned beef and pastrami products. Loaf items include braunschweiger, kielbasa, head cheese, olive, oval spiced ham, minced, and pickle and pimento. Thumann also offers a wide variety of beef and pork hot dogs and such sausage products as bratwurst, hot and sweet Italian sausage, knockwurst, pork sausage links, ring kielbasa, and hickory-smoked sliced bacon. In addition, Thumann produces about two-dozen varieties of turkey and chicken products. The Thumann's label is found on the usual complement of deli cheeses as well, including American, hot pepper jack, mozzarella, Muenster, provolone, sharp cheddar, swiss lace, baby swiss, and domestic swiss cheese, as well as cream cheese. In order to cater to changing consumer tastes, Thumann has also introduced a line of natural meat products free of antibiotics, growth hormones, and a host of common additives.

The Thumann's label also adorns a line of packaged salads (including potato, egg, macaroni, and tuna, as well as cole slaw) and such condiments as mustards, horseradish sauce, ham glaze, sauerkraut, pickles, sweet roasted peppers, and gourmet onions in sauce. To ensure quality, all raw materials undergo X-ray analysis and infrared scanning to verify leanness and quality, and the final products receive a similar scanning to make sure they meet Thumann's specifications. The company is owned and operated by the third generation of the Thumann and Burke families.

POST–WORLD WAR II ORIGINS

Thumann Inc. was founded by Henry F. Thumann Sr. He was born in Germany around 1911 and raised on a farm where he learned the family's meat product recipes, which relied on the leanest cuts of meat. He immigrated to the United States at the age of 17, and became an apprentice butcher. In addition to mastering that trade, he learned the food business, in particular food distribution. He became a distributor for Boar's Head, a deli company that would one day become his chief competitor in the New York City area. Boar's Head was well entrenched in the market. Its founder, Frank Brunckhorst, had been delivering deli meats to delicatessens and grocery stores by horse and wagon since 1905. In 1933 Brunckhorst opened his own processing plant in Brooklyn.

Across the New York Harbor in New Jersey, one of his former distributors, Thumann, would begin to produce his own line of deli products to rival Boar's Head. According to company sources, Thumann had been sharing meats he had made using his family's recipes with friends at dinner, and encouraged by their response, he decided to sell the items to the public. Thus, in 1949 he opened his first meat-processing plant in Wallington, New Jersey, located between midtown Manhattan and Passaic, New Jersey. He had just five employees and two trucks to deliver his deli products in northern New Jersey, where his products, which did not make use of fillers or an abundance of artificial ingredients, found a ready market.

SECOND GENERATION JOINS THE BUSINESS

Thumann essentially copied the way Boar's Head conducted its business, down to the red, black, and gold color scheme of the delivery trucks. In the early days, to drum up business, he and his wife Frieda were also known to sell their meats door to door, and she even drove a delivery truck as needed. Thumann's business grew steadily through word of mouth and soon he was assisted by a second generation, his son Henry G. Thumann and the husband of his daughter Linda, Robert F. Burke Sr. The operation was also relocated to a facility in Carlstadt, New Jersey.

For years, the Thumann's brand competed on a local basis, as Boar's Head did, promoting its products to retailers rather than direct to consumers. Thumann relied mostly on its reputation for high-quality and superior taste to drive sales, supplemented by posters, clocks, and other promotional items bearing the Thumann's logo and mouth-watering images of deli products. For the most part Thumann was dominant in

northern New Jersey, whereas Boar's Head was the major deli brand across the river in New York City, but both sold on either side of the Hudson River and Thumann did not consider Boar's Head a significant threat to its business.

The deli-counter industry underwent a major shift in the mid-1970s when the federal government mandated inspections of meatpacking plants. One consequence of this new regimen was to allow provisioners to sell across state lines. Thumann, which had saturated its own market, was not quick to move into new markets, nor was it ready for an influx of competition from provisioners located in parts of the country where labor was considerably less expensive than the metropolitan New York City area, thus providing its competitors with an edge as they attempted to invade Thumann's territory. Moreover, the consumption of processed meats was declining amid consumer concerns over salt content, cholesterol, and carcinogens. As a result, after years of strong growth, Thumann experienced a drop in sales in the late 1970s.

CONSUMER ADVERTISING BEGINS, CIRCA 1985

Boar's Head had begun advertising direct to consumers soon after out-of-state markets opened up, and enjoyed success in creating brand awareness in the deli case where previously products had been unbranded. Thumann's pride in the quality of its products in some respects worked against the company. As Burke, then Thumann's general manager, told the *Record* in a 1987 article, "Why spend a lot on advertising when you were the accepted standard in the industry." It was not until the mid-1980s that Thumann finally began to advertise to consumers, although it was with some reluctance that Henry Thumann, still serving as president, approved the expenditures. Although the company claimed the move was not made because it was losing market share to Boar's Head, it nevertheless admitted that it had reached a sales plateau and there was a clear need to stimulate the brand.

In 1985 Thumann began spending money on television and radio commercials. The initial television effort was amateurish, featuring a pair of Thumann employees dressed as medieval trumpeters who were to herald the "king of hams." One of Thumann's employees, a shipping clerk named Thomas Lewandowski Jr., the son of Henry Thumann's first employee, was a trained audio engineer and rock musician who overhead two company managers in the men's room discussing an upcoming radio ad. He was certain that he could do a better job in his home studio. He received permission from Burke to take off two days, and returned to Carlstadt with three radio spots. The clerk was soon made vice-president of advertising and given a reserved parking spot.

Lewandowski developed a folksy ad campaign to support the Thumann's brand, and kept costs down by doing most of the work on the radio spots. In some cases, he wrote the copy, sang the parts of the jingle while accompanying himself, and did the mixing and engineering. In addition, print ads and billboards were developed to work in coordination with the radio spots. The brand's main selling point was its low salt content and refusal to use the flavor enhancer monosodium glutamate. During the first full year of the new advertising campaign, Thumann spent about $2 million.

MODERNIZATION OF THE BRAND

The company also invested in other ways to develop the brand. The logo was modernized as was the clock sign that adorned the walls of countless New Jersey delis. Thumann also repainted its fleet of more than 200 delivery trucks, removing the gold lettering that had become closely associated with Boar's Head. A booklet replete with high production values was created to detail product offerings to retailers and a newsletter was launched to improve communications with the company's network of about 175 independent distributors. Thumann also provided them with business cards and hosted seminars to help improve sales techniques. The company even staged its own food show to promote its products. Not only did Thumann fend off competition in New Jersey, it made further inroads in the primary market of Boar's Head in New York City. As a result of these efforts Thumann's began again to enjoy some sales growth. Revenues improved from $54.3 million in 1985 to $58.6 million the following year.

Efforts to brand the deli counter continued in the 1990s. Upscale supermarkets also began to tout specialty meat brands such as Thumann's in their own circulars. Store signage gained even more prominence, as Thumann called attention to products that were low in salt or 98 percent fat free. The company also looked to improve sales by outfitting a promotional bus, on which sales associates could taste products and receive training. Distributors also provided samples of Thumann products in stores on a regular basis to attract more attention from consumers, and in some locations television monitors played Thumann's promotional infomercial in continuous 90-minute loops. Nevertheless, Thumann's remained a regional specialty brand while Boar's Head was becoming more of a commercial brand, distributed more widely and gaining more national recognition. To help maintain its place in the New York City market and possibly pull away sales from Boar's Head, Thumann signed Major League Baseball's popular New York Yankees manager, Joe Torre, as a spokesperson.

NEW CENTURY BRINGS NEW GENERATION OF LEADERSHIP

As Thumann's entered the second half of its first century in business and began the new millennium, it remained very much a family business that clung to tradition as much as possible. A third generation took the helm in Robert F. Burke Jr., but the company avoided e-mail and interoffice memos as much as possible, preferring face-to-face communications. Rather than squeeze out extra profits by automating the production process, Thumann continued to rely on expert butchers to prepare meats for processing and many items were still packaged by hand to avoid unnecessary damage. In one of the few concessions to the modern workplace, Thumann invested in a new enterprise resource planning system to cut down on a blizzard of paperwork and make processing activities faster and more accurate.

The area in which Thumann had always been ahead of the market was its emphasis on quality, the company's key selling point for decades. In 2007 Thumann's entire product line was certified gluten free by the Gluten-Free Certification Organization. Thumann also introduced a line of all-natural deli products, made with sea salt, pure cane sugars, and other natural ingredients while eschewing additives, antibiotics, and growth hormones. The initial four products included turkey breast, chicken breast, black forest ham, and top-round roast beef. They proved popular and the line was soon supplemented with six additional products: smoked turkey breast, smoked chicken breast, pastrami, corned beef, and pork and beef frankfurters.

FOUNDER DIES: 2009

In May 2009 Henry F. Thumann died at the age of 98. The company he founded was still in family hands and had grown into a super-regional company, generating about $115 million in annual revenues. His grandson was in charge and a great-grandson was waiting in the wings to possibly carry on the family tradition, especially if Robert Burke Jr. had his wish. Regarding the passing of the torch, Burke told *Food and Drink* in the fall of 2008, "It's a special thing because it is something that my family built and I want to continue to carry the quality tradition. There is a little bit more pride involved when it's a family business." He also indicated that he wanted to build on the legacy and continue to take the Thumann's name to new markets.

Ed Dinger

PRINCIPAL COMPETITORS

Boar's Head Provisions Co., Inc.; Dietz & Watson, Inc.; Hormel Foods Corporation.

FURTHER READING

"Corporate Spotlight on Thumann's," *American Executive,* February 2006.

Levin, Jay, "Deli Company Founder, Henry F. Thumann Sr., 98," *West Paterson Herald News,* May 16, 2009.

Linsen, Mary Ann, "The Name Dropping," *Progressive Grocer,* November 1993, p. 10.

Sasson, Victor E., "A Dispatch from the Cold-Cuts War," *Record* (N.J.), July 26, 1987, p. B1.

Tiflis, Fernie, "Not Just a Name," *Food and Drink,* Fall 2008, p. 54.

Tigre S.A. Tubos e Conexões

───────■───────

Rua dos Borrorós 84
Joinville, Santa Catarina 89239-290
Brazil
Telephone: (55 47) 3441-5000
Toll Free: (877) 751-5371
Fax: (55 47) 3441-5388
Web site: http://www.tigre.com.br

Public Company
Founded: 1941
Employees: 5,400
Sales: BRL 2.3 billion ($1.25 billion) (2008)
NAICS: 326130 Laminated Plastics Plate, Sheet, and
Shape Manufacturing

■ ■ ■

Tigre S.A. Tubos e Conexões is the Latin America leader in the manufacture of polyvinyl chloride (PVC) pipes and fittings and accessory products. It offers complete systems of hot and cold water, drains, sewers, electricity, telecommunications, and gas, and fixed and portable solutions for irrigation. Many of its plants are in Brazil, but there are several in other countries, including one in the United States. Tigre is also the leader in its field in Chile and Argentina. In addition, the company leads Brazil in the production of brushes and door and window frames made of PVC. Although a public company, Tigre is not listed on any stock exchange.

PVC PIPES AND OTHER PLASTIC PRODUCTS: 1941–82

Tigre got its name from a small factory in Joinville, Santa Catarina, that João Hansen Jr. opened in 1941 to make combs of ox horn. The next year this facility began making Sawa pipes. Soon plastic products began to arrive in Brazil. Tigre turned to the new material and purchased a mold injector in order to produce combs, cigarette holders, cups, plates, toys, and fans. In those days the few fans available were imported and expensive, so women were delighted to be able to buy affordable ones made of plastic. Tigre turned out a "painting school" set of 40 different models that proved a great success.

By the end of the 1950s Tigre had an array of plastic products, both extruded and injected. Then Hansen made the decision to invest in a product absolutely new for this era—PVC pipes and joints for water and sewage installations. Many considered this idea absurd, because plastic seemed too fragile to replace pipes made of galvanized iron. This decision resulted in Tigre's continued leadership in the field in which it had embarked, which came to include electrical pipes as well.

The company was quick to consolidate its gains in civil construction generally. It advertised to the public on radio and offered samples to motorists with "advice" such as, "Now that you're going to the beach, try to rust this pipe." During the 1970s Tigre was the first company in the construction sector to advertise on television. By the end of the decade it enjoyed 60 percent of its market sector. A plant established in Camaçari, Bahia, in 1982 to manufacture PVC pipes also became the center for distributing Tigre products throughout northeastern Brazil.

FAMILY PROBLEMS: 1988–95

As with so many Brazilian family enterprises, Tigre eventually hit a snag over the question of succession. The heir apparent was João Hansen III, the founder's elder son. João III became superintendent of the company but left in 1988 after constant quarrels with his father and devoted himself to financial investments and a hotel in Porto Seguro, Bahia.

João III's brother, Carlos Roberto, was named leader of Tigre by his father, who was in failing health, in 1991. João Jr. bequeathed the two brothers equal shares in JHJ, the family holding company, but Carlos Roberto was allotted two-thirds of the voting shares. After he died in an airplane accident in Colombia in 1994, his father was too ill to resume control, and so João III again took the reins.

The prodigal son made it clear to Tigre's directors and managers that he was in complete charge of the enterprise. He fired the two executives closest to his brother. One of them, advised by the Brazilian unit of the U.S. consultant McKinsey & Company, Inc., had recommended a restructuring of the company intended to launch it into new businesses and in other countries as well as Brazil, with the objective of directing it to the manufacture of products with greater aggregate value. João Hansen III suspended this project.

Instead of pursuing new business, Hansen gave priority to shoring up Tigre's position in its existing market, where it had weakened in the past few years. Its sales had fallen from $330 million in 1992 to $310 million in 1993, and its market share from 45 percent to 36 percent. In order to better compete, Tigre cut its prices by an average of 30 percent. To be able to do so, it also cut costs, firing 500 workers and 25 of the 50 top managers, and reducing the number of items manufactured from 3,700 to 2,500. A plant that made architectural profiles, purchased for $10 million only a year earlier, was sold. A sale of 100 properties brought in $40 million.

The 48-year-old Hansen stressed the need for new blood in the company, saying he did not want any executives around him older than himself. In order to bring Tigre into closer contact with customers, the top executives were moved to São Paulo, with only line managers remaining in Joinville. New directors were appointed for the company's four customer areas: dealers, public organs, agriculture, and industry. Tigre's sales rose to $367 million in 1994, and its profit grew almost 15 percent.

THE SUCCESSION STRUGGLE: 1995–2001

João Hansen Jr., founder of the firm, died in January 1995. His surviving son, João III, did not long outlast him at Tigre. Within months, Rosane Hansen, his sister-in-law, had exercised her control of the voting shares of JHJ to oust him, make herself chairman of the board, and also to move the holding company back to Joinville. The new president, Francisco Amaury Olsen, was the only one of Carlos Roberto's inner circle to have survived João's purge and the only one to remain in Joinville after the unpopular move to São Paulo. A personal friend of Rosane, he had spent 27 years at Tigre, beginning as office boy and rising to industrial director.

João Hansen III sold his 25 percent of the company in 1997 to Previ, a pension fund for the employees of Banco do Brasil (Bradesco), Brazil's leading bank. He then bought a share of a rival company named Fortilit. Tigre was also facing a formidable challenge from a manufacturer named Akros. Here again, the problem was in large part personal. In 1976 João Hansen Jr. had fired Tigre's general manager, Ninfo König, in the course of a dispute that almost came to blows. König, with three partners, two of them also Tigre executives, then founded Akros, which became Tigre's only competitor in pipe fittings and accessories and was, in 1996, on the verge of opening its own PVC pipe factory. By 2000 both Akros and Fortilit were controlled by Amanco Brasil Ltda., which held 30 percent of the market compared to 60 percent for Tigre. This competition was cutting into Tigre's profits.

The Hansen family continued to be at loggerheads. Eliseth, João's sister, had demanded a revision in her inheritance after her husband's business affairs fell into disarray. She had been bequeathed preferred stock only in JHJ, although she had also received four other businesses, farms, a yacht, a helicopter, and other properties valued at $200 million. Her lawsuit was backed by her mother but opposed by Rosane Hansen, her sister-in-law, and by Bradesco. As of 2001, Previ held 25 percent of the capital in Tigre, and Bradesco Capitalização held

KEY DATES

1941: Tigre factory opens, making combs of ox horn.

1960: Tigre manufactures an array of plastic products.

1980: The company holds 60 percent of its market sector in Brazil.

1994-95: Death of Tigre's founder and his son creates havoc.

1997: Joao Hansen III sells his share of the company to a bank pension fund.

2000: Tigre's sales pass BRL 1 billion ($550 million); acquisitions abroad enhance Tigre's presence outside Brazil.

2006: One-quarter of Tigre's sales come from other countries.

2007: Tigre opens its first U.S. plant, in Janesville, Wisconsin.

2008: Tigre has a manufacturing presence in eight countries besides Brazil.

18 percent, with the rest owned by two companies representing Rosane and her three children.

ACQUISITIONS IN BRAZIL AND ABROAD: 1997–2000

Despite these distractions, Tigre had substantially raised its revenues in the previous five years, passing BRL 1 billion ($550 million) in 2000. Production had almost tripled in quantity during this period. The company, in the past two years, had spent BRL 200 million ($110 million) in acquisitions and expansion, including entry into new and promising areas, such as gas pipelines, telecommunications, basic sanitation, and the manufacture of polyvinyl doors and windows. Although principally still a pipe extruder, Tigre had also increased its injection blow-molding lines. Both its extrusion and injection molding capacities were dedicated mostly to processing PVC.

Pincéis Tigre, a brush manufacturer with more than 75 years in business, was acquired in 1997. The factory turned out over 2,000 products, including brushes and accessories both for painting buildings and for artistic painting. Indaiatuba, São Paulo, became the site of a factory producing Claris brand window and door frames, and, beginning in 1998, profiles made of PVC

as well. Claris became the Brazilian leader in its field in 1999.

Tigre was also rapidly expanding to other South American countries. Since 1977 it had held a 49 percent share of Tubopar Tubos Paraguayos S.A. & Cia., which dominated PVC production in Paraguay. In Argentina, Tigre opened a PVC pipe plant in Pilar in 1998. The following year it purchased Argentine pipe fitting manufacturer Santorelli S.A. Santorelli made pipe fittings for the sewage sector and had a distribution network that Tigre could use to sell its plastics products made in Brazil, such as high density polyethylene water tanks. In 2000 Tigre purchased a controlling interest in Plasmar S.A., the leading company in its field in Bolivia.

Tigre's participation was even larger in Chile. The company's purchase of Fanaplas S.A. in 1997 gave it a 15 percent share in the Chilean plastic pipe market. Two years later, it acquired three more companies there: Plástica Veintiuno S.A., Industrias Saladillo S.A., and Reifox Industrial Ltda. These additions expanded its range of products in Chile to water- and sewage-system fittings. By 2006 sales outside Brazil represented one-quarter of Tigre's total.

CONTINUED GROWTH IN THE EARLY 21ST CENTURY

Tigre was voted Brazil's best company in the field of construction materials in both 2005 and 2006 by the business magazine *Exame*. Its Claris line of doors and windows had in less than three years grown to account for about one-fifth of all its sales. Growth was strongest in infrastructure, light construction, and exports. Tigre had five plants in Brazil and one each in Argentina, Bolivia, Chile, and Paraguay.

Tigre opened its first U.S. plant in 2007, producing pipe fittings in Janesville, Wisconsin. The company was already selling fittings in the United States under the Schedule brand and products for sewage, drainage, and ventilation under the DWW label. In 2008 it inaugurated its sixth Brazilian plant, for extrusion and injection blow mold accessory products such as toilet seats, lids, and tanks. A second phase called for the addition of glues, solvents, lubricant paste, and rubber rings. This facility, in Pouso Alegre, Minas Gerais, was named Plena and was to have a portfolio of 200 products, including bathroom mirrors and cabinets, showers, hoses, and similar articles for the bathroom and laundry area.

The rivalry with Amanco had taken a new turn with that company's acquisition by the Mexican chemicals producer Mexichem S.A. in 2007. Mexichem purchased PVC Plastubos, a Brazilian manufacturer, in

2008. Tigre responded by acquiring Plástica S.A., one of the three largest manufacturers of PVC pipes and fittings in Peru, a country in which Mexichem also was active. Tigre had a manufacturing presence in eight countries outside Brazil, including Colombia and Ecuador. At this time it held more than 50 percent of the Brazilian market, while Mexichem had 32 percent.

Tigre's revenues reached BRL 2.3 billion ($1.25 billion) in 2008, an increase of about 20 percent over the previous year, and its productive capacity grew about 30 percent. Units abroad represented 35 percent of total volume. Tigre was the leader in pipes and fittings in Chile and Argentina as well as Brazil. The company was present in about 40 countries. For 2009 it was planning to spend about BRL 100 million ($54 million) in the development of new products and innovation in processes and solutions for property, infrastructure, and irrigation. New plants were to be opened in Pernambuco, Brazil; Montevideo, Uruguay; and Resistencia, Argentina.

Evaldo Dreher, vice-president of Tigre, succeeded Olsen as president in 2009. In his 13 years as vice-president, Dreher was credited with the growing internationalization of the company.

Robert Halasz

PRINCIPAL SUBSIDIARIES

Comércio e Representações Tigre Ltda.; Máquinas Tigre S.A.; Pincéis Tigre S/A; Plasmar S.A. (Bolivia); Tigre Argentina S.A.; Tigre Chile S.A.

PRINCIPAL COMPETITORS

Amanco Brasil Ltda.

FURTHER READING

Caetano, José Roberto, "Um mico na vida do tigre," *Exame,* April 4, 2001, pp. 66–69.

Costa, Flávio, "Agora, a dona é quem manda," *Exame,* May 10, 1995, p. 58.

———, "O filho pródigo fala grosso," *Exame,* June 8, 1994, pp. 52–53.

Costa, Sandra Mara, "Brazil's Tigre Snags Santorelli," *Plastics News,* August 23, 1999, p. 48.

———, "Pipe Maker Adding Windows to Lineup," *Plastics News,* July 28, 1997, p. 42.

Lamounier, André, "Vingança é prato que se come frio," *Exame,* February 28, 1996, p. 41.

Martins Gomes, Clezia, "A fera que se deu bem," *Exame Melhores e Maiores,* July 2005, pp. 176, 178.

Martins Gomes, Clezia, and Rodrigo Garutti, "Além das fronteiras," *Exame Melhores e Maiores,* July 2006, pp. 186, 188.

"Pipe Producer Tigre to Grow in Americas," *Plastics News,* July 25, 2005, p. 8.

"Tigre compra concorrente peruana da Mexichem," *Valor Econômico,* February 11, 2008.

"Tigre lança marca de acessórios Plena," *Jornal do Comércio,* April 8, 2008.

"A Tigre ruge," *Exame,* August 31, 1994, p. 49.

Uni-President Enterprises Corporation

301 Chung Cheng Road
Yung Kang, 710
Taiwan
Telephone: (886 6) 253 2121
Fax: (886 6) 253 2661
Web site: http://www.uni-president.com.tw

Public Company
Incorporated: 1967 as President Enterprises Corporation
Employees: 67,625
Sales: TWD 288,592 million ($1.46 billion) (2007)
Stock Exchanges: Taiwan
Ticker Symbol: 1216
NAICS: 311511 Fluid Milk Manufacturing; 311119 Other Animal Food Manufacturing; 311211 Flour Milling; 311225 Fats and Oils Refining and Blending; 311514 Dry, Condensed, and Evaporated Dairy Product Manufacturing; 311812 Commercial Bakeries; 312111 Soft Drink Manufacturing

■ ■ ■

Uni-President Enterprises Corporation (UPEC) is Taiwan's largest diversified foods manufacturing group and one of the largest in the Asian region. The company is also one of the most ambitious—its strategy calls for the company to grow into the world's largest food company, with a sales target of more than $120 billion by 2017. Toward this end, the company has been building up a presence in the mainland China market. The company's operations there are grouped under the umbrella of its Hong Kong Stock Exchange-listed subsidiary Uni-President China Holdings. Through subsidiary Wyndham Foods, the company is present in the United States; the company also operates businesses in Vietnam, the Philippines, Indonesia, and elsewhere.

In Taiwan, the company is the leading producer of fresh milk and dairy products through its Uni-President, Rui-Sui, and other brands. UPEC is also a major producer of instant noodles, milled flour, tea, soft drinks, prepared foods and ready-made meals, packaged meats, animals and fish feeds, among many others. Uni-President also holds the Taiwanese franchise for 7-Eleven convenience stores, with 2,800 stores in operation, as well as a majority stake in Philippine Seven Corp., the 7-Eleven franchise holder in that country. UPEC also opened its first 7-Eleven stores in Shanghai in 2009. UPEC is listed on the Taiwan Stock Exchange and generated revenues of TWD 289 billion ($1.46 billion) in 2007. The company is led by CEO Chang-Sheng Lin, President Chih Hsien Lo, and Chairman Chin-Yen Kao.

ORIGINS IN TAIWAN FOOD AND FEED GROUP

UPEC had its start in 1967 as a producer of flour and animal feed in Yanshing Village, in the Tainan region of Taiwan. Founded by Wu Hsui Chi and Kao Chin-Yen, the company, then called President Enterprises Corporation, was ambitious from the start. Through the end of the 1960s and into the early 1970s, the company's stated goal was to open at least one new factory each year. Toward this end, the company formed a technology partnership with Japan's Nisshin Food Products

Co., enabling the Taiwanese company to expand it production of feed and flour. The group's feed production rose to 20,000 metric tons by 1969, and then to 100,000 metric tons by 1973.

Recognizing growth opportunities in the Taiwanese government's drive to industrialize the island's economy, the company entered the food manufacturing market in 1969, establishing the basis of its future Foods Group. In that year, the company established a new factory and by 1970 had launched its own brand of instant noodles, Tong Yi Mien. The company also introduced its Li Bi Lung E brand of wheat germ that year. The company continued to expand its range of instant noodle products through the 1970s, quickly becoming the leader in that staple foods segment in Taiwan.

Other components of the later UPEC group were put into place during the 1970s. The group built a new factory for the production of vegetable oils and animal fats in 1971 and added a second feed factory that year. The company also established the Uni-President brand, starting with the launch of its first soy-based products in 1972. Also in that year, the company adopted a division structure, setting up separate units for its flour, animal feed, and oils businesses. The group's Foods operations took off in the 1970s as well, starting with the construction of a canning plant in Daying. This led to the launch of the group's first beverage products, including orange, guava, and asparagus juice drinks.

INTERNATIONAL STEPS

The company then moved into the dairy market, acquiring a factory from China Dairy Industry Corp. in Chaiautou. The company then formed a technical cooperation agreement with Japan's Meiji Dairies Corporation. This led to the construction of a new dairy facility, in Sinshih, which began production in 1977. By this time, the company had established its first foreign businesses. The company entered Thailand, where it launched production of instant noodles, in 1972. In 1975, the company entered the United States, establishing an instant noodle factory there as well. These expansion efforts came in support of the increasingly international growth of the company's Tong Yi brand, which entered the Hong Kong market in 1975, before establishing itself as one of the major noodle brands in the Asian region.

The company continued to roll out new products during the decade, adding soy and other sauces, ketchup, pickles, and tea, among others. In 1977, the company launched construction of a new baked goods factory in Jungli, launching its own lines of breads, pastries, and confectionery. These operations were regrouped into a new Bakery division, established in 1980. Toward the end of the 1970s, the company also became determined to enter the retail sector. In 1979, the group acquired the franchise to operate 7-Eleven convenience stores in Taiwan. The company opened its first 14 stores that year. The company's 7-Eleven business, which initially operated in partnership with Southland, grew to become one of Taiwan's major retailers, with more than 2,800 stores in operation across the island.

During the 1980s, the company targeted further expansion, including the development of a vertical integration model, as well as a broader diversification of its operations. In 1981, for example, the company formed a partnership with Jui Yue, the exclusive distributor of General Electric products in Taiwan, to distribute GE's semiconductors to the island's rapidly growing high-technology industries. Closer to its core operations, the company launched its own vending machine business, and by 1985 had placed more than 1,000 machines. The group's 7-Eleven operations also grew strongly, opening the 100th store in 1986. In that year, the group's 7-Eleven business was spun off into its own company, President Chain Store Corporation.

GROWTH AND EXPANSION

The company parlayed its food production and retail experience into an extension into the restaurant sector, opening Taiwan's first Kentucky Fried Chicken outlet in 1985. The company also launched its own retail bakery operations during the 1980s. By 1988, the company had developed a new second-generation bakery format, which launched with 66 stores that year. By 1990, the group's Uni-President Bakery chain had reached 300 franchised stores. The 7-Eleven chain, in the meantime, reached 500 stores that year.

The 1980s also saw the expansion of the company's feed operations. The company added fish and shrimp feed operations, and even began to export its technologies. In 1986, for example, the company signed a technical partnership to import its shrimp feed technology to Indonesia. The company's international sales expanded as well, and included the launch of tomato paste in Australia in 1984 and canned fruit juices in the United States in 1986.

The company maintained a steady pace of its new product launches, adding new lines of ready-made meals, such as the Tong Yi Imperial Big Meals introduced in 1983. Through the decade, the company added such products as Low-Lactose Premium Milk, launched in 1986; the group's patented Tong Yi Thick Rice Noodle in 1987; and the company's first infant formula products under the Uni-President brand in 1988. By then, the company had gone public, listing its shares on the Taiwan Stock Exchange in 1987.

By the beginning of the 1990s, the group dominated much of the Taiwanese food market as the island's largest integrated food company. The company's instant noodle sales, for example, claimed as high as a 50 percent market share. While the company continued to seek further growth in Taiwan, including acquiring rival food producers, the company targeted its international growth as a means for ensuring its future expansion.

The international expansion effort took the company to the United States in 1990, where it paid $325 million to acquire Wyndham Foods. That company, which had been formed in 1985 as a grouping of several regional bakeries in the Midwest, had become the third largest producer of cookies in the United States, with a focus on the low-priced cookie segment. The U.S. bakery business was renamed as President Baking Co. Inc. The company later sold the U.S. operation, in 1998.

INTERNATIONAL ACQUISITIONS CONTINUE

Other international acquisitions followed through the decade, as the company established a presence throughout much of the Asia-Pacific region, with a focus on the Thai, Vietnamese, Filipino, and Indonesian markets. In 1994, for example, the company established Uni-President Thailand Co., which began producing fruit juices and other beverages, as well as instant noodles. By the end of the decade, the company had marketing and distribution operations in India, Australia, New Zealand, and Burma (Myanmar), as well as in Africa and the Central and South American markets.

The focus of the company's international expansion naturally turned toward mainland China. The group established its first operations, building a factory in Beijing and launching production of its Tong Yi noodle brand in 1991. Through that decade, the company opened a string of new factories in a number of strategic mainland markets. Building a presence on the mainland proved difficult, as the group faced rising competition, as well as a degree of resistance because of its roots in Taiwan. By 2001, however, the company's mainland operations had begun to show profits for the first time.

The company officially changed its name in 2000, becoming Uni-President Enterprises Corporation (UPEC). In the new decade, the company continued to explore new food segments, such as organic foods, setting up Uni-President Organics Corp. in 2000. The company explored new international markets as well. In 2001, UPEC set up an animal and fish feed plant in Vietnam, and then formed an instant noodle manufacturing joint venture with RFM Corporation in the Philippines.

Back at home, however, UPEC had begun to face a challenge for its dominance of the instant noodle market. In 1999, the company's effort to acquire a 33 percent stake in one of its major domestic rivals, Tingyi, was thwarted when the stake went to Japan's Sanyo instead. A new threat emerged in the new decade when another major Taiwanese rival, Ting Hsin, announced plans to begin importing instant noodles from its mainland operations. Ting Hsin, which had entered the mainland several years before UPEC, had succeeded in gaining the lead in that market. The threat of facing lower-priced imported noodles forced UPEC to follow suit.

GLOBAL ASPIRATIONS

UPEC continued to invest in the Chinese mainland in the 21st century, investing some $1.7 billion and building a network of 46 factories there before the middle of the decade. As its mainland businesses became profitable, the company announced its intention to regroup these operations under a single holding company, Uni-President China Holdings, with an eye toward a future listing on the Hong Kong exchange. That public offering finally took place in December 2007.

Through the decade UPEC continued to seek out the blockbuster deal that would establish the company as a truly major player in the Chinese food market. That deal proved elusive, however. In 2004, for example, the company's negotiations to form a major fruit juice joint venture with Shanghai Bright Dairy & Food failed. The company also lost out on a bid to acquire the 7-Eleven franchise for the important Beijing area. Meanwhile, in Taiwan, UPEC failed in a bid to merge with the number-two instant noodle player, Wei Lih. That deal was struck down by the country's Fair Trade Commission.

Despite these setbacks, UPEC's ambitions remained high, as the company announced its aspirations for becoming the world's largest food group with projected annual sales of more than $120 billion by as early as 2017 compared to annual sales of less than $1.5 billion in 2007. To move in this direction, the company acquired mainland carbonated drinks trader Foshan Sanshui Jianlibao in 2005; at the end of 2008, the company announced its plans to launch carbonated beverage production in the mainland. The company also acquired stakes in a number of other mainland food producers, including more than 10.5 percent of fruit juice group Yantai North Andre Juice Co.

At the same time, UPEC's retail operations also received a boost, as the company gained a franchise to open its first 7-Eleven stores in the Shanghai region. The first four stores opened in Shanghai's Xuhui, Luwan, and Pudong New Area districts in April 2009. From its position as Taiwan's leading food products

corporation, UPEC sought to position itself among the global majors in the 21st century.

M. L. Cohen

PRINCIPAL SUBSIDIARIES

Datungying Industrial Co.; Jinmailang Beverage Co. (China); Philippine Seven Corporation (50.4%); Tong Ang Co.; Uni-President Glass Industrial Co; Uni-President China Holdings Ltd. (Hong Kong); Uni-President Cold-Chain Corporation; Uni-President Organics Corporation; Uni-President Vietnam Ltd.; Wyndham Foods Inc. (USA); Zhangjiagang President Nissin Food Co., Ltd. (China); Zhongshan President Enterprises Co., Ltd. (China).

PRINCIPAL DIVISIONS

Beverage Division; Bread Division; Dairy Product Division; Food Division; Frozen Prepared Foods Division; Ice Cream Division; International Division; Meat Division; Sauce and Seasoning Division; Tea Beverage Division.

PRINCIPAL OPERATING UNITS

Dairy and Beverage Group; General Foods Group; Health Group; Instant Food Group.

PRINCIPAL COMPETITORS

Shandong Qingyuan Foodstuff Company Ltd.; Shaanxi Land-Reclamation Agriculture and Industry and Commerce General Corp.; Guangdong Wenshi Food Group Company Ltd.; Henan Lingang Industrial and Trade Co.; Hebei Hualong Food Group Company Ltd.; Jilin Deda Company Ltd.; Unilever (China) Ltd.; Guangzhou Food Enterprise Group Company Ltd.; Xiamen Xiangyu Group Company Ltd.; Heilongjiang Feihe Dairy Industrial Company Ltd.; Jilin Cereals, Oils and Foodstuffs Imp. and Exp. Company Ltd.

FURTHER READING

Kovac, Matt, "What Isn't Cooking at Uni-President," *Business Week,* November 8, 2004, p. 25.

"Taiwan-Based Food Conglomerate Secures Stake in Juice Maker," *AsiaPulse News,* March 24, 2005.

"Taiwan's Uni-President to Invest More in Philippines," *AsiaPulse News,* July 22, 2002.

Thu, Thanh, "Firm's Hormone Feed Excuse Hard to Swallow," *Vietnam Investment Review,* January 29, 2007, p. 10.

"Ting Hsin, President to Import Instant Noodles from Mainland Affiliates," *Taiwan Economic News,* December 21, 2001.

"Uncertainty Surrounds Taiwan Merger Block," *AsiaLaw,* October 2008.

"Uni-President Aims to Be World's Largest Foods Company," *Alestron,* April 25, 2003.

"Uni-President Buys into Tait," *Taiwan Economic News,* November 8, 2006.

"Uni-President China Debuts on SEHK," *Alestron,* December 18, 2007.

"Uni-President China Holdings Ltd.," *China Law & Practice,* February 2008.

"Uni-President Injects CNY240mn into Jianlibao," *Alestron,* December 19, 2008.

"Uni-President No. 1 Producer of Fish Food in Vietnam," *Taiwan Economic News,* July 19, 2006.

"Uni-President Strengthens Juice Business," *Sinocast China Business Daily News,* December 15, 2008.

"Uni-President to List Mainland Business in HK in Dec.," *Alestron,* November 28, 2007.

"Uni-President to List Moneymaking Firm on Mainland Stock Mart," *Taiwan Economic News,* June 20, 2002.

U.S. Silica Company

106 Sand Mine Road
Berkeley Springs, West Virginia 25411-0187
U.S.A.
Telephone: (304) 258-2500
Toll Free: (800) 243-7500
Fax: (304) 258-8295
Web site: http://www.u-s-silica.com

Private Company
Incorporated: 1987
Employees: 650
Sales: $185 million (2007 est.)
NAICS: 212322 Industrial Sand Mining

■ ■ ■

U.S. Silica Company is a privately held, Berkeley Springs, West Virginia-based industrial minerals company. It produces ground and unground silica, fine silica, aplite, kaolin, magnesium silicate, and a variety of filtration sands and gravels. These products are used to make flat glass, glass containers, fiberglass insulation, textile fiberglass; building products such as asphalt shingles and sealant, clay bricks, grouts, and mortars; pool filtration media; molds for foundries; materials employed in wastewater treatment facilities and drinking water systems; fillers and extenders in the production of paints, sealants, polishes and cleansers, epoxy, rubber, and other products; and as a necessary absorbent in chromatography.

The company also produces sand used by golf courses for bunkers and in the construction and maintenance of tees, fairways, and greens. In addition to Berkeley Springs, U.S. Silica plants are located in Mapleton Depot, Pennsylvania; Rockwood, Michigan; Mauricetown, New Jersey; Ottawa, Illinois; Pacific, Missouri; Montpelier, Virginia; Jackson, Tennessee; Mill Creek, Oklahoma; Columbia, South Carolina; Dubberly, Louisiana; Hurtsboro, Alabama; and Kosse, Texas.

ORIGINS

U.S. Silica was formed in 1987 through the merger of Berkeley, West Virginia-based Pennsylvania Glass Sand Corporation, Ottawa Silica Company, and Pacific Coast Resources. The lineage of these enterprises dates back to the 1800s. Pennsylvania Glass Sand was incorporated in Delaware in August 1899 with a capital of $100,000. The company established its headquarters in Lewistown, Pennsylvania, a major source for Oriskany sandstone that produced glass sand, and maintained sales offices in Philadelphia and Pittsburgh. The company operated several quarries and mills in central Pennsylvania, but would also look to West Virginia, which offered sandstone with an exceptionally high silica content, ideally suited for use in making the highest-quality glass. In 1903 the company acquired the mill of the Hancock White Sand Company, which had first quarried the Warm Springs Ridge of Morgan County, West Virginia, in the Berkeley Springs area, during the 1860s. The Oriskany sandstone it produced was of such high quality that several other quarries were also established to extract it, along with Tuscarora sandstone, which also produced an excellent glass sand.

Pennsylvania Glass Sand rebuilt the Hancock mill in 1905. The sand rock from the nearby Hancock quarry was brought there in mine cars, crushed, screened, washed, and dried. The float sand and clay byproducts were sold to firebrick factories, the lower quality sand sold for building or engine sand, and screened out pebbles found use in pebble asphalt roofing. The remaining glass sand was 99.6 percent silica, ideal for glass manufacturers. In 1906 Pennsylvania Glass Sand opened another quarry in Berkeley Springs, some four miles from Hancock, and opened a second plant there. By 1929 Pennsylvania Glass Sand had taken over all of the quarry operations on the ridge and in time would become the only major glass sand producer in the state.

By the early 1940s Pennsylvania Glass Sand was generating revenues of nearly $5.5 million. That amount increased to about $20 million by the mid-1960s. A steady business, the company attracted the attention of International Telephone and Telegraph Corporation (ITT), which in January 1968 purchased Pennsylvania Glass Sand for $112 million in stock. The deal provided diversity for ITT and opportunity for Pennsylvania Glass Sand, whose chairman, Earle Andrews, told the press at the time, "We are confident that the association with ITT will enable us to explore areas that hitherto have been out of reach for our company." Maintaining its headquarters in Berkeley Springs, Pennsylvania Glass Sand remained part of the ITT family until 1985. By this juncture Pennsylvania Glass Sand was generating annual revenues of $83.5 million, but it became expendable when the parent company initiated an asset redeployment program that called for the corporate giant to divest $1.7 billion worth of assets in order to focus on core business areas. Thus, in 1985 Pennsylvania Glass Sand was sold to Los Angeles-based United States Borax & Chemical Corporation.

U.S. SILICA FORMED

A year after acquiring Pennsylvania Glass Sand, Borax became the largest producer of glass sand in the United States when it paid $46 million for Ottawa Silica Company. Founded in Ottawa, Illinois, in 1900, Ottawa Silica maintained facilities in Illinois, Connecticut,

Texas, Michigan, California, and Louisiana, and generated annual sales of $48 million. Although Pennsylvania Glass Sand and Ottawa offered similar products, they complemented one another because there was little geographic overlap in markets. Along with another Borax unit, Pacific Coast Resources, they were brought together under the U.S. Silica Company banner in June 1987.

U.S. Silica remained a part of Borax until 1995. By this time the company employed 725 people at its 13 facilities, producing 4.8 million tons of silica and posting sales of $115 million in 1994. Borax's corporate parent, RTZ Corp PLC, did not believe U.S. Silica was compatible with its international orientation, considering it too regional in scope, despite its rank as the second largest supplier of industrial sand in the United States. As a result, U.S. Silica found itself on the block in 1995. In November of that year a buyer was found in New York City-based D. George Harris & Associates (DGH&A), which agreed to pay $120 million in cash and deferred payments that could total as much as an additional $20 million. Not included in the transaction was the U.S. Silica subsidiary Floridin Co., which controlled Florida mineral reserves and an attapulgite processing plant, as well as a California mine and an associated Nevada facility. These assets were sold off piecemeal.

DGH&A was the investment arm of chemical entrepreneur D. George Harris. Established in 1988, it primarily financed management buyouts of international chemical companies. Harris Chemical Group, an inorganic chemical company, was brought together in 1993. A year later Harris Specialty Chemicals was created to participate in the specialty chemicals sector. George Harris considered U.S. Silica a good fit with his other interests, telling the press, "U.S. Silica is an excellent complement to our existing inorganic chemical business, and gives us a platform for further growth in the extractive minerals industry." Although Harris served as chairman of a holding company, USS Holdings Inc., U.S. Silica would operate as an independent company and its management team led by President Richard Goodell remained in place. The company's headquarters remained in Berkeley Springs.

With the financial backing of Harris, as well as J.P. Morgan Partners LP, which bought a stake to make it a portfolio company, U.S. Silica embarked on an expansion program, spurred by acquisitions. In 1998 the company acquired Jackson, Tennessee-based Nicks Silica, a regional sand supplier to the ceramic, fiberglass, and construction industries as well as to golf courses. Annual sales were about $4 million. Later in 1998 U.S. Silica added Wayne, Pennsylvania-based George F. Petti-

KEY DATES

1899: Pennsylvania Glass Sand is incorporated.
1900: Ottawa Silica Company founded.
1968: International Telephone and Telegraph Corporation acquires Pennsylvania Glass Sand.
1985: United States Borax & Chemical Corporation acquires Pennsylvania Glass Sand.
1986: Borax acquires Ottawa Silica Co.
1987: Pennsylvania Glass Sand, Ottawa Silica Co., and Pacific Coast Resources are merged to form U.S. Silica Company.
1995: U.S. Silica is sold to D. George Harris & Associates for parent company USS Holdings.
1999: USS Holdings renamed Better Minerals and Aggregates Company (BMAC).
2003: BMAC sells aggregates unit.
2007: U.S. Silica changes owners twice.
2008: Golden Gate Capital acquires U.S. Silica.

nos (GFP), producer of silica sand used in the construction industry. It also served as a reseller of other products used in the foundry industry. GFP brought with it quarries and processing facilities in Berlin, New Jersey, and Hamilton, Ontario, as well as annual sales of about $15 million.

FURTHER ACQUISITIONS

More acquisitions followed in 1999. Philadelphia, Pennsylvania–area Better Materials Corporation was purchased, adding a pair of argillite crushed-stone quarries and three bituminous asphalt plants. They served eastern Pennsylvania and central and southern New Jersey contractors, landfill operators, road builders, and ready-mix concrete plants. A month later U.S. Silica acquired five New Jersey operations of Connecticut's Unimin Corporation. Facilities in Cedar Lake, Mauricetown, and Port Elizabeth produced industrial sand, while a resin-coated sand facility was located in Holly City, and commercial sand was produced in Upper Township. In the meantime, parent company USS Holdings began acquiring aggregate assets, including Commercial Stone Co. Inc., a producer of aggregates and asphalt paving materials, in November 1999. Because of the company's expanding scope into aggregates, its name was changed from USS Holdings to Better Minerals and Aggregates Company (BMAC). U.S. Silica and Stone Materials became the two operat-

ing companies. Stone Materials later changed its name to Better Materials Corporation.

At the onset of the 21st century, U.S. Silica reorganized its assets somewhat, selling George F. Pettinos (Canada) Ltd. to Stake Technology Ltd. in April 2000. BMAC underwent a deeper restructuring effort. In 2003 Better Materials was sold for $152 million in stock plus the assumption of $3 million in debt to a subsidiary of Hanson Building Materials America Inc., part of Hanson plc, an international building materials company. What remained of BMAC, namely U.S. Silica, was left to face a number of challenges on its own. The company's financial performance was not outstanding, it was a capital-intensive business, and in recent years it had to contend with product liability issues.

For several decades it was known that prolonged exposure to silica dust could lead to the incurable condition known as silicosis. Lungs scarred by the dust while working in glassmaking, sand blasting, metal foundries, and mines had difficulty removing oxygen from the air. Pennsylvania Glass Sand had warned industry buyers about the dangers of silica dust since 1976, and a year later began printing warnings on bags containing silica-based materials. While silica-related deaths were on the decrease at the end of the century, the number of liability lawsuits began to increase sharply so that in the early years of the new century it became difficult to secure insurance.

According to the *Charleston Daily Mail* in October 2003, which quoted U.S. Silica's chief executive, John Ulizio: "The number of times U.S. Silica has been sued this year has tripled from the year before. It's 164 times more than just six years ago." Due to the uncertain outcomes of the deluge of lawsuits and the other factors challenging U.S. Silica, BMAC had its securities downgraded in 2003 by credit rating agency Standard & Poor's. It was under these difficult conditions that the company initiated a restructuring program that concluded successfully in August 2004 with a reduction in debt and lower interest costs, a situation that management hoped would better position U.S. Silica to target the more profitable segments of the industrial minerals industry.

OWNERSHIP CHANGES

In July 2007 George Harris died at the age of 74 and U.S. Silica underwent a flurry of ownership changes. The business was put on the block prior to the death of Harris, with Wachovia Securities facilitating the sale. New York City-based Harvest Partners LLC bought U.S. Silica for about $200 million in August 2007, outbidding New York hedge fund Harbinger Capital Partners.

A little more than two months later, Harvest sold the property to Harbinger for slightly less than $300 million, according to press reports, turning a quick and substantial profit. Harbinger's ownership lasted about a year, when it too sold the property, albeit not with the same results as Harvest. In November 2008, Harbinger sold U.S. Silica to San Francisco-based Golden Gate Capital for $200 million. Golden Gate also arranged for $137 million in debt financing and a revolving credit facility that, according to Ulizio, "will enable U.S. Silica to continue to focus on its core end-markets, while also investing in the production of sand for fast-growing end-markets such as frac sand for natural gas drilling and low-iron sand for solar applications." Whether the company would be successful in those endeavors remained to be seen, but what was not in question was that the need for silica remained unchanged and that U.S. Silica continued to be one of the leading providers of it and other industrial minerals.

Ed Dinger

PRINCIPAL COMPETITORS

Unimin Corporation; Carmeuse North America B.V.; Fairmont Minerals, Ltd.

FURTHER READING

Casper, Sherree, "U.S. Silica Offices Will Close," *Martinsburg (W.Va.) Journal,* November 10, 2007.

"D. George Harris Buys U.S. Silica for U.S. $120 Million," *Industrial Specialties News,* November 13, 1995.

"Golden Gate Capital Completes $337M Acquisition of U.S. Silica," *TendersInfo,* November 28, 2008.

Grimsley, G. P., *West Virginia Geological Survey,* Wheeling, W.Va.: Wheeling News Litho Co., 1916.

"Hanson to Acquire U.S. Producer for $152 Million," *Pit & Quarry,* May 2003, p. 12.

"I.T.T. Set to Buy Silica Supplier," *New York Times,* January 30, 1968.

"Mineral Co., Sinks Lower," *Loan Market Week,* August 11, 2003, p. 8.

"Mississippi Sees Increase in Silica Lawsuits," *Charleston Daily Mail,* October 20, 2003.

"N.Y. Buyout Shop Seeks Silica Producer," *Alternative Investment News,* November 5, 2007.

"U.S. Silica Company," *Foundry Management & Technology,* August 2008, p. 64.

"U.S. Silica Expands Construction and Foundry Business," *Industrial Specialties News,* August 10, 1998.

Vaisala Oyj

———————■———————

Vanha Nurmijärventie 21
Vantaa, Fin-01670
Finland
Telephone: (358 9) 894 91
Fax: (358 9) 8949 2227
Web site: http://www.vaisala.com

Public Company
Incorporated: 1936 as Vilho Väisälä Oyj
Employees: 1,200
Sales: EUR 242 million ($341 million) (2008)
Stock Exchanges: NASDAQ OMX Helsinki
Ticker Symbol: VAIAS
NAICS: 334513 Instruments and Related Product
    Manufacturing for Measuring, Displaying, and
    Controlling Industrial Process Variables

■ ■ ■

With customers in more than 100 countries, Vaisala Oyj is a Finland-based global environmental measurement company with operations in the United States, France, the United Kingdom, Germany, Sweden, the United Arab Emirates, China, India, Malaysia, Australia, and Japan. About 97 percent of revenues come from exports. The company's business is divided into three areas: Meteorology, providing the professional meteorological market with measurement, data management, and early warning equipment; Weather Critical Operations, serving customers involved with defense, airports, roads, and wind energy; and Controlled Environment, focusing on clean rooms and chambers, building automation, and other needs of industrial customers. Vaisala's weather measurement products include barometric pressure, carbon dioxide, dew point, and humidity instruments.

The company also offers weather stations and systems geared specifically for roads, aviation, and rail; lightning detection systems; sounding equipment used to observe upper air weather; wind profiling equipment to observe air quality and measure airport conditions; and weather radar systems. Products serving industrial customers include humidity calibrators, moisture in natural gas and oil instruments, dew point instruments, oxygen analyzers, barometric pressure instruments, carbon dioxide instruments, and wind sensors. Vaisala units also offer repair and calibration services.

ORIGINS

Vaisala was founded by Professor Vilho Väisälä, who was born in the provincial town of Joensuu in 1889 when Finland was still part of the Russian Empire. Väisälä earned a degree in mathematics from the University of Helsinki in 1912. He also studied physics and received a licentiate's degree and a doctorate from the same institution, despite a civil war caused by the upheaval in Russia. In 1919, the same year Väisälä received his doctorate, the independent Republic of Finland emerged. While pursuing his postgraduate education, Väisälä was employed by the Central Meteorological Institute, working his way from assistant to the director of the aerological department by the time he received his doctorate. He made major contributions to the kite method of observing the atmosphere and also developed the anemograph to document wind speed and direction.

In 1931 Väisälä began development of a radiosonde (a miniature radio transmitter of weather data) for use in weather balloons, an idea that was already being pursued by scientists in Germany, France, and the Soviet Union. The disposable radio transmitting instrument, light and about the size of a cigarette pack, was ready to present to the international meteorological community in 1935 and was quickly adopted by all of the Scandinavian countries. In 1936 Väisälä established Vilho Väisälä Oyj to manufacture the instrument. It was also in July of that year that the first radiosonde was sold in the United States to the Massachusetts Institute of Technology, which bought 25 of the devices for use in studying hurricanes and tropical storms in Caribbean waters. A year later the radiosonde won a gold medal at the 1937 Paris World Fair.

In the late 1930s war broke out in Europe and the demand for radiosondes for military purposes increased. Väisälä not only had to contend with the loss of key employees to the military, he faced difficulties in securing raw materials, including aluminum, silver, brass, copper, celluloid, porcelain, batteries, and radio tubes. Despite the difficulties, he managed to ramp up production during the war years of the 1940s, with three-quarters of his radiosondes sold directly to the military. Most of the others were sold to Sweden, which was ostensibly a neutral country, but was ideally situated to provide weather data used by the Allies in determining bombing missions. During this time Väisälä reorganized his business, in 1944 creating Mittari Oy (Meter Ltd.) to manufacture the radiosondes and V. Väisälä Oy to sell them. He also established a subsidiary in Sweden.

POSTWAR GROWTH

The war came to an end for Finland in 1944 when it was defeated by the Soviet Union, which soon expressed an interest in Väisälä's radiosonde. With an order in hand from the Soviet Union, he was able to operate his companies during the difficult postwar years. He then faced competition from U.S. producers, who did not have to contend with the same constant short supply of raw materials and capital, but he correctly assumed that the market for radiosondes would only continue to grow as accurate weather forecasts grew in importance for both military and commercial applications.

Väisälä was able to build a new plant in 1946 and increase production enough to meet the demand where he could best compete, in the Scandinavian market. He also improved efficiencies, allowing him to lower the price of the radiosonde to create a competitive edge. Even when Väisälä had to contend with a shortage of electrical power so severe that it threatened the very existence of the company, he found a way to carry on, sending workers home to assemble radiosondes. They returned the next day to the plant to deliver the finished products and pick up more parts. The business carried on this way until power was restored.

Not only did Väisälä skillfully manage his business, in 1948 he was appointed professor of meteorology at the University of Helsinki and soon became the head of the department. With the university providing him with a salary, the financial picture at Mittari Oy improved and the company was able to establish a meteorological research institute at the University of Helsinki, essentially a tax-free way to create a research and development unit. Hence, all the pieces were in place for Väisälä to expand his business internationally. Because of his new post, Väisälä dissolved V. Väisälä Oy in 1949, which was replaced by a limited partnership called Kommandittiyhtio Väisälä, in which he was a general partner. In this way he did not have to explain to the university how he could simultaneously hold down two full-time jobs. He also took the opportunity to restructure the operation, bringing in two of his brothers to run the company, thus freeing him up to pursue further development of the radiosonde and meteorological research. When one of them died suddenly, a nephew, a young engineer named Pentti Väisälä, was brought in.

The growth of the radiosonde market following the war was even greater than Väisälä had hoped. Instead of a limited number of researchers and meteorologists buying radiosondes, weather stations all over the world sprang up, taking soundings at least twice each day, creating a demand for the accurate and disposable radiosondes. The days of selling the instrument to a limited number of people, many of whom Väisälä knew personally, were soon forgotten, and the more global, impersonal market that emerged was not to his liking but one in which his young nephew thrived. Vilho Väisälä had the scientific credentials to attract new business, but it was Pentti Väisälä who then maintained the business relationships. He was also especially good at

KEY DATES

1931: Vilho Väisälä begins development of a radiosonde for use in weather balloons.
1936: Vilho Väisälä Oyj is established in Finland to manufacture radiosondes.
1944: Mittari Oy (Meter Ltd.) is formed to manufacture radiosondes and V. Väisälä Oy to sell them.
1949: Vilho Väisälä dissolves V. Väisälä Oy, which is replaced by a limited partnership called Kommandittiyhtio Väisälä.
1955: Pentti Väisälä restructures the business, forming a new limited liability company, Vaisala Oy.
1960: Vaisala introduces first automatic radiosonde receiver.
1969: Vilho Väisälä dies.
1979: United Kingdom subsidiary is formed.
1985: Tycho Technologies Inc. is acquired in the United States.
1990: Subsidiary in France opens.
1994: Subsidiary in China opens.
2000: Jenoptik Impulsphysik GmbH and Dimension SA are acquired.
2004: The Vaisala Weather Transmitter, a single instrument capable of measuring six key weather parameters, is introduced.
2007: Business is reorganized based on market segments.

marketing the radiosonde, and by the mid-1950s the Väisälä instrument was used all over the world. The most lucrative markets, the United States, Western Europe, and then the Soviet Union, were closed, however, because of the military value of weather forecasts. The major military powers preferred to develop their own instruments rather than be dependent on a small Finnish company.

LEADERSHIP TRANSITION BEGINS

In 1955 Vilho Väisälä turned 65 and took steps to turn over the reins of the company to his nephew, charging him with the task of reorganizing the business in light of changing conditions. It had become apparent that in order for Kommandittiyhtio to remain viable in a geopolitically unstable world, it had to establish

subsidiaries in key overseas markets. Moreover, almost 20 years had passed since any major improvements had been made to the radiosonde. Although a new model had been in development since the end of the war, it had taken longer to perfect than expected, making it imperative that the company make greater investments in research and development to prepare for the future.

Pentti Väisälä restructured the business by eliminating Mittari Oy, shelving Kommandittiyhtio for possible future use, and forming a new limited liability company, Vaisala Oy. The name did not contain umlauts, part of an effort to pursue an international strategy, as Penntti Väisälä explained in a company document: "Everything manufactured by our company, the hardware, will be called Vaisala, without the dots over the letter 'a.' But the relevant software, i.e. the methods of graphical computation, the Väisälä Sounding System, etc., and expressions related to theory or other mental activity, will still be printed with the original dots, however."

Pentti Väisälä was also determined to dominate the niche that lay between the military and major civilian meteorological markets. The company's inexpensive radiosonde was a natural fit, but he was also interested in developing other suitable products, not just improvements to the radiosonde, and gave serious consideration to becoming involved in portable radio and mobile phone manufacturing. Even before this reorganization, the company had moved to a plant in Vintaa, Finland, close to a new international airport as well as new University of Helsinki research facilities, again part of a plan to expand globally.

While the company's radiosonde had always been regarded as one of the best instruments of its type on the market, the sounding system was little more than adequate. The greatest drawback was an inability to track the flight of the instrument in darkness or even overcast conditions. The most urgent need was for a better-designed and more accurate wind-measuring instrument. The company made a concerted effort in the second half of the 1950s to address this problem and in 1960 the company introduced the first automatic radiosonde receiver. In the meantime, Penntti Väisälä was looking to establish subsidiaries in markets where Vaisala could compete, finally settling on South Africa and Argentina. Companies were established in 1959, and three years later manufacturing plants opened in both countries.

PENNTTI VÄISÄLÄ DIES

Much of the groundwork needed to achieve Penntti Väisälä's vision was done, but in March 1963 he unexpectedly fell ill and subsequently died at the age of

42. It was a shocking development for the company, but one that also played a role in the future development of Vaisala. Penntti Väisälä had been interested in diversifying the company, pursuing such products as mobile telephones for truck drivers and electronic microphones for scientists, but new management decided the wiser course was to focus solely on meteorological instruments. In keeping with this philosophy, Vaisala in 1965 unveiled the world's first transistorized radiosonde and in 1969 introduced its first weather satellite image receiver.

More innovative meteorological instruments followed in the 1970s, but the company would do without its founder. In the summer of 1969 he suffered a stroke and in August of that year died at the age of 79. What had once been a minor element of the company, the Väisälä Sounding System, became the foundation for much of the company's research and development efforts, as it evolved into a sophisticated system that could measure temperature, humidity, pressure, wind speed and direction, as well as levels of ozone and radioactivity in the atmosphere. In 1973 the company introduced the world's first humidity sensor using thin-film technology. Vaisala's first airport meteorological system was installed in 1975, followed two years later by the first automatic road weather stations.

The groundwork was also laid to produce instruments for the growing environmental measurement market. The company also continued to turn out radiosondes, manufacturing its one-millionth unit in 1975. The 1970s also saw Vaisala further its global ambitions. A U.K. subsidiary was established in 1979, leading to the opening of a sales office a year later, and plans were laid to start a company in the United States, a long cherished dream to establish a presence in North America where an important market had been closed to Vaisala due to Cold War national security concerns.

INTERNATIONAL EXPANSION

During the 1980s Vaisala not only gained a foothold in North America but in other parts of the world as well. A subsidiary was formed in Japan in 1983, and two years later Vaisala acquired Tycho Technologies Inc., a U.S. manufacturer of upper air wind profilers, thus laying the foundation for Vaisala Inc., the company's U.S. subsidiary. Also during the course of the decade Vaisala established subsidiaries in Germany and Australia in 1986 and bolstered its U.K. operation in 1989 with the acquisition of British Thermal Mapping International Ltd., which specialized in road and runway thermal measurement instruments and forecast models. On the product development front, Vaisala in 1983 introduced a new radiosonde, model RS80, which set a new

standard for upper air weather observation. Two years later the company introduced its BAROCAP silicon barometric pressure sensor technology, and in 1987 offered its DEWCAP surface acoustic wave dew point sensor technology.

Growth continued for Vaisala in the final decade of the century. Subsidiaries were established in France in 1990 and China in 1994, the same year that Vaisala became a public company and was listed on the Helsinki Stock Exchange (later merged with the Stockholm Stock Exchange to become OM HEX, which in 2008 was acquired by the NASDAQ to become NASDAQ OMX Helsinki). Vaisala also grew through external means. In 1996 it acquired another U.S. company, Artais Weather Check Inc., an Ohio company that manufactured airport automated weather observing systems. A pair of U.S. businesses were acquired in 1999: Handar Inc., a Texas maker of surface weather instruments; and AIR Inc., a Boulder, Colorado-based developer of sounding systems.

Technological advancements made in the 1990s included the 1996 introduction of Global Positioning System (GPS) technology into upper air measurements. In 1997 a carbon dioxide sensor using silicone technology was added, as was a dew point sensor for industrial applications that relied on thin film technology. Due to the increasing range of its products, Vaisala in the course of the decade divided its operations into three divisions: the Upper Air Division, where the radiosonde and sounding systems business was housed; the Surface Weather Division, focusing on instruments for highways and runways; and the Sensor System Division, which focused on the company's Humicap technologies to measure humidity levels for industrial applications.

GROWTH CONTINUES IN THE 21ST CENTURY

Vaisala's expansion was unimpeded as it entered the new century. Jenoptik Impulsphysik GmbH of Germany, maker of airport weather systems, and France's Dimension SA, a lightning detection equipment company, were acquired in 2000. The following year the Meteorological Systems Unit of Radian International LLC was acquired, adding profiler technology. In 2002, Tucson, Arizona-based Global Atmospherics Corporation was purchased and its lightning detection equipment operation combined with that of Dimension SA. Vaisala's growing portfolio of technologies allowed it in 2004 to introduce the Vaisala Weather Transmitter, a single instrument capable of measuring six key weather parameters. While the company was generally broadening its scope, it elected in 2004 to discontinue a line of ammonia detection instruments, introduced just three years earlier to serve the needs of the food industry.

Vaisala completed two more U.S. acquisitions in 2005. In July of that year it bought Minneapolis, Minnesota-based CLH Inc., provider of airport weather observing systems. At the end of the year Vaisala acquired Westford, Massachusetts-based Sigmet Corporation, a radar signal processor and application software developer. Spread in a number of directions, Vaisala in 2007 initiated a strategy to focus on markets with the greatest growth potential, leading to a reorganization based on market segments: Meteorology, Weather Critical Operations, and Controlled Environment. The company remained willing to acquire additional properties if they became available, in late 2008 buying a Kansas company, Aviation Systems Maintenance, Inc., to strengthen its position in the U.S. airport market. Despite instability in the global economy in 2009, Vaisala remained well positioned to maintain its strong growth on a long-term basis.

Ed Dinger

PRINCIPAL OPERATING UNITS

Meteorology; Weather Critical Operations; Controlled Environment.

PRINCIPAL COMPETITORS

Mettler Toledo International Inc.; Siemens Aktiengesellschaft; Thermo Fisher Scientific Inc.

FURTHER READING

Michelsen, Karl-Erik, *Global Innovator: The Story of Vaisala*, Finland: Vaisala, 2006.

"Vaisala Acquires Global Atmospheric Inc.," *Bulletin of the American Meteorological Society*, October 2002.

"Vaisala Group to Acquire CLH Inc.," *Airline Industry Information*, July 5, 2005.

"Vaisala Oyj Acquires US Software Company SIGMET Corporation," *Nordic Business Report*, December 23, 2005.

"Vaisala Oyj Is Discontinuing Its Ammonia Measurement Business," *Europe Intelligence Wire*, March 26, 2004.

"Vaisala Refines Its Strategy and Focuses on Key Market Segments," *TendersInfo*, November 6, 2008.

Visa Inc.

---

900 Metro Center Boulevard
Foster City, California 94404
U.S.A.
Telephone: (650) 432-3200
Fax: (650) 432-7436
Web site: http://www.visa.com

Public Company
Incorporated: 1970 as National BankAmericard Inc.
Employees: 5,479
Sales: $1.48 billion (2007)
Stock Exchanges: New York
Ticker Symbol: V
NAICS: 522320 Financial Transactions Processing, Reserve, and Clearinghouse Activities

■ ■ ■

Visa Inc. operates as the largest payments company in the world with nearly 1.6 billion cards in circulation and annual worldwide Visa purchases totaling about $4 trillion. The company's retail electronic payments network had 16,600 financial institution customers and processed over 52 billion transactions during that same time period. Visa offers its customers the VisaNet processing network; credit, debit, and prepaid/commercial solutions; security services; money transfer; chip technology; and mobile payments and services. The company claims to be the most recognized financial services brand in the world and has exclusive partnerships with the Federation Internationale de Football Association (FIFA) and the Olympic Games. Visa Inc.

does not issue cards; it secures revenues primarily through fees paid by financial institutions based on payment volume and fees paid for processing transactions.

COMPANY ORIGINS

The driving force behind Visa's explosive growth was Dee Ward Hock. Born in 1930, the son of a lineman for Utah Power & Light Company, Hock was raised in North Ogden, Utah. He attended a local junior college, married his childhood sweetheart soon after school, and worked in a slaughterhouse and for a brick mason. In the early 1950s, Hock joined the consumer finance department of Pacific Finance Company and soon became a local branch manager.

In 1965 Hock began working for National Bank of Commerce in Seattle, eventually becoming assistant vice-president. At the same time, Bank of America was in the process of licensing BankAmericard, its credit card operation, to other banks. National Bank became one of BankAmericard's first licensees, and Hock was promoted to manager of the bank's credit card program. However, many of the new licensee banks complained of delayed payment transfers and lack of adequate measures to prevent user fraud. At a meeting of over 100 bank licensees in 1968, Hock prodded the members to restructure the entire credit card operation. Hock was elected head of the committee to resolve recurring problems.

Hock influenced an industry with a history dating back to 1914 when the first customer charge card was issued by Western Union. This card provided many different services, including deferred payment for preferred

COMPANY PERSPECTIVES

■

Fifty years ago, Visa had a vision to offer individuals and businesses a better alternative to cash and checks. Visa's founder, Dee Hock, believed "digital money" could transform currencies and commerce, dismantling economic barriers and transcending national borders by freeing people and businesses to buy and sell with ease and security. Today, we connect hundreds of millions of people, governments and businesses in more than 170 countries. Together, they have used our credit, debit and prepaid products and services to pay for goods and services safely and reliably. As we move toward an increasingly interconnected world, we believe that we have an opportunity to extend the value of Visa to new users of our products, to drive convenient and efficient global commerce and to accelerate economic growth.

customers. Over the years, a variety of hotels, gasoline companies, and department stores issued their customers charge cards, but the first card accepted by a number of different merchants, the Diners Club Card, was introduced in 1950. Merchants were reimbursed for transactions made with the Diners Club Card by deducting a small fee. Customers were billed monthly for the charges they incurred on the card and were required to pay the full amount of the invoice upon receipt.

In 1951 Franklin National Bank on Long Island issued the first bank-based charge card. The card was accepted only by local merchants, but soon more than 100 other banks were issuing cards. Merchants were charged a fee by the issuing bank for any transaction made with the card, and no fee or interest was charged to cardholders who paid the entire bill upon receipt. However, since these early bank card systems served only a bank's local area, profits remained low.

Bank of America issued its BankAmericard in 1958. The card was successfully marketed throughout the entire state of California. One new factor essential to its success was the credit service. BankAmericard provided its customers with the option of paying the balance of the account in installments, with a monthly finance charge on the remaining balance, rather than requiring a full payment upon receipt of the bill. Of course, the customer could still pay the full balance of the account for the month without any finance charge.

Soon Bank of America was forming licensing agreements with banks outside of California that allowed them to issue the BankAmericard. At approximately the same time, a consortium of banks from Illinois, California, and a number of East Coast states established another bank card association and began to issue Master Charge (later MasterCard). In light of the success of these two bank card licensing associations, most local and regional banks terminated their independent bank card programs and joined either BankAmericard or Master Charge. By 1970, over 1,400 banks offered one of the two cards, and total consumer charges on the cards amounted to $3.8 billion.

CONSORTIUM REVAMPS BANKAMERICARD

The success of Bank of America's credit card operation was accompanied by problems, which Hock, in his capacity as head of the banks' committee, was responsible for solving. He urged the member banks to take control of the BankAmericard program, and in 1970 they created National BankAmericard Inc. (NBI), a consortium of banks that issued the BankAmericard. This independent, nonstock membership corporation purchased the entire bank card operation from Bank of America over the next few years and then began to administer and develop the BankAmericard system. Hock was chosen to lead the new organization.

Hock headed an entirely domestic bank card system. Outside the United States, BankAmericard was issued by Bank of America's licensee banks in over 15 countries. In 1974 Hock negotiated the sale of all foreign credit card operations held by Bank of America to IBANCO, a group of bank licensees that formed a multinational, nonstock corporation to administer and develop the international operations of the BankAmericard program. He then made the entire domestic BankAmericard system a subsidiary of IBANCO, and served as this group's chief executive officer.

When it came to Hock's attention that in many foreign countries there was resistance to issuing a card associated with Bank of America, despite the fact that the association was nominal only, he decided to change the name of the card and the company. In 1976 BankAmericard was renamed the Visa card. Hock chose the name "Visa" because it implied no national identification, it was relatively easy to pronounce in any language, and it made no reference to a bank, which Hock thought might limit how customers perceived they could use the card. Concurrently, NBI was renamed Visa U.S.A., and IBANCO became Visa International.

Under Hock's leadership, customer billings for the Visa card rose dramatically, and worldwide name recognition grew at an astronomical rate. The first Visa Classic card was issued in 1977, and in 1979 Visa Travelers Cheques were introduced. Also in 1979, Visa management began to encourage merchants to use an electronic transaction-authorizing system whenever a purchase was made with the card. Visa terminals read a magnetic stripe on the card and automatically requested authorization, thereby reducing retail store fraud by almost 85 percent. The Visa Premiere card was introduced in 1981, and in 1983 the Visa Classic card was redesigned to include a hologram for added security against user fraud. In 1977 Visa's market share of the bank card business was 40 percent and MasterCard International's was 60 percent. By 1983, the market share proportions of each company had reversed, with Visa's billings amounting to $59 billion and Master-Card's billings at $42 billion.

CONTINUED EXPANSION

In 1983 Hock implemented one of the most important and far-reaching services known in the credit card industry: a global network of automated teller machines (ATMs) that allowed Visa cardholders to obtain cash at locations far away from the banks or credit unions that originally issued them the card. The network provided a cash-dispensing service for travelers carrying the Visa card; after inserting the card into an ATM, the customer received cash from a bank account or from a previously established line of credit. Most of the ATMs were situated initially in places convenient for travelers, such as airports and tourist attractions, but soon ATMs were placed in banks themselves, gas stations, grocery stores, and innumerable other locations.

Visa's ATM network was not well received by the banking industry, since many banks operated their own network of ATMs. The Plus System Inc., located in Denver, was owned by 34 banks, all of which were Visa members, and had approximately 950 various financial institutions that operated ATMs which accepted only the Plus card. The banks each invested up to $150,000 to exclude customers who banked with competitors. Thus, while the Plus System and other similar ATM networks worked hard to ensure exclusivity for their members, Hock was implementing a network that would be accessible to customers of all 15,000 member banks of Visa.

Hock retired as president of Visa in 1984 and was succeeded by Charles T. Russell, vice-president and longtime employee of the company. Russell immediately worked to defuse the animosity between Visa and its member banks over the ATMs. During that year, the Visa ATM network was the first to complete a transnational transaction. Visa continued its phenomenal growth under the leadership of Russell. In 1986 Visa and MasterCard took a 73 percent share of the $275 billion worldwide charge card market, and their combined transactions totaled $3.9 billion, far more than any other financial services company.

IMPROVING THE COMMUNICATIONS NETWORK

In January 1987 Visa won a contract to operate Interlink, the largest retailer, or point-of-sale (POS), network that accepted debit cards in restaurants and stores in the United States. Already managing the California-based Interlink network of transactions since 1984, Visa was ahead of the competition in the burgeoning POS business. In February of the same year, it reached an agreement to pay $5 million for a 33 percent share in the Plus System of ATMs. By adding the 13,000 machines from Plus, the second largest ATM network in the nation, Visa provided its cardholders with access to almost one-third of the 68,000 ATMs in the United States. The Plus System was acquired completely by Visa in 1993.

One of Russell's most important strategies to maintain Visa's market share involved a commitment to improve the company's communications network. Having started VisaNet in 1972, a comprehensive communications and data processing network, Russell directly supervised a $16 million transformation of the system from that of credit card transaction to general purpose electronic payment, capable of dealing with most types of consumer banking transactions. Aware that the continued success of Visa was dependent upon the connection between its e-mail systems and data processing networks, Russell initiated a comprehensive redesign of the company's data centers.

In 1992 Visa converted its Basingstoke, England, and McLean, Virginia, data centers into global "supercenters" capable of processing worldwide volume from either location. This setup was made possible because Visa incorporated transoceanic fiber-optic cables to upgrade its international communications network. As a result of these improvements, a significant increase in volume occurred while the cost per transaction decreased. In 1992 the number of transactions on VisaNet reached a record 807 per second. The network was then capable of processing 1,100 transactions per second at less than a penny per transaction.

BECOMING THE MARKET LEADER

By 1992, Visa's Gold Card, previously the Premiere Card, had become the most widely used and best recognized credit card in the world. Indeed, by all measures of success, 1993 was a banner year for Visa. Total worldwide billings under the Visa name amounted to over $500 billion; more than 300 million cards were issued to customers around the world; more than six billion card and check transactions were made, with traveler's checks alone growing to a worldwide sales volume of more than $16 billion; and Visa operated more than 160,000 ATMs in 60 nations.

An aggressive marketing campaign conducted against Visa by MasterCard in 1991 and 1992 appeared to pay off by March 1993. For the first time in 14 years, MasterCard reported a gain in its U.S. market share for charge card spending, up to 26.8 percent, while Visa's market share decreased from 45.3 percent to 45.1 percent. The competition between Visa and MasterCard, however, was friendly because almost all the banks that owned the MasterCard association also belonged to the Visa association, and no one bank benefited from a gain in market share by one at the expense of the other.

Visa's primary competitor for both the U.S. and international markets was American Express. Whereas the Diners Club card held a 2.2 percent market share of U.S. charge card spending in 1992 and the Sears Discover card a 6.5 percent share, American Express maintained a 19.4 percent share and was working hard to increase it. Both Visa and American Express intensified the competition for a larger U.S. market share by using the concept of "ambush advertising" in their commercials. Visa, as one of the major sponsors of the 1992 Olympics, used its television ads to remind viewers that the Visa card was more widely accepted than American Express. American Express, for their part, featured an Olympic theme while using a clever play on the word *visa* to promote its own card at Visa's expense.

American Express's advertising did not gain any market share for the company. In fact, American Express lost ground in the early and mid-1990s, with its global market share falling to 13.4 percent in 1992 and down to 10.4 percent in 1995. In addition, merchants who accepted the card fell over the same period. In an effort to increase market share, American Express introduced a bank credit card of its own. Visa, however, thwarted this attempt in the United States by establishing an internal bylaw that banned its members from issuing the American Express card.

When the battle for market share refocused in Western Europe, Visa attempted to introduce a similar bylaw for its European member banks in 1996. American Express had arranged with several banks in Portugal, Greece, and Israel to offer its card and fought the proposed bylaw through the European Commission. When Europe's competition commissioner announced that Brussels would not accept the bylaw, Visa backed down. In June 1996 it decided not to restrict member banks in Europe from issuing cards that competed with Visa.

OVERCOMING CHALLENGES

In the mid-1990s Visa developed new products and services that met with varying degrees of consumer enthusiasm. In 1994 the company acquired Interlink, which provided Visa with an online banking service it could offer around the world. A joint venture with Microsoft to offer home banking services and create related software did poorly against Intuit and other competitors in its first few years.

Much more popular was Visa's debit card, a payment option that gained a great deal of momentum in the 1990s. Payments made with a debit card were withdrawn from the holder's checking account and no interest payments were levied. Visa invested heavily in another new payment option, the chip-based "smart card," with much less satisfying results. Although Visa had endorsed the chip technology in 1992, it did not offer the card until 1996. Named Visa Cash, the card electronically stored money to be used as cash. Consumers could load money onto the card by transferring money from a checking account to the card at an ATM. To encourage member banks to transfer from magnetic stripe cards to the new technology, Visa instituted the Partner Program in 1997. Tests with the card, however, were not encouraging. In a 1998 trial by Citibank and Chase Manhattan on the Upper West Side of Manhattan, consumers rarely loaded their cards a second time. "Smart cards are a technology chasing a business case," Richard Speer, CEO of the financial consulting firm Speer & Associates, told the *New York Times* in 1998.

Visa encountered some setbacks in 1997 related to new shopping services on the Internet. Visa and Yahoo, the largest Internet search engine at that time, had reached an agreement to jointly develop an Internet shopping site. Yahoo canceled the agreement in September 1997, however, which cost Visa an estimated $20.5 million. The same year Visa postponed the full introduction of a secure Internet purchasing system. The system, dubbed the Secure Electronic Transaction (SET) protocol, would make electronic money transactions safe through the use of encryption, digital certificates, and digital signatures. In August 1997 Visa began the world's largest pilot program for secure electronic commerce using the SET protocol.

In 1998 federal regulators filed an antitrust suit against Visa and MasterCard, charging that their bylaws preventing member banks from issuing competing cards were creating an uncompetitive marketplace. Visa fought the suit, claiming intense market competition existed. "We believe the suit filed today by federal regulators will fail in a court of law," Paul Allen, executive vice-president and general counsel for Visa U.S.A., said in a press release. "Because, when it comes right down to it, consumers have unlimited choices when it comes to credit cards."

In the late 1990s, Visa's focus was on developing its foreign operations, increasing its debit activity, and improving its technological infrastructure. Despite problems with its electronic cash card, the introduction of its SET protocol, and the federal antitrust suit, Visa operated the largest and strongest consumer payment system in the world.

MOVING INTO THE 21ST CENTURY

The early years of the new millennium were filled with litigation and change. Visa and MasterCard's antitrust suit from 1998 went to trial in 2000. In 2001, a U.S. district judge ruled that both companies violated antitrust laws. The Supreme Court rejected Visa's appeal in 2004. After the ruling, American Express and Discover filed suit against Visa and MasterCard, claiming they had lost revenues because of Visa and Master-Card's actions. In November 2007, Visa agreed to pay $2.1 billion in damages to American Express. The company settled with Discover in October 2008.

Meanwhile, Visa prepared itself for an initial public offering worth approximately $19 billion. During 2007, the company restructured its operations, merging together Visa International, Visa Canada, and Visa U.S.A. to form Visa Inc. One year later, Visa went public on the New York Stock Exchange in the largest public offering in U.S. history to date and one of the largest in the world. Visa planned to use a portion of the proceeds to pay for its costly legal fees and settlements.

International growth remained a cornerstone in Visa's strategy during this time period. While nearly one-third of consumer spending in the United States involved a credit or debit card transaction, these cards were used in less than 10 percent of total consumer spending transactions in Asia, the Middle East, Central and South America, and Eastern Europe. Visa Chairman and CEO Joseph Saunders believed the company was well positioned to tap into these growth markets, especially in India where the company was running tests for electronic bill payment via cell phone.

The U.S. economy was rocky at best during 2007 and 2008, but Visa remained somewhat shielded from significant losses seen in the credit market. The company earned revenues from processing fees, so when a customer failed to pay a bill, the issuing bank was responsible for the loss. Even so, Visa earned more when customers spent more. At the same time, new competitors such as Paypal Inc. and Revolution Money Inc. were offering new payment options for consumers and merchants. With competition looking to capture some of Visa's market share, the company focused heavily on technological advancements in the payment industry.

Despite these challenges, Visa was fairly secure in its position as the leading payments company in the world. During 2007, the company's VisaNet system processed over 81 billion authorization, clearing, and settlement transactions. By 2008, there were 1.6 billion Visa cards in circulation and the company's total volume had reached $4 trillion. An October 2008 *Forbes* article summed up Visa's situation as the company looked toward a new decade. "Visa is bulletproof to bad credit," the article claimed, "but not to new rivals and new ways to pay. That leaves boss Joe Saunders to revamp a business built on plastic or go the way of the rabbit ears antenna."

Thomas Derdak
Updated, Susan Windisch Brown;
Christina M. Stansell

PRINCIPAL SUBSIDIARIES

Advanced Resolution Services, Inc.; Debit Processing Services, Inc.; Gerencia y Administracion, Sociedad Anonima (Guatemala); Inovant LLC; Integrated Solutions Concepts, Inc.; Interlink Network, Inc.; New Stone Ventures LLC; PLUS System, Inc.; SET Secure Electronic Transaction LLC; Servicios Visa International Ltda. (Chile); VCA Inovant Investments Inc. (Canada); Visa Canada Corporation; Visa CEMEA (UK) Ltd.; Visa Consolidated Support Services (India) Private Ltd.; Visa Do Brasil Empreendimentos Ltda.; Visa Holdings, Inc.; Visa Information Systems (Shanghai); Visa International (Asia Pacific), LLC; Visa International (Asia Pacific) Korea Ltd.; Visa International Holdings LLC; Visa International (Holland) B.V.; Visa International (Mexico) S.A. DE C.V.; Visa International (Venezuela) S.A.; Visa International Service Association; Visa Land Management, Inc.; Visa Land Management II, Inc.; Visa Land Management III, LLC; Visa Land Management IV, LLC; Visa Management Services Limited (United Kingdom); Visa Risk Ltd. (United Kingdom); Visa Resource Management Ltd. (Jersey); Visa Sub-Saharan Africa (Proprietary) Ltd. (fka_Micawber_656 [Proprietary] Ltd.) (South Africa); Visa Support Services (Singapore) Pte Ltd.; Visa U.S.A. Inc.; Visa Worldwide (Cayman) Co.; Visa Worldwide (Japan) Co., Ltd.; Visa Worldwide LLC; Visa Worldwide Pte. Ltd. (Singapore); White Pike Financial Services International B.V. (Netherlands).

PRINCIPAL COMPETITORS

American Express Company; Discover Financial Services; MasterCard Inc.

FURTHER READING

Bray, Chad, "Discover Settles Lawsuit with Visa and Master-Card," *Wall Street Journal,* October 15, 2008, p. C3.

Dash, Eric, "Visa Agrees to Pay Amex $2.1 Billion to Settle Suit," *New York Times,* November 8, 2007.

Desmond, Edward, "Yahoo: Still Defying Gravity on the Web," *Fortune,* September 8, 1997, p. 154.

Fitch, Stephanie, "Hard Charger," *Forbes,* October 27, 2008.

Garfield, Bob, "AMEX vs. Visa—Round 2: The Agony of Ambushing," *Advertising Age,* July 20, 1992, p. 44.

Hansell, Saul, "Got a Dime? Citibank and Chase End Test of Electronic Cash," *New York Times,* November 4, 1998, p. C1.

Louis, Arthur M., "Visa Stirs Up the Big Banks—Again," *Fortune,* October 3, 1983, pp. 196–203.

"A Punch-Up in Plastic," *Economist,* June 8, 1996, pp. 77–78.

Sidel, Robin, "Visa's $19 Billion IPO Swipe," *Wall Street Journal,* February 26, 2008, p. C1.

"Visa, Mastercard Settle with Government," *Wall Street Journal,* January 5, 2007, p. C2.

Welch Foods Inc.

■

3 Concord Farms
575 Virginia Road
Concord, Massachusetts 01742
U.S.A.
Telephone: (978) 371-1000
Fax: (978) 371-3879
Web site: http://www.welchs.com

*Wholly Owned Subsidiary of National Grape Cooperative
Association*
Founded: 1869
Employees: 1,170
Sales: $685 million (2008 est.)
NAICS: 311411 Frozen Fruit, Juice, and Vegetable
Processing

■ ■ ■

Based in Concord, Massachusetts, Welch Foods Inc., a cooperative, is the manufacturing and marketing arm of the 1,350-member National Grape Cooperative Association. Using Concord and Niagara grapes, the company offers a wide variety of juice, juice concentrates, powdered drinks, jellies, jams, spreads, dried fruit, and other snacks, including fresh grapes packaged under the Welch's label. The company also blends grapes with other fruits and produces cocktails, non-grape juices, and sparkling juices. In addition, Welch's sells peanut butter, jams, jellies, and preserves under the BAMA label.

Welch's Foodservice Division provides single-serve and multi-serve versions of its products to restaurants,

hotels, schools, healthcare facilities, military facilities, and other institutional customers. Welch's draws on 48,000 acres of vineyards located in Michigan, New York, Ohio, Pennsylvania, Washington, and Ontario, Canada. In addition to its headquarters, the company maintains a technology center in Billerica, Massachusetts, and plants in Michigan, New York, Pennsylvania, and Washington, as well as sales offices in the United States, Hong Kong, and London, England. All told, Welch Foods products are sold in more than 50 countries and territories.

SACRAMENTAL ROOTS

The man behind the Welch's name was Thomas Bramwell Welch, an Englishman turned New Jersey dentist and physician who was also a religious man. He served as communion steward for his church and because he did not believe in serving wine to parishioners, he sought a way to bottle grape juice so that it would not ferment into wine. He relied on a pair of innovations from the mid-1800s: the Concord grape and pasteurization. The Concord grape had been developed in Concord, Massachusetts, by Ephraim Wales Bull, who devoted 35 years of his life to crossbreeding grapes until he created a sweet and palatable variety. After winning the top prize at the Boston Horticultural Society exhibition in 1853, the Concord grape gained worldwide popularity. Welch became the first person to successfully bottle juice made from the grape by immersing the bottled juice into boiling water to kill the microorganisms, a technique developed by scientist Louis Pasteur. Thus, the grape juice remained grape juice rather than becoming wine, and beginning in 1869

Welch was able to offer "unfermented sacramental wine" to his church without fear that their lips would touch alcohol.

In 1870 Welch and his son, Charles Edgar Welch, began selling "Dr. Welch's Unfermented Wine" on a small scale. Like his father, Charles then studied dentistry and returned home to New Jersey to set up a practice as well as to sell grape juice. Meanwhile, his father had grown disenchanted with the grape juice business, finding it difficult to overcome the reluctance of clergy and laity to give up the traditional wine, but he was unable to persuade the younger Welch to abandon the juice venture. Charles Welch also began manufacturing dental supplies, a business he sold in 1886, while continuing to practice dentistry and produce juice. Drugstores and grocers began carrying the product, leading to a change in name to the more consumer-friendly "Dr. Welch's Grape Juice" in 1890. A turning point for the company came in 1893 when the juice became a hit at the Chicago World's Fair, prompting another name change. The "Dr." was dropped and the product became known as "Welch's Grape Juice." The business was then known and incorporated as the Welch Grape Juice Company. It became a public stock company, but the Welch family retained control.

OPERATION MOVES TO WESTERN NEW YORK

Charles Welch then decided to focus his attention on grape juice, and ended his dentistry practice. In 1896 he reinvested in the company and moved his pressing operations from New Jersey to Watkins, New York, closer to a ready supply of Concord grapes, which thrived in areas that experienced cold winters followed by balmy summers. A year later he moved again to Westfield, New York, located between Buffalo and Cleveland on the southern shores of Lake Erie, the heart of the Western New York grape belt. The company continued to focus on grape juice. The extent of its innovation was the 1907 introduction of a four-ounce bottle of juice, the "Welch Junior," aimed at children.

Nevertheless, business thrived, leading Welch to purchase a second processing plant in North East, Pennsylvania, near Erie, in 1911, followed three years

later by a plant in Canada. A second product category was not added until 1918 when the company introduced Grapeade, in reality grape jam. It was an ideal product for use by American troops during World War I, and when those soldiers returned home from the war, they spurred an increase in demand for the product. To keep up with growing production needs, the company bought a processing plant in Lawton, Michigan, in 1919, and built a plant in Springdale, Arkansas, to supply emerging markets in the Southwest.

Thomas Welch died in 1903 and Charles Welch passed away while on vacation in Florida in 1926. One of his sons, Edgar, took the helm, and under his direction the company expanded beyond grape products, introducing Welch's Homogenized Tomato Juice in 1927. A year later his brother, Paul R. Welch, a Columbia Law School graduate, succeeded him as president. Turning over the business to the next generation proved difficult, however, leading to discord between Welch's sons and the sale of a controlling interest in the business. In 1928 a major block of stock was acquired by a group of Nashville investors, headed by Paul M. Davis, president of the American National Company, and the following year the syndicate gained control of Welch Grape Juice Company.

Although under new ownership, the company remained under the leadership of Paul Welch until 1945. The brand continued to grow, due in part to health claims for grape juice that could not be substantiated. In 1943 Welch Grape Juice Company was charged by the Federal Trade Commission with misrepresenting the benefits of grape juice, such as claims of the ability to reduce fat without exercise or change in diet, treat acidosis, prevent anemia, and relieve constipation.

JACOB KAPLAN GAINS CONTROL

Control of Welch's passed to Jacob M. Kaplan in 1945, when he acquired 40 percent of its common stock. Kaplan was a wealthy New York businessman who after leaving school in Boston at the age of 16 had made a fortune in the molasses industry. As the president of Hearns Department Store, Kaplan established a lucrative wine and liquor department following the repeal of Prohibition in 1933. In order to create a supply of wine he bought a Brockton, New York, grape-processing plant in 1933 and formed the National Grape Corporation, which evolved into the National Grape Cooperative Association in 1945. In the postwar economic boom, both National Grape and Welch's enjoyed strong growth. The latter, headed by Kaplan as president, topped $20 million in annual sales in 1947 and for the first time in company history posted earnings in excess of $1 million.

KEY DATES

1869: Dr. Thomas B. Welch pasteurizes grape juice for sacramental use.
1870: Welch begins selling bottled grape juice.
1893: Welch's grape juice is popular at Chicago's World Fair.
1918: Grapeade, a jam product, is introduced.
1929: Company acquired by Nashville investor group.
1945: Jacob M. Kaplan gains control of Welch Grape Juice Company.
1949: Frozen grape juice concentrate is introduced.
1956: National Grape Cooperative Association acquires company from Kaplan.
1983: Headquarters moved to Concord, Massachusetts.
1994: BAMA brand acquired.
2001: Fruit snacks line introduced.
2005: Organic grape juice introduced.

The processor developed another important new product in 1949, introducing frozen grape juice concentrate.

Kaplan increased his ownership of Welch's to 90 percent in 1952, and sold it to National Grape through an unusual arrangement. He provided the cooperative with long-term, no-interest paper equal to 10 percent of Welch's annual sales. Once those certificates equaled $15 million they could be used to purchase Welch's from Kaplan. In this way, National Grape made Welch's into its manufacturing and marketing subsidiary, completing the deal in 1956 when it paid $28.6 million for the business. Kaplan used much of the money he received for a wide variety of philanthropic endeavors he pursued until his death at the age of 95 in 1987.

When Kaplan sold the business to National Grape, Welch's was generating $37 million in annual sales. Much of the growth was driven by television advertisements on popular children's programs. Welch's became an early sponsor of the *Howdy Doody Show* in 1951, and in 1956 became a sponsor of Walt Disney's *Mickey Mouse Club.* Moreover, a grape juice concession stand was established at Disneyland. Welch's grape juice would also sponsor another popular children's show, *The Flintstones,* in 1962.

In 1964 longtime Kaplan lieutenant Raymond T. Ryan took over as Welch's president. After graduating from Pace College in 1933 he began managing property for Kaplan and assisted him in the purchase of the Brockton grape-processing plant, an experience that provided him with a background in the grape business. He put that knowledge to use in 1945 when Kaplan made him executive vice-president at Welch's to oversee operations as well as to serve as a liaison with grape growers. He stayed on after Kaplan sold Welch's to National Grape. As president of Welch's from 1964 to 1970, Ryan expanded the Westfield facility to support the introduction of a line of fruit spreads and non-grape drinks. Revenues increased 21 percent to $70 million during his tenure. He was replaced in January 1970 by R. Craig Campbell.

LAUNCHING NEW PRODUCTS

Over the next 20 years Welch's continued to introduce new products: red grape juice and white grape juice and canisters of powdered drink in the 1970s, sparkling grape juice in the early 1980s, and squeezable jellies and preserves in 1985. The company also moved its headquarters back to Concord, leaving Westfield, New York, in 1983, primarily to allow marketing executives to be closer to their customers. The brand began to lose its way, however, as the eating habits of Americans shifted. Welch's was slow to adjust to the trend of lighter and infrequent breakfasts that led to a steady decrease in the market for jams and jellies, an erosion of about 1 percent each year. Revenues dipped to $220 million in 1991, prompting a turnaround program.

The company looked to launch new products as well as to pursue acquisitions. In 1990 Welch's acquired organic food manufacturer Cascadian Farm. BAMA, a jam and jelly brand popular in the South, was added in 1994. BAMA was clearly a better fit with Welch's, and in 1996 Cascadian Farm was sold to allow the company to focus on the core brands. A year later Welch's repackaged its lines, the first change in look in a dozen years, in an effort to revitalize its place on supermarket shelves.

New product launches were also a key element in the company's revival. In 1996 Welch (by this time known as Welch Foods to reflect the expanding scope of the company) enjoyed its most successful product launch to date with the Juicemakers line of juice concentrate that did not require freezing. Annual sales increased to a record $572.7 million in fiscal 1997. A major factor in this improvement was the company's success in broadening the distribution of its products to a wider range of retailers, from convenience stores on one end of the spectrum to giant mass merchant Wal-Mart on the other. Wal-Mart named Welch Foods its "Grocery Vendor of the Year" in 1997. The company also helped to make its case by sponsoring studies that allowed it to tout the health benefits of grape juice.

Welch Foods continued to enjoy steady growth in the late 1990s. It introduced a plastic can that allowed frozen concentrate to be defrosted in a microwave oven, and a frozen fat-free fruit smoothie drink. A 32-ounce plastic jelly jar was also unveiled in 1999, and a licensing agreement with C.H. Robinson brought Welch's products into the supermarket produce section. As a result of these changes and the continuing benefits of the efforts initiated earlier in the 1990s, the company outperformed the industry, increasing sales to $631 million and net earnings to $70.5 million to close the 1990s.

NEW CONCERNS IN THE 21ST CENTURY

The new century started off well for Welch Foods, spurred by a slate of new products. A squeezable raspberry spread was introduced in 2000, as well as Welch's Fresh Grapes in the produce section of more than 30 supermarket chains. A year later a line of fruit snacks and single-serve drinks in ten-ounce plastic bottles were introduced. Welch Foods turned its attention overseas in 2002, establishing a presence in the United Kingdom and forging an alliance with South Korea's Nong Shim, a major consumer products company. However, consumers at this time were becoming increasingly interested in organic products, energy drinks, and vitamin water, and while its competitors had been quick to adapt to this new trend, Welch Food had been slow to respond. Although Welch Foods introduced organic grape juice in 2005, the company realized that it had lost favor with many consumers.

After a disappointing fiscal 2006, when Welch Foods paid its growers $47 million, about 40 percent less than three years earlier, a new management team was installed, led by CEO David J. Lukiewski, who had joined the company in 1995 as vice-president of sales. Under his leadership, Welch Foods sought to regain its relevance with consumers. The company emphasized the health benefits of grapes and emulated Ocean Spray by introducing five new dried fruit flavors in the fall of 2007. It also introduced grape juice with fiber and grape juice with calcium. Moreover, Welch Foods increased its marketing budget to launch a "Superfruit" ad campaign in late 2008. While the company faced some challenges in carving out a position with a new generation, the Welch's brand retained a great deal of value that could be used to great effect in the effort. Leading the way would be a new CEO, Brad Irwin, replacing Lukiewski, who retired in October 2008. The former president of Cadbury Adams North America LLC, Irwin assumed his new post in February 2009.

Ed Dinger

PRINCIPAL DIVISIONS

Welch's Foodservice.

PRINCIPAL COMPETITORS

Apple & Eve L.L.C.; Ocean Spray Cranberries, Inc.; The J.M. Smucker Company; Tropicana Products, Inc.

FURTHER READING

Abelson, Jenn, "New Recipe for Success," *Boston Globe,* June 1, 2008, p. G1.

Burton, Jonathan, "All Juiced Up," *Chief Executive,* May 1998, p. 24.

Chazzanof, William, *Welch's Grape Juice: From Corporation to Co-Operative,* Syracuse, N.Y.: Syracuse University Press, 1977, 405 p.

"Edgar T. Welch, Ex-Head of Grape Juice Company," *New York Times,* June 27, 1963.

"Farm Group Buys Welch Juice Co.," *New York Times,* August 27, 1956.

Johnston, Paul A., "Grape Harvest," *Barron's National Business and Financial Weekly,* December 12, 1955, p. 15.

"Paul Welch, Leader of Grape Juice Firm," *New York Times,* November 23, 1952.

Saxon, Wolfgang, "Jacob Kaplan, Philanthropist, Is Dead," *New York Times,* July 20, 1987.

World Kitchen, LLC

5500 North Pearl Street, Suite 400
Rosemont, Illinois 60018-5303
U.S.A.
Telephone: (847) 233-8600
Toll Free: (800) 999-3436
Fax: (847) 678-9424
Web site: http://www.worldkitchen.com

Private Company
Incorporated: 1998 as Corning Consumer Products
    Company
Employees: 2,900
Sales: $1.3 billion (2008 est.)
NAICS: 327215 Glass Product Manufacturing Made of
    Purchased Glass; 327212 Other Pressed and Blown
    Glass and Glassware Manufacturing; 332211 Cut-
    lery and Flatware (Except Precious) Manufacturing

■ ■ ■

World Kitchen, LLC, is a privately held company based
in Rosemont, Illinois, that controls a stable of well-
known brands of glass, glass ceramic, and metal
cookware; bakeware; cutlery; and tableware. These
include Baker's Secret, Chicago Cutlery, CorningWare,
Corelle, EKCO, Magnalite, Olfa, Pyrex, Revere, and
Visions. World Kitchen products are widely distributed,
available at major department stores, specialty retailers,
mass merchants, hardware stores, catalog showrooms,
supermarket chains, and online, as well as at 14 CorningWare Corelle Revere factory stores, which also carry
some non–World Kitchen merchandise. The company

maintains manufacturing facilities and distribution
centers in the United States, Canada, and the Pacific
Rim. Since its creation, World Kitchen has struggled to
consolidate its holdings and at one point was
restructured under Chapter 11 bankruptcy protection.

19TH-CENTURY ORIGINS IN CORNING INC.

The foundation for World Kitchen was Corning
Consumer Products Company (CCPC), a spinoff of
Western New York's Corning Inc. Corning was
established in Cambridge, Massachusetts, in 1851 when
Amory Houghton bought into the Bay State Glass
Company. Houghton eventually purchased the Brooklyn
Flint Glass Company and in 1864 moved the business
from Brooklyn, New York, to Corning, New York,
which was better suited for glass making because of its
proximity to an abundance of coal and wood, imperative for the manufacturing of glass. Corning Glass
Works, as the company was then known, proved to be
an innovator. In the early 1900s its researchers
developed a heat-resistant glass, borosilicate. Initially
used to produce a shatterproof lantern used by railway
signalmen, borosilicate would be used to produce Pyrex,
used at first to make laboratory equipment but then in
1915 incorporated into a line of bakeware products.

Kitchenware was never a priority for Corning,
which was involved in optical glass, ribbon glass used to
make electronic components, photosensitive glass, and
later television tubes. Nevertheless, Corning occasionally
produced products for everyday household use. During
World War II the company developed durable glass

tableware for the U.S. Navy, and work in glass ceramics led to the 1950s introduction of Corning Ware cookware, which proved highly popular with consumers because it could be used for baking and broiling as well as on the stove top. Corelle dinnerware was introduced in 1970 and transparent glass ceramic cookware followed in 1981. Corning's housewares products were then supplemented with the 1988 acquisition of Revere Ware Corporation, a company whose roots in housewares reached back to 1892 when Revere Copper and Brass began producing teakettles. Revere Ware cookware was then introduced in 1939.

Although a major technology firm, often on the cutting edge, Corning stumbled in the 1990s, leading to bankruptcy in 1995. A new management team installed in 1997 elected to focus the company's resources on its communications, environmental, and advanced materials business. As a result a number of assets were divested, including the housewares business (a contributor of $639 million in revenues in 1996), which attracted several suitors. A deal was struck to sell the unit in August 1997 to the New York-based private investment firm AEA Investors for $975 million, but due to a downturn in the housewares sector AEA backed out. At the end of a ten-month search, the unit was finally sold for a reported $603 million in April 1998 to Borden Inc., which was privately held by the investment firm of Kohlberg Kravis Roberts & Co. (KKR).

Gaining its independence was considered to be advantageous to CCPC, which had never been given much financial support from its corporate parent. Under the leadership of Peter Campanella, who had run the unit for Corning Inc., the company devoted its first year to establishing itself in the market as an independent company while improving its systems and reorganizing its sales operation. Although sales declined about 10 percent to $580 million in 1998, due in large measure to economic problems in Asia, CCPC was able to invest in product development and still service its debt

through ample cash flow. A year later, however, the company took on an excessive amount of debt when management and its corporate parent decided to create a kitchenware giant.

ADDING EKCO GROUP AND GENERAL HOUSEWARES

In August 1999 CCPC reached an agreement to acquire Ekco Group Inc. for $300 million and General Housewares Corporation for another $145 million. Ekco had a long history in the housewares industry. It was founded in Chicago in 1888 by Edward Katzinger, who started out manufacturing commercial baking pans. He adopted the Ekco label, but the company was known as Edward Katzinger Company until 1944 when it elected to adopt the Ekco Products Company name. By this stage, Ekco was involved through subsidiaries in a wide variety of kitchenware products, including cutlery, flatware, kitchen tools, egg beaters, strainers, and can openers.

Ekco remained independent until 1965 when it merged with American Home Products Corporation, a major pharmaceutical and consumer products company. American Home kept Ekco until 1984, when it was sold to Packaging Corp. of America, a Tenneco Inc. unit. Ekco changed hands again just three years later when Centronics Corporation acquired the business. Once known as Centronics Data Computer, Ekco's parent company had been a technology leader in the 1970s, specializing in dot-matrix printers, but overwhelmed by imports the company reinvented itself in the 1980s as a kitchenware company. In April 1988, Centronics adopted the name Ekco Group Inc. It was this entity that would be acquired by CCPC a decade later.

The other CCPC acquisition, General Housewares Corporation, was founded in 1967 by Jack Muller, a General Foods marketing executive who at the age of 43 decided to strike out on his own and had the financial backing of Laird Incorporated even before he had an industry to pursue. Out of desperation to find inspiration, Muller visited Macy's flagship department store in Manhattan. He began his quest at the top floor and was still bereft of ideas by the time he descended to the basement where Macy's sold housewares products. Almost by default he decided to pursue this category. His initial focus was on enamel cookware, followed by tabletop giftware and a few side ventures that did not fare as well, such as novelty candles, kitchen stools, and outdoor grills.

In the late 1970s General Housewares introduced the Magnalite Professional line of cast aluminum and magnesium skillets and bakeware. In the 1980s the company added the upscale line of Chateau enamel

KEY DATES

1888: Edward Katzinger Company (later renamed Ekco Housewares Company) is founded.

1892: Revere Copper and Brass begins making teakettles.

1915: Corning Inc. introduces bakeware.

1930: Chicago Cutlery established.

1967: General Housewares Corporation established.

1988: Corning acquires Revere Ware Corporation.

1998: Corning spins off Corning Consumer Products Company (CCPC).

1999: CCPC acquires Ekco Group and General Housewares Corp.

2000: CCPC is renamed World Kitchen, Inc.

2002: World Kitchen files for Chapter 11 bankruptcy protection.

2003: Company emerges from bankruptcy.

2006: Name changed to World Kitchen, LLC.

pots, and in 1988 completed a major acquisition, purchasing Chicago Cutlery, established in 1930 by Alfred Paulson, who started out conditioning knives for butchers and packing houses and then developed his own line of professional knives. They did not become available to the public until 1969, but quickly gained a reputation as a topnotch brand. Chicago Cutlery and Magnalite cookware became the focus of General Housewares in the early 1990s.

Added to the mix through an acquisition in 1992 was OXO International, maker of specialty kitchen tools, followed two years later by the purchase of Olfa Products Corporation, the exclusive North American distributor of the high-performance cutting tools produced by Japan's Olfa Corporation. In the mid-1990s General Housewares suffered through a period of poor financial performance, leading to the sale of non-strategic interests and a shift in focus from manufacturing to distribution. Chicago Cutlery was the only line the company then manufactured for itself. The turnaround was completed in 1998, and a year later General Housewares was picked up by CCPC.

WORLD KITCHEN NAME ADOPTED

In January 2000 the enlarged CCPC was renamed World Kitchen, Inc. While the World Kitchen name was advertised to the financial and trade community, it was not applied to any products. Rather, the company planned to continue to promote the stable of brands it had accumulated from CCPC, Ekco, and General Housewares. The administrative, sales, and marketing operations of the three companies were consolidated, and the products were organized within six categories: tabletop, bakeware, range-top cookware, cutlery, kitchenware, and cleaning. A month later Campanella turned over the reins to a new chief executive officer, Nathaniel Stoddard, a former executive with the Canadian home appliance manufacturer Camco Inc.

Stoddard took over a company generating $900 million in annual sales but one that still had not fully integrated its diverse operations. At the same time, World Kitchen had to support a new line of Cuisinart kitchenware products it had licensed through Conair Corporation. It soon became apparent that cleaning products were not a good fit and in September 2000 the Ekco Cleaning Inc. unit was divested. The sale helped to lessen World Kitchen's debt load but only modestly. The company continued to owe $760 million, an amount that became a millstone around the neck of every company CEO. In January 2000, after less than a year on the job, Stoddard resigned. He was succeeded as CEO by Steve Lamb, the former chief operating officer of CNH Global N.V., an agricultural and construction supplier that resulted from the merger of Case Corp. and New Holland N.V. in 1999. Lamb was well familiar with the difficulties of the integration process, but he too had to contend with managing the company's heavy debt.

Lamb launched an effort to cut costs, taking steps to consolidate manufacturing and outsourcing some operations, while lowering inventories and distribution charges. He also closed 30 unprofitable company-owned factory stores. The company's debt continued to mount, however, reaching $812 million and preventing him from truly executing the business plan. In May 2002 World Kitchen sought Chapter 11 bankruptcy protection in order to reorganize its finances, however, before filing it had already secured support for a restructuring plan from parties holding 80 percent of the company's debt. That plan called for the debt to be reduced to $373 million.

EMERGING FROM BANKRUPTCY

While World Kitchen was in bankruptcy Lamb was replaced as CEO in October 2002 after 21 months on the job. His replacement was James Sharman, the company's fourth chief executive in less than three years. Sharman had joined World Kitchen in April 2001 as senior vice-president of household products and supply-chain management after serving as CEO of Chicago-based Rubicon Technology, a manufacturer and distributor of synthetic crystal. Under his watch, in February 2003, World Kitchen emerged from bankruptcy protection. As part of the restructuring, J.P. Morgan Chase & Co. converted $189 million of its loans to an 80 percent interest in the company, while KKR and its affiliates exchanged their bonds and loans for a 12 percent stake. Thus, World Kitchen cut its debt by about half. It also received a new board of directors as it pursued a revised business plan that was already in place.

In May 2003 World Kitchen raised $275 by selling OXO International to Helen of Troy, maker of Vidal Sassoon hair care products, the funds intended to further pay down debt as well as invest in World Kitchen's primary kitchen lines. Other cost-cutting measures were also taken to improve the company's position, including the 2004 closure of the Ekco plant in Massillon, Ohio, which eliminated 200 jobs, or about 9 percent of the domestic workforce. The loss of OXO made World Kitchen a less desirable company, however, when an investment firm was hired in 2005 to help sell World Kitchen. While many of the individual brands were desirable, the goal was to sell World Kitchen as a single unit. There were no takers.

In 2006 the company changed its name to World Kitchen, LLC, and once again changed chief executives. In May of that year Joseph T. Mallof took over for Sharman, who World Kitchen maintained had led the company through a successful turnaround and positioned it to enjoy long-term growth. The former CEO of CIBA Vision Corporation, Mallof brought 25 years of marketing and international experience to the job. He appeared to enjoy a strong start as demonstrated by his inclusion among trade publication *HFN*'s "Power 100" of the most influential people in the home industry. Reviewing his efforts after a year in the job, *HFN* opined in June 2007, "Mallof has shown a keen understanding of the company's core audience as well as the need to draw newcomers to its stable of venerable brands."

Helping in the efforts to curry favor with younger consumers was a deal struck with Food Network star Giada De Laurentiis to apply her name to a new line of Pyrex baking dishes. Pyrex also added silicone grips and enlarged handles to appeal to an aging population. World Kitchen's CorningWare brand introduced a new, extremely lightweight product line using laminated glass to retain its relevance in the marketplace. In addition, the company continued to make efforts to cut costs, as demonstrated by the 2008 closing of a Niagara Falls

warehouse. The company for the most part maintained a low profile, and as a private company was not obligated to divulge its financial results. Mallof remained CEO of the company in mid-2009, three years after assuming the post, a length of term exceeding his predecessors, and an indication that, at the least, he had the support of his board of directors. Whether World Kitchen had indeed achieved a successful turnaround and was pursing a pattern of growth remained to be seen, however.

Ed Dinger

PRINCIPAL OPERATING UNITS

Baker's Secret; Chicago Cutlery; CorningWare; Corelle; EKCO; Magnalite; Olfa; Pyrex; Revere; Visions.

PRINCIPAL COMPETITORS

Newell Rubbermaid Inc.; SEB S.A.; Tupperware Brands Corporation.

FURTHER READING

Porter, Thyra, "Another CEO at World Kitchen," *HFN*, October 21, 2002, p. 1.

———, "Lamb Executing an About-Face at World Kitchen," *HFN*, January 28, 2002, p. 4.

———, "Lamb Taking Command at World Kitchen," *HFN*, March 5, 2001, p. 47.

———, "World Kitchen, in Chapter 11, Vows to Keep Brands," *HFN*, June 3, 2001, p. 1.

———, "World Kitchen Moves to Cut Costs," *HFN*, April 9, 2001, p. 14.

———, "World Kitchen Sells Ekco Cleaning to Focus on Other Categories," *HFN*, September 25, 2000, p. 89.

———, "World Kitchen Wants to Sell, Does Anyone Want to Buy?" *HFN*, March 7, 2005, p. 3.

———, "World Kitchen's Global Quest," *HFN*, January 15, 2001, p. 10.

———, "World Kitchen's Growing Saga," *HFN*, June 10, 2002, p. 4.

Thau, Barbara, "Corning Consumer Takes on the World," *HFN*, January 17, 2000, p. 1.

———, "Corning to Acquire Ekco, GHC," *HFN*, August 9, 1999, p. 1.

———, "Corning to Shutter Ekco, GHC, Headquarters," *HFN*, October 11, 1999, p. 81.

———, "Corning Updates Brand Image, Marketing," *HFN*, May 10, 1999, p. 48.

Cumulative Index to Companies

Applied Signal Technology, Inc., 87 35–38

Applied Technology Solutions *see* RWD Technologies, Inc.

Aprilia SpA, 17 24–26

AptarGroup, Inc., 69 38–41

Aqua Alliance Inc., 32 52–54 (upd.)

aQuantive, Inc., 81 30–33

Aquarion Company, 84 12–16

Aquarius Platinum Ltd., 63 38–40

Aquent, 96 8–11

Aquila, Inc., 50 37–40 (upd.)

AR Accessories Group, Inc., 23 20–22

ARA *see* Consorcio ARA, S.A. de C.V.

ARA Services, II 607–08 *see also* Aramark.

Arab Potash Company, 85 10–13

Arabian Gulf Oil Company *see* National Oil Corp.

Aracruz Celulose S.A., 57 45–47

Aral AG, 62 12–15

ARAMARK Corporation, 13 48–50; 41 21–24 (upd.)

Arandell Corporation, 37 16–18

Arapuã *see* Lojas Arapuã S.A.

ARBED S.A., IV 24–27; 22 41–45 (upd.) *see also* Arcelor Gent.

Arbeitsgemeinschaft der öffentlich-rechtlichen Rundfunkanstalten der Bundesrepublik *see* ARD.

The Arbitron Company, 38 56–61

Arbor Drugs Inc., 12 21–23 *see also* CVS Corp.

Arby's Inc., 14 32–34

Arc International, 76 29–31

ARCA *see* Appliance Recycling Centers of America, Inc.

Arcadia Group plc, 28 27–30 (upd.)

Arcadis NV, 26 21–24

Arçelik A.S., 100 31–34

Arcelor Gent, 80 9–12

Arch Chemicals, Inc., 78 17–20

Arch Coal Inc., 98 5–8

Arch Mineral Corporation, 7 32–34

Arch Wireless, Inc., 39 23–26

Archer Daniels Midland Company, I 419–21; 11 21–23 (upd.); 32 55–59 (upd.); 75 30–35 (upd.)

Archie Comics Publications, Inc., 63 41–44

Archon Corporation, 74 23–26 (upd.)

Archstone-Smith Trust, 49 27–30

Archway Cookies, Inc., 29 29–31

ARCO *see* Atlantic Richfield Co.

ARCO Chemical Company, 10 110–11 *see also* Lyondell Chemical Co.

Arcor S.A.I.C., 66 7–9

Arctco, Inc., 16 31–34

Arctic Cat Inc., 40 46–50 (upd.); 96 12–19 (upd.)

Arctic Slope Regional Corporation, 38 62–65

ARD, 41 25–29

Arden Group, Inc., 29 32–35

Áreas S.A, 104 18–21

Arena Leisure Plc, 99 43–46

Arena Resources, Inc., 97 41–44

ARES *see* Groupe Ares S.A.

AREVA NP, 90 25–30 (upd.)

Argentaria Caja Postal y Banco Hipotecario S.A. *see* Banco Bilbao Vizcaya Argentaria S.A.

Argon ST, Inc., 81 34–37

Argos S.A. *see* Cementos Argos S.A.

Argosy Gaming Company, 21 38–41 *see also* Penn National Gaming, Inc.

Argyll Group PLC, II 609–10 *see also* Safeway PLC.

Arianespace S.A., 89 70–73

Ariba, Inc., 57 48–51

Ariens Company, 48 32–34

ARINC Inc., 98 9–14

Aris Industries, Inc., 16 35–38

Aristocrat Leisure Limited, 54 14–16

Aristokraft Inc. *see* MasterBrand Cabinets, Inc.

The Aristotle Corporation, 62 16–18

AriZona Beverages *see* Ferolito, Vultaggio & Sons.

Arjo Wiggins Appleton p.l.c., 34 38–40

Ark Restaurants Corp., 20 25–27

Arkansas Best Corporation, 16 39–41; 94 35–40 (upd.)

Arkema S.A., 100 35–39

Arkla, Inc., V 550–51

Arla Foods amba, 48 35–38

Arlington Tankers Ltd., 101 35–38

Armani *see* Giorgio Armani S.p.A.

Armco Inc., IV 28–30 *see also* AK Steel.

Armor All Products Corp., 16 42–44

Armor Holdings, Inc., 27 49–51

Armour *see* Tommy Armour Golf Co.

Armstrong Air Conditioning Inc. *see* Lennox International Inc.

Armstrong Holdings, Inc., III 422–24; 22 46–50 (upd.); 81 38–44 (upd.)

Army and Air Force Exchange Service, 39 27–29

Arnhold and S. Bleichroeder Advisers, LLC, 97 45–49

Arnold & Porter, 35 42–44

Arnold Clark Automobiles Ltd., 60 39–41

Arnoldo Mondadori Editore S.p.A., IV 585–88; 19 17–21 (upd.); 54 17–23 (upd.)

Arnott's Ltd., 66 10–12

Aro Corp. *see* Ingersoll-Rand Company Ltd.

Arotech Corporation, 93 53–56

ArQule, Inc., 68 31–34

ARRIS Group, Inc., 89 74–77

Arriva PLC, 69 42–44

Arrow Air Holdings Corporation, 55 28–30

Arrow Electronics, Inc., 10 112–14; 50 41–44 (upd.)

Arsenal Holdings PLC, 79 30–33

The Art Institute of Chicago, 29 36–38

Art Van Furniture, Inc., 28 31–33

Artesyn Technologies Inc., 46 35–38 (upd.)

ArthroCare Corporation, 73 31–33

Arthur Andersen & Company, Société Coopérative, 10 115–17 *see also* Andersen.

The Arthur C. Clarke Foundation, 92 9–12

Arthur D. Little, Inc., 35 45–48

Arthur J. Gallagher & Co., 73 34–36

Arthur Lundgren Tecidos S.A., 102 25–28

Arthur Murray International, Inc., 32 60–62

Artisan Confections Company, 103 23–27

Artisan Entertainment Inc., 32 63–66 (upd.)

Arts and Entertainment Network *see* A&E Television Networks.

Art's Way Manufacturing Co., Inc., 101 39–42

Artsana SpA, 92 13–16

Arval *see* PHH Arval.

Arvin Industries, Inc., 8 37–40 *see also* ArvinMeritor, Inc.

ArvinMeritor, Inc., 54 24–28 (upd.)

AS Estonian Air, 71 38–40

Asahi Breweries, Ltd., I 220–21; 20 28–30 (upd.); 52 31–34 (upd.)

Asahi Denka Kogyo KK, 64 33–35

Asahi Glass Company, Ltd., III 666–68; 48 39–42 (upd.)

Asahi Komag Co., Ltd. *see* Komag, Inc.

Asahi National Broadcasting Company, Ltd., 9 29–31

Asahi Shimbun, 9 29–30

Asanté Technologies, Inc., 20 31–33

ASARCO Incorporated, IV 31–34; 40 220–22, 411

Asatsu-DK Inc, 82 16–20

Asbury Automotive Group Inc., 60 42–44

Asbury Carbons, Inc., 68 35–37

ASC, Inc., 55 31–34

ASCAP *see* The American Society of Composers, Authors and Publishers.

Ascend Communications, Inc., 24 47–51 *see also* Lucent Technologies Inc.

Ascendia Brands, Inc., 97 50–53

Ascential Software Corporation, 59 54–57

Ascom AG, 9 32–34

ASDA Group Ltd., II 611–12; 28 34–36 (upd.); 64 36–38 (upd.)

ASEA AB *see* ABB Ltd.

ASG *see* Allen Systems Group, Inc.

Ash Grove Cement Company, 94 41–44

Ashanti Goldfields Company Limited, 43 37–40

Ashdown *see* Repco Corporation Ltd.

Asher's Chocolates, Inc., 103 28–31

Ashland Inc., 19 22–25; 50 45–50 (upd.)

Ashland Oil, Inc., IV 372–74 *see also* Marathon.

Ashley Furniture Industries, Inc., 35 49–51

Ashtead Group plc, 34 41–43

Ashworth, Inc., 26 25–28

Avado Brands, Inc., 31 39–42
Avalon Correctional Services, Inc., 75 40–43
AvalonBay Communities, Inc., 58 11–13
Avantium Technologies BV, 79 46–49
Avaya Inc., 104 22–25
Avco Financial Services Inc., 13 63–65 *see also* Citigroup Inc.
Avecia Group PLC, 63 49–51
Aveda Corporation, 24 55–57
Avedis Zildjian Co., 38 66–68
Avendt Group, Inc. *see* Marmon Group, Inc.
Aventine Renewable Energy Holdings, Inc., 89 83–86
Avery Dennison Corporation, IV 251–54; 17 27–31 (upd.); 49 34–40 (upd.)
Aviacionny Nauchno-Tehnicheskii Komplex im. A.N. Tupoleva, 24 58–60
Aviacsa *see* Consorcio Aviacsa, S.A. de C.V.
Aviall, Inc., 73 42–45
Avianca Aerovías Nacionales de Colombia SA, 36 52–55
Aviation Sales Company, 41 37–39
Avid Technology Inc., 38 69–73
Avionics Specialties Inc. *see* Aerosonic Corp.
Avions Marcel Dassault-Breguet Aviation, I 44–46 *see also* Groupe Dassault Aviation SA.
Avis Group Holdings, Inc., 6 356–58; 22 54–57 (upd.); 75 44–49 (upd.)
Avista Corporation, 69 48–50 (upd.)
Aviva PLC, 50 65–68 (upd.)
Avnet Inc., 9 55–57
Avocent Corporation, 65 56–58
Avon Products, Inc., III 15–16; 19 26–29 (upd.); 46 43–46 (upd.)
Avondale Industries, Inc., 7 39–41; 41 40–43 (upd.)
AVTOVAZ Joint Stock Company, 65 59–62
AVX Corporation, 67 41–43
AWA *see* America West Holdings Corp.
AWB Ltd., 56 25–27
Awrey Bakeries, Inc., 56 28–30
AXA Colonia Konzern AG, III 210–12; 49 41–45 (upd.)
Axcan Pharma Inc., 85 25–28
Axcelis Technologies, Inc., 95 36–39
Axel Johnson Group, I 553–55
Axel Springer Verlag AG, IV 589–91; 20 50–53 (upd.)
Axsys Technologies, Inc., 93 65–68
Aydin Corp., 19 30–32
Aynsley China Ltd. *see* Belleek Pottery Ltd.
Azcon Corporation, 23 34–36
Azelis Group, 100 44–47
Azerbaijan Airlines, 77 46–49
Azienda Generale Italiana Petroli *see* ENI S.p.A.
Aztar Corporation, 13 66–68; 71 41–45 (upd.)

AZZ Incorporated, 93 69–72

B

B&G Foods, Inc., 40 51–54
B&J Music Ltd. *see* Kaman Music Corp.
B&Q plc *see* Kingfisher plc.
B.A.T. Industries PLC, 22 70–73 (upd.) *see also* Brown and Williamson Tobacco Corporation
B. Dalton Bookseller Inc., 25 29–31 *see also* Barnes & Noble, Inc.
B.F. Goodrich Co. *see* The BFGoodrich Co.
B.J. Alan Co., Inc., 67 44–46
The B. Manischewitz Company, LLC, 31 43–46
B.R. Guest Inc., 87 43–46
B.W. Rogers Company, 94 49–52
B/E Aerospace, Inc., 30 72–74
BA *see* British Airways plc.
BAA plc, 10 121–23; 33 57–61 (upd.)
Baan Company, 25 32–34
Babbage's, Inc., 10 124–25 *see also* GameStop Corp.
The Babcock & Wilcox Company, 82 26–30
Babcock International Group PLC, 69 51–54
Babolat VS, S.A., 97 63–66
Baby Lock USA *see* Tacony Corp.
Baby Superstore, Inc., 15 32–34 *see also* Toys 'R Us, Inc.
Bacardi & Company Ltd., 18 39–42; 82 31–36 (upd.)
Baccarat, 24 61–63
Bachman's Inc., 22 58–60
Bachoco *see* Industrias Bachoco, S.A. de C.V.
Back Bay Restaurant Group, Inc., 20 54–56; 102 34–38 (upd.)
Back Yard Burgers, Inc., 45 33–36
Backus y Johnston *see* Unión de Cervecerias Peruanas Backus y Johnston S.A.A.
Bad Boy Worldwide Entertainment Group, 58 14–17
Badger Meter, Inc., 22 61–65
Badger Paper Mills, Inc., 15 35–37
Badger State Ethanol, LLC, 83 33–37
BAE Systems Ship Repair, 73 46–48
Bahamas Air Holdings Ltd., 66 24–26
Bahlsen GmbH & Co. KG, 44 38–41
Baidu.com Inc., 95 40–43
Bailey Nurseries, Inc., 57 59–61
Bain & Company, 55 41–43
Baird & Warner Holding Company, 87 47–50
Bairnco Corporation, 28 42–45
Bajaj Auto Limited, 39 36–38
Baker *see* Michael Baker Corp.
Baker and Botts, L.L.P., 28 46–49
Baker & Daniels LLP, 88 17–20
Baker & Hostetler LLP, 40 55–58
Baker & McKenzie, 10 126–28; 42 17–20 (upd.)
Baker & Taylor Corporation, 16 45–47; 43 59–62 (upd.)

Baker Hughes Incorporated, III 428–29; 22 66–69 (upd.); 57 62–66 (upd.)
Bakkavör Group hf., 91 35–39
Balance Bar Company, 32 70–72
Balchem Corporation, 42 21–23
Baldor Electric Company, 21 42–44; 97 63–67 (upd.)
Baldwin & Lyons, Inc., 51 37–39
Baldwin Piano & Organ Company, 18 43–46 *see also* Gibson Guitar Corp.
Baldwin Richardson Foods Company, 100 48–52
Baldwin Technology Company, Inc., 25 35–39
Balfour Beatty Construction Ltd., 36 56–60 (upd.)
Ball Corporation, I 597–98; 10 129–31 (upd.); 78 25–29 (upd.)
Ball Horticultural Company, 78 30–33
Ballantine Books *see* Random House, Inc.
Ballantyne of Omaha, Inc., 27 56–58
Ballard Medical Products, 21 45–48 *see also* Kimberly-Clark Corp.
Ballard Power Systems Inc., 73 49–52
Ballistic Recovery Systems, Inc., 87 51–54
Bally Manufacturing Corporation, III 430–32
Bally Total Fitness Corporation, 25 40–42; 94 53–57 (upd.)
Balmac International, Inc., 94 58–61
Bâloise-Holding, 40 59–62
Baltek Corporation, 34 59–61
Baltika Brewery Joint Stock Company, 65 63–66
Baltimore & Ohio Railroad *see* CSX Corp.
Baltimore Aircoil Company, Inc., 66 27–29
Baltimore Gas and Electric Company, V 552–54; 25 43–46 (upd.)
Baltimore Orioles L.P., 66 30–33
Baltimore Technologies Plc, 42 24–26
The Bama Companies, Inc., 80 13–16
Banamex *see* Grupo Financiero Banamex S.A.
Banana Republic Inc., 25 47–49 *see also* Gap, Inc.
Banc One Corporation, 10 132–34 *see also* JPMorgan Chase & Co.
Banca Commerciale Italiana SpA, II 191–93
Banca Fideuram SpA, 63 52–54
Banca Intesa SpA, 65 67–70
Banca Monte dei Paschi di Siena SpA, 65 71–73
Banca Nazionale del Lavoro SpA, 72 19–21
Banca Serfin *see* Grupo Financiero Serfin, S.A.
Banco Bilbao Vizcaya Argentaria S.A., II 194–96; 48 47–51 (upd.)
Banco Bradesco S.A., 13 69–71
Banco Central, II 197–98; 56 65 *see also* Banco Santander Central Hispano S.A.
Banco Central del Paraguay, 100 53–56
Banco Comercial Português, SA, 50 69–72

CB Richard Ellis Group, Inc., 70 45–50 (upd.)

CBI Industries, Inc., 7 74–77 *see also* Chicago Bridge & Iron Company N.V.

CBN *see* The Christian Broadcasting Network, Inc.

CBOT *see* Chicago Board of Trade.

CBP *see* Corporation for Public Broadcasting.

CBRL Group, Inc., 35 82–85 (upd.); 86 65–70 (upd.)

CBS Corporation, II 132–34; 6 157–60 (upd.); 28 69–73 (upd.) *see also* CBS Television Network.

CBS Television Network, 66 44–48 (upd.)

CBSI *see* Complete Business Solutions, Inc.

CCA *see* Corrections Corporation of America.

CCA Industries, Inc., 53 86–89

CCC Information Services Group Inc., 74 68–70

CCG *see* The Clark Construction Group, Inc.

CCH Inc., 14 95–97

CCM Inc. *see* The Hockey Co.

CDC *see* Control Data Corp.

CDC Corporation, 71 97–99

CDI Corporation, 6 139–41; 54 46–49 (upd.)

CDL *see* City Developments Ltd.

CDW Computer Centers, Inc., 16 85–87; 52 67–70 (upd.)

Ce De Candy Inc., 100 92–95

CEC Entertainment, Inc., 31 94–98 (upd.)

CECAB *see* Groupe CECAB S.C.A.

Cedar Fair Entertainment Company, 22 130–32; 98 41–45 (upd.)

CEDC *see* Central European Distribution Corp.

Cegedim S.A., 104 69–73

Celadon Group Inc., 30 113–16

Celanese Corp., I 317–19 *see also* Hoechst Celanese Corp.

Celanese Mexicana, S.A. de C.V., 54 50–52

Celebrate Express, Inc., 70 51–53

Celebrity, Inc., 22 133–35

Celera Genomics, 74 71–74

Celestial Seasonings, Inc., 16 88–91 *see also* The Hain Celestial Group, Inc.

Celestica Inc., 80 59–62

Celgene Corporation, 67 97–100

CellStar Corporation, 83 64–67

Cementos Argos S.A., 91 99–101

CEMEX S.A. de C.V., 20 123–26; 59 111–16 (upd.)

CEMIG *see* Companhia Energética De Minas Gerais S.A.

Cencosud S.A., 69 92–94

Cendant Corporation, 44 78–84 (upd.) *see also* Wyndham Worldwide Corp.

Centel Corporation, 6 312–15 *see also* EMBARQ Corp.

Centennial Communications Corporation, 39 74–76

Centerior Energy Corporation, V 567–68

Centerplate, Inc., 79 96–100

Centex Corporation, 8 87–89; 29 93–96 (upd.)

Centocor Inc., 14 98–100

Central and South West Corporation, V 569–70

Central European Distribution Corporation, 75 90–92

Central European Media Enterprises Ltd., 61 56–59

Central Florida Investments, Inc., 93 137–40

Central Garden & Pet Company, 23 108–10; 58 57–60 (upd.)

Central Hudson Gas And Electricity Corporation, 6 458–60

Central Independent Television, 7 78–80; 23 111–14 (upd.)

Central Japan Railway Company, 43 103–06

Central Maine Power, 6 461–64

Central National-Gottesman Inc., 95 87–90

Central Newspapers, Inc., 10 207–09 *see also* Gannett Company, Inc.

Central Parking System, 18 103–05; 104 74–78 (upd.)

Central Soya Company, Inc., 7 81–83

Central Sprinkler Corporation, 29 97–99

Central Vermont Public Service Corporation, 54 53–56

Centrica plc, 29 100–05 (upd.)

Centuri Corporation, 54 57–59

Century Aluminum Company, 52 71–74

Century Business Services, Inc., 52 75–78

Century Casinos, Inc., 53 90–93

Century Communications Corp., 10 210–12

Century Telephone Enterprises, Inc., 9 105–07; 54 60–63 (upd.)

Century Theatres, Inc., 31 99–101

Cenveo Inc., 71 100–04 (upd.)

CEPCO *see* Chugoku Electric Power Company Inc.

Cephalon, Inc., 45 93–96

Cepheid, 77 93–96

Ceradyne, Inc., 65 100–02

Cerebos Gregg's Ltd., 100 96–99

Cerner Corporation, 16 92–94; 94 111–16 (upd.)

CertainTeed Corporation, 35 86–89

Certegy, Inc., 63 100–03

Cerveceria Polar, I 230–31 *see also* Empresas Polar SA.

Ceské aerolinie, a.s., 66 49–51

Cesky Telecom, a.s., 64 70–73

Cessna Aircraft Company, 8 90–93; 27 97–101 (upd.)

Cetelem S.A., 21 99–102

CeWe Color Holding AG, 76 85–88

ČEZ a. s., 97 112–15

CF Industries Holdings, Inc., 99 89–93

CG&E *see* Cincinnati Gas & Electric Co.

CGM *see* Compagnie Générale Maritime.

CH2M HILL Companies Ltd., 22 136–38; 96 72–77 (upd.)

Chadbourne & Parke, 36 109–12

Chadwick's of Boston, Ltd., 29 106–08

Chalk's Ocean Airways *see* Flying Boat, Inc.

The Chalone Wine Group, Ltd., 36 113–16

Champion Enterprises, Inc., 17 81–84

Champion Industries, Inc., 28 74–76

Champion International Corporation, IV 263–65; 20 127–30 (upd.) *see also* International Paper Co.

Championship Auto Racing Teams, Inc., 37 73–75

Chancellor Beacon Academies, Inc., 53 94–97

Chancellor Media Corporation, 24 106–10

Chanel SA, 12 57–59; 49 83–86 (upd.)

Channel Four Television Corporation, 93 141–44

Chantiers Jeanneau S.A., 96 78–81

Chaoda Modern Agriculture (Holdings) Ltd., 87 96–99

Chaparral Steel Co., 13 142–44

Charal S.A., 90 117–20

Chargeurs International, 6 373–75; 21 103–06 (upd.)

Charisma Brands LLC, 74 75–78

The Charles Machine Works, Inc., 64 74–76

Charles River Laboratories International, Inc., 42 66–69

The Charles Schwab Corporation, 8 94–96; 26 64–67 (upd.); 81 62–68 (upd.)

The Charles Stark Draper Laboratory, Inc., 35 90–92

Charles Vögele Holding AG, 82 63–66

Charlotte Russe Holding, Inc., 35 93–96; 90 121–25 (upd.)

The Charmer Sunbelt Group, 95 91–94

Charming Shoppes, Inc., 8 97–98; 38 127–29 (upd.)

Charoen Pokphand Group, 62 60–63

Chart House Enterprises, Inc., 17 85–88; 96 82–86 (upd.)

Chart Industries, Inc., 21 107–09

Charter Communications, Inc., 33 91–94

Charter Financial Corporation, 103 96–99

Charter Manufacturing Company, Inc., 103 100–03

ChartHouse International Learning Corporation, 49 87–89

Chas. Levy Company LLC, 60 83–85

Chase General Corporation, 91 102–05

The Chase Manhattan Corporation, II 247–49; 13 145–48 (upd.) *see also* JPMorgan Chase & Co.

Chateau Communities, Inc., 37 76–79

Chattanooga Bakery, Inc., 86 75–78

Chattem, Inc., 17 89–92; 88 47–52 (upd.)

Chautauqua Airlines, Inc., 38 130–32

Computervision Corporation, 10 240–42

Compuware Corporation, 10 243–45; 30 140–43 (upd.); 66 60–64 (upd.)

Comsat Corporation, 23 133–36 *see also* Lockheed Martin Corp.

Comshare Inc., 23 137–39

Comstock Resources, Inc., 47 85–87

Comtech Telecommunications Corp., 75 103–05

Comverse Technology, Inc., 15 124–26; 43 115–18 (upd.)

Con Ed *see* Consolidated Edison, Inc.

Con-way Inc., 101 130–34

ConAgra Foods, Inc., II 493–95; 12 80–82 (upd.); 42 90–94 (upd.); 85 61–68 (upd.)

Conair Corporation, 17 108–10; 69 104–08 (upd.)

Conaprole *see* Cooperativa Nacional de Productores de Leche S.A. (Conaprole).

Concentra Inc., 71 117–19

Concepts Direct, Inc., 39 93–96

Concha y Toro *see* Viña Concha y Toro S.A.

Concord Camera Corporation, 41 104–07

Concord EFS, Inc., 52 86–88

Concord Fabrics, Inc., 16 124–26

Concurrent Computer Corporation, 75 106–08

Condé Nast Publications, Inc., 13 177–81; 59 131–34 (upd.)

Cone Mills LLC, 8 120–22; 67 123–27 (upd.)

Conexant Systems, Inc., 36 121–25

Confluence Holdings Corporation, 76 118–20

Congoleum Corporation, 18 116–19; 98 52–57 (upd.)

CONMED Corporation, 87 117–120

Conn-Selmer, Inc., 55 111–14

Connecticut Light and Power Co., 13 182–84

Connecticut Mutual Life Insurance Company, III 236–38

The Connell Company, 29 129–31; 104 83–87 (upd.)

Conner Peripherals, Inc., 6 230–32

Connetics Corporation, 70 64–66

Connors Bros. Income Fund *see* George Weston Ltd.

Conn's, Inc., 67 128–30

ConocoPhillips, IV 399–402; 16 127–32 (upd.); 63 104–15 (upd.)

Conrad Industries, Inc., 58 68–70

Conseco Inc., 10 246–48; 33 108–12 (upd.)

Conso International Corporation, 29 132–34

CONSOL Energy Inc., 59 135–37

Consolidated Delivery & Logistics, Inc., 24 125–28 *see also* Velocity Express Corp.

Consolidated Edison, Inc., V 586–89; 45 116–20 (upd.)

Consolidated Freightways Corporation, V 432–34; 21 136–39 (upd.); 48 109–13 (upd.)

Consolidated Graphics, Inc., 70 67–69

Consolidated Natural Gas Company, V 590–91; 19 100–02 (upd.) *see also* Dominion Resources, Inc.

Consolidated Papers, Inc., 8 123–25; 36 126–30 (upd.)

Consolidated Products, Inc., 14 130–32

Consolidated Rail Corporation, V 435–37

Consorcio ARA, S.A. de C.V., 79 113–16

Consorcio Aviacsa, S.A. de C.V., 85 69–72

Consorcio G Grupo Dina, S.A. de C.V., 36 131–33

Constar International Inc., 64 85–88

Constellation Brands, Inc., 68 95–100 (upd.)

The Consumers Gas Company Ltd., 6 476–79; 43 154 *see also* Enbridge Inc.

Consumers Power Co., 14 133–36

Consumers Union, 26 97–99

Consumers Water Company, 14 137–39

The Container Store, 36 134–36

ContiGroup Companies, Inc., 43 119–22 (upd.)

Continental AG, V 240–43; 56 67–72 (upd.)

Continental Airlines, Inc., I 96–98; 21 140–43 (upd.); 52 89–94 (upd.)

Continental Bank Corporation, II 261–63 *see also* Bank of America.

Continental Cablevision, Inc., 7 98–100

Continental Can Co., Inc., 15 127–30

Continental Corporation, III 239–44

Continental General Tire Corp., 23 140–42

Continental Grain Company, 10 249–51; 13 185–87 (upd.) *see also* ContiGroup Companies, Inc.

Continental Group Co., I 599–600

Continental Medical Systems, Inc., 10 252–54

Continental Resources, Inc., 89 161–65

Continucare Corporation, 101 135–38

Continuum Health Partners, Inc., 60 97–99

Control Data Corporation, III 126–28 *see also* Seagate Technology, Inc.

Control Data Systems, Inc., 10 255–57

Controladora Comercial Mexicana, S.A. de C.V., 36 137–39

Controladora Mabe, S.A. de C.V., 82 74–77

Converse Inc., 9 133–36; 31 134–38 (upd.)

Conzzeta Holding, 80 76–79

Cook Group Inc., 102 93–96

Cooker Restaurant Corporation, 20 159–61; 51 82–85 (upd.)

Cookson Group plc, III 679–82; 44 115–20 (upd.)

CoolBrands International Inc., 35 119–22

CoolSavings, Inc., 77 120–24

Coop Schweiz Genossenschaftsverband, 48 114–16

Coopagri Bretagne, 88 53–56

Cooper Cameron Corporation, 20 162–66 (upd.); 58 71–75 (upd.)

The Cooper Companies, Inc., 39 97–100

Cooper Industries, Inc., II 14–17; 44 121–25 (upd.)

Cooper Tire & Rubber Company, 8 126–28; 23 143–46 (upd.)

Cooperativa Nacional de Productores de Leche S.A. (Conaprole),92 60–63

Coopers & Lybrand, 9 137–38 *see also* PricewaterhouseCoopers.

Coors Company *see* Adolph Coors Co.

Copa Holdings, S.A., 93 164–67

Copart Inc., 23 147–49

Copec *see* Empresas Copec S.A.

The Copley Press, Inc., 23 150–52

Coppel, S.A. de C.V., 82 78–81

The Copps Corporation, 32 120–22

Cora S.A./NV, 94 134–37

Corbis Corporation, 31 139–42

Corby Distilleries Limited, 14 140–42

The Corcoran Group, Inc., 58 76–78

Cordis Corporation, 19 103–05; 46 104–07 (upd.)

Cordon Bleu *see* Le Cordon Bleu S.A.

Corel Corporation, 15 131–33; 33 113–16 (upd.); 76 121–24 (upd.)

Corelio S.A./N.V., 96 87–90

CoreStates Financial Corp, 16 111–15 *see also* Wachovia Corp.

Corinthian Colleges, Inc., 39 101–04; 92 64–69 (upd.)

The Corky McMillin Companies, 98 58–62

Cornelsen Verlagsholding GmbH & Co., 90 141–46

Corning Inc., III 683–85; 44 126–30 (upd.); 90 147–53 (upd.)

Corporación Geo, S.A. de C.V., 81 95–98

Corporación Interamericana de Entretenimiento, S.A. de C.V., 83 87–90

Corporación Internacional de Aviación, S.A. de C.V. (Cintra), 20 167–69

Corporación José R. Lindley S.A., 92 70–73

Corporación Multi-Inversiones, 94 138–42

Corporacion Nacional del Cobre de Chile, 40 121–23

The Corporate Executive Board Company, 89 166–69

Corporate Express, Inc., 22 152–55; 47 88–92 (upd.)

Corporate Software Inc., 9 139–41

Corporation for Public Broadcasting, 14 143–45; 89 170–75 (upd.)

Correctional Services Corporation, 30 144–46

Corrections Corporation of America, 23 153–55

Correos y Telegrafos S.A., 80 80–83

Corrpro Companies, Inc., 20 170–73

Luby's, Inc., 17 290–93; 42 233–38 (upd.); 99 266–273 (upd.)

Lucas Industries Plc, III 554–57

Lucasfilm Ltd., 12 322–24; 50 320–23 (upd.)

Lucent Technologies Inc., 34 257–60

Lucille Farms, Inc., 45 249–51

Lucky-Goldstar, II 53–54 *see also* LG Corp.

Lucky Stores Inc., 27 290–93

Ludendo S.A., 88 237–40

Lufkin Industries, Inc., 78 198–202

Lufthansa *see* Deutsche Lufthansa AG.

Luigino's, Inc., 64 248–50

Lukens Inc., 14 323–25 *see also* Bethlehem Steel Corp.

LUKOIL *see* OAO LUKOIL.

Luminar Plc, 40 296–98

Lunar Corporation, 29 297–99

Lunardi's Super Market, Inc., 99 274–277

Lund Food Holdings, Inc., 22 326–28

Lund International Holdings, Inc., 40 299–301

Lush Ltd., 93 305–08

Lutheran Brotherhood, 31 318–21

Luxottica SpA, 17 294–96; 52 227–30 (upd.)

LVMH Moët Hennessy Louis Vuitton SA, 33 272–77 (upd.) *see also* Christian Dior S.A.

Lycos *see* Terra Lycos, Inc.

Lydall, Inc., 64 251–54

Lyfra-S.A./NV, 88 241–43

Lyman-Richey Corporation, 96 265–68

Lynch Corporation, 43 273–76

Lynden Incorporated, 91 322–25

Lyondell Chemical Company, IV 456–57; 45 252–55 (upd.)

Lyonnaise des Eaux-Dumez, V 655–57 *see also* Suez Lyonnaise des Eaux.

M

M&F Worldwide Corp., 38 293–95

M-real Oyj, 56 252–55 (upd.)

M.A. Bruder & Sons, Inc., 56 207–09

M.A. Gedney Co., 51 230–32

M.A. Hanna Company, 8 345–47 *see also* PolyOne Corp.

M. DuMont Schauberg GmbH & Co. KG, 92 213–17

M.E.P.C. Ltd. *see* MEPC plc.

M.H. Meyerson & Co., Inc., 46 280–83

M.R. Beal and Co., 102 244–47

M. Shanken Communications, Inc., 50 324–27

M6 *see* Métropole Télévision S.A..

Maatschappij tot Exploitatie van de Onderneming Krasnapolsky *see* Grand Hotel Krasnapolsky N.V.

Mabe *see* Controladora Mabe, S.A. de C.V.

Mabuchi Motor Co. Ltd., 68 241–43

Mac Frugal's Bargains - Closeouts Inc., 17 297–99 *see also* Big Lots, Inc.

Mac-Gray Corporation, 44 271–73

The Macallan Distillers Ltd., 63 246–48

MacAndrews & Forbes Holdings Inc., 28 246–49; 86 253–59 (upd.)

MacArthur Foundation *see* The John D. and Catherine T. MacArthur Foundation.

Mace Security International, Inc., 57 230–32

The Macerich Company, 57 233–35

MacGregor Golf Company, 68 244–46

Mack-Cali Realty Corporation, 42 239–41

Mack Trucks, Inc., I 177–79; 22 329–32 (upd.); 61 179–83 (upd.)

Mackay Envelope Corporation, 45 256–59

Mackays Stores Group Ltd., 92 218–21

Mackie Designs Inc., 33 278–81 *see also* LOUD Technologies, Inc.

Macklowe Properties, Inc., 95 251–54

Maclean Hunter Publishing Limited, IV 638–40; 26 270–74 (upd.) *see also* Rogers Communications Inc.

MacMillan Bloedel Limited, IV 306–09 *see also* Weyerhaeuser Co.

Macmillan, Inc., 7 284–86

The MacNeal-Schwendler Corporation, 25 303–05

MacNeil/Lehrer Productions, 87 296–299

Macquarie Bank Ltd., 69 246–49

Macromedia, Inc., 50 328–31

Macrovision Solutions Corporation, 101 314–17

Macy's, Inc., 94 284–93 (upd.)

MADD *see* Mothers Against Drunk Driving.

Madden's on Gull Lake, 52 231–34

Madeco S.A., 71 210–12

Madeira Wine Company, S.A., 49 255–57

Madelaine Chocolate Novelties, Inc., 104 280–83

Madge Networks N.V., 26 275–77

Madison Dearborn Partners, LLC, 97 258–61

Madison Gas and Electric Company, 39 259–62

Madison-Kipp Corporation, 58 213–16

Madrange SA, 58 217–19

Mag Instrument, Inc., 67 240–42

Magazine Luiza S.A., 101 318–21

Magellan Aerospace Corporation, 48 274–76

MaggieMoo's International, 89 312–16

Magma Copper Company, 7 287–90 *see also* BHP Billiton.

Magma Design Automation Inc., 78 203–27

Magma Power Company, 11 270–72

Magna International Inc., 102 248–52

MagneTek, Inc., 15 287–89; 41 241–44 (upd.)

Magneti Marelli Holding SpA, 90 286–89

Magyar Telekom Rt, 78 208–11

MAI Systems Corporation, 11 273–76

Maid-Rite Corporation, 62 235–38

Maidenform, Inc., 20 352–55; 59 265–69 (upd.)

Mail Boxes Etc., 18 315–17; 41 245–48 (upd.) *see also* U.S. Office Products Co.

Mail-Well, Inc., 28 250–52 *see also* Cenveo Inc.

MAIN *see* Makhteshim-Agan Industries Ltd.

Maine & Maritimes Corporation, 56 210–13

Maine Central Railroad Company, 16 348–50

Maines Paper & Food Service Inc., 71 213–15

Maison Louis Jadot, 24 307–09

Majesco Entertainment Company, 85 225–29

The Major Automotive Companies, Inc., 45 260–62

Make-A-Wish Foundation of America, 97 262–65

Makhteshim-Agan Industries Ltd., 85 230–34

Makita Corporation, 22 333–35; 59 270–73 (upd.)

Malayan Banking Berhad, 72 215–18

Malaysian Airline System Berhad, 6 100–02; 29 300–03 (upd.); 97 266–71 (upd.)

Malcolm Pirnie, Inc., 42 242–44

Malden Mills Industries, Inc., 16 351–53 *see also* Polartec LLC.

Malév Plc, 24 310–12

Mallinckrodt Group Inc., 19 251–53

Malt-O-Meal Company, 22 336–38; 63 249–53 (upd.)

Mammoet Transport B.V., 26 278–80

Mammoth Mountain Ski Area, 101 322–25

Man Aktiengesellschaft, III 561–63

MAN Roland Druckmaschinen AG, 94 294–98

Management and Training Corporation, 28 253–56

Manatron, Inc., 86 260–63

Manchester United Football Club plc, 30 296–98

Mandalay Resort Group, 32 322–26 (upd.)

Mandom Corporation, 82 205–08

Manhattan Associates, Inc., 67 243–45

Manhattan Group, LLC, 80 228–31

Manheim, 88 244–48

Manila Electric Company (Meralco), 56 214–16

Manischewitz Company *see* B. Manischewitz Co.

Manitoba Telecom Services, Inc., 61 184–87

Manitou BF S.A., 27 294–96

The Manitowoc Company, Inc., 18 318–21; 59 274–79 (upd.)

Mannatech Inc., 33 282–85

Mannesmann AG, III 564–67; 14 326–29 (upd.); 38 296–301 (upd.) *see also* Vodafone Group PLC.

Mannheim Steamroller *see* American Gramophone LLC.

Millennium & Copthorne Hotels plc, 71 231–33

Millennium Pharmaceuticals, Inc., 47 249–52

Miller Brewing Company, I 269–70; 12 337–39 (upd.) *see also* SABMiller plc.

Miller Industries, Inc., 26 293–95

Miller Publishing Group, LLC, 57 242–44

Milliken & Co., V 366–68; 17 327–30 (upd.); 82 235–39 (upd.)

Milliman USA, 66 223–26

Millipore Corporation, 25 339–43; 84 271–276 (upd.)

The Mills Corporation, 77 280–83

Milnot Company, 46 289–91

Milton Bradley Company, 21 372–75

Milton CAT, Inc., 86 268–71

Milwaukee Brewers Baseball Club, 37 247–49

Mine Safety Appliances Company, 31 333–35

Minebea Co., Ltd., 90 298–302

The Miner Group International, 22 356–58

Minera Escondida Ltda., 100 293–96

Minerals & Metals Trading Corporation of India Ltd., IV 143–44

Minerals Technologies Inc., 11 310–12; 52 248–51 (upd.)

Minnesota Mining & Manufacturing Company, I 499–501; 8 369–71 (upd.); 26 296–99 (upd.) *see also* 3M Co.

Minnesota Power, Inc., 11 313–16; 34 286–91 (upd.)

Minntech Corporation, 22 359–61

Minolta Co., Ltd., III 574–76; 18 339–42 (upd.); 43 281–85 (upd.)

The Minute Maid Company, 28 271–74

Minuteman International Inc., 46 292–95

Minyard Food Stores, Inc., 33 304–07; 86 272–77 (upd.)

Miquel y Costas Miquel S.A., 68 256–58

Mirage Resorts, Incorporated, 6 209–12; 28 275–79 (upd.) *see also* MGM MIRAGE.

Miramax Film Corporation, 64 282–85

Mirant Corporation, 98 243–47

Miroglio SpA, 86 278–81

Mirror Group Newspapers plc, 7 341–43; 23 348–51 (upd.)

Misonix, Inc., 80 248–51

Mississippi Chemical Corporation, 39 280–83

Misys PLC, 45 279–81; 46 296–99

Mitchell Energy and Development Corporation, 7 344–46 *see also* Devon Energy Corp.

Mitchells & Butlers PLC, 59 296–99

Mitel Corporation, 18 343–46

MITRE Corporation, 26 300–02

MITROPA AG, 37 250–53

Mitsubishi Bank, Ltd., II 321–22 *see also* Bank of Tokyo-Mitsubishi Ltd.

Mitsubishi Chemical Corporation, I 363–64; 56 236–38 (upd.)

Mitsubishi Corporation, I 502–04; 12 340–43 (upd.)

Mitsubishi Electric Corporation, II 57–59; 44 283–87 (upd.)

Mitsubishi Estate Company, Limited, IV 713–14; 61 215–18 (upd.)

Mitsubishi Heavy Industries, Ltd., III 577–79; 7 347–50 (upd.); 40 324–28 (upd.)

Mitsubishi Materials Corporation, III 712–13

Mitsubishi Motors Corporation, 9 349–51; 23 352–55 (upd.); 57 245–49 (upd.)

Mitsubishi Oil Co., Ltd., IV 460–62 *see also* Nippon Mitsubishi Oil Corp.

Mitsubishi Rayon Co. Ltd., V 369–71

Mitsubishi Trust & Banking Corporation, II 323–24

Mitsubishi UFJ Financial Group, Inc., 99 291–296 (upd.)

Mitsui & Co., Ltd., I 505–08; 28 280–85 (upd.)

Mitsui Bank, Ltd., II 325–27 *see also* Sumitomo Mitsui Banking Corp.

Mitsui Marine and Fire Insurance Company, Limited, III 295–96

Mitsui Mining & Smelting Co., Ltd., IV 145–46; 102 274–78 (upd.)

Mitsui Mining Company, Limited, IV 147–49

Mitsui Mutual Life Insurance Company, III 297–98; 39 284–86 (upd.)

Mitsui O.S.K. Lines Ltd., V 473–76; 96 282–87 (upd.)

Mitsui Petrochemical Industries, Ltd., 9 352–54

Mitsui Real Estate Development Co., Ltd., IV 715–16

Mitsui Trust & Banking Company, Ltd., II 328

Mitsukoshi Ltd., V 142–44; 56 239–42 (upd.)

Mity Enterprises, Inc., 38 310–12

MIVA, Inc., 83 271–275

Mizuho Financial Group Inc., 25 344–46; 58 229–36 (upd.)

MN Airlines LLC, 104 321–27

MNS, Ltd., 65 236–38

Mo och Domsjö AB, IV 317–19 *see also* Holmen AB

Mobil Corporation, IV 463–65; 7 351–54 (upd.); 21 376–80 (upd.) *see also* Exxon Mobil Corp.

Mobile Mini, Inc., 58 237–39

Mobile Telecommunications Technologies Corp., 18 347–49

Mobile TeleSystems OJSC, 59 300–03

Mocon, Inc., 76 275–77

Modell's Sporting Goods *see* Henry Modell & Company Inc.

Modern Times Group AB, 36 335–38

Modern Woodmen of America, 66 227–29

Modine Manufacturing Company, 8 372–75; 56 243–47 (upd.)

MoDo *see* Mo och Domsjö AB.

Modtech Holdings, Inc., 77 284–87

Moen Incorporated, 12 344–45

Moët-Hennessy, I 271–72 *see also* LVMH Moët Hennessy Louis Vuitton SA.

Mohawk Industries, Inc., 19 274–76; 63 298–301 (upd.)

Mohegan Tribal Gaming Authority, 37 254–57

Moksel *see* A. Moksel AG.

MOL *see* Mitsui O.S.K. Lines, Ltd.

MOL Rt, 70 192–95

Moldflow Corporation, 73 227–30

Molex Incorporated, 11 317–19; 14 27; 54 236–41 (upd.)

Moliflor Loisirs, 80 252–55

Molinos Río de la Plata S.A., 61 219–21

Molins plc, 51 249–51

The Molson Companies Limited, I 273–75; 26 303–07 (upd.)

Molson Coors Brewing Company, 77 288–300 (upd.)

Monaco Coach Corporation, 31 336–38

Monadnock Paper Mills, Inc., 21 381–84

Monarch Casino & Resort, Inc., 65 239–41

The Monarch Cement Company, 72 231–33

Mondadori *see* Arnoldo Mondadori Editore S.p.A.

Mondragón Corporación Cooperativa, 101 347–51

MoneyGram International, Inc., 94 315–18

Monfort, Inc., 13 350–52

Monnaie de Paris, 62 246–48

Monnoyeur Group *see* Groupe Monnoyeur.

Monoprix S.A., 86 282–85

Monro Muffler Brake, Inc., 24 337–40

Monrovia Nursery Company, 70 196–98

Monsanto Company, I 365–67; 9 355–57 (upd.); 29 327–31 (upd.); 77 301–07 (upd.)

Monsoon plc, 39 287–89

Monster Cable Products, Inc., 69 256–58

Monster Worldwide Inc., 74 194–97 (upd.)

Montana Coffee Traders, Inc., 60 208–10

The Montana Power Company, 11 320–22; 44 288–92 (upd.)

Montblanc International GmbH, 82 240–44

Montedison S.p.A., I 368–69; 24 341–44 (upd.)

Monterey Pasta Company, 58 240–43

Montgomery Ward & Co., Incorporated, V 145–48; 20 374–79 (upd.)

Montres Rolex S.A., 13 353–55; 34 292–95 (upd.)

Montupet S.A., 63 302–04

Moody's Corporation, 65 242–44

S-K-I Limited, 15 457–59

S.A.C.I. Falabella, 69 311–13

S.A. Cockerill Sambre *see* Cockerill Sambre Group.

s.a. GB-Inno-BM *see* GIB Group.

S.C. Johnson & Son, Inc., III 58–59; 28 409–12 (upd.); 89 382–89 (upd.)

SAA (Pty) Ltd., 28 402–04

Saab Automobile AB, 32 386–89 (upd.); 83 334–339 (upd.)

Saab-Scania A.B., I 197–98; 11 437–39 (upd.)

Saarberg-Konzern, IV 196–99 *see also* RAG AG.

Saatchi & Saatchi plc, I 33–35; 33 328–31 (upd.)

SAB *see* South African Breweries Ltd.

Sabanci Holdings *see* Haci Omer Sabanci Holdings A.S.

Sabaté Diosos SA, 48 348–50 *see also* OENEO S.A.

Sabena S.A./N.V., 33 376–79

SABIC *see* Saudi Basic Industries Corp.

SABMiller plc, 59 352–58 (upd.)

Sabratek Corporation, 29 410–12

Sabre Holdings Corporation, 26 427–30; 74 286–90 (upd.)

Sadia S.A., 59 359–62

Safe Flight Instrument Corporation, 71 321–23

SAFECO Corporation, III 352–54

Safeguard Scientifics, Inc., 10 473–75

Safelite Glass Corp., 19 371–73

SafeNet, Inc., 101 438–42

Safeskin Corporation, 18 467–70 *see also* Kimberly-Clark Corp.

Safety 1st, Inc., 24 412–15

Safety Components International, Inc., 63 342–44

Safety-Kleen Systems Inc., 8 462–65; 82 314–20 (upd.)

Safeway Inc., II 654–56; 24 416–19 (upd.); 85 362–69 (upd.)

Safeway PLC, 50 401–06 (upd.)

Saffery Champness, 80 324–27

Safilo SpA, 40 155–56; 54 319–21

SAFRAN, 102 363–71 (upd.)

Saga Communications, Inc., 27 392–94

The Sage Group, 43 343–46

SAGEM S.A., 37 346–48 *see also* SAFRAN.

Sagicor Life Inc., 98 337–40

Saia, Inc., 98 341–44

SAIC *see* Science Applications International Corp.

Sainsbury's *see* J Sainsbury PLC.

Saint-Gobain *see* Compagnie de Saint Gobain S.A.

Saks Inc., 24 420–23; 41 342–45 (upd.)

Salant Corporation, 12 430–32; 51 318–21 (upd.)

Salem Communications Corporation, 97 359–63

salesforce.com, Inc., 79 370–73

Salick Health Care, Inc., 53 290–92

Salix Pharmaceuticals, Ltd., 93 384–87

Sallie Mae *see* SLM Holding Corp.

Sally Beauty Company, Inc., 60 258–60

Sally Industries, Inc., 103 377–81

Salomon Inc., II 447–49; 13 447–50 (upd.) *see also* Citigroup Inc.

Salomon Worldwide, 20 458–60 *see also* adidas-Salomon AG.

Salt River Project, 19 374–76

Salton, Inc., 30 402–04; 88 343–48 (upd.)

The Salvation Army USA, 32 390–93

Salvatore Ferragamo Italia S.p.A., 62 311–13

Salzgitter AG, IV 200–01; 101 443–49 (upd.)

Sam Ash Music Corporation, 30 405–07

Sam Levin Inc., 80 328–31

Samick Musical Instruments Co., Ltd., 56 297–300

Sam's Club, 40 385–87

Sam's Wine & Spirits, 96 366–69

Samsonite Corporation, 13 451–53; 43 353–57 (upd.)

Samsung Electronics Co., Ltd., 14 416–18; 41 346–49 (upd.)

Samsung Group, I 515–17

Samuel Cabot Inc., 53 293–95

Samuels Jewelers Incorporated, 30 408–10

San Diego Gas & Electric Company, V 711–14 *see also* Sempra Energy.

San Diego Padres Baseball Club L.P., 78 324–27

San Francisco Baseball Associates, L.P., 55 340–43

San Miguel Corporation, 15 428–30; 57 303–08 (upd.)

Sanborn Hermanos, S.A., 20 461–63

Sanborn Map Company Inc., 82 321–24

SanCor Cooperativas Unidas Ltda., 101 450–53

The Sanctuary Group PLC, 69 314–17

Sandals Resorts International, 65 302–05

Sanders Morris Harris Group Inc., 70 285–87

Sanders\Wingo, 99 386–389

Sanderson Farms, Inc., 15 425–27

Sandia National Laboratories, 49 345–48

Sandoz Ltd., I 671–73 *see also* Novartis AG.

Sandvik AB, IV 202–04; 32 394–98 (upd.); 77 367–73 (upd.)

Sanford L.P., 82 325–29

Sanitec Corporation, 51 322–24

Sankyo Company, Ltd., I 674–75; 56 301–04 (upd.)

Sanlam Ltd., 68 331–34

SANLUIS Corporación, S.A.B. de C.V., 95 362–65

The Sanofi-Synthélabo Group, I 676–77; 49 349–51 (upd.)

SanomaWSOY Corporation, 51 325–28

Sanpaolo IMI S.p.A., 50 407–11

Sanrio Company, Ltd., 38 413–15; 104 404–07 (upd.)

Santa Barbara Restaurant Group, Inc., 37 349–52

The Santa Cruz Operation, Inc., 38 416–21

Santa Fe Gaming Corporation, 19 377–79 *see also* Archon Corp.

Santa Fe International Corporation, 38 422–24

Santa Fe Pacific Corporation, V 507–09 *see also* Burlington Northern Santa Fe Corp.

Santa Margherita S.p.A. *see* Industrie Zignago Santa Margherita S.p.A.

Santos Ltd., 81 360–63

Sanwa Bank, Ltd., II 347–48; 15 431–33 (upd.)

SANYO Electric Co., Ltd., II 91–92; 36 399–403 (upd.); 95 366–73 (upd.)

Sanyo-Kokusaku Pulp Co., Ltd., IV 327–28

Sao Paulo Alpargatas S.A., 75 347–49

SAP AG, 16 441–44; 43 358–63 (upd.)

Sapa AB, 84 342–345

Sappi Limited, 49 352–55

Sapporo Holdings Limited, I 282–83; 13 454–56 (upd.); 36 404–07 (upd.); 97 364–69 (upd.)

Saputo Inc., 59 363–65

Sara Lee Corporation, II 571–73; 15 434–37 (upd.); 54 322–27 (upd.); 99 390–398 (upd.)

Sarnoff Corporation, 57 309–12

Sarris Candies Inc., 86 347–50

The SAS Group, 34 396–99 (upd.)

SAS Institute Inc., 10 476–78; 78 328–32 (upd.)

Sasol Limited, IV 533–35; 47 340–44 (upd.)

Saturn Corporation, 7 461–64; 21 449–53 (upd.); 80 332–38 (upd.)

Satyam Computer Services Ltd., 85 370–73

Saucony Inc., 35 386–89; 86 351–56 (upd.)

Sauder Woodworking Co., 12 433–34; 35 390–93 (upd.)

Saudi Arabian Airlines, 6 114–16; 27 395–98 (upd.)

Saudi Arabian Oil Company, IV 536–39; 17 411–15 (upd.); 50 412–17 (upd.)

Saudi Basic Industries Corporation (SABIC), 58 325–28

Sauer-Danfoss Inc., 61 320–22

Saul Ewing LLP, 74 291–94

Saur S.A.S., 92 327–30

Savannah Foods & Industries, Inc., 7 465–67 *see also* Imperial Sugar Co.

Savers, Inc., 99 399–403 (upd.)

Sawtek Inc., 43 364–66 (upd.)

Saxton Pierce Restaurant Corporation, 100 373–76

Sbarro, Inc., 16 445–47; 64 339–42 (upd.)

SBC Communications Inc., 32 399–403 (upd.)

SBC Warburg, 14 419–21 *see also* UBS AG.

Sberbank, 62 314–17

SBI *see* State Bank of India.

Simon Transportation Services Inc., 27 403–06

Simplex Technologies Inc., 21 460–63

Simplicity Manufacturing, Inc., 64 353–56

Simpson Investment Company, 17 438–41

Simpson Thacher & Bartlett, 39 365–68

Simula, Inc., 41 368–70

SINA Corporation, 69 324–27

Sinclair Broadcast Group, Inc., 25 417–19

Sine Qua Non, 99 419–422

Singapore Airlines Limited, 6 117–18; 27 407–09 (upd.); 83 355–359 (upd.)

Singapore Press Holdings Limited, 85 391–95

Singer & Friedlander Group plc, 41 371–73

The Singer Company N.V., 30 417–20 (upd.)

The Singing Machine Company, Inc., 60 277–80

Sir Speedy, Inc., 16 448–50

Sirius Satellite Radio, Inc., 69 328–31

Sirti S.p.A., 76 326–28

Siskin Steel & Supply Company, 70 294–96

Sistema JSFC, 73 303–05

Six Flags, Inc., 17 442–44; 54 333–40 (upd.)

Sixt AG, 39 369–72

SJW Corporation, 70 297–99

SK Group, 88 363–67

Skadden, Arps, Slate, Meagher & Flom, 18 486–88

Skalli Group, 67 349–51

Skandia Insurance Company, Ltd., 50 431–34

Skandinaviska Enskilda Banken AB, II 351–53; 56 326–29 (upd.)

Skanska AB, 38 435–38

Skechers U.S.A. Inc., 31 413–15; 88 368–72 (upd.)

Skeeter Products Inc., 96 391–94

SKF see Aktiebolaget SKF.

Skidmore, Owings & Merrill LLP, 13 475–76; 69 332–35 (upd.)

SkillSoft Public Limited Company, 81 371–74

skinnyCorp, LLC, 97 374–77

Skipton Building Society, 80 344–47

Skis Rossignol S.A., 15 460–62; 43 373–76 (upd.)

Skoda Auto a.s., 39 373–75

Skyline Chili, Inc., 62 325–28

Skyline Corporation, 30 421–23

SkyMall, Inc., 26 439–41

SkyWest, Inc., 25 420–24

Skyy Spirits LLC, 78 348–51

SL Green Realty Corporation, 44 383–85

SL Industries, Inc., 77 383–86

Sleeman Breweries Ltd., 74 305–08

Sleepy's Inc., 32 426–28

SLI, Inc., 48 358–61

Slim-Fast Foods Company, 18 489–91; 66 296–98 (upd.)

Slinky, Inc. see Poof-Slinky, Inc.

SLM Holding Corp., 25 425–28 (upd.)

Slough Estates PLC, IV 722–25; 50 435–40 (upd.)

Small Planet Foods, Inc., 89 410–14

Smart & Final LLC, 16 451–53; 94 392–96 (upd.)

Smart Balance, Inc., 100 398–401

SMART Modular Technologies, Inc., 86 361–64

SmartForce PLC, 43 377–80

Smarties see Ce De Candy Inc.

SMBC see Sumitomo Mitsui Banking Corp.

Smead Manufacturing Co., 17 445–48

SMG see Scottish Media Group.

SMH see Sanders Morris Harris Group Inc.; The Swatch Group SA.

Smith & Hawken, Ltd., 68 343–45

Smith & Nephew plc, 17 449–52; 41 374–78 (upd.)

Smith & Wesson Corp., 30 424–27; 73 306–11 (upd.)

Smith Barney Inc., 15 463–65 see also Citigroup Inc.

Smith Corona Corp., 13 477–80

Smith International, Inc., 15 466–68; 59 376–80 (upd.)

Smith-Midland Corporation, 56 330–32

Smithfield Foods, Inc., 7 477–78; 43 381–84 (upd.)

SmithKline Beckman Corporation, I 692–94 see also GlaxoSmithKline plc.

SmithKline Beecham plc, III 65–67; 32 429–34 (upd.) see also GlaxoSmithKline plc.

Smith's Food & Drug Centers, Inc., 8 472–74; 57 324–27 (upd.)

Smiths Industries PLC, 25 429–31

Smithsonian Institution, 27 410–13

Smithway Motor Xpress Corporation, 39 376–79

Smoby International SA, 56 333–35

Smorgon Steel Group Ltd., 62 329–32

Smucker's see The J.M. Smucker Co.

Smurfit-Stone Container Corporation, 26 442–46 (upd.) ; 83 360–368 (upd.)

Snap-On, Incorporated, 7 479–80; 27 414–16 (upd.)

Snapfish, 83 369–372

Snapple Beverage Corporation, 11 449–51

SNC-Lavalin Group Inc., 72 330–33

SNCF see Société Nationale des Chemins de Fer Français.

SNEA see Société Nationale Elf Aquitaine.

Snecma Group, 46 369–72 see also SAFRAN.

Snell & Wilmer L.L.P., 28 425–28

SNET see Southern New England Telecommunications Corp.

Snow Brand Milk Products Company, Ltd., II 574–75; 48 362–65 (upd.)

Soap Opera Magazine see American Media, Inc.

Sobeys Inc., 80 348–51

Socata see EADS SOCATA.

Sociedad Química y Minera de Chile S.A.,103 382–85

Società Finanziaria Telefonica per Azioni, V 325–27

Società Sportiva Lazio SpA, 44 386–88

Société Air France, 27 417–20 (upd.).

Société BIC S.A., 73 312–15

Societe des Produits Marnier-Lapostolle S.A., 88 373–76

Société d'Exploitation AOM Air Liberté SA (AirLib), 53 305–07

Société du Figaro S.A., 60 281–84

Société du Louvre, 27 421–23

Société Générale, II 354–56; 42 347–51 (upd.)

Société Industrielle Lesaffre, 84 356–359

Société Luxembourgeoise de Navigation Aérienne S.A., 64 357–59

Société Nationale des Chemins de Fer Français, V 512–15; 57 328–32 (upd.)

Société Nationale Elf Aquitaine, IV 544–47; 7 481–85 (upd.)

Société Norbert Dentressangle S.A., 67 352–54

Société Tunisienne de l'Air-Tunisair, 49 371–73

Society Corporation, 9 474–77

Sodexho SA, 29 442–44; 91 433–36 (upd.)

Sodiaal S.A., 19 50; 36 437–39 (upd.)

SODIMA, II 576–77 see also Sodiaal S.A.

Soft Sheen Products, Inc., 31 416–18

Softbank Corporation, 13 481–83; 38 439–44 (upd.); 77 387–95 (upd.)

Sojitz Corporation, 96 395–403 (upd.)

Sol Meliá S.A., 71 337–39

Sola International Inc., 71 340–42

Solar Turbines Inc., 100 402–06

Sole Technology Inc., 93 405–09

Solectron Corporation, 12 450–52; 48 366–70 (upd.)

Solo Cup Company, 104 424–27

Solo Serve Corporation, 28 429–31

Solutia Inc., 52 312–15

Solvay & Cie S.A., I 394–96; 21 464–67 (upd.)

Solvay S.A., 61 329–34 (upd.)

Somerfield plc, 47 365–69 (upd.)

Sommer-Allibert S.A., 19 406–09 see also Tarkett Sommer AG.

Sompo Japan Insurance, Inc., 98 359–63 (upd.)

Sonae SGPS, S.A., 97 378–81

Sonat, Inc., 6 577–78 see also El Paso Corp.

Sonatrach, 65 313–17 (upd.)

Sonera Corporation, 50 441–44 see also TeliaSonera AB.

Sonesta International Hotels Corporation, 44 389–91

Sonic Automotive, Inc., 77 396–99

Sonic Corp., 14 451–53; 37 360–63 (upd.); 103 386–91 (upd.)

Sonic Innovations Inc., 56 336–38

Sonic Solutions, Inc., 81 375–79

SonicWALL, Inc., 87 421–424

Index to Industries

Accounting

American Institute of Certified Public
  Accountants (AICPA), 44
Andersen, 29 (upd.); 68 (upd.)
Automatic Data Processing, Inc., III; 9
  (upd.); 47 (upd.)
BDO Seidman LLP, 96
BKD LLP, 96
CROSSMARK, 79
Deloitte Touche Tohmatsu International,
  9; 29 (upd.)
Ernst & Young, 9; 29 (upd.)
FTI Consulting, Inc., 77
Grant Thornton International, 57
Huron Consulting Group Inc., 87
KPMG International, 33 (upd.)
L.S. Starrett Co., 13
McLane Company, Inc., 13
NCO Group, Inc., 42
Paychex, Inc., 15; 46 (upd.)
PKF International 78
Plante & Moran, LLP, 71
PRG-Schultz International, Inc., 73
PricewaterhouseCoopers, 9; 29 (upd.)
Resources Connection, Inc., 81
Robert Wood Johnson Foundation, 35
RSM McGladrey Business Services Inc.,
  98
Saffery Champness, 80
Sanders\Wingo, 99
Schenck Business Solutions, 88
StarTek, Inc., 79
Travelzoo Inc., 79
Univision Communications Inc., 24; 83
  (upd.)

Advertising & Other Business Services

ABM Industries Incorporated, 25 (upd.)
Abt Associates Inc., 95
AchieveGlobal Inc., 90
Ackerley Communications, Inc., 9
ACNielsen Corporation, 13; 38 (upd.)
Acosta Sales and Marketing Company,
  Inc., 77
Acsys, Inc., 44
Adecco S.A., 36 (upd.)
Adia S.A., 6
Administaff, Inc., 52
The Advertising Council, Inc., 76
The Advisory Board Company, 80
Advo, Inc., 6; 53 (upd.)
Aegis Group plc, 6
Affiliated Computer Services, Inc., 61
AHL Services, Inc., 27
Allegis Group, Inc., 95
Alloy, Inc., 55
Amdocs Ltd., 47
American Building Maintenance
  Industries, Inc., 6
American Library Association, 86
The American Society of Composers,
  Authors and Publishers (ASCAP), 29
Amey Plc, 47
Analysts International Corporation, 36
aQuantive, Inc., 81
The Arbitron Company, 38
Ariba, Inc., 57
Armor Holdings, Inc., 27
Asatsu-DK Inc., 82
Ashtead Group plc, 34
The Associated Press, 13
Avalon Correctional Services, Inc., 75
Bain & Company, 55

Barrett Business Services, Inc., 16
Barton Protective Services Inc., 53
Bates Worldwide, Inc., 14; 33 (upd.)
Bearings, Inc., 13
Berlitz International, Inc., 13
Bernard Hodes Group Inc., 86
Bernstein-Rein, 92
Big Flower Press Holdings, Inc., 21
Billing Concepts, Inc., 26; 72 (upd.)
Billing Services Group Ltd., 102
The BISYS Group, Inc., 73
Booz Allen Hamilton Inc., 10; 101 (upd.)
Boron, LePore & Associates, Inc., 45
The Boston Consulting Group, 58
Bozell Worldwide Inc., 25
BrandPartners Group, Inc., 58
Bright Horizons Family Solutions, Inc., 31
Broadcast Music Inc., 23; 90 (upd.)
Buck Consultants, Inc., 55
Bureau Veritas SA, 55
Burke, Inc., 88
Burns International Services Corporation,
  13; 41 (upd.)
Cambridge Technology Partners, Inc., 36
Campbell-Ewald Advertising, 86
Campbell-Mithun-Esty, Inc., 16
Cannon Design, 63
Capario, 104
Capita Group PLC, 69
Cardtronics, Inc., 93
Career Education Corporation, 45
Carmichael Lynch Inc., 28
Cash Systems, Inc., 93
Cazenove Group plc, 72
CCC Information Services Group Inc., 74
CDI Corporation, 6; 54 (upd.)
Cegedim S.A., 104
Central Parking System, 18; 104 (upd.)
Century Business Services, Inc., 52

Aerospace

Airlines

Beverages

Bio-Technology

Chemicals

Givaudan SA, 43

Great Lakes Chemical Corporation, I; 14 (upd.)

GROWMARK, Inc., 88

Guerbet Group, 46

H.B. Fuller Company, 32 (upd.); 75 (upd.)

Hauser, Inc., 46

Hawkins Chemical, Inc., 16

Henkel KGaA, III; 34 (upd.); 95 (upd.)

Hercules Inc., I; 22 (upd.); 66 (upd.)

Hoechst A.G., I; 18 (upd.)

Hoechst Celanese Corporation, 13

Huls A.G., I

Huntsman Corporation, 8; 98 (upd.)

IMC Fertilizer Group, Inc., 8

Imperial Chemical Industries PLC, I; 50 (upd.)

International Flavors & Fragrances Inc., 9; 38 (upd.)

Israel Chemicals Ltd., 55

Kemira Oyj, 70

KMG Chemicals, Inc., 101

Koppers Industries, Inc., I; 26 (upd.)

Kwizda Holding GmbH, 102 (upd.)

L'Air Liquide SA, I; 47 (upd.)

Lawter International Inc., 14

LeaRonal, Inc., 23

Loctite Corporation, 30 (upd.)

Loos & Dilworth, Inc., 100

Lonza Group Ltd., 73

The Lubrizol Corporation, I; 30 (upd.); 83 (upd.)

Lyondell Chemical Company, 45 (upd.)

M.A. Hanna Company, 8

MacDermid Incorporated, 32

Makhteshim-Agan Industries Ltd., 85

Mallinckrodt Group Inc., 19

MBC Holding Company, 40

Melamine Chemicals, Inc., 27

Methanex Corporation, 40

Mexichem, S.A.B. de C.V., 99

Minerals Technologies Inc., 52 (upd.)

Mississippi Chemical Corporation, 39

Mitsubishi Chemical Corporation, I; 56 (upd.)

Mitsui Petrochemical Industries, Ltd., 9

Monsanto Company, I; 9 (upd.); 29 (upd.)

Montedison SpA, I

Morton International Inc., I; 9 (upd.); 80 (upd.)

The Mosaic Company, 91

Nagase & Company, Ltd., 8

Nalco Holding Company, I; 12 (upd.); 89 (upd.)

National Distillers and Chemical Corporation, I

National Sanitary Supply Co., 16

National Starch and Chemical Company, 49

NCH Corporation, 8

Nippon Soda Co., Ltd., 85

Nisshin Seifun Group Inc., 66 (upd.)

NL Industries, Inc., 10

Nobel Industries AB, 9

NOF Corporation, 72

Norsk Hydro ASA, 35 (upd.)

North American Galvanizing & Coatings, Inc., 99

Novacor Chemicals Ltd., 12

Nufarm Ltd., 87

NutraSweet Company, 8

Occidental Petroleum Corporation, 71 (upd.)

Olin Corporation, I; 13 (upd.); 78 (upd.)

OM Group, Inc., 17; 78 (upd.)

OMNOVA Solutions Inc., 59

Penford Corporation, 55

Pennwalt Corporation, I

Perstorp AB, I; 51 (upd.)

Petrolite Corporation, 15

Pfizer Inc., 79 (upd.)

Pioneer Hi-Bred International, Inc., 41 (upd.)

PolyOne Corporation, 87 (upd.)

Praxair, Inc., 11

Quaker Chemical Corp., 91

Quantum Chemical Corporation, 8

Reichhold Chemicals, Inc., 10

Renner Herrmann S.A., 79

Rhodia SA, 38

Rhône-Poulenc S.A., I; 10 (upd.)

Robertet SA, 39

Rohm and Haas Company, I; 26 (upd.); 77 (upd.)

Roussel Uclaf, I; 8 (upd.)

RPM International Inc., 8; 36 (upd.); 91 (upd.)

RWE AG, 50 (upd.)

S.C. Johnson & Son, Inc., III; 28 (upd.); 89 (upd.)

The Scotts Company, 22

SCP Pool Corporation, 39

Sequa Corp., 13

Shanghai Petrochemical Co., Ltd., 18

Sigma-Aldrich Corporation, I; 36 (upd.); 93 (upd.)

Sociedad Química y Minera de Chile S.A., 103

Solutia Inc., 52

Solvay S.A., I; 21 (upd.); 61 (upd.)

Stepan Company, 30

Sterling Chemicals, Inc., 16; 78 (upd.)

Sumitomo Chemical Company Ltd., I; 98 (upd.)

Takeda Chemical Industries, Ltd., 46 (upd.)

Teknor Apex Company, 97

Terra Industries, Inc., 13

Tessenderlo Group, 76

Teva Pharmaceutical Industries Ltd., 22

Tosoh Corporation, 70

Total Fina Elf S.A., 24 (upd.); 50 (upd.)

Transammonia Group, 95

Ube Industries, Ltd., 38 (upd.)

Union Carbide Corporation, I; 9 (upd.); 74 (upd.)

United Industries Corporation, 68

Univar Corporation, 9

The Valspar Corporation, 32 (upd.); 77 (upd.)

VeraSun Energy Corporation, 87

Vista Chemical Company, I

Witco Corporation, I; 16 (upd.)

Yule Catto & Company plc, 54

WD-40 Company, 87 (upd.)

Zakłady Azotowe Puławy S.A., 100

Zeneca Group PLC, 21

Conglomerates

A.P. Møller - Maersk A/S, 57

ABARTA, Inc., 100

Abengoa S.A., 73

Acciona S.A., 81

Accor SA, 10; 27 (upd.)

Ackermans & van Haaren N.V., 97

Adani Enterprises Ltd., 97

Aditya Birla Group, 79

Administración Nacional de Combustibles, Alcohol y Pórtland, 93

AEG A.G., I

Al Habtoor Group L.L.C., 87

Alcatel Alsthom Compagnie Générale d'Electricité, 9

Alco Standard Corporation, I

Alexander & Baldwin, Inc., 10, 40 (upd.)

Alfa, S.A. de C.V., 19

Alfa Group, 99

Algar S/A Emprendimentos e Participações, 103

Alleghany Corporation, 60 (upd.)

Allied Domecq PLC, 29

Allied-Signal Inc., I

AMFAC Inc., I

Andrade Gutierrez S.A., 102

The Anschutz Company, 73 (upd.)

The Anschutz Corporation, 36 (upd.)

Antofagasta plc, 65

Apax Partners Worldwide LLP, 89

APi Group, Inc., 64

Aramark Corporation, 13

ARAMARK Corporation, 41

Archer Daniels Midland Company, I; 11 (upd.); 75 (upd.)

Arkansas Best Corporation, 16

Associated British Ports Holdings Plc, 45

BAA plc, 33 (upd.)

Barlow Rand Ltd., I

Barratt Developments plc, 56 (upd.)

Bat Industries PLC, I

Baugur Group hf, 81

BB Holdings Limited, 77

Berjaya Group Bhd., 67

Berkshire Hathaway Inc., III; 18 (upd.); 42 (upd.); 89 (upd.)

Block Communications, Inc., 81

Bond Corporation Holdings Limited, 10

Brascan Corporation, 67

BTR PLC, I

Bunzl plc, 31 (upd.)

Burlington Northern Santa Fe Corporation, 27 (upd.)

Business Post Group plc, 46

C. Itoh & Company Ltd., I

C.I. Traders Limited, 61

Camargo Corrêa S.A., 93

Cargill, Incorporated, II; 13 (upd.); 40 (upd.); 89 (upd.)

CBI Industries, Inc., 7

Charoen Pokphand Group, 62

Chemed Corporation, 13

Chesebrough-Pond's USA, Inc., 8

Construction

Electrical & Electronics

Financial Services: Banks

Financial Services: Excluding Banks

Rathbone Brothers plc, 70
Raymond James Financial Inc., 69
Resource America, Inc., 42
Robert W. Baird & Co. Incorporated, 67
Ryan Beck & Co., Inc., 66
Safeguard Scientifics, Inc., 10
St. James's Place Capital, plc, 71
Salomon Inc., II; 13 (upd.)
Sanders Morris Harris Group Inc., 70
Sanlam Ltd., 68
SBC Warburg, 14
Schroders plc, 42
Scottrade, Inc., 85
SEI Investments Company, 96
Shearson Lehman Brothers Holdings Inc., II; 9 (upd.)
Siebert Financial Corp., 32
Skipton Building Society, 80
SLM Holding Corp., 25 (upd.)
Smith Barney Inc., 15
Soros Fund Management LLC, 28
Spear, Leeds & Kellogg, 66
State Street Boston Corporation, 8
Stephens Inc., 92
Student Loan Marketing Association, II
Sun Life Financial Inc., 85
T. Rowe Price Associates, Inc., 11; 34 (upd.)
Teachers Insurance and Annuity Association-College Retirement Equities Fund, 45 (upd.)
Texas Pacific Group Inc., 36
3i Group PLC, 73
Total System Services, Inc., 18
TradeStation Group, Inc., 83
Trilon Financial Corporation, II
United Jewish Communities, 33
The Vanguard Group, Inc., 14; 34 (upd.)
VeriFone Holdings, Inc., 18; 76 (upd.)
Viel & Cie, 76
Visa Inc., 9; 26 (upd.); 104 (upd.)
Wachovia Corporation, 12; 46 (upd.)
Waddell & Reed, Inc., 22
Washington Federal, Inc., 17
Waterhouse Investor Services, Inc., 18
Watson Wyatt Worldwide, 42
Western Union Financial Services, Inc., 54
WFS Financial Inc., 70
Working Assets Funding Service, 43
World Acceptance Corporation, 57
Yamaichi Securities Company, Limited, II
The Ziegler Companies, Inc., 24; 63 (upd.)
Zurich Financial Services, 42 (upd.); 93 (upd.)

Food Products

A. Duda & Sons, Inc., 88
A. Moksel AG, 59
Adecoagro LLC, 101
Agri Beef Company, 81
Agway, Inc., 7
Ajinomoto Co., Inc., II; 28 (upd.)
Alabama Farmers Cooperative, Inc., 63
The Albert Fisher Group plc, 41
Alberto-Culver Company, 8; 36 (upd.); 91 (upd.)
Alfred Ritter GmbH & Co. KG, 58

Alfesca hf, 82
Allen Brothers, Inc., 101
Allen Canning Company, 76
Alpine Confections, Inc., 71
Alpine Lace Brands, Inc., 18
American Crystal Sugar Company, 11; 32 (upd.)
American Foods Group, 43
American Italian Pasta Company, 27; 76 (upd.)
American Licorice Company, 86
American Maize-Products Co., 14
American Pop Corn Company, 59
American Rice, Inc., 33
Amfac/JMB Hawaii L.L.C., 24 (upd.)
Amy's Kitchen Inc., 76
Annie's Homegrown, Inc., 59
Archer-Daniels-Midland Company, 32 (upd.)
Archway Cookies, Inc., 29
Arcor S.A.I.C., 66
Arla Foods amba, 48
Arnott's Ltd., 66
Artisan Confections Company, 103
Asher's Chocolates, Inc., 103
Associated British Foods plc, II; 13 (upd.); 41 (upd.)
Associated Milk Producers, Inc., 11; 48 (upd.)
Atkinson Candy Company, 87
Atlantic Premium Brands, Ltd., 57
August Storck KG, 66
Aurora Foods Inc., 32
Auvil Fruit Company, Inc., 95
Awrey Bakeries, Inc., 56
B&G Foods, Inc., 40
The B. Manischewitz Company, LLC, 31
Bahlsen GmbH & Co. KG, 44
Bakkavör Group hf., 91
Balance Bar Company, 32
Baldwin Richardson Foods Company, 100
Baltek Corporation, 34
The Bama Companies, Inc., 80
Bar-S Foods Company, 76
Barbara's Bakery Inc., 88
Barilla G. e R. Fratelli S.p.A., 17; 50 (upd.)
Barry Callebaut AG, 71 (upd.)
Baxters Food Group Ltd., 99
Bear Creek Corporation, 38
Beatrice Company, II
Beech-Nut Nutrition Corporation, 21; 51 (upd.)
Beer Nuts, Inc., 86
Bel/Kaukauna USA, 76
Bellisio Foods, Inc., 95
Ben & Jerry's Homemade, Inc., 10; 35 (upd.); 80 (upd.)
Berkeley Farms, Inc., 46
Bernard Matthews Ltd., 89
Besnier SA, 19
Best Kosher Foods Corporation, 82
Bestfoods, 22 (upd.)
Better Made Snack Foods, Inc., 90
Bettys & Taylors of Harrogate Ltd., 72
Birds Eye Foods, Inc., 69 (upd.)
Blue Bell Creameries L.P., 30
Blue Diamond Growers, 28

Bob's Red Mill Natural Foods, Inc., 63
Bobs Candies, Inc., 70
Bolton Group B.V., 86
Bonduelle SA, 51
Bongrain S.A., 25; 102 (upd.)
Booker PLC, 13; 31 (upd.)
Borden, Inc., II; 22 (upd.)
Boyd Coffee Company, 53
Brach and Brock Confections, Inc., 15
Brake Bros plc, 45
Bridgford Foods Corporation, 27
Brigham's Inc., 72
Brioche Pasquier S.A., 58
British Sugar plc, 84
Brossard S.A., 102
Brothers Gourmet Coffees, Inc., 20
Broughton Foods Co., 17
Brown & Haley, 23
Bruce Foods Corporation, 39
Bruegger's Corporation, 63
Bruster's Real Ice Cream, Inc., 80
BSN Groupe S.A., II
Bumble Bee Seafoods L.L.C., 64
Bunge Brasil S.A. 78
Bunge Ltd., 62
Bourbon Corporation, 82
Burns, Philp & Company Ltd., 63
Bush Boake Allen Inc., 30
Bush Brothers & Company, 45
The C.F. Sauer Company, 90
C.H. Robinson Worldwide, Inc., 40 (upd.)
C.H. Guenther & Son, Inc., 84
Cabot Creamery Cooperative, Inc., 102
Cactus Feeders, Inc., 91
Cadbury Schweppes PLC, II; 49 (upd.)
Cagle's, Inc., 20
Cal-Maine Foods, Inc., 69
Calavo Growers, Inc., 47
Calcot Ltd., 33
Callard and Bowser-Suchard Inc., 84
Campagna-Turano Bakery, Inc., 99
Campbell Soup Company, II; 7 (upd.); 26 (upd.); 71 (upd.)
The Campina Group, 78
Campofrío Alimentación S.A, 59
Canada Bread Company, Limited, 99
Canada Packers Inc., II
Cape Cod Potato Chip Company, 90
Cargill, Incorporated, II; 13 (upd.); 40 (upd.); 89 (upd.)
Carnation Company, II
The Carriage House Companies, Inc., 55
Carroll's Foods, Inc., 46
Carvel Corporation, 35
Castle & Cooke, Inc., II; 20 (upd.)
Cattleman's, Inc., 20
Ce De Candy Inc., 100
Celestial Seasonings, Inc., 16
Cemoi S.A., 86
Central Soya Company, Inc., 7
Cerebos Gregg's Ltd., 100
Chaoda Modern Agriculture (Holdings) Ltd., 87
Charal S.A., 90
Chase General Corporation, 91
Chattanooga Bakery, Inc., 86
Chef Solutions, Inc., 89

Health & Personal Care Products

Health Care Services

Hotels

Insurance

Legal Services

Manufacturing

Materials

Mining & Metals

Paper & Forestry

Personal Services

Petroleum

Publishing & Printing

Retail & Wholesale

Rubber & Tires

Telecommunications

Textiles & Apparel

Utilities

Waste Services

Geographic Index

Canada

United States

America's Favorite Chicken Company, Inc., 7
American & Efird, Inc., 82
American Airlines, I; 6 (upd.)
American Apparel, Inc., 90
American Axle & Manufacturing Holdings, Inc., 67
American Banknote Corporation, 30
American Bar Association, 35
American Biltrite Inc., 16; 43 (upd.)
American Brands, Inc., V
American Building Maintenance Industries, Inc., 6
American Business Information, Inc., 18
American Business Products, Inc., 20
American Campus Communities, Inc., 85
The American Cancer Society, 24
American Capital Strategies, Ltd., 91
American Cast Iron Pipe Company, 50
American Civil Liberties Union (ACLU), 60
American Classic Voyages Company, 27
American Coin Merchandising, Inc., 28; 74 (upd.)
American Colloid Co., 13
American Commercial Lines Inc., 99
American Crystal Sugar Company, 9; 32 (upd.)
American Cyanamid, I; 8 (upd.)
American Eagle Outfitters, Inc., 24; 55 (upd.)
American Ecology Corporation, 77
American Electric Power Company, Inc., V; 45 (upd.)
American Equipment Company, Inc., 104
American Express Company, II; 10 (upd.); 38 (upd.)
American Family Corporation, III
American Financial Group Inc., III; 48 (upd.)
American Foods Group, 43
American Furniture Company, Inc., 21
American General Corporation, III; 10 (upd.); 46 (upd.)
American General Finance Corp., 11
American Girl, Inc., 69 (upd.)
American Golf Corporation, 45
American Gramaphone LLC, 52
American Greetings Corporation, 7; 22 (upd.); 59 (upd.)
American Healthways, Inc., 65
American Home Mortgage Holdings, Inc., 46
American Home Products, I; 10 (upd.)
American Homestar Corporation, 18; 41 (upd.)
American Institute of Certified Public Accountants (AICPA), 44
American International Group, Inc., III; 15 (upd.); 47 (upd.)
American Italian Pasta Company, 27; 76 (upd.)
American Kennel Club, Inc., 74
American Lawyer Media Holdings, Inc., 32
American Library Association, 86
American Licorice Company, 86
American Locker Group Incorporated, 34

American Lung Association, 48
American Maize-Products Co., 14
American Management Association, 76
American Management Systems, Inc., 11
American Media, Inc., 27; 82 (upd.)
American Medical Alert Corporation, 103
American Medical Association, 39
American Medical International, Inc., III
American Medical Response, Inc., 39
American Motors Corporation, I
American National Insurance Company, 8; 27 (upd.)
American Nurses Association Inc., 102
American Pad & Paper Company, 20
American Pharmaceutical Partners, Inc., 69
American Pop Corn Company, 59
American Power Conversion Corporation, 24; 67 (upd.)
American Premier Underwriters, Inc., 10
American President Companies Ltd., 6
American Printing House for the Blind, 26
American Re Corporation, 10; 35 (upd.)
American Red Cross, 40
American Reprographics Company, 75
American Residential Mortgage Corporation, 8
American Restaurant Partners, L.P., 93
American Retirement Corporation, 42
American Rice, Inc., 33
American Safety Razor Company, 20
American Science & Engineering, Inc., 81
American Seating Company 78
American Skiing Company, 28
American Society for the Prevention of Cruelty to Animals (ASPCA), 68
The American Society of Composers, Authors and Publishers (ASCAP), 29
American Software Inc., 25
American Standard Companies Inc., III; 30 (upd.)
American States Water Company, 46
American Stores Company, II; 22 (upd.)
American Superconductor Corporation, 97
American Technical Ceramics Corp., 67
American Technology Corporation, 103
American Tourister, Inc., 16
American Tower Corporation, 33
American Vanguard Corporation, 47
American Water Works Company, Inc., 6; 38 (upd.)
American Woodmark Corporation, 31
AmeriCares Foundation, Inc., 87
Amerigon Incorporated, 97
AMERIGROUP Corporation, 69
Amerihost Properties, Inc., 30
AmeriSource Health Corporation, 37 (upd.)
AmerisourceBergen Corporation, 64 (upd.)
Ameristar Casinos, Inc., 33; 69 (upd.)
Ameritech Corporation, V; 18 (upd.)
Ameritrade Holding Corporation, 34
Ameriwood Industries International Corp., 17
Amerock Corporation, 53

Ameron International Corporation, 67
Ames Department Stores, Inc., 9; 30 (upd.)
AMETEK, Inc., 9
AMF Bowling, Inc., 40
Amfac/JMB Hawaii L.L.C., I; 24 (upd.)
Amgen, Inc., 10; 30 (upd.); 89 (upd.)
AMICAS, Inc., 69
Amkor Technology, Inc., 69
Amoco Corporation, IV; 14 (upd.)
Amoskeag Company, 8
AMP Incorporated, II; 14 (upd.)
Ampacet Corporation, 67
Ampco-Pittsburgh Corporation 79
Ampex Corporation, 17
Amphenol Corporation, 40
AMR Corporation, 28 (upd.); 52 (upd.)
AMREP Corporation, 21
Amscan Holdings, Inc., 61
AmSouth Bancorporation, 12; 48 (upd.)
Amsted Industries Incorporated, 7
AmSurg Corporation, 48
Amtran, Inc., 34
Amway Corporation, III; 13 (upd.); 30 (upd.)
Amy's Kitchen Inc., 76
Amylin Pharmaceuticals, Inc., 67
Anacomp, Inc., 94
Anadarko Petroleum Corporation, 10; 52 (upd.)
Anaheim Angels Baseball Club, Inc., 53
Analex Corporation, 74
Analog Devices, Inc., 10
Analogic Corporation, 23
Analysts International Corporation, 36
Analytic Sciences Corporation, 10
Analytical Surveys, Inc., 33
Anaren Microwave, Inc., 33
Anchor Bancorp, Inc., 10
Anchor BanCorp Wisconsin, Inc., 101
Anchor Brewing Company, 47
Anchor Gaming, 24
Anchor Hocking Glassware, 13
Andersen, 10; 29 (upd.); 68 (upd.)
Anderson Trucking Service, Inc., 75
The Anderson-DuBose Company, 60
The Andersons, Inc., 31
Andin International, Inc., 100
Andis Company, Inc., 85
Andrew Corporation, 10; 32 (upd.)
The Andrews Institute, 99
Andrews Kurth, LLP, 71
Andrews McMeel Universal, 40
Andronico's Market, 70
Andrx Corporation, 55
Angelica Corporation, 15; 43 (upd.)
AngioDynamics, Inc., 81
Anheuser-Busch InBev, I; 10 (upd.); 34 (upd.); 100 (upd.)
Anixter International Inc., 88
Annie's Homegrown, Inc., 59
Annin & Co., 100
AnnTaylor Stores Corporation, 13; 37 (upd.); 67 (upd.)
ANR Pipeline Co., 17
The Anschutz Company, 12; 36 (upd.); 73 (upd.)
Ansoft Corporation, 63